November 12–16, 2014
Istanbul, Turkey

Association for
Computing Machinery

Advancing Computing as a Science & Profession

ICMI'14

Proceedings of the 2014 International Conference on Multimodal Interaction

Sponsored by:

ACM SIGCHI

Supported by

SAP Innovation Center Turkey, Openstream, US National Science Foundation, Boğaziçi University, TÜBİTAK, and Turkish Airlines

Association for
Computing Machinery

Advancing Computing as a Science & Profession

The Association for Computing Machinery
2 Penn Plaza, Suite 701
New York, New York 10121-0701

ISBN: 978-1-4503-2885-2 (Digital)

ISBN: 978-1-4503-3387-0 (Print)

Additional copies may be ordered prepaid from:

ACM Order Department
PO Box 30777
New York, NY 10087-0777, USA

Phone: 1-800-342-6626 (USA and Canada)
+1-212-626-0500 (Global)
Fax: +1-212-944-1318
E-mail: acmhelp@acm.org
Hours of Operation: 8:30 am – 4:30 pm ET

Printed in the USA

ICMI 2014 Chairs' Welcome

Welcome to Istanbul and to the 16th edition of the ACM International Conference on Multimodal Interaction, ICMI 2014. ICMI is the premier international forum for multidisciplinary research on multimodal human-human and human-computer interaction, interfaces, and system development. The conference focuses on theoretical and empirical foundations, component technologies, and combined multimodal processing techniques that define the field of multimodal interaction.

As in the previous years, in 2014, we had a strong number of submissions: 127 long and short paper submissions (82 long papers and 45 short papers) and 16 demonstration papers. From these submissions, we accepted 23 papers for oral presentation and 28 papers for poster presentation. We have an acceptance rate of 18% for oral presentations and an overall acceptance rate of 40% for short and long papers combined. Of the 16 demonstration papers, 10 were accepted.

This year, the conference will host four invited keynote talks from thought leaders in academia and industry. They are Yvonne Rogers (University College London, UK), Cafer Tosun (SAP Innovation Center, Turkey), Peter Robinson (Cambridge University, UK), and Alexander Waibel (Carnegie Mellon University, USA and Karlsruhe Institute of Technology, Germany). In addition to these keynotes, we will host a plenary talk by the recipient of the *Sustained Accomplishment Award*, presented for the first time by the ICMI Advisory Board.

A number of satellite events will be held along with the main conference. The ICMI program includes three multimodal grand challenges and a doctoral consortium. The challenges are designed to stimulate the community with standardized corpora competition, and new research questions. The doctoral consortium extends our commitment to the emerging generation of researchers. ICMI will be followed by five workshops, which are selected from the nine workshop proposals we received.

The Doctoral Consortium, co-chaired by Marco Cristani and Justine Cassell, is organized on the first day of the conference. In this special session, a highly-accomplished mentor team and selected senior PhD students gather around a round table to discuss research plans and progress of each student. This combination of peer and expert evaluation aims to promote the next generation of multimodal interaction researchers, and to strengthen the ICMI community. Accepted students receive a travel grant and registration waiver to attend both the Doctoral Consortium event, and the main conference. From among 19 applications, 14 students were accepted for participation and to receive travel funding. The organizers thank the U.S. National Science Foundation (award IIS 1443097) and conference sponsors for the financial support to make this happen.

The Multimodal Grand Challenges were introduced to ICMI in 2012. This year's challenges are co-chaired by Hatice Gunes and Dirk Heylen and include the Third Multimodal Learning Analytics Challenge, the Second Emotion Recognition In The Wild Challenge and the Mapping Personality Traits Challenge (MAPTRAITS). All three Grand Challenges will be presented on Wednesday, November 12nd, and a summary session will take place on Friday, November 14th, during the main conference.

The workshops in this year's program take place on the final day of the conference, and include the Workshop on Multimodal, Multi-Party, Real-World Human-Robot Interaction, the Workshop on Understanding and Modeling Multiparty, Multimodal Interactions, the Workshop on Roadmapping the Future of Multimodal Interaction Research including Business Opportunities and Challenges, 2nd International Workshop on Emotion Representations and Modelling in Human-Computer Interaction Systems, and 7th Workshop on Eye Gaze in Intelligent Human Machine Interaction: Eye-Gaze and Multimodality. Carlos Busso and Alexandros Potamianos are co-chairing this year's workshops.

The main conference program includes a Demonstrations & Exhibits session, co-chaired by Lale Akarun and Kazuhiro Otsuka, which is intended to showcase innovative implementations, systems, and technologies demonstrating new ideas about interactive multimodal interfaces.

The general themes that dominated this year's accepted papers focused on social interaction, multimodal fusion and integration, affect and cognitive modeling, discourse and dialogue modeling, and analysis of nonverbal behaviors such as gestures, body pose and gaze. Other prominent themes include mobile interaction, human-robot interaction, healthcare and assistive technologies, ubiquitous and pervasive environments. Finally, we have several papers on the theme of "urban interactions," which we have added to the main themes of ICMI as a new area with growing interest.

The review process for the short and long papers was organized using the PCS submission and review system, as in the previous years. The quality of the review process was high, thanks to 23 Senior Program Committee (SPC) members who helped the Program Chairs in defining the Technical Program Committee, and in finding excellent reviewers for each paper. Overseen by the Program Chairs, each SPC member has been assigned a maximum of six papers, based on their preferences in a bidding process and their expertise. The SPC members distributed the papers to members of the Technical Program Committee and volunteer reviewers. Once reviews were submitted, the SPCs provided meta-reviews, which, along with the reviews, were sent to the authors for a rebuttal — a step which allows authors to clarify their intentions and results in higher quality final reviews. In a final step, all papers and their reviews were discussed in detail by the Program Chairs on a two-day remote meeting, in order to decide on the list of accepted submissions. We are indebted to the contributions of our reviewers and program and area chairs. The program was formed by grouping papers into main topics of interest for this year's conference. Following the trend in previous ICMI events and many other academic meetings, to minimize paper consumption, we decided to distribute the conference proceedings electronically, and did not print paper proceedings.

ICMI traditionally gives outstanding paper awards. The Program Chairs pre-selected the top-ranked paper submissions based on the reviews and meta-reviews and identified the nominees for both the *Outstanding Paper Award* and *Outstanding Student Paper Award*. An Outstanding Paper Award committee was created with internationally renowned researchers in multimodal interaction. The committee reviewed these top-ranked papers carefully and selected the recipients of the *Outstanding Student Paper Award* and the *Outstanding Paper Award*.

Beginning this year, the ICMI Advisory Board established three new awards. The *Sustained Accomplishment Award* is presented to a scientist who has made innovative and long-lasting contributions to our field. The Award acknowledges an individual who has demonstrated vision in shaping the field, with a sustained record of research that has influenced the work of others. The *Ten-Year Technical Impact Award* is presented to a group of scientists for contributing a seminal paper published in ICMI (or conferences and workshops that evolved into ICMI). For its first edition, this award is given to a paper published 10 years or more in the past. Finally, the *Community Service Award* is presented to an individual for making sustained organizational contributions with positive impact on the ICMI community. The awardees for all categories are announced at the conference banquet.

As in previous editions, ICMI 2014 has been organized with the support of ACM and SIGCHI. In addition, considerable support has been provided by our generous sponsors. We have two diamond sponsors (SAP Innovation Center Turkey and NSF), and one gold sponsor (Openstream). We have received additional infrastructure and logistics support from Boğaziçi University, where the conference takes place. Turkish Airlines was our official airline. For Dr. Robinson's keynote, we thank the ACM Distinguished Speakers Program. We are grateful for the support extended by all these organizations.

The chairs would like to thank our colleagues on the conference organization committee for their contributions and for the great dialogue that made this organization into a smooth and enjoyable experience: Alexandros Potamianos, Carlos Busso, Kazuhiro Otsuka, Lale Akarun, Dirk Heylen, Hatice Gunes, Marco Cristani, and Justine Cassell; our Publication Chairs Alessandro Vinciarelli and Zakia Hammal, our Publicity Chairs Toyoaki Nishida and Nicu Sebe, our Sponsorship Chair Aytül Erçil, and our Local Organization Chair, Hazım Kemal Ekenel. We thank Julien Epps, the General Chair of ICMI 2013, and the ICMI Advisory Board for their support and guidance. We thank all Senior Program Committee members, Doctoral Consortium Program Committee members, Doctoral Consortium mentors, and volunteer reviewers who contributed time and effort to the review process and made it possible to develop such a high quality technical program. Finally, we thank our colleagues at Sheridan Communications, Ashley Cozzi (ACM), Cem Tuncel (BROS) Bilge Yüksel (BROS), Alen Demirel (BROS) and Hasan Küçük (BROS) for their support in the ICMI'14 organization.

Albert Ali Salah
ICMI'14 General Chair
Boğaziçi University, Turkey

Jeffrey Cohn
ICMI'14 General Chair
University of Pittsburgh, USA

Björn Schuller
ICMI'14 General Chair
University of Passau, Germany / Imperial College London, UK

Oya Aran
ICMI'14 Program Chair
Idiap Research Institute, Switzerland

Louis-Philippe Morency
ICMI'14 Program Chair
University of Southern California, USA

Philip R. Cohen
ICMI'14 Program Chair
Adapx, USA

Table of Contents

Poster Session

Session Chairs: Oya Aran *(Idiap Research Institute)* & Louis-Philippe Morency *(University of Southern California)*

Keynote Address 2

Session Chair: Louis-Philippe Morency *(University of Southern California)*

Oral Session 3: Affect and Cognitive Modeling

Session Chair: Sharon Oviatt *(Incaa Designs)*

Oral Session 4: Nonverbal Behaviors

Session Chair: Bülent Sankur *(Boğaziçi University)*

Doctoral Spotlight Session

Session Chair: Marco Cristani *(University of Verona)*

The Second Emotion Recognition In The Wild Challenge

MLA'14 Workshop & Challenge Presentations

(Co-located presentations may be found at enter doi link to workshop proceedings*)*

MAPTRAITS'14 Workshop & Challenge Presentations

(Co-located presentations may be found at enter doi link to workshop proceedings*)*

Workshop Overviews

ICMI 2014 Conference Organization

General Chairs: Albert Ali Salah *(Boğaziçi University, Turkey)*
Jeffrey Cohn *(University of Pittsburgh, USA)*
Björn Schuller *(University of Passau, Germany and Imperial College London, UK)*

Program Chairs: Oya Aran *(Idiap Research Institute, Switzerland)*
Louis-Philippe Morency *(University of Southern California, USA)*
Philip R. Cohen *(Adapx, USA)*

Workshop Chairs: Alexandros Potamianos *(University of Crete, Greece)*
Carlos Busso *(The University of Texas at Dallas, USA)*

Demo Chairs: Kazuhiro Otsuka *(NTT Communication Science Laboratories, Japan)*
Lale Akarun *(Boğaziçi University, Turkey)*

Multimodal Grand Challenge Chairs: Dirk Heylen *(University of Twente, The Netherlands)*
Hatice Gunes *(Queen Mary University of London, UK)*

Doctoral Consortium Chairs: Marco Cristani *(University of Verona, Italy)*
Justine Cassell *(Carnegie Mellon University, USA)*

Publication Chairs: Zakia Hammal *(Carnegie Mellon University, USA)*
Alessandro Vinciarelli *(University of Glasgow, UK)*

Publicity Chairs: Nicu Sebe *(University of Trento, Italy)*
Toyoaki Nishida *(Kyoto University, Japan)*

Sponsorship Chair: Aytül Erçil *(Sabancı University, Turkey)*

Local Organization Chairs: Hazım Kemal Ekenel *(Istanbul Technical University, Turkey)*
Hande Alemdar *(Boğaziçi University, Turkey)*

Senior Program Committee: Bert Arnrich *(Boğaziçi University, Turkey)*
Dan Bohus *(Microsoft Research, USA)*
Mary Czerwinski *(Microsoft Research, USA)*
Sidney D'Mello *(University of Notre Dame, USA)*
Vanessa Evers *(University of Twente, the Netherlands)*
Roland Goecke *(University of Canberra, Australia)*
Jonathan Gratch *(University of Southern California, USA)*
Ashish Kapoor *(Microsoft Research, USA)*
Samuel Kaski *(Aalto University, Finland)*

Senior Program Committee (continued):

Stefan Kopp *(University of Bielefeld, Germany)*
Simon Lucey *(Carnegie Mellon University, USA)*
Nadia Magnenat-Thalmann *(Nanyang Technological University, Singapore)*
Kenji Mase *(Nagoya University, Japan)*
Konstantinos Moustakas *(University of Patras, Greece)*
Shrikanth Narayanan *(University of Southern California, USA)*
Anton Nijholt *(University of Twente, the Netherlands)*
Sharon Oviatt *(Incaa Designs, USA)*
Catherine Pelachaud *(CNRS-LTCI, Télécom-ParisTech, France)*
Bülent Sankur *(Boğaziçi University, Turkey)*
Metin Sezgin *(Koç University, Turkey)*
Gualtiero Volpe *(University of Genova, Italy)*
Stefanos Zafeiriou *(Imperial College London, UK)*
Yu Zheng *(Microsoft Research Asia, China)*

Doctoral Consortium Program Committee:

Henry Been-Lirn Duh *(National University of Singapore, Singapore)*
Dick Bulterman *(Vrije Universiteit, the Netherlands)*
Daragh Byrne *(Carnegie Mellon University, USA)*
Sylvain Castagnos *(LORIA, France)*
Andrea Cavallaro *(Queen Mary University of London, UK)*
Dong Seon Cheng *(Hankuk University of Foreign Studies, Korea)*
Sidney D'Mello *(University of Notre Dame, France)*
Federico Fontana *(University of Udine, Italy)*
Hatice Gunes *(Queen Mary University of London, UK)*
Riad Hammoud *(BAE Systems, UK)*
Hayley Hung *(TU Delft, the Netherlands)*
Shuqiang Jiang *(Institute of Computing Technology, China)*
Marc Erich Latoschik *(Würzburg University, Germany)*
Nadia Magnenat-Thalmann *(Nanyang Technological University, Singapore)*
David McGookin *(Heriot-Watt University, UK)*
Vittorio Murino *(Istituto Italiano di Tecnologia, Italy)*
Andreas Pusch *(Würzburg University, Germany)*
Davide Rocchesso *(IUAV, Italy)*
Nicu Sebe *(University of Trento, Italy)*
Roberto Vezzani *(University of Modena, Italy)*

ICMI 2014 Additional Reviewers

Samer Al Moubayed
Vicent Alabau
Francesc Alías Pujol
Miguel Alonso-Arevalo
Robin Aly
Nese Alyuz
Sean Andrist
Lisa Anthony
Nontas Antonakos
Mobolaji Ayoade
Felipe Bacim
Tadas Baltrušaitis
Timo Baumann
Aryel Beck
Christian Becker Asano
Hrvoje Benko
Kirsten Bergmann
Jonas Beskow
Nadia Bianchi-Berthouze
Brigitte Bigi
Guido Bologna
Brennon Bortz
Nigel Bosch
Frank Broz
Andreas Bulling
Hendrik Buschmeier
Qin Cai
Sergio Canazza
George Caridakis
Sait Celebi
Lei Chen
Liming Chen
Silvia Chiappa
Phil Cohen
Cristina Conati
Daniel Davison
Iwan de Kok
Celso de Melo
Roelof de Vries
Cenk Demiroğlu
Hamdi Dibeklioğlu
Trinh Minh Tri Do
Anastasios Drosou
Andrew Duchowski
Bruno Dumas
Aaron Elkins
Yu Enokibori
Julien Epps
Engin Erzin
Taner Eskil
Anna Esposito
Florian Eyben
Gaelle Ferre
Anthony Fleury
Mary Ellen Foster
Takeshi Furuhashi
Jorge Gallego Perez
Daniel Gatica-Perez
Patrick Gebhard
Guillaume Gibert
Ran Gilad-Bachrach
Dorota Glowacka
Jon Ander Gomez Adrian
Joseph Grafsgaard
Dimitris Grammenos
David Griol
Hatice Gunes
Yuki Hayashi
Takatsugu Hirayama
Mohammed Hoque
Hung-Hsuan Huang
Eva Hudlicka
Hayley Hung
Wolfgang Hürst
Tanveer Iftekhar
Bihan Jiang
Michael Johnston
Kristiina Jokinen
Michiel Joosse
Kyriaki Kalimeri
Kouichi Katsurada
Casey Kennington
Felix Kistler
Markus Koskela
Irene Kotsia
Aleksandra Krolak
Ayşe Küçükyılmaz
Tsvi Kuflik
Denis Lalanne
Joe LaViola
Jonathan Le Roux
Iolanda Leite
Luis Leiva
Bruno Lepri
Vincent Levesque
Haifeng Li
David Lindlbauer
Tong Liu
Manja Lohse
Patrick Lucey
Nadia Mana
Maurizio Mancini
Erik Marchi
Ioannis Marras
Brais Martinez
Stefano Masneri
Roderick McCall
David McGee
Gregor Mehlmann
Cetin Mericli
Wolfgang Minker
Teruhisa Misu
Gelareh Mohammadi
Junya Morita
Emily Mower Provost
Mihalis A. Nicolaou
Radoslaw Niewiadomski
Iason Nikolas
Pedro Nogueira
David Novick
Mohammad Obaid
Catharine Oertel
Shogo Okada
Eva Oliveira
Rieks op den Akker
George Papagiannakis
Chris Papapavlou
Stavros Petridis
Martin Pielot

Isabella Poggi
Ronald Poppe
Benjamin Poppinga
Gerasimos Potamianos
Shaolin Qu
Jose Francisco Quesada Moreno
Bayu Rahayudi
Shyam Sundar Rajagopalan
Norbert Reithinger
Elisa Ricci
Laurel D. Riek
Peter Robinson
Luis Rodríguez
Teresa Romão
Ognjen Rudovic
Maha Salem
Georgia Sandbach
Allison Sauppé
Kai Schadenberg
Stefan Scherer
David Schlangen
Tim Schwartz
Thibaud Senechal
Hui Shi
Enrique Sánchez-Lozano
Candace Sidner
Gabriel Skantze
Yale Song
Stefan Steidl
Rainer Stiefelhagen
Yusuke Sugano
Daniel Thalmann
Khiet Truong
Jack Valmadre
Michel Valstar
Giovanna Varni
Radu-Daniel Vatavu
Brian Vaughan
Torben Wallbaum
Yilun Wang
Lei Wei
Felix Weninger
Jason D. Williams
Graham Wilson
Christian Wolf
Bo Xiao
Kazunori Yamada
Yingxiang Yang
Anil Yüce
Cristina Zaga
Cha Zhang
Yin Zhou
Gottfried Zimmermann

ICMI 2014 Sponsor & Supporters

Sponsor:

SIGCHI

Supporters:

SAP INNOVATION CENTER TURKEY

Openstream® Making Communications Smarter

NSF

BOĞAZİÇİ ÜNİVERSİTESİ 1863 150TH YIL | YEAR

TÜBİTAK

TURKISH AIRLINES A STAR ALLIANCE MEMBER

Bursting our Digital Bubbles: Life Beyond the App

Yvonne Rogers
UCLIC, University College London, London, UK

Abstract

30 years ago, a common caricature of computing was of a frustrated user sat staring at a PC hands hovering over a keyboard and mouse. Nowadays, the picture is very different. The PC has been largely overtaken by the laptop, the smartphone and the tablet; more and more people are using them extensively and everywhere as they go about their working and everyday lives. Instead the caricature has become one of people increasingly living in their own digital bubbles - heads-down glued to a mobile device, pecking and swiping at digital content with one finger. How can designers and researchers break out of this app mindset to exploit the new generation of affordable *multimodal* technologies, in the form of physical computing, internet of things, and sensor toolkits, to begin creating more diverse heads-up, hands-on, arms-out user experiences? In my talk I will argue for a radical rethink of our relationship with future technologies. One that inspires us, through shared devices, tools and data, to be more creative, playful and thoughtful of each other and our surrounding environments.

Categories and Subject Descriptors
H.5.2 User Interfaces

Keywords: Digital bubble; Mindful technology; vision; creative technology, HCI

Short Bio

Yvonne Rogers is a Professor of Interaction Design, the director of UCLIC and a deputy head of the Computer Science department at UCL. Her research interests are in the areas of ubiquitous computing, interaction design and human-computer interaction. A central theme is how to design interactive technologies that can enhance life by augmenting and extending everyday, learning and work activities. This involves informing, building and evaluating novel user experiences through creating and assembling a diversity of pervasive technologies.

Yvonne is also the PI at UCL for the Intel Collaborative Research Institute on Sustainable Connected Cities (ICRI Cities) which was launched in October 2012 as a joint collaboration with Imperial College. She was awarded a

prestigious EPSRC dream fellowship rethinking the relationship between ageing, computing and creativity.

She is a visiting professor at the Open University and Indiana University. She has spent sabbaticals at Stanford, Apple, Queensland University, University of Cape Town, University of Melbourne, QUT and UC San Diego.

Central to her work is a critical stance towards how visions, theories and frameworks shape the fields of HCI, cognitive science and Ubicomp. She has been instrumental in promulgating new theories (e.g., external cognition), alternative methodologies (e.g., in the wild studies) and far-reaching research agendas (e.g., "Being Human: HCI in 2020" manifesto). She has also published a monograph (2012) called "HCI Theory: Classical, Modern and Contemporary."

From 2006-2011, Yvonne was professor of HCI in the Computing Department at the OU, where she set up the Pervasive Interaction Lab. From 2003-2006, she was a professor in Informatics at Indiana University. Prior to this, she spent 11 years at the former School of Cognitive and Computing Sciences at Sussex University.

Yvonne was one of the principal investigators on the UK Equator Project (2000-2007) where she pioneered ubiquitous learning. She has published widely, beginning with her PhD work on graphical interfaces to her recent work on public visualizations and behavioral change. She is one of the authors of the definitive textbook on Interaction Design and HCI now in its 3rd edition that has sold over 150,000 copies worldwide and has been translated into 6 languages. She is a Fellow of the British Computer Society and the ACM's CHI Academy.

ICMI '14, Nov 12-16 2014, Istanbul, Turkey
ACM 978-1-4503-2885-2/14/11.
http://dx.doi.org/10.1145/2663204.2669984

Managing Human-Robot Engagement with Forecasts and... *um...* Hesitations

Dan Bohus
Microsoft Research
One Microsoft Way
Redmond, WA, 98052
+1-425-706-5880
dbohus@microsoft.com

Eric Horvitz
Microsoft Research
One Microsoft Way
Redmond, WA, 98052
+1-425-706-2127
horvitz@microsoft.com

ABSTRACT
We explore methods for managing conversational engagement in open-world, physically situated dialog systems. We investigate a self-supervised methodology for constructing forecasting models that aim to anticipate when participants are about to terminate their interactions with a situated system. We study how these models can be leveraged to guide a disengagement policy that uses linguistic hesitation actions, such as filled and non-filled pauses, when uncertainty about the continuation of engagement arises. The hesitations allow for additional time for sensing and inference, and convey the system's uncertainty. We report results from a study of the proposed approach with a directions-giving robot deployed in the wild.

Categories and Subject Descriptors
H.1.2 **[Models and Principles]:** User/Machine System – *Human Information Processing*; H.5.2 **[Information Interfaces and Presentation]**: Multimedia Information Systems – *Audio input/outputs;* User Interfaces – *Natural Language*; I.4.8 **[Scene Analysis]**: Tracking, Sensor Fusion

General Terms
Algorithms, Human Factors

Keywords
Engagement; hesitation actions; filled pauses; forecasting models; human-robot interaction; multimodal interaction; self-supervision.

1. INTRODUCTION
Situated, multimodal interactive systems typically grapple with multiple uncertainties as they perceive, infer, and act. In addition to challenges with speech recognition, such systems face uncertainties in the visual space, and in the multimodal inferences they make such as tracking the location of users, their focus of attention, gestures, engagement, floor control actions, and intentions. Beyond real-time inferences about the state of world, the systems may leverage the ability to forecast future states, and use such forecasts for planning and decision making. For instance, in making a decision about taking a turn in a multiparty conversation, a robot or virtual agent may need to consider who is likely to start talking next and when? Similarly, the ability to anticipate that people are about to enter or leave a conversation, or that their focus of attention may shift, can help support the planning of verbal and gestural outputs in a manner that leads to more fluid interactions.

We explore the construction and use of forecasting models that enable interactive systems to make inferences about the near-term future. In particular, we investigate a self-supervised approach to constructing these models that does not require manual annotations. Furthermore, we investigate the use of linguistic hesitation actions that can signal the system's state of confusion and generate additional time for collecting evidence and resolving uncertainties. We explore the use of forecasts and hesitations both separately and together, showing how forecasts can guide hesitations.

While the proposed forecasting and hesitation mechanisms are applicable to a variety of interaction problems, we explore their use in the context of managing conversational disengagement in a physically situated interactive system. Starting with a conservative, heuristic model for disengagement, we present methods for learning a forecasting model that is guided by this heuristic and that aims to anticipate whether participants will terminate their interactions with the system. We show how this self-supervised model can guide disengagement policies that use hesitations when situations of high uncertainty about the future arise. Specifically, if the model indicates that participants might disengage, the system may insert a filled pause, *"So ... "*, and, as it collects more evidence, the next contribution can be generated accordingly, for instance: *"Anything else I can do for you?"* if the participants remain engaged, or *"Well, I'll catch you later then."* if they disengage.

We begin with a review of related work. Next, in Section 3, we motivate and articulate the open-world disengagement challenge. We outline the proposed approach in Section 4, present empirical results in Section 5, and discuss limitations, lessons learned and future opportunities in Section 6. Section 7 summarizes the paper.

2. RELATED WORK
The ability to establish and maintain an open communication channel is a foundational competency for spoken language interaction. In physically situated settings, participants committed

ICMI '14, November 12 - 16 2014, Istanbul, Turkey.

ACM 978-1-4503-2885-2/14/11…$15.00
http://dx.doi.org/10.1145/2663204.2663241

to an interaction typically enter into and maintain a certain spatial orientation, or *f-formation* [1], and actively signal and manage their conversational engagement by a variety of verbal and non-verbal cues, including gaze, gesture and body language.

Several strands of research have investigated various aspects of the engagement process in situated interactive systems. Sidner and colleagues [2] showed that people direct their attention to a robot more often if the robot performed engagement behaviors. A model of engagement for human-robot interaction based on connection events is proposed and implemented in [3]. In [4] a model of engagement based on proxemics was proposed and evaluated with a receptionist robot. In our own previous work, we have proposed a computational model for managing engagement with a situated agent in multiparty, open-world settings [5]. Furthermore, in [6], we have showed how, by starting with a conservative heuristic for detecting when people are initiating their engagement with a conversational agent, we can learn to predict this event from visual features. In this work, we focus instead on the problem of *disengagement*, and show how a similar, self-supervised forecasting approach can be used to anticipate when participants are about to finish their interactions. In addition, we conduct an online evaluation of the learned model, and investigate how it can guide disengagement policies that leverage hesitation actions to mitigate situations of high uncertainty.

Hesitations and disfluencies abound in conversational speech, and have previously been the object of linguistic investigation. For instance, [7] discusses the use of filled pauses like *uh* and *um* and, based on a corpus analysis, conclude that they are used to signal short (*uh*) or long (*um*) production pauses. In [8], a survey of previous analyses of fillers and hesitations is presented, indicating that fillers occur in situations where speakers are uncertain about choices they need to make, and that they facilitate understanding and allow listeners to assess the speaker's level of confidence.

In human-computer interaction, methods have been proposed for detecting filled pauses during speech recognition [9, 10], and for modeling and producing them during synthesis [11]. In efforts more closely related to this work, filled pauses have also been used in incremental natural language generation systems. For instance, results from a Wizard of Oz study [12] indicate that an incremental natural language generation system leveraging filled pauses, as well as overt and covert self-corrections, can achieve shorter response times and is perceived as more efficient than a non-incremental generator, even though it produces longer utterances. [13] presents an analysis of types of user reactions occurring while pausing by using filled pauses, gaze, and syntactic completeness. Reinforcement learning methods for guiding incremental generation of natural language were shown to avoid long waiting times and minimize the use of fillers and self-corrections [14].

We use filled pauses as hesitation devices to endow a system with the ability to generate additional time for perception and decision making, as well as to display the uncertainty the system has. In distinction to prior efforts, we operate in the more complex setting of a multimodal, physically situated interactive system. Our focus is on uncertainties and decisions related to managing engagement. The generation of filled pauses is driven by a learned model that uses multimodal information to continuously forecast whether participants are about to terminate their interactions with the system. Finally, we conduct and report results from an end-to-end, in-the-wild study of the proposed approach with a deployed human-robot interactive system.

3. PROBLEM

We focus on the problem of managing conversational engagement, defined in [2] as "the process by which two (or more) participants establish, maintain and end their perceived connection during interactions they jointly undertake". As an experimental platform, we use Directions Robot [15], a system that couples a platform of physically situated interaction [16] with a Nao humanoid robot [17]. The system uses language synchronized with gestures to provide directions to people's offices, conference rooms, and other public areas inside our building; a video is available at http://sdrv.ms/15Yay8V. The robot is deployed in an open space, in front of the elevators on the 3rd floor, in a standing setup shown in Figure 1. The usual traffic in this area includes people with offices on the floor, as well as visitors, who come to see people or attend meetings in the building, and who are often unfamiliar with the surroundings.

Managing engagement in physically situated settings is a challenging multimodal problem. Engagement is a mixed-initiative, jointly coordinated process, involving multiple signals across different channels, including proxemics and body orientation, eye gaze, head and hand gestures, verbal and non-verbal behaviors. The open-world deployment of the Directions Robot brings additional challenges: interactions often involve groups of people, and are sometimes driven by actual needs and often by curiosity about the robot. People come and go at will, and their focus of attention is often shared between the robot and other people in a group, bystanders, or people passing by.

The Directions Robot manages engagement via a computational model previously described in [5]. For every person in the scene, the robot reasons about the engagement *state*, *actions,* and *intentions*, and makes engagement decisions based on these inferences. The *engagement state* captures whether or not a person is engaged in an interaction with the system. The *engagement intention* reflects whether or not the person wants to be engaged with the system. Finally, *engagement actions* model whether a person is performing a maintaining or disengaging action (if engaged), or an initiating action versus no action (if not engaged).

In a previous set of experiments [15], we explored the use of heuristic and machine-learned models for inferring engagement actions performed by people in the scene. In addition to bringing to the fore some of the challenges with managing engagement that we have already outlined, the study also highlighted a tradeoff between making early, incorrect disengagement decisions, versus being more conservative, and making these decisions too late. We found that, when using a model that we had learned from data, the robot would sometimes disengage abruptly if a participant would turn their attention towards another person in their group, or towards the direction that the robot was pointing to while it provided directions. Such head turns and motions resemble the beginning of disengagements. Committing false-positive errors on detecting disengagement is very costly as the robot disengages and bids the user a goodbye inappropriately, while the user expects the conversation to continue. A more conservative approach for inferring disengagement (such as a heuristic rule used in the study) may largely avoid such false positives, but can in turn lead to late disengagement decisions. As a result, the robot sometimes tries to continue the dialog while the participants are leaving.

4. APPROACH

Motivated in part by lessons learned from this initial user study, we investigate methods for managing disengagement decisions that address this tradeoff. We present a methodology where the system

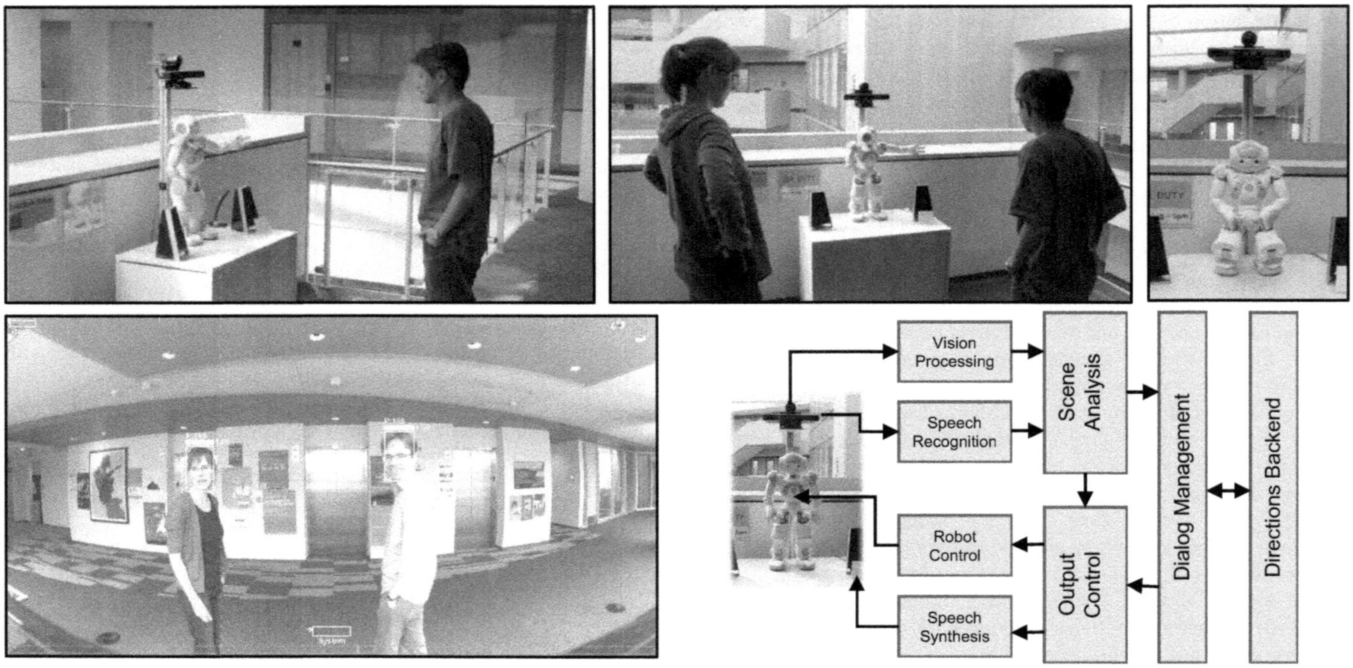

Figure 1. Directions Robot, from top-left to bottom-right: robot interacting with one participant; robot interacting with two participants; robot in offline position; sample view from system camera; system diagram.

automatically learns, in a self-supervised manner, to *forecast* whether participants will shortly disengage. This prediction is accomplished by starting with a conservative heuristic for detecting disengagement, and learning to predict when this heuristic will signal disengagement *ahead of time*, from available real-time multimodal features. In addition to this forecasting model, we explore the use of *hesitation actions* such as filled and non-filled pauses, in situations of high uncertainty about the future. Producing filled pauses can reflect the system's state, allow for more time for gathering evidence, and mitigate disengagement decisions that may have a high cost. We describe the details of the approach below.

4.1 Forecasting Disengagement

The forecasting model for disengagement aims to assess the likelihood that a participant will disengage with the system within some small time interval or *lookahead* (*e.g.*, 5 seconds) into the future. We expect that the ability to forecast disengagement can inform better decision-making, and help avoid late contributions.

The self-supervised methodology for training this predictive model relies on initially running the system with a heuristic rule for assessing disengagement that is conservative, or high-precision: the rule aims to commit no false positives, *i.e.*, it only indicates disengagement when it has indeed happened, at the cost of potentially being late. We construct this heuristic by leveraging features that capture how close the participant is, whether a participant is stationary or moving, and whether or not a participant is attending to the robot.

As an example, Figure 2 shows a trace of key variables for a participant, over time. The top three plots show the location of the face in the x dimension (A), the width of the face (B), and the probability that the participant's attention is on the system computed via a probabilistic model (C). These raw streams are used to compute measures of proximity, stability, and attention, which are in turn used via a heuristic rule (see more details in the next section) to estimate the probability of disengagement – shown in Figure 2.D. Based on interaction data collected by the system, we

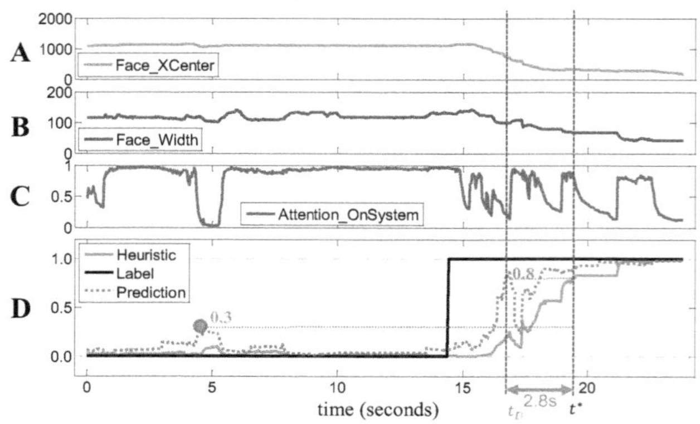

Figure 2. User trace. A: location of face, B: width of face, C: inferences about attention of user on system, and D: heuristic inference, labels, and forecasting model

can automatically define a target label for the forecasting model at every frame: the label (also shown in Figure 2.D) is 1 if the conservative heuristic signals disengagement with probability > 0.8 within the lookahead window (in this case 5 seconds), and 0 otherwise. The disengagement forecasting model is trained to predict this label at every frame, from existing features. The probability of future disengagement computed by running a trained forecasting model is also shown in Figure 2.D.

4.2 Disengagement Policy with Hesitations

The second focus of this work is the study of a disengagement policy that relies on hesitation actions such as filled and non-filled pauses to mitigate high-cost disengagement decisions. The central idea is that, in situations of high uncertainty about the future engagement state of the participants, instead of issuing the next dialog contribution, the system can instead produce a hesitation, *e.g.*, slowly saying *"So ... "* as a non-committal linguistic action that leaves the options open for either continuing or finishing the engagement.

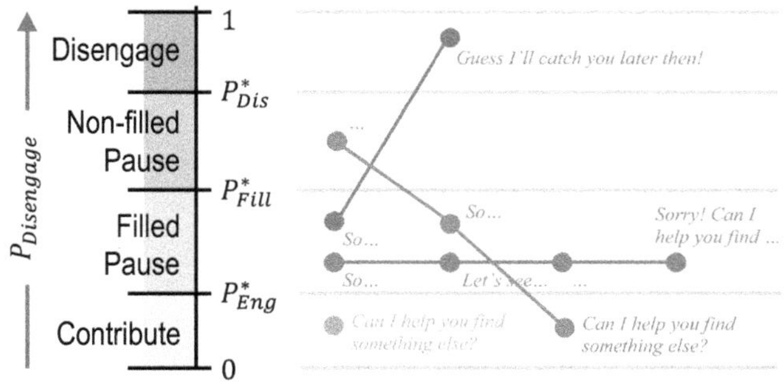

Figure 3. Disengagement policy with hesitation actions.

The disengagement policy chooses among four possible actions by comparing the probability of disengagement against three predefined thresholds, as shown in Figure 3. As with the standard policy, the probability of disengagement is compared at every frame against a disengagement threshold, and, if it exceeds the threshold ($P_D > P^*_{Dis}$), the system disengages. In addition, every time the system is about to take a turn, a decision is made about whether a filled or non-filled pause should be triggered instead. If the probability of disengagement is low, *i.e.* smaller than a corresponding engagement threshold ($P_D < P^*_{Eng}$), the system takes the turn and generates its next contribution. If the probability of disengagement falls the middle range ($P^*_{Eng} < P_D < P^*_{Dis}$), the new policy triggers instead a hesitation action, in the form of a filled or a non-filled pause. Filled-pauses, *i.e., "So...,"* or *"Let's see...,"* accompanied by an extended arm gesture toward the participant are produced when the probability of disengagement is smaller than a preset filled-pause threshold ($P^*_{Eng} < P_D < P^*_{Fill}$); non-filled pauses are produced otherwise ($P^*_{Fill} < P_D < P^*_{Dis}$).

The filled and non-filled pauses are hesitation actions that allow the system to buy more time, at a relatively low cost. As the hesitation action is being produced, the system can gather additional evidence over time that will hopefully lead to resolving the uncertainty: the system will eventually figure out whether or not the participants are disengaging and can perform the correct action. The expected cost of these hesitations is lower compared to a potentially incorrect engaging or disengaging action. In addition, the production of a filled pause also conveys to the user the system's difficulty with making a choice [8] at this time.

If the uncertainty persists, the policy re-runs, and may produce a succession of hesitations. If the probability of disengagement remains in the filled-pause region and the system should take a turn, the system produces up to two successive filled pauses, *i.e., "So...," "Let's see...,"* followed by a non-filled pause, and eventually a contribution if the uncertainty still persists (blue trace in Figure 3) If the probability of disengagement drops back into the engaging region after the system produced a hesitation, and more than 2 seconds have elapsed since, the system inserts an overt self-repair—*"Sorry!"* before issuing its next contribution, to share a reflection with the user about the hesitation, and prior uncertainty and its resolution. We believe the apology can help further mitigate the costs of the filled pause.

5. EXPERIMENTS AND RESULTS

We now describe the experiments conducted with the proposed approach. The test-bed for these experiments is the *Directions Robot,* a robotic system deployed in the wild that can interact with one or multiple participants via natural language, and provide directions to people and offices in our building. The system combines a Nao humanoid robot with off-board sensors and computation. A high-resolution wide-angle camera and a Kinect sensor are placed above the robot, and a multi-core desktop computer runs the software infrastructure and controls the robot. The software subsumes components for making inferences from audio-visual signals (*e.g.*, face tracking, speech recognition, *etc.*) and combines them with interaction planning, decision making, and output generation. In addition, the robot leverages directory information and a building map framework to construct spoken directions. A video is available at http://sdrv.ms/15Yay8V.

5.1 Baseline Inference and Policy

The baseline system was equipped with a conservative inference model for assessing disengagement. This model was manually crafted, taken into account lessons learned from a previous user study [15]. It constructed an estimate for the probability that a participant is disengaging by combining three continuous scores (in the 0-1 interval), capturing three signals of engagement: *proximity* (*P*), *stability* (*S*), and *attention persistence* (*A*), according to the equation below:

$$P_D = 1 - P \cdot (1 - (1 - S) \cdot (1 - A))$$

This heuristic requires that proximity is high and at least one of stability or attention is high in order for the user to be considered engaged. If the proximity score is low, or alternatively if both stability and attention are low, the probability of disengagement moves towards one. The scores for proximity, stability and attention persistence were computed by applying a sigmoid transform to a base feature. For proximity, the base feature was the size of the tracked face. For stability, the base feature measured the ratio between the max horizontal excursion of the face throughout the last one second and the size of the face. Finally, for attention persistence the base feature was computed by averaging over the past two seconds the probability that the user is attending to the system. The latter probability is computed by a machine learned model that uses face tracking and head pose information. The parameters of each sigmoid normalization function were manually tuned to ensure a conservative inference model, which aims to minimize the false-positive rate.

The default policy for making engagement control decisions relies on the computed probability of disengagement: when this exceeds a preset threshold, the robot disengages with the participant. The interaction is terminated when the last participant is being disengaged. The final disengagement action performed by the robot depends on the current dialog state. If disengagement occurs near the beginning of the dialog, the robot terminates the interaction without any speech or gesture: this covers mostly cases when the engagement was incorrectly initiated with a person going by. If the disengagement occurs in the middle of the dialog, the robot says "*Well, guess I'll catch you later then!*" communicating its surprise at the early disengagement. Finally, if the engagement terminates after directions were given, a simple salutation such as *"Bye bye!"* is performed, accompanied by a hand-waving gesture. In addition, when interrupting its own speech to terminate an interaction, the robot produces a synthetic disfluency (if the break did not occur on a word boundary) to further indicate its surprise, followed by a final, *"Oops! Guess I'll catch you later then."*

Given challenges with tracking multiple participants in open-world settings, the vision system may sometimes lose track of an engaged participant. In this case, to avoid an immediate termination of engagement, the participant is persisted in an *invisible* mode for a short period, giving the tracker a chance to recover. While the participant is in this invisible mode, the heuristic rule increases the probability of disengagement from the last known value towards one, ensuring that the disengagement threshold is reached in five seconds since the face was lost. If the track is still not recovered at that point, the system disengages with the invisible participant. The baseline policy is adjusted to avoid producing any verbal contributions if all engaged participants are in this invisible state. Since lost faces often occur when people turn and leave abruptly, this policy reduces the chances of the robot issuing a late verbal contribution, while people are trying to disengage.

5.2 Forecasting Disengagement

5.2.1 Data

The data for constructing the forecasting model for disengagement was collected by running the baseline system described above for a period of 5 days. Throughout this time, the robot initiated 133 interactions. The resulting dataset for training the forecasting model contained 158 user traces (due to the multiparty interaction setting, there are more user traces than interactions), and ~126K frames or data-points.

5.2.2 Labels and Features

For each frame in a user trace, labels indicating whether disengagement would occur (according to the baseline heuristic) within a future time window were automatically constructed, as described in Section 4.1. We explored the use of models with different lookaheads, ranging from 3 to 6 seconds. We also investigated the use of different classes of features, spanning multiple knowledge sources and modalities:

- *FaceLocation* (51 features): the horizontal location and the size of the tracked face, and derived feature streams capturing statistics of these signals such as average, slope, standard deviation, excursion over past time windows ranging from 250ms to 8 seconds. In addition, we added the base stability feature that was used in the baseline heuristic.
- *TrackingConfidence* (18 features): the tracking confidence score, and derived feature streams capturing the average and slope of this signal over past time windows; in addition we used information about whether the face was currently invisible, and for long this situation persisted.
- *Focus-of-Attention* (19 features): the probability that the user is attending to the system produced by the attention inference model, together with derived streams capturing un-weighted and time-based exponentially weighted averages, as well as the slope of this signal across past time windows.
- *Interaction/Dialog* (116 features): features that encode the current dialog state as well as derived features that describe and how long the system has been in that state; the dialog state generally corresponds to the system's semantic output, *e.g., DoYouNeedHelp, LocationConfirm, WhatAreYouLookingFor*. We also include here turn-taking information such as whether the system or a user is currently speaking, and related timing information. Finally, we include the total number of people detected in the scene and the number of users engaged in the interaction.
- *BaselineHeuristic* (1 feature): the baseline heuristic described above was also considered as a feature.

5.2.3 Model Training and Selection

We trained logistic regression and boosted decision tree models, with various parameterizations: for logistic regression we explored the use of different L1 and L2 regularization weights, while for boosted trees we changed the number of leaves (2, 4, 8), the number of trees constructed (500, 1000, 2000), and the learning rate. We identified the best logistic regression and boosted tree model across these different parameterizations for each specified lookahead.

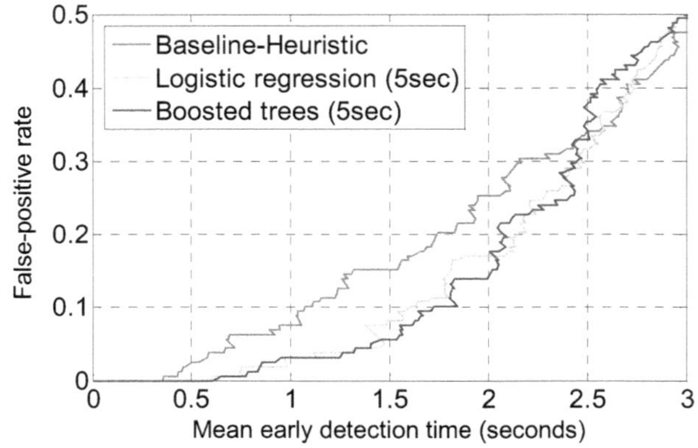

Figure 4. False-positive rate versus mean early-detection-time at different thresholds.

Each of these models implements a particular tradeoff between the false-positive rate and how early the future disengagement may be detected. To illustrate this, consider again the trace representing the predictions from a given model shown in Figure 2.D. By applying a disengagement threshold, such as 0.8, a correct prediction of disengagement is made 2.8 seconds ahead of the moment that the heuristic signals disengagement. We refer to this time as the *early-detection-time*. If we use a lower disengagement threshold, the prediction might be made even earlier. At the same time, lowering the threshold too much, for instance to 0.3, can lead to false-positives, as marked by the red dot in Figure 2.D.

For each of the pre-selected models, we conducted an analysis where we varied the disengagement threshold and plotted the mean early-detection-time versus the false-positive rate. In this analysis, false positives were defined as any detection earlier than 6 seconds before the heuristic detection; if a user engaged and disengaged multiple times, we considered only the first disengagement event on the user trace. Figure 4 shows the plots for the heuristic baseline, and the best performing logistic regression and boosted trees models. Based on this analysis, we selected the 5-second lookahead logistic regression model. In an effort to keep the false-positives to a minimum, we chose a high disengagement threshold, based on a methodology that aimed to minimize false-positives: we incrementally lowered the threshold from 1.0, until a first false-positive error at a large early-detection-time was found.

Finally, for the chosen model setup, we also investigated how performance varies when using different subsets of features. The frame-based classification error and mean squared error attained by using different subsets of the features are shown in Table 1.

Table 1. Performance with different feature sets

Model	Classification error	Mean squared error
Majority Baseline	**24.9%**	**0.1880**
Heuristic based model (H)	13.9%	0.1134
Focus-of-Attention (A)	17.0%	0.1249
FaceLocation (L)	16.3%	0.1265
TrackingConfidence (C)	18.8%	0.1468
Interaction/Dialog (D)	21.3%	0.1526
A+L	13.5%	0.1057
A+L+C	11.7%	0.0955
A+L+C+D	11.5%	0.0924
Full model (A+L+C+D+H)	**10.9%**	**0.0863**

Training a model using the manually engineered baseline heuristic as a feature produces a model (H) that outperforms the models trained on any of the other feature classes in isolation: focus-of-attention (A), face-location (L), tracking-confidence (C) and interaction/dialog (D). Of these, the focus-of-attention and location features seem to be most informative. Adding them together leads to a model (A+L) that already exceeds the model based on the heuristic (H). Adding the other two feature classes (tracking-confidence and interaction/dialog) further improves performance—see A+L+C+D model in Table 1. Finally, the results indicate that the manually constructed heuristic contains information orthogonal to the models constructed with the other feature classes, as adding it as a feature yields further performance gains for the Full model.

5.3 In-the-Wild Study

The performance assessment presented above indicates that the forecasting model can indeed anticipate disengagement, as signaled by the conservative heuristic, while maintaining a low false-positive rate. In order to understand the effect of this model and hesitation-based policy on the end-to-end system, we deployed the selected model in the live system, and ran an observational user study. To tease apart the effects of the forecasting model and of the hesitation policy, we implemented and contrasted four different conditions for managing disengagement:

- *Baseline (B)*: the system uses the baseline, conservative heuristic for inferring disengagement and the baseline policy.
- *Baseline+Hesitations (B+H)*: the system uses the baseline heuristic for inferring disengagement in conjunction with the hesitation-action policy.
- *Forecast (F)*: the system uses the forecasting model for disengagement, and the baseline policy.
- *Forecast+Hesitations (F+H)*: the system uses the forecasting model for disengagement, and the hesitation-action policy.

The study ran for 19 days, and each time an interaction was initiated, the robot randomly chose one of the four conditions above to use for disengagement. Throughout this time, the robot initiated 589 interactions. 80 of them were eliminated from the analysis: 19 due to various crashing bugs, and 61 due to false initiations of engagement. The remaining corpus contains 509 interactions: 133 (26.1%) in the *Baseline* condition, 123 (24.2%) in the *Baseline+Hesitations* condition, 125 (24.6%) in the *Forecast* condition, and 128 (25.1%) in the *Forecast+Hesitations* condition.

During the user study, we found a subtle bug that postponed the termination of the interaction by a single frame for the F and F+H conditions, in situations where the probability computed by the forecasting model exceeded the disengagement threshold. We believe this very small delay does not affect the results.

We focused the assessment on the system's behavior during the final moments of the interaction, when the last engaged participant was disengaging. The goal was to identify situations where the system continued the dialog inappropriately while participants were leaving, but also situations where the system terminated the interaction too early, prior to the moment participants wished to disengage. An inherent tradeoff exists between these categories: when using a conservative disengagement model and policy, the robot can avoid incorrect, early disengagements, but this comes at the expense of producing more late disengagements, *i.e.*, the system will tend to continue the interaction *after* participants have already terminated their engagement, as they are on their way out. Also, the system often interrupts itself on these contributions, as the disengagement model finally indicates that users are leaving. We expect that, with use of the forecasting model and hesitations, the number of late disengagements would be reduced, without a significant increase in the number of early disengagements.

To identify late disengagements, we developed a tagging scheme that focused on the last system contribution that was not a departure salutation, and identified whether this contribution was produced late with respect to the engagement state of the participants. A contribution was denoted late if it was started after the last engaged participant broke the f-formation and terminated their engagement – *LateStart*, or if it was started correctly, while at least one participant was engaged, but continued after the last participant had left the engagement – *LateContinue*. Otherwise, if at least one participant maintained engagement throughout the system's contribution, the contribution was denoted *OnTime*.

The annotations were performed by a professional tagger, who had access to the video and audio of the interactions from the system's viewpoint, as shown in Figure 1. If the last contribution was a *LateStart*, the annotator also inspected the previous contributions, in order to identify the earliest one that might have been started or continued late. In addition, the annotator also identified early disengagements, *i.e.*, situations when the system stops the conversation early, before the participants actually disengaged; these were assessed at the moment the system started its departure salutation or finished the interaction non-verbally.

To gain a better understanding of the effect of the hesitation actions, we also instructed the annotator to inspect each hesitation action produced (including the non-filled pauses), and mark whether it was acceptable or costly in terms of perceived awkwardness and overall influence on the interaction, when viewed in context. We asked the annotator to write down their observations about how costly hesitation actions influenced the interactions. This analysis aimed to shed more light on classes of problems that occur with hesitation actions, and to identify other aspects that should be taken into account when constructing hesitation policies.

With respect to the perceived naturalness and cost to the interaction, a complex interplay exists between the verbal outputs and hesitations produced by the robot, the timing of their production with respect to the engagement status of the participants, and the broader dialog and situational context. From a disengagement perspective, we considered interactions that contain a late contribution that tries to advance the dialog while participants are disengaging to be unnatural or costly. There are two types of dialog acts however that we believe are less costly if produced even while participants are disengaging. One of them is the *NoProblem* dialog act. Oftentimes, after receiving directions, people thank the robot, and leave. If the thank you is confidently understood, the robot responds with a *no-problem* dialog act, rendered by saying *"You're welcome!"*, or *"No problem!"* This contribution is acceptable even when participants are on their way out as it does not attempt to move the dialog forward and can be seen as a closure. Such closures at a distance occur naturally among people after a disengagement. We denote these contributions *Late(NoProblem)*.

At the onset, we also started with the assumption that the filled pause dialog act – *Late(Hesitation)*, is less costly than a regular dialog act when produced during moments of disengagement. For instance, *"So...,"* followed often by a departure salutation like *"Well, guess I'll catch you later!"* generally has a lower cost than issuing a contribution that tries to advance the dialog. Subsequent data inspection and the annotator analysis revealed however that filled pauses produced late were sometimes judged as costly / awkward; often this had to do with the filled pause causing the disengaging participants to turn their attention back to the system, and sometimes even stop in their tracks. We therefore further

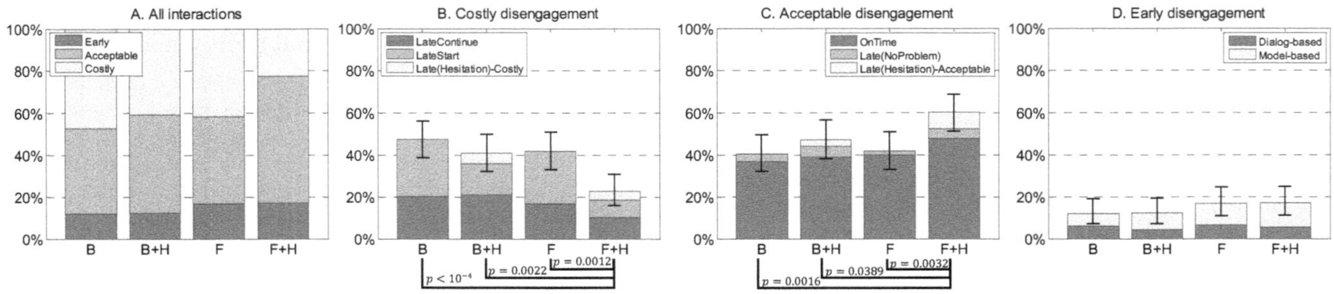

Figure 5. Breakdown of disengagement types.

decomposed these *Late(Hesitation)* acts into *Late(Hesitation)-Costly*, and *Late(Hesitation)-Acceptable*.

Overall, we believe there are various cost differences between interactions that end with a *LateContinue*, *LateStart*, *Late(No-Problem)*, *Late(Hesitation)-Acceptable*, *Late(Hesitation)-Costly*, or with an *OnTime* output. As such, for completeness, we present the corresponding statistics for each of these classes across conditions in Table 2. As a simplifying first order approximation, we considered as *Costly* disengagements the interactions with disengagements ending with a *LateContinue*, *LateStart* and *Late(Hesitation)-Costly* contributions. We also grouped together as *Acceptable* disengagements the ones with *OnTime*, *Late(No-Problem)* and *Late(Hesitation)-Acceptable* contributions. Finally, the third, *Early* disengagement class captures the interactions where the system terminated the engagement prematurely. With this grouping, the proportions of interactions in each of these categories across the four conditions are shown in Table 2 and Figure 5, together with the 95% confidence bounds. Statistically significant differences at a level below 0.05, based on a chi-squared test are shown with the corresponding *p*-values in Figure 5.

When comparing the baseline and forecasting model conditions, no significant differences are observed in the percentage of *Acceptable* disengagements. The percentage of *Costly* disengagements decreases slightly when using the forecasting model, but the difference appears at the expense of a corresponding increase in *Early* disengagements.

Using the hesitations-based policy leads however to larger reductions in the percentages of *Costly* disengagements: 47.4% (B) > 40.7% (B+H), and 41.6% (F) > 22.7% (F+H). The smallest percentage of *Costly* disengagements is attained when using the forecasting disengagement models in conjunction with the hesitation policy (F+H). The results indicate that a large proportion of these gains stem from reducing the number of *LateStart* contributions. As Table 5 indicates, the reductions in *Costly* disengagements when using the hesitation policy happen largely in conjunction with corresponding increasing in the *Acceptable* disengagements, rather than the *Early* ones. The decomposition of *Acceptable* disengagements in Table 5 indicates that in part, the gains observed when using the hesitation policy, *i.e.* when moving from B to B+H, or F to F+H, correspond to interactions where hesitations are inserted late in a manner that does not appear costly to the interaction – the *Late(Hesitation)-Acceptable* line.

Finally, with respect to *Early* disengagements, these can be triggered not only by false-detections of disengagement by the inference model, but also by speech recognition errors: for instance, the system asks *"Is there anything else?"* the participant responds *"Yes"*, and this is misunderstood as *"No"*; the system then terminates the interaction and bids the user goodbye. We report these incorrect *Dialog-based* terminations separately. The results

Disengagement type	B	B+H	F	F+H
Costly	**47.4%**	**40.7%**	**41.6%**	**22.7%**
LateContinue	20.3%	21.1%	16.8%	10.2%
LateStart	27.1%	14.6%	24.8%	8.6%
Late(Hesitation)-Costly	0.0%	4.9%	0.0%	3.9%
Acceptable	**40.6%**	**47.2%**	**41.6%**	**60.2%**
On-time	36.8%	39.0%	40.0%	47.7%
Late(NoProblem)	3.8%	4.9%	1.6%	4.7%
Late(Hesitation)-Acceptable	0.0%	3.3%	0.0%	7.8%
Early	**12.0%**	**12.2%**	**16.8%**	**17.2%**
Dialog-based	6.0%	4.1%	6.4%	5.5%
Model-based	6.0%	8.1%	10.4%	11.7%

Table 2. Breakdown of disengagement types

indicate that with the forecasting model (F and F+H conditions) leads to a slightly increased percentage of *Model-based* early (compared to the B and B+H conditions); the observed differences do not reach statistical significance.

This analysis indicates that overall, the hesitation-based policies based on the forecasting model led to better behaviors on disengagement. However, these policies may also sometimes inadvertently trigger filled and non-filled pauses during the dialog, at times when participants are not disengaging. We therefore also took a closer look at the hesitations triggered by the system. Recall that the annotator tagged each hesitation as costly or not. We eliminated from the analysis below a set of 15 hesitation actions that were triggered in succession within a single interaction, where the robot incorrectly continued an engagement with a person that was close to the robot but involved in a conversation with someone else. Over the remaining hesitation actions, 81% were judged acceptable. This proportion was larger when using the forecasting model than when using the baseline heuristic: 86% (F+H) > 63% (B+H). A significantly larger number of hesitations were triggered when using the forecasting model: 130 (F+H) > 38 (B+H).

The annotator's observations revealed several classes of problems. Perhaps not unexpected, the production of hesitations actions at inopportune moments keeps the participants waiting too long for an answer that they expect to get immediately, or appears awkward, *e.g.*, when produced after a departure salutation from the user. At other times, the production of a filled pause appears to interrupt the users. Finally, sometimes, filled pauses produced while participants are actually disengaging can cause them to turn their attention back to the system, and sometimes stop in their tracks – the already discussed *Late(Hesitation)-Costly* case. An inspection of the *Late(Hesitation)* actions produced by the robot while participants were disengaging showed that 60% (6 out of 10 total) were costly when using the baseline heuristic (B+H), whereas on 33% (5 out of 15 total) were costly when using the forecasting model (F+H).

6. DISCUSSION

Below, we discuss limitations of this study, and future directions that remain to be explored.

Although the results indicate improvements in disengagement behaviors, recall that the baseline heuristic was designed to be conservative in order to avoid false disengagements and provide reliable labels. Future work should assess how the proposed approach fares in comparison to models learned based from labeled ground truth, or models manually tuned by other experts. Forecasting the actual moment of disengagement, as opposed to the estimate a conservative heuristic can provide automatically, may also be a more challenging learning problem. Finally, future work should assess the performance of the conservative heuristic and forecasting model against manually labeled ground truth.

One advantage of the approach we have described is that it does not require manual supervision. The system learns by itself, guided by a conservative heuristic, and tunes its behaviors to the specifics of its environment. Future work should investigate whether the type of conservative heuristic that we have constructed generalizes well to other settings, or whether it needs to be adapted. Even if some tuning is required for new environments, adapting the heuristic might still be less costly than performing manual annotations.

Another area of future exploration is the setting of thresholds: while the disengagement threshold P_{Dis}^{*} was based on a method that aimed to minimize false positives, the other thresholds for disengagement in the conservative heuristic, or for producing filled and non-filled pauses were chosen in a fairly arbitrary manner—by observing the behavior of the forecasting model on a few interactions, and were kept the same for both the baseline (B+H) and forecasting conditions (F+H). Better results may be attained with tuning, for both the baseline heuristic and forecasting model.

Perhaps even more importantly, the analysis of the form, function, and impact / cost of hesitation actions is a task that clearly deserves additional attention. The impact of a hesitation in dialog depends both on its form and on many contextual factors. Our study was constrained by the speech synthesis engine, but future work should investigate the use of other fillers, like *um* or *uh*, which might be more appropriate during disengagement as they don't carry the interrogative and floor release function that a prolonged "*So…*" sometimes does. Hesitations implemented as non-filled pauses, perhaps accompanied by appropriate non-verbal behaviors may generally constitute a lower cost option than filled pauses. Future work should also investigate how the choice of hesitations may be contextualized based on other aspects of the situation at hand.

7. CONCLUSION

We have investigated a self-supervised methodology for constructing forecasting models for disengagement, and proposed the use of disengagement policies that leverage linguistic hesitation actions to mitigate uncertainty. An initial study of the proposed approach with a directions-giving robot deployed in the wild shows that the joint use of forecasts and hesitations can help manage disengagement, and points to several interesting directions for future work. We believe that the study of policies for introducing hesitations is ripe for future exploration and that mastery of such policies will help systems to engage in more seamless, natural interactions with people in open-world settings.

ACKNOWLEDGMENTS

We thank Rebecca Hanson for assistance with data annotation, Anne Loomis Thompson and Nick Saw for project contributions, and the anonymous reviewers for their feedback.

8. REFERENCES

[1] Kendon, A. 1990. Spatial organization in social encounters: the F-formation system, *Conducting Interaction: Patterns of behavior in focused encounters*, Studies in International Sociolinguistics, Cambridge University Press.

[2] Sidner, C.L., Lee, C., Kidd, C.D., Lesh, N. and Rich, C., 2005. Explorations in engagement for humans and robots, *Artificial Intelligence*, 166 (1-2), pp. 140-164.

[3] Rich, C., Ponsler, B., Holroyd, A., and Sidner, C.L., 2010. Recognizing engagement in human-robot interaction, in *Proc. of HRI'2010*, Osaka, Japan.

[4] Michalowski, M.P., Sabanovic, S., and Simmons, R., 2006. A spatial model of engagement for a social robot, in *9th IEEE Workshop on Advanced Motion Control*, pp. 762-767.

[5] Bohus, D., and Horvitz, E., 2009. Models for Multiparty Engagement in Open-World Dialog, in *Proc. of SIGdial'2009*, London, UK.

[6] Bohus, D., and Horvitz, E., 2009. Learning to Predict Engagement with a Spoken Dialog System in Open-World Settings, in *Proc. of SIGdial'2009*, London, UK.

[7] Clark, H.H., and Fox Tree, J.E., 2002. Using uh and um in spontaneous speaking, *Cognition*, 84(1):73-111, May, 2002.

[8] Corley, M., and Stewart, O.W., 2008. Hesitation disfluencies in spontaneous speech: The meaning of *um*, *Language and Linguistics Compass*, 4, 589-602.

[9] Goto, M., Itou, K., and Hayamizu, S., 1999. A Real-time Filled Pause Detection System for Spontaneous Speech Recognition, in *Proc. of Eurospeech'99*, Budapest, Hungary.

[10] An, G., Brizan, D.G., and Rosenberg, A., 2013. Detecting laughter and filled pauses using syllable-based features, in *Proc. of Interspeech'2013*, Lyon, France.

[11] Adell, J., Bonafonte, A., and Escudero, D., 2010. Synthesis of filled pauses based on a disfluent speech model, in *Proc. of ICASSP'2010*, Dallas, TX.

[12] Skantze, G., and Hjalmarsson, A., 2010. Towards incremental speech generation in dialogue systems, in *Proc. of SIGDial'2010*, Tokyo, Japan.

[13] Skantze, G., Hjalmarsson, A., and Oertel, C., 2013. Exploring the effects of gaze and pauses in situated human-robot interaction, in *Proc. of SIGDial'2013*, Metz, France.

[14] Dethlefs, N., Hastie, H., Reiser, V., and Lemon, O., 2012. Optimizing Natural Language Generation for Decision Making for Situated Dialogue, in *Proc. of INLG'2012*, 49-58, Utica, IL.

[15] Bohus, D., Saw, C.W., and Horvitz, E., 2014. Directions Robot: In-the-Wild Experiences and Lessons Learned, in *Proc. of AAMAS'2014*, Paris, France.

[16] Bohus, D., and Horvitz, E., 2009. Dialog in the Open World: Platform and Applications, in *Proc. of ICMI'2009*, Boston, MA.

[17] Gouaillier, D., Hugel, V., Blazevic, P., Kilner, C., Monceaux, J., Lafourcade, P., Marnier, B., Serre, J., Maisonnier, B. 2009. Mechatronic design of NAO humanoid. *In Proceedings of ICRA'09*, Kobe, Japan.

Written Activity, Representations and Fluency as Predictors of Domain Expertise in Mathematics

Sharon Oviatt
Incaa Designs
11140 N.E. Wing Point Dr.
Bainbridge Island, WA. 98110
oviatt@incaadesigns.org

Adrienne Cohen
University of Washington
Adrienne.o.cohen@gmail.com

ABSTRACT

The emerging field of multimodal learning analytics evaluates natural communication modalities (digital pen, speech, images) to identify domain expertise, learning, and learning-oriented precursors. Using the Math Data Corpus, this research investigated students' digital pen input as small groups collaborated on solving math problems. Compared with non-experts, findings indicated that domain experts have an opposite pattern of accelerating total written activity as problem difficulty increases, a lower written and spoken disfluency rate, and they express different content—including a higher ratio of nonlinguistic symbolic representations and structured diagrams to elemental marks. Implications are discussed for developing reliable multimodal learning analytics systems that incorporate digital pen input to automatically track the consolidation of domain expertise. This includes prediction based on a combination of activity patterns, fluency, and content analysis. New MMLA systems are expected to have special utility on cell phones, which already have multimodal interfaces and are the dominant educational platform worldwide.

Categories and Subject Descriptors

H5.2 Information interfaces and presentation: User interfaces—user-centered design, interaction styles, evaluation/methodology.

General Terms

Experimentation, Design, Performance, Human Factors

Keywords

Collaborative problem solving; domain expertise; Math Data Corpus; digital pen; written activity; disfluency; multimodal learning analytics

1. INTRODUCTION

Multimodal learning analytics (MMLA) is an emerging field within learning analytics [3] that analyzes natural communication modalities such as speech, writing, gesturing, facial expressions, and physical activity patterns [12; 18]. It aims to identify domain expertise and changes in expertise rapidly, reliably, and objectively, and also to identify critical learning-oriented precursors. MMLA supports a rich systems-level view that is grounded in converging multimodal data on how students communicate, collaborate, and solve problems during learning activities. It has the potential to improve our understanding of how students learn, and to create better resources for supporting learning with new curricula and digital tools. MMLA techniques could be especially useful for guiding the design of new educational technologies (e.g., pen, multimodal, tangible) that are not limited by keyboards. In the long-term, multimodal learning analytics is expected to yield more sensitive, reliable, objective, and richly contextualized metrics of learning-oriented behavior than existing learning analytics methods, as well as ones that can be analyzed more unobtrusively and automatically in field settings like classrooms.

One especially important advantage of MMLA techniques is that they can be used to assess both *interpersonal* and *computer-mediated* learning activities, since they are based on natural communication modalities [22; 18]. In comparison, most existing learning analytics methods involve click-stream analysis, which only is applicable in computer-mediated learning contexts. They typically require keyboard input, which is a critical disadvantage since cell phones with multimodal interfaces have become the dominant educational technology platform worldwide. Most cell phones now have multimodal interfaces that support input using a combination of speech, touch and multi-touch, gesture, virtual keyboard, sensors, and pen input [12]. To evaluate learning when using these devices, new MMLA techniques will be required that are capable of collecting and analyzing these types of multimodal input.

1.1 Emergence of Pen System Capabilities

Among the most recent additions to cell phone input during 2013 is written input, based either on stylus or fingertip writing. The focus on written input emphasizes "content creation" within applications, which makes a permanent ink trace rather than ephemeral touch-based gesturing. For example, the Samsung Galaxy Note cell phone with S-pen input [21] supports precise, pressure sensitive, and speedy note-taking, sketched information, annotations on photos or diagrams, collaborative whiteboard applications, and other functions. Pen input also supports writing in Asian and other world languages (e.g., Chinese, Japanese, Urdu) that do not have easy-to-type compact Roman alphabets. Instead, such languages have complex and spatially intensive character sets with diacritics, logograms, and similar features that are not adequately supported by keyboards. Samsung's hardware uses multiple touch technologies to sense the proximity and pressure sensitivity of the stylus, which maintains the simultaneous ability to recognize multi-touch gestural control of the interface.

During 2013, Google also released MyScript software for Android smart phones and mobile internet search [7]. It includes

ICMI'14, November 12–16, 2014, Istanbul, Turkey.

ACM 978-1-4503-2885-2/14/11…$15.00.
http://dx.doi.org/10.1145/2663204.2663245

MyScript Notes, *MyScript Calculator* for handwritten math content and formulas, and the recent beta release of *MyScript Stylus* aimed at collecting and recognizing handwritten input in 54 languages. These collective capabilities are designed to replace physical and virtual keyboards on mobile devices with multimodal pen and touch input—including interactive handwriting recognition of multilingual, numeric, and symbolic content. These new pen-based capabilities support stylus input on capacitive or multi-touch screens, which improves the sophistication of multimodal interfaces on cell phones. As a result of these developments, pen input can be used for basic applications like email, web browsing, SMS and MMS, text editing, calendar entries, etc. These emerging Google pen input and recognition capabilities emphasize accommodating language needs in developing regions, where cell phone expansion currently is centered.

A related development during 2013 is the Livescribe 3 pen [8], based on Anoto's digital pen and paper technology. This new Livescribe pen is now the size of a regular pen, rather than a chunky mini-computer. It includes a capacitive stylus on the opposite end from the ink tip, which can be used to write directly on cell phones or laptops. In addition, the ink tip end still has a high-speed infrared camera and can be used to write on a digital paper notebook. On the Livescribe 3, this writing can be transmitted and displayed directly on a cell phone or laptop screen. Whether writing on paper or a device screen, the written content can be viewed, collected with accompanying speech (e.g., class lecture during note-taking), transmitted (e.g., emailed and shared), content searched, recognized and displayed as text, or otherwise processed. The new Liverscibe pen's functionality is more tightly integrated with accompanying mobile devices (e.g., iPhone, iPad, Android devices forthcoming), and it also depends on tight coupling with them for system processing.

Anoto digital pens and paper [1] recently have been adopted as part of integrated multimedia classroom systems in the Korean public schools. In this large-scale implementation, Symphony software is used to integrate students' digital pen and paper input with interactive whiteboards to create an interactive learning environment. Pen input tools are especially well suited for expressing Asian languages, mathematics symbols and formulas, and spatial content central to educational curricula (e.g. diagramming). Together, these recent pen system developments create an unprecedented opportunity for designing new educational technologies that incorporate pen input for the worldwide market. They will in turn generate a need for related learning analytics techniques that are capable of evaluating students' written activity and content during educational activities.

1.2 Pen Input and Improved Cognition

Recent research has revealed that computer interfaces can be designed with input capabilities that substantially facilitate people's ability to produce domain-appropriate ideas, solve problems correctly, and make accurate inferences about information [17; 14]. The magnitude of these effects in different studies has ranged from 9% to 38%. These findings generalize across different content domains (e.g., mathematics, science, everyday reasoning), student populations and ability levels (e.g., low and high performers), types of thinking and reasoning, computer hardware, and evaluation metrics. This recent work identified advantages of pen input for facilitating human cognition, which is largely due to their expressive power and flexibility in conveying all types of representation, especially spatial ones (e.g., diagrams, symbols).

In one study, students were asked to produce as many appropriate science hypotheses as they could while using different computer interfaces and also non-digital tools. They expressed 56% more *nonlinguistic* content when using a pen interface, compared with a non-digital pen. More strikingly, they simultaneously generated 38.5% more appropriate science hypotheses, and a linear regression indicated that knowledge of students' level of nonlinguistic communication predicted 72% of the variance in their production of appropriate science ideas [17; 13]. In contrast, when the same students used keyboard input they produced 41% more *linguistic* content, and regression analyses revealed that students' higher rate of linguistic communication had a *negative* predictive relation with their ability to generate ideas. In this case, knowledge of students' level of linguistic communication predicted 62% of the variance in their *lack of ability* to produce appropriate science hypotheses.

In another study focused on problem solving, students solved 13% more problems correctly when using a pen interface, compared with keyboard input that included a supplementary pen. Related analyses confirmed that when students made diagrams and marks before solving a problem, this nonlinguistic content was associated with 25-36% higher solution scores, compared with matched problems in which they did not diagram or mark [17]. A further study on inferential reasoning discovered that the same students solving the same inference problems constructed more Venn diagrams, and also 14% more *correct* Venn diagrams, when using a pen interface compared with an analogous non-digital pen. The pen interface also stimulated a 9.4% higher percentage of correct inferences about the content displayed [18; 14]. In summary, pen input improves users' expressive power, especially the ability to convey spatial content, which substantially facilitates human cognition. For this reason, pen interfaces and multimodal ones that incorporate them can provide far better computational "thinking tools" and an improved foundation for educational technologies, compared with existing keyboard-based interfaces.

1.3 Identification of Domain Expertise

Related literature on prediction of domain expertise and learning has included linguistic and discourse analysis, content and concept analysis, diagram analysis, uncertainty detection, sentiment analysis, acoustic-prosodic analysis, and other related techniques. This work has determined that experts express more domain specific technical terms, lexical certainly, and positive affect [5; 9; 20; 24]. They take more time to plan before initiating a task [11], and their subsequent spoken language is more concise (i.e., lower ratio words to concepts) and less disfluent [6; 20; 24. They also speak at a faster rate with altered peak slope [6]. This past work has focused mainly on *text and speech.*

Relatively little work has investigated writing or combined multimodal input as information sources for evaluating expertise and learning, even though multimodal information is known to improve robustness [13]. In addition, writing is associated with type II reflective reasoning, deliberative problem-solving, and self-regulated behavior and learning [14]. As a result, writing and representational content may provide more reliable predictors of domain expertise than nonverbal audio-visual sources. The latter are known to be prone to systematic biases in human judgment associated with type I reasoning, especially under high cognitive load [23]. Some research on writing and expertise has shown that experts make more structured diagrams [11], and higher-

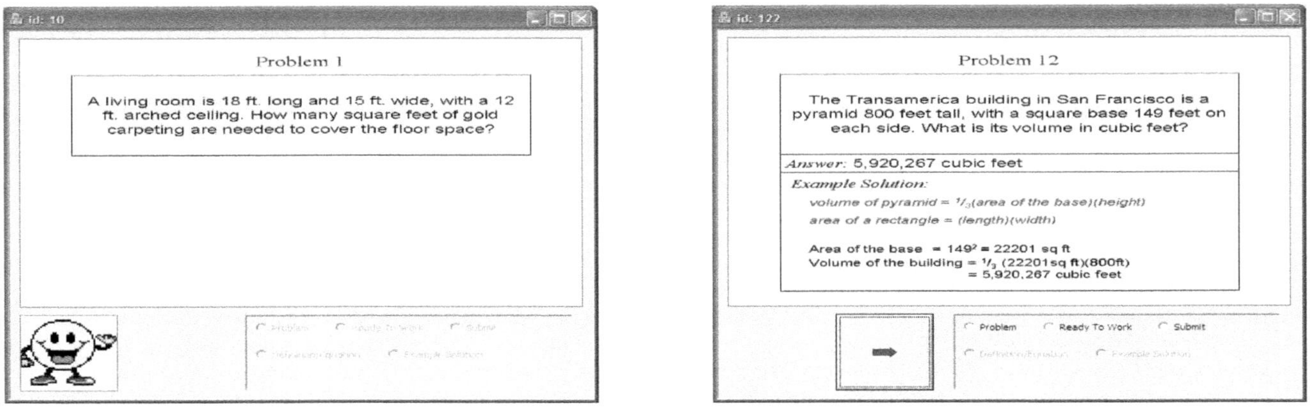

(a) Interface displaying an easy math problem.

(b) Interface displaying a very hard math problem, answer, and example solution.

Figure 1. Computer monitor displaying easy math problem (left) & very hard problem (right) with answer and worked solution

performing math students express more symbols and increase their diagramming more as tasks become more difficult [15]. Other work has shown that expertise in math is associated with fewer and briefer pauses when writing formulas, reflecting increased chunking of domain information in working memory [4].

Recent work has begun to investigate digital pen and multimodal information sources as potentially fertile avenues for identifying domain expertise and correct problem solving. This work analyzed multimodal communication patterns (digital pen, speech, images) in collaborating student groups as they solved math problems together in the Math Data Corpus [18]. Findings revealed that in 96-97% of cases the correctness of a group's in-progress solution was predictable in advance based on students' written content [16]. A linear regression also revealed that 65% of the variance in individual students' domain expertise rankings could be accounted for based on analysis of their written work content. Perhaps surprisingly, a multimodal analysis based on both written and spoken solution contributions correctly predicted the dominant domain expert in a student group 100% of the time. That is, MMLA analysis of students' written and spoken *activity patterns*, in particular their *volume of answer contributions irrespective of answer correctness*, was a strikingly reliable predictor of domain expertise [16].

1.4 Research Goals

One implication of the research described above is that digital pen input may be a promising avenue for stimulating cognition, and also monitoring student progress during learning activities. With respect to pedagogical goals, it could enable timely intervention when student work is progressing incorrectly, or assist in identifying student expertise levels so productive learning groups could be formed. The objective of this work is to investigate written activity, representational content, and fluency for possible indices to reliably distinguish domain expertise from non-expertise in mathematics. The Math Data Corpus and its richly coded representational content was adopted as a test-bed for exploring MMLA predictors of domain expertise.

2. METHOD

2.1 Student Participants

Participants were 18 high school students, 9 female and 9 male, between 15 to 17 years old. All had recently completed Introductory Geometry at a local high school. They represented a range of geometry skills from low to high performers. Participants were paid volunteers and native English speakers. During data collection, small groups of three students apiece jointly solved problems. Each group was matched on gender and geometry skill level to facilitate reciprocal collaboration.

2.2 Math Tasks

During each session, students engaged in authentic problem solving and peer tutoring as they worked on 16 geometry and algebra problems, four apiece representing easy, moderate, hard, and very hard difficulty. These math word problems varied along dimensions known to make them difficult [10].

2.3 Data Collection Procedure

Each of the six student groups met for two sessions, during which students could view the problems on a tabletop computer screen. The sessions were facilitated by a system that presented problems with accompanying visuals, terms and equations related to solving the problems, worked examples, and solutions. This system was controlled by a simulation environment during data collection [2].

One student in the group was designated as the leader for a given session, and the leader switched on the group's second session which resulted in 12 sessions with 12 different leaders. Each group was instructed to exchange information as they worked on solving the problems so everyone understood the solution and could explain it if asked. To ensure that all students participated fully, they were told that each participant would be randomly asked to explain the group's math solutions as they worked. The leader was responsible for coordinating the group's activity and interacting with the system. She could request the system to: (1) display the problem, (2) provide definitions of math terms, if needed, (3) provide formulas, (4) turn off, to avoid distracting students while working, (5) collect the group's answer, (6) show the correct solution after the answer was submitted, and (7) provide sample solutions. Usually during each problem, one student proposed a solution to the others, which was discussed among them. Once agreed upon and all students understood how to solve it, the leader submitted the group's answer to the computer. Afterwards, the system displayed the correct answer, so students could check their solution. If correct, a student sometimes was called upon by the computer to explain the solution. If not correct, the leader could ask for a worked example before moving to a new problem.

While working, students used a calculator, digital pen, and large sheets of digital paper. They were told that they could write with the digital pens just like a normal pen on paper, and they could erase by crossing out. None of the students had used a digital pen before. After instructions, each group was given three sample math problems for orientation to the problems, computer, and materials. Each group session lasted 60-90 minutes.

2.4 Multimodal Data Collection

During each session, twelve data streams were collected involving multimodal input from video cameras, digital pens, and close-talking microphones. Figure 2 illustrates high-resolution data collected from five camera views. Digital audio recordings also were collected of each participant's speech using close-talking microphones. A fourth audio recording was collected using an omni-directional microphone above the table. Each participant's writing was collected using Nokia digital pens and Anoto digital paper. The pens provided unique identification for each student. Technical details of multimodal data collection are described elsewhere [18].

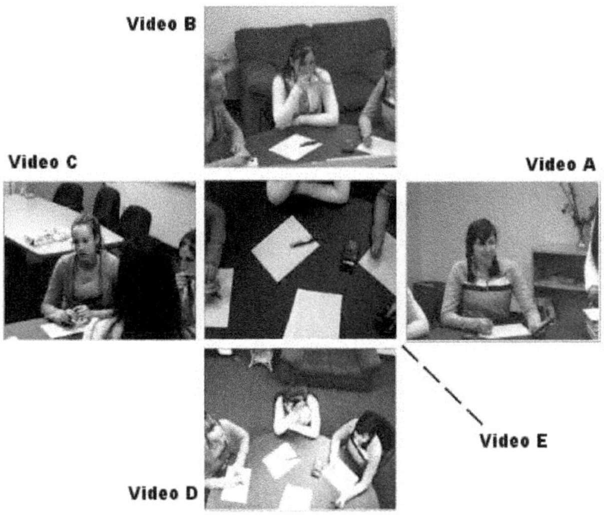

Figure 2. Synchronized views from all five cameras at same moment in time during data collection. Videos A, B and C show close-up views of individual students, video D a wide-angle view, and video E top-down view of tabletop artifacts.

2.5 Data Coding & Performance Metrics

2.5.1 Segmentation of Problems

Data were segmented into start and end of all 16 problem-solving episodes.

2.5.2 Correctness of Problem Solution

Each submitted problem solution was scored for correctness.

2.5.3 Oral Initiator of Problem Solution

The student who first orally proposed the group's problem solution was scored for every problem, as well as whether their solution was correct or not.

2.5.4 Cumulative Expertise Rating

To assess domain expertise, each student's cumulative problem-solving performance was calculated across their two sessions. When a student was the oral initiator of a group solution, the following numeric values were assigned: total number of easy problems solved versus missed (+1 or -1 pt.), moderate problems (+2 or -2 pts.), hard problems (+3 or -3 pt.), and very hard problems (+4 or -4 pt.). Based on totals, the dominant expert in each group was identified. All students were rank ordered by expertise.

2.5.5 Written Representations

The start time, end time, semantic content, and total number of representations written by each student was coded for all task-relevant language (e.g., words, abbreviations), numbers, symbols (e.g., π), diagrams, and elemental marks (e.g., line to connect label with diagram part, underlining answer). This content was coded within problem boundaries. For details, see Oviatt, Cohen & Weibel [18], Appendix B.

2.5.6 Written Disfluencies

All writing involving content corrections, misspellings and malformed symbols, or retracing over past writing was coded for type and number of episodes. This included crossing out past written content to delete it, rewriting new content, overwriting to change past content, and writing next to previous ink to add information to it. The scope of disfluencies ranged from a single digit to a whole problem solution. A rate or percentage of written disfluencies was calculated per 100 written representations.

2.5.7 Spoken Disfluencies

Spoken disfluencies were coded by expert and non-expert students during intervals when they were asked to explain how they had solved a given math problem. Spoken disfluencies were coded as all content corrections, verbatim lexical repetitions, non-word fillers (e.g., "um" ,"ah") and discontinued grammatical constructions (e.g., "I think… I'm going to…"), and a rate or percentage of spoken disfluencies then was calculated per 100 spoken words.

3. RESULTS

Data were available for analysis on 18 individual students and 12 group sessions. This included 192 problem episodes and 576 problems completed by individual students (144 at each difficulty level). Data also were available on 10,595 coded written representations.

In this math domain, 80.3% of students' written content was nonlinguistic representations, including numeric (45.7%), symbolic (25.7%), diagrammatic (7.0%), and marking (1.9%). Spatial representations (diagrams, marks) totaled 8.9% of all writing. Linguistic content was 19.7% of all writing. During math problem solving, numbers, symbols, and diagrams were the representations that increased in volume as problems became more difficult, whereas linguistic content and marks did not. In this regard, diagrams, symbols and numbers were the "workhorses" that helped students to think about and solve increasingly difficult math problems.

3.1 Written Activity Patterns

The total number of written representations averaged 294.3 per session. Figure 3 shows that students' total writing increased steadily between easy and very hard tasks. Expert students wrote an average of 51.4 representations on easy problems, 63.1 on moderate ones, 62.9 on hard, but increased their writing substantially to 87.6 on very hard problems. In contrast, non-expert students averaged 61.7 representations on easy problems, which they increased to 75.9 on moderate, 81.8 on hard, and 86.3 on very hard problems. Overall, non-expert students averaged 15.3% more total written representations.

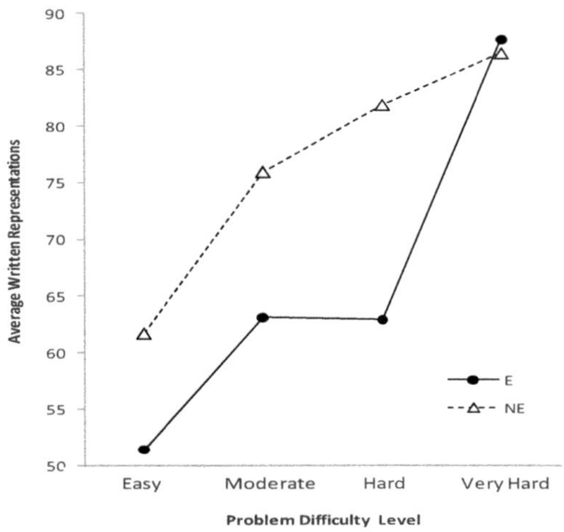

Figure 3. Average total written representations per session for experts (E) vs. non-experts (NE) by problem difficulty

Figure 3 shows a distinctive difference between non-expert and expert students in their total amount of written activity with increased problem difficulty. Non-experts increased their written activity most between easy to moderate problems (14.2), with only a small increase between hard to very hard ones (4.5). In contrast, experts accelerated their written activity most between hard to very hard problems (24.7), with just a small increase between easy to moderate ones (11.7). A comparison of students with the highest versus lowest cumulative expertise scores (i.e., experts vs. non-experts) confirmed that 90% conformed with the predicted within-subject pattern, which was statistically significant by Wilcoxon Signed Ranks test, T+=53 (N=10), $p < .01$, one-tailed. These findings underscore characteristic differences between the groups in when they accelerate written activity. These distinctively different patterns are summarized in Figure 4.

3.2 Type Written Representations

As shown in Figure 5, expert students had a higher ratio of using nonlinguistic symbolic representations (i.e., symbols, numbers, diagrams) to linguistic or non-symbolic ones (i.e., elemental marks), compared with non-experts. They also were more responsive to increasing these representations as problems became more difficult. Figure 6 also shows that experts' had a higher ratio of structured diagrams to elemental marks, a difference between groups that expanded with task difficulty and was especially pronounced on very hard problems. In addition, non-experts had a 134% higher rate than experts of making elemental marks. Whereas 80% of experts rarely or never made these simpler marks (i.e., less than 3 instances total), the majority or over 62% of non-experts did express them.

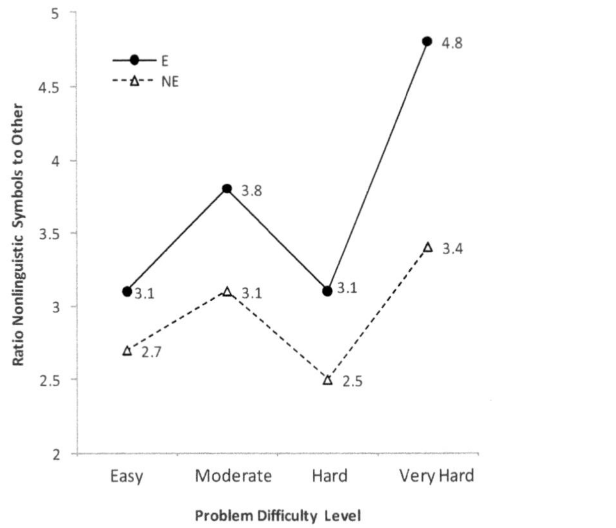

Figure 5. Ratio of nonlinguistic symbols to linguistic and non-symbolic content for experts (E) vs. non-experts (NE) by problem difficulty

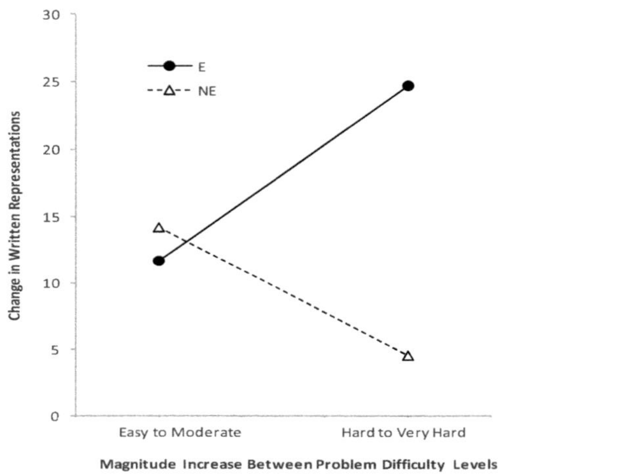

Figure 4. Increase in total written representations between easy to moderate and hard to very hard tasks for experts (E) versus non-experts (NE)

3.3 Written Disfluencies

Written disfluencies were relatively common in this domain, averaging 5.9% of all written representations. The majority of disfluencies were content corrections, which typically involved either crossing out and rewriting or overwriting previous content. The second most common type of disfluency involved retracing

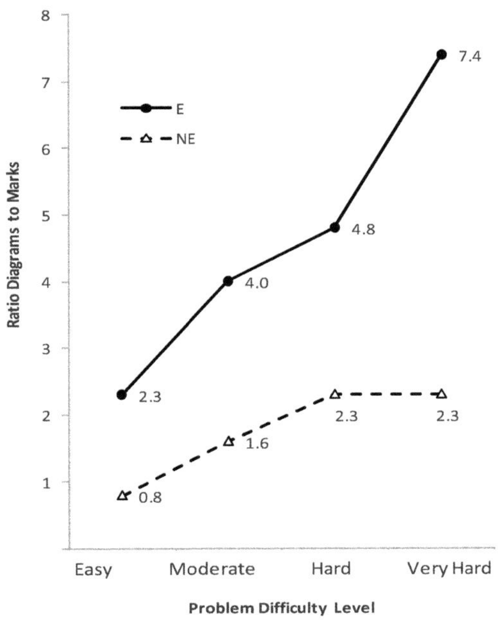

Figure 6. Ratio of diagrams to marks for experts (E) vs. non-experts (NE) by problem difficulty

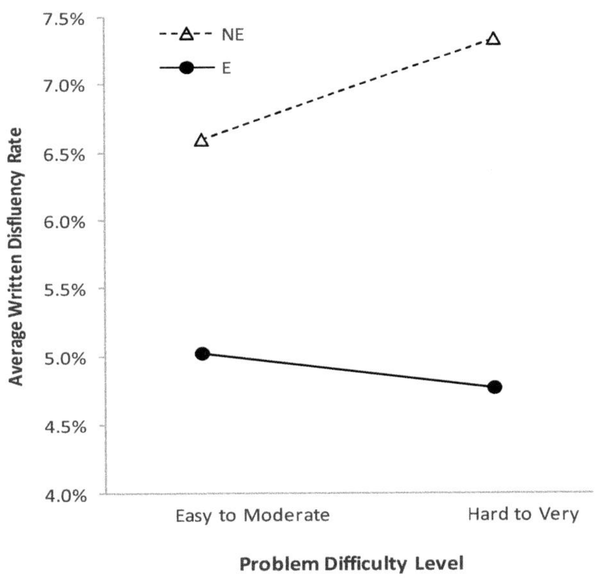

Figure 7. Written disfluency rate for experts (E) vs. non-experts (NE) by problem difficulty

parts of previously written ink content. As shown in Figure 7, non-expert students had a 42% higher written disfluency rate than experts, with the difference between groups accentuated on harder problems. Students who were not domain experts averaged 6.59% disfluencies on easy to moderate problems, increasing to 7.34% on hard to very hard problems. In contrast, domain experts averaged an overall lower 5.02% rate on the same easy-moderate problems, and actually decreased to 4.77% on hard-very hard problems. Although there was considerable variability between individual students in average written disfluency rates, a comparison of students with the highest versus lowest cumulative expertise scores confirmed that 70% conformed with the predicted within-subject pattern of non-experts *increasing* vs. experts *decreasing* in their disfluency rate on more difficult problems, Wilcoxon Signed Ranks test T+=42 (N=10), $p < .04$, one-tailed.

3.4 Spoken Disfluencies

For comparison with written disfluencies, the spoken disfluency rate per 100 words was calculated for both expert and non-expert students during intervals when they were asked to explain how a math problem had been solved. The spoken disfluency rate averaged lower than the written one for this same group of students. However, there was a substantially higher rate in non-expert students (mean= 4.3%), compared with experts (2.1%), paired t test=3.03 (df, 5), $p < .015$, one-tailed. Overall, students classified as non-experts exhibited a striking 103% higher rate of spoken disfluencies than experts.

4. DISCUSSION

The present findings contribute to the emerging body of research on designing reliable multimodal learning analytics techniques, in particular ones that incorporate digital pen data, which aim to automatically assess consolidation of domain expertise during learning activities. They identify distinguishing markers of domain expertise based on analysis of students' digital pen input while solving math problems, including that non-experts have a 42% higher rate of written disfluences than domain experts. In this mathematics domain involving student learners, written disfluencies were common, occurring on about 6% of all written representations. Written disfluencies most frequently involved content corrections, in which a student crossed out and rewrote content, or retraced over previously written ink. These disfluent events could be identified automatically more easily than predictors requiring content analysis. The most sensitive way to use disfluencies for identifying domain expertise would be to track them within subjects as problems become more difficult, since non-experts' written disfluency rate *increased* but experts' rate *decreased* with greater difficulty.

Compared with written disfluencies, spoken disfluencies during problem explanation phases actually distinguished experts from non-expert students far better. In fact, non-expert students produced a striking 103% higher rate of spoken disfluencies overall. Since spoken disfluencies were sampled during problem explanation phases when students had to summarize how their numeric computations were calculated in some detail, it's likely that students experienced higher cognitive load when composing these explanations. As a result, this type of content may have been especially sensitive in distinguishing between the two student groups.

In addition, a distinctive and large magnitude difference was evident between non-experts and experts in their total written activity as problems became more difficult. Whereas non-experts increased their written activity most between *easy to moderate problems*, in contrast experts accelerated their written activity most between *hard to very hard problems*. This opposite pattern between the groups, most clearly illustrated in Figure 4, reveals characteristic differences in *when* domain experts versus non-experts accelerate their written activity. This difference most likely reflects that non-experts become most engaged trying to solve easy problems because they believe they are within their repertoire, whereas their engagement declines on harder problems when they lose confidence that they can solve them. In contrast, domain experts are least engaged on the easy problems, which they sometimes solve in their head without writing at all. Instead, they expend a high level of effort writing on the hardest problems that they are confident they can solve. Irrespective of its basis, this opposite pattern of written activity on problems varying in difficulty is a salient marker distinguishing domain experts from non-experts, and one that also does not require content analysis. These findings underscore the *nonlinear* nature of increases in total writing as students solve harder problems. Whereas examining the average for all students creates the impression that writing increases linearly with difficulty, closer examination of students varying in expertise disconfirms that a linear model fits either group.

Domain experts have a higher ratio of nonlinguistic symbolic representations (i.e., symbols, numbers, diagrams) and structured diagrams to elemental marks. In this respect, experts are more adept at constructing and using representational tools that are well matched with a problem domain, which reflects better meta-cognitive skills. These findings replicate and extend past work showing that experts express more symbols when solving math problems [15]. They also construct more structured diagrams, especially as tasks become harder [11; 15], whereas non-experts make twice as many elemental marks [19]. An absence of elemental marks in particular is a good predictor of expertise, since experts rarely or never made them.

Digital pen input has been relatively neglected, both as an interface and as a means of collecting student data and transparently assessing learning progress. This is unfortunate, since writing is a reflective modality associated with the read-write cycle, and pen input also supports mobile and field use in contexts like classrooms. Unlike video and speech, it is easy to record high-quality writing in classrooms. And unlike speech, students are more likely to communicate using pen input in classroom settings. Since written work and its content evaluation is customary practice in classrooms settings, MMLA techniques based on analysis of writing also may incur fewer privacy concerns than collection of speech or visual images. In the case of mathematics, writing is an especially valuable means of collecting and analyzing students' work, which is full of spatial diagrams, symbols and digits.

Recent major pen system developments by Samsung, Google, Livescribe, and others create an unprecedented opportunity to design new educational technologies that incorporate pen input as a "content creation" tool for the worldwide market. These developments focus on pen input for cell phones, which currently are the dominant educational platform worldwide. Advances such as these generate a parallel need for multimodal learning analytics techniques that are more appropriately matched with the multimodal interfaces on cell phones, and that improve upon the reliability and interpretability of existing click-stream learning analytics methods. This research identifies aspects of written activity, fluency, and representational content that may be valuable individually or in combination with other predictors for reliably identifying domain expertise and learning during educational activities. Future research will need to assess the generality of these findings in other domains and cultural contexts, and to confirm them in situated classrooms and with larger datasets.

5. ACKNOWLEDGMENTS

This research was supported by Incaa Designs (http://www.incaadesigns.org/).

6. REFERENCES

[1] Anoto (2013) http://www.anoto.com/lng/en/pageTag/page:home/; retrieved Oct. 31, 2013.

[2] Arthur, A., Lunsford, R., Wesson, M. & Oviatt, S.L. (2006) Prototyping novel collaborative multimodal systems: Simulation, data collection and analysis tools for the next decade, *Eighth International Conference on Multimodal Interfaces (ICMI'06),* ACM: New York, 209-226.

[3] Baker, R. & Yacef, K. (2009). The state of educational data mining in 2009: A review and future visions, *Journal of Educational Data Mining,* 1:3-17.

[4] Cheng, P. C. H., & Rojas-Anaya, H. (2007). Measuring mathematical formula writing competence: An application of graphical protocol analysis. In D. S. McNamara & J. G. Trafton (Eds.), *Proceedings of the 29th Conference of the Cognitive Science Society*, Austin, TX: Cognitive Science Society, 869-874.

[5] D'Mello, S., Craig, S., Witherspoon, A., McDaniel, B. & Graesser, A. (2008). Automatic detection of learner's affect from conversational cues, *User Modeling and User Adapted Interaction*, 18(1-2), 45-80.

[6] Dral, J., Heylen, D. & op den Akker, R. (2008). Detecting uncertainty in spoken dialogues: An explorative research to the automatic detection of a speakers' uncertainty by using prosodic markers. In *Sentiment analysis: Emotion, metaphor, ontology and terminology*, Marrakech, Morocco, 72-78.

[7] Google (2013) https://play.google.com/store/apps/details?id=com.visionobjects.notesmobile&hl=en; retrieved Oct. 31, 2013.

[8] Livescribe (2013) http://www.livescribe.com/en-us/smartpen/ls3/; retrieved Oct. 31, 2013.

[9] Liscombe, J., Hirschberg, J. & Vendetti, J. (2005). Detecting certainness in spoken tutorial dialogs, *Proceedings of Interspeech 2005-Europeech*, Lisbon, Portugal.

[10] Lunsford, R., Oviatt, S. & Arthur, A. (2006). Toward open-microphone engagement for multiparty interactions, *International Conference on Multimodal Interaction,* ACM: New York, 273-280.

[11] Martin, L. & Schwartz, D. (2009). Prospective adaptation in the use of external representations, *Cognition and Instruction,* 27(4), 370-400.

[12] Oviatt, S. (2012). Multimodal interfaces. In J. Jacko (Ed.) The *Human-Computer Interaction Handbook:Fundamentals, Evolving Technologies and Emerging Applications, 3rd ed.* LEA: N.J., 18, 405-430.

[13] Oviatt, S. (2002). Breaking the robustness barrier: Recent progress on the design of robust multimodal systems.In M. Zelkowitz (Ed.) *Advances in Computers*, Academic Press, 56, 305-341.

[14] Oviatt, S.L. (2013). *The Design of Future Educational Interfaces*, Routledge Press.

[15] Oviatt, S., Arthur, A., Brock, Y. & Cohen, J. (2007). Expressive pen-based interfaces for math education. In C. Chinn, G. Erkens & S. Puntambekar (Eds.) *Proceedings of the Conference on Computer Supported Collaborative Learning, International Society of the Learning Sciences,* 8(2), 569-578.

[16] Oviatt, S. & Cohen, A. (2013). Written and multimodal representations as predictors of expertise and problem-solving success in mathematics, *Second Intl. Grand Challenge Workshop on Multimodal Learning Analytics*, Sydney Australia, December 2013.

[17] Oviatt, S.L., Cohen, A., Miller, A., Hodge, K. & Mann, A. (2012) The impact of interface affordances on human ideation, problem solving and inferential reasoning, *ACM Transactions on Computer Human Interaction,* 19 (3).

[18] Oviatt, S., Cohen, A. & Weibel, N. (2013). Multimodal learning analytics: Description of math data corpus for ICMI grand challenge workshop, *2nd Intl. Challenge Workshop on Multimodal Learning Analytics*, Sydney, December 2013.

[19] Oviatt, S., Mann, A. & Cohen, A. (2010). Supporting students' thinking marks: Designing accessible interfaces for science education, *American Association for Educational Research,* New Orleans, LA.

[20] Purandare, A. & Litman, D. (2008). Content-learning correlations in spoken tutoring dialogs at word, turn, and discourse levels, *Proceedings of 21st Intl. FLAIRS Conference*, Coconut Grove, FL.

[21] Samsung (2013) http://www.samsung.com/us/topic/the-next-big-thing-is-here/; retrieved Oct. 31, 2013

[22] Scherer, S., Weibel, N., Oviatt, S. & Morency, L.P. (2012). Multimodal prediction of expertise and leadership in learning groups, *Proc, of International Workshop on Multimodal Learning Analytics*, ACM: N.Y.

[23] Wigboldus, D., Sherman, J., Franzese, H. & Knippenberg, A. (2004). Capacity and comprehension: Spontaneous stereotyping under cognitive load, *Social Cognition,* 22 (3), 292-309.

[24] Worsley, M. & Blikstein, P. (2010). Toward the development of learning analytics: Student speech as an automatic and natural form of assessment, *AERA Conference.*

Analysis of Respiration for Prediction of "Who Will Be Next Speaker and When?" in Multi-Party Meetings

Ryo Ishii
NTT Communication Science Laboratories, NTT Corporation
3-1, Morinosato-Wakamiya, Atsugi-shi Kanagawa, Japan
ishii.ryo@lab.ntt.co.jp

Kazuhiro Otsuka
NTT Communication Science Laboratories, NTT Corporation
3-1, Morinosato-Wakamiya, Atsugi-shi Kanagawa, Japan
otsuka.kazuhiro@lab.ntt.co.jp

Shiro Kumano
NTT Communication Science Laboratories, NTT Corporation
3-1, Morinosato-Wakamiya, Atsugi-shi Kanagawa, Japan
kumano.shiro@lab.ntt.co.jp

Junji Yamato
NTT Communication Science Laboratories, NTT Corporation
3-1, Morinosato-Wakamiya, Atsugi-shi Kanagawa, Japan
yamato.junji@lab.ntt.co.jp

ABSTRACT

To build a model for predicting the next speaker and the start time of the next utterance in multi-party meetings, we performed a fundamental study of how respiration could be effective for the prediction model. The results of the analysis reveal that a speaker inhales more rapidly and quickly right after the end of a unit of utterance in turn-keeping. The next speaker takes a bigger breath toward speaking in turn-changing than listeners who will not become the next speaker. Based on the results of the analysis, we constructed the prediction models to evaluate how effective the parameters are. The results of the evaluation suggest that the speaker's inhalation right after a unit of utterance, such as the start time from the end of the unit of utterance and the slope and duration of the inhalation phase, is effective for predicting whether turn-keeping or turn-changing happen about 350 ms before the start time of the next utterance on average and that listener's inhalation before the next utterance, such as the maximal inspiration and amplitude of the inhalation phase, is effective for predicting the next speaker in turn-changing about 900 ms before the start time of the next utterance on average.

Categories and Subject Descriptors

H.1.2 [User/Machine systems]: Human information processing

Keywords

Respiration, multi-party meetings, next-speaker prediction, speaking-timing prediction, gaze behavior

ICMI '14, November 12 - 16 2014, Istanbul, Turkey
Copyright 2014 ACM 978-1-4503-2885-2/14/11 ...$15.00
http://dx.doi.org/10.1145/2663204.2663271.

1. INTRODUCTION

Face-to-face communication is one of the most basic forms of communication in daily life and group meetings are used for conveying information, understanding others' intentions, and making decisions. Smooth communication similar to face-to-face communication is desired in remote human-to-human and human-agent communication. Therefore, ways to automatically analyze multi-party meetings have been actively researched in recent years [8, 21].

Turn-changing, the situation where the speaker changes, is especially important. The participants need to predict the end of the speaker's utterance and who will start speaking next and to consider a strategy for good timing with respect to who will speak next in multi-party meetings. If a model can predict the next speaker and the start time of the next speaker's first utterance, the model will lay the foundation for the development of natural conversational systems in which conversational agents speak with natural timing and of teleconference systems that avoid utterance collisions with time delays by apprising who will speak to participants.

Studies in social psychology have reported that nonverbal and verbal behavior, such as gaze behavior and prosody, have an important association with the next speaker and start time of the next utterance [15, 24]. For automatically detecting or predicting who becomes the next speaker at the time of turn-changing in the engineering field, several studies have proposed using voice information and gaze behavior to predict the next speaker [9, 13] and the start time of the next utterance [9, 10]. It is hoped that the associations between other types of information and the next speaker and the start time will be demonstrated. In addition, it is desirable that more robust and high-precision prediction models be realized by using mulitimodal information. With the goal of building a high-performance prediction model, we are investigating the role of participants' respiration, which no previous research has examined in multi-party meetings.

It is known that utterances and respiration have a close relation. In order to speak, we must breathe out and need to take breaths to continue speaking for a long time. When starting an utterance, the next speaker inhales deeply. Moreover, a person's attitude about an utterance is frequently represented figuratively as breathing. For example, keeping as low a profile as possible to not be yielded the turn is often referred to metaphorically as "to hold one's breath" or "to save one's breath".

In this work, as a first attempt to deal with respiration, we performed a fundamental study of the relationships between respiration, the next speaker and the start time in multi-party meetings. First, we collected participants' respiration data using a band respiratory sensor and utterances. The results of the analysis reveal that a speaker inhales more rapidly and quickly right after the end of a unit of utterance in turn-keeping. The next speaker takes a bigger breath toward speaking in turn-changing than listeners who will not become the next speaker. Based on the results of the analysis, to evaluate how effective the parameters are, we constructed models for predicting whether turn-keeping or turn-changing happen and models for predicting the next speaker. For the former, the parameters are the speaker's inhalation right after a unit of utterance, such as the start time from the end of unit of utterance, and the slope and time duration of the inhalation phase. For the latter, they are the listener's respiration before the next speaking, such as the maximal inspiration and amplitude of the inhalation phase. The results of the evaluation suggest that speaker's inhalation is effective for predicting whether turn-keeping or turn-changing happen and the listener's inhalation is effective for predicting the next speaker before the start time of next speaking. Furthermore, we discuss new possibilities of multimodal processing to predict the next speaker and the start time using gaze behavior along with respiration.

This paper is organized as follows. Section 2 reviews related work and highlights our approach. Section 3 describes the corpus data for the analysis in multi-party meetings. Section 4 shows the results of the analysis of the relationships between respiration, and next speaker, and start time. Section 5 covers the preliminary investigation of a prediction model using respiration. Section 6 discusses the probability of a multimodal approach. Section 7 concludes the paper and mentions future work.

2. RELATED WORK

Most of the work related to elucidating the mechanism of the delivery of the turn in conversation has been performed in the field of social psychology. Sacks et al. [24] proposed a turn-changing model, in which turn-changing can only happen at transition relevance points near the end of utterances.

Several studies have explored the idea of automatically detecting whether turn-changing takes place or not in multi-party meetings by speech processing [3, 4, 6, 11, 17, 18, 25] and visual nonverbal behaviors such as gaze behavior [3, 4, 11] and physical motion [3, 4, 5] near the end of an utterance. In addition to the prediction of turn-changing, some studies have tried to predict who will become the next speaker at the time of turn-changing and the start time of the next utterance. Kawahara et al. [13] proposed a next-speaker detection model using prosody and gaze information in three-person poster conversation. Ishii et al. [9, 10] proposed a prediction model that features three processing steps to predict whether turn-changing or turn-keeping will occur, who will be the next speaker in turn-changing, and the timing of the start of the next speaker's utterance using gaze transition patterns, which have an n-gram of gaze objects including mutual gaze information. With the advent of these proposed prediction model for the next speaker and the start time of the next utterance using voice information and gaze behavior, it is hoped that the association between other types of information and the next speaker and the start time will be demonstrated. Further, the realization of more robust and high-precision prediction models is desirably conducted with multimodal information.

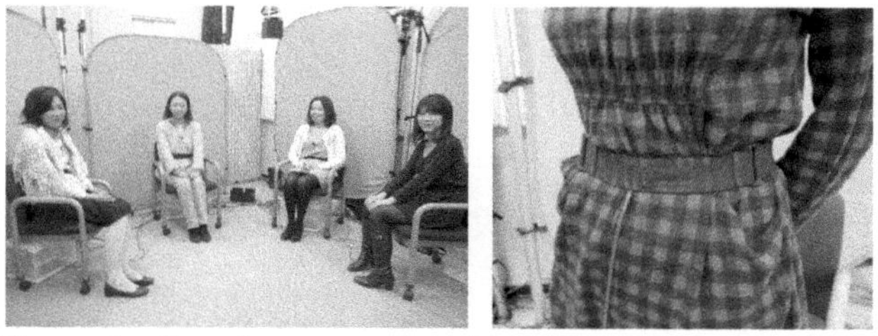

Figure 1: Sample scene of multi-party meeting and band respiratory sensor wrapped on participant's body.

With the goal of building a model for predicting the next speaker and the start time of the next utterance, we here focus on the respiration of biological signal, which has not been examined in previous work on prediction models for turn-changing, next speaker, and the start time of next utterance in multi-party meetings.

Several preliminary studies of two-persons dialogs have investigated the differences in respiration in speaking and listening situations and differences between the inhalation length and the length of following utterance [19, 23, 26]. No research has investigated the relationship between respiration and turn-changing in multi-party meetings. The fact that the sound of the intake of breath that can be heard is used for automatic speech separation in call center systems [7]. However, the sound cannot always be heard and the intake of breath cannot always be detected by speech processing. Monitoring respiration with a band respiratory sensor provides information about the intake of breath, which is not detected by speech processing, as well as many other kinds of information, such as the deepness, duration, and momentum of respiration.

Recently, it has become possible to easily monitor respiration with miniature sensors embedded in clothing [1] and image-based techniques with an RGB camera [22] or Kinect [27]. In the future, we will be able to monitor respiration in multi-party meetings, and it is expected that it will become simpler and easier to do so. Therefore, our research will contribute as basic knowledge for future progress.

In this paper, as initial research of respiration, we demonstrate the relationships between respiration and turn-changing, the next speaker, and the start time in multi-party meetings.

3. CORPUS DATA

3.1 Data collection of multi-party meetings

To collect a conversation corpus in multi-party meetings for the analysis of respiration, we recorded four natural four-persons meetings held by four groups of four different persons (16 people in total) for ten minutes. The four participants were in their 20's and 30's, and this was the first time they had met. They faced each other and sat down (See Fig. 1). They argued and gave opinions in response to highly divisive questions like "Is marriage the same as love?" and needed to draw a conclusion within ten minutes.

We recorded the participants' voices with a pin microphone attached to their chest and made a video recording of the entire scene and took bust shots of each participant (recorded at 30 Hz). We recorded each participant's respiration information using a NeXus-10 MARKII [20]. The respiration sensor of the system records the depth of breathing with the belt wrapped around participant's body (See Fig. 1) and outputs a value of the degree of breathing depth (called the "RSP value" hereafter) at 128 Hz. A high RSP value means that the person keeps taking air into the lungs. In contrast, a low RSP value means the absence of air in the lungs. During our experiment, we collected four meetings whose length was about 12 minutes each (total of about 50 minutes) and built a multimodal corpus consisting of the following verbal and nonverbal behaviors and biological information from the recorded data:

- Gaze object: The gaze object was annotated manually using bust-up and overhead views from the videos per frame by skilled annotator. The objects of gaze were the four participants (hereafter denoted as P1, P2, P3, and P4) and others, i.e., the hall or ceiling.
- Utterance: We built the utterance unit using the inter-pausal unit (IPU) [16]. The utterance interval was extracted manually from the speech wave. The portion of an utterance followed by 200 ms of silence was used as the unit of one uuterance. From the created IPU, supportive responses [12] were excluded and an utterance unit continued by the same person was considered as one utterance turn. And pairs of IPUs that adjoined in time and groups of IPUs at the time of turn-keeping and turn-changing were created. Data for speech overlap situations, i.e., when a listener interrupted during a speaker's utterance or two or more participants spoke simultaneously in turn-changing, were excluded from the pairs of IPUs for analysis. Eventually the numbers of the created groups of IPUs were 906 at the time of turn-keeping and 148 at the time of turn-changing.
- Respiration: NeXus-10 MARKII outputs the RSP value that indicates the degree of depth of respiration. The RSP value has a different magnitude for each participant. To correct for the individual differences, the RSP value of each participant was normalized by the mean value μ and standard deviation value δ of each participant. Specifically, the RSP value of each participant was normalization on the basis of the values of $\mu + \delta$ and $\mu - \delta$ of each participant. In this way, we can treat each participants RSP value data for the analysis on the same scale.

All the above mentioned data were integrated for 30Hz for visual display using the NTT Multimodal Meeting Viewer (called "NTT MM-Viewer") that we developed. The viewer enables us to annotate the multimodal data frame by frame and observe the data intuitively.

4. ANALYSIS

We analyzed how the respiration of the speaker, listener, and next speaker quantitatively differ in turn-changing and turn-keeping. We considered that if the analysis revealed differences in the speaker's respiration between turn-changing and turn-keeping or the differences of respiration between next speaker in turn-changing and listener in turn-changing and turn-keeping, respiration could be used as a good feature to predict the next speaker and the start time of the next utterance.

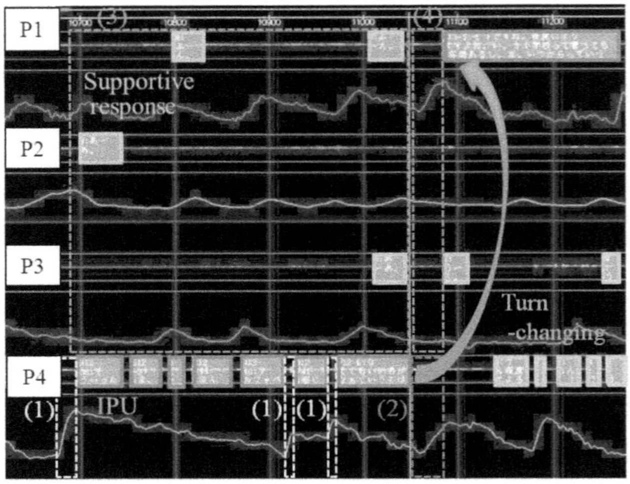

Figure 2: Sample scene in the situation that turn-changing from P4 to P1 happens.

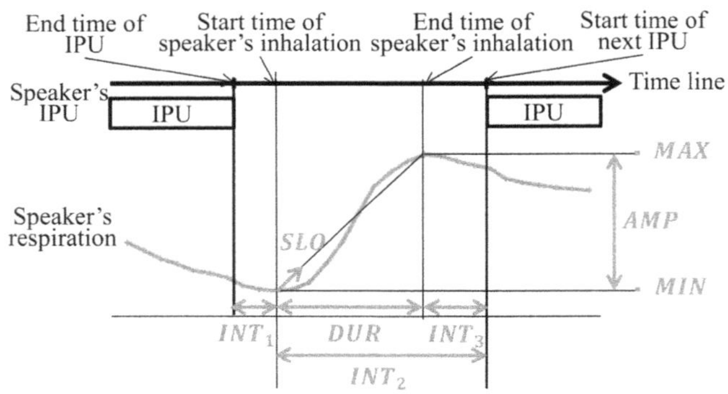

Figure 3: Analytic parameters of speaker's inhalation right after end of IPU.

4.1 Preliminary analysis of speaker's respiration

With the corpus data obtained with the NTT MM-Viewer, we performed a preliminary study of the analysis of differences in a speaker's respiration between turn-changing and in turn-changing before analyzing them in detail. Fig. 2 shows a sample scene of turn-changing from P4 to P1 after several turn-keepings by P4. The wave shows the RSP value. The green box shows the supportive response and the blue box shows the IPU. P4, who is the speaker in turn-keeping, takes a breath quickly (duration of increasing RSP value is very short) right after the end of the IPU (See Fig. 2 (1)). It is assumed that the speaker takes a breath to make up for the deficient oxygenation on speaking on a regular basis. In contrast, when P4 stops speaking in turn-changing, she doesn't take a breath as quickly (See Fig. 2 (2)). Therefore, the speaker's inhalation just after the end of the IPU is assumed to differ in turn-changing and in turn-keeping. We focused on the speaker's inhalation just after end of the IPU for the analysis.

We compare the differences in extracting the inhalation phase of the speaker right after the end of the IPU between turn-changing and turn-keeping. To extract the inhalation phase in detail, we extracted a point where two RSP values right before the point continuously decreased and two RSP values right after the point continuously increased as the

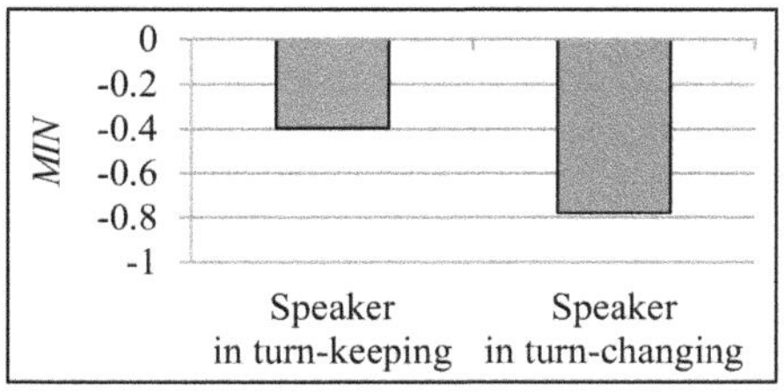

Figure 4: MIN of speaker's inhalation phase right after end of IPU.

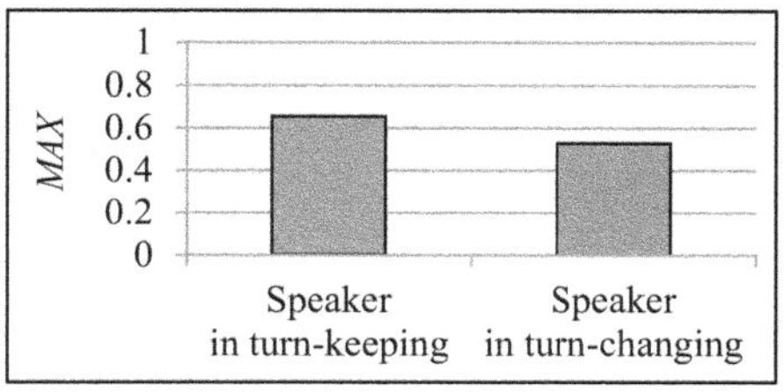

Figure 5: MAX of speaker's inhalation phase right after end of IPU.

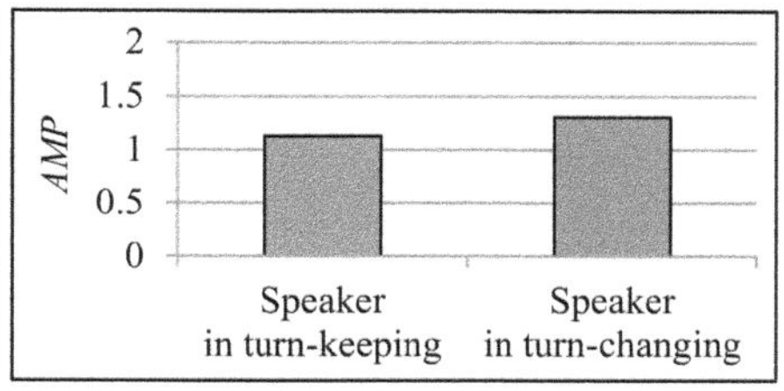

Figure 6: AMP of speaker's inhalation phase right after end of IPU.

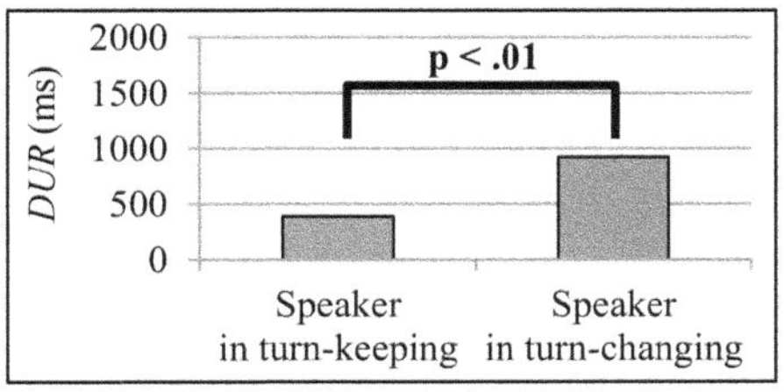

Figure 7: DUR of speaker's inhalation phase right after end of IPU.

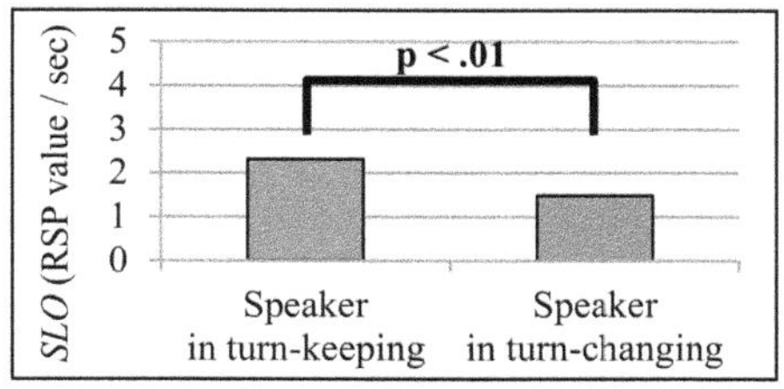

Figure 8: SLO of speaker's inhalation phase right after end of IPU.

start of the inhalation phase. We extracted a point after the start of the inhalation phase where two RSP values right before the point continuously increased and two RSP values right after the point continuously decreased as a the end of the inhalation phase. Before this extraction, we performed a smoothing process whose window length was three frames to eliminate micro noise in RSP value waveforms and thereby prevent erroneous extraction. At this time, the data that did not have an inhalation phase, i.e., speaker didn't take a breath, in turn-keeping was excluded from the analysis. The analysis data are 402, which is 40.2% of all 906 data in turn-keeping and 148 in turn-changing.

We use the following inhalation-phase parameters for the speaker to compare differences between inhalations in detail (See Fig. 3).

- MIN: RSP value at the start of inhalation phase, i.e., minimum RSP value of inhalation phase.
- MAX: RSP value at the end of inhalation phase, i.e., maximum RSP value of inhalation phase.
- AMP: Amplitude of RSP value of inhalation phase.
- DUR: Duration of inhalation phase.
- SLO: Mean value of slope of RSP value per second during inhalation phase.
- INT_1: Interval between end time of speaker's IPU and start time of inhalation.
- INT_2: Interval between start time of inhalation and start time of next IPU.
- INT_3: Interval between end time of inhalation and start time of next IPU.

We analyzed these parameters in turn-changing and turn-keeping.

4.2 Results of analysis of speaker's inhalation right after end of IPU

We calculated the mean value of MIN, MAX, and AMP of the speaker for each participant in turn-changing and turn-keeping. Then, we calculated the mean value of the mean values of all participants. These average values are shown in Fig. 4, 5, and 6. We used a paired t-test to statistically verify whether the MIN, MAX, and AMP in turn-changing are significantly different from them in turn-keeping. The results suggested that there are no significant differences in MIN, MAX, and AMP between turn-changing and turn-keeping. This reveals that there are no differences in MIN, MAX, and AMP of the speaker's inhalation right after the end of the IPU between turn-changing and turn-keeping.

The mean value of the mean values of DUR, the duration of the inhalation phase, of the speaker for each participant in turn-changing and turn-keeping is shown in Fig. 7. A paired t-test suggested that there is a significant difference in DUR between turn-changing and turn-keeping ($t(30) = 3.08, p < .01$). This reveals that the DUR of the speaker's inhalation right after the end of the IPU is shorter in turn-keeping than in turn-changing.

The mean value of the mean values of SLO of the speaker for each participant in turn-changing and turn-keeping is shown in Fig. 8. A paired t-test suggested there is a significant difference in SLO between turn-changing and turn-keeping ($t(30) = 2.96, p < .01$) which indicates that SLO of the speaker's inhalation right after end of IPU is larger in turn-keeping than in turn-changing.

The mean value of the mean values of INT_1 of the speaker for each participant in turn-changing and turn-keeping is shown in Fig. 9. A paired t-test suggested that there is a significant difference in INT_1 between turn-changing and turn-keeping ($t(30) = 2.04$, $p < .10$). This reveals that INT_1 of the speaker's inhalation right after the end of the IPU is shorter in turn-keeping than in turn-changing.

The results for INT_2 and INT_3 are similar to the result of INT_1. The mean value of the mean values of INT_2 and INT_3 of the speaker for each participant in turn-changing and turn-keeping is shown in Fig. 10 and 11. A paired t-test suggested that there is a significant difference in INT_2 and INT_3 between turn-changing and turn-keeping ($t(30) = 3.83$, $p < .01$ for INT_2; $t(30) = 3.52$, $p < .01$ for INT_3). This reveals that INT_2 and INT_3 of the speaker's inhalation right after the end of the IPU are shorter in turn-keeping than in turn-changing.

The above results suggest that the speaker takes a breath more quickly (i.e., the duration of the inhalation phase is shorter and the slope of the RSP value of inhalation is larger)

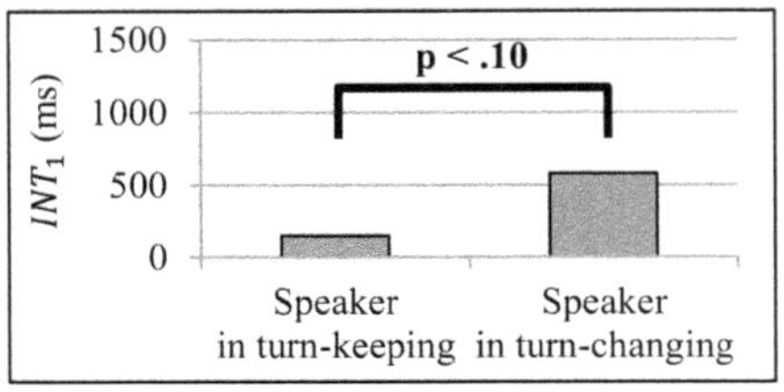

Figure 9: INT_1 of speaker's inhalation phase right after end of IPU.

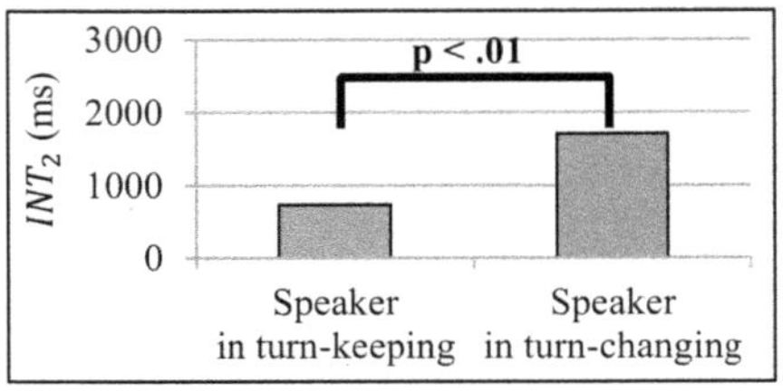

Figure 10: INT_2 of speaker's inhalation phase right after end of IPU.

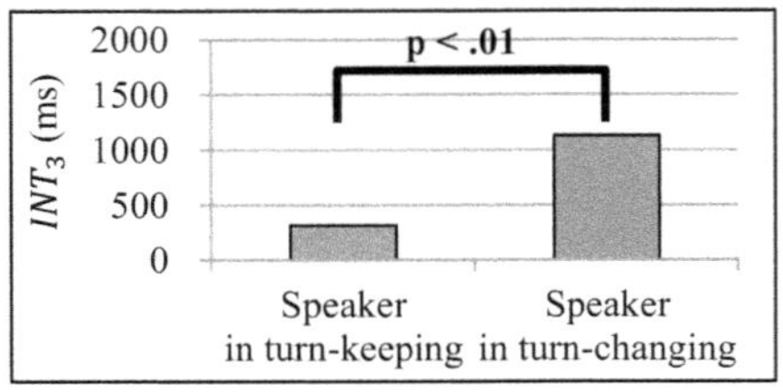

Figure 11: INT_3 of speaker's inhalation phase right after end of IPU.

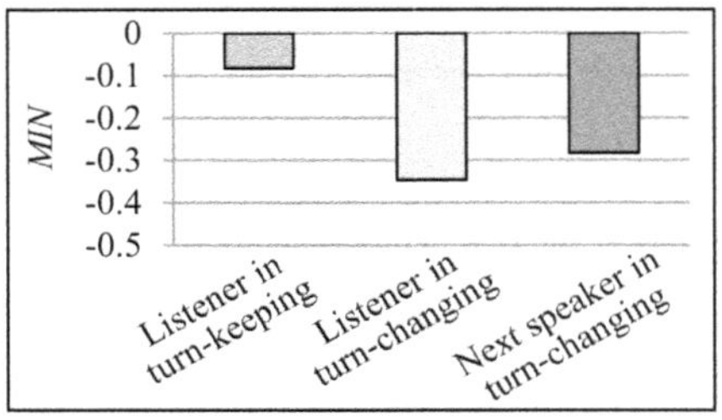

Figure 12: MIN of inhalation phase of listener and next speaker right after end of IPU.

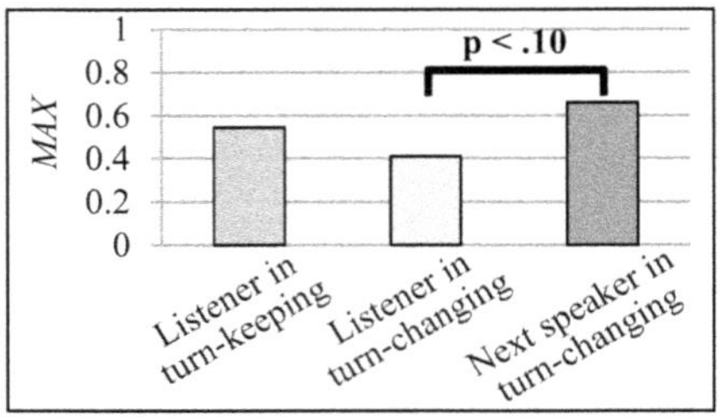

Figure 13: MAX of inhalation phase of listener and next speaker right after end of IPU.

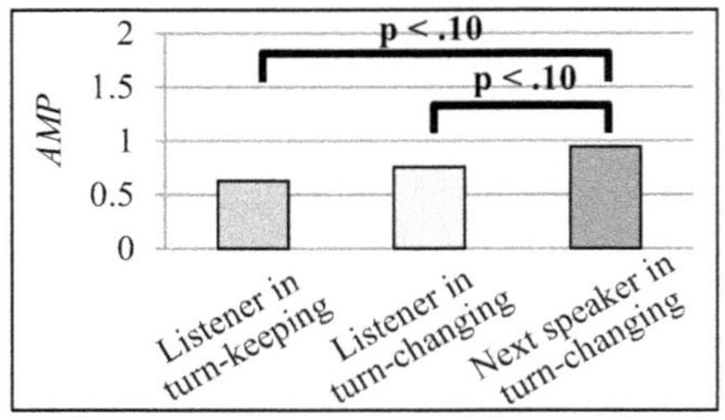

Figure 14: AMP of inhalation phase of listener and next speaker right after end of IPU.

and immediately after the end of IPU (i.e., the interval between the end time of speaker's IPU and the start time of speaker's inhalation is shorter) in turn-keeping than in turn-changing. They also indicate that the speaker starts to speak after inhaling sooner in turn-keeping than the next speaker starts to speak after inhaling in turn-changing.

4.3 Preliminary analysis of listener's and next speaker's respiration

Using the corpus data obtained with the NTT MM-Viewer, we performed a preliminary study of the differences in respiration between listeners in turn-keeping, listeners in turn-changing, and the next speaker in turn-changing before analyzing them in detail.

Fig. 2 (3) shows sample data of a listener's respiration in turn-keeping. Fig. 2 (4) shows sample data of the next speaker's and listeners' respiration in turn-changing. In Fig. 2 (3), all three listeners' respiration is extremely stable. In contrast, the next speaker takes a big breath right before starting to speak, as shown in Fig. 2 (4). It is assumed that the next speaker takes a big breath to make up the deficit of oxygen attendant on speaking and listeners' respiration is extremely stable because they don't need to take a breath for speaking. We focused on the inhalation of the next speaker before the start of the next utterance in turn-changing and the respiration of listeners in turn-changing and turn-keeping. If we find differences in inhalation between the next speaker in turn-changing and in the inhalation of listeners in turn-changing and turn-keeping, these inhalations will contribute to predicting the next speaker and start time of the next utterance.

The average start time of the next speaker's inhalation in turn-changing is 297 ms before the end of the speaker's IPU. On that account, we treat the data in the term between 60 frames (2000 ms) before the end of speaker's IPU and the time right before the start of the next speaker's IPU as analysis data. We extract the inhalation phase that has the largest AMP of all inhalations during the interval of analysis. The extracted inhalation of the next speaker in turn-changing, practically, is inhalation right after the start to speak. We compare the differences in the parameter of extracted inhalation between the next speaker in turn-changing and that of the listeners in turn-changing and turn-keeping. The method of extracting the inhalation is the same as in subsection 4.1. The analysis data are 906 in turn-keeping and 148 in turn-changing.

4.4 Results of analysis of respiration of listeners and next speaker

We calculated the mean value of the mean values of MIN, MAX, and AMP of listeners in turn-keeping and turn-changing and the next speaker in turn-changing for each participant. The mean value is shown in Fig. 12, 13 and 14. We performed a repeating one-way factorial analysis of variance to determine whether the condition of listeners in turn-keeping and in turn-changing and next speaker in turn-changing affected the MIN, MAX, and AMP.

The results suggested the condition has no significant effect on MIN. However, they suggested the condition has a significant trend in MAX ($F(2, 45) = 2.60$, $p < 0.1$) and AMP ($F(2, 45) = 2.73$, $p < 0.1$). Next, multiple comparisons using the Tukey-Kramer method were performed to confirm the differences between pairs of individual criteria. Results for MAX suggested significant differences only between the listeners in turn-changing and the next speaker in turn-changing ($p < .10$). Results for AMP suggested significant differences only between the listeners in turn-keeping and the next speaker in turn-changing ($p < .10$) and between the listeners in turn-changing and the next speaker in turn-changing ($p < .10$). This reveals that MAX of the next speaker is larger than that of the listener in turn-keeping and that AMP of the next speaker in turn-changing is larger than that of listeners in turn-keeping and turn-changing.

The mean value of the mean values of DUR of listeners in turn-keeping and turn-changing and the next speaker in turn-changing for each participant is shown in Fig. 15. A

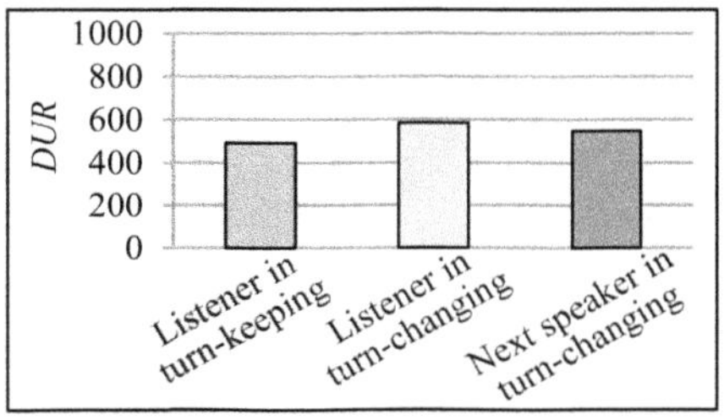

Figure 15: DUR of inhalation phase of listener and next speaker right after end of IPU.

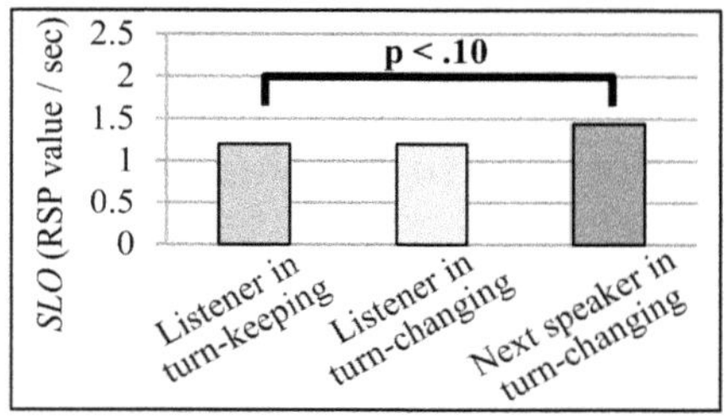

Figure 16: SLO of inhalation phase of listener and next speaker right after end of IPU.

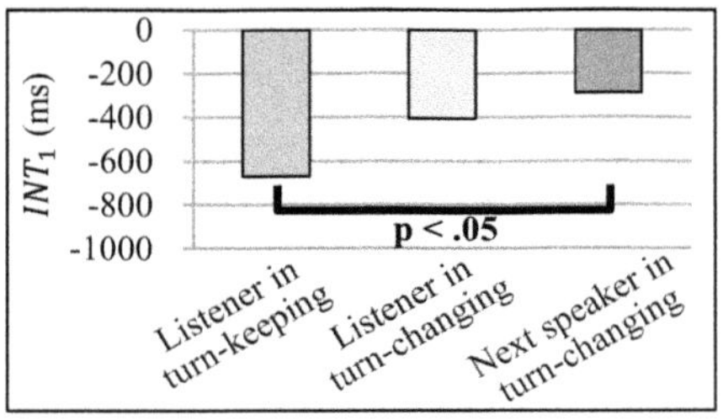

Figure 17: INT_1 of inhalation phase of listener and next speaker right after end of IPU.

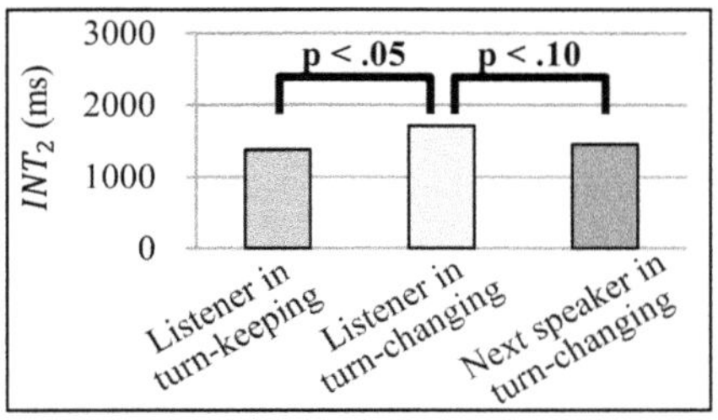

Figure 18: INT_2 of inhalation phase of listener and next speaker right after end of IPU.

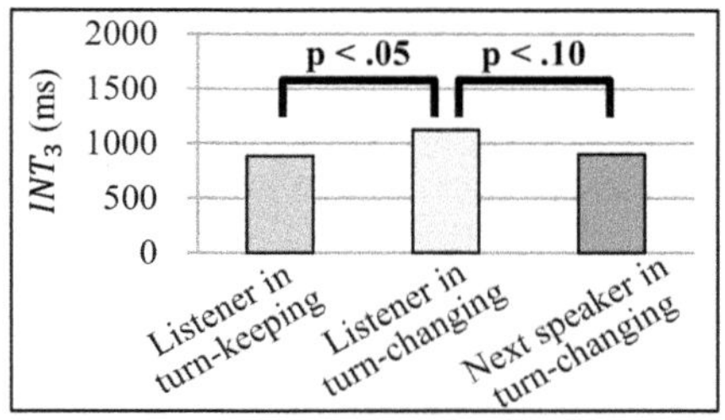

Figure 19: INT_3 of inhalation phase of listener and next speaker right after end of IPU.

repeating one-way factorial analysis of variance suggested that the condition of listeners in turn-keeping and in turn-changing and the next speaker in turn-changing did not have a significant effect, indicating that there is no difference in DUR of listeners between turn-keeping and turn-changing and the next speaker in turn-changing.

The mean value of the mean values of SLO of listeners in turn-keeping and turn-changing and the next speaker in turn-changing for each participant is shown in Fig.16. A repeating one-way factorial analysis of variance showed that the condition of listeners in turn-keeping and turn-changing and the next speaker in turn-changing has a significant trend ($F(2, 45) = 2.85$, $p < .10$). Results of multiple comparisons using the Tukey-Kramer method performed to confirm differences between pairs of individual criteria suggested significant differences only between the listeners in turn-keeping and the next speaker in turn-changing ($p < .10$), These results reveal that the SLO of the next speaker in turn-changing is larger than that of listeners in turn-keeping.

The mean value of the mean values of INT_1 of the listeners and next speaker for each participant is shown in Fig. 17. A repeating one-way factorial analysis of variance suggested that the condition of listeners in turn-keeping and in turn-changing and the next speaker in turn-changing has a significant effect on the INT_1 ($F(2, 45) = 3.62$, $p < .05$). This reveals that INT_1 of the speaker's inhalation right after the end of the IPU is shorter in turn-keeping than in turn-changing. Multiple comparisons using the Tukey-Kramer method were performed to confirm the differences between pairs of individual criteria. Results for INT_1 suggested a significant difference only between the listeners in turn-keeping and the next speaker in turn-changing ($p < .05$).

The results for INT_2 and INT_3 are similar to the result for INT_1. The mean value of the mean values of INT_2 and INT_3 of the listeners and next speaker for each participant are shown in Fig. 18 and 19. A repeating one-way factorial analysis of variance suggested that the condition of listeners in turn-keeping and in turn-changing and the next speaker in turn-changing has a significant effect on INT_2 and INT_3 ($F(2, 45) = 3.64$, $p < .05$ for INT_2; $F(2, 45) = 3.76$, $p < .05$ for INT_3). Multiple comparisons using the Tukey-Kramer method were performed to confirm the differences between pairs of individual criteria. Results for INT_2 suggested significant differences only between the listeners in turn-keeping and the listener in turn-changing ($p < .05$) and between the listeners in turn-changing and the next speaker in turn-changing ($p < .10$). Results for INT_3 suggested significant differences only between the listeners in turn-keeping and the listeners in turn-changing ($p < .05$) and between the listeners in turn-changing and the next speaker in turn-changing ($p < .10$).

The above results for INT_1 reveal that the start time of the listeners' inhalation in turn-keeping is longer before the end of the speaker's IPU than the start time of the next speaker's inhalation in turn-changing and that INT_2 and INT_3 of the inhalation of the listeners in turn-keeping and the next speaker in turn-changing is shorter than that of the listener in turn-changing.

These results suggest that the next speaker takes a bigger breath more quickly and deeply in turn-changing than the listeners in turn-keeping (i.e., the amplitude and slope of RSP value of inhalation is larger and the interval between the end of the speaker's IPU and start of the next speaker's inhalation), and the next speaker takes a bigger breath than the listeners in turn-changing (i.e., the maximum and amplitude of RSP value of inhalation is larger). They also suggest that the interval between the start time of next speaker's utterance and next speaker's inhalation in turn-changing and the interval between the start time of speaker's utterance and the next speaker's inhalation in turn-keeping is shorter than the interval between the start time of the next speaker's utterance and listeners' inhalation in turn-changing.

5. PRELIMINARY INVESTIGATION OF PREDICTION MODEL USING RESPIRATION

5.1 Prediction of turn-keeping or turn-changing using speaker's respiration

We discuss the prediction of who will start to speak next and when using respiration. The analysis results in subsection 4.2 suggest that the DUR, SLO, and INT_1 of the speaker's inhalation right after the IPU are different between turn-keeping and turn-changing. To investigate the effectiveness of DUR, SLO, and INT_1 of the speaker's inhalation right after the IPU for the prediction of whether turn-keeping or turn-changing happens, we constructed a prediction model based on a support vector machine (SVM), in which the method is SMO [14] implemented in the Weka data mining tool [2], and evaluated the performance of the model. The settings of the SVM are RBF (radial basis function) kernel with C ($C = 1.0$) as the default parameter. The data used in the SVM contains the turn states of turn-changing and turn-keeping as a class and DUR, SLO and INT_1 of the speaker's inhalation as features.

We employed the ten-fold cross validation with 296 data, which includes 148 data that was taken by sampling from 402 data in turn-changing to remove the bias of the number of data and 148 data used in Section 4.2 in turn-changing. The accuracy rate of the prediction model is 78.7%. This suggests that parameters DUR, SLO, and INT_1 of the speaker's inhalation right after the IPU contribute to predicting whether turn-keeping or turn-changing happens. The result of the analysis of the INT_3 in Section 4.2 suggests that a prediction model using DUR, SLO, and INT_1 of speaker's inhalation right after a unit of utterance has the potential to predict whether turn-keeping or turn-changing happens about 350 ms before the start time of the next utterance in turn-keeping and about 1150 ms before the start time of the next utterance in turn-changing on average.

In this evaluation of the model, we removed the data on turn-keeping when the inhalation by the speaker didn't happen. A future challenge is to conduct an investigation of the prediction model with all of turn-keeping data, including the removed data, in detail. Then, we plan to make better use of the listeners' inhalation because the inhalation parameters such as AMP and INT_1 are different between the listener in turn-keeping and the next speaker in turn-changing, as shown in Section 4.4.

5.2 Prediction of next speaker using listener's respiration

From the analysis results in subsection 4.4, the MAX and AMP of the listener's and next speaker's inhalation before the next speaker's utterance are different in turn-changing. To investigate the effectiveness of MAX and AMP of the three listener's inhalation before the next utterance for the prediction of the next speaker in turn-changing, we constructed a prediction model based on the SVM as previously explained and evaluated the performance of the model. The data used in the SVM contains the next speaker as a class and the parameters MAX and AMP of each three listener's inhalation as features. The data used in the SVM contains the next speaker as a class and the parameters of MAX and AMP of each three listener's inhalation as features.

We employed ten-fold cross validation with the 148 turn-changing data used in Section 4.4. The accuracy rate of the prediction model is 40.8%. The chance level is 33.3% because there are the three next-speaker candidates in turn-changing. This suggests that the MAX and AMP parameters of the listeners' inhalation contribute to predicting the next speaker in turn-changing. From the results of the analysis of INT_3, a prediction model using MAX and AMP of listener's inhalation has the potential to predict the next speaker about 900 ms before the start time of the next utterance in turn-changing on average. In future work, we plan to devise a prediction model that can predict the next speaker and start time well by making better use of the more detailed parameters of the listeners' inhalation.

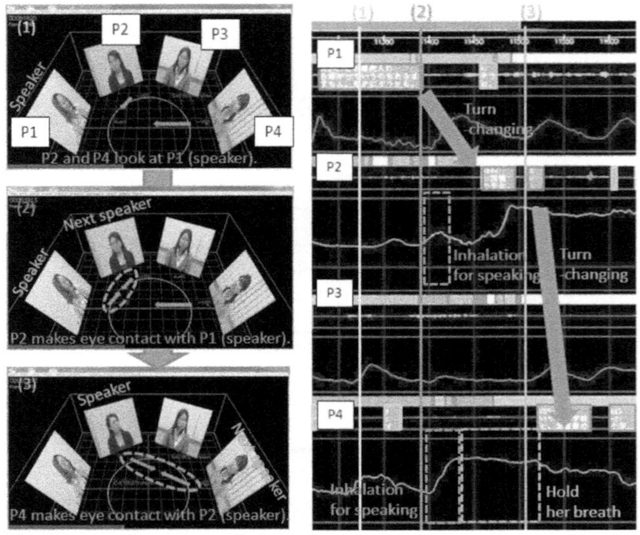

Figure 20: Analysis of the relationship between multimodal information such as respiration and gaze behavior and the next speaker.

6. DISCUSSION: MULTIMODAL APPROACH

Some previous work [9, 10] has demonstrated that gaze behavior plays a crucial role in deciding the who will be the next speaker in multi-party meetings. In particular, the speaker looks at a listener to yield the turn and the listener who becomes the next speaker makes eye contact with the speaker to grab the turn. Here we discuss the possibility of multimodal processing of gaze behavior with respiration for the prediction model.

Fig. 20 shows a conversational scene of turn-changing from P1 to P2 and from P2 to P4. First, P2 and P4, who are listeners, look at P1, who is the speaker, near the end of the speaker's IPU (See Fig. 20 (1)). Then, P1 looks at P2 for a turn-yielding cue and eye contact happens. Soon after that, P2 takes a breath quickly and deeply. Meanwhile, P4 takes a breath quickly and deeply too. After that, P2 starts to speak before P4 does because P2 receives the turn from P1 via the eye contact. Thereafter, P4 makes eye contact with P2 and starts to speak i.e., grabs the turn.

There are two interesting things in this scene. One is that a listener (P2) who made eye contact with the speaker started to speak first right after the two listeners (P2 and P4) had taken a breath quickly and deeply to start to speak. The other is that the listener (P4) who had taken a breath to start to speak and could not start to speak first held her breath for a couple of seconds. The results mean that the listener (P4) tried to take every opportunity to start to speak and the speaker's (P2) gaze toward her (P4) played the role of the trigger of the start of her (P4) speaking. Therefore, it is reasonable to suppose that the use of the multimodal information such as gaze behavior and respiration will contribute to developing a prediction model of higher order.

7. CONCLUSION AND FUTURE WORK

We performed a fundamental study on how effective respiration is for the prediction of the next speaker and the start time of the next utterance. The results of the analysis reveal that a speaker inhales more rapidly and quickly right after the end of a unit of utterance in turn-keeping. The next speaker takes a bigger breath toward speaking in turn-changing than listeners who will not become the next speaker. We constructed prediction models to evaluate how effective the parameters are. The results of the evaluation suggest that the speaker's inhalation right after a unit of utterance, such as the start time from the end of the unit of utterance and the slope and duration of the inhalation phase, is effective for predicting whether turn-keeping or turn-changing happen about 350 ms before the start time of the next utterance on average and that listener's inhalation before the next utterance, such as the maximal inspiration and amplitude of inhalation phase, is effective for predicting the next speaker in turn-changing about 900 ms before the start time of the next utterance on average. Moreover, multimodal processing using gaze behavior in addition to respiration will open up new possibilities for predicting the next speaker and the start time.

In future work, with the goal of achievement highly accurate prediction, we plan to explore a high performance prediction model using both the speaker's and listeners' respiration and multimodal information such as gaze behavior.

8. REFERENCES

[1] Athos "Athos". https://www.liveathos.com/.

[2] R. R. Bouckaert, E. Frank, M. A. Hall, G. Holmes, B. Pfahringer, P. Reutemann, and I. H. Witten. WEKA–experiences with a java open-source project. J. Machine Learning Research, 11:2533–2541, 2010.

[3] L. Chen and M. P. Harper. Multimodal floor control shift detection. In ICMI, pages 15–22, 2009.

[4] I. de Kok and D. Heylen. Multimodal end-of-turn prediction in multi-party meetings. In ICMI, pages 91–98, 2009.

[5] A. Dielmann, G. Garau, and H. Bourlard. Floor holder detection and end of speaker turn prediction in meetings. In ISCA, pages 2306–2309, 2010.

[6] L. Ferrer, E. Shriberg, and A. Stolcke. Is the speaker done yet? faster and more accurate end-of-utterance detection using prosody in human-computer dialog. In ICSLP, volume 3, pages 2061–2064, 2002.

[7] T. Fukuda, O. Ichikawa, and M. Nishimura. Combining feature space discriminative training with long-term spectro-temporal features for noise-robust speech recognition. In Annu. Conf. Int. Speech Communication Association, pages 229–232, 2011.

[8] D. Gatica-Perez. Analyzing group interactions in conversations: a review. In MFI, pages 41–46, 2006.

[9] R. Ishii, K. Otsuka, S. Kumano, M. Matsuda, and J. Yamato. Predicting next speaker and timing from gaze transition patterns in multi-party meetings. In ICMI, pages 79–86, 2013.

[10] R. Ishii, K. Otsuka, S. Kumano, and J. Yamato. Analysis and modeling of next speaking start timing based on gaze behavior in multi-party meetings. In ICASSP, pages 694–698, 2014.

[11] K. Jokinen, H. Furukawa, M. Nishida, and S. Yamamoto. Gaze and turn-taking behavior in casual conversational interactions. J. TiiS, 3(2):12, 2013.

[12] N. Jovanovic, R. op den Akker, and A. Nijholt. Addressee identification in face-to-face meetings. In Conf. European Chapter of the ACL, 2006.

[13] T. Kawahara, T. Iwatate, and K. Takanashii. Prediction of turn-taking by combining prosodic and eye-gaze information in poster conversations. In ISCA, 2012.

[14] S. S. Keerthi, S. K. Shevade, C. Bhattacharyya, and K. R. K. Murthy. Improvements to platt's smo algorithm for svm classifier design. Neural Computation, 13(3):637–649, 2001.

[15] A. Kendon. Some functions of gaze direction in social interaction. ActaPsychologica, 26:22–63, 1967.

[16] H. Koiso, Y. Horiuchi, S. Tutiya, A. Ichikawa, and Y. Den. An analysis of turn-taking and backchannels based on prosodic and syntactic features in japanese map task dialogs. In Language and Speech, volume 41, pages 295–321, 1998.

[17] K. Laskowski, J. Edlund, and M. Heldner. A single-port non-parametric model of turn-taking in multi-party conversation. In ICASSP, pages 5600–5603, 2011.

[18] G.-A. Levow. Turn-taking in mandarin dialogue: Interactions of tones and intonation. In SIGHAN, 2005.

[19] D. H. McFarland. Respiratory markers of conversational interaction. J. Speech, Language and Hearing Research, 44(1):128–143, 2001.

[20] MIND MEDIA "NeXus-10 MARKII". http://www.mindmedia.info/CMS2014/products/systems/nexus-10-mkii.

[21] K. Otsuka. Conversational scene analysis. IEEE Signal Processing Magazine, 28:127–131, 2011.

[22] Philips "Vital Signs Camera", 2014. http://www.vitalsignscamera.com/.

[23] A. Rochet-capellan, G. Bailly, and S. Fuchs. Is breathing sensitive to the communication partner? In Speech Prosody, pages 613–617, 2014.

[24] H. Sacks, E. A. Schegloff, and G. Jefferson. A simplest systematics for the organisation of turn taking for conversation. Language, 50:696–735, 1974.

[25] D. Schlangen. From reaction to prediction experiments with computational models of turn-taking. In ISCA, pages 17–21, 2006.

[26] A. L. Winkworth, P. J. Davis, R. D. Adams, and E. Ellis. Breathing patterns during spontaneous speech. J. Speech, Language and Hearing Research, 38(1):124–144, 1995.

[27] J. Xia and R. A. Siochi. A real-time respiratory motion monitoring system using kinect: proof of concept. Med Phys, 39(5):2682–5, 2012.

A Multimodal In-Car Dialogue System That Tracks The Driver's Attention

Spyros Kousidis
Bielefeld University
PO-Box 10 01 31
33501 Bielefeld, Germany
spyros.kousidis@uni-bielefeld.de

Casey Kennington
CITEC, Bielefeld University
PO-Box 10 01 31
33501 Bielefeld, Germany
ckennington@cit-ec.uni-bielefeld.de

Timo Baumann
Hamburg University
Vogt-Kölln-Strasse 30
22527 Hamburg, Germany
baumann@informatik.uni-hamburg.de

Hendrik Buschmeier
CITEC, Bielefeld University
PO-Box 10 01 31
33501 Bielefeld, Germany
hbuschme@uni-bielefeld.de

Stefan Kopp
CITEC, Bielefeld University
PO-Box 10 01 31
33501 Bielefeld, Germany
skopp@uni-bielefeld.de

David Schlangen
Bielefeld University
PO-Box 10 01 31
33501 Bielefeld, Germany
david.schlangen@uni-bielefeld.de

ABSTRACT

When a passenger speaks to a driver, he or she is co-located with the driver, is generally aware of the situation, and can stop speaking to allow the driver to focus on the driving task. In-car dialogue systems ignore these important aspects, making them more distracting than even cell-phone conversations. We developed and tested a "situationally-aware" dialogue system that can interrupt its speech when a situation which requires more attention from the driver is detected, and can resume when driving conditions return to normal. Furthermore, our system allows driver-controlled resumption of interrupted speech via verbal or visual cues (head nods). Over two experiments, we found that the situationally-aware spoken dialogue system improves driving performance and attention to the speech content, while driver-controlled speech resumption does not hinder performance in either of these two tasks.

Categories and Subject Descriptors

H.5.2 [**User Interfaces**]: Information Systems

Keywords

Spoken Dialogue Systems; Incremental Dialogue; In-car Dialogue; Speech Output Generation; Multimodal

1. INTRODUCTION

Vehicles are increasingly being equipped with added functionality to help the driver increase efficiency while driving, such as navigation systems and hands-free phones. However, such systems are a distraction to the driver; using the interfaces often requires some visual attention of the driver, for example, to look up a route or to find a phone number. One potential solution to this is to use spoken dialogue systems (SDS) which can understand driver commands and perform tasks. Even though this keeps the driver's visual attention on the road, it has been shown that even hands-free devices do not improve driver performance [10, 11, 12, 23]. Furthermore, simply paying attention to speech was found to induce an additional cognitive load on the driver [7]. However, according to [8], driver performance is not hindered when drivers speak to passengers, perhaps due to a shared situational awareness; the driving and traffic are, at times, topics of conversation. It was indeed found that passengers adopt strategies that relieve the driver from attending to the conversation in difficult driving situations [9]. In short, *co-location* is a requirement for risk-free in-car interaction, regardless of the interface. Most in-car systems (spoken or otherwise) do not address this, adding to the potentially already high cognitive load of the driver.

In this paper, we present our recent work on addressing this shortcoming. We have implemented a "situationally-aware" dialogue system that can react when the driving environment requires more attention from the driver. This is accomplished through *incremental* dialogue, specifically dialogue output (following [6], this term covers incremental language and speech generation here) which can interrupt its speech when a "dangerous" driving situation is detected, and flexibly resume when driving conditions become safe again. Our system delivers calendar events, informing the driver via speech about upcoming schedule items. We tested our system using a variation of a standard driving task, and found that it improved both driving performance and recall, compared to a non-adaptive baseline system. In a more recent experiment, our system yielded control of the decision to resume speaking optionally to the driver, who could signal return of attention to the spoken information, via speech or head nods. We found that this did not impact the users' driving performance or recall of information negatively. This shows that an in-car dialogue system that is situationally aware (both to extra-conversational events as well as to the dialogue) is safer and more effective than a system that has no notion of the driving conditions.

In the following section we describe the incremental and multimodal functions of our dialogue system, followed by the description of the system setup in Section 3. We then explain two experiments: one which compares performance in driving and memory

ICMI'14 November 12–16 2014, Istanbul, Turkey

ACM ACM 978-1-4503-2885-2/14/11 ...$15.00.
http://dx.doi.org/10.1145/2663204.2663244.

tasks under non-adaptive and adaptive speech conditions (Section 4); and a more recent one where we tested the effects of multimodal user control in the same tasks (Section 5). We then present and discuss our results in Section 6, and conclude in Section 7.

2. MULTIMODAL INCREMENTAL DIALOGUE

In general, (SDS) have three aspects: input via automatic speech recognition (ASR) which is the main input modality, dialogue management (DM) which makes decisions based on the input, and output in the form of natural language generation (NLG) which produces spoken utterances via speech synthesis (TTS). A multimodal SDS can handle other sources of information, such as gaze and gestures, which can be used to aid in interpreting the intent of the speaker as in [15], and help the DM make more informed decisions on how to act. In this paper, we use a multimodal SDS by incorporating information about the driving situation, ASR, and head nods into the DM decision.

An SDS that processes input *incrementally* produces behaviour that is perceived by human users to be more natural than systems that end-point on larger sentence-length segments or use a turn-based approach (such as phone-based dialogue systems) [1, 25, 24]. Incremental dialogue has seen improvements in speech recognition where intermediate results are provided before an utterance is complete [2], and speech synthesis where parts of an utterance yet to be realised can be altered, even while the utterance prefix is in progress [6]. This approach to interactive dialogue is necessary in real-time interactive systems, such as in-car dialogue, as the dialogue system can act and react immediately to changes in the driving situation.

Our SDS consists of many incremental components and is able to integrate many multimodal features. In the following, we describe the most relevant components used in this study, namely incremental language generation and head nod detection.

Incremental Output Generation.

Making the output of an in-car SDS situationally aware requires its output generation modules, speech synthesis and natural language generation, to be able to (1) timely and plausibly interrupt and resume speech output, and (2) to flexibly adapt or even reformulate the content of its utterances, taking into account a preceding delivery interruption.

Both requirements call for incremental processing in these modules. On the level of speech synthesis, incrementality allows for shorter response times (i.e., it can resume faster) as the system can start speech output while still synthesising the rest of an utterance [6]. It also enables changes to the prosody of an ongoing utterance [4], allowing the system to add a prosodic marker to signal the system's awareness to the word preceding the interruption. On the level of natural language generation, incrementality makes it possible to change those parts of an utterance that have not been delivered yet. The continuation of an interrupted utterance can thus differ from planned but yet undelivered parts by choosing a continuation point that, e.g., re-states some of the context but does not repeat more than is needed.

Our work builds on the existing incremental output generation system of [6] that fulfils the requirements specified above and is partially available in the open source incremental dialogue processing toolkit INPROTK ([5], see below)[1]. It consists of incremental components for speech synthesis and natural language generation that are integrated in such a way that timely interruptions and adaptive continuations are possible.

The system's language generation component creates utterances in two processes [6]. The first process plans the overall utterance by laying out a sequence of chunks which determine what will be said, and when; the second, which is based on the SPUD microplanning framework [26], computes how each of these chunks is realised linguistically. Utterances are incrementally generated chunk by chunk. Adaptations to an ongoing utterance are therefore constrained to the chunk level as well. The chunk-planning process can change the sequence of chunks, repeat one or several chunks, or leave some out. The microplanning process can change how a chunk is realised, e.g., by inserting or leaving out cue words, by providing information that has been mentioned before, or by making information conveyed implicitly explicit – or vice versa. Our system made use of adaptations resulting from both processes.

Incremental speech synthesis [4] performs all computationally expensive processing steps, such as waveform synthesis, as late as possible while performing prosodic processing (which has non-local effects) as early as necessary [3], resulting in fast response times with as little impact on quality as possible. Ongoing synthesis can be changed, and adapted prosodically with minimal latency, and provides detailed progress information on various linguistic levels. Our system uses the incremental capabilities to stop synthesis at word boundaries when interrupted and to generate new sentence onset intonations for continuations.

Multimodal Dialogue with Head Nods.

A new addition to our SDS is the incorporation of head nods as an additional modality. Head nods in human–human interaction are the most prominent head gesture, especially in situations of active listening [27]. In dyadic interaction, head nods signal understanding/agreement and prompt the speaker to continue, among other functions [22]. These properties suggest the head nod gesture as a good alternative to speech for a natural prompt from the driver to the in-car system.

Our head nod detection component uses the output of a head tracking software (described below) that utilises a standard webcam. The software estimates the head posture from the position and orientation of the face mask shown in Figure 1. Head posture is defined by the standard translation (x, y, z) and rotation $(pitch, yaw, roll)$ axes. In addition to the head posture, the head tracking software reports a percentage value representing the tracking confidence.

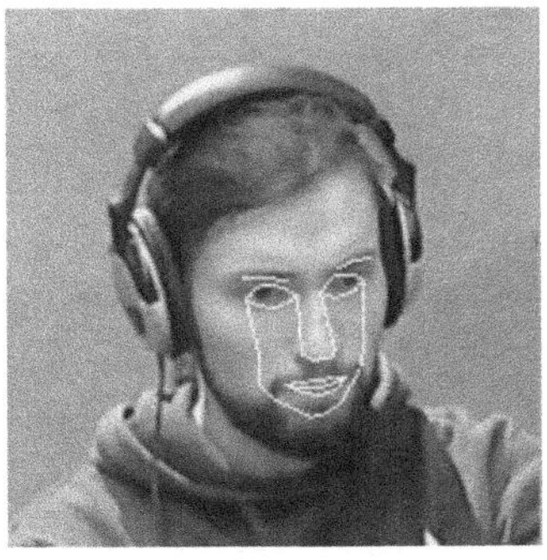

Figure 1: Face capture frame from the face tracking software FaceAPI.

Algorithm 1 shows our simple algorithm that detects head nods incrementally based on the raw pitch rotation angle (see Figure 2) and the tracking confidence. We calculate the energy of the head pitch rotation at each sample (30 Hz), and open a new "window" (candidate of a head nod) if the energy and confidence both exceed their pre-set thresholds. If enough high-energy points extend the window beyond a *minimum duration*, the algorithm reports an (ongoing) head nod. If no new high energy points extend the window any more, the algorithm reports that the head nod ceased. This al-

[1] `http://inprotk.sourceforge.net`

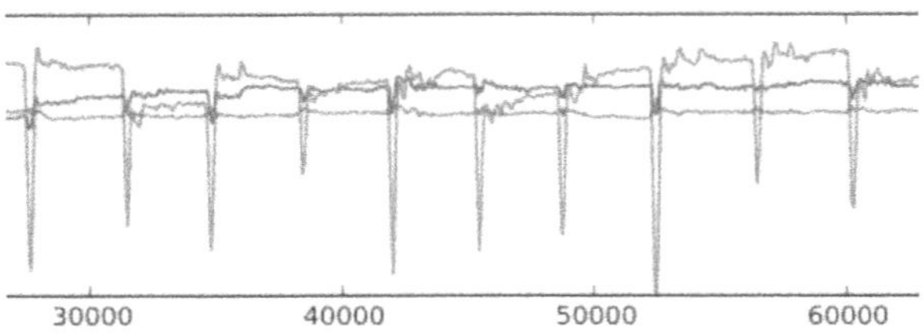

Figure 2: Head rotation angles as detected by our real-time head nod detection software. The pitch rotation angle spikes (red) signify instances of head nods.

gorithm is rather simple and would most probably be unsuitable for spontaneous human–human dialogue, where the form of head nods is much more varied [18]. However, we qualitatively evaluated that the algorithm worked well for head nods that are presented to the system, as they are *displayed* by the participants, rather than being spontaneous. The parameters of the algorithm were fine-tuned for each participant before experiments.

3. MULTIMODAL SYSTEM SETUP

Hardware.

Our driving simulation scenario consists of a 40-inch 16:9 screen with a Thrustmaster PC Racing Wheels Ferrari GT Experience steering wheel and pedal. Audio is presented to the participant via Sennheiser headphones (see Figure 3). To recognise speech, we used a Sennheiser ME 2 lavalier microphone and for head nod detection, we used a Logitech C270 webcam.

Figure 3: View of experiment setup: a driving simulation, interfaced with a steering wheel and pedal, is shown on the large screen. Speech is presented to the participant via headphones

Software.

For the driving simulator, we used the OpenDS Toolkit [21][2]. We developed our own simple driving scenarios (derived from the "ReactionTest" task, distributed together with OpenDS) that specified the driving task and timing of the concurrent speech, as described below. For head tracking, we used SeeingMachines FaceAPI[3] which sent head posture data to our head nod detection algorithm described above. Our incremental SDS was built on the framework of INPROTK [5] (our speech output – NLG and TTS – componens are part of this), with recent extensions allowing for multimodal coupling of distributed components which we denote INPROTK_S [16]. We make use of an incremental automatic speech recogniser (a variant of Sphinx as part of INPROTK [2]) to recognise specific words. For DM, we integrated OpenDial [20][4] into INPROTK_S.

Algorithm 1 Head Nod Detection: the DETECT_HEAD_NOD procedure is called every time new data is received from FaceAPI. The four variables that are used for thresholds and housekeeping are described before the procedure.

```
confidence_threshold # head confidence threshold (%)
velocity_sample # max time jump for calculating velocities (ms)
min_duration # min duration for buffer before detecting a nod (ms)
buffer # energy buffer for time jump (samples)
procedure DETECT_HEAD_NOD(frame)
    if frame.confidence < confidence_threshold:
        return
    end if
    if frame.time – lastframe.time < velocity_sample:
        velocity =frame.head_rotation – lastframe.head_rotation
        energy = 100*velocity^2
         # (scale to deal with small numbers)
    else energy = 0
    end if
    if energy > energy_threshold:
        buffer.append(frame)
    end if
    if buffer.length > min_duration:
        send_headnod_event() # (head nod detected)
    end if
    lastframe = frame
end procedure
```

Connecting All Components with mint.tools.

Our overall system setup is depicted in Figure 4. The three hardware components (and their software), which comprise three modalities of driving scenario events, speech, and head nods, were plugged into three corresponding workstations (all used Ubuntu 12.04, except the one running the FaceAPI software, which run on MS Windows 7). An important aspect of our setup is how the various software components communicate with each other across the network. For this, we used the *mint.tools* architecture [19], which utilises the Robotics Service Bus (RSB) message passing architecture [28] and the InstantIO/InstantReality framework, facilitating real-time data passing and logging[5,6].

FaceAPI sent raw data (via InstantIO) to a process running our implemented algorithm that detected head nods, which in turn passed head nod events via RSB to INPROTK_S. To make our system situationally aware, we modified OpenDS to pass real-time data (e.g. car position/velocity/events in the simulation, such as a gate becoming visible or a lane change) to INPROTK_S (via InstantIO). Finally, ASR and NLG were controlled by INPROTK_S directly. Further information was sent from INPROTK_S (e.g., input events such as head nods or detected speech, DM decisions, text used for NLG) to the logger (via InstantIO). Running on a dedicated fourth workstation, the logger wrote all data (with timestamps) sent over InstantIO from any of the components to a compressed file in XML format, which we used for post analysis. We want to further add that with *mint.tools*, one can use the XML log file to replay the recorded interaction in real-time.

In the following we describe two experiments. Experiment 1 was performed in previous work presented in [14], but as the setup is a precursor, and the results are directly comparable to the work done

[2] http://www.opends.eu/

[3] http://www.seeingmachines.com/product/faceapi/

[4] http://opendial.googlecode.com/

[5] https://code.cor-lab.de/projects/rsb

[6] http://www.instantreality.org/

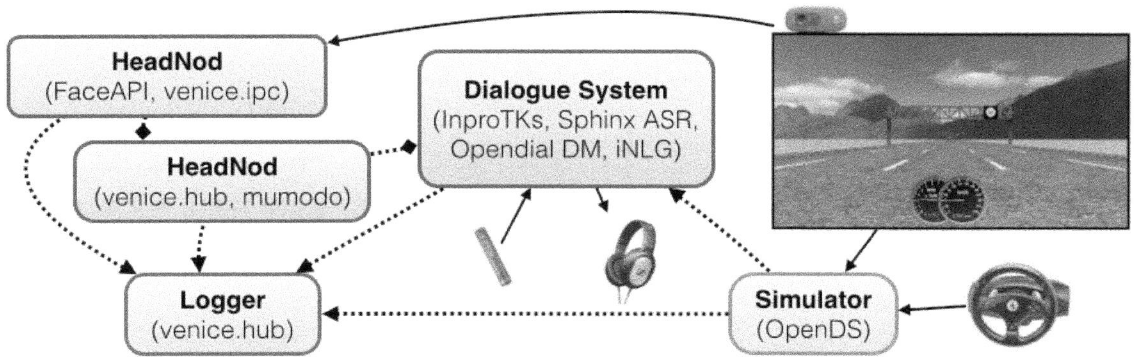

Figure 4: Overview of our system: solid lines denote connections between hardware and software components, colours denote the workstations (in this case 4) that we used. Dashed lines denote network connections between components, arrows denote InstantIO connections, diamonds denote RSB connections.

in this paper, we also provide a description here. Experiment 2 builds on Experiment 1, with added control over the SDS given to the driver.

4. EXPERIMENT 1: ESTABLISHING ADAPTIVE SPEECH

The goal of this experiment is two-fold: first, we want participants to be able to perform a driving task as a responsible driver would; second, we want to explore how well they pay attention to and recall speech during driving, under two possible presentations of speech: the *adaptive* presentation, in which the speech of the SDS is interrupted when a "dangerous" situation is detected in the driving scene, and later resumed after the dangerous situation is no longer present. This mimics a situated dialogue participant who is aware of the physical surroundings and driving conditions; and the *non-adaptive* presentation, a non-incremental system that does not stop speaking when a dangerous driving condition is detected. In order to simulate these conditions, we use a combination of two tasks: a driving task and a memory task, which we explain in detail below.

The Driving Task.

For the driving task we used a variant of the standard lane-change task (LCT [13]). It requires the driver to react to a green light positioned on a signal gate above the road (see Figure 5). The driver, otherwise instructed to remain in the middle lane of a straight, 5-lane road, must move to the lane indicated by the green light, remain there until a tone is sounded, and then return again to the middle lane. OpenDS gives a *success* or *fail* result to this task depending on whether the target lane was reached within 10 seconds (if at all) and the car was in the middle lane when the signal became visible. In addition, OpenDS reports a *reaction time*, which is the time between the moment the signal to change lane becomes visible and the moment the lane has been reached. A lane-change trial simulates a "dangerous" situation on the road.

We added a second component to the task, which was to change the speed from 40 km/h (the default speed that the car maintained without the gas pedal being pressed) to 60 km/h during the lane change. This speed is lower than the maximum speed, so that the right position of the gas pedal had to be found and the speed be monitored continuously.

The Memory Task.

We tested the attention of the drivers to the generated speech using a simple true/false memory task. The dialogue system generated calendar-entry utterances such as *"am Samstag den siebzehnten Mai 12 Uhr 15 bis 14 Uhr 15 hast du 'gemeinsam Essen im Westend mit Martin'"* (on Saturday the 17th of May from 12:15-14:15 you are meeting Martin for lunch). These utterances (spoken by a female voice) always had 5 information tokens (chosen at random from a database) in a specified order: day, time, activity, location, and partner. Three seconds after the utterance was complete, and while no driving distraction occurred, a true/false confirmation question about one of the uttered tokens was asked by a male voice, e.g. *"Richtig oder falsch? – Freitag"* (Right or wrong? – Friday). The subject was then required to answer true or false by pressing one of two respective (labelled) buttons on the steering wheel. The token of the confirmation question was chosen randomly.

In the case of an interruption/resumption, tokens spoken after the resumption can be more easily remembered than those given before the interruption. By giving the early tokens (day and time) a higher probability of occurrence, we biased the design *against* the adaptive system since the question tends to refer to tokens spoken *before* the interruption more often than not.

Figure 5: From the perspective of the driver, a gate is shown with a green lane signal over the right-most lane.

Interaction Between Tasks.

Figure 6 shows how the task unfolds over time when changing the lane: all red-dashed lines represent pre-set event triggers (that are invisible to the driver) or simply events of the simulation that trigger unique messages to be sent to the SDS. At the t_1 marker, a trigger is sent to the DM to start speaking. A random delay (0–4 seconds for the non-adaptive, 4–7 seconds for the adaptive setting) is inserted before the speech begins in order to vary the type of token that is spoken during the exact moment of interruption or steering. At t_2, the gate is in view (as seen from Figure 5) and a gate light is visible. In the adaptive setting, at this point the speech would be

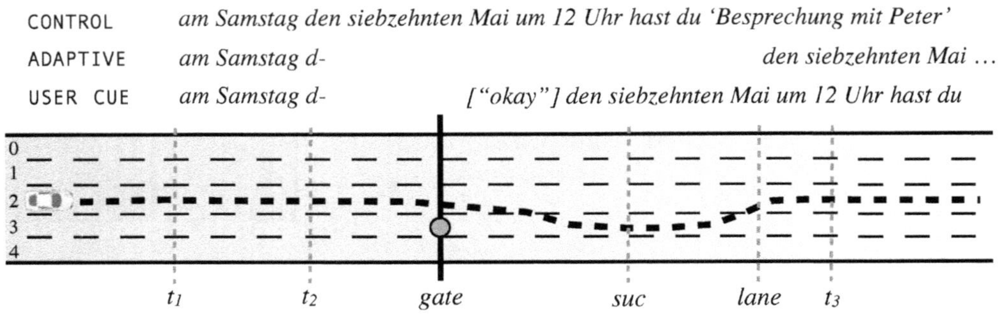

Figure 6: Top view of driving task: as the car moves to the right over time, speech begins at t_1, the gate with the lane-change indicator becomes visible at t_2, where in the adaptive version speech pauses. If a successful lane change is detected at *suc*, then speech resumes at *lane*, otherwise it resumes at t_3. All red-dotted lines denote events sent from OpenDS to the Dialogue Manager. CONTROL and ADAPTIVE were used in Experiment 1, whereas ADAPTIVE and USER CUE were used in Experiment 2. In USER CUE, the participant speaks "okay", triggering a continuation in the speech before the end of the lane-change.

interrupted; in the non-adaptive setting the speech would continue until complete. At *suc*, the target lane has been reached (the tone signal is sounded), but the speech does not resume yet. At *lane*, the car has returned to the middle lane, at which point the adaptive speech would continue the interrupted utterance. In case the task was not completed correctly (e.g. the target lane change did not happen), a time-out at t_3 would trigger the adaptive speech to continue. Three seconds after the calendar event speech is completed, the true/false question is asked. There is ample time for the participant to press the yes/no button before any other distraction (on the road or from speech) occurs.

A single driving scenario consisted of 44 gates, with 11 gates each for the following conditions: speech with no lane change, lane change with no speech, non-adaptive speech with lane change, and adaptive speech with lane change. Each of these gates was followed by two empty gates, in order to clearly separate the effects of successive trials. The order of the gate types was randomly shuffled and unique for each participant. This, combined with the random silence before speech, makes the events (speech or lane-change) to be perceived as occurring completely randomly.

Procedure.

Figure 3 shows a participant during the driving simulation experiment. First, each participant signed a consent form and was then seated in the chair in front of the steering wheel and screen (seat adjustments made, if necessary). The participant was then given headphones to put on, after which the audio levels were tested and the task was explained. Following this, the OpenDS scene was started, showing the driving simulation on the large screen, at which point the participant was instructed to control the steering wheel and pedal. In the beginning of the simulation, 10 signal gates were presented for practice in using the controls and performing the driving task. During this practice stretch of road an experimenter was sitting next to the participant in order to clarify any questions that could be asked during this phase (the simulation could be paused, if necessary, to answer difficult questions or make adjustments). When the participant confirmed that he or she had understood the task, the experimenter left the scene.

Immediately after the practice gates, without any interruption, a clearly marked "START" gate signalled the beginning of the experiment, followed by the sequence of 44 gates described previously. The end of the experiment was signalled with a clearly marked "FINISH" gate, at which point the simulation stopped. In total, the driving simulation took around 30 minutes, including practice time. The participant was then given a post-task questionnaire to fill out.

In total, 17 participants (8 male, 9 female, aged 19–36) participated in the study. All of the participants were native German speakers affiliated with Bielefeld University and holders of a driving license (for normal automobiles). Two participants had previous experience with driving simulators and only one had previous experience with SDS.

5. EXPERIMENT 2: ADAPTIVE SPEECH WITH DRIVER CONTROL

For this experiment, the driving task and the memory task were the same as in Experiment 1, but the interaction between them and the presentation of the gates were altered. This difference is explained in the following.

Interaction Between Tasks: Added Driver Control.

In this experiment, participants were presented with two different systems. *System A* interrupted speech at the beginning of a lane-change task and continued after the task was complete, as described before. *System B* had the added functionality of allowing the participant to cue the SDS to continue speaking after its speech had been interrupted. The cue could be given in three ways, either by saying "okay" or by saying "weiter" (continue), which were the only two words we allowed our SDS to react to. The participant could also perform a simple head nod. Cues from the driver were only allowed while the calendar event was interrupted (i.e., the driver could not cue the system to begin a new calendar event). The participant could also make no cue at all, allowing the system to function normally (as in System A) by resuming the speech after the lane change was completed. This simple alteration gives the driver the option of controlling when the continuation of the calendar event speech is started. Figure 6 gives an example of how giving a cue ("okay") could play out over time during a lane-change task.

Procedure.

In this experiment, participants were seated, audio levels were tested, head-nod detection parameters were fine-tuned, and finally the task was explained. As in the previous experiment, 10 training gates without calendar events were used to familiarise the participants to the driving task. Another 4 gates with calendar events were added in order to familiarise participants with controlling the speech resumption by means of speech and head nod cues. Each participant had to complete one session of System A and one of System B (20 gates each). Half of the participants were presented with System A first, then System B, the other half in the opposite order. When System B was presented first, participants were presented with 10 + 4 training gates as described above, followed by the main task ("START" , 20 task gates, "FINISH"). Immediately afterwards, OpenDS was restarted and participants were presented with System A ('START", 20 gates, "FINISH"). When system A was presented first, the ASR and head nod tests, as well as the 4 training gates occurred after System A was completed and immediately before System B was started. Figure 7 shows the system presentations graphically.

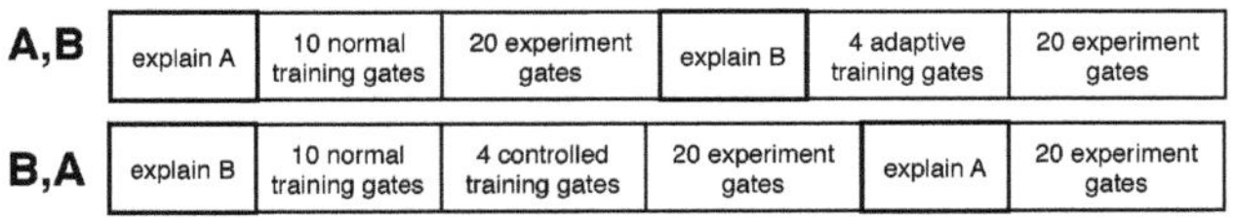

Figure 7: Experiment 2 procedure for varied system presentation. System B responded to driver cues, System A did not.

In this second study 10 native German speakers (3 female and 7 male) participated, two of whom had no drivers license, half had previous experience with SDS and half had previous experience with driving simulators. One participant was familiar with the specific system, having participated in Experiment 1.

6. RESULTS

We present here the results from both experiments for comparison. The results from Experiment 1 have been previously reported in [17] and in more detail in [14].

6.1 Experiment 1

In our first experiment, we found that listening to speech from a system that is not co-located adversely affects the performance in both the driving task and the memory task. In contrast, a system that is adaptive and aware of the driving conditions leads to participants' performance that is equivalent to the control conditions of performing either task in isolation. The *error rate* quantifies the percentage of unsuccessful trials in the driving (e.g., target lane not reached in time) and memory task (e.g., wrong or no answer given; see Figure 8). Statistical significance was tested using a Generalised Linear Mixture Model (GLMM) for estimating the probability of a successful/unsuccessful response as a function of within-subject factors CONDITION and TIME as well as many between subject factors (e.g., AGE, GENDER). In both the driving and memory tasks the effect of CONDITION was found to be significant ($p < 0.05$) while no significant effect was found for any of the between-subject factors. These findings validated our hypotheses and are consistent with previous research.

Interestingly, the majority of participants in the first experiment stated (in the post-experiment questionnaire) their preference towards the non-adaptive system, as they considered the system's interruption to be a hindrance. Some stated that they would like to be able to control the system in some way (giving rise to Experiment 2). There were further results in Experiment 1 that are not of interest here and for which we refer the reader to [14].

6.2 Experiment 2

In the second experiment, we provided the participants with the option to trigger resumption of the output using either speech or head nods. We wanted to test whether this type of control would affect performance, as well as how it would be adopted by the participants. We find almost identical performance in both systems in the memory task, and no significant difference in the driving task (see Figure 9). Significance was tested with the same method (GLMM) as in Experiment 1.

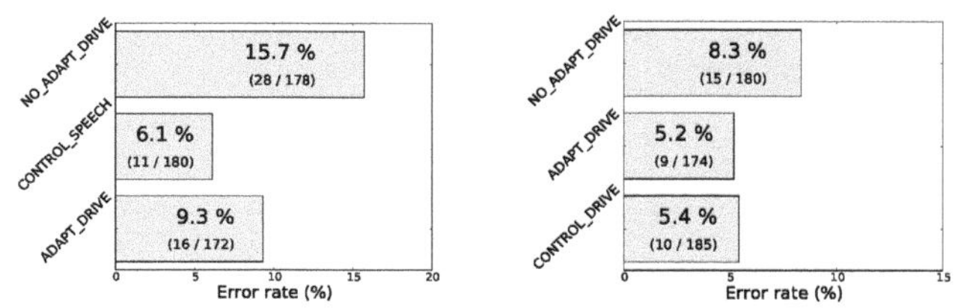

(a) Memory task (b) Driving task

Figure 8: Error rates in the two tasks in Experiment 1. For both tasks, there were significant differences between the adaptive and non-adaptive conditions, with no significance between adaptive and control conditions.

Therefore, we find no evidence that our introduction of control of the system speech resumption degrades performance compared to a system that decides by itself. We note that participants made wide use of the functionality (see below), asking the system to resume when they felt comfortable with their tasks or concentrating on the driving task more when they needed to.

As expected, the vast majority (9 out of 10) of the participants stated their preference towards the system that allows user control, and specifically by speech rather than head nods. The latter finding is implicit, as head nods were used less than speech when both options were available (the detection of head nods and the automatic speech recognition performed roughly equally well). Noting that half of the participants had previous experience with SDS, we could interpret this as an effect of collective familiarity with SDS that is just not there for "head gesture interfaces" yet; that is, the general public may not be as accustomed to systems understanding gestures, as opposed to systems understanding speech, at least in some contexts such as in-car systems. Since our findings from Experiment 2 are novel, we present them in more detail below.

Effect of User Control.

We present here results of a preliminary analysis of the effect of *usage* of user control on the performance in both task. As the usage was optional, we firstly look at amount of usage, followed by the error rate in both tasks, as shown in Table 1. Note that SPEECH and HEAD NOD only refer to correctly detected events that actually triggered the resumption. The low scores in the TIME-OUT condition represent an aggregation of errors and added cognitive load due to mis-recognitions. We have found no evidence that user-guided resumption of speech can lead to decreased performance in either task. As mentioned in the previous section, speech was the preferred option compared to head nods.

We further investigated the effect of the *time* of the system speech resumption on the main variables, regardless of whether the participant controlled the resumption or not (Figure 10). For both tasks, there appears to be an optimal time for the speech to resume, or conversely, two inappropriate times. Recall that the system speech

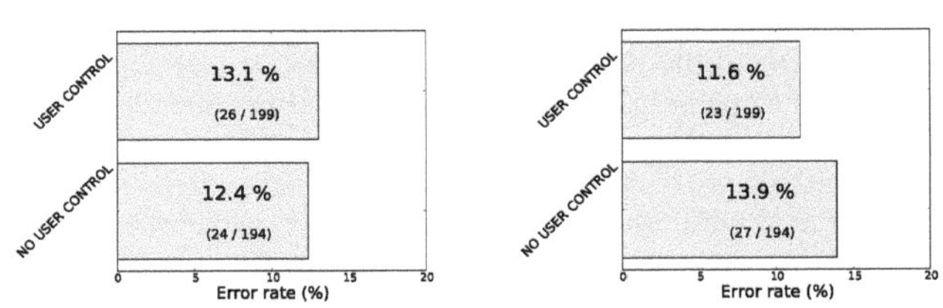

(a) Memory task (b) Driving task

Figure 9: Error rates in the two tasks in Experiment 2.

Table 1: Error rate in two tasks by type of evens triggering resumption of system speech.

		Error rate (%)	
Resume by	Usage (%)	Driving task	Memory task
Speech	46.7	7.5	11.8
Head Nod	9.0	5.5	5.5
Return to lane	25.1	2	14
Time-out	18.6	35	18.1

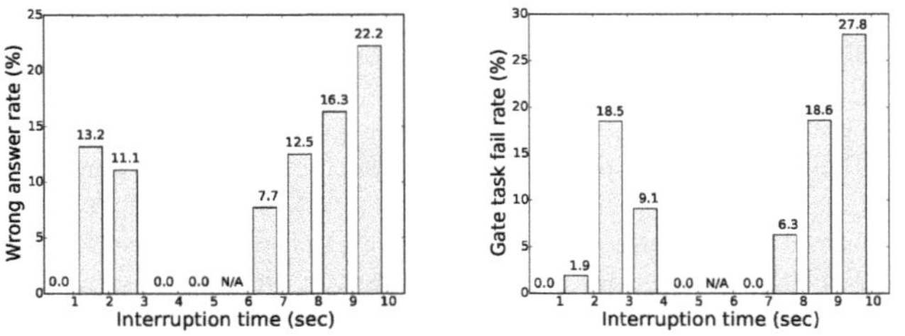

(a) Memory task

(b) Driving task

Figure 10: Error rates in the two tasks by duration of system speech interruption.

interrupts as soon as the signal indicating a lane change becomes visible. An early "peak" appears around 2-3 seconds, which coincides roughly with the main action of the driving task, which is to accelerate and steer in order to reach the target lane. After this time, the driving task becomes much easier: it is relatively easy to maintain 60 km/h after first stabilizing the car velocity at that level and there is nothing to do other than wait for the tone signal to return to the middle lane. This is reflected by the valley in the middle region in both tasks, during which no errors occur. The error rates begin to scale up again after 6 seconds, where again several effects and factors aggregate: second or third attempts after mis-recognitions of speech or nods, longer mid-utterance silence time that affects recall, and resumptions after a failure in the driving task has been registered.

It would be possible to further refine the system behaviour to avoid re-starting the speech at sub-optimal times. This can be implicitly coded by monitoring the steering and acceleration, in order to estimate the cognitive load of the driving task in real time. Such estimation (which we defer to future work) would also be a more realistic approach to triggering speech interruptions as well. Here we have assumed that the system "knows" when to stop speaking.

Individual Differences.

Although the overall performance in the memory task is roughly equal for the two systems, we see in Figure 11 that individual participants' performances vary in the direction of the effect. However, these differences are for the most part relatively small; they amount to 1–2 gates per participant/system.

In the case of the driving task, we also notice (see Figure 12) that individual participants can be affected in either direction or not at all. Interestingly, participants who do not perform well at the driving task do not coincide with those that have no driver's license or experience with driving simulators. Further, performance does not correlate across the two tasks (i.e., individual participants may perform well in either, neither, or both tasks). Participants in general put more effort and attention on the driving task, which is the desired behaviour. Giving drivers control over the speech delivery did not hinder their driving performance.

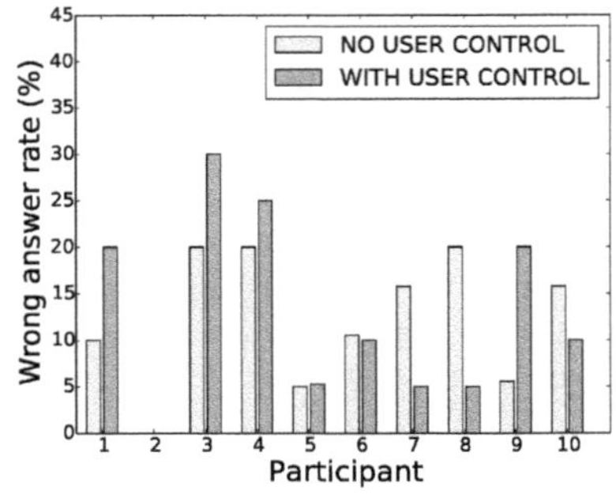

Figure 11: Effect of system type (with/without user control) on individual participant's performance in the memory task

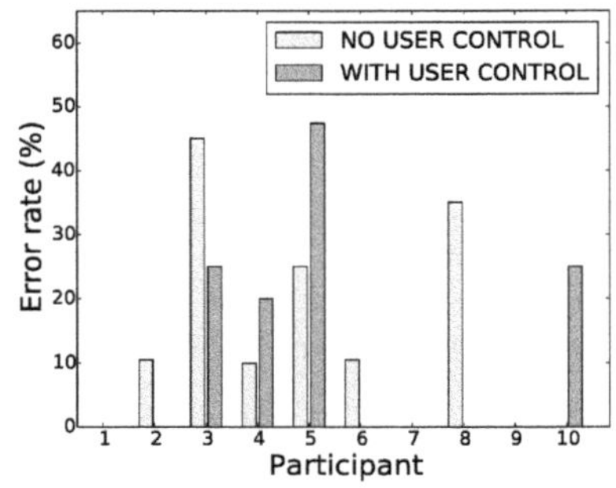

Figure 12: Effect of system type (with/without user control) on individual participant's performace in the driving task

7. CONCLUSIONS

We have presented the latest developments of our co-located, situationally-aware multimodal in-car dialogue system. Our explorations so far have shown that situational awareness is indeed a significant property for in-car systems that are safe, as well as more efficient in their own goal (as represented by the memory task). Further, we have added the functionality of yielding control to the driver using natural human interaction modalities (speech and head gestures). In our experiments, we did not find any evidence that this by itself has any effect on performance, but further work is required in this direction. We found that participants were much more comfortable speaking than nodding, and were forgiving of mis-recognitions in speech more than in head nods. In future work, we will further investigate the best division of labour between such modalities.

8. ACKNOWLEDGEMENTS

This research was partly supported by the Deutsche Forschungsgemeinschaft (DFG) in the CRC 673 "Alignment in Communication", the Center of Excellence in "Cognitive Interaction Technology" (CITEC), and a PostDoc grant by Daimler and Benz Foundation to Timo Baumann. The authors would like to thank Oliver Eickmeyer and Michael Bartholdt for helping implement the system setup, as well as Gerdis Anderson and Fabian Wohlgemuth for assisting as experimenters. Thanks also to the anonymous reviewers.

9. REFERENCES

[1] G. Aist, J. Allen, E. Campana, L. Galescu, C. A. G. Gallo, S. Stoness, M. Swift, and M. Tanenhaus. Software architectures for incremental understanding of human speech. In *Proc. Interspeech*, pages 1922–1925, 2006.

[2] T. Baumann, M. Atterer, and D. Schlangen. Assessing and Improving the Performance of Speech Recognition for

Incremental Systems. In *Proc. NAACL-HLT*, pages 380–388, 2009.

[3] T. Baumann and D. Schlangen. Evaluating prosodic processing for incremental speech synthesis. In *Proc. Interspeech*, pages 438–441, 2012.

[4] T. Baumann and D. Schlangen. Inpro_iss: A component for just-in-time incremental speech synthesis. In *Proc. ACL 2012 System Demonstrations*, pages 103–108, 2012.

[5] T. Baumann and D. Schlangen. The InproTK 2012 release. In *NAACL-HLT Workshop SDCTD*, pages 29–32, 2012.

[6] H. Buschmeier, T. Baumann, B. Dosch, S. Kopp, and D. Schlangen. Combining incremental language generation and incremental speech synthesis for adaptive information presentation. In *Proc. SIGDIAL2012*, pages 295–303, 2012.

[7] V. Demberg, A. Sayeed, A. Mahr, and C. Müller. Measuring linguistically-induced cognitive load during driving using the ConTRe task. In *Proc. Automotive'UI*, pages 176–183, 2013.

[8] F. A. Drews, M. Pasupathi, and D. L. Strayer. Passenger and cell-phone conversations in simulated driving. *Proc. HFES 48th Annual Meeting*, pages 2210–2212, 2004.

[9] F. A. Drews, M. Pasupathi, and D. L. Strayer. Passenger and cell phone conversations in simulated driving. *Journal of Experimental Psychology: Applied*, 14(4):392–400, 2008.

[10] J. He, A. Chaparro, B. Nguyen, R. Burge, J. Crandall, B. Chaparro, R. Ni, and S. Cao. Texting while driving: Is speech-based texting less risky than handheld texting? In *Proc. Automotive'UI 13*, pages 124–130, 2013.

[11] W. J. Horrey and C. D. Wickens. Examining the impact of cell phone conversations on driving using meta-analytic techniques. *Human Factors*, 48:196–205, 2006.

[12] Y. Ishigami and R. M. Klein. Is a hands-free phone safer than a handheld phone? *Journal of Safety Research*, 40(2):157–164, 2009.

[13] ISO. Road vehicles – Ergonomic aspects of transport information and control systems – Simulated lane change test to assess in-vehicle secondary task demand. ISO 26022:2010, 2010.

[14] C. Kennington, S. Kousidis, T. Baumann, H. Buschmeier, S. Kopp, and D. Schlangen. Better driving and recall when in-car information presentation uses situationally-aware incremental speech output generation. In *Proc. AutoUI*, 2014.

[15] C. Kennington, S. Kousidis, and D. Schlangen. Interpreting situated dialogue utterances: An update model that uses speech, gaze, and gesture information. In *Proc. SIGDIAL2013*, pages 173–182, 2013.

[16] C. Kennington, S. Kousidis, and D. Schlangen. InproTKS: A toolkit for incremental situated processing. *Proc. SIGDIAL2014: Short Papers*, pages 84–88, 2014.

[17] S. Kousidis, C. Kennington, T. Baumann, H. Buschmeier, S. Kopp, and D. Schlangen. Situationally aware in-car information presentation using incremental speech generation: Safer, and more effective. In *Proc. EACL 2014 Workshop on Dialogue in Motion*, pages 68–72, 2014.

[18] S. Kousidis, Z. Malisz, P. Wagner, and D. Schlangen. Exploring annotation of head gesture forms in spontaneous human interaction. In *Proc. TiGeR*, 2013.

[19] S. Kousidis, T. Pfeiffer, and D. Schlangen. MINT.tools: Tools and adaptors supporting acquisition, annotation and analysis of multimodal corpora. In *Proc. Interspeech 2013*, pages 2649–2653, 2013.

[20] P. Lison. Probabilistic dialogue models with prior domain knowledge. In *Proc. SIGDIAL2012*, pages 179–188, 2012.

[21] R. Math, A. Mahr, M. M. Moniri, and C. Müller. OpenDS: A new open-source driving simulator for research. In *GMM-Fachbericht-AmE 2013*, 2013.

[22] E. Z. McClave. Linguistic functions of head movements in the context of speech. *Journal of Pragmatics*, 32(7):855–878, 2000.

[23] S. P. McEvoy, M. R. Stevenson, A. T. McCartt, M. Woodward, C. Haworth, P. Palamara, and R. Cercarelli. Role of mobile phones in motor vehicle crashes resulting in hospital attendance: A case-crossover study. *BMJ*, 331(7514):428, 2005.

[24] G. Skantze and A. Hjalmarsson. Towards incremental speech generation in dialogue systems. In *Proc. SIGDIAL2010*, pages 1–8, 2010.

[25] G. Skantze and D. Schlangen. Incremental dialogue processing in a micro-domain. In *Proc. EACL*, pages 745–753, 2009.

[26] M. Stone, C. Doran, B. Webber, T. Bleam, and M. Palmer. Microplanning with communicative intentions: The SPUD system. *Computational Intelligence*, 19:311–381, 2003.

[27] P. Wagner, Z. Malisz, and S. Kopp. Gesture and speech in interaction: An overview. *Speech Communication*, 57:209–232, 2014.

[28] J. Wienke and S. Wrede. A middleware for collaborative research in experimental robotics. In *Proc. 2011 IEEE/SICE SII2011*, pages 1183–1190, 2011

Deep Multimodal Fusion: Combining Discrete Events and Continuous Signals

Héctor P. Martínez
Institute for Digital Games
University of Malta, 2080
Msida, Malta
hector.p.martinez@um.edu.mt

Georgios N. Yannakakis
Institute for Digital Games
University of Malta, 2080
Msida, Malta
georgios.yannakakis@um.edu.mt

ABSTRACT

Multimodal datasets often feature a combination of continuous signals and a series of discrete events. For instance, when studying human behaviour it is common to annotate actions performed by the participant over several other modalities such as video recordings of the face or physiological signals. These events are nominal, not frequent and are not sampled at a continuous rate while signals are numeric and often sampled at short fixed intervals. This fundamentally different nature complicates the analysis of the relation among these modalities which is often studied after each modality has been summarised or reduced.

This paper investigates a novel approach to model the relation between such modality types bypassing the need for summarising each modality independently of each other. For that purpose, we introduce a deep learning model based on convolutional neural networks that is adapted to process multiple modalities at different time resolutions we name *deep multimodal fusion*. Furthermore, we introduce and compare three alternative methods (convolution, training and pooling fusion) to integrate sequences of events with continuous signals within this model. We evaluate deep multimodal fusion using a game user dataset where player physiological signals are recorded in parallel with game events. Results suggest that the proposed architecture can appropriately capture multimodal information as it yields higher prediction accuracies compared to single-modality models. In addition, it appears that pooling fusion, based on a novel *filter-pooling* method provides the more effective fusion approach for the investigated types of data.

Categories and Subject Descriptors

H.1.2 [**Information Systems**]: User/Machine Systems—*Human factors*; I.2.1 [**Artificial Intelligence**]: Applications and Expert Systems—*Games*

ICMI'14, November 12–16, 2014, Istanbul, Turkey.

http://dx.doi.org/10.1145/2663204.2663236.

General Terms

Algorithms, Experimentation, Human Factors

Keywords

Deep Learning; Multimodal Fusion; Sequence Classification; Sequence Fusion; Auto-encoders; Convolutional Neural Networks; Pooling Method; Physiology; Behaviour

1. INTRODUCTION

The different sources of information that form a multimodal dataset are usually presented on a variety of formats related to their abstraction level. We can distinguish two particular formats that are common across multiple domains: *continuous signals* and sequences of *discrete events*. Continuous signals are often captured by hardware devices such as cameras, microphones and physiological sensors that monitor a human or the environment at a high and fixed sampling rate and a low abstraction level. On the other hand, sequences of discrete events are processed by software (e.g. a logged action in a virtual environment) or annotated by experts (e.g. a facial action unit), they are more infrequent than continuous recordings but they hold more abstract and complex information that characterises the user's behaviour or context. Capturing the relation between these two streams of data can provide valuable information that is not visible on each modality independently. For example, an increment in skin conductance (SC) can indicate an increment in arousal but a facial action unit indicating a smile or a frown can connect that heightened state of arousal to excitement or anger. However, integrating automatically these signals is not trivial due to their different formats and abstraction levels. Most studies resort to feature- or model-level fusion [16], i.e. the signals are reduced independently prior to their fusion (see [21, 12] among others). This process, however, neglects the low-level interactions among modalities which leads to models of lower expressivity.

In this paper we introduce *deep learning* as a general methodology for *data-level fusion*. Rather than reducing each modality independently (feature-level fusion) our approach generates a set of multimodal features, thereby, maintaining core properties of the dissimilar signals and resulting to fused models of higher accuracy. While deep learning has been applied for automatic feature extraction [8, 9, 13] the integration of multiple modalities with different time resolutions has been far from trivial. Towards this aim this paper introduces an augmented convolutional neural network (CNN) that integrates signals at different layers according to their sampling rate. CNNs reduce the time resolution of their input signals as they pass through convolution and pooling layers, increasing the abstraction level of the information and, thereby, making them the ideal model for the fusion task at hand.

Based on the CNN model, we evaluate three different approaches to fuse sequences of discrete events with continuous signals. The first approach, namely *convolution fusion*, consists of transforming the sequence of events into a *pulse signal* that is one when the event is occurring and zero otherwise. This signal can be simply introduced as the input to a convolutional layer. The second approach, namely *training fusion*, utilises the fused signal that is created when combining information from the original continuous signals and the sequence of discrete events. This fused signal is produced by a single-layer CNN that models the effect discrete events have on the continuous signals and vice-versa. In this approach, the sequences of events are not directly added to a convolutional layer, but they are used to stir the training process. The third approach, namely *pooling fusion*, introduces the sequence of discrete events into a pooling layer resulting in a novel *filter-pooling* method that attenuates the outputs of a convolutional layer within time intervals when events are not occurring. This method complements training fusion by highlighting the patterns detected by a CNN when the interaction among modalities is potentially occurring.

We evaluate and compare the three approaches on a dataset that includes a physiological signal (skin conductance) and two different sequences of events (collecting pellets and colliding with enemies in a 3D prey/predator game). After extracting multimodal features with the CNN, we use a single-layer perceptron to predict six different affective states. The results of this initial study show that convolutional neural networks can be adapted to create multimodal features with a high predictive power. Pooling fusion appears to be the most promising fusion approach. Even though the filter-pooling layers hinder information when events do not occur, when combined with standard average-pooling layers the pooling fusion approach outperforms the other two fusion approaches and any single-modality modelling attempts. Convolution fusion also yields high prediction accuracies but it shows lower robustness. Finally, the training fusion does not appear to be able to capture information specific to both modalities within the space of topologies explored.

2. RELATED WORK

Sequences of discrete events and continuous signals are often found together in many different domains but this combination is particularly prominent in human-computer interaction studies. The interaction with the computer is often characterised by a series of events that give a context to multiple other modalities that generate continuous streams of data. Successfully fusing context with other modalities appears to be the key to automatically understand user experience [1].

In this domain, McQuiggan et al. [12] used statistical summarisation (i.e. extracted averages, standard deviations and other simple statistical features) to reduce continuous signals such as heart rate and skin conductance. In addition, different events arising from the interaction with a 3D learning environment where processed with ad-hoc metrics such as the time spent on a task (duration of the event or time between events) or a list of locations visited. On a similar basis, statistical summarisation was used to reduce several physiological features and game events in [10, 21]. Although these simple approaches yield models of acceptable prediction accuracies, the exact relation among modalities remains largely unknown. The method proposed in this paper attempts to improve the accuracy and expressiveness of these models by exploiting the low temporal relation among modalities.

Data-level fusion of events and continuous signals has been achieved before using frequent sequence mining [11]; however, this approach requires transforming the continuous signals into sequences of events. For instance, in [11] a skin conductance signal is converted into a sequence of significant increments and decrements of the signal. This transformation requires ad-hoc preprocessing which discards part of the information present in the raw signal. Deep learning approaches investigated in this paper, on the other hand, are defined for continuous signals and therefore do not require ad-hoc preprocessing.

Deep learning has already been applied to a number of human-computer interaction tasks such as facial expression recognition [17], speech recognition [8] and modelling of physiological signals [9]; however, all these studies develop methods tailored for single-modality atemporal or continuous data, and therefore are not suited for series of events that are central to this paper. Likewise, some studies have explored the fusion of dissimilar modalities that are either atemporal (e.g. text and images [19], images and sound [14]) or well synchronised (e.g. video and sound [13]). The main approach followed in these studies consists of processing each modality individually and combining them at a higher representation level. By doing so, however, the low level interactions between modalities may be hindered, which, in turn, signals the necessity of new deep learning approaches to data level multimodal fusion. This paper proposes alternative deep fusion mechanisms for eliminating the drawbacks of current multimodal fusion practice reported above.

3. METHOD

In order to facilitate the extraction of information across sequences of discrete events and continuous signals, we define a new architecture for convolutional neural networks to handle inputs at different time resolutions. As CNNs are naturally suited for continuous signals but no discrete events, we propose three different approaches to integrate sequences of events with other continuous modalities. In this section we describe the basics of CNNs and detail the proposed enhancements. In addition, we briefly describe the modelling mechanism used to test the prediction power of the variant CNNs.

3.1 Convolutional Neural Networks

Convolutional (or time-delay) neural networks [8] are feed-forward neural networks designed to deal with large input spaces as those seen in image classification tasks. CNNs are constructed by stacking alternatively *convolutional layers* and *pooling layers*. A convolutional layer consists of a number of neurons that process sequentially consecutive patches of the input signal, i.e. this layer convolves a set of neurons along the temporal dimension of the input signal. Each neuron defines one local feature which is extracted at every position of the input signal; the resulting values cre-

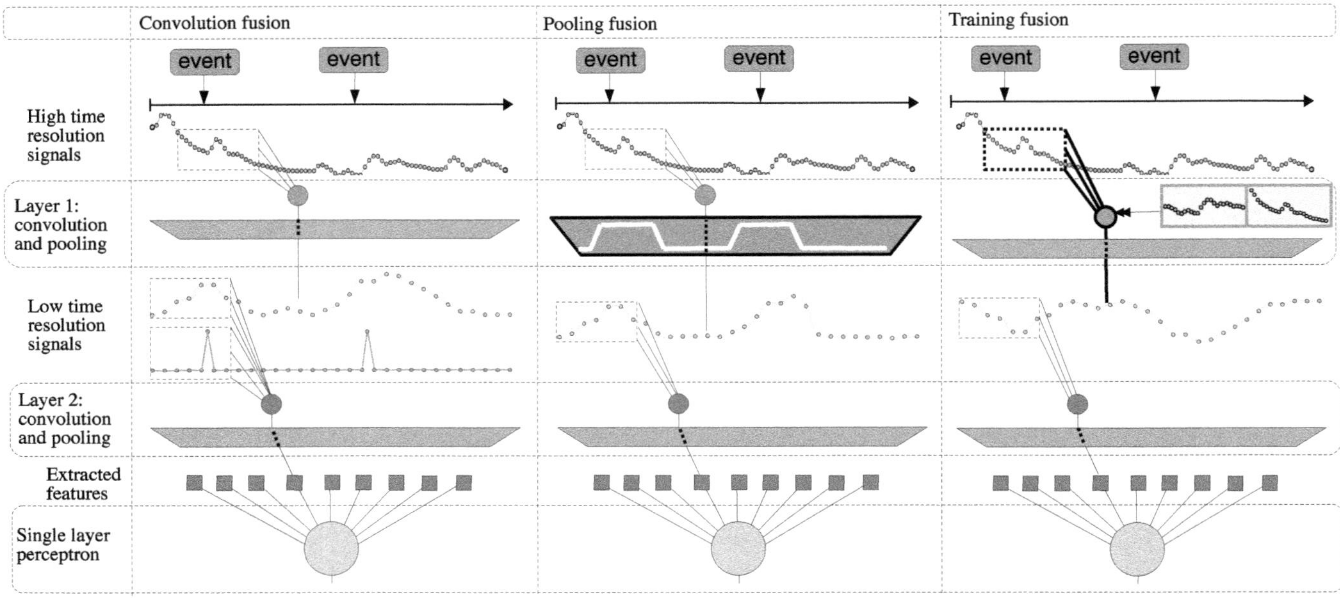

Figure 1: Three approaches to deep multimodal fusion via convolutional neural networks. The example CNNs illustrated present two layers with one neuron each. The first convolutional layer receives as input a continuous signal at a high time resolution, which is further reduced by a pooling layer. The resulting signal (feature map) presents a lower time resolution. The second convolutional layer can combine this feature map with additional modalities at the same low resolution. In the convolution fusion network (left figure), the two events are introduced at this level as a pulse signal. In the pooling fusion network (middle figure), the events are introduced as part of the first pooling layer, resulting in a filtered feature map. Finally, in the training fusion network (right figure), the events affect the training process of the first convolutional layer, leading to an alternative feature map.

ate a new signal referred to as *feature map*. A pooling layer reduces the dimensionality of the feature maps generated by a convolutional layer. It typically applies a simple statistical function (e.g. average or maximum value) to non-overlapping patches of the feature maps. By stacking several convolutional and pooling layers, CNNs can effectively reduce the input signals to a small set of features. The experimenter must define the topology of the network including the number of neurons and the number of inputs for each neuron in each convolutional layer, and the number of inputs and function used by the pooling layer. Once those parameters are fixed, the neurons can be automatically trained to minimise the loss of information in the feature extraction process.

The pooling layers perform a very simple processing task, and thus the extracted features are mainly defined by the convolutional layers, and more concretely, their neurons. By analysing the weights of each neuron, one can derive the characteristics of the input that every feature is capturing. When the input to the neuron is a 1-dimensional signal (e.g. skin conductance), the weights of the neuron can be plotted in a temporal order to reveal the input patterns that yield higher output values (e.g. see [9]).

We train each convolutional layer using *denoising autoencoders* [5, 4]. This approach consists of feeding the outputs of the convolutional layer into a *decoder* that reconstructs the original input signal; by means of gradient-descent, the weights of each neuron are adjusted iteratively to achieve a minimal reconstruction error, i.e. a minimal discrepancy between the signal reconstructed by the decoder and the original input signal [9]. The neurons of each convolutional layer are trained patch-wise, i.e. by considering the input at each position (one patch) in the sequence as one example. This allows faster training than training convolutionally, but may yield translated versions of the same filter. This is the same idea as the process followed by PCA but with the advantage of bypassing the linearity assumption [20]. Alternative training methods such as restricted Boltzmann machines present a more complex theoretical background but have not produced better results in practice. Thus, we opt for the simplest method.

3.1.1 Dealing with multiple time resolutions

Standard CNN architectures process all inputs at the first layer after all data samples have been reduced to the same dimensions. Then the neurons of the first convolutional layer scan the input signals sample-by-sample along time. When the signals present different number of samples per unit of time, however, this process is not applicable as the scanning process requires a different pace for each modality.

The CNN architecture can be adapted by allowing modalities with different sampling rates to feed into different layers (see Figure 1). Consequently, the signals with a higher sampling rate are processed earlier by a convolutional and a pooling layer that transform them into a feature map with the same time resolution as the signals with lower sampling rates. Alternatively, one could simply undersample all the signals to the lowest sampling rate (which can be seen as a form of a pooling layer). However, using also a convolutional layer can potentially reduce the information loss because consecutive outputs of a convolutional layer are very similar when entering the pooling layer. In addition, the

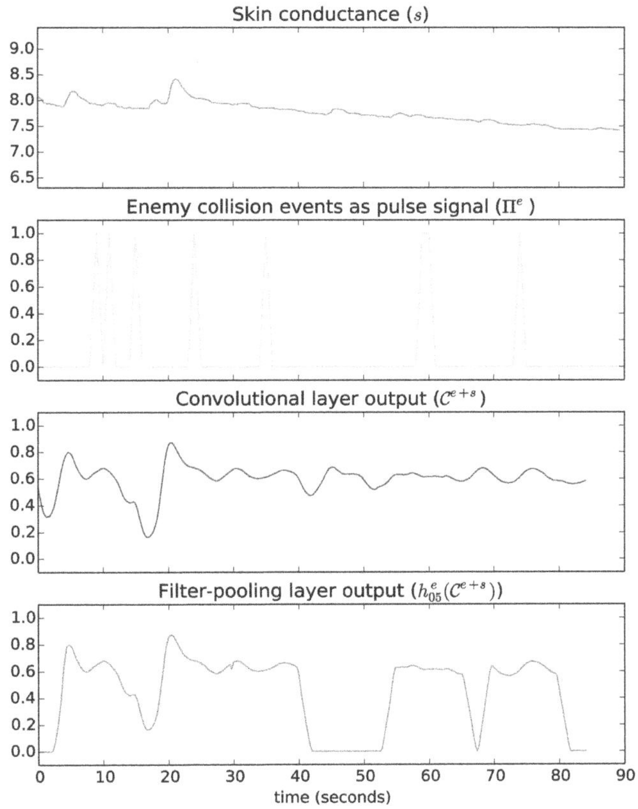

Figure 2: Signals captured in one game through the three approaches for fusion. The top figure shows the raw skin conductance signal. The second figure depicts the sequence of enemy collision events. The third figure shows the output of a convolutional layer with one neuron applied to the SC signal. The bottom figure depicts the output of a filter-pooling layer applied to the previous convolutional layer.

convolutional layers increase the complexity of the information as the time resolution is reduced, which may facilitate modality fusion at the same abstraction level. Consider for instance the example of skin conductance and pellet collection events; matching one of those events with the exact value of SC on an exact millisecond might not provide interesting information. Alternatively, if SC is first processed by a convolutional layer, it may detect spikes on the signal caused by a pellet collection event.

A disadvantage of using this architecture is that global relations might be missed (e.g. if the final game score is related to the maximum value of the SC). Nevertheless, we expect that the local temporal relations among the modalities are more informative in most domains.

3.1.2 Convolution fusion

With the architecture presented above, the simplest solution to introduce a sequence of events is to transform it into a continuous signal at the appropriate sampling rate. We choose a pulse signal that equals one only when the event was recorded and zero otherwise (see Figure 1 and Figure 2).

3.1.3 Training fusion

Training fusion is inspired by the idea that the continuous signals may present specific patterns when discrete events are occurring, that are not that common otherwise. On that basis, the events are used to select specific parts of the continuous signals. A new subset of data is created by extracting patches within a given time window centred at each event (in this paper the window is 5, 10 and 15 seconds). The resulting dataset is used to train a single-layered CNN that is specialised on the patterns of variation in the continuous signals around the events. We expect that, to some degree, this model characterises both the changes that are produced in the continuous signals when events occur and the variations in the continuous signals that prompt events.

Once trained, the single-layered CNN is convolved over the raw continuous signal to generate a new set of signals based on the variation patterns seen around the events (see Figure 2). As we are using a CNN to further process the resulting signals, this approach can be interpreted as an alternative training of the first layer of the network (see Figure 1).

3.1.4 Pooling fusion

An alternative approach to introduce discrete event information into the CNN is through the pooling layers. This is achieved by defining a new pooling method (denoted as *filter-pooling*) that attenuates the input signal (i.e. the output of the previous convolutional layer) around a sequence of events given. The result is a new signal where the patterns within a given window (in this paper 5, 10 and 15 seconds) centred at the events are highlighted (see Figure 2 and Figure 1)). This fusion approach makes multimodal patterns more salient for the next layer of the CNN. In this paper we use a simple filter that equals 1 within the time window selected and decays linearly to zero (or increases linearly from zero) within two seconds after (or before) the window.

3.2 Modelling

Once the CNN is trained as described in the previous section, it can be used to produce a number of multimodal features (see Figure 1). We test whether these features are more informative than single-modality features by training a single layer perceptron (SLP) to predict a series of target outputs. As the dataset used in this paper contains pairwise preferences indicating different affective states, we employ a *preference learning* variant of backpropagation to train the SLP (see Section 3.2.1). In addition, as the CNN creates features that capture any characteristic of the input signals regardless of the prediction target, *automatic feature selection* (see Section 3.2.2) is an essential process towards distinguishing which of those features can assist the creation of the prediction model. These experiments are performed using the *Preference Learning Toolbox* [2].

3.2.1 Preference Learning

Preference learning [3] is a subfield of machine learning that deals with the problem of learning orders. When these orders are specified as pairs of data samples, the learning problem consists of creating a model that outputs higher values for the samples preferred on each pair and lower for the non-preferred. Backpropagation [18] on its basic form optimises an error function iteratively across a number of epochs by adjusting the parameters of a neural network (i.e.

value of each weight and threshold) proportionally to the derivative (gradient) of the error with respect to the parameter. In this paper we use the *regularised least squares* error function, designed for learning from pairwise preferences [15].

3.2.2 Feature Selection

Feature selection (FS) consists of a search scheme to test alternative combinations of input features and a heuristic to determine their relevance. Opposed to other dimensionality reduction methods such as principal component analysis [20] and *Fisher's projection* [7] that project the feature space into a space of lower dimensionality, FS eliminates dimensions (features) from the original space maintaining the physical meaning of the inputs to the model. We consider that this is a key feature for multiple domains, as it is necessary to analyse the mappings captured by the models learned.

In this paper we used *sequential forward feature selection* (SFS) [21, 6], a bottom-up search procedure where one feature is added at a time to the current feature set. The feature to be added is selected from the subset of the remaining features such that the new feature set generates the maximum value of an objective function over all candidate features for addition. The objective function used in this paper is the training accuracy of an ANN model on the evaluated dataset.

4. DATASET

The dataset used to evaluate the proposed methodology was gathered during an experimental game survey in which 36 participants played four pairs of different variants of the same video-game. The test-bed game named *Maze-Ball* is a 3D prey/predator game that features a ball inside a maze controlled by the arrow keys. The goal of the player is to maximise her score in 90 seconds by collecting a number of pellets scattered in the maze while avoiding enemies that wander around. A number of eight different game variants were presented to the players. The games were different with respect to the virtual camera profile used which determines how the virtual world is presented on screen. We expected that different camera profiles would induce different experiences and affective states which would, in turn, reflect on the physiological state of the player making possible to predict the players' affective self-reported preferences using information extracted from their physiology. Each participant played one pair of variants in both orders and other two pairs with different game variants. The games played by each participant are assigned in such a way that, in total, 4 preference instances should be obtained for each pair of the game variants in both orders (2 preference instances per playing order).

Skin conductance was recorded during each game session using the IOM biofeedback device at 31.25Hz. While other off-the-self devices offer higher sampling rates, previous studies have shown that accurate predictors of affect can be constructed for this device. Following previous work on training convolutional models of affect from SC [9], we further reduced the signal by 8 after applying a mean filter of the same length, to produce approximately 2.5 recordings per second. In addition, pellet collection and collision with enemies are logged. After each pair of games, the players filled-in a questionnaire reporting which of the games induced higher levels of *anxiety*, *challenge*, *excitement*, *fun*, *frustration* and *relaxation*. The answers "none of the two" and "both equally" are also included in their options (4 alternative forced choice questionnaire). The details of the Maze-Ball game design and the experimental protocol followed are already well reported in the literature and can be found in [21, 10].

5. RESULTS

In order to evaluate the proposed methodology, we compare single and multiple modality features created with CNNs. As seen in previous work [9] the topology of the network is critical to create accurate prediction models, however, the exhaustive evaluation of all combinations is intractable. After preliminary experiments with the single modalities, we fix the topology of the CNN to two layers with 5 neurons each; each neuron has 20 inputs for each input feature map (either an input modality or the output of the previous pooling layer). The learning rate, number of epochs and corruption level are adjusted for each experiment independently.

The outputs of the CNNs are used as inputs for the single layer perceptron. For each experimental condition, we run SFS 10 times, and for each of those runs we evaluate the best set of features using the 3-fold cross validation accuracy of a SLP. This procedure may hinder partially the generality of the created models, as the average cross-validation accuracy is used to guide the feature selection search. However, the comparison between single and multiple modalities, and across fusion approaches is fair because all experiments follow the same procedure.

Significance in this paper is calculated using a two-tailed unpaired t-test.

5.1 Fusing Skin Conductance with Pellet Collection

The best models that rely on training fusion applied to pellet collection events and SC ($\mathcal{C}^{p+s}$) outperform the single-modality models built on SC (s) only on *anxiety* and *frustration* (see Figure 3a). This suggests that this approach captures low amount of event-specific information. This is also supported by the small differences across trained neurons (see Figure 4). As it can be observed, the weights of the five neurons are very similar for the alternative time windows (5, 10 and 15). In fact, the difference with respect to a model built on the complete dataset (i.e. using every interval in the SC signal, hence ignoring events) is also very small.

Interestingly, the convolution fusion approach that introduces pellet collection events as a pulse signal ($\Pi^p + s$) yields prediction accuracies significantly higher than $\mathcal{C}^{p+s}$ only for *challenge* and *fun* (p-value < 0.01), and only higher than the single-modality approach for *challenge* and *anxiety* (p-values < 0.01) as depicted in Figure 3a which indicates that this approach did not fuse physiological and contextual information satisfactorily either. Models based only on the event signal (Π^p) yield poor prediction accuracies which indicates that either the pellet collection event is not relevant for prediction on its own, or that the nature of the pulse signal complicates the feature extraction task for convolutional neural networks.

When the $\mathcal{C}^{p+s}$ signals are combined with a filter-pooling layer ($h^p_{t_w}(\mathcal{C}^{p+s})$), we observe significant improvements (p-values < 0.01) in prediction accuracy for all affective states except *frustration* with respect to the unfiltered version (see

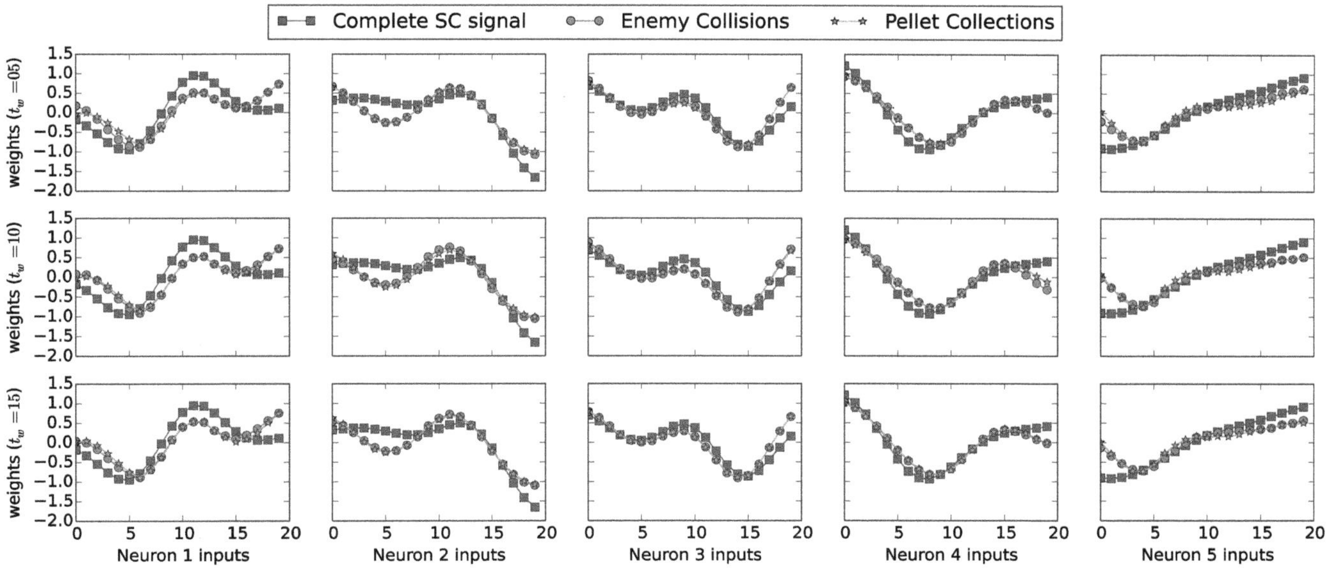

Figure 4: Example models built with the training fusion approach. Each frame shows the weight values of the same neuron from three independent CNNs: one trained with patches around pellet collection events, another trained with patches around enemy collision events and the last one trained with the complete SC signal. Each row of frames corresponds to the 5 neurons in the same network, trained using a time window t_w centred at the given event.

Figure 3b). Furthermore, these models outperform the other approaches significantly in all affective states except *fun* (no significant difference compared to single-modality), and *challenge* and *fun* (no significant difference compared to $\Pi^p + s$). This suggests that incorporating the contextual information as a filter-pooling layer, facilitates the fusion process when compared to the use of convolution fusion.

Finally, when the filtered $\mathcal{C}^{p+s}$ signals are combined with the raw SC signal into the same model ($h^p_{t_w}(\mathcal{C}^{p+s}) + s$), further improvements are observed, notably for *frustration* and *anxiety* (p-value < 0.01), and *fun* (p-value < 0.05) (see Figure 3c). This suggests that the information carried by the SC signal in intervals when no events are triggered is also relevant for prediction of particular states. It thus appears that the combination of filter-pooling and standard average-pooling methods can provide a mixture of single and multiple modality signals that yield more accurate multimodal predictors.

The time window values used to define the filter in the pooling layer signals $\mathcal{C}^{p+s}$ do not show a consistent variation across affective states. This pattern was expected as the physiological manifestations of each emotion may be salient within different time intervals around the events.

5.2 Fusing Skin Conductance with Enemy Collision

Predictors using enemy collision events as a pulse signal together with the raw SC signal ($\Pi^e + s$) show significantly higher accuracies (p-values < 0.01) than predictors using the $\mathcal{C}^{e+s}$ signals or a single modality (s or$\Pi^{\ e}$) for *fun, excitement, frustration* and *anxiety*, and no difference in the remaining two affective states (see Figure 5a). As observed by the heightened prediction accuracies of several models based on$\Pi^{\ e}$, it appears that the pulse signal based on enemy collisions yields more informative features than the pellet collection signal, which also contributes to more accurate convolution fusion models. As also seen in the previous set of experiments, training fusion models ($\mathcal{C}^{e+s}$) do not consistently outperform the single skin conductance signal. In fact, the differences between the neurons trained using SC values around enemy collision events and pellet collection events are minimal (Figure 4). Therefore, it appears that the training fusion approach captured only a minimal amount of information about the events in this dataset.

Adding a filter-pooling layer, improves the accuracy of models based on $\mathcal{C}^{e+s}$ in all affective states (p-values < 0.01), and it even results in accuracies higher than$\Pi^{\ e} + s$ for *anxiety* (p-value < 0.01), *challenge* (p-value < 0.01) and *relaxation* (p-value $= 0.03$) as depicted in Figure 5b. These results further validate the appropriateness of using the filter-pooling layer as a method to fuse sequences of events with continuous signals.

Similarly to the experiments with pellet collection events, adding the raw SC as an additional input ($h^e_{t_w}(\mathcal{C}^{e+s}) + s$) yields further improvements (see Figure 5c). These improvements lead to accuracies above (p-values < 0.02) or equal to $\Pi^e + s$ in all affective states, making this combination the most robust method for fusion identified across all experiments of this paper. As before, the optimal time window is dependent on the affective state.

When comparing the results for the same time window value, we can observe some accuracy decrements when the raw signal is added (e.g. compare $h^e_{05}(\mathcal{C}^{e+s})$ to $h^e_{05}(\mathcal{C}^{e+s})+s$ for *excitement*). This is caused by the fixed topology used in both experiments that forces the second model to ignore information from $h^e_{05}(\mathcal{C}^{e+s})$ in favour of the added s signal. While the new information introduced by s is in general relevant, some of the ignored information may have been key for the prediction. A simple and sensible solution consists of increasing the number of neurons as the number of inputs

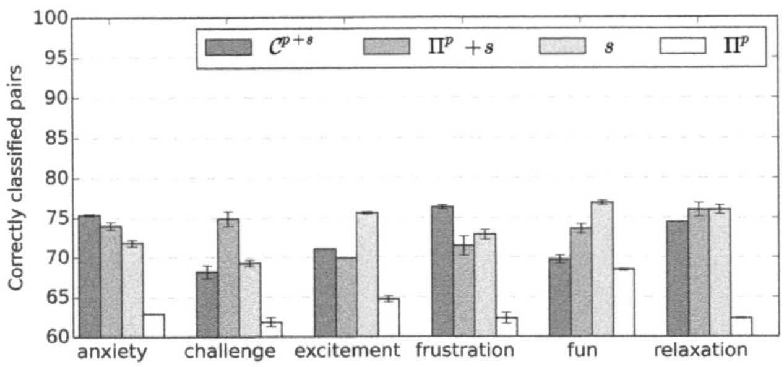

(a) Single modalities (s andΠ ^{p}), convolution fusion ($s + \Pi^p$) and training fusion ($\mathcal{C}^{p+s}$)

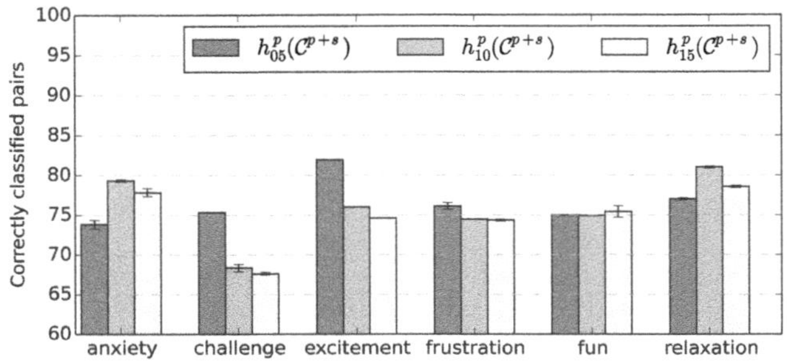

(b) Pooling fusion ($h^p_{t_w}(\mathcal{C}^{p+s})$)

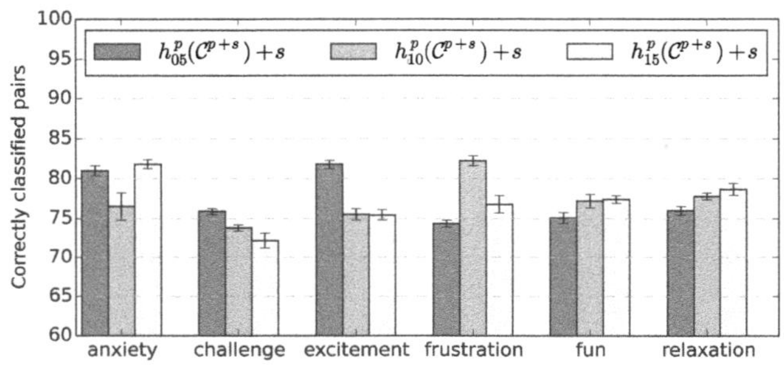

(c) Pooling fusion combined with raw SC ($h^p_{t_w}(\mathcal{C}^{p+s}) + s$)

Figure 3: Pellet collection events and skin conductance. Average classification accuracy of 10 single-layer perceptrons trained on a set of features selected using sequential feature selection. The pool of available features is created by convolutional neural networks that take one or more of the following signals as input: a SC signal (s), a pulse signal representing the pellet collection events (Π^p), a fusion signal produced by a single-layered CNN ($\mathcal{C}^{p+s}$) and a fusion signal produced by a CNN with a filter-pooling layer ($h^p_{t_w}(\mathcal{C}^{p+s})$) with time window t_w.

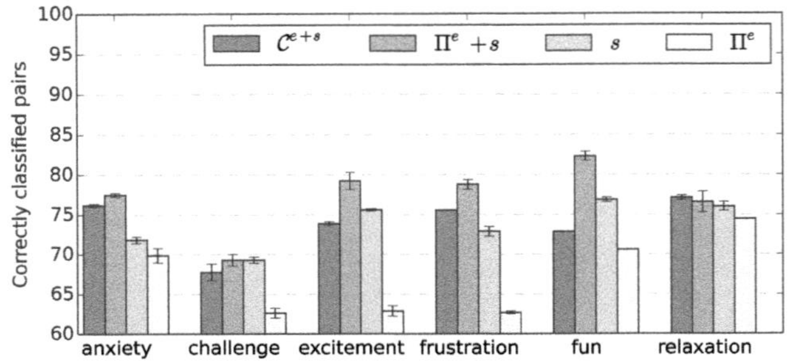

(a) Single modalities (s andΠ ^{e}), convolution fusion ($s + \Pi^e$) and training fusion ($\mathcal{C}^{e+s}$)

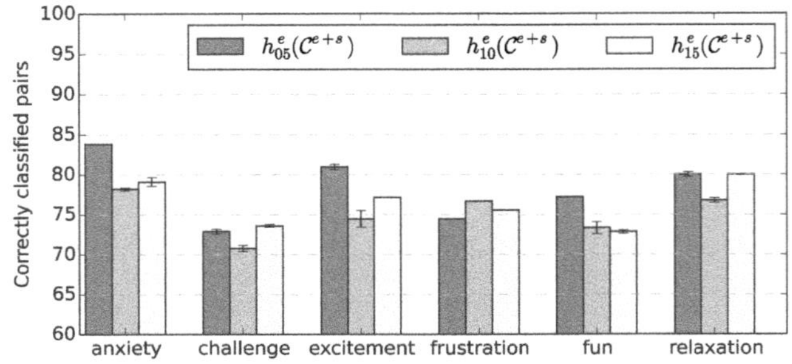

(b) Pooling fusion ($h^e_{t_w}(\mathcal{C}^{e+s})$)

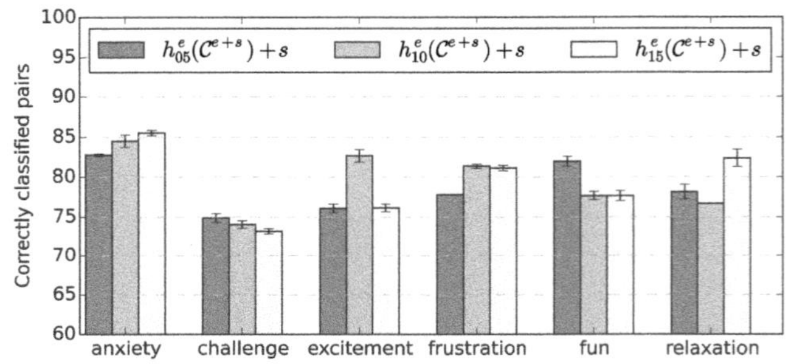

(c) Pooling fusion combined with raw SC ($h^e_{t_w}(\mathcal{C}^{e+s}) + s$)

Figure 5: Enemy collision events and skin conductance. Average classification accuracy of 10 single-layer perceptrons trained on a set of features selected using sequential feature selection. The pool of available features is created by convolutional neural networks that take one or more of the following signals as input: a SC signal (s), a pulse signal representing the enemy collision events (Π^e), a fusion signal produced by a single-layer CNN ($\mathcal{C}^{e+s}$) and a fusion signal produced by a CNN with a filter-pooling layer ($h^e_{t_w}(\mathcal{C}^{e+s})$) with time window t_w.

increase. This will naturally allow the CNN to extract more patterns from each modality.

6. CONCLUSIONS

In this paper we introduce deep learning as a method for fusing sequences of discrete events and continuous signals. In particular, we define a convolutional neural network architecture to integrate modalities with different time resolutions and propose three different approaches to integrate information from the continuous signals and the sequences of events. We evaluate these using a dataset that contains game events and physiological signals.

The first fusion approach, *convolution fusion*, consists of injecting events as a pulse signal into a convolutional layer. This method yielded high prediction accuracies specially when the events appeared to be informative as a standalone modality. Nevertheless, models based on a single-modality could outperform them, suggesting that the convolutional network cannot extract all the relevant information associated with the events.

The second fusion approach, *training fusion*, is based on training a single-layer convolutional network to distinguish the effects of events in the continuous signals. This method appears to fail to capture information across modalities as—regardless of the events presented and time interval used—the resulting CNNs found similar patterns in the dataset studied. The prediction accuracies also suggest that this method is weaker than convolution fusion.

The third method, *pooling fusion*, adds information about events through a pooling layer that filters the output of a convolutional layer connected to a continuous signal. This method boosts the prediction accuracies of training fusion models suggesting the successful integration of information from continuous signals and the sequences of events. As a side effect of this pooling method, patterns found on the continuous signal when no events occur are attenuated. However, we show that a combination of this new pooling method with standard average-pooling yields models that can combine single modality and multimodality information leading to more accurate predictions than any of the other methods evaluated. It appears that the filter-pooling layer is responsible for the entire improvement on accuracy, and therefore it is likely to yield the same results if used independently of training fusion. Future work will investigate this hypothesis and explore the new space of parameters introduced by this pooling method, including the type of filter and the window size.

While our experiments are restricted to unidimensional signals, the architecture introduced in this paper is general and can be applied to other multimodal datasets including, for instance, video recordings. Future work will focus on validating these methods in such datasets as well as extending the current evaluation to a larger number of modalities, prediction models, feature selection mechanisms and network topologies.

7. ACKNOWLEDGMENTS

This research was supported, in part, by the ILearnRW (project no: 318803) FP7 ICT EU project.

8. REFERENCES

[1] L. Barrett, B. Mesquita, K. Ochsner, and J. Gross. The experience of emotion. *Annual review of psychology*, 58:373, 2007.

[2] V. E. Farrugia, H. P. Martínez, and G. N. Yannakakis. The preference learning toolbox. Technical Report IDG-2014-01, Institute of Digital Games, University of Malta, 2014.

[3] J. Fürnkranz and E. Hüllermeier. *Preference learning*. Springer, 2010.

[4] G. Hinton and R. Salakhutdinov. Reducing the dimensionality of data with neural networks. *Science*, 313(5786):504–507, 2006.

[5] G. E. Hinton and R. S. Zemel. Autoencoders, minimum description length, and helmholtz free energy. In *Advances in neural information processing systems (NIPS)*, 1994.

[6] A. Jain and D. Zongker. Feature selection: evaluation, application, and small sample performance. *IEEE transactions on pattern analysis and machine intelligence*, 19(2):153–158, 1997.

[7] W. Krzanowski. The performance of fisher's linear discriminant function under non-optimal conditions. *Technometrics*, 19(2):191–200, 1977.

[8] Y. LeCun and Y. Bengio. Convolutional networks for images, speech, and time series. In *The handbook of brain theory and neural networks*, volume 3361. Cambridge, MA: MIT Press, 1995.

[9] H. P. Martínez, Y. Bengio, and G. N. Yannakakis. Learning deep physiological models of affect. *Computational Intelligence Magazine, IEEE*, 9(1):20–33, 2013.

[10] H. P. Martínez and G. N. Yannakakis. Genetic search feature selection for affective modeling: a case study on reported preferences. In *Proceedings of international workshop on Affective interaction in natural environments (AFFINE)*, pages 15–20. ACM, 2010.

[11] H. P. Martínez and G. N. Yannakakis. Mining multimodal sequential patterns: a case study on affect detection. In *Proceedings of International Conference on Multimodal Interfaces (ICMI)*, pages 3–10. ACM, 2011.

[12] S. Mcquiggan, B. Mott, and J. Lester. Modeling self-efficacy in intelligent tutoring systems: An inductive approach. *User Modeling and User-Adapted Interaction*, 18(1):81–123, 2008.

[13] J. Ngiam, A. Khosla, M. Kim, J. Nam, H. Lee, and A. Y. Ng. Multimodal deep learning. In *Proceedings of the 28th International Conference on Machine Learning (ICML-11)*, pages 689–696, 2011.

[14] P. O'Connor, D. Neil, S.-C. Liu, T. Delbruck, and M. Pfeiffer. Real-time classification and sensor fusion with a spiking deep belief network. *Frontiers in neuroscience*, 7, 2013.

[15] T. Pahikkala, E. Tsivtsivadze, A. Airola, J. Järvinen, and J. Boberg. An efficient algorithm for learning to rank from preference graphs. *Machine Learning*, 75(1):129–165, 2009.

[16] M. Pantic and L. Rothkrantz. Toward an affect-sensitive multimodal human-computer interaction. *Proceedings of the IEEE*, 91(9):1370–1390, 2003.

[17] S. Rifai, Y. Bengio, A. Courville, P. Vincent, and M. Mirza. Disentangling factors of variation for facial expression recognition. In *Proceedings of European Conference on Computer Vision (ECCV)*, 2012.

[18] D. Rumelhart. *Backpropagation: theory, architectures, and applications*. Lawrence Erlbaum, 1995.

[19] N. Srivastava and R. Salakhutdinov. Multimodal learning with deep boltzmann machines. In F. Pereira, C. Burges, L. Bottou, and K. Weinberger, editors, *Advances in Neural Information Processing Systems 25*, pages 2222–2230. Curran Associates, Inc., 2012.

[20] S. Wold, K. Esbensen, and P. Geladi. Principal component analysis. *Chemometrics and intelligent laboratory systems*, 2(1):37–52, 1987.

[21] G. Yannakakis, H. Martínez, and A. Jhala. Towards affective camera control in games. *User Modeling and User-Adapted Interaction*, 20(4):313–340, 2010.

The Additive Value of Multimodal Features for Predicting Engagement, Frustration, and Learning during Tutoring

Joseph F. Grafsgaard[1], Joseph B. Wiggins[1], Alexandria K. Vail[1],
Kristy Elizabeth Boyer[1], Eric N. Wiebe[2], James C. Lester[1]

[1]Department of Computer Science [2]Department of STEM Education
North Carolina State University, Raleigh, NC, USA

{jfgrafsg, jbwiggi3, akvail, keboyer, wiebe, lester}@ncsu.edu

ABSTRACT
Detecting learning-centered affective states is difficult, yet crucial for adapting most effectively to users. Within tutoring in particular, the combined context of student task actions and tutorial dialogue shape the student's affective experience. As we move toward detecting affect, we may also supplement the task and dialogue streams with rich sensor data. In a study of introductory computer programming tutoring, human tutors communicated with students through a text-based interface. Automated approaches were leveraged to annotate dialogue, task actions, facial movements, postural positions, and hand-to-face gestures. These dialogue, nonverbal behavior, and task action input streams were then used to predict retrospective student self-reports of engagement and frustration, as well as pretest/posttest learning gains. The results show that the combined set of multimodal features is most predictive, indicating an additive effect. Additionally, the findings demonstrate that the role of nonverbal behavior may depend on the dialogue and task context in which it occurs. This line of research identifies contextual and behavioral cues that may be leveraged in future adaptive multimodal systems.

Categories and Subject Descriptors
H.1.2 [**User/Machine Systems**]: Human factors; H.5.m [**Information Interfaces and Presentation (e.g., HCI)**]: Miscellaneous

General Terms
Human Factors

Keywords
Affect; multimodal; engagement; frustration; facial expression; gesture; posture; tutorial dialogue

ICMI'14, November 12 - 16, 2014, Istanbul, Turkey

http://dx.doi.org/10.1145/2663204.2663264

1. INTRODUCTION
Combining multiple modalities to predict affect has been found to produce a "consistent, but modest" effect [4]. A majority of such studies aimed to predict basic emotions, which have been the focus of much research over the past several decades. However, recent attempts to apply affective computing techniques to naturalistic domains have considered a broader range of affective states, such as anxiety, boredom, confusion, excitement, and interest [1–3, 10, 12, 13, 18, 24]. With this renewed focus on applying multimodal techniques to affect recognition and understanding, it is important to investigate the relative benefit of multimodal feature sets across non-basic affective states.

Prior studies have examined learning-centered affective states through self-reports and observer judgments [1–3, 13]. Multimodal features such as dialogue, facial expression, posture, and task actions were used to predict momentary affective states, such as boredom, confusion, excitement, and frustration. While these studies have provided insight into moments of judged and self-reported affect, they were not designed to identify how these moments contribute to an overall sense of whether a student is engaged, frustrated, or learning. For instance, if a student is frustrated throughout the majority of a tutoring session, this affective state may be accompanied by cohesive moments of dialogue, nonverbal behavior, and task activity.

A central problem in multimodal interaction for tutoring lies in understanding how observed behavior is associated with persistent affective states. This may be addressed by an approach that analyzes tutorial modalities (e.g., dialogue, nonverbal behavior, task actions) with students' retrospective self-reports of affect. Such an approach is already used in investigations of affect in clinical psychology and inspired the work reported here. In studies of anxiety and depression, nonverbal behavior is examined over a period of time to identify differences in behavior due to psychological conditions [10, 12, 18]. Similarly, learning-centered affective states that occur throughout a tutoring session may coincide with differences in observable behavior.

To address this problem, this paper reports on the first study to investigate how multimodal feature sets can be used to predict whole-session retrospective self-reports of affect and learning gain within human-human tutoring. Multimodal feature sets were constructed from input streams of dialogue, nonverbal behavior, and task actions in computer-mediated one-on-one tutoring. The nonverbal behavior input stream included automatically tracked facial expression, hand-to-face gestures, and posture. Unimodal, bimodal, and trimodal feature sets were used to predict retrospective self-reports of engagement and frustration during the tutoring session and learning gain. The complete trimodal feature set was most predictive of each of the three tutoring outcomes, and bimodal features with dialogue were most predictive of each tutoring outcome. Importantly, the findings demonstrate that the role of nonverbal behavior may depend on the dialogue and task context in which it occurs. These results provide a promising direction for investigating multimodal feature sets in affective tutorial interaction. Future adaptive multimodal interfaces may leverage such detailed task-contextualized features to disambiguate affective behavior and improve user outcomes.

2. RELATED WORK

Several studies have examined multimodal features in learning-centered affect. Two studies have examined multimodal features in order to predict judged affective states. Kapoor & Picard aimed to classify teachers' labels of interest in children's gameplay with Fripple Place, a constraint-satisfaction game [13]. A mixture of Gaussian processes was used to achieve 87% accuracy with combined modalities of facial expression, posture, and task. In a later study, D'Mello & Graesser produced expert judgments of six affective states (boredom, confusion, engagement/flow, frustration, delight, surprise, and neutral) in interactions with the AutoTutor intelligent tutoring system [3]. A multimodal feature set of dialogue, facial expression, and posture performed best at classifying the affective states, with Cohen's K of 0.33 for fixed emotion judgments and 0.39 for spontaneous ones.

In another line of research with the Wayang Outpost intelligent tutoring system, multimodal features were observed and categorized for their occurrence across learning-centered affective states [24]. This investigation included modalities of head movement, gaze, gesture, facial expression, posture, and vocalizations. This work was followed up with efforts to predict self-reported affective states (confidence, excitement, frustration, and interest) during interactions with Wayang Outpost [1]. Multiple sensor streams were used, including facial expression tracked by the MindReader system, pressure-sensitive mouse, skin conductance bracelet, and pressure-sensitive chair. Stepwise regression models were constructed across feature combinations, with best fit models achieving effect sizes from $r = 0.54$ to 0.83. A follow-up validation study was also conducted with a new set of students from a different school and a lower age group [2]. The validation results showed that the previously used features were only partially generalizable to the new population, with reduced accuracies for most features.

In contrast to these prior studies, this paper presents an analysis of how modalities of dialogue, nonverbal behavior, and task action are predictive of students' whole-session retrospective self-reports of affect. This approach identified observed behaviors that are associated with engagement, frustration, and learning throughout tutoring sessions. Studies in this vein may provide significant insight into persistent tutoring-centric phenomena that analyses of moment-by-moment states would not.

3. MULTIMODAL TUTORING CORPUS

The corpus consists of computer-mediated tutorial dialogue for introductory computer science collected during the 2011-2012 academic year. Students (N=67) and tutors interacted through a web-based interface that provided learning tasks, an interface for computer programming, and textual dialogue.

3.1 JavaTutor Study

The participants were university students in the United States, with average age of 18.5 years (*stdev*=1.5). The students voluntarily participated for course credit in an introductory engineering course, but no prior computer science knowledge was assumed or required. Recordings of the sessions included database logs, webcam video, skin conductance, and Kinect depth video. For logistical reasons, video and physiology were recorded only at the student workstations. The present analysis examines the database logs, webcam video, and Kinect depth video from the first lesson as a multimodal tutoring corpus. The JAVATUTOR interface is shown in Figure 1.

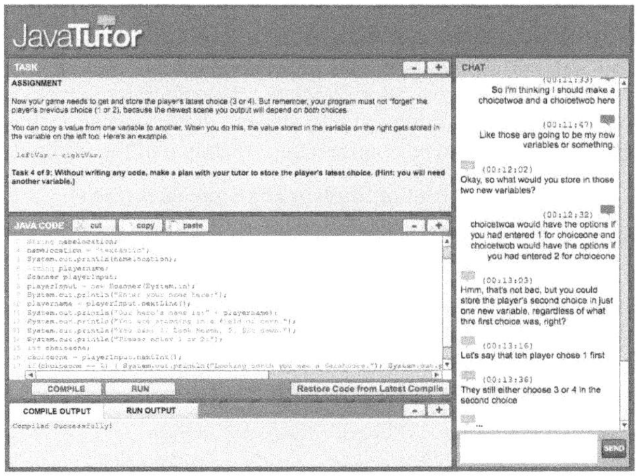

Figure 1. The JAVATUTOR interface

Before each session, students completed a content-based pretest. After each session, students answered a post-session survey and posttest (identical to the pretest). The post-session survey items included the User Engagement Survey (UES) [17] and the NASA-TLX workload survey [11], which included an item for Frustration Level. The survey items for retrospective self-report of engagement and frustration are shown in Figure 2. For more information on the UES, see a recent study validating the survey in another task-oriented domain [23].

User Engagement Survey (Likert items):

I lost myself in this learning experience.
I was so involved in my learning task that I lost track of time.
I blocked out things around me when I was working.
When I was working, I lost track of the world around me.
The time I spent working just slipped away.
I was absorbed in my task.
During this learning experience I let myself go.
Working on this task was worthwhile.
I consider my learning experience a success.
My learning experience was rewarding.
I would recommend using JavaTutor to my friends and family.
I was really drawn into my learning task.
I felt involved in this task.
This learning experience was fun.

Frustration Level (0-100 scale):

How insecure, discouraged, irritated, stressed, and annoyed were you?

Figure 2. Retrospective student affect survey items

3.2 Dialogue Acts

Student-tutor dialogue provides a rich source of data. Analyzing the dialogue transcripts can shed light on the effectiveness of tutoring strategies and participation of the student. Additionally, certain dialogue moves are related to student task progress and learning, as a tutor may need to provide more or less help.

The corpus was previously manually annotated using a fine-grained dialogue act annotation scheme [21]. A J48 decision tree classifier was constructed from these labels, producing an accuracy of 80.11% (Cohen's $K = 0.79$) on a held-out test set. This automatic dialogue act classifier [20] provided annotations of over 8,300 tutor and student messages across the corpus.

Due to space constraints, only the dialogue acts relevant to the results of the analysis are presented (see Table 1 and Table 2). The dialogue acts provide coverage of statements, questions, answers, and feedback of both tutors and students. Within these main categories, there are specific dialogue acts for tutors and students. For instance, tutor dialogue acts include more types of statements and questions, while student dialogue acts include feedback on the student's current understanding of the material.

Table 1. Subset of Student Dialogue Acts (DAs)

Student DA Label	Examples
AEX Extra Domain Answer	*Pretty good, just a lot of homework.* *I am great.*
E Explanation	*Once you respond with a name...* *I need a write statement.*
FNU Not Understanding Feedback	*I'm not sure if this is right...* *I'm not sure, I guess it would because it is Java?*
FU Understanding Feedback	*Oh, alright. Makes sense.* *Ohh, I see!*
GRE Greeting	*Hello!* *See you next time.*
O Observation	*See, the comment was ignored by Java.* *As you see, we have a bug.*
QI Information Question	*Why doesn't it stop on the next line in this case?* *How does that work?*

3.3 Nonverbal Behavior

We examined nonverbal behavior modalities as potential indicators of learning-centered cognitive-affective states across tutoring sessions. Recent advances in nonverbal behavior tracking were leveraged to recognize facial expression, hand-to-face gestures, and body posture. Due to human data collection error, the multimodal tutoring corpus includes nonverbal data for sixty-three of the sixty-seven students (N=63).

3.3.1 *Facial Expression*

The corpus includes facial expression annotations from the Computer Expression Recognition Toolbox (CERT) [15]. This tool recognizes fine-grained facial movements, or facial *action units (AUs)*, detailed in the Facial Action Coding System [6]. CERT finds faces in a video frame, locates facial features for the nearest face, and outputs weights for each tracked facial action unit using support vector machines. A recent article provides a detailed description of the technology used in CERT [25].

Based on the results of a validation study of CERT output, we adopt the method of mean-centering the output of CERT [8]. The validation study showed that this adjustment to CERT output produced excellent aggregate agreement with manual FACS annotations on a subset of five action units, while unadjusted CERT output did not. Also in accordance with that study [8], we use a mean-centered output threshold of 0.25 for presence of a facial action unit. This higher threshold may reduce false positives compared to the default threshold of any positive value. Additionally, we examine the five action units that were previously validated: AU1 (Inner Brow Raiser), AU2 (Outer Brow Raiser), AU4 (Brow Lowerer), AU7 (Lid Tightener), and AU14 (Mouth Dimpler).

Table 2. Subset of Tutor Dialogue Acts (DAs)

Tutor DA Label	Examples
ACK Acknowledgement	*Okay.* *I see.*
AWH WH-Question Answer	*The string PlayerName.* *That depends on the development.*
AYN Yes/No Answer	*Yes.* *No, sir.*
E Explanation	*Once you respond with a name...* *I need a write statement.*
FO Other Feedback	*That's fine.*
OEX Extra Domain Other	*Calc is hard.* *I want to thank you for helping us out.*
QEX Extra Domain Question	*How are classes going?* *How are you today?*
QO Open Question	*How can you fix it?* *How could you solve this problem?*
R Reassurance	*We have plenty of time.* *One thing: the more mistakes you make, the more you will learn.*

3.3.2 *Posture*

Postural features were created using depth image recordings from the Kinect sensor. A posture tracking algorithm identified distances of the head, upper torso, and lower torso. This posture tracking algorithm was previously found to be 92.4% accurate versus manual labels [7].

Head distances were then used to discretize postural distance (PosNear, PosMid, and PosFar), based on workstation-specific median distances and standard deviation. One standard deviation closer or farther than the median (across subjects) was considered "near" or "far," respectively.

Additionally, postural movements were labeled based on acceleration of the head tracking point. The absolute sum of frame-to-frame acceleration was accumulated in a rolling one-second window at each frame. The average amount of acceleration in a one-second interval was computed across all students. If acceleration in the present interval was above average, it was marked as a postural movement, PosMove; otherwise, it was marked as NoMove.

3.3.3 Gesture

Hand-to-face gestures were also tracked in the Kinect depth sensor recordings. A gesture detection algorithm recognized one or two hands touching the lower face. This algorithm relies on surface propagation from the center of the head, with pixel distances from the center used to identify a round (i.e., normal head shape) or an oblong shape (i.e., surface extends beyond the head) formed by the surface pixels. The hand-to-face gesture detection algorithm was previously found to be 92.6% accurate compared to manual labels [7]. Examples of detected hand-to-face gestures are shown in Figure 3.

Figure 3. Examples of detected hand-to-face gestures

3.4 Multimodal Features

The automatically recognized dialogue acts and nonverbal behaviors were combined with task action features in order to form the multimodal tutoring corpus. As students worked on programming tasks, the database logged dialogue messages, typing, and task progress. Tutorial dialogue occurred at any time during the sessions, with student and tutor messages sent asynchronously (StudentMessage and TutorMessage, respectively). Each of these student and tutor messages has an associated dialogue act label, as described in Section 3.2. These dialogue events comprise the Dialogue data stream.

The Task data stream consists of student task actions. As a student completed the programming task, he or she would press a compile button to convert the Java program code into a format that is ready to run. These compile attempts may be successful (CompileSuccess) or fail due to an error in the program code (CompileError). The student would also run his or her program (RunProgram) in order to test the output and interact with it. The student may also be working on the program code (Coding), or have stopped coding (StopCoding) at each moment.

The Nonverbal data stream consists of student facial expression, hand-to-face gestures, and posture. Each of the nonverbal behaviors were tracked at all times, so they were combined in parallel (i.e., each interval records the presence or absence of facial expression, gesture, and posture).

These data streams were discretized into one-second intervals. The most recent event of a given type (dialogue, nonverbal, task) was used as the current value at each interval. For instance, if a student had been coding but stopped after half a second into the current interval, the task action would be assigned to StopCoding. These one-second time intervals were used to calculate relative duration following a specific dialogue event or task action, or during a particular nonverbal behavioral display. Thus, each possible feature has a single numerical value (relative duration) for each student session. The simplest feature sets constructed in this way (the *unimodal* sets) consist of a single data stream. The average relative durations of each feature in the unimodal Task feature set are shown in Table 3.

Table 3. Average relative duration in the Task feature set

	Avg. Relative Duration (%)
Coding	18
StopCoding	25
CompileSuccess	9
CompileError	4
RunProgram	44

The *bimodal* feature sets each consist of the Cartesian product of two unimodal feature sets. This resulted in three bimodal feature sets: Dialogue × Nonverbal, Dialogue × Task, and Nonverbal × Task. Similarly, the complete *trimodal* feature set consists of the Cartesian product of all three unimodal feature sets, Dialogue × Nonverbal × Task. A final feature set combined all three bimodal feature sets through set union. This Bimodal Union feature set allows for comparison of the combined bimodal feature sets versus the complete trimodal feature set.

4. MULTIMODAL FEATURE ANALYSIS

This paper presents two levels of analysis: 1) comparison of feature set performance in predicting tutorial outcomes; and 2) comparison of the most predictive features across feature sets. These were performed for each of the three tutoring outcomes: engagement, frustration, and learning gain.

4.1 Model Construction

Model averaging was used to identify the most generalizable features in models with bimodal or trimodal feature sets and to reduce the feature space [19]. This approach produces average coefficient estimates and standard error across a wide range of models. Ratios of absolute value of the coefficient estimate versus standard error were also computed. These ratios provided a tradeoff between predictive weight and numerical stability, as estimates with lower standard error varied less across models. The features were then sorted using the ratios and the top twenty were selected for use in model building. (In the case of unimodal feature sets, all features were used and model averaging was not performed.) Predictive models were built using forward stepwise linear regression. Features were selected to optimize the leave-one-out cross-validated R^2 value of each model.

4.2 Engagement

The predictive models of engagement across feature sets, shown in Table 4, display a clear advantage of the trimodal feature set combining dialogue, nonverbal behavior, and task actions (D×N×T). The next best model uses the bimodal feature set combining dialogue and task actions (D×T). The union of bimodal feature sets (Bimodal Union) performs worse than D×T, but it uses fewer parameters. The trimodal feature set explains 50% more variance in retrospective self-reported engagement compared to the next best model (D×T) and uses fewer parameters.

Table 4. Engagement Feature Sets

Feature Set	R^2	# parameters
Unimodal Feature Sets		
DIALOGUE	0.048	3
NONVERBAL	-0.030	2
TASK	0.006	4
Bimodal Feature Sets		
DIALOGUE × NONVERBAL	0.146	3
DIALOGUE × TASK	0.187	9
NONVERBAL × TASK	0.112	5
Trimodal Feature Sets		
BIMODAL UNION	0.157	7
DIALOGUE × NONVERBAL × TASK	0.282	6

The two predictive models of retrospective self-reported engagement incorporating all three modalities of dialogue, nonverbal behavior, and task actions are shown in Table 5. There is slight overlap between the models (features that occur in both models are in bold type). The combination of student observational statements (O-STUDENT) and stopping coding was a negative predictor of engagement in both models. This may indicate moments when the student stopped working on the task in order to make a comment, which is consistent with loss of focus on the task. Mouth dimpling (AU14) was also involved in negatively predictive features in both models. This facial action unit has been associated with frustration and mental effort in prior analyses [8, 14]. Open questions from the tutor (QO-TUTOR) with no student brow lowering (NoAU4) were positively predictive of engagement in the model with the combined bimodal feature set (Bimodal Union). Brow lowering has been previously associated with confusion, frustration, and mental effort [5, 8, 9, 14]. Thus, this may highlight moments when the student was not perplexed by a tutor question. In the model with the trimodal feature set, student informational questions (QI-STUDENT) with outer brow raising (AU2) and running the program were positively predictive of engagement. This may indicate some interest in how the program operates, with the student actively engaging in discussion with the tutor.

A sequence of tutoring events related to engagement is shown in Figure 4. The left image shows the student coding the program. The middle shows when the student had stopped coding and read a yes/no answer from the tutor. In the right image, the student has returned to coding the program.

Figure 4. Sequence related to engagement

Table 5. Engagement Feature Comparison

Feature	β	p
BIMODAL UNION, $R^2 = 0.157$		
O-STUDENT, STOPCODING	-0.310	0.002
QEX-TUTOR, **AU14**	-0.283	0.005
GRE-STUDENT, COMPILESUCCESS	-0.275	0.007
FO-TUTOR, **AU2**	-0.247	0.061
FO-TUTOR, AU7	-0.195	0.137
QO-TUTOR, NOAU4	0.269	0.008
INTERCEPT	0.003	1
DIALOGUE × NONVERBAL × TASK, $R^2 = 0.282$		
AEX-STUDENT, **AU14**, RUNPROGRAM	-0.333	0.003
O-STUDENT, AU1, **STOPCODING**	-0.201	0.082
TYPINGMESSAGE, AU4, CODING	-0.197	0.110
AYN-TUTOR, POSNEAR, **STOPCODING**	0.256	0.014
QI-STUDENT, **AU2**, RUNPROGRAM	0.707	<0.001
INTERCEPT	0.076	1

4.3 Frustration

A comparison of predictive models of retrospective self-reported frustration across unimodal, bimodal, and trimodal feature sets is shown in Table 6. As with the models of engagement, there is a clear advantage of the trimodal feature sets. The trimodal feature sets greatly improve upon the bimodal feature sets, with the complete trimodal feature set (DIALOGUE × NONVERBAL × TASK) explaining more than three times the variance of the best bimodal feature set (DIALOGUE × TASK). The union of bimodal features (BIMODAL UNION) also explains over two times the variance of the individual bimodal feature sets, demonstrating an additive effect across the combined feature sets.

Table 6. Frustration Feature Sets

Feature Set	R^2	# parameters
Unimodal Feature Sets		
DIALOGUE	-0.033	1
NONVERBAL	-0.010	2
TASK	-0.033	1
Bimodal Feature Sets		
DIALOGUE × NONVERBAL	0.019	2
DIALOGUE × TASK	0.137	2
NONVERBAL × TASK	0.134	5
Trimodal Feature Sets		
BIMODAL UNION	0.347	7
DIALOGUE × NONVERBAL × TASK	0.520	5

Both predictive models of retrospective self-reported frustration that include all three modalities of dialogue, nonverbal behavior, and task actions are shown in Table 7. Interestingly, both models provide only positive predictors of frustration. There is also a fair degree of overlap between the models (shared features are indicated in bold). In both models, higher frustration is predicted by students providing feedback on their current understanding when working on the program. Students often did this after receiving tutor input on how the program works. So, this type of dialogue act may confirm that they understood the new information given by the tutor. However, the underlying trend may be that students had just received help from the tutor in order to remove a misconception. Thus, the students may feel frustration partially due to the lingering misconception.

Table 7. Frustration Feature Comparison

Feature	β	p
BIMODAL UNION, $R^2 = 0.347$		
FNU-STUDENT, **POSNEAR**	0.141	0.210
FNU-STUDENT, AU14	0.202	0.042
QEX-TUTOR, **STOPCODING**	0.260	0.013
STUDENTMESSAGE, RUNPROGRAM	0.260	0.008
OEX-TUTOR, POSMOVE	0.323	0.003
FU-STUDENT, CODING	0.456	<0.001
INTERCEPT	0	1
DIALOGUE × NONVERBAL × TASK, $R^2 = 0.520$		
R-TUTOR, NOAU1, **STOPCODING**	0.091	0.549
FU-STUDENT, NOAU2, **CODING**	0.336	<0.001
OEX-TUTOR, AU7, **STOPCODING**	0.429	0.006
FU-STUDENT, POSNEAR, CODING	0.451	<0.001
INTERCEPT	0	1

Another prominent pattern in both models is the emphasis on moments when the student was coding the program or had stopped coding. The moments of coding aligned with student feedback on his or her current level of understanding (FU-STUDENT). On the other hand, moments when the student stopped coding were associated with tutor messages. These tutor messages were related to off-topic statements (OEX) or questions (QEX), and reassurance (R). In such instances, the tutor is focusing on off-task discussion. Therefore, these features may be related to moments when the student stopped coding and received off-task tutor messages (with causality in either direction).

A sequence of tutoring events related to frustration is shown in Figure 5. First, the student encounters a compile error. The tutor then directs the student on how to fix the problem. Second, the student reports her understanding of the directive and implements the solution. Third, the tutor tells the student to compile and she does so successfully.

COMPILEERROR — FU-STUDENT, POSNEAR, CODING — COMPILESUCCESS

Figure 5. Sequence related to frustration

4.4 Normalized Learning Gain

Normalized learning gain (or percent learning gain) measures how much a student learned relative to what he or she could have learned [16]. This accounts for relative differences in learning between students who scored high or low on the pretest. Normalized learning gain was computed with the following formula if posttest score was greater than pretest score:

$$NLG = \frac{Posttest - Pretest}{1 - Pretest}$$

Otherwise, normalized learning gain was computed as follows:

$$NLG = \frac{Posttest - Pretest}{Pretest}$$

The predictive models of normalized learning gain are shown in Table 8, containing all three modalities of dialogue, nonverbal behavior, and task actions. In contrast with the affective tutoring outcomes, a unimodal feature set has significant predictive power, as the DIALOGUE unimodal feature set is predictive of learning. This underscores the important role of tutorial dialogue in the process of learning. Despite the significant predictive power of the best bimodal feature set (DIALOGUE × NONVERBAL), the complete trimodal feature set (D×N×T) still explains around sixteen percent more variance in learning gains.

The trimodal feature comparison models of normalized learning gain are shown in Table 9. These models overlap on the mouth dimpling facial action unit (AU14), which is a negative predictor of learning in both models. In viewing the tutoring session videos, AU14 appeared to correspond with moments when students were expending mental effort or thinking about the task. In the BIMODAL UNION model, AU14 coincides with tutor extra-domain questions. In the complete trimodal model (D×N×T), AU14 co-occurs with students running the program and remarking on lack of understanding in one trimodal feature, and with student stopping coding and tutor answers to complicated questions (not a "yes" or "no" answer) in another trimodal feature. In each case, the presence of AU14 may involve a reaction to a recent event in the tutoring session, whether it is the behavior of the program or messages from the tutor.

Table 8. Normalized Learning Gain Feature Sets

Feature Set	R^2	# parameters
Unimodal Feature Sets		
DIALOGUE	0.370	10
NONVERBAL	0.037	3
TASK	-0.034	1
Bimodal Feature Sets		
DIALOGUE × NONVERBAL	0.465	6
DIALOGUE × TASK	0.407	13
NONVERBAL × TASK	0.243	10
Trimodal Feature Sets		
BIMODAL UNION	0.460	5
DIALOGUE × NONVERBAL × TASK	0.544	8

On the side of positive predictors of learning, facial action unit features were involved in both models. In the BIMODAL UNION model, learning is positively predicted by student outer brow raising (AU2) with tutor feedback that is not distinctly positive or negative (FO-TUTOR). In the complete trimodal model (D×N×T), the positive predictors that included facial action units were tutor open questions (QO-TUTOR) after stopping coding with brow lowering (AU4), and tutor acknowledgements with no brow lowering (NOAU4) during coding. In the first case, the student may be effortfully considering the tutor's question. In the second case, the student may be continuing work on the task with no hesitation due to the tutor acknowledgement message. Both the positive and negative predictors of normalized learning gain demonstrate the importance of upper and lower face expression recognition in task-oriented multimodal systems.

Table 9. Normalized Learning Gain Feature Comparison

Feature	β	p
BIMODAL UNION, $R^2 = 0.460$		
O-STUDENT, **STOPCODING**	-0.478	<0.001
QEX-TUTOR, **AU14**	-0.341	0.001
GRE-STUDENT, **COMPILESUCCESS**	-0.314	0.002
FO-TUTOR, AU2	0.295	0.002
INTERCEPT	0.002	1
DIALOGUE × NONVERBAL × TASK, $R^2 = 0.544$		
FNU-STUDENT, **AU14**, RUNPROGRAM	-0.415	<0.001
AWH-TUTOR, **AU14**, **STOPCODING**	-0.311	0.001
E-TUTOR, POSMOVE, CODING	-0.213	0.019
FU-STUDENT, AU1, **COMPILESUCCESS**	-0.171	0.053
E-STUDENT, NOMOVE, RUNPROGRAM	0.132	0.160
ACK-TUTOR, NOAU4, CODING	0.205	0.028
QO-TUTOR, AU4, **STOPCODING**	0.231	0.011
INTERCEPT	0.002	1

A sequence of events related to learning is shown in Figure 6. In the first image, the student is testing his program. Further in the session, the student has begun coding more of the program. In the second image, the student has stopped coding and displayed AU4 as the tutor asked an open-ended question. The third image shows the student at a farther postural distance after successfully compiling the program.

RUNPROGRAM — QO-TUTOR, AU4, STOPCODING — COMPILESUCCESS

Figure 6. Sequence related to normalized learning gain

5. DISCUSSION

This paper has presented an in-depth comparison of multimodal feature sets related to engagement, frustration, and learning in computer-mediated human tutoring. The results show a distinct additive effect of features across modalities of dialogue, nonverbal behavior, and task actions. Each set of models found an improvement from unimodal to bimodal features and from bimodal to trimodal features.

Prior work has demonstrated mixed results in applying multimodal feature sets to prediction of affect. Often, a particular feature set is useful for one affective state, but not another [4]. However, most prior multimodal studies of tutoring did not involve a strong dialogue component [1, 2, 13]. In the present multimodal tutoring corpus, student-tutor dialogue plays a very significant role in predicting tutoring outcomes. A majority of features involve dialogue in the models built on a union of bimodal features, which had the potential to select nonverbal behavior and task features instead. Additionally, dialogue was the only unimodal feature set that was strongly predictive of a tutoring outcome—in this case, normalized learning gain. The importance of adaptive dialogue has also been shown in studies that examined the advantages of one-to-one tutoring [22].

While dialogue was of primary importance in these findings, the nonverbal behavior and task modalities also provided additional explanatory power. Task actions were fairly straightforward (e.g., the student was working on the task or not), but nonverbal behaviors co-occurred with specific task contexts. For instance, both presence of brow lowering (AU4) and its absence (NOAU4) appeared as positive predictors of normalized learning gain. The task contexts associated with these predictions were tutor utterance (QO vs. ACK) and student task actions (STOPCODING vs. CODING). The first feature (QO-TUTOR, AU4, STOPCODING) describes a moment when a student has stopped coding, has been posed an open-ended question by the tutor, and is thoughtfully reflecting on the question (as evidenced by brow lowering). The second feature (ACK-TUTOR, NOAU4, CODING), in contrast, may highlight a moment when the student is focused on implementing the program after receiving an acknowledgment from the tutor. AU4 may be absent in this context because the student knows how to modify the program and is making the changes with certainty. Similarly, a near postural position (POSNEAR) was predictive of both higher engagement and higher frustration. The divergent contexts of POSNEAR were student/tutor utterance (AYN-TUTOR vs. FU-STUDENT) and student task actions (STOPCODING vs. CODING). In the first case (AYN-TUTOR, STOPCODING), it seems that the student may sit near and stop coding while reading the tutor answer, which may reflect focused concentration. In the second case (FU-STUDENT, CODING), the student may be responding to tutor help and continuing work on the task, in which case the student may be having difficulty with the task, in turn associated with frustration.

Some nonverbal behaviors were more consistently predictive of tutoring outcomes. Mouth dimpling (AU14) appeared in multiple predictive features as an indicator of lower engagement, higher frustration, and reduced learning gain. Additionally, postural movement (POSMOVE) was associated with lower learning gain and increased frustration. Despite the alignment of these nonverbal behaviors toward negative affect, it is important to note that they were conditioned upon specific tutorial contexts. Thus, further analyses are necessary to infer generalizable situations in which these nonverbal behaviors occur.

6. CONCLUSION

It has long been hypothesized that combining multiple modalities improves multimodal interfaces' interpretive capabilities. In the study reported here, human tutors communicated with students through a text-based interface. Automated approaches were leveraged to annotate dialogue, task actions, facial movements, postural positions, and hand-to-face gestures. These dialogue, task progress, and nonverbal behavior input streams were then used to predict retrospective student self-reports of engagement and frustration, as well as pre/post-test learning gains. The overall finding is that the complete trimodal feature set is most predictive of each of the three tutoring outcomes. Additionally, the affective models showed large improvements from unimodal to bimodal and bimodal to trimodal feature sets. Dialogue played a large role in predicting learning gain, so the magnitude of improvement due to multimodal features was less for this outcome, though the bimodal and trimodal feature sets did outperform unimodal dialogue. Close examination of model features revealed that bimodal features with dialogue were most predictive of each tutoring outcome and that the role of nonverbal behavior may depend on the dialogue and task context in which it occurs.

These results presented here suggest a promising direction for investigating multimodal feature sets in affective tutorial interaction. Detailed task-contextualized multimodal information can provide insight not only into the moment-by-moment affective states experienced by users, but also on the states that may pervade the users' retrospective perception of their interaction. Future adaptive multimodal interfaces may leverage this detailed task-contextualized information to disambiguate affect and intervene effectively.

ACKNOWLEDGEMENTS

This work is supported in part by the North Carolina State University Department of Computer Science along with the National Science Foundation through Grants DRL-1007962 and IIS-1409639. Any opinions, findings, conclusions, or recommendations expressed in this report are those of the participants, and do not necessarily represent the official views, opinions, or policy of the National Science Foundation.

REFERENCES

[1] Arroyo, I., Cooper, D.G., Burleson, W., Woolf, B.P., Muldner, K. and Christopherson, R.M. 2009. Emotion Sensors Go To School. *14th International Conference on Artificial Intelligence in Education*, 17–24.

[2] Cooper, D.G., Muldner, K., Arroyo, I., Woolf, B.P. and Burleson, W. 2010. Ranking Feature Sets for Emotion Models used in Classroom Based Intelligent Tutoring Systems. *Proceedings of the 18th International Conference on User Modeling, Adaptation, and Personalization*, 135–146.

[3] D'Mello, S.K. and Graesser, A.C. 2010. Multimodal Semi-automated Affect Detection From Conversational Cues, Gross Body Language, and Facial Features. *User Modeling and User-Adapted Interaction*. 20, 2, 147–187.

[4] D'Mello, S.K. and Kory, J. 2012. Consistent but Modest: A Meta-Analysis on Unimodal and Multimodal Affect Detection Accuracies from 30 Studies. *Proceedings of the 14th ACM International Conference on Multimodal Interaction*, 31–38.

[5] D'Mello, S.K., Lehman, B., Pekrun, R. and Graesser, A.C. 2014. Confusion Can Be Beneficial for Learning. *Learning & Instruction*. 29, 153–170.

[6] Ekman, P., Friesen, W. V. and Hager, J.C. 2002. *Facial Action Coding System*. A Human Face.

[7] Grafsgaard, J.F., Fulton, R.M., Boyer, K.E., Wiebe, E.N. and Lester, J.C. 2012. Multimodal Analysis of the Implicit Affective Channel in Computer-Mediated Textual Communication. *Proceedings of the 14th ACM International Conference on Multimodal Interaction*, 145–152.

[8] Grafsgaard, J.F., Wiggins, J.B., Boyer, K.E., Wiebe, E.N. and Lester, J.C. 2013. Automatically Recognizing Facial Expression: Predicting Engagement and Frustration. *Proceedings of the 6th International Conference on Educational Data Mining*, 43–50.

[9] Grafsgaard, J.F., Wiggins, J.B., Boyer, K.E., Wiebe, E.N. and Lester, J.C. 2013. Automatically Recognizing Facial Indicators of Frustration: A Learning-Centric Analysis. *Proceedings of the 5th International Conference on Affective Computing and Intelligent Interaction*, 159–165.

[10] Harrigan, J.A. and O'Connell, D.M. 1996. How Do You Look When Feeling Anxious? Facial Displays of Anxiety. *Personality and Individual Differences*. 21, 2, 205–212.

[11] Hart, S.G. and Staveland, L.E. 1988. Development of NASA-TLX (Task Load Index): Results of Empirical and Theoretical Research. *Human Mental Workload*. P.A. Hancock and N. Meshkati, eds. Elsevier Science. 139–183.

[12] Joshi, J., Goecke, R., Parker, G. and Breakspear, M. 2013. Can Body Expressions Contribute to Automatic Depression Analysis? *Proceedings of the 10th IEEE International Conference and Workshops on Automatic Face and Gesture Recognition*, 1–7.

[13] Kapoor, A. and Picard, R.W. 2005. Multimodal Affect Recognition in Learning Environments. *Proceedings of the 13th Annual ACM International Conference on Multimedia*, 677–682.

[14] Littlewort, G., Bartlett, M.S., Salamanca, L.P. and Reilly, J. 2011. Automated Measurement of Children's Facial Expressions during Problem Solving Tasks. *Proceedings of the IEEE International Conference on Automatic Face and Gesture Recognition*, 30–35.

[15] Littlewort, G., Whitehill, J., Wu, T., Fasel, I., Frank, M., Movellan, J.R. and Bartlett, M.S. 2011. The Computer Expression Recognition Toolbox (CERT). *Proceedings of the IEEE International Conference on Automatic Face and Gesture Recognition*, 298–305.

[16] Marx, J.D. and Cummings, K. 2007. Normalized Change. *American Journal of Physics*. 75, 1, 87–91.

[17] O'Brien, H.L. and Toms, E.G. 2010. The Development and Evaluation of a Survey to Measure User Engagement. *Journal of the American Society for Information Science and Technology*. 61, 1, 50–69.

[18] Scherer, S., Stratou, G., Mahmoud, M., Boberg, J., Gratch, J., Rizzo, A. and Morency, L.-P. 2013. Automatic Behavior Descriptors for Psychological Disorder Analysis. *Proceedings of the 10th IEEE International Conference and Workshops on Automatic Face and Gesture Recognition*, 1–8.

[19] Symonds, M.R.E. and Moussalli, A. 2010. A Brief Guide to Model Selection, Multimodel Inference and Model Averaging in Behavioural Ecology using Akaike's Information Criterion. *Behavioral Ecology and Sociobiology*. 65, 1, 13–21.

[20] Vail, A.K. and Boyer, K.E. 2014. Adapting to Personality Over Time: Examining the Effectiveness of Dialogue Policy Progressions in Task-Oriented Interaction. *Proceedings of the 15th Annual SIGDIAL Meeting on Discourse and Dialogue*, 41–50.

[21] Vail, A.K. and Boyer, K.E. 2014. Identifying Effective Moves in Tutoring: On the Refinement of Dialogue Act Annotation Schemes. *Proceedings of the 12th International Conference on Intelligent Tutoring Systems*, 199–209.

[22] VanLehn, K., Graesser, A.C., Jackson, G.T., Jordan, P., Olney, A. and Rosé, C.P. 2007. When Are Tutorial Dialogues More Effective Than Reading? *Cognitive Science*. 31, 1, 3–62.

[23] Wiebe, E.N., Lamb, A., Hardy, M. and Sharek, D. 2014. Measuring Engagement in Video Game-based Environments: Investigation of the User Engagement Scale. *Computers in Human Behavior*. 32, 123–132.

[24] Woolf, B.P., Burleson, W., Arroyo, I., Dragon, T., Cooper, D.G. and Picard, R.W. 2009. Affect-Aware Tutors: Recognising and Responding to Student Affect. *International Journal of Learning Technology*. 4, 3-4, 129–164.

[25] Wu, T., Butko, N.J., Ruvolo, P., Whitehill, J., Bartlett, M.S. and Movellan, J.R. 2012. Multi-Layer Architectures for Facial Action Unit Recognition. *IEEE Transactions on Systems, Man and Cybernetics, Part B: Cybernetics*. 42, 4, 1027–1038.

Computational Analysis of Persuasiveness in Social Multimedia: A Novel Dataset and Multimodal Prediction Approach

Sunghyun Park, Han Suk Shim*, Moitreya Chatterjee*, Kenji Sagae, and Louis-Philippe Morency
Institute for Creative Technologies
University of Southern California
12015 Waterfront Dr., Los Angeles, CA 90094
{park, hshim, mchatterjee, sagae, morency}@ict.usc.edu

ABSTRACT

Our lives are heavily influenced by persuasive communication, and it is essential in almost any types of social interactions from business negotiation to conversation with our friends and family. With the rapid growth of social multimedia websites, it is becoming ever more important and useful to understand persuasiveness in the context of social multimedia content online. In this paper, we introduce our newly created multimedia corpus of 1,000 movie review videos obtained from a social multimedia website called ExpoTV.com, which will be made freely available to the research community. Our research results presented here revolve around the following 3 main research hypotheses. Firstly, we show that computational descriptors derived from verbal and nonverbal behavior can be predictive of persuasiveness. We further show that combining descriptors from multiple communication modalities (audio, text and visual) improve the prediction performance compared to using those from single modality alone. Secondly, we investigate if having prior knowledge of a speaker expressing a positive or negative opinion helps better predict the speaker's persuasiveness. Lastly, we show that it is possible to make comparable prediction of persuasiveness by only looking at thin slices (shorter time windows) of a speaker's behavior.

Categories and Subject Descriptors

H.4.3 **[Information Systems Applications]**: Communications Applications.
J.4 **[Computer Applications]**: Social and Behavioral Sciences.

General Terms

Algorithms, Performance, Experimentation, Human Factors.

Keywords

Persuasion; persuasiveness; multimodal; prediction; social multimedia; POM corpus; persuasive opinion multimedia corpus.

1. INTRODUCTION

Our daily lives are heavily influenced by persuasive communication. Making a convincing case in the courtroom [41], seeking patients' compliance to medical advice [29], advertising and selling products in business [24] and even interacting with our friends and family all have persuasion at the core of the interaction.

ICMI '14, November 12 - 16 2014, Istanbul, Turkey
Copyright 2014 ACM 978-1-4503-2885-2/14/11...$15.00.
http://dx.doi.org/10.1145/2663204.2663260

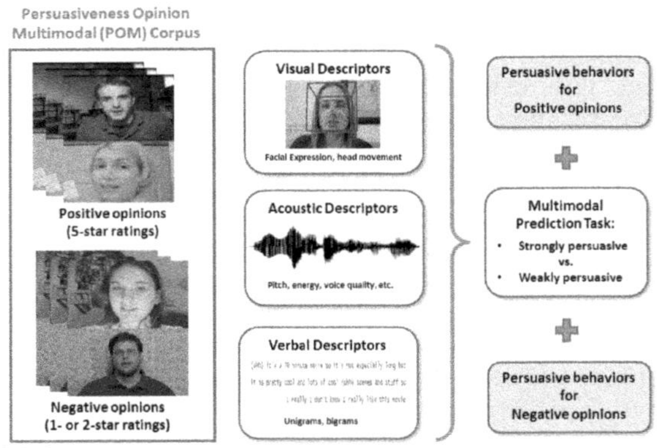

Figure 1. Overview of our multimodal approach in predicting persuasiveness in social multimedia.

With the advent of the Internet and the recent growth of social networking sites, more and more of our daily interaction is taking place in the online domain. Whereas the communication modality used online was predominantly text in the past, there is now an explosion of online content in the form of videos, making it more important and useful to understand persuasiveness in the context of online social multimedia content. What makes some people persuasive in online multimedia and influential in shaping other people's opinions and attitudes while others are ignored? This is the key question that we would like to start addressing with this paper.

While there has been a considerable amount of research on persuasion in the traditional sense, there has been very limited work investigating persuasion from the computational perspective and from the context of social multimedia. However, recent progress in computer vision and audio signal processing technologies [10, 13, 26, 27] is enabling automatic extraction of various visual and acoustic behavioral cues without having to depend on costly and time-consuming manual annotations, making it more feasible to tackle the problem from a more computational standpoint.

In this paper, we introduce our newly created Persuasive Opinion Multimedia (POM) corpus consisting of 1,000 movie review videos obtained from a social multimedia website called ExpoTV.com, which we plan to make freely available to the research community. Our experimental analysis revolves around the following 3 main research hypotheses. Firstly, we study if computational descriptors derived from verbal and nonverbal behavior can be predictive of persuasiveness. We further analyze the combination of descriptors from multiple communication modalities (audio, text and visual)

* The indicated authors made equal contribution to this work.

for predicting persuasiveness and compare with using single modality alone. Secondly, we investigate differences when speakers are expressing a positive or negative opinion and if having that prior knowledge helps in persuasiveness prediction. Lastly, we test if it is possible to make comparable prediction of persuasiveness by only looking at thin slices (i.e., shorter time windows) of a speaker's behavior.

In the next section, we give a brief overview of the literature that gave theoretical ground and motivation to our work, followed by our specific contributions. In Section 3, we outline our main research hypotheses, and Section 4 introduces our novel multimedia dataset designed for investigating persuasiveness in social multimedia. We give explanations on the design of our computational descriptors in Section 5 and experiments in Section 6. We report our results in Section 7 with discussions, and we conclude in Section 8.

2. THEORETICAL BACKGROUND

Persuasion in human communication has been a very hot topic for research over the past decades due to its wide applicability and substantial implications, and there is a plethora of sources in the literature that cover the topic in much breadth and depth. In this section, we give a brief review of past research that are only immediately relevant to our study. For an overview and history on persuasion research, interested readers are referred to other recent comprehensive texts such as [8, 28, 31].

In social psychology, the dual process models of persuasion [6, 32] have gained much attention and wide acceptance over the past decades. According to the models, there are two different routes we take when processing information that can influence our attitudes. One route is based on cognition that is more systematic and effortful while the other is based on peripheral or heuristic cues such as credibility or attractiveness of the message source. Our work in this paper can be seen in light of the dual process models with the focus on the peripheral route of information processing.

Modality Influence & Human Perception

Human communication is comprised of multiple modalities including verbal, acoustic and visual channels, and it is apparent that each modality has its own separate influence on human perception. Mehrabian [22] even goes as far to claim that our perception of an individual is determined 7% by his/her verbal content, 38% by his/her tone of voice, and 55% by his/her facial and bodily cues. Although his claim is arguable in our research context, it is obvious that multimodal analysis is an inevitable step to have a better understanding of human behavior and perception. In particular, Chaiken et al. [5] showed different influences on persuasion and comprehension when a message was delivered through the written, audiotaped or videotaped modality. Worchel et al. [42] also studied the effects on persuasion with different types of media, communicators, and positions of the message.

Acoustic Perspective

Showing the importance of acoustic cues in human speech, Stern et al. [40] reported that natural speech was more persuasive and taken more favorably than computer-synthesized speech. In addition, Mehrabian and Williams [23] reported that more intonation and higher speech volume contributed to perceived persuasiveness, Pittam [33] studied the relationship between nasality and perceived persuasiveness with a group of Australian speakers, Burgoon et al. [3] found a positive correlation between vocal pleasantness and perceived persuasiveness, and Pearce and Brommel [30] reported different effects of vocalic cues from conversational and dynamic speech styles on the perception of credibility and persuasiveness depending on the listener's preconceived notion of the speaker.

Verbal and Para-Verbal Perspective

Para-verbal cues are consistently found by many researchers to have a strong relationship with our perception of persuasiveness. For instance, Mehrabian and Williams [23] reported that higher speech rate and less halting speech contributed to perceived persuasiveness, Miller et al. [25] reported that a rapid speech rate positively influenced persuasion, and Pearce and Brommel [30] reported that dynamic and conversational styles (with varying characteristics in pitch, volume and use of pauses) had different effects on the perception of credibility and persuasiveness.

There are many components in the verbal domain that have strong relationship with persuasiveness [15, 44]. However, for the purpose of our work, we are not concerned with the validity or quality of argumentation in the textual data, and we are interested only at the level of finding key words that are informative in differentiating between strongly persuasive and weakly persuasive speakers.

Visual Perspective

Independent of text and voice, our facial expressions and bodily gestures convey much information as well. In relation to persuasion research, Mehrabian and Williams [23] found that more eye contact, smaller reclining angles, more head nodding, more gesticulation and more facial activity yielded significant effects for increasing perceived persuasiveness. LaCrosse [19] also found a similar set of nonverbal behavior related to persuasiveness that he calls affiliative nonverbal behavior. Moreover, Burgoon et al. [3] found that greater perceived persuasiveness correlated with kinesic / proxemic immediacy, facial expressiveness, and kinesic relaxation. Rosenfeld [36] found that the level of persuasiveness was positively correlated with positive head nods and negatively correlated with self-manipulations.

Thin Slice Prediction

Ambady and Rosenthal [1] showed that much inference is possible just by observing "thin slices" of nonverbal behavior, and Curhan and Pentland [9] applied the idea in a simulated employment negotiation scenario where they found that certain speech features within the first five minutes of negotiation were predictive of the overall negotiation outcome in the end. It is quite likely that the same idea can apply in the context of persuasiveness perception.

Contributions

To our knowledge, our new corpus is the first multimedia dataset created with the intention of studying persuasiveness in social multimedia. Furthermore, the main novelty of our work lies in investigating computational models of persuasiveness that take advantage of all 3 communicative modalities.

3. RESEARCH HYPOTHESES

Motivated by findings from past research outlined in the pervious section, our study presented in this paper was designed to specifically address the following three main hypotheses.

Computational Descriptors (Unimodal vs. Multimodal): As reviewed in the previous section, past research points to various cues in verbal and nonverbal behavior that influence human perception of persuasiveness. We hypothesize that we can capture such indicators of persuasiveness through computational descriptors to predict whether a speaker in social multimedia is

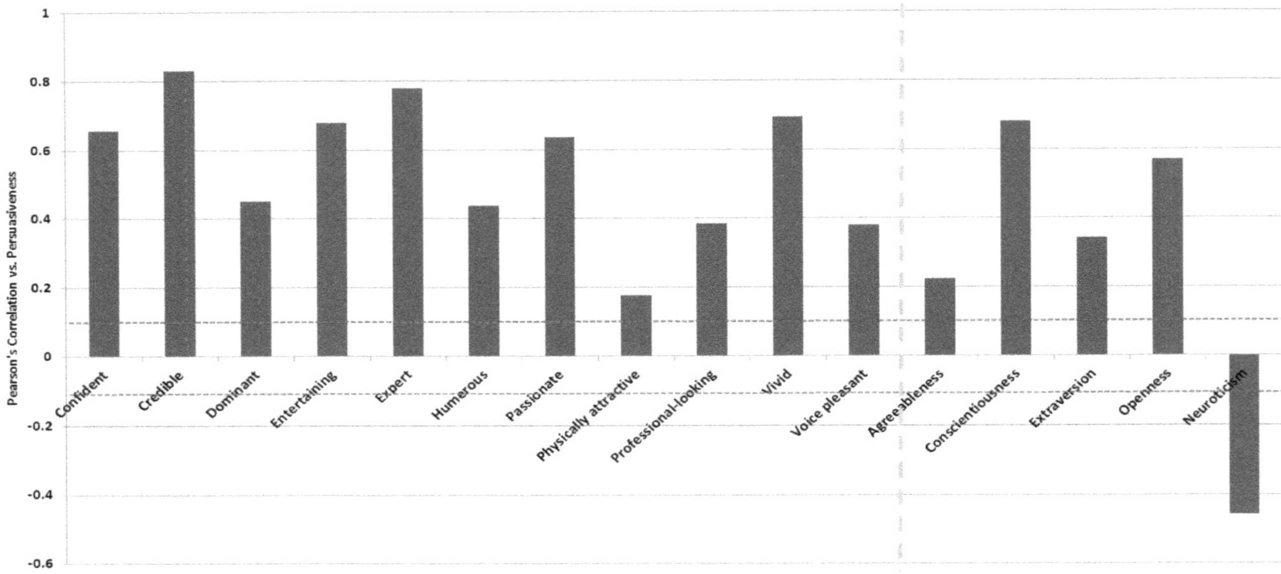

Figure 2. Pearson's correlation coefficients between persuasiveness and high-level and personality attributes (after taking the mean of 3 repeated annotations). The red line indicates statistical significance at $p < 0.001$, and the grey line visually divides the personality dimensions from other attributes.

strongly persuasive or weakly persuasive. In particular, we hypothesize that combining computational descriptors derived from multiple modalities of communication can make more accurate prediction than using those from a single modality alone from the acoustic, verbal or visual channel.

Hypothesis 1 (H1): Multimodal computational descriptors of verbal and nonverbal behavior perform better than unimodal descriptors in predicting a speaker's persuasiveness in social multimedia.

Prior Knowledge of Opinion Polarity: Persuasion can happen in a variety of context, and it is likely that we change our behavior depending on the context in our persuasion attempt. We hypothesize that if it is known in advance whether a speaker is trying to persuade one in favor of or against something, computational models can better capture the difference between persuasive and unpersuasive contents to make a more informed and better prediction.

Hypothesis 2 (H2): Persuasive behavior changes with opinion polarity and having prior knowledge of this sentiment polarity helps better predict a speaker's persuasiveness.

Thin Slice Prediction: In trying to persuade others, we may convey varying degrees of information in different stages of our persuasion attempt. For instance, we may tend to put more emphasis in the very beginning or we may typically want to close our speech with more impact close to the end. Combined with the idea of thin slices, we hypothesize that by looking at verbal and nonverbal behavior at specific shorter time periods, we can still make comparable prediction of persuasiveness of a speaker in social multimedia compared to making prediction based on the entire length of the speaker's behavior in video.

Hypothesis 3 (H3): Computational descriptors derived from a thin slice time period can make comparable prediction of a speaker's persuasiveness compared to those derived from the entire length of his/her video.

4. PERSUASIVE OPINION MULTIMEDIA CORPUS

Since there is currently no suitable corpus in the research community to study persuasiveness in the context of online social multimedia (currently the most relevant one to our knowledge is a dataset of online conversational videos by Biel et al. [2]), we found ExpoTV.com to be a good source to create a new corpus for our research topic. We plan to make our new Persuasive Opinion Multimedia (POM) corpus freely available to the research community. ExpoTV.com is a popular website housing videos of product reviews. Each product review has a video of a speaker talking about a particular product, as well as the speaker's direct rating of the product on an integral scale from 1 star (for most negative review) to 5 stars (for most positive review). This direct rating is useful for the purpose of our study because the star rating has close relationship with the direction of persuasion. For instance, the speaker in a 5-star movie review video would most likely try to persuade the audience in favor of the movie while the speaker in a 1-star movie review video would argue against watching the movie. Our corpus includes only movie review videos for the consistency of context. Since we were interested in exploring the difference in behavior between the cases when a speaker is trying to persuade the audience positively and negatively, we collected a total of 1,000 movie review videos as follows:

- **Positive Reviews:** 500 movie review videos with 5-star rating (315 males and 185 females).
- **Negative Reviews:** 500 movie review videos with 1 or 2-star rating, consisting of 216 1-star videos (151 males and 65 females) and 284 2-star videos (212 males and 72 females). We included 2-star videos due to a lack of 1-star videos on the website.

Each video in the corpus has a frontal view of one person talking about a particular movie, and the average length of the videos is about 94 seconds with the standard deviation of about 32 seconds. The corpus contains 372 unique speakers and 600 unique movie titles, including all types of common movie genres.

Table 1. Krippendorff's alpha agreement for our attributes.

Attribute	Kripp. alpha	Attribute	Kripp. alpha
Confident	0.73	Passionate	0.75
Credible	0.69	Professional-looking	0.70
Dominant	0.67	Vivid	0.68
Entertaining	0.68	Voice pleasant	0.67
Expert	0.70	Phys. Attractive	0.76
Humorous	0.74	**Persuasive**	**0.68**
Agreeableness	0.68	Openness	0.66
Conscientiousness	0.70	Neuroticism	0.64
Extraversion	0.73		

4.1 Subjective Annotations

Amazon Mechanical Turk (AMT) [21], which is a popular online crowdsourcing platform, was used to obtain subjective evaluations of the speaker in each video. A total of 50 native English-speaking workers based in the United States participated in the evaluation process online, and the task was evenly distributed among the 50 workers. To minimize gender influence, the task was distributed such that the workers only evaluated the speakers of the same gender. We note that although our primary focus was in investigating persuasiveness, various other high-level attributes including personality were also evaluated, making the corpus more widely applicable for other related research topics.

4.1.1 Persuasiveness & High-Level Attributes

For each video in the corpus, we obtained 3 repeated annotations on the level of persuasiveness of the speaker by asking the workers to give direct rating on the speaker's persuasiveness on a Likert scale from 1 (very unpersuasive) to 7 (very persuasive). In addition to persuasiveness, we also obtained evaluations on various high-level attributes, many of which past research suggests for having close relationship with our perception of persuasiveness. The high-level attributes were evaluated similarly as persuasiveness on a 7-point Likert scale with 1 being the least descriptive of the attribute and 7 being the most descriptive. For evaluating personality, a 10-item version of the Big Five Inventory [35] was used to assess the personality of the speaker in each video. We note that we also have self-assessed personality of the workers who performed the evaluations so that a deeper analysis can be possible by investigating the relationship between the personality of the perceiver and the perceived.

- **High-Level Attributes:** confident, credible, dominant, entertaining, expert, humorous, passionate, physically attractive, professional-looking, vivid, and voice pleasant.
- **Personality Dimensions (Big Five Model):** agreeableness, conscientiousness, extraversion, openness, and neuroticism.

4.1.2 Analysis

Due to variability in human perception and judgment, taking the mean or majority vote of repeated evaluations would be a sensible method of obtaining final labels. For our study, we used the mean score of 3 repeated Likert-scale evaluations as the final measure. Table 1 summarizes the mean agreement measured with Krippendorff's alpha between our final measure and each coder. The agreement is generally high around 0.70. Figure 2 shows the correlations between persuasiveness and other attributes when using our final measures, and many of the high-level attributes show a strong correlation with persuasiveness, which is consistent with past research in the literature [8, 28, 31]. It is particularly interesting to see which traits are not correlated or inversely correlated. The fact that physical attractiveness is only weakly correlated is most likely due to our design of the same-gender evaluation. Neuroticism is inversely correlated. Some of the most strongly correlated traits are credibility, confidence, and expertise.

To validate the persuasiveness measure, we included in the annotation tasks two questions related to the annotators' interest in watching the reviewed movies. For the first question, annotators were shown the synopsis of the movie and were asked, "How interested are you in watching this movie?" This first question was before watching the review. Then after watching the review, the annotators were asked the following second question, "After seeing this movie review, how interested are you in watching this movie?", with a scale ranging from -3 (much less interested than before) to +3 (much more interested than before). The annotators were also asked another question to note whether they have seen the movies before. Out of 3000 annotation tasks (1000 movies multiplied by 3 for repeated annotations), 1089 were marked by annotators who have seen the movies, and excluding those, our validity analysis shows a strong correlation between the persuasiveness score rating and the annotators' interest after watching the movie reviews, 0.69 and 0.54 for positive and negative reviews respectively.

4.1.3 Transcriptions

Using AMT and 18 participants from the same worker pool for the subjective evaluations, we obtained verbatim transcriptions, including pause-fillers and stutters. Each transcription was reviewed and edited by in-house experienced transcribers for accuracy.

Table 2. Overview of our computational multimodal descriptors

Acoustic
• Formants: F1 ~ F5 • Mel frequency cepstral coefficients: MFCC 1 ~ 24 • Pitch / Fundamental frequency (F0) • Voice qualities: normalized amplitude quotient (NAQ), parabolic spectral parameter (PSP), maxima dispersion quotient (MDQ), quasi-open quotient (QOQ), difference between the first two harmonics (H1-H2), and peak-slope
Verbal and Para-Verbal
• Unigrams • Bigrams • Verbal fluency qualities: articulation rate, pause, pause-filler, speech disturbance ratio, and stutter
Visual
• Emotions: anger, contempt, disgust, fear, joy, sadness, and surprise • Valence: negative, neutral, and positive • Facial Action Units: AU1, AU2, AU4, AU5, AU6, AU7, AU9, AU10, AU12, AU14, AU15, AU17, AU18, AU20, AU23, AU24, AU25, AU26, and AU28 • Eye gaze movements: displacement in x and y axes • Head movements: displacement and rotation in x, y and z axes • Approximated posture: displacement in the z-axis
Statistical Functionals (acoustic and visual descriptors only)
mean, median, percentiles (10th, 25th, 75th, and 90th), ranges (between min and max, 10th and 90th percentiles, and 25th and 75th percentiles) skewness, standard deviation

5. COMPUTATIONAL DESCRIPTORS

In this section, we give details on the extraction and computational encoding of multimodal descriptors as potential candidates for capturing persuasiveness. Except for most of the verbal and para-verbal descriptors, which depended on manual transcriptions for feature extraction, all other descriptors were extracted and encoded automatically using various acoustic and visual tracking tools. All the computational descriptors that we used are summarized in Table 2.

5.1 Acoustic Descriptors

Following common approaches for conducting automatic speech analysis [39], we extracted various speech features related to pitch, formants, voice qualities and mel-frequency cepstral coefficients (MFCCs) using a publicly available software called Covarep [10]. The raw feature values were then used to compute common statistical descriptors including mean, median, percentiles, ranges, skewness, and standard deviation. The encoded features were then used to explore their feasibility in capturing persuasiveness in acoustic signals of speech.

- Formants: The information of acoustic resonance of the human vocal track, called formant, is commonly used for speech recognition and emotion recognition. We explored formants F1 through F5.
- Mel frequency cepstral coefficients (MFCC): Also widely used for speech and emotion recognition are MFCCs, and we explored MFCC 1~24.
- Pitch (F0), also referred to as the fundamental frequency, is closely tied to the affective aspect of speech [4].
- Voice Qualities: Many studies show a strong relation between voice quality features and perceived emotion [14], and it is widely used for emotion recognition in speech. We used various voice quality descriptors including normalized amplitude quotient (NAQ), parabolic spectral parameter (PSP), maxima dispersion quotient (MDQ), quasi-open quotient (QOQ), difference between the first two harmonics (H1-H2), and peak-slope. For more details, readers are referred to [16, 17, 37].

5.2 Verbal and Para-Verbal Descriptors

From the verbatim transcriptions of the dataset, we extracted all standard unigram and bigram features commonly used in natural language processing, with the only difference in that the term frequencies were normalized by the video length. In addition, we observed a set of frequent para-verbal cues that could be associated with the level of persuasiveness.

- Articulation rate: Articulation rate is the rate of speaking in which all pauses are excluded from calculation and was computed by taking the ratio of the number of spoken words in each video to the actual time spent speaking.
- Pause: We computed this descriptor by counting all instances of silence during speech that are greater than 0.5 seconds in length, normalized by the total length of the video. FaceFX software [12] was used to automatically extract and encode this descriptor.
- Pause-filler: Pause-fillers are sounds that are used to fill the pause in speech, such as "um" or "uh." This descriptor was computed by counting all instances of pause-fillers, normalized by the total number of words spoken in each video.
- Speech disturbance ratio: Pause-fillers and stuttering can be considered as the same category of speech disturbance [20]. We computed speech disturbance ratio by counting the number of speech disturbance instances (pause-fillers and stutter), normalized by the total number of words spoken in each video.

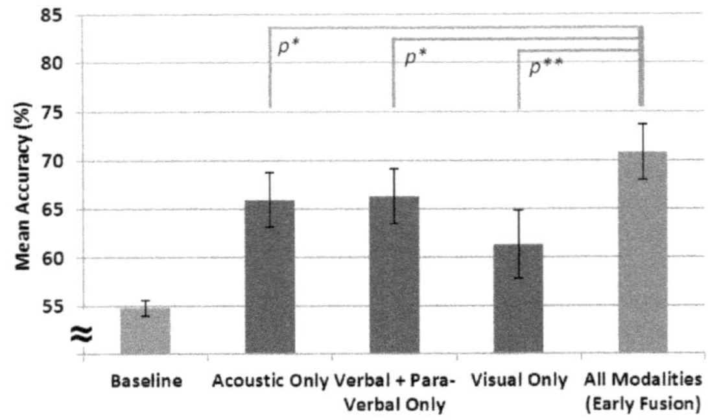

Figure 3. Persuasiveness prediction results for unimodal and multimodal models when using both positive and negative reviews combined ($p^* < 0.05$ and $p^{**} < 0.01$).

- Stutter: For this descriptor, we counted all instances of stuttering in each video, normalized by the number of words spoken in the video.

5.3 Visual Descriptors

Using readily available visual tracking technologies [13, 26, 27], we extracted various raw features from the face and the head movement of each speaker in the video. Similarly as the acoustic descriptors, we computed the same statistical descriptors to explore their usefulness in indicating persuasiveness.

- Discrete Emotions: The level of anger, contempt, disgust, fear, joy, sadness, and surprise.
- Valence: The level of high-level valence including negative, neutral and positive valence.
- Facial Action Units: The level of movements in various facial areas as codified by Facial Action Coding System (FACS) [11] including AU1, AU2, AU4, AU5, AU6, AU7, AU9, AU10, AU12, AU14, AU15, AU17, AU18, AU20, AU23, AU24, AU25, AU26, and AU28.
- Eye gaze movements: The gaze movement in the x and y axes
- Head movements: The head displacement and rotation in the x, y and z axes.
- Approximated posture: The movement in the z axis (toward or away from the camera).

6. EXPERIMENTS

This section gives details on the experimental methodology, particularly on our prediction models and the experimental conditions we designed to test our research hypotheses.

6.1 Experimental Conditions

In order to address the first hypothesis (H1), we trained and tested the prediction models and performed feature selection in the following groups depending on the communication modality:

- Acoustic descriptors only.
- Verbal and para-verbal descriptors only.
- Visual descriptors only.

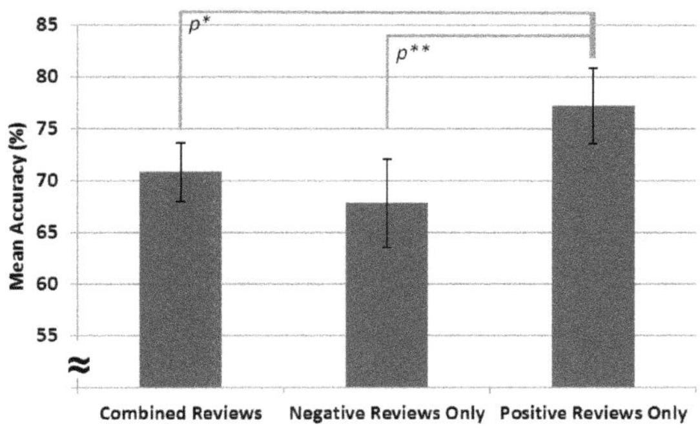

Figure 4. Persuasiveness prediction results for sentiment-independent and sentiment-dependent conditions using all modalities (p* < 0.05 and p < 0.01).**

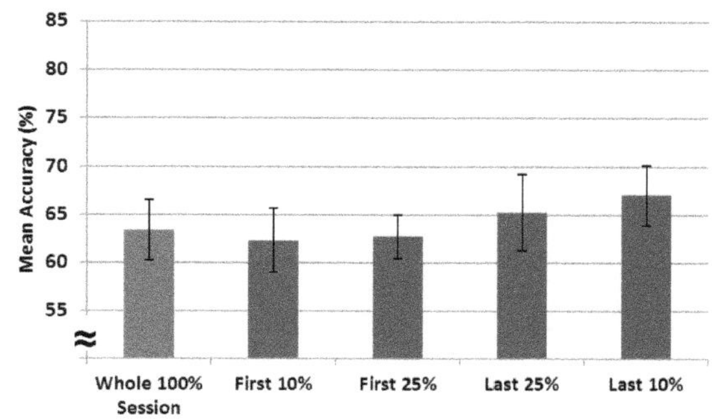

Figure 5. Persuasiveness prediction results using acoustic and visual descriptors in thin slices (shorter time windows).

- Early fusion: All types of descriptors together.

To address the second hypothesis (H2), we also performed our experiments in 3 different groups depending on the sentiment (opinion polarity) of the reviews:

- Positive reviews only (sentiment-dependent).
- Negative reviews only (sentiment-dependent).
- Both review types combined (sentiment-independent).

To address the third hypothesis (H3), we performed additional experiments with the acoustic and visual descriptor groups by computing the descriptors separately within different thin slices. More specifically, we divided each review video into 4 different thin slices of first 10%, first 25%, last 25% and last 10% of the video and repeated the same experiments. We did not use verbal and para-verbal descriptors for this because most of them were derived from manual transcriptions that did not have timestamp information.

6.2 Persuasiveness Labels

The ground-truth persuasiveness score of equal to or greater than 5.5 was taken as persuasive speakers and the score of equal to or less than 2.5 weakly persuasive speakers. After taking this step, we ended up with a total of 300 videos, specifically 157 videos of positive reviews (75 persuasive and 82 unpersuasive) and 143 videos of negative reviews (62 persuasive and 81 unpersuasive). We note that this selection process was done so that we could primarily focus on investigating behavioral differences between strongly persuasive and weakly persuasive videos. We keep as future work the regression analysis.

6.3 Methodology

For all experiments, we used the support vector machine (SVM) classifier with the radial basis function kernel as the prediction models [7]. The experiments were performed with 10-fold cross-validation (CV). Each CV experiment had 1 fold testing and 3-fold validation (among 9 training folds) for automatic selection of hyper parameters (i.e., gamma and C parameters for SVM). We repeated the experiments 3 times with randomly and newly separated folds. It is worth emphasizing that our folds were created such that no 2 folds contained samples from the same speaker or the same movie title. These restrictions assure user-independent experiments for better generalizability of our prediction models and results. Our evaluation metric is the averaged accuracy over all folds.

For feature selection, we mainly used the Information Gain (IG) metric [43]. We note that we performed feature selection only using the training samples from each cross-validation experiment. None of the test samples were used for feature selection. That is, we performed 10 separate feature selections using only the training samples for each 10 iterations during cross-validation testing. In order to keep the feature space to roughly 1/10th of the sample size, we selected top 30 features as determined by the IG score.

7. RESULTS AND DISCUSSIONS

In this section, we report and discuss our results testing our 3 main research hypotheses described in Section 3, followed by descriptor analysis.

7.1 Multimodal vs. Unimodal (H1)

Figure 3 shows the prediction accuracy results with the combined movie review condition, the persuasiveness predictors trained by fusing the descriptors from all 3 modalities together performed better with a statistical significance compared to each type of unimodal predictors, confirming our first research hypothesis. Specifically, our multimodal predictors predicted persuasiveness with a mean accuracy of 70.84%, and paired-sample t-tests showed that the performance was statistically significance compared to acoustic only predictors that performed at 65.97% ($p < 0.05$), verbal and para-verbal only predictors that performed at 66.29% ($p < 0.05$), and visual only predictors at 61.35% ($p < 0.01$). The baseline or the majority vote accuracy when always siding with the class label with more samples was at 54.83%.

Our results suggest that visual, acoustic and verbal descriptors are complementing each other during the persuasiveness assessment of online multimedia content. Our multimodal predictor is able to identify this complementarity as shown by other statistically significant results.

7.2 Prior Knowledge of Sentiment (H2)

Figure 4 shows the prediction accuracy results for the multimodal predictors with all 3 modalities across different conditions of positive reviews only, negative reviews only, and all reviews combined. The predictors trained and tested using only the positive reviews performed best at 77.24%, and paired-sample t-tests show statistical significance compared to those trained and tested using only the negative reviews which performed at 67.84% ($p < 0.01$) and those using the combined reviews which performed at 70.84% ($p < 0.05$).

This result partially confirms our second hypothesis and suggests that our computational descriptors can capture indicators of persuasiveness far better when the speakers are trying to persuade to watch a movie compared to when they are trying to persuade you against it, with the prediction performance falling somewhere between the two when using both kinds of reviews together. This

Table 3. Top computational descriptors for positive and negative reviews which were automatically selected using Information Gain.

Positive Reviews	Info Gain	Negative Reviews	Info Gain
		Acoustic	
MFCC4: stddev	0.12	MFCC3: mean	0.12
MFCC4: range (min ~ max)	0.11	MFCC3: median	0.12
MFCC2: range (10th ~ 90th perc.)	0.11	MFCC3: 75th perc.	0.10
MFCC4: range (10th ~ 90th perc.)	0.10	F3: 10th perc.	0.10
MFCC8: skew	0.10	F4: median	0.09
		Verbal and Para-Verbal	
pause	0.13	pause	0.11
articulation rate	0.08	articulation rate	0.09
n-grams: in, things, there are, very, one, well, is the, you, say, movie that, even though, will be, movie its, deleted, a pretty, a lot, and they're, movie in, good movie, don't know, you should, character, that I'm		n-grams: make, to make, it but, not even, even, just, the film, night, do not, character, premise, out, movie this, end, terrible, real, kids, but if, at all, writing, feels, poor, yourself	
		Visual	
posture: 10th perc.	0.13	gaze movement x-axis (left/right): range	0.14
posture: 25th perc.	0.12	gaze movement x-axis: range (25th ~ 75th perc.)	0.13
posture: mean	0.12	head rotation in all x, y, z axes: range (25th ~ 75th perc.)	0.13
head movement z-axis: 90th perc.	0.12	head rotation in all x, y, z axes: range (10th ~ 90th perc.)	0.12
posture: median	0.11	AU12: stddev.	0.12

may be explained by the imbalance of sentiment or opinion polarity in our dataset. Due to the lack of 1-star movie reviews on ExpoTv.com, we included 2-star reviews to match the number of positive reviews in our dataset. It is quite possible that the 2-star review videos convey weaker verbal and nonverbal cues than the two extremes of 1-star and 5-star review videos, making the prediction with negative reviews more difficult than the positive reviews.

7.3 Thin Slice Prediction (H3)

Figure 5 shows the accuracy results of the predictors using both the acoustic and visual modalities across different thin slices. Using the whole length of each review yielded the mean prediction accuracy of 63.41%, and the figure shows that the performance is comparable across all thin slices. This result is a typical demonstration of the idea of thin slices, and it suggests that we can still make much inference on a speaker's persuasiveness just by looking at the very beginning or end of the movie review. Although not conclusive, another interesting finding is that there seems to be mild tendency that more verbal and nonverbal indicators of persuasiveness are present or stronger toward the end of the video.

7.4 Descriptor Analysis

Table 3 summarizes a short analysis highlighting top descriptors that have been discriminative in separating strongly persuasive and weakly persuasive speakers.

From the acoustic modality, MFCC descriptors in the low frequency regions stand out for predicting persuasive speakers in both positive and negative reviews, which are expected to perform better than high frequency regions due to denser resolutions and being more robust to noise. Although MFCC features are heavily used in speech recognition and analysis, they unfortunately do not give room for much interpretation.

Consistent with the literature described in Section 2, para-verbal descriptors of pause and articulate (speech) rate proved to show much discriminative power in separating speakers who are perceived as persuasive and those who are not. The unigram and bigram descriptors also look reasonable in that they tend to be more positive with words such as "will be," "a pretty," "a lot," "good movie" and "you should" for positive reviews. On the other hand, for negative reviews, the words tend to be a little more negative such as "it but," "not even," "do not," "terrible," and "poor."

From the visual modality, the descriptors from the approximated posture were predominant followed by those from head displacement movement for positive reviews. For negative reviews, the descriptors from gaze movement and head rotation showed most predictive power. Although not shown as top descriptors, AU1 (inner brow raiser) was a notable facial descriptor for indicating persuasiveness in the positive reviews, and AU12 (lip corner puller), AU14 (dimpler) and AU20 (lip stretcher) were among the next top descriptors in the negative review condition.

8. CONCLUSIONS & FUTURE WORK

We introduced a novel multimedia corpus specifically designed to study persuasiveness in the context of social multimedia. We presented our computational approach in using verbal and nonverbal behavior from multiple modalities of communication to predict a speaker's persuasiveness in online social multimedia content and showed that having prior knowledge of the speaker's sentiment has partial influence in better predicting the level of persuasiveness. Furthermore, we demonstrated that the idea of thin slices can be used to observer a short window of a speaker's behavior in the beginning and toward the end to achieve comparable prediction compared to observing the entire length of the video.

Interesting future directions include investigating more ways of computationally capturing various indicators of persuasiveness and better algorithmic methods of fusing information from multiple modalities. Our results will provide a baseline for all future studies using this new corpus for carrying out deeper analysis of understanding the relationship between persuasiveness and relevant high-level attributes including personality.

9. ACKNOWLEDGMENTS

This material is based upon work supported by the National Science Foundation under Grant No. IIS-1118018 and the U.S. Army. The content does not necessarily reflect the position or the policy of the Government, and no official endorsement should be inferred.

We thank the USC Annenberg Graduate Fellowship Program for supporting the first author's graduate studies.

10. REFERENCES

[1] Ambady, N. and Rosenthal, R. 1992. Thin slices of expressive behavior as predictors of interpersonal consequences: A meta-analysis. *Psychological Bulletin* 111, 2 (Mar 1992), 256-274.

[2] Biel, J., Teijeiro-Mosquera, L., and Gatica-Perez, D. 2012. FaceTube: Predicting personality from facial expression of emotion in online conversational video. In *Proc. of the 14th ACM Int'l Conf. on Multimodal Interaction.* ICMI '12, 53-56.

[3] Burgoon, J., Birk, T., and Pfau, M. 1990. Nonverbal behaviors, persuasion, and credibility. *Human Communication Research* 17, 1 (Sept. 1990), 140-169.

[4] Busso, C., Lee, S. and Narayanan, S. 2009. Analysis of emotionally salient aspects of fundamental frequency for emotion detection. *IEEE Transactions on Audio, Speech, and Language Processing*, 17, 4 (May 2009), 582-596.

[5] Chaiken, S. and Eagly, A. 1983. Communication modality as a determinant of message persuasiveness and message comprehensibility. *Journal of Personality and Social Psychology* 34, 4 (Oct. 1976), 605-614.

[6] Chaiken, S., Liberman, A., and Eagly, A. Heuristic and systematic information processing within and beyond the persuasion context. In J. Uleman and J. Bargh (Eds.), *Unintended Thought: Limits of Awareness, Intention, and Control* (pp. 212-252). New York: Guildford Press.

[7] Chang, C.-C. and Lin, C.-J. 2011. LIBSVM: A library for support vector machine. *ACM Transactions on Intelligent Systems and Technology* 2, 3 (Apr. 2011), 27:1-27:25.

[8] Crano, W. and Prislin, R. 2006. Attitudes and persuasion. *Annual Review of Psychology* 57 (Jan. 2006), 345-374.

[9] Curhan, J. and Pentland, A. 2007. Thin slices of negotiation: Predicting outcomes from conversational dynamics within the first 5 minutes. *Journal of Applied Psychology* 92, 3 (May 2007), 802-811.

[10] Degottex, G., Kane, J., Drugman, T., Raitio, T., and Scherer, S. 2014. COVAREP - A collaborative voice analysis repository for speech technologies. In *Proc. of the 39th Int'l Conf. on Acoustics, Speech, and Signal Processing*. ICASSP '14.

[11] Ekman, P. and Rosenberg, E. 1997. *What the Face Reveals: Basic and Applied Studies of Spontaneous Expression Using the Facial Action Coding System (FACS)*, Oxford University Press, New York, NY.

[12] FaceFX. http://www.facefx.com/

[13] FACET. http://www.emotient.com/cert

[14] Gobl, C. and Chasaide, A. 2003. The role of voice quality in communication emotion, mood and attitude. *Speech Communication* 40, 1-2 (Apr. 2003), 189-212.

[15] Hosman, L. 2002. Language and persuasion. In J. Dillard and M. Pfau (Eds.), *The Persuasion Handbook: Developments in Theory and Practice* (pp. 371-390). New York: Sage.

[16] Kane, J., Scherer, S., Aylett, M., Morency, L.-P., and Gobl, C. 2013. Speaker and language independent voice quality classification applied to unlabeled corpora of expressive speech. In *Proc. of the 38th Int'l Conf. on Acoustics, Speech, and Signal Processing*. ICASSP '13, 7982-7986.

[17] Kane, J., Scherer, S., Morency, L.-P., and Gobl, C. 2013. A comparative study of glottal open quotient estimation techniques. In *Proc. of the 14th Annual Conf. of the Int'l Speech Communication Association*. Interspeech '13, 1658-1662.

[18] Krippendorff, K. 2004. *Content Analysis: An Introduction to Its Methodology.* Sage, Beverly Hills, CA.

[19] LaCrosse, M. 1975. Nonverbal behavior and perceived counselor attractiveness and persuasiveness. *Journal of Counseling Psychology* 22, 6 (Nov. 1975), 563-566.

[20] Mahl, G. 1956. Disturbances and silences in the patient's speech in psychotherapy. *The Journal of Abnormal and Social Psychology* 53, 1 (Jul. 1956), 1-15.

[21] Mason, W. and Suri, S. Conducting behavioral research on Amazon's Mechanical Turk. *Behavior Research Methods 44*, 1 (Mar. 2012), 1-23.

[22] Mehrabian, A. 1971. *Silent messages*. Wadsworth Publishing Company, Inc., Belmont, CA.

[23] Mehrabian, A. and Williams, M. 1969. Nonverbal concomitants of perceived and intended persuasiveness. *Journal of Personality and Social Psychology* 13, 1 (Sept. 1969), 37-58.

[24] Meyers-Levy, J. and Malaviya, P. 1999. Consumers' processing of persuasive advertisements: An integrative framework of persuasion theories. *Journal of marketing* 63, 4 (Oct. 1999), 45-60.

[25] Miller, N., Maruyama, G., Beaber, R., and Valone, K. 1976. Speed of speech and persuasion. *Journal of Personality and Social Psychology* 34, 4 (Oct. 1976), 615-624.

[26] Morency, L.-P., Whitehill, J., and Movellan, J. 2008. Generalized adaptive view-based appearance model: Integrated framework for monocular head pose estimation. In *Proc. of the 8th Int'l Conf. on Automatic Face and Gesture Recognition*. FG '08, 1-8.

[27] OKAO Vision. http://www.omron.com/r_d/coretech/vision/okao.html

[28] O'Keefe. 2002. *Persuasion: Theory and Research.* Sage, Thousand Oaks, CA.

[29] O'Keefe, D. and Jensen, J. 2007. The relative persuasiveness of gain-framed loss-framed messages for encouraging disease prevention behaviors: A meta-analytic review. *Journal of Health Communication* 12, 7 (Oct. 2007), 623-644.

[30] Pearce, W. and Brommel, B. 1972. Vocalic communication in persuasion. *Quarterly Journal of Speech* 58, 3 (1972), 298-306.

[31] Perloff, R. 2010. *The Dynamics of Persuasion: Communication and Attitudes in the Twenty-First Century*. Routledge, New York, NY.

[32] Petty, R. and Cacioppo, J. 1986. *Communication and Persuasion: Central and Peripheral Routes to Attitude Change*. New York: Springer-Verlag.

[33] Pittam, J. 1990. The relationship between perceived persuasiveness of nasality and source characteristics for Australian and American listeners. *The Journal of Social Psychology* 130, 1 (1990), 81-87.

[34] Pornpitakpan, C. 2004. The persuasiveness of source credibility: A critical review of five decades' evidence. *Journal of Applied Social Psychology* 34, 2 (Feb. 2004), 243-281.

[35] Rammstedt, B. and John, O. Measuring personality in one minute or less: A 10-item short version of the Big Five Inventory in English and German. Journal of Research in Personality, 41, 1 (Feb. 2007), 203-212.

[36] Rosenfeld, H. 1966. Approval-seeking and approval-inducing functions of verbal and nonverbal responses in the dyad. *Journal of Personality and Social Psychology* 4, 6 (Dec. 1966), 597-605.

[37] Scherer, S., Kane, J., Gobl, C., and Schwenker, F. Investigating fuzzy-input fuzzy-output support vector machines for robust voice quality classification. *Computer Speech and Language* 27, 1 (Jan. 2013), 263-287.

[38] Scherer, S., London, H., and Wolf, J. 1973. The voice of confidence: Paralinguistic cues and audience evaluation. *Journal of Research in Personality* 7, 1 (June 1973), 31-44.

[39] Schuller, B., Steidl, S., Batliner, A., Schiel, F., and Krajewski, J. 2011. The Interspeech 2011 speaker state challenge. In *Proc. of the 12th Annual Conf. of the Int'l Speech Communication Association*. Interspeech '11, 3201-3204.

[40] Stern, S., Mullennix, J., and Wilson, S. 2002. Effects of perceived disability on persuasiveness of computer-synthesized speech. *Journal of Applied Psychology* 87, 2 (Apr. 2002), 411-417.

[41] Voss, J. 2005. The science of persuasion: An exploration of advocacy and the science behind the art of persuasion in the courtroom, *Law and Psychology Review* 29 (2005), 301-327.

[42] Worchel, S., Andreoli, V., and Eason, J. 1975. Is the medium the message? A study of the effects of media, communicator, and message characteristics on attitude change. *Journal of Applied Social Psychology* 5, 2 (June 1975), 157-172.

[43] Yang, Y. and Pedersen, J. 1997. A comparative study on feature selection in text categorization. In *Proc. of the 14th Int'l Conf. on Machine Learning*. ICML '97, 412-420.

[44] Young, J., Martell, C., Anand, P., Ortiz, P., and Gilbert, H. 2011. A microtext corpus for persuasion detection in dialog. In *Proc. of the AAAI-11 Workshop on Analyzing Microtext*, 80-85.

Deception Detection Using a Multimodal Approach

Mohamed Abouelenien
Computer Science and Engineering
University of Michigan
Ann Arbor, MI 48109, USA
zmohamed@umich.edu

Verónica Pérez-Rosas
Computer Science and Engineering
University of North Texas
Denton, TX 76207, USA
vrncapr@umich.edu

Rada Mihalcea
Computer Science and Engineering
University of Michigan
Ann Arbor, MI 48109, USA
mihalcea@umich.edu

Mihai Burzo
Mechanical Engineering
University of Michigan, Flint
Flint, MI 48502, USA
mburzo@umich.edu

ABSTRACT

In this paper we address the automatic identification of deceit by using a multimodal approach. We collect deceptive and truthful responses using a multimodal setting where we acquire data using a microphone, a thermal camera, as well as physiological sensors. Among all available modalities, we focus on three modalities namely, language use, physiological response, and thermal sensing. To our knowledge, this is the first work to integrate these specific modalities to detect deceit. Several experiments are carried out in which we first select representative features for each modality, and then we analyze joint models that integrate several modalities. The experimental results show that the combination of features from different modalities significantly improves the detection of deceptive behaviors as compared to the use of one modality at a time. Moreover, the use of non-contact modalities proved to be comparable with and sometimes better than existing contact-based methods. The proposed method increases the efficiency of detecting deceit by avoiding human involvement in an attempt to move towards a completely automated non-invasive deception detection process.

Categories and Subject Descriptors

I.2 [**Artificial Intelligence**]: Miscellaneous

Keywords

multimodal; deception; thermal

1. INTRODUCTION

DePaulo et al. [2], define the act of deception as a deliberate attempt to mislead others. As deception occurs on a daily basis through explicit lies, misrepresentations, or omissions, it has attracted the interest of researchers from multiple research fields. Also with a growing number of multimodal communications, the need arises for efficient and enhanced methodologies to detect deceptive behaviors.

Previous attempts on detecting deceit were usually conducted using physiological sensors and trained experts. However, a major drawback for these strategies is that human judgment on different cases is usually biased and achieves poor classification accuracy [1]. Moreover, these approaches require a large amount of time and effort for analysis.

Psychological and theoretical approaches [3] have also been proposed in order to increase human capability of detecting deceptive behavior. Additionally, efforts were exerted to collect behavioral clues that can be indicative of deception. However, these clues can also be results of other states such as the fear of being caught in a lie [2]. For instance, travelers in airports that are the subjects of custom verifications where deception often occurs, can also be stressed due to long flights, fear of flights, and many other reasons.

While it was reported that audible and verbal clues are better deception indicators compared to visual clues [1], recent studies argued that a sudden increase in the blood flow in the periorbital area of the face, which results from spontaneous lies can be detected using thermal imaging. This is especially true when a person tries to find an answer to unexpected questions and unanticipated events [24].

This paper addresses the problem of automatic deception detection using a multimodal approach. The paper makes two important contributions. First, we create a new dataset with the participation of 30 subjects. The subjects were asked to discuss two different topics – ("Abortion" and "Best Friend," described in detail below) – in both truthful and deceptive manners, while they were recorded using a microphone, a thermal camera, and several physiological sensors. Second, in order to automate and improve the detection of deceptive behaviors, avoid human efforts and the limitations associated with individual methods, and increase the efficiency of the decision making process, we build a multimodal system that integrates features extracted from three different modalities. Features are extracted from the linguistic responses of the subjects, thermal recordings of the face, and physiological measures obtained from several sensors. We

ICMI'14, November 12–16, 2014, Istanbul, Turkey.

http://dx.doi.org/10.1145/2663204.2663229.

report the individual performance of each modality as well as the performance of various modality combinations. To our knowledge, this is the first attempt to detect deceptive behaviors by integrating these modalities.

This paper is organized as follows. Section 2 surveys some of the related work. Section 3 describes the data collection process and our experimental design. Section 4 illustrates the feature extraction process utilized for each modality. Section 5 discusses our experimental results. Finally, concluding remarks and future work are provided in Section 6.

2. RELATED WORK

While most of the earlier research on the deception detection task focused on analyzing physiological responses such as skin conductance, blood pressure pulse, and respiration rate, there have been important efforts on identifying deceptive behavior in scenarios where contact-based measurements are not available. For instance, researchers have studied verbal behaviors exhibited by people while deceiving [5, 23]. Speaking rate, energy, pitch, range as well as the identification of salient topics have been found useful to distinguish between deceptive and non-deceptive speech [4]. Linguistic clues such as self references or positive and negative words have been used to profile true tellers from liars [8]. Other work has focused on analyzing the number of words, sentences, self references, affect, spatial and temporal information associated with deceptive content [16].

Several efforts have also been presented with the use of non-invasive measurements such as thermal imaging. Researchers investigated the relation between measurements extracted from the subjects' faces and states of deception. Pavlidis et al. [10] developed a high definition thermal imaging method to detect deceit from the facial area claiming to reach a performance close to that of the polygraph tests. Warmelink et al. [25] used thermal imaging as a lie detector in airports. They extracted the maximum, minimum, and average temperatures from the thermal images to detect deceit. With 51 participants, their system was able to detect lying participants with accuracy above 60%. However, interviewers outperformed the system with above 70% accuracy. Pavlidis and Levine [11, 12] applied thermodynamic modeling on thermal images to transform the raw thermal data from the periorbital area to blood flow rates to detect deception. Merla and Romani [7] investigated the correlation between different emotional conditions, such as stress, fear, and excitement, and facial thermal signatures using thermal imaging.

In order to specify which thermal areas have higher correlation to deceptive behaviors, facial regions of interest were specified. Rajoub and Zwiggelaar [17] analyzed thermal faces by creating two regions of interest by manually identifying the corners of the eyes and tracking these regions over the recorded video frames. Their deception detection system performed well on within-subject data but not on across-subject scenarios. Pollina et al. [15] extracted the minimum and maximum temperatures from video frames recorded of subjects in states of deceptions and truthfulness. They focused on the eyes region of the face and reported a significant change in the surface skin temperature between the two states. Jain et al. [6] employed a thermal camera with face detection, tracking, and landmark detections systems to detect and track landmarks on the regions of interest in the face area. The method calculated the average temperature of the 10% hottest pixels of a window that includes both tear ducts. Pavlidis et al. [13] observed distinct non-overlapping facial thermal patterns resulting from different activities and detected an increase in the blood flow around the eyes when subjects act deceptively. Tsiamyrtzis et al. [21] used tandem tracking and noise suppression methods to extract thermal features from the periorbital area without restriction on the face movements of the subjects in order to improve deception detection rates. Sumriddetchkajorn and Somboonkaew [20] introduced an infrared system to detect deception by converting variation in the thermal periorbital area to relative blood flow velocity and by deducing the respiration rate from the thermal nostril areas. Park et al. [9] employed a functional discriminant analysis to separate between deceptive and non-deceptive behaviors using the average maximum temperature of the periorbital region of the subjects' faces during their answers to specific questions. To be able to only extract measurements from the periorbital area, subjects were not allowed to move or tilt their faces.

3. EXPERIMENTAL SETUP

We build upon previous work on deception detection, in particular we use protocols similar to those previously used in psychology and physiology. The hypothesis, verified in these earlier works and in ours, is that as a person acts/speaks deceptively, there will be subtle changes in his or her physiological and behavioral response. Additionally, during our experiments, we avoided any bias towards certain topics by using two different topics. Furthermore, we did not interfere with the responses of the participants. The sole purpose of the interviewer was to hand the subjects the topic they had to discuss in a deceptive or truthful manner. Our scenarios are more difficult for the detection of deception as compared to other question-based scenarios.

3.1 Equipment and data acquisition

We acquired measurements using a thermal camera FLIR Thermovision A40 with a resolution of 340x240 and a frame rate of 60 frames per second, as well as four biosensors including: blood volume pulse (BVP sensor), skin conductance (SC sensor), skin temperature (T sensor), and abdominal respiration (BR sensor). Each session was also video recorded (with audio) using a Logitech Web Cam.

During each recording session we obtained thermal measurements of participants' faces using the software provided with the thermal camera, namely, the Flir ThermaCam Researcher. Also, four sensors were attached to the non-dominant hand of the participants. Two skin conductance electrodes were placed on the second and third fingers whereas the skin temperature and blood volume blood volume sensors were placed at the thumb and index fingers respectively. The respiration sensor was placed comfortably around the thoracic region. The output of each sensor was obtained from a multimodal encoder connected to the main computer using an USB interface device. We recorded the combined output using the Biograph Infinity Physiology suite[1], which allowed us to visualize and control the data acquisition process.

[1]http://www.thoughttechnology.com/physsuite.htm

3.2 Participants

The human subjects consisted of 30 graduate and undergraduate students. The sample consisted of 5 female and 25 male participants, all expressing themselves in English, from several ethnic backgrounds (Asian, African-American, Caucasian, and Hispanic), with ages ranging between 22 and 38 years.

3.3 Collecting truthful and deceptive responses

The participation in the study consisted of sitting at the recording station while connected to the physiological sensors. Thermal recordings and physiological measurements were obtained during each part of the experiment.

First, we described the experimental system and procedure to be followed by the participants and instructed them to respond either truthfully or deceptively, depending on the topic being run. Then, we attached the sensors to the non-dominant hand and setup the thermal camera. Participants were asked to avoid any excessive movements with their head or hands in order to keep to a minimum measurement uncertainties. The reason of movement restrictions was to obtain high quality data from the cameras and reduce the amount of possible disturbances with the physiological sensors.This is particularly important for the temperature and the skin conductance measurements, since they are obtained using sensors that need to be in permanent contact with participant's skin. For this study we have decided to use wired sensors due to their cost, reliability and robustness but wireless sensors can also be used.

In order to elicit deceptive and truthful responses, we designed the following two topics, for which participants were asked to speak freely for about 2-3 minutes.

Abortion (AB) In this experiment participants were asked to provide a truthful and a deceptive opinion about their feelings regarding abortion. Participants were asked to imagine a topic where they took part in a debate on abortion. The experiment session consisted of two independent recordings for each case, when the participant was either telling the truth or lying. In the first part of the experiment, the participant had to defend his or her point of view regarding abortion, while in the second part the participant was asked to lie about what she or he really thinks about abortion.

Best Friend (BF) In this experiment participants were asked to provide both a true description of their best friend, as well a deceptive description about a person they cannot stand. Thus, in both cases, a person was described as the participant's best friend, but in only one of the cases the description was truthful. The experiment session consisted of two independent recordings for each case, when a given participant was either telling the truth or lying.

4. METHODOLOGY

After the data collection, we obtained a total of 30 truthful and 30 deceptive observations for each topic to form a total of 120 responses, including their corresponding audio/visual, thermal and physiological sensors recordings. The deception detection process involves two steps: discriminant feature extraction and classification.

4.1 Multimodal features

The raw data was processed to obtain a set of features to represent each modality.

4.1.1 Physiological features

We obtained physiological features by processing the raw signal from each sensor. We used the Biograph Infiniti Physiology suite to obtain physiological assessments for temperature, heart rate, blood volume pulse, skin conductance, and respiration rate. More specifically, using the raw output from each sensor, we calculated the mean, standard deviation, and power mean. We also obtained the same descriptors for each two-seconds epoch length. In addition to this, we obtained features derived from inter beat intervals (IBI) measurements such as minimum and maximum amplitude and their intervals. The final set consists of 60 physiological features.

4.1.2 Linguistic features

We obtained linguistic features which represent the participant's use of language when they are either telling the truth or lying. To represent the linguistic component we obtained manual transcriptions of the recorded statements. We then extracted two different sets of features.

First, we used a bag-of-words representation of the transcripts to derive unigram counts, which are then used as linguistic features. We started by building a vocabulary consisting of all the words occurring in the transcripts. We then removed those words that have a frequency below 10 (value determined empirically on a small development set). The remaining words represent the unigram features, which are then associated with a value corresponding to the frequency of the unigram inside each video transcription. Second, in order to obtain features that represent psychological processes occurring while people are providing truthful or deceptive statements, we opted for using the Linguistic Inquiry and Word Count (LIWC) lexicon, which is a resource developed for psycholinguistic analysis [14] and has been widely used to aid deceit identification in written sources [8, 18]. In particular, we used the 2001 version of the dictionary, which contains about 70 word classes relevant to psychological processes (e.g., emotion, cognition), which in turn are grouped into four broad categories[2] namely: linguistic processes, psychological processes, relativity, and personal concerns. We extracted frequency counts of words occurring in the transcripts belonging to the different lexicon word classes. We performed separate evaluations using each of the four broad LIWC categories, as well as using all the categories together. The classification results for truthful and deceptive responses, obtained with a decision tree classifier implemented as described in Section 5 are shown in Table 1.

Motivated by the results shown in Table 1, which indicate that the combination of the Linguistic Processes and unigrams attained the best overall accuracy for the best friend and abortion topics, we decided to keep only these features for the remaining analysis. Note that we also attempted to use unigrams and higher order n-grams (bigrams and trigrams) in combinations with the different LIWC categories but evaluations did not show any improvements over the use of unigrams. The final feature set for both topics consisted of 214 linguistic features.

[2]http://www.liwc.net/descriptiontable1.php

	Topic		
Features	AB	BF	AB+BF
LIWC:Linguistic Processes	55.00%	66.66%	**63.33%**
LIWC:Psychological Processes	40.00 %	58.33%	57.50%
LIWC:Personal Concerns	58.33%	41.66%	49.16%
LIWC:Relativity	48.33%	65.00 %	60.00%
LIWC:All	53.33%	65.00%	60.83%
Unigrams	56.66%	65.00%	59.16%
Ling.Proc.+Uni	**56.66%**	**70.00%**	62.50%

Table 1: Deceptive and truthful statements classification using LIWC categories and unigrams. Results are obtained using leave-one-out cross-validation

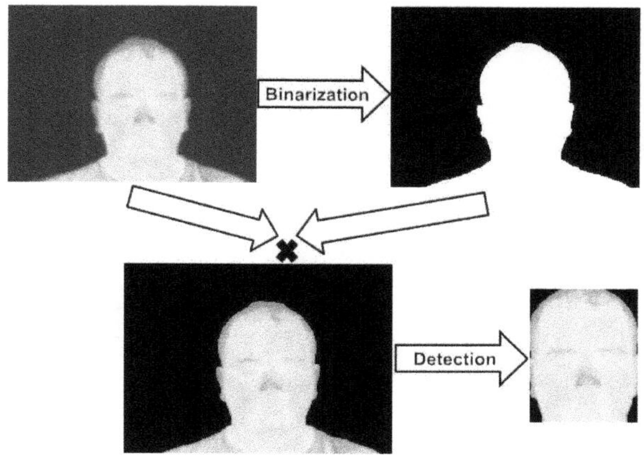

Figure 1: An overview of the thermal face detection process.

4.1.3 Thermal features

We decided to use the whole facial area to extract meaningful features that can discriminate between deceptive and non-deceptive behaviors. In order to do this, we first detected the facial areas of the subjects, followed by creation of heat maps of the detected faces. We tried the Viola-Jones face detection algorithm [22] to detect the faces directly from the thermal images but were not satisfied with the results due to a large number of undetected faces. Hence, we automatically isolated the subjects' faces from the background using image binarization given that the heat emitted from the background was always assumed to be of lower intensity compared to the skin temperature. Higher values of the frames' pixels indicate higher temperatures, which corresponds to lighter colors in the frames. The binarization process converts the pixels of each frame into black and white by thresholding the values of the pixels into either (0) for black or (1) for white using Otsu's method [19]. The thresholding process relies on the pixels intensities to minimize the intra-class variance of the white and black pixels.

The binarization process results in a holistic shape of white pixels of the upper body including face, neck, and shoulder areas. The binarized image is then multiplied by the original image to eliminate the background, i.e., the upper body is retained when multiplied by 1 while the background pixels are blackened. Using relative measurements, we were able to locate the neck area assuming that it always has the least width of non-zero pixels. Hence, we were able to detect the facial area while completely eliminating the background including the corners found in the cropped face images. All the eliminated parts have black (zero-valued) pixels. The face detection process is shown in Figure 1.

Following the face detection process, we extracted the maximum pixel value corresponding to the highest face temperature, the minimum pixel value corresponding to the lowest face temperature, the average of the pixels values of the face, the maximum/minimum pixels range which measures the difference between the maximum and minimum temperatures, and histogram of 120 bins over the pixels values in the facial area to form a total of 124 thermal features for each image. We uniformly sampled 200 frames from each video response. The extracted features were averaged over this number of frames for each subject. These measurements along with the histogram create a complete heat map that defines the heat distribution on the face. We aim at detecting variations in this heat map when any of the subjects acts deceptively.

Different subjects can have varying skin temperatures in normal conditions. These variations can manipulate the thermal maps and negatively affect the deception detection performance. To treat different subjects fairly, we used the first 50 seconds of each video recording as the thermal baseline for each subject. During this time, each subject was sitting on a chair without performing any activity or verbal responses. The same set of 124 features were extracted and averaged over this time frame. Hence, thermal correction is created by dividing the extracted features from the subjects' responses by their thermal baseline. This normalization process indicates whether there is a shift in the thermal map towards higher temperatures, i.e. higher pixel values, when the subjects respond deceptively regardless of the inter-personal temperature variations.

4.2 Deception classification

The feature extraction process generates a feature vector for each modality for each subject. Feature-level fusion is then employed by concatenating the features extracted from the three modalities for each subject. The concatenated feature vectors are used to train a decision tree classifier as recommended in [16] using the statistical toolbox in Matlab R2013a in order to detect deceptive instances. The classification process employs a leave-one-out cross validation scheme and the average overall and per class accuracies are reported. To clarify whether the integration of features from different modalities in fact improves the performance, we conducted our experiments using features from individual modalities as well as in combination. Additionally, we also report the performance of an across-topic learning scheme, where the classifier is trained with features extracted from one topic while tested on the other. The across-topic analysis is conducted to explore the capability of detecting deception when the training and test data is drawn from different topics.

5. EXPERIMENTAL RESULTS

Given our set of a total of 120 instances for each of the three modalities (two per subject per topic), we started by

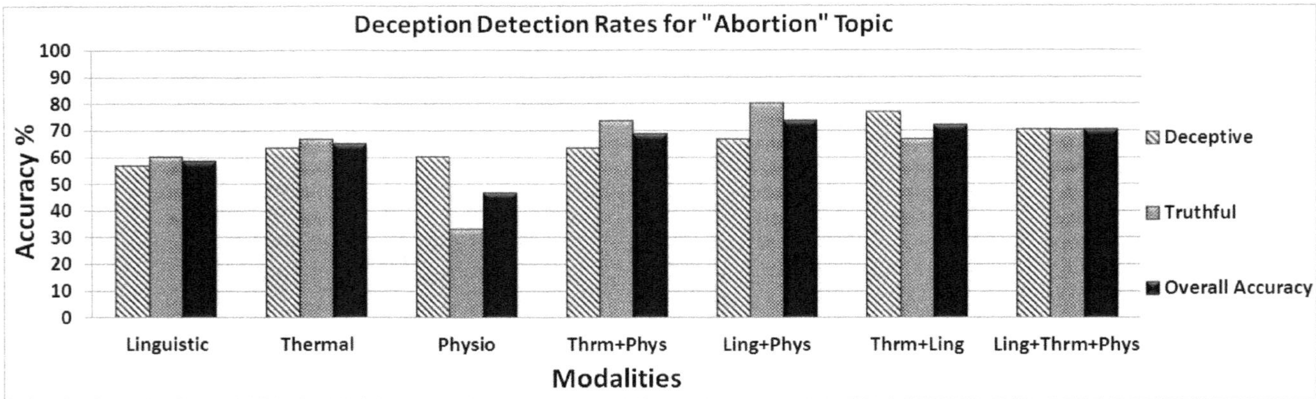

Figure 2: Deception, truthfulness, and overall accuracy percentages for individual and integrated modalities using features extracted from the abortion topic.

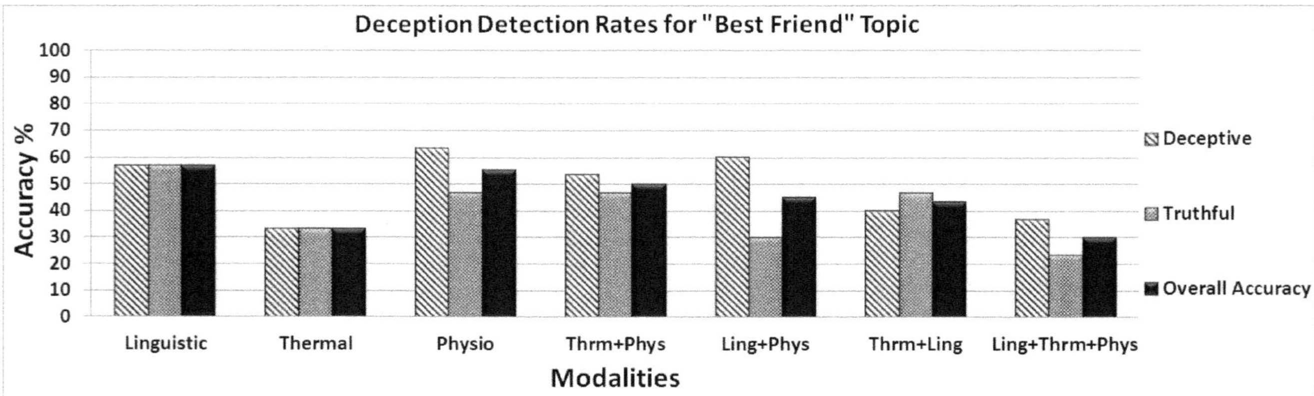

Figure 3: Deception, truthfulness, and overall accuracy % for individual and integrated modalities using features extracted from the "Best Friend" topic.

evaluating the performance of the features extracted from each topic, followed by the the evaluation of the features of both topics combined. We compared the performance of individual modalities to their combinations. This is followed by evaluating the performance of the across-topic learning process to investigate whether a trained model can identify deceit in different domains.

5.1 Individual and integrated modalities

Figure 2 shows deception and truthfulness detection rates in addition to the overall accuracy using different modalities for the abortion topic. The figure indicates that overall the combination of different modalities improves the performance compared to individual ones. The thermal modality achieved the highest performance of the individual modalities with above 60% for each class as well as for the overall accuracy. The linguistic features exhibit close performance while the physiological features achieved the lowest performance. While there is an improvement in the deception detection using the physiological features, the performance of the truthful class is deteriorated significantly.

A clear improvement in performance can be seen for several modality combinations. In particular the combination of all three modalities achieves a consistent 70% accuracy among all classes. The combination of linguistic and thermal features exceeds 70% accuracy for the deceptive class as well as for the overall accuracy. The combination of linguistic and physiological features leads also to a similar overall performance with a drop and an improvement in the performances of the deceptive and the truthful classes, respectively. The improvement in the overall accuracy using this combination of modalities results in an error rate reduction of 53% as compared to the use of one modality at a time.

The performance of the features extracted from the best friend topic is significantly lower than the first topic using different modalities as can be seen in Figure 3. In the abortion topic, subjects had a conclusive opinion whether to support it or not. Therefore, their responses were clearly either deceptive or truthful. However, the subject's responses on the best friend topic were mixed with positive and negative statements. For example, while truthfully describing their best friend, subjects sometimes mentioned things they don't like about their best friend such as "He is kind of lazy." Our analysis indicates that inclusion of some negative statements and/or memories in the truthful responses affect the quality of the extracted features, especially the thermal and physiological features. This is supported by the improved performance of the deceptive class compared to the truthful one for most modalities.

Additionally, Figure 3 shows that different combinations

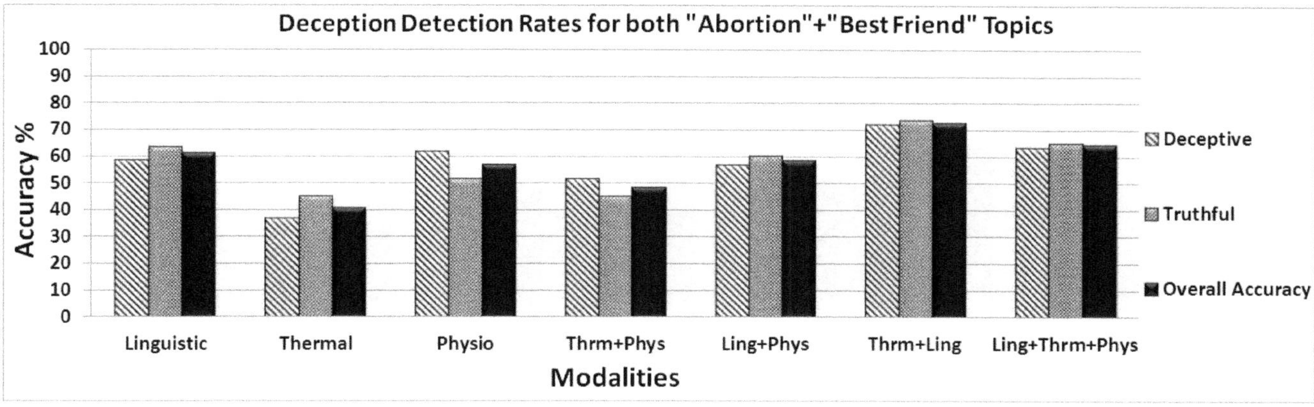

Figure 4: Deception, truthfulness, and overall accuracy percentages for individual and integrated modalities using features extracted from both the abortion and best friend topics.

of modalities achieve an accuracy that is equal to or lower than that of binary random guessing. The performance of individual modalities for this topic is sometimes better than their combinations as seen with the linguistic features. The deception detection rate using physiological and linguistic features is able to rise above 50%, but it does not improve over the use of linguistic features by themselves.

Figure 4 illustrates the performance of the features extracted from both topics together for all modalities. The linguistic and physiological features exhibit improved performance compared to their per-topic performance. This indicates that as the number of instances increases, even with data from different topics, the trained model shows considerable increase in its capability of discriminating between deceptive and truthful instances. However, although the thermal features here demonstrate improved performance compared to the best friend topic, their overall accuracy does not exceed that of random guessing and does not reach that of the abortion topic. Given the obvious difference in the performance of thermal features for both topics, the increase in the number of instances is not able to reconcile this large difference. On the other hand , the difference in performance using the linguistic and physiological features for both topics is not significant and hence, integrating features from both topics further improve the accuracy.

The use of multimodal features further enhances the classification accuracy. In particular, the integration of all three modalities together in addition to the integration of the thermal and linguistic features obtain higher accuracy in comparison to all other combinations as well as all individual modalities. Although the best performing single modalities are linguistic and physiological, the combination of thermal and linguistic modalities exceeds 70% for both classes and for the overall accuracy. The decision tree model was able to select its nodes and classification rules using a combination of thermal and linguistic features, which was more discriminative between the deceptive and truthful classes as compared to features obtained from the individual modalities. Furthermore, the improvement in accuracy obtained by using the linguistic-thermal combination is statistically significant (t-test $p< 0.05$) over the use of single modalities, i.e linguistic and thermal. The overall accuracy of this combination is additionally better than the accuracy of any individual or combined modalities for the individual topics.

These results suggest two important remarks. First, enlarging the data size with features from different deceptive topics is useful. Second, integrating features from multiple modalities can significantly improve the performance. In fact, the improvement obtained from the thermal and linguistic features can move us towards automated non-invasive deception detection methods.

5.2 Across-topic learning

Figures 5 and 6 illustrate the deceptive and truthful detection rates and the overall accuracy for the across-topic learning process using individual and combined modalities. In this learning scheme, the classifier is trained using features from one topic and then tested on the other topic. For example, the classifier is trained using the best friend features and tested using abortion features in Figure 5 and viceversa for Figure 6. In both cases, it can be noticed that the linguistic modality creates a large imbalance between the detection rate of the deception and truthfulness classes. While one class has a significantly improved performance, the other class suffers a deteriorated performance, which indicates the failure of the learning process. Moreover, the same trend is observed whenever the linguistic features are added to features extracted from other modalities. This trend is not observed with the thermal and physiological individual modalities as well as the combined modalities that exclude the linguistic features.

The disposition of the results can be explained with the dependency of the linguistic features on the corresponding topic. For instance, the unigrams extracted from abortion depend on words that are mostly related to this particular topic such as "illegal," "health," "baby," etc. These features are not related to the other topic and, hence, does not support the learning process.

Surprisingly, the across-topic learning scheme improves the detection rates for the thermal and physiological modalities except when the abortion topic is tested in Figure 5 with the combination of the thermal and physiological features. This can be attributed, as discussed earlier, to the abortion features having higher quality compared to the features obtained for the best friend topic. The deception detection rate is improved and the truthful class accuracy is deteriorated using thermal features in Figure 5, however, the overall accuracy remains the same at 65%. On the other hand,

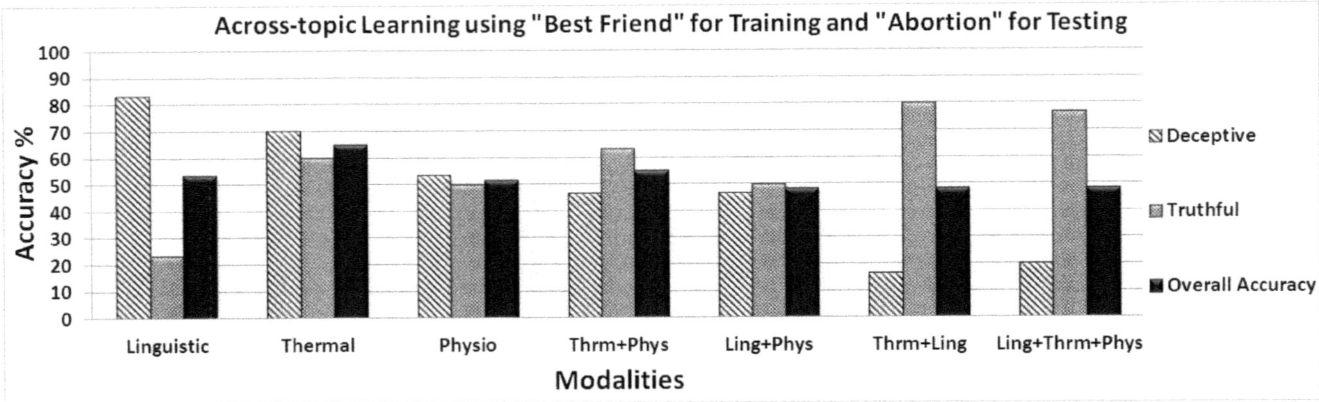

Figure 5: Deception, truthfulness, and overall accuracy percentages for individual and integrated modalities using across-topic learning. best friend features are used for training and abortion features are used for testing.

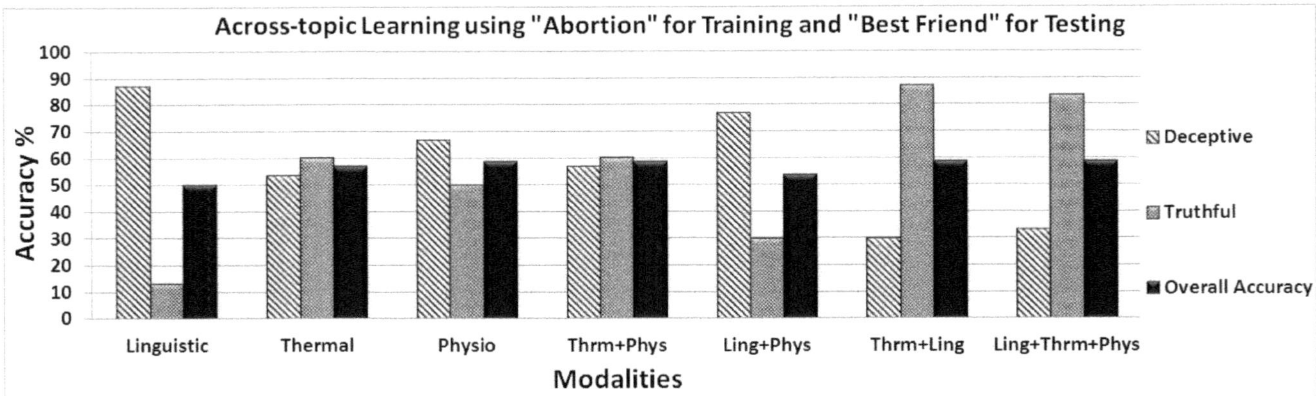

Figure 6: Deception, truthfulness, and overall accuracy percentages for individual and integrated modalities using across-topic learning. Abortion features are used for training and best friend features are used for testing.

training the classifier with the abortion thermal features in Figure 6 significantly improves the performance of the best friend topic to 70.1% overall accuracy.

6. CONCLUSIONS AND FUTURE WORK

This paper introduced a novel multimodal system to detect deceptive behaviors by integrating features from linguistic, thermal, and physiological modalities. The paper also contributed a new dataset consisting of deceptive and truthful responses. The proposed method is a step towards a completely automated non-invasive deception detection process.

Experimental results suggested that features extracted from linguistic and thermal modalities can potentially be good indicators of deceptive behaviors. Moreover, creating a multimodal classifier by integrating features from different modalities proved to be superior compared to learning from individual modalities. In particular, the integration of thermal and linguistic features resulted in a significant performance gain.

Additionally, our experiments showed that the quality of the extracted features is topic-related. In some topics, emotions and memories could negatively affect the quality of the features and reduce their capability of discriminating between deceptive and truthful behaviors. A disadvantage of using linguistic features existed when the system attempted to detect deceit on a completely new topic that was not used to train the classifier. However, this is not a problem for the thermal and physiological features, which can improve the performance of detecting deceit in a new topic if high quality features were provided for the training process. These trends indicate that a larger dataset needs to be collected using multiple topics and events in order to further improve the performance.

In the future, we are planning to collect a larger dataset with a variety of new topics and scenarios. Additionally, we will investigate the integration of additional modalities such as visual features. We also plan to extract more sophisticated features from different modalities. For instance, we will divide the thermal faces into regions of interest to analyze which parts of the face provide the highest discriminatory features. For the linguistic modality, we plan to explore the use of syntactic stylometry in order to capture deeper syntax patterns associated with deceptive statements. Furthermore, we are investigating the use of automatically extracted action units, which will be used to identify facial behaviors associated with deception.

7. ACKNOWLEDGMENTS

This material is based in part upon work supported by National Science Foundation awards #1344257 and #1355633, by grant #48503 from the John Templeton Foundation, and by DARPA-BAA-12-47 DEFT grant #12475008. Any opinions, findings, and conclusions or recommendations expressed in this material are those of the authors and do not necessarily reflect the views of the National Science Foundation, the John Templeton Foundation, or the Defense Advanced Research Projects Agency.

8. REFERENCES

[1] C. F. J. Bond and B. M. DePaulo. Accuracy of deception judgments. *Personality and Social Psychology Review*, 10:214–234, 2006.

[2] B. M. Depaulo, B. E. Malone, J. J. Lindsay, L. Muhlenbruck, K. Charlton, H. Cooper, B. M. Depaulo, B. E. Malone, D. O. Psychology, J. J. Lindsay, L. Muhlenbruck, and K. Charlton. Cues to deception. *Psychological Bulletin*, pages 74–118, 2003.

[3] P. A. Granhag and M. Hartwig. A new theoretical perspective on deception detection: On the psychology of instrumental mind-reading. *Psychology, Crime & Law*, 14(3):189–200, 2008.

[4] J. Hirschberg, S. Benus, J. Brenier, F. Enos, S. Friedman, S. Gilman, C. Gir, G. Graciarena, A. Kathol, and L. Michaelis. Distinguishing deceptive from non-deceptive speech. In *In Proceedings of Interspeech 2005 - Eurospeech*, pages 1833–1836, 2005.

[5] D. Howard and C. Kirchhübel. Acoustic correlates of deceptive speech: an exploratory study. In *Proceedings of the 9th international conference on Engineering psychology and cognitive ergonomics*, EPCE'11, pages 28–37, Berlin, Heidelberg, 2011. Springer-Verlag.

[6] U. Jain, B. Tan, and Q. Li. Concealed knowledge identification using facial thermal imaging. In *2012 IEEE International Conference on Acoustics, Speech and Signal Processing (ICASSP)*, pages 1677–1680, March 2012.

[7] A. Merla and G. Romani. Thermal signatures of emotional arousal: A functional infrared imaging study. In *29th Annual International Conference of the IEEE Engineering in Medicine and Biology Society, EMBS.*, pages 247–249, Aug 2007.

[8] M. Newman, J. Pennebaker, D. Berry, and J. Richards. Lying words: Predicting deception from linguistic styles. *Personality and Social Psychology Bulletin*, 29, 2003.

[9] K. K. Park, H. W. Suk, H. Hwang, and J.-H. Lee. A functional analysis of deception detection of a mock crime using infrared thermal imaging and the concealed information test. *Frontiers in Human Neuroscience*, 7, 2013.

[10] I. Pavlidis, N. L. Eberhardt, and J. A. Levine. Human behavior: Seeing through the face of deception. *Nature*, 415(6867):35–35, 2002.

[11] I. Pavlidis and J. Levine. Monitoring of periorbital blood flow rate through thermal image analysis and its application to polygraph testing. In *Proceedings of the 23rd Annual International Conference of the IEEE Engineering in Medicine and Biology Society.*, volume 3, pages 2826–2829, 2001.

[12] I. Pavlidis and J. Levine. Thermal image analysis for polygraph testing. *IEEE Engineering in Medicine and Biology Magazine*, 21(6):56–64, Nov 2002.

[13] I. Pavlidis, J. Levine, and P. Baukol. Thermal imaging for anxiety detection. In *IEEE Workshop on Computer Vision Beyond the Visible Spectrum: Methods and Applications.*, pages 104–109, 2000.

[14] J. Pennebaker and M. Francis. Linguistic inquiry and word count: LIWC, 1999. Erlbaum Publishers.

[15] D. Pollina, A. Dollins, S. Senter, T. Brown, I. Pavlidis, J. Levine, and A. Ryan. Facial skin surface temperature changes during a "concealed information" test. *Annals of Biomedical Engineering*, 34(7):1182–1189, 2006.

[16] T. Qin, J. K. Burgoon, J. P. Blair, and J. F. Nunamaker. Modality effects in deception detection and applications in automatic deception-detection. In *Proceedings of the 38th Hawaii International Conference on System Sciences*, 2005.

[17] B. Rajoub and R. Zwiggelaar. Thermal facial analysis for deception detection. *IEEE Transactions on Information Forensics and Security*, PP(99):1–1, 2014.

[18] V. Rubin. On deception and deception detection: Content analysis of computer-mediated stated beliefs. *Proceedings of the American Society for Information Science and Technology*, 47(1):1–10, 2010.

[19] M. Sezgin and B. Sankur. Survey over image thresholding techniques and quantitative performance evaluation. *Journal of Electronic Imaging*, 13(1):146–168, 2004.

[20] S. Sumriddetchkajorn and A. Somboonkaew. Thermal analyzer enables improved lie detection in criminal-suspect interrogations. In *SPIE Newsroom: Defense & Security*, 2011.

[21] P. Tsiamyrtzis, J. Dowdall, D. Shastri, I. Pavlidis, M. Frank, and P. Eckman. Lie detection - recovery of the periorbital signal through tandem tracking and noise suppression in thermal facial video. In *SPIE Conference on Sensors and Command Control Communications and Intelligence Technologies for Homeland Security and Homeland Defense IV*, pages 555–566, 2005.

[22] P. Viola and M. Jones. Robust real-time face detection. *International Journal of Computer Vision*, 57(2):137–154, 2004.

[23] A. Vrij, P. Granhag, and S. Porter. Pitfalls and Opportunities in Nonverbal and Verbal Lie Detection. *Psychological Science in the Public Interest*, 11(3):89–121, Dec. 2010.

[24] A. Vrij, S. Leal, P. Granhag, S. Mann, R. Fisher, J. Hillman, and K. Sperry. Outsmarting the liars: The benefit of asking unanticipated questions. *Law and Human Behavior*, 33(2):159–166, 2009.

[25] L. Warmelink, A. Vrij, S. Mann, S. Leal, D. Forrester, and R. Fisher. Thermal imaging as a lie detection tool at airports. *Law and Human Behavior*, 35(1):40–48, 2011.

Multimodal Interaction for Future Control Centers

An Interactive Demonstrator

Ferdinand Fuhrmann
Institute for Information and Communication Technologies
JOANNEUM RESEARCH
Graz, Austria
ferdinand.fuhrmann@joanneum.at

Rene Kaiser
Institute for Information and Communication Technologies
JOANNEUM RESEARCH
Graz, Austria
rene.kaiser@joanneum.at

ABSTRACT

This interactive demo exhibits a visionary multimodal interaction concept designed to support operators in future control centers. The applied multi-layered hardware and software architecture directly supports the operators in performing their lengthy monitoring and urgent alarm handling tasks. Operators are presented with visual information on three completely configurable levels of screen displays. Gesture interaction via skeleton and finger tracking acts as the main control interaction principle. We particularly developed a special sensor-equipped chair as well as an audio interface allowing for speaking and listening in isolation without any wearable device.

Categories and Subject Descriptors

H.5.2 [**User Interfaces**]: Input devices and strategies

Keywords

user interface; multimodal interaction; HCI; control centers

1. INTRODUCTION AND CONCEPT

Control rooms play an important role for monitoring and manipulating external processes in the industry or public infrastructure. The technological advancement results in larger amounts of information, which is monitored by fewer people. However, most of the current interfaces in such control rooms depend on text-centered displays. Moreover, increasing sensor data is often implemented by adding additional interfaces – and yet another keyboard and mouse. This leads to complex and counter-intuitive interaction systems, which hinder efficient, thus time-saving workflows while increasing the cognitive load of the operators.

We developed an innovative interaction concept for future control centers with special emphasis on a human-centered design process. By utilizing a range of novel hardware components for this application domain, we want to implement concepts for a more intuitive and efficient human-computer interaction. Our vision of future interaction paradigms relates to a context-dependent interaction, which gives the operator more room to interact with the available devices. By considering the cognitive and physiological capabilities of the operators and the length of work shifts of typically 8-12 hours, we aim to facilitate (a) faster recognition of events, (b) faster reaction towards events, (c) faster workflows, and (d) a better overview of the overall process.

Figure 1: Control center setup with two workplaces and specific components highlighted.

Figure 1 shows an overview of our concept. Operators largely perform their routine tasks by interacting with contact-free sensors. The large video wall offers a shared overview of the whole process to be monitored. Multiple depth sensors are tracking the location of operators in the control room, allowing for gestural interaction with the system. The tablet permits the user to manually adjust process parameters and display fine-grained information, both on site and remotely.

2. DEMO SETUP

We constructed a prototype system for and evaluating our multimodal interaction concept. This interactive demonstrator consists of a single work station of a future control center. Demo users can take the seat of a traffic monitoring operator and experience the system's interaction principles and their multimodal combinations. For that matter, the system is able to play-back different software scenarios, simulating typical real-world situations. The specific aims of the interaction concept are thereby directly incorporated

ICMI'14, November 12–16, 2014, Istanbul, Turkey.
ACM 978-1-4503-2885-2/14/11.
http://dx.doi.org/10.1145/2663204.2669620.

into the user's workflow. By interacting with the system the demo user can learn about the hypothesized benefits for the real operators and their workflows, while judging and reflecting on the intuitiveness and accurateness of the individual interaction components and their multimodal combination. In the following, we describe the main components of the presented demonstration system.

2.1 Visualization

Our concept limits the amount of displays to a 3-stage intelligent visualization, consisting of a single general view display, a single fixed-mounted wide-screen for each work station, as well as one mobile screen (tablet). For the general view display we use a 65" Ultra-HD monitor (the demo may use a projector instead). Each work station is further equipped with a 29" 21:9 aspect ratio screen, which enables the parallel inspection of multiple media sources such as video cameras, event lists, or detailed zooms on the general view. For the mobile device we opted for a state-of-the-art 12" tablet computer. Here, the rather big size guarantees both a rich-in-detail visualization of the content to inspect as well as accurateness as a touch input device.

The software system is based on a sensor data simulator and comprises several data processing and visualization components, including a *stripe image* visualization (compressed video overview), and a *function wheel*, offering a context-dependent set of actions to the operator. The latter is used as main menu for interacting with the system, hence representing the main control interface between the operator and the system. Given the problem-at-hand, the function wheel automatically adjusts its content, presenting the most plausible control elements to the operator.

2.2 Gesture control

Regarding the gesture interaction we distinguish between *macro* and *micro* gestural interaction. The former is driven by Microsoft's Kinect V2 sensor, enabling the tracking of the full human skeleton. Here, gestures are used to transfer information from one display to another, always down the hierarchy. For instance, the operator may drag a specific event appearing on the general view display to her/his work station display for further processing. Micro gestures are based on the Leap Motion sensor, which is able to track finger positions with reasonable accuracy [1]. These sensors are mounted on the armrest of the operator's chair, thus guaranteeing an ergonomic handling. The chair itself is further equipped with an inertial measurement unit (IMU), evaluating the rotation with respect to the room. Hence, if the operator uses fingers as a pointing device, the system is able to calculate the pointing position inside the room model. Furthermore, a vibrating element is mounted in the back of the chair which gives tactile feedback in case an object is targeted for interaction, which cannot give visual or acoustic feedback to indicate that it has been selected.

2.3 Audio interface

The demo's audio interface components can be divided into the audio playback and capturing system. The playback system consists of two parametric loudspeaker arrays, which emit spatially focused sound. We use two Acouspade ultrasonic[1] speakers. The arrays are placed on the desk of the work station in a typical stereo arrangement. To ensure that each speaker's sound beam is always exactly pointing to the respective ear of the operator, the speakers are mounted on motor-driven automatic alignment units. We built our own prototypes of these alignment systems using two stepper motors – one for the azimuth and one for the elevation angle. These units are steered using data from a head tracking device, which captures the operator's head position and rotation. Here, we again use the Kinect V2, mounted on top of the work station screen.

Figure 2: Workstation with Kinect sensor and acoustic interface highlighted.

The audio capturing system consists of a microphone array which is used for applying a beamforming algorithm. The beamformer implements an automatic alignment of the microphones' sensitivity in space towards the human speaker, hence enhancing the target speech while suppressing noise and other unwanted sounds from the neighboring work stations. We particularly use an adaptive generalized sidelobe canceller (GSC) [2], a robust variant of the Minimum Variance Distortionless Response (MVDR) beamformer. Furthermore, we constructed an array consisting of 8 microphones to ensure an effective signal bandwidth up to approximately 10 kHz, which is sufficient for the transmission of telephone audio and other acoustical messages (e.g. sound notifications). See Figure 2 for an illustration of the concepts behind the acoustical part of the interface.

Acknowledgement

This work has been performed within the FUSINC project[2], supported by the Austrian Ministry for Transport, Innovation and Technology.

References

[1] H. Fürntratt. Finger pointing accuracy on leap motion sensor. In *Interfaces and Human Computer Interaction (IHCI)*, 2014.

[2] O. Hoshuyama, A. Sugiyama, and A. Hirano. A robust adaptive beamformer for microphone arrays with a blocking matrix using constrained adaptive filters. *IEEE Transactions on Signal Processing*, 47(10):2677–2684, Oct. 1999.

[1] `http://www.ultrasonic-audio.com/products/acouspade.html`

[2] `http://www.joanneum.at/en/digital/reference-projects/fusinc.html`

Emotional Charades

Stefano Piana*
stefano.piana@dist.unige.it

Alessandra Staglianò*
alessandra.stagliano@unige.it

Francesca Odone*
francesca.odone@unige.it

Antonio Camurri*
antonio.camurri@unige.it

ABSTRACT
This is a short description of the Emotional Charades serious game demo. Our goal is to focus on emotion expression through body gestures, making the players aware of the amount of affective information their bodies convey. The whole framework aims at helping children with autism to understand and express emotions. We also want to compare the performances of our automatic recognition system and the ones achieved by humans.

1. INTRODUCTION
Bodily expressions convey important affective information that can be captured and analyzed by automatic systems. Studies from experimental psychology (de Meijer[2], Wallbott [8], Boone & Cunningham [1]) and from humanistic theories (Laban effort [5, 4]) have confirmed the important role of body gestures in emotion expression, identifying a set of emotion related dimensions that characterize the different emotions. The framework for automatic emotion recognition from body gestures, presented in our previous papers [6, 7], we exploit in this demo is based on such ideas, since the movement features we use to represent body gestures are strongly inspired by these dimensions. In this work we focus on the big six emotions [3]: Happiness, Sadness, Anger, Surprise, Disgust, and Fear. Emotional Charades is a two-player game demonstration based on this automatic emotion recognition framework, that encourages the players in expressing a number of emotions using only body gestures, discarding facial expressions and voice. The demo is based on the new Microsoft Kinect 2 `http://www.microsoft.com/en-us/kinectforwindows/` and on the Eyesweb platform `http://www.infomus.org/eyesweb`.

2. EMOTION RECOGNITION
The real time framework we developed for automatic emotion recognition takes in input a stream of 3D coordinates, estimated by the Kinect skeleton, representing the movements of a set of upper-body joints, and returns an estimate of the emotion expressed by the subject. It detects gesture primitives segmenting the streams of coordinates according to low values of the kinetic energy and extracts movement-related features (e.g. contraction index, symmetry, impulsiveness) from the segments. Then, it computes first order statistics of the features for each segment, and concatenates them in a single feature vector. Linear SVM is used to classify this feature vector, basing the answer on models trained with data of people expressing the six emotions with their body. The data for the training, validation, and test of the models were collected in Casa Paganini.

3. THE GAME
Rules
In this demo, two players are provided with a computer and a Microsoft Kinect 2 each, and they do not see each other. Figure 1 shows the first screen of the game seen by both the players. When the game starts, Player1 will decide which emotion to express, and then she will move her body in front of the sensor to do it. Player2 will see the moving silhouette of Player1, as in Figure 2, and, just observing the body movements, will try to guess the correct emotion. The computer will try to do the same. The guesses of both the computer and Player2 will be shown to Player1 and she will say whether Player2 or the computer gave the correct answer. The pictures shown in this description are taken from a first revision of the demo, working with the previous version of Kinect. The demo that will be presented will use Kinect 2.

Points
This is a collaborative game, so Player1 will gain more points if both the computer and Player2 give the correct answer. In particular, Player1 will gain 2 points if both Player2 and the computer are correct, 1 point if only one of them is correct, and no points if they are both wrong. Player2 will gain 2 points if her answer is the only one correct, 1 point if the computer gives the same answer as her (whether it is correct or wrong), and no points if only the computer gives the correct answer. The game goes on with inverted roles. On the splashscreen there is a counter that compares the rate of correct answers given by the human and the machine. Figure 3 shows a visual description of the game, a full video of which can be seen at `https://www.youtube.com/watch?v=_CHbLzvVh-A`.

*DIBRIS, University of Genova, 16145 Genova, Italy

ICMI '14 Nov 12-16 2014, Istanbul, Turkey
ACM 978-1-4503-2885-2/14/11.
http://dx.doi.org/10.1145/2663204.2669622

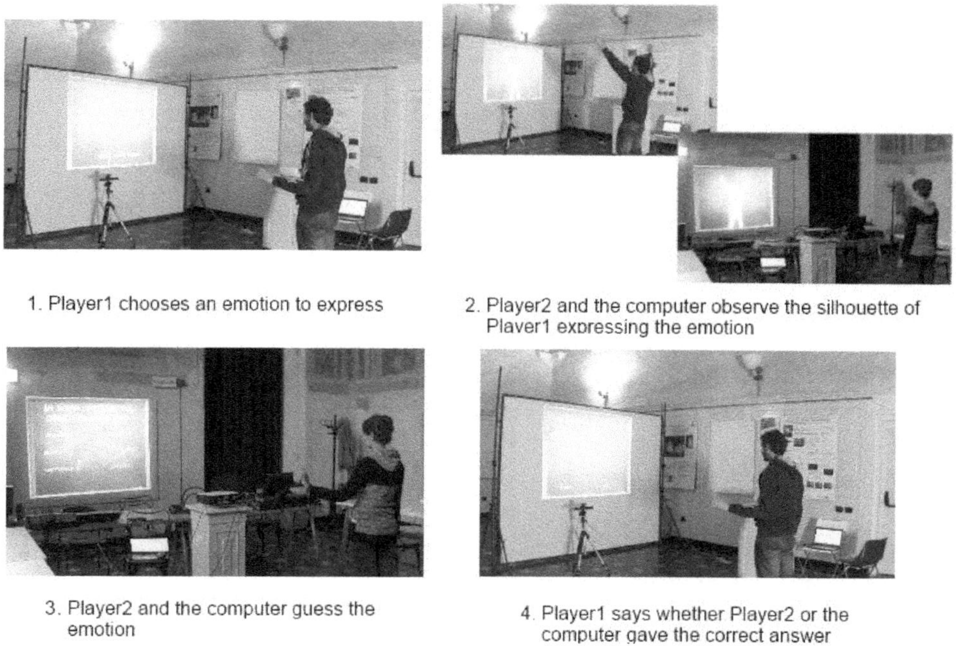

Figure 3: A description of the different steps of Emotional Charades.

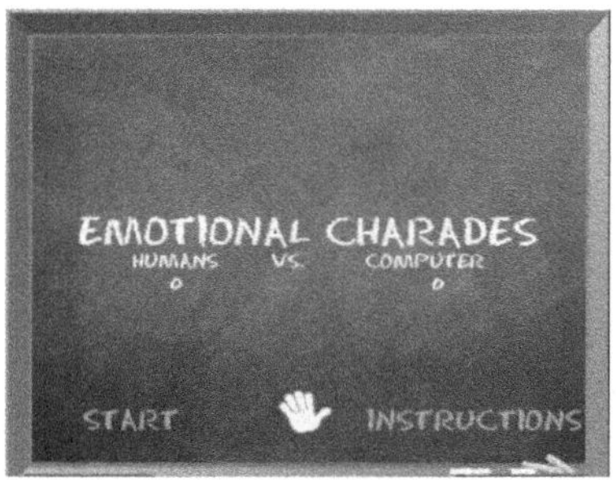

Figure 1: First screen of Emotional Charades.

Figure 2: The silhouette of the player that is expressing the chosen emotion.

Acknowledgements

The research leading to these results has received funding from the European Community's Seventh Framework Programme (FP7/2007-2013) under grant agreement No. 289021 (ASC-Inclusion).

4. REFERENCES

[1] R. T. Boone and J. G. Cunningham. Children's decoding of emotion in expressive body movement: The development of cue attunement. *Developmental psychology*, 34:1007–1016, 1998.

[2] M. de Meijer. The contribution of general features of body movement to the attribution of emotions. *Journal of Nonverbal Behavior*, 13(4):247–268, 1989.

[3] P. Ekman. Universals and cultural differences in facial expressions of emotion. In *Nebraska symposium on motivation*. University of Nebraska Press, 1971.

[4] R. Laban. *Modern Educational Dance*. Macdonald & Evans, London, 1963.

[5] R. Laban and F. C. Lawrence. *Effort*. Macdonald & Evans, London, 1947.

[6] S. Piana, A. Staglianò, A. Camurri, and F. Odone. A set of full-body movement features for emotion recognition to help children affected by autism spectrum condition. In *IDGEI International Workshop*, 2013.

[7] S. Piana, A. Staglianò, F. Odone, A. Verri, and A. Camurri. Real-time automatic emotion recognition from body gestures. to appear in IDGEI 2014 proceedings.

[8] H. G. Wallbott. Bodily expression of emotion. *European Journal of Social Psychology*, 28:879–896, 1998.

Glass Shooter: Exploring First-Person Shooter Game Control with Google Glass

Chun-Yen Hsu, Ying-Chao Tung, Han-Yu Wang,
Silvia Chyou, Jer-Wei Lin, Mike Y. Chen
Mobile and HCI Research Lab, National Taiwan University
{hcythomas0125,tony61507,huw12313212,silvia.chyou,evin92}@gmail.com,
mikechen@csie.ntu.edu.tw

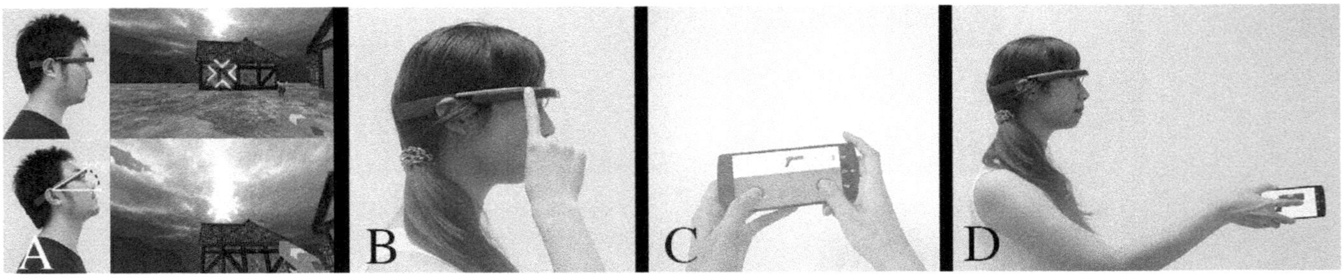

Figure 1: We implement multiple possible control methods for "Glass Shooter". (A) Our demos uses head mounted gyroscope to control the first-person viewport. (B) We designed a set of gestures on the touchpad strip: Players can move forward by touching the front half of the touchpad, and move backward by touching the rear half. Weapons can be fired by using taps. (C) Smartphones as virtual controller: two virtual joysticks and buttons to move and to change the viewport and to fire weapons; (D) Considering smart phone as a small gun: the player can use her phone orientation to aim the target.

ABSTRACT

Smart Glasses offer the opportunity to use head mounted sensors, such as gyroscope and accelerometers, to enable new types of game interaction. To better understand game play experience on Smart Glasses, we recruited 24 participants to play four current games on Google Glass that uses different interaction methods, including gyroscope, voice, touchpad, and in-air gesture. Study results showed that participants were concerned with comfort and social acceptance. Also, their favorite input method was gyroscope, and their favorite game type was First-Person Shooter (FPS) game. Hence, we implemented a FPS game on Google Glass using gyroscope for changing the viewport, and divide FPS controls into four categories: (a)Viewport Control, (b)Aim Control, (c)Fire Control, (d) Move Control. We implemented multiple control method in each category to evaluate and explore glass game control design.

Categories and Subject Descriptors

K.8.0. [**Personal Computing**]: General Games

General Terms

Human Factor

ICMI'14, November 12–16, 2014, Istanbul, Turkey.
ACM 978-1-4503-2885-2/14/11.
http://dx.doi.org/10.1145/2663204.2669623

Keywords

Google Glass, Wearable Devices, Game Design, Head Mounted Display, Multi-Modal, Mobile Phone, Gestures.

1. INTRODUCTION

Smart Glasses provide several new features, such as always available display, head mounted sensors, and first-person viewport. These novel elements do not exist in the traditional game platforms. How to apply these techniques to create a relevant game experience on Smart Glasses is still an unexplored area.

To better understand game design for Smart Glasses, we invited 24 users to play 4 existing games [5] on the most popular Smart Glasses, Google Glass. The four games have been selected to span different game types and control styles. Our study showed three design challenges that are not discussed in the current game design guidelines: "Limited control", "Eye strain" and "Social acceptance". Moreover, after playing these 4 selected glass games, most participants expressed that they prefer to play First-Person Shooter(FPS) game on Google Glass.

In this demo, we focus on the issue "Limited control". Compared with other gaming platforms, Smart Glasses lack traditional input method like mouse, keyboard, joystick, or touch screen. However, there are some non-traditional wearable sensors such as camera, touchpad, microphone, gyroscope, and accelerometer.

Considering traditional game design and new features on Smart Glasses, we implement a game, "Glass Shooter", a FPS game with multiple control styles on Google Glass. With "Glass Shooter", we can collect user feedback of different control schemes and understand user preference to evaluate an ideal FPS game on Google Glass.

2. CONTROL

There are four main controls in FPS games: (a)Viewport Control, (b)Aim Control, (c)Fire Control, (d)Move Control. With "Viewport Control", users can change camera's perspective and observe the surrounding environment. "Aim Control" is about how players moving the crosshair. Furthermore, users open fire with "Fire Control" and move their avatars through "Move Control" in the game.

To extend the diversity of our input controls, we design control methods not only with input manners available on Google Glass, but also with possible game control methods on Smart Phones.

According to previous work[1, 3, 2, 6], using head orientation as a viewport control is undoubtedly intuitive (see Figure 1.A).Therefore, in this work, we only explore the remaining control problems on "Aim Control", "Fire Control", and "Move Control". First, we supposed 3 different Aim Control schemes to test which would be the most favorite control for users. Three different Aim Control schemes are listing below:

1. Viewport aiming scheme: The crosshair is always at the center of the viewport. Player can aim the enemy by using their head to move their viewport. In other words, player is using head orientation to aim the target.
2. Gun aiming scheme: Considering your smart phone as a small gun. The player can use the phone orientation to aim the target. The crosshair will be controlled by the direction of the phone.(see Figure 1.D)
3. Phone joystick scheme: Using smart phone as a joystick to move the crosshair on the glass screen.(see Figure 1.C)

We also bring up 4 different Fire Controls as below:

1. Phone trigger scheme: Using touch screen on a mobile phone as the fire trigger. Players can just open fire by tapping their phone touchscreen.
2. Glass tapping scheme: Player uses fingers to tap on glass touchpad to open fire. (see Figure 1.B)
3. Voice control scheme: Player uses voice control, such as the sound of "Bang", to open fire.
4. Eye winking scheme: Player uses intentional eye winking as a fire trigger.

We propose 4 Move Control schemes:

1. Head gesture scheme: We implement the system from the work of Hinkel et al.[4] in our FPS game control system.
2. Glass touchpad: We designed a set of gestures on the touchpad strip. Players can move forward by touching the front half of the touchpad, and move backward by touching the rear half.
3. Phone controller scheme: Using virtual joystick on Smart Phone to move the character.
4. On track moving scheme: There exist possibilities that controlling player's movement is not completely suitable for glass game. Therefore, we design a pre-defined track for player in this scheme, and the avatar will move on the track automatically. So the player can focus on aiming and fighting, rather than the movement control.

3. CONCLUSION AND FUTURE WORK

We have recruited 24 players to play 4 different built-in games on google glass. Through the investigations, we observed three main categories of challenges we may meet when developing glass games, which are "Limited control", "Eye strain" and "Social acceptance" respectively. In this work, we cast our focus mainly on discussing "limited control", for different types of controlling methods we encounter in a first-person shooter game on Google Glass. Therefore, after referring to both previous game design and glass features, we've classified the control issues among FPS glass game into four main categories as follows: "Viewport Control", "Aim Control", "Fire Control," and last but not least, the "Move Control". For all these four terms of controls mentioned above, we've proposed several methods in each category.

In the following months, we are planning to conduct a series of user studies to clarify which method is the most suitable for each four class of controls. With these user studies, we can develop a more intuitive controlling method for FPS games on Google Glass. Furthermore, we will also move on to discuss the "Eye Strain" and "Social Acceptance" problems we brought up before to accomplish the complete study of FPS games on Google Glass.

4. ACKNOWLEDGEMENTS

We thank our advisor Prof. Mike Y. Chen and the faculty and staff of National Taiwan University. We should also like to express our gratitude towards all players and testers who have helped us in our many (buggy) iterations.

5. REFERENCES

[1] J. Arun Kulshreshth, Joseph J. LaViola. Evaluating performance benefits of head tracking in modern video games. In *SUI'13*, 2013.

[2] J. Corey Pittman, Joseph J. LaViola. Exploring head tracked head mounted displays for first person robot teleoperation. In *IUI'14*, 2014.

[3] K. T. Dingyun Zhu, Tom Gedeon. Exploring camera viewpoint control models for a multi-tasking setting in teleoperation. In *CHI'11*, 2011.

[4] J. B. Hinkel. Head-guided wheelchair control system. In *ASSETS '10*, 2010.

[5] Glass Mini-Games. `http://developers.google.com/glass/samples/mini-games`.

[6] D. J. R. Stefan Greuter. Controlling viewpoint from markerless head tracking in an immersive ball game using a commodity depth based camera. In *DS-RT '11*, 2011.

Orchestration for Group Videoconferencing

An Interactive Demonstrator

Wolfgang Weiss
Institute for Information and Communication Technologies
JOANNEUM RESEARCH
Graz, Austria
wolfgang.weiss@joanneum.at

Rene Kaiser
Institute for Information and Communication Technologies
JOANNEUM RESEARCH
Graz, Austria
rene.kaiser@joanneum.at

Manolis Falelakis
Department of Computing
Goldsmiths, University of London
London, UK
m.falelakis@gold.ac.uk

ABSTRACT

In this demonstration we invite visitors to join a live videoconferencing session with remote participants across Europe. We demonstrate the behavior of an automatic decision making component in the realm of social video communication. Our approach takes into account several aspects such as the current conversational situation, conversational metrics of the past, and device capabilities, to make decisions on the visual representation of available video streams. The combination of these cues and the application of automatic decision making rules results into commands of how to mix and how to compose the available video streams for each conversation node's screen. The demo's features are another step towards optimally supporting users in communication within various communication contexts and adapting the user interface to the users' needs.

Categories and Subject Descriptors

H.5.m [**Information Interfaces and Presentation (e.g. HCI)**]: Miscellaneous

Keywords

Videoconferencing; communication orchestration; automatic decision making; video mediated group communication

1. INTRODUCTION

Mediated communication via audio and video pervades slowly but continuously our daily life, mainly driven by the availability of broadband services and mobile devices. One important aspect in our life is social communication with our friends. This type of communication is featured by certain characteristics, for example people could join and leave continuously, the dynamic of the conversation might change over time and the network capabilities might change. Current video communication systems for social communication have limited intelligence to adapt to specific communication situations. We hypothesize that taking into account conversational metrics and other parameters such as device capabilities and to adapt the visual representation of the videoconferencing client accordingly helps the user to get immersed by the communication experience.

The Vconect project[1] investigates novel ways of supporting mediated audio-visual communication for ad-hoc groups. One problem implied by such video communication setups is that for each participant, there are multiple video streams available as options for being currently shown, i.e. when there are n participants and each is equipped with 1 camera, $n-1$ exterior video streams are candidates for being displayed at each client (no self-view assumed). The question is how to optimally deal with them. An intuitive, but not always scalable option, is to show each user all video streams side by side on one screen (referred to as tiled layout). We set out to investigate more sophisticated solutions with the aim of achieving better communication support through intelligent camera selection. When taking into account further parameters such as conversational metrics [1] which represent the dynamics of a conversation, and the capabilities and size of the client it is possible to select a suitable visual layout and the corresponding video streams. A component which automatically executes a mixing process of different video streams is known as a *Virtual Director* [2]. In the realm of communication this is mostly referred to as *Orchestration* [4].

Subsequently, we discuss the architecture and influencing parameters of the decision making component which intelligently switches between visual representations and executes the video mixing process for each user. The final section highlights what users can expect and describes the demo in detail.

2. ORCHESTRATION

Communication Orchestration is the decision making process which controls the mixing process of all available video streams. It can be compared to compiling a live TV transmission, but in the case of video conferencing it has to address communication rather than narrative needs. Orchestration is a reasoning process which operates in real-time for each location participating in the communication. It builds upon the audio and video processing infrastructure and executes camera control and audio-visual composition (cf. [4]).

Vconect's Orchestration Engine automatically produces camera selections and visual layout changes by reasoning on

[1]`http://www.vconect-project.eu/`

ICMI'14, November 12–16, 2014, Istanbul, Turkey.
ACM 978-1-4503-2885-2/14/11.
http://dx.doi.org/10.1145/2663204.2669624.

audio-visual cue streams from its participants. The system is implemented as a three step process:

Cue extraction: Audio-visual streams are processed by analysis modules in the system underneath and low level cues are extracted in real-time. An example for a low level cue is "voice activity".

Fusion and interpretation: Low-level cues from all locations are aggregated in the Semantic Lifting module of the Orchestration Engine. In this processing step, higher-level semantic events that concern the communication as a whole, such as a "turn-shift", are generated while properties of the state of the interaction at each point, such as "active speaker" or "crosstalk", are evaluated continuously. The module aims to achieve a computational interpretation of the current communication situation on a semantic level that can directly be evaluated by the decision making components. The Semantic Lifting module also calculates conversation metrics such as "turn shifts per active participants" or the "active participation duration per each participant" based on a sliding temporal window. These conversation metrics allow to identify monologue situations or to identify the "heatedness" of a discussion.

Decision making: The application of mixing rules that result in the selection of camera streams and the adaptation of the visual layout is made by the decision making modules. For each screen one separate instance reasons based on high-level events and conversation metrics received from Semantic Lifting and other modules. This process allows to select the optimal visual layout in combination with the necessary video streams for each user and gives best support in communication by respecting the given limitations.

The two latter components are part of the Orchestration Engine which is a central, server-side software component. The logic is implemented declaratively using forward-chaining rules of the JBoss Drools[2] reasoning engine. Detailed examples of rules already incorporated into the system together with challenges about their implementation were reported in [3].

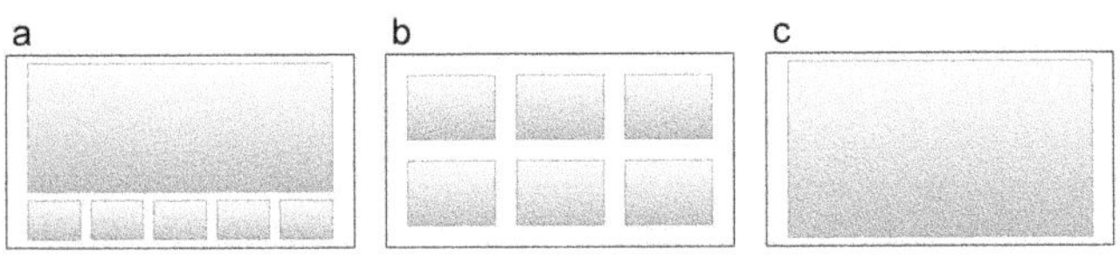

Figure 1: (a) Layout with focus on one person and with smaller tiles for all other participants. (b) Tiled view layout. (c) Full screen layout.

3. THE DEMO

This demo shows the capabilities of a video conferencing system for social communication that takes into account various system parameters as well as conversation metrics to select the optimal visual layout for each participant. The content for the regions of each layout is selected by the mixing rules of the decision making process. It usually puts the currently active speaker in the main view and the other participants in the smaller previews.

Figure 1a illustrates a layout with focus on one person and with smaller tiles for all other participants. This is suitable for most situations when the screen size is big enough and the number of participants does not exceed more then 10 people and the conversation is in a low or normal pace. If the conversation gets more heated (animated), meaning there is a high number of turn shifts between the participants within the analysis time window, it would be beneficial for the user to see all involved participants on the screen. This visual layout is illustrated in figure 1b but this can only be applied if certain other parameters allow a switch e.g. there needs to be enough space on the users' screen. A single full screen layout which has only one video stream (see figure 1c) will be chosen when there is a monologue detected by a participant. Another reason for a single full screen layout would be if the the screen size is very small.

Interested persons have the possibility at the live demo to use one videoconferencing node on site to join a video conferencing session together with four remote participants. The remote participants are located in different countries. Video streams are transmitted in HD quality from all participants, and also the audio quality is very high. Users can experience a videoconferencing system which automatically selects a suitable visual layout and the right video streams to optimally support users in communication. It is also possible to manually select the visual layout so that the automatic decision making system can be easily compared.

4. ACKNOWLEDGMENTS

The research leading to these results has received funding from the European Community's Seventh Framework Programme (FP7/2007-2013) under grant agreement no. ICT-2011-287760. We thank all partners who contributed to the Vconect system for supporting this demo.

5. REFERENCES

[1] F. Hammer, P. Reichl, and A. Raake. The well-tempered conversation: interactivity, delay and perceptual VoIP quality. In *IEEE International Conference on Communications*, ICC'05, pages 244–249, 2005.

[2] R. Kaiser and W. Weiss. *Media Production, Delivery and Interaction for Platform Independent Systems: Format-Agnostic Media*, chapter Virtual Director. Wiley, 2014.

[3] R. Kaiser, W. Weiss, M. Falelakis, S. Michalakopoulos, and M. Ursu. A Rule-Based Virtual Director Enhancing Group Communication. In *2012 IEEE International Conference on Multimedia and Expo Workshops*, ICMEW'12, pages 187–192, July 2012.

[4] M. F. Ursu, M. Groen, M. Falelakis, M. Frantzis, V. Zsombori, and R. Kaiser. Orchestration: TV-like Mixing Grammars Applied to Video-communication for Social Groups. In *21st ACM International Conference on Multimedia*, MM '13, pages 333–342, 2013.

[2]`https://www.jboss.org/drools/`

Integrating Remote PPG in Facial Expression Analysis Framework

H. Emrah Tasli Amogh Gudi Marten den Uyl
Vicarious Perception Technologies, Amsterdam, The Netherlands

ABSTRACT

This demonstration paper presents the FaceReader framework where human face image and skin color variations are analyzed for observing facial expressions, vital signs including but not limited to average heart rate (HR), heart rate variability (HRV) and also the stress and confidence levels of the person. Remote monitoring of the facial and vital signs could be useful for wide range of applications. FaceReader uses active appearance modeling for facial analysis and novel signal processing techniques for heart rate and variability estimation. The performance has been objectively evaluated and psychological guidelines for stress measurements are incorporated in the framework for analysis.

Categories and Subject Descriptors

H.4 [**Information Systems Applications**]: Miscellaneous

General Terms

Demonstration

1. INTRODUCTION

Remote monitoring of facial and vital signs via a conventional off-the-shelf video camera using ambient light for detecting the photo-plethysmographic (PPG) signals and 3D modeling of the face is a very challenging task. For this purpose we demonstrate the FaceReader framework where human facial expressions and human vital signs are remotely observed for measuring the physical and psychological state of a person. The framework offers a non-invasive, passive monitoring of the signals for various purposes including, but not limited to, medical monitoring and diagnosis, user experience analysis and market research. With the help of 3D facial landmark modeling, head pose of the person can be accurately detected and the proposed measurements could be robustly performed during a natural state of head movement while the person is still facing the camera.

PPG based techniques depends on the reflectance properties of human skin for measuring the changes in oxygen saturation of the blood. The underlying principle is that the variations in blood flow due to heart beats would change the volume and the oxygen saturation of the blood in the vessels, which affects the skin reflectance. Remote measurement of such signals is useful for various reasons, e.g. attachment of a sensor could violate the hygienic conditions and cause discomfort. It could also be useful for measuring engagement between people under a stimuli. The most common way to acquire information about people's emotional responses is to use self-report measures. Marketing researchers will ask the consumers' opinion about a product. Self-report measures are problematic because of socially desirable answers, where people feel too uncomfortable to report their true feelings and instead provide a desirable answer. Furthermore, people often lack insight into their own affective responses, and the reliability of the answer decrease as the time between the emotional experience and the questions increase. Alternatively, physiological information is less sensitive to socially desirable answers, and has the important benefit that it can be collected continuously. Emotion researchers therefore often rely on physiological signals to study people's responses. The most commonly used measures are heart rate, and its variability. There is also a strong correlation between such responses and the level of endured stress [4], [6].

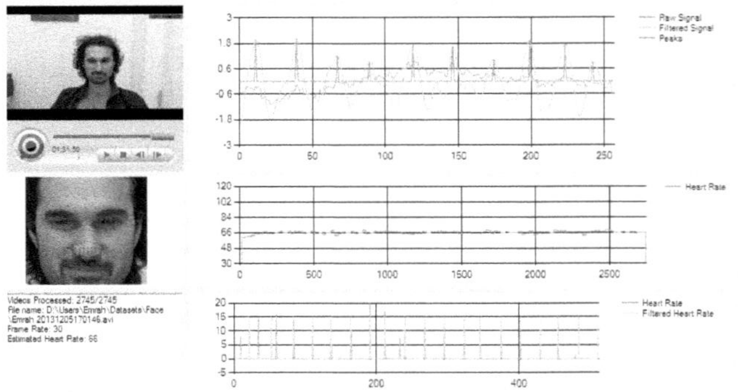

Figure 1: Heart rate monitoring could supply real-time feedback on the subject

2. METHOD

The facial landmark estimation is achieved using the active appearance modeling (AAM) technique [2] that has been improved and integrated in the FaceReader framework [3]. Using the selected facial regions, skin color changes are tracked for observing the periodic components caused by the blood volume changes at each heart beat. The details of the method is further explained in a prior work [7].

ICMI'14, November 12–16, 2014, Istanbul, Turkey.
ACM 978-1-4503-2885-2/14/11.
http://dx.doi.org/10.1145/2663204.2669626.

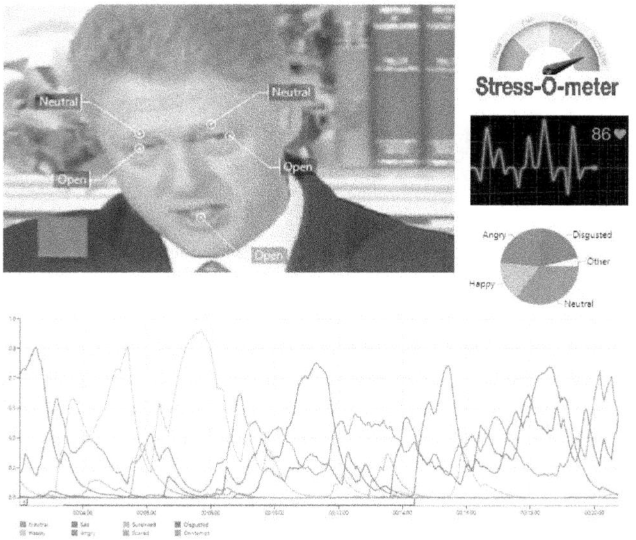

Figure 2: The reliability of verbal communication could be better evaluated with the accompanying physical and psychological analysis

2.1 Facial Expression Analysis

Apart from being the channel to identify other people, the human face provides a number of signals essential for interpersonal communication in our social life. The face houses the speech production center and is used to regulate the conversation by gazing or nodding, and to interpret what is said by lip reading. It is the direct and naturally preeminent means of communicating and understanding one's affective state and intentions solely based on a displayed facial expression. Personality, attractiveness, age and gender information can be extracted from one's facial appearance. Analysis of facial signals would be highly beneficial in many different fields such as security, behavioral science, medicine, communication, education, and human-machine interaction.

FaceReader is currently capable of automatically modeling an unknown face, in real-time, using a 3D face model with over 500 keypoints. Seven most prominent universal facial expressions are classified according to the following emotional states: anger, disgust, fear, joy, sadness, surprise and contempt, plus a neutral state. Furthermore, Facial Action Coding System (FACS) decomposes the face into 46 individual Action Units (AUs). FaceReader can automatically detect the 20 most commonly occurring AUs (see Figure 3).

2.2 Vital Signs Analysis

Body temperature, heart rate, blood pressure, and respiration rate are considered to be the vital signs, and are crucial in determining one's physical and psychological state. Remote monitoring of the changes in these signals supplies a strong medical indications for diagnostic purposes. These signs are further integrated into the facial expressions for a multimodal analysis [8].

3. EXPERIMENTS AND DEMO

The performance of the automatic facial expression recognition is tested on the Radboud Faces Database [5]. In order to validate the performance of the remote heart rate measurements, estimated remote PPG signal is compared with

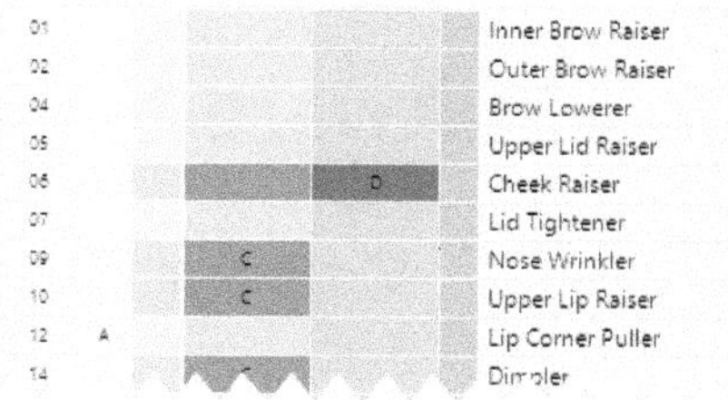

Figure 3: Examples of some action units with different levels of activation intensity

a ground truth signal from a contact PPG sensor. To our best knowledge, there is no publicly available dataset with ground truth PPG measurements that could be used to verify the performance of RPPG methods. Therefore, we have created a new dataset for evaluating RPPG measurements, where the ground truth PPG is provided and synced with the captured video [7]. In the demo session we provide a live demonstration with real-time facial expression feedback and heart-rate measurements.

4. CONCLUSION

Automatic facial expression recognition with the extended capability of vital signs measurement offers a complete framework for understanding one's physical and psychological state. This can be used in a wide range of applications, creating a valuable research and commercial commodity. For more information, please visit [1]

5. REFERENCES

[1] VicarVision FaceReader 6 product description. http://www.vicarvision.nl/facereader/productdescription. Accessed: 2014-08-05.

[2] T. F. Cootes, G. J. Edwards, and C. J. Taylor. Active appearance models. *Pattern Analysis and Machine Intelligence, IEEE Transactions on*, 2001.

[3] M. J. den Uyl and H. van Kuilenburg. The FaceReader: Online facial expression recognition. In *International Conference on Methods and Techniques in Behavioural Research*, 2005.

[4] N. Hjortskov, D. Rissén, A. K. Blangsted, N. Fallentin, U. Lundberg, and K. Søgaard. The effect of mental stress on heart rate variability and blood pressure during computer work. *European journal of applied physiology*, 2004.

[5] O. Langner, R. Dotsch, G. Bijlstra, D. H. Wigboldus, S. T. Hawk, and A. van Knippenberg. Presentation and validation of the radboud faces database. *Cognition and Emotion*, 2010.

[6] J. Taelman, S. Vandeput, A. Spaepen, and S. Huffel. Influence of mental stress on heart rate and heart rate variability. *4th European conference of the international federation for medical and biological engineering*, 2009.

[7] H. E. Tasli, A. Gudi, and M. den Uyl. Remote PPG based vital sign measurement using adaptive facial regions. In *International Conference on Image Processing*, 2014.

[8] H. E. Tasli and P. Ivan. Turkish presidential elections trt publicity speech facial expression analysis. In *arXiv preprint arXiv:1408.3573*, 2014.

Context-Aware Multimodal Robotic Health Assistant

Vidyavisal Mangipudi
Openstream Inc
USA
visal@openstream.com

Raj Tumuluri
Openstream Inc
USA
raj@openstream.com

ABSTRACT
Reduced adherence to medical regimen has led to poorer health, more frequent hospitalization and costs the American economy over $290 Billion annually. EasyHealth Assistant (EHA) is a context aware and interactive robot that helps patients receive their medication in the prescribed dosage at the right time. Additionally, EHA features multimodal elements such as Face Recognition, Speech Recognition + TTS, Motion Sensing and MindWave (EEG) interactions that were developed using W3C MMI Architecture and Markup Languages. EHA improves the Caregiver/ Doctor – Patient collaboration with tools like Remote control and Video conference. It also provides the Caregivers with real-time statistics and allows easy monitoring of medical adherence and health vitals, which should result in improved outcome for the patient.

Categories and Subject Descriptors
I.4.m **[Image Processing and computer vision]:** Feature measurements, Applications, Miscellaneous, H.5.2 **[User Interactions]:** Voice I/O, I.2.9 **[Robotics]:** Sensors, I.2.10 [**Vision and Scene Understanding**]: Video Analysis, D.2.2 [**Design Tools and Techniques**]: State Charts.

Keywords
Multimodal Interaction Architecture; Robot; Health Assistant; Context Aware; Human-Machine Interface, W3C, Arduino, Face Recognition.

1. INTRODUCTION
The EasyHealth Assistant (EHA) is a context-aware multimodal robot that securely houses and dispenses medication for multiple patients. The non-operational version of this working prototype was introduced at ICMI '13. It has since evolved from a bare bones concept with primitive implementation to a prototype with many multimodal interactions. EHA is designed to engage patients by reminding them to abide by their medical plan and by keeping them connected to their caregiver and physician. In order to do this effectively, EHA uses Text-To-Speech (TTS), Speech recognition, Face Recognition, Motion sensing and Mindwave (EEG) interactions. The robot also features a Bluetooth component that enables EHA to connect to third party health devices such as a Blood Pressure Monitor or wearable electronics like fitness trackers. In the interest of keeping the caregiver and physician informed, EHA sends real time updates concerning the patient's adherence, vital readings and any new developments with the patient. The robot can also have a video call with the physician or the caregiver with the touch of a button. There are many existing medication adherence apps and products; however, none of them engage the patient due to lack of interaction.

ICMI '14, Nov 12-16, 2014, Istanbul, Turkey.
ACM 978-1-4503-2885-2/14/11.
http://dx.doi.org/10.1145/2663204.2669627

2. PHYSICAL DESIGN OF EHA
EHA is a static robot (does not move around) which has a revolving head and three passive Infrared Motion (PIR) sensors. The camera, display, microphone and speakers from a phone are located on the revolving head. When motion is detected, the head turns in the corresponding direction and faces the user.

One of the core functions of EHA is the dispensing of medication to the correct user at the prescribed time. The servos, motors, PIR sensors and Wi-Fi connectivity are controlled using an Arduino microcontroller.

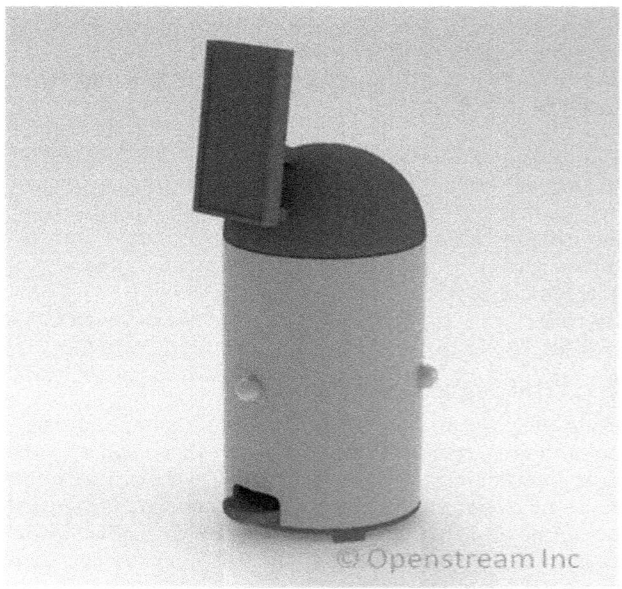

Figure 1. Design of the first functional prototype.

APPLICATON FLOW IN DEMO

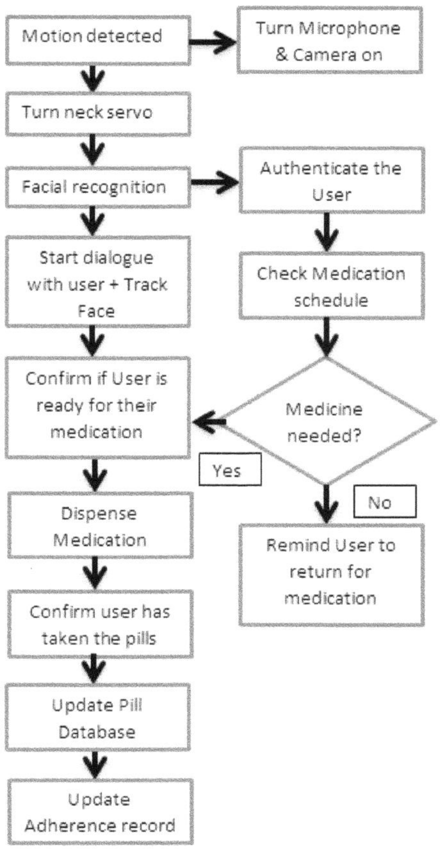

Figure 4. Sample flow of high level events in the demo.

3. MOTION DETECTION

There are three PIR sensors located 120° apart to allow for a full range of motion sensing. The 'motion detected' event is the trigger which begins the interaction between the user and EHA. When motion is detected, the robot turns to face the direction of motion and launches face recognition and face tracking.

FACE RECOGNITION

4. FACE RECOGNITION

The Face recognition engine serves the purpose of authenticating the identity of the user. The authentication of the user gives EHA context for any upcoming interaction, such as reminding the user if it is time to take their medication or if the caregiver has changed their regimen. Lastly, the face recognition improves the quality of the interaction as it can now refer to the user with her first name.

5. FACE TRACKING

Face tracking is one of the features, which allows EHA to respond to the users movements in a more human manner. Once motion is detected and the head turns in the corresponding direction, the camera locates the location of the user and sends commands to the neck servo to face the user squarely. As the user moves around, EHA will continue to track their face and adjust its head accordingly.

6. TTS AND SPEECH RECOGNITION

EHA is equipped with TTS and local speech recognition to make the interaction with the user more natural. The speech recognizer uses a lead word to reduce false positive recognition and end of speech recognition to simulate a normal conversation.

7. MINDWAVE HEADSET

There are two modes for EHA; a passive mode, where the user provides commands and the robots executes them, and an active mode where EHA initiates and drives the interaction. Once paired with the NeuroSky Mindwave headset, EHA asks binary questions in a logical progression and a redundant manner. The user has to voluntarily blink for an affirmative response. This method of interaction is capable of communicating with individuals that are incapable of speech or are disabled in a way that prevents from using normal interaction.

8. BLUETOOTH INTEGRATION

EHA is equipped to read directly from HDP & other compatible health-monitoring devices & medical instrumentation obviating the need for user to enter the readings manually off the instrument-displays.

9. ACKNOWLEDGMENTS

We thank all the team members of Openstream Inc. who helped in the design and development of the first prototype, especially Ankita and Chandra.

10. REFERENCES:

1. Easy Health Assistant use case video http://youtu.be/x2Tte0QyTiA

2. Openstream Easy Health Assistant Mindwave Demo http://youtu.be/aEgdRU-yM2o

3. Poor Medication adherence costs $290 Billion Annually: http://mobilehealthnews.com/3901/poor-medication-costs-290-billion-a-year/

WebSanyog: A Portable Assistive Web Browser for People with Cerebral Palsy

Tirthankar Dasgupta
Indian Institute of Technology Kharagpur
tirtha@cse.iitkgp.ernet.in

Manjira Sinha
Indian Institute of Technology Kharagpur
manjira@cse.iitkgp.ernet.in

Gagan Kandra
Indian Institute of Technology Kharagpur
gagankandra@gmail.com

Anupam Basu
Indian Institute of Technology Kharagpur
anupam@cse.iitkgp.ernet.in

ABSTRACT

The paper presents design and development of WebSanyog, an Android based web browser that helps people with severe form of spastic cerebral palsy and highly restricted motor movement skills to access web contents.The target user group has acted as our design advisers through constant interaction during the whole process. Features like, auto scanning mechanism, predictive keyboard and intelligent link parser make the system suitable for our target users. The browser is primarily developed for mobile and tablet based devices keeping in mind the portability issue.

Categories and Subject Descriptors

K.4.2 [**Social Issues**]: Assistive technologies for persons with disabilities; H.1.2 [**User/Machine Systems**]: Human factors

Keywords

Web Browser; Cerebral Palsy; Portability; Scanning based Systems; Mobile Devices

1. INTRODUCTION

People with severe speech and motor impairment (SSMI), such as in spastic cerebral palsy face difficulty in using conventional computer peripherals like keyboard, mouse, which demand fine motor controls. Due to their dysarthia, voice command is also not a viable option. Therefore, they are restricted from accessing the vast information repository of the World Wide Web (WWW). The unavailability of Augmentative and Alternative Communication(AAC) options dedicated to facilitate web access for such users motivated us to pursue the development of the system. Particularly, in a developing country like India, in spite of the fact that 2.21% of the population posses some kind of disability, the social support system for such people has not yet properly shaped and the high procurement cost of available accessible devices make them unaffordable for an average person. Therefore, we aim to develop a portable, low cost, web access system dedicated to people with cerebral palsy and SSMI. We have named the system as WebSanyog, where Web stands for WWW and *Sanyog* is a *Sanskrit* term meaning communication.

Our design and development process involved the target user group for continuous inputs. We have interacted with persons from Indian Institute of Cerebral Palsy (IICP) Kolkata. They are at level five for both Gross Motor Functional Classification System and Manual Ability Classification System. According to their feedbacks the problem has two dimensions: firstly, the available tools and technologies have to imported for Indian environment, therefore support and maintenance is difficult along with the procurement cost; second, no assistive browsers are available for mobile platforms.

ICMI'14, November 12–16, 2014, Istanbul, Turkey.
ACM 978-1-4503-2885-2/14/11.
http://dx.doi.org/10.1145/2663204.2669628.

2. WORKING OF WEBSANYOG

Based on the design suggestions by the users, the browsing system was developed for 7-10 inch tablets running on either Windows or Android OS. We have described the issues with tablet design later. The browser GUI is divided into three panels: the browsing window, the frequently sued navigational tasks and a panel for the browsing task (refer to figure 1). The system consists of the following modules that contains a number of novel and salient features:

Scanning Mechanism and Access Switches: Based on the preference of the focus user group, our system employ a virtual scanning mechanism that can be operated in a semi automatic manner with the aid of access switches. These switches are specially designed hardware that can be operated through nay body parts such as lips, hands, and feet [3]. The switches are connected to computer via standard USB mouse. They are manufactured locally in India and come at a price of only $10-20 per pair. The working of a special access switch is illustrated in Figure 1 At present our system has a 2D row-column scanning control.

The Alphabetic Keyboard with Predictive Engine and Iconic Keyboard: To facilitate the text entry, we have integrates a customized virtual scanning keyboard [2]

Figure 1: Illustration of the special access switch integrated with a tablet

with a predictive engine that has been developed based on the AOL query logs.

One of the challenges faced by the target users is that the ease of a scanning keyboard comes at an increase time cost for typing out long query strings. To optimize the efficiency trade-off, we have designed an iconic keyboard that uses the standard iconic stamps used in communication by the focus users to generate string queries.

Domain Specific Content Search: We have incorporated two domain specific content searches namely education and entertainment. Browsing a query with these domain search options automatically redirects the search in the Wikipedia and YouTube respectively, therefore saving time and effort. In future, we are trying to incorporate also news search domain. These domains were selected based on the users search references.

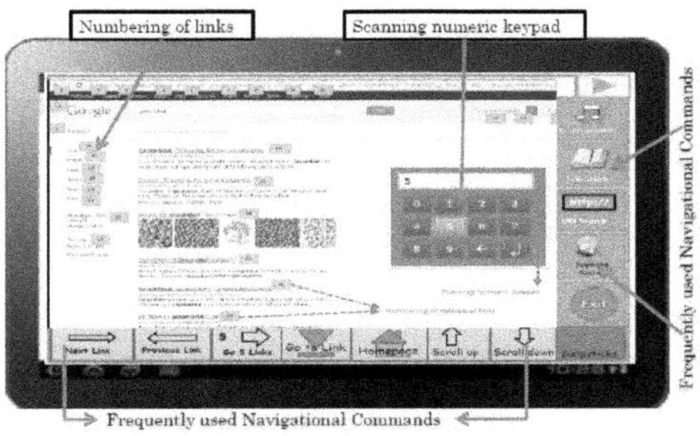

Figure 2: Illustration of the browser in a tablet device

We have observed that the Windows based desktop version is compatible to the Windows based tablets manufactured by HP, Dell and Lenovo. However, Windows based tablets are too expensive (costs around $500) as compared to Android based tablets (ranges between $50- $150). On the other hand, the JAVA based ADT framework for Android platform offers limited features as compared to its Windows based desktop counterpart. This is one of the challenges faced by us during the development of the tablet interface. Further, due to the reduced screen size of the tablets (typically 7 to 10 inch screen), a lot of users have claimed for poor visibility of items.

We have also implemented a glass pane over the top of the browser that allows any touch or click events to be captured by the glass pane. A glass pane is essentially a normal window with transparent background property. Therefore, any window present behind the glass window will be visible to the viewer, but any input event will be registered to the glass pane. As a result of this, whenever a user touches the tablet screen, the touch event is captured by the glass pane. The glass pane then identifies the browser item which is presently in focus and transfers the touch event to that item. Thus, whenever a user touches on any coordinate of the screen, a touch event will be generated to only that item on which the scanning mechanism is focused. This significantly reduce the hassles in carrying a mesh of cables everywhere along with the access switches. An important advantage of the touch-screen based tablets is that the device can be use to simulate the working of an access switch to the CP user. For this, we have used the JAVA glass pane API over the top of the browser. A glass pane is essentially a normal window with transparent background property. Therefore, any window present behind the glass window will be visible to the viewer, but any input event will be registered to the glass pane. As a result of this, whenever a user touches the tablet screen, the touch event is captured by the glass pane. The glass pane then identifies the browser item which is presently in focus and transfers the touch event to that item. Thus, whenever a user touches on any coordinate of the screen, a touch event will be generated to only that item on which the scanning mechanism is focused. This significantly reduce the hassles in carrying a mesh of cables everywhere along with the access switches.

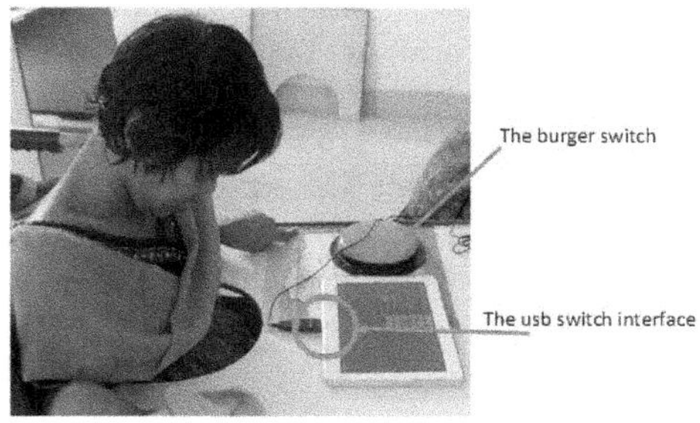

Figure 3: Evaluating the browser with target users

3. CONCLUSIONS

We present the development of WebSanyog, a portable assistive web browsing interface for people with CP. The browser has a number of novel features like, access through special switches, an iconic query generation system, and an intelligent web content access techniques. Both, Desktop and tablet versions of the browser has been evaluated by our target users. Results shows that the performance of our proposed browser is better than the existing techniques. However, it would be premature to conclude anything concrete based only on the current experimental results. Hence, a more rigorous testing of the system different group of participants and over a larger number of sessions is required to establish a concrete claim.

4. REFERENCES

[1] www.advancedperipheral.com.

[2] G. Lesher, B. Moulton, and D. J. Higginbotham. Techniques for augmenting scanning communication. *Augmentative and Alternative Communication*, 14(2):81–101, 1998.

[3] C. E. Steriadis and P. Constantinou. Designing human-computer interfaces for quadriplegic people. *ACM Transactions on Computer-Human Interaction (TOCHI)*, 10(2):87–118, 2003.

The hybrid Agent MARCO

Demo description

Nicolas Riesterer*
riestern@cs.uni-freiburg.de

Christian Becker-Asano
basano@cs.uni-freiburg.de

Julien Hué
hue@cs.uni-freiburg.de

Christian Dornhege
dornhege@cs.uni-freiburg.de

Bernhard Nebel
nebel@cs.uni-freiburg.de

ABSTRACT

We present MARCO, a hybrid, chess playing agent equipped with a custom-built robotic arm and a virtual agent's face displaying emotions. MARCO was built to investigate the hypothesis that hybrid agents capable of displaying emotions make playing chess more personal and enjoyable. In addition, we aim to explore means of achieving emotional contagion between man and machine.

Categories and Subject Descriptors

I.2.9 [**Computing Methodologies**]: Artificial Intelligence—*Robotics*

General Terms

Chess; Robotics; Human-agent interaction; Hybrid agent; Affective Computing

1. INTRODUCTION

Our robotic system combines ideas from several previous research projects that enabled humans to play chess against the machine. "Gambit", for example, is an engineer's solution to an autonomous chess-playing robotic system [8]. Although it does not feature an anthropomorphic design, it includes a "natural spoken language interface" to communicate with the human opponent. It outperformed all robotic opponents at the 2010 AAAI Small Scale Manipulation Challenge, but no data on human players' enjoyment is available. An emotional iCat was programmed as a chess opponent as well [7], but this robotic chess system depended on the human player's assistance to move its chess pieces. A 'hybrid system" similar to ours is called "Turk-2" [9] and features an abstract talking head together with a simple robotic arm.

Figure 1: The pan-tilt-roll agent display, the robotic arm, the digital chess board with a chess clock, and a Kinect sensor for human player tracking

Our MARCO system combines[1] a rotating display that presents a virtual agent's face with a custom build robotic arm to resemble an autonomous opponent for chess. The virtual face can express a variety of emotions that are driven by the WASABI affect simulation architecture [4] in combination with the TSCP chess engine [6].

2. SYSTEM DESCRIPTION

The complete setup is presented in Figure 1. The hardware used comprises a 5.6 inch pan-tilt-roll display to present the virtual agent's face, a robotic arm to move the chess pieces, and a digital chess board (DGT USB Rosewood) with a digital chess clock. A Kinect RGBD camera is used by the "NovA - Nonverbal Behavior Analyzer" [2] to track the human player's nonverbal behavior for online and offline analysis.

*All authors share the following affiliation: Albert-Ludwigs-Universität Freiburg, Department of Computer Science, Georges-Köhler-Allee 052, 79110 Freiburg, Germany

[1]See `https://www.becker-asano.de/media/video/RoboChessICMIDemo.mp4` for a video of MARCO.

ICMI'14, November 12–16, 2014, Istanbul, Turkey.
ACM 978-1-4503-2885-2/14/11..

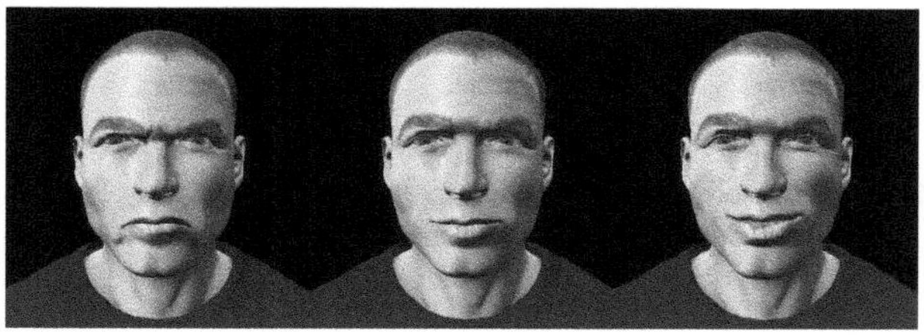

Figure 2: The virtual agent expressing *anger*, *neutral*, and *joy* (left to right)

The pan-tilt-roll display features a physical resolution of 640×480 pixels at 16bit color depth. It is mounted in upright orientation at a height that gives the impression that the virtual agent could potentially overlook the complete chess board. Three Dynamixel AX-12A servos are connected to an Arduino-based control board to change the display orientation during the game along all three axes. Thus, the agent can look up from the board into the human player's direction or even physically "shake its head".

The robotic arm is based on the "WidowX Robotic Arm Kit Mark II" [1] available from Trossen Robotics. The rotational base remained unchanged, but the arm itself was extended and the gripper modified. Five Dynamixel servos of four different families move the robot's arm. For the base and wrist two MX-28 servos are used. An MX-64 servo moves the robot's elbow and an MX-106 servo its shoulder. The gripper is opened and closed by an AX-12A servo. The gripper jaws were built to grab the Staunton chess pieces on the DGT board regardless of their height or size. With a maximum reach of $550mm$ the robotic arm can pick and place all pieces on all 64 squares of the $480mm \times 480mm$ DGT tournament chess board.

The software architecture behind MARCO consists of five main components that are linked together to form the chess playing agent:

- The DGT board connected via USB to detect moving pieces
- The TSCP chess engine for position evaluation and move calculation
- The emotion engine WASABI to simulate MARCO's emotions
- The robotic arm to move the chess pieces on the board
- The MARC framework to create the agent's visual appearance on the pan-tilt-roll display

The main information flow originates, on the one hand, from the DGT chess board detecting when pieces are lifted or put down, and, on the other hand, from the chess engine that calculates MARCO's next move based on the updated board information. The result is sent as movement commands to the robotic arm and the virtual agent receives a behavior description expressed in terms of the behavior markup language (BML) [11].

The MARC framework [5] is used to animate the virtual agent, which is displayed on the pan-tilt-roll display next to the robotic arm. Emotional facial expressions (see Fig. 2 for examples) that are part of the BML description are processed by the MARC framework to create lip-sync animations of emotional verbal utterances. Thanks to the integration of the open-source text-to-speech synthesis OpenMARY [10] the agent's emotion also influences the agent's auditory speech. A very similar technical setup was used to realize an empirical study on the effect of emotions displayed by the same virtual agent during a memorization task [3].

3. SUMMARY

We introduced MARCO, a chess playing hybrid agent equipped with a robotic arm and a rotatable screen displaying a virtual agent capable of emotional facial expressions.

This setup is inspired by previous agent systems that (more or less successfully) enhanced the chess playing experience. We believe that our hybrid agent enables us to study how virtual and robotic parts can be best combined to achieve and study emotional contagion between man and machine in the context of chess. Therefore, we aim to analyze for differences in a human player's nonverbal reactions to the hybrid agent using the "NovA" framework [2].

4. REFERENCES

[1] `http://www.trossenrobotics.com/widowxrobotarm`.

[2] T. Baur, I. Damian, F. Lingenfelser, J. Wagner, and E. André. Nova: Automated analysis of nonverbal signals in social interactions. In *Human Behavior Understanding*, LNCS, pages 160–171, 2013.

[3] C. Becker-Asano, P. Stahl, M. Ragni, J.-C. Martin, M. Courgeon, and B. Nebel. An affective virtual agent providing embodied feedback in the paired associate task: system design and evaluation. In *Intelligent Virtual Agents (IVA 2013)*, pages 406–415, 2013.

[4] C. Becker-Asano and I. Wachsmuth. Affective computing with primary and secondary emotions in a virtual human. *Autonomous Agents and Multi-Agent Systems*, 20(1):32–49, 2010.

[5] M. Courgeon, J.-C. Martin, and C. Jacquemin. MARC: a Multimodal Affective and Reactive Character. In *Proc. 1st Workshop on AFFective Interaction in Natural Environements*, 2008.

[6] T. Kerrigan. Tom kerrigan's simple chess program. `http://www.tckerrigan.com/Chess/TSCP`.

[7] I. Leite, C. Martinho, A. Pereira, and A. Paiva. icat: an affective game buddy based on anticipatory mechanisms. In *Procs of the 7th Intl. joint conference on Autonomous agents and multiagent systems*, AAMAS '08, pages 1229–1232, 2008.

[8] C. Matuszek, B. Mayton, R. Aimi, M. Deisenroth, L. Bo, R. Chu, M. Kung, L. LeGrand, J. Smith, and D. Fox. Gambit: An autonomous chess-playing robotic system. In *Robotics and Automation (ICRA)*, pages 4291–4297, 2011.

[9] L. Sajó, Z. Ruttkay, and A. Fazekas. Turk-2, a multi-modal chess player. *International Journal of Human-Computer Studies*, 69(7–8):483–495, 2011.

[10] M. Schröder. OpenMARY sources. https://github.com/marytts/marytts, 2013.

[11] H. Vilhjálmsson, et. al. The behavior markup language: Recent developments and challenges. In *Intelligent Virtual Agents*, LNCS, pages 99–111. Springer Berlin Heidelberg, 2007.

Towards Supporting Non-linear Navigation in Educational Videos

Kuldeep Yadav
Xerox Research Centre, India
Bangalore, India
kuldeep.r@xerox.com

Kundan Shrivastava
Xerox Research Centre, India
Bangalore, India

Om Deshmukh
Xerox Research Centre, India
Bangalore, India
om.deshmukh@xerox.com

ABSTRACT

MOOC participants spend most of their time watching videos in a course and recent studies have found that there is a requirement of non-linear navigation system for educational videos. We propose a system that provides efficient and non-linear navigation in a given video using multi-modal dimensions (i.e. customized word-cloud, image cloud) derived from video content. The end-to-end system is implemented and we demonstrate capabilities of the proposed system using any given YouTube or MOOC video.

Categories and Subject Descriptors

H.5.1 [**Multimedia Information Systems**]: Video

Keywords

Video Navigation; MOOCs; Word-cloud; Image cloud

1. INTRODUCTION

Various studies have found that most of the people in MOOCs use non-linear navigation for the course content [1, 2]. Bulk of the MOOC material is in the form of video content. On an average, certificate earners skip 22% of the content. A study performed on the Edx platform found that certificate earning students spend only about 4.4 minutes on a 12 to 15 minute video. Further, participants keep referring to video content at different time intervals for specific queries. For instance, it has been observed that students often go back to lecture videos while doing assignments. Consider an example, Alice is enrolled in Probability and Statistics course on Coursera. In one of the lectures, instructor discussed an interesting example about rolling a dice that clearly explained a certain concept. While doing assignment, Alice realizes that she needs to revisit that lecture, specifically the part of video (say point of interest) where instructor discussed that example. A recent study shows that there is a point of interest every 2 minutes in a given educational video [2].

Consider the following two prominent navigation techniques currently available: (a) YouTube and other related systems provide visual snapshot in response to users' mouse roll-over event on a video timeline. Such a visual snapshot is not sufficient in majority of these cases due to reasons such as limited screen text, lack of localized context and limited size of the visual snapshot; (b) The video player in EdX provides text transcripts of the video alongside and allows the user to click on any of the words in the text transcripts. As a result of this click, the video navigates to the time corresponding to the occurrence of that particular word. Neither of these techniques provide any aggregate localized information about the content nor do they support non-linear navigation based on the content. Thus, a user ends up spending significant time in finding/navigating to the different points of interests in a video.

This paper presents a multi-modal system for efficiently navigating through a video. Specifically, we design a customized word-cloud that uses location, color, and 3-D depth to provide handles for content summarization/indexing and navigation along with the traditional font size feature. The x-coordinate of the word location implies the mean temporal occurrence of the word in the video, the y-coordinate implies the spread of the word across the video, the color implies the emphasis the speaker puts on the word as captured by the acoustic stress, and the 3-D depth captures the image/screenshot type corresponding to the occurrence of the word in the video. The relative font size of the word retains the traditional indicator of frequency of the occurrence of the word in the video. We provide two other time-localized multimedia dimensions to further aid the navigation: (a) image cloud which presents visuals corresponding to a selected word in the word-cloud, and (b) read-out-loud of prominent words as the user rolls over the video timeline.

All the above dimensions aid the user in quickly navigating or finding a point of interest in a given video. Further, we have implemented these dimensions as an end-to-end system which works with any given YouTube and MOOC video. We performed an initial evaluation of the system with 6 participants and found that proposed system results in nearly $10x$ reduction of navigation time as compared to YouTube. A large-scale user study of the effectiveness of the system is underway. While we have developed this system with the educational domain in mind, we believe this system has applicability across a wide variety of video content.

2. SYSTEM DESCRIPTION

Figure 1 shows the block diagram of the proposed system for efficient video navigation. The input to the system is a video and two optional parameters: a time stamp in the video (say X seconds) and a "time interest window" around the specified time stamp. When the optional parameters are not specified, the entire video is considered for analysis.

Text and Time-stamp Extraction: In this step, the audio stream from the video is extracted using ffmpeg library. Following this,

ICMI'14, November 12–16, 2014, Istanbul, Turkey.
ACM 978-1-4503-2885-2/14/11.
http://dx.doi.org/10.1145/2663204.2669630.

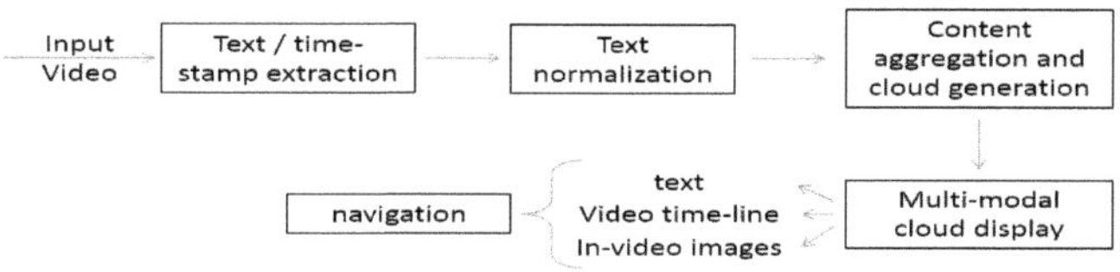

Figure 1: Block diagram of proposed system

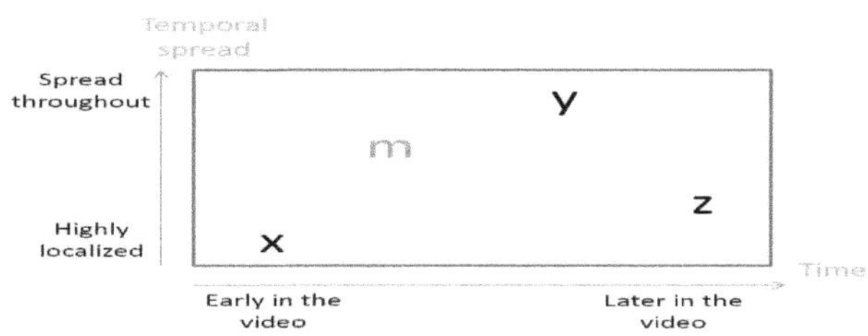

Figure 2: Structure of customized word cloud where word placement is derived from combination of features such as temporal spread, word spread, auditory stress and in-video images

the audio stream is analyzed by an Automatic Speech Recognition (ASR) system which hypothesizes the spoken text and the time stamps of each word in the text. Several of the educational videos are accompanied with time-aligned subtitles for closed captioning purpose.

Text Normalization: Spoken text is normalized in following ways: (a) Stop words such as "a", "an", "the", "of", etc are removed because they carry little information about the topic being discussed (b) Stemming: It is the process of transforming a given word to its *root* form. For example, "finding", "find", "finds" should all be transformed to "find". One of the main advantages of stemming is that it reduces the number of dimensions. Often times, standard stemming tools do not always transform a given word to its correct root form, for example "course", "courses" map to the stem "cours". This is still advantageous because the number of dimension is reduced and all the related words still transform to the same stem. In context of our system, such nonsensical words can lead to reduced readability and poorer user experience. In the "content aggregation" section, we describe how this problem has been overcome.

Content Aggregation and Cloud Generation: In a word-cloud, typically the frequency of the words is used as the indicator of prominence of the word and this is translated into either a bigger and/or thicker font or a brighter colour. While, we use the frequency of the word as the initial prominence indicator, one of the novelties of the proposed system lies in using other aspects of the delivery of the word(s) in determining their relative prominence and their relative placement in the word cloud as explained below.

- Reverse Stemming: As mentioned above, stemming can lead to some stems which may be nonsensical (e.g., "course", "courses" are stemmed to "cours"). To increase readability, the original word form has to be displayed. But, stemming is a many-to-one process and hence, it is not invertible. To overcome this, we choose the most frequent original word form of the stemmed word in the word document as the representative word (for e.g., if in the original transcript "course" occurred 3 times and "courses" occurred 4 times leading to a frequency count of 7 for the stem "cours", we choose "courses" as the representative for the stem "cours").

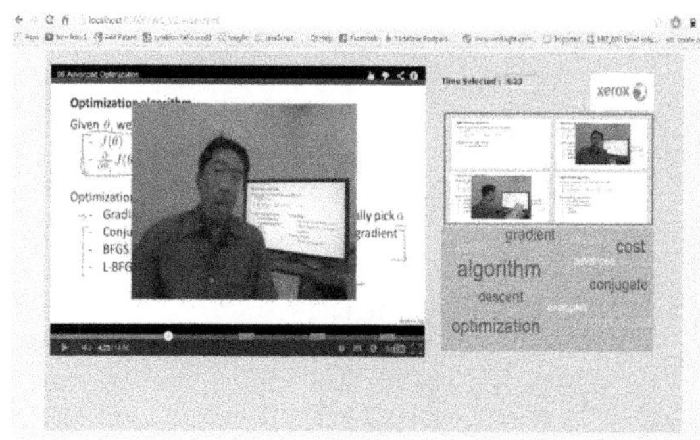

Figure 3: End-to-end System Demonstration Snapshot

- Mean-time of Occurrence: We estimate the mean-time of occurrence for every word using the time-aligned subtitles or ASR output. This mean time, relative to the total duration of the video, is indicative of which part of the video is this word most discussed in. We use the placement of the words on the x-axis of the 2-dimensional word cloud to indicate this relative time occurrence. For e.g., in Figure 2 words towards the left side (like "x") would have occurred earlier in the video than words towards the right side (like "z").
- Temporal Spread: We also estimate how spread out the word is in the document based on their time stamps,. For example if the word occurs regularly throughout the document, it will have a much higher variance than a word which occurs only in the beginning. We use the placement of the words on the y-axis of the word cloud to indicate this relative temporal spread. For e.g., in Figure 2 words towards to the top (like "y") would have occurred over a wider span of time in the video than words towards the bottom (like "x"). Observe that the top-left and top-right corners will not be occupied by any words.

In educational videos, whenever instructor wants to convey an important concept, she tend to verbally stress words indicative of the concepts. Furthermore, we use the colour of the word to represent the emphasis, which also aid in quick navigation to important concepts. For example, word "m" in Figure 2 is shown as more emphasized on an average than the other words.

Multi-modal Cloud Display: The proposed system uses multi-modal cloud display (word & images) to enable efficient navigation. Whenever user clicks or roll-over on any particular word of the 2-dimensional cloud, the time-instances of the occurrences of the word in the video are highlighted on the video timeline (red bars in the video as shown in figure), the in-video images at the corresponding times are shown in a separate window as shown in Figure 3. Clicking on any of these images will take the user to the corresponding time in the video. Often times users remember the visual events from the lecture and showing images would further aid the user in quickly navigating to the region of interest.

3. REFERENCES

[1] Guo, P. J., & Reinecke, K., Demographic differences in how students navigate through MOOCs. Proceedings of the first ACM conference on Learning@ scale conference,2014.

[2] Kim, J., Guo, P. J., Seaton, D. T., Mitros, P., Gajos, K. Z., & Miller, R. C.,Understanding in-video dropouts and interaction peaks inonline lecture videos. Proceedings of the 1st ACM conference on Learning@ scale conference, 2014.

Detecting Conversing Groups with a Single Worn Accelerometer

Hayley Hung*
TU Delft
Delft, The Netherlands
h.hung@tudelft.nl

Gwenn Englebienne*
University of Amsterdam
Amsterdam, The Netherlands
g.englebienne@uva.nl

Laura Cabrera-Quirós
TU Delft
Delft, The Netherlands
l.c.cabreraquiros@tudelft.nl

ABSTRACT

In this paper we propose the novel task of detecting groups of conversing people using only a single body-worn accelerometer per person. Our approach estimates each individual's social actions and uses the co-ordination of these social actions between pairs to identify group membership. The aim of such an approach is to be deployed in dense crowded environments. Our work differs significantly from previous approaches, which have tended to rely on audio and/or proximity sensing, often in much less crowded scenarios, for estimating whether people are talking together or who is speaking. Ultimately, we are interested in detecting who is speaking, who is conversing with whom, and from that, to infer socially relevant information about the interaction such as whether people are enjoying themselves, or the quality of their relationship in these extremely dense crowded scenarios. Striving towards this long-term goal, this paper presents a systematic study to understand how to detect groups of people who are conversing together in this setting, where we achieve a 64% classification accuracy using a fully automated system.

Categories and Subject Descriptors

H.1.2 [**Models and Principles**]: User/Machine Systems—*Human Information Processing*; H.3.1 [**Information Storage and Retrieval**]: Content Analysis and Indexing—*Indexing Methods*; G.3 [**Probability and Statistics**]: Time Series Analysis

Keywords

Human behavior; human factors; wearable sensors; data mining

1. INTRODUCTION

In this paper, we propose to detect conversing groups automatically in dense crowds during social gatherings using only a single worn accelerometer per person. Our long term goal with such a set-up is to be able to analyse socially relevant behaviour in such gatherings to understand if people enjoyed themselves, the type of mood of the event, whether people would come again, *etc.* This requires us to try to get a deeper understanding of what is happening in the crowd in terms of the social interactions and relationships between the people. By taking inspiration from findings in social psychology, we aim to address such problems while maintaining privacy and minimising additional effort of the user.

To that end, in this paper, we go significantly beyond prior work where the state of the art addressed whether socially relevant actions during conversations, such as speaking, could be estimated from just a single body worn accelerometer [13]. Our aim is to try to understand deeply the problems and opportunities of automatically analysing social behaviour using such an approach, as a starting point for other systems that may wish to embellish with more sensors, or indeed to strip down to as few sensors as possible.

Importantly for research in estimating social attributes such as dominance[15], leadership [16], or cohesion [14], one of the most informative features is typically based on the management of turns (turn-taking patterns) within a group. Therefore, the ability to automatically detect where a conversing group is, and when someone is speaking, are vital action units from which semantically higher level social concepts can be inferred.

Specifically in this paper, we address the task of estimating whether two people are conversing in dense crowded social gatherings by just measuring the movement via a body worn accelerometer. It is worth considering this modality as in such scenarios, relying on proximity alone to make robust detections is challenging as the detections are bursty. Audio data would be contaminated by significant background noise from all conversations happening at the gathering making robust audio processing too challenging. Moreover, the use of audio can be considered privacy invasive to wearers.

Prior work has used infrared (IR) sensors to detect the proximity of others as a proxy for interaction [4, 11] in much less crowded scenarios which showed poor accuracies when accumulated over short periods (5 minutes) [4]. The lack of reliability of IR sensors is partially caused by how people choose to place themselves in a space which can depend on the shape of a room or its furniture for example [22]. Under such scenarios audio sensors have been used to detect conversational interactions [5, 4, 11, 20] robustly.

The Scenario Challenges.

As already mentioned, in this paper, we address the problem of addressing socially relevant behaviour in dense crowded social gatherings such as the conference pictured in Fig. 1. Note that this image captures just a small corner of the entire space of the event, which in this case consisted of 300 participants. In such social settings, groups can tend to form, merge, and split, but still remain together spatially as different social networks with common acquaintances

*H. Hung and G. Englebienne contributed equally to this work.

ICMI'14, November 12–16, 2014, Istanbul, Turkey.
Copyright 2014 ACM 978-1-4503-2885-2/14/11 ...$15.00.
http://dx.doi.org/10.1145/2663204.2663228.

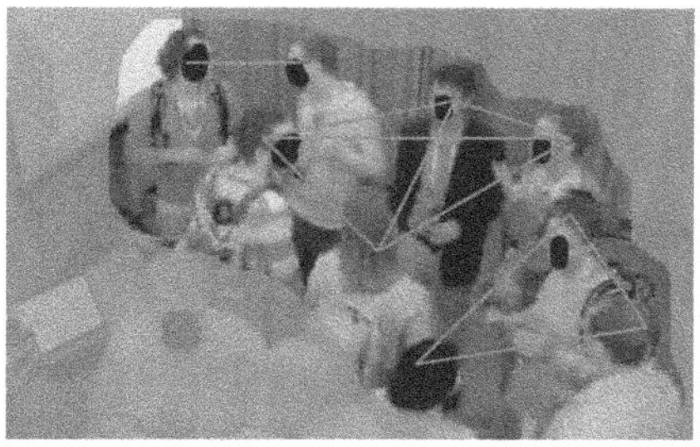

Figure 1: The complexity of crowded social encounters.

are found in the same physical space. For large groups (> 5 people) sustaining a single informal conversation is not possible [8]. However, perhaps due to the familiarity of the group members with each other, they may tend to orientate themselves towards the entire group, while gazing at the few people they are actually talking to. An example of this is shown in the crowded social gathering in Fig. 1 where the highlighted group are all acquainted with each other. Although there are 3 different conversing groups (shown by the red lines), the people still try to remain quite open to starting a conversation or including one of the others in their conversation at any moment. Therefore relying on physical cues such as just directed proximity and body orientation also does not address the problem sufficiently well. Using radio-based sensors to detect proximity allows for slightly less direction-specific detections. However, when events are densely crowded, it is likely that more people will be detected as being proximate than are actually participating in a conversation, or indeed could potentially converse together.

Despite these challenges, the automated analysis of interactive behaviour has many potential applications, of both scientific and commercial nature. For example, wearable sensors can be used for the analysis of individual and social behaviour in large crowds, for on-line evaluation of the success-rate of social events such as conferences or trade fairs, for the inclusion of social factors in handling people logistics in massive crowds such as at large sport events.

An important requirement for such a device is that wearers must not feel as if their privacy is invaded. Therefore, it must be unobtrusive and their raw speech should not be recorded.

Robust wireless transmission of real-time measurements is challenging in situations with many nodes in a restricted area. It is clear that additional sensors such as extra accelerometers on different parts of the body, gyroscopes or a magnetic compass would provide additional information, at the cost of increased bandwidth requirements and device price, and that this could lead to improved recognition rates. In this work, we focus on showing how surprisingly informative the lowly accelerometer is.

The practical appeal of such a system is that the use of a single sensor significantly reduces the power consumption. In addition, unlike mobile-based applications, designing for incentivised uptake (to compensate for increased battery usage and consent to the access of private personal data) is not necessary. One can imagine such a device could be easily attached to a conference badge, for example without further intervention from the wearer.

Theoretical Issues.

Experimentally, since our aim is to carry out a systematic study of how to detect conversing groups, we provide here a more formal definition by social psychologist Adam Kendon [17] of what we precisely mean by this. Kendon made clear distinctions between differing taxonomies of interacting groups. Co-located and co-ordinated group behaviour were named focused encounters when for example, people gathered together to perform in a marching band, play football, or watch a match. Within the set of all possible focused encounters are a specific type, called F-formations which define a small group of people who spatially and orientationally arrange themselves to facilitate conversation. An F-formation arises when

> "two or more individuals in close proximity orient their bodies in such a way that each of them has an easy, direct and equal access to every other participant's transactional segment, and when they maintain such an arrangement, they can be said to create an F-formation" [6](p.243).

Importantly, this definition makes explicit the fact that it is not necessary for someone to speak at all while being in an F-formation. However, other behaviours during participation in an F-formation, which for example correspond to listening, are still clearly important parts of being in a conversation. Moreover, findings in social psychology also suggest that other co-ordinated body motions also exist when people are in an F-formation, which are not necessarily directly related to the management of the turn-taking itself (*e.g.* simultaneous shifts of posture [17] or behavioural mimicry [3]). It is also important to highlight that while a conversing group might imply a cluster of multiple F-formations who are spatially close, here, the definition refers more specifically to one conversation happening for which all members of the F-formation are equally engaged as either the speaker(s) or listener(s).

Novel Contributions.

The contributions of this paper are: (i) we demonstrate method of using accelerometers alone to model and automatically detect instantaneous conversation-related social actions online, through a systematic analysis of streaming accelerometer readings, which out-performs the state of the art [13]; (ii) We show that the synchronicity as expressed through the mutual information between these social actions is indicative of whether people are part of the same F-formation, (iii) we show that even using imperfect recognition of such social actions results in good F-formation recognition, while direct computation of the mutual information between people's raw acceleration utterly fails to do the same.

2. RELATED WORK

2.1 Activity and Action Recognition

The majority of related work on human activity recognition using accelerometers have tended to concentrate on non-social activities such as fall detection [7, 33], ordinary daily activities including walking, running, sitting, climbing the stairs [19], daily household activities including eating or drinking, vacuuming or scrubbing, lying down [1], or to identify modes of transport taken [31]. Classifying these types of activities is possible with excellent performance. However, the aim of this paper is to measure behaviour for which the link between the activity and the behaviour is not as direct. That is, the movements associated with speaking for example, are physical manifestations of the cognitive process of speaking but do not directly produce the spoken behaviour [17].

Matic et al. also used acceleration to detect speaking status by strapping an accelerometer to the chest so that vibrations directly caused by speaking could be detected [23]. This essentially limited the possibility to interpret the verbal content of a conversation but would be much less practical to implement in a crowded social setting. In [13] an initial study was carried out to see if socially relevant actions during conversations such as speaking and laughing could be detected. In those experiments, the class data was pre-segmented and a fixed window size was used. We improved upon that work by demonstrating the feasibility of measuring the same behaviours from continuous accelerometer data and parameters trained on each class explicitly, leading to significant improvements in the performance.

2.2 Detecting Conversing Groups

There has been much prior research on analysing and estimating aspects of social behaviour using wearable sensors on both the small group scale with 2-6 people in a room [18, 10] and on larger scale, with 50 - 100 participants [9]. To our knowledge, most automated analysis of face-to-face scenarios have been carried out on small groups (2-6 people [18, 10]). Studies which have analysed larger groups of people (10-200) have used sensors such as bluetooth and/or infrared (IR) to detect when people are close together, as a proxy for interaction [21, 26, 9, 4, 11], or audio [32] However, these studies were often carried out over weeks, sometimes also exploiting other communication methods such as call frequency. [26, 9]. Moreover, it is expected that at any moment in time, the number of detected neighbours is in general far fewer than would occur in crowded situations. More systematic evaluation of conversation detection and the level of formality of the conversation was analysed by Matic et al. using both proximity and orientation sensors from a mobile phone [24]. Again, experiments were carried out in uncrowded situations.

Wearable sensors have been used as a means of supporting cooperative activities in working environments [29, 26], analysing the diffusion of political opinions or ideas [21], influence and centrality [4], or affiliation [12] amongst many others. In contrast, we focus on the detection of immediate aspects of interpersonal communication in crowded situations, at shorter timescales (and therefore relying on fewer measurements,) that require a reasonable estimation accuracy.

One of the most similar prior works that measured social behaviour using wearable sensors was proposed by Choudhury [4]. She carried out initial experiments to detect social interaction using infrared sensors attached to a "sociometer" device. This was worn on the shoulder blade of each participant for around 10 days. Experimental results showed that using infrared sensors as a proxy for interaction was quite inaccurate when trying to measure spontaneous interactions over short time scales, but performed better when accumulated over 10 days or more. Choudhury also obtained significantly better results at shorter time scales of one minute, but this was using the recorded audio signal from each device. In these experiments, the behaviour of 25 individuals was recorded, as a result of 3 different recorded time periods.

The primary distinguishing factor of our work is that the methods we propose are intended to address the specific challenges of analysing social behaviour in crowded and noisy environments, whereas most prior work, with the exception of Gips [11], have operated in less densely crowded environments. Gips [11] built on the work of Choudhury by using accelerometer readings to measure interactions using the "Uberbadge" [27]. Similar to the "sociometer", the "Uberbadge" contains an accelerometer and an IR transceiver but the badge was hung around the neck. Gips used accelerometer readings to extract the mutual information in the motion energy (MIME) to find interacting participants, rather than using an audio signal. Such a feature can find synchronous behaviour but could also find erroneous occurrences, for example if one person is following another down a corridor, or they are queuing. Unfortunately, while Gips provided an analysis of the extracted features with factors such as the affiliation of the participants at an event, no performance evaluation was made. So it is not clear how well the MIME feature performed on the various data sets that were tested on.

Olguin et al. [26] measured the behaviour of 22 colleagues in a company over one month using their "sociometric badge". The badge contained a number of different sensors and devices that are also used in conjunction with sensors within the wearer's mobile phone. For detecting and measuring social interactions, bluetooth was used to communicate between the wearers' mobile phone and the devices of others who were probably within an appropriate distance for conversation. In addition, a microphone for measuring non-verbal cues related to excitement and interest, and infrared (IR) sensors with a 30 degrees and 1m range of sensitivity for measuring interaction were also used. This badge was worn around the neck. The IR sensor readings were used as a proxy for interaction but was not evaluated explicitly during these experiments. Finally, an audio signal recorded from the badge was used to detect when someone was speaking. For a more detailed overview of existing methods that use wearable sensors for analysing social behaviour, we refer the reader to the recent book chapter by Olguin et al. [25].

In summary, all prior work listed above has tended to use IR sensors as a proxy for interaction, and used microphones for detecting when people are speaking. In contrast, we propose to do both using just one tri-axial accelerometer per person. Moreover, we explicitly address the problem of detecting F-formations [17] to ensure a clear labelling strategy in the presence of complex ambiguous data. So far, this has also not been addressed by existing research work.

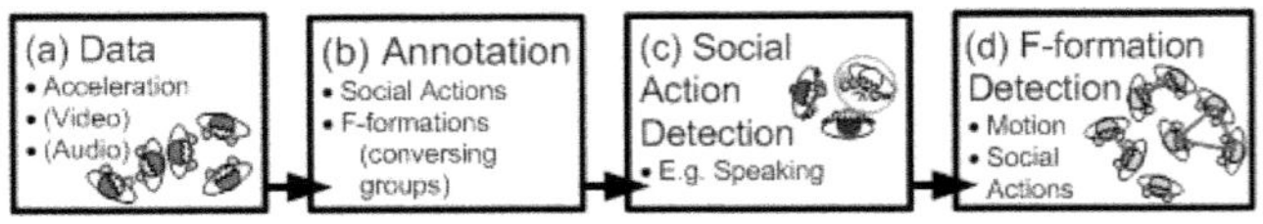

Figure 2: Flow diagram showing the experiments that were carried out in the rest of the paper.

3. OUR APPROACH

Figure 2 shows a flow diagram of our experiments. First the data is described in Section 4.1. Then in Section 4.2 the annotations for both social actions and F-formations will be described. Section 5 describes the methodology, experiments and resuts for estimating social actions. Section 6 describes how the social action labels are used to detect F-formations, the experimental procedure, and finally discusses the results. We conclude in Section 7.

4. DATA

4.1 The Scenario

For our experiments, we use the data presented in Hung et al. [13] where a social event was organised to obtain natural behaviour and in a dense crowded environment. A total of 32 student volunteers from different universities took part in the data collection. The volunteers were briefed that the aim of the event was to play a quiz game in teams, where the quiz was designed to span a wide variety of topics so that only diverse teams could be competitive. To form competitive teams, the volunteers had to (i) meet new people from different backgrounds, and (ii) form teams of four people to play the quiz. To increase motivation, prises (personal music players and book vouchers) were awarded to the top 3 winning teams.

Each participant wore a sensor pack hung around the neck, which contained a triaxial accelerometer, proximity sensor, and an indoor positioning device. The proximity and position information was not used in these experiments though investigating the combination of such modalities as well as the trade-offs are left for feature work. 12 wireless microphones were randomly distributed amongst the participants and three overhead fish-eye cameras recorded the experimental area (5m $\times$ 6m). All participants were requested to stay within this marked area during the recording. Both audio and video data was used only to collect ground truth labels for training the classifiers. An example snapshot of the scene is shown in Figure 3.

Unfortunately, of the 12 subjects wearing microphones, only 10 had accelerometer data due to a firmware bug. The behaviour of these subjects was already annotated every 2s for the actions: *speaking*, *laughing*, *gesturing* (either hand or head), *stepping* (or walking) and *drinking*. An additional 17 subjects wore working accelerom-

Figure 3: Overhead snapshot of the scenario used in our data.

eters but wore no microphone and so no ground truth annotations were recorded for these people. We carried out experiment with both fully annotated social action data (**10 person data**), and the partially annotated social action data **26 person data**.

4.2 Data Annotation

We used the 10 minute mingling part of the event as annotated by Hung et al. [13] for which annotations of social actions were already available. We extended the work of Hung et al. [13] by manually annotating for F-formations. The F-formations were annotated as follows. This involved manually associating each person in the video with their corresponding sensor readings and then labelling the social actions appropriately. The same 10 minute segment for all 32 subjects was annotated every 2s, depending on whether people were in the same F-formation or not, leading to 300 time frames of annotated data. Unfortunately only 26 subjects had working accelerometer data. Annotating those with missing data was important for understanding the affect that these people might have on the behaviour of those with working accelerometers.

5. ESTIMATING SOCIAL ACTIONS

5.1 Method

Similar to Hung et al. [13], we extract spectral features from the accelerometer readings and evaluate how well a Hidden Markov Model (HMM, [30]) and random forests (RF,[2]) models these. Unlike the work of Hung et al. [13], who attempted to label pre-segmented data sequences as corresponding to an action or not, in this work, we perform segmentation and classification simultaneously. These tasks are different, but they are clearly related: we can use an HMM to solve both cases, the difference is in the meaning of the states: in [13], the states of the HMM model different aspects of an action, such as its onset or final phase. The optimal number of states is, therefore, related to the action to be recognised, and not intrinsically limited. In this work, there are only two states: whether the action is being performed in the current time slot or not. This task is clearly more challenging, as the model needs to recognise both on the segment boundaries and the corresponding actions.

We have, therefore, modified the earlier approach by modelling the emission probabilities of the "action" and "non-action" states with mixtures of Gaussians instead of single Gaussians. Whereas the complex distribution of the observations was handled by many states in "action" and "non-action" HMMs, in this work the complexity is handled by the mixture elements within the "action" and "non-action" states of a single HMM. The resulting model is equally powerful in terms of its capacity to model the complex distributions of the observations, but is slightly less powerful in its capacity to model the transitions between parts of an action. For example, if we imagine that the action of speaking consists of an onset, varying behaviours during speech, and termination, the current model is oblivious to the order of these phases even though it correctly models each.

Table 1: Summary of social action estimation performance using continuous data. (see text for details)

HMM-based

Action	Class Prop.	length (s)	elem.	Prec.	Rec.	F1	Acc.
Gesturing	0.67	5	1	0.70	0.62	0.66	0.67
Stepping	0.09	5	3	0.32	0.28	0.30	0.85
Drinking	0.05	2.5	1	0.20	0.19	0.19	0.88
Laughing	0.03	3.5	2	0	0	0	0.97
Speaking	0.42	3.5	2	0.85	0.84	.84	0.50

Random-forest-based

Action	Class Prop.	length (s)	Trees	Prec.	Rec.	F1	Acc.
Gesturing	0.67	5	500	0.58	0.56	0.57	0.83
Stepping	0.09	5	500	0.54	0.53	0.53	0.91
Drinking	0.05	5	1000	0.43	0.43	0.43	0.95
Laughing	0.03	5	1000	0.23	0.24	0.23	0.96
Speaking	0.42	5	500	0.69	0.68	0.69	0.76

As the expressiveness of the transition model decreases, the question arises whether a standard classifier, without transition model, is not more suitable. To test this, we have compared the HMM's performance to a powerful ensemble method, random forests [2], trained on the individual time slices.

5.2 Results

We performed our experiments on the accelerometer readings of 26 participants from [13]. We replicated the feature extraction of Hung et al., by processing the signal from the three-dimensional acceleration readings by computing a Discrete Fourier Transform of the acceleration along each dimension individually, and used log-spaced bins of varying size, so as to obtain a higher resolution for the low frequencies.

Different actions have varying degrees of complexity and different durations. It makes sense, therefore, to use different numbers of mixture elements and different lengths for the windows used for feature extraction (for the HMM), and different numbers of trees for the random forests. Table 1 lists the number of mixture elements and the window lengths in seconds used for the different gestures (fourth and third columns respectively). These numbers were chosen based on cross-validated selection using pre-segmented data. The table further lists the precision, recall, F1 measure and accuracy (columns five to eight). The listed parameters in columns three and four were trained on cross-validated pre-segmented data.

From these results, we note that the HMM performs better at recognising *gesturing* and *speaking*, which are longer-duration actions in our dataset, while the random forest is better at recognising *stepping*, *drinking* and *laughing*. in this work we focus on the analysis of F-formations from the obtained actions, but in practice, of course, there is no problem with choosing the best tool for the task and applying different models for the different actions.

Notice how *stepping*, *drinking* and *laughing* are not recognised well at all by the HMM, although the random forest performs quite a bit better despite the class imbalance. In particular, *stepping* is remarkably badly recognised. This is due to the definition of *stepping* used in the data, which can consist both of walking or *stepping*, but also of switching one's weight from one foot to another during a conversation. Although relevant, this form of body language is very challenging to detect with our current model. *Drinking* and *laughing* suffer from the small dataset and few positive examples. Table 1 shows the performance, allowing up to a 2 seconds shift of the an-

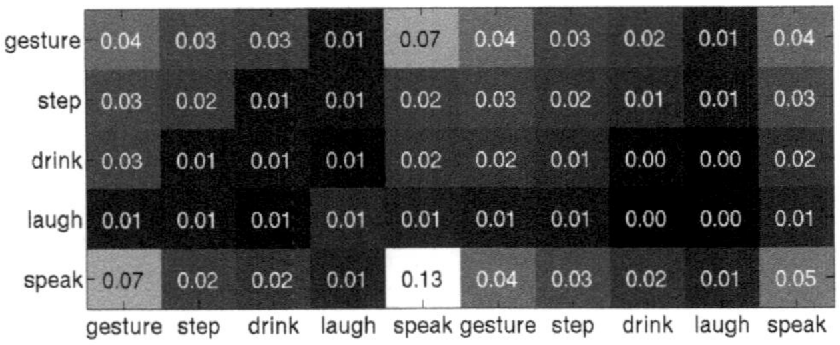

Figure 4: Matrices showing the average mutual information for each pair of social actions for people who were annotated to be in the same F-formation (left) and not in the same F-formation (right) over a 20s window.

notations either way. The resulting figures show that *gesturing* and *speaking* are segmented and recognised much better than random but that, as expected from the few positive examples of these classes, *stepping*, *drinking* and *laughing* perform badly.

6. IDENTIFYING PAIRWISE F-FORMATION MEMBERSHIP

6.1 Method

To understand more about the problem of automatically identifying F-formations, we hypothesised that people have strongly co-ordinated behaviour during conversations that would highlight the moments when they were conversing compared to times when they are not. Furthermore, motivated from findings in social psychology[17], we hypothesise that in addition to the co-ordination of speaking turns, other socially relevant behaviours could also be indicative of being in an F-formation. Moreover, when the accuracy in estimating speaking status is reduced, the use of other socially relevant conversational behaviours could enhance the performance.

To verify this hypothesis, we adjusted the method of Wyatt et al. [32], who applied this method on audio data. Mutual information is calculated over a window for both social action streams. The pair are labelled as being in an F-formation using a threshold on the mutual information value (trained on separate data). So pairs of people whose binary streams yield a higher mutual information are considered to be more likely to be talking together.

To illustrate how each social action can indicate who is in an F-formation with whom, we plotted the mean mutual information per ground-truth-labelled action pair, differentiated by whether they were in the same F-formation or not. Figure 4 shows a colour-coded matrix of the within-group and without-group mean mutual information per pair of social actions. Light colours indicate where pairs of actions have higher mean mutual information. The left half of the figure shows the mean mutual information of actions for people in the same F-formation and the right half shows the same information for people in different F-formations. We see that overall, the mean mutual information between actions of pairs of people in the same group tend to be higher than those of people in different groups. As expected, speaking from both people yields the highest mean mutual information. However, it is worth highlighting that other action pairs also have higher mutual information within the same F-formation. Note that these results highlight patterns for the dyads that exist in this labelled data.

Interestingly, we also see that pairwise speaking activity for both participants also yields the highest mean mutual information for people who are not in the same F-formation. In fact, the mutual information for two speakers is almost twice as high as the next

Table 2: F-formation estimation accuracy using the mean MI. GT: ground truth, RF: Random forest.

Win. Size (s)	5s	10s	20s	40s	80s
10 person GT	0.51	0.59	0.62	0.62	0.57
10 person RF	0.51	0.56	0.63	**0.64**	0.60
26 person RF	0.49	0.50	0.50	0.50	0.50

ranked action pairs (speaking and gesturing) in the in-group case. This suggests that although speaking is a key characteristic of people being in a conversation together, other social actions also contribute to the dynamics of activities that are indicative of F-formations.

From the analysis shown in Figure 4, we chose a simple late fusion approach by taking the mean mutual information for every possible action pair in a given window.

6.2 Experimental Results

To experimentally validate the F-formation detection, the performance was cross-validated by a leave-one-pair out approach. For a given pair of people and window size, the mutual information threshold was trained using the labelled binary social action streams of all other pairs of the remaining people. The threshold was selected by finding the value that maximised the classification accuracy from the training data. For the 10 annotated people, at any one time, there were far fewer instances of pairs of people in the same F-formations than in different F-formations. Therefore, to handle the significant imbalance in the classes, the smaller class was reweighted during training and testing. All the presented results are therefore presented based on upsampling the smaller class to be identical in size.

6.2.1 Using Ground Truth Social Actions

To understand what the upper bound of the performance of the F-formation detector would be, we first present results using the ground truth labels of the social actions. Figure 5 summarises the classification accuracy for detecting people being in the same F-formation for different window sizes. Lighter colours indicate better performance. In practice, the optimal window size can also be trained for, but we wanted to analyse how differing window sizes might affect performance when using ground truth compared to estimated social actions.

The first thing to note is that the best accuracy of 0.65 is obtained when using the mutual information of speaking activity of both participants using a 20s window. There appears to be a peak in performance of the *speaking- speaking* action pair at this window length, after which the performance decreases. This suggests that within 20s, turn exchanges were sufficiently captured to obtain discriminative mutual information between the two binary streams. However, the performance of the *speaking-gesturing* action pair increases with longer window lengths, which on further investigation of the social action label estimates can be explained by *gesturing* occurring more sparsely than *speaking*. Importantly, all the remaining social actions, with the exception of *laughing* all pair with other social actions to produce F-formation estimates which are better than the random baseline (50% classification accuracy). This may be due to there being very few examples of *laughing* in the data. Moreover, peaks in performance of different social action pairs occur at varying window lengths, which is in keeping with the nature of some social actions being longer than others. Overall, in line with prior work [32], speaking status is very important for identifying conversing groups. However, our experiments show that other social actions are also informative of being in an F-formation but their infrequence in the labelled data suggests that more data is needed to further investigate this result. To understand how the performance might improve by incorporating the mutual information between all social action

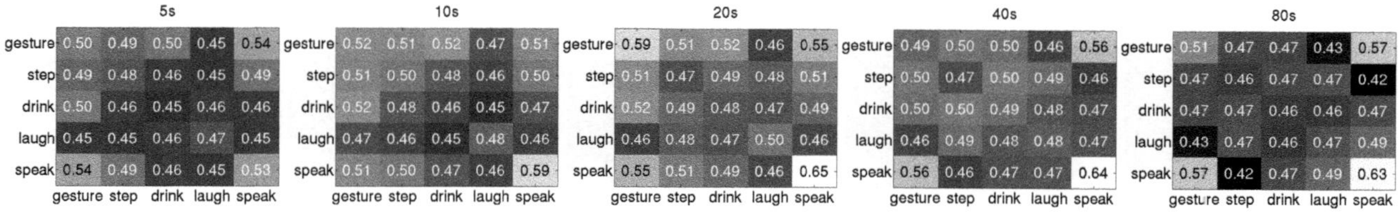

Figure 5: Ground-truth social action labels: F-formation detection performance in terms of classification accuracy per action pair using the 10 people from the fully annotated data.

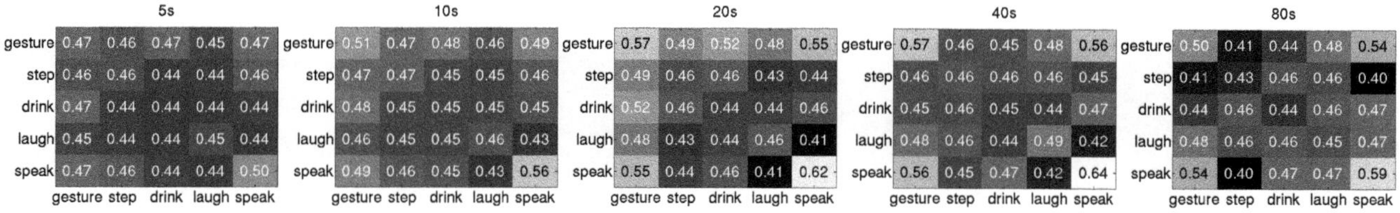

Figure 6: Estimated social action labels using the random forests method: F-formation detection performance in terms of classification accuracy per social action pair for the 10 people from the fully annotated data.

pairs. The same cross-validated experiments were carried out using the mean mutual information of all action pairs over a given window. The balanced classification accuracy is shown in Table 2 for the same window sizes. In the first row, a peak classification accuracy of 0.62 is achieved for the 20s and 40s window. This is a reduction in performance compared to just the *speaking-speaking* action pair. Given that other social action pairs can be indicative of F-formation membership, this suggests that more complex classifiers and more data for these other social actions are required to understand the problem more deeply.

6.2.2 Using Estimated Social Actions

Results on the Fully Annotated 10-person Data.

Having seen what the upper bound on performance is when using the ground truth labels, we now present the performance results when using the social actions as estimated using the Random Forest method as described in Section 5. We present just results with this method since its social action estimation performance was better than the HMMs. Again, we initially carried out tests by observing the performance differences for different action pairs. The results are summarised in Figure 6. If we compare the performance when using the ground truth social action labels with the estimates from the random forest, the performance is comparable but achieves the best accuracy (0.64) when using a 40s window and the *speaking-speaking* social action pair. Comparing this to the results using the ground truth labels of the social actions, where the best performance of 0.65 classification accuracy was obtained using a 20s window, we see that significantly longer window sizes are necessary, probably to account for the noisier estimates of the social actions. Note that the colour coding is normalised across Figures 6, 7 and 5 for easier comparison.

In terms of the performance when using the mean mutual information of all action pairs, the results are summarised in Table 2 again in terms of the class-balanced classification accuracy. In the second row, the best performance (0.64) is again obtained with a 40s window. However, now a more comparable performance of 0.63 classification accuracy is also achieved with the 20s window, which is also quite competitive compared to the results when using the ground truth labels. This suggests that when the social action estimates are more noisy, then exploiting other social action streams becomes more useful. Using the mean MI values across all social action pairs leads to an equal or slight increase in performance over any single action pair for all window sizes. This suggests again that considering other social action pairs is beneficial.

Table 3: Frequency of occurrence (in seconds) of different group sizes for both data sets.

	1	2	3	4	5
all 32 persons	1528	2624	2210	1300	126
26-person data	1694	3150	1736	874	10
10-person data	2848	1576	0	0	0

Results on the 26 person data.

We performed F-formation estimation on the full set of people (with working sensor readings) during the same 10 minute interval. Since not everyone was wearing a microphone, this data was generated from the 10-person training data only. The results for each action pair and using the mean of the MI are shown in Figure 7 and Table 2 respectively. In both cases, the performance of the F-formation detection drops to below the random baseline. There are a number of possible explanations for this.

First, the social action performance could be worse given that the size of the training data is significantly less than the test set. Second, a deeper analysis of the data reveals very different distributions of each group size instance in the 10person and 26 person data (see Table 3). Note that the table also shows statistics for those who were not labelled to be in any F-formation and are therefore singletons.

As shown in Table 3, the distribution of group sizes was substantially different. It is also likely that in the 10-person data, many of the singletons and some of the dyads were people talking others who were not wearing microphones and therefore not annotated for social actions. Likewise in the 26-person data, only the data from those who had accelerometer readings were used to generate the distribution. By comparing with the statistics for all 32 subjects, we see that there were deviations between the true and estimated F-formation sizes. Note that these differences do not affect the F-formation estimation performance because it was trained on pairwise mutual information values. However, there are clearly more groups of size 3-5 and therefore estimating differing F-formation sizes is a much more challenging task. It is likely that the mutual information between dyads is much higher because both have to be constantly actively involved in the conversation. On the other hand, for smaller group sizes, the behaviour is perhaps less strongly co-ordinated.

We investigated further by computing the accuracy per group size, as shown in Figure 8 for 40s and 80s window lengths. We can see that above random performance is mostly concentrated in the groups of size 2. This further suggests that different group sizes should be treated differently during training and testing and indeed could

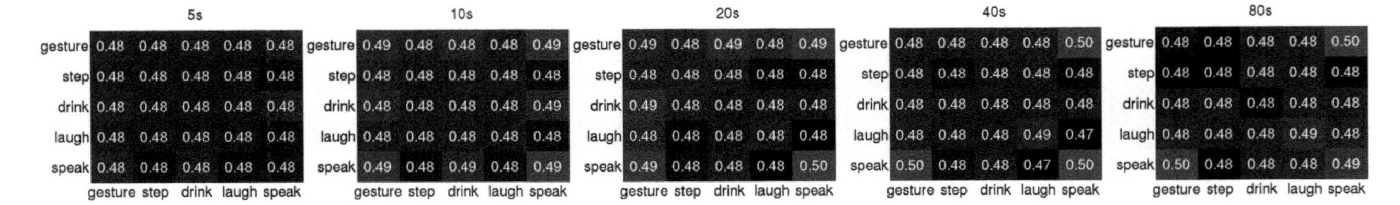

Figure 7: F-formation detection performance in terms of classification accuracy per social action pair, using action pairs estimated with random forests for all 26 people from the 10 minute interval annotated for F-Formations.

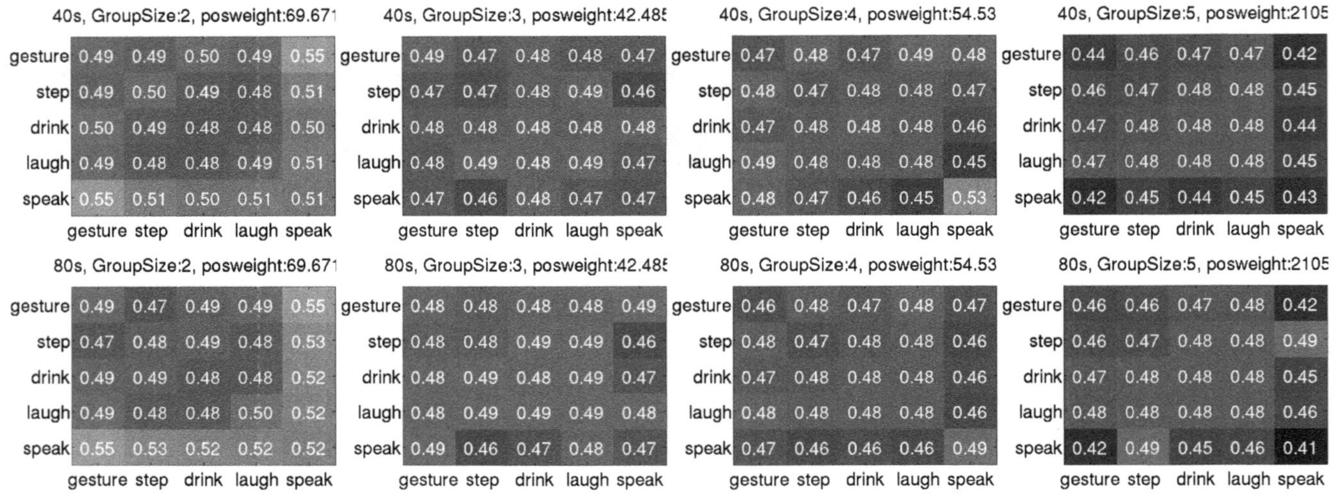

Figure 8: F-formation detection performance in terms of class balanced classification accuracy per action pair in different group sizes. Posweight shows the ratio of the number of negative to positive data points for each corresponding group size.

depend on certain action pairs more than others.

6.2.3 *Ground Truth vs. Estimated Social Actions*

On comparing the performance of the F-formation detection using ground truth compared to estimated labels, in Figures 5 and 6, a general decrease in performance is observed except for the *gesturing-gesturing* social action pair at the 40s window length. This shows that each of the defined social actions have a salient and measurable meaning in the co-ordination of behaviour in F-formations. The exception is due to errors in the social action estimate: closer inspection of the estimated social actions revealed that *gesturing* is most often mistaken for speaking, which is the single most informative action in the data.

When using the true labelled social actions, taking the mean mutual information did not improve the performance over considering the mutual information of any individual action pair. In comparison, taking the mean mutual information tended to improve the performance of the F-formation detection using estimated social actions. Also when using both the estimated labels, taking the mean of the mutual information of all social action pairs led a reduced latency in obtaining above close to the best performance. This suggests that in the presence of noisy labels, relying on multiple action pairs rather than a single one to improve accuracy and latency is a sensible choice. It also suggests that combining multiple action pairs at shorter time scales can provide stronger evidence for F-formations.

6.3 Social Actions vs. Motion

It is not clear whether it is purely the co-ordination of motion rather than specific social actions that indicate whether people are in an F-formation or not. We carried out additional experiments where we calculated the mutual information on the raw tri-axial motion signal per person. Since the mutual information is sensitive to the binning choice when approximating a probability distribution, we wanted to chose a more stable method of estimating the mutual information from continuous data. To this end, we used the implementation of the mutual information proposed by Peng et al. [28] for both these experiments, and those with binary streams. For the motion data, this method approximates the distribution of the data using kernel density estimation.

Table 4: F-formation accuracy from raw acceleration

Window Size (s.)	10-person data	26-person data
5	0.55	0.52
10	**0.56**	0.51
20	**0.56**	0.51
40	0.55	0.50
80	0.52	0.48

We carried out the same experiments calculating the mutual information on the magnitude of the raw acceleration streams. The results are shown in Table 4. Here we see that for the 10-person data, the performance does not surpass the social action approach, which suggests that there is something salient about the social actions that provides clear distinctions between behaviour which is relevant to conversations, and other motion which does not. For the 26-person data, the motion features alone do provide some discrimination, which suggests that the reason that our social action approach did not work is possible related to not having enough data for training the social actions.

There are, of course, other ways of pre-processing the motion features before calculating the mutual information for every pair. However, more complex representations of the motion features could have resulted indirectly in more semantically meaningful representations of the motion that would go beyond treating it as the raw signal, thus defeating the purpose of this particular comparative study.

7. CONCLUSIONS

In this paper, we have demonstrated that complex social behaviour related to conversations can be estimated using just a single body-worn accelerometer. The goal of the paper was to understand how the co-ordinated body movements can be indicative of being in a conversation. Thus far, it has been used to augment audio-based sensing of conversations in less crowded and acoustically clean situations. First, we have shown improved social action estimation performance on non pre-segmented data over prior work [13]. Second, we have also shown that it is possible to detect F-formations by measuring the co-ordination of automatically extracted conversationally relevant behaviours. Importantly, we have highlighted that using noisy estimates of speaking activity alone to detect F-formations is informative but that taking into account other conversationally related behaviours leads to an improved performance. A best classification accuracy of 64% was achieved for the *speaking-speaking* social action pair where mutual information between these streams was accumulated over a 40s window for the fully annotated 10-person data. Combining multiple social actions to estimate F-formation membership showed slightly improved results and warrants further investigation. However, when considering the 26-person data, overall F-formation estimation performance dropped below the random baseline. Further investigation showed that this was because more different group sizes were taken into account than in the 10-person data where only dyads were present. Future work will investigate how to develop methods that take into account group size.

8. ACKNOWLEDGEMENTS

Thanks to Matthew Dobson, Claudio Martella, and Maarten van Steen (VU University of Amsterdam) for the use of their wearable sensors and assistance during the data collection. We also thank Jeroen Kools and Ben Kröse (University of Amsterdam) for their help during the data collection and the annotation process. This work was partially supported by the Delft Technology Fellowship, European Commission under contract number FP7-ICT-600877 (SPENCER) and grant agreement number 601033 - MOnarCH, the Dutch National Program COMMIT, and the Costa Rican Institute of Technology and is affiliated with the Delft Data Science consortium.

9. REFERENCES

[1] L. Bao and S. Intille. Activity recognition from user-annotated acceleration data. *Pervasive Computing*, pages 1–17, 2004.

[2] L. Breiman. Random forests. *Machine learning*, 45(1):5–32, 2001.

[3] T. L. Chartrand and J. A. Bargh. The chameleon effect: the perception-behavior link and social interaction. *Journal of Personality and Social Psychology*, 76(6):893–910, 1999.

[4] T. Choudhury. *Sensing and Modeling Human Networks*. PhD thesis, 2004.

[5] T. Choudhury and A. Pentland. Characterizing Social Networks using the Sociometer. In *PROCEEDINGS OF NAACOS 2004*, 2004.

[6] T. M. Ciolek and A. Kendon. Environment and the Spatial Arrangement of Conversational Encounters. *Sociological Inquiry*, 50(3-4):237–271, 1980.

[7] C. Doukas, I. Maglogiannis, P. Tragas, D. Liapis, and G. Yovanof. Patient fall detection using support vector machines. *Artificial Intelligence and Innovations 2007: from Theory to Applications*, pages 147–156, 2007.

[8] R. Dunbar, N. Duncan, and D. Nettle. Size and structure of freely forming conversational groups. *Human Nature*, 6(1):67–78, 1995.

[9] N. Eagle and A. S. Pentland. Reality mining: sensing complex social systems. *Personal Ubiquitous Computing*, 10(4):255–268, 2006.

[10] D. Gatica-Perez. Automatic nonverbal analysis of social interaction in small groups: A review. *Image and Vision Computing*, 27(12):1775–1787, 2009.

[11] J. Gips. Social Motion: Mobile Networking Through Sensing Human Behavior. Master's thesis, 2006.

[12] J. Gips and A. Pentland. Mapping Human Networks. In *PerCom*, pages 159–168. IEEE Computer Society, 2006.

[13] H. Hung, G. Englebienne, and J. Kools. Classifying Social Actions with a Single Accelerometer. In *Ubicomp*, pages 207–210. ACM, 2013.

[14] H. Hung and D. Gatica-Perez. Estimating cohesion in small groups using audio-visual nonverbal behavior. *Multimedia, IEEE Transactions on*, 12(6):563–575, 2010.

[15] D. Jayagopi, H. Hung, C. Yeo, and D. GaticaPerez. Modeling dominance in group conversations from non-verbal activity cues. *IEEE Transactions on Audio, Speech and Language Processing*, 2008.

[16] D. B. Jayagopi and D. Gatica-Perez. Mining Group Nonverbal Conversational Patterns Using Probabilistic Topic Models. *IEEE Transactions on Multimedia*, 12(8):790–802, 2010.

[17] A. Kendon. *Conducting Interaction: Patterns of Behavior in Focused Encounters*. Cambridge University Press, 1990.

[18] T. Kim, A. Chang, L. Holland, and A. Pentland. Meeting mediator: enhancing group collaborationusing sociometric feedback. In *CSCW*, pages 457–466, 2008.

[19] J. R. Kwapisz, G. M. Weiss, and S. A. Moore. Activity recognition using cell phone accelerometers. *ACM SIGKDD Explorations Newsletter*, 12(2):74–82, 2011.

[20] C.-C. Lian and J. Y.-j. Hsu. Probabilistic Models for Concurrent Chatting Activity Recognition. In *IJCAI*, pages 1138–1143, 2009.

[21] A. Madan, K. Farrahi, D. Gatica-Perez, and A. Pentland. Pervasive sensing to model political opinions in face-to-face networks. *Pervasive Computing*, pages 214–231, 2011.

[22] P. Marshall, Y. Rogers, and N. Pantidi. Using F-formations to analyse spatial patterns of interaction in physical environments. In *Proceedings of the ACM 2011 conference on Computer supported cooperative work*, CSCW '11, pages 445–454, New York, NY, USA, 2011. ACM.

[23] A. Matic, V. Osmani, A. Maxhuni, and O. Mayora. Multi-modal mobile sensing of social interactions. In *Pervasive computing technologies for healthcare (PervasiveHealth), 2012 6th international conference on*, pages 105–114. IEEE, 2012.

[24] A. Matic, V. Osmani, and O. Mayora-Ibarra. Analysis of social interactions through mobile phones. *Mobile Networks and Applications*, 17(6):808–819, 2012.

[25] D. O. Olguin, A. Madan, M. Cebrian, and A. Pentland. Mobile Sensing Technologies and Computational Methods for Collective Intelligence. In N. Bessis and F. Xhafa, editors, *Next Generation Data Technologies for Collective Computational Intelligence*, Studies in Computational Intelligence, pages 575–597.

[26] D. O. Olguín, B. N. Waber, T. Kim, A. Mohan, K. Ara, and A. Pentland. Sensible Organizations: Technology and Methodology for Automatically Measuring Organizational Behavior. *IEEE transactions on systems, man, and cybernetics-Part B: Cybernetics*, 2009.

[27] J. A. Paradiso, J. Gips, M. Laibowitz, S. Sadi, D. Merrill, R. Aylward, P. Maes, and A. Pentland. Identifying and facilitating social interaction with a wearable wireless sensor network. *Personal and Ubiquitous Computing*, 14(2):137–152, 2010.

[28] H. Peng, F. Long, and C. Ding. Feature selection based on mutual information: criteria of max-dependency, max-relevance, and min-redundancy. *IEEE Transactions on Pattern Analysis and Machine Intelligence*, 27:1226–1238, 2005.

[29] A. S. Pentland, T. J. Kim, et al. *Enhancing distributed collaboration using sociometric feedback*. PhD thesis, Massachusetts Institute of Technology, 2011.

[30] L. Rabiner. A Tutorial on Hidden Markov Models and Selected Applications in Speech Recognition. *PROCEEDINGS OF THE IEEE*, 77(2):257, 1989.

[31] S. Reddy, M. Mun, J. Burke, D. Estrin, M. Hansen, and M. Srivastava. Using mobile phones to determine transportation modes. *ACM Transactions on Sensor Networks (TOSN)*, 6(2):13, 2010.

[32] D. Wyatt, T. Choudhury, and J. Bilmes. Conversation detection and speaker segmentation in privacy-sensitive situated speech data. In *In Proc. of Interspeech*, 2007.

[33] T. Zhang, J. Wang, P. Liu, and J. Hou. Fall detection by embedding an accelerometer in cellphone and using KFD algorithm. *Int. Journal of Computer Science and Network Security*, 6(10):277–284, 2006.

Identification of the Driver's Interest Point using a Head Pose Trajectory for Situated Dialog Systems

Young-Ho Kim
Computer Science and Engineering
Texas A&M University
College Station, TX, 77843
yhkim@cse.tamu.edu

Teruhisa Misu
Honda Research Institute USA
425 National Avenue
Mountain View, CA, 94040
tmisu@hra.com

ABSTRACT

This paper addresses issues existing in situated language understanding in a moving car. Particularly, we propose a method for understanding user queries regarding specific target buildings in their surroundings based on the driver's head pose and speech information. To identify a meaningful head pose motion related to the user query that is among spontaneous motions while driving, we construct a model describing the relationship between sequences of a driver's head pose and the relative direction to an interest point using the Gaussian process regression. We also consider time-varying interest point using kernel density estimation. We collected situated queries from subject drivers by using our research system embedded in a real car. The proposed method achieves an improvement in the target identification rate by 14% in the user-independent training condition and 27% in the user-dependent training condition over the method that uses the head motion at the start-of-speech timing.

Categories and Subject Descriptors:
H.1.2[MODELS AND PRINCIPLES]: User/Machine Systems ; I.2.6[ARTIFICIAL INTELLIGENCE]: Learning

Keywords: Situated Dialog Systems; Multimodal interaction; Modeling a head pose trajectory; Identification of the interest point

1. INTRODUCTION

Recent advances in sensing technologies have enabled researchers to explore applications that require a clear awareness of a system's dynamic contact on physical surrounding. Cohen et al. [3] collected and analyzed interaction in a moving car, where *situated interactions* often take place. One of their insights was that drivers frequently use referring expressions about their surroundings (e.g., *What is that restaurant?*). They also found that drivers do not necessarily present position cues (e.g., "on the right", or "right ahead") in a query, but simply say "what's that". In fact, about half of the utterances do not include specific position information. Instead, drivers used multi-modal cues such as head pose movements or gestures to indicate their target. Based on these insights, Misu et al. [12] constructed a system that uses head pose based on the assumption that drivers look at the target point of interest (POI). However, they showed that using head pose information at the start of speech timing does not necessarily contribute to POI identification. Their analysis shows that this is mainly because (1) drivers do not keep looking at the target, because making a query about surroundings is a secondary task compared to looking forward for their primary task of driving, and (2) POI is represented as a point (pair of latitude and longitude), and the difference between a head direction and the POI direction is not necessarily zero. In this paper, we consider tracking the change sequence (trajectory) of the head pose. We believe that will lead to robust inference of a POI identification during a short time frame rather than one instant capture.

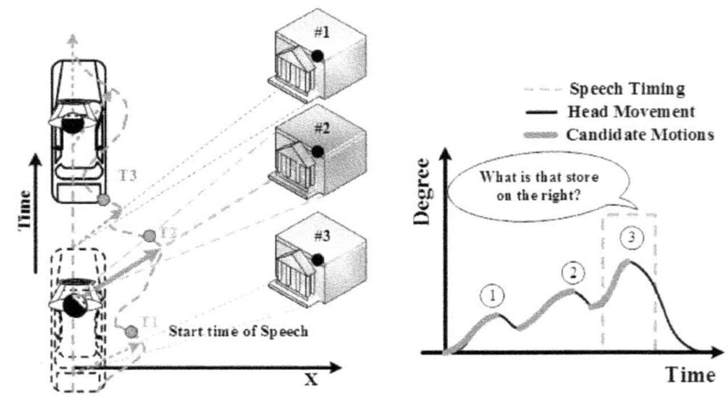

(a) Uncertainty of the user head pose direction: a timing and an observation point

(b) Time-varying interest point about one query

Figure 1: Several problems of understanding situated head movement: uncertainty of the user head pose movement and time-varying interest point

However, using head pose trajectory is not straightforward due to the following problems:

1. There is a discrepancy between a driver's head pose direction and speech timing (Fig. 1(a)).
2. A driver's looking motion is not consistent because of different velocities and accelerometer readings (Fig. 1(a)).
3. There exists spontaneous varied head pose movements while driving: it is difficult to link one query to a specific pattern (Fig. 1(b)).
4. The looking pattern might be user dependent.

To solve these problems, we model a driver's looking motion that is a relationship between the driver's head pose

ICMI'14, November 12–16, 2014, Istanbul, Turkey.

http://dx.doi.org/10.1145/2663204.2663230.

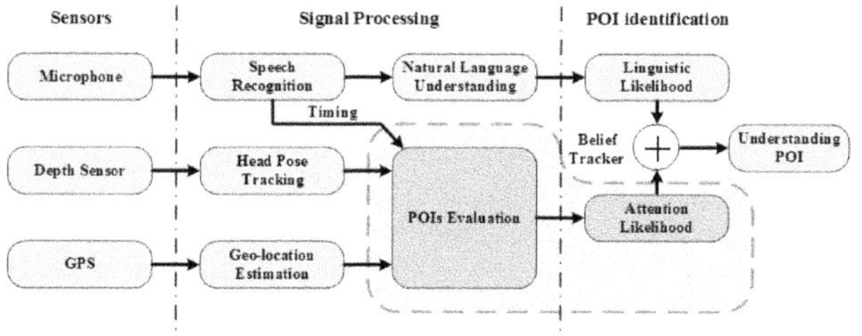

Figure 2: Townsurfer system diagram: sensors, signal processing, and POI identification. We focus on the POIs evaluation (the circle)

and the target POI direction by using the Gaussian Process Regression (GPR) over time. This facilitates adaptation to a specific user. Then, we incorporate a kernel density estimation in the time frame to find a head movement that is most closely related to the utterance.

2. RELATED WORK

Doshi and Trivedi [5] demonstrated that head pose movement is enough to predict drivers' lane-change activities. Their findings include that head pose is a better cue than (noisy) eye gaze information to detect task-oriented (user-driven) activities. Our research utilizes their findings and focuses on detecting users' intended target based on head motions.

Fletcher and Zelinsky [7] proposed a method of detecting driver inattention based on the eye gaze-road event correlation. While their method focuses on fixation of the eye gaze to classify whether a driver sees some objects or not, we utilize trajectory information of the user head pose.

Several works [2, 8, 9] have used timing to enhance natural interaction with systems. They confirmed that the system's reference resolution performance is enhanced by taking the user's eye fixation into account. However, their results are not directly applied to an interaction in a rapidly changing environment while driving where eye fixations are unusual activities. Estimation of user intention from eye gaze trajectory is done in several studies [4], usually conducted in indoor simulation where estimation of eye gaze is easy.

3. TOWNSURFER SYSTEM

Fig. 2 shows an overview of our system. The system considers three main input modalities: speech, head pose, and geo-location. Speech is the modality that triggers interactions (= POIs evaluation). The system lists candidate POIs based on the geo-locations at the speech timing. Then, the attention likelihoods for each candidate is calculated based on the head-pose trajectory evaluation model. Finally, the POI identification is done by selecting the POI with maximum POI likelihood, which is calculated by combining the attention likelihood with linguistic likelihood [12, 13, 15]. In this paper, we focus on POIs evaluation (the red circle in Fig. 2) to achieve a better attention likelihood calculation.

The system hardware uses a 3D depth sensor, a GPS, and a microphone. These sensors are installed in our Honda Pilot experimental car. We employ a head pose estimation module [6] that works for 30Hz with filtering.

4. APPROACH

4.1 Overview and Preliminary Results

To model a relationship between the user head motion trajectory and the POI positions, we use two measurements:

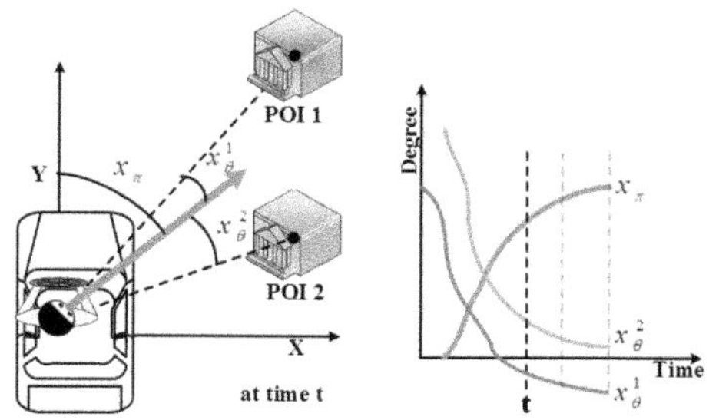

(a) x_π with x_θ^r, at time t (b) x_π with x_θ^r over time

Figure 3: x_π is the head direction degree. x_θ is the relative POI degree

One is the degree between the car forward direction and the face direction, which is called x_π. Another is the relative degree between the face direction and each POI direction, which is called x_θ. The relationship of these two is illustrated in Fig 3(a). When x_θ is small, we can presume that the driver is more likely to be interested in the POI. However, timing is an important factor. For example, in Fig. 3(b), the degree x_θ^1 is smaller then x_θ^2 at time t, but the driver might be on the way to see the POI-2. Thus, we expect x_θ can be small at the end of the looking motion. In addition, x_θ might not be zero. Thus, we will consider the whole motion sequence to handle the motion variation (Sec 4.3). Moreover, since the head motion and speech activity do not necessarily occur simultaneously, we need to select a head motion that relates most closely to the utterance in Fig 1(b). We thus model the relationship between the head pose sequence and the start of speech timing (Sec 4.5).

As a preliminary way to represent a trajectory, we define two categorized trajectories as a vector sequence. Let $x_\pi(t) \in \mathbb{R}$ be the head pose degree at time t. We also let $\Delta x_\pi(t) \in \mathbb{R}$ be the head pose velocity at time t. The moving patterns are defined as h-th meaningful head trajectory, which is $\mathbf{H_h} = (\mathbf{x}_\pi, \mathbf{\Delta x}_\pi)_h$, $h \in [1, H]$, where $\mathbf{x}_\pi = (x_\pi(t_1), ..., x_\pi(t_j))$ and $\mathbf{\Delta x}_\pi = (\Delta x_\pi(t_1), ..., \Delta x_\pi(t_j))$, H is the number of a head pose movement sequence, $j > 0$. Let $x_\theta(t) \in \mathbb{R}$ be the relative degree of the POI and the face direction at time t. Then, each head trajectory, H_h, has r-th candidate POI lists, $\mathbf{P_h^r} = (x_\theta(t_1), ..., x_\theta(t_{j'}))$, where $j > j'$ and $r \in [1, R]$. R is the number of a relative POI degree sequence.

4.2 Looking Motion Detection

The system detects candidate head pose motions that might be related to the driver query. We assume that a meaningful motion occurs before and during the driver query. The system collects candidate POIs from the database based on distance between a car (Pos_{car}) and j-th POI ($Pos_{poi(j)}$). γ is a threshold. Then, the system checks whether current head pose is increasing-decreasing with respect to positive-negative head pose, respectively. If the condition is true, then we collect the pair of point sequences as a meaningful trajectory at the end of speech time.

However, the collected candidate motion sequences $\mathbf{H_h}$ and $\mathbf{P_h^r}$ are not always complete trajectories ($x_\pi(t_1) \neq 0$). In addition, there are different lengths and sampling rates of each trajectory. To overcome these problems, we use the normalization idea proposed in [10]. In our case, because $\mathbf{P_h^r}$ is related to the variation of $\mathbf{H_h}$, $\mathbf{P_h^r}$ can be simply normalized by a reference head trajectory $\mathbf{H_h}$. Thus, we first simply normalize the change scale of $\mathbf{P_h^r}$ by $H_r^j - H_r^1$ for all r to scale target $\mathbf{P_h^r}$ to be the same change scale as $\mathbf{H_h}$. Moreover, we use a normalized discretized time frame, L. The patterns are normalized by $\frac{x_\pi(t_j)-x_\pi(t_1)}{x_\pi(t_j)}$ as a percentage of the complete trajectory.

4.3 Learning a Likelihood Model using GPR

We use the GPR to model POI likelihood (= probability of x_θ given x_π). The model is defined by $x_\theta = f(t) + \epsilon$, where $\epsilon \sim N(0, \sigma^2)$ and $f(t)$ with mean function $m(t) = \mathbb{E}[f(t)] = 0$ and a covariance function $k(t,t') = \mathbb{E}[(f(t) - m(t))(f(t') - m(t'))]$. We chose a kernel function, $k(t_i, t_j)$, as an exponential kernel [14]. When we have an observation vector $(\mathbf{t}, \mathbf{x}_\theta) = \{(t_1, x_\theta(t_1)), ..., (t_n, x_\theta(t_n))\}$, then a zero-mean multivariate Gaussian with a $n \times n$ kernel matrix, $\mathbf{K}'$ with Gaussian noise, is $\mathbf{K}' = \mathbf{K} + \sigma^2\mathbf{I}$. The following posterior density for a test point t^*, $P(x_\theta^*|t^*, \mathbf{t}, \mathbf{x}_\theta)$, is with the mean $\mu(t^*)$ and interpolation variance $\mathbb{V}'(t^*)$:

$$\begin{aligned} \mu(t^*) &= \mathbf{k}(t^*)^T \mathbf{K}'^{-1} \mathbf{z}, \\ \mathbb{V}'(t^*) &= \mathbf{k}(t^*)^T \mathbf{K}'^{-1} (\mathbf{x}_\theta - \mu(t^*))^T (\mathbf{x}_\theta - \mu(t^*)). \end{aligned} \tag{1}$$

where $\mathbf{k}(t^*)$ is the covariance vector between the queries $\mathbf{t}^*$ and the observation $\mathbf{t}$. We consider the interpolation variance $\mathbb{V}'$ that has informative uncertainty measure, which facilitates the model learning with a few training samples with data variability. Detailed GPR is in [14] [11].

4.4 POI Likelihood of the Head Pose Motion

In Sec. 4.3, we defined the model for two classes (motion to look at right and left), χ_k, $k \in [1, 2]$. Using the model, we evaluate the probability density of a normalized test pattern, $\mathbf{x}_\theta$ to measure similarity as a form of likelihood in the given training class:

$$L_h^r(k) = \frac{1}{J} \sum_{i=1}^{J} p(x_\theta^*(i) | \hat{t}(i)^*, \chi_k), \tag{2}$$

where J is the number of time frame.

4.5 Timing Model of Head Pose Motion

Let $\mathbf{T} = (T_1, ..., T_H)$ be an independent sample drawn from the distribution of timing deviation between the start of speech T_{start} and the end time of h-th head pose sequence t_j^h where $T_h = t_j^h - T_{start}$, $h \in [1, H]$. Then we employ kernel density estimation (KDE) for an unknown density f. The shape of the function $\hat{f}_B(x) = \frac{1}{hB}\sum_{i=1}^{h} K(\frac{x-T_i}{B})$ is estimated where B is a bandwidth. We choose a kernel function, K, as a Epanechnikov kernel [1]. The timing model is demonstrated in Fig. 4(b). Once we have $\hat{f}_B(x)$, we can get the weight of each head trajectory. That is $\omega_h = \delta \cdot \hat{f}_B(t_h)$ for $h \in [1, H]$, where δ is a normalization factor. Then, the the head motion likelihood toward POIs is defined by the weighted sum $\sum_{h=1}^{H} \omega_h \cdot L_h^r(k)$.

5. EXPERIMENTS

5.1 Data Collection

We collected data using a test route that passes through downtown Mountain View. We manually constructed our database containing 250 POIs (restaurants and companies) in this area. Each POI database entry has geo-location (latitude and longitude). We collected data from 15 subjects drivers. They were asked to drive the test route and make any queries about surrounding buildings. Each subject made two round trips using the test routes (four sessions for each subject). In total, we collected 464 queries with a target POI. The user-intended POIs were manually annotated by confirming the intended target POI based on the speech recorded during the test sessions.

5.2 Baseline and Proposed Approaches

We use the two baseline methods used in the paper [12]. One is capturing the instant value of x_θ at the start of speech timing. The second is a Gaussian mixture model (GMM)-based method that uses a start of speech time to capture the POIs distance from the car position. Additionally, we employ two baselines that use x_θ or GMM at a peak-heading (end-of-the-motion) timing t_j from Sec. 4.2. To carefully investigate the effects of 1) using trajectory and 2) timing information, we evaluate two variations of the proposed method. One picks the end timing t_j of the head pose sequence that has the closest timing between the end time t_j and T_{start}. Another uses the timing model based on head pose sequence. In summary, we compare the following methods.

1. Use x_θ at the **S**tart-of-speech timing/ **P**eak-of-heading timing, **(BASE-S/ BASE-P)**; the likelihood calculation is that the smaller x_θ of POIs is the higher score.
2. Use distance to the POI at the **S**tart-of-speech timing/ **P**eak-of-heading timing, **(GMM-S/ GMM-P)**; the likelihood calculation is based on the trained distance modeled by GMM [12].
3. Use GPR (with or without timing weight) for the likelihood calculation

We judge the system successfully understands a user query when the likelihood of the target (user-intended) POI is the highest. The chance rate, given by the average of the inverse number of candidate POIs in the POI look-up, is 10.0%.

We have two training conditions: *user-independent* and *user-dependent*. In the *user-independent* condition, models (GPR, GMM parameters, KDE function for timing) are trained based on user-based cross-validation, where data from 14 subjects is used to train the model and the data from the remaining subject is used to test it. The *user-dependent* condition uses session-based cross-validation. Three of four sessions by a subject are used for training. The remaining session is used for evaluation. All training data is complemented by stable data, which consists of 40 complete trajectories by another subject.

5.3 Analysis of Results

We first analyzed the effect of using head pose trajectory by comparing BASE-S, BASE-P, and GPR. Table 1 shows the success rates of the above-mentioned methods. Using peak-of-heading timing shows 12% improvement over the method, which uses start-of-speech timing in the *user-independent* condition. Considering trajectory patterns in GP is improved by 3%. These results support the hypothesis that a head trajectory pattern is still useful to improve the system even in the *user-dependent* case.

Next, we evaluate the timing effects in Table 1. Using timing information degraded the performance from 55.7% to 52.5% in the *user-independent* condition. We see a similar result in BASE-P. This indicates that the timing model might be user-dependent.

	BASE-S	BASE-P	GMM-S	GMM-P	GPR
w/o timing	40.8	52.8	34.0	33.3	55.7
w/ timing		50.4		33.3	52.5

Table 1: Comparison of success rate (%) in the user-independent condition

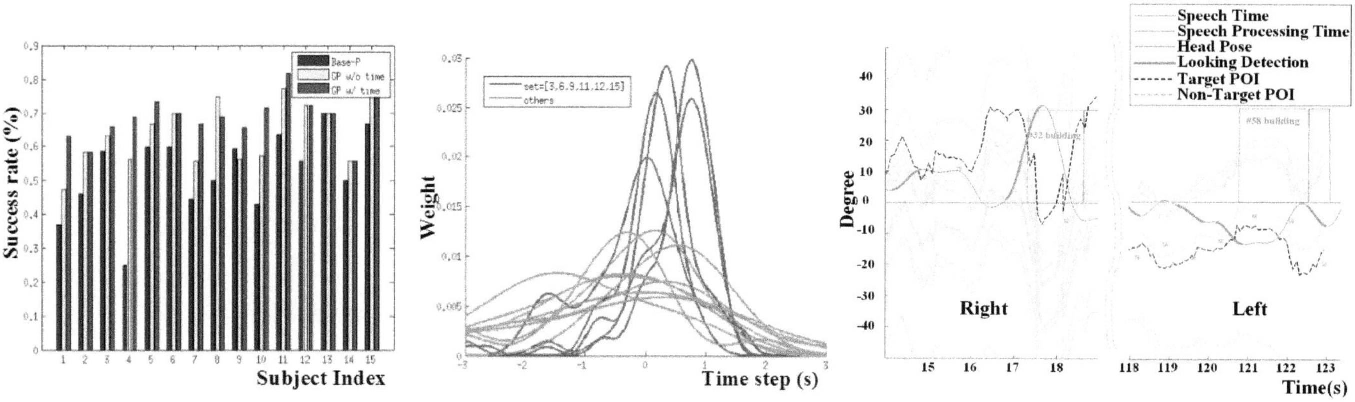

(a) Success rate per each driver (the user-dependent training condition):BASE-P and GPR w/ or w/o timing

(b) Kernel density estimation results of 15 users that shows two groups: consistent timing and non-consistent timing

(c) This shows the real signal: speech timing, speech processing timing, x_θ, and x_π over time. Right and Left head pose motions are shown separately.

Figure 4: 4(a) and 4(b) show the timing model of the user-dependent training condition. 4(c) demonstrates the results of the real signal.

	BASE-S	BASE-P	GMM-S	GMM-P	GPR
w/o timing	40.4	53.2	41.8	41.1	63.5
w/ timing		53.6		42.9	67.7

Table 2: Comparison of success rate (%) in the user-dependent condition

We then evaluate the methods in the user-dependent training condition. The results are shown in Table 2. In this condition, using the GPR method shows outstanding improvement (10%) over the BASE-P. Additionally, combining timing information with the GPR method achieves a success rate of 67.7%, outperforming the method that does not use timing information (63.5%). Considering that this performance (67.7%) is achieved with a fewer number of training data compared to the user-independent condition (52.5 % in Table 1), this indicates that the speech timing and the head pose motion have user-dependent patterns. While a 67.7% in success rate is not satisfactory, the success rate goes to 81.2% if we consider 2nd rank in the *user-dependent* case. The performance will be still higher when we combine the attention likelihood with linguistic likelihood (*c.f,* Fig. 2).

Finally, we compared the consistency of speech timing and improvement by using timing information. Success rates per user (Fig. 4(a)) and kernel density estimation results per user (Fig. 4(b)) is illustrated. We can see that our GPR-based method with timing is generally more effective for users with non-consistent timing. Actually, the performances of subjects number 1,4,7, and 10 are increased remarkably.

Fig. 4(c) demonstrates the results of the looking motion detection with several POIs in a query. There are several motion patterns; moreover, POIs are not necessarily smooth and at a certain value at the time of facing the target POI.

6. CONCLUSION

We addressed the identification of the driver's interest point using the head pose movement for situated dialog systems. We focused on two issues: (1) modeling the uncertain user head pose patterns, and (2) optimizing the driver's time-varying interest point.

The effectiveness of the proposed methods was confirmed based on evaluation using user-independent and dependent training conditions. We achieved an approximately 68% success rate, rising to about 81% success when including 2nd rank POI identification.

7. REFERENCES

[1] A. W. Bowman and A. Azzalini. *Applied Smoothing Techniques for Data Analysis.* Oxford Press, USA, 1997.

[2] J. Chai and Z. Prasov. Fusing eye gaze with speech recognition hypotheses to resolve exophoric reference in situated dialogue. In *Proc. EMNLP*, 2010.

[3] D. Cohen, A. Chandrashekaran, I. Lane, and A. Raux. the HRI-CMU corpus of situated in-car interactions. In *Procddings of IWSDS*, pages 201–212, 2014.

[4] J. Dodane, T. Hirayama, H. Kawashima, and T. Matsuyama. Estimation of user interest using time delay features between proactive content presentation and eye movements. In *Proc. Affective Computing and Intelligent Interaction*, 2009.

[5] A. Doshi and M. Trivedi. Head and Eye Gaze Dynamics during Visual Attention Shifts in Complex Environments. *Journal of Vision*, 12.

[6] G. Fanelli, J. Gall, and L. Van Gool. Real time head pose estimation with random regression forests. In *Computer Vision and Pattern Recognition (CVPR)*, pages 617–624, June 2011.

[7] L. Fletcher and A. Zelinsky. Driver inattention detection based on eye gaze - road event correlation. *Internation Journal of Robotic Research*, 28(6):774–801, 2009.

[8] R. Iida, M. Yasuhara, and T. Tokunaga. Multi-modal reference resolution in situated dialogue by integrating linguistic and extra-linguistic clues. In *Proc. IJCNLP*, pages 84–92, 2011.

[9] C. Kennington, S. Kousidis, and D. Schlangen. Interpreting situated dialogue utterances: an update model that uses speech, gaze, and gesture information. In *Proc. SIGDIAL*, 2013.

[10] K. Kim, D. Lee, and I. Essa. Gaussian Process Regression Flow for Analysis of Motion Trajectories. In *Proceedings of International Conference on Computer Vision*, Nov. 2011.

[11] Y.-H. Kim, D. A. Shell, C. Ho, and S. Saripalli. Spatial Interpolation for Robotic Sampling: Uncertainty with two Models of Variance. In *Proceedings of International Symposium on Experimental Robotics*, Quebec, Canada, 2012.

[12] T. Misu, A. Raux, R. Gupta, and I. Lane. Situated Language Understanding at 25 Miles per Hour. In *Proceedings of A Workshop*, Dec. 2014.

[13] T. Misu, A. Raux, I. Lane, J. Devassy, and R. Gupta. Situated Multi-modal Dialog System in Vehicles. In *Proceedings of International Conference on Multimodal Interaction*, 2013.

[14] C. E. Rasmussen and C. K. I. Williams. *Gaussian Processes for Machine Learning.* MIT Press, Cambridge, MA, USA, 2006.

[15] A. Raux and Y. Ma. Efficient Probabilistic Tracking of User Goal and Dialog History for Spoken Dialog Systems. In *Proceedings of Interspeech*, page 801, Aug.

An Explorative Study on Crossmodal Congruence Between Visual and Tactile Icons Based on Emotional Responses

Taekbeom Yoo
POSTECH
Pohang, Korea
taekbeomyoo@postech.ac.kr

Yongjae Yoo
POSTECH
Pohang, Korea
dreamseed@postech.ac.kr

Seungmoon Choi
POSTECH
Pohang, Korea
choism@postech.ac.kr

ABSTRACT

Tactile icons, brief tactile stimuli conveying abstract information, have found their use in various applications, and their use with visual elements is increasing on touchscreen user interfaces. However, effective design guidelines of tactile icons for crossmodal use have not been established. This paper addresses this problem by investigating the congruence between visual and tactile icons based on the hypothesis that emotional agreement between the icons improves congruence. The validity of this hypothesis was examined in three experiments. In Exp. I, we selected common visual icons and estimated their emotional responses using the circumplex model of affect. Tactile icons to be used as a pair were designed in Exp. II by varying their amplitude, frequency, and envelope (rhythm). Their emotional responses were also evaluated. In Exp. III, the congruence of 192 crossmodal icons made by combining the visual icons (8) and the tactile icons (24) was evaluated, and these congruence scores were compared with the valence and arousal scores of the two unimodal icons obtained in Exp. I and II. Experimental results suggested that the congruence of a crossmodal icon highly depends on the agreement in the emotional responses between its visual and tactile icons. This finding provides feasibility to the development of general design guidelines and heuristics for crossmodal icons that rely on the relationship between the emotional responses from the individual modalities. Our approach is expected to advance the current practice that associates the physical parameters between the different senses with better intuitiveness and simplicity.

Categories and Subject Descriptors

H.5.1 [**Information Interfaces and Presentation**]: Multimedia Information Systems; H.5.2 [**Information Interfaces and Presentation**]: User Interfaces—*Haptic I/O; User-centered design*

Keywords

crossmodal; visual icon; tactile icon; congruence; emotion; affect

ICMI'14, November 12–16, 2014, Istanbul, Turkey.

http://dx.doi.org/10.1145/2663204.2663231.

1. INTRODUCTION

Touchscreen is a versatile platform for multimodal human-computer interaction (HCI), providing simultaneous touch input and visual output. Its well-recognized drawback is the lack of programmable haptic feedback, and researchers have put a great amount of effort to improve on it. Common approaches use mechanical vibration [5], electrovibration [2], and surface friction modulation [20], even kinesthetic feedback by translating the touchscreen itself [30]. However, relatively less attention has been paid to how to design tactile feedback that feels seamless with the visual content. In this context, this paper proposes a framework for the design of *emotionally congruent crossmodal icons* that combine visual and tactile icons displayed on a touchscreen, as well as an explorative assessment of its feasibility.

1.1 Related Work

Tactile icons, also called tactons [3], refer to short tactile stimuli that are associated with abstract meanings. Tactile icons are not only valuable to users with visual impairments, but have also found adequate use cases in which the user's visual attention is unavailable and/or sound feedback is inappropriate. Most research on tactile icons used vibrotactile stimuli, exploring their design space to establish effective design heuristics and guidelines. Many design variables have been examined, such as amplitude, frequency, duration, waveform, envelope, rhythm, and body site [33, 4, 32, 17, 22]. The main performance measures involved were the discriminability, identifiability, and memorability of tactile icons [27]. Tactile icons are now used in a variety of applications, e.g., for improved key entry on a touchscreen [13], eyes-free navigation [9], and haptic warnings during driving [6].

Research efforts have also progressed to crossmodal interaction. Crossmodal interaction uses different senses to provide the same information, while multimodal interaction can encode different but coordinated information into multiple senses [12]. To our knowledge, research on crossmodal icons involving the tactile sense was initiated by Hoggan and her colleagues [12, 14]. Their first work pertained to those combining audio and tactile icons, focusing on the transfer of the pre-learned knowledge about audio (or tactile) icons to the learning of tactile (or audio) icons [12]. This work was extended to crossmodal icons that involve all of the visual, auditory, and tactile senses using congruence as the criterion [14]. In this context, *congruence* was defined as an intuitive harmony or match between the percepts of feedback from different modalities. Using eight visual buttons and four types of tactile feedback, as well as the sound feedback produced by the vibrotactile actuator itself, the congruence between the visual and tactile elements was evaluated to find the visual and tactile *physical* features that allow for high congruence. This pioneering work inspired our present study.

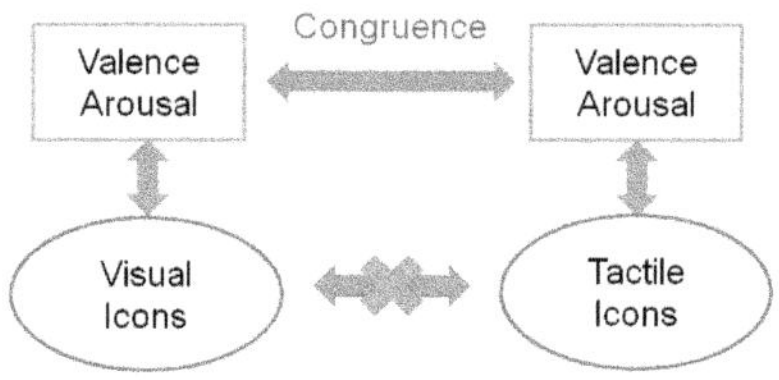

Figure 1: Proposed framework for studying the crossmodal congruence of visuotactile icons.

The research status on crossmodal icons including tactile feedback cannot be said mature at the moment. The most critical difficulty arises from the huge space of design parameters and their possible interplays. To tackle this problem, we propose a framework that is based on the emotional responses of visual and tactile icons. In fact, there has been increasing interest in understanding the emotional responses that synthetic tactile stimuli can elicit. For example, six emoticons used in instant messaging were matched to intuitively-designed tactile icons to enrich user experience [25]. It was also demonstrated that four distinctive emotions can be communicated using a simple haptic knob [31]. Using a rotating cylinder that stimulated the user's finger, Salminen et al. assessed the effects of several physical parameters on emotional responses in terms of pleasantness, arousal, approachability, and dominance [28]. They also conducted a similar study for thermal stimuli [29]. In [24], a few methods that induce the tactile sensation of movement, e.g., saltation, using three distant actuators were compared for their effects on pleasantness, arousal, and continuity. Besides, a small robotic creature was able to inform its emotional state through haptic responses, better in valence than arousal [36]. Despite these endeavors, comprehensive and thorough knowledge necessary to account for the relationships between the various parameters of tactile stimuli and their resulting emotional responses still lacks for competent design. This is in spite of the prevalence of tactile displays in HCI.

1.2 Proposed Framework

In this study, we investigate the feasibility of a new approach to understanding the crossmodal congruence between visual and tactile icons. The main idea is to introduce an additional layer that explicitly associates the emotional responses of visual and tactile icons. To this end, we rely on the circumplex of affect, a widely-used dimensional model of emotion [26]. This model is based on the hypothesis that each basic emotion can be represented using bipolar continua, e.g., valence (pleasant vs. unpleasant) and arousal (aroused vs. relaxed) [11]. A third dimension, dominance (dominant vs. submissive), is also frequently used [18].

Figure 1 further depicts our research concepts. As discussed in [14], the physical features that describe visual and tactile icons are greatly diverse. They include, for visual icons, color, shape, size, depth, and texture, and for tactile icons, waveform, amplitude, frequency, envelope, and duration, to just name a few. This large number of associated physical variables can make it unfruitful to find design guidelines and heuristics for congruent crossmodal icons by empirically matching between the parameters. Our approach attempts to reduce the dimensionality of the search space by introducing an *emotional layer*. We also expect that congruence could be better explained between the emotional dimensions of vision and touch, and their intuitiveness would facilitate the design process.

Another motivation behind our envisioned approach is the emergence of *emotional icons*. While traditional icons convey the states or actions of computing, emotional icons represent the user's emotional states (the former will be called *objective icons* for distinction). The use of emotional icons is becoming more and more popular, especially in computer-based personal communications such as e-mails, text messages, and social networking services (SNSs). If a crossmodal icon is objective, users are likely to understand its associated meaning by looking at its visual icon; vision greatly outperforms touch for recognition. The role of its tactile pair may remain negligible for objective information, regardless of its design or congruence to the visual icon. Tactile icons are by nature far more difficult to indicate objective information, and icon-meaning association for tactile icons generally requires a considerable amount of learning [10, 27]. If a crossmodal icon is emotional, however, its tactile icon is expected to have much elevated influence on users' emotional responses to the crossmodal icon. Touch is the most private, affective, sensual, and empathetic among the five human senses [23]. As a consequence, our proposed framework may be better suited to understanding the crossmodal congruence when the visual icon is emotional than when it is objective.

1.3 Paper Overview

We carried out three user experiments in order to answer the following two research questions:

Q1: *Can the proposed emotion-based framework account for the congruence between visual and tactile icons?*

Q2: *Which of emotional and objective icons are more appropriate for the emotion-based framework?*

In Exp. I (Section 2), we conducted an internet survey to select eight visual icons, four emotional and four objective, and evaluated their valence and arousal in a controlled experiment. In Exp. II (Section 3), we designed 24 amplitude-modulated vibrotactile stimuli by varying their amplitude (2), frequency (2), and envelope (6). The valence and arousal of the 24 tactile icons were then rated. In Exp. III (Section 4), participants assessed the degrees of congruence between the 8 visual icons and the 24 tactile icons, so a total of 192 crossmodal icons. These results were then compared to the results of Exp. I and II to find answers to the two research questions. All the experiments were more exploratory than hypothesis-driven to examine the feasibility of our new emotion-based approach. Also note that our visual and tactile icons were tailored to our research aims and disparate from those used in [14].

We consider that the contributions of this study are: (1) Proposition of a new emotion-based framework for the design of congruent crossmodal visuotactile icons; (2) Investigation of the effects of the amplitude, frequency, and envelope of tactile icons on emotional responses using the valence-arousal space and associated design guidelines (Exp. II); (3) Confirmation of the feasibility of the new emotion-based approach (Exp. III); and (4) Derivations of some design guidelines for emotionally congruent crossmodal visuotactile icons (Exp. III).

2. EXPERIMENT I: VISUAL ICONS

The aims of Exp. I reported in this section were to determine the visual icons to be used in Exp. III and then to evaluate their valence and arousal.

2.1 Methods

2.1.1 Selection of Visual Icons

In order to select a set of visual icons to use in Exp. III, we first collected many visual icons from various sources available on the

Table 1: Visual icons selected in Exp. I.

ID	Icon	Meaning	Weight Emotional	Weight Objective
V1		Thumbs up	72.2	27.8
V2		Thumbs down	–	–
V3		Smiley face	70.6	29.4
V4		Long face	76.3	23.7
V5		Chat, talk	47.8	52.2
V6		Edit	–	–
V7		Find	27.5	72.5
V8		Mail, message	30.6	69.4

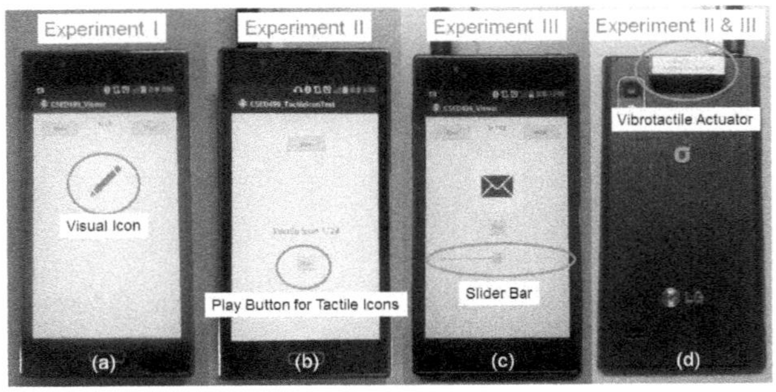

Figure 2: Smart phone with a vibrotactile actuator used in all experiments. The left three pictures show the GUIs used in Exp. I–III. The right picture shows the back panel.

internet. Using this initial set, we carried out a web-based survey with 22 participants to select representative visual icons. The selection focused on two classes of visual icons, one group that conveys objective information (e.g., search, mail arrival, etc.) and the other group that signifies subjective emotion (e.g., happy, sad, etc.). This was to investigate our hypothesis for the research question Q2 that visual icons representing emotional responses may match tactile icons better if the tactile icons elicit similar emotional responses. In the survey, participants rated each icon with two weights for its emotional and objective content so that the sum of the two weights was to be 100.

Based on the survey results, we selected eight visual icons that are all used frequently in SNS, as shown in Table 1. The first three icons we chose had higher weights for emotion (V1–thumbs up, V3–smiley face, and V4–long face). Then we added V2 (thumbs down) as a pair of V1. We also selected three objective icons (V5–chat, talk, V7–find, search, and V8–mail, message) on the basis of the survey results. Another icon (V6–edit, write) frequently used in the same context was added to the set, completing the eight icons. It was interesting that V5 resulted in almost even emotional and objective weights. Since V5 is used to initiate chats with people, its emotional implication seems to be as strong as its functional meaning. Using these eight visual icons, we carried out a within-subjects controlled experiment to assess their valence and arousal.

2.1.2 *Apparatus*

To comply with the context of our research, all experiments used a smart phone (LG-F160S, 4.7" touchscreen). The visual icons were displayed on the touchscreen of the smart phone, one at a time, all in the same size of 2.06×2.06 cm (250×250 pixel). In Exp. I, a graphical user interface (GUI) showed only a visual icon with previous and next buttons (Figure 2(a)).

2.1.3 *Participants*

Participants were 18 volunteers who were regular users of a smart phone and SNS (9 male and 9 female; 18–26 years old with a mean 21.6), without known sensorimotor impairment. They were paid $3 after the experiment.

2.1.4 *Procedure*

Before the experiment, the experimenter explained the concepts associated with valence, arousal, and emotion with examples to each participant. The participant was allowed to ask any questions in this period. The participant then signed on an informed consent form and started the experiment.

In the experiment, each participant rated the valence and arousal of the eight visual icons rendered on the smart phone one after another. This was done using an answer sheet, which showed both a horizontal line (for valence) and a vertical line (for arousal) and their crossing point (the neutral point on both axes). Both lines were 6.4-cm long. The participant was asked to look at each visual icon, decide its perceived valence and arousal, and then mark the corresponding point within the 2D valence-arousal square.

The experiment consisted of two blocks of trials, and each visual icon was tested once in each block. The first block was to enable the participants to experience all the icons and decide their range and scale of rating. The data of the first block were discarded, and only the data of the second block were used in data analysis. The order of presenting the icons was randomized for each participant within each block.

Each participant completed the experiment in 20 min. After the experiment, we linearly scaled the participants' valence and arousal ratings recorded on the answer sheet to scores between -100 and 100. These scaled scores were used in data analysis.

2.2 Results and Discussion

The results of Exp. I are visualized in Figure 3, which shows the mean valence and arousal scores averaged across the participants for the eight visual icons. The ranges of standard errors (SEs) were 2.7–6.8 for valence and 4.9–9.6 for arousal. These values were relatively large, but it was expected in subjective scaling of emotions. Individual SEs are not shown for visibility.

For the emotional icons, V1 and V3 resulted in highly pleasant responses (valence score 63.5 and 67.2), while their negative pairs V2 and V4 led to quite unpleasant responses (-54.7 and -62.2). The arousal scores of the four emotional icons were relatively similar to each other (23.3–47.4), indicating that they were moderately exciting. The valence scores of the four objective icons were all positive but distributed in a much narrower range (12.7–26.4). Their arousal scores (-1.2–26.9) also had a relatively small variance, and were generally lower than those of the emotional icons.

One-way repeated-measures ANOVA showed that visual icon was statistically significant for both valence ($F(7,119) = 76.30, p < 0.0001$) and arousal ($F(7,119) = 3.57, p = 0.0016$). We also conducted Tukey's test for post-hoc multiple pairwise comparisons. It identified three statistically different groups for valence: {V1, V3},

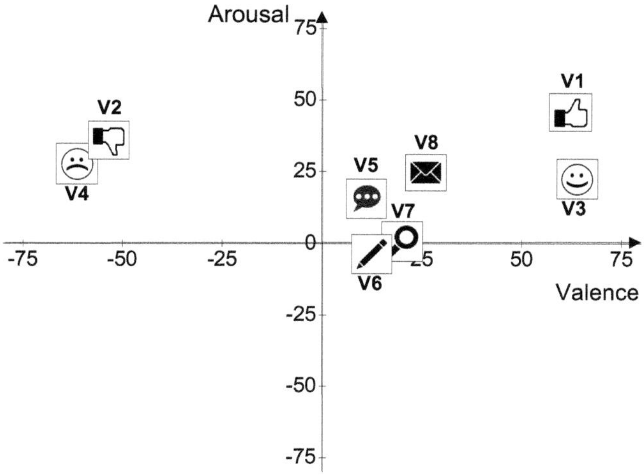

Figure 3: Mean valence and arousal scores of the visual icons.

{V2, V4}, and {V4, V5, V6, V7}.[1] For arousal, only {V1} and {V6, V7} showed significant pairwise differences.

Therefore, the results of Exp. I can be summarized as follows: (1) The emotional and objective icons belonged to different clusters in the valence dimension; (2) The emotional icons were either highly pleasant or highly unpleasant, and were similarly arousing; (3) The objective icons were moderately pleasant with similar scores. They also resulted in similar arousal scores; and (4) The arousal scores of the emotional icons were generally higher than for the objective icons, but with only the two pairs of statistically significant differences.

Overall, Exp. I demonstrated that the eight visual icons are good representatives of the emotional characteristics of emotional and objective icons, adequately reflecting our intent. Also note that we tried to minimize the arousal differences among the icons by drawing them in the same size and color (black and white) [35, 8]. An alternative set could be those including a large number of visual icons that are rather densely and uniformly distributed in the valence-arousal space. However, it would increase the number of visual icons, which subsequently hampers a full factorial design of visual and tactile icons in Exp. III for thorough exploration. For this reason, we needed to keep the total number of crossmodal icons reasonable, and made the number of visual icons (8) much less than the number of tactile icons (24; see Section 3). This decision indeed put more emphasis on tactile icons as their emotional characteristics are far less understood than those of visual icons.

3. EXPERIMENT II: TACTILE ICONS

In Exp. II, we designed a large number of tactile icons by varying three variables that were expected to affect the emotional responses of tactile icons and then measured users' emotional responses on the valence-arousal space.

3.1 Methods

3.1.1 Design of Tactile Icons

For the design of tactile icons, we relied on the previous literature and pilot tests in order to find a set of tactile icons that were likely

[1]This notation means that any icon in a set S_1 and any icon in a set S_2 have a statistically significant pairwise difference at a significance level $\alpha = 0.05$, but any two icons in the same set S_1 or S_2 do not.

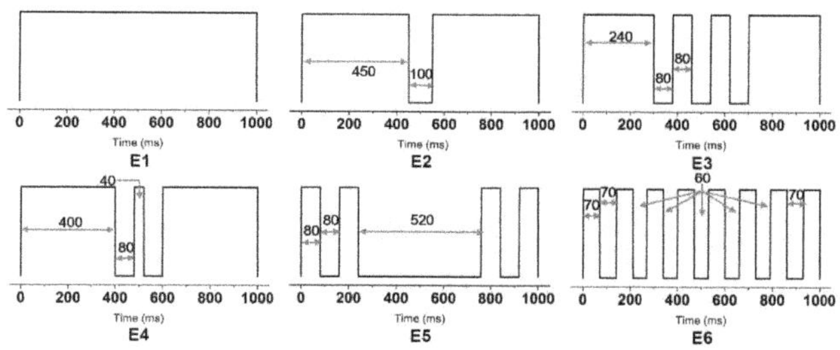

Figure 4: Signal envelopes used for tactile icon design.

to vary systematically in both valence and arousal. To this end, we combined 2 amplitudes (weak and strong), 2 frequencies (100 and 250 Hz), and 6 envelopes (Figure 4), as follows:

$$x(t) = A\,E(t)\,\sin(2\pi F t), \qquad (1)$$

where $x(t)$ is the vibration waveform, t is the time, A is the amplitude, $E(t)$ is the envelope function, and F is the frequency. This method, called amplitude modulation, is effective in designing easily distinguishable tactile icons [33, 32], as well as in controlling their perceptual impression (e.g., rough or smooth) [22]. The actual amplitudes were adjusted so that weak and strong vibrations had measured amplitudes around 1.5 and 3.0 G[2], respectively, when the smart phone was grasped in a user's hand. The measurements were made along the main vibration direction (left and right in Figure 2) using an external miniature accelerometer attached to the smartphone. In addition, all the tactile icons were 1-s long. This duration is sufficient for stable perception, not affected by temporal tactile summation [34], and also corresponds to a medium value for tactile icons (generally several hundred ms to 2 s [32]). These 24 tactile icons are denoted by A{w or s}F{100 or 250}E{1–6} hereafter.

The three parameters were chosen based on the following rationale: (1) *Amplitude*: As the perceived intensity of a tactile stimulus increases with its amplitude, increasing the amplitude was expected to increase the arousal of the tactile icon; (2) *Frequency*: The signal frequency affects the perceptual quality of tactile stimuli in systematic manner, as well established in [15]. At a high frequency (e.g., 250 Hz), the stimuli are mediated by the Pacinian (PC) channel and perceived as smooth vibrations [5]. At a low frequency (e.g., 100 Hz), responses from the RA (rapidly adapting) channel play an important role, leading to rougher sensations [5]. Hence, we expected that signal frequency would be relevant to the valence of tactile icons; and (3) *Envelope*: In our design using amplitude modulation, envelope is the only factor that determines the rhythm of a tactile icon. Not only rhythm is the most effective design variable for highly discriminable tactile icons [32], but it also continuously changes the subjective impression of vibrotactile stimuli from smooth vibrational sensations to rough, fluttering ones [22]. As such, we hypothesized that valence would be the highest with E1 and the lowest with E6. We also confirmed that the 24 tactile icons could be easily recognized by conducting pilot experiments.

3.1.2 Participants

We recruited 18 healthy participants for this experiment (9 male and 9 female; 19–25 years old with an average 21.0). They were regular users of a smart phone and SNS. They were paid $5 after the experiment.

[2]Gravitational acceleration unit.

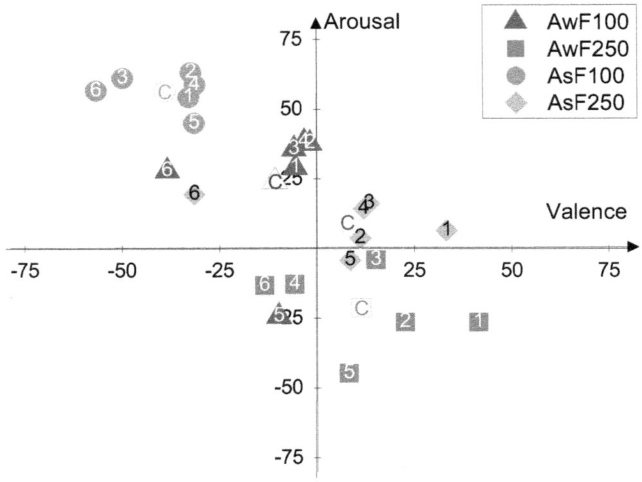

Figure 5: Mean valence and arousal scores of the tactile icons. A number *i* inside each symbol represents the envelope (E*i*) used for that tactile icon. The centroids of the four amplitude-frequency clusters are marked with C within their symbols.

3.1.3 Apparatus

A wide-band vibrotactile actuator (TactileLabs, Haptuator II; bandwidth 100–500 Hz) was attached on the back panel of the smart phone, as shown in Figure 2(d). The actuator was connected to the phone using its audio output through a custom power amplifier. The tactile icons were generated by the actuator. A GUI displayed a play button that allowed the participant to feel the tactile icons repeatedly (Figure 2(b)), without visual icons.

3.1.4 Procedure

The experimental procedure was almost identical to that of Exp. I. The only exception was that participants evaluated the valence and arousal of the 24 tactile icons while holding the smart phone in their non-dominant hand. The experiment took about 30 min for each participant.

3.2 Results and Discussion

Experimental results are summarized in the valence-arousal space shown in Figure 5. Each symbol represents the mean valence and arousal scores across the participants for the corresponding tactile icon. SEs ranged from 6.1 to 14.2 for valence and from 4.5 to 12.5 for arousal, but they are not drawn for clarity.

Visual inspection of Figure 5 suggested four clusters of the tactile icons depending on their amplitude and frequency. The centroids of the clusters were (-10.8, 24.2) for AwF100, (11.3, -21.3) for AwF250, (-39.0, 56.5) for AsF100, and (7.8, 9.3) for AsF250. We also conducted a three-way repeated-measures ANOVA with the three independent factors of amplitude, frequency, and envelope. It verified the following findings: (1) *Amplitude*: Increasing the amplitude of a tactile icon decreased its valence ($F(1,17) = 20.00, p = 0.0003$), but increased its arousal ($F(1,17) = 48.49, p < 0.0001$), both with statistical significance. While the latter was well expected, the former may also be relevant to the fact that increasing the amplitude of a vibrotactile stimulus decreases its perceived pitch [19]; (2) *Frequency*: Increasing the frequency of a tactile icon increased its valence ($F(1,17) = 15.07, p = 0.0012$), but decreased its arousal ($F(1,17) = 36.35, p < 0.0001$), both with statistical significance. The former was well anticipated. The latter is likely to have also resulted from the fact that the perceived intensity of a vibrotactile stimulus decreases with its frequency if its amplitude remains constant in an acceleration unit [16]; and (3) *Envelope*: The envelope of a tactile icon had a significant effect on both its valence and arousal ($F(5,85) = 6.66, p < 0.0001$ and $F(5,85) = 5.62, p = 0.0002$). Varying the stimulus envelope from E1 (a constant 1-s pulse) to E6 (eight short-duration pulses) generally decreased their valence, but its effect on arousal was not clearly observed. Tukey's test for post-hoc pairwise comparisons showed that for valence {E1, E2, E3, E4, E5} and {E6} and for arousal {E1, E2, E3, E4, E6} and {E5} had significant differences ($p < 0.05$). E6 consisted of many short pulses, which could have made it distinctive from the other icons in terms of valence. E5 had two short pulses at both its start and end with a long intermediate recess. This seems to have made it less arousing (more relaxing) than the others.

Interaction terms between the main factors were significant only with amplitude × frequency ($F(1,17) = 12.10, p = 0.0029$) and frequency × envelope ($F(5,85) = 2.60, p = 0.0308$) for valence and amplitude × envelope ($F(5,85) = 2.52, p = 0.0354$) for arousal. The first significant interaction term was caused by the similar mean valence scores of AwF250 and AsF250 (11.3 and 7.8), but interpretations of the latter two terms were not clear.

The above results can be compiled to the following *guidelines for the design of tactile icons with desired emotional responses*: (1) To increase the valence of a tactile icon, one can decrease its amplitude or increase its frequency, and vice versa; (2) To increase the arousal of a tactile icon, one can increase its amplitude or decrease its frequency, and vice versa; and (3) The valence of a tactile icon can also be increased by changing its envelope from one consisting of many short pulses to a long constant envelope. It is noted that guidelines (1) and (2) should be accepted with care. Increasing amplitude or frequency to be much higher than the tested range (3.0 G or 250 Hz, respectively) saturates increase in perceived intensity or pitch, resulting in no salient effects on emotional responses.

There were a few other observations that deserved discussion. First, the range of the mean valence scores obtained with the tactile icons (-56.6–41.5) was generally narrower than that for the visual icons (-62.2–67.2), despite the substantial variances in the three parameters of tactile icons. Second, the range of the mean arousal scores was generally wider for the tactile icons (-44.8–63.4) than for the visual icons (-1.2–47.4). It is reminded that the arousal of the visual icons was controlled by presenting them in the same size and color in Exp. I. Lastly, the tactile icons were mostly distributed in the second and fourth quadrants of the valence-arousal space. This implies that our icon set did not include those highly pleasant and highly aroused or highly unpleasant and highly relaxed. Designing such tactile icons might be challenging, given the contradictory effects of amplitude and frequency on valence and arousal observed in Exp. II and the general correlation existing between valence and arousal [1].

4. EXPERIMENT III: CROSSMODAL CONGRUENCE

Using the visual and tactile icons designed and analyzed in Exp. I and II, we carried out Exp. III to investigate the degree of congruence between the visual and the tactile icons.

4.1 Methods

4.1.1 Participants

The participants of Exp. II also participated in this experiment. Since most people do not have prior experiences of evaluating the properties of various tactile stimuli, we kept the same participants

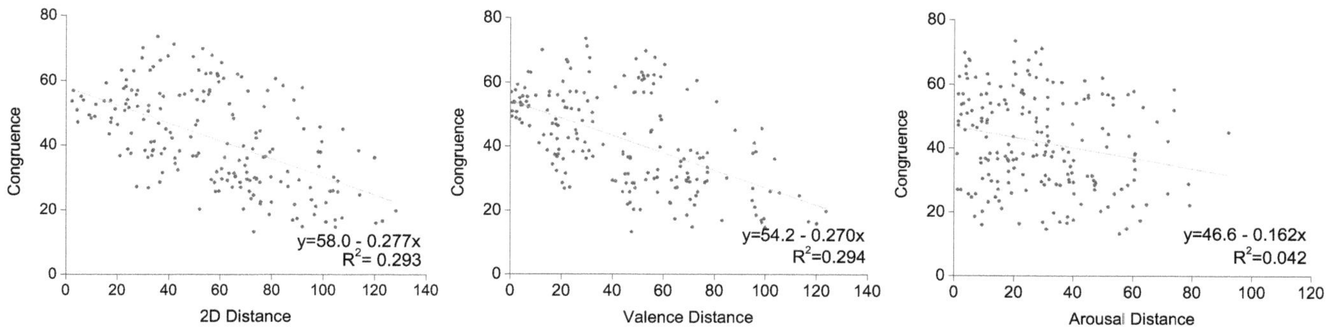

Figure 6: Scatter plots with the regression results of congruence.

to minimize the need for familiarization steps with the tactile icons. The participants were paid $10 after the experiment.

4.1.2 Apparatus

In this experiment, the touchscreen of the smart phone presented both a visual icon and a play button for a tactile icon, as shown in Figure 2(c). The GUI also included a slider bar to obtain participants' responses for crossmodal congruence.

4.1.3 Procedure

The crossmodal icons used in this experiment were made by pairing one of the 8 visual icons and one of the 24 tactile icons, designed and assessed in Exp. I and II, respectively. Each participant perceived all of the 192 ($= 8 \times 24$) crossmodal icons and rated their degree of congruence. The participant was instructed to perceive each crossmodal icon and evaluate the degree of harmony between its visual and tactile stimuli based on their own criteria. Then the participant entered a congruence score using the slider bar, which was scaled to a 0–100 range by the experimental program for data analysis. The other procedure was the same as that of Exp. I and II. Each participant could complete the experiment in one hour.

4.2 Results and Discussion

The main aim of this experiment was to explore the relationships between the emotional responses of visual and tactile icons and their user-perceived congruence. Therefore, we looked at correlations between the relevant variables. Let (v_V, a_V) be the valence and arousal scores of a visual icon measured in Exp. I and (v_T, a_T) be those of a tactile icon measured in Exp. II. For each pair of a visual and a tactile icon, we computed the 2D Euclidian distance of their valence and arousal scores, $\|(v_V, a_V) - (v_T, a_T)\|$, as well as the valence distance $|v_V - v_T|$ and the arousal distance $|a_V - a_T|$.[3] Each of these terms were compared with the congruence scores measured in Exp. III, resulting in the correlation coefficients (Pearson's r) shown in Table 2.

All of the correlation coefficients were negative, indicating that the congruence improved as the differences in the emotional responses decreased. When all the crossmodal icons were included in the analysis, the 2D distance and the valence distance had moderate correlations (r =-0.54 and -0.54), while the arousal distance had quite a weak correlation (-0.22).[4] We also broke the analysis down

[3]What metrics are the most psychologically valid in the valence-arousal space is an open research problem [11]. Under this uncertainty, we used the simplest distance functions, as is generally done in the emotion recognition literature (e.g., [21]), without normalization between the valence-arousal scores of the visual and tactile icons. We tried a few normalization methods, but the main results remained the same.

[4]These interpretations of correlation follow the categorization in [7].

Table 2: Correlations to congruence scores.

Icons	2D Distance	Valence Distance	Arousal Distance
All	-0.54	-0.54	-0.22
Emotional	-0.67	-0.69	-0.11
Objective	-0.72	-0.79	-0.40

to the emotional and objective icons. For only the emotional icons, the congruence score was more strongly correlated with the 2D distance (-0.67) and the valence distance (-0.69), but was not correlated with the arousal distance (-0.11). For the objective icons, the 2D distance and the valence distance were strongly correlated with the congruence score (-0.72 and -0.79). Interestingly, the arousal distance was also moderately correlated (-0.40).

Scatter plots are shown in Figure 6 for the all-icon cases. The congruence scores ranged from 13.3 to 73.6 with a mean 41.9. The results of linear regression analysis were also shown, and their linear terms were all statistically significant ($p < 0.05$). This is another evidence for our hypothesis that individual emotional responses can account for crossmodal congruence. Results for the emotional icons only and for the objective icons only were also similar, but are not shown here due to the limited space.

Further insights can be gained in Figure 7, where each visual icon is paired with its three most congruent tactile icons. For the two positive emotional visual icons (V1 and V3) with high positive valence and moderately active arousal, no tactile icons with similar emotional responses existed. All the tactile icons with the highest congruence were those of F250, which feel more pleasant than those of F100, and were among the closest to the visual icons in the valence-arousal space. These tactile icons were preferred to those with more similar arousal but more dissimilar valence (AwF100E1–E3), suggesting that the perceptual weight of valence used in congruence judgment could have been greater than that of arousal.

For the two negative emotional visual icons (V2 and V4) that had high negative valence and moderately active arousal, our experiment included many tactile icons, mostly of F100, in that area of the valence-arousal space. Consequently, V2 and V4 were matched with the tactile icons of F100 with negative valence. In particular, the tactile icons most congruent to V4 (long face) was those highly unpleasant and highly aroused (all AsF100). Further, comparison between V1–V2 and V3–V4 indicated that V3–V4 were matched with tactile icons with more extreme arousal scores, which seem reasonable to the emotional nature of V3–V4.

The objective visual icons (V5–V8) had moderate or weak positive valence and weak positive or neutral arousal. As can be seen

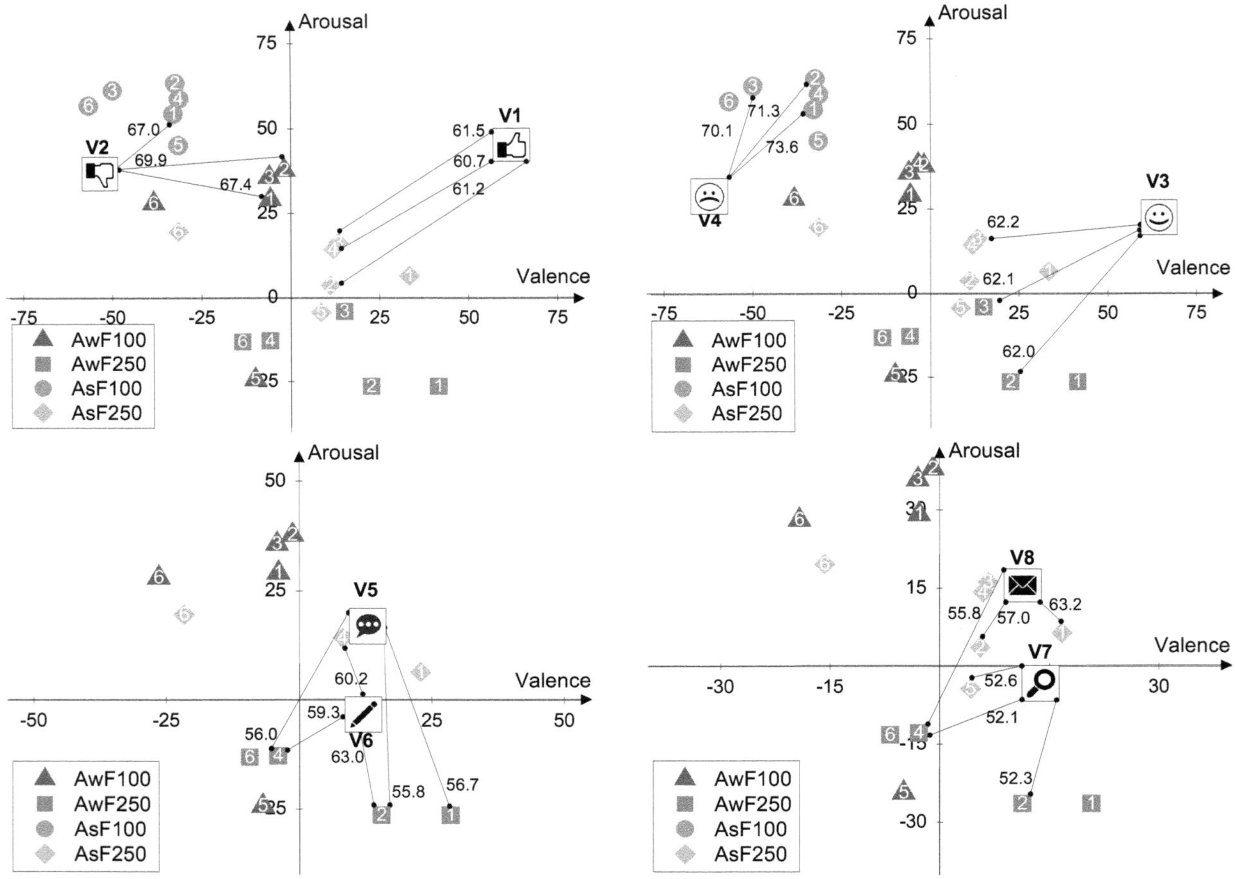

Figure 7: Top three most congruent tactile icons for each visual icon. Each figure is zoomed-in for visibility. The number on the line connecting a tactile and a visual icon is the mean congruence score of that pair.

in Figure 7, this region of valence-arousal space was densely populated by both the objective visual icons and the tactile icons used in our experiments. This seems to have contributed to the strong or moderate correlations of the objective icons between all the valence-arousal distances and the congruence scores (Table 2). Also, all the three most congruent tactile icons were those of F250, implying that the participants favored more pleasant tactile icons for the objective icons. Overall, these results appear to be in good agreement with the nature of objective icons.

Based on the above results, the answers to our two research questions can be summarized as follows:

Q1: *Can the proposed emotion-based framework account for the congruence between visual and tactile icons?*
Yes, the individual emotional responses of the visual and tactile icons were strongly or moderately correlated to their crossmodal congruence.

Q2: *Which of emotional and objective icons are more appropriate for the emotion-based framework?*
Both types of icons are, albeit the latter being somewhat against our initial expectation.

Lastly, we present the *design guidelines for emotionally-congruent visuotactile crossmodal icons* that were elicited from our results: (1) *Emotional icons*: The emotional responses of emotional icons need to be made as close to those of tactile icons as possible. In case that this requirement cannot be satisfied because of wide-spread emotional responses of emotional icons, high priority should be imposed on valence than arousal for crossmodal matching; and (2) *Objective icons*: The valence of objective icons is moderate or weak positive, and its arousal is close to neutral. The valence and arousal of tactile icons need to reside in the same region, and pleasant tactile icons should have greater preference.

5. CONCLUSIONS

This paper presented an explorative study that examined the validity of an emotion-based framework for the design of congruent visuotactile crossmodal icons using their valence-arousal emotional responses as a means for association. Three user experiments were carried out, and they led to some useful design guidelines for tactile icons with desired emotional characteristics and those for crossmodal visuotactile icons with a high degree of congruence.

This work also enabled us to identify further research issues, including (1) how to design tactile icons with both highly positive valence and arousal or both highly negative valence and arousal; (2) the individual effects of various physical parameters of tactile icons on emotional response and their interaction; (3) the validity of the emotion-based framework for a larger range of visual icons; and (4) elucidation of the factor effects by hypothesis-driven experiments. We plan to look into these topics in the near future.

6. ACKNOWLEDGMENTS

This work supported in part by an ITRC NIPA-2014-H0301-14-1014 from NIPA and a grant 2013R1A2A2A01016907 from NRF.

7. REFERENCES

[1] N. Alvarado. Arousal and valence in the direct scaling of emotional response to film clips. *Motivation and Emotion*, 21:323–348, 1997.

[2] O. Bau, I. Poupyrev, A. Israr, and C. Harrison. Teslatouch: Electrovibration for touch surfaces. In *Proc. of UIST*, pages 283–292, ACM, 2010.

[3] S. Brewster and L. M. Brown. Tactons: Structured tactile messages for non-visual information display. In *Proc. of AUIC*, pages 15–23, ACM, 2004.

[4] L. M. Brown, S. A. Brewster, and H. C. Purchase. Multidimensional tactons for non-visual information presentation in mobile device. In *Proc. of MobileHCI*, pages 231–238, ACM, 2006.

[5] S. Choi and K. J. Kuchenbecker. Vibrotactile display: Perception, technology, and applications. *Proceedings of the IEEE*, 101(9):2093–2104, 2013.

[6] J. Chun, I. Lee, G. Park, J. Seo, S. Choi, and S. H. Han. Efficacy of haptic blind spot warnings applied through a steering wheel or a seatbelt. *Transportation Research Part F: Traffic Psychology and Behaviour*, 21:231–241, 2013.

[7] C. Dancey and J. Reidy. *Statistics without Maths for Psychology*. Prentice Hall, 2011.

[8] B. H. Detenber and B. Reeves. A bio-informational theory of emotion: Motion and image size effects on viewers. *J. of Communication*, 46 (3):66–84, 1996.

[9] L. R. Elliott, J. B. van Erp, E. S. Redden, and M. Duistermaat. Field-based validation of a tactile navigation device. *IEEE Trans. on Haptics*, 3(2):78–87, 2010.

[10] M. Enriquez and K. MacLean. The role of choice in longitudinal recall of meaningful tactile signals. In *Proc. of HAPTICS*, pages 49–56, IEEE, 2008.

[11] H. Gunes and M. Pantic. Automatic, dimensional, and continuous emotion recognition. *Int. J. of Synthetic Emotions*, 1(1):68–99, 2010.

[12] E. Hoggan and S. A. Brewster. Designing audio and tactile crossmodal icons for mobile devices. In *Proc. of ICMI*, pages 162–169, ACM, 2007.

[13] E. Hoggan, S. A. Brewster, and J. Johnston. Investigating the effectiveness of tactile feedback for mobile touchscreens. In *Proc. of CHI*, pages 1573–1582. ACM, 2008.

[14] E. Hoggan, T. Kaaresoja, P. Laitinen, and S. Brewster. Crossmodal congruence: The look, feel and sound of touchscreen widgets. In *Proc. of ICMI*, pages 157–164. ACM, 2008.

[15] I. Hwang and S. Choi. Perceptual space and adjective rating of sinusoidal vibrations perceived via mobile device. In *Proc. of HAPTICS*, pages 1–8. IEEE, 2010.

[16] I. Hwang, J. Seo, M. Kim, and S. Choi. Vibrotactile perceived intensity for mobile devices as a function of direction, amplitude, and frequency. *IEEE Trans. on Haptics*, 6(3):352–362, 2013.

[17] K. E. MacLean. Foundations of transparency in tactile information design. *IEEE Trans. on Haptics*, 1(2):84–95, 2008.

[18] A. Mehrabian. Pleasure-arousal-dominance: A general framework for describing and measuring individual differences in temperament. *Current Psychology*, 14:261–292, 1996. 4.

[19] J. W. Morley and M. J. Rowe. Perceived pitch of vibrotactile stimuli: Effects of vibration amplitude, and implications for vibration frequency coding. *The J. of Physiology*, 431:403–416, 1990.

[20] J. Mullenbach, D. Johnson, J. Colgate, and M. Peshkin. Activepad surface haptic device. In *Proc. of HAPTICS*, pages 407–414, IEEE, 2012.

[21] M. A. Nicolaou, H. Gunes, and M. Pantic. Continuous prediction of spontaneous affect from multiple cues and modalities in valence-arousal space. *IEEE Trans. on Affective Computing*, 2(2):92–105, 2011.

[22] G. Park and S. Choi. Perceptual space of amplitude-modulated vibrotactile stimuli. In *Proc. of WHC*, pages 59–64, IEEE, 2011.

[23] M. Paterson. *The Senses of Touch: Haptics, Affects and Technologies*. Bloomsbury Academic, 2007.

[24] J. Raisamo, R. Raisamo, and V. Surakka. Comparison of saltation, amplitude, modulation, and a hybrid method of vibrotactile stimulation. *IEEE Trans. on Haptics*, 6(4):517–521, 2013.

[25] L. Rovers and H. van Essen. HIM: A framework for haptic instant messaging. In *Proc. of CHI*, pages 1313–1316. ACM, 2004.

[26] J. A. Russell. A circumplex model of affect. *J. of Personality and Social Psychology*, 39(6):1161–1178, 1980.

[27] J. Ryu, J. Chun, G. Park, S. Choi, and S. H. Han. Vibrotactile feedback for information delivery in the vehicle. *IEEE Trans. on Haptics*, 3(2):138–149, 2010.

[28] K. Salminen, V. Surakka, J. Lylykangas, J. Raisamo, R. Saarinen, R. Raisamo, J. Rantala, and G. Evreinov. Emotional and behavioral responses to haptic stimulation. In *Proc. of CHI*, pages 1555–1562, ACM, 2008.

[29] K. Salminen, V. Surakka, J. Raisamo, J. Lylykangas, J. Pystynen, R. Raisamo, K. Mäkelä, and T. Ahmaniemi. Emotional responses to thermal stimuli. In *Proc. of ICMI*, pages 193–196, ACM, 2011.

[30] M. Sinclair, M. Pahud, and H. Benko. Touchmover: Actuated 3D touchscreen with haptic feedback. In *Proc. of ITS*, pages 287–296, ACM, 2013.

[31] J. Smith and K. E. MacLean. Communicating emotion through a haptic link: Design space and methodology. *Int. J. of Human-Computer Studies*, 65(4):376–387, 2007.

[32] D. Ternes and K. E. MacLean. Designing large sets of haptic icons with rhythm. *Lecture Notes on Computer Science (EuroHaptics 2008)*, 5024:199–208, 2008.

[33] J. B. F. van Erp and M. M. Spape. Distilling the underlying dimensions of tactile melodies. In *Proc. of Eurohaptics*, pages 111–120, 2003.

[34] R. T. Verrillo and R. L. Smith. Effect of stimulus duration on vibrotactile sensation magnitude. *Bulletin of Psychonomic Review*, 8:112–114, 1976.

[35] J. Walters, M. J. Apter, and S. Svebak. Color preference, arousal, and the theory of psychological reversals. *Motivation and Emotion*, 6(3):193–215, 1982.

[36] S. Yohanan and K. E. MacLean. Design and assessment of the haptic creature's affect display. In *Proc. of HRI*, pages 473–480, ACM, 2011.

Why We Watch the News: A Dataset for Exploring Sentiment in Broadcast Video News

Joseph G. Ellis
Electrical Engineering
Columbia University
New York City, NY
jge2105@columbia.edu

Brendan Jou
Electrical Engineering
Columbia University
New York City, NY
bjou@ee.columbia.edu

Shih-Fu Chang
Electrical Engineering
Columbia University
New York City, NY
sfchang@ee.columbia.edu

ABSTRACT

We present a multimodal sentiment study performed on a novel collection of videos mined from broadcast and cable television news programs. To the best of our knowledge, this is the first dataset released for studying sentiment in the domain of broadcast video news. We describe our algorithm for the processing and creation of person-specific segments from news video, yielding 929 sentence-length videos, and are annotated via Amazon Mechanical Turk. The spoken transcript and the video content itself are each annotated for their expression of positive, negative or neutral sentiment.

Based on these gathered user annotations, we demonstrate for news video the importance of taking into account multimodal information for sentiment prediction, and in particular, challenging previous text-based approaches that rely solely on available transcripts. We show that as much as 21.54% of the sentiment annotations for transcripts differ from their respective sentiment annotations when the video clip itself is presented. We present audio and visual classification baselines over a three-way sentiment prediction of positive, negative and neutral, as well as person-dependent versus person-independent classification influence on performance. Finally, we release the News Rover Sentiment dataset to the greater research community.

Categories and Subject Descriptors

I.2.10 [**Artificial Intelligence**]: Vision and Scene Understanding; I.2.7 [**Artificial Intelligence**]: Natural Language Processing–*Discourse*

Keywords

Sentiment Analysis; Video Processing; News Video; Multimodal Processing; Audio Processing; Person Naming

1. INTRODUCTION

Text-based sentiment analysis has become a hot topic in recent years [14], spurred on in particular by the important use cases of automatic political polling, advertisement recommendation, and more. Using sentiment analysis we are able to gauge the public's opinion about topics that would have been impossible to gain widespread opinion data about 10 to 15 years ago cheaply and without interaction. This amount of opinion mining has been made possible by the influx of readily available on-line text data from social media and blog sources such as Twitter, Facebook, and Blogger. However, much of the opinion mining analysis is done in domains that have heavily polarized lexicons and obvious sentiment polarity. For example, a very popular domain for sentiment analysis is movie and product reviews, where the text available is heavily polarized and there is little room for ambiguity. Statements like "I absolutely loved this movie" or "the acting was terrible", have very clear and polarized sentiment that can be attributed to them.

However, in more complicated domains, such as news video transcripts or news articles, the sentiment attached to a statement can be much less obvious. For example, take the statement that has been relevant in the news in the past year, "Russian troops have entered into Crimea". This statement by itself is not polarizing as positive or negative and is in fact quite neutral. However, if it was stated by a U.S. politician it would probably have very negative connotations and if stated by a Russian politician it could have a very positive sentiment associated with it. Therefore, in more complicated domains such as news the text content is often not sufficient to determine the sentiment of a particular statement. For some ambiguous statements it is important to take into account the way that words are spoken (audio) and the gestures and facial expressions (visual) that accompany the sentence to be able to more accurately determine the sentiment of the statement.

Visual and audio elements of a statement can be useful in determining the overall sentiment of a video statement. However, the way that people portray positive, sarcastic, negative, and other feelings can be very different. Many people have difficulty grasping whether someone that they just met was being sarcastic or completely serious with something that he/she had just stated. This is a common phenomenon and happens because people portray emotions in a variety of different ways that are unique to a single person. Therefore, we propose to take advantage of these person-specific actions by focusing on person-specific models that are trained and tested using only videos of a single person. With the advent of video-based social media such as Instagram, Vine, and YouTube finding enough data to build person-specific models is not infeasible.

ICMI'14, November 12–16, 2014, Istanbul, Turkey.

ACM 978-1-4503-2885-2/14/11 ...$15.00.
http://dx.doi.org/10.1145/2663204.2663237.

News provides an interesting opportunity for us to not only study micro-level sentiment trends, but also macro-level trends. By analyzing the sentiment of speakers and the way that topics are covered by different channels, shows, and people, we can address public opinion and media opinion towards topics. Many interesting macro-level experiments can be carried out using sentiment analysis on news broadcasts. For example, we can determine whether the sentiment that a news channel uses in their coverage of a topic effects the companies that choose to advertise on their shows. We could also address regional biases, channel biases, and the changes in how a topic is covered over time.

The specific contributions of this work are as follows:

- The release of a video dataset in the novel domain of video news, annotated for multimodal sentiment
- A study demonstrating the importance of the audio and visual components of a statement in determining sentiment in news video.
- Baseline audio and visual classifiers and experiments for the dataset are presented.
- Experiments demonstrating improved performance with person-specific audio and visual sentiment classification models compared to global models.

2. RELATED WORK

Text analysis has been used prevalently in social analytics in the past. The authors in [14] present an overview of the field of text-based sentiment analysis up to the state of the art. Recently deep learning techniques have also been applied in the field of text analysis, and have obtained results with high accuracy [18].

There has also been an interest recently in combining multimodal signals (audio, visual, and text) for analysis of sentiment in videos. Emotion recognition by video and audio analysis has been studied extensively, however almost all of this work has been done on heavily controlled datasets that are created for benchmarking performance of algorithms. Popular challenges and datasets have improved performance in controlled scenarios [19, 16]. Recently, however with the advent of video social media sites such as YouTube, Vine, Instragram, and Vimeo, work has begun to perform sentiment analysis "in the wild". This has proven to be much more challenging. While the benchmark datasets have been curated to have very clear sentiment/emotion and little noise, the same can not be said about videos found in social media and television. The field was first pioneered by the authors of [11], where they utilized product reviews in YouTube to show that by using audio and visual features, in conjunction with text features, a higher sentiment classification accuracy can be achieved. Each of the videos within this dataset were labeled on an entire video level, and tri-modal (negative, neutral, positive) sentiment annotation and classification was performed. In [15], sentiment annotation and classification is performed on the utterance level. This is a more natural setting for sentiment analysis, because the sentiment displayed by a person can change between sentences or utterances even if the topic remains the same. Finally, in [22] the more complicated domain of on-line video movie reviews is analyzed using bi-directional long short term memory recurrent neural networks with linguistic, visual and audio features. Recently, a research challenge addressing the recognition of human emotion in the wild was organized, with very promising results [3]. Researchers have also tackled interesting problems such as the "desire to watch again" of a user given their facial expressions in unconstrained on-line content viewing [10]. The engagement of viewers while watching television using their facial expressions [6] and trying to predict movie ratings based on the expressions of viewers throughout a movie [12] have been studied. The authors of [19], state that higher accuracies for visual emotion classification can be obtained if the identity of the person during test time is known beforehand. We will also build off of the ideas in [19], and show the usefulness of person-specific classifiers. We can see that many interesting applications and techniques for emotion and sentiment recognition from video content have been proposed and explored recently.

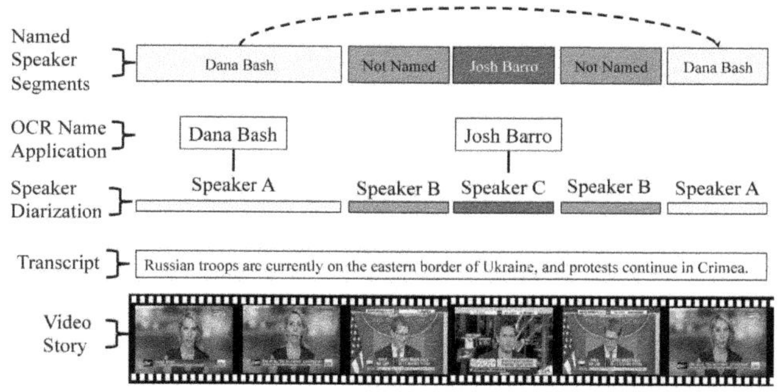

Figure 1: Speaker naming algorithm for video news. Names are detected on-screen using OCR and are used to label speaker segments generated by speaker diarization.

3. NEWS VIDEO SENTIMENT DATASET

In this section we discuss the data collection scheme that was used to create this dataset.

3.1 News Processing Overview

News video is a distinct and interesting domain that is ripe for sentiment mining and analysis due to the variety of opinions that are portrayed within the news. For the past two years, we have been recording up to 12 news programs simultaneously from 100 possible channels and storing and processing the videos. A detailed look at our framework for processing videos in its entirety can be seen here [8].

3.2 Mining Speakers from the News

In this work we create a study dataset with two particular goals. First, the dataset that we create should have an accurate transcript of the words and sentences that are spoken in each video, and this will be automatically created without difficult manual transcribing. Secondly, the dataset would be a diverse representation of the type of people that appear within news programs (politicians, anchors, reporters, etc.), with sufficient spoken sentence videos for each person. After recording the full length programs, removing the commercials, and then segmenting the programs into separate news "stories" [8], we automatically find sections of the

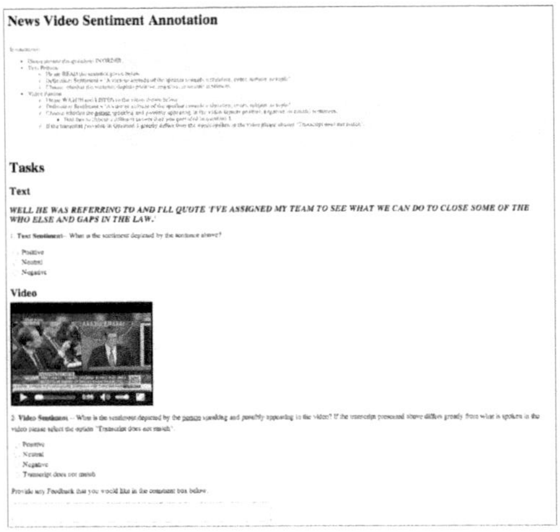

Figure 2: Example Amazon Mechanical Turk Interface. This is an example of the Amazon Mechanical Turk interface used to collect annotations, both the text and video annotation questions and instructions can be seen.

video where particular people of interest are speaking. The speaker naming algorithm presented in this section builds off of the work in [8]. The closed caption transcript associated with each video story accurately transcribes what is stated in the story, but can lag the timing of what is said anywhere between 5-25 seconds. To create an accurate time-aligned transcript of the video we first perform speech recognition on the entire video segment, and then align the associated closed-caption transcript using a modified minimum-edit distance algorithm. This algorithm results in 91.5% precision in the alignment of the transcript to what is said in the sentence level videos used in this experiment. Videos without a properly aligned transcript are removed from the dataset and are not used in the experiments presented later in the paper. Once the time-alignment is completed, we then perform speaker diarization [7] on the audio portion of each video story to determine when each speaker begins and ends speaking throughout the story. To "name" the speech portions we find when a person name appears on-screen, and apply that name as a label to that speech portion. The intuition behind this idea is that when a person is speaking, oftentimes their name will appear in a specific location on the screen (usually in the lower left corner). We first mine the specific "name location" for each separate program by performing OCR on the screen and then comparing the detected OCR text to a list of common first names from the Social Security Name database. Once we find the "name location(s)" on the screen where names most frequently appear for each program we use all of the detected text in this portion as a person name, and apply it as a label to the time-overlapping speech-segment. Once all of the names found are applied to the overlapping speech segments, we find any speaker clusters (the collections of similar speech segments created by speaker diarization) that have only one name applied to them and label these portions of the video according to that name. Finally, we extract the portions of a video that constitute one full sentence within each named speaker portion and add this video to our study. This process is illustrated in Figure 1. We are able to extract from each video specific segments of a person speaking and label them with their appropriate name.

We randomly sampled 198 videos from the dataset to see how many of the videos were named properly and found that 170 out of 198 (85.85%) videos were properly named. The most common error cases occurred during free-flowing debates where it becomes very difficult to detect a change of speaker.

3.3 Dataset Statistics

The videos used for this dataset were recorded and processed between August 13, 2013 and December 25, 2013, and are taken from a large variety of American news programs and channels. A breakdown of the dataset by person, with their occupation and amount of videos within the study can be seen in Table 1. We limit the length of the videos used in the study to be between 4 and 15 seconds long. This is done because it can be difficult to decipher sentiment for very short videos with little speech, and videos longer than 15 seconds could have multiple statements with opposing sentiment.

4. SENTIMENT ANNOTATION

In this section we will discuss our sentiment annotation methodology and how we used Amazon Mechanical Turk to obtain over 3000 unique annotations, and also discuss some interesting statistics of the Turk annotators.

4.1 Annotation Methodology

To obtain sentiment labels for each video we employed a three-way sentiment annotation scheme, where each video was labeled as either positive, negative, or neutral. We utilized Amazon Mechanical Turk to crowd-source the annotation of sentiment in the videos. To prove that the audio and visual components can alter the sentiment implied by a given statement we created an interface that began by showing a sentence to the "turker", a worker on Amazon Mechanical Turk, and asked them to determine the sentiment portrayed by the sentence. Once the turker has labeled the sentence, they are then prompted to watch a video in which the same sentence they previously annotated is spoken by someone in the news and evaluate the sentiment of the video. The turker is told to treat each annotation as a separate entity, and evaluate the sentiment present in the video independently from that of the transcript. We also provided an option to the turker to state that the sentence annotated from the text portion does not match what is said in the video, and we collect these videos and remove them from the overall dataset. An example Amazon Mechanical Turk Human Intelligence Task can be seen in Figure 2.

4.2 Annotation Statistics

We had 72 total annotators provide annotations for our dataset through Mechanical Turk. The number of annotations provided by each user ranged from as little as one annotation, to as many as 343 unique annotations. These annotations were captured over a two week period in April, 2014. We did not collect any personal data from the annotators, as we avoided collecting any data that would make a particular turker identifiable. A histogram breakdown of

Table 1: **Dataset statistics by person. The dataset is categorized into occupation, category of news television appearances, and number of videos within each sentiment class.**

Person	Category	Occupation	Negative Videos	Neutral Videos	Positive Videos
Jay Carney	Politician	White House Press Secretary	36 (31.85%)	61 (53.98%)	16 (14.15%)
John Kerry	Politician	U.S. Secretary of State	35 (44.30%)	34 (43.03%)	10 (12.65%)
Goldie Taylor	Pundit/Analyst	Author, Opinion Writer	63 (59.43%)	29 (27.35%)	14 (13.20%)
Josh Barro	Pundit/Analyst	Editor at Business Insider	68 (44.15%)	63 (40.90%)	23 (14.93%)
Dana Bash	Reporter	Capitol Hill Correspondent	36 (23.84%)	100 (66.22%)	15 (9.93%)
Jim Acosta	Reporter	White House Correspondent	27 (23.07%)	79 (67.52%)	11 (9.40%)
Chris Cillizza	Pundit/Analyst	MSNBC Political Analyst	16 (16.84%)	63 (66.31%)	16 (16.84%)
C. Amanpour	Reporter	International Correspondent	22 (19.29%)	72 (63.15%)	20 (17.54%)

the number of annotations provided by the annotators can be seen in Figure 3.

5. ANNOTATION RESULTS

For each video we received annotations from three distinct turkers and used a majority voting scheme to decide the label of the videos. If there was no majority label across the three annotations that particular example is removed from the study due to sentiment ambiguity, approximately 6% of the video annotations fell into this category. In total we collected 929 majority-vote sentiment labels for videos used in this study.

Our study shows that by watching and listening to the statement portrayed by a person the perceived sentiment can change quite frequently compared to the original sentiment perception based solely on the transcript associated with the video. The majority-voted sentiment label changed between the original text annotation and the video annotation in 21.54% of the annotations. Therefore, for many examples in our study text is insufficient to fully understand the sentiment portrayed, and it is necessary to take into account the way that the sentence content is delivered by the speaker. The breakdown of sentiment in the videos by neutral, negative, and positive sentiment categories can be seen in Table 2. The breakdown of sentiment labels remains reasonably consistent throughout the dataset between text and video sentiment even though over 20% of the annotated labels differ between the text and video. This is because there are roughly equal amounts of annotations that change from neutral in the text to positive or negative in the video and vice-versa. It is also interesting to note that most of the differences in sentiment labels between the two modalities consist of one label being neutral and the other label being positive or negative.

When we study the sentiment breakdown of each person's video and group them by occupation we can see that people within the same occupation have a similar percentage of videos in each sentiment category. John Kerry and Jay Carney both portray neutral sentiment in a large portion of their videos, especially Jay Carney who, as the White House Press Secretary, is often tasked with holding news conferences about breaking news events which he portrays a calm and controlled demeanor. John Kerry on the other hand is often criticizing the actions of other countries, which can be seen in his slightly higher proportion of negative videos. Jim Acosta and Dana Bash are both on-site reporters for their respective news channels, and are therefore tasked with giving an un-biased description of the particular news events happening that day. This is why they both have around two-thirds of their videos labeled under the neutral sentiment category. Finally, the talk-show political pundits such as Josh Barro and Goldie Taylor are often brought onto television programs to give their opinions and react strongly towards a given topic. This is why we see both exhibiting a relatively large percentage of their videos being deemed positive or negative compared to the other occupations.

Table 2: **Percentage of sentiment examples in each class for both transcript and video annotations.**

Sentiment	Video	Transcript
Negative	32.61%	34.23%
Neutral	53.92%	53.96%
Positive	13.45%	11.79%

6. FEATURE EXTRACTION

We model our baseline feature extraction algorithm off of the baseline feature set in the AVEC 2011 challenge [16], with some slight modifications for our domain. We chose this feature set because the AVEC 2011 challenge is a commonly referenced benchmark dataset and is still actively used for evaluation today.

6.1 Audio Features

Our audio features are extracted independently from each sentence-level video using the openSMILE [5] "emotion base" feature set tuned for emotion recognition. The feature set consists of 988 features, consisting of a variety of low level feature descriptors with functionals applied to them over the entire sentence length video (Mel Frequency Cepstral Coefficients, pitch, etc.).

6.2 Visual Features

Extracting visual features from news video presents some unique challenges not present in other datasets. For example, in news video frames can often be split with multiple faces on screen. However we only want to analyze the sentiment portrayed by the "speaking" face. Another difficult scenario appearing in the news is that a reporter or pundit will be speaking, but on-screen a different video would be shown with a large variety of possible alternate content (on-site scenes, picture of people of interest, etc).

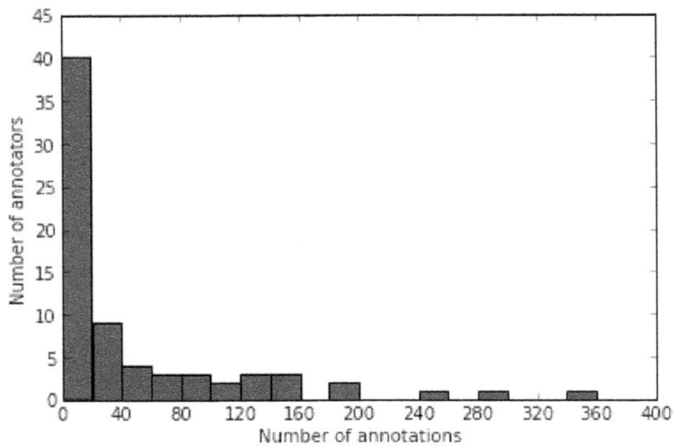

Figure 3: Histogram of annotations per annotator. We can see that many annotators supply few annotations, while approximately 20 provided annotations in large numbers throughout the project.

6.2.1 *Visual Speaker Detection*

We take inspiration for our visual speaker detection algorithm from [4]. We sample frames in each news video at 10 frames/sec, and on each sub-sampled frame we detect faces using the OpenCV implementation of the Viola-Jones face detector [21]. Using these detected faces we refine the face detections by forming coherent face tracks across the entire video by exploiting the temporal and spatial consistency of the tracks within each successive frame using optical-flow. After this we are left with a consistent set of face images belonging to one identity for the duration of the time that this face appears within the video. For each of the faces within a track we then extract seven landmark points on the detected face [20], and then affine warp and resize the faces to a fixed 200×200 pixel resolution such that the facial landmarks appear at the same point for each face.

Once all of the aligned face tracks are generated from a particular video we find the face track that corresponds to the speaker within the video. We extract the mouth region from each aligned face within a face track and perform a normalized cross-correlation comparison between two mouth patches in successive frames. We then compute the median cross-correlation score between successive faces to obtain a "speaking" score for each face track. We threshold the score for each to determine if it represents a visual speaker. If multiple visual speakers are detected within a video at different times we choose the face that appeared on screen longer as the detected visual speaker. Using this methodology, we have determined that visual speakers appear in 455 out of the 929 videos that appeared in this dataset. The amount of videos in which a visual speaker was detected in each person specific video set is shown in Table 3.

6.2.2 *Face Features*

Following the AVEC 2011 Challenge [16] we extract dense Local Binary Patterns (LBP) [13] on the 200×200 pixel face images of detected visual speakers. LBP has proven to be a useful feature for a variety of tasks concerning humans faces, such as emotion [17] and person recognition [1].

We first divide each image into 10×10 evenly spaced image sections (20×20 pixel image patches), and extract uniform LBP patches from each section. A histogram of the LBP features are taken over each image patch resulting in 100 59-dimensional LBP histograms for each face image. The histograms are then concatenated together for each image, resulting in a 5900-dimensional feature representation for each face within our dataset. These visual features will be used as the baseline visual feature set for our video classification analysis.

Table 3: Number of videos per person in which a visual speaker is detected.

Person	# of Videos
Jay Carney	44
John Kerry	37
Goldie Taylor	70
Josh Barro	64
Dana Bash	71
Jim Acosta	56
Chris Cillizza	85
Christiane Amanpour	28

We also present an alternate visual feature representation pipeline based on Block-Based-Bag-of-Words (BBoW) [9]. First, we separate the image into four quadrants, top left, top right, bottom left, and bottom right. Next, within each quadrant we extract LBP histograms in the same manner as described above from each quadrant. Within the LBP features extracted from every image in a particular quadrant we use k-means clustering to generate a codebook, and then quantize the features into a Bag of Words representation for each quadrant. The quantized features from each quadrants are then concatenated together to create the representation for each image. Codebook sizes of 50, 200, and 1000 are used in this implementation, and each codebook is created using the complete representation of features from each quadrant (over 3 million LBP histogram features).

7. SENTIMENT CLASSIFICATION

In this section, we explore text, audio, and visual classification of the sentiment of the news videos. We provide results demonstrating the accuracy of global models trained on all of the people in the dataset and person-specific models.

7.1 Text Classification

We performed sentiment classification from the transcript annotations obtained from Amazon Mechanical Turk using one of the state-of-the-art deep-learning based text sentiment analysis algorithms [18]. We first perform true-casing on news transcripts, because the news transcripts use only capitalized letters and then use the true-cased transcripts for text sentiment classification. The positive, negative, and neutral classification accuracy of [18] on our corpus is 45.6%. This low level of accuracy shows that news domain transcripts are quite ambiguous with regard to sentiment. There is much room for improvement by incorporating the multimodal information also present within the video.

We believe that the classification accuracy is particularly low due to several reasons. First, it must be stressed that this classification accuracy was achieved using the text system "out-of-the-box" and no domain adaptation to the news

Table 4: Video sentiment classification accuracy.

Feature Set	Accuracy
AVEC Raw LBP	31.47%
BBoW 50-dim codebook	44.41%
BBoW 200-dim codebook	37.94%
BBoW 1000-dim codebook	33.48%

transcripts was done. It is believed that some domain adaptation would improve the results considerably. Second, the grammar in news transcripts is often not perfect, because the transcripts are manually typed during the news program. This could also lead to degraded performance because the sentences are not well formed. Both of these issues are not the focus of this work.

7.2 Global Models

We trained sentiment models using all of the data present in the dataset independent of person identity.

7.2.1 Audio Classification

For audio classification, we used the raw features from openSMILE to train a linear SVM classifier using libSVM [2]. We use four-fold cross-validation to tune the SVM cost parameter, and report here the average accuracy of the four-fold cross-validation. We split each set of person videos into four-folds and use three of the folds across all of the people for training and one for test. We do this so that we know the accuracy of the trained global model on each person, and to insure that training examples exist for each person in each training fold. The four-fold training classification accuracy for audio classification across the entire dataset is 56.57%. random guess model for this classification is 33.33%, and the dominant class guess for this dataset is neutral with 53.92%. The audio classification accuracy of the global model for each particular person in our dataset can be seen in Table 5.

7.2.2 Video Classification

The results in the video classification utilize the 455 videos in which we detected speaking faces. In the same fashion as the audio classification we trained a linear SVM classifier and report the average accuracy over four-fold classification over our four different feature extraction algorithms. The videos are split in the same way as described in Sec. 7.2.1. We label all of the extracted frames within a video with the sentiment label of the video and then train a frame-level classifier for sentiment. We then carry out a majority vote classification over the frames in each video to determine the sentiment on a video-level during test. The results can be seen in Table 4. We can see that our Block-Based Bag of Words feature representation outperforms the LBP standard feature extraction method on this dataset, and performs the best with a small codebook size of 50 codewords per quadrant (200 codewords across the whole face). We believe that the small codebook performs well because we have few label categories (positive, negative, and neutral) and there is high inter-image similarity because all the images are aligned faces. The video classification accuracy of the best performing global model for each particular person in our dataset can be seen in Table 6. The visual model accuracy is not directly comparable to the audio model accuracies, because the visual model was only tested on the subset of videos in which visual speakers were detected.

Table 5: Classification accuracy (%) for audio-based person-specific and global sentiment classifiers.

Person	Global	Person-Specific
Global	56.57	62.56
Jay Carney	58.92	64.17
John Kerry	42.10	48.68
Goldie Taylor	54.80	59.61
Josh Barro	50.00	59.21
Dana Bash	59.45	66.21
Jim Acosta	63.79	67.24
Chris Cillizza	60.86	66.30
C. Amanpour	59.82	65.17

7.3 Person-Specific Models

Although most of the previous work in the field of multimodal sentiment has been done by creating global models that apply to all people, there are some inherent advantages to training classifiers for specific people. People have their own unique ways of displaying anger, happiness, sarcasm, and sentiment in both auditory and visual ways. In the age of social media it is possible to gather large amounts of video for one person, and we show that taking into account person-specific classification can improve or achieve comparable performance with our global models.

The dataset was separated into smaller single-person video sets based on the names applied during the named multimodal speaker diarization algorithm described in Sec. 3.2. We randomly sampled videos from our dataset and found that our naming algorithm has an accuracy of 85.85%. The incorrectly named videos within each person-specific video set will alter slightly the learned classifiers and results, but since these outliers are a small minority we do not expect the effect on results to be drastic. This also demonstrates the feasibility of automatically mining person video data and building person-specific classifiers. The entire processing pipeline from raw-video content to predicted sentence-level video sentiment can be seen in Figure 4.

7.3.1 Audio Classification

The audio classification scheme described in Sec. 7.2.1 followed in exactly the same way, but person-specific models are trained and tested only using the videos that are labeled as one particular person within our dataset. The results can be seen in Table 5.

We can see that building the person-specific classifiers improves the results of classification in every case. We postulate that this occurs for two reasons. First, we are able to take into account person-specific quirks in the audio segment that within a person can be descriptive for sentiment, but are lost when compared across the whole dataset. Second, due to the imbalance of sentiment label classes within each person we are able to take into account the likelihood of a person demonstrating positive, negative, or neutral sentiment when only using their videos as training data compared to the global models. Based on the results we can see that building person-specific sentiment models can achieve similar or improved results over the global model with less data and therefore faster training time.

Table 6: Classification accuracy (%) for visual-based person-specific and global sentiment classifiers.

Person	Global	Person-Specific
Global	44.41	56.85
Jay Carney	36.36	34.09
John Kerry	50.00	52.77
Goldie Taylor	55.88	42.64
Josh Barro	51.56	59.37
Dana Bash	35.29	48.52
Jim Acosta	28.57	66.07
Chris Cillizza	55.95	67.85
C. Amanpour	25.00	85.71

It is also interesting to note that some person-specific models produce the same classification accuracy as the dominant label classification strategy within person. For example, the audio person-specific classifier for reporters, such as Dana Bash or Jim Acosta that has the highest accuracy across the cross-validation folds is the one that classifies every video as "neutral". This shows that it is quite difficult to learn sentiment models for on-site reporters/correspondents, something that is very intuitive because they are expected to give an un-biased description of news events.

7.3.2 Video Classification

The video classification scheme described in Sec. 7.2.2 is replicated in exactly the same way, but models are trained and tested using only the person-specific data. We use the best performing model, which was our block-based bag of words with a codebook size of 50. The results can be seen in Table 6. We can see that the results improve in most cases, and in some cases greatly using the person-specific models. Due to the fact that each frame extracted from the training set videos is used for building the classifiers, the visual classifier is trained with a larger set of data making it more robust for the person-specific classifiers as compared to the person-specific audio classifiers. Due to the majority voting scheme within video tracks, this method is also robust to spurious classifications, because the results of the classification on each frame are effectively averaged out over the entire duration of the video. The visual model performance is not directly comparable to the audio model performance, because the visual model was only tested on the subset of videos in which visual speakers were detected.

8. CONCLUSIONS

In this work we describe an algorithm for extracting named speech segments from broadcast news videos, which are then used in a framework for joint sentiment annotation of text and video content using Amazon Mechanical Turk. Using this data we have performed a study detailing the added value of seeing and hearing a statement delivered when determining sentiment in comparison to simply reading the sentence. In particular we show that 21.54% of annotations differ when users are given only the text content compared to the full video. These results imply that when dealing with complicated domains for sentiment analysis such as spoken news video, it is important to take into account the video content and not focus solely on text.

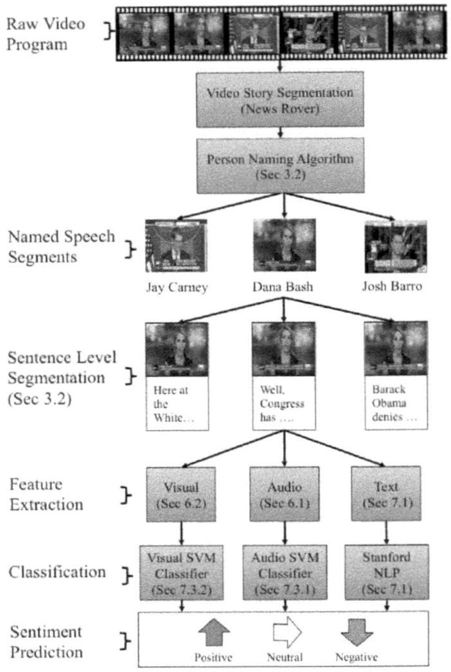

Figure 4: Full News Rover sentiment processing pipeline. Here we represent the ingestion of content into our system from a raw-video program to predicted sentence-level sentiment.

The News Rover Sentiment dataset has been presented and baseline classification algorithms benchmarked on this dataset. We think this dataset presents a rich opportunity for the research community to tackle difficult video-based sentiment analysis questions "in the wild". The News Rover Sentiment dataset described in this paper is available at `www.ee.columbia.edu/dvmm/newsrover/sentimentdataset`. Because it was automatically created using the algorithms for naming and visual speaker detection described in this work it contains some noise. Therefore, we have manually inspected the dataset and provide a "clean" dataset with videos of only properly named visual speakers as well. The same classification algorithms are performed on this dataset, and results on the "clean" dataset can be seen on the provided website, and can be used for benchmarking against.

9. FUTURE WORK

We hope to expand this work by fusing the multimodal features for sentiment classification on this dataset, and transferring current state-of-the-art techniques to this domain. We believe that gains can be made in text-based sentiment classification on the news transcripts by developing techniques that are robust to errors in grammar and are more domain specific. In the future we will pursue a fusion method for the person-specific and global models to leverage the "big-data" advantages of a global model, while still learning person-specific features. Finally, once reliable sentiment classifiers are built then macro-level experiments exploring news program trends will be carried out.

10. REFERENCES

[1] T. Ahonen, A. Hadid, and M. Pietikainen. Face description with local binary patterns: Application to face recognition. *IEEE Transactions on Pattern Analysis and Machine Intelligence*, 2006.

[2] C.-C. Chang and C.-J. Lin. LIBSVM: A library for support vector machines. *ACM Transactions on Intelligent Systems and Technology*, 2011.

[3] A. Dhall, R. Goecke, J. Joshi, M. Wagner, and T. Gedeon. Emotion recognition in the wild challenge (emotiw) challenge and workshop summary. In *International Conference on Multimodal Interaction*, 2013.

[4] M. Everingham, J. Sivic, and A. Zisserman. Taking the bite out of automatic naming of characters in TV video. *Image and Vision Computing*, 2009.

[5] F. Eyben, M. Wöllmer, and B. Schuller. Opensmile: The munich versatile and fast open-source audio feature extractor. In *ACM Multimedia*, 2010.

[6] J. Hernandez, Z. Liu, G. Hulten, D. Debarr, K. Krum, and Z. Zhang. Measuring the engagement level of tv viewers. In *IEEE Automatic Face and Gesture Recognition*, 2013.

[7] M. Huijbregts. *Segmentation, Diarization, and Speech Transcription: Suprise Data Unraveled*. PhD thesis, University of Twente, 2008.

[8] B. Jou*, H. Li*, J. G. Ellis*, D. Morozoff, and S.-F. Chang. Structured exploration of who, what, when, and where in heterogeneous multimedia news sources. In *ACM Multimedia*, 2013.

[9] Z. Li, J. Imai, and M. Kaneko. Robust face recognition using block-based bag of words. In *International Conference on Pattern Recognition*, 2010.

[10] D. McDuff, R. E. Kaliouby, D. Demirdjian, and R. W. Picard. Predicting online media effectiveness based on smile responses gathered over the internet. In *IEEE Automatic Face and Gesture Recognition*, 2013.

[11] L.-P. Morency, R. Mihalcea, and P. Doshi. Towards multimodal sentiment analysis: Harvesting opinions from the web. In *International Conference on Multimodal Interaction*, 2011.

[12] R. Navarathna, P. Lucey, P. Carr, E. Carter, S. Sridharan, and I. Matthews. Predicting movie ratings from audience behaviors. In *IEEE Winter Conference on Applications of Computer Vision*, 2014.

[13] T. Ojala, M. Pietikäinen, and T. Mäenpää. Multiresolution gray-scale and rotation invariant texture classification with local binary patterns. *IEEE Transactions on Pattern Analysis and Machine Intelligence*, 2002.

[14] B. Pang and L. Lee. Opinion mining and sentiment analysis. *Foundations and Trends in Information Retrieval*, 2(1-2), 2008.

[15] V. Perez-Rosas, R. Mihalcea, and L.-P. Morency. Utterance-level multimodal sentiment analysis. In *Association for Computational Linguistics*, 2013.

[16] B. Schuller, M. F. Valstar, F. Eyben, G. McKeown, R. Cowie, and M. Pantic. Avec 2011-the first international audio/visual emotion challenge. In *Affective Computing and Intelligent Interaction*, 2011.

[17] C. Shan, S. Gong, and P. W. McOwan. Facial expression recognition based on local binary patterns: A comprehensive study. *Image and Vision Computing*, 2009.

[18] R. Socher, A. Perelygin, J. Wu, J. Chuang, C. D. Manning, A. Y. Ng, and C. Potts. Recursive deep models for semantic compositionality over a sentiment treebank. In *Empirical Methods in Natural Language Processing*, 2013.

[19] U. Tariq, K.-H. Lin, Z. Li, X. Zhou, Z. Wang, V. Le, T. Huang, X. Lv, and T. Han. Recognizing emotions from an ensemble of features. *IEEE Transactions on Systems, Man, and Cybernetics, Part B: Cybernetics*, 2012.

[20] M. Uřičář, V. Franc, and V. Hlaváč. Detector of facial landmarks learned by the structured output SVM. In *International Conference on Computer Vision Theory and Applications*, 2012.

[21] P. Viola and M. J. Jones. Robust real-time face detection. *International Journal of Computer Vision*, 2004.

[22] M. Wollmer, F. Weninger, T. Knaup, B. Schuller, C. Sun, K. Sagae, and L.-P. Morency. Youtube movie reviews: Sentiment analysis in an audio-visual context. *IEEE Intelligent Systems*, 2013.

Dyadic Behavior Analysis in Depression Severity Assessment Interviews

Stefan Scherer
USC Institute for Creative Technologies
12015 Waterfront Dr.
Playa Vista, CA
scherer@ict.usc.edu

Zakia Hammal
Carnegie Mellon University
5000 Fifth Avenue
Pittsburgh, PA
zakia_hammal@yahoo.fr

Ying Yang
University of Pittsburgh
Biomedical Science Tower
Pittsburgh, PA 15213
yiy17@pitt.edu

Louis-Philippe Morency
USC Institute for Creative Technologies
12015 Waterfront Dr.
Playa Vista, CA
morency@ict.usc.edu

Jeffrey F. Cohn
University of Pittsburgh
210 S. Bouquet St.
Pittsburgh, PA 15260
jeffcohn@cs.cmu.edu

ABSTRACT

Previous literature suggests that depression impacts vocal timing of both participants and clinical interviewers but is mixed with respect to acoustic features. To investigate further, 57 middle-aged adults (men and women) with Major Depression Disorder and their clinical interviewers (all women) were studied. Participants were interviewed for depression severity on up to four occasions over a 21 week period using the Hamilton Rating Scale for Depression (HRSD), which is a criterion measure for depression severity in clinical trials. Acoustic features were extracted for both participants and interviewers using COVAREP Toolbox. Missing data occurred due to missed appointments, technical problems, or insufficient vocal samples. Data from 36 participants and their interviewers met criteria and were included for analysis to compare between high and low depression severity. Acoustic features for participants varied between men and women as expected, and failed to vary with depression severity for participants. For interviewers, acoustic characteristics strongly varied with severity of the interviewee's depression. Accommodation - the tendency of interactants to adapt their communicative behavior to each other - between interviewers and interviewees was inversely related to depression severity. These findings suggest that interviewers modify their acoustic features in response to depression severity, and depression severity strongly impacts interpersonal accommodation.

ICMI'14, November 12 - 16 2014, Turkey

http://dx.doi.org/10.1145/2663204.2663238.

General Terms

H.1.2 User/Machine Systems; H.5.m Miscellaneous; J.4 Social and Behavioral Sciences

Keywords

Depression; Dyadic Interaction; Accommodation; Voice Quality

1. INTRODUCTION

Diagnosis and assessment of depression is almost entirely informed by what patients, their families, or caregivers report. Standardized procedures for incorporating nonverbal behavior and voice characteristics, in particular, are lacking. Their absence is especially salient for depression, a mood disorder for which disruption in emotion experience, communication, and self-regulation are key features [1, 69, 14, 20]. Within the past decade, significant progress has been made in linking voice characteristics to emotion [26, 39, 61, 2, 68], turn-taking, reciprocity [19, 55], and a broad range of interpersonal outcomes [38, 54]. There is strong reason to believe that automatic analysis of voice characteristics could provide a powerful tool to assist in detection and assessment of depression over the course of treatment and recovery. Improved measurement and understanding of the relation between depression and voice characteristics could aid early detection, and lead to better understanding of mechanisms and improved interventions. The lower vocal tract is innervated by the vagal nerve, and thus provides important information about the peripheral physiology of depression [51, 56]. Because depression is one of the most prevalent mental health disorders [44] and a leading cause of disability worldwide [52], the potential contribution of improved measurement is great.

The timing, amplitude, and acoustic features of speech have been investigated [63, 60]. Several investigations have revealed reduced speech variability and monotonicity in loudness and pitch [50, 13, 47, 25], reduced speech [33], reduced articulation rate [11], and increased pause duration [63, 6] when compared to non-depressed comparison participants.

Varied switching pause duration was found to be correlated with depression severity in a within-subject analysis [66]. Findings for acoustic features in general have found depression effects, as well. These effects include increased tension in the vocal tract and the vocal folds in between-subject studies [13, 59], and speech characteristics related to psychomotor retardation [22, 62]. Yang et al. [66], however, found no differences in fundamental frequency (f_0) in relation to depression severity.

With two notable exceptions, previous work has focused on depressed participants and ignored the interview context and their interviewers in particular. Scherer et al. [58] studied suicidal adolescents who were depressed and their interviewers. Suicidal adolescents had more breathy voice qualities than non-suicidal comparison participants, interviewers' acoustic characteristics were correlated with these changes. Backchannels provided by the interviewer were more breathy when they were interviewing suicidal adolescents. Yang et al. [66] found that interviewer, but not interviewee, f_0 mean and variability showed a strong relationship with severity of depression. Interviewers used lower and more variable f_0 when speaking with participants who were more depressed than they did when speaking with participants who were less depressed.

A number of factors might account for the discrepancy with respect to acoustic features between the different studies. The participants in Yang et al., study all met criteria for Major Depressive Disorder and were studied with respect to change in severity over time. Other studies have compared depressed and non-depressed participants. Perhaps most important, the analysis of acoustic characteristics by Yang et al. was limited to f_0. Other work has more comprehensively analyzed acoustic features. To investigate whether the reduced feature set in Yang et al. may have accounted for this discrepancy, we analyze their recordings using more comprehensive, state of the art procedures to assess voice characteristics related to both prosody as well as voice quality, collected in a freely available speech signal processing toolbox [16]. Further, we address the dyadic analysis of acoustic and nonverbal accommodation, which represents the major novelty of this study.

2. METHODS AND MATERIALS

2.1 Participants

Fifty-seven depressed participants (34 women, 23 men) were recruited from a clinical trial for treatment of depression. They ranged in age from 19 to 65 years (mean = 39.65) and were Euro- or African-American (46 and 11, respectively). At the time of study intake, all met DSM-IV [1] criteria [21] for Major Depressive Disorder (MDD). Although not a focus of this report, participants were randomized to either anti-depressant treatment with a selective serotonin re-uptake inhibitor (SSRI) or Interpersonal Psychotherapy (IPT). Both treatments are empirically validated for treatment of depression [37].

2.2 Observational Procedures

Symptom severity was evaluated on up to four occasions at 1, 7, 13, and 21 weeks by ten clinical interviewers (all female). Interviewers were not assigned to specific participants, and they varied in the number of interviews they conducted. Four interviewers were responsible for the bulk of the interviews. The median number of interviews per interviewer was 14.5; four conducted six or fewer. Interviews were conducted using the Hamilton Rating Scale for Depression (HRSD) [34], which is a criterion measure for assessing severity of depression. Interviewers all were expert in the HRSD and reliability was maintained above 0.90. HRSD scores of 15 or higher are generally considered to indicate moderate to severe depression; and scores of 7 or lower to indicate a return to normal [24]. We used these cut-off scores to define the two conditions of high depression and low depression in this study. Subjects scoring between cut-off scores 7 and 15 were excluded from the analysis.

Interviews were recorded using four hardware synchronized analogue cameras and two unidirectional microphones. Two cameras were positioned approximately 15° to the participant's left and right to record their shoulders and face. A third camera recorded a full body view while a fourth recorded the interviewer's shoulders and face from approximately 15° to their right. Audio was digitized at 48 kHz and later down-sampled to 16 kHz for speech processing. Missing data occurred due to missed appointments, or technical problems. Technical problems included failure to record audio or video, audio or video artifacts, and insufficient amount of data. To be included for analysis, we required a minimum of 20 speaker turns with at least 3 seconds in length and at least 50 seconds of vocalization in total. Thus, the final sample was 61 sessions from 36 participants; 47 score high on HRSD and 14 low.

2.3 Preprocessing

To attenuate noise as well as to equalize intensity, Adobe Audition II [54] was used to reduce noise level and equalize intensity. An intermediate level of 40% noise reduction was used to achieve the desired signal-to-noise ratio without distorting the original signal. Each pair of recordings was transcribed manually using Transcriber software [7] and then force-aligned using CMU Sphinx III [2] post-processed using Praat [8]. Because session recordings exceeded the memory limits of Sphinx, it was necessary to segment recordings prior to forced alignment. While several approaches to segmentation were possible, we segmented recordings at transcription boundaries; that is, whenever a change in speaker occurred. Except for occasional overlapping speech, this approach resulted in speaker-specific segments. Forced alignment produced a matrix of four columns: speaker (which encoded both individual and simultaneous speech), start time, stop time, and utterance. To assess the reliability of the forced alignment, audio files from 30 sessions were manually aligned and compared with the segmentation yielded by Sphinx. Mean error (s) for onset and offset, respectively, were .097 and .010 for participants and .053 and .011 for interviewers.

The forced alignment timings were used to identify speaker-turns and speaker diarization for the subsequent automatic feature extraction (cf. Section 2.4).

2.4 Acoustic Features

For the processing of the speech signals, we use the freely available COVAREP toolbox, a collaborative speech analysis repository available for Matlab and Octave [16][1]. COVAREP provides an extensive selection of open-source ro-

[1] `http://covarep.github.io/covarep/`

bust and tested speech processing algorithms enabling comparative and cooperative research within the speech community.

The extracted acoustic features were chosen based on previous encouraging results in classifying voice patterns of suicidal adolescents and distressed adults [58, 59] as well as the features' relevance for characterizing voice qualities on a breathy to tense dimension [57, 42]. Below we introduce the utilized speech features in more detail.

2.4.1 *Fundamental Frequency (f_0)*

In [18], a method for fundamental frequency f_0 tracking and simultaneous voicing detection based on residual harmonics is introduced. The method is especially suitable in noisy and unconstrained conditions. The residual signal $r(t)$ is calculated from the speech signal $s(t)$ for each frame using inverse filtering, for all times t. In particular, we utilize a linear predictive coding (LPC) filter of order $p = 12$ estimated for all Hanning windowed speech segments. Each speech segment has the length of 25 ms and is continuously shifted by 5 ms. This process removes strong influences of noise and vocal tract resonances. For each $r(t)$ the amplitude spectrum $E(f)$ is computed, revealing peaks for the harmonics of f_0, the fundamental frequency. Then, the summation of residual harmonics (SRH) is computed as follows [18]:

$$SRH(f) = E(f) + \sum_{k=2}^{N_{harm}} [E(k \cdot f) - E((k - \frac{1}{2}) \cdot f)], \quad (1)$$

for $f \in [f_{0,\min}, f_{0,\max}]$, with $f_{0,min} = 50$, $f_{0,max} = 500$, and $N_{harm} = 5$. The frequency f for which $SRH(f)$ is maximal $f_0 = \arg\max_f(SRH(f))$ is considered the fundamental frequency of the investigated speech frame. By using a simple threshold $\theta = 0.07$, the unvoiced frames can be discarded as in [18]. Unvoiced samples, i.e. times when no vocal fold vibration is present, are not analyzed for any of the extracted features.

2.4.2 *Maxima Dispersion Quotient (MDQ) and Peak Slope (PS)*

The Maxima Dispersion Quotient (**MDQ**) and the Peak Slope (**PS**) measure involve a dyadic wavelet transform using $g(t)$, a cosine-modulated Gaussian pulse similar to that used in [12] as the mother wavelet:

$$g(t) = -cos(2\pi f_n t) \cdot exp\left(-\frac{t^2}{2\tau^2}\right) \quad (2)$$

where the sampling frequency $f_s = 16$ kHz, $f_n = \frac{f_s}{2}$, $\tau = \frac{1}{2f_n}$ and t is time. The wavelet transform, $y_i(t)$, of the input signal, $x(t)$, at the ith scale, s_i, is calculated by:

$$y_i(t) = x(t) * g\left(\frac{t}{s_i}\right) \quad (3)$$

where $*$ denotes the convolution operator and $s_i = 2^i$. This functions essentially as an octave band zero-phase filter bank. For the PS feature [40], the speech signal is used as $x(t)$ in Eq. (3). Maxima are measured across the scales, on a fixed-frame basis, and a regression line is fit to these maxima. The slope of the regression line for each frame provides the peakSlope value. The feature is essentially an effective correlate of the spectral slope of the signal. Finally, the measurement of the maxima dispersion quotient (MDQ, [41]) uses the Linear Prediction (LP) residual as $x(t)$ in Eq. (3). Then using the GCIs, located using SE-VQ, the dispersion of peaks in relation to the GCI position is averaged across the different frequency bands and then normalized to the local glottal period. For tense voice, where the sharp closing of the glottis is analogous to an impulse excitation the maxima are tightly aligned to the GCI, whereas for laxer phonation the maxima become highly dispersed.

2.4.3 *Normalized Amplitude Quotient (NAQ)*

The normalized amplitude quotient (**NAQ**) feature is derived from the glottal source signal estimated by iterative adaptive inverse filtering (IAIF, [4]). The output is the differentiated glottal flow. The normalized amplitude quotient (NAQ, [5]) is calculated using:

$$\text{NAQ} = \frac{f_{ac}}{d_{peak} \cdot T_0}, \quad (4)$$

where d_{peak} is the negative amplitude of the main excitation in the differentiated glottal flow pulse, while f_{ac} is the peak amplitude of the glottal flow pulse and T_0 the length of the glottal pulse period.

NAQ is a direct measure of the glottal flow and glottal flow derivative and as an amplitude based parameter, was shown to be more robust to noise disturbances than parameters based on time instant measurements and has, as a result, been used in the analysis of conversational speech [10], which is frequently noisy. The parameter, however, may not be as effective as a voice quality indicator when a speaker is using a wide f_0 range [29].

2.4.4 *Quasi Open Quotient (QOQ)*

The quasi-open quotient (**QOQ**, [32]) is also derived from amplitude measurements of the glottal flow pulse and is a frequently used correlate of the open quotient OQ, i.e. the period the vocal folds are open. OQ is a salient measurement of the glottal pulse, thought to be useful for discriminating breathy to tense voice [35, 36, 64]. OQ can be defined as the duration of the glottal open phase normalized to the local glottal period. The quasi-open period is measured by detecting the peak in the glottal flow and finding the time points previous to and following this point that descend below 50% of the peak amplitude. The duration between these two time-points is divided by the local glottal period to get the QOQ parameter.

Below the investigated speech parameters are specified with subscripts $_P$ and $_I$ to specify if they relate to participants or interviewers speech respectively.

2.5 Accommodation Analysis

Accommodation, also described under the terms convergence [27] [53], entrainment [9], or mimicry [54], refers to the tendency of interactants to adapt their communicative behavior to each other.

To measure the synchrony in the development of the extracted speech parameters for each interactant we utilized the standard Pearson correlation coefficient $\rho \in [-1, 1]$, that measures linear dependencies between two sets of observations x and y:

$$\rho_{xy} = \frac{\sum_{i=1}^{N}(x_i - \mu_x)\sum_{i=1}^{N}(y_i - \mu_y)}{(N-1)\sigma_x\sigma_y}, \quad (5)$$

where $|x| = |y| = N$ the length of the observation set, μ_x the mean value of x (respectively μ_y), σ_x the standard deviation of x (respectively σ_y), and $x_i \in x \quad \forall i = 1, ..., N$ (respectively y_i). For large $\rho_{xy} > 0$ we have strong linear dependencies, which indicates a synchronous behavior of the prosodic parameters over the analyzed fragment. Small values $\rho_{xy} < 0$ indicate strong asynchronous developments of the observed parameters. For values close to zero no linear correlation is observed, i.e. a state of maintenance is present.

Within this study, we investigate correlation between participants' and interviewers' speech characteristics using a time-aligned moving average approach [15]. Interviews were subdivided into successive segments of 50 seconds with 10 second shifts (i.e. 40 seconds overlap). For each segment, characteristics for both the participant and the respective interviewer are computed. This results in a time series of observations for both the interviewer and the participant. A Pearson correlation ρ was computed for each observed feature for each interview.

The observed accommodation between the participants' and interviewers' acoustic parameters are denoted as ρ with the respective acoustic parameter as subscripts.

3. DATA ANALYSES AND RESULTS

We investigated the acoustic characteristics of participants, interviewers, and the accommodation between participants and interviewers during high depression severity and low severity, respectively.

3.1 Condition Effects on Participant Behavior

Do acoustic characteristics of participants vary with depression severity? In particular, we investigate acoustic parameters characterizing the participants' voice quality on a breathy to tense dimension.

Table 1: Participant acoustic parameter correlation. P for participants.

	$f_{0,P}$	MDQ$_P$	PS$_P$	NAQ$_P$	QOQ$_P$
$f_{0,P}$	1	.711**	.614**	-.402**	-.520**
MDQ$_P$		1	.400**	-.020	-.315**
PS$_P$			1	-.507**	-.540**
NAQ$_P$				1	.847**
QOQ$_P$					1

Because speech parameters were highly correlated (Table 1[2]), they were analyzed using MANOVA. Depression severity, sex, and their interaction were included as covariates. There was no effect for depression severity (F(5, 55) = 1.759, p = .137) or sex-by-depression severity interaction (F(5, 55) = 0.964, p = .448). There was a significant effect for sex (F(5, 55) = 5.339, p < .01).

Follow-up F tests revealed significant sex effects for all speech parameters with the exception of NAQ$_P$. As expected, fundamental frequency was higher for women than for men. Further, significantly more breathy voice characteristics were observed as measured with MDQ$_P$, and more tense voice characteristics as measured using PS$_P$ as well as QOQ$_P$, for details see Table 2

[2]All p-values of statistical tests < .05 and < .01 are denoted with * and ** respectively.

Table 2: Follow-up F test results for participant behavior depending on sex.

	Women		Men	
	μ	σ	μ	σ
$f_{0,P}$	191.77	26.24	145.05	38.26**
MDQ$_P$	0.130	0.007	0.121	0.010**
PS$_P$	-0.422	0.034	-0.465	0.028**
QOQ$_P$	0.380	0.072	0.444	0.082*

3.2 Condition Effects on Interviewer Behavior

Do acoustic characteristics of interviewers vary with depression severity?

Table 3: Interviewer acoustic parameter correlation. I for Interviewer.

	$f_{0,I}$	MDQ$_I$	PS$_I$	NAQ$_I$	QOQ$_I$
$f_{0,I}$	1	.579**	.546**	-.134	-.239*
MDQ$_I$		1	.202	.442**	.281**
PS$_I$			1	-.224*	-.208
NAQ$_I$				1	.934**
QOQ$_I$					1

Speech parameters for interviewers were highly correlated (Table 3) and were analyzed using MANOVA. Depression severity, sex, and their interaction were included as covariates. There was a significant effect of depression severity on interviewers' acoustic characteristics (F(5, 55) = 2.609, p = .035). There was a marginally significant effect for sex (F(5, 55) = 2.121, p = .077) and no sex-by-depression severity interaction (F(5, 55) = 0.189, p = .966).

Table 4: Follow-up F test results for interviewer behavior depending on depression severity and sex.

	High Severity		Low Severity	
	μ	σ	μ	σ
PS$_I$	-0.407	0.022	-0.383	0.027**
NAQ$_I$	0.099	0.022	0.086	0.015
	Women		**Men**	
	μ	σ	μ	σ
$f_{0,I}$	195.10	26.24	170.41	38.26*
MDQ$_I$	0.130	0.007	0.125	0.010*

Follow-up F tests for the individual speech parameters revealed significant effects for breathier voice quality as measured by PS$_I$ and a trend to more breathy voice as measured with NAQ$_I$. Effects for other parameters failed to reach significance. PS$_I$ and NAQ$_I$ per condition and their standard errors are visualized in Figure 1; for details see Table 4.

Several follow-up F tests for effects of participant sex on interviewers were significant. Fundamental frequency of the interviewer and breathiness were higher when the participant was a woman (cf. Table 4)

3.3 Accommodation Between Interactants

Does accommodation vary with depression severity?

As discussed in Section 2.5 we compute Pearson's ρ for all speech parameters. The extracted accommodation parameters were moderately correlated (cf. Table 5). As above,

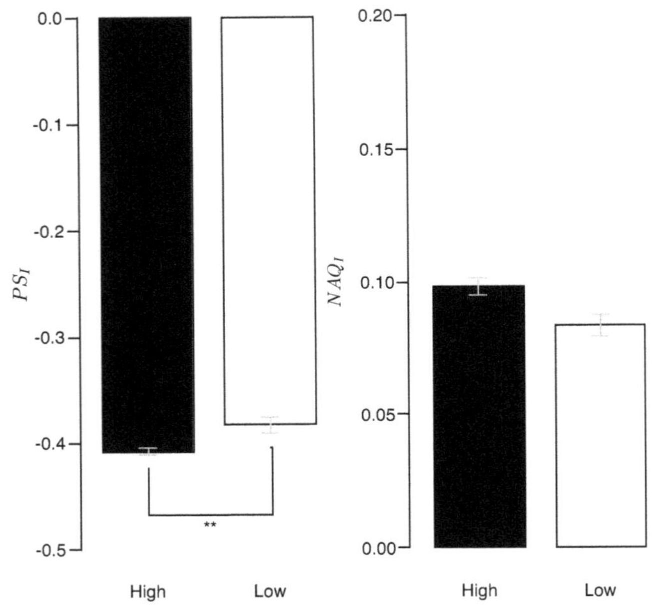

Figure 1: Acoustic Features of Interviewer Speech Characteristics. Observed acoustic features of interviewers across conditions high depression severity (High) vs. low severity (Low). The displayed whiskers signify standard errors and the bracket show significant results with ** ... p < .01.

Table 5: Correlation of acoustic accommodation measurements between participants and interviewers. ρ for the observed accommodation.

	ρ_{f_0}	ρ_{MDQ}	ρ_{PS}	ρ_{NAQ}	ρ_{QOQ}
ρ_{f_0}	1	.362**	.194	.279*	.269*
ρ_{MDQ}		1	-.024	.236*	.033
ρ_{PS}			1	.318**	.532**
ρ_{NAQ}				1	.479**
ρ_{QOQ}					1

they were analyzed using MANOVA with depression severity, sex, and sex-by-depression severity interaction entered as covariates. The effect of depression severity was significant ($F(5, 55) = 2.508$, $p = .037$). There was no main effect or interaction for sex ($F(5, 55) = 1.648$, $p = .16$; and $F(5, 55) = 1.195$, $p = .320$, respectively).

Table 6: Follow-up F test results for interactant accommodation depending on depression severity.

	High Severity		Low Severity	
	μ	σ	μ	σ
ρ_{PS}	0.160	0.300	0.350	0.281*
ρ_{QOQ}	0.093	0.274	0.269	0.331**

Follow-up F tests for the individual speech variables and the observed accommodation measured as Pearson's ρ revealed significant effects for higher accommodation for low depression severity for ρ_{PS} and ρ_{QOQ}. Effects for other parameters failed to reach significance, for details see Table 6.

The observed accommodation for ρ_{PS} and ρ_{QOQ} per condition and the standard errors are visualized in Figure 2.

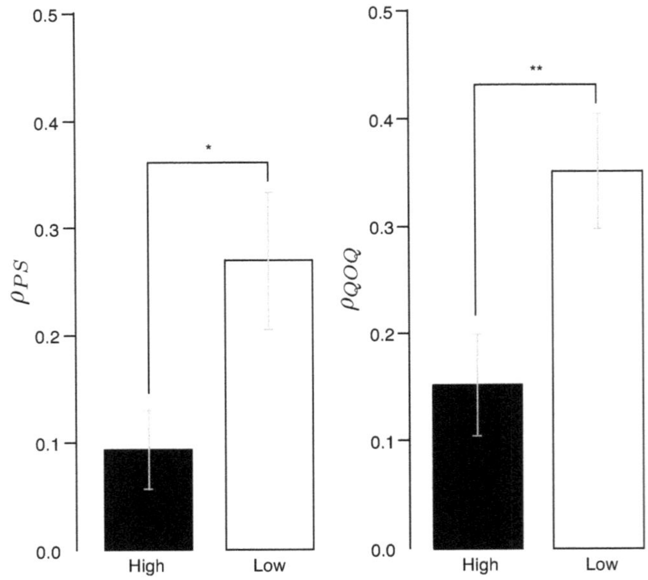

Figure 2: Acoustic Accommodation between Participants and Interviewers. Observed acoustic accommodation as measured as Pearson's ρ between participants and interviewers across conditions high depression severity (High) vs. low severity (Low). The displayed whiskers signify standard errors and the brackets show significant results with * ... p < .05 and ** ... p < .01.

4. DISCUSSION

We investigated acoustic characteristics in depressed participants and their interviewers. The participants varied in their level of depression severity (that is, high versus low). For participants, of the five acoustic parameters evaluated, none varied with depression severity. The only obtained effects were expected ones for sex. Women for example had higher fundamental frequency. These findings for sex effects are consistent with [45]. The lack of findings for depression effects could be due to several factors. A methodological reason may be that we used only a subset of the data used by [66], as well as the use of SSRI might have influenced speech characteristics. Further, most previous findings for f_0 effects in depression were from comparisons with non-depressed participants [3]. Because participants with depression differ in many ways from those without depression [46], such results lack specificity for depression. Those studies that have investigated change in depression severity over time have reported very small effect sizes that depended on large numbers of participants [49]. Small effect sizes are unlikely to have much utility for machine learning.

Another factor may be differences in participant characteristics across studies. With the exception of [66], previous work has compared depressed with non-depressed participants [13, 59, 65]; whereas we made comparisons within a depressed sample. All participants met criteria for Major Depression Disorder, all had histories of multiple, protracted episodes, and they varied only in their current level of severity. People with chronic history of depression may be very different than those that have never been depressed or only depressed in a limited way. High trait neuroticism and low trait extraversion, for instance, are much more likely in people with histories of chronic depression [46] These differences may contribute to relative stability in acoustic parameters robust to variation in depression severity.

Other factors may have been context related. In [59], participants were interviewed by virtual humans rather than humans and the interviews included broader range of questions [31, 17]. The latter may have occasioned more diversity in vocal samples, and vocal timing varied markedly from that with human interviewers. Accommodation was not possible with the virtual humans. [48] studied depressed adolescents in extended conversations with their two parents. In [65], participants were involved in human-computer interaction tasks. These factors, too, may explain the differences across studies. Greater attention is needed to the observational contexts and individual differences in studies.

Consistent with previous findings [66], interviewer acoustic characteristics showed a strong relationship with severity of depression. In particular, interviewers exhibited significantly more breathy voice characteristics when interacting with highly depressed participants. Our findings extend the findings of Yang et al. [66] who found that interviewer f_0 mean and variability were strongly related to depression severity. The obtained results can be explained by the increased felt empathy towards the interviewee. As previously investigated, breathy voice qualities were associated with sad emotion, friendly attitude, and intimate interpersonal relation in perceptual experiments [30]. Further, Scherer et al. have previously reported more breathy voice qualities in interviewers' voice and back-channels when interviewing suicidal adolescents [58]. Findings such as these suggest that depression effects are bidirectional and that nonverbal behavior in the non-depressed interactant could provide a sensitive barometer of depression. Behavioral differences of interviewers may be more indicative of a participant's condition than the participant's own behavior [67]. This further underlines the importance to investigate the behaviors jointly within dyadic HRSD interviews as argued in [23].

We utilized a time-aligned moving average approach to assess acoustic accommodation within dyadic HRSD screening interviews between the interviewer and the participant. This approach overcomes the issue of asynchronously observed speech in dyadic interactions and enables the investigation of accommodation between the interactants [15]. With respect to the accommodation between interactants, we identified a main effect of depression severity on PS and QOQ (cf. Section 2.4). They both were inversely correlated with depression severity. Hence, accommodation is significantly increased for interviews where the participants have low depression severity. These findings are consistent with the hypothesis that a function of depression is to attenuate interpersonal coordination in the service of social isolation [28]. Further, prosodic accommodation has been found to be perceptually correlated with increased perceived flow of conversation, speaker engagement, and liking [15].

We found accommodation effects, a remaining research question is how these effects are achieved. We might assume that the direction of effects is from participant to interviewer. That is, interviewers are responding to the participants' restricted acoustic characteristics. Alternatively, there may be dynamic adjustments made over the course of the interviews. Participants and interviewers may each be both cause and effect of the other person's behavior [43]

5. CONCLUSIONS

We investigated acoustic characteristics of depressed participants and their interviewers in a clinical interview to assess depression severity. All participants met stringent criteria for Major Depressive Disorder and had histories of multiple and often lengthy episodes. They differed in whether their symptoms were high or low at the time of the interview. We found no variation in acoustic characteristics in relation to severity for the participants. We found strong effects in interviewers of participants' depression severity, and we found strong accommodation effects. To the best of our knowledge, this study is the first to reveal accommodation for acoustic parameters related to depression severity.

Acknowledgements

This work was supported in part by US National Institutes of Health grants MH096951 and MH051435 to the University of Pittsburgh. This work is supported by DARPA under contract (W911NF-04-D-0005) and U.S. Army RDECOM. The content does not necessarily reflect the position or the policy of the Government, and no official endorsement should be inferred.

6. REFERENCES

[1] *Diagnostic and statistical manual of mental disorders.* American Psychiatric Association, Washington, DC, 1994.

[2] Cmu sphinx: Open source toolkit for speech recognition. Technical report, Carnegie Mellon University, Undated.

[3] S. Alghowinem, R. Goecke, M. Wagner, J. Epps, M. Breakspear, and G. Parker. From joyous to clinically depressed: Mood detection using spontaneous speech. In *Proceedings of International Florida Artificial Intelligence Research Society Conference (FLAIRS 2012)*, pages 141–146, 2012.

[4] P. Alku, T. Bäckström, and E. Vilkman. Glottal wave analysis with pitch synchronous iterative adaptive inverse filtering. *Speech Communication*, 11(2-3):109–118, 1992.

[5] P. Alku, T. Bäckström, and E. Vilkman. Normalized amplitude quotient for parameterization of the glottal flow. *Journal of the Acoustical Society of America*, 112(2):701–710, 2002.

[6] M. Alpert, E. R. Pouget, and R. R. Silva. Reflections of depression in acoustic measures of the patient's speech. *Journal of Affective Disorders*, 66(1):59–69, 2001.

[7] C. Barras, E. Geoffrois, Z. Wu, and M. Liberman. Transcriber: development and use of a tool for assisting speech corpora production. *Speech Communication special issue on Speech Annotation and Corpus Tools*, 33:5–22, 2001.

[8] P. Boersma. Praat, a system for doing phonetics by computer. *Glot International*, 5(9):341–345, 2001.

[9] S. Brennan. Lexical entrainment in spontaneous dialog. *Proceedings of ISSD*, pages 41–44, 1996.

[10] N. Campbell and P. Mokhtari. Voice quality: The 4th prosodic dimension. In *Proceedings of the 15th international congress of phonetic sciences (ICPhS'03)*, pages 2417–2420. ICPhS, 2003.

[11] M. Cannizzaro, B. Harel, N. Reilly, P. Chappell, and P. J. Snyder. Voice acoustical measurement of the severity of major depression. *Brain and Cognition*, 56(1):30–35, 2004.

[12] C. d'Alessandro and N. Sturmel. Glottal closure instant and voice source analysis using time-scale lines of maximum amplitude. *Sadhana*, 36(5):601–622, 2011.

[13] J. K. Darby, N. Simmons, and P. A. Berger. Speech and voice parameters of depression: a pilot study. *Journal of Communication Disorders*, 17(2):75–85, 1984.

[14] R. J. Davidson, editor. *Anxiety, Depression, and Emotion*. Oxford University Press, 2000.

[15] C. De Looze, S. Scherer, B. Vaughan, and N. Campbell. Investigating automatic measurements of prosodic accommodation and its dynamics in social interaction. *Speech Communication*, 58:11–34, 2014.

[16] G. Degottex, J. Kane, T. Drugman, T. Raitio, and S. Scherer. Covarep - a collaborative voice analysis repository for speech technologies. In *Proceedings of IEEE International Conference on Acoustics, Speech and Signal Processing (ICASSP 2014)*, pages 960–964, 2014.

[17] D. DeVault, R. Artstein, G. Benn, T. Dey, E. Fast, A. Gainer, K. Georgilia, J. Gratch, A. Hartholt, M. Lhommet, G. Lucas, S. Marsella, F. Morbini, A. Nazarian, S. Scherer, G. Stratou, A. Suri, D. Traum, R. Wood, Y. Xu, A. Rizzo, and L.-P. Morency. Simsensei: A virtual human interviewer for healthcare decision support. In *Proceedings of Autonomous Agents and Multiagent Systems (AAMAS)*, pages 1061–1068, 2014.

[18] T. Drugman and A. Abeer. Joint robust voicing detection and pitch estimation based on residual harmonics. In *Proceedings of Interspeech 2011*, pages 1973–1976. ISCA, 2011.

[19] S. Duncan. Some signals and rules for taking speaking turns in conversations. *Journal of Personality and Social Psychology*, 23(2):283–292, 1972.

[20] R. Elliott, R. Zahn, J. F. W. Deakin, and I. M. Anderson. Affective cognition and its disruption in mood disorders. *Neuropsychopharmacology*, 36:153–182, 2011.

[21] M. B. First, R. L. Spitzer, M. Gibbon, and J. B. W. Williams. *Structured clinical interview for DSM-IV axis I disorders*. Biometrics Research Department, New York State Psychiatric Institute, New York, patient edition edition, 1995.

[22] A. J. Flint, S. E. Black, I. Campbell-Taylor, G. F. G. Gailey, and C. Levinton. Abnormal speech articulation, psychomotor retardation, and subcortical dysfunction in major depression. *Journal of Psychiatric Research*, 27(3):309–319, 1993.

[23] G. N. Foley and J. P. Gentile. Nonverbal communication in psychotherapy. *Psychiatry*, 7(6):38–44, 2010.

[24] J. C. Fournier, R. J. DeRubeis, S. D. Hollon, S. Dimidjian, J. D. Amsterdam, R. C. Shelton, and F. J. Antidepressant drug effects and depression severity: A patient-level meta-analysis. *Journal of the American Medial Association*, 303(1):47–53, 2010.

[25] D. J. France, R. G. Shiavi, S. E. Silverman, M. K. Silverman, and D. M. Wilkes. Acoustical properties of speech as indicators of depression and suicidal risk. *IEEE Transactions on Biomedical Engineering*, 47(7):829–837, 2000.

[26] R. W. Frick. Communicating emotion: The role of prosodic features. *Psychological Bulletin*, 97(3):412–429, 1985.

[27] H. Giles, N. Coupland, and J. Coupland. Accommodation theory: Communication, context, and consequence. *Contexts of accommodation: Developments in applied sociolinguistics*, pages 1–68, 1991.

[28] J. M. Girard, J. F. Cohn, M. H. Mahoor, S. M. Mavadati, Z. Hammal, and D. P. Rosenwald. Nonverbal social withdrawal in depression: Evidence from manual and automatic analyses. *Image and Vision Computing Journal*, 2014.

[29] C. Gobl and A. N. Chasaide. Amplitude-based source parameters for measuring voice quality. In *Proceedings of ISCA Tutorial and Research Workshop on Voice Quality: Functions, Analysis and Synthesis (VOQUAL'03)*, pages 151–156. ISCA, 2003.

[30] C. Gobl and A. Ní Chasaide. The role of voice quality in communicating emotion, mood and attitude. *Speech Communication*, 40:189–212, 2003.

[31] J. Gratch, R. Artstein, G. Lucas, S. Scherer, A. Nazarian, R. Wood, J. Boberg, D. DeVault, S. Marsella, D. Traum, A. Rizzo, and L.-P. Morency. The distress analysis interview corpus of human and computer interviews. In *Proceedings of Language Resources and Evaluation Conference (LREC)*, 2014.

[32] T. Hacki. Klassifizierung von glottisdysfunktionen mit hilfe der elektroglottographie. *Folia Phoniatrica*, pages 43–48, 1989.

[33] J. A. Hall, J. A. Harrigan, and R. Rosenthal. Nonverbal behavior in clinician-patient interaction. *Applied and Preventive Psychology*, 4(1):21–37, 1995.

[34] M. Hamilton. A rating scale for depression. *Journal of Neurology and Neurosurgery*, 23:56–61, 1960.

[35] H. Hanson, K. Stevens, H. Kuo, M. Chen, and J. Slifka. Towards models of phonation. *Journal of Phonetics*, (29):451–480, 2001.

[36] N. Henrich, C. d'Alessandro, and B. Doval. Spectral correlates of voice open quotient and glottal flow asymmetry: theory, limits and experimental data. *Proceedings of EUROSPEECH, Scandanavia*, pages 47–50, 2001.

[37] S. D. Hollon, M. E. Thase, and J. C. Markowitz. Treatment and prevention of depression. *Psychological Science in the Public Interest*, 3(2):38–77, 2002.

[38] J. Jaffe, B. Beebe, S. Feldstein, C. L. Crown, and M. Jasnow. Rhythms of dialogue in early infancy. *Monographs of the Society for Research in Child Development*, 66:1–8, 2001.

[39] P. N. Juslin and P. Laukka. Communication of emotions in vocal expression and music performance:

Different channels, same code? *Psychological Bulletin*, 129:770–814, 2003.
[40] J. Kane and C. Gobl. Identifying regions of non-modal phonation using features of the wavelet transform. *Proceedings of Interspeech, Florence, Italy*, pages 177–180, 2011.
[41] J. Kane and C. Gobl. Wavelet maxima dispersion for breathy to tense voice discrimination. *IEEE Transactions on Audio Speech and Language processing*, Under Review.
[42] J. Kane, S. Scherer, M. Aylett, L.-P. Morency, and C. Gobl. Speaker and language independent voice quality classification applied to unlabelled corpora of expressive speech. In *Proceedings of International Conference on Acoustics, Speech, and Signal Processing (ICASSP)*, pages 7982–7986. IEEE, 2013.
[43] D. A. Kenny, L. Mannetti, A. Pierro, S. Livi, and D. A. Kashy. The statistical analysis of data from small groups. *Journal of Personality and Social Psychology*, 83(1):126–137, 2002.
[44] R. Kessler, W. Chiu, O. Demler, and E. E. Walters. Prevalence, severity, and comorbidity of 12-month dsm-iv disorders in the national comorbidity survey replication. *Archives of General Psychiatry*, 62:617–627, 2005.
[45] D. H. Klatt and L. C. Klatt. Analysis, synthesis, and perception of voice quality variations among female and male talkers. *Journal of the Acoustical Society of America*, 87(2):820–857, 1990.
[46] R. Kotov, W. Gamez, F. Schmidt, and D. Watson. Linking big personality traits to anxiety, depressive, and substance use disorders: A meta-analysis. *Psychological Bulletin*, 136(5):768–821, 2010.
[47] J. Leff and E. Abberton. Voice pitch measurements in schizophrenia and depression. *Psychological Medicine*, 11(4):849–852, 1981.
[48] L.-S. Low, N. C. Maddage, M. Lech, L. B. Sheeber, and N. B. Allen. Detection of clinical depression in adolescents? speech during family interactions. *IEEE Transactions on Biomedical Engineering*, 58(3):574–586, 2010.
[49] J. C. Mundt, A. P. Vogel, D. E. Feltner, and W. R. Lenderking. Vocal acoustic biomarkers of depression severity and treatment response. *Biological Psychiatry*, 72(7):580–587, 2012.
[50] A. Nilsonne. Speech characteristics as indicators of depressive illness. *Acta Psychiatrica Scandinavica*, 77(3):253–263, 1988.
[51] J. P. O'Reardon, P. Cristancho, and A. D. Peshek. Vagus nerve stimulation (vns) and treatment of depression: To the brainstem and beyond. *Psychiatry*, 3(5):54–63, 2006.
[52] W. H. Organization. The global burden of disease: 2004 update. World Health Organization, 2008.
[53] J. Pardo. On phonetic convergence during conversational interaction. *The Journal of the Acoustical Society of America*, 119:2382, 2006.
[54] A. Pentland. *Honest signals: How they shape our world*. MIT Press, Cambridge, 2008.
[55] B. S. Reed. Speech rythm across turn transitions in cross-cultural talk-in-interaction. *Journal of Pragmatics*, 42(4):1037–1059, 2010.
[56] A. D. Rubin and R. T. Sataloff. Vocal fold paresis and paralysis. *Otolaryngologic Clinics of North America*, 40(5):1109–1131, 2007.
[57] S. Scherer, J. Kane, C. Gobl, and F. Schwenker. Investigating fuzzy-input fuzzy-output support vector machines for robust voice quality classification. *Computer Speech and Language*, 27(1):263–287, 2013.
[58] S. Scherer, J. P. Pestian, and L.-P. Morency. Investigating the speech characteristics of suicidal adolescents. In *Proceedings of International Conference on Acoustics, Speech, and Signal Processing (ICASSP)*, pages 709–713. IEEE, 2013.
[59] S. Scherer, G. Stratou, J. Gratch, and L.-P. Morency. Investigating voice quality as a speaker-independent indicator of depression and ptsd. In *Proceedings of Interspeech 2013*, pages 847–851. ISCA, 2013.
[60] D. Schrijvers, W. Hulstijn, and B. G. Sabbe. Psychomotor symptoms in depression: a diagnostic, pathophysiological and therapeutic tool. *Journal of Affective Disorders*, 109(1-2):1–20, 2008.
[61] B. Schuller, A. Batliner, S. Steidl, and D. Seppi. Recognising realistic emotions and affect in speech: State of the art and lessons learned from the first challenge. *Speech and Communication*, 53(9/10):1062–1087, 2010.
[62] T. Shimizu, N. Furuse, T. Yamazaki, Y. Ueta, T. Sato, and S. Nagata. Chaos of vowel /a/ in japanese patients with depression: a preliminary study. *Journal of Occupational Health*, 47(3):267–269, 2005.
[63] C. Sobin and H. A. Sackheim. Psychomotor symptoms of depression. *American Journal of Psychiatry*, 154(1):4–17, 1997.
[64] R. Timcke, H. von Leden, and P. Moore. Laryngeal vibrations: measurements of the glottic wave. Part 1: The normal vibratory cycle. *Archives of Otolaryngology - Head and Neck surgery*, 68(1):1–19, 1958.
[65] J. R. Williamson, T. F. Quatieri, B. S. Helfer, R. Horwitz, B. Yu, and D. D. Mehta. Vocal biomarkers of depression based on motor incoordination. In *Proceedings of the 3rd ACM international workshop on Audio/visual emotion challenge*, AVEC '13, pages 41–48. ACM, 2013.
[66] Y. Yang, C. Fairbairn, and J. F. Cohn. Detecting depression severity from vocal prosody. *IEEE Transactions on Affective Computing*, 4(2):142–150, 2013.
[67] M. Yarczower, J. E. Kilbride, and A. T. Beck. Changes in nonverbal behavior of therapists and depressed patients during cognitive therapy. *Psychological Reports*, 69(3):915–919, 1991.
[68] Z. Zeng, M. Pantic, G. Roisman, and T. S. Huang. A survey of affect recognition methods: Audio, visual, and spontaneous expressions. *IEEE Transactions Pattern Analysis and Machine Intelligence*, 31(1):31–58, 2009.
[69] A. J. Zlochower and J. F. Cohn. Vocal timing in face-to-face interaction of clinically depressed and nondepressed mothers and their 4-month-old infants. *Infant Behavior and Development*, 19:373–376, 1996.

Touching the Void – Introducing CoST: Corpus of Social Touch

Merel M. Jung[1], Ronald Poppe[2], Mannes Poel[1], Dirk K. J. Heylen[1]
[1]University of Twente, P.O. Box 217, 7500 AE, Enschede, The Netherlands
[2]University of Utrecht, P.O Box 80125, 3508 TC, Utrecht, The Netherlands
m.m.jung@utwente.nl, r.w.poppe@uu.nl, m.poel@utwente.nl, d.k.j.heylen@utwente.nl

ABSTRACT

Touch behavior is of great importance during social interaction. To transfer the tactile modality from interpersonal interaction to other areas such as Human-Robot Interaction (HRI) and remote communication automatic recognition of social touch is necessary. This paper introduces CoST: Corpus of Social Touch, a collection containing 7805 instances of 14 different social touch gestures. The gestures were performed in three variations: gentle, normal and rough, on a sensor grid wrapped around a mannequin arm. Recognition of the rough variations of these 14 gesture classes using Bayesian classifiers and Support Vector Machines (SVMs) resulted in an overall accuracy of 54% and 53%, respectively. Furthermore, this paper provides more insight into the challenges of automatic recognition of social touch gestures, including which gestures can be recognized more easily and which are more difficult to recognize.

Categories and Subject Descriptors

H.5.2 [**User Interfaces**]: Haptic I/O; I.5.2 [**PATTERN RECOGNITION**]: Design Methodology—*Classifier design and evaluation*

General Terms

Measurement, Performance

Keywords

Social touch; Touch corpus; Touch gesture recognition

1. INTRODUCTION

Touch behavior is one of the important non-verbal forms of social interaction as are visual cues such as facial expressions and body gestures [16]. In interpersonal interaction, touch is important for establishing and maintaining social interaction [5]. Also, touch is used to generate and communicate both positive and negative emotions as well as to express intimacy, power, and status [5, 7]. The positive effects of touch on well-being, such as stress reduction, are extensively described in the literature (for a review see [4]). Furthermore, it is known that tactile interaction may affect compliance and liking [5, 7]. Touch behavior is seen in many different forms of social interaction: a handshake as a greeting, a high-five to celebrate a joint accomplishment, a tap on the shoulder to gain someone's attention, a comforting hug from a friend, or holding hands with a romantic partner.

The human sense of touch consists of physiological inputs from various receptors: receptors in the skin register pressure, pain and temperature while receptors in the muscles, tendons and joints register body motion [5]. However, just equipping a robot or interface with touch sensors is not enough. Automatic recognition of social touch is necessary to transfer the tactile modality from interpersonal interaction to other areas such as Human-Robot Interaction (HRI) and remote communication [5, 6]. Providing tactile social intelligence to robots and virtual agents can open up opportunities for various applications. If a robot can understand social touch behavior, the robot can respond accordingly – resulting in richer and more natural interaction. One of these applications is robot therapy in which robots are used to comfort people in stressful environments such as children in hospitals and elderly people in nursing homes [15].

Some promising attempts have been made to recognize different touch gestures for specific applications. However, recognition rates depend on the degree of similarity between the gestures. In order to engage in tactile interaction with a robot or an interface, there is a need for reliable recognition of a wide range of social touch gestures. A Robust touch gesture recognition system should be real-time and generalizable across users. Because there is a need for touch datasets, we have recorded a corpus of social touch gestures to characterize various touch gestures and work towards reliable recognition. The main contributions of this paper are a Corpus of Social Touch (CoST) and the insights from a first exploration into the recognition of these touch gestures.

The remainder of the paper is organized as follows: the next section discusses related work on recognition of social touch; Section 3 presents CoST; classification results of the gestures from a subset of the data are presented and discussed in Sections 4 and 5, respectively; The paper concludes in Section 6.

2. RELATED WORK

Previous attempts to sense, classify and interpret social touch behavior include the development and deployment of

ICMI'14, November 12–16, 2014, Istanbul, Turkey.

ACM 978-1-4503-2885-2/14/11 ...$15.00.
http://dx.doi.org/10.1145/2663204.2663242

several animal and humanoid robots, as well as the use of touch for other applications such as remote communication. One approach is to focus on building an artificial skin for robots that simulate the human somatosensory system using touch sensors [3]. To allow for physical interaction between humans and robots, Naya et al. intended to cover a robot with sheets of pressure sensitive ink. Five different touch gestures: 'pat', 'scratch', 'slap', 'stroke' and 'tickle', were performed on a single 44×44 gridded sensor sheet [12]. The absolute pressure values and total touch surface were found to be discriminative features for the touch gestures 'pat', 'scratch' and 'slap' using the k-nearest neighbor method. 'Stroke' and 'tickle' could be distinguished using temporal differences in pressure and touch surface using Fisher's linear discriminant method. Combining the results of two classifications using different classifiers and features resulted in an overall accuracy of 87% between subjects. Silvera-Tawil and colleagues developed an artificial skin to enable tactile HRI based on the principle of Electrical Impedance Tomography to measure pressure [13]. Six touch gestures: 'pat', 'push', 'scratch', 'slap', 'stroke' and 'tap' were performed on a flat surface covered with the artificial skin. Classification of the gestures using the LogitBoost algorithm resulted in overall accuracies of 91% within a single subject and 74% between multiple subjects. The same six touch gestures were performed by the same participants on the back of a single person who acted as a human classifier resulting in an average performance of 86%. In a follow-up study, Silvera-Tawil et al. compared human touch recognition on the arm with automatic recognition on a full-sized mannequin arm covered with the artificial skin [14]. Nine gestures: 'no-touch', 'pat', 'pull', 'push', 'scratch', 'slap', 'stroke', 'squeeze', and 'tap' were classified by human receivers and the LogitBoost algorithm. Human recognition ($M = 90\%$) was higher than automatic classification using leave-one-subject-out cross-validation ($M = 71\%$).

Another approach is to focus on the embodiment of a specific robot which can be covered with sensors. *The Huggable* is a robotic companion in the form of a teddy bear [15]. In an initial study nine touch gestures: 'contact', 'pat', 'pet', 'poke', 'rub', 'scratch', 'slap', 'squeeze' and 'tickle' were performed on an arm of the robot equipped with temperature sensors (thermistors), proximity sensors (electric field sensors) and pressure sensors (Quantum Tunneling Composite sensors) [15]. Using a neural network to classify 199 gesture instances showed that some touch gestures such as 'rub' and 'squeeze' could be recognized from the sensor data, however, 'slap' could not be recognized. *The Sensate Bear* platform was developed to explore the feasibility of real-time classification of social touch before integration with *The Huggable* teddy bear [10]. To sense social touch, the body of the robot bear was covered with capacitive sensors to register proximity and contact area as well as to distinguish between humans and objects. Real-time classification of four gestures showed that 'foot-rub' and 'head-pat' could be accurately recognized while 'hug' and 'tickle' were more problematic. 'Hugs' were difficult to sense because sensing through clothing was not possible while 'tickle' was difficult to recognize because of the large variation in body locations. *Haptic Creature* is a robot that resembles a small lap animal which can sense and react to touch input [1, 17]. A first study into the recognition of four touch gestures – 'pat', 'poke', 'slap' and 'stroke' – performed by a single participant was based on the data of the force sensing resistors which were attached all over the body of the *Haptic Creature* [1]. Accuracies ranged from 11% to 77% depending on the sensor density of the part of the body that was touched. Cooney et al. used a mock-up of a humanoid robot to study affectionate touch behavior towards the mock-up [2]. Two types of touch sensors using photo-interrupters were incorporated in the upper body of the humanoid mock-up: one for detecting perpendicular movement (i.e. towards and from the body surface) such patting and the other for detecting lateral movement (i.e. parallel to the body surface) such as rubbing. Both computer vision (using Microsoft Kinect) and the touch sensors were used to recognize twenty different touch interactions such as 'pat head', 'rub back' and 'shake hand'. Also, the performance of two classifiers: Support Vector Machines (SVMs) with radial basis function kernel and the k-nearest neighbor method were compared using leave-one-subject-out cross-validation. Overall accuracies showed that the SVM classifiers consistently outperformed the k-nearest neighbor method. Recognition for the SVMs of touch gestures using only vision (78%) performed better than using only touch (72%) while the combination of both modalities yielded the best performance (91%).

Aside from tactile HRI, the recognition of social touch can also be used for other types of interfaces which can, for example, enable remote communication. *Emoballoon* is a balloon interface for social touch which contains a barometric pressure sensor and a microphone [11]. Seven different touch gestures: 'grasp', 'hug', 'press', 'punch', 'rub', 'slap' and 'no-touch' were classified using SVMs with the radial basis function kernel resulting in an overall accuracy of 75% between participants and 84% within participants. In a study of Huisman et al. on communicative mediated touch, participants wore a tactile sleeve containing a pressure sensitive input layer and an output layer consisting of vibrotactile motors [9]. Subjects received six different touch gestures: 'hit', 'poke', 'press', 'rub', 'squeeze' and 'stroke' on the vibrotactile display of the sleeve which they had to imitate using the sleeve's input layer. Comparison of the duration and contact area used for the prerecorded gestures and the imitated gestures showed that people had difficulty with the precise replication of the touch duration and touch surface. Participants were not directly asked to classify the gestures, however, human classification of the gestures based on video recordings of the imitated gestures showed that the received gesture often differed from the imitated gesture especially for the gestures 'rub' and 'stroke'.

In summary, development of an artificial skin to provide future robots with a sense of touch is beneficial but brings extra design requirements such as flexibility and stretchability to cover curved surfaces and moving joints [13, 14]. In the short term, the use of a fully embodied robot covered with sensors has the advantage of providing information about body location which can be used to recognize touch [2, 10]. However, this can cause problems ensuring adequate sensor density on all body parts [1]. Furthermore, Silvera-Tawil et al. showed that comparable accuracies can be achieved using partial embodiment in the form of an arm covered with artificial skin [13, 14]. Automatic classification on several sets of touch gestures, ranging from 4 to 20 different gestures, performed on various robots, robot skins and interfaces yielded mixed results. For example, recognition varied per gesture [10, 15] and location [1]. Human classification of touch gestures outperformed automatic classification [13, 14]. However, human gesture recognition of mediated touch was found to be more difficult [9].

In order to work towards more robust gesture recognition, further research on the characteristics of touch gestures is needed. One central problem is that there is no gesture data set available for research and benchmarking. This work focuses on improving touch gesture recognition instead of on embodiment of a robot/ interface by collecting a data set containing a relatively large set of touch gestures.

3. COST: CORPUS OF SOCIAL TOUCH

To address the need for social touch datasets, we recorded a corpus of social touch gestures. The data set is publicly available[1]. CoST consists of sensor data from 31 participants performing 3 variations (normal, gentle and rough) of 14 different touch gestures. Each gesture was performed 6 times on a sensor grid wrapped around a mannequin arm. The arm was chosen as the contact surface because it is one of the least invasive body areas to be touched [8] and presumably a neutral body location to touch others. The data from the pressure sensor consists of a pressure value (i.e. intensity) per channel (i.e. location) at 135 fps (i.e. temporal resolution).

3.1 Touch gestures

The touch gestures (see Table 1) were taken from the touch dictionary of [17]. The list of gestures was adapted to suit interaction with an artificial human arm. Touch gestures involving physical movement of the arm itself, for example lift, push and swing, were omitted because the movement of the mannequin arm could not be sensed by the pressure sensor grid. In the instructions of the gesture to perform, the participants were shown the name of the gesture and not the definition from [17]. Instead, they were shown an example video before the start of the data collection in which each gesture was demonstrated. During the data collection, 14 different touch gestures were performed 6 times in 3 variations, resulting in 252 gesture instances per participant. The order of gestures was pseudo-randomized into three blocks using the following rule: each instruction was given two times per block but the same instruction was not given twice in succession. A single fixed list of gestures was constructed using this criterion. This list and the reversed order of the list were used as instructions in a counterbalanced design. After each touch gesture, the participant had to press a key to see the next gesture. The keystrokes were used for segmentation afterwards. Figure 1 shows the evolution over time of the summed pressure for a gesture instance of each class. Figure 2 and Figure 3 show the evolution over time of the summed pressure for the gesture 'rough grab' performed by a single participant and multiple different participants, respectively. These examples illustrate the variation in duration and intensity of a gesture, within participants and between participants.

3.2 Setup

For the sensing of the gestures, an 8×8 pressure sensor grid (from *plug-and-wear*, www.plugandwear.com) was connected to a Teensy 3.0 USB Development Board (by *PJRC*, www.pjrc.com). The sensor is made of textile consisting of

[1]Data available on request, contact *m.m.jung@utwente.nl*

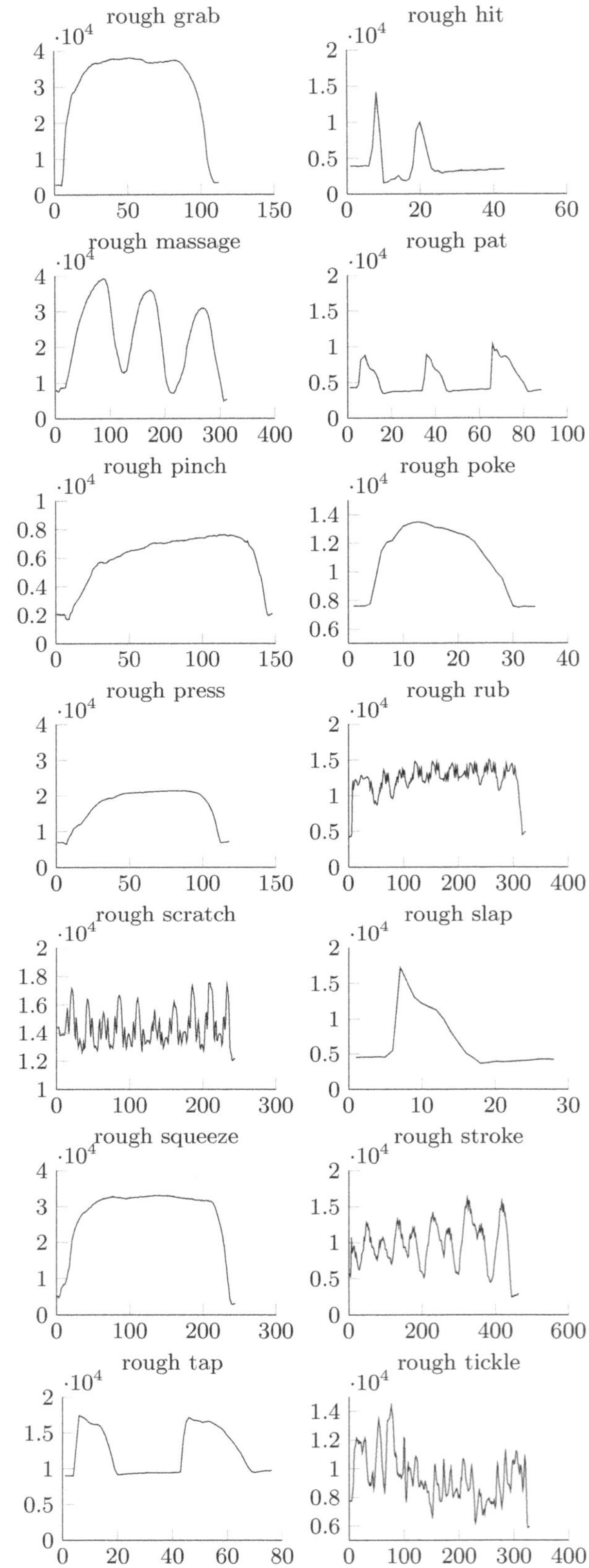

Figure 1: Summed pressure (y-axis) over time (x-axis) for a gesture instance of each class.

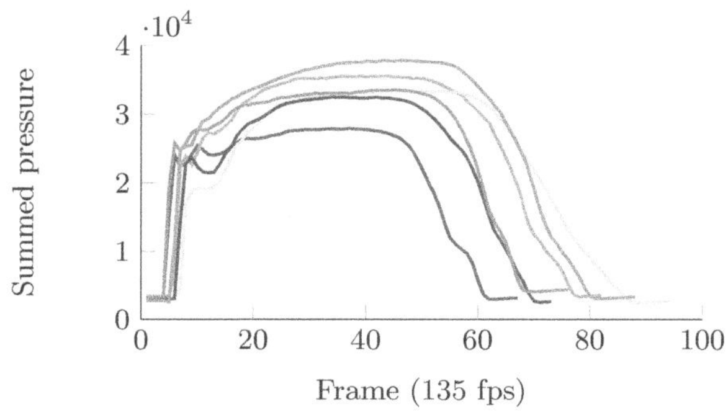

Figure 2: Summed pressure per frame of a 'rough grab' performed six times by a single participant.

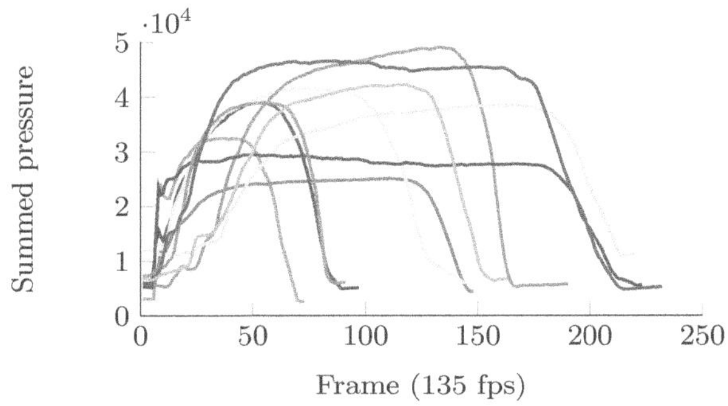

Figure 3: Summed pressure per frame of a 'rough grab' performed by multiple different participants.

Table 1: Touch dictionary adapted from [17].

Gesture label	Gesture definition
Grab	Grasp or seize the arm suddenly and roughly.
Hit	Deliver a forcible blow to the arm with either a closed fist or the side or back of your hand.
Massage	Rub or knead the arm with your hands.
Pat	Gently and quickly touch the arm with the flat of your hand.
Pinch	Tightly and sharply grip the arm between your fingers and thumb.
Poke	Jab or prod the arm with your finger.
Press	Exert a steady force on the arm with your flattened fingers or hand.
Rub	Move your hand repeatedly back and forth on the arm with firm pressure.
Scratch	Rub the arm with your fingernails.
Slap	Quickly and sharply strike the arm with your open hand.
Squeeze	Firmly press the arm between your fingers or both hands.
Stroke	Move your hand with gentle pressure over arm, often repeatedly.
Tap	Strike the arm with a quick light blow or blows using one or more fingers.
Tickle	Touch the arm with light finger movements.

five layers. The two outer layers are protective layers made of felt. Each outer layer is attached to a layer containing eight strips of conductive fabric separated by non-conductive strips. Between the two conductive layers is the middle layer which comprises a sheet of piezoresistive material. The conductive layers are positioned orthogonally so that they form an 8 by 8 matrix. One of the conductive layers is attached to the power supply while the other is attached to the A/D converter of the Teensy board. The sensors' detectable pressure ranges from 1.8×10^{-3} to > 0.1 MPa at an ambient temperature of 25 °C. After A/D conversion, the pressure values of the 64 channels range from 0 to 1023 (i.e., 10 bits). Sensor data was sampled at 135 Hz. The sensor was attached to the forearm of a full size rigid mannequin arm consisting of the left hand and the arm up to the shoulder (see Figure 4). The mannequin arm was fastened to the table to prevent it from slipping. Video recordings were made during the data collection as verification of the sensor data and the instructions given. The instructions for which gesture to perform had been scripted and were displayed to the participants on a PC monitor.

Figure 4: Set-up showing the pressure sensor (the black fabric) wrapped around the mannequin arm and the computer monitor displaying the instructions.

3.3 Participants

A total of 32 people volunteered to participate in the data collection. Data of one participant was omitted due to technical difficulties. The remaining participants, 24 male and 7 female, all studied or worked at the University of Twente. The age of the participants ranged from 21 to 62 years ($M = 34, SD = 12$) and 29 were right-handed.

3.4 Preprocessing

The raw data was checked and segmented before feature extraction. Each subset of variations consists of 14 gestures $\times$ 6 repetitions $\times$ 31 people = 2604 gestures in total. Coarse segmentation was based on the key strokes of the participants marking the end of a gesture. As segmentation between keystrokes still contained many frames from before and after the gesture, the data was further segmented. Removing these additional frames is especially important to reduce noise in the calculation of features which use a time

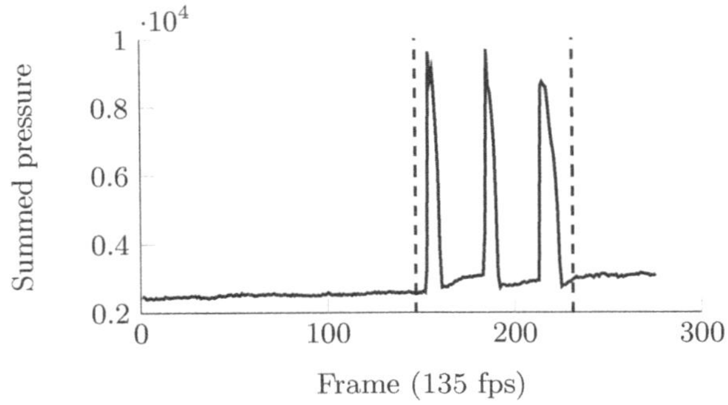

Figure 5: Segmentation of a 'rough pat' based on pressure difference indicated by the dashed lines.

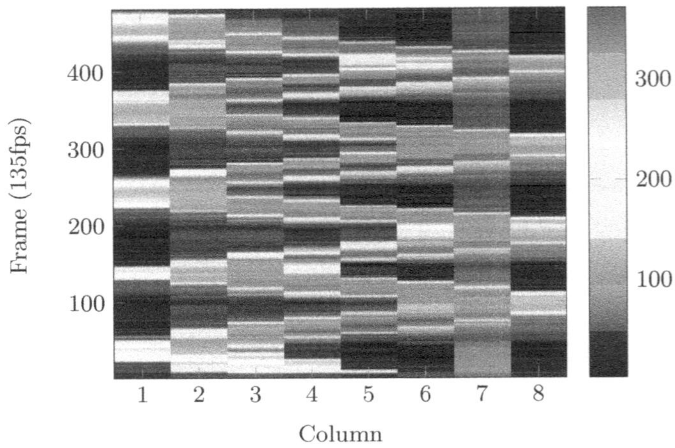

Figure 6: A 'rough stroke'. Mean pressure per sensor grid column over time visualizes the displacement in the opposite direction (i.e. the rows).

component, such as averaging over frames and the total amount of frames of a gesture instance. Further segmentation was based on the change in the gesture's intensity, that is, the summed pressure over all 64 channels. Parameters were optimized by visual inspection and kept constant for the whole data set. See Figure 5 for an example of the segmentation of a 'rough pat'.

The automatic segmentation was inspected visually to ensure that all gestures were captured. Inspection of the segmented data showed that six gestures instances could not be automatically segmented because there were only small differences in pressure during the gesture. The video recordings revealed that an instance of a 'rough stroke' was performed too fast to be distinguishable from the sensors' noise. The other five gesture instances were accidentally skipped. One other notable gesture instance of a 'normal squeeze' was of much longer duration (over a minute) than all other instances. The video footage showed that instead of a single squeeze, all 14 different touch gestures were practiced again on the sensor grid, while the data recording was already started. All seven gesture instances were removed from the dataset. See Table 2 for total of gesture instances per variation after preprocessing.

Table 2: Gesture instances per variation and in total of the CoST dataset after preprocessing.

	Variation			
	Gentle	Normal	Rough	Total
Recorded	2604	2604	2604	7812
Data loss	1× massage, 1× pat, 1× stroke	1× tickle, 1× squeeze	1× rub, 1× stroke	7
Data	2601	2602	2602	7805

4. RECOGNITION OF TOUCH GESTURES

For the first exploration into the recognition of social touch gestures from the CoST dataset, the rough touch gestures were used because of the favorable signal-to-noise ratio. The rough gesture subset consisted of 2602 gesture instances.

4.1 Feature extraction

From the sensor data, 28 features were extracted. Features are numbered between brackets.

Mean pressure was calculated by the mean pressure of all channels averaged over time (1).

Maximum pressure is the maximum channel value of the gesture (2).

Pressure variability indicates the differences in pressure applied during the gesture. The variability over time was calculated by the mean absolute pressure differences summed over all channels (3).

Mean pressure per column was calculated over time, resulting in eight features (4-11).

Mean pressure per row was calculated over time, resulting in eight features (12-19).

Contact area was calculated per frame as the percentage of sensor area (i.e. the number of channels divided by the total numbers of channels) that exceed 50% of the maximum pressure. Two features were calculated: the mean of the contact area over time (20) and the contact area of the frame with the maximum overall pressure (i.e. the highest summed pressure over all channels) (21).

Peak count is the number of positive crossings of the threshold. Two ways to calculate the threshold were used, resulting in two features: one threshold is defined as 50% of the frame with the maximum summed pressure (22), the other is defined as the mean of the summed pressure over time (23).

Displacement indicates whether the area of contact is static during a gesture or whether the hand moves across the contact area (i.e. dynamic). Figure 6 shows an example of a dynamic gesture (a 'rough stroke'). The position of the center of mass is used to calculate the movement on the contact surface in both the x-axis and the y-axis. Four features were calculated, both the mean over time and the summed absolute difference of the center of mass on the x-axis (24-25) and the y-axis (26-27).

Duration is the time used to make contact with the surface to perform the gesture which is measured in frames at 135 fps (28).

To visualize similarities within and between gestures, a normalized distance matrix between the summed pressure over time of the gestures was calculated using the dynamic time warping algorithm to indicate the difficulty of the clas-

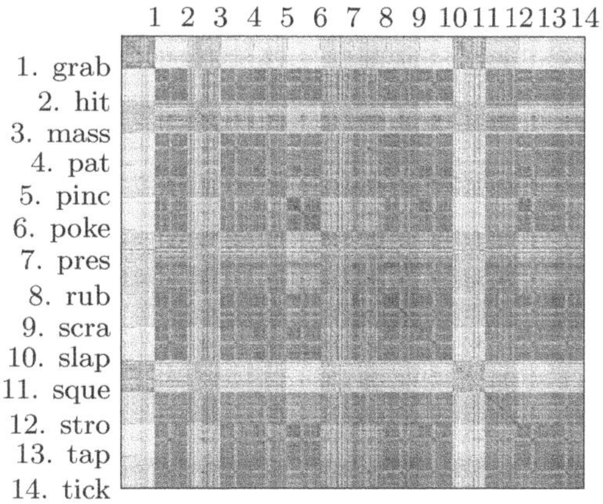

Figure 7: Normalized distance matrix of the summed pressure over time for all rough gesture instances. Darker areas indicate smaller differences.

sification problem (see Figure 7). Darker areas indicate smaller differences between two gesture instances. See Figure 8 for the mean pressure of all channels averaged over time (feature 1) and the duration (feature 28) plotted per gesture class. It can be seen from the figure that there is a lot of overlap between gesture classes and a large spread within classes.

4.2 Classification

The features from Section 4.1 were used for classification using MATLAB® (release 2013b). First, Gaussian Bayesian classifiers were used as baseline performance for gesture recognition. Second, the more complex SVM classifiers were used for comparison. The results of the classification were evaluated using leave-one-subject-out cross-validation. The baseline of classifying a sample into the correct class is $1/14 \approx 7\%$.

4.2.1 Bayesian classifiers

The mean and covariance for each class were calculated from the training data. The parameters for the multivariate normal distribution were used to calculate the posterior probability of the test sample belonging to the given class. Samples were assigned to the class with the maximum posterior probability. The summed results of the 31-fold cross-validation are displayed in a confusion matrix in Table 3. Between participants, the correct rate over all classes ranged from 24% to 75% ($M = 54\%, SD = 12\%$).

4.2.2 Support Vector Machine classifiers

We treated the classification of touch gestures as a multi-class problem using the one-vs.-all approach using the linear kernel with the default parameter of $C = 1$. Using this approach, models were trained for every gesture versus all other gestures. A test sample was classified for all models as belonging to the gesture class or the other class. There were 3 possible scenarios: (1) the test sample was classified as belonging to only one gesture class, in that case the test sample was assigned to that respective class, (2) the test sample was classified as belonging to multiple gesture classes, in that case the test sample was assigned to the class with the maximum distance to the hyperplane, (3) the test sample was never classified as belonging to the gesture class, in that case the test sample was assigned to the class with the minimum distance to the hyperplane. The summed results of the 31-fold cross-validation are displayed in a confusion matrix in Table 4. Between participants the correct rate over all classes ranged from 32% to 75% ($M = 53\%, SD = 11\%$).

Table 3: Confusion matrix of the Bayesian classifiers [Overall accuracy = 54%]. ***Legend*** **– classification of gesture instances into a class: ≥ 10% , ≥ 50% .**

Predicted class	grab 1	hit 2	mass 3	pat 4	pinc 5	poke 6	pres 7	rub 8	scra 9	slap 10	sque 11	stro 12	tap 13	tick 14
1	121	0	1	0	0	0	18	2	0	0	73	0	0	0
2	0	116	0	26	0	6	1	0	0	53	0	0	31	0
3	7	0	127	0	2	1	0	18	12	0	7	1	0	8
4	0	17	3	43	0	5	0	4	4	18	0	14	26	5
5	2	2	12	4	125	18	15	5	5	2	26	5	1	3
6	0	7	0	7	16	131	15	0	1	2	1	0	18	3
7	8	3	0	6	25	8	115	11	5	2	14	4	3	0
8	0	2	17	4	0	0	2	76	16	0	0	33	4	10
9	0	1	3	4	0	1	1	18	96	0	0	8	0	40
10	0	25	0	20	0	0	0	0	1	93	0	1	17	0
11	46	1	7	2	17	1	15	0	1	1	65	2	1	0
12	0	1	9	4	0	1	2	37	11	1	0	109	3	3
13	0	11	0	61	1	13	2	0	0	12	0	2	78	5
14	2	0	7	5	0	1	0	14	34	2	0	6	4	109
sum	186	186	186	186	186	186	186	185	186	186	186	185	186	186

Table 4: Confusion matrix of the SVM classifiers [Overall accuracy = 53%]. ***Legend*** **– classification of gesture instances into a class: ≥ 10% , ≥ 50% .**

Predicted class	grab 1	hit 2	mass 3	pat 4	pinc 5	poke 6	pres 7	rub 8	scra 9	slap 10	sque 11	stro 12	tap 13	tick 14
1	123	0	5	0	1	0	14	1	0	0	67	0	0	0
2	0	123	0	22	0	4	0	0	0	64	0	1	23	0
3	3	0	126	0	4	1	2	18	8	0	10	1	0	6
4	0	27	0	80	1	4	9	4	6	18	0	4	39	5
5	9	5	3	2	129	54	18	0	1	0	33	0	2	0
6	0	4	1	0	13	86	17	0	0	1	0	0	11	1
7	1	2	1	6	9	5	68	5	2	3	2	1	3	1
8	0	0	22	2	2	0	26	62	12	0	2	25	3	8
9	4	0	6	3	3	6	0	23	102	3	1	5	2	46
10	1	14	0	14	0	1	2	2	0	82	1	5	14	0
11	42	0	3	0	9	0	13	1	0	0	65	2	0	0
12	1	0	7	6	11	1	11	55	14	2	3	135	4	3
13	0	11	0	45	3	20	6	2	1	13	2	3	81	4
14	2	0	12	6	1	4	0	12	40	0	0	3	4	112
sum	186	186	186	186	186	186	186	185	186	186	186	185	186	186

4.2.3 Comparison of classifiers

Overall accuracy of both classifiers was more than 7 times higher than classification by random guessing (1/14). However, there were large difference between gestures and participants. The correct rate per gesture for both the Bayesian classifiers and the SVMs are listed in Table 5. The mean correct rates and the standard deviations of the two classifiers were almost equal ($M = 54\%, SD = 14\%$ vs. $M = 53\%, SD = 14\%$). Differences between the two classifiers were calculated by subtracting the correct rate per gesture of the Bayesian classifiers from the correct rates of the SVMs, the differences ranged from -20% to 25% ($M = 1\%, SD = 12\%$). The most notable differences were seen for the gestures 'poke' and 'press' which were classified much more accurately ($\geq 20\%$) using Bayesian classifiers while 'pat' was classified much more accurately ($\geq 20\%$) using SVMs.

The most frequent confusion was between the following gestures: 'grab' and 'squeeze'; 'hit', 'pat', 'slap' and 'tap'; 'rub' and 'stroke'; 'scratch' and 'tickle'. Confusion between 'grab' and 'squeeze' can be explained by the similarity in contact area, use of the whole hand, and the duration of the gesture. Furthermore, it can be argued that 'grab' is

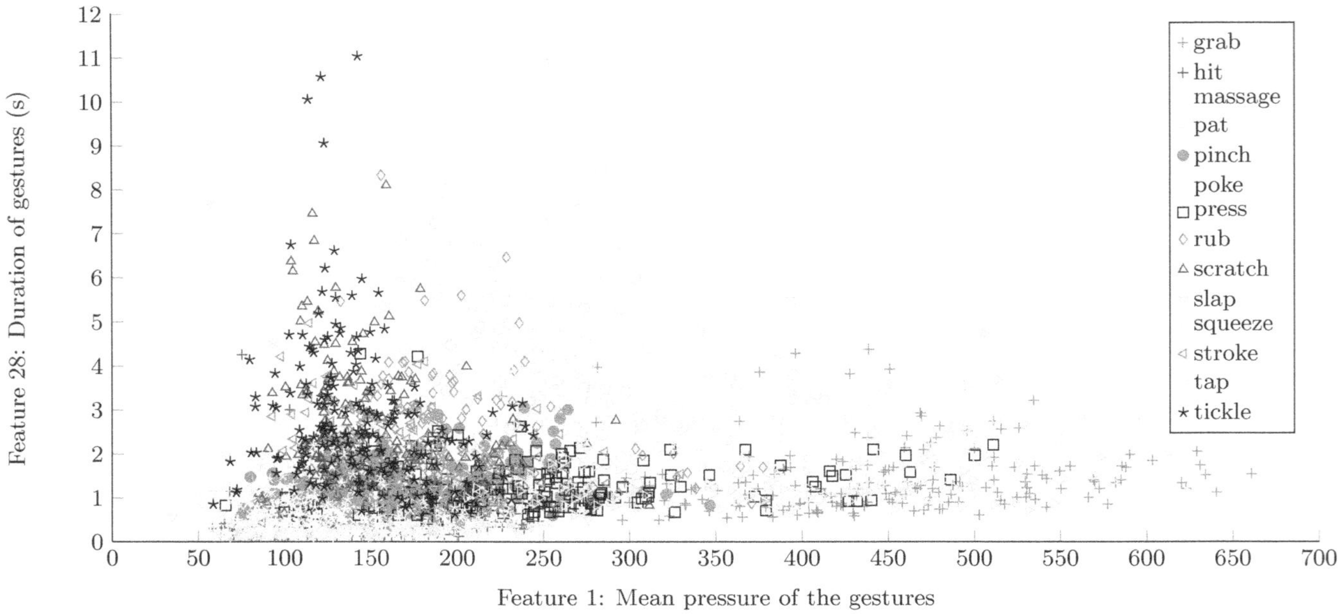

Figure 8: Feature 1 and feature 28 plotted per gesture class. Best viewed in color.

Table 5: Comparison of accuracy per gesture for both classifiers. ***Legend*** **– accuracy: $\geq 50\%$, $\geq 70\%$.**

Gesture	grab	hit	mass	pat	pinc	poke	pres	rub	scra	slap	sque	stro	tap	tick
Bayes	.65	.62	.68	.23	.67	.70	.62	.41	.52	.50	.35	.59	.42	.59
SVM	.66	.66	.68	.43	.69	.46	.37	.34	.55	.44	.35	.73	.44	.60
Difference	-.01	-.04	.00	-.20	-.02	.24	.25	.07	-.03	.06	.00	-.14	-.02	-.01

part of the 'squeeze gesture'. 'Hit', 'pat', 'slap' and 'tap' show similarities in duration, contact area and possibility of having been repeated several times during one gesture instance. In contrast, differences in pressure are expected between 'hit' and 'slap' compared to 'pat' and 'tap'. Both 'rub' and 'stroke' are prolonged gestures in which a back and forth movement is expected, however higher pressure levels are expected for 'rub'. 'Scratch' and 'tickle' are both characterized by a frequent change of direction and long duration. However, for 'tickle', pressure levels are expected to be lower and more variability in direction is expected instead of the back and forth movement of 'scratch'. The inclusion of touch gesture variants could have increased the difficulty of differentiating between gestures because pressure is one of the main characteristics on which the classification was based. Instructions to perform the touch gestures in gentle, normal and rough variations, could have encouraged subjects to use pressure levels to differentiate between gesture variants (e.g. 'gentle pat' vs. 'rough pat') rather than between gesture classes (e.g. 'pat' vs. 'slap'). However, in natural settings force differences can be expected between subjects based on personal characteristics such as physical strength but also within subjects based on the social context.

The correct rate per participant of the leave-one-subject-out cross-validation for both the Bayesian classifiers and the multi-class SVMs are listed in Table 6. The mean correct rates and standard deviations of the two classifiers were almost equal ($M = 54\%, SD = 12\%$ vs. $M = 53\%, SD = 11\%$). Differences between the two classifiers were calculated by subtracting the correct rate per participant of the Bayesian classifiers from the correct rates of the SVMs, the differences ranged from -8% to 14% ($M = 1\%, SD = 6\%$).

5. DISCUSSION

Classification of 14 gesture classes resulted in a maximum overall accuracy of 54% which is less than reported in related studies which reported mostly accuracies $> 70\%$. However, direct comparison of gesture recognition between studies based on reported accuracies is difficult because of differences in gesture sets, sensors, and classification protocols. Some reported accuracies were the result of a best-case scenario intended to be a proof of concept [1, 12]. While other studies focused on the location of the touch rather than the gesture, such as distinguishing between 'head-pat' and 'foot-rub' [10] or 'handshake' and 'back-pat' [2]. Although it could be argued that some gestures will be more suitable for particular body locations. Also, within subjects results were generally better than between subjects [11, 13]. However, some studies have used a subset of the gesture set in this paper which makes comparison possible. Recognition of a subset of the gestures was evaluated with Bayesian classifiers following the same procedure as used for the full gesture set described in Section 4.2.1. Using the gesture set of [1]: 'pat', 'poke', 'slap' and 'stroke', resulted in an overall accuracy of 79% which is comparable with the overall accuracy of 77% reported by Chang et al. on the area with the largest sensor density. Recognition of the gesture set of [12]: 'pat', 'scratch', 'slap', 'stroke' and 'tickle', resulted in an overall accuracy of 69%. This result is less than the overall accuracy of 87% reported by Naya et al., however these results were achieved by combining the maximum accuracies per class of two classifiers. Recognition of the gesture set of [9]: 'hit', 'poke', 'press', 'rub', 'squeeze' and 'stroke' resulted in an overall accuracy of 77% however, direct com-

Table 6: **Comparison of accuracy per participant for both classifiers.** *Legend* – **colors:** $\geq 50\%$, $\geq 70\%$.

Participant	1	2	3	4	5	6	7	8	9	10	11	12	13	14	15	16
Bayes	.52	.69	.71	.56	.75	.48	.58	.54	.57	.75	.64	.50	.61	.35	.49	.36
SVM	.52	.56	.68	.64	.75	.50	.58	.49	.64	.75	.65	.51	.48	.35	.46	.44
Difference	.00	.13	.03	-.08	.00	-.02	.00	.05	-.07	.00	-.01	-.01	.13	.00	.03	-.08

Participant	17	18	19	20	21	22	23	24	25	26	27	28	29	30	31
Bayes	.49	.58	.50	.38	.57	.62	.24	.68	.45	.63	.54	.44	.51	.52	.49
SVM	.51	.51	.51	.36	.43	.62	.32	.65	.44	.62	.55	.32	.55	.46	.50
Difference	-.02	.07	-.01	.02	.14	.00	-.08	.03	.01	.01	-.01	.12	-.04	.06	-.01

parison was not possible because accuracies per class were not provided.

Preliminary classification results of the normal and gentle gestures indicate similar performance to the rough gesture variants. Bayesian classifiers (normal: $M = 56\%, SD = 11\%$; gentle: $M = 47\%, SD = 11\%$) outperformed the SVMs (normal: $M = 48\%, SD = 10\%$; gentle: $M = 41\%, SD = 10\%$). The gentle gestures were more difficult to distinguish which was expected due to the lower signal-to-noise ratio.

6. CONCLUSION

In order to work towards reliable recognition of social touch gestures this paper introduces a Corpus of Social Touch (CoST) to fill the void of available touch data. This paper describes CoST, a data set consisting of 14 different touch gestures as well a first exploration into the automatic recognition of the social touch gestures of CoST. Classification of the rough variations showed that 14 gesture classes could be classified with an overall accuracy of 54% and 53% using Bayesian classifiers and SVMs respectively. Results were more than 7 times higher than chance ($1/14 \approx 7\%$) but less than results reported in related literature. The difference can partly be explained by the use of different sets of touch gestures, within person classification and the use of different types of sensors. Classification of a subset of gesture classes used in other studies resulted in overall accuracies which were more similar to the accuracies reported in the literature. Future work will include further analysis of the CoST dataset as well as optimization of the gesture recognition.

7. ACKNOWLEDGMENTS

This publication was supported by the Dutch national program COMMIT.

8. REFERENCES

[1] J. Chang, K. MacLean, and S. Yohanan. Gesture recognition in the haptic creature. In *Proceedings of the International Conference EuroHaptics, (Amsterdam, The Netherlands)*, pages 385–391. 2010.

[2] M. D. Cooney, S. Nishio, and H. Ishiguro. Recognizing affection for a touch-based interaction with a humanoid robot. In *Proceedings of the International Conference on Intelligent Robots and Systems (IROS), (Vilamoura, Portugal)*, pages 1420–1427, 2012.

[3] R. S. Dahiya, G. Metta, M. Valle, and G. Sandini. Tactile sensing — from humans to humanoids. *Transactions on Robotics*, 26(1):1–20, 2010.

[4] T. Field. Touch for socioemotional and physical well-being: A review. *Developmental Review*, 30(4):367–383, 2010.

[5] A. Gallace and C. Spence. The science of interpersonal touch: an overview. *Neuroscience & Biobehavioral Reviews*, 34(2):246–259, 2010.

[6] A. Haans and W. IJsselsteijn. Mediated social touch: a review of current research and future directions. *Virtual Reality*, 9(2-3):149–159, 2006.

[7] M. J. Hertenstein, J. M. Verkamp, A. M. Kerestes, and R. M. Holmes. The communicative functions of touch in humans, nonhuman primates, and rats: a review and synthesis of the empirical research. *Genetic, Social, and General Psychology Monographs*, 132(1):5–94, 2006.

[8] R. Heslin, T. D. Nguyen, and M. L. Nguyen. Meaning of touch: The case of touch from a stranger or same sex person. *Journal of Nonverbal Behavior*, 7(3):147–157, 1983.

[9] G. Huisman, A. Darriba Frederiks, B. Van Dijk, D. Heylen, and B. Kröse. The tasst: Tactile sleeve for social touch. In *Proceedings World Haptics Conference (WHC), (Daejeon, Korea)*, pages 211–216, 2013.

[10] H. Knight, R. Toscano, W. D. Stiehl, A. Chang, Y. Wang, and C. Breazeal. Real-time social touch gesture recognition for sensate robots. In *Proceedings of the International Conference on Intelligent Robots and Systems (IROS), (St. Louis, MO)*, pages 3715–3720, 2009.

[11] K. Nakajima, Y. Itoh, Y. Hayashi, K. Ikeda, K. Fujita, and T. Onoye. Emoballoon a balloon-shaped interface recognizing social touch interactions. In *Proceedings of Advances in Computer Entertainment (ACE), (Boekelo, The Netherlands)*, pages 182–197. 2013.

[12] F. Naya, J. Yamato, and K. Shinozawa. Recognizing human touching behaviors using a haptic interface for a pet-robot. In *Proceedings of the International Conference on Systems, Man, and Cybernetics (SMC), (Tokyo, Japan)*, volume 2, pages 1030–1034, 1999.

[13] D. Silvera-Tawil, D. Rye, and M. Velonaki. Touch modality interpretation for an eit-based sensitive skin. In *Proceedings of the International Conference on Robotics and Automation (ICRA), (Shanghai, China)*, pages 3770–3776, 2011.

[14] D. Silvera-Tawil, D. Rye, and M. Velonaki. Interpretation of the modality of touch on an artificial arm covered with an eit-based sensitive skin. *The International Journal of Robotics Research*, 31(13):1627–1641, 2012.

[15] W. D. Stiehl, J. Lieberman, C. Breazeal, L. Basel, L. Lalla, and M. Wolf. Design of a therapeutic robotic companion for relational, affective touch. In *Proceedings of International Workshop on Robot and Human Interactive Communication (ROMAN), (Nashville, TN)*, pages 408–415, 2005.

[16] A. Vinciarelli, M. Pantic, H. Bourlard, and A. Pentland. Social signals, their function, and automatic analysis: a survey. In *Proceedings of the international conference on Multimodal interfaces (ICMI), (Chania, Crete, Greece)*, pages 61–68, 2008.

[17] S. Yohanan and K. E. MacLean. The role of affective touch in human-robot interaction: Human intent and expectations in touching the haptic creature. *International Journal of Social Robotics*, 4(2):163–180, 2012.

Unsupervised Domain Adaptation for Personalized Facial Emotion Recognition

Gloria Zen, Enver Sangineto
University of Trento
Trento, Italy

Elisa Ricci
FBK — Trento, Italy
University of Perugia — Perugia, Italy

Nicu Sebe
University of Trento
Trento, Italy

ABSTRACT

The way in which human beings express emotions depends on their specific personality and cultural background. As a consequence, person independent facial expression classifiers usually fail to accurately recognize emotions which vary between different individuals. On the other hand, training a person-specific classifier for each new user is a time consuming activity which involves collecting hundreds of labeled samples. In this paper we present a personalization approach in which only unlabeled *target-specific* data are required. The method is based on our previous paper [20] in which a regression framework is proposed to learn the relation between the user's specific sample distribution and the parameters of her/his classifier. Once this relation is learned, a target classifier can be constructed using only the new user's sample distribution to transfer the personalized parameters. The novelty of this paper with respect to [20] is the introduction of a new method to represent the source sample distribution based on using only the Support Vectors of the source classifiers. Moreover, we present here a simplified regression framework which achieves the same or even slightly superior experimental results with respect to [20] but it is much easier to reproduce.

Categories and Subject Descriptors

I.2.10 [**Vision and Scene Understanding**]: [Video Analysis]; H.1.2 [**User/Machine Systems**]: [Human factors, Human information processing]

General Terms

Human factors

Keywords

Facial Expression Recognition; Action Unit Detection; Unsupervised Domain Adaptation

ICMI November 12-16th, 2014, Istanbul, Turkey
Copyright 2014 ACM 978-1-4503-2885-2/14/11 ...$15.00
http://dx.doi.org/10.1145/2663204.2663247.

Figure 1: Sample frames of spontaneous neutral (odd rows) and painful (even rows) facial expressions taken from the PAINFUL dataset. The frames illustrate how human expressions like pain can be exhibited in many different ways, depending on the individual's appearance or personality.

1. INTRODUCTION

There is a long debate in the psychological community on the universality of emotions and on the impact of culture and other environmental aspects on the way human beings express their feelings [8]. Even if the degree of importance of the environment is not yet clear, it is commonly accepted that factors such as the cultural background, gender, age or specific personality traits play a strong role in influencing the modalities and the intensity in which emotions are shown by different people. For instance, the way in which happiness or pain is expressed usually varies, on average, between women and men, introvert and extrovert persons, citizens of different countries, etc. On the other hand, this large variability of behaviors is one of the reasons for which common emotion recognition classifiers usually drop their performance when tested with subjects not belonging to the training set [23, 15]. However, collecting a large number of user-specific labeled data for training a personalized classifier is a time consuming and expensive activity and becomes practically infeasible for easy-to-use Human Computer Interface (HCI) systems.

In this paper we focus on facial expression recognition, which is one of the main modalities in which people express emotions [23] and we show how a user-specific classifier can be built using only unlabeled target data. The method we propose does not make any assumption on the specific features used to represent the emotions and on the facial expression scenario we adopted in our experiments. As a consequence, it can be applied to different input data types (e.g., audio, accelerometer data, physiological signals, text, etc.) as well as different verbal or non-verbal human communication modalities (e.g. voice recognition, gesture recognition, etc.).

Our idea is based on the framework proposed in [20], where a regression function is learned which associates the (unlabeled) distribution of the user's data in the feature space with the hyperplane parameters of her/his personalized classifier. More specifically, given a set of N *source* users, with their associated *labeled* training samples, a set of corresponding N source linear classifiers (linear SVMs) $C_1, ..., C_N$ is learned. Each classifier C_i is defined by its decision hyperplane $(\mathbf{w}_i, b_i)$. Then, a regression function $f(\cdot)$ is trained which relates the shape of the *unlabeled* data distribution of the i-th source user with her/his specific hyperplane $(\mathbf{w}_i, b_i)$. Once $f(\cdot)$ is learned, labeled data are not necessary any more. Hence, given a new *target* user and her/his *unlabeled* collection of samples, applying $f(\cdot)$ to the new data distribution, the target-specific classifier's parameters can be obtained.

In this paper we build on this idea and we make the following contributions. (1) We simplify the whole framework, e.g., using a scalar Support Vector Regression (SVR) for learning $f(\cdot)$ instead of the Multi-output SVR proposed in [20], which makes the approach easier to be reproduced. (2) More importantly, restricting the chosen classifiers to be linear SVMs, we propose to represent the *source* data distributions by means of the corresponding Support Vectors, which are related with $(\mathbf{w}_i, b_i)$ via the Karush-Kuhn-Tucker (KKT) condition. This makes stronger the geometric relation between $(\mathbf{w}_i, b_i)$ and our non-parametric representation of the source data. We show in Sec. 4 that, using the proposed Support Vector-based representation, we obtain comparable or even better results than [20] on the same benchmarks.

Following [20], we tested our method on different benchmarks and in different application scenarios. In the first scenario we trained a patch-based *facial expression recognition* system based on Local Binary Pattern Histograms (LBPH) [1] and we used the recently proposed PAINFUL dataset [14], which collects videos of real patients with shoulder injuries. The way and the intensity in which the patients spontaneously show pain while performing motion activities largely varies between one person and the other (see Fig. 1). This is witnessed by the experimental results reported in [10], where the authors use the same benchmark and show that person-dependent testing (no training samples of the testing subject used for training) achieves a largely lower performance than a person-independent cross validation. In the second set of experiments, we used the more commonly adopted Extended Cohn Kanade (CK+) face dataset [13] and we trained an *Action Unit detection* system based on facial landmark detection and SIFT extraction. Even if the tasks and the adopted features in the two scenarios are different, we show in Sec. 4 that our approach is able to outperform both a non-personalized classifier and other state-of-the-art unsupervised personalization methods. More importantly, our training strategy is significantly faster (and simpler to implement) than other domain adaptation approaches, most of which are based on time consuming retraining strategies. In Sec. 4 we show that we can compute the target classifier in significantly shorter time, and we believe that this is a important aspect for user personalization in real HCI applications.

2. RELATED WORK

In this section we briefly review the literature related to both single-frame (static) facial expression analysis and domain adaptation/transfer learning techniques.

Single Frame Facial Expression Analysis. Frame-level methods to detect AU occurrence and facial expressions (e.g. happiness, sadness, fear) analyze individual frames [15, 23]. This is typically done first performing face registration, then extracting geometric or appearance features representing each frame, and finally feeding the visual descriptors into static classifiers (e.g. SVM, Boosting, Random Forests). Face registration is commonly achieved through the localization of anatomically salient facial points [19], while in the feature extraction phase both geometric descriptors (e.g. containing information of landmark locations) and appearance features capturing texture changes (e.g. LBPH, SIFT) are typically used.

While state-of-the-art frame-level approaches achieve very accurate recognition in controlled conditions (i.e. frontal face images and posed emotions), the performance significantly degrade in more realistic settings. To address this issue, recent works have focused on recognizing spontaneous facial emotions such as pain [7, 12, 21] and on coping with the challenges of person-specific facial appearance variability [18]. However, most of these works are based on generic detectors, i.e. on classifiers learned with a dataset which is supposed to be representative of all the possible sources of variability (acquisition conditions, differences among individuals, etc.). Unfortunately, having at disposal only datasets of few thousands of images, generalization to arbitrary people appearance and environmental conditions is hard to achieve. In particular, to cope with the issue of facial appearance variability among different people, few recent works have proposed domain adaptation approaches which leverage from unlabeled data depicting the user of interest to learn personalized classifiers. For instance, in [4] an extension of the popular AdaBoost algorithm is proposed for creating user-specific pain recognition models. In [5] an approach based on Kernel Mean Matching [9] named Selective Transfer Machine (STM) is presented for person-specific AU detection. While very accurate recognition results are obtained, STM is very slow at training time. On the other hand to be used in many real world applications, such HCI systems, adaptation algorithms are required to be computationally efficient. Our method is mainly motivated by this need and our experiments (reported in Sec. 4) confirm that it is much faster than [5], being its accuracy comparable or even slightly better.

Transfer learning. Domain adaptation and transfer learning approaches have recently become popular as a means to alleviate the problem of the scarceness of (annotated) training samples for the target domain. In [16] a taxonomy of domain adaptation approaches is presented. According to the type of information which is transferred from the source to the target domain, these methods can be categorized into *instance-transfer*, *features-transfer* and *parameter-transfer* approaches.

Feature-transfer involves finding a shared feature space in which both the source and target data are represented. For instance, in [6] the input features space is augmented originating in a novel descriptor composed of a shared, a source-specific and a target-specific part.

Parameter transfer techniques aim to discover a set of shared parameters or priors between the source and the target models. In Adaptive-SVMs [22] the classifier parameters are obtained training an SVM on the target domain and imposing a regularization term which forces these parameters to be similar to the previously learned source task classifier(s). However, the parameter transfer approaches usually require labeled target data. In our facial expression analysis scenario, this means annotated data for every new user (i.e. users not belonging to the training set) and it is practically infeasible in most applications.

When the target data are unlabeled, instance-transfer approaches are commonly adopted. For instance, in [9] a sample reweighting algorithm is introduced. Gretton et al. propose to compare the centroids of the source and the target distributions and to estimate the weights of the source samples in order to reduce this discrepancy. These weights are then used to assign importance to the source samples when training a model for the target domain. The approach presented in [5] develops from a similar idea. The main drawback of these methods is that computing the difference between the means of the source and the target data distributions in the Reproducing Kernel Hilbert Space may poorly approximate the real distance between distributions. In this paper we circumvent this problem by learning the relation between the "shape" of each user-specific data distribution and the corresponding classifier parameters.

3. REGRESSION-BASED PARAMETER TRANSFER

In this section we present our Support Vector-based Transductive Parameter Transfer (SVTPT) method. This approach is a general framework and it is independent from the types of features and from the applicative scenario. In Sec. 4 we show how this framework can be instantiated with different input modalities (visual descriptors) and classification tasks.

Let $\mathcal{X}, \mathcal{Y}$ be, respectively, a feature space and a label space. In this paper we consider $\mathcal{Y} = \{-1, 1\}$ but generalizing our approach to a multiclass setting is straightforward. We assume that N *labeled source* datasets $D_1^s, ..., D_N^s$, $D_i^s = \{\mathbf{x}_j^s, y_j^s\}_{j=1}^{n_i^s}$, and an *unlabeled target* dataset $X^t = \{\mathbf{x}_j^t\}_{j=1}^{n^t}$, $\mathbf{x}_j^s, \mathbf{x}_j^t \in \mathcal{X}$, $y_j^s \in \mathcal{Y}$, are available. Moreover, let denote $X_i^s = \{\mathbf{x}_j^s\}_{j=1}^{n_i^s}$ the set of points in D_i^s obtained by discarding the label information. D_i^s contains all the training samples specific to the i-th source person, while X^t is the (unlabeled) set of samples of the target individual for whom we aim to construct a personalized classifier.

We assume that the vectors in X_i^s are generated by a marginal distribution P_i^s defined on $\mathcal{X}$ and similarly the vectors X^t are generated by P^t. We generally assume that: $P^t \neq P_i^s$ and $P_i^s \neq P_j^s$ $(1 \leq i, j \leq N,\ i \neq j)$. Finally, we call $\mathcal{P}$ the space of all the possible distributions on $\mathcal{X}$ and we assume that P^t, P_i^s are drawn from $\mathcal{P}$ according to the meta-distribution Π, i.e. $P^t, P_i^s \sim \Pi$ $(1 \leq i \leq N)$.

Our goal is to learn a classifier on the target data X^t without acquiring labeled information. The approach we propose is based on three main phases (Fig. 2). First, a set of source-specific classifiers is learned, one for each training set D_i^s. In the second phase a regression algorithm is adopted in order to learn the relation between the marginal distributions P_i^s and the source classifiers' parameter vectors $\boldsymbol{\theta}_i$. Finally, the desired target classifier $\boldsymbol{\theta}^t$ is obtained by applying the learned distribution-to-classifier mapping and using as input the distribution P^t. In the following, the three phases are described in details.

Source Training Phase 1. In the first phase, each source dataset D_i^s is used to train a classifier solving an optimization problem as:

$$\boldsymbol{\theta}_i = \min_{\boldsymbol{\theta} \in \Theta} \mathcal{R}(\boldsymbol{\theta}) + \lambda_L L(\boldsymbol{\theta}, D_i^s) \tag{1}$$

where $\boldsymbol{\theta}_i$ is the parameter vector associated to the learned classifier, Θ is the parameter space, $\mathcal{R}(\cdot)$ a regularizer and $L(\cdot)$ is the empirical risk weighted with λ_L. Each $\boldsymbol{\theta}_i$ is a personalized classifier (called "ideal" classifier in [5]) because it was trained using the *user specific* data D_i^s. Specifically, in this paper we use a set of linear SVM classifiers, thus $\boldsymbol{\theta}_i = [\mathbf{w}_i', b_i]$, $\mathbf{w}_i \in I\!R^M$, $b_i \in I\!R$, defines a hyperplane in the feature space $\mathcal{X} \equiv I\!R^M$ (see Fig. 2) and it can be estimated by solving:

$$\min_{\mathbf{w}, b} \frac{1}{2}||\mathbf{w}||^2 + \lambda_L \sum_{j=1}^{n_i^s} l(\mathbf{w}'\mathbf{x}_j^s + b, y_j^s) \tag{2}$$

where $l(\cdot)$ is the hinge loss.

Source Training Phase 2. In the second phase, we use a regression approach to learn a mapping $f : \mathcal{P} \rightarrow \Theta$. The intuition here is that each hyperplane, defined by $\boldsymbol{\theta}_i$, depends on the distribution P_i^s generating the data points X_i^s. Thus, if using the source data we are able to learn the relationship between the "shape" of the underlying distribution and its corresponding hyperplane, then, for computing the optimal hyperplane on the target data, we do not need label information any more and we can simply apply the learned mapping $f(\cdot)$, i.e. $\boldsymbol{\theta}^t = f(P^t)$.

Of course, we do not know P_i^s $(1 \leq i \leq N)$ neither P^t, thus we need to approximate both types of distributions using empirical data at disposal. P^t can be approximated using X^t. Similarly, P_i^s can be approximated using X_i^s. However, P_i^s can be approximated also using only the Support Vectors obtained solving (2) for the i-th source classification task. Let $V_i = \{\mathbf{v}_j\}_{j=1}^{m_i}$ be the Support Vectors associated with $\boldsymbol{\theta}_i$ $(V_i \subseteq X_i^s)$. The distribution generating V_i is generally different from the distribution generating X_i^s. In fact V_i does not include those points which are far from the decision hyperplane. Thus approximating P_i^s using V_i introduces an error. Anyway, using V_i instead of X_i^s brings two advantages for our regression framework. The first is that there is a well-known relation between the Support Vectors and the decision hyperplane, given by the KKT condition:

$$\mathbf{w}_i = \sum_{j=1}^{m_i} \alpha_j y_j \mathbf{v}_j, \tag{3}$$

where y_j is the label associated with $\mathbf{v}_j$ and α_j the corresponding Lagrange multiplier obtained solving (2). Note that we do not have labels for the target task, thus (3) cannot be directly used to compute $\mathbf{w}^t$. The KKT condition guarantees the existence of a relation between V_i and $\boldsymbol{\theta}_i$

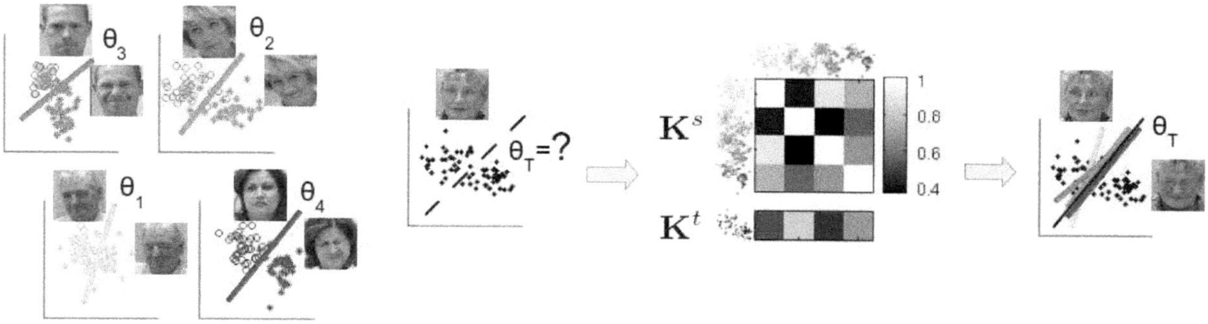

Figure 2: Overview of the training phase. Left: different linear classifiers are learned using labeled source datasets. The goal is to learn a target classifier $\boldsymbol{\theta}^t$ using unlabeled samples. Middle: the source kernel matrix $\mathbf{K}^s$ and the target kernel vector $\mathbf{K}^t$ are computed (see Algorithm 1). Right: $\boldsymbol{\theta}^t$ (black line) is obtained applying the regression function. See the text for more details.

which makes the estimate of our regression function more robust.

The second advantage in using V_i in place of X_i^s to approximate P_i^s is the speed-up and the storage saving we can obtain being usually $m_i < n_i^s$. We show in Sec. 4 that indeed using V_i we obtain slightly more accurate results with a faster training phase.

Let Z_i be the set of points chosen to approximate P_i^s, where either $Z_i = V_i$ or $Z_i = X_i^s$. Given a training set $\mathcal{T} = \{(Z_i, \boldsymbol{\theta}_i)\}_{i=1}^N$ we propose to learn a mapping:

$$\widehat{f} : 2^{\mathcal{X}} \rightarrow \Theta \tag{4}$$

which approximates $f(\cdot)$. The function $\widehat{f}(\cdot)$ is a vector-valued set function, i.e. a function which takes as input a set of points X ($X \subseteq \mathcal{X}$) and outputs a vector $\boldsymbol{\theta} = [\mathbf{w}', b]$. If $\mathcal{X} \equiv I\!R^M$, i.e. $\boldsymbol{\theta}$ is a $M+1$ dimensional vector, $\widehat{f}(\cdot)$ can be learned using $M+1$ independent scalar regressors $\widehat{f}_k(X)$:

$$\widehat{f}(X) = (\widehat{f}_1(X), ..., \widehat{f}_k(X), ..., \widehat{f}_{M+1}(X))' \tag{5}$$

We compute each $\widehat{f}_k(\cdot)$ using the well-known ϵ-insensitive Support Vector Regression framework proposed by Vapnik, which, in our setting, can be formulated as follows. Each $\widehat{f}_k(\cdot)$ $(1 \leq k \leq M+1)$ is defined by a set of parameters $\boldsymbol{\pi}_k = (\mathbf{b}_k, c_k)$:

$$\widehat{f}_k(X) = \langle \phi_k(X), \mathbf{b}_k \rangle + c_k, \tag{6}$$

where $\mathbf{b}_k$ and c_k is the weight vector and the bias, respectively, $\phi_k(X)$ is a nonlinear mapping of X to a higher-dimensional space and $\langle X_1, X_2 \rangle$ is a scalar product defined in such a space. In turn $\boldsymbol{\pi}_k$ can be found by minimizing:

$$\min_{\boldsymbol{\pi}} \frac{1}{2} ||\boldsymbol{b}_k||^2 + \lambda_E \sum_{i=1}^{N} |\boldsymbol{\theta}_{ik} - \widehat{f}_{\boldsymbol{\pi}}(Z_i)|_\epsilon \tag{7}$$

where $\boldsymbol{\theta}_{ik}$ is the *scalar* value corresponding to the k-th dimension of $\boldsymbol{\theta}_i$, $(Z_i, \boldsymbol{\theta}_i) \in \mathcal{T}$, λ_E is a weight for the empirical risk and $|e|_\epsilon = max(0, |e| - \epsilon)$ is the ϵ-insensitive loss function. The parameter ϵ regulates the accuracy of the approximation.

Eq. (7) can be transformed into the dual problem:

$$\max_{\{\beta_i^k\}} -\frac{1}{2} \sum_{i,l=1}^{N} \beta_i^k \beta_l^k \kappa(Z_i, Z_l) + \sum_{i=1}^{N} \boldsymbol{\theta}_{ik} \beta_i^k - \epsilon \sum_{i=1}^{N} |\beta_i^k| \tag{8}$$

such that:

$$\sum_{i=1}^{N} \beta_i^k = 0, \ |\beta_i^k| \leq \lambda_E \ (k = 1, ..., M+1). \tag{9}$$

In (8) $\{\beta_i^k\}$ is the set of Lagrange multipliers and $\kappa(Z_i, Z_l) = \langle Z_i, Z_l \rangle$ is the kernel function. Note that the same kernel can be used for all $k = 1, ...M+1$, since $\kappa(Z_i, Z_l)$ estimates the similarity between Z_i and Z_l which is independent from the value of k. In this dual form, (6) becomes:

$$\widehat{f}_k(X) = \sum_{i=1}^{N} \beta_i^k \kappa(Z_i, X) + c_k. \tag{10}$$

From the above formulas, it is clear that both when we compute the parameters of the regression function $\widehat{f}_k(\cdot)$ using (8)-(9) and when this function is applied to a new input using (10), i.e. $\widehat{f}_k(X^t)$, the only thing we need is the kernel function $\kappa(\cdot, \cdot)$, which must be defined for every pair of subsets of $\mathcal{X}$, while the direct definition of the mapping functions $(\phi_k(X), k = 1, ..., M+1)$ is no more necessary.

It is important to note that $\kappa(\cdot, \cdot)$ is defined on *sets* of points and not on feature vectors (i.e., single points) as common kernel functions are. In other words, we need a kernel for estimating the similarity between distributions empirically represented by a set of data points. To this aim we use the non-parametric distribution kernel recently proposed in [2]. This kernel is based on a (single point) Density Estimate kernel and it is defined as follows:

$$\kappa(X_i, X_l) = \frac{1}{nm} \sum_{p=1}^{n} \sum_{q=1}^{m} \kappa_{\mathcal{X}}(\mathbf{x}_p, \mathbf{x}_q), \tag{11}$$

where $X_i = \{\mathbf{x}_p\}_{p=1}^n$, $X_l = \{\mathbf{x}_q\}_{q=1}^m$ and $\kappa_{\mathcal{X}}(\cdot, \cdot)$ is a normalized Gaussian kernel defined on the feature space $\mathcal{X}$.

Target Training Phase. Finally, once $\widehat{f}_k(\cdot)$ is computed using (8)-(9) for every $k = 1, ..., M+1$, in the last phase of our method, we plug (10) into (5) and we apply $\widehat{f}(\cdot)$ to the target data set X^t, obtaining the desired parameter vector of the target classifier:

$$\boldsymbol{\theta}^t = \widehat{f}(X^t). \tag{12}$$

In Algorithm 1 we summarize the whole *training* procedure. Note that the two source training phases need to be computed only once using all the source datasets. Then, for every new target dataset, only the target training phase

Algorithm 1 The proposed SVTPT approach.

Input: The sets $D_1^s, ..., D_N^s$, X^t and the regularization parameters λ_L, λ_E, ϵ.

Source Training Phase 1:
Compute $\{\boldsymbol{\theta}_i = (\mathbf{w}_i, b_i)\}_{i=1}^N$ using (2).
Source Training Phase 2:
Create a training set $\mathcal{T} = \{Z_i, \boldsymbol{\theta}_i\}_{i=1}^N$, where $Z_i = V_i$ or $Z_i = X_i^s$.
Compute the source kernel matrix $\mathbf{K}^s$, $\mathbf{K}_{il}^s = \kappa(Z_i, Z_l)$ using (11)
Given $\mathbf{K}^s$, $\mathcal{T}$, for every $k = 1, ..., M+1$ solve (8)-(9).
Target Training Phase:
Compute the target kernel vector $\mathbf{K}^t$, $\mathbf{K}_i^t = \kappa(Z_i, X^t)$ using (11)
Given $\mathbf{K}^t$, compute $(\mathbf{w}^t, b^t) = \widehat{f}(X^t)$ using (10) and (5).

Output: $\mathbf{w}^t, b^t$

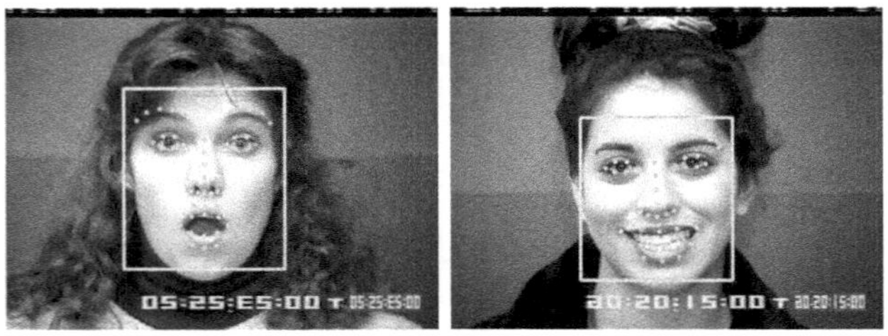

Figure 3: Sample frames of the CK+ dataset. The green rectangles show the cropped part of the image and the dots are the detected facial landmarks (better seen at a high magnification).

needs to be repeated. Thus, when a new target user is introduced into the system, computational times for domain adaptation only depend on the target training phase. Finally, note that all the optimization problems involved in our approach (i.e. (2) and (8)) can be computed with any standard SVM solver. We used the well know LIBSVM library. The whole procedure is shown in Fig. 2.

Testing phase. Once $\boldsymbol{\theta}^t$ has been computed, the test procedure is standard as in classification with linear SVMs. Given a new target feature vector $\mathbf{x}$, the corresponding label y is predicted using: $y = sign((\mathbf{w}^t)'\mathbf{x} + b^t)$.

3.1 Discussion

In this paper we propose to learn the relation between the "shape" of each user-specific data distribution and the corresponding classifier parameters. It is worth noting that, generally speaking, the parameters of a linear classifier (e.g., $\boldsymbol{\theta}_i$ or $\boldsymbol{\theta}^t$) depend not only on the marginal distribution (P_i^s or P^t) but also on the relative distributions of the positives and negatives inside P_i^s and P^t. However, since the classification task is the same for all the users, our assumption is that this relative distributions of positives and negatives inside every user's data is relatively constant and can be learned using source users. We are currently working on extending the experiments with other datasets and our finding is that, as far as data are sufficiently linearly separable, our assumption holds. Representing P_i^s using Support Vectors helps because the classifier parameters are related to the Support Vectors via the KKT condition.

4. EXPERIMENTS

In this section we present two series of experiments to demonstrate the effectiveness of the proposed SVTPT approach in two different applications: AU detection and pain recognition. We deliberately choose these in order to compare SVTPT with our previous work [20] and with the only two other transductive domain adaptation methods for facial expression analysis we are aware of: STM [5] and Transductive AdaBoost (TA) [4]. For the sake of comparison, we adopt the same datasets and features presented in [20, 4, 5]. The performances are evaluated using the F_1 score, defined as $F_1 = \frac{2 \cdot recall \cdot precision}{recall + precision}$, and the Area Under ROC Curve (AUC). Note that the results reported for the other methods we compare with and for our previous work [20] were previously published in [20]. In this paper we are simply restating them for ease of comparison between methods.

4.1 Facial Action Unit Detection

4.1.1 Experimental setup

In this series of experiments we consider the Extended Cohn-Kanade (CK+)[1] dataset [13]. CK+ contains a set of frontal faces depicting spontaneous and posed expressions. The dataset includes 593 videos from 123 users. The number of videos per user ranges from 1 to 11. The video length varies from 4 to 71 frames. Sample frames are shown in Fig. 3.

We followed the same experimental protocol adopted in [5, 20], implementing the same feature extraction pipeline. First, for each frame the face and the facial landmarks are detected, then the face is aligned, cropped and resized to 200×200 pixels. For this pre-processing step, we use the code of [5], available at the author's website[2]. Subsequently, we select 16 landmarks from which we extract SIFT descriptors using OpenCV from 36×36 pixel regions around them. Finally, the descriptors are concatenated and dimensionality is reduced using Principal Component Analysis. We retain 90% of the energy, resulting in feature vectors of size 51. As discussed in [20], we select the most frequent AUs and each AU detection is considered as an independent binary classification problem. Following [5, 20], our experiments are conducted using a leave-one-subject-out evaluation scheme.

4.1.2 Results

We compare our approach with a generic SVM classifier learned on the entire source data, Transductive SVM (TSVM) [11] and domain adaptation-based methods: Kernel Mean Matching (KMM) [9], Domain Adaptation SVM (DASVM) [3] and STM [5]. We also compare with the Transductive Parameter Transfer (TPT) in [20] when the Density Estimate Kernel is used for comparing data distributions. The values concerning the performance of the baseline methods are taken from [5, 20]. The SVTPT parameters (Algorithm 1) have been set with cross-validation. The results are shown in Tables 1 and 2. For the proposed SVTPT method *SVs* means that we use only the support vectors ($Z_i = V_i$) for computing $\mathbf{K}^s$ and $\mathbf{K}^t$ (see Algorithm 1). We also report the results obtained when all the source data points are used, i.e. $Z_i = X_i^s$ (*All*).

[1]http://www.pitt.edu/~emotion/ck-spread.htm
[2]http://humansensing.cs.cmu.edu/intraface/

Table 1: Performance on CK+ dataset. Comparison of different methods based on F_1 Score.

AU	SVM	TSVM [9]	KMM [11]	DASVM [3]	STM [5]	TPT [20]	SVTPT All	SVTPT SVs
1	61.1	56.8	44.9	57.7	74.0	74.4	73.2	74.9
2	73.5	59.8	50.8	64.3	76.2	84.2	81.7	82.4
4	62.7	51.9	52.3	57.7	69.1	66.3	64.5	74.2
6	75.7	47.8	70.1	68.2	79.6	74.8	77.2	74.3
12	76.7	59.6	74.5	59.0	77.2	85.1	83.0	84.6
17	76.0	61.7	53.2	81.4	84.3	76.1	79.0	84.3
Avg	70.9	56.3	57.6	64.7	74.8	76.8	76.7	**79.1**

Table 2: Performance on CK+ dataset. Comparison of different methods based on AUC.

AU	SVM	TSVM [9]	KMM [11]	DASVM [3]	STM [5]	TPT [20]	SVTPT All	SVTPT SVs
1	79.8	69.9	68.9	72.6	88.9	88.2	87.8	89.6
2	90.8	69.3	73.5	71.0	87.5	92.6	92.8	93.9
4	74.8	63.4	62.2	79.9	81.1	84.3	84.5	88.6
6	89.7	60.5	87.7	94.7	94.0	91.7	91.1	91.5
12	88.1	76.0	89.5	95.5	92.8	97.1	96.3	97.5
17	90.3	73.1	66.6	94.7	96.0	94.3	94.4	94.1
Avg	85.6	68.7	74.7	83.1	90.1	91.3	91.3	**92.7**

When support vectors are used for approximating the source data distributions, our approach outperforms all the other methods considering both the AUC and the F_1 score. In particular, SVTPT outperforms the TPT method presented in [20]. This result confirms the intuition that using only Support Vectors for representing the source distributions is more effective than using all the data points (see Sec. 3). In other words, considering only SVs allows to exclude data points which are far away from the hyperplanes and that could be misleading in an unsupervised domain adaptation process. In this sense, the proposed approach comes as an improvement of the method presented in [20]. Among the other baselines, TSVM performs poorly. We ascribe this to the fact that all the source samples are retained during training and the resulting classifier can be wrongly biased when samples from irrelevant individuals are included. KMM, DASVM and STM, instead, re-weight and possibly retain only important data. Among them, STM is the most successful. However, SVTPT and TPT achieve even better performance than STM, probably due to a more effective representation of similarity between data distributions.

4.2 Pain Expression Recognition

4.2.1 *Experimental Setup*

The PAINFUL[3] dataset is part of the UNBC-McMaster Shoulder Pain Expression Archive Database [14] and is composed of 200 video sequences of 25 patients with shoulder injuries. The videos depicts the patients while performing a series of active and passive range-of-motion tests with either their affected limb or the unaffected one. The facial expressions of the patients are fully spontaneous. The annotation of the video is on a frame basis (48398 frames are labeled by experts using the Prkachin and Solomon Pain Intensity, PSPI, metric system [17]). Some frames are shown in Fig. 4.

To compare our results with [4, 20] we compute the same features. For each frame we use the ground truth eye locations provided in the database to crop and warp the face region into a 128×128 pixel image. The resulting image is divided into 8×8 blocks and LBPH features [1] are computed. We adopt *uniform* $LBP^{u2}_{8,1}$, where *u2* means "uniform" and $(8, 1)$ represents 8 sampling points on a circle of radius 1. For each block a 59-dimensional feature vector is obtained. These vectors are then concatenated resulting into a descriptor of $8 \times 8 \times 59 = 3776$ dimensions. For dimensionality reduction Principal Component Analysis is applied retaining 90% of the variance and obtaining for each frame a feature vector of size 334.

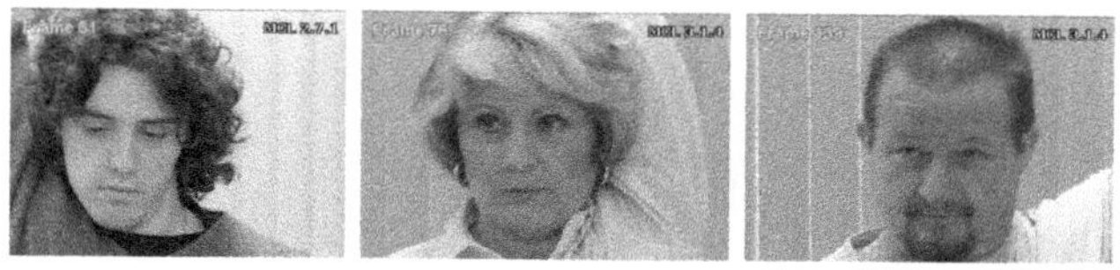

Figure 4: Sample frames of the PAINFUL dataset. Spontaneous facial expressions of patients under shoulder mobility tests are shown.

Table 3: Performance on PAINFUL dataset, AUC. (*) Results obtained on 30% of data points, see text for details.

AdaBoost [4]	TTA [4]	TSVM [11]	STM* [5]	TPT [20]	SVTPT All	SVTPT SVs
76.9	76.5	69.8	76.8	76.7	76.7	**78.4**

Following [4, 20], our experiments are conducted using a leave-one-subject-out evaluation scheme. However, since there is no pain exhibited in the videos of one subject (i.e. PSPI score is equal to 0 for all the frames), we excluded the videos of this person from the experiments because he cannot be used as a source. Hence, the final number of subjects considered, both at training and at testing time, is 24. Nevertheless, using the non-pain user only as a target, we got slightly better results.

4.2.2 *Results*

In order to allow a comparison of our results with [4, 20], we evaluate the performance using AUC and we compare against: a generic classifier (AdaBoost) trained using only the source samples (no domain adaptation), Transductive Transfer AdaBoost (TTA) [4], TSVM [11], STM [5] and TPT with Density Estimate Kernel [20]. For TTA and AdaBoost we report the performances published by Chen et al. in [4], and for TPT we report the performances published in [20], while for TSVM and STM we used the codes publicly available[4,5]. Both for TSVM and STM and for TPT and SVTPT, the system's parameters have been set with cross-validation. Table 3 reports the results. As in the case of the CK+ dataset, our approach outperforms all the baseline methods and, concerning SVTPT, a significant improvement in terms of AUC is obtained in the *SVs* case. This confirms again the efficiency of using SVs w.r.t. considering all the data points in our learning from distribution framework, as was initially proposed in [20]. Note that for the case of STM, the results are reported using randomly subsampled 30% of the data points for training. We stopped at this percentage value because the computational time for training a classifier on each subject was over 1 day (see Tab. 6 below) and the time complexity growth is more than linear with respect to the number of training points. Note that this computational

[3] http://www.pitt.edu/~emotion/um-spread.htm

[4] http://svmlight.joachims.org/

[5] http://humansensing.cs.cmu.edu/software.html

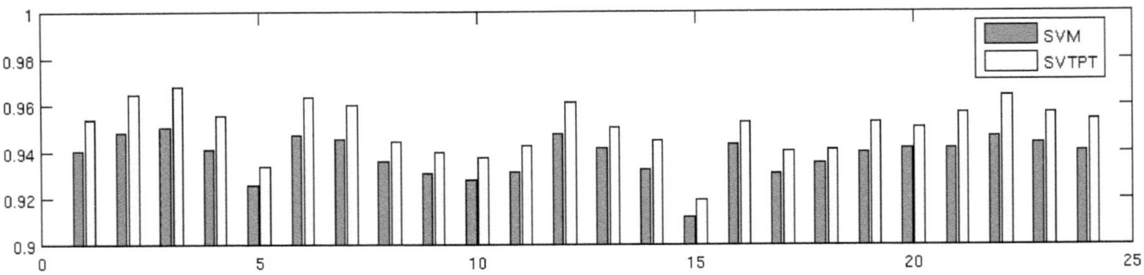

Figure 5: PAINFUL dataset. Similarity of the classifiers θ_i^{SVM} and θ_i^{SVTPT}, with respect to the *personalized* classifiers θ_i, $i = 1, ..., 24$, obtained respectively with SVM and our method (SVTPT) (see the text for details).

Table 4: PAINFUL dataset. (Upper part) Average time cost for training a target classifier for different methods. (Lower part) details on average time costs for different phases of our method.

Method	Data%	Variable to be computed	Training on source	Training on target
SVM	100%	θ^{SVM}	25'	-
TSVM	100%	θ^{TSVM}	-	$1h$ 50'
STM	30%	θ^{STM}	-	$> 1day$
SVTPT All	100%	θ^{SVTPT}	47.1"	0.8"
SVTPT SVs	100%	θ^{SVTPT}	44.1"	0.5"
SVTPT	100%	θ_i; i=1,..,N	37"	-
	100%	$\mathbf{K}^s$ All	10"	-
	100%	$\mathbf{K}^s$ SVs	7"	-
	100%	β_i^k; $1 \leq i \leq N$; $1 \leq k \leq M+1$	0.1"	-
	100%	$\mathbf{K}^t$ All	-	0.8"
	100%	$\mathbf{K}^t$ SVs	-	0.5"

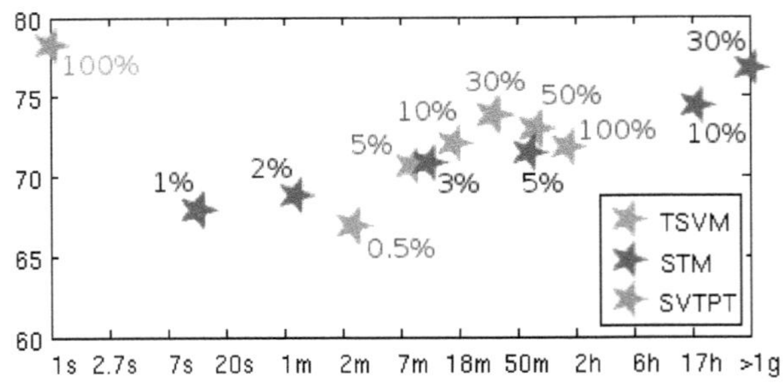

Figure 6: PAINFUL dataset. Performance (AUC) vs average time (in logarithmic scale) for training a target classifier with different unsupervised personalization methods: (red) TSVM [11], (blue) STM [5] and (green) SVTPT. Results for [5, 11] are reported considering different percentage of source data samples. Our method allows the best performance in the shortest time, considering 100% of the data points.

time must be multiplied by 24, the number of leave-one-subject-out cross validation iterations.

In the rest of the experiments, if not otherwise explicitly stated, we refer as SVTPT to indicate our method when training is performed using only Support Vectors (SVs). In order to further validate our approach, in Fig. 5 we show the similarity of the classifiers θ_i^C (where: $C \in \{SVM, SVTPT\}$) with respect to the *personalized* classifiers θ_i for each of the 24 users of the PAINFUL dataset. The personalized classifiers θ_i are trained with labeled data points of only the i-th user (see Eq.(2)). Conversely, each θ_i^{SVTPT} is obtained with the proposed method, as output of our regression function, while θ_i^{SVM} is a generic classifier trained with all and only the data points of the remaining 23 source users. The similarity is computed as $S_i^C = exp(-||\theta_i^C - \theta_i||_2)$, thus the larger its value, the more similar is the classifier to the personalized one. Fig. 5 shows that θ_i^{SVTPT} is closer to θ_i for each of the 24 users of the PAINFUL dataset.

The last part of our experiments is dedicated to compare SVTPT with respect to the state-of-the-art approaches whose code is available on line (i.e. TSVM and STM) in terms of computational times. In Fig. 6 we report the performance versus the target training time cost of SVTPT and the baseline methods. In [4] Chen et al. report the training time for TTA on PAINFUL (17.6 minutes) but they do not mention the workstation they used, thus the results are not directly comparable. Our experiments were run on a 4 Cores 2.40GHz CPU machine. It is clear from this plot that both TSVM and STM do not scale well as the number of training samples increases. For instance, using only 10% of the source samples, TSVM needs 17 minutes on average for training a personalized classifier, STM 18 hours and SVTPT only less than a second. Even if the accuracy of all the methods are comparable in this challenging dataset, our proposed approach largely outperforms all the other algorithms with respect to the computational cost. We believe that time efficiency is crucial in real world multimedia applications where the construction of a personalized classifier needs to be fast to attract real users.

In Table 4 (upper part) we report the computational costs for the different methods during the two phases: (i) *source training*, which involves only source data, and (ii) *target training*, in which also target data are used. In Table 4 (lower part) we report the computational costs of the main SVTPT operations (see Algorithm 1). SVTPT is the only method whose computational cost is split between these two phases, and the most expensive operations (i.e. computation of $\mathbf{K}^s$ and θ_i) are executed only once, as they are target independent. Note that, in a HCI setting, the computational cost of the second phase is the only one perceived by a new user. Conversely, other personalization methods, such as TSVM and STM are based on *training* a new classifier for each target user, an operation which is generally more costly then applying a pre-learned regression function. Moreover, the STM iterative optimization steps do not scale well with large datasets. Finally, the generic SVM classifier does not have any computational cost at target training time, as no personalization is performed. However, training the generic SVM is more costly then SVTPT, taking about 25 minutes versus less than 1 minute. The reason is that the computational complexity of the SVM solvers varies between $O(m^2)$ and $O(m^3)$, with m the number of training data points. In the case of PAINFUL dataset, training 1 classifier over $\sim 45k$ data samples is more costly than training N source classifiers, with an average of $\sim 1.9k$ data samples each.

4.3 Conclusions

In this paper we proposed a novel domain adaptation approach for facial expression analysis which deals with the inter-individual variability of expressing emotions by learning a set of personalized facial expression classifiers. With our approach a classifier for a new target individual is inferred without the need of acquiring labeled data. The proposed method relies on a regression framework to learn a mapping between a marginal distribution of the datapoints associated to a given person and the parameters of her/his personalized classifier. This distribution is represented by the set of Support Vectors of the linear classifier in the source case and by all the unlabeled data points in the target case. While we tested our method on facial analysis problems (AU detection and pain recognition), its formulation is completely general and potentially applicable to many other (visual or non-visual) domain adaptation problems. We showed that our system achieves state-of-the-art accuracy on public benchmarks while being different orders of magnitude faster than other unsupervised domain adaptation approaches.

5. ACKNOWLEDGMENTS

This work was partially supported by the European 7th Framework Program, under grant VENTURI (FP7-288238) and the Active Ageing at Home cluster project.

6. REFERENCES

[1] T. Ahonen, A. Hadid, and M. Pietikäinen. Face description with local binary patterns: Application to face recognition. *IEEE Trans. on PAMI*, 28(12):2037–2041, 2006.

[2] G. Blanchard, G. Lee, and C. Scott. Generalizing from several related classification tasks to a new unlabeled sample. In *NIPS*, 2011.

[3] L. Bruzzone and M. Marconcini. Domain adaptation problems: A DASVM classification technique and a circular validation strategy. *IEEE Trans. on PAMI*, 32(5):770–787, 2010.

[4] J. Chen, X. Liu, P. Tu, and A. Aragones. Learning person-specific models for facial expression and action unit recognition. *Pattern Recognition Letters*, 34(15):1964–1970, 2013.

[5] W.-S. Chu, F. De La Torre, and J. F. Cohn. Selective transfer machine for personalized facial action unit detection. In *CVPR*, 2013.

[6] H. Daume. Frustratingly easy domain adaptation. In *Proc. of Association for Computational Linguistics*, pages 256–263, 2007.

[7] H. Dibeklioğlu, T. Gevers, A. A. Salah, and R. Valenti. A smile can reveal your age: Enabling facial dynamics in age estimation. In *ACM Multimedia*, 2012.

[8] P. Ekman. Universals and cultural differences in facial expressions of emotion. In *Proc. Nebraska Symp. Motivation*, 1971.

[9] A. Gretton, A. Smola, J. Huang, M. Schmittfull, K. Borgwardt, and B. Schölkopf. Covariate shift by kernel mean matching. *Dataset shift in machine learning*, 3(4):5, 2009.

[10] Z. Hammal and J. F. Cohn. Automatic detection of pain intensity. In *ICMI*, 2012.

[11] T. Joachims. Transductive inference for text classification using support vector machines. In *ICML*, 1999.

[12] G. Littlewort, M. S. Bartlett, and K. Lee. Faces of pain: automated measurement of spontaneous facial expressions of genuine and posed pain. In *ICMI*, 2007.

[13] P. Lucey, J. F. Cohn, T. Kanade, J. Saragih, Z. Ambadar, and I. Matthews. The Extended Cohn-Kanade Dataset (CK+): A complete dataset for action unit and emotion-specified expression. In *CVPR Workshops (CVPRW)*, 2010.

[14] P. Lucey, J. F. Cohn, K. M. Prkachin, P. E. Solomon, S. W. Chew, and I. Matthews. Painful monitoring: Automatic pain monitoring using the unbc-mcmaster shoulder pain expression archive database. *Image Vision Comput.*, 30(3):197–205, 2012.

[15] A. Martinez and S. Du. A model of the perception of facial expressions of emotion by humans: Research overview and perspectives. *Journal of Machine Learning Research*, 13:1589–1608, 2012.

[16] S. J. Pan and Q. Yang. A survey on transfer learning. *IEEE Trans. on Knowledge and Data Engineering*, 22(10):1345–1359, 2010.

[17] K. M. Prkachin and P. E. Solomon. The structure, reliability and validity of pain expression: Evidence from patients with shoulder pain. *Pain*, 139(2):267–274, 2008.

[18] O. Rudovic, V. Pavlovic, and M. Pantic. Context-sensitive conditional ordinal random fields for facial action intensity estimation. In *ICCV Workshops*, 2013.

[19] E. Sangineto. Pose and expression independent facial landmark localization using dense SURF and the Hausdorff distance. *IEEE Trans. on PAMI*, 35(3):624–638, 2013.

[20] E. Sangineto, G. Zen, E. Ricci, and N. Sebe. We are not all equal: Personalizing models for facial expression analysis with transductive parameter transfer. In *ACM Multimedia*, 2014.

[21] M. F. Valstar, M. Pantic, Z. Ambadar, and J. F. Cohn. Spontaneous vs. posed facial behavior: automatic analysis of brow actions. In *ICMI*, 2006.

[22] J. Yang, R. Yan, and A. G. Hauptmann. Adapting svm classifiers to data with shifted distributions. In *IEEE International Conference on Data Mining (ICDM) Workshops*, 2007.

[23] Z. Zeng, M. Pantic, G. I. Roisman, and T. S. Huang. A survey of affect recognition methods: Audio, visual, and spontaneous expressions. *IEEE Trans. on PAMI*, 31(1):39–58, 2009.

Predicting Influential Statements in Group Discussions using Speech and Head Motion Information

Fumio Nihei
Seikei University
Musashino, Tokyo 180-8633 Japan
dm146211@cc.seikei.ac.jp

Yukiko I. Nakano
Seikei University
Musashino, Tokyo 180-8633 Japan
y.nakano@st.seikei.ac.jp

Yuki Hayashi
Osaka Prefecture University
Sakai, Osaka 599-8531 Japan
hayashi@kis.osakafu-u.ac.jp

Hung-Hsuan Huang
Ritsumeikan University
Kusatsu, Shiga 525-8577 Japan
huang@fc.ritsumei.ac.jp

Shogo Okada
Tokyo Institute of Technology
Yokohama, Kanagawa 226-8502 Japan
okada@dis.titech.ac.jp

ABSTRACT

Group discussions are used widely when generating new ideas and forming decisions as a group. Therefore, it is assumed that giving social influence to other members through facilitating the discussion is an important part of discussion skill. This study focuses on influential statements that affect discussion flow and highly related to facilitation, and aims to establish a model that predicts influential statements in group discussions. First, we collected a multimodal corpus using different group discussion tasks; in-basket and case-study. Based on schemes for analyzing arguments, each utterance was annotated as being influential or not. Then, we created classification models for predicting influential utterances using prosodic features as well as attention and head motion information from the speaker and other members of the group. In our model evaluation, we discovered that the assessment of each participant in terms of discussion facilitation skills by experienced observers correlated highly to the number of influential utterances by a given participant. This suggests that the proposed model can predict influential statements with considerable accuracy, and the prediction results can be a good predictor of facilitators in group discussions.

Categories and Subject Descriptors

H5.3 [Information Interfaces and Presentation]: Group and Organization Interfaces - Synchronous interaction.

General Terms

Human Factors, Design, Measurement.

Keywords

Influential statements; group discussion; facilitation; nonverbal information.

ICMI'14, November 12–16, 2014, Istanbul, Turkey.

http://dx.doi.org/10.1145/2663204.2663248

1. INTRODUCTION

Group discussions are team activities designed to form decisions and generate new ideas. Project managers are required to lead project members in group discussions. Therefore, management schools include group discussion activities as part of their management education programs. Younger employees are also required to perform well as team members in group discussions. In such situations, it has become common to use group discussions as assessment tools for group performance and for individual social competence. Group discussions are also used in job recruitment processes where recruiters observe discussions by a group of candidates and choose good discussion performers. Nevertheless, in current human resource management, there is no common standard to assess discussion skills. In practical situations, subjective impressions by senior managers or experienced recruiters are matched in many cases; however, it is more reasonable to consult explicit and objective measures.

Moreover, social dynamics in group discussions are also important aspects of group activities. In argument analysis [1], the flow of a discussion is represented as a tree or a graph in which the relationship between statements are illustrated. Argument trees are also useful in finding important statements that affect the flow of the discussion. For example, such statements may introduce a new idea and be followed by other opinions about it. In this study, we call such utterances *influential statements*. It is also assumed that participants good at facilitating discussions produce influential statements more frequently than other group members. Thus, it is expected for influential statements to be useful for tracking the flow of the discussion as well as for predicting the communication skill of each participant.

Based on the discussion above, this study addresses the following issues:

- Discuss and review the types of group discussion tasks that are used in human resource management, especially in job recruiting processes
- Collect multimodal group discussion corpus using various sensing technologies
- Define influential statements in group discussions and annotate them
- Establish a model that predicts influential statements based on prosodic features as well as attention and head motion information by the speaker and other group members

- Evaluate the model by investigating whether the number of influential statements correlates with facilitation skill assessments by experienced observers

The remainder of this paper is organized as follows. Previous corpus studies on group discussions are reviewed in Section 2. Section 3 explains how we built our group discussion corpus, and Section 4 describes how we analyzed the discussion flow. Based on the analysis, a prediction model for influential statements is proposed and evaluated in Section 5.

2. RELATED WORK

In psychological studies, it was found that vocal and visual perceptions affect the judgment of interviewers with regard to applicants in job interviews [2]. Interviewers also infer applicant personality traits from the mood and social attitudes of the applicants [3]. In computational approaches, hand gestures and postures were used to predict personality and employability [4]. On the basis of these studies, the TARDIS (Training young Adult's Regulation of emotions and Development of social Interaction Skills) project built a scenario-based serious game simulation platform [5]. This project incorporated social signal modules that recognize various nonverbal social cues, such as posture, gesticulation, voice activity, smiles, and laughter, and use them to interpret an applicant's social attitudes. However, these studies did not consider social dynamics in group discussions.

Group discussions have been studied in the research field of multimodal interaction. Many group discussion corpora have been collected using different task settings and various audio/visual equipment, such as AMI corpus [6] and ISL corpus [7]. We compared 14 group discussion corpora reviewed in [8] in terms of task, corpus size, equipment used, data collected, and annotations. The number of group members ranged from four to nine, and in many corpora, it was four. Corpus size varied; the number of collected conversations ranged from 40 to 100, and the total amount of time ranged from ten to 100 hours. Most of the corpora added verbal and nonverbal annotations, such as transcription, speech segmentation, gesture, gaze direction, and posture. We designed our corpus collection experiment based on these previous studies.

There have been also many studies that used these corpora. Many such studies attempted to estimate the characteristics of individual participants using audio, visual, and multimodal features. Some studies proposed models for predicting influential persons in group interactions [9, 10]. Based on the influence model, Dong et al. [11] predicted the functional roles of participants, such as orienter, seeker, and giver [12]. Studies with similar motivation proposed models for estimating dominance in group discussions [13-16]. In their series of studies, Sanchez-Cortes et al. [8] also proposed a model for predicting emergent leadership, and found that dominance and leadership were highly correlated. Audio-visual nonverbal features were also used for predicting self-reported personality traits [17, 18], as well as personality impressions from external observers [19]. These features were also used for characterizing behavioral patterns in group interaction [20]. Whereas the goal of these studies is to predict the characteristics of individual participants, the purpose of this study is to detect influential events that contribute to group discussions and affect the flow of the discussion.

On the other hand, research on argument analysis provides knowledge on how to analyze the flow of a discussion, and this can be applied to visualize the discussion in order to identify important statements in the discussion. Toulmin's model for argumentation [1] is broadly used in argumentation support systems [21, 22], and argumentation state graphs can be illustrated using this model. Prakken [23] proposed an argumentation model and illustrated persuasion dialogue using dialogue trees. In analyzing group discussions, we were also influenced by an annotation scheme for persuasion dialogues by Georgila et al. [24].

Figure 1. Snapshot of corpus collection experiment.

3. GROUP DISCUSSION CORPUS

In order to collect verbal and nonverbal communicative behaviors in group discussion situations, we conducted a multimodal corpus collection experiment in which groups of four people discussed three different topics.

3.1 Data Collection Environment

We set up a 4.5 m × 4.5 m experimental space enclosed by curtains; experimenters and PCs for controlling devices were placed behind these curtains in order to avoid distracting the participants of the experiments. At the center of this space, we placed a 1.2 m × 1.2 m table with one participant sitting on each side of the table. A snapshot of the experiment is shown in Figure 1, and the layout of the data collection environment is illustrated in Figure 2. The following describes the measured data and the devices used in the experiment.

(a) Motion capture: a total of 12 infrared cameras for the OptiTrack motion capture system [1] were set around the participants as shown in Figure 2. Each participant wore a cap to which reflective markers were attached. Each cap was recognized as an object, and its position and rotation in the x, y, and z coordinates were measured. The reflective markers were also placed on the subject's shoulders, elbows, wrists, and middle fingers. Thus, four markers were placed on each arm.

(b) Head acceleration: accelerometers (ATR-Promotions: WAA-010) were attached to the back of each participant's head, more specifically, to each participant's cap. These sensors can measure head acceleration and angular velocity in the x, y, and z coordinates at 30 fps. The measured data were sent to a server machine through Bluetooth. The server machine received and saved the data with a timestamp.

(c) Kinect sensor data: four Kinect sensors were used to obtain skeleton data and depth image of each participant's upper body.

[1] https://www.naturalpoint.com/optitrack/

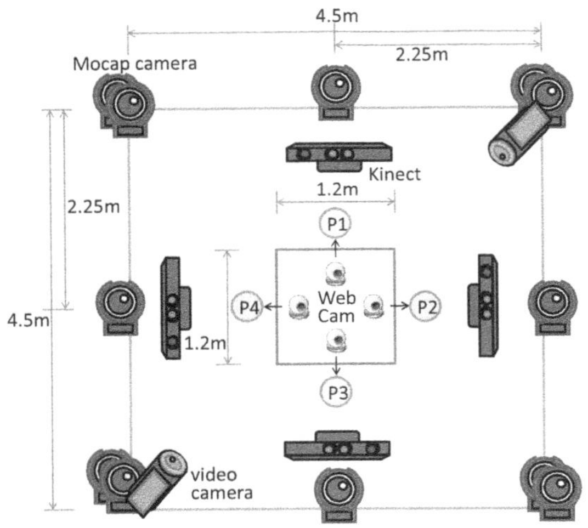

Figure 2. Data collection environment.

Each Kinect sensor was placed on a pole approximately 2 m from each participant. The resolution of the depth image was 320 × 240 pixels, and 8-bit values were saved with the timestamp.

(d) Eye tracking: each participant wore eye-tracking glasses (Tobii Glasses[2]) that allowed us to measure precise eye gaze data synchronized between the four participants. During measurement, data were stored in an SD card via a recording assistant device. Eye gaze data and scene videos from the participants' perspective were extracted from the SD card using a specific analysis software after the experimental session. Then, we created movies where the gaze points were overlaid on the scene image. The image resolution was 640 × 480 pixels, and the frame rate was 30 fps. The movies were also used to synchronize data between participants.

(e) Video: two video cameras (SONY HDR-CX630V) were set to record an overview of the communication from opposite directions. In addition, four web cameras (Logicool HD Pro Webcam C920t) were placed in the center of the table to record close-up front face images of each participant. The resolution of the image was 1280 × 720 and the frame rate was 30 fps. The distance between a web camera and each participant was approximately 1 m.

(f) Audio: all participants wore a hands-free headworn microphone (Audio-technica HYP-190H) to record speech data individually. Speech input from each microphone was sent to a PC via an audio interface, and recorded in four channels using a recording software. Further, we created mix down audio for four participants in the WAV format.

(g) Personality traits: NEO-FFI was used to measure participant personality. NEO-FFI is a questionnaire that consists of 60 items, each of which is graded on a five-point scale based on the well-known Big Five personality traits: Extraversion, Agreeableness, Neuroticism, Openness to experience, and Conscientiousness.

3.2 Experiment Design

We conducted a corpus collection experiment using a set of the audio-visual devices described in the previous section.

3.2.1 Categories of group discussion tasks

To form the basis of our experiment design, we reviewed and categorized group discussion tasks used in recruiting by consulting a job search support center at a university. A list of the discussion themes is described below:

Free discussion: a discussion theme is given to the applicants, who are requested to freely discuss it. In many cases, the theme is general and sometimes abstract, for example, "What would you like to do if you could start over your campus life?"

In-basket: this is typically called a "survival task" [25]. A list of items is shown to the applicants, and their task is to rank the items in order of importance. One of the main purposes of this task is to prioritize items in a reasonable way under time pressure.

Case study: in many cases of this type of discussion, data, conditions, and documents are provided. The applicants are requested to create ideas and plans considering the information provided by the materials, for example, "Determine the products that should be sold at your new shop."

Debate: applicants are separated into two groups, to which conflicting stances are assigned. Unlike a formal debate, in recruiting, the order of the speaker is not determined, and any applicant can speak freely at any time, for example, "Discuss the pros and cons of nuclear power plants."

In our survey, we noticed that in-baskets and case studies are used frequently in recruiting in Japanese companies. For in-basket tasks, applicant skills to logically and clearly state the preferred item order are evaluated. Another requirement for this type of task is to resolve any disagreements that might arise among participants regarding the item order, and reach an agreement. Thus, it is expected that the applicants' communication skills be evaluated through in-basket discussions. For case studies, where task conditions are predefined, analytical skills are required in order to propose important discussion points. It is also necessary to elicit opinions and ideas from other members, as well as lead the discussion to form a plan agreeable to all members. With the purpose of collecting a corpus that allows the systematic analysis of the different skill types that evolve in group discussions and of the argument structure, we adopted in-baskets and case studies as our experimental tasks. We set up one in-basket task and two case study tasks, and a group of four people was engaged in all these tasks. Therefore, these three discussion corpora are comparable to each other without concerning the subjects' individual differences and/or the experimental environment.

3.2.2 Discussion tasks

The three discussion tasks used in the experiment are described below. As indicated in the previous section, the first task is an in-basket task, and the remaining two are case study tasks.

(a) Celebrity guest selection (in-basket): the participants were asked to pretend that they were the executive committee members for a school festival, and were choosing the guest of the festival. Their discussion task was to decide the ranked order of 15 celebrities by considering cost and audience attraction. For the first five minutes, each participant was requested to read the instructions and decide alone (that is, without interacting with other members) the order of the 15 celebrities. Subsequently, the participants were engaged in a discussion to determine the ranked order as a group.

[2] http://www.tobii.com/en/eye-tracking-research/global/products/hardware/tobii-glasses-eye-tracker/

Table 1. Basic statistics for utterances in three discussion corpora

		Total	AV	S.D.
Celebrity guest selection (N = 32)	Num. of utterances	3978	124.3	56.1
	duration (sec)	6447.3	201.5	119.2
Booth planning for school festival (N = 36)	Num. of utterances	5105	141.8	75.4
	duration (sec)	8825.4	245.1	163.1
Travel plans for foreign friends (N = 36)	Num. of utterances	5239	145.5	80.7
	duration (sec)	8395.9	233.2	162.2
Total (N = 104)	Num. of utterances	14322	137.2	70.7
	duration (sec)	23668.6	226.6	148.2

(b) Booth planning for a school festival (case study): the participants were instructed to discuss and create a plan for a small booth intended to sell food or drinks at the school festival. The participants were given a map that indicated the location of other booths, as well as possible places for opening their own booth. They also had a document that showed data for the distribution of visitors' age and the number of visitors by time. The participants were instructed to review these documents for five minutes before starting the discussion. Then, based on the data shown in the documents, the participants were allowed to discuss for 20 minutes where to open their booth and the type of goods they would sell.

(c) Travel planning for foreign friends (case study): the participants were instructed to create a two-day travel plan for foreign friends visiting Japan on vacation. The discussion time allowed was 20 minutes, and there was no time granted to think individually.

3.2.3 Experimental procedure

We recruited 40 Japanese university students (29 male and 11 female) to participate in the experiment, and divided them into 10 groups of four people. In some groups, one of the participants had prior experience in job searching. The participants did not know each other. Before starting the discussion sessions, all participants completed the NEO-FFI questionnaire and signed a consent form. It was explained to the participants that their manner of speaking and the content of their speech would be evaluated so that they understood these were serious tasks.

Each group had three discussion sessions in Japanese where each of the three tasks listed in Section 3.2.2 was discussed. In order to cancel out the effect of task order, the order of the task was randomized. The participants were also instructed that one member of their group would report the results of their discussion for one minute as a representative of the group. A timer was placed on each of the two poles so that the participants could see the remaining time. The timers rang at the start and end time of the discussion to notify the participants. After completing all sessions, the participants were paid 3,000 yen.

3.3 MATRICS Corpus

From the experiment described above, we created the MATRICS (MultimodAl (Task-oriented) gRoup dIsCuSsion) corpus. The total duration of the MATRICS corpus was approximately 10 hours (ten groups × three sessions of 55 min each). All audio and visual data were synchronized using the start buzzer, and various sensing data were synchronized using the timestamp assigned to each record. The accuracy of the timestamp was guaranteed by synchronizing all the computers that received sensor data through access to a unique NTP server in the same local network.

In order to generally compare corpus size between the three types of discussions, we extracted spoken utterances using a speech processing tool in a speech recognition system [26] that can detect speech segments based on zero-crossing number and power (level). When more than 200 ms of silence were observed, such silence was identified automatically as the utterance boundary. Because audio data for four sessions were lost due to device failure and operation errors, we obtained 104 audio files of individual speakers (32 files for the Celebrity guest selection, 36 for Booth planning, and 36 for Travel planning. Table 1 lists the basic statistics for the number and the duration of utterances for the three types of discussion tasks. The size of the Celebrity guest selection corpus was slightly smaller than the other two given that this session was five minutes shorter than the others; however, the average and standard deviation for the number and length of utterances did not vary significantly depending on the task. As a result, we collected over 14,000 utterances.

For the rest of this paper, we focus on the Booth planning corpus because this task includes different discussion phases, such as proposing an idea, discussing the proposed idea, and forming a decision, and thus, this task is suitable for analyzing influential statements in different discussion phases.

4. ANALYZING DISCUSSIONS

4.1 Influence Analysis

In order to identify important and influential statements in group discussions, we need to discuss first the definition of influential statements. In argument analysis, a discussion stream is illustrated as a tree or a graph [23]. The size of a branch indicates the size of the argument, and a large branch is assumed to influence the discussion. A similar idea can be applied to online discussion boards and re-tweets in Twitter. It is reasonable to assume that the more responses or re-tweets a message receives, the more influential it is. We follow this idea and define the influence level of a given utterance as the number of subsequent utterances that are related to it. Advantages and disadvantages, clarification, agreement, and alternatives are regarded as being related and subsequent to a preceding utterance.

Note that, for the purpose of analyzing the influence of statements, shorter speech intervals are not useful as the unit of analysis, and it is better to identify a sequence of speech intervals by the same speaker as one statement. Therefore, in the analysis of influence, we processed audio signals from each participant headset microphone using a speech recognition system [26], and identified a speech interval as an utterance when more than 1,500 ms of silence were observed in the speech signal[3].

[3] For this reason, the number of utterances was different from the numbers shown in Table 1.

Table 2. Correlation between frequency of influential statements and facilitation ability assessment

	F1	F2	F3	F4	F5	F6	F7	FA
NU	.661	.692	.614	.687	.571	.592	.604	.658
NIU	.671	.704	.661	.695	.577	.619	.655	.682

Then, we counted the number of utterances directly or indirectly related to a given utterance. Suppose that there is a sequence of utterances A, B, and C by different speakers. If utterance B is related to utterance A and utterance C is related to utterance B, then utterance A has two related turns, B and C. Thus, we assume that the number of related utterances indicates the degree of influence of a given utterance. If there is another utterance by the same speaker, we do not count it as a related utterance. In this case, the influence score of utterance A is two. We annotated 2,428 utterances contained in eight booth-planning case study discussions[4], and counted the number of related utterances for each of them. Then, the count was assigned to the utterance as the influence score.

In order to create a binary classification model for predicting influential utterances, each utterance was labeled as influential or non-influential. In this study, if the influence score is equal to or larger than two, the utterance is categorized as influential. If the score is less than two (zero or one), the utterance is categorized as non-influential. A good reason for this threshold is that each utterance can obtain at least one subsequent related utterance by designating the next speaker. In particular, such utterances construct an adjacency pair, for example, as question-answer, and in such a case, the next speaker has an obligation to respond to the preceding utterance. If an utterance has more than one related utterance, this suggests that the utterance receives non-obligatory reactions from other participants.

4.2 Video Assessment by Experienced Observers

We assume that the more facilitation skills a participant has, the more frequently such person makes influential statements. To test this hypothesis and ensure the validity of our discussion analysis in Section 4.1, we asked experienced observers to assess the facilitation ability of the participants by watching group discussion videos. If evaluation by an experienced observer correlates with the frequency of influential statements in the discussion analysis, the validity of our discussion analysis is supported.

To evaluate facilitation ability, we created a questionnaire that consists of seven items scored with a five-point scale. The seven items are: (F1) start a discussion or a new topic (F2) lead the discussion at many points (F3) propose discussion points (F4) aggregate and summarize member opinions (F5) attempt to maintain the discussion on topic and restore the discussion to topic if group members digressed (F6) be conscious of the structure of the discussion and consider time pressure (F7) attempt to elicit opinions from other members. These seven items are closely related to Pianesi et al.'s Functional Role Coding Scheme (FRCS) [27] and Bales' Interaction Process Analysis [12].

[4] We did not analyze one of the booth-planning discussions because a part of the sensor data were lost due to device failure.

For video observation, each video was divided into three parts. Since the entire discussion lasted 20 min, the length of each part was approximately 7 min. We recruited 21 observers with recruiting experience, and assigned them one of the three parts of each discussion (the observers were not assigned two parts in the same discussion) in order to assess each participant's facilitation ability by completing the aforementioned questionnaire. Thus, 28 scoring data were obtained for each video part (seven observers × four participants). The assignment and the order of the videos were randomized among the observers.

4.3 Correlation between Influential Statements and Facilitation Ability

In order to investigate the correlation between the number of influential statements and the facilitation assessment, we defined the following measures:

Number of Utterances [NU]: total number of utterances that a given participant made in a session

Number of Influential Utterances [NIU]: total number of influential utterances made by a given participant in a session

We calculated Person's correlation coefficients between these values and the facilitation assessment for seven items (F1 to F7), and the average score (FA) of the seven items. Table 2 shows the results. NIU has the higher correlation with all types of facilitation measures compared to NU. In particular, for F7, which evaluates coordination skill, the correlation with NIU (0.655) is much higher than that with NU (0.604). This suggests that facilitation ability does not mean talkative only [28]. Even if a participant speaks a lot of non-influential statements, expert observers might not evaluate such a person as the discussion leader. These results support the concept that influential utterance is a good predictor of facilitation ability, and that predicting influential utterances is useful for understanding the stream of discussion with group dynamics. We use the 7-items average scores (FA) for further analysis.

5. PREDICTING INFLUENTIAL STATEMENTS

Using the MATRICS corpus from Section 3 and the annotation of influential statements from Section 4, this section proposes a model for predicting influential statements.

5.1 Feature Definition and Extraction

In this study, we focus on attention direction and head movement as visual features, and on intensity and duration of speech and pause as audio features. Figure 3 illustrates these types of information during an influential statement. In this figure, P1 speaks an influential statement, and P3 and P4 look at P1 while moving their heads with speech signals. However, P2 does not look at P1, and does not move or speak.

Based on the observation above, we defined nine audio features and ten visual features. They were assigned to each utterance as an instance, whereas to calculate feature values, the audio and visual data from two seconds before the beginning of the utterance to three seconds after the end of the utterance were used. This is because other participant reactions were expected to occur before, and specifically, after the utterance. Therefore, if there is an utterance made by others, 2 sec before or 3 sec after the utterance, data obtain during this time interval were included into

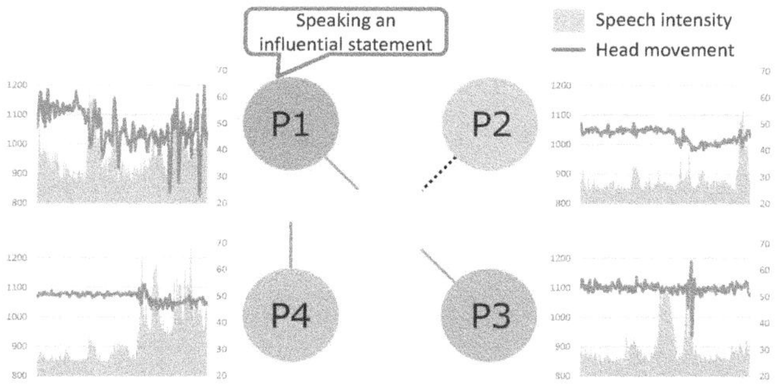

Figure 3. Multimodal signals during an influential statement.

the feature values. The descriptions of the features are given below.

5.1.1 Visual features

For visual information, we set up two features for attention, and eight features for head movement.

(A) Features for visual attention: these features were assigned semi-automatically; the direction of attention was estimated approximately by processing each participant's front face video data from web cameras using a vision-based face tracker (FaceAPI) by mainly considering rotation along vertical axis, and were manually corrected subsequently[5]. The following feature values were normalized by the utterance duration.

Number of attention shifts (NumOfAS): number of attention shifts by the speaker during his/her utterance.

Number of attention received from more than one participant (NumOfAR_P > 1): frequency of receiving attention from at least two other participants in the group during the speaker's utterance.

(B) Features for head movement: for each frame *i*, the composite acceleration for x, y, and z axes (HMA_i) was computed by equation (1) using accelerometer data.

$$HMA_i = \sqrt{x_i^2 + y_i^2 + z_i^2} \quad (1)$$

Then, the average of the current speaker's HMA_i (HMA_ave), variance (HMA_var), maximum value (HMA_max), and minimum value (HMA_min) were computed per utterance and used as feature values.

For the head acceleration of non-speakers (participants who do not have a speaking turn), the sum of their HMA_i was calculated for each frame *i*. Then, the average of the summed HMA_i (O'sHMA_ave), variance (O'sHMA_var), maximum value (O'sHMA_max), and minimum value (O'sHMA_min) were computed per utterance and used as feature values.

5.1.2 Audio features

For audio information, we set up nine features for intensity and duration of speech and pause. Intensity was measured every 10 ms using Praat [29] speech analysis software.

[5] Because the goal of this paper is to establish prediction models, it would be better to use larger and more accurate data. However, approximately 20% of the face tracking data were missed because of tracking errors. Therefore, for this study, we annotated participant head direction in a semi-automatic manner.

Table 3. Differences in feature values between influential and non-influential utterances

	Influential	Non-Influential	t(df) = t-value * : p<.05 ** : p<.01
NumOfAS	0.16	0.1199	t(2426) = 4.377**
NumOfAR_P>1	2.263	1.154	t(351.7) = 3.801**
HMA_ave	1057	1063	t(411.3) = -2.73**
HMA_var	1572	1350	t(2426) = 2.209*
HMA_max	1196	1178	t(2426) = 3.579**
HMA_min	873	900.9	t(2426) = -3.208**
O'sHMA_ave	3198	3203	t(2426) = -1.205
O'sHMA_var	3443	3607	t(474.5) = -0.9543
O'sHMA_max	3382	3375	t(2426) = 0.9245
O'sHMA_min	2945	2966	t(2426) = -1.968*
SI_ave	39.41	36.64	t(421.3) = 13.49**
SI_var	96.29	76.66	t(2426) = 9.724**
SI_max	64.05	62.14	t(2426) = 4.571**
SI_min	25.69	25.61	t(2426) = 1.638
SPR	1.382	1.157	t(2426) = 2.488*
OI_ave	104.9	104.2	t(486.8) = 1.363
OI_var	262.3	216.1	t(2426) = 4.751**
OI_max	152.9	146.8	t(427.5) = 4.903**
OI_min	79.33	80.03	t(473.1) = -4.014**

For the speaker's audio features, the average (SI_ave), variance (SI_var), maximum value (SI_max), and minimum value (SI_min) of the intensity of the speaker's voice per utterance were computed. In addition, we computed the time ratio of the speaking time to the accumulated pause length within an utterance (SPR). To calculate this feature, silence longer than 200 ms within the utterance was detected using a speech processing tool, and the speaking time was calculated by subtracting the pause length from the entire utterance duration.

For the non-speakers' audio features, the sum of the intensity for non-speakers was calculated. Then, the average (OI_ave), variance (OI_var), maximum value (OI_max), and minimum

Table 4. Performance of prediction models

Class	Precision	Recall	F-Measure
SVM	0.718	0.763	0.74
Random Forests	0.728	0.687	0.707
Logistic Regression	0.701	0.71	0.705

value (OI_min) of the summed intensity per utterance were computed.

In order to select useful features for predicting influential statements, we examined the difference between influential and non-influential statements with respect to these features. Table 3 shows the results of the t-test used to compare the average of each feature value between influential and non-influential utterances. The differences in the two visual attention features are statistically significant. During an influential utterance, the speaker more frequently shifted his/her attention (NumOfAS) and received more attention from others (NumOfAR_P>1) compared to non-influential utterances. Thus, both attention features may be useful in prediction. For head movement features, the differences in HMA_ave, HMA_var, HMA_max, HMA_min, and O'sHMA_min were statistically significant. Since the HMA value decreased often according to head motion, the minimum values become smaller when the head moves. Therefore, HMA_min and O'sHMA_min for influential utterances were smaller for influential utterances than for non-influential utterances. In addition, all speech features, with the exception of SI_min and OI_ave, were also significant. Influential statements were uttered with a louder voice (SI_ave) and with more varied intensity (SI_var) than non-influential statements. Voice intensity from other participant responses varied more for influential utterances than for non-influential utterances (OI_var).

These results suggest that the speakers of influential statements make more frequent attention shifts with more motion variations and speak with louder voice. During such an influential utterance, non-speaker participants pay more attention to the speaker with more head motion variations and respond to the speech with more variation in loudness.

5.2 Prediction Models

Since the number of influential and non-influential utterances was unbalanced, we re-sampled the data in order to use an equal number of instances for both classes. Thus, 600 utterances were used in creating models. Three different classification methods were used: Support Vector Machines (SVM) using RBF kernel with parameter C = 2.125 and gamma = 1.0, Random Forests, and Logistic Regression. We used leave-one-out cross validation for model evaluation. We report precision, recall, and F-measure (harmonic mean of precision and recall) for each model in Table 4. Among these three models, the SVM model performed best. Both precision and recall rate are over 0.7, and F-measure is 0.74. These results suggest that although the model does not look at the linguistic stream of argument, the model helps to predict how influential the current speaker's statement will be in future discussions by looking at the speaker's behavior and the non-speakers' reaction.

In Section 4.3, we discussed the correlation between influential statements and facilitation ability, and discovered that a participant who makes influential statements more frequently than other members provides a good impression of their facilitation ability. To confirm the validity of this finding using the prediction model, we calculated NIU based on the prediction results of influential statements using the SVM model, and ranked the participants according to their estimated NIU values. We also ranked the participants according to their real NIU values as calculated in Section 4.3. The matched ratio between the ranked order based on the facilitation ability scores (FA) rated by the experienced observer and estimated/real NIU are shown in Table 5. As the table indicates, 87.5% of the participants ranked highest for facilitation ability had the highest estimated NIU values among all participants. Moreover, the average matched ratio using the estimated NIU is 0.625, which is equal to the matched ratio using the real NIU. This suggests that the estimated NIU can predict the ranking of facilitation ability as accurately as the real NIU. Intriguingly, the estimated NIU predicts the highest and lowest ranked participants more accurately than the real NIU. This suggests that our proposed model is particularly useful in predicting the best performer and the poorest performer. Whereas the goal of this study is not to estimate facilitation ability, we still believe that this result is sufficiently strong to claim that predicting influential statements significantly contributes to characterizing participants in group discussions. Facilitation ability estimation is one good example.

Table 5. Matched ratio with human assessment of facilitation ability

Ranking by human assessment	Matched ratio with ranking by real NIU	Matched ratio with ranking by estimated NIU
1	0.75	0.875
2	0.625	0.375
3	0.5	0.5
4	0.625	0.75
all	0.625	0.625

6. CONCLUSIONS AND FUTURE DIRECTION

This study constructed comparable group discussion corpus in different task settings, and proposed a model for predicting influential statements in group discussions using our case-study-type corpus. The performance of the proposed model was 0.74 in its F-measure. We also found that a person who makes influential statements more frequently than other group members is more likely to provide a better impression of his/her discussion facilitation ability. Because facilitation skills are part of leadership, there is a good possibility that the model can contribute to predicting leadership [30].

In terms of future direction, we note that the data size of this analysis is not sufficiently large (32 participants in eight conversations), and it is necessary to evaluate our model using other types of discussions, such as in-basket tasks. If the model is useful in other types of discussion, this could suggest the versatility of the model. Our corpus is perfectly designed for such a research purpose. Second, another direction to confirm the usefulness of the proposed model is to implement an automatic influential statement detection mechanism because all the features used in the model can be obtained automatically. For longer-term issues, in the current analysis, linguistic information is not used. Even if we can see that the statement is influential, it is also necessary to know the content of the statement: advantages, disadvantages, clarification, etc. Our model and analysis need to be improved by considering utterance content. Finally, it is also indispensable to continue developing the MATRICS corpus. Presently, we have not integrated all the sensor data. In particular, eye tacking data and Kinect sensor data are expected to enrich the corpus. There is also a possibility to share the corpus with other researchers as the basis of multimodal interaction studies.

7. ACKNOWLEDGMENTS

This work was supported by JSPS KAKENHI Grant Number 25280076.

8. REFERENCES

[1] Toulmin, S. E. 2003. *The Uses of Argument*: Cambridge University Press.

[2] Motowidlo, T. D. a. S. J. 1999. Why visual and vocal interview cues can affect interviewers' judgment and predict job performance, *Journal of Applied Psychology*, 84(6): p. 986-993.

[3] Hareli, S. and Hess, U. 2010. What emotional reactions can tell us about the nature of others: An appraisal perspective on person perception, *Cognition & Emotion*, 24(1): p. 128–140.

[4] Nguyen, L. S., et al. 2013, Multimodal analysis of body communication cues in employment interviews, in *Proceedings of the 15th ACM on International conference on multimodal interaction*, ACM: Sydney, Australia, p. 437-444.

[5] Anderson, K., et al. 2013. The TARDIS Framework: Intelligent Virtual Agents for Social Coaching in Job Interviews, in *Advances in Computer Entertainment*. p. 476-491.

[6] Jovanovic, N., Akker, R. o. d., and Nijholt, A. 2006 A corpus for studying addressing behavior in multi-party dialogues, in *Language Resources and Evaluation*. p. 5-23.

[7] Burger, S., MacLaren, V., and Yu, H. 2002, The ISL meeting corpus: the impact of meeting type on speech style, in *International conference on spoken language processing, Interspeech-ICSLP*.

[8] Sanchez-Cortes, D., et al. 2013. Emergent leaders through looking and speaking: from audio-visual data to multimodal recognition, *Journal on Multimodal User Interfaces*, 7(1-2): p. 39-53.

[9] Otsuka, K., et al. 2006. Quantifying interpersonal influence in face-to-face conversations based on visual attention patterns, in *CHI '06 Extended Abstracts on Human Factors in Computing Systems (CHI EA '06). ACM*, New York, NY, USA.

[10] Basu, S., et al. 2001. Towards measuring human interactions in conversational settings, in *IEEE CVPR Workshop on Cues in Communication*.

[11] Dong, W., et al. 2007. Using the influence model to recognize functional roles in meetings, in *the 9th ACM international conference on Multimodal interfaces*.

[12] Bales, R. F. 1970. *Personality and interpersonal behavior.*: New York: Holt, Rinehart and Winston.

[13] Rienks, R., et al. 2006. Detection and application of influence rankings in small group meetings, in *ICMI '06 Proceedings of the 8th international conference on Multimodal interfaces (ICMI06)*, p. 257 - 264.

[14] Hung, H., et al. 2008. Investigating Automatic Dominance Estimation in Groups From Visual Attention and Speaking Activity, in *the 10th international conference on Multimodal interface (ICMI '08)*, p. 233-236.

[15] Jayagopi, D. B., et al. 2009. Modeling Dominance in Group Conversations Using Nonverbal Activity Cues, *IEEE Transactions on Audio, Speech, and Language Processing*, 17(3): p. 501 - 513.

[16] Escalera, S., et al. 2010. Automatic Detection of Dominance and Expected Interest, *EURASIP Journal on Advances in Signal Processing*, Volume 2010.

[17] Lepri, B., et al. 2012. Connecting meeting behavior with extraversion - a systematic study, *IEEE Transactions on Affective Computing*, 3(4): p. 443–455.

[18] Staiano, J., et al. 2011, Automatic modeling of personality states in small group interactions, in *ACM Multimedia*, p. 989–992.

[19] Aran, O. and Gatica-Perez, D. 2013, One of a Kind: Inferring Personality Impressions in Meetings, in *the 15th ACM on International conference on multimodal interaction (ICMI2013)*, p. 11-18.

[20] Jayagopi, D. B., et al. 2012. Linking Speaking and Looking Behavior Patterns with Group Composition, Perception, and Performance, in *the 14th ACM international conference on Multimodal interaction (ICMI2012)*, p. 433-440.

[21] Gordon, T. F. and Karacapilidis, N. I. 1997, The Zeno Argumentation Framework, in *International Conference on Artificial Intelligence and Law*, p. 10-18.

[22] Verheij, B. 2003. Artificial argument assistance for defeasible argumentation, *Artificial Intelligence*, 150(1-2): p. 291-324.

[23] Prakken, H. 2008. A formal model of adjudication dialogues, *Artificial Intelligence and Law*, 16(3): p. 305-328.

[24] Georgila, K., et al. 2011, An Annotation Scheme for Cross-Cultural Argumentation and Persuasion Dialogues, in *the SIGDIAL 2011 Conference*, p. 272-278.

[25] Kickul, J. and Neuman, G. 2000. Emergent Leadership Behaviors: The Function of Personality and Cognitive Ability in Determining Teamwork Performance and KSAs, *Journal of Business and Psychology*, 15(1): p. 27-51.

[26] Julius http://julius.sourceforge.jp/.

[27] Pianesi, F., et al. 2008. Multimodal support to group dynamics, *Personal and Ubiquitous Computing*, 12: p. 181-195.

[28] Mast, M. S. 2002. Dominance as expressed and inferred through speaking time, *Human Communication Research*, 28(3): p. 420-450.

[29] Praat http://www.fon.hum.uva.nl/praat/.

[30] Sanchez-Cortes, D., et al. 2010. Identifying Emergent Leadership in Small Groups using Nonverbal Communicative Cues, in *International Conference on Multimodal Interfaces and the Workshop on Machine Learning for Multimodal Interaction (ICMI-MLMI'10)*.

The Relation of Eye Gaze and Face Pose: Potential Impact on Speech Recognition

Malcolm Slaney
Microsoft Research
Mountain View, CA USA
malcolm@ieee.org

Andreas Stolcke
Microsoft Research
Mountain View, CA USA
Andreas.Stolcke@microsoft.com

Dilek Hakkani-Tür
Microsoft Research
Mountain View, CA USA
dilek@ieee.org

ABSTRACT

We are interested in using context to improve speech recognition and speech understanding. Knowing what the user is attending to visually helps us predict their utterances and thus makes speech recognition easier. Eye gaze is one way to access this signal, but is often unavailable (or expensive to gather) at longer distances. In this paper we look at joint eye-gaze and facial-pose information while users perform a speech reading task. We hypothesize, and verify experimentally, that the eyes lead, and then the face follows. Face pose might not be as fast, or as accurate a signal of visual attention as eye gaze, but based on experiments correlating eye gaze with speech recognition, we conclude that face pose provides useful information to bias a recognizer toward higher accuracy.

Categories and Subject Descriptors

I.2.7 [**Natural Language Processing**]: Speech recognition and synthesis

General Terms

Evaluation

Keywords

Speech recognition; eye gaze; face pose; language models

1. MOTIVATION

Several research groups have demonstrated improved speech recognition with access to a user's eye-gaze information [1, 6]. But eye-gaze information is difficult to obtain at a distance. In this paper we wish to demonstrate the utility of face-pose information as a proxy for eye-gaze information.

Eye gaze information will always be the better source of information. The fovea is highly specialized for gathering information, and is the portion of the eye with the highest spatial resolution. It is certainly possible to glimpse information from the corner of one's eye, but that is probably not how most people read information.

The system we envision combines a screen with speech recognition. Explicit pointing will always be valuable, using gestures, touch or a pointing device. This paper deals with eye-gaze and face-pose information because one must look at an object before you can point at it. This information makes the recognizer's job easier because intent and visual history are both important contextual information for a recognizer.

Our hypothesis is that the orientation of the face, or its pose, is a proxy or an approximation of eye gaze. While one can certainly gaze in a wide range of directions without moving one's head, the natural action appears to be that the eyes move first, and then the head follows. We wish to characterize the temporal course of the head-pose signal, and its accuracy. Both the eye-gaze and the face-pose signals function as a spotlight, effectively selecting certain words on the screen and potentially biasing the speech recognizer's language model (LM).

2. EXPERIMENTAL SETUP

We collected joint data using a Tobii REX for eye-gaze data, and a Microsoft Kinect for face-pose data. Users were asked to read text at random locations on a large screen, thus insuring that the user was focused on the task at hand.

Our two sensors have conflicting requirements. The eye-gaze hardware works best with close distances so it can capture an image of the user's eyes with high resolution, while the face-pose software wants to see more of the body so it can reliably detect the user and identify the face. We wanted to collect simultaneous eye-gaze and face-pose data, so we had a narrow range of user-to-screen distances so as to satisfy the requirements of both devices.

Figure 1 depicts our overall experiment setup. A large (132cm diagonal) display shows text to the user, who stands at a distance of 74cm from a 40 dots per inch (dpi) screen. A Kinect is mounted above the display and looks down on the user, and a REX is mounted at the bottom of the display and looks up at the user's eyes. The user's speech utterances were collected with a headset-mounted noise-cancelling microphone but are not analyzed in this paper. Instead, we compare the relation between eye gaze and face pose in our data with data from a previous experiment that examined the relationship between eye-gaze and speech-recognition performance.

ICMI'14, November 12–16, 2014, Istanbul, Turkey.
Copyright 2014 ACM 978-1-4503-2885-2/14/11:.$15.00.
http://dx.doi.org/10.1145/2663204.2663251.

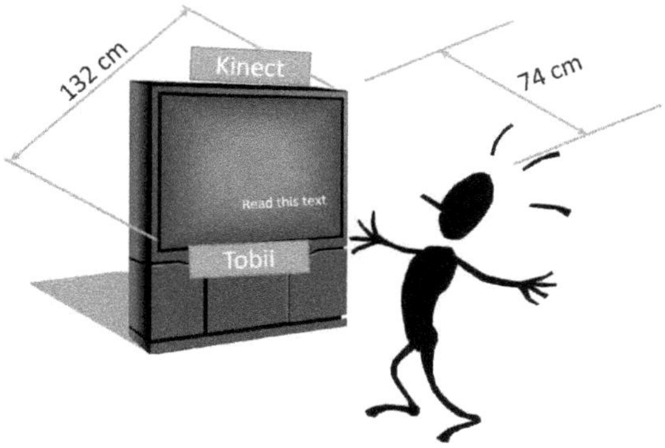

Figure 1: Our basic experimental setup. A user sees a blank screen, and then seeks and reads text placed at random on the screen.

2.1 Tobii REX Eye Tracker

The Tobii REX is an inexpensive eye-tracking sensor that detects infrared glints using a small camera. The specifications for the REX state that it is useful for screen-to-eye distances between 40 and 90cm. In our setup, we got position updates at about 30Hz in pixel coordinates. We used the vendor-supplied software to calibrate the eye-gaze calculations for each user. Our display was larger than their specification allowed, and we were at the limit of their depth range. Thus the calibration software often complained that it was not able to get a good look at all of the points used for calibration. But since we are mostly interested in temporal information, as opposed to precise pixel locations, this was judged to be sufficient for our purposes.

2.2 Microsoft Kinect

The Microsoft Kinect, on the other hand, is a general device for collecting body skeleton information. The Face-Tracking toolkit that is part of the Developer's Toolkit (version 1.8) uses depth and color image data to track one or more faces. Kinect includes a full body tracker, and a special mode in the Kinect for Windows device that only needs the user's upper body for tracking. In this near-range mode the Kinect has a practical range from 80cm to 250cm. The Kinect software returns the location of a face, in meters relative to the camera location, and the 3-D pose of the face as angles relative to the camera coordinate system. The camera has a vertical field of view of 43° We also received face-pose information at a rate of about 30Hz.

The Kinect provides head positions and angles, and does not include any provision for calibration. We needed to transform these positions and angles into screen coordinates. The ultimate solution is a two-camera approach suggested by Huang [3]. Instead, we implemented a simpler solution by putting the camera on the same plane as the screen, thus reducing parallax effects, and then using an affine transform to perform the final mapping into screen coordinates. To effect this transformation we asked the user to turn their head towards 8 different points around the outskirts of the display. We used the face-pose information provided by the Kinect, and simple geometric transformations to transform the raw Kinect data into the camera's imaging plane (which was slightly tilted with respect to the display.) We then found an optimum affine transform that transformed the points in the camera plane to pixels in the computer's world. Again, this transformation is not general, but was deemed sufficiently accurate for this paper's purposes.

2.3 Automatic Speech Recognition

We use a state-of-the-art large vocabulary speech recognizer in our experiments [2, 6]. The acoustic models incorporate the latest advances in context-dependent deep neural networks (DNN) for estimating senone likelihoods. The language model (LM) is a general-purpose backoff 4-gram model with a vocabulary of about 400K words. This generic LM (GLM) was trained on a wide variety of sources ranging from transcribed speech from deployed ASR applications, such as voice search, to text from a diverse set of web resources. The GLM was not tailored or adapted to the tasks of our study.

To study the potential benefit of context information for speech recognition we performed LM adaptation experiments in an N-best rescoring framework [5]. We generated lists of the 100 best hypotheses for each utterances, using the GLM. The baseline word error rate was 43.8%. The best achievable (oracle) error rate, by rescoring the 100 best hypothesis, was 22.5%.

Besides the generic LM, we also investigated a second, stronger baseline system in which we derive an utterance-specific bigram LM from the full-screen contents, irrespective of eye-gaze information. This LM is restrictive since there are roughly one thousand words on a single page. The utterance-specific whole-page LM was combined with the GLM via log-linear score combination at the utterance level. This corresponds to a log-linear interpolation of the two LMs [4], but without normalizing the combined probability distribution. We estimated the linear weights for GLM and utterance-specific LM log probabilities on one half of the test speakers and applied to the other half, in a jack-knifing experiment. The N-best hypotheses were rescored with the combined LM and the new 1-best hypotheses extracted.

Finally, we built context-dependent utterance-specific LMs, based on the estimated location of the user's attention before and during the time of each utterance. To build the context-conditioned LM, we collected words appearing on the screen at the appropriate times and locations. We then found bigrams by sorting the word locations into reading order, and combining words into bigrams if they are on the same line and adjacent to each other. From the bigrams thus collected, another utterance-specific LM was estimated, and combined with both baseline LMs (GLM and whole-page LM) via log-linear score combination, again using jack-knifing for weight estimation.

2.4 Display Experiment

Before collecting speech we asked 6 users to calibrate themselves for both the eye gaze and face trackers. In addition to helping us map angles to pixels on the screen, this calibration procedure allowed us to get basic information about the static performance of the system and our users. Users were aware that we were tracking both their head pose and eye gaze, but were not aware of our specific hypothesis.

After calibration we asked each user to perform 20 to 30 speech-reading trials. Before each trial, users were told to look at the center of the screen, where a circle was fixed. Then after a few seconds a short text utterance (a few words from a news headline) with a 6mm high font was displayed somewhere at random on the screen. This appeared suddenly so there was an orienting response by the user. We also added a short 2cm arrow to the center circle to indicate the direction of the text. We did not enforce a specific gaze location at the start of an experiment. And there was likely both head and eye movement as the user prepared for each trial. The utterance starts some number of seconds after the text appears, and we are interested in the time till the eye gaze and face pose estimates are stable.

3. RESULTS

We would like to relate eye gaze and face pose to speech-recognition performance. This is difficult for a number of reasons, including task and cognitive issues, but also due to simple physical effects. We assume a user absorbs information from within a visual spotlight that moves over time. In addition the sensors have their own physical limitations, which we can model as (Gaussian) noise added to each measurement. Finally, there is some function that relates the probability of a user's comfortable head positions to their desired eye-pose direction. This probability function is certainly related to physical considerations like maintaining comfortable positions, while not shaking the head too much, or too fast. We model the spotlight size as a sum of independent factors: fovea size, eye-tracking error, and if necessary comfortable head-eye orientations.

We compare eye-gaze and face-pose information in three ways. Most simply, we look at the basic sensor error and can quantify the "noise." Secondarily, we look at the time delay between eye gaze and face pose information. Finally, we translate these numbers into a perplexity measure by which we can characterize speech-recognition performance.

3.1 Noise

As part of our calibration procedure, we asked users to stare at a moving dot on the screen. When the dot is not moving, and the user's head is still, we can use the eye-gaze and face-pose information to estimate the inherent noise in the sensor. For the eye gaze, at this screen size the variance was 65^2 pixels. While for the face pose, again given the geometry we used in this study, the variance of the sensor noise was 58^2 pixels. These numbers are important as we look at the optimum spotlight when adjusting the speech recognizer's language model.

3.2 Temporal Characteristics

The temporal patterns of eye gaze and face pose are certainly different. We hypothesize that eyes are faster to orient and then the face catches up. Here we only investigate the delay between eye-gaze and face-pose orientation; the full spectral–temporal relationship between these two signals is beyond the scope of this paper.

We asked subjects to read aloud text phrases we put at random locations onto an otherwise blank screen. Users were told that they could look at the center of the screen for an indication of where the string had appeared, but most users were actively scanning during the experiment.

Since the text was relatively small given the distance (0.5° visual height), users need to orient their eyes onto the text to perform the task. We also observed that users turned their heads toward the text. Thus we characterized the user's eye and facial orientation in terms of their average location when reading the text, and measured the distance to this average location over time. Before the spoken utterance, the distance should be much larger than it is during the utterance. Figure 2 shows an example of this behavior, quantified by the normalized distances from the final average fixation point. We can look for the time of orientation by correlation of the sensor signal with a unit step that goes from +1 to -1 at a variable point in time. With this simple correlation we could estimate the orientation time.[1]

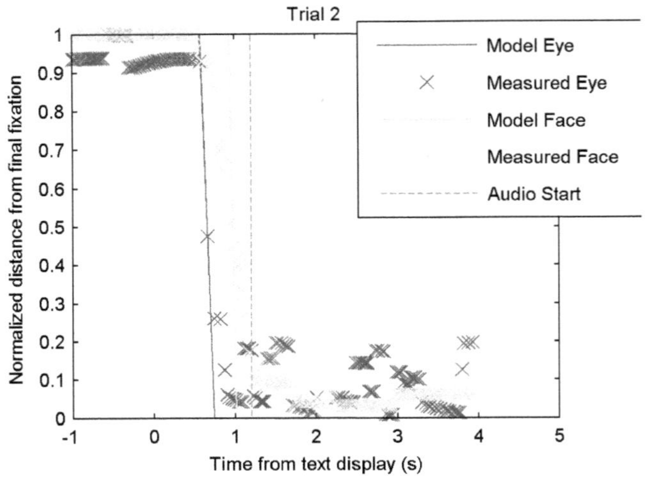

Figure 2: Normalized distance to the text for eye-gaze and face-pose signals during one trial.

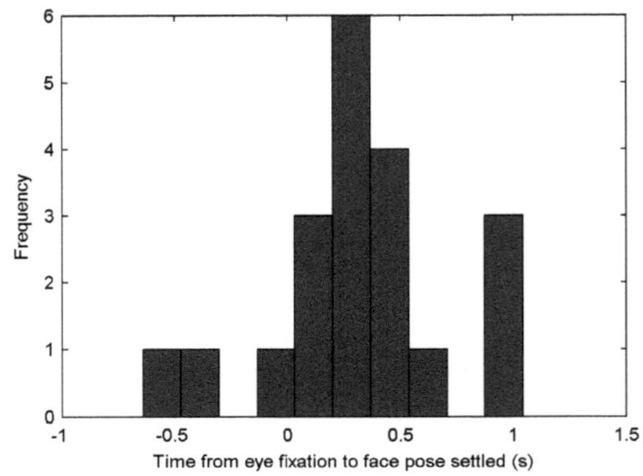

Figure 3: Distribution of the time delay between the eye-gaze fixation on the text and the eventual face orientation to the neutral position.

Because of the random nature of the task, and the user's eye-gaze and head orientation, we found 20 trials where we got a clear signal from both sensors. A histogram of the difference in orientation time between the two sensors is shown in Figure 3. In most cases, the head trailed the eyes by 0.3 seconds. But there were still cases where the head was pointed in the right location before the text appeared, and then eyes had to move to catch up to the head pose.

[1]We also looked at using logistic regression to model the data, but found that noise in the data made it hard to precisely estimate the transition time.

3.3 Perplexity

In a previous study [6] we used a desktop display to measure the effect of eye gaze on speech-recognition performance and LM perplexity during a speech-reading task. The display had a diagonal of 24", 77 dpi, 17 pixels per line of text, eye-tracking noise with variance 9.6^2 pixels, and the user sat 30" from the screen. Figure 4 shows speech recognition difficulty for this reading task when using eye-gaze information to adjust the recognizer's language model. Difficulty is expressed in terms of perplexity, which is a measure of how good the language model is at predicting the next word, given the words it has already seen. Lower perplexity means the language model thinks fewer words are possible, thus reducing the complexity of the speech recognizer's task, and increasing performance. But too small a spotlight removes needed information. Thus the optimum spotlight size was 200 pixels, and reduced the speech-recognition error by about 20%. We would like to know how face-pose information might translate into this domain.

To make the speech-recognizer's job easier, our spotlight should be as small as possible, including all necessary words on the screen, in spite of any sensor errors. In the eye-tracking case there are two components to the spotlight: a cognitive/reading effect and the sensor noise. The same idea holds for face-pose data, but there is also a component that corresponds to the short-term discrepancy between face pose and eye-gaze as the eyes and head adjust to a new task. We do not have an estimate of this variable, except as shown in Section 3.2 that there is a 0.3 second delay.

We use the eye-tracking ASR experiment to guage the impact of using face pose to bias a recognizer. The noise due to the face sensor is higher, but overall has a small effect on the overall perplexity. The spotlight in the desktop display has a radius of 200 pixels, or approximately 5° of arc. The face-sensor noise was 58^2 pixels on a larger display, suggesting a noise of approximately 3° degrees. Overall, this represents less than a factor of two increase in potential spotlight size. This certainly affects perplexity, but as can be seen in Figure 4 the modified perplexity is higher, but still an improvement over the whole-screen perplexity. Thus face pose adds information to the speech recognizer, and, based on the prior study, has the potential to improve recognition accuracy. We hope to verify this in a future experiment that uses the face-pose signal directly for biasing the speech recognizer.

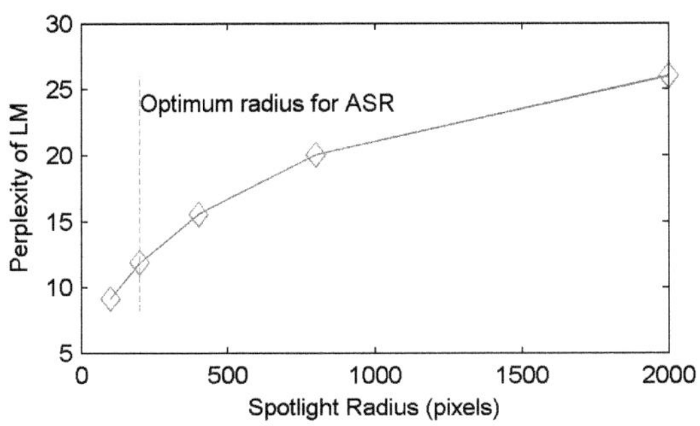

Figure 4: LM perplexity as a function of spotlight radius for the desktop screen, independent of modality.

4. CONCLUSIONS

We demonstrated the viability of face-pose information as a proxy for eye-gaze information. Eye-gaze information reduces the difficulty of the recognition task by a factor of two, in terms of language model perplexity. While eye gaze usually preceeds face orientation and current face sensors are not as accurate as eye trackers, face-pose information has the potential to also significantly reduce LM perplexity.

We have quantified eye-gaze and face-pose information in a joint experiment, where we jointly measure both signals from a single user. While face pose can not tell the whole story, it has similar errors, and a slight delay from the eye-gaze signal. This resulting perplexity reduction is important because it directly impacts speech-recognition performance. Speech recognition will be challenging in the large-display scenarios we envision because of multiple users, reverberent environments, and large microphone-to-user distances.

We need to perform further studies to quantify the effect that face pose information has on the visual spotlight needed for language modeling. This study shows that the errors are manageable, and suggest that there is a significant reduction in perplexity when using face-pose information. By this study we demonstrated the value of these new more ASR experiments using face-pose information.

5. REFERENCES

[1] N. J. Cooke and M. Russell. Gaze-contingent automatic speech recognition. In *Signal Processing*, pages 369–380, 2008.

[2] L. Deng, J. Li, J.-T. Huang, K. Yao, D. Yu, F. Seide, M. Seltzer, G. Zweig, X. He, and J. Williams. Recent advances in deep learning for speech research at microsoft. In *Proceedings of the 2013 IEEE International Conference on Acoustics, Speech, and Signal Processing (ICASSP)*, 2013.

[3] J.-B. Huang, Q. Cai, Z. Liu, N. Ahuja, and Z. Zhang. Towards accurate and robust cross-ratio based gaze trackers through learning from simulation. In *Proceedings of the Symposium on Eye Tracking Research and Applications*, ETRA '14, pages 75–82, New York, NY, USA, 2014. ACM.

[4] D. Klakow. Log-linear interpolation of language models. In *Proceedings of the International Conference on Spoken-Language Processing (ICSLP)*, page 1695, 1998.

[5] M. Ostendorf, A. Kannan, S. Austin, O. Kimball, R. Schwartz, and J. R. Rohlicek. Integration of diverse recognition methodologies through reevaluation of n-best sentence hypotheses. In *Proceedings of the workshop on Speech and Natural Language (HLT '91)*, pages 83–87. Association for Computational Linguistics, 1991.

[6] M. Slaney, R. Rajen, A. Stolcke, and P. Parthasarathy. Gaze enhanced speech recognition. In *Proceedings of IEEE International Conference onAcoustics, Speech and Signal Processing (ICASSP)*, 2014.

Speech-Driven Animation Constrained by Appropriate Discourse Functions

Najmeh Sadoughi[1], Yang Liu[2], Carlos Busso[1]
1. Multimodal Signal Processing (MSP) Laboratory
2. Human Language Technology Research Institute
The University of Texas at Dallas, Richardson TX 75080, USA
Emails: nxs137130@utdallas.edu, yangl@hlt.utdallas.edu, busso@utdallas.edu

ABSTRACT

Conversational agents provide powerful opportunities to interact and engage with the users. The challenge is how to create naturalistic behaviors that replicate the complex gestures observed during human interactions. Previous studies have used rule-based frameworks or data-driven models to generate appropriate gestures, which are properly synchronized with the underlying discourse functions. Among these methods, speech-driven approaches are especially appealing given the rich information conveyed on speech. It captures emotional cues and prosodic patterns that are important to synthesize behaviors (i.e., modeling the variability and complexity of the timings of the behaviors). The main limitation of these models is that they fail to capture the underlying semantic and discourse functions of the message (e.g., nodding). This study proposes a speech-driven framework that explicitly model discourse functions, bridging the gap between speech-driven and rule-based models. The approach is based on *dynamic Bayesian Network* (DBN), where an additional node is introduced to constrain the models by specific discourse functions. We implement the approach by synthesizing head and eyebrow motion. We conduct perceptual evaluations to compare the animations generated using the constrained and unconstrained models.

Categories and Subject Descriptors

H.5.2 [**Information Interfaces and Presentation**]: User Interfaces—*Conversational Agent*

Keywords

Conversational Agent; Head motion; Eyebrow movement; dynamic Bayesian network; Discourse function

1. INTRODUCTION

Conversational agents (CAs) provide powerful opportunities to better interact and engage with the users. They can communicate verbal and nonverbal information, which can be close to natural human interactions. CAs with naturalistic behaviors can be used in mobile interfaces, devices for the hearing impaired, animated movies, animations, intelligent tutoring systems, and entertainment industry. The challenge is to generate avatars with appropriate naturalistic nonverbal behaviors, responding to the underlying flow of the interaction.

Nonverbal behaviors are expressed through the body posture, hand gestures, head movements, eyebrow movements, facial expression and gaze [15]. People use these behaviors to highlight their emotional state, portray their thoughts, refer to concrete objects, illustrate abstract ideas, and clarify the intended semantic content. In order to create believable CAs, a precise and deep understanding of the relationship between speech and gestures is required. McNeill [20] mentioned that 90% of gestures occur when people are speaking. Moreover, speech and gestures are synchronized at different levels (i.e., phonemes, words, phrases, sentences) [10]. Gestures such as raising the eyebrows, nodding the head, shaking the head and frowning are timely aligned with their underlying verbal message. A CA should capture this complex coupling between gestures and speech.

Previous work on CAs are mainly divided into two categories: rule-based systems [2, 10, 15, 19], and data-driven systems [3, 5, 9, 16–18]. Rule-based systems usually define rules about the behaviors based on the contextual information during the dialog. Data-driven systems rely on recorded data to synthesize behaviors. An appealing approach to drive the animation is speech. Speech conveys rich information that a CA can leverage to synthesize naturalistic behaviors. Prosodic information conveyes the intonation and emphasis which is important to model the variability and complexity of the timings of the behaviors. However, when only speech is used to drive the animation, the behaviors may not capture the contextual information, ignoring the discourse functions of the gestures (nodding for affirmation, shaking head for negation, frowning for disapproval). This study addresses this limitation by proposing a framework for speech-driven animations that explicitly models the underlying discourse functions.

This paper presents our preliminary attempt to bridge the gap between speech-driven approaches and rule-based systems, exploiting the advantages of both methods. The paper proposes to constrain a speech-driven animation system by the underlying discourse function of the message, providing more appropriate behaviors. The models are built upon the *dynamic Bayesian network* (DBN) proposed in Mariooyiad and Busso [18], which captures the relationship between

ICMI'14, November 12–16, 2014, Istanbul, Turkey.
Copyright 2014 ACM 978-1-4503-2885-2/14/11 ...$15.00.
Replace this line with the http://dx.doi.org/10.1145/2663204.2663252.

head movements, eyebrow movements and speech prosody features. We propose to add an extra variable reflecting the discourse function, which constrains the synthesized behaviors. We present perceptual evaluations to compare the constrained and unconstrained speech driven models.

2. RELATED WORK

Some of the frameworks for CA proposed in previous studies depend on carefully designed rules to synthesize appropriate gestures. Cassell et al. [10] designed a system with specific rules to generate facial expressions, head movements, and hand gestures, which were synchronized with speech [10]. In their follow up work, they designed the *behavior expression animation toolkit* (BEAT), which receives text as input to generate appropriate gestures and speech for the animation [11]. Kopp et al. designed a unified framework named *behavior markup language* (BML), for generating animations based on rules [15]. This effort allows other researches working on *embodied conversational agents* (ECAs) to use this language to combine various rules to generate behaviors (gaze, facial expression, head and hand movements). Marsella et al. [19] designed a system to synthesize animations that relies on speech and its transcription. They conducted acoustic and syntactic analysis on the inputs, generating animations based on some predefined behavior mapping. After synthesizing the gestures, they proposed heuristic rules to remove conflicting behaviors. They showed that animations generated using their approach are perceived more appropriate than prosody driven beats.

Studies have shown the relationship between head movements, eyebrow movements and speech [8,13]. Graf et al. [13] showed that head movements and facial expressions are correlated with speech prosody features. They showed that despite variations of amplitude and direction of head movements, the timing of these movements are correlated with prosodic features. They also identified correlation between the rise of eyebrows and prosodic features. These studies have motivated us to drive facial animations using speech as an alternative approach to rule-based methods [5–7,12].

Brand [3] proposed a mapping approach from HMMs to generate animations from speech. Cao et al. [9] designed a framework based on a generative model to synthesize facial expression with appropriate lip synchronization using speech prosody features. Busso et al. [5,6] synthesized head movements, using HMMs and vector quantization to generate head movements based on speech prosody features. Mariooryad and Busso [18], proposed a framework based on DBNs to model the relationship between head movement, eyebrow movement, and speech. This generative model synthesized head and eyebrow movements using prosody features. Le et al. [16] proposed a live speech-driven head, gaze, and eyelid motion synthesis framework. They designed a *Gaussian mixture model* (GMM) to capture the static kinematic properties of head movement and speech prosody features. Then, they used a gradient descent scheme to find the optimum mapping for head motion synthesis. Levine et al. [17] designed a framework based on *conditional random fields* (CRFs) to use speech prosody features to find the kinematic properties of joint movements.

Rule-based systems define certain predefined behaviors which are not likely to capture the rich and complex relationship and variability between modalities. If we rely solely on rule-based systems, the animation will tend to display repetitive behaviors, with desynchronization between gestures and speech. Data-driven systems have the potential to capture variations of behaviors observed in the corpus, and to produce gestures that are timely synchronized with speech. Several studies have used speech prosodic features to generate facial behaviors. Although prosody is directly affected by emphasis, and emotional state of the speaker, the generated behaviors may not properly respond to the underlying discourse function in the dialog (e.g., nodding for affirmation, shaking head for negation, frowning for disapproval). This study proposes a systematic framework to incorporate the benefits of rule-based systems and speech-driven animation by constraining the models with appropriate discourse functional classes.

3. DATABASE AND ANNOTATION

The study relies on the *interactive emotional dyadic motion capture* (IEMOCAP) corpus [4]. This database comprises dyadic interactions between two actors (a female and a male), during improvisation and scripted scenarios. The scenarios are designed to evoke different emotional reactions from the actors. The corpus consists of five sessions (10 actors), and includes motion capture data, videos, and audio recordings of the interactions. This study only uses the improvisation scenarios for the first session.

The study aims to constrain speech-driven models by the underlying discourse functions. For this purpose, it is important to annotate the data with discourse function classes. The annotation was conducted with ANVIL [14], which is a flexible tool to annotate multiple events in the video. We started with the segmentation boundaries of the speaking turns available in the IEMOCAP corpus. Some segments were split to better localize the behaviors. The discourse function classes selected for the study were inspired by previous studies [19,22]. Instead of a full semantic analysis of the input transcription, Marsella et al. [19] considered only semantic classes that tend to generate gestures. In our study, we also restrict the set to discourse function classes which we expect to produce nonverbal behaviors. The toolkit GRETA lists an extensive set of mappings between discourse function rules and distinct configurations for facial expressions and head movements [22]. From the list, we select the following discourse function classes for annotation: *affirmation*, *negation*, *question*, *statement* (opinion-statement), *contrast*, *uncertain*, *appreciation*, *request*, *command*, *suggest*, *warn*, and *inform*. However, we did not have enough samples for all of these classes. Therefore, this study only considers four dialog act classes: *affirmation* (90 turns), *negation* (53 turns), *question* (112 turns), and *statement* (158 turns). These classes are prone to generate gestures, and therefore provide the perfect starting point to study the role of discourse functions in the synthesis of behaviors for CA.

4. STATISTICAL ANALYSIS

We conduct a statistical analysis on the data, before constraining the speech-driven models by the four discourse function classes selected in Section 3. The purpose of the analysis is to identify whether the behaviors observed for each discourse function class present characteristic patterns. The study focuses on head and eyebrow motion, so this analysis considers only these gestures. For head motion, we study pitch, yaw, and roll movements and their circular

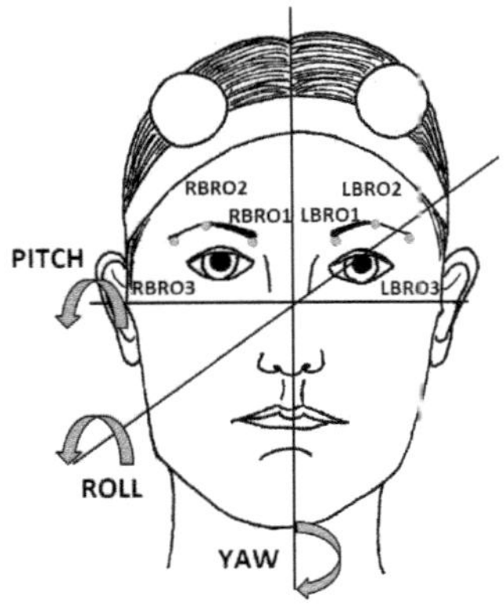

Figure 1: The movements analyzed in this paper.

Table 1: Features that are significantly different for each discourse function class (ANOVA). Figure 1 describes the features for head and eyebrow motion.

Question vs. Non-Question	
Pitch	$F(1,452) = 8.58$, $p = 0.004$
Roll	$F(1,452) = 7.05$, $p = 0.008$
Pitch Velocity	$F(1,452) = 7.05$, $p = 0.008$
Affirmation vs. Non-Affirmation	
LBRO3	$F(1,464) = 7.87$, $p = 0.005$
RBRO3	$F(1,464) = 10.42$, $p = 0.001$
Pitch Velocity	$F(1,464) = 6.74$, $p = 0.0097$
Negation vs. Non-Negation	
Yaw	$F(1,419) = 5.17$, $p = 0.023$
Pitch Velocity	$F(1,419) = 4.99$, $p = 0.026$
Statement vs. Non-Statement	
Pitch Velocity	$F(1,470) = 4.30$, $p = 0.038$

velocity. For eyebrow motion, we study the position and velocity of the markers placed on the eyebrows: LBRO1, LBRO2, LBRO3, RBRO1, RBRO2, and RBRO3 (see Fig. 1).

The analysis separately considers the four discourse function classes. For a given class (e.g., *question*), we group all the turns that do not belong to that class (e.g., *non-questions*). The patterns on the features for these two groups are then compared (*question* versus *non-question*). Table 1 reports the one way *analysis of variance* (ANOVA) results for the features that are found significantly different for each discourse function class. We assert significance when $p < 0.05$. Since the features have different dynamic ranges, we also estimate the standard deviation of the features. This measure characterizes changes in the dynamic range of the features induced by a discourse function class. Then, we estimate a one-way ANOVA over these values and we report the results in Table 2.

The results show that there are significant differences between the mean and standard deviation of *Yaw* for *negation* versus *non-negation*. This result is expected since people tend to shake their head for disagreement. Likewise,

Table 2: Features in which their standard deviations are significantly different for each discourse function class (ANOVA). Figure 1 describes the features for head and eyebrow motion.

Question vs. Non-Question	
Pitch	$F(1,452) = 7.33$, $p = 0.0071$
Roll	$F(1,452) = 5.37$, $p = 0.0210$
Affirmation vs. Non-Affirmation	
Yaw	$F(1,464) = 9.45$, $p = 0.0022$
Roll	$F(1,464) = 19.94$, $p = 10^{-5}$
LBRO1	$F(1,464) = 6.47$, $p = 0.0113$
LBRO3	$F(1,464) = 5.69$, $p = 0.0174$
RBRO1	$F(1,464) = 6.95$, $p = 0.009$
RBRO3	$F(1,464) = 7.84$, $p = 0.005$
Pitch Velocity	$F(1,464) = 21.36$, $p = 4.93 \times 10^{-6}$
Yaw Velocity	$F(1,464) = 12.74$, $p = 3.94 \times 10^{-4}$
Negation vs. Non-Negation	
Yaw	$F(1,419) = 7.42$, $p = 0.0067$
Roll Velocity	$F(1,419) = 8.75$, $p = 0.0033$
Yaw Velocity	$F(1,419) = 53.21$, $p = 1.51 \times 10^{-12}$
RBRO3	$F(1,419) = 6.19$, $p = 0.0132$
Statement vs. Non-Statement	
Roll Velocity	$F(1,470) = 4.46$, $p = 0.0351$

there are significant differences in *Pitch Velocity* for *affirmation* vs. *non-affirmation*. People tend to nod their head for agreement. Also, features describing head movements present statistical differences when people ask questions.

There are few differences in the features for *statement*. Therefore, we expect that models constrained by this discourse function class may not produce perceptive changes on the behaviors. Therefore, we exclude this class for the analysis. Likewise, we exclude the class *negation* since we only have 53 turns which are not enough to train the DBN models (Sec. 5).

5. SPEECH-DRIVEN ANIMATION

This section introduces the acoustic and visual features used to synthesize the behaviors from speech. It also describes the framework to synthesize the CA.

5.1 Mapping between Facial Markers & FAPs

We use the toolkit Xface [1] to generate the animations using the facial markers. Xface is an open source software complying with the MPEG-4 standard. Xface accepts *facial animation parameters* (FAPs) as input. There are 68 FAPs defined in the MPEG-4 standard, where two of them correspond to high-level parameters (visemes and emotions), and the others are low-level parameters. The FAPs are defined in terms of displacement of *facial feature points* (FPs) with respect to their reference position [23]. Most of the facial markers in the IEMOCAP database were selected following the locations of the FPs. Therefore, it is possible to establish a linear transformation from facial markers to FAPs. In particular, we use the approach described in Mariooryad and Busso [18].

5.2 Acoustic Features

The acoustic features to drive the facial animation correspond to prosodic features: fundamental frequency (F0) and the *RMS* energy. We also include their first and second derivatives forming a 6D feature vector. F0 contours have discontinuities during unvoiced regions, which introduce undesired breaks in the input signal. We address this problem by interpolating the F0 contour. Another challenge in modeling acoustic and facial features is the differences in the time resolution. The sampling frequency for the speech signal is 16 KHz, where the acoustic features are extracted from short-time windows every 16.67 ms (60 frames per second). The sampling rate for the motion capture data is 120 Hz. We address this problem by upsampling the acoustic features to 120 Hz. Therefore, the acoustic and facial features are aligned.

5.3 Speech-Driven Models using DBN

The baseline system to model the relationship between facial behaviors and speech correspond to one of the approaches proposed by Mariooryad and Busso [18]. They designed three DBNs, which make different assumptions on the relationship between speech and facial features (eyebrow and head motions). The study demonstrated that the *jDBN3* model, described in Figure 2(a), achieved the best performance using both objective and subjective evaluations. Therefore, we selected this model as our baseline system (i.e., unconstrained models). The node *Speech* represents the acoustic features. The node *Head&Eyebrow* corresponds to a joint variable describing the configuration of head and eyebrow positions. These two nodes are connected to the parent node $H_{h\&e}$, which is a discrete state space variable defining possible speech-gesture configurations (i.e., codebook). During training, all the variables are provided to the system. During synthesis, only the *Speech* variable is available, and the $H_{h\&e}$ node is estimated from the model.

We build upon the *jDBN3* model to incorporate constraints on discourse function classes. We propose to add an extra observation node, *Discourse_ Function*, which is a binary variable indicating the presence or absence of a given discourse function class. Figure 2(b) describes this model, which is referred to as *C-jDBN3*. The addition of this variable provides a novel framework to effectively constrain the model by the underlying discourse function. The *Discourse_Function* node affects the distribution of the hidden states. During inference, introducing evidences about the presence of the discourse function will constrain the model by increasing the posterior probability of appropriate hidden states associated with that discourse class.

Notice that separate models are used to model each of the discourse function classes. The reason for not modeling all of the discourse classes together is the limited data available for the evaluation. The framework is implemented with the Bayes Net Toolbox for MATLAB [21].

5.3.1 Inference

Inference in the *C-jDBN3* is based on Forward-Backward algorithm. The observation variables during learning and inference are different. During learning, we have full observation which includes *Speech*, *Head&Eyebrow*, and *Discourse_Function*. During synthesis, the observation is limited to *Speech* and *Discourse_Function*. The learning inference uses full observation probability (Equation 1), and the synthesis inference uses partial observation probability (Equation 2).

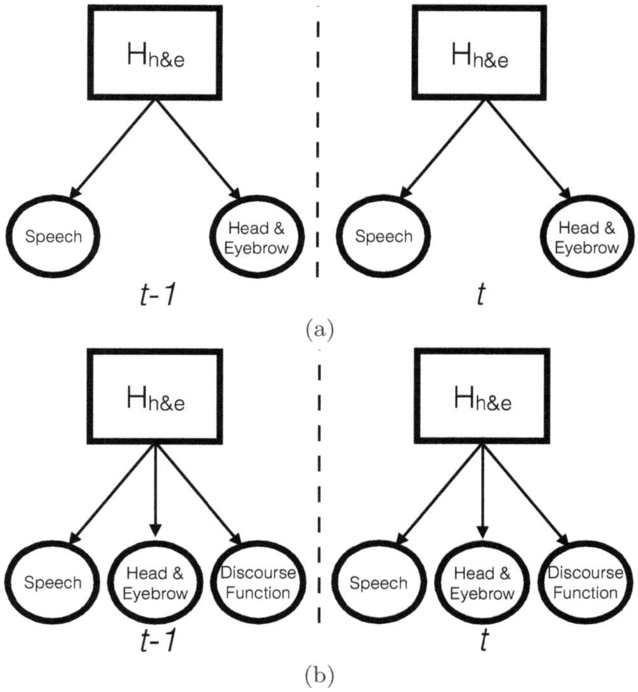

Figure 2: Illustration of (a): *jDBN3*, and (b): *C-jDBN3*. $H_{h\&e}$ represents a single, hidden state space variable, *Speech* represents the prosodic features extracted from speech, *Head&Eyebrow* represents the head and eyebrow features, and *DiscourseFunction* represents the constraint applied to the model.

$$O_t^F(i) = P(Speech_t | H_{h\&e_t} = i) \cdot P(Head\&Eyebrow_t | H_{h\&e_t} = i) \cdot P(Discourse\_Function_t | H_{h\&e} = i) \quad (1)$$

$$O_t^P(i) = P(Speech_t | H_{h\&e_t} = i) \cdot P(Discourse\_Function_t | H_{h\&e} = i) \quad (2)$$

5.3.2 Synthesis

After inference with partial observation, the expected values of head and eyebrow features are derived according to Equation 3. These trajectories are used to synthesize the movements using either the unconstrained models (*jDBN3*) and the constrained models (*C-jDBN3*). $\gamma(i)$ is the posterior probability of the ith state generating the observation, and $\mu_{h\&e}(i)$ is the mean of head and eyebrow features for the ith state.

$$E\left[Head\&Eyebrow | Speech, Discourse\_Function\right] = \sum_{i=1}^{n} \mu_{h\&e}(i)\gamma(i) \quad (3)$$

With the *C-jDBN3* model, the *Discourse_Function* node changes the posterior probability of the hidden states given the observation, affecting in a principled manner the ex-

Model	Constraint	States#	Params#	Train Turns#
C-jDBN3	Question	6	527	95
jDBN3	Question	6	521	95
C-jDBN3	Affirmation	6	527	74
jDBN3	Afirmation	6	521	74

Table 3: This table shows the specifications for training the two models, constrained and unconstrained one, for (*affirmation* and *question*).

pected value of head and eyebrow movements. The model generates appropriate movements according to the specific discourse function class.

After finding the expected value for head and eyebrow motion, we implement an interpolation scheme to remove abrupt transitions or jerky movements. The approach selects key points, which are used to interpolate the trajectory. More details about this smoothing approach are given in Mariooryad and Busso [18].

Notice that we synthesize the expected eyebrow and head movements given the observation. Therefore, the behaviors synthesized using these models do not produce movements spanning the same dynamic range as the original behaviors in the database. As a result, some of the movements are not visually perceived in Xface. We address this problem by scaling the behaviors to recover the original standard deviation observed over the training data. The calculated scaling factor is then downscaled by 0.4, since a test data might not include the whole range of movements appeared in the training set. This constant factor is selected empirically. Note that this process only scales the trajectories. It does not interfere with the correlation between the synthesized and original behaviors.

6. EXPERIMENTS AND RESULTS

To assess the performance of the constrained model *C-jDBN3*, we demonstrate that the model can create naturalistic behaviors. We compare the results of the *C-jDBN3* models with the videos synthesized with the *jDBN3* model. For comparison, we also create animations with the actual sequences directly extracted from the motion capture data. We refer to these videos as *original*. The videos for *C-jDBN3* and *jDBN3* are created as follows. First, we implement a five-fold cross-validation scheme, where in each fold four partitions are used to train the models, and one partition is used to create the animations. This scheme maximizes the usage of the data, preserving separate partitions for training and testing the models. Second, we balance the number of samples used for training the *C-jDBN3* models (e.g., same number of samples for *question* and *non-question* classes). Notice that there are more samples not belonging to the discourse function class. Therefore, we randomly select samples to balance the number of samples for both conditions. Third, we use the same set of sentences to train *C-jDBN3* and *jDBN3* models. Table 3 reports the configuration settings for the models.

6.1 Subjective Evaluation of the results

Our aim is to analyze how the synthesized animation using the *C-jDBN3* models are perceived in comparison with the ones generated with the unconstrained *jDBN3* models. We define a perceptual evaluation task in which each evaluator watches two videos with the same audio file, but with different animations. We consider three conditions: *C-jDBN3*, *jDBN3* and *original*. Therefore, the task requires 3 evaluations per sentence (*C-jDBN3* versus *jDBN3*, *C-jDBN3* versus *original*, and *jDBN3* versus *original*). After watching a pair of videos, the evaluator is asked to answer three preference questions: (1) which video do you prefer? (2) which video looks more natural? (3) in which video do the behaviors of the avatar look more appropriate with respect to the context?

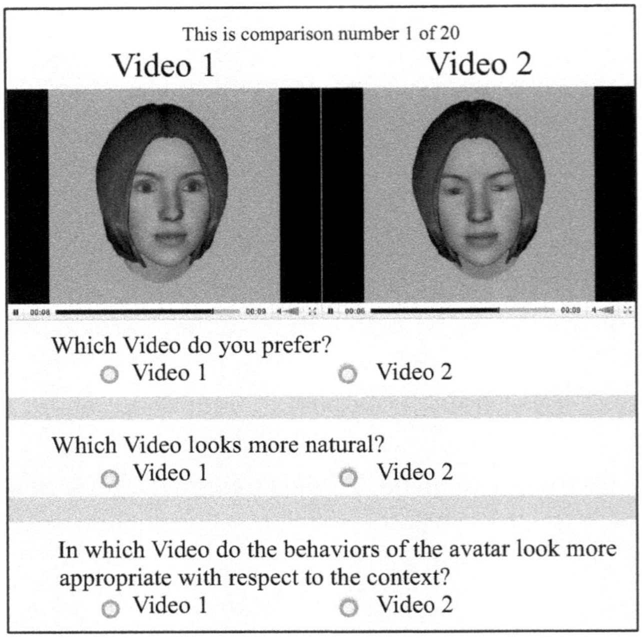

Figure 3: The interface used for the perceptual evaluation.

For each discourse function class (*question*, *affirmation*), we selected 20 different sentences for the evaluations. Therefore, the evaluations consider 60 comparisons per discourse function class. To reduce fatigue, we split these 60 comparison into three sets with 20 comparisons. Each evaluator completes one of these sets. We rely on crowdsourcing for the perceptual evaluation – *Mechanical Turk* (MT). Figure 3 shows the *graphical user interface* (GUI) to evaluate the people's preference in pairwise comparisons. We recruit 60 different evaluators. Each comparison is evaluated by 10 evaluators. The position of the videos (left or right) are randomized for each evaluator. The agreement between the evaluators is low given the subtle differences between the generated videos (it is a difficult task).

A common problem observed when using crowdsourcing is noisy data provided by cheaters (evaluators interested in the payments who do not care about the task). We address this problem by setting a threshold on the duration of the evaluation of each pair of videos (see Equation 4). If the duration of the task is less than T, we discard the evaluations, since it is unlikely that the evaluators watched both videos before providing their preferences (the evaluation is not reliable). This threshold discarded 6% of the comparison pairs for *Question*, and 10.1% of the comparisons for

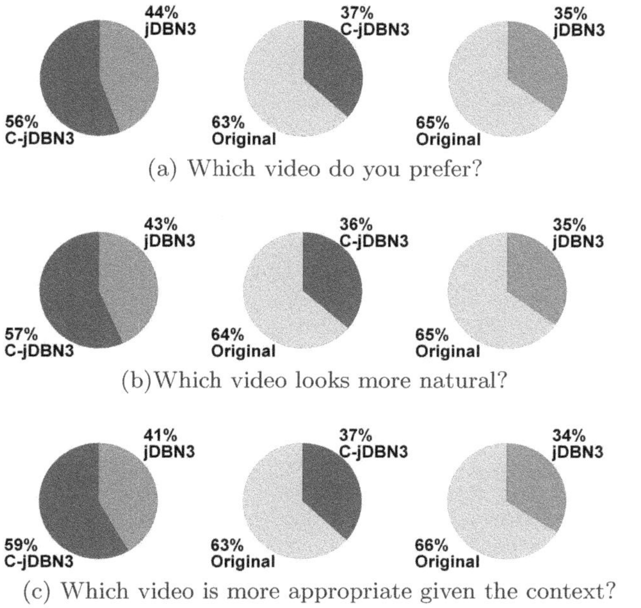

(a) Which video do you prefer?

(b)Which video looks more natural?

(c) Which video is more appropriate given the context?

Figure 4: The result of perceptual evaluation for the pairwise comparison tasks where the constraint is *Question.*

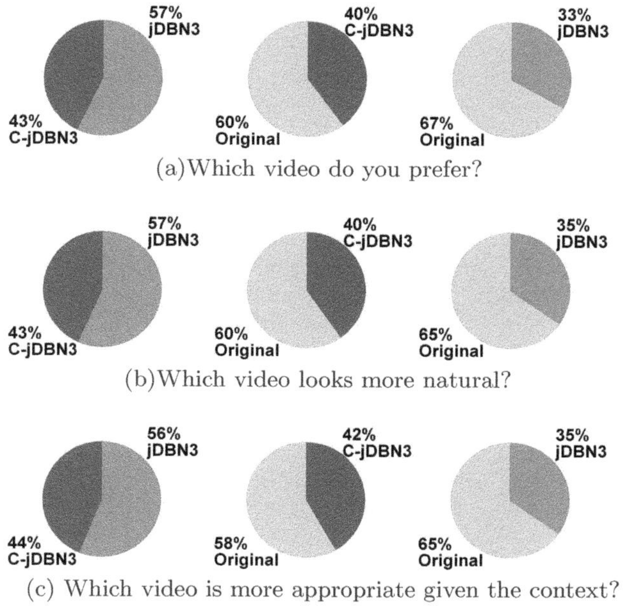

(a)Which video do you prefer?

(b)Which video looks more natural?

(c) Which video is more appropriate given the context?

Figure 5: The result of perceptual evaluation for the pairwise comparison tasks where the constraint is *Affirmation.*

Affirmation. For consistency, we recollected the perceptual evaluations for these pairs.

$$T = 2 \times duration_{video} + 3(seconds) \quad (4)$$

To evaluate the results from MT, we conducted an informal evaluation with two evaluators from our laboratory following the same approach. The inter-evaluator agreement in controlled conditions was similar to the ones achieved with MT. Therefore, we conclude that the data from MT is reliable.

Figure 4 and 5 shows the results of the perceptual evaluation. These figures gives the preference for each pairwise comparison. Figure 4 gives the results when *C-jDBN3* is constrained by *question*, and Figure 5 gives the results when *C-jDBN3* is constrained by *Affirmation*. In these two figures, the first, second and third rows correspond to the results of the first, second and third questions, respectively.

For the discourse function class *question*, Figure 4(a) shows that in 56% of the times the evaluators preferred the animations generated with *C-jDBN3* over the ones generated with *jDBN3*. There is a 95.5% probability that this proportion is greater than chances (50%). From the second question (Fig. 4(b)), the evaluators considered 57% of the times the animations generated with the *C-jDBN3* model more natural than the ones generated with the unconstrained *jDBN3* model. There is a 97.6% probability that the proportion for this comparison is greater than chances. Finally, the evaluators considered in 59% of the time that the *C-jDBN3* model was more appropriated than the ones generated with *jDBN3*. There is a 99.45% probability that the proportion for this comparison is greater than chances. Figure 4 also shows that the *C-jDBN3* model is more selected than the unconstrained models when they are compared with the original sequences (indirect comparison).

For the discourse function class *affirmation*, the results are not conclusive. Figure 5(a) shows that the evaluators preferred *C-jDBN3* 43% of the times over the animations generated with *jDBN3*. Similar results are observed for the question about naturalness (Fig. 5(b)) and appropriateness (Fig. 5(c)). These results are not consistent with the indirect evaluations, where we compare the synthesized models with the animations generated with the original data. This indirect comparisons indicate that the constrained models are selected more frequently than the unconstrained models. Our future work will continue to explore the benefits of using constrained models for *affirmation*.

7. CONCLUSIONS AND DISCUSSION

This paper proposed to constrain speech-driven animation models by the underlying discourse functions. We focus on head and eyebrow motion. The statistical analysis demonstrated significant changes in these behaviors across discourse function classes (*affirmation*, *negation*, *question*, and *statement*). This analysis implies that, in addition to speech, other important factors should be included to synthesize natural behaviors. Then, we proposed a DBN, where a variable was added to constrain the behaviors. Perceptual evaluations for the discourse function class *question* showed that the animations with constrained models are perceived more preferable, natural and appropriate than the animations with the unconstrained models. For the class *affirmation*, the results are not conclusive. Although in the direct comparison the evaluators preferred the unconstrained models over the constrained models, indirect comparisons with the original videos reveal a different trend. When evaluators compared the synthesized animations with the original animations, the constrained models were selected more often than the unconstrained models. This result may be due to lack of samples to train the DBN models. The statistical analysis revealed that patterns for eyebrow movements change for *affirmation*. However, the perceptual contribution of eyebrow movements in the synthesized animations is less dominant than the perceptual contribution of head motion [18]. Furthermore, eyebrows have subtle movements which can be captured by increasing the number of parameters. We expect that a better parametrization of eyebrows may help in producing distinctive behaviors that evaluators can perceive.

This study validates the idea of constraining speech-driven models by the discourse function. We need more data to further explore this research direction. We are currently collecting motion capture recordings where the scenarios are carefully designed to elicit specific discourse functions. The corpus will play a key role in extending the proposed constrained speech-driven models. It will offer the opportunity to consider other relevant discourse function classes such as *contrast*, *negation*, *warn*, and *uncertain*. The perceptual evaluation reveals that the raters preferred the animation with the *original* sequences over the ones synthesized with the DBN models (see Fig. 4 and 5). We expect that future improvements on the proposed models can help in reducing this gap.

8. ACKNOWLEDGMENTS

This work was funded by NSF (IIS 1352950).

9. REFERENCES

[1] K. Balci. Xface: MPEG-4 based open source toolkit for 3D facial animation. In *Conference on Advanced Visual Interfaces (AVI 2004)*, pages 399–402, Gallipoli, Italy, May 2004.

[2] E. Bevacqua, M. Mancini, R. Niewiadomski, and C. Pelachaud. An expressive ECA showing complex emotions. In *Proceedings of the Artificial Intelligence and Simulation of Behaviour (AISB 2007) Annual Convention*, pages 208–216, Newcastle, UK, April 2007.

[3] M. Brand. Voice puppetry. In *Proceedings of the 26th annual conference on Computer graphics and interactive techniques (SIGGRAPH 1999)*, pages 21–28, New York, NY, USA, 1999.

[4] C. Busso, M. Bulut, C. Lee, A. Kazemzadeh, E. Mower, S. Kim, J. Chang, S. Lee, and S. Narayanan. IEMOCAP: Interactive emotional dyadic motion capture database. *Journal of Language Resources and Evaluation*, 42(4):335–359, December 2008.

[5] C. Busso, Z. Deng, M. Grimm, U. Neumann, and S. Narayanan. Rigid head motion in expressive speech animation: Analysis and synthesis. *IEEE Transactions on Audio, Speech and Language Processing*, 15(3):1075–1086, March 2007.

[6] C. Busso, Z. Deng, U. Neumann, and S. Narayanan. Natural head motion synthesis driven by acoustic prosodic features. *Computer Animation and Virtual Worlds*, 16(3-4):283–290, July 2005.

[7] C. Busso, Z. Deng, U. Neumann, and S. Narayanan. Learning expressive human-like head motion sequences from speech. In Z. Deng and U. Neumann, editors, *Data-Driven 3D Facial Animations*, pages 113–131. Springer-Verlag London Ltd, Surrey,United Kingdom, 2007.

[8] C. Busso and S. Narayanan. Interrelation between speech and facial gestures in emotional utterances: a single subject study. *IEEE Transactions on Audio, Speech and Language Processing*, 15(8):2331–2347, November 2007.

[9] Y. Cao, W. Tien, P. Faloutsos, and F. Pighin. Expressive speech-driven facial animation. *ACM Transactions on Graphics*, 24:1283–1302, October 2005.

[10] J. Cassell, C. Pelachaud, N. Badler, M. Steedman, B. Achorn, T. Bechet, B. Douville, S. Prevost, and M. Stone. Animated conversation: Rule-based generation of facial expression gesture and spoken intonation for multiple conversational agents. In *Computer Graphics (Proc. of ACM SIGGRAPH'94)*, pages 413–420, Orlando, FL,USA, 1994.

[11] J. Cassell, H. H. Vilhjálmsson, and T. Bickmore. Beat: the behavior expression animation toolkit. In *Life-Like Characters*, pages 163–185. Springer, 2004.

[12] Z. Deng, C. Busso, S. Narayanan, and U. Neumann. Audio-based head motion synthesis for avatar-based telepresence systems. In *ACM SIGMM 2004 Workshop on Effective Telepresence (ETP 2004)*, pages 24–30, New York, NY, October 2004. ACM Press.

[13] H. P. Graf, E. Cosatto, V. Strom, and F. J. Huang. Visual prosody: Facial movements accompanying speech. In *Proc. of IEEE International Conference on Automatic Faces and Gesture Recognition*, pages 396–401, Washington, D.C., USA, May 2002.

[14] M. Kipp. ANVIL - a generic annotation tool for multimodal dialogue. In *European Conference on Speech Communication and Technology (Eurospeech)*, pages 1367–1370, Aalborg, Denmark, September 2001.

[15] S. Kopp, B. Krenn, S. Marsella, A. N. Marshall, C. Pelachaud, H. Pirker, K. R. Thórisson, and H. Vilhjálmsson. Towards a common framework for multimodal generation: The behavior markup language. In *Intelligent virtual agents*, pages 205–217. Springer, 2006.

[16] B. H. Le, X. Ma, and Z. Deng. Live speech driven head-and-eye motion generators. *IEEE transactions on visualization and computer graphics*, 18(11):1902–1914, 2012.

[17] S. Levine, P. Krähenbühl, S. Thrun, and V. Koltun. Gesture controllers. *ACM Transactions on Graphics (TOG)*, 29(4):124, 2010.

[18] S. Mariooryad and C. Busso. Generating human-like behaviors using joint, speech-driven models for conversational agents. *IEEE Transactions on Audio, Speech and Language Processing*, 20(8):2329–2340, October 2012.

[19] S. Marsella, Y. Xu, M. Lhommet, A. Feng, S. Scherer, and A. Shapiro. Virtual character performance from speech. In *Proceedings of the 12th ACM SIGGRAPH/Eurographics Symposium on Computer Animation*, pages 25–35. ACM, 2013.

[20] D. McNeill. *Hand and Mind: What gestures reveal about thought.* The University of Chicago Press, Chicago, IL, USA, 1992.

[21] K. Murphy. Bayes net toolbox for matlab. https://code.google.com/p/bnt/, October 2007.

[22] I. Poggi, C. Pelachaud, F. Rosis, V. C. B., and Carolis. Greta. a believable embodied conversational agent. *Multimodal Intelligent Information Presentation*, pages 3–25, 2005.

[23] A. Tekalp and J. Ostermann. Face and 2-d mesh animation in MPEG-4. *Signal Processing: Image Communication*, 15(4):387–421, January 2000.

Many Fingers Make Light Work: Non-Visual Capacitive Surface Exploration

Martin Halvey
Department of Computer and Information Sciences
University of Strathclyde, Glasgow, G1 1XQ, UK
martin.halvey@strath.ac.uk

Andrew Crossan
ITT Group, School of Engineering and Built Environment
Glasgow Caledonian University, Glasgow, G4 0BA, UK
andrew.crossan@gcu.ac.uk

ABSTRACT
In this paper we investigate how we can change interactions with mobile devices so we can better support subtle low effort intermittent interaction. In particular we conducted an evaluation with varying interaction techniques which looked at non-visual touch based exploration of information on a capacitive surface. The results of this evaluation indicate that there is very little difference in terms of selection accuracy between the interaction techniques that we implemented and a slight but significant time reduction when using multiple fingers to search, over one finger. Users found locating information and relating information to physical landmarks easier than relating virtual locations to each other. In addition it was found that search strategy and interaction varied between tasks and also at different points in the task.

Categories and Subject Descriptors
H.5.2 User interfaces: Input devices and strategies (e.g. mouse, touchscreen)

Keywords
Non-visual; touch; multi-touch; exploration; wearable;

1. INTRODUCTION
Recent innovations in mobile interaction and input technologies have led to huge advances in the usability of mobile devices. Technologies such as capacitive touchscreens have opened the door to engaging and aesthetic interfaces that have contributed to an explosion in their usage and in the range of functionality on offer. In spite of these advances however, the way that people interact with these devices has changed very little, with users still selecting from arrays of onscreen buttons as with a desktop interface. Touchscreens allow the user to interact through a small but high resolution screen and directly manipulate widgets and icons. Despite the ease with which it is possible to scroll and resize objects with quick flicks of the finger, they are poorly designed for many common tasks and restrict users to at most a few small single point cursors on screen. The simple act of clicking a button can be a frustrating process as the device must interpret the user's intention by translating an onscreen finger position (that may obscure the target) to a single pixel position. Phones resort to techniques, such as predictive text models for typing tasks, for example, to attempt to work around this issue. Problems with lighting conditions combined with the lack of tactile feedback can affect target selection, and if the user is on the move, focusing visual attention on the small screen can interfere with the more important task of safely avoiding obstacles. These issues in some ways make today's mobile devices more difficult to use while on the move than previous generations of mobile phones that used physical buttons.

ICMI '14, November 12 - 16 2014, Istanbul, Turkey

http://dx.doi.org/10.1145/2663204.2663253

More recent developments look to improve this mobile interaction mechanism through the use of new technologies. Wearable devices such as Google's Glass and Samsung's Watch[1] are seen by many as the future of mobile interaction. Interfaces such as Apple's Siri software are exploring speech recognition to improve mobile input. However, despite the wealth of research in the area [1, 3, 11, 12] developing optimum mobile inputs for different scenarios is still an open problem. For example Google Glass[2] attempts to achieve this through augmenting vision. However, augmenting vision may have problems as it requires special potentially expensive and visible hardware; it may be distracting and may not facilitate low levels of engagement. Glass also relies heavily on voice input, which is potentially error prone and not always appropriate. An alternative to visual interaction would be to shift to more continuous multimodal forms of interaction that are more suited to use on the move, while pushing the boundaries of currently available touch technology to its full potential to allow more expressive interaction.

In this paper we will begin to look at one method of fundamentally altering the 'on the move' interaction mechanisms to better support subtle, low effort, intermittent interaction. We begin to examine the process of shifting to non-visual feedback which facilitates variable levels of engagement. We promote closed loop interaction by investigating different non-visual touchscreen input techniques for exploring an audio space. In particular we compare single-finger point, multi-finger point, and multi-finger area cursor interactions for basic search and spatial awareness tasks. The rest of the paper is organised as follows. The next section outlines related work. This is followed by an outline of the experiment conducted, including apparatus, tasks, interaction techniques and procedure. This is followed by an outline of the results that have a mix of qualitative and quantitative results. These results inform a discussion session, which is followed up with conclusions and future work.

2. RELATED WORK
With the rapid advances in the technologies being integrated into mobile devices, the way we interact with these devices is starting to change to better support 'on the move' interaction. In this

[1] http://www.bbc.co.uk/news/technology-23961692

[2] www.google.com/glass

section we will outline the evolution of some of these technologies, with particular attention being paid to touch and non-visual interaction. With the advent of capacitive touchscreens, popularised initially by the iPhone, gesture has now become a dominant modality for input. Capacitive touchscreens allow basic, general purpose functionality like target selection and scrolling to be performed through direct manipulation quickly and effortlessly. Before the iPhone, resistive touchscreens with a stylus mediating the contact were the norm for on the move interaction. However, the whole ethos of capacitive touchscreens was that they were designed to allow users to interact directly using their fingertips. The phone gathers data from a range of capacitive sensors distributed over the screen and reduces these data to one or more single pixel points of contact. This suits the traditional desktop style interactions where target selection from a range of visible targets is the common task. However, we believe that by reducing the data from the capacitive sensor array to single point cursors, much useful and expressive input potential is lost. Further to this, fingertip interaction on a touchscreen introduces its own problems. Siek et al. [19] describes the 'fat finger' problem where targeting on a touchscreen can be difficult as the user's finger obscures the target as they touch it on the screen. There are also issues caused by taking the users contact area on the touchscreen and translating it to a single cursor point on the screen. The system must take a distributed and potentially moving contact area and infer the user's intent. Rogers et al. [16] note that the centroid of the contact area is often used to determine screen position when targeting on a touchscreen as it is relatively simple to calculate, and demonstrates how to improve this through knowledge of the approach of the finger. The targeting issue is often illustrated through typing tasks on an onscreen keyboard. Typing on a touchscreen has been shown to be slower and more error prone than physical keyboards with the lack of tactile feedback often cited as the main contributing factor. These targeting issues become more problematic on smaller screens such as mobile phones, with many keyboards resorting to predictive text models to help manage the high error rate. Despite these limitations touch technologies are a growing area of interest as they are currently expanding beyond the traditional phone interactions. For example Nintendo have recently released their Wii U[3] console that uses a controller with inbuilt capacitive touchscreen. From a mobile perspective, there has also been much interest in touchscreens for non-visual interactions in other areas, for in-car interfaces for example [4].

2.1 Extending the use of touch input

Much of the research looking to improve touchscreen interaction has looked to either improve the accuracy of targeting or improve the management of errors. Baudisch [2] examines different cursor control and display techniques for managing the fat finger problem, particularly for devices with very small screens. One interesting and novel theme of Baudisch's work is his exploration of back of the device interaction. Here they entirely avoid obscuring the screen by interacting with a separate surface. Many of the interaction techniques explored, however, remain very similar to traditional situations despite the different requirements with the visual channel required for use. Williamson and Murray-Smith developed the Stane interface which allows the user to tap and scrape different textures on the device to interact [14]. The different textures also allow the device to be explored entirely non-visually with scraping gestures being classified by a neural network. Lyons et al. [13] developed Facet, a multi-display wrist worn system consisting of multiple independent touch-sensitive segments joined into a bracelet. Facet allows users to control how applications use segments alone and in coordination. Applications can expand to use more segments, collapse to encompass fewer, and be swapped with other segments. Yang et al. created Magic Finger [23], which is a small device worn on the fingertip, which supports always-available input. Magic Finger senses touch through an optical mouse sensor, enabling any surface to act as a touch screen. This inverts the relationship between finger and surface, as the finger is the instrument rather than the surface. Kane et al. [10] present three new access overlays with the intention of improving the accessibility of large touch screen interfaces, specifically looking at interactive table tops. Two of the proposed techniques were faster than Apple Voiceover[4] and were preferred by users. Applications of these overlays include board games and maps. Touch interaction with table top surfaces in particular still utilise visual feedback and can do so in interesting ways. Much of the work presented thus far looks at providing new devices or in the case of Baudish using a new part of the device, in the work presented here we concentrate on utilising a wider range of the hand for gesture interaction using already existing devices. In a similar vein Wobbrock et al. [22] found for table tops that in many cases visual feedback was required. They conducted an evaluation to try and ascertain user preferences for gestures on table top surfaces. They found that users rarely care about the number of fingers they employ, that one hand is preferred to two, that desktop interactions strongly influence users' mental models, and that some commands elicit little gestural agreement. There are many examples of novel touch interactions for table tops that use visual feedback. Rock & Rails [20] combines three shape gestures with traditional touch based gestures to increase control, avoid occlusions and separate constraints in 2D manipulation tasks. The bubble cursor [9] is a target acquisition technique based on area cursors where the cursor dynamically resizes its activation area depending on the proximity of surrounding targets, so that only one target is selectable at any time.

2.2 Exploiting Capacitive Sensors More Fully

As outlined in the introduction and mentioned in the previous section the potential for capacitive surface interaction has not been fully explored, and as such they present many opportunities for new interactions. However, there has been some movement towards exploring this area. Sato et al. [17] show how by augmenting everyday objects with capacitive surfaces, specific gestures and the way these gestures are performed can be recognised reliably. One other advantage with capacitive sensing is that it provides a mechanism to sense proximity as well as contact. SNOUT [24] is an interface overlay designed for occasional no-hand or one-handed use of handheld capacitive touch devices. Nose taps, speech-to-text and the accelerometer are used for interaction with the device. Rogers et al. [16] exploit this with finger touch where the interaction includes not only the contact position of the screen but also the direction and angle of the user's finger as they touch the screen. Multi touch gestures have been pushed heavily as a selling point for Apple's mobile products, but the fact that visual feedback plays such an important role interaction generally restricts these interactions to the finger

[3] http://www.nintendo.com/wiiu

[4] http://www.apple.com/accessibility/osx/voiceover/

tips so as not to block the screen. This leads to the rich potentially expressive information about the rest of the user's hand being thrown away as the interaction gets reduced to a few single pixels on the screen.

2.3 "One the Move" Interaction

Beyond capacitive surfaces there is also a host of technologies that now look to solve the on the move interaction problem through other means. One recent area of research explores in-air interactions in mobile situations. Agrawal [1] describes a system that allows users to draw gestures in the air to interact with a mobile device. Kim et al. [11] and Cheng et al. [3] use a wrist based device to detect whole hand gestures allowing users to access a range of functionality through different hand postures. Leap Motion[5] is a commercially available device that offers in air whole hand gestures in a desktop setting. Much of the research about making information more accessible on the move has concentrated on representing the information through the auditory or tactile channels rather than through vision [5], we look at this in the next section.

2.4 Non-Visual Interaction

From the non-visual perspective, an early example of interaction design for use on the move would be the Nomadic Radio system that allows users to browse a range of content on the move [18]. Previous work has also looked at developing mechanisms for hands-free whole body interaction [6-8]. Results demonstrate how wrist and head rotation along with foot tapping can be sensed and used as input techniques in a mobile setting. Using these techniques, users could search and select information in a mobile setting entirely hands and eyes free combining a few relatively low bandwidth input channel. However, a number of issues were raised about the social acceptability of performing unusual interactions in public [15]. Results show that interactions with a visible device are preferable to gestures where devices are hidden [15, 21]. Costanza [5] avoids this issue using EMG for discreet almost invisible gesturing that allows low bandwidth communication. There are a number of techniques, including haptics etc. that are no outlined here due to space constraints.

In this paper we look to build on the successful approaches outlined in this section by demonstrating far more expressive and continuous control to improve browsing, organising and selecting data. Rather than simple target selection, exploiting whole hand interaction, which we begin to move towards in this work, will allow subtle probing and filtering of the information space to narrow down the information presented.

3. EVALUATION

In this paper, we investigate different input techniques for allowing a user to interact non-visually with a mobile touch surface. A single point of contact is most often used when making touchscreen selections. However, when interacting with a screen, the user can obtain an overview of the interaction space quickly and effectively through a visual glance. If we are working with a touch surface, this glance is not available. A single point exploration of the space can turn searching for the appropriate target into a long and frustrating temporal task. We therefore explore techniques to better support exploration of the space. We first allow multiple points of contact, allowing the user to use more of their whole hand. By distributing the search task among several fingers, it is hoped that targets will be found more quickly and with less effort. Secondly, interactions with a screen necessarily rely on the finger tips. This allows the user to specify the closest approximation of a point on the screen while minimising the finger obscuration of the target. When interacting with a surface instead of a screen, there is no need to worry about obscuring the target. We therefore allow the user to vary the size of their cursor on the screen by using a smaller or larger contact area. It is envisaged that this will allow a user to approximate the 'glance' through using a large contact area with the surface and receiving a wide but unfocussed view of the workspace. Small contact areas can then be used for fine grained selection allowing a small but focused area of the workspace to be presented. The goal of this study is to examine how these techniques are used in searching an audio space.

3.1 Experimental Tasks

Three different tasks were used for evaluation. Firstly, locating a target on the surface is a fundamental interaction. Secondly, we test if users can build up a spatial awareness of the targets on the screen by asking them to locate the two closest targets. Finally we ask the users to compare target location with a physical landmark. Details of each of these tasks are outlined below. These tasks are designed to determine whether the user can accurately build up a mental model of the relative positions of the targets in the interaction space non-visually, and how their methods change when allowed to use multiple points of contact as opposed to a single point. Each task involved 3 targets, 3 were chosen as it was the smallest number we could use for some of the tasks which involved comparisons as outlined below.

3.1.1 Locate

Participants are presented with an audio space with 3 targets. The targets are an audio loop of a voice saying 'Alpha', 'Bravo' and ''Charlie' respectively. The task set is for the user to find the 'Alpha' target, with 'Bravo' and 'Charlie' acting as distractors. Searching and locating a target within the space is a basic task that must be performed for a non-visual interface and we would envisage this to be an important task for a large number of interactions with the touch surface.

3.1.2 Closest Targets

The three targets (again 'Alpha', 'Bravo' and 'Charlie') are placed in the audio space. The task is for the user to find the two closest targets. The user must therefore locate the targets and then make judgments about their relative positions. This task tests the user's ability to make spatial judgments between virtual objects. This would be crucial to allow a user to build up a mental model of the distribution of targets within the audio space.

3.1.3 Closest Edge

Three targets are placed in the environment. The task set is to find the target closest to a named edge. An equal number of 'Top', 'Bottom', 'Left' and 'Right' judgments are given. Physical landmarks have been shown to provide a useful mechanism for guiding a non-visual search. This task examines a user's ability to make spatial judgments about virtual and physical objects.

3.2 Targets

In each of these tasks, users will be searching for audio targets. Each target has a sound associated with it. Each sound used is a looped recording of a person saying a word from the phonetic alphabet. There are three targets so we use 'Alpha', 'Bravo' and

[5] www.leapmotion.com

'Charlie' for each of the targets. When the user is not touching the screen or is far away from the targets, no sound will be heard. As a user approaches a target and they get within hearing range (which varies depending on the cursor width), the target sound will start playing. When far away, the audio volume will be low and as the user approaches the target, the audio volume increases reaching a maximum when over the target. The full range of audio volumes allowed by android is used, with the volume at maximum directly over the target and continuously dropping off to zero as the user moves further away from the target. The volume reaches zero at one cursor width distance from the target. Audio latency was not experimentally measured; however, there was no noticeable latency present when interacting.

3.3 Interaction Techniques

The three different interaction techniques implemented, are outlined below and are shown in Figure 1.

3.3.1 Single Point Touch

Here, the user will explore with a single point of contact. This method acts as a baseline control and is similar to non-visual accessible mobile systems like Apple's VoiceOver[6]. As the user gets closer to a target, the audio volume increases with the sound played at full volume when inside the target. The targets and interaction points are both modelled as circles of fixed size. Values for target radius and interaction point radius were set through pilot testing and at 30 pixels and 100 pixels respectively. Outside a range of 130 pixels, the target cannot be heard.

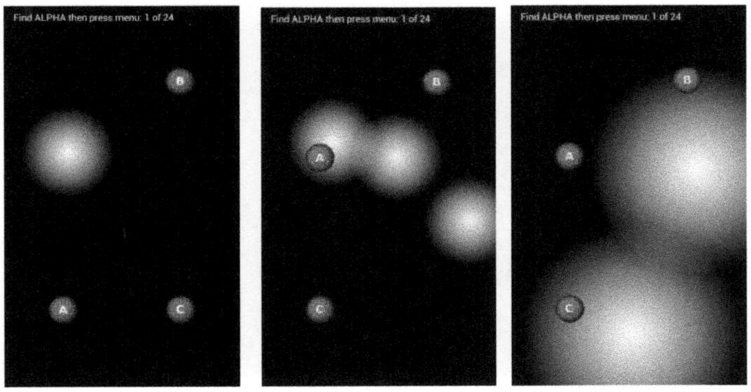

Figure 1: Visual example of the three interaction techniques. From left to right, single touch, multi-touch with 3 points of contact and multi-touch area with 2 points of contact.

3.3.2 Multi-Point Touch

In the second condition, the participant can interact with multiple fingers. Each finger corresponds to an interaction point on the screen. The target size and cursor with are identical to the single point condition. The audio volume of a target is set using the closest interaction point only.

3.3.3 Multi-Area Touch

The capacitive surface allows not only multiple points of contact, but also can be used to gain insight into the contact area of the user's finger with the screen. Most of this information is hidden in the firmware layer of the phone, however, using standard Android API calls, it is possible to approximate by getting the size of contact area from a touch event using a call to getSize(),with the touch points modelled as circles and the size varying as the radius of the circle. The size value returned is processed further using:

$$Radius\ on\ screen = (40 \times getSize)^2$$

These values were set through pilot testing to allow a wide range of different usable contact areas. This additional information allows the user to control the level of focus in their search with a large contact area allowing a broad area of the audio space to be played to the user, and a smaller contact point being used to present a smaller more focused area of the space to the user.

3.4 Experimental Procedure

The experiment was a 3 x 3 design (interaction x task). The order of interaction technique was counterbalanced to avoid order effects. For each interaction technique block each participant completed the three tasks in the order Locate, Closest Targets, Closest Edge. Participants were given 8 training tasks for each technique/task combination, for the first 4 of those tasks visual and audio feedback was provided and for the final 4 only audio feedback was provided, just like in the experimental tasks. For each interaction technique we measured task completion time, accuracy and a screen trace of user interactions. There were 24 trials for each task giving 216 per participant trials in total. In the 'Locate' and 'Closest Targets' conditions, the targets were spaced randomly around a 3x5 regular grid on the screen. The same 24 position sets were used for each technique to maintain the same level of difficulty in each condition, but presented in a random order. For 'Closest Edge', the target distances from the chosen edge were varied between 80 and 180 pixels with the difference in target distance for each trial ranging between 20 and 60 pixels. Again, the same 24 position sets were used for each trial presented in a random order to maintain the same level of difficulty between trials. Participants completed a NASA TLX workload estimation form after each condition. Participants were instructed to hold the device in their non-dominant hand in portrait mode and interact with the phone in their dominant hand. They could support their arms anyway they wished. Audio feedback was given through headphones. Evaluations took place in a quiet office environment.

3.5 Apparatus

The experimental software was developed in Android. The experimental software ran on a Samsung Galaxy S2.

3.6 Participants

12 participants (10 male, 2 female) aged between 24 and 52 (mean 31.4) took part in the evaluation. All 12 participants had touch screen phones, 9 either owned or had used a tablet, 5 had used a table top and 11 had used touch screen kiosks. All participants were instructed to hold the device in portrait in their non-dominant hand, and to interact with the fingers of the dominant hand. All were right handed and received a £10 Amazon voucher for their participation in the evaluation.

4. RESULTS

As much of the data analysed showed significant differences for Levene's Test, non-parametric statistical tests were used. The independent variables were analysed using a Friedman's analysis of variance by ranks, with pairwise comparisons made using a Wilcoxon test. Task and interaction technique were the independent variables.

[6] http://www.apple.com/accessibility/osx/voiceover/

4.1 Errors

Table 1: Accuracy (%) for closest and closest edge tasks for each interaction technique

	Single Point	Multi-touch	Multi-area
Closet Targets	84.85	85.61	84.85
Closest Edge	75.38	75.00	71.21

For the closest targets and closest edge tasks, we calculated the accuracy of the user responses, the results are shown in Table 1. It was found that task accuracy was not effected by interaction technique ($\chi^2(2)=0.743$, $p=0.690$). However, there was a significant difference for task ($z=-5.647$, $p<0.001$), with participants being less accurate at identifying the closest edge.

Table 2: Mean (std. dev.) error x, y and total distance error in pixels for locate task for each interaction technique

	Single Point	Multi-touch	Multi-area
X error	31.923 (33.195)	32.900 (31.340)	32.030 (25.644)
Y error	37.640 (61.064)	33.080 (35.300)	38.540 (37.578)
Error	54.710 (65.359)	52.890 (40.075)	55.740 (38.366)

For the locate task, we measured how close in pixels the user located Alpha to be, we analysed the distance from Alpha in the x direction, y direction and total error. Neither X-error ($\chi^2(2)=0.582$, $p=0.747$) or Y-error ($\chi^2(2)=4.211$, $p=0.122$) was significant. Total error was found to be significant (χ^2 $(2)=7.045$, $p=0.030$), however pairwise comparisons of techniques revealed no significant differences.

4.2 Time to Detection

A summary of the average completion times is in Table 3. Interaction technique was found to significantly affect completion time (χ^2 $(2)=19.670$, $p<0.001$). Pairwise comparisons showed that multi-touch was significantly faster than single point ($z=-3.459$, $p=0.001$) and multi-area ($z=-3.642$, $p<0.001$). Task was also found to have a significant affect (χ^2 $(2)=523.467$, $p<0.001$), with pairwise comparisons showing that all tasks were significantly different at $p<0.001$.

Table 3: Average task time for each task and interaction technique combination, measure is in milliseconds

	Single Point	Multi-touch	Multi-area
Locate	9784.18 (4867.855)	8999.86 (4816.794)	9620.22 (5627.442)
Closest	20881.93 (10023.673)	18584.20 (10852.074)	20036.22 (11419.397)
Closest Edge	11873.79 (6952.276)	11415.40 (6055.607)	12330.604 (7849.816)

4.3 Subjective Workload

Responses to the NASA TLX were evaluated using a repeated measures ANOVA, the entire calculated score rather than the individual scales were used. Interaction technique was not found to be significant ($F_{2,20}=0.590$, $p=0.563$), although the trend was that across almost all differentials that the multi-point touch technique had the lowest workload. Task was found to be significant ($F_{2,20}=14.546$, $p<0.001$), with locating the two closest points having the highest workload across all differentials. Pairwise comparisons with a Bonferroni adjusted alpha showed that this task was significantly different from locate ($p<0.001$) and closest edge ($p=0.013$). The average responses to each of the scales for task and interaction technique are shown in Figure 2 and Figure 3 respectively.

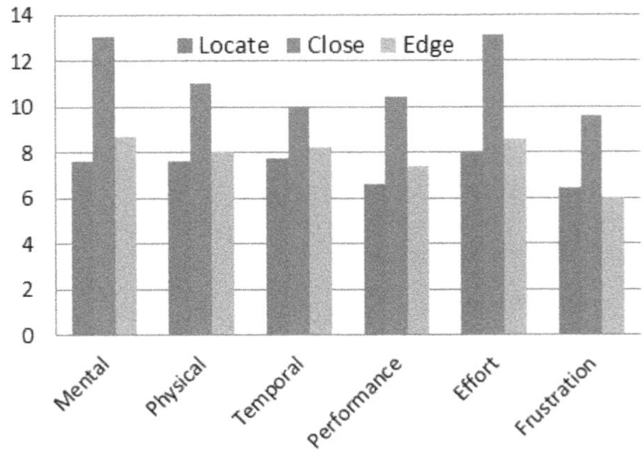

Figure 2: Average TLX responses for each differential per task

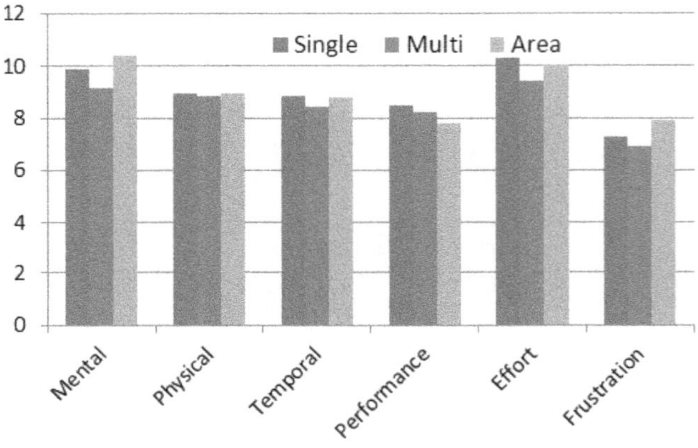

Figure 3: Average TLX responses for each differential per interaction technique.

4.4 Cursor Trace Analysis

Cursor trace analysis was carried out to attempt to identify the techniques that participants adopted using each of the techniques to answer each of the tasks. Here we visualise the cursor traces to categorise the techniques adopted by each of the participants. We also analyse the number of fingers used, the size of interaction points in the area cursor condition and the speed and distribution of the cursors during each exploration.

4.4.1 General Exploration Techniques

The users adopted different techniques for each of the different tasks set. We will discuss these in turn. Locating at least one target was a fundamental task in all of the conditions. In the 'Locate' and 'Closest Targets' conditions, there were no physical cues to guide the exploration. In the large majority of cases, users started at the top of the screen and worked their way down. This was the same regardless of interaction technique. Increasing the number of points available to the user allowed them to adapt their search. In the single point condition, users generally started at the top-left and zig-zagged right and left downwards until they found a point of interest. This resulted in a search where the users searched first the upper half of the screen and then the lower half in a logical manner (an example is shown in Figure 4 (a)).

When multiple interaction points were available, most users took advantage of the additional interaction points and adapted their search. Two users almost exclusively chose to continue to use one point of contact, even when given the option of using multiple. The general multi-finger technique adopted was to place three or four fingers across the screen and move downwards until a target was found. This had the effect of parallelising the horizontal search between a number of fingers (as shown in Figure 4(b)). Determining the closest targets was generally seen as the most challenging task. This task combined the locate task with a relative position judgment between the different targets, requiring the user to build and maintain a mental model of the target distribution within the workspace. In Figure 5(a) we see how the user zig-zags down the screen in single point mode until all targets are located and then the user moves directly between two targets rapidly to get the answer. In the multi-point mode, the same participant uses the standard multi-finger locate technique then places multiple fingers on the targets to make the decision.

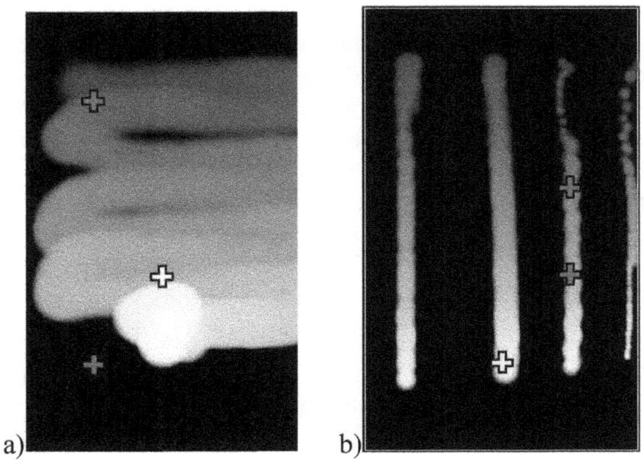

Figure 4: Typical cursor traces in the Locate task using Single (a) and multiple (b) fingers. Darker colours show earlier in the search. The white cross indicates the target to be found

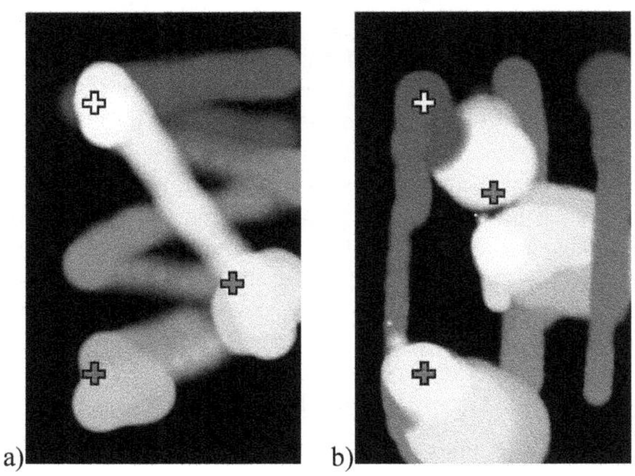

Figure 5: Typical cursor traces in the Closest Points task using Single (a) and Multiple (b) fingers. Darker colours show earlier in the search. The white cross indicates the target to be found

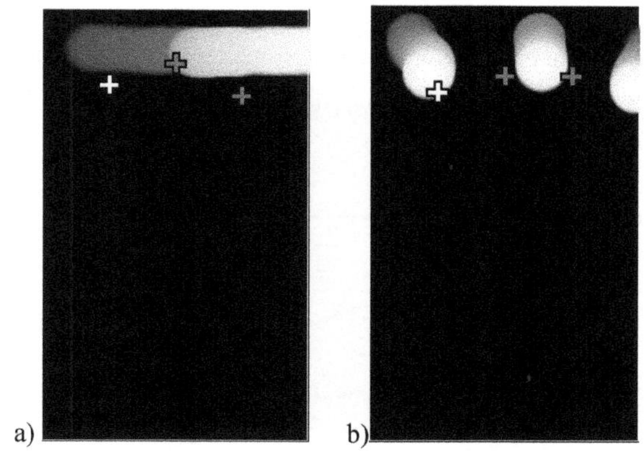

Figure 6: Typical cursor traces in the Closest Edge task using Single (a) and multiple (b) fingers. Darker colours show earlier in the search. The white cross indicates the target to be found

When given a physical cue as to the location to start the search - as was the case in the 'Closest Edge' condition – participants used it to guide the search starting point. In the single cursor condition, the technique used almost exclusively was to move back and forth along the appropriate edge rapidly gradually moving further from the edge until points of interest were detected. This was the same technique for horizontal and vertical edges. Again 10 participants used multiple contact points during the 'Closest Edge' condition when given the choice. For the top or bottom edge three or four fingers were spread across the screen in a horizontal line at the edge with the user moving away from the edge until they found a point of interest. Orientation affected how multiple fingers were used. For side edge conditions, participants still used multiple fingers but moved them up and down along the edge of the phone as in the single point condition.

4.4.2 Multiple Fingers When Locating

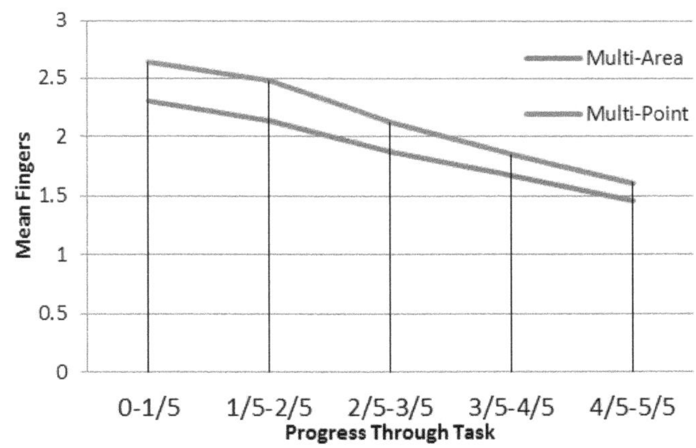

Figure 7: Mean number of fingers on the screen as the Locate task progresses by dividing each task into 5th

If we look at the number of fingers used in the Locate task, we see differing numbers of fingers used as each trial progressed. We split each trial into 5ths, Normalising the time taken to complete the task. 0->1/5th represents the start of the search with 4/5ths -> 5/5th being the end. By looking at the number of fingers used as each task progresses, we see that in the multi-cursor conditions, people used more fingers at the start of the exploration. By using multiple fingers at the start, they were able to search in parallel.

As the target is located, they reduce the number of fingers to perform a finer-grained search over a smaller area (see Figure 7).

4.4.3 Finger Velocity across the Screen

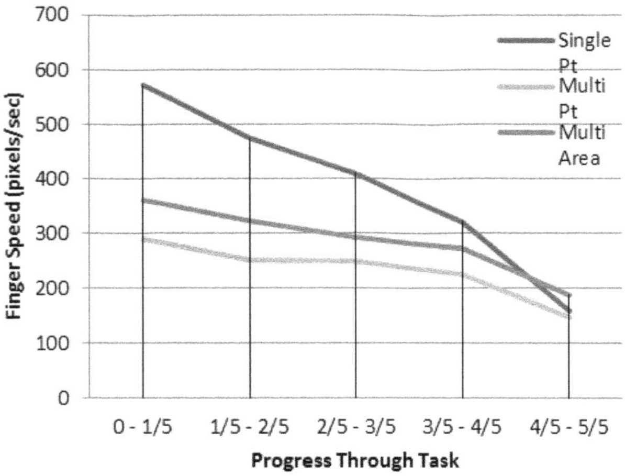

Figure 8: Mean finger speed across the screen for all techniques in the Locate task.

Again if we split the search session into fifths we can see the difference in behaviour of speed of movement across the surface. Looking at mean finger velocity over the screen, we see a large difference between the single-point condition and the multi-point conditions. Figure 8 shows that when multiple fingers were used, the user moved more slowly over the screen. Although the user was able to spread multiple fingers over the screen to search a wider area, they were compensated with the restrictions in the single point mode by moving much faster over the screen.

4.4.4 Cursor Size

a) b)

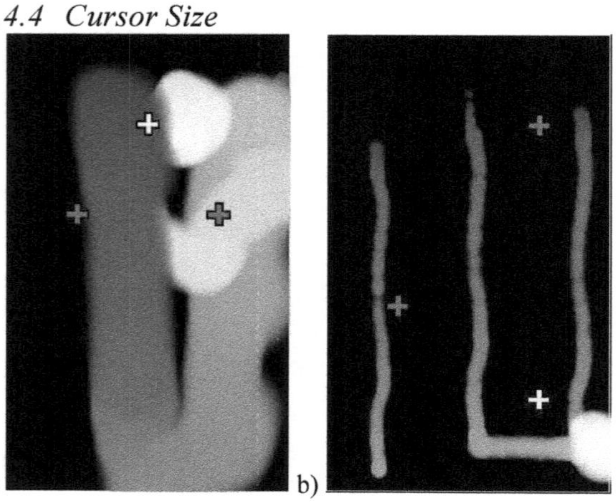

Figure 9: Screen shots of 2 users choosing different area cursor sizes, a) shows a large contact area while b) shows a small contact area.

When examining how participants used the variable cursor width in the 'Multi-Area' cursor condition, it was not clear that it was used as part of the search. Participants tended to keep the cursor size approximately the same throughout. Each participant had their own preferred size of cursor; however, this is most likely down to factor such as the size of fingers and whether the participants interacted using the very tip or the flat of the finger. Figure 9 shows two extremes, these participants used very different contact areas with the screen resulting in differing cursor widths, but were consistent between tasks.

5. Discussion

In this experiment we compared three different input techniques for interacting with a capacitive touch surface non-visually. The task set asked participants to locate audio targets on the surface, judge relative distance between targets and judge the position of targets relative to a fixed physical edge. Searching the space and locating the target is the fundamental interaction fundamental to each of these tasks. Using each of these interaction mechanisms, users were able to locate the target to an accuracy of approximately 50 pixels within 10 seconds. Non-visual exploration will always be slower than using visual exploration, however here we target mobile scenarios where vision may be unsuited. Further, this study used an unstructured space with targets appearing randomly throughout the screen. For any system that uses these techniques, we would expect a structured, predictable space that we would expect to reduce time to target. From this perspective, combining the touch surface with audio targets can be seen as a successful mechanism for interaction. We were further able to demonstrate that different techniques were used by participants when single or multi-point interactions were used. For a single finger search, the user zig-zagged left and right down the surface. When using multiple fingers, by far the most common technique was to spread three or four fingers in a line near the top of the screen and move downwards. Results show this method lead to slightly faster search times in the Multi-Point condition than in the Single-Point condition. This could be due to the fact that the search task is being parallelised between the fingers reducing the need to move side to side. This time difference was somewhat offset by the fact that users moved a single point on the surface faster than when the more cumbersome multiple-points were in contact. There was no effect detected on the targeting error.

The area cursor technique was included to allow both a broad view and a focused view of the space. The broad view is an attempt to replace the visual glance that we rely on for everyday interactions with mobile devices. The focused view was intended to allow for more fine-grained interactions. However, from the cursor trace data; there is no evidence that participants used the cursor sizing as an intentional input mechanism. Participant's maintained relatively constant cursor sizes throughout the study although these varied between participants. In this instance either through a lack of perceived usefulness, or through lack of previous exposure to a novel interaction technique, it was not used by these participants. It is still an open question whether any performance benefits can be gained by this technique. Multiple fingers on the surface served a similar purpose creating a cursor distributed across multiple points on the surface. There is evidence that users placed more fingers on the screen during the initial search phase. Towards the end of the search as the target was located, fewer fingers were used showing transition from a broad search to a narrower focused search

When asked after the experiment, participants stated a preference for the single finger condition. This was a lab-based study where users were sat at a desk with phone in hand. This is a familiar situation for phone usage and the fact that they were able to move their finger over the screen in a posture and manner similar to everyday usage may have influence their opinions. Similar performance was seen in each of the given task for each of the cursor techniques. It remains to be seen whether when mobile, the ability to ground multiple fingers on the surface will have a steadying effect on the hand and easy mobile interaction. Of the given tasks, judging the spatial relationships between the virtual targets was the most difficult this is borne out by the additional time required to complete the task as well as the NASA TLX results. Participants did however manage to successfully complete the task with a good degree of accuracy (~85% in all conditions). Multiple fingers here reduced the need to move between he targets when located, but did not lead to any performance gains.

6. CONCLUSION

We conducted a study to examine the performance of three different input techniques aimed at eventually allowing non-visual low effort interactions in a mobile setting. Results showed that participants were comfortable searching an audio space using one or multiple fingers on a capacitive surface with multiple fingers showing a significant reduction in time for locating a target. Participants still stated a preference for the more familiar single point of contact interaction. These results along with the analysis of the strategies employed by the participants when using one or multiple fingers on a touch surface will aid designers of mobile or wearable system who consider similar interaction styles. Future work will look to extend this lab study to a more realistic mobile setting with the device located either in pocket or worn on a sleeve or belt. We will also look again at the question of the use of area cursors as this remains an open question. With appropriate training, this technique may still provide a mechanism that will allow both an overview of the space to be gained while still allowing accurate selection. This is the first in a series of studies where we will look to push the boundaries of capacitive touch input. By allowing the user to exploit more of their whole hand, we aim to develop discrete, low effort interactions that will benefit on the move interactions for mobile and wearable devices.

7. REFERENCES

[1] Agrawal, S., Constandache, I., Gaonkar, S., Roy Choudhury, R., Caves, K. and DeRuyter, F. Using mobile phones to write in air. ACM MobileHCI 2011, 15-28.

[2] Baudisch, P. and Chu, G. Back-of-device interaction allows creating very small touch devices. ACM CHI 2009, 1923-1932.

[3] Cheng, J., Bahle, G. and Lukowicz, P. A simple wristband based on capacitive sensors for recognition of complex hand motions. IEEE Sensors 2012, 1-4.

[4] Colby, R. Considerations for the Development of Non-Visual Interfaces for Driving Applications, Doctoral dissertation, Virginia Polytechnic Institute and State University (2012).

[5] Costanza, E., Inverso, S. A. and Allen, R. Toward subtle intimate interfaces for mobile devices using an EMG controller. ACM CHI 2005, 481-489.

[6] Crossan, A., Brewster, S. and Ng, A. Foot tapping for mobile interaction. BritishHCI 2010, 418-422.

[7] Crossan, A., McGill, M., Brewster, S. and Murray-Smith, R. Head tilting for interaction in mobile contexts. ACM MobileHCI 2009, 6.

[8] Crossan, A., Williamson, J., Brewster, S. and Murray-Smith, R. Wrist rotation for interaction in mobile contexts. ACM MobileHCI 2008, 435-438.

[9] Grossman, T. and Balakrishnan, R. The bubble cursor: enhancing target acquisition by dynamic resizing of the cursor's activation area. ACM CHI 2005, 281-290.

[10] Kane, S. K., Morris, M. R., Perkins, A. Z., Wigdor, D., Ladner, R. E. and Wobbrock, J. O. Access overlays: improving non-visual access to large touch screens for blind users. ACM UIST 2011, 273-282.

[11] Kim, D., Hilliges, O., Izadi, S., Butler, A. D., Chen, J., Oikonomidis, I. and Olivier, P. Digits: freehand 3D interactions anywhere using a wrist-worn gloveless sensor. ACM UIST 2012, 167-176.

[12] Lumsden, J. and Brewster, S. A paradigm shift: alternative interaction techniques for use with mobile & wearable devices. Proc. of the 2003 conference of the Centre for Advanced Studies on Collaborative research. IBM Press, 2003, 197-210.

[13] Lyons, K., Nguyen, D., Ashbrook, D. and White, S. Facet: a multi-segment wrist worn system. ACM UIST 2012, 123-130.

[14] Murray-Smith, R., Williamson, J., Hughes, S. and Quaade, T. Stane: synthesized surfaces for tactile input. ACM CHI 2008, 1299-1302.

[15] Rico, J. and Brewster, S. Usable gestures for mobile interfaces: evaluating social acceptability. ACM CHI 2010, 887-896.

[16] Rogers, S., Williamson, J., Stewart, C. and Murray-Smith, R. Fingercloud: uncertainty and autonomy handover incapacitive sensing. ACM CHI 2010, 577-580.

[17] Sato, M., Poupyrev, I. and Harrison, C. Touché: enhancing touch interaction on humans, screens, liquids, and everyday objects. ACM CHI 2012, 483-492.

[18] Sawhney, N. and Schmandt, C. Nomadic radio: speech and audio interaction for contextual messaging in nomadic environments. ACM transactions on Computer-Human interaction (TOCHI), 7(3) (2000), 353-383.

[19] Siek, K. A., Rogers, Y. and Connelly, K. H. Fat finger worries: how older and younger users physically interact with PDAs. Interact 2005, 267-280.

[20] Wigdor, D., Benko, H., Pella, J., Lombardo, J. and Williams, S. Rock & rails: extending multi-touch interactions with shape gestures to enable precise spatial manipulations. ACM CHI 2011, 1581-1590.

[21] Williamson, J. R., Crossan, A. and Brewster, S. Multimodal mobile interactions: usability studies in real world settings. ACM ICMI 2011, 361-368.

[22] Wobbrock, J. O., Morris, M. R. and Wilson, A. D. User-defined gestures for surface computing. ACM CHI 2009, 1083-1092.

[23] Yang, X., Grossman, T., Wigdor, D. and Fitzmaurice, G. Magic finger: always-available input through finger instrumentation. ACM UIST 2012, 147-156.

[24] Zarek, A., Wigdor, D. and Singh, K. SNOUT: one-handed use of capacitive touch devices. ACM AVI 2012, 140-147.

Multimodal Interaction History and its use in Error Detection and Recovery

Felix Schüssel[1] Frank Honold[1] Miriam Schmidt[3]
Nikola Bubalo[2] Anke Huckauf[2] Michael Weber[1]

[1]Institute of Media Informatics
[2]Institute of Psychology and Education
[3]Institute of Neural Information Processing
Ulm University, Germany
felix.schuessel frank.honold michael.weber
nikola.bubalo anke.huckauf miriam.k.schmidt @uni-ulm.de

ABSTRACT

Multimodal systems still tend to ignore the individual input behavior of users, and at the same time, suffer from erroneous sensor inputs. Although many researchers have described user behavior in specific settings and tasks, little to nothing is known about the applicability of such information, when it comes to increase the robustness of a system for multimodal inputs. We conducted a gamified experimental study to investigate individual user behavior and error types found in an actually running system. It is shown, that previous ways of describing input behavior by a simple classification scheme (like simultaneous and sequential) are not suited to build up an individual interaction history. Instead, we propose to use temporal distributions of different metrics derived from multimodal event timings. We identify the major errors that can occur in multimodal interactions and finally show how such an interaction history can practically be applied for error detection and recovery. Applying the proposed approach to the experimental data, the initial error rate is reduced from 4.9% to a minimum of 1.2%.

Categories and Subject Descriptors

H.5.2 [**Information Interfaces and Presentation**]: User Interfaces—*Theory and methods, Input devices and strategies, Interaction styles*

General Terms

Theory, Human Factors

Keywords

HCI; Multimodal Interaction; User Behavior; Interaction History; Input Error Detection and Recovery

ICMI'14, November 12–16, 2014, Istanbul, Turkey.
Copyright 2014 ACM 978-1-4503-2885-2/14/11 ...$15.00.
http://dx.doi.org/10.1145/2663204.2663255.

1. INTRODUCTION

Multimodal systems do already exist and are a topic of research for some time, but the fusion of multimodal inputs from users is still defined a priori, assuming more or less error-free sensor inputs. Thus, errors stemming from sensor inputs at runtime (e.g. speech recognition) can neither be detected nor avoided. An important aspect may be the multimodal input behavior of users measured over a prolonged period of time, for which we use the generic term *interaction history*. In order to create a robust system, which has an error rate acceptable by the users, this factor could be of utmost importance. Studies in literature [1,2,5,7–9], that have dealt with multimodal input behavior, show distinct interindividual differences, but, to our knowledge, were purely descriptive in nature. Little is known about which information, drawn from a user's interaction history, is actually relevant to achieve an increased robustness of a system as well as how such information can be applied in the first place. In our study we pursue these questions by conducting an experiment in which participants had to solve a visual search task by multimodal interaction. Subsequently, we analyzed the users input behavior and the system's errors. The objective is, to provide an rationale of how the former can be a practical remedy for the later on an individual scale. The results show how versatile the system's errors can be and how they can be avoided. Moreover, only an individualized look at each user's interaction history seems to be a promising approach to success.

In the next section, we present related work that leads to our main research questions (Sec. 3). Section 4 describes the conducted experiment and data acquisition. In the results section we use the gathered data to take a deeper look at how an interaction history looks like, what kind of errors can occur in multimodal systems, and how this information can be used to detect and recover from such errors instantly during system operation. At the end of the results section, we show how this can be practically realized in an actual system and give results from our data. Section 6 summarizes our findings and gives an outlook on future research.

2. RELATED WORK

There has been a number of research in recent years, investigating the user's input behavior in multimodal interaction.

In the following, we summarize related work, regarding the modalities taken into account, the tasks at hand, and the findings relevant for the work presented here.

In [7–9] speech and pen input behavior is investigated according to different aspects. The task at hand in all three publications is a major flood, where users had to coordinate emergency resources using a map display. The subtasks involved multimodal placing of items ("place a barge here", while pointing at a location), specification of movement routes and several others. Each experiment itself was conducted using Wizard of Oz (WoZ) technique. Oviatt et al. were the first to coin the term *multimodal integration pattern* [6]. Such an integration pattern typifies a user's combined use of different input modes (e.g. speech and pen), which can either be sequential or simultaneous. According to [6], a combination is sequential, if there is no temporal overlap of the multimodal signal intervals, while it is simultaneous, when they do overlap. These temporal gaps are calculated using the on- and offsets of the two involved modalities where an overlap gives a negative temporal gap. In addition, the users can be categorized as being either predominantly sequential or simultaneous integrators, if 60% or more of the users multimodal integrations belong to the same category. If a user shows less preference for one type of integration, it is categorized as being non-dominant. In [8] the consistency of users within their dominant pattern is reported to be very high (97%) and quite resistant against selective reinforcement via manipulated error rates of the opposite pattern. The generated errors were of unspecific type, i.e. the users were only told, that the system was unable to understand the previous input. In [7] the consistency of integration patterns is reported to be 93.5% and Oviatt et al. conclude, that even if users like the ability to use multimodal inputs, they don't always do, when given the choice. In [9] it is shown for the same tasks and modalities, that integration patterns are even stable over time (three sessions over a time period of four to six weeks).

Integration patterns are also investigated in [3, 4], were machine learning based approaches to predict a user's integration pattern were presented, based on the data of [7]. It is shown that 15 samples per user are enough to predict a user's integration pattern with an accuracy of 81%, so integration patterns can be detected relatively fast, even in an automated way.

Lee and Billinghurst [5] performed an experiment involving speech and gesture for a multimodal augmented reality system, where users had to alter the color, shape, and position of 3D objects. The results of their WoZ experiment show that speech input usually consists of short commando-like inputs. Referring to input timings, in 94% of all multimodal inputs, gesture was preceding speech input and the gesture was held several seconds longer after the speech input was finished. Although Lee and Billinghurst did not explicitly analyze it, their reported data clearly suggests a dominant simultaneous integration pattern for most of the users.

Dey et al. investigated speech and multi-touch input for the manipulation of digital photos [1]. The users had to perform a fixed sequence of manipulation tasks, where touch input was limited to selection of photos and issuing a fixed increase or decrease of the size by performing a pinch gesture. Speech input was also limited to a fixed set of commands, like "rotate clockwise", or "zoom in". In contrast to the WoZ experiments mentioned before, a completely autonomous system was realized. For the chosen tasks, multimodal input was less popular than unimodal input using a touch only interface for comparison. Dey et al. did not calculate integration patterns as defined by Oviatt et al., but instead measured the temporal gap between the onsets of speech and touch input. Most users performed the speech command after the touch command (72%) with a large overall variance of about $\pm$ 1500 milliseconds. Further insights, e.g. on the inter-individual differences between users, or the intra-individual consistency in input behavior of a single user, are not reported.

In [2] speech and single touch inputs are investigated for the task of placing different object types on a specific location of a map from a military scenario. The main measures, that may be relevant, are the input order (touch before speech, or speech before touch) and the time distances between the two modalities. The analyzed 11 participants split up into two groups, namely those, that always started with speech input (7), and those that always started with touch input (4). None of them changed the input order during the experiment. Regarding the time distances between the two inputs, touch-first participants exhibited significantly lower temporal gaps to the speech input, than speech-first participants exhibited to the touch input. User's individual consistency was not analyzed. In contrast to the findings of Oviatt et al., where typically simultaneous integration patterns were much more often observed, here, all of the inputs were sequential ones. Haas et al. [2] conclude that this may be due to the fact, that their tasks involved much shorter (command-like) speech inputs than those of Oviatt et al.

In summary, all these experiments show different, but quite consistent user behavior, that highly depends on the involved modalities and tasks. Not only did the participants use the same input order most of the time, they also tend to do this in a temporally consistent way, as shown in Oviatt's integration pattern experiments. It remains unclear, if input orders, onset distances, integration patterns or some other measures are the adequate representation of a user's interaction history. As Oviatt et al. already suggested in [9], it should be possible to use this information to become more robust. To our knowledge, this has not yet been done till now and it is a remaining open research question, how an interaction history might practically be used for this purpose.

3. RESEARCH QUESTIONS

The primary goals of this article can be separated into three parts. (1) How does an interaction history look like and what are the individual user differences? I.e. which representation of typical user behavior should be used, independent of the underlying task or modalities at hand? (2) In order to increase the robustness of a system, we must take a deeper look into the types of errors that can occur during multimodal input. And finally (3), how can an interaction history be actually used to detect, or even resolve, different error types in a multimodal input system?

4. METHODS

In order to answer these questions, we performed an experiment that involved speech and touch input. As suggested by the related work, users should not be limited to multimodal inputs only, but should also be able to use unimodal inputs. To keep the participants motivated over a lot of similar inputs, we decided to create a gamified task.

4.1 Tasks and System

The participants were presented with a matrix of numbered geometric shapes at the center of the screen, which could either be red, blue or green (see Figure 1). A timer, indicating the remaining time left and money to be won in that round, was shown on the side of the screen corresponding to the participants dominant hand, while three big round buttons in the three aforementioned colors were depicted on the other side. The difficulty of the task was modified by the size of the matrix and thus the number of presented objects (e.g. 3x3, 4x4, 5x5). On each screen, there was one unique object with a unique combination of color and shape at a random position, while all other objects shared color and shape at least once. The participants were asked to indicate the location and color of this unique item as quickly as possible, enforced by a ticking clock sound and the decrease of the time/money bar. They could do so either by using exclusive touch (touching of the object plus the corresponding color button), exclusive speech (naming the position number of the object and its color), or a combination of those modalities (touching the object and naming its color or vice versa). The faster the participants completed the task successfully the more money they earned. When they indicated a false location or color, they did not get any money for this particular turn.

Figure 1: A user in front of the system indicating the individual item's location using touch and its color by using speech.

The experiment was realized as a fully functional system with components for automatic speech recognition (ASR), touch input, and input fusion, which provided the actual application with input events. The ASR component was realized using the Microsoft Speech API (SAPI 5.4)[1] with a speech grammar for recognizing all required utterances (colors "red", "green", "blue" and/or locations as numbers from 1 to 25). In order to maximize the performance of the ASR component, a dedicated voice headset microphone was used and there were differently trained speech profiles for the recognition of male and female voices. Touch input was realized using the Multi-Touch SDK[2] from PQLabs. Both input components provide the input fusion component with single events for color or location, containing temporal on- and offsets, together with a confidence value. The fusion component itself is realized as described in [10] and fuses the single incoming inputs to one complete and crisp event (color+location) that is passed on to the application. The application reacts accordingly to the input with positive or negative audiovisual feedback and proceeds to the next task.

[1]http://msdn.microsoft.com/en-us/library/ee125663
[2]http://multitouch.com/sdk.html

4.2 Participants

42 volunteers, 33 male and 9 female, participated in the experiment and were paid according to their success in the game (between 10.75 and 16.30 Euro). 88.1% of the participants were right handed. The average age in the participant pool is 27.17 (standard deviation, SD = 9.18) with the youngest participant being 16 and the oldest being 63. 95.2% had prior experience with multi-touch interfaces like smartphones or tablets. One participant's data was not usable, because of an extreme low speech recognition rate.

4.3 Experimental Procedure

Each participant was welcomed and asked to fill out an introductory questionnaire consisting of basic demographic information (e.g. sex, age, handedness, occupation). Consequently each participant was introduced to the system and the game mechanics through trial runs for all possible multimodal combinations before the actual experiment started. An interaction history is something that is built from interactions in the past before it is actually applied. That is why we decided to split the experiment into two separate blocks.

The first block of the experiment ("history" block) was comprised of 90 trials, which in turn were segmented into three parts with increasing task difficulty. All tasks within the first block had to be solved with a specific modality combination (e.g. location-touch + color-speech) to build up the corresponding interaction history for all possible combinations. The second block of the experiment ("free interaction" block) entailed 45 trials with randomized difficulty in which the participant had a free choice of which modalities to use.

After the experiment, the participants were asked for their preferred kind of interaction and could give feedback on the experiment. Finally they were paid and the intentions behind the study were explained.

4.4 Data Recording

All system components (ASR, touch, fusion and application) contributed to a central XML-based log file with all their relevant events. Video was recorded from a third person's perspective (cf. Figure 1) and frontal from on top of the screen. Audio was recorded separately from the headset microphone and the system's audio output.

4.5 Acquired Variables and Labeling of Data

From each participant's log file the following variables were extracted: On- and offsets of actual single inputs; event times of single input events; the modality combination of complete inputs (speech-only, touch-only, location-touch + color-speech, color-speech + location-touch).

In addition to these automatically sampled variables, the data was semi-automatically labeled for the following information: system behavior as intended by user; error type; actual intended input (when part of the event-log).

5. RESULTS

With 41 successful participants, a total of 5535 tasks could be analyzed using IBM SPSS® Statistics and Matlab® from MathWorks. The following sections show the results related to the research questions from Section 3.

5.1 Interaction History and Individual Differences

The data from the "history" block is used as basis for interaction history analysis. It contains 90 tasks for each of the 41 users, that were instructed to use one of the four modality combinations throughout the entire block. From these overall 3690 interactions, those 3317 where the intended inputs were correctly recognized by the system represent the actual interaction history discussed in this section.

5.1.1 Integration Patterns and Input Order

As the related work suggests, multimodal integration patterns may be a distinctive measure for any user's multimodal interaction behavior. Table 1 shows the integration patterns for the users that performed the location input via touch and the color input via speech. While all 11 users can be categorized as being either simultaneous or sequential integrators (i.e. more than 60% of inputs where uttered in the respective manner), the average consistency of 82.9% is considerably lower than the 93.5% found in [7] and 95% in [9]. for pen and speech input. In fact, there are some users (e.g. user 9) who perform about a third of their inputs in the opposite way as their overall categorization suggests. Calculation of integration patterns of the other modality combinations (location-speech + color-touch, touch-only, and speech-only) showed similar results with moderate internal consistency, except for speech-only inputs, as they naturally can only be performed in a sequential manner.

	User	% simultaneous constructions	% sequential constructions
SIM integrators	37	**100.0**	0.0
	29	**93.4**	6.6
	17	**92.0**	7.9
	1	**91.7**	8.3
	25	**84.6**	15.4
	21	**82.5**	17.5
	5	**82.2**	17.8
	13	**64.5**	35.5
SEQ integrators	9	32.8	**67.2**
	33	27.5	**72.5**
	41	1.2	**98.8**

Average Consistency: 82.9%

Table 1: Simultaneous and sequential integrators with modality combination color-speech + location-touch. The average consistency is considerably lower compared to those reported in literature [7,9].

At least for the modalities and relatively short inputs of our experiment, it seems that integration patterns are not distinctive enough to be used as a basis for adaption of multimodal systems' temporal thresholds, as suggested in [9]. E.g. even if a predominantly simultaneous integrator such as user no. 5 performs a sequential input, the system should usually accept it, otherwise almost every fifth input (17.8%) would be falsely rejected.

Regarding the order of inputs, as the other scheme used to classify users found in the related work, our data shows no clear distinctiveness either. Similar to integration patterns, we divided participants into groups that predominantly started with color (>60% of all inputs), and those that predominantly started with location. Four users showed no dominant order, while 15 predominantly started with color and 22 with location inputs. Overall 24.4% of the 41 participants showed a consistency of less than 80%.

These results indicate, that a more detailed analysis of the data is required, and that there may be no simple way that can be used to represent typical user behavior. This holds for both concepts known so far (integration patterns and input orders).

5.1.2 Individual Distributions of Different Metrics

The underlying basis for the classification of integration patterns is the distribution of *temporal gaps* between the two single inputs of a multimodal utterance. I.e. the time difference between the offset of the first input and the onset of the second input. But there are other metrics that can be used as well. Figure 2 shows the actual distributions of the *temporal gaps* and the *onset distances* between the location and color inputs for the same users as in Table 1. As one can see, these distributions are highly different between users with varying means and standard deviations.

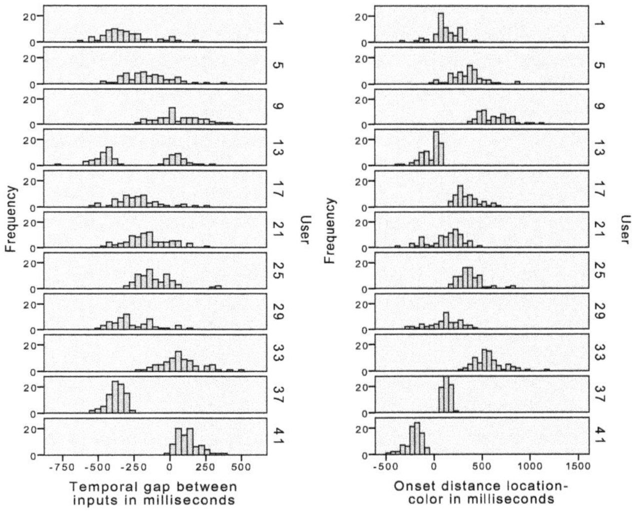

Figure 2: Histograms for users with modality combination color-speech + location-touch clearly show the individuality of users.

There are a number of metrics that can be built from the two single events (color and location) with their respective onsets and offsets. Constructing all meaningful measures from the onset and offset information results in 13 different variants of metrics for the interaction history data, as shown in Table 2. Note that all these metrics can be created for all four modality combinations, including speech- and touch-only inputs. The metric called *Integration Index* is different from the other metrics, as it does not simply depend on the absolute distances between two timestamps, but is a relative measure for the position (center) of one input related to the whole time interval of the other input. This way, it comprises more information than the other metrics.

Metric	Illustration	13 variants, depending on
Temporal Gap (Offset – Onset)		Input sequence Color relative Location relative
Onset Distance		Input sequence Color relative
Offset Distance		Input sequence Color relative
Total Duration		Earliest onset and latest offset
Center Distance		Input sequence Color relative
Integration Index	-1 0 +1	Relative to longest input Color relative Location relative

Table 2: All metrics and their variants created from the onset and offset information. Redundant variants are not listed.

But which metric is the best for which modality combination? Or in other words: which one does describe the individuality of users best? There are two relevant aspects here, namely the ability of a metric to *differentiate* between users, and the *consistency* of values within a metric for a specific user. These aspects can be derived from two features of a metric: the mean values and the standard deviations. Hence, a metric with larger differences of means and a lower standard deviations across users should be preferred. Metrics can be compared by calculating the standard deviation of all means, and the mean of all standard deviations, at least for metrics with a similar range of values. As an example, Figure 3 shows the comparison between the different variants of the Integration Index for the touch-only modality. The location relative version shows a larger standard deviation of means and a lower mean of standard deviations, and thus could describe best the individuality between the users. While this may give some hints, which metrics (or variants) should be preferred for which modalities, the decision finally depends on how well a metric performs when used as an interaction history to increase the robustness of an actual multimodal input system.

Note that we found no clear evidence of significant changes in metrics' distributions for the different difficulty levels. The differences we found, e.g. a reduced temporal gap between events, seem to stem from learning effects, as participants tend to get faster in the course of time. So we decided not to differentiate between difficulties of the tasks.

In addition to these user-related metrics, the actual event distance between two single inputs is also calculated. In contrast to the metrics based on onsets and offsets of actual user utterances, this value is calculated from the actual time the system received the input events. Due to sensor processing times, there may be a significant delay before the system actually becomes aware of the input's onset and offset values. E.g. the mean delay of the ASR component before raising an input event was 642 milliseconds (SD = 229). In contrast, the touch input component only took about 1.6 milliseconds, before an event was raised. These delays are of special importance, when the interaction history should be used in a system with online processing.

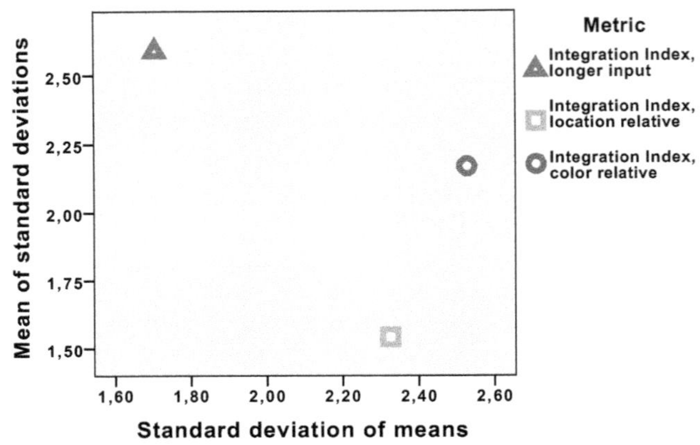

Figure 3: Comparison of the three Integration Index variants for the touch-only modality. The location relative Integration Index does describe user individuality best.

5.2 Error Types of Multimodal Interaction

Within the "free interaction" block (consisting of 1845 trials), the implemented system performed quite robustly. But video analysis and manual labeling reveal, that there were still situations, in which the system did not behave as intended by the users. This kind of error occurred on average in 4.9% (90 cases) of all inputs, ranging up to 17.8% for some individuals. This overall very good performance can be attributed to the efforts spent on making sensory inputs (esp. speech inputs) as robust as possible. E.g. the users had to use a dedicated high quality headset microphone for voice input, different speech recognition profiles were used for female and male participants and there was effectively no ambient noise. In a more realistic setting, one could expect a considerably higher error rate. Taking a deeper look, we can identify multiple types of errors that can occur on multimodal inputs depending on erroneous sensor inputs:

False negatives: This happens, when a sensor does not react at all, or is too unconfident on the intended input. The user has to repeat the input using the same or even other modalities.

False positives: This happens, when a sensor reacts upon an action of the user that was not intended as input. This can even trigger a totally wrong action.

Conflicts: This is a special case of the false positive error, where an input of the user is disturbed by a false positive from another sensor. Lacking any information to resolve it, the current system implementation discards both contradicting inputs, so that the user has to repeat the intended input.

Misunderstandings: The system reacts on an intended input in an unintended way. This happens, when a sensor misinterprets an input. As with false positives, this can trigger a totally wrong action.

Other: This category contains unclear error types, like a combination of two or more errors from above, as well as user initiated errors. These can be for example self corrections, that are missed by the system, or incomplete inputs by the user.

Figure 4 shows the frequency for each error type within the "free interaction" block of our experiment. This certainly does not allow to draw a conclusion on the frequency distribution in other tasks and systems, but still we claim that these types cover all relevant sensory errors that can occur in any multimodal interaction. The question remains, how an interaction history can be used to prevent or at least recover from such errors.

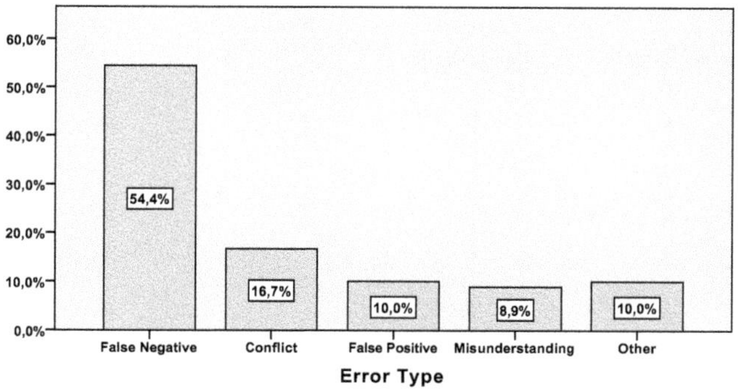

Figure 4: Frequency per error type within the "free interaction" block. False negative is by far the most occurring error.

5.3 Applying the Interaction History

In the following sections, we show how an interaction history (as described above) can be applied to the different types of errors. Note, that whenever a user's individual history is not known for a specific modality combination, we use the the averaged history values of all other users (for the same modality combination).

5.3.1 False Negatives

To give a typical example, imagine the following situation: The user performs a touch input to specify the location, and a speech input to specify the color of the target object. A false negative occurs, when the speech input is not detected by the ASR component, so this part of the multimodal input is missing. In order to detect such false negatives, the event distances of the history can be used:

Whenever a single input event is raised, calculate the maximum event distance of every possible multimodal input combination from the interaction history. When no further input is recognized up to that maximum time, a false negative is assumed.

Figure 5 shows the results for the data, that contains 54 cases of this error. As shown, 87.8% of all false negative inputs are correctly detected and 4.9% of "normal" inputs are misjudged as being false negatives. While the detection of false negatives is a mandatory step, their recovery requires additional steps. One idea is to "ask" all respective sensory components, to re-process their input data within the time frame of the earliest onsets and latest offsets contained in the interaction history. Using this *back-channelling* approach, the common one-way processing of input from sensors to the application is substantially enhanced, because it may be possible to detect the missed input with increased sensitivity. Although this is out of the scope of this paper and deserves further research.

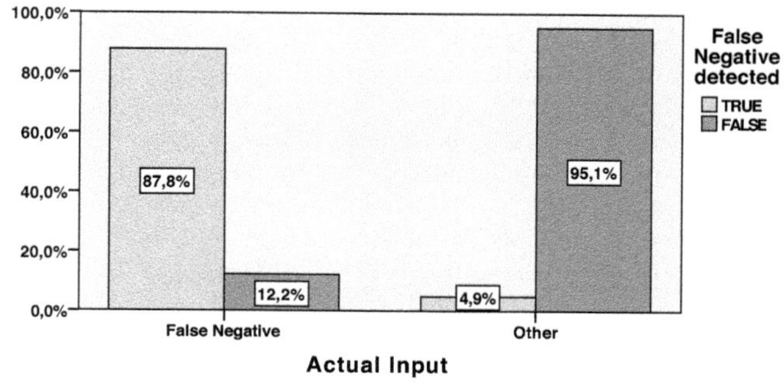

Figure 5: Detection rate of false negatives for actual false negatives and all other inputs within the "free interaction" block. While 87.8% of the false negatives are correctly detected, only 4.9% of the other inputs are misjudged.

5.3.2 False Positives

When the ASR component wrongly detects a location input (e.g. based on some nonverbal utterance of the user) while the user performs a touch input to specify the color, a typical false positive error occurred. As both inputs can be successfully fused to form a complete input, the system triggers a wrong input. The interaction history can be used to detect such false positives as follows:

Whenever a complete input is detected, verify the accordance to the interaction history for this kind of modality combination. As a starting point, we use *min* and *max* values of the metrics stored in the interaction history. If the complete input exhibits a non-typical temporal relation, the single input with the lower confidence value is assumed to be a false positive.

Figure 6 shows the results for our data set, that contains only nine cases. As depicted, only one false positive error is detected correctly (11.1%), while at the same time, some of the not erroneous inputs are falsely identified as being false positives (1.2%, or 21 cases). This is due to the fact that false positives not necessarily occur in an unusual temporal relation, while some of the intended inputs do. The proposed solution to cope with false positives is to ignore the input with the lower confidence and wait for the next one.

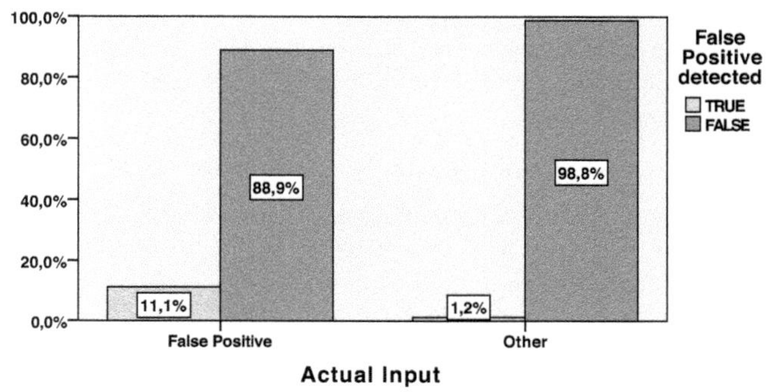

Figure 6: Detection rate of false positives for actual false positives and all other inputs within the "free interaction" block. While only 11.1% of the false positives are correctly detected, 1.2% of the other inputs are misjudged.

5.3.3 Conflicts

A typical example of a conflict is given by the following situation: The ASR component wrongly detects a location input (a false positive), before the user performs a touch input to specify the location and an intended speech input for the color. As the input fusion component already is able to detect such conflicts from semantically contradicting inputs (two different locations from different sensors, cf. [10]), the interaction history can directly be used to resolve the conflict. First, we need a measure to compare the possible alternatives. For this purpose, we propose to calculate the relative conformity with the interaction history. Given the value I_m of a pair of inputs for a specific metric m and the *mean*, *min* and *max* values H_m^{mean}, H_m^{min} and H_m^{max} of the history for this metric, the conformity is defined as:

$$\text{con}(I_m) = \begin{cases} 1 - \dfrac{|H_m^{mean} - I_m|}{H_m^{mean} - H_m^{min}} & \text{if } I_m \leq H_m^{mean} \\ 1 - \dfrac{|H_m^{mean} - I_m|}{H_m^{max} - H_m^{mean}} & \text{if } I_m > H_m^{mean} \end{cases}$$

Put concretely: The conformity of an input is 1.0 if it exactly meets the mean of the history, becomes 0.0 at the min and max boundaries, and negative outside.

But conformity with the interaction history is not the only measure that should be taken into account. In addition, the confidence of a single input should also be considered. For example, touch inputs are usually much more certain, than speech inputs. To account for this, we multiply the conformity value with the confidence C_{si} of the doubtful single input event, that is provided by the respective sensor component. So the final possibility value p for each input pair is computed as:

$$p = \max(\text{con}(I_m)) * C_{si},$$

where max() simply selects the highest conformity of all considered metrics. The input combination with the higher possibility value p is then assumed to be the intended input.

When applied to all found conflicts of the "free interaction" block, most conflicts (88.9%, 16 out of 18) can be successfully resolved using the approach described above. Only one conflict was wrongly resolved, while another one could not be resolved at all, because both alternatives where not valid according to the interaction history. In this case, both conflicting inputs can either be ignored, or the user could be asked for a solution.

5.3.4 Misunderstandings

When the ASR component misunderstands a location input while the user performs a touch input to specify the color, a typical misunderstanding occurred. As both inputs can be successfully fused to form a complete input, the system triggers a wrong input. These types of errors (8 cases in our data) are the only ones, that cannot be detected using an interaction history, because their temporal relations are totally valid and don't differ from normal inputs.

5.3.5 Putting the Pieces Together

As demonstrated in the previous sections, an interaction history can be used to detect (and partially recover from) false negatives, false positives and conflicts. In the results shown above, the different methods were applied to all inputs to show their general performance in retrospect. In an actual running system, obviously this is not the case. In fact, the different error types occur at different points in time and so should their detection and recovery. But when should an actual system execute the detection of the different error types in its multimodal input processing? The logical order, in which errors are detected can be conceptualized as a *cascading process* and is visualized in Figure 7.

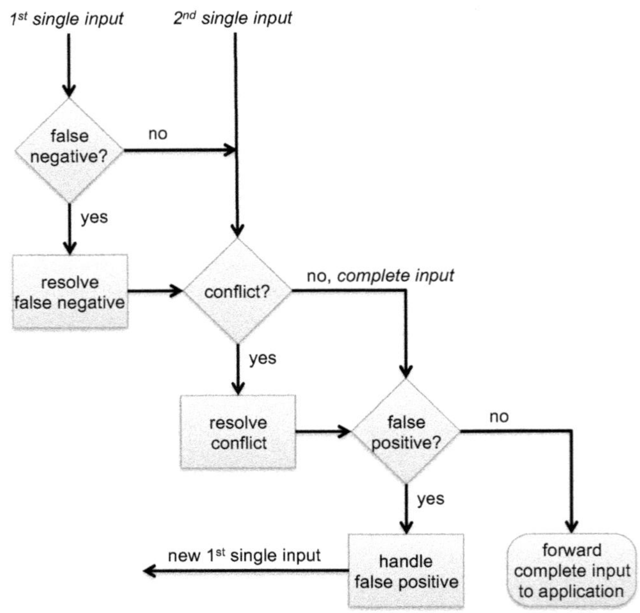

Figure 7: The error detection and recovery can be conceptualized as a cascading process that performs stepwise error detection and recovery.

The process works as follows: Whenever a potential *1st single input* (e.g. a location event) of a multimodal input occurs, the process starts by trying to detect a false negative as described in Section 5.3.1. When a false negative is detected (e.g. a missing event for the color), the proposed back-channeling must be invoked in order to resolve the false negative. When the resolve is completed successfully or a *2nd single input* event occurs, the fusion of both single inputs may reveal a conflict error. A possible conflict is then resolved as described in Section 5.3.3. When a solution is found, or if there was no conflict at all, the *complete input* (e.g. color: red + location: 4) is tested for being a false positive, as described in Section 5.3.2. Handling a detected false positive, results in restarting the process with the most confident single input as a new 1st single input. Finally, if no false positive is detected, the complete input seems to be valid and can be forwarded to the application.

This cascading process was applied on the data of the experiment in a stepwise manner. The overall rate of inputs where the system does not behave as intended, decreases from initially 4.9% to 1.2%. Due to the fact that the handling strategies (for false negatives and false positives) cannot be tested on the recorded data, 7.2% of all tasks remain undecided.

6. SUMMARY AND OUTLOOK

Our experimental data shows, that integration patterns as defined by Oviatt et al. are oversimplified to be suited as a representation of multimodal input interaction history, at least for the tasks of our study. The overall consistencies are much lower (82.9%) and show a more divergent characteristic per user than reported in [7,9]. The same holds for another user classification based on the order of inputs [1,2,5]. None of these simple measures showed enough consistency, that promising error detection, based on them, could be expected. Instead, we suggest that temporal distributions (in various metrics based on multimodal event timings) should be used as interaction history, as they hold much more information than the classification-based approaches known so far. The presented metrics clearly show individual differences between users (variances of means between participants are high), while retaining meaningful coherence per user (means of variances are low).

The identified four major errors, that can occur in multimodal input systems, all stem from failures of sensor components: false negatives, false positives, conflicts, and misunderstandings. We presented specific approaches for error detection and recovery (for 3 of the 4 error types). We showed the practical applicability of input interaction history for the purpose of error detection and recovery in multimodal systems. Using these approaches for error detection and recovery, we were able to correctly detect about 88% of the false negatives and conflicting inputs of our data. For the presented experimental data, the overall error rate can be reduced from 4.9% to a minimum of 1.2%. But there remain 7.2% of interactions, whose outcome as false or correct cannot be told with final certainty. It depends on the performance of the mentioned recovery strategies (e.g. backchanneling for false negatives) and needs further research.

As the proposed process deals with multimodal inputs on an abstract level it is supposed to be generally applicable to any multimodal system. By including the individual history, the interaction with a system can be more pleasing for a user, because typical errors, as presented here, can be detected and resolved. Therefore the full potential of multimodal interaction can be really exploited.

A next step in our research is to evaluate how well specific metrics are suited for detecting certain error types in particular modalities. Currently, the lab conditions where optimized for the recording of interaction histories, having obvious drawbacks when it comes to error recovery (low overall error rate). Thus, a dataset with an overall higher error rate is needed to have a greater database for spotting significant differences between the metrics.

We are currently implementing the presented error detection and recovery in a follow up system, together with complete realization of the online error handling strategies presented here. To get the needed data with an overall higher error rate, we are going to increase the degree of realism in our experimental setup (e.g. adding background noise).

7. ACKNOWLEDGMENTS

We would like to thank Thilo Hörnle and Reinhard Schwegler for technical support and Sasha Meudt for providing the ATLAS tool for reviewing the recordings. This work originates in the SFB/TRR 62 "Companion-Technology for Cognitive Technical Systems" funded by the German Research Foundation (DFG).

8. REFERENCES

[1] P. Dey, S. Madhvanath, A. Ranjan, and S. Das. An exploration of gesture-speech multimodal patterns for touch interfaces. In *Proc. of the 3rd Int. Conference on Human Computer Interaction*, IndiaHCI '11, pages 79–83, New York, 2011. ACM.

[2] E. C. Haas, K. S. Pillalamarri, C. C. Stachowiak, and G. McCullough. Temporal binding of multimodal controls for dynamic map displays: a systems approach. In *Proc. of the 13th international conference on multimodal interfaces*, ICMI '11, pages 409–416, New York, 2011. ACM.

[3] X. Huang and S. L. Oviatt. Toward adaptive information fusion in multimodal systems. In S. Renals and S. Bengio, editors, *Machine Learning for Multimodal Interaction, MLMI 2005, Edinburgh, UK*, volume 3869/2006 of *Lecture Notes in Computer Science*, pages 15–27. Springer, 2005.

[4] X. Huang, S. L. Oviatt, and R. Lunsford. Combining user modeling and machine learning to predict users' multimodal integration patterns. In S. Renals, S. Bengio, and J. G. Fiscus, editors, *Machine Learning for Multimodal Interaction, MLMI 2006, Bethesda, USA*, volume 4299/2006 of *LNCS*, pages 50–62. Springer, 2006.

[5] M. Lee and M. Billinghurst. A wizard of oz study for an ar multimodal interface. In *Proc. of the 10th international conference on Multimodal interfaces*, ICMI '08, pages 249–256, New York, 2008. ACM.

[6] S. Oviatt, P. Cohen, L. Wu, J. Vergo, L. Duncan, B. Suhm, J. Bers, T. Holzman, T. Winograd, J. Landay, J. Larson, and D. Ferro. Designing the user interface for multimodal speech and pen-based gesture applications: state-of-the-art systems and future research directions. *Human-Computer Interaction*, 15(4):263–322, 2000.

[7] S. Oviatt, R. Coulston, and R. Lunsford. When do we interact multimodally?: cognitive load and multimodal communication patterns. In *ICMI '04: Proc. of the 6th international conference on Multimodal interfaces*, pages 129–136, New York, 2004. ACM.

[8] S. Oviatt, R. Coulston, S. Tomko, B. Xiao, R. Lunsford, M. Wesson, and L. Carmichael. Toward a theory of organized multimodal integration patterns during human-computer interaction. In *ICMI '03: Proc. of the 5th international conference on Multimodal interfaces*, pages 44–51, New York, 2003. ACM.

[9] S. Oviatt, R. Lunsford, and R. Coulston. Individual differences in multimodal integration patterns: what are they and why do they exist? In *CHI '05: Proc. of the SIGCHI conference on Human factors in computing systems*, pages 241–249, New York, 2005. ACM.

[10] F. Schüssel, F. Honold, and M. Weber. Using the transferable belief model for multimodal input fusion in companion systems. In F. Schwenker, S. Scherer, and L.-P. Morency, editors, *Multimodal Pattern Recognition of Social Signals in HCI*, volume 7742 of *LNCS*, pages 100–115. Springer Berlin Heidelberg, 2013.

Gesture Heatmaps: Understanding Gesture Performance with Colorful Visualizations

Radu-Daniel Vatavu
University Stefan cel Mare of Suceava
Suceava 720229, Romania
vatavu@eed.usv.ro

Lisa Anthony
Department of CISE
University of Florida
Gainesville, FL 32611 USA
lanthony@cise.ufl.edu

Jacob O. Wobbrock
Information School | DUB Group
University of Washington
Seattle, WA 98195-2840 USA
wobbrock@uw.edu

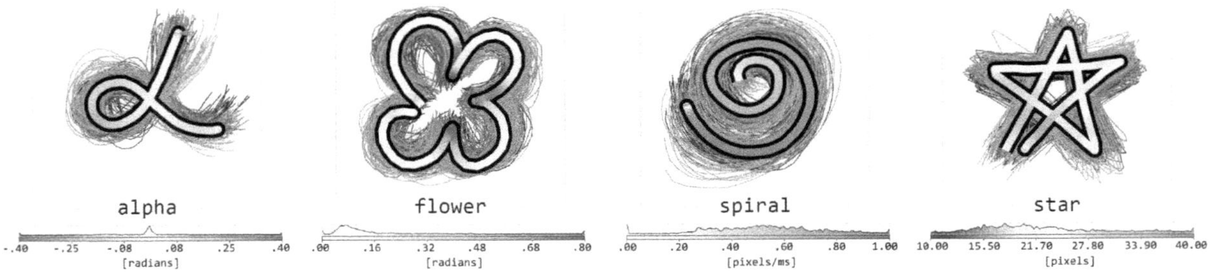

Figure 1. Gesture heatmap examples illustrating user variation during gesture articulation measured as *localized* absolute and relative turning angles ("alpha" and "flower"), articulation speed ("spiral"), and shape distance error from a template ("star"). NOTE: Heatmaps were generated with our tool, GHoST (Gesture HeatmapS Toolkit).

ABSTRACT

We introduce *gesture heatmaps*, a novel gesture analysis technique that employs color maps to visualize the variation of local features along the gesture path. Beyond current gesture analysis practices that characterize gesture articulations with single-value descriptors, *e.g.*, size, path length, or speed, gesture heatmaps are able to show with colorful visualizations how the value of any such descriptors vary along the gesture path. We evaluate gesture heatmaps on three public datasets comprising 15,840 gesture samples of 70 gesture types from 45 participants, on which we demonstrate heatmaps' capabilities to (1) explain causes for recognition errors, (2) characterize users' gesture articulation patterns under various conditions, *e.g.*, finger versus pen gestures, and (3) help understand users' subjective perceptions of gesture commands, such as why some gestures are perceived easier to execute than others. We also introduce *chromatic confusion matrices* that employ gesture heatmaps to extend the expressiveness of standard confusion matrices to better understand gesture classification performance. We believe that gesture heatmaps will prove useful to researchers and practitioners doing gesture analysis, and consequently, they will inform the design of better gesture sets and development of more accurate recognizers.

Keywords

Gesture heatmaps; features; recognition; user study; toolkits.

Categories and Subject Descriptors

H.5.2 [**Information Interfaces & Presentation**]: User Interfaces.

ICMI '14, November 12 - 16 2014, Istanbul, Turkey

ACM 978-1-4503-2885-2/14/11...$15.00.
http://dx.doi.org/10.1145/2663204.2663256.

1. INTRODUCTION

As touch-screen interfaces continue to be the dominant form of interaction with mobile devices, it is important to consider best practices for supporting smooth and accurate touch and gesture-based interfaces. One can consider the problem space in two parts: that of the best ways to support user needs, expectations, and abilities in the design of the gestures themselves [19,30,31,33], and that of the best ways to recognize gestures through the design of recognition algorithms [3,28,34]. Both components would benefit from a broader understanding of *how users actually articulate gestures*. Previous work has examined this question from several angles, such as users' consensus for multi-stroke gesture production [2], analysis of the articulation characteristics of specific user groups [14], the effect of gesture implementer on articulation [27], and explorations of how gestures vary relative to each other [29]. Several tools have been developed to enable designers to assess recognition performance and analyze users' gestures [2,5,18,29]. However, researchers and practitioners still lack adequate tools to readily visualize and explore gesture articulation patterns.

We introduce *gesture heatmaps* (see Figure 1), a novel gesture analysis technique that employs color maps to visualize the variation of local features along the gesture path. Gesture heatmaps go beyond today's gesture analysis practices that employ single-value descriptors to characterize gesture articulation, *e.g.*, size, path length, or speed [2,14,27,29,31] by providing rich visualizations of how such descriptors vary along the gesture path. We demonstrate the use of gesture heatmaps with three case studies involving public datasets comprising 15,840 samples of 70 gesture types from 45 participants. Specifically, we show how gesture heatmaps are able to (1) explain causes for recognition errors, (2) characterize users' gesture performance under various articulation conditions, *e.g.*, finger versus pen gestures, and (3) help designers understand users' subjective perceptions of gestures, such as why some gestures are perceived easier to execute than others. To this end, we also introduce new concepts, such as the *chromatic confusion matrix* that extends the standard confusion matrix with gesture heatmaps.

The contributions of this paper are: (1) the introduction of a novel gesture visualization technique, *gesture heatmaps*, that focuses on exposing variations in local features along the gesture path; (2) an exploration of gesture heatmaps with public datasets, uncovering new findings related to the relationship between users' gesture articulation patterns, recognizers' classification performance, and users' subjective perceptions about gesture commands; and (3) a tool to compute gesture heatmaps and chromatic confusion matrices, the Gesture HeatmapS Toolkit (GHoST). Our work enables a deeper understanding of users' gesture articulation patterns, which subsequently will be useful to researchers and practitioners for improving touch and gesture interaction by designing better gesture sets and more accurate gesture recognizers.

2. RELATED WORK

We review in this section techniques and tools for analyzing users' gesture articulation patterns. We also point to relevant literature employing heatmaps for visualizing scientific data.

2.1 Techniques to study gesture articulation

Understanding the way users articulate stroke gestures is essential to designing good gesture sets and developing robust recognizers. To this end, researchers have proposed several techniques and, in many cases, delivered companion toolkits to support analysis of users' gesture articulation patterns [2,14,18,27,29]. These previous techniques employed geometric and kinematic features to characterize gesture articulations [2,14,29], used gesture descriptors to group gestures into perceptually-similar classes [18,30,31], and analyzed articulation consensus across users [2,33]. For example, several tools are available to assist in designing highly-recognizable gesture sets. The Gesture Design Tool [18] informs designers about classification errors by computing and presenting distance and confusion matrices. MAGIC [5] is another tool designed to assist practitioners to record motion gestures and visualize recognition performance measures on those gestures.

Researchers have employed feature analysis to characterize users' gesture articulation patterns and to uncover particular aspects of stroke gesture input under various articulation conditions. For example, Tu et al. [27] compared finger and pen gestures using geometric and kinematic features and found that finger-drawn gestures were larger and faster than pen gestures, but similar in articulation time and proportional shape distance. Kane et al. [14] compared gesture articulations of blind and sighted users, and reported significant differences in gesture speed, size, and shape. Anthony et al. [2] analyzed user consensus for multi-stroke articulation in terms of preferred number of strokes, stroke ordering, and stroke direction, which they measured as agreement rates [33]. They reported high agreement within users (.91), lower agreement between users (.55), and pointed to several connections between gesture complexity and consensus of gesture articulation. Agreement rates can now be computed automatically with the GEsture Clustering toolKit (GECKo) [2]. Vatavu et al. [29] introduced relative accuracy measures to characterize the degree by which single and multi-stroke gesture articulations vary from templates stored in the training sets of gesture recognizers. The authors delivered the Gesture RElative Accuracy Toolkit (GREAT) that computes geometric, kinematic, and articulation relative accuracy measures [29]. The gesture recognition literature also contains many features [6,24,32] that can be used to further characterize users' gesture articulations in more depth. For example, Rubine's statistical classifier [24] employs a set of 11 geometric and kinematic features, Blagojevic et al. [6] described 114 features, and Willems et al. [32] employed the g-48 gesture set to recognize multi-strokes using SVM and MLP classifiers.

Researchers have also looked at people's perceptions about gesture commands in order to identify perceptually-similar classes [19, 22,30,31]. For example, Long et al. [19] investigated the visual similarity of pen gestures and derived a computable model for perceptual similarity using gesture features, such as curviness, that correlated R^2=.56 with user-reported similarity. Vatavu et al. [31] found that subjects were highly consistent in estimating the execution difficulty of single-stroke gestures, leading to two estimation rules based on production time that approximated absolute and relative perceived difficulty with 75% and 90% accuracy, respectively. Recently, Rekik et al. [22] extended the study to include multi-stroke gestures. Subjects were also consistent in their perception of gesture scale (*e.g.*, large versus small gestures), which is predictable with 90% accuracy using a rule based on the area size of the gesture bounding box [30].

2.2 Using heatmaps to inform design

Heatmaps are a common technique to visualize users' interactive behavior, most frequently in terms of mouse cursor movement and eye gaze [12,21], but also for touch patterns on mobile devices [16,25]. The ultimate goal of heatmap analysis in HCI is to pinpoint usability problems, to allow designers to understand their users' interaction patterns and improve their designs. For example, Huang et al. [12] showed that mouse cursor position closely relates to eye gaze, and used heatmaps of click and cursor movement positions to understand and improve the way people use search engines. Navalpakkam and Churchill [21] employed both cursor and eye gaze heatmaps in a study devoted to measuring and predicting aspects of users' web experience, such as frustration and reading struggles. Heatmaps have also been used to visualize touch patterns on mobile devices. For instance, Lettner and Holzmann [16] suggested the use of heatmaps to visualize users' touch paths on mobile devices in order to detect usability issues, *e.g.*, significantly more touches in the vicinity of a target may indicate users having problems acquiring that target from the first attempt. Schaefers et al. [25] employed heatmaps of touch points to uncover users' preferred patterns for articulating swipe gestures on mobile devices.

3. GESTURE HEATMAPS

Pseudo-coloring numerical data represents a standard information visualization technique to display scalar values in a non-numerical way [8,20]. The goal is to present the viewer with an overall image of the variation within the data and, consequently, to allow understanding of complex numerical information with the use of appropriate colors. A color map (*e.g.*, the rainbow map), is employed to compute the color of each value point in the data by means of interpolation. Color maps usually exploit perceptual cues with their selected range of colors. For example, "warm" orange and red colors usually indicate more magnitude in the data, while "cold" colors, such as green and blue, are used to encode data values with smaller magnitudes. We build on the large literature of heatmap visualization and its applications to different areas of study [8,21,23,25,26] to introduce gesture heatmaps to provide thorough characterization of users' gesture articulation patterns with the use of appropriately colored rendering of localized gesture features. In this section, we present technical details of how to construct a colorful heatmap for stroke gestures in order to render values of localized gesture features, and we discuss several color scheme choices that we believe are best suited for this goal.

3.1 Computing gesture heatmaps

We use gesture heatmaps to visualize the variation that is present during articulation of stroke gestures, such as the shape error of gesture candidates with respect to predefined templates [28,34], differences in articulation speed within and between users [29], or the amount of shape deformation that users naturally apply to the geometry of the gesture shape during articulation under various conditions [2,29]. Consequently, gesture heatmaps are computed from gesture samples captured from users, such as those used to train recognizers [3,28,34]. Let T denote such a dataset composed of gestures represented as a series of 2-D points with timestamps:

$$\{p_i = (x_i, y_i, t_i) \in \mathbb{R}^2 \times \mathbb{R}^+ \mid i = 1..n\} \quad (1)$$

We assume that all the gestures in the set have been normalized with respect to their sampling rate and their location in the plane, *i.e.*, all the gestures have the same number of points n, and were translated to origin so that their centroids are now $(0, 0)$. The gesture re-sampling step is required by the gesture task axis extraction algorithm that aligns individual points belonging to different gestures [29], as we explain further in the paper. In this work, we use n=64 sampling points to represent gestures, a value that was used in the $1 recognizer [34]. The translation-to-origin pre-processing step is required so that the geometrical features that we compute are invariant to the specific location where gestures have actually been produced on the interactive touch-screen area, *i.e.*, we make sure that the feature values we work with are translation-invariant. These two pre-processing steps are straightforward to implement, and pseudo-code for implementing them has already been made available in the gesture recognition literature [3,28,34]. Note that we do not normalize gestures with respect to scale or rotation (which are other common gesture pre-processing techniques, usually executed before gesture recognition [3,28,34]), because we want to capture the full amount of shape deformation that users naturally produce during articulation.[1]

Let f be a gesture feature defined at each point p_i of the gesture path. For example, $f(p_i)$ may be the local turning angle or the local articulation speed at point p_i. We discuss in detail the features that we use in the Case Studies section of the paper. Let $\mathcal{C}$ be a color map represented as an array of colors, $\{\mathcal{C}_i \mid i = 1..|\mathcal{C}|\}$, that we assume already sorted in ascending order in terms of users' perceptions of the relative differences between different colors [1,11,17]. Perceptual ordering of colors means that the first entries in the color map are intuitively perceived as having "less" amount of magnitude (*e.g.*, usually expressed with brightness or saturation) when compared with subsequent colors in the map. We discuss our choices for color maps in the next section. Using interpolation between consecutive colors in the array, we can create fine-resolution transitions between these colors and, consequently, we can assume that $\mathcal{C}$ contains a sufficient number of entries. Each feature value is then mapped to a color from $\mathcal{C}$ using a linear interpolation technique:

1. Normalize the value of the feature $f(p_i)$ in $[0..1]$:

$$f_{norm}(p_i) = \frac{f(p_i) - \min\limits_{i=1..n} f(p_i)}{\max\limits_{i=1..n} f(p_i) - \min\limits_{i=1..n} f(p_i)} \quad (2)$$

2. Use the normalized feature value to index the color map, $\mathcal{C}_{\lfloor f_{norm} \cdot |\mathcal{C}| \rfloor}$. For example, if the normalized feature value is .721 and the color map contains 600 distinct colors, the corresponding color will be $\mathcal{C}_{\lfloor .721 \times 600 \rfloor} = \mathcal{C}_{\lfloor 432.6 \rfloor} = \mathcal{C}_{432}$.

The colors corresponding to feature values for consecutive points p_i and p_{i+1} on the gesture path are used to render the stroke segment $[p_i p_{i+1}]$ with a linear color gradient interpolating the colors of its two extremities using arc-length as the interpolation parameter. The result is a smooth color gradient going from the first to the last point of the gesture path reflecting changes in the feature values. Please note that heatmap colors need to be rendered on top of an actual gesture shape, which would ideally be the *representative* articulation of that gesture type. The literature offers several options for selecting this representative articulation, such as using a predefined template [27] or the gesture task axis [29] in one of its forms: designer-defined, centroid of all gestures, or the sample closest to the centroid [29] (p. 282). In this work, we adopt the latter approach, and choose the shape of the gesture heatmap to be the sample from the dataset that is closest to the centroid of all gestures of the same type. Figure 2 illustrates the representative gesture shape of a set of samples with speed values mapped to colors.

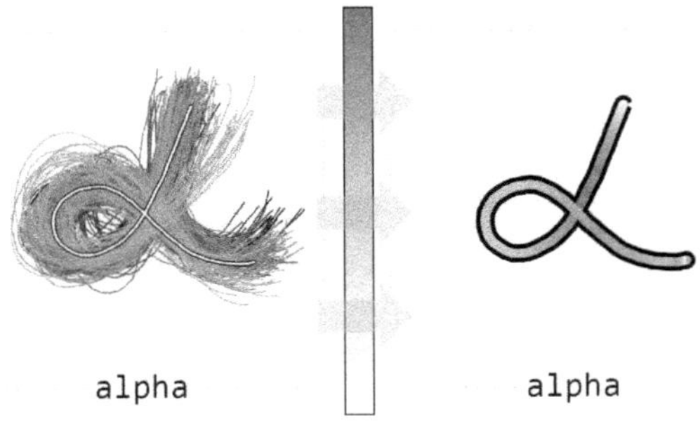

Figure 2: A representative shape of a gesture set (in yellow in the left image) is rendered with colors to highlight variation in a gesture feature (right). In this example, the heatmap shows variation in speed for the "alpha" symbol, measured from 220 samples from 11 participants [31]. Note how speed increases during the straight parts, and decreases during the loop.

3.2 Color schemes

Traditionally, heatmap visualizations have employed the *rainbow color scheme*, which has become the prevalent color map in the information visualization community [8]. At the same time, some work has shown that the pseudo-colors of the rainbow map do not represent the optimal choice to visualize data effectively [8,17,23]. For example, Borland and Taylor II [8] pointed to several usability problems for the rainbow color map, such as the lack of perceptual ordering of the colors of the light spectrum, the uncontrolled variation in luminance for these colors, and potential misleads that may occur during data interpretation. Despite these problems, the rainbow color map is still heavily used to display data in the scientific community, even by information visualization researchers [8].

Beyond rainbow colors, alternative color schemes have been proposed to better exploit people's capacity to perceive differences between hues and luminance. Moreland [20] lists criteria for good color maps, such as the ability of the heatmap to maximize perceptual resolution, to provide intuitive perception of color order, and to produce aesthetically pleasing images. One simple coloring scheme is represented by *graylevel scales* that use shades of gray to encode levels of amplitude in the data. The graylevel scale is effective because the human visual system is sensitive to changes in luminance that can be interpreted accordingly as changes in the amplitude of data values. However, brightness perception has been found to be dependent on context, such as the brightness of the surrounding area, making the same color appear differently in different contexts, which is known as the simultaneous contrast effect [26]. Moreland [20] explored *diverging color maps* that transition from one color to another by passing through an unsaturated color, such as white, and showed the advantages of these color maps compared to the rainbow color scheme. Light and Bartlein [17] suggested alternatives for the rainbow colors, such as a modified spectral color scheme, colors pro-

[1] However, depending on the purpose of the study, gestures could undergo normalization by scale and/or rotation [3,28,34].

duced by single-hue progressions (*e.g.*, from white to purplish-blue), and diverging progression between two hues (*e.g.*, from blue to gray, or the orange-white-purple diverging scheme). Finally, the ColorBrewer web site and application [1] provides hand-crafted color scheme suggestions for visualizing sequential (grayscale), diverging, and qualitative data.

Informed by the aforementioned literature, we adopted in this work the following color schemes to visualize our gesture heatmaps:

❶ Diverging color map. Two different colors are used to indicate the minimum and maximum magnitude of the values present in the data. The leftmost color of the scale, corresponding to the minimum magnitude, changes gradually into a neutral color (*e.g.*, white) positioned at the center of the scale, and then gradually turns into the second, rightmost color, corresponding to the maximum magnitude in the data. This type of double-ended color scheme is useful to visualize ratio data (*i.e.*, data that has a clear zero point), by indicating on which side of zero a given value lies. This color scheme represents our default choice for gesture heatmap visualizations of features that have values located on both sides of an explicit zero point, such as turning angle, curvature, acceleration, etc. Because diverging color maps lack a natural order of colors, it is common practice to choose extremity colors that are usually associated with low/high and cold/hot connotations [20]. Examples are red and yellow colors associated to warm and blue and green to cold, which seems to be a perception invariant across subjects and cultures [11]. We adopted one of the hand-crafted color schemes available on ColorBrewer [1] that employs blue and red diverging colors. (See Figure 1 on the first page showing local turning angles for the "alpha" symbol.)

❷ Sequential (grayscale) color map. This color map interpolates colors gradually from light to dark, with dark denoting the maximum magnitude in the data. It is our default choice for visualizing features whose values do not contain a significant midpoint, such as features represented by values that are all located on one side of the zero point. Examples from our case study features would be speed or Euclidean shape distance values that are always positive. In this case, the visualization literature recommends using a sequence of lightness steps combined with a single hue to visualize such data [17]. We used again ColorBrewer [1] to select two hand-crafted sequential schemes with green and orange hues. (See the "flower" and "spiral" gesture heatmaps of Figure 1 showing the variation in relative turning angle and articulation speed along the gesture path.)

❸ Rainbow color map. Despite being criticized in the literature [8,17,23], we decided to implement this color scheme as well due to its popularity and wide adoption even in the information visualization community [8]. Cold colors (blue and green) encode low magnitude in the data, while warm colors (orange and red) are mapped to high-magnitude values. (See the "star" gesture heatmap of Figure 1 computed to show the Euclidean shape distance.)

4. CASE STUDIES

Gesture heatmaps are general visualizers of any feature that is ultimately the designer's choice. Here we illustrate the use of gesture heatmaps with three case studies that cover important aspects of gesture interaction design: (1) we reveal causes of erroneous classification by using gesture heatmaps to visualize the gesture articulation shape distance used by the $1 gesture recognizer [34]; (2) we show how gesture heatmaps can be used to understand people's subjective perceptions about gesture commands by visualizing the articulation speed for the execution difficulty datasets [31]; (3) we employ gesture heatmaps to characterize users' gesture articulation differences between finger and pen gestures on the MMG multistroke gesture dataset [3,4]. Overall, we provide results from 15,840 gesture samples of 70 gesture types from 45 participants.

4.1 Understanding gesture recognition errors

We show in the following how gesture heatmaps can point to causes leading to recognition errors that cannot otherwise be revealed with today's standard measures for assessing recognition performance, such as error rates and confusion matrices. Being highly visual in nature, gesture heatmaps highlight "hot" parts of a gesture shape that exhibit high variance, helping practitioners to optimize their gesture shapes and maximize recognition performance. For this case study, we employ the dataset of Wobbrock et al. [34] on which the performance of the $1 gesture recognizer was evaluated[2]. We only report results for the subset of gestures articulated at fast speed, as they had the highest rate of recognition errors [34] (p. 165). This dataset is composed of 1,600 samples of 16 distinct gesture types articulated by 10 participants for 10 times each.

The performance of a gesture recognizer is evaluated today using accuracy or error rates [3,18,24,28,34]. High recognition accuracy (and, implicitly, low recognition errors) signal a high-performing gesture recognizer. These measures are useful to understand recognition performance overall and to compare recognition performance between experimental conditions, *e.g.*, the $1 recognizer was found 7% more accurate than Rubine's recognizer, and equally accurate as the Dynamic Time Warping cost function [34] (p. 165). To find out more about recognition performance, practitioners can compute recognition rates per gesture type that indicate poorly-recognized gestures, *e.g.*, see the performance of the "circle" and "question mark" symbols in Figure 3 with 75% and 92% recognition rates[3], significantly lower than the performance of the other gesture types ($\chi^2(15)=196.184$, $p<.01$). Practitioners can also resort to confusion matrices that characterize error rates in more depth by showing how often one gesture type is misrecognized for another. For example, Figure 4 reveals that the 8% error rate of "question mark" is mostly caused by the "right square bracket" and "right curly brace" symbols. Long et al. [18] showed that practitioners can successfully employ these numbers to select highly-recognizable gestures for their applications. However, numbers only are not informative enough to explain the *cause* of recognition errors. Recognition percentages are valuable means to sum up the level of performance,

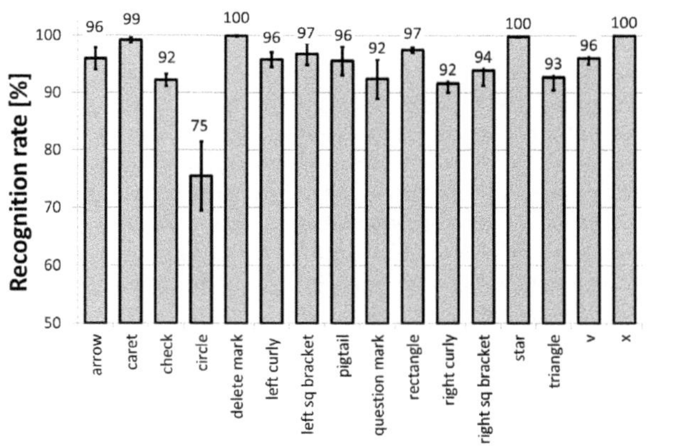

Figure 3: User-independent recognition rates for the gestures of the $1 dataset computed with $1's Euclidean cost function [34].

[2] http://depts.washington.edu/aimgroup/proj/dollar/

[3] We compute and report average recognition rates for the Euclidean cost function and the Nearest-Neighbor classification technique (*i.e.*, the $1 recognizer) in the user-independent scenario using the methodology from [28] (p. 275). We vary the number of training participants P and training samples per gesture type T in a geometric progression from 1 to 8 (*i.e.*, $P = 1, 2, 4, 8$, and $T = 1, 2, 4, 8$). All gestures were re-sampled to n=64 points, uniformly scaled, and translated to origin, as in [3,28,34].

	↗	∧	✓	○	X	{	[	ℓ	?	□	}	]	☆	△	V	X
↗	.96	.01	.00	.00	.00	.00	.00	.02	.00	.00	.00	.00	.01	.00	.00	.00
∧	.00	.99	.00	.00	.00	.00	.00	.00	.01	.00	.00	.00	.00	.00	.00	.00
✓	.00	.00	.92	.00	.00	.00	.00	.00	.00	.00	.00	.00	.00	.00	.08	.00
○	.00	.00	.00	.75	.00	.00	.01	.00	.00	[illegible]	.00	.00	.00	.13	.01	.00
X	.00	.00	.00	.00	1.00	.00	.00	.00	.00	.00	.00	.00	.00	.00	.00	.00
{	.00	.00	.00	.00	.00	.96	.03	.00	.00	.00	.01	.00	.00	.00	.00	.00
[	.00	.00	.00	.00	.00	.03	.97	.00	.00	.00	.00	.00	.00	.00	.00	.00
ℓ	.02	.02	.00	.00	.00	.00	.00	.96	.00	.00	.00	.00	.00	.00	.00	.00
?	.00	.01	.01	.00	.00	.00	.00	.00	.92	.00	.02	.03	.00	.00	.00	.00
□	.00	.00	.00	.02	.00	.00	.00	.00	.00	.97	.00	.00	.00	.00	.00	.00
}	.00	.00	.00	.00	.00	.01	.00	.00	.01	.00	.92	.06	.00	.00	.00	.00
]	.00	.00	.00	.00	.00	.00	.00	.00	.02	.00	.04	.94	.00	.00	.00	.00
☆	.00	.00	.00	.00	.00	.00	.00	.00	.00	.00	.00	.00	1.00	.00	.00	.00
△	.00	.00	.00	.07	.00	.00	.00	.00	.00	.00	.00	.00	.00	.93	.00	.00
V	.00	.00	.04	.00	.00	.00	.00	.00	.00	.00	.00	.00	.00	.00	.96	.00
X	.00	.00	.00	.00	.00	.00	.00	.00	.00	.00	.00	.00	.00	.00	.00	1.00

Figure 4: Standard confusion matrix (user-independent) for the $1 gesture set and $1's Euclidean cost function [34].

but they cannot tell us why a recognizer has troubles with a certain gesture. Knowing more about the *why* of recognition errors will help us to more intelligently design gesture sets and choose recognizers not likely to encounter the same types of recognition errors. Next, we show how gesture heatmaps uncover causes of recognition errors, while we introduce the chromatic confusion matrix.

The $1 recognizer computes the sum of Euclidean distances between points to discriminate between gesture types [34] (p. 162). This cost function can also be interpreted as a feature, *i.e.*, the relative shape error between candidate p and template q [29] (p. 280):

$$ShE(p,q) = \sum_{i=1}^{n} \|p_i - q_i\| \quad (3)$$

Because shape error is computed at each point on the gesture path, we can visualize it using gesture heatmaps for which the color of each point is in direct correspondence with the shape error between the two gestures at that point precisely. We generated heatmaps for all the gesture types in the $1 dataset and arranged them in the form of a confusion matrix so that heatmap colors reflect the amount of shape error between a candidate and a template; see Figure 5. The candidate shown for each gesture type is actually the user-independent gesture task axis of Vatavu et al. [29], computed from all the samples available in the set for that gesture type (in our case, 100 articulations = 10 participants × 10 executions).

Note how gesture heatmaps provide more information than the standard confusion matrix about the cause of recognition errors. For instance, the diagonal of the chromatic matrix shows candidates compared to gestures of the same type for which shape errors are low (an expected result) and, therefore, all color hues are mostly blue. However, color intensity increases toward "hot" hues, such as orange and red, for those gesture parts of the candidate that are most dissimilar from their corresponding parts on the template, and decrease toward "cold" green and blue hues for similar gesture parts. For instance, the cause of the "question mark" symbol being misrecognized as right curly and square braces appears more clear now: the shape of the question mark superimposes almost perfectly on the shapes of these other gestures, which causes low shape error values between their corresponding points, shown by the high proportion of blue segments in that pairing. The same can be said for other gesture pairs, such as "circle" and "triangle", left and right "curly braces", "curly braces" and "square brackets", "v" and "check", etc. Shape errors are low for these gesture types because they follow the same articulation direction (*e.g.*, going from top to bottom for braces, brackets, and the question mark), while their specific shape characteristics (*e.g.*, the upper curl of the question mark or the middle curly point of the curly braces) are sometimes overtaken in magnitude by the variation induced by different users articulating these shapes (which can be seen in the background gestures shown for each candidate heatmap). On the other hand, we can easily identify the most dissimilar gestures in the set, such as "delete mark", "star", or x", that present large shape errors for almost all their parts (reflected with orange and red hues).

When we know the features that might impact the performance of a recognizer, such as shape error being critical to the way $1 recognizes gestures, gesture heatmaps enable us to visually compare those features quickly for candidate gesture sets, and re-design the shape of gesture pairs which will be too similar for this recognizer. For example, once practitioners have identified the causes leading to recognition errors, they can proceed to rectify these causes, without necessarily having to remove a particular gesture from the set [18]. For example, the articulation direction of the "circle" can be reversed so that it won't conflict any longer with that of the "triangle", knowing (and seeing now concretely) that the $1 recognizer matches points in their order of input. Also, the shape design of the curly braces can specifically include a more pointed curl, which will slightly shift the centroid of these shapes toward the left, increasing therefore the shape error with respect to the "question mark" and "right square bracket" symbols. The same approach could be adopted for the second part of the "check" symbol, making it even longer to better disambiguate it from the "v" shape. Such changes acting only on some parts of the gesture shape can improve recognition accuracy, without removing that gesture from the set, as was the only option with previous approaches [18].

4.2 User perception of execution difficulty

We next show how gesture heatmaps are valuable in uncovering connections between objective articulation performance (*e.g.*, execution speed), and people's subjective perceptions about the gestures they articulate, usually collected as Likert ratings [31,33]. Prior work by Vatavu et al. [31] found that people's perceptions about the execution difficulty of stroke gestures can be reliably estimated using kinematic measurements on the gesture path. The authors reported 96% positive correlation between perceived difficulty and articulation time, and 87% negative correlation with articulation speed. The longer it takes people to articulate a gesture shape or the slower they are during articulation, the more likely people will rate that shape as more difficult to produce. However, there is no explanation in that work of the causes of these high correlations. In the following, we point to possible explanations for this phenomenon by visualizing articulation speed values[4] for the gesture types used in the execution difficulty work. There are two gesture datasets reported in [31] composed of 5,040 and 4,400 samples of 38 distinct gesture types collected from 25 participants with 20 executions each[5]. We employ one dataset to derive possible causes for the difficulty perception phenomenon, which we validate on the gestures belonging to the second set.

Figure 6 shows gesture heatmaps generated for localized articulation speed measured at each point p_i as the ratio of the path length

[4] We focus on the articulation speed because time heatmaps are not interesting for this analysis, as time increases monotonically along the gesture path. However, local speed values change according to the gesture shape.

[5] http://www.eed.usv.ro/~vatavu/index.php?menuItem=downloads

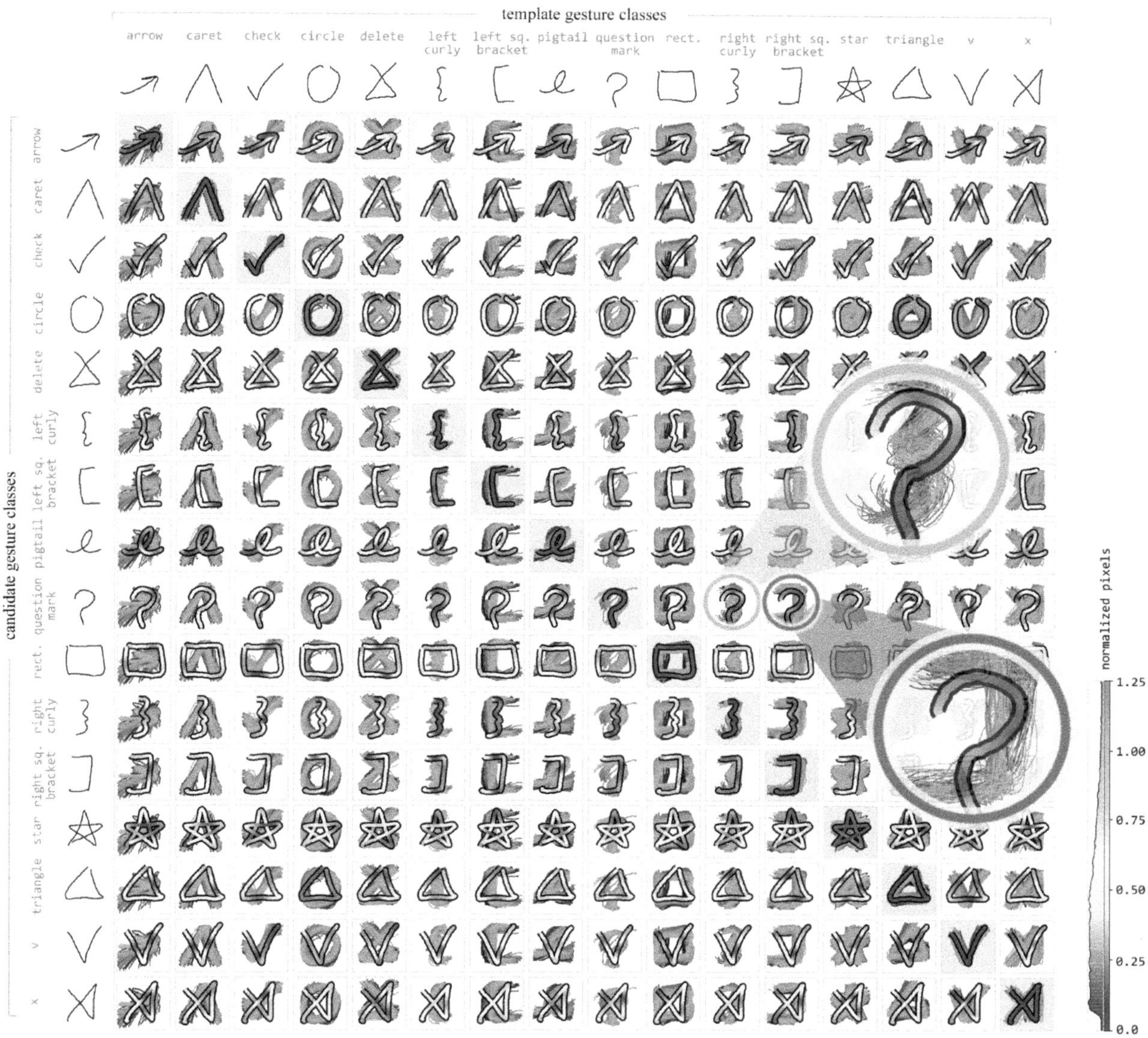

Figure 5: Gesture heatmaps for the 16 gestures of the $1 dataset [34] showing the Shape Error [29,34] between candidates and templates in the form of a *chromatic confusion matrix*. NOTES: Cold colors (*e.g.*, blue and green) show small shape errors between candidates and templates, which may cause recognition errors. The matrix was generated with our toolkit, GHoST, in the user-independent scenario. The scale shows values in normalized pixel values (*i.e.*, all gestures were scaled down to [0,1]×[0,1]).

between points p_{i-1} and p_{i+1} and the corresponding time duration:

$$s_i = \frac{\|p_{i-1} - p_i\| + \|p_i - p_{i+1}\|}{t_{i+1} - t_{i-1}} \tag{4}$$

Each gesture has a ranking number showing its position in the list of all gestures in ascending order by perceived execution difficulty. These rankings are median values computed from the ratings collected from participants [31] (p. 96). Note how our speed gesture heatmaps actually show with colors the bell-shaped velocity profiles observed in motor control studies [10], with speed increasing along the stroke path until it reaches its midpoint, after which speed starts to decrease. Please note however that motor control theory's definition of a "stroke" is different from that commonly accepted in HCI as the path between two consecutive touch-down and touch-up events (see also [13]). For example, the "strike" gesture (index 16, Figure 6, left), although being a unistroke, is actually decomposable into six distinct ballistic movements, according to models in motor control theory. Looking at the heatmaps of the first dataset (Figure 6, left) we see that shapes with few such fundamental movements are rated less difficult to execute, such as "circle" (one ballistic movement), digit "3" (two movements), "6" (one movement), letter "m" (three movements), "sail" (four movements), and so on. The heatmaps of these gestures use hot orange and red colors showing fast articulation speeds. As the gesture shape becomes more complex with more turning points, relative articulation speed decreases as our gesture heatmaps correctly reflect with brighter colors. When we look at the gestures of the second dataset (Figure 6), we see that these observations hold true: complex trajectories that need to be articulated with more ballistic strokes are shown in brighter colors corresponding to slower relative speeds, as users have to continuously accelerate and decelerate along the gesture path. These speed patterns may be one reason why people perceive these gestures as more difficult to execute. For example, the "spiral" shape (index 8, Figure 6, right) allows continuous acceleration, while the "star" requires five decelerations along its path.

Figure 6: Gesture heatmaps showing articulation speed values for the two execution difficulty datasets of Vatavu et al. [31]. NOTES: Brighter colors show slow speeds, which correlated negatively with perceived difficulty [31], and thus indicate gesture parts that make gestures difficult to articulate. Numbers in the top-left corner show gesture ranking in ascending order of perceived difficulty.

We believe these observations are useful to explain, at least partially, the complexity of the difficulty perception phenomenon reported in [31]. While we do not provide the decisive answer to this question in this work (nor is it our goal) because of the complexity of this phenomenon (*e.g.*, the effect of practice, familiarity, writer speed, etc.), we believe we open new paths toward new gesture discoveries. For example, we think that gesture heatmaps may be used to spot ballistic strokes, which we believe to be in connection with Isokoski's approach for measuring geometric complexity [13], hopefully leading to advances in assessing gesture complexity. Also, ballistic movements could lead to a more suitable segmentation of a gesture shape into primitives, which may be used to increase the performance of the Curves Lines Corners (CLC) model [9] for estimating gesture production time by considering actual user-generated interruptions in the gesture path instead of decomposition of that path into standard geometric primitives. While we only point at these fruitful lines of work, we are eager to see how researchers will use our gesture heatmaps to explain more subtle connections between user perception and gesture articulation.

4.3 Finger versus stylus gestures

We next show how gesture heatmaps can reveal more discoveries about users' gesture articulation patterns and how these discoveries connect to previous work, as we look at the effect of gesture implementer (*i.e.*, finger or stylus) on articulation. Previous work [27] found that gesture implementer has no influence on the values of the proportional shape distance for single-stroke gestures. Another study [4] found recognition differences between multi-stroke gestures articulated with a finger versus a stylus, *i.e.*, higher recognition accuracy with the $N recognizer was seen on gestures made with a finger. Because recognizers like $1, $N, and $P [3,4,28,34] employ the shape distance as the recognizer cost function, variations in this feature have the potential to impact recognition accuracy significantly. Therefore, in this case study, we use Shape Error gesture heatmaps (eq. 3) to understand more about the articulation differences caused when employing the finger versus the stylus. We employ the MMG dataset [4] composed of 9,600 samples of 16 distinct multi-stroke gestures collected from 20 participants using either the finger or the stylus[6]. Because gestures in this set vary in terms of stroke ordering and stroke direction [4,29], we computed Shape Error with the $P alignment technique that minimizes the sum of Euclidean distances between pairs of points [28].

[6]https://depts.washington.edu/aimgroup/proj/dollar/ndollar.html

Gesture heatmaps showed in Figure 7 indicate differences in the accuracy (in terms of Shape Error) at which users produce gestures with the finger versus the pen. For example, finger articulation of "D" and "P" show the most concentrated regions of high shape error (Figure 7, left, orange and red), while the articulations of the same shapes using the stylus are displayed in green and yellow, indicating much lower shape error with this implementer. In contrast, "H" and "N" articulated by a stylus show the highest shape errors, but again do not exhibit high shape error when articulated by the finger. These gesture types are also among the most highly-confused pairs by the $N-Protractor recognizer [4] (p. 120). Mann-Whitney U tests confirmed significant differences (at $p<.01$) between the mean Shape Errors for 12 out of all 16 gesture types (exceptions were "arrowhead", "asterisk", "five point star", and "X").

Beyond pointing to overall differences between articulations (*e.g.*, there is more shape error when articulating "P" with the finger than the pen), gesture heatmaps can also point to localized "hot" spots on the gesture shape that exhibit large shape errors. For example, strokes' start and end points are shown with more intense colors, *e.g.*, see "arrowhead", "line", "I", "asterisk", etc., showing that large shape errors occur frequently at these locations. This observation connects to the concern in the sketching community to remove hooks that occur at the end of strokes (caused by users lifting the stylus off of the surface) in order to increase recognition accuracy of sketch input [15] (p. 11). This finding may inform the designer to replace a multi-stroke gesture with the single-stroke equivalent where applicable, *e.g.*, "N" can be articulated with three strokes (as it was in the MMG set), but also as a single-stroke. We believe that "hot" point scrutiny will help practitioners understand better how users articulate gestures, and thus, improve their gesture set designs.

5. CONCLUSION

We introduced in this work gesture heatmaps as a practical visualization technique to aid researchers during gesture analysis. To this end, we release the Gesture HeatmapS Toolkit (GHoST) as open source software[7] that computes heatmap visualizations for both user-dependent and independent scenarios, and exports results as `.csv` and `.bmp` files. Future work will explore animations and motion features [7] for stroke gestures. It is one of the goals of this work to encourage researchers to explore gesture heatmaps in order to uncover new findings about users' gesture articulation behavior, to design better gesture sets, and to develop more accurate recognizers.

[7]http://depts.washington.edu/aimgroup/proj/dollar/ghost.html

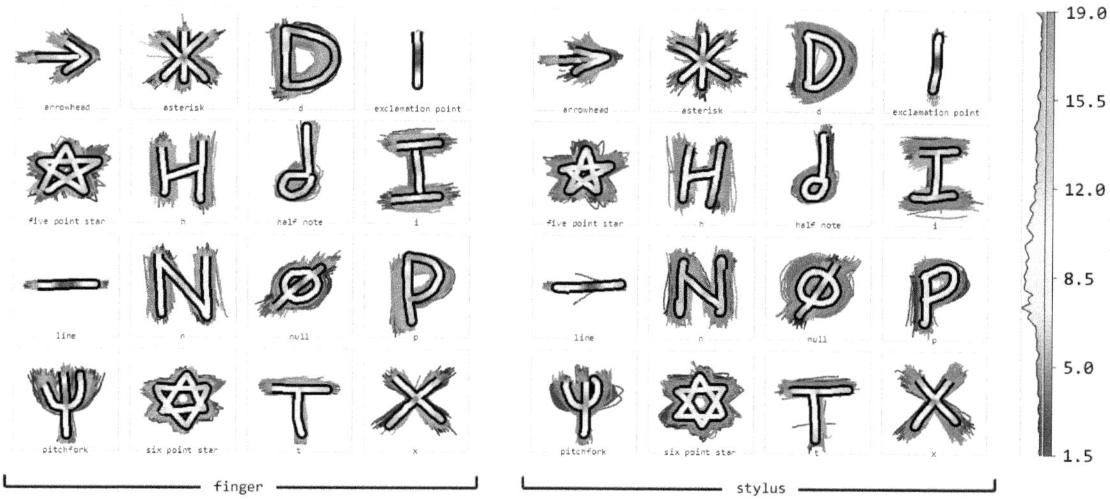

Figure 7: Shape error heatmaps for gestures articulated with the finger and the stylus [3,4]. Note how gesture heatmaps point to localized "hot" spots on the gesture shape that exhibit large shape errors, such as strokes' start and end points (orange and red).

6. REFERENCES

[1] ColorBrewer: Color advice for maps. http://colorbrewer2.org/.

[2] Anthony, L., Vatavu, R.-D., and Wobbrock, J. O. Understanding the consistency of users' pen and finger stroke gesture articulation. In *GI'13* (2013), 87–94.

[3] Anthony, L., and Wobbrock, J. O. A lightweight multistroke recognizer for user interface prototypes. In *GI'10* (2010), 245–252.

[4] Anthony, L., and Wobbrock, J. O. $N-Protractor: A fast and accurate multistroke recognizer. In *GI'12* (2012), 117–120.

[5] Ashbrook, D., and Starner, T. MAGIC: A motion gesture design tool. In *CHI '10*, ACM (2010), 2159–2168.

[6] Blagojevic, R., Chang, S. H.-H., and Plimmer, B. The power of automatic feature selection: Rubine on steroids. In *SBIM'10*, Eurographics Association (2010), 79–86.

[7] Bobick, A. F., and Davis, J. W. The recognition of human movement using temporal templates. *IEEE TPAMI 23*, 3 (March 2001), 257–267.

[8] Borland, D., and Taylor II, R. M. Rainbow color map (still) considered harmful. *IEEE CGA 27*, 2 (March 2007), 14–17.

[9] Cao, X., and Zhai, S. Modeling human performance of pen stroke gestures. In *CHI '07*, ACM (2007), 1495–1504.

[10] Djioua, M., and Plamondon, R. Studying the variability of handwriting patterns using the kinematic theory. *Hum Mov Sci. 28*, 5 (2009), 588–601.

[11] Hardin, C., and Maffi, L. (Eds.) *Color Categories in Thought and Language*. Cambridge University Press, 1997.

[12] Huang, J., White, R. W., and Dumais, S. No clicks, no problem: Using cursor movements to understand and improve search. In *CHI '11*, ACM (2011), 1225–1234.

[13] Isokoski, P. Model for unistroke writing time. In *CHI '01*, ACM (2001), 357–364.

[14] Kane, S. K., Wobbrock, J. O., and Ladner, R. E. Usable gestures for blind people: understanding preference and performance. In *CHI '11*, ACM (2011), 413–422.

[15] LaViola, Jr., J. J. Sketching and gestures 101. In *ACM SIGGRAPH 2006 Courses*, SIGGRAPH '06, ACM (2006).

[16] Lettner, F., and Holzmann, C. Heat maps as a usability tool for multi-touch interaction in mobile applications. In *MUM '12*, ACM (2012), 49:1–49:2.

[17] Light, A., and Bartlein, P. J. The end of the rainbow? color schemes for improved data graphics. *EOS Transactions of the American Geophysical Union 85*, 40 (2004), 385–391.

[18] Long, Jr., A. C., Landay, J. A., and Rowe, L. A. Implications for a gesture design tool. In *CHI '99*, ACM (1999), 40–47.

[19] Long, Jr., A. C., Landay, J. A., Rowe, L. A., and Michiels, J. Visual similarity of pen gestures. In *CHI '00* (2000), 360–367.

[20] Moreland, K. Diverging color maps for scientific visualization. In *ISVC '09*, Springer (2009), 92–103.

[21] Navalpakkam, V., and Churchill, E. Mouse tracking: Measuring and predicting users' experience of web-based content. In *CHI '12*, ACM (2012), 2963–2972.

[22] Rekik, Y., Vatavu, R.-D., and Grisoni, L. Understanding users' perceived difficulty of multi-touch gesture articulation. In *ICMI '12*, ACM (2014).

[23] Rogowitz, B. E., and Treinish, L. A. Data visualization: The end of the rainbow. *IEEE Spectr. 35*, 12 (Dec. 1998), 52–59.

[24] Rubine, D. Specifying gestures by example. *SIGGRAPH Comput. Graph. 25*, 4 (July 1991), 329–337.

[25] Schaefers, K., Ribeiro, D., and de Barros, A. C. Beyond heat maps: Mining common swipe gestures. In *MUM'13* (2013).

[26] Stone, M. Representing colors as three numbers. *IEEE Comp. Graph. Appl. 25*, 4 (2005), 78–85.

[27] Tu, H., Ren, X., and Zhai, S. A comparative evaluation of finger and pen stroke gestures. In *CHI '12*, ACM (2012), 1287–1296.

[28] Vatavu, R.-D., Anthony, L., and Wobbrock, J. O. Gestures as point clouds: A $P recognizer for user interface prototypes. In *ICMI '12*, ACM (2012), 273–280.

[29] Vatavu, R.-D., Anthony, L., and Wobbrock, J. O. Relative accuracy measures for stroke gestures. In *ICMI'13*, ACM (2013), 279–286.

[30] Vatavu, R.-D., Casiez, G., and Grisoni, L. Small, medium, or large?: Estimating the user-perceived scale of stroke gestures. In *CHI '13*, ACM (2013), 277–280.

[31] Vatavu, R.-D., Vogel, D., Casiez, G., and Grisoni, L. Estimating the perceived difficulty of pen gestures. In *INTERACT'11*, Springer (2011), 89–106.

[32] Willems, D., Niels, R., van Gerven, M., and Vuurpijl, L. Iconic and multi-stroke gesture recognition. *Pattern Recognition 42*, 12 (2009), 3303–3312.

[33] Wobbrock, J. O., Morris, M. R., and Wilson, A. D. User-defined gestures for surface computing. In *CHI '09*, ACM (2009), 1083–1092.

[34] Wobbrock, J. O., Wilson, A. D., and Li, Y. Gestures without libraries, toolkits or training: A $1 recognizer for user interface prototypes. In *UIST '07*, ACM (2007), 159–168.

Personal Aesthetics for Soft Biometrics: a Generative Multi-resolution Approach

Cristina Segalin
Dept. of Computer Science
University of Verona, Italy
cristina.segalin@univr.it

Alessandro Perina
Dept. of Pattern Analysis and Computer Vision (PAVIS)
Istituto Italiano di Tecnologia(IIT), Italy
alessandro.perina@iit.it

Marco Cristani
Dept. of Computer Science
University of Verona, Italy
marco.cristani@univr.it

ABSTRACT

Are we recognizable by our image preferences? This paper answers affirmatively the question, presenting a soft biometric approach where the preferred images of an individual are used as his personal signature in identification tasks. The approach builds a multi-resolution latent space, formed by multiple Counting Grids, where similar images are mapped nearby. On this space, a set of preferred images of a user produces an ensemble of intensity maps, highlighting in an intuitive way his personal aesthetic preferences. These maps are then used for learning a battery of discriminative classifiers (one for each resolution), which characterizes the user and serves to perform identification. Results are promising: on a dataset of 200 users, and 40K images, using 20 preferred images as biometric template gives 66% of probability of guessing the correct user. This makes the "personal aesthetics" a very hot topic for soft biometrics, while its usage in standard biometric applications seems to be far from being effective, as we show in a simple user study.

Categories and Subject Descriptors

K.6.5 [**Computing Milieux**]: Security and Protection—*authentication, unauthorized access*; I.5.4 [**Computing methodologies**]: Pattern Recognition—*pattern analysis*

Keywords

Soft biometrics; computational aesthetics; Counting Grid

1. INTRODUCTION

Soft biometric traits are human characteristics that provide some information about the identity of an individual, that differ from standard biometric patterns since they are not intrusive and do not require explicit cooperation for their extraction - they can be fully imperceptible [2].

Soft biometrics can be divided into *physical/physyiological* (age, gender, ethnicity, height, EEG signals etc.) and *behavioral* biometrics, that is, encoding a characteristic linked to the behavior of a person [9]. This last class can be further partitioned into *authorship-based* (linked to style peculiarities of the individual - how she/he writes a book), *motor skill-based* (how a person performs a particular physical task), *purely behavioral* (how a person solves a mentally demanding task) and *HCI-based biometrics* [24].

HCI-based biometrics are based on the idea that every person has a unique way to interact with a personal computer. For example, some methods investigated the possibility of identifying a person considering mouse or keystrokes dynamics [17, 19]; some other approaches focused on how people use Internet, like chatting [18] or browsing histories [14].

Very recently, a brand-new HCI-based biometric trait emerged, exploiting the "personal aesthetics" of people, that is, those image preferences that distinguish people from each other [9]. The approach assumes that, given a set of preferred images, it is possible to extract a set of features individuating discriminative visual patterns; these patterns can be used as biometric template, and employed for identification.

The motivations of why focusing on pictures to encode the identity of an individual are many: from one side, taking pictures is the action most commonly performed with mobile phones (82% of the users from USA), followed by exchanging text messages (80% of the users) and accessing the Internet (56% of the users) [4]. Furthermore, 56% of the American Internet users either post online original pictures and videos (46% of the total Internet users) or share and redistribute similar material posted by others (41% of the total Internet users). In this scenario, the use of the *liking* mechanisms, that is, online actions allowing users to publicly express preference for a given picture, has become pervasive and massive, becoming a social mass phenomenon [20]. On the other side, psychology and neuroscience have investigated the role of personal characteristics on aesthetic preferences [8], finding that there are remarkable ties between aesthetic appreciation and personality [6]. This latter, being a stable characteristic of humans, ensures that personal aesthetics are somewhat *permanent*, a desirable property for soft biometric traits [2].

In this paper, this novel promising direction is followed, proposing a generative embedding approach for managing the personal aesthetics soft biometrics. The general assumptions of the approach are that, for a given set of users, we have a pool of images preferred by each one of them; we

ICMI'14, November 12–16, 2014, Istanbul, Turkey.
Copyright 2014 ACM 978-1-4503-2885-2/14/11 ...$15.00.
http://dx.doi.org/10.1145/2663204.2663259 .

also suppose that these images have been chosen from a potentially infinite set of images and that the amount of liked images shared by more than a user is minimal. These assumptions are crucial for the effectiveness of the approach, but reasonable, as we will see in the following.

The approach consists in an initialization stage, followed by the enrollment stage and finally the identification stage. In the initialization stage, a low-dimensional multi-resolution latent space is learned, consisting of a set of Counting Grids (CGs) [16]: each CG is a 2D space (a flattened torus), where visually similar pictures are mapped nearby; each CG is characterized by a particular resolution, that in rough words models how much visually similar should be the images in order to be close on the grid. Having multiple resolutions means to evaluate differently grained similarity relations among images.

In the enrollment stage, a collection of preferred pictures of an individual in the gallery set is mapped into the multi-resolution CG, resulting in an ensemble of *embedding* maps, one for each resolution. These embedding maps are then fed into discriminative classifiers: in particular, for each resolution grain (that is, for each embedding map) a classifier is instantiated, learned in one-VS-all modality.

In the identification stage, test images (one, or more than one) are projected into the CGs, forming another set of embedding maps which are then classified, producing a joint prediction; this last is used to provide the identity of the user. Please note that the approach allows to use a varying number of images both for the enrollment and the identification stage, providing a flexible soft-biometrics mechanism.

The proposed approach is very expressive: it allows to understand "visually" the kind of images liked by a user, and how such images distinguish him from other persons, in a very compact and economic way, using directly the CGs. This overcomes one of the limitations of [9], where the images are treated directly in the original feature space, and analyzed through LASSO regression as classifier; in the case of high number of features, this would lead to overfitting issues. As second, methodological contribution, an intrinsic limitation of Counting Grids has been circumvented, that is, their model selection (how to select a particular resolution [16]). This problem has been faced by considering various CG resolutions, capturing the diverse mappings they generate; this results in a multi-resolution image analysis, which has proven to be better than focusing on a single resolution. More importantly, the CG modeling allows to get impressive identification performances, definitely beating the state of the art. Comparative tests have been performed on the only real dataset currently available in the literature [9], composed by 40000 images which belong to 200 users chosen at random from the Flickr community. For each user, 200 preferred images (his "favorites") have been retained.

As identification performance, using 20 preferred test images as biometric signature gives 66% of probability of guessing the correct user (state of the art was 25%), promoting personal aesthetics as a promising soft biometric modality, with performances quite close to what one can expect from a classic biometric signature. Anyway, the assumption of having an infinite number of images that the user can select from (that is, the entire Flickr repository) is an essential hypothesis for making our approach effective; in order to demonstrate this fact, we set up a user study which analyzes a random subset of users; each user is asked to select a number of preferred images from a finite pool of available test images, as it could happen in a standard biometric approach where the user has to select a signature from a finite number of alternatives (a password). In this case, the available aesthetical variability diminishes dramatically, and as a consequence, identification performances drop.

Summarizing, the contributions of this work are

- a novel approach for personal aesthetics, which is a very recent soft biometric trait;
- a novel methodology for Counting Grids modeling, solving the problem of the model selection;
- new state of the art and impressive results, doubling in some cases the state of the art performances;
- a critical study of the limitations of the personal aesthetics.

The rest of the paper is organized as follows: in Sec. 2 a summarization of the Counting Grid generative model is reported; in Sec. 3 the proposed approach is detailed, explaining how it can be customized for the identification tasks. The approach is thoroughly tested in Sec. 4, and, finally, conclusions are given and future perspectives are envisaged in Sec. 5.

2. MATHEMATICAL BACKGROUND: THE COUNTING GRID MODEL

The Counting Grid (CG) is a recent generative model [16] aimed at analyzing image collections. It assumes that images are i.i.d. random variables represented as histograms (or bags-of-features) $\{c_z\}_{z=1,\dots,Z}$, where each c_z is a counting variable which enumerates the occurrences of the z−th feature.

In its two-dimensional version[1], a CG π is a 2D finite discrete grid (a flattened torus), spatially indexed by $\mathbf{i} = (x, y) \in [1 \dots E] \times [1 \dots E]$, and containing normalized counts of features $\{\pi_{\mathbf{i},z}\}$, indexed by $z = 1, \dots, Z$. Therefore, $\sum_z \pi_{\mathbf{i},z} = 1$ for every $\mathbf{i}$ on the grid. Under this model, an image (i.e. its BoF $\{c_z\}$) is generated by selecting a certain location $\mathbf{k}$, calculating the distribution $h_{\mathbf{k},z} = \frac{1}{S^2} \sum_{\mathbf{i} \in W_{\mathbf{k}}} \pi_{\mathbf{i},z}$ by averaging all the words counts within the window $W_{\mathbf{k}}$ (of dimensions $S \times S$ and such that $\mathbf{k}$ is its upper left corner) and then drawing features counts from this distribution. In practice, a small window is located in the grid, averaging the feature counts within it to obtain a local probability mass function over the features, and then generating from it an appropriate number of features in the bag $\{c_z\}$. In other words, unlike a straightforward embedding (e.g. PCA) that links an image with a point location, the CG forces the image to link with a small window of locations. Simply speaking, a CG could be think as a mixture model, where the components are overlapping windows indexed by $\mathbf{k}$.

This said, it appears clear that the position of the window $\mathbf{k}$ in the grid is a latent variable; given $\mathbf{k}$, the likelihood of $\{c_z\}$ is

$$p(\{c_z\}|\mathbf{k}) = \prod_z (h_{\mathbf{k},z})^{c_z} = \frac{1}{S^2} \prod_z \Big(\sum_{\mathbf{i} \in W_{\mathbf{k}}} \pi_{\mathbf{i},z} \Big)^{c_z}. \quad (1)$$

[1] N-dimensional in general, here we focus on 2 dimensions.

Given that the size $E \times E$ of a Counting Grid is usually small compared to the number of images, this also forces windows linked to different images to overlap, and to co-exist by finding a shared compromise in the feature counts located in their intersection. The overall effect of these constraints is to produce locally smooth transitions between strongly different feature counts by gradually phasing features in/out in the intermediate locations. In practice, local neighborhoods in the grid represent similar concepts and images mapped in close locations are somehow similar.

To learn a Counting Grid, the likelihood over all training images T needs to be maximized, and this can be written as

$$p(\{\{c_z^t\}, \mathbf{k}^t\}_{t=1}^T) \propto \prod_{t=1}^{T} \prod_{z=1}^{Z} \Big(\sum_{\mathbf{i} \in W_{\mathbf{k}^t}} \pi_{\mathbf{i},z} \Big)^{c_z^t}. \quad (2)$$

The sum over $\mathbf{k}$ makes it difficult to perform assignment to the latent variables (i.e., the components of the mixture) and so to estimate the model parameters; this is the same that happen with mixtures of Gaussians, hidden Markov models etc.; therefore, it is necessary to employ an EM algorithm. The procedure is a bit complicated and involves different variational distributions; for this study it is only necessary to quote the posterior distribution, calculated in the E step,

$$p(\mathbf{k}^t | \{c_z^t\}) = q_{\mathbf{k}}^t \propto \exp \sum_z c_z^t \cdot \log h_{\mathbf{k},z} \quad (3)$$

which is a probabilistic mapping of the t-th bag to the grid windows $\mathbf{k}$. This mapping is usually peaky, i.e. each image tends to map to a few nearby locations in the grid. For details on the learning algorithm and on its efficiency, the reader can refer to the original paper [16].

3. THE PROPOSED APPROACH

The proposed three-stage approach is sketched in Fig. 1. The initialization step is applied on a training set made by generic images: it consists on creating a bag of features for each image, and learning the multiscale Counting Grid. In the enrollment stage, the preferred images of each user x_u, $u = 1, \dots, U$ of the gallery set are mapped on the CG latent space, and the resulting maps (one for each CG scale) are fed into a discriminative classifier. In the identification stage, the test images of a probe subject are transformed into bags of features, and embedded into the CGs; the resulting maps are given as input to all the U gallery classifiers, producing U identification scores. These scores are used to decide the best gallery user.

3.1 Initialization Stage: Creating the Bags of Features

For the sake of comparison, in this work the dataset used in [9] has been considered; it is composed by 40000 images belonging to 200 users, chosen at random from the Flickr website. For each user, the 200 last "favored" pictures have been retained (the act of favoring an image consists in clicking on a specific icon close to the liked image in the main Flickr interface). Repeated images across users are less than the 0.05%.

From each image $\mathbf{x}_t$, the same set of cues of [9] has been extracted, composed by 19 types of features resulting in a 111-dimensional real vector (see Table 1); the goal is to manage highly heterogeneous image features, letting them smoothly interact in the CG.

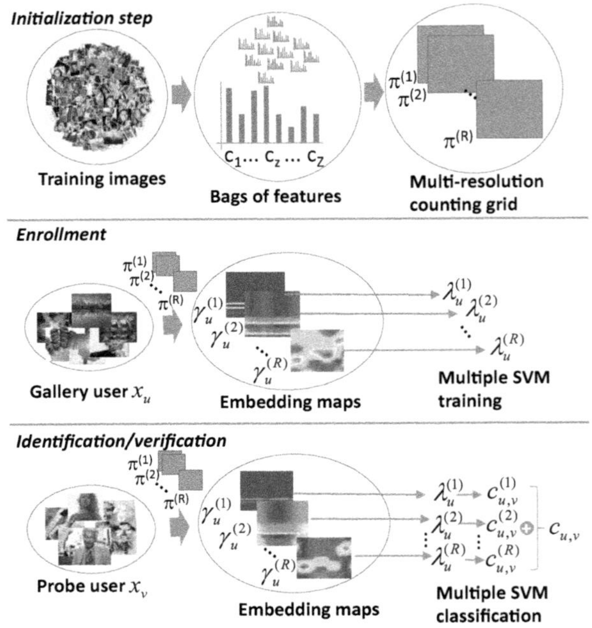

Figure 1: The proposed approach, composed by three stages: *initialization*, where the multi-resolution Counting Grid is learnt; *enrollment*, where the classifiers for each user are trained, and *identification* stages, where unknown personal aesthetics are matched with the gallery.

The features are organized in two families: on one side, are reported the cues that focus on aesthetic aspects [3, 11]: in practice, they encode low-level global image properties. On the other side, there are the *content-based* features, which individuate local image patterns representing semantic entities (cars, chairs and the like); to this end, robust probabilistic object detectors have been employed [5] (for a complete list of all the detectable objects, see Table. 1); other than the number of objects in an image, the object area (that is, the bounding box of the detected object) is also retained. In the case of multiple instances of the same object, the average area is considered. Faces have been extracted adopting the standard Viola-Jones face detection algorithm [23]. Finally, the GIST descriptor [15] for scene categorization has been considered.

It is worth noting that each feature extracted in the proposed approach indicates the level of presence of a particular cue, i.e. an intensity count. This is needed for the modeling with the Counting Grid. For this reason, features working on angular measures (as those modeling the Hue channel in the HSV color space) have been discarded. For more details on the features, see [9]. Since the range values are very heterogeneous, each feature is normalized across all training images to have zero mean and unit standard deviation. The same normalization is then applied to the features extracted from test data.

3.2 Initialization Stage: Multi-resolution Counting Grid Training

Given the bags of features, the extent E of the classical Counting Grid and its window size S, a multi-resolution CG is learned. In practice this amounts to learn $R = E - S$

Category	Name	L	Short Description
Perceptual	Use of light	1	Average pixel intensity of V channel [3]
	HSV statistics	3	Mean of S channel and standard deviation of S, V channels [11]
	Emotion-based	3	Amount of *Pleasure*, *Arousal*, *Dominance* [11, 22]
	Circular Variance	1	*Circular variance* of the H channel in the IHLS color space [12]
	Colorfulness	1	Colorfulness measure based on Earth Mover's Distance (EMD) [3, 11]
	Color Name	11	Amount of *Black*, *Blue*, *Brown*, *Green*, *Gray*, *Orange*, *Pink*, *Purple*, *Red*, *White*, *Yellow* [11]
	Entropy	1	Image entropy [10]
	Wavelet textures	12	Level of spatial graininess measured with a three-level (L1,L2,L3) Daubechies wavelet transform on the HSV channels [3]
	Tamura	3	Amount of *Coarseness*, *Contrast*, *Directionality* [21]
	GLCM-features	12	Amount of *Contrast*, *Correlation*, *Energy*, *Homogeneity* for each HSV channel [11]
	Edges	1	Total number of edge points, extracted with Canny [10]
	Level of detail	1	Number of regions (after mean shift segmentation) [1, 7]
	Regions	1	Average *size* of the regions (after mean shift segmentation) [1, 7]
	Low depth of field (DOF)	3	Amount of focus sharpness in the inner part of the image w.r.t. the overall focus [3, 11]
	Rule of thirds	2	Mean of S,V channels in the inner rectangle of the image [3, 11]
	Image parameters	1	Aspect ratio of the image [3, 10]
Content	Objects	28	Objects detectors [5]: in particular, here are the objects for which detectors are available: *people*, *plane*, *bike*, *bird*, *boat*, *bottle*, *bus*, *car*, *cat*, *dog*, *table*, *horse*, *motorbike*, *chair*. In all the cases we kept the number of instances and their average bounding box *size*
	Faces	2	Number and *size* of faces after Viola-Jones face detection algorithm [23]
	GIST descriptors	24	Level of openness, ruggedness, roughness and expansion for scene recognition [15].

Table 1: Summary of all features. The column 'L' indicates the feature vector length for each type of feature.

Counting Grids, starting at resolution $r = 1$ (the lowest resolution level) with the window of size $E - 1$, decreasing the window size of one pixel at each time, until the minimum size S (the highest resolution level $r = R$) is reached. At each resolution level r (except the first one), the prior parametrization for $\pi^{(r)}$ is the CG learnt at the previous step, i.e., $\pi^{(r-1)}$. At the first resolution level, the initialization is random. In simple words, the size of the window S determines how smoothed is the latent space where the images coexist: the larger is the window, the smoother is the mapping, and the larger is the neighborhood where similar images could be mapped. In practice, operating with a large window size corresponds to heavily smooth the images, capturing solely their main characteristics, while at the smaller scale, all the details of an image contribute to determine a precise location in the grid. Therefore, having a set of multi-resolution CGs corresponds to analyze the images at a different level of detail, from a coarse to a fine grain.

For the sake of visualization, the Counting Grids can not be directly visualized (each location contains a distribution of features), but it is possible to create an image mosaic using those images $\{c_z^t\}$ which give the highest posterior at each location $\mathbf{k}$, i.e., $p(\mathbf{k}^t|\{c_z^t\})$, at a given resolution level r. In Fig. 2, on the left, the Counting Grid with $E = 45$ at resolution $r = R$ ($S = 10$, maximum resolution) is reported. As visible, close images are visually similar, and semantic topics do emerge[2].

3.3 Enrollment Stage

Once the multi-resolution Counting Grid is learnt, the images of each gallery user can be mapped within it, obtaining R maps, one for each resolution. The generative embedding occurs by calculating a posterior probability at each location $\mathbf{k}$; once we have fixed a user u and a resolution r the posterior is

$$\gamma_u^{(r)} = \sum_{t \in T_u} p(\mathbf{k}^t|\{c_z^t\}, \pi^{(r)}) \tag{4}$$

where T_u identifies the set of images of the user u: T_u can have different cardinalities, depending on how many gallery images are available for user u. Roughly speaking, the main idea is to sum all the mappings of the images belonging to a given user, thus highlighting the zones of the latent space where the images have been located. The presence of Counting Grids at multiple scale allows to map the preferences of the user from a very rough resolution (on the Counting Grids obtained with large windows) until the finest resolution (the Counting Grid being learned with a small sized window), where the map is usually peaked.

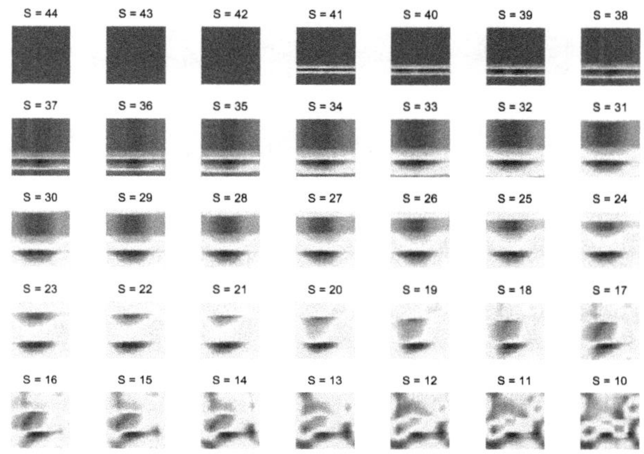

Figure 3: Embedding maps for user 38 of Fig. 2. Starting from the lowest resolution (r=1, S=44) and going towards higher resolutions, the maps show refined blobs and areas, identifying more precisely semantic areas, easily interpretable, on the grid.

A graphical explanation of the mapping process is shown in Fig. 2 and Fig. 3; in Fig. 2, together with the collage of the CG, on the left are reported the embedding maps of a single resolution level (the maximum, i.e., r=R) for three subjects, together with some random images preferred by them. One can notice two facts: 1) given a user, looking at his map and at the CG collage as reference, does allow to easily understand which kind of images are his preferred; 2) comparing the maps of different users, one can understand possible similarities: first two users from the top appear to share much the same preferences, while the third one has radically diverse tastes. This fact is confirmed by checking the random pictures of the users, on the right[3].

In Fig. 3 are reported the R mappings for the user 38 of Fig. 2. Starting from very blurred and unstructured maps corresponding to the lower resolutions, going toward higher

[2]A larger figure is reported in the additional material, also depicting different CGs at different resolution

[3]The complete set of images of these users are reported in the additional material.

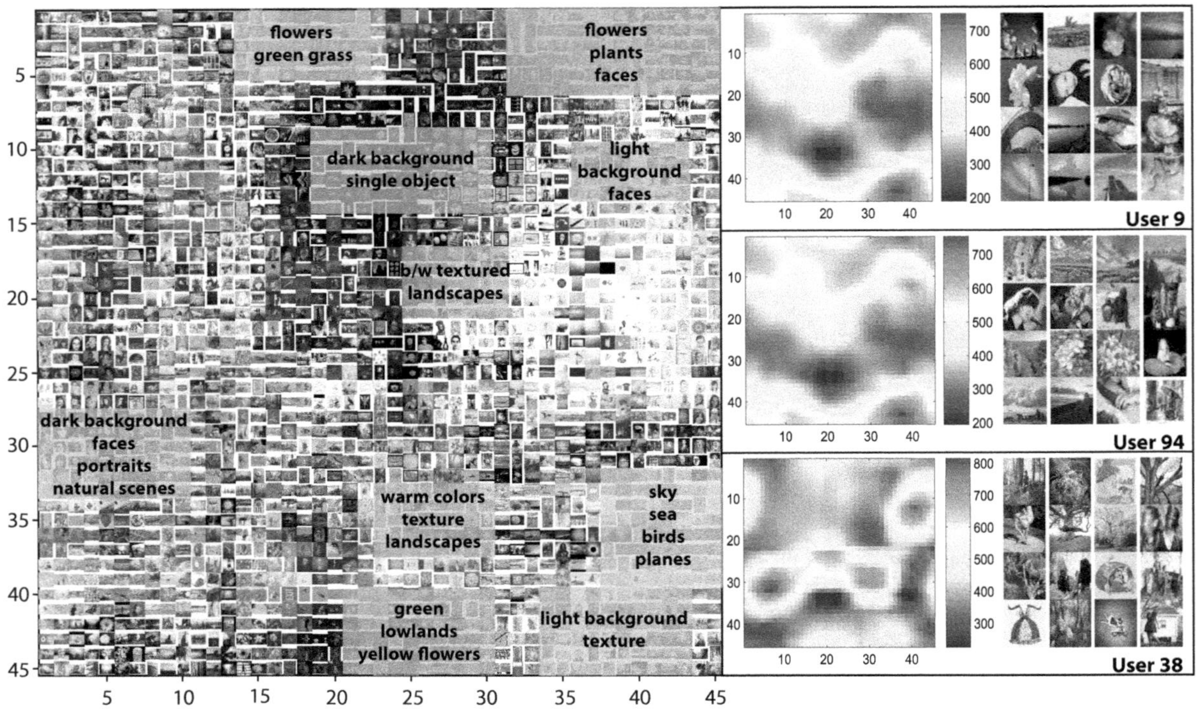

Figure 2: Counting grid at resolution $r = R$: on the left, the grid is visualized as a collage of images that, at a given location k, exhibit the highest posterior probability $p(\mathbf{k}^t|\{c_z^t\})$. On the right, the embedding maps of a single resolution level (r=R) are reported for three subjects, together with some random images preferred by them.

resolution maps, blobs and distinct areas start to emerge, refining the "semantic" knowledge of the preferences a user exhibits.

After the mapping step, the maps $\{\gamma_u^{(r)}\}_{r=1,\ldots,R}$ can be used as ID template for user u; to this sake, a battery of discriminative classifiers $\{\lambda_u^{(r)}\}_{r=1,\ldots,R}$ are learnt (one for each resolution). In this study, Support Vector Machines with radial basis functions have been employed: in particular, SVMs take as positive samples the maps $\{\gamma_u^{(r)}\}_r$, while as negative samples the maps of all the other gallery users. This step concludes the enrollment stage.

3.4 Identification Stage

In the identification stage, all the probe images of a user v are first encoded as bags of features. Subsequently, they are mapped on the multi-resolution CG, and the resulting maps $\{\gamma_v^{(r)}\}_{r=1,\ldots,R}$ are used as input of the SVMs related to the gallery user u; they classify the maps producing R scores $\{c_{u,v}^{(r)}\}_{r=1,\ldots,R}$ that, once mediated, provide a single classification score $c_{u,v}$. In other words, each user produces R probe maps; each of them is given as test input to the correspondent SVM of the gallery user, providing a confidence score (the distance from the separating hyperplane). Averaging these scores over all the resolutions gives the final confidence score. In the identification case, a confidence score is associated to each gallery user; this allows to rank the scores, keeping the highest ranked user as the best match with the probe.

4. EXPERIMENTAL EVALUATION

The general aim of the experiments is to explore to which extent the personal aesthetics signature is effective in a soft-biometrics context; to this aim, and for the sake of comparability, the same experiments carried out in [9] have been taken into account, for what concerns the identification task[4]. In addition, several experiments have been performed, to investigate the peculiarities of our proposal. In all the experiments, the Flickr dataset has been divided into a training and testing partitions, each composed by 100 preferred images. The training partition has been used to learn the Counting Grid, to produce the embedding maps of the gallery users and to learn the gallery SVMs. The testing partition has been used to select the probe images, mapping them into the CG and producing the probe embedding maps.

The first experimental scenario considers an identification task: here the soft-biometric system wants to recognize the user of a Flickr account, given a pool of unknown preferred images - all liked by the same individual - against a set of gallery users. The second set of experiments is aimed to individuate the limitations of personal aesthetics, and in particular what happens when the users are forced to select from a relatively small number of test images and not from a potentially infinite set as the Flickr repository could be considered.

In both the cases, the parametrization of the multi-resolution Counting Grid is the same: the CG size has been fixed at $E = 45$ pixels, while the (smallest) window size has been set to $S = 10$; this generates a set of 35 maps per user. The extraction of the image features takes 60 minutes per user (100 images), on a not optimized MATLAB code run on a 3.4 GHz processor with 16 Giga of RAM (the long time is

[4]The verification experiments in [9] have also been taken into account, not reported here for the lack of space, essentially confirming the superiority of our approach.

due to the object detectors). The learning of the Counting Grid at a single resolution takes in total 2 minutes, while the mapping + SVM training operation requires 3 seconds for $N = 100$ images of the same user, on the same computer. Regarding the variability of the results in relation to the E and S values, the proposed approach maintains similar performance when the ratio between E and S (also dubbed "capacity" in [16]) is bounded in the interval [3,5]. Even if E and S respect the capacity ratio, performances seem to decrease when $E < 10$ and $E > 70$.

4.1 Identification Results

The results of the identification tasks have been carried out following the protocol of [9], for a fair comparison; cross-validation has been performed using 2-fold scheme, repeating each experiment 20 times and shuffling the gallery/probe partition of each user. We also crossvalidated the parameters C and g of the SVM classifier obtaining the best configuration with $C = 1000$ and $g = 0.001$.

Given a probe signature built from an image or a set of images, the goal is to guess the gallery user who tagged them. To do that, the SVM classification (averaged) confidence score produced by each of the gallery classifiers has been analyzed. Hopefully, the gallery user with highest score is the one related to the user who originally selected as favorite the photo or the set of photos. To evaluate the recognition capability the Cumulative Matching Characteristic (CMC) curve has been computed [13]; the CMC is a widely-known performance measure in the field of person recognition/identification. Given a probe signature of a user and the matching confidence score, the curves tells the rate at which the correct user is found within the first k matches, with all possible k spanned on the x-axis. Fig. 4 shows various CMC curves for the dataset, where the curves have been obtained by averaging the CMC curves of the 20 different experiments with different gallery/probe splits. In particular, four different CMCs are reported, varying the number of test images used to compose the probe signature of a user, while keeping the number of images used to build the gallery signature fixed to 100. In practice, it is assumed to have 1, 5, 20 and 100 images which have been faved by the same unknown user.

Table 2 reports the CMC mean values (plus standard deviations) for the different ranks, for a quantitative analysis. We also reported the normalized area under the CMC curve (nAUC) as global performance measure.

As visible, the proposed approach definitely overcomes the performance of [9], at every signature cardinality, at each rank. As expected, having more images as test does improve systematically the identification performances. In particular one can note that, having 20 images as test signature allows to reach an average probability of guessing the correct user at the first rank of 0.66, which is definitely above the chance. The probability raises at 0.88 if we check the event of having the correct user within the first 5 ranked users.

Another experiment consisted in fixing the number of test images to 100 and varying the cardinality of the gallery signature, that is, the number of images used to compose the embedded maps fed into the SVM classifiers.

The curves are reported in Fig. 5, and the diverse rank values are listed in Table. 3.

Even in this case the proposed approach sets the new best performance, once again exhibiting higher performance when increasing the number of images adopted to build the gallery signature.

To explore the identification performance while diminishing the number of resolutions employed to learn the CG rep-

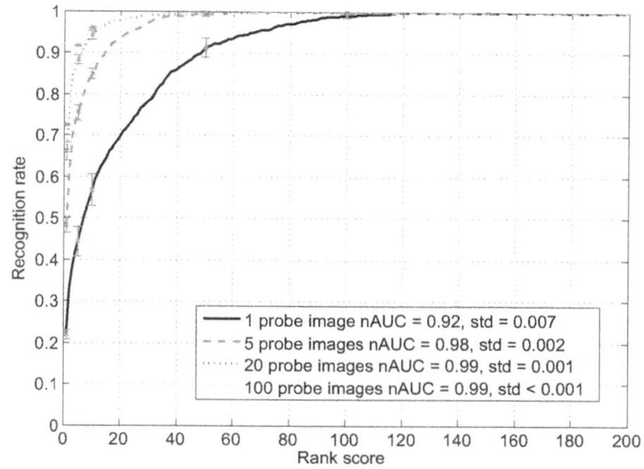

Figure 4: Cumulative Matching Characteristic curve for our approach, while varying the number of test images used to compose the probe signature. The normalized area under the curve (nAUC) is also reported.

T_{te}	Met.	rank 1	rank 5	rank 20	rank 50	nAUC
1	[9]	0.06	0.18	0.40	0.82	0.76
	our	**0.22±0.01**	**0.44±0.04**	**0.70±0.04**	**0.91±0.02**	**0.92±0.007**
5	[9]	0.14	0.39	0.68	0.96	0.89
	our	**0.48±0.02**	**0.75±0.02**	**0.94±0.01**	**0.99±<0.01**	**0.98±0.002**
20	[9]	0.25	0.62	0.88	0.99	0.96
	our	**0.66±0.02**	**0.88±0.01**	**0.98±<0.01**	**1.00±<0.01**	**0.99±0.001**
100	[9]	0.35	0.79	0.97	0.99	0.98
	our	**0.73±<0.01**	**0.92±<0.01**	**0.98±<0.01**	**1.00±<0.01**	**0.99±0.000**

Table 2: Recognition results, varying the number T_{te} of images that compose the *probe* signatures (and fixing the number of gallery images T_{tr} to 100 for each user). The rank numbers are the x-axis values of the CMC curve we focus on. In practice, the reported values represent the average probability of having the correct match within the first 1-5-20-50 signatures, considering different number of probe images.

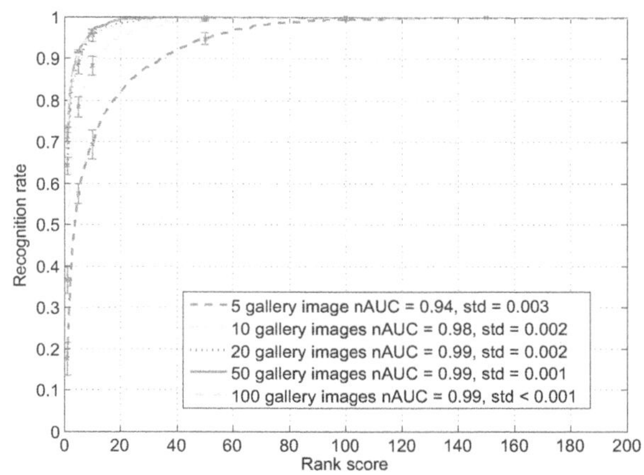

Figure 5: Cumulative Matching Characteristic curve for our approach, while varying the number of train images used to compose the gallery signature. The normalized area under the curve (nAUC) is also reported.

T_{tr}	Met.	rank 1	rank 5	rank 20	rank 50	nAUC
5	*our*	**0.17±0.04**	**0.57±0.02**	**0.82±0.02**	**0.95±0.01**	**0.94±0.003**
	[9]	0.07	0.23	0.49	0.88	0.81
10	*our*	**0.37±0.03**	**0.78±0.02**	**0.95±0.01**	**0.99±<0.01**	**0.98±0.002**
	[9]	0.11	0.32	0.62	0.94	0.87
20	*our*	**0.64±0.02**	**0.89±0.02**	**0.98±0.01**	1.00±<0.01	**0.99±0.002**
	[9]	0.15	0.44	0.74	0.97	0.91
50	*our*	**0.70±0.02**	**0.99±<0.01**	1.00±<0.01	**0.99±0.001**	**0.92±<0.01**
	[9]	0.22	0.57	0.83	0.99	0.94
100	*our*	**0.73±<0.01**	**0.92±<0.01**	**0.98±<0.01**	1.00±<0.01	**0.99±<0.01**
	[9]	0.35	0.79	0.97	0.99	0.98

Table 3: Recognition results, varying the number T_{tr} of images that compose the *gallery* signatures (and fixing the number of probe images T_{te} to 100 for each user). The rank numbers are the x-axis values of the CMC curve we focus on.

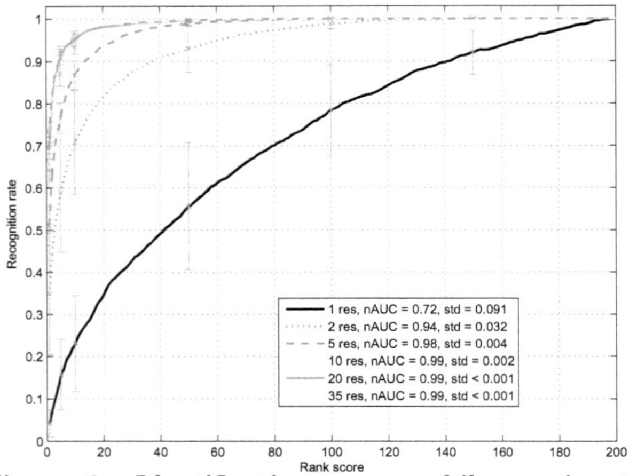

Figure 6: Identification scores while varying the number of resolution employed.

resentation, another test has been performed. In this case 1, 2, 5, 10, 20 and 35 different resolutions have been considered (keep in mind that 35 is the number of resolutions used so far for producing the above results). In the case of a single resolution, all the S windows size between 10 and $E-1 = 44$ have been independently evaluated, calculating the recognition performance while using 100 images of gallery and 100 of probe. The resulting identification scores have been averaged, providing also the standard deviation values. For evaluating higher numbers of resolutions, different windows size have been sampled without replacement (depending on the cardinality being evaluated) and ranked in descending order. After that, the window with the largest size has been learned with random initialization; the obtained CG has been used as prior for the second ranked one and so on. The experiments have been repeated 35 times, reporting the average recognition score. Results are portrayed in Fig. 6.

As expected, increasing the number of resolution levels does augment the identification capabilities.

4.2 Limitations of our approach

So far, all the works on personal aesthetics did the general assumption that all the images selected from the users, both of training and testing, were not overlapping, that is, no common preferred images are shared among users. In the dataset used so far this hypothesis holds, being the number of repeated images less than the 0.2%. But this is not always the case, especially when a much larger number of users is occurring, or when the images to select come from a restricted number of available pictures. In this last experiment we take into account this situation with a user study: as first operation we build a "reduced" test dataset, by sampling one image from each pool of the 200 originally liked images of all the 200 users, clearly avoiding repeated images. These 200 images have been organized on a web interface, where the users can select them. Then, 16 users of the original dataset have been asked to select from this interface 5, 10, 20 images. After that, the selected images have been used as a test signature for our approach, and compared with the gallery signatures (which for simplicity have been kept equal to the experiments of the previous section), generating three different CMC curves. As comparison, we use the test signatures coming from the original test images of the dataset, and not from the reduced set. The results are shown in Fig.7, which show that the images coming from the reduced dataset have obviously less discriminative power than the ones coming from the original one: this is because of the less aesthetical variability contained within, and to the possible number of images which have been selected by more than one user. In this sense, it is interesting to note that, while increasing the number of images used for building the signature from 5 to 20, the performance of the reduced dataset slightly diminish, while in the original case they obviously augment.

5. CONCLUSIONS

So far, aesthetical preferences have been considered in computer science as underlying a common sense of beauty; in fact, the literature focused on the design of methods aimed at evaluating a general "computational aesthetics" of pictures. With the approach of [9], personal aesthetic preferences started to emerge as peculiar features capable of characterizing the identity of a person. In this paper, a second approach in this brand new field is proposed, which consists in a generative embedding strategy: a generative step (the mapping on the Counting Grids) is followed by a discriminative step (the SVM training). This way, exploiting the advantages of hybrid generative/discriminative approaches, the compact and interpretable CG representation becomes a feature for a discriminative classifier, resulting in the new state of the art on a dataset of 200 users and 40K images. This papers presents also one of the main limitation of our approach, that is, the images selected by the user have to come from a large (potentially infinite) set of images, with no images shared among users; when this assumption holds no more, we have two problems emerging: the first is that the variability of the test signatures irremediably diminishes, as the number of images to select from is smaller, and the second is that the number of images which can be chosen by more than a user is no more negligible. This suggests that, for a valid biometric application (and not solely a soft biometric one), different (and more structured) multimodal interaction paradigms would be necessary.

6. REFERENCES

[1] D. Comaniciu and P. Meer. Mean shift: a robust approach toward feature space analysis. *IEEE Trans. on Pattern Analysis and Machine Intelligence*, 24(5):603 – 619, 2002.

[2] A. Dantcheva, C. Velardo, A. D'angelo, and J.-L. Dugelay. Bag of soft biometrics for person identification. *Multimedia Tools and Applications*, 51(2):739–777, 2011.

[3] R. Datta, D. Joshi, J. Li, and J. Wang. Studying aesthetics in photographic images using a

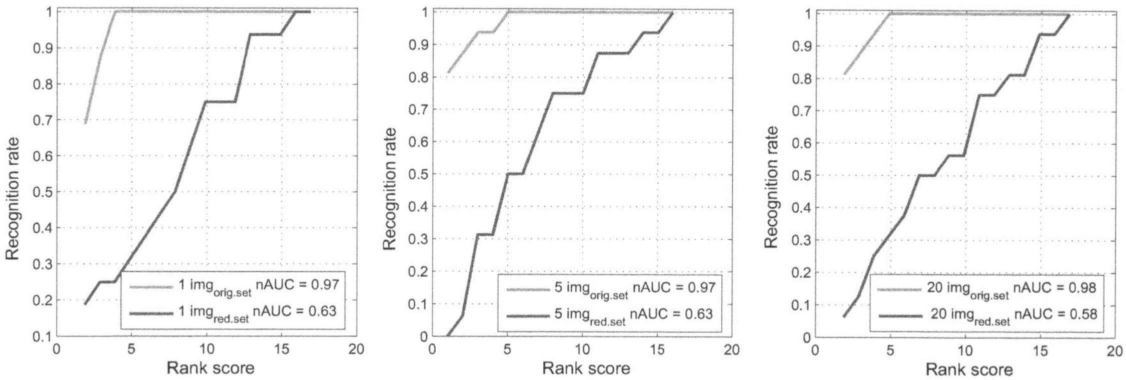

Figure 7: Identification performance while using the original test dataset ($\text{img}_{\text{orig. set}}$) and the reduced dataset ($\text{img}_{\text{red. set}}$).

computational approach. In *European Conference on Computer Vision*, volume 3953, pages 288–301. Springer Berlin / Heidelberg, 2006.

[4] M. Duggan and L. Rainie. Cell phone activities 2012. *Pew Research Center*, 2012.

[5] P. Felzenszwalb, R. Girshick, D. McAllester, and D. Ramanan. Object detection with discriminatively trained part-based models. *IEEE Trans. on Pattern Analysis and Machine Intelligence*, 32:1627–1645, 2010.

[6] A. Furnham and J. Walker. The influence of personality traits, previous experience of art, and demographic variables on artistic preference. *Personality and Individual Differences*, 31(6):997–1017, 2001.

[7] C. Georgescu. Synergism in low level vision. In *International Conference on Pattern Recognition*, pages 150–155, 2002.

[8] D. Joshi, R. Datta, E. Fedorovskaya, Q. T. Luong, J. Wang, J. Li, and J. Luo. Aesthetics and emotions in images. *Signal Processing Magazine, IEEE*, 28(5):94–115, 2011.

[9] P. Lovato, M. Bicego, C. Segalin, A. Perina, N. Sebe, and M. Cristani. Faved! Biometrics: Tell Me Which Image You Like and I'll Tell You Who You Are. *IEEE Trans. on Information Forensics and Security*, 9(3):364–374, March 2014.

[10] P. Lovato, A. Perina, N. Sebe, O. Zandonà, A. Montagnini, M. Bicego, and M. Cristani. Tell me what you like and I'll tell you what you are: discriminating visual preferences on flickr data. In *Computer Vision–ACCV 2012*, pages 45–56. Springer, 2013.

[11] J. Machajdik and A. Hanbury. Affective image classification using features inspired by psychology and art theory. In *International Conference on Multimedia*, pages 83–92. ACM, 2010.

[12] K. Mardia and P. Jupp. *Directional Statistics*. Wiley, 2009.

[13] H. Moon and P. J. Phillips. Computational and performance aspects of PCA-based face-recognition algorithms. *Perception-London*, 30(3):303–322, 2001.

[14] L. Olejnik, C. Castelluccia, A. Janc, et al. Why johnny can't browse in peace: On the uniqueness of web browsing history patterns. In *5th Workshop on Hot Topics in Privacy Enhancing Technologies (HotPETs 2012)*, 2012.

[15] A. Oliva and A. Torralba. Modeling the shape of the scene: A holistic representation of the spatial envelope. *International Journal of Computer Vision*, 42(3):145–175, 2001.

[16] A. Perina and N. Jojic. Image analysis by counting on a grid. In *Computer Vision and Pattern Recognition (CVPR), 2011 IEEE Conference on*, pages 1985–1992. IEEE, 2011.

[17] M. Pusara and C. E. Brodley. User re-authentication via mouse movements. In *Proceedings of the 2004 ACM workshop on Visualization and data mining for computer security*, pages 1–8. ACM, 2004.

[18] G. Roffo, C. Segalin, A. Vinciarelli, V. Murino, and M. Cristani. Reading between the turns: Statistical modeling for identity recognition and verification in chats. In *Advanced Video and Signal Based Surveillance (AVSS), 2013 10th IEEE International Conference on*, pages 99–104. IEEE, 2013.

[19] M. Rybnik, M. Tabedzki, and K. Saeed. A keystroke dynamics based system for user identification. In *Computer Information Systems and Industrial Management Applications, 2008. CISIM'08. 7th*, pages 225–230. IEEE, 2008.

[20] J. Suler. Image, word, action: Interpersonal dynamics in a photo-sharing community. *CyberPsychology & Behavior*, 11(5):555–560, 2008.

[21] H. Tamura, S. Mori, and T. Yamawaki. Texture features corresponding to visual perception. *IEEE Trans. on Systems, Man and Cybernetics*, 8(6), 1978.

[22] P. Valdez and A. Mehrabian. Effects of color on emotions. *Journal of Experimental Psychology: General*, 123(4):394, 1994.

[23] P. Viola and M. Jones. Rapid object detection using a boosted cascade of simple features. In *IEEE Conference on Computer Vision and Pattern Recognition*, pages 511–518, 2001.

[24] R. V. Yampolskiy and V. Govindaraju. Behavioural biometrics: a survey and classification. *International Journal of Biometrics*, 1(1):81–113, 2008.

Synchronising Physiological and Behavioural Sensors in a Driving Simulator

Ronnie Taib
National ICT Australia
13 Garden Street
Eveleigh NSW Australia
ronnie.taib@nicta.com.au

Benjamin Itzstein
National ICT Australia
13 Garden Street
Eveleigh NSW Australia
benjamin.itzstein@nicta.com.au

Kun Yu
National ICT Australia
13 Garden Street
Eveleigh NSW Australia
kun.yu@nicta.com.au

ABSTRACT

Accurate and noise robust multimodal activity and mental state monitoring can be achieved by combining physiological, behavioural and environmental signals. This is especially promising in assistive driving technologies, because vehicles now ship with sensors ranging from wheel and pedal activity, to voice and eye tracking. In practice, however, multimodal user studies are confronted with challenging data collection and synchronisation issues, due to the diversity of sensing, acquisition and storage systems. Referencing current research on cognitive load measurement in a driving simulator, this paper describes the steps we take to consistently collect and synchronise signals, using the Orbit Measurement Library (OML) framework, combined with a multimodal version of a cinema clapperboard. The resulting data is automatically stored in a networked database, in a structured format, including metadata about the data and experiment. Moreover, fine-grained synchronisation between all signals is provided without additional hardware, and clock drift can be corrected post-hoc.

Categories and Subject Descriptors

H.5.1 [**Information interfaces and presentation (e.g., HCI)**]: Multimedia Information Systems - *Artificial, augmented, and virtual realities; Evaluation/methodology.*

General Terms

Measurement, Reliability, Experimentation.

Keywords

Multimodal data synchronisation; data collection and storage; physiological and behavioural sensors; driving simulator; cognitive load.

1. INTRODUCTION

With the advent of cheaper and simpler sensors, the multimodal interaction research community and human-computer interaction practitioners at large have started to explore richer interfaces, by fusing a larger number of signals. Behavioural signals such as speech, gesture or facial expressions, which were until recently the basis of a majority of multimodal systems are now complemented by a mixture of behavioural and physiological sensors. They include gaze tracking and pupil dilation (e.g. using eye tracking glasses (ETG)), galvanic skin response (GSR), heart rate, blood volume pulse (BVP), muscular activity (EMG) and electroencephalography (EEG). Complex set-ups, such as functional magnetic resonance imaging (fMRI) scanners are also starting to be used in non-medical studies related to psychology and cognition. Environmental sensors, such as ambient temperature and noise, are also useful for ensuring experimental control conditions are maintained.

ICMI'14, November 12–16, 2014, Istanbul, Turkey.

http://dx.doi.org/10.1145/2663204.2663264

The benefits of fusing multiple sensor signals are to increase reliability, range, complementarity and sensitivity, as some sensors may not be accurate at all levels of activity, or may have a lower signal-to-noise ratio for the specific quantity to be studied. Cross-referencing signals improves pattern recognition, especially when external noise is present, or when discriminating similar conditions. The low cost and miniaturisation of many sensors also make them available not only to researchers, but to the consumer market, promising interesting deployments of multimodal systems.

However, the new sensors come with heavy requirements, especially in terms of annotation and analysis complexity. Physiological sensors are typically acquired in tens to thousands of Hertz, and often across multiple channels, such as in the case of EEG. Depending on the hardware or vendor, pre-processing may be available and offer high level features of interest to the researchers. But even so, the data rate and format are usually not compatible with other sensors. Practically speaking, fine-grained synchronisation of mixed signals is almost impossible with modern low-cost sensors, or comes at the expense of extremely long and tedious manual annotations.

This paper is based on several years of experimental work in our team, which have led to the creation of a usable, low-cost, synchronisation methodology for a wide range of sensors. It relies on the OML framework, and we describe its integration in our latest research on cognitive load measurement in a driving simulator. We discuss the major hurdles that researchers in our domain face, how we addressed them, and how our methodology can benefit other research community.

2. BACKGROUND

2.1 Physiological and Behavioural Sensors

As far as multimodal interaction is concerned, sensors are used to provide insights into human activity (behavioural sensor) or physiological reactions. In this paper, we distinguish the two in terms of conscious vs. unconscious process, whereby eye gaze is a behavioural process, whereas pupil dilation is a physiological signal, for example.

From the Polhemus used by Bolt et al. in early speech and gesture fusion, to the Kinect or Google Glass, it seems impossible to write a comprehensive list of behavioural sensors which have been used to capture human activity, often to allow interaction with machines or other humans.

Even more variety can be found in physiological sensors, including much wider ranges of quality and cost. These are progressively being adopted by the human-computer interaction (HCI) community, for their ability to represent the user's psychological state, possibly in real-time. While this psychophysiological inference is complex and still open to research, multimodal fusion of physiological inputs and task space measures are promising to improve the robustness and complexity of the user representation [1], leading to finer models of human activity.

Nowadays, different biometrical sensors are often utilised together to gather appropriate data and investigate the behavioural or physiological patterns of drivers. The most popular devices utilised include electroencephalogram (EEG) sensors and the eye trackers or front camera, due to their high sensitivity and convenience for live monitoring [2], [3]. Heart rate and skin conductance level were considered reflective of cognitive load changes, and in many studies they were studied together [4], [5]. Many devices are capable of monitoring electrocardiogram (ECG) and measuring skin conductance (GSR) at the same time, such as the commonly used Vitaport Temec BV, MEDAC or Procomp Infiniti. Some other sensors used involve detection of the electrooculography (EoG) or electromyography (EMG) changes of the eye or facial muscles [6], [7], and gestures of the hand [8]. However, any single sensor used in current driver monitoring systems, is not capable of reliably detecting a driver's mental or physical status under all circumstances. For example, hand movement detectors are reported capable of detecting early stages of fatigue [8], however some false alerts may occur if the driver is driving along a straight lane. Eye tracking cameras determine a driver's fatigue state via the pupil and eyelid movements, which is sometimes sensitive to illumination and distance of the camera to the eye [9], [10].

Combined usage of the sensors aims to improve the sensitivity and accuracy of driver mental state monitoring, and an increasing number sensors have been integrated and deployed in studies, due to the fact that physiological sensors are becoming cheaper and transportable. They are even making their way into other field studies such as the evaluation of museum interfaces [11]. However, HCI researchers and practitioners are faced with practical issues:

- **Quality:** reliable (quantitative) measurements
- **Ease of use:** deployability, portability/mobility
- **Cost:** sensor, consumables, maintenance
- **Usability:** ease of use, subjective experience/preference

These aspects are often tightly coupled, so the selection of sensors generally comes down to a trade-off between purchase cost and signal quality. This can happen to the detriment of the ease of use and ancillary costs, in particular:

- **Storage costs** can be high when sensors provide large volumes of (uncompressed) data. Conversely, some sensors may only provide compressed data losing important information. An example are the raw eye video feeds provided by SMI's Eye Tracking Glasses, which only provide a 1Hz sampling rate;
- **Annotation requirements** may be high when the signal is analog and the sensor does not provide pre-processing for high-level features. For example, audio and video recordings are typically useful to capture the context of the experiment, but very time consuming to annotate for fine-grained annotation, such as for multi-participant multimodal input analysis [12]. Any manual annotation requirement precludes the use of the sensor in real-time systems;
- **Processing requirements** may be high when pre-processing is performed on an acquisition computer instead of within the sensor's hardware. This, combined with the number of computer ports required by the sensor, may preclude the use of many sensors on the same computer;
- **Deployment complexity** is increased because more time and procedures are required to deploy all the sensors. Interferences between different sensors may exist, and failure of one single sensor may result in the invalidity of all the data;
- **Synchronisation** between multiple signals is difficult to perform *post hoc*, because signals are often not timestamped consistently across vendors. Moreover, timestamps are sometimes too coarse, inexistent, or subject to clock differences and drifts between acquisition machines.

This latter aspect is the main topic addressed by this paper.

2.2 Data Logging and Synchronisation

The preferred output of a multimodal data logging system would keep all data universally timestamped, i.e. along the same timeline, as proposed in [13]. However, the limited processing power of acquisition machines, and to some extent the bandwidth and storage costs, impose that multiple computers be used for data collection. To facilitate data aggregation and to address the synchronisation requirement imposes that these machines be networked and that attention be paid to differences in their clocks. Hardware solutions such as multi-relay cooperation scheme [14] or GPS disciplined oscillators are effective but require additional, often complex and costly hardware, and may not function indoors. In this paper we focus on low-cost software solutions.

A framework for multimodal data collection and synchronisation was proposed by [15]. It relies on the Network Time Protocol (NTP), the standard clock synchronisation protocol used on the Internet. A limitation is that it uses proprietary timestamping of data, such as video frames. Also, the target signals (video, audio and electronic pens) could be synchronised with an accuracy of up to 120ms in only 80% of the cases. Furthermore, their pen data suffered large synchronisation offsets of up to 120 seconds, which could not be corrected *post hoc*. In other research, a distributed fusion architecture using a central track file was used to collate multiple sensor data, with variable sampling rates, in a vehicular environment [16]. However, they did not specifically address synchronisation and instead relied on fast network data transfer to a central location. While this may work satisfactorily in a car, with streaming sensors, a larger computer network may adversely affect synchronisation and the approach doesn't readily apply to buffered or processed sensor data.

Looking at standard ways to perform these functions, and with better synchronisation, we found two main technologies able to provide data transfer and centralised storage, in consistent format.

The MQ Telemetry Transport (MQTT) is an open source protocol defining broker-based message passing, and offers complex features such as message queuing and selectable levels of quality.

While it is designed to be open, simple, lightweight and easy to implement [17], [18], and offers application programming interfaces (API) for a multitude of languages, we found that the protocol comes with many business-oriented features which may not be relevant or easy to deploy for user study experimenters. Furthermore, its message passing technology has heavy dependencies, especially IBM WebSphere. Most importantly, while the quality of service can be tuned to regulate message ordering for example, the protocol does not seem to include any timestamping or specific support to synchronise messages at a fine level.

Another option is the Orbit measurement library (OML) framework [19] which can be used as a reporting system for any sort of set-up requiring moving sampled data from decentralised sensing devices to a centralised storage database. It offers automatic timestamping facilities, and implementations in multiple programming languages allowing easy integration with various sensors, even if they come with different APIs.

The OML framework consists of a lightweight client library through which instrumented applications report individual sensor readings, and a data collection server which automatically stores them in a database for later analysis, using a consistent format. We found that the server installation using Linux packages was trivial and involved few dependencies. Further to its simplicity, OML is an open standard and seems to be adopted by an increasingly wider community.

3. USE-CASE: EXPERIMENT DESIGN

3.1 Experiment Overview

The user study used here as a test bed for the OML logging examines the performance of drivers under varying levels of cognitive load. The study is carried out in a simulator, as we are eliciting potentially dangerous levels of inattention. The main task is related to real-life driving on a 2x1 lane country road, with some surrounding traffic present. Secondary tasks involving mental recall and processing are used to control the level of cognitive load experienced by the participant, and are carefully crafted to:

- Be easily conducted while driving;
- Induce scalable levels of cognitive load;
- Resemble everyday mental processes while driving.

The experiment was conducted in five sub-sessions of about 5 minutes each. Since the focus of this initial experiment was to validate the data collection and synchronisation framework, we only recruited six volunteer participants. All had to own a driving license, because traffic rules applied during the experiment, and we didn't want cognitive load generated by inexperienced drivers. Participants were also restricted to those not requiring glasses or contact lenses, due to a limitation in the eye tracking system.

The driving simulator itself is a low-fidelity simulator, composed of a real car driving seat, Logitech Driving Force GT gaming steering wheel and pedals, and three monitors (1920x1080 pixels each), as pictured in Figure 1. The Unity3D game engine was used to implement a customized virtual driving environment matching the task design requirements.

Figure 1: Driving simulator

Emphasis was placed on creating immersive realistic conditions, through the use of ordinary tourism cars, coaches and trucks, as well as items of scenery such as a farm building or cows. The car model, e.g. acceleration, grip and noise, was tuned to provide as realistic a handling as possible. Unity3D provides some fine rendering features, making the experience more immersive, including realistic sky, water bodies and reflections on the car hood. It also generates sound for passing cars and wind on the windshield, based on vehicle speeds.

3.2 Sensors

The sensors used in the experiment were relatively low cost, and easy to use. They all had different sampling rates and numbers of channels, and could not be run concurrently on the same computer because of their computing requirements (EEG and ETG in particular), so the data acquisition was spread across several networked machines. An example of an acquisition client is shown in Figure 2. A comprehensive list of sensors is provided in Table 1, along with the actual location of these sensors shown in Figure 3.

Figure 2: Sensor acquisition machine (OML client)

A microphone and camera pointing at the participant's face were also recording the general interaction and facial expressions. Our goal is to provide mental state detection in real-time, without the need for manual annotation. Hence this microphone and camera are only used as a reference in our analysis.

Table 1: Sensors and characteristics.

Sensor	Sample rate	Data streams	Device
Eye tracking glasses (ETG) 1	30 Hz	3 channels: gaze direction, pupil dilation, blinks	SMI ETG
EEG headset 2	128 Hz	14 channels EEG, 2 axis gyroscope	Emotiv Epoc
GSR (weak hand fingers) 3	512 Hz	2 channels: galvanic skin response, blood volume pulse	Procomp Infiniti
BVP (ear lobe) 4			
4 Pressure sensors on seat pan, 6 on backrest 5	500 Hz	18 channels: pressure and distance for posture, ambient temperature, vibration	3x Phidget 8/8/8
3 Distance sensors for head, 6 1 for chest, 7 2 for legs 8			
Temperature (beside seat)			
Vibration (see Section 4.3)			
Simulator events	50 Hz	10+ channels	Unity3D C# interface
Annotations (by experimenter)	125 Hz	1 channel: key logging	Keyboard

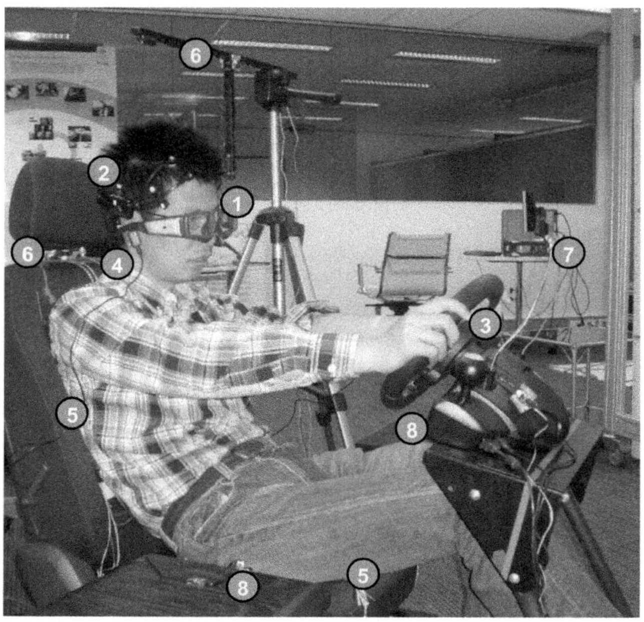

Figure 3: Sensor placements

The prominent practical issues we encountered and address in this paper include:

- Inconsistent acquisition methods: polling vs. event based, leading to a mix of regular streaming samples vs. sporadic samples, according to the sensor used;
- Diverse API programming and languages;
- Eclectic data formats reported by the devices, often geared towards manual review, not automated analysis;
- Most devices introduce internal sub-sampling, buffering and other mechanisms, that may obscure the true time of each data point. We assumed that these are negligible for our purpose, i.e. below 10ms;
- Some devices provide timestamping, based on the local computer clock, others on their internal clock, and others yet didn't provide any timestamping at all.

These issues were addressed through the development of custom parsers and the integration within the OML framework, as detailed in the following sections.

4. OML DEPLOYMENT

4.1 Integration of OML into User Study

OML clients were coded in C#, using the respective API of each sensor. Each client created a reporting thread to read data (pushed from some sensors, and polled from others) and used the OML client API to transfer the readings to the OML server for persistent storage. All sensors described in Table 1 were assigned an OML client, with the exception of the ETG, which did not provide a working API for real-time data acquisition. The eye tracking data had to be imported *post hoc* into the OML database, and the scene video and audio captured by the ETG were stored in files.

Due to the processing requirements of the various sensor drivers and APIs, the data collection had to be spread across a number of computers, as detailed in Table 2.

Table 2: Experiment network topology

Computer	Sensors
Windows PC 1	Simulator events, driver behaviour, live keyboard annotations
Windows PC 2	EEG, GSR & BVP, posture, temperature, vibration
Windows PC 3	Eye tracking glasses (eye tracking, scene video and microphone)
Linux server	[OML server]

Once pushed into an OML client, the data becomes a *measurement point*, which is automatically attributed a timestamp by the client, and gets linked to the current experiment, by way of a unique ID mechanism. This is convenient for our user study because metadata (experiment domain, application name and sender ID) gets automatically saved along with the raw sensor data, ensuring safe management of the data, and hence best practice in terms of data archival, without additional effort.

Every measurement point is transmitted as a single OML message over Transmission Control Protocol (TCP) and stored in the database on the server. Two standard timestamps are automatically appended to every measurement:

- oml_client_ts: the message send time, based on the client system clock;
- oml_server_ts: the message reception time, based on the server system clock.

For our data collection purposes, the OML server was configured with a PostgreSQL back-end, on a shared Linux server. A positive side-effect of storing the user study data in a centralised database is that we can leverage near real-time access to structured time series data, and so are able to realise a number of benefits:

- Visualisation of signals, for monitoring activity and to ensure sensor quality remains stable, throughout the experiment. This proved important for example to detect when the BVP sensor moved slightly out of place on a participant's earlobe. While not apparent to the experimenters, because the move was small, the impact on signal quality was significant;
- Feature extraction for immediate use in classification and prediction models;
- Data sets are automatically organised and stored in a consistent documented format, including metadata about the experiment.

Figure 4 shows a web-based session visualisation tool we developed, that can dynamically calculate and display any combination of time series features, for any session, by running SQL queries on raw data stored on the OML server, in real-time or *post hoc*.

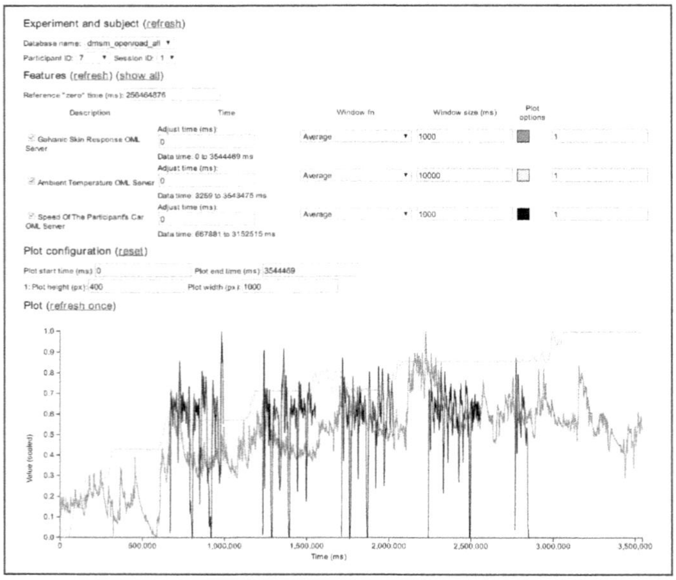

Figure 4: Visualisation tool, showing GSR, car speed and ambient temperature

4.2 Synchronisation Challenges

Generally speaking, synchronising clocks is a difficult problem, with a large body of research and development attached to it. Concrete solutions are provided in many applications, and generally require some trade-offs between accuracy and cost, depending on the needs of the application.

From the perspective of an HCI practitioner wanting to run user studies with multiple sensors, three primary synchronisation challenges exist:

- **Lack of sensor timing:** Some sensors do not provide accurate (if any) timestamping, nor any API allowing real-time data acquisition. This is the case for the version of the ETG glasses and software we were using. Moreover, these sensors may have uncertain or unreliable sample times, as their timestamps are relative to an unspecified start time and clock. For example, we found that the scene video, audio, and eye data, all being captured on the same ETG device for the same period, will vary in overall duration, sometimes in the order of several seconds. Data file creation and modification times are often the only time reference available for some sensors, and these do not provide much precision. In essence, we have no inherent indication of when the first sample was captured and of any systematic drift that occurred over the recordings;
- **Acquisition machine clock:** The network time protocol (NTP) is a well-established mechanism for fine-grained synchronisation of computers over networks. Unfortunately, while usually reliable on Linux machines, the Windows Time Service implementation of the protocol does not guarantee synchronisation with a time server with an accuracy any better than 5 minutes. In practice, the delay is usually much lower, but we will show in the coming sections how a computer clock may apply many corrections to synchronise to a server, introducing substantial jitter in the clock, hence dramatically affecting readings;
- **Lag in the sensor and driver:** Most sensors, especially cheaper ones, will have some lag between the time when an event occurs (and is sensed) and when it becomes available within the API. This is due to a combination of delay in the embedded electronics, software processing by the driver, and possibly multiple buffering stages. This information is usually not readily available, and extremely difficult to ascertain without using metrology equipment. In this paper, we assume that this delay is typically under 10 ms, hence below the target accuracy we set to achieve.

The next two sections detail how we addressed the first two issues, by respectively introducing a multimodal synchronisation event, and using OML to adjust timestamps *post hoc*.

4.3 Multimodal Synchronisation Event

In order to address absent system timings, and provide a control measure in this study, we designed a multimodal synchronisation event which appears on at least one OML-connected sensor for each system clock (on PC 1 and PC 2), as well as for the sensors which are not connected to OML (ETG, audio and video on PC 3). The event is also designed so that it generates clear signal patterns that would not be readily confused with ordinary behaviour in the experiment and could be automatically identified from the signal with some heuristics. For example, tapping on an accelerometer typically produces a sharp high spike in the signal.

In between each task of the experiment, (approximately every 7-10 minutes), the participants were instructed to perform a set of synchronisation actions *simultaneously*, as described in Table 3. This set was repeated 5 times in a row, at a 1 second interval roughly, to make it easily distinguishable in the signal.

Table 3: Synchronisation event actions

Simultaneous action	Targeted sensor
Tap the NumLock key with the provided vibration sensor in the right hand 	PC 1: keyboard annotations PC 2: Phidgets (vibration) Additionally: PC 2: Microphone PC 3: ETG (microphone)
Observe the NumLock light key with the ETG camera	PC 3: ETG (scene video)
Blink eyes deliberately	PC 3: ETG (eye tracking) PC 4: Face video
Tap the gyroscope on the EEG headset with the left hand 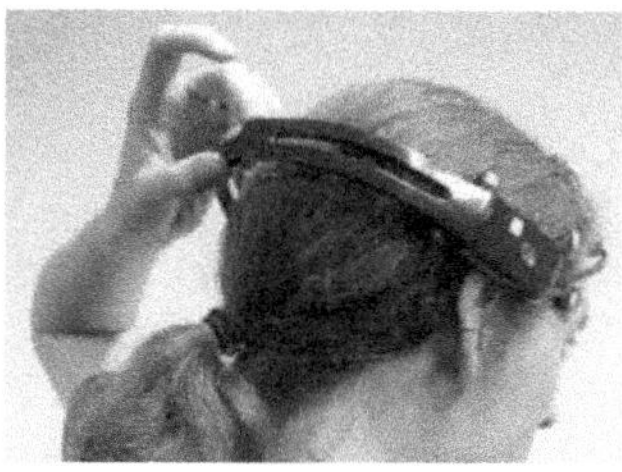	PC 2: Emotiv EPOC (EEG/gyro)

Recording just one of these synchronisation sequences is sufficient to align all targeted data streams at a given point in time, simultaneously correcting any offsets due to differences in clocks. However, for redundancy and to identify and minimise the effect of any clock drift over the period of the experiment, we chose to periodically repeat the synchronisation sequence after each task. While we cannot rely on participants to perfectly align the simultaneous actions, we assume that they will all occur within 30ms, which is the threshold at which humans can typically perceive coincidence between events [20].

4.4 Synchronisation without External Event

During the experiments, the clocks of PCs 1-4 were being actively synchronised to a time server by the Windows Time Service. At the beginning of the experiments all PC clocks agreed, as observed by the experimenters, however, plotting the signals corresponding to a multimodal synchronisation event unveiled a very important issue. Throughout the experiment, PC 2 significantly skewed its clock, in an effort to synchronise with the time server, making its clock tick at a different pace from the OML server and other PCs.

Figure 5 zooms on the second multimodal synchronisation event for one participant. The onset time of the initial spike was manually adjusted to align with the other signals. That lag was 104s for PC 2 and 0.7s for PC 3. Given that the ETG data on PC 3 was timestamped based on file modification time, such a static offset, of order 1 second, was expected.

After accounting for the clock offset PC 1 and PC 3 were relatively in sync, as can be seen by the aligned NumLock presses (E: large yellow spikes) and ETG blinks (D: red spikes). Since it couldn't be timestamped in real-time, ETG couldn't be synchronised by our system, and was only used it to assess delay/drift between machines during manual validation.

However, the EEG activity, calculated as the total energy on all the EEG channels (A: black), EEG gyro (B: blue) and vibration sensor (C: green), all captured on PC 2, are running quite ahead. In the short 4 second synchronisation event pictured here, the signals on PC 2 moved 1200ms ahead of the rest, as can be seen by their 5th peak being shifted to the right compared to the yellow spike.

Figure 5: Client times, with PC 2 signals running ahead

Figure 6 shows the same event, using the OML server time, i.e. the arrival times of reported measurements, with no adjustments. Clearly, they are well aligned, which confirms that the PC 2 clock is dramatically drifting. The slight lag observed between the yellow spikes and the other peaks can be explained by the fact that the NumLock press event (D: yellow) gets detected by the computer hardware when the key is being pressed half way down or so. The vibration peak (C: green) is observed when the key reaches its fully depressed position, hence the sensor gets stopped suddenly. The lagging EEG gyroscope (B: blue) and activity (A: black) suggests that this oml_client_ts (s) on the headset with a slight delay.

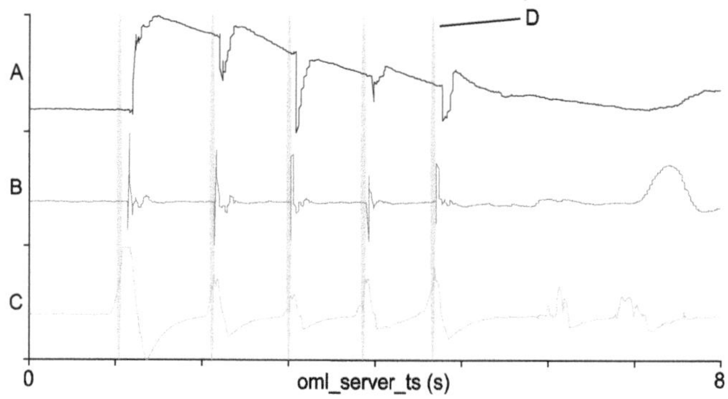

Figure 6: Server times, with PC 2 signals running ahead

Based on these results, it would be tempting to simply use the server timestamp as a reference for all the experimental data, and this would in fact provide an accuracy of the order of 100ms or better on a high quality local area network. However, we will find in the next two sections that other issues exist, but can be addressed by the framework.

5. SYNCHRONISATION CORRECTION

5.1 Timestamp Fusion

The server timestamp is dependent on the packet transmission time, hence the conditions of the network. When looking closely at the curves in Figure 5 and Figure 6, it can be noted that the former exhibits sharper features than the latter, for the same event. This can be explained by small fluctuations in the network, as well as potential buffering within the TCP stack.

The way to address this issue is to use the server timestamp to correct the synchronisation of the client timestamps, globally. In addition to the two standard OML timestamps introduced in Section 4.1 (oml_client_ts and oml_server_ts), we added a custom timestamp to our measurements:

- client_sample_ts: an educated guess of the time the data sample was captured, based on the system clock of the client, and the behaviour of the API and sensors, e.g. back-dating buffered samples via linear interpolation.

In a high performance real-time system, where samples are processed as soon as they are captured and the clocks are in sync, we would expect that client_sample_ts and oml_client_ts should be very similar to each other.

In an OML set-up including several clients, any drifting clock will become apparent when compared to the rest of the cohort. The timestamp for that clock can be adjusted according to the rest of the clocks. In the unlikely situation where all clocks would drift, the final timestamps would not represent absolute time correctly, but would at least all be aligned, which is paramount for any fine-grained HCI analysis.

5.2 Offset Correction

As noted before, the first event in Figure 5 and Figure 6 has been manually aligned to allow drift comparison. This relative time offset between computer clocks is easily measured by comparing the signals, using their original client timestamps (client_sample_ts). Figure 7 illustrates this, where the tap vibrations (green) are dramatically ahead of the NumLock press (black dots) and eye blinks (blue triangles).

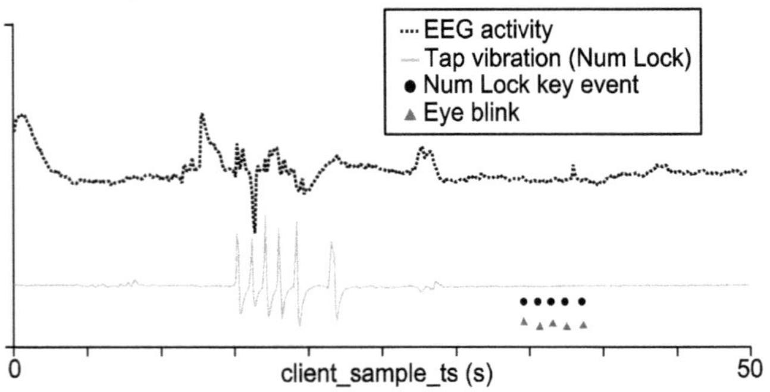

Figure 7: Offset between client clocks

More generally, by comparing oml_client_ts time to oml_server_ts for a measurement, any difference greater than 100ms (network transmission time) is likely due to an offset in the client's clock.

Detecting the spikes in the multimodal synchronisation event will also provide concrete confirmation of that offset if needed, as well as determining offset of non-OML connected data streams.

5.3 Drift Correction

A benefit of collecting multiple timestamps is that they can be used to quantify the amount of lag and drift on each individual clock in the system. In the case studies in section 4.4 where the clock of PC 2 appeared to be fast, we can actually get a much more precise insight into the situation by examining the difference between the client and server clock. The blue line in Figure 8 represents that difference over the one hour duration of the experiment. The line essentially reflects the correction pattern that the Windows Time Service was applying to the PC 2 local clock, throughout the experiment. It is made of series of linear corrections, getting the clock to alternatively tick too fast and too slow until convergence can be achieved. Clearly, the signals captured on PC 2 would continuously move ahead and behind the rest of the signals for no apparent reason should that pattern not be unveiled.

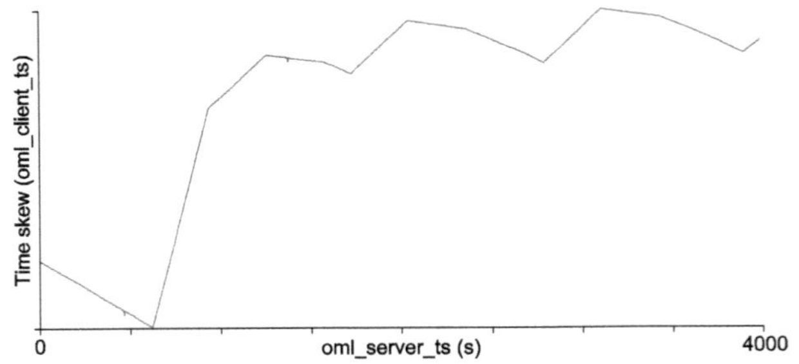

Figure 8: Clock drift pattern over the full experiment session

Once unveiled, though, it can be used to apply linear correction for each of the sections, hence completely repair the signal. At this stage, the process is manual, but it could be automated in the future, since the blue line can be obtained automatically.

6. DISCUSSION

Based on a combination of standard tool (OML) and empirical method (multimodal synchronisation event) we managed to provide synchronisation between a large number of heterogeneous sensor signals. This was achieved at very low cost, and improved synchronisation accuracy over traditional methods by an order of magnitude or more. We successfully implemented simple heuristic filters to detect tap vibrations and deliberate blinks from the data stored in the OML database. However, most of our participants tapped on the EEG gyroscope lightly, so the signal-to-noise ratio was quite low. We will explore ways to increase that ratio in the future, simply by instructing them to tap stronger, or providing a mechanical aid for tapping on the sensor.

Interestingly, we found that the EEG activity seemed to be a more robust indicator of the tapping activity. We are planning to explore whether this is due to the participant focusing on this specific task, hence producing specific brain activity, or whether it is simply due to the mechanical sensitivity of the EEG pads when the headset gets tapped on (even lightly).

We unveiled the dangers of relying on automatic clock synchronization, through Windows Time Service. Using Meinberg NTP software for Windows could reduce the observed client clock offset, but the protocol introduces drift by nature. We proposed a way to repair such errors *post hoc*.

In this paper, we assumed that the latency between raw sample capture and that data becoming available via the API is stable throughout the experiment. We will be on the look out for more research results in this field. We are planning to explore the user-to-user variation during the multimodal synchronisation event, to quantify the accuracy and consistency of this method.

7. CONCLUSION

This paper identified a set of key requirements for data collection in experiments where multiple physiological and behavioural sensors are being used. These requirements are low storage cost, minimal manual annotation, limited processing power, data synchronisation, and easy deployment. These typically impose that multiple networked machines must be used to pre-process and store the signals. Past research addressed the issue by using the network time protocol (NTP) and manual annotations, but these are limited by varying unreliability in some operating systems such as Windows, and also produce synchronisation accuracies of the order of 1 second at best.

We tested a set-up centred around the Orbit measurement library (OML) framework, in the context of a driving simulator, with multiple physiological and behavioural sensors in use. The framework provided simple-to-deploy data transfer, centralised storage and timestamping features. We showed that a severely drifting clock on an acquisition computer could be corrected effectively by cross referencing the timestamps of the server and several clients. Further levels of correction could be applied, leading to well under 100ms precision.

However, cheaper sensors may not come with real-time API so we also designed a multimodal synchronisation event, inspired from cinema clapperboards, whereby multiple signals get physically aligned. A benefit of that event over traditional manual synchronisation (e.g. using video recordings) is that it generates signal patterns that can be identified automatically using simple heuristic-based data filters.

In conclusion, the OML framework and multimodal synchronisation event can help HCI practitioners make the most of multiple low cost sensors. They can provide synchronisation support at least an order of magnitude more accurate than traditional systems, and can be deployed easily on operating systems with varying levels of clock reliability. Most importantly, they can dramatically decrease the need for manual annotations.

8. ACKNOWLEDGMENTS

The authors would like to thank the user study participants for their time and patience. NICTA is funded by the Australian Government through the Department of Communications and the Australian Research Council through the ICT Centre of Excellence Program.

9. REFERENCES

[1] S. H. Fairclough, "Fundamentals of physiological computing," *Interacting with Computers*, vol. 21, no. 1–2, pp. 133–145, Jan. 2009.

[2] M. Bartels and S. P. Marshall, "Measuring cognitive workload across different eye tracking hardware platforms," presented at the Proceedings of the symposium on eye tracking research and applications, 2012, pp. 161–164.

[3] D. De Waard and V. Studiecentrum, *The measurement of drivers' mental workload.* Groningen University, Traffic Research Center, 1996.

[4] J. Engström, E. Johansson, and J. Östlund, "Effects of visual and cognitive load in real and simulated motorway driving," *Transportation Research Part F: Traffic Psychology and Behaviour*, vol. 8, no. 2, pp. 97–120, 2005.

[5] J. Son, Y. Lee, and M.-H. Kim, "Impact of traffic environment and cognitive workload on older drivers' behavior in simulated driving," *International Journal of Precision Engineering and Manufacturing*, vol. 12, no. 1, pp. 135–141, 2011.

[6] M. Akin, M. B. Kurt, N. Sezgin, and M. Bayram, "Estimating vigilance level by using EEG and EMG signals," *Neural Computing and Applications*, vol. 17, no. 3, pp. 227–236, 2008.

[7] R. N. Khushaba, S. Kodagoda, S. Lal, and G. Dissanayake, "Driver drowsiness classification using fuzzy wavelet-packet-based feature-extraction algorithm," *Biomedical Engineering, IEEE Transactions on*, vol. 58, no. 1, pp. 121–131, 2011.

[8] T. C. Chieh, M. M. Mustafa, A. Hussain, E. Zahedi, and B. Majlis, "Driver fatigue detection using steering grip force," presented at the Research and Development, 2003. SCORED 2003. Proceedings. Student Conference on, 2003, pp. 45–48.

[9] S. Hu and G. Zheng, "Driver drowsiness detection with eyelid related parameters by Support Vector Machine," *Expert Systems with Applications*, vol. 36, no. 4, pp. 7651–7658, 2009.

[10] R. F. Knipling, W. W. Wierwille, and I. America, *Vehicle-based drowsy driver detection: Current status and future prospects.* National Highway Traffic Safety Administration, Office of Crash Avoidance Research, 1994.

[11] A. J. Karran, S. H. Fairclough, and K. Gilleade, "Towards an adaptive cultural heritage experience using physiological computing," in *CHI '13 Extended Abstracts on Human Factors in Computing Systems*, Paris, France, 2013, pp. 1683–1688.

[12] S. Oviatt and A. Cohen, "Written and multimodal representations as predictors of expertise and problem-solving success in mathematics," in *Proceedings of the 15th ACM on International conference on multimodal interaction*, Sydney, Australia, 2013, pp. 599–606.

[13] A. L. Thompson and D. Bohus, "A framework for multimodal data collection, visualization, annotation and learning," in *Proceedings of the 15th ACM on International conference on multimodal interaction*, Sydney, Australia, 2013, pp. 67–68.

[14] J. Zhang, J. Jia, Q. Zhang, and E. M. K. Lo, "Implementation and Evaluation of Cooperative Communication Schemes in Software-Defined Radio Testbed," in *INFOCOM, 2010 Proceedings IEEE*, 2010, pp. 1–9.

[15] A. M. Arthur, R. Lunsford, M. Wesson, and S. Oviatt, "Prototyping novel collaborative multimodal systems: simulation, data collection and analysis tools for the next decade," in *Proceedings of the 8th international conference on Multimodal interfaces*, Banff, Alberta, Canada, 2006, pp. 209–216.

[16] A. Amditis, A. Polychronopoulos, I. Karaseitanidis, G. Katsoulis, and E. Bekiaris, "Multiple sensor collision avoidance system for automotive applications using an IMM approach for obstacle tracking," in *Proceedings of the Fifth International Conference on Information Fusion, 2002*, 2002, vol. 2, pp. 812–817 vol.2.

[17] IBM and Eurotech, "MQTT v3.1 Protocol Specification." IBM, 19-Aug-2010.

[18] V. Lampkin, W. T. Leong, L. Olivera, S. Rawat, N. Subrahmanyam, and R. Xiang, *Building Smarter Planet Solutions with MQTT and IBM WebSphere MQ Telemetry.* 2012.

[19] O. Mehani, G. Jourjon, T. Rakotoarivelo, and M. Ott, "An Instrumentation Framework for the Critical Task of Measurement Collection in the Future {I}nternet," *Computer Networks*, vol. 63, pp. 68–83, Apr. 2014.

[20] B. Dainton, "Temporal Consciousness," in *The Stanford Encyclopedia of Philosophy*, Spring 2014., E. N. Zalta, Ed. 2014.

Data-Driven Model of Nonverbal Behavior for Socially Assistive Human-Robot Interactions

Henny Admoni
Department of Computer Science
Yale University
New Haven, CT 06520 USA
henny@cs.yale.edu

Brian Scassellati
Department of Computer Science
Yale University
New Haven, CT 06520 USA
scaz@cs.yale.edu

ABSTRACT

Socially assistive robotics (SAR) aims to develop robots that help people through interactions that are inherently social, such as tutoring and coaching. For these interactions to be effective, socially assistive robots must be able to recognize and use nonverbal social cues like eye gaze and gesture. In this paper, we present a preliminary model for nonverbal robot behavior in a tutoring application. Using empirical data from teachers and students in human-human tutoring interactions, the model can be both *predictive* (recognizing the context of new nonverbal behaviors) and *generative* (creating new robot nonverbal behaviors based on a desired context) using the same underlying data representation.

Categories and Subject Descriptors

I.2.9 [**Artificial Intelligence**]: Robotics

Keywords

Human-robot interaction; nonverbal behavior; tutoring

1. INTRODUCTION

Socially assistive robotics (SAR) focuses on building robots that help people through interactions that are inherently social [5]. Application areas for SAR include tutoring [8, 9], autism therapy [13], and elder care [16]. Social robots augment traditional human-human interactions in these areas by providing additional interactions that are impractical, time-consuming, or impossible to achieve with a person.

For example, a social robot can act as a peer tutor, helping students practice skills or solidify knowledge through one-on-one interactions outside of the classroom. By presenting itself as a peer, the robot can encourage students to practice previously-learned knowledge by re-teaching it to the robot. In this way, the robot provides educational support beyond what a classroom teacher has time for, and with potentially more consistent quality than a human peer.

ICMI '14 November 12–16 2014, Istanbul, Turkey
Copyright 2014 ACM 978-1-4503-2885-2/14/11 ...$15.00.
http://dx.doi.org/10.1145/2663204.2663263.

Figure 1: Screenshots from human-human teaching interaction videos. The student (top) displays gaze to the referent, while the teacher (bottom) displays gaze to the partner and a deictic gesture to the map.

For social robots to be effective communicators, they must understand the *context* of their human partner's communication, that is, the communicative goal or perspective. In the tutoring robot example, for instance, the robot must be able to recognize whether its partner is referring to a location in the environment, asking a question, or explaining some knowledge. Similarly, social robots must be able to convey the context of their own communication effectively.

The cues to understanding such context can come from speech, but often come from nonverbal behaviors like eye gaze [3] and gesture [10]. Gestures, for instance, reflect ideas that are not necessarily conveyed in speech [6], and teachers frequently use gestures to ground their spoken utterances to the objects of instruction [1, 12]. Eye gaze is critical for joint attention—simultaneous attention toward a particular object or location—which is fundamental for learning [15]. Therefore, the effectiveness of the tutoring robot, or any socially assistive robot, depends on its ability to recognize and utilize the nonverbal context clues that people use naturally.

In this work, we take a *data-driven* approach, using empirical data from human-human interactions to build a model of nonverbal robot behaviors. By training on previously-observed human behavior, we take advantage of the frequency and ease with which people use nonverbal behaviors to design more communicative robot behaviors.

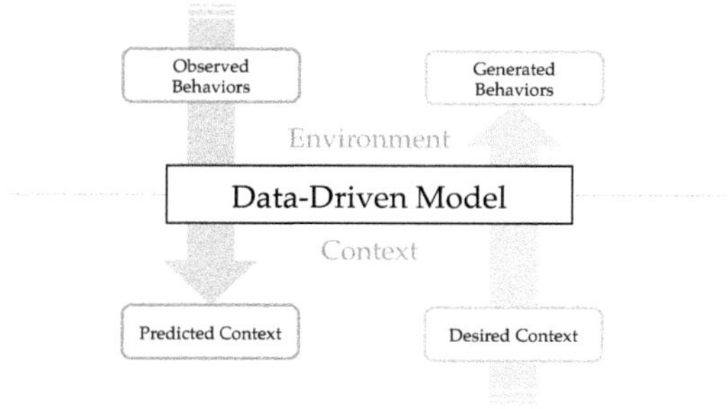

Figure 2: The model performs both context prediction (blue) and behavior generation (green).

Other work uses a similar data-driven approach for nonverbal behavior modeling. Researchers have generated robot behavior, such as gaze aversions [2] and narrative gestures [7], by analyzing videos of people conversing or telling stories. For virtual agents, empirical observation has driven gesture formation for iconic gestures [4] and narrative performance [11, 14].

However, much of this previous work focuses exclusively on the speaker's behaviors. In contrast, our work considers the behaviors of *both* interaction partners simultaneously. Tutoring is an activity with bi-directional communication—the teacher makes a statement, the student asks a question, the teacher replies, the student confirms—and peoples' nonverbal behavior is influenced by the behavior of their partner. For instance, joint reference is a common social behavior that involves one person deictically referring to an object or location, then repeatedly glancing between that referent and the partner's face to confirm that their partner understands the reference. With a view of both partners' behaviors, joint reference can emerge naturally from our model.

Our work also hinges on the idea that a model for nonverbal behavior should be simultaneously *predictive* and *generative*. In other words, the model should be able to both predict (or classify) the context of a newly observed set of nonverbal behaviors, and generate a set of nonverbal behaviors given a context of communication (Figure 2), without needing to collect and train on different sets of data. Some other work has this capability (such as [4]), but we elevate this to a central requirement for our system.

In this paper, we introduce the context and features that comprise our model and describe our preliminary data collection of real-world human-human teaching interactions. We then describe our model in terms of these features, detailing how it can both predict new contexts and generate new behaviors. We evaluate the model and show that it is effective at both of these tasks. We conclude with ideas for extensions of this model.

2. HUMAN-HUMAN INTERACTION

To create a model of nonverbal behavior, we first collected examples of nonverbal behavior during tutoring (Figure 1). We recruited two pairs of participants (mean age 22), randomly assigning one as teacher and the other as student, and recorded their interaction as the teacher taught the student how to play a board game called TransAmerica.

In TransAmerica, players must place game pieces representing railroad tracks along a grid overlaid on a map of the United States. Players score points for successfully building a track network that connects the cities specified in their randomly-selected hand of cards. We chose this game specifically because teaching the game involves spatial references, which encourage deictic gestures and demonstrations in addition to statements of facts and rules.

Neither student nor teacher had played the board game previously. Before the recorded interaction, the teacher was given a lesson on the game from an experimenter for approximately five minutes. The teacher was also provided with a rule sheet that described all of the rules of the game.

We audio- and video- recorded both teacher and student during this interaction, which lasted approximately five minutes per dyad. We then manually coded these recordings for five *predictors*: the *teacher's gaze*, the *teacher's gestures*, the *teacher's deictic references*, the *student's gaze*, and the *student's gestures* (Table 1). The student's deictic reference was infrequent, so we did not code for that predictor. We also coded the *context* of each utterance.

Values for gaze follow previous work [7], and represent possible gaze locations: to the *partner*, to the *referent* of current speech (regardless of who is speaking), to one's *own gesture*, or to some *other* location in the environment.

Values for gesture include those from established categorizations as well as additional values specific to physically-based teaching tasks. *Iconic*, *metaphoric*, *deictic*, and *beat* gestures are defined as in the literature [10]. *Demonstrations* involve physical movements that mimic the topic of speech. *Functional* movements are not intended for communication, but are used to accomplish game-related tasks such as dealing cards. Actions outside of these categories, such as brushing hair behind an ear, were categorized as *other*.

The deixis category encodes gesture types—*pointing* to a single target, *sweeping* over a range of targets, and *holding*—as well as gesture locations—the game *map*, *cards*, *playing pieces*, and *box*. Though every deixis value must have an associated gesture, not every gesture must have a deixis value. Deixis values can occur with any gesture, especially demonstrations and functional gestures.

The nine contexts each represent a particular kind of communication, and contexts are determined based on both speech and nonverbal behaviors. Contexts are mutually exclusive, though two sets of identical nonverbal behaviors may be classified as different contexts, for instance based on different speech during those behaviors.

The *rules* context indicates communication about the rules of the game. *Fact* contexts involve communication about facts that don't include game rules, such as "The name of the game is TransAmerica." An *expository* context indicates communication that elaborates on previous statements without providing new rules or facts. *Question* and *reply* contexts involve asking questions or providing direct answers, respectively. *Deixis* indicates communication that refers to physical locations or nearby objects. *Confirmation* contexts involve confirmation-seeking questions or statements such as "do you understand?" *Backchannel* contexts are utterances that indicate a listener's attention. *Filler* are non-meaningful communications that stand in for silence, often at the beginning of a new phrase.

We developed the list of contexts before examining the human-human interaction data, so that we would not be swayed by individual preferences for certain contexts. Interestingly, we did not note a single instance of confirmation context in the interactions we annotated, despite their ex-

Name	Values
Gaze (A)	partner, referent, own gesture, other
Gesture (E)	iconic, metaphoric, deictic, beat, demonstration, functional, other
Deixis (D)	point {map, own cards, partner cards, box}, sweep {map, box}, hold {cards, game piece, box}
Context (C)	backchannel, deixis, expository, fact, filler, question, reply, rules

Table 1: Model parameters and their values.

pected appearance in a teaching task. It is possible that a more experienced teacher might employ confirmation seeking behaviors, even though our current participants did not.

3. NONVERBAL BEHAVIOR MODEL

A model of nonverbal behavior should be able to classify the context given new observations of nonverbal behavior, as well as generate appropriate behaviors to suit a desired context (Figure 2).

We discretized the human-human interaction recordings into one-second segments. Each segment provides one observation $o \in O$, which is described by a tuple of predictors $o = \{a_T, e_T, d_T, a_S, e_S\}$ where $a_T, a_S \in A$ are the type of eye gaze exhibited by the teacher and student, respectively, $e_T, e_S \in E$ are the types of gestures exhibited by the teacher and student, respectively, and $d_T \in D$ is the deictic referent of the teacher's gesture in that segment. We chose one-second segments after observing the interactions, though the level of data granularity is flexible and may be adjusted for different applications.

Sometimes it is useful to take history into account, as well. An observation with history,

$$o_h = \{a_{T_t}, e_{T_t}, d_{T_t}, a_{S_t}, e_{S_t}, a_{T_{t-1}}, e_{T_{t-1}}, d_{T_{t-1}}, a_{S_{t-1}}, e_{S_{t-1}}\}$$

is defined by predictor values at current time t and predictor values from the previous time step $t-1$, if available. The set of observations including history is O_h.

Using this formulation, we can represent each observation as a point in high-dimensional space.

3.1 Predicting Context

Given a set of observations of nonverbal behavior, our system can predict the context of the communication. To do so, observations from the human-human interactions were used to train a prediction algorithm using k-nearest neighbors. In this algorithm, predictors are attributes and context is the class label. We can denote this as $label\,(o_h) = c$ for observation o_h and context c. Note that *label* is not a function, since identical observations can have different contexts.

To classify the context of a new observation, the algorithm performs operation

$$nclosest : (O_h, o_{new}, k) \rightarrow K \tag{1}$$

which takes a set of observations O_h, a new observation o_{new}, and a positive integer k and returns a set $K = \{o_{h_1}, \ldots, o_{h_k}\}$ containing the k closest observations to o_{new}.

Because the predictor values are categorical, rather than continuous, our KNN algorithm uses the Hamming distance to identify nearest neighbors. For each existing observation $o_{old} = \{x_1, \ldots, x_n\}$, the algorithm calculates the distance D between o_{old} and the new observation $o_{new} = \{y_1, \ldots, y_n\}$,

$$D = \sum_{i=1}^{n} h(x_i, y_i), \quad h(a,b) = \begin{cases} 0 & \text{if } a = b \\ 1 & \text{if } a \neq b \end{cases} \tag{2}$$

Once it has evaluated the k nearest neighbors, the model assigns o_{new} a context based on a majority vote of the contexts of the observations in K. Ties are resolved by selecting randomly. Since there may be several different behaviors applicable in the same context, we extend the context assignment to o_{new} such that the probability of context assignment is proportional to the number of observations with that context in K. In other words, the probability of assigning o_{new} a context c is $p(c) = \frac{count(label(o_h)=c)}{k}$ for each $o_h \in K$, where $count(x)$ is a function that returns the number of instances of x in the data.

We empirically determined that $k = 2$ was the most accurate value for our data, though k may vary by application. Our model examines the two most similar examples of previous behavior to judge a new behavior's context.

3.2 Generating Behavior

Given a context, the model can also select appropriate nonverbal behaviors. It does so by finding the largest cluster of examples for the context, then selecting the nonverbal behaviors that are most common in that cluster.

Mathematically, given a desired context $c_{des} \in C$, the model searches over all observations $o \in O$ for

$$\{\{a_T, e_T, d_T, a_S, e_S\} \mid \; count\,(label(o) = c_{des}) > count\,(label(o) = c_i)\,, c_{des} \neq c_i\} \tag{3}$$

Since this can yield multiple qualifying sets of behavior, the model can weight its behavior choice based on the frequency of observations containing that behavior for the desired context. This allows behavior variability in proportion to observed examples.

In effect, the model is replicating the most common behaviors it has observed for a given context. This follows the idea that people learn to communicate by mimicking observed behavior in given situations.

This behavior generation algorithm is amnesic because it does not account for history. To account for behavior from the previous time step, we use the history-aware representation of an observation, o_h. The process for generating new context (equation 3) remains the same, except that every step now uses o_h instead of o.

4. MODEL EVALUATION

Given a new observation containing the five predictors, how accurate is the model at identifying the correct context? We performed a 10-fold cross validation: combining all observations from both dyads, this validation segmented the data into 10 groups, trained the model on nine of those groups, and calculated the accuracy of context predictions using data from the remaining, untrained group (Figure 3a). On average, cross-validation accuracy was 45.9%. This value is significantly better than chance, which is 11.1% for nine classifications. It is also better than simply predicting the most common classification—rules—which only leads to an accuracy of 37.5% using the cross-validated model. Table 2 shows a confusion matrix for the cross-validated model.

Given a context, how well does the model generate gaze and gesture behaviors? To test this, we compared the rec-

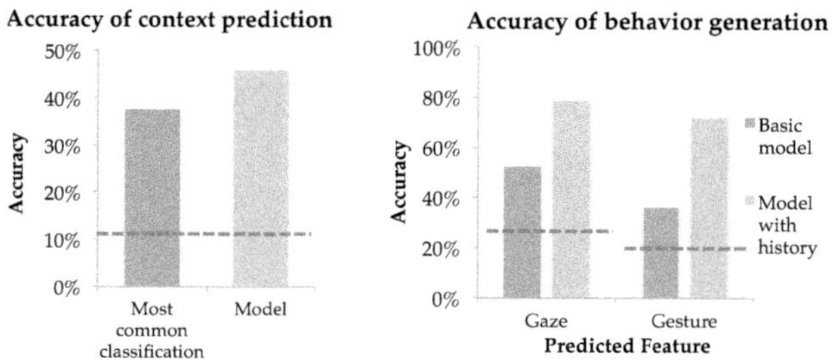

(a) Accuracy of predicting context given behavior observations.

(b) Accuracy of generating new behaviors given context.

Figure 3: Results of model evaluation. The dashed line indicates chance.

10	13	23	1	11	2	2	21
4	14	16	0	6	4	0	15
6	13	59	3	29	8	3	28
1	0	4	0	1	2	0	1
1	13	36	2	32	1	3	22
5	6	7	2	8	26	0	5
1	2	4	0	1	1	2	4
7	19	47	3	25	6	3	72

Table 2: A confusion matrix for context prediction with the cross-validated model. Variable order is listed in Table 1.

orded human behavior for each observation in our data set against the most likely behavior generated by the algorithm for that observation's context (Figure 3b). When using the amnesiac generation method (that is, behavior generation that ignores any history), our system matches actual human gaze behavior 52.0% of the time, and human gesture behavior 36.0% of the time. This is an improvement over randomly selecting behavior values, which would yield 25.0% accuracy for gaze and 14.3% accuracy for gesture. Taking a single time-step of history into account significantly improves performance. The historically mindful generation method yields 78.8% accuracy for gaze behaviors and 72.0% accuracy for gestures.

5. DISCUSSION & FUTURE WORK

The next step in evaluating the model is to generate real robot behaviors and to measure how those behaviors are received in a human-robot interaction. We plan to use the generative portion of the model to create robot behaviors for a tutoring task similar to the one in this experiment. We will measure participants' acceptance and information recall when interacting with a robot using the current model versus a robot using a heuristic model or one that exhibits limited nonverbal behavior.

Given annotated data, our model is adaptable to new users and new tasks. However, data annotation remains a challenge. Manual annotations take time, and automatic annotations are not yet robust enough to correctly identify all of the features used by the model, particularly the context. However, automatic gaze and gesture detectors may ease some of the burden of manual annotation.

As a data-driven model, the effectiveness of the system depends on the quality of the data provided. This paper uses a small data corpus (two dyadic interactions), which we plan to increase for future evaluations. Even with this small corpus, however, the model can successfully predict and generate reasonable nonverbal behavior. While many nonverbal behaviors are consistent across people, atypical social behavior might necessitate a re-seeding of the model with new observations of that behavior.

We developed the model for a subset of the nonverbal behaviors that people use to communicate. Extending the model to include other features, such as head pose, might yield even greater accuracy and expressiveness.

6. ACKNOWLEDGMENTS

This work is supported by NSF grants 1117801 and 1139078.

7. REFERENCES

[1] M. W. Alibali and M. J. Nathan. Teachers' gestures as a means of scaffolding students' understanding: Evidence from an early algebra lesson. *Video Research in the Learning Sciences*, pages 349–365, 2007.

[2] S. Andrist, X. Z. Tan, M. Gleicher, and B. Mutlu. Conversational gaze aversion for humanlike robots. In *Proceedings of the 10th International Conference on Human-Robot Interaction (HRI '14)*. ACM, 2014.

[3] M. Argyle and M. Cook. *Gaze and Mutual Gaze.* Cambridge University Press, Oxford, England, 1976.

[4] K. Bergmann and S. Kopp. Modeling the production of coverbal iconic gestures by learning bayesian decision networks. *Applied Artificial Intelligence*, 24:530–551, 2010.

[5] D. Feil-Seifer and M. J. Matarić. Defining socially assistive robotics. In *Proceedings of the 9th International IEEE Conference on Rehabilitation Robotics*, 2005.

[6] S. Goldin-Meadow. The role of gesture in communication and thinking. *Trends in Cognitive Sciences*, 3(11):419 – 429, 1999.

[7] C.-M. Huang and B. Mutlu. Learning-based modeling of multimodal behaviors for humanlike robots. In *Proceedings of the 2014 ACM/IEEE International Conference on Human-Robot Interaction*, pages 57–64. ACM, 2014.

[8] T. Kanda, R. Sato, N. Saiwaki, and H. Ishiguro. Friendly social robot that understand human's friendly relationships. In *Proceedings of the 2004 IEEE/RSJ International Conference on Intelligent Robots and Systems*, pages 2215–2222, 2004.

[9] J. M. Kory, S. Jeong, and C. L. Breazeal. Robotic learning companions for early language development. In *Proceedings of the 15th ACM on International Conference on Multimodal Interaction (ICMI '13)*, pages 71–72, New York, NY, USA, 2013. ACM.

[10] D. McNeill. *Hand and Mind: What Gestures Reveal about Thought.* The University of Chicago Press, Chicago, 1992.

[11] M. Neff, M. Kipp, I. Albrecht, and H.-P. Seidel. Gesture modeling and animation based on a probabilistic re-creation of speaker style. *ACM Transactions on Graphics*, 27(1):5:1–5:24, Mar. 2008.

[12] W.-M. Roth. Gestures: Their role in teaching and learning. *Review of Educational Research*, 71(3):365–392, 2001.

[13] B. Scassellati, H. Admoni, and M. Matarić. Robots for use in autism research. *Annual Review of Biomedical Engineering*, 14:275–294, 2012.

[14] M. Stone, D. DeCarlo, I. Oh, C. Rodriguez, A. Stere, A. Lees, and C. Bregler. Speaking with hands: Creating animated conversational characters from recordings of human performance. In *Proceedings of ACM SIGGRAPH*, pages 506–513, New York, NY, USA, 2004. ACM.

[15] M. Tomasello and M. J. Farrar. Joint attention and early language. *Child Development*, 57(6):1454–1463, 1986.

[16] K. Wada and T. Shibata. Living with seal robots—its sociophsychological and physiological influences on the elderly at a care house. *IEEE Transactions on Robotics*, 23(5):972–980, October 2007.

Towards Automated Assessment of Public Speaking Skills Using Multimodal Cues

Lei Chen
Educational Testing Service (ETS)
660 Rosedale Rd
Princeton, NJ, USA
LChen@ets.org

Gary Feng
ETS
660 Rosedale Rd
Princeton, NJ, USA
GFeng@ets.org

Jilliam Joe
ETS
660 Rosedale Rd
Princeton, NJ, USA
JJoe@ets.org

Chee Wee Leong
ETS
660 Rosedale Rd
Princeton, NJ, USA
CLeong@ets.org

Christopher Kitchen
ETS
660 Rosedale Rd
Princeton, NJ, USA
CKitchen@ets.org

Chong Min Lee
ETS
660 Rosedale Rd
Princeton, NJ, USA
CLee001@ets.org

ABSTRACT

Traditional assessments of public speaking skills rely on human scoring. We report an initial study on the development of an automated scoring model for public speaking performances using multimodal technologies. Task design, rubric development, and human rating were conducted according to standards in educational assessment. An initial corpus of 17 speakers with 4 speaking tasks was collected using audio, video, and 3D motion capturing devices. A scoring model based on basic features in the speech content, speech delivery, and hand, body, and head movements significantly predicts human rating, suggesting the feasibility of using multimodal technologies in the assessment of public speaking skills.

Categories and Subject Descriptors

H.5.1 [**Information interfaces and presentation**]: General—*Multimedia Information Systems*

Keywords

Multimodal Presentation Assessment, Public Speaking, Multimodal Corpus, Body Tracking, Educational Applications

1. INTRODUCTION

Oral communication is consistently rated as one of the most valued workforce skills in national surveys [8], and its importance is reflected in the Common Core State Standards for K12 education. Public speaking is the epitome - and evidently the most feared form [12] - of oral communication that is often overlooked in educational assessment.

ICMI'14, November 12–16, 2014, Istanbul, Turkey.

http://dx.doi.org/10.1145/2663204.2663265.

A successful public speaking performance is distributed across multiple modalities - e.g., the speech content, voice and intonation, facial expressions, head poses, hand gestures, and body postures. While current rubrics for evaluating public speaking performances attend to both verbal and non-verbal aspects, virtually all existing assessments require human rating [14]. In this paper, we describe research using multimodal sensing, namely motion tracking, head tracking, and speech processing, toward developing an automated assessment system for scoring presentation skills.

The remainder of the paper is organized as follows: Section 2 reviews the previous research on (a) analyzing presentation performance by using oral and multimodal cues and (b) multimodal corpus using Kinect tracking device. Section 3 describes the multimodal presentation corpus we created, including tasks, data recording methods, and the human scoring process. Section 4 describes experiments predicting presentation skills using multimodal features extracted from audio, video, and motion data. Finally, Section 5 summarizes the findings of the paper and discuss future research directions.

2. PREVIOUS RESEARCH

A number of publications described research prototypes of using audio and video cues to evaluate presentation skills. [13] conducted an audio/visual analysis on a political speech corpus and found some clues related to speaking performance rating. [7] developed a presentation coaching system by using Automatic Speech Recognition (ASR), prosody analysis, and image processing. A marker-based computer vision object tracking method was used for head tracking. However, marker-based and video-only methods for tracking body movements tend to be cumbersome and error-prone.

The emergence of 3D motion tracking devices such as the Microsoft Kinect has greatly facilitated multimodal research. [11] proposed building a public speaking evaluation system. Students participating in a scientific presentation course were recorded by using a Kinect device. [1] created a public speaking skill training system with a combination of advanced multimodal sensing and virtual human technologies. Meanwhile, a virtual audience would respond to the quality of the presentation in real time to provide feedback and training opportunities. In addition, affective computing has been utilized to analyze public speaking, especially focusing on speakers' stress responses [4, 5].

Two observations can be drawn from the literature. With regard to the technology, there is a convergence on 3D sensors such as Kinect in combination with audio/video recording as the basis for evaluating presentation performances. With regard to applications, there is much interest in designing interactive systems for training presentation skills. We believe the multimodal technology can transform traditional human-scored public speaking assessments [14] and make them more reliable and cost-efficient.

Our primary research question, therefore, is whether machine-generated multimodal features can predict human scores based on a well-designed rubric for public speaking performance. The aforementioned multimodal research [11, 1] has so far been based on non-standardized scoring rubrics and human scoring process, leaving it vulnerable to reliability threats. In addition, the content of the speech, which is central in traditional public speaking assessments, is seldom taken into account in these studies. We apply natural language processing techniques on speech transcripts as an initial attempt to calculate content-related features.

3. MULTIMODAL CORPUS

3.1 Tasks

Four public speaking tasks were developed. Tasks B and C were modeled after prepared informational speeches, in which the speaker was given a pre-prepared slide deck and up to 10 minutes to prepare for the presentation. Task B was a business presentation, where the speaker was to present a financial report. Task C is a simulated teaching task on the topic targeting middle school students. The other two tasks were persuasive and impromptu speeches. No visual aids were provided for Task D and Task E.

3.2 Multimodal Data Collection

A Microsoft Kinect for Windows Version 1 device was used to record 3D body motions. Brekel Pro Body Kinect tracking software (v1.30 64 bit version) was used to record 48 body joints and stored the motions in the Biovision hierarchical data format (BVH). A JVC Everio GZ-HM35BUSD digital camcorder was used for audio/video recording. The camcorder was mounted together with Kinect on a tripod. The raw video resolution used UXP high definition setting and was saved in the MTS format. Both Kinect and camcorder were placed 6ft away from the front of the speaking zone that was marked on the ground. For Tasks B and C, a SMART Board projector system was used to show the PowerPoint slides.

Speakers were 17 volunteers recruited from an education assessment company, with 10 male participants and 7 female participants. 7 of the participants were experienced public speakers from the Toastmasters Club. The rest varied widely in their experience in public speaking. The participants' time was covered by the employer so they did not additional compensation. After being familiarized with the recording equipment, participants were informed that they were expected to speak for 4 to 5 minutes for Task B and C and 2 to 3 minutes for Task D and E. For Tasks B and C, which involved PowerPoint slides, they were given 10 minute to prepare for their presentation. They were not allowed to bring notes during the presentation. In Task D and E, the participants were given no preparation time. They would start speaking as soon as they were given the topic of the impromptu speech. Before each recording, the speaker was asked to clap, which served as a signal synchronizing the multimodal data. Some data were lost due to equipment failures. In total, we obtained 56 presentations with complete multimodal recordings.

3.3 Data Processing

After getting raw recordings from our lab sessions, the following steps were taken to process the data for further analysis. The motion and video data streams were synchronized. The HD video files were converted to another format (with a higher compression rate) for playing back, e.g., in Xvid or *H*.263 codec. The audio channel from the video was extracted for several speech processing procedures, including (a) manual transcription, (b) using P2FA [16] forced alignment tool to obtain time stamps for all transcribed words (and phonemes), (c) using Praat [2] acoustics analysis software to extract pitch and intensity measurements. In addition, nonverbal features related to hand movements, body locomotion, and head orientation, were computed. More details will be provided in Section 4.1.

3.4 Human Rating

A key emphasis of our research is a valid and comprehensive assessment of the public speaking skills. To this end we designed the human rating process according to the standard practice in educational assessment. We began with a construct analysis of skills involved in public speaking and a review of existing assessments and rubrics. The final rubric was based on the Public Speaking Competence Rubric (PSCR) [14] due to its psychometric properties. According to their study using five trained faculty member raters on 45 speech presentations by college students, the *intraclass correlation coefficients* (ICCs; a measure of variance in scores associated with raters) across the 10 dimensions and holistic score ranged from .37 to .93, making it one the most reliable human-scored instruments for assessing public speaking performance.

Using the PCSR tailored to our tasks, human raters scored these presentation videos on 10 dimensions, such as vocal expression (VE), which measures the efficiency of using vocal expression and paralinguistic cues to engage the audience, and nonverbal behavior (NVB), which measures the effect of using nonverbal behaviors to reinforce verbal messages, as well as overall holistic scores.

Five raters were recruited from the same educational assessment company. Two expert raters had background in oral communication/public speaking instruction at the higher education level. The other three (non-expert raters) had extensive experience in scoring essays, but not in scoring public speaking performances. For reliability purposes, the presentations were double-scored. The scoring process was organized in two phases. Phase 1 involved working with the two expert raters in order to develop criterion scores for a randomly selected subset of presentation videos. The criterion videos and scores were used to train non-expert raters in Phase 2. During the training, non-expert raters review exemplar videos from the criterion set and discuss with expert raters in order to come to the same scores. The process continued until they could reliably rate the criterion set. In

Phase 2 expert and non-expert raters worked together to score the remainder of the presentations. Each presentation was randomly assigned to an expert and a non-expert rater, who scored independently. Regarding holistic scores, between human raters, ICC is 0.385 and Pearson correlation is 0.385. The following adjudication process was used to generate final scores. If two raters agree with each other, the score will be used as the final score. Otherwise, a third rater (expert) will be brought in to make the final judgment. In our experiments described in Section 4, we focused on the final holistic scores after the adjudication process.

4. EXPERIMENTS

4.1 Multimodal Features

We focused on three types of features, namely speech delivery, speech content, and non-verbal behaviors. For speech delivery, we included features widely used in automated speech scoring. In particular, following the feature extraction method described in [3], we used speech and transcription to generate a series of features on the multiple dimensions of speaking skills, e.g., speaking rate, prosodic variations, pausing profile, and pronunciation.

Features of the content of speech were extracted using a syntactic complexity analyzer tool [9] on speech transcripts. This is a crude first attempt because speech transcripts differ importantly from written texts.This tool counts the frequencies of 9 types of syntactic structures, e.g., verb phrases (VP), T-units (T), clauses (C), etc., and computes 14 syntactic complexity feature values, such as the mean length of clause (MLC), verb phrases per T-unit (VP/T), etc. A complete list of the features can be found in [9].

For non-verbal features, we focused on the amount of locomotion, hand movements, and head orientation. The locomotion was indexed by the hip movement from the Kinect data. A basic feature set was extracted based on the mean and standard deviation (SD) of the hip and hand movement speeds and the log-transformed values. The orientation of the head is an approximation of the speaker's attention to the audience. Head poses were tracked by using GAVAM head tracker [10] from the video data. Unreliable data (with confidence less than 7) were marked as missing. The head features consist the mean, SD, as well as mean/SD on the log scale, of the horizontal and vertical head movements.

Given the modest size of the corpus, we chose to proceed with a simple feature selection process, by taking the top features from each category based on the Pearson correlation with the human rating scores on the entire data set [1], as seen in Table 1 on the next page.

4.2 Predicting Human Holistic Scores

We run a standard machine learning experiment for using these multimodal features to predict human judged holistic scores. In particular, we run a leave-one-out cross-validation among all of subjects ($n = 17$). In each fold, presentations from 16 subjects were used to train a regression model and then the trained model was applied to the presentations from the remaining subjects. Two regression approaches were utilized, including Random Forest (RF) and Support Vector Machine (SVM) using a polynomial kernel. We used the implementations provided by R caret package [6]. Hyper parameters of these machine learning models were automatically tuned by using a 5-fold cross-validation on the training set. The whole process was repeated for 17 times to obtain the machine predicted scores for all of the presentations. Table 2 reports on the correlation between the human rated holistic scores and machine predicted ones.

[1]If we have a large-sized data set, such feature selection will be conducted on the training set only.

Table 2: Regression models of using multimodal features to predict final holistic scores

Feature set	Random Forest (RF)	SVM
lexical	0.283	0.220
speech	0.312	0.372
visual	0.202	0.132
lexical + speech	0.383	0.377
multimodal	0.416	0.447

By using the lexical features, speech features, and visual features from videos and motions tracked by Kinect, respectively, we find that each modality provides information for predicting overall presentation performance. Among the three modalities, the speech channel provides the most information. After combining both lexical and speech features together, for the RF model, we saw a performance increase. However, such gain was not observed for the SVM model. On the basis of the verbal model (using both lexical and speech features), adding visual features makes the multimodal model achieve the highest performance. The correlation has been increased from 0.383 to 0.416 for the RF model and from 0.377 to 0.447 for the SVM model.

5. DISCUSSIONS

We reported an initial study toward building an automated multimodal scoring model for public speaking assessments. Based on our multimodal presentation corpus, we found that simple multimodal features of the speech content, speech delivery (fluency, pronunciation, and prosody), and nonverbal behaviors (head, body, and hand motions) together significantly predict human scores on the presentation performance. The result is promising as a first step toward an automated assessment of public speaking skills. The study extends prior research (e.g., [11, 1]) with better grounding in construct definitions, more rigorous human scoring process, and the incorporation of content features along with speech and non-verbal features. This interim report based on our initial corpus only explored a few basic features and modeling techniques. Limitations notwithstanding, our on-going research continues to focus on expanding the multimodal corpus, developing advanced features such as gesture recognition, and building more robust scoring models for the multimodal presentation assessment.

6. REFERENCES

[1] L. Batrinca, G. Stratou, A. Shapiro, L.-P. Morency, and S. Scherer. Cicero-towards a multimodal virtual audience platform for public speaking training. In *Intelligent Virtual Agents*, pages 116–128, 2013.

[2] P. Boersma and D. Weeninck. Praat, a system for doing phonetics by computer. Technical Report 132, University of Amsterdam, Inst. of Phonetic Sc., 1996.

[3] L. Chen, K. Zechner, and X. Xi. Improved pronunciation features for construct-driven assessment

Feature	Category	Description	r_{HS}
W	transcript	# words	0.417
S	transcript	# sentences	0.382
VP	transcript	# verb phrases	0.457
C	transcript	# clauses	0.439
T	transcript	# T-units	0.454
DC	transcript	# dependent clauses	0.298
CT	transcript	# complex T-units	0.298
CP	transcript	# coordinate phrases	0.305
CN	transcript	# complex nominals	0.339
DC	transcript	# dependent clauses per clause	0.298
MLC	transcript	mean length of clause	−0.112
DC.C	transcript	dependent clauses per clause	−0.173
T.S	transcript	T-units per sentence	0.302
SpeakRate	fluency	speaking rate in words per second	0.463
UttLenVar	fluency	Mean deviation of the lengths (words) in chunks	0.447
Pausing	fluency	Mean of pauses' lengths within clauses	−0.466
Pronunciation	pronunciation	Goodness of pronunciation [15, 3]	0.436
Prosody	prosody	Mean deviation of the prosodic units	0.326
HipMvLgSd	body	Hip movement (in log scale) SD	−0.328
LHMvLgSd	body	left hand movement (in log scale) SD	−0.393
RHMvLgSd	body	right hand movement (in log scale) SD	−0.275
FaceUpDownLgMean	head	Face Y-axis angle (in log scale) mean	−0.261
FaceUpDownSd	head	Face Y-axis angle SD	−0.254
FaceLeftRighMean	head	Face X-axis angle mean	−0.176
FaceLeftRightSd	head	Face X-axis angle SD	−0.158

Table 1: A list of multimodal features used in our experiment; Pearson correlations (rs) between the features and human rated holistic scores were reported in the last column.

of non-native spontaneous speech. In *NAACL-HLT*, 2009.

[4] T. Giraud, M. Soury, J. Hua, et al.. Multimodal expressions of stress during a public speaking task: Collection, annotation and global analyses. In *Affective Computing and Intelligent Interaction (ACII), 2013 Humaine Association Conference on*, pages 417–422. IEEE, 2013.

[5] A. Kleinsmith and N. Bianchi-Berthouze. Affective body expression perception and recognition: A survey. *Affective Computing, IEEE Transactions on*, 4(1):15–33, 2013.

[6] M. Kuhn. Building predictive models in r using the caret package. *Journal of Statistical Software*, 28(5):1–26, 2008.

[7] K. Kurihara, M. Goto, J. Ogata, Y. Matsusaka, and T. Igarashi. Presentation sensei: a presentation training system using speech and image processing. In *Proceedings of the 9th international conference on Multimodal interfaces*, pages 358–365. ACM, 2007.

[8] P. C. Kyllonen. Measurement of 21st century skills within the common core state standards. In *Invitational Research Symposium on Technology Enhanced Assessments. May*, pages 7–8, 2012.

[9] X. Lu. Automatic analysis of syntactic complexity in second language writing. *International Journal of Corpus Linguistics*, 15(4):474–496, 2010.

[10] L.-P. Morency, J. Whitehill, and J. Movellan. Monocular head pose estimation using generalized adaptive view-based appearance model. *Image and Vision Computing*, 28(5):754–761, 2010.

[11] A.-T. Nguyen, W. Chen, and M. Rauterberg. Online feedback system for public speakers. In *IEEE Symp. e-Learning, e-Management and e-Services*. Citeseer, 2012.

[12] C. B. Pull. Current status of knowledge on public-speaking anxiety. *Current opinion in psychiatry*, 25(1):32–38, 2012.

[13] S. Scherer, G. Layher, J. Kane, H. Neumann, and N. Campbell. An audiovisual political speech analysis incorporating eye-tracking and perception data. In *LREC*, pages 1114–1120, 2012.

[14] L. M. Schreiber, G. D. Paul, and L. R. Shibley. The development and test of the public speaking competence rubric. *Communication Education*, 61(3):205–233, 2012.

[15] S. M. Witt. *Use of Speech Recognition in Computer-assisted Language Learning*. PhD thesis, University of Cambridge, 1999.

[16] J. Yuan and M. Liberman. Speaker identification on the scotus corpus. In *Proc. of Acoustics*, 2008.

Increasing Customers' Attention using Implicit and Explicit Interaction in Urban Advertisement

Matthias Wölfel[+,×] and Luigi Bucchino[+]
[+] School of Design, University Pforzheim, Pforzheim, Germany
[×] School of Digital Media, University Furtwangen, Furtwangen, Germany
matthias@wolfel.de, mail@luigibucchino.com

ABSTRACT
Online advertising campaigns are gaining customers' attention in comparison to advertisement campaigns in the urban space. How to bring back users' attention to advertisement in the urban space by using implicit and explicit interactions of the user is investigated in this publication. We have used age, gender and position estimates to automatically customize the advertisement campaign and 3D gestures to allow the customer to interact with the shown content. To evaluate the overall acceptability and particular aspects of such kind of targeted and interactive advertisement we have developed a prototypical implementation and placed it into a crowded shopping mall. In total 98 random visitors of the mall have experienced the system and answered a questionnaire afterwards.

Categories and Subject Descriptors
H.1.2 [**Models and Principles**]: User/Machine Systems – *Human factors*

General Terms
Design, Human Factors

Keywords
Interaction Design, Human-Computer-Interaction, Hybrid Space, Interactive Advertisement, User Attention, Public Displays

1. INTRODUCTION
In contrast to online advertising campaigns, advertisement in the urban space is losing attention due to the novel possibilities of personalized, individualized and interactive online campaigns. The emergence of hybrid urban spaces as the digital augmentation of space, merging the borders between physical and virtual space, allows to integrate these new possibilities in the urban context. This leads to a novel perception of urban space where the former coherent urban tissue becomes opened to customized placements of advertisement. Publicly placed targeted advertising apparently is supposed to have other impacts on the human mindset than those of classical billboard or shop window advertising. But can it be used to good effect and bring back customers' focus?

We believe that how this digital content is integrated into the urban environment, and the way of how we interact with it will significantly impact the effectiveness and acceptability of such systems. Hybrid, digitally augmented or replaced, advertisements apparently are supposed to require other interaction paradigms as known from traditional human-computer-interaction approaches in which the digital is clearly separable and not seamlessly integrated into the environment.

2. INTERACTION PARADIGMS FOR PUBLIC TARGETED ADVERTISEMENT
While the new technological possibilities of advertisement offer great value and have already started to change our personal and professional lives (in particular in the online world), we are mainly still using interaction paradigms derived for graphical user interfaces using a keyboard and a mouse.

Selecting an icon by pointing to it is likely the most widely used interaction principle to interface with virtual content. While not only well adapted, but even a better fit for touch input this interaction principle has to be called into question for touchless interfaces [1]. This type of interfaces observes and interprets the poses and gestures of users in 3D space by RGB, depth or other type of sensors [2]. Touchless input is the preferred choice to interface with digital content in the public due to hygienic reasons. Pointing to an object on a flat screen with three-dimensions of freedom (excluding rotation) is neither very natural nor effective: the arm gets tired after a very short time, it is not precise and takes longer than touching on a screen [3]. Using unique 3D gestures to select different functionalities, however, would be faster and more natural. Using 3D gesture recognition [4], instead of a graphical interface, no reference (a cursor on screen or an avatar) would be needed. Music, for instance, could be accessed by touching both ears with the hands to start playing; both arms straight in front of the body and raising or lowering one arm would change the volume respectively.

3. RELATED WORK
The idea of interactive advertisement is, of course, not new. The following examples show concepts of university prototypes and commercially used systems.

3.1 Interactive Display Window Concept
The Interactive Display Window Concept [5] by students of the Hyper Island Design School developed an interactive showcase for an Australian street wear label. The system is tracking the location of persons. The video sequences in the showcase are adjusted to the

ICMI '14, November 12 – 16, 2014, Istanbul, Turkey.

ACM 978-1-4503-2885-2/14/11…$15.00
http://dx.doi.org/10.1145/2663204.2663268

position of a single passer-by. The video shows a model in a rendered 3D room which shows different patterns on the walls. The virtual model presents street wear for young people about dynamic movements of the model (break dance, jumps). The model, the room design and the camera perspective react on the position of passers-by. The principal aim is the joy of interaction and to get attention, not the presentation of clothes.

3.2 Interactive Display Window

The English telecommunication provider Orange aimed to get more attention to their shop windows. After closing time, passers-by could read news on the screen, watch cinema trailers, play mini-games or could surf on the orange website [6]. The interaction was not obvious, however, at the first use. The user had to become active for using and experiencing it. He/she had to realize that his/her hand was tracked and that it could be used to control a cursor just like a mouse.

3.3 Interactive Shop Window

The Interactive Shop Window of the Fraunhofer Heinrich-Hertz Institute [7] offers the use of a display behind the showcase glasses by simple gestures. Via finger gestures digital objects can be moved, zoomed and virtual pages can be turned. Small cameras recognize the position of the face, eyes and hands as well as the position of each finger. The fingers, however, are treated like cursor movements.

As in the previous example, the user imitates the mouse behaviour of computers and does not use natural gestures like swiping the hand to flip a page.

The given example demonstrates that, for novel interfaces – those which are required for interactive urban advertisement – we cannot just take the given principles for granted, but we have to think twice and validate if these principles still hold. In addition we have to think about how they change the environment and context, in which they will be used.

4. INTERACTING WITH URBAN ADVERTISEMENT

Public displays are still widely assumed to be non-interactive and compete for audience attention with other stimuli in the environment. The audience, therefore, is initially passing, without noting that the content is targeted to them and that it is possible to actively interact with it. If it stays unnoticed that the content is automatically adapting to particular features of the user (e.g. gender, age, walking speed) or the environment (e.g. weather, traffic), it is not dramatic and its purpose might be still fulfilled. However, if the interaction possibilities cannot be communicated, they are not used and, therefore, cannot fulfill their original purpose. To get the attention of passers-by, the interactive advertisement needs to (1) first get noticed, (2) demonstrate its interactivity, and (3) motivate to interact with it [8].

On one hand, calls-to-action (e.g. touch to start) or attract loops (e.g. a repeating video) are "visual noisy" and therefore are not a proper fit. Just think about the distraction provided by the array of flickering neon signs in the main street of Ginza, Tokyo! On the other hand, relying only on targeted content (according to age and gender) is increasing attention, but not as much as it possibly could otherwise. In addition the individualization often stays unnoticed. Therefore, a less obtrusive way which still attracts significant attention is preferable. It comes in handy that humans are well trained to recognize human motion and to realize if somebody is following and copying the movements (kinesthetic-visual matching [9]). By matching the movements of a person walking by with a virtual mannequin on a screen this person gets temporary irritated, stops, turns his/her face to the virtual mannequin and realizes that he/she can control it. This irritation, however, often happens after passing the display (landing effect [10]). In this case the virtual mannequin stops following at the display boarder waiting for the passers-by to turn and come back. The resampling of the movements can now be used to let the mannequin pose (inadvertent interaction).

Whether it is possible to change the content and how is still unclear at this point, because no visual information is given on how to interact with the system and what 3D gestures are expected to interface the system (invisibility dilemma [11]). This is in contrast to pointing (no matter if controlled by mouse, finger or in 3d space): The icons provide visual hints, people are assuming – if properly designed – that you can select them by pointing to it and people have already got accustomed to it. The previous statements would favor to stick with pointing, but there are other drawbacks as already discussed in Section 2. Therefore, a *learning phase* on how to use the system is required. A brief tutorial video can demonstrate what 3D gestures are possible and what they are used for. Learned once, this information has not to be given again for the same user.

5. EVALUATION

In the following we report on the evaluation of our approach: We were preliminary interested whether such kind of system could already be applied "in the wild" and whether it would be accepted by the potential target audience and fulfills its purpose. A short-term field study has allowed us to collect and analyze a large set of data. This does, however, not allow for a prediction of the long-term

Figure 1: Demonstrating the different possible 3D gestures. Opening the menu by moving the hand up and down. Changing the top to the next one by swiping the arm. By turning the body the virtual mannequin turns with you.

effect on the user and his long-term buying behavior, but it is already a good indicator. Furthermore, we asked the users to fill out a questionnaire after the experiment.

5.1 Setup

An "interactive display", realized by projection with a beamer on a canvas, replaces the traditional shop window in its size (3x2 meters) and function. Instead of a window mannequin, a virtual fashion model is presented. Even though 3D models would have given us more "visual possibilities" (e.g. exactly following the movement of the user) than composed recordings of real humans, we decided for the latter. This decision is based on two reasons: the *uncanny valley*[1] [12] and that 3D real-time rendering of fabric is a tremendous effort.

We have used two sensors located next to the display: An RGB camera with successive pattern analysis to estimate the age and gender group (boy, girl, woman or man). This information has been used to switch the shown mannequin to the according group. A Kinect™ and the software Kinetic Space [4] to get the position, orientation and the 3D gestures. The position and orientation are used by the system to let the mannequin resemble the movements of the person in front of the screen. The gestures (see examples in Figure 1) are used to change the dress of the mannequin and to switch the automatically determined age and gender group:

- Raising and lowering the hand: A menu appears (sliding down from the top). Now you can use one of the following gestures to navigate in the menu.
- Sliding the right hand to left in front of the head: The next top slides into the image and gets pulled on the virtual mannequin.
- Sliding the right hand to left in front of the belt: The next bottom slides into the image and gets pulled on the virtual mannequin.
- Sliding the left hand to right in front of the head: The previous top slides into the image and gets pulled on the virtual mannequin.
- Sliding the left hand to right in front of the belt: The previous bottom slides into the image and gets pulled on the virtual mannequin.

5.2 Participants

The participants were randomly selected visitors of the shopping mall *Schlössle Gallerie*[2] located in Pforzheim, Germany and recruited on site free of charge. This method has the disadvantage that people without interest in the shown content or system in general could simply walk away without answering the questionnaire – this group, however, might be immune to advertisement anyway.

In total, 98 participants (58 female, 40 male) used the system and filled out a questionnaire. None of them have ever used an interactive shopping window before. 30 participants were in the range between 10 and 20 years, 25 between 20 and 30, 12 between 30 and 40 and 15 above 50.

[1] The uncanny valley describes the response of revulsion among some humans when artificial human features look and move almost, but not exactly, like natural human beings.

[2] Link to the shopping mall "Schlössle Gallerie" in Pforzheim, Germany, http://www.schloessle-galerie.de/

6. RESULTS

We have expected that the different age and gender groups would show large variation in the given scores. The scores, however, were nearly similar (a maximum difference of 0.4 for age groups and 0.3 difference between male and female) with one exception: A 69 year old woman, voted the system very negative, while all others were quite positive (also the ones of the same age group). Due to this finding results are presented without differentiation of age or gender. Most people found that the system feels natural, is fun to be used and innovative – a key aspect in advertisement.

The score range for all questions, followed the rules of a forced choice Likert scale, went from (1) strongly agree, (2) agree, (3) disagree to (4) strongly disagree.

6.1 Targeted Advertisement

We have been keen to know whether our study group would vote targeted advertisement favorable or not. We separated between online and public advertisement. With "online" we refer to the Internet services provided by Amazon (customers also bought), Google (paid search queries), etc. while "public" was what the study group has been experienced in our demonstrator.

In average people agreed (a score of 2.0 for online and 1.6 for public) that targeted advertisement is useful with a clear preference to public. Nine persons, out of 98, voted online more useful as public while 33 voted public more useful. More than the average voted public and online (private) equally.

6.2 Information and Buying Interest

But does the proposed targeted advertisement system provide better information and raise buying interests? Except for the previously mentioned outlier, all asked persons at least partly agreed that they get better informed with such kind of system. A system which provides better information seems not be directly transferred into buying interests: While 31 participants strongly agreed to get better informed, only 19 strongly agreed to have a higher buying interest in the presented products. Five persons even strongly disagreed that their buying interest was raised.

6.3 Personal Issues

Touching public user interfaces might feel uncomfortable because the surface feels dirty and people are afraid that microorganisms from contaminated people can be transferred during use [13]. 19 participants of our study strongly agreed and 20 agreed to feel some form of disgust touching public interfaces and thus, independent of the content, have a negative user experience. Some reported that they would not touch a public interfaces to interact if they don't have to. They would, for instance, touch an interface to get a train ticket but not to get more information of an ad.

In this respect it would be preferable that a public interface is touch free. It might, however, have other disadvantages: it might collect personal data because of the needed sensor technology and the persons might feel uncomfortable to use it if watched by others. The former concern was strongly agreed by 11 participants, they did not, however, transfer their bad feeling onto the presented products. The latter issue was not confirmed: The vast majority did not feel uncomfortable using the defined gestures, 12 agreed (3 strongly agreed) to feel embarrassed. In a crowded place, the investigated interface, might not be used by those kind of people.

7. CONLUSSION

In this paper we presented a novel approach to advertisement in the urban environment. In a case study we could confirm that by using implicit user interaction, content can be tailored to increase passers-by attention. Gender and age are already good indicators what is paid attention to. In our experiments gender and age estimations have not been very reliable for various reasons. We found that a misclassification, however, is not dramatic as long as the feature of tailoring is unknown. If these features, however, were known and the passer-by got wrongly classified, people got either disappointed or amused. It is, therefore, preferable to show targeted content only, if the confidence of the classifiers is high, and to show general content otherwise.

The possibility to control the mannequins pose by moving his/her own body is obvious to all users. The possible poses of the mannequin need to be restricted to not show strange poses or completely mess up the visualization. Changing the closes of the mannequins by 3D gestures provides a more natural user interface than pointing gestures, even though a learning stage is required. In addition the 3D gestures helped to foster the *honeypot effect* [14] that describes the effect to people being attracted by persons already interacting with a device. The 3D gestures were correctly detected most of the time (above 95%). If a misclassification happened or the gesture was not registered, most people corrected or repeated them without thinking about it. The 3D gestures to control the system have to be carefully designed to avoid gestures, which are believed by the users to contradict their role in society. Crossing the threshold between passively observing and actively interacting requires a higher level commitment from the passers-by. Persons are only willing to spend their time and effort if they see themselves benefiting. Our design of the system – a mannequin following and resampling the passers-by – fostered the willingness to spend more time with the advertisement and to interact with it. If this is true in other cultures has to be investigated.

A feature many people asked for was a further personalization of the shown mannequins: some would prefer to see their own face instead of the model or that it would resemble their body shape. They felt irritated or amused that the "mirror" was showing a different person.

Even though privacy is widely discussed lately and this tech-nology might be a risk that systems acquire information about the users, which they would rather keep privately for themselves, only little concerns about this issue can be confirmed. To maintain the status quo the passers-by have to be informed what data is collected, what it is used for and if it gets stored.

Other benefits of such systems are lower logistic work because decoration elements and outfits won't need to be transported or mannequins be decorated. Detailed outfit demonstrations are also possible because the virtual mannequins can be seen from all angles and poses. In addition a whole collection can be shown and individually combined by the user to fit his/her personal taste.

In combination with other urban computing applications [15] targeted advertising in urban space can go far beyond the possibilities demonstrated in this publication. It can react to local weather and news, analyze your emotional state or exchange data with your smartphone to either identify you or to push additional information to it. A whole array of novel possibilities. What is possible, however, is not necessarily socially and legally permissible. Consumers will soon have to decide what they are willing to accept. While some might be turned off by constant deeply personalized advertisement in public space, others will enjoy the greater relevance of the new offers presented to them.

8. REFERENCES

[1] M. Wölfel. U. Gehmann, and M. Zampella, "Rethinking Interaction Design for Hybrid Urban Space," In Proc. of UrbanIxD Symposium September 2014

[2] Q. Pu, S. Gupta, S. Gollakota, S. Patel, "Whole-home gesture recognition using wireless signals." In Proceedings of the 19th annual international conference on Mobile computing & networking, ACM, pages 27-38, September 2013

[3] U. Bröckl, A. Harter, and A. S. Skrenkovic, „Eine Variante von Fitts Gesetz zum Vergleich von 2D- und 3D-Interaktion." In: Reiterer, H. & Deussen, O. (Editors), Mensch & Computer, Oldenbourg Verlag, pages 313-322, 2012

[4] M. Wölfel, „Kinetic Space: 3D-Gestenerkennung für dich und mich," Konturen, Ausgabe 31, p. 58-63, 2012

[5] B. Areilza, G. Engström, J.O. Silva, L. Lima, and M. Wallander, "Interactive Display Window Concept." URL: http://vimeo.com/ 18499643 [8.04.13], 2010

[6] O. Schwede "Interaktives Schaufenster begeistert Passanten." URL: http://invidis.de/2008/01/poi-nach-ladenschluss-bei-orange/ [8.04.13], 2008

[7] P. Chojecki, "Interactive Shop Window: Ein interaktiver Schaufensterbummel" URL: http://www.hhi.fraunhofer.de/de/ infocenter/projekt-des-monats/archiv-2012/das-interaktive-schaufenster.html [8.04.13], 2011

[8] J. Müller, F. Alt, D. Michelis, and A. Schmidt, "Requirements and design space for interactive public displays." In Proc. of ACM Multimedia '10, ACM, pages 1285-1294, 2010

[9] R.W. Mitchell, "Kinesthetic-Visual Matching and the Self-Concept as Explanations of Mirror-Self-Recognition." Journal for the theory of social behaviour 27.1 (1997): 17-39.

[10] J: Müller, Robert Walter, Gilles Bailly, Michael Nischt, Florian Alt, „Looking Glass: A Field Study on Noticing Interactivity of a Shop Window" In CHI '12: Proceedings of the 2012 ACM Conference on Human Factors in Computing Systems. Austin, TX, USA, May 5-10, 2012. ACM, New York, NY, USA. ISBN 978-1-4503-1015-4

[11] M. Kranz, P. Holleis and A. Schmidt "Embedded interaction: Interacting with the internet of things", Internet Computing, IEEE, 14(2), 46-53, 2010

[12] M. Mori, K.F. MacDorman, N. Kageki, "The Uncanny Valley [From the Field]," Robotics & Automation Magazine, IEEE, vol.19, no.2, pp.98,100, June 2012

[13] K. Chairman, K. Elizabath Mathew, C. Padmalatha, and A. J. A. Ranjit Singh. "Beware of pathogenic microbes in public utility devices." Journal of Microbiology & Biotechnology Research 1 (3): 85-90, 2011.

[14] H. Brignull, and Y. Rogers "Enticing people to interact with large public displays in public spaces." In Proceedings of INTERACT'03, Zurich, pp. 17-24, 200

[15] Y. Zheng, L. Capra, O. Wolfson, H. Yang. "Urban Computing: concepts, methodologies, and applications." ACM Transaction on Intelligent Systems and Technology. 5(3), 2014

System for Presenting and Creating Smell Effects to Video

Risa Suzuki, Shutaro Homma, Eri Matsuura, Ken-ichi Oakada
Keio University
3-14-1 Hiyoshi, Kohoku-ku, Yokohama-shi, Kanagawa-ken, Japan
{risa, honma, matsuura, okada}@mos.ics.keio.ac.jp

ABSTRACT

Olfaction has recently been gaining attention in information and communication technology, as shown by attempts in theaters to screen videos while emitting scents. However, because there is no current infrastructure to communicate and synchronize odor information with visual information, people cannot enjoy this experience at home. Therefore, we have constructed a system of smell videos which could be applied to television (TV), allowing viewers to experience scents while watching their videos. To solve the abovementioned technical problems, we propose using the existing system for broadcasting closed caption. Our system's implementation is mindful of both video viewers and producers, allowing the system on the viewer end to disperse odorants in synchronization with videos, and allowing producers to add odor information to videos. We finally verify the system's feasibility. We expect that this study will make smell videos become common, and people will enjoy ones in daily life in the near future.

Categories and Subject Descriptors

H.5.1 [**Information Interfaces and Presentation**]: Multimedia Information Systems – *artificial, augmented, and virtual realities*.

General Terms

Design, Human Factors.

Keywords

Olfactory information; human computer interaction; multimedia; closed caption; authoring tool.

1. INTRODUCTION

Interaction with computer via five senses of human (eyesight, hearing, smell, taste, and touch) has gathered attention. In five senses, olfactory stimulation has a strong, direct connection to human emotion and memory. Therefore, some attempts to integrate videos with odors have been done. Videos accompanied by odors increase viewer concentration and retention of the video [13]. Furthermore, odors added to videos enable to increase viewer immersion. To take advantage of these phenomena, some "smell films" have been shown such as *Willy Wonka and the Chocolate Factory* [8], and other smell videos have been attempted in specialized theaters in theme parks. However, people cannot enjoy smell videos at home. Many people have probably at least once imagined that aromas were emitted from an image of delicious-looking food on the TV. In this study, we propose a system to allow smell video to become a reality also on TV. To this end, we think smell supports must exist on both viewer and producer end. TV sets on the viewer end need to be able to receive smell programs and emit odors. On the other hand, producers need to make videos that incorporate olfactory information. We therefore address both sides of this system and propose the style to enjoy smell video in daily life.

In Section 2, we introduce current studies on videos with odor components. In Section 3, we propose our smell video system. Section 4 explains the system's implementation, and Section 5 assesses its feasibility. Finally, in Section 6, we present our conclusions.

2. RELATED WORK

The challenges of emitting odors in a movie theater have started since 1950s. The travelogue film *Behind the Great Wall* was released in 1959, accompanied by "AromaRama." The system piped odors through the air-conditioning system of a theater. In the next year, *Scent of Mystery* was released, and the invention known as "Smell-O-Vision" was introduced. This film was whodunit story, and odors were used as clues to identify a murder. Audiences smelled from a network of tubes to each individual seat. In these attempts, odors were diffused and lingering in the air, so that different kinds of odors were mixed. Smell films gathered attention, but mixture of motion pictures and synthetic odors was not acceptable [7, 15, 19]. With improved technology, we can have an experience with 4D world along with a development of 3D images recently. 4D is three dimensions plus odor, and it became widely known by the film *Spy Kids: All the Time in the World in 4D* released in 2011 [17]. Audiences could have some opportunities to "smell" not only view the scenes in the movie. They received the Aromascope cards that eight numbers were outlined. When a number was showed in the screen through the movie, they scratched and sniffed the same number in the card. Eight odors were not mixed each other, but audiences had to scratch the card when they were absorbed in the film, so it was difficult to make them feel the scenes alive.

In recent years, the research to eject odors through the display screen has been done. Tomono et al. used a thin LED display panel and presented odors from the tiny pores of the panel [14]. Matsukura et al. also proposed the screen to present odors, but they gave users an odor through the airflow by fans placed at the corner of the screen [9]. In addition, the systems to emit odors while displaying videos have also been studied. Nakamoto et al. constructed a remote communication system via the Internet,

ICMI '14, November 12 - 16 2014, Istanbul, Turkey
Copyright 2014 ACM 978-1-4503-2885-2/14/11…$15.00
http://dx.doi.org/10.1145/2663204.2663269

enabling to transmit and receive odor information with a video [2]. The SubSmell system developed by Pornpanomchai et al. can emit odor while displaying video [12]. Here, the kind of odor and the time of emission are coordinated by the SubSmell logo, which is an odor emission cue according to color, presented on the corner of the screen. These systems would assume that odor information is treated on the PC not on TV. When odors are emitted with some programs on TV, viewers can enjoy them in their own homes and can feel a high realistic sensation of the scenes. For example, when items like perfume are advertised on TV commercials with their scents, viewers can smell and may purchase them, because Ward et al. indicate that odor is something the customer cannot ignore [20]. However, this smell TV has not come true. To make it a reality, it is necessary to propose the way of transmission of odor information since there are some strict TV broadcast standards. However, existing ideas of emitting odors with videos have not taken into account TV broadcast. In addition, existing studies are specific to odor emission. Though they proposed the way of synchronizing odor with video, they have not proposed the way of creating smell effects for video. A perspective of smell video production, not only smell video playback, is necessary to become common.

3. SYSTEM FOR PRESENTING AND CREATING SMELL EFFECTS TO VIDEO

We propose a system to synchronize odors with videos, which will enable viewers at home to enjoy watching and smelling videos like on TV. In this study, we approach three difficulties which existing researches have not dealt with: odor mixing, smell video applied to TV, and smell video production.

First, we solve the odor mixing problem. In some attempts of smell film, odors were diffused in the air, and a theater was filled with them. When multiple different odors were emitted, audiences smelled the mixture of them and felt unpleasant. This problem is one of the reasons why smell films have not become common yet [8]. To address the difficulty, we adopt pulse ejection, which is the way of emitting odors for very short durations [11]. By setting the time and the intensity, we control the amounts of emitted odorants particularly. Since very small amounts of odorants are emitted, the pulse ejection enables to switch different odors instantly, with no action like scratching cards in the attempt of *Spy Kids*. Then, it eliminates the problem of mixing odors, and smell video can raise realistic sensation which viewers feel.

Second, we think about the feasibility of smell TV because smell video will be expected to become common if we can watch one on TV at home. As pointed out in the previous section, however, existing systems to emit odors with videos have not considered applying to TV. We therefore construct a system for smell TV corresponding to current TV standards. Since TV is now almost ubiquitous and TV broadcasting follows a standardized system, it is not easy to change the standard to incorporate a dedicated channel for sending odor information. Hence we use closed caption to synchronize odors with videos. Closed caption is a TV system that displays audio captions for viewers to read at the bottom of the screen, and is available at the viewers' discretion by pressing the remote-control button. Most TVs have decoders of them as a standard feature. By using the existing closed captions channel, the need for new infrastructure can be avoided. We propose the way to send the odor information by inserting into closed-captioned data. In recent years, digital telecast become common, and TV can be connected to the Internet. However, we

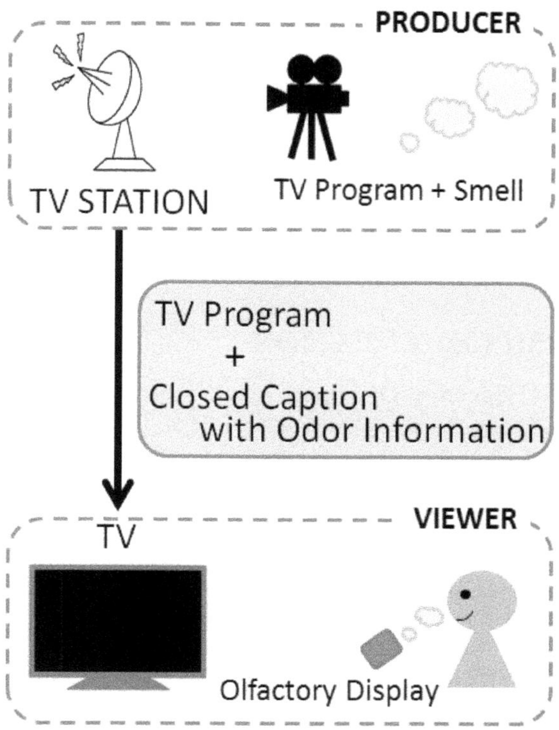

Figure 1. Flow of our system

choose the system of closed caption, because it is easily editable and already synchronized with video. Closed captions are simple data strings, so that it is easy to edit them to insert odor information. In addition, since closed captions are displayed on the screen in time with each scene, our system doesn't require a new structure for synchronization. Thus, it is easy to introduce odor into existing TV with our system.

The last point of this study is adding odors to videos. There have been few studies to focus on production of smell videos, but we think that it is necessary to construct the system to produce smell videos in order to become popular. We propose the style that people enjoy smell videos by creating smell effects for themselves. If smell TV comes true, seeing smell videos will become so common. When people watch or produce videos at home, they may want to enjoy them with odors. We therefore provide the way to create smell effects for videos easily and the new way to enjoy videos. To add matched odor for each scene, producers need to set kind of odor and ejection time while watching the video and smelling the odors. In addition, we propose that odor intensity is also set to represent more realistic scenes. The odor information can be saved as a closed-captioned data file format automatically. By synchronizing odors with videos using closed-captioned data, our system allow people not only to produce but to share smell videos on the website like YouTube, since most video-sharing sites have a function of uploading closed-captioned data.

Then, we introduce our system, taking application to TV for example. Figure 1 shows the flow of the system, incorporating both producer and viewer end. Producers of smell videos of course need to create smell effects for their programs, setting kind, timing, and intensity of each odor. While kind and timing are required to present a sense of realism [5], odor intensity is required to present a sense of perspective. Producers must create these effects, which are represented in strings and inserted into the closed-captioned data. Then, the data is broadcasted. On the viewer end, the odor information is extracted from the closed-captioned data, and it is sent to the olfactory display, allowing viewers to smell the odor synchronized with the scene in the video. In this system, the olfactory display which is capable of pulse ejection is used. We think that the above system, using closed-captioned data, will make smell TV a reality and make smell video accessible for people, who will be able to enjoy odors with videos in daily life. Furthermore, our system allow for the further development of interaction through olfaction.

4. IMPLEMENTATION

4.1 Olfactory Display

The olfactory display we use in our system is "Fragrance of Jet for Mobile." It is worn around the neck as shown in Figure 2-A, and only the user can smell the emitted odors. Figure 2-B shows a plane view of it, and Figure 2-C shows a side view. This device adopts the thermal method used in ink-jet printers to emit odors. It has an ejection head, storing one large tank and three small tanks. Each of the tank stores an odorant, thus four kinds of odors can be contained. Odorants are emitted in picoliter (pl) quantities from small holes in the head on the wind by a fan. The average ejection quantity from one large tank's hole is 7.3 pl and one small tank's hole is 4.7 pl. There are 255 minimum holes in the head connected to the large tank and 127 minimum holes in the head connected to the small ones. Since this device can emit odorants from multiple holes at one time, the ejection intensity is controlled by the number of holes, of which the range is 0-255 in large tank or 0-127 in small tanks. In addition, the time of ejection can be controlled by 667 microseconds, the unit time. Hence, shown in Figure 3, the total ejection quantity for one pulse is determined by the ejection time and the ejection quantity per unit time, which is determined by the average ejection quantity of using tank (7.3 pl or 4.7 pl) and the number of holes. The device is capable of this pulse ejection, allowing it to emit odors in a manner to avoid sensory adaptation [6]. Since pulse ejection can also prevent odors from lingering in the air, the device can also emit different odors for each scene and switch odors quickly. It is therefore suitable for presenting odors with videos.

In this study, we use the wearable olfactory display in order that only a viewer can smell odors. If a normal free-standing, rather than wearable, olfactory display is used, odors may permeate the vicinity as is the case in movie theaters. However, with the wearable olfactory display, these problems can be avoided. It can make a personal enjoyable space to smell. For example, a TV viewer in the living room can smell odors from a TV program, not disturbing what others in the same room are doing like reading magazines. The wearable olfactory display is also optimal when producing smell videos. It is easy for producers to use a computer to add odors because they need not change their postures to smell odors while watching videos. In addition, the device does not disperse a large amount of odorants into the air and not leave behind smells, so it is not necessary to prepare a dedicated room to create smell effects for video.

4.2 System of Synchronizing Smell with Video Using Closed Caption

When viewers watch smell videos, odors are emitted in time with their scenes. In this study, the smell effects are synchronized with

Figure 2-A. Wearable olfactory display

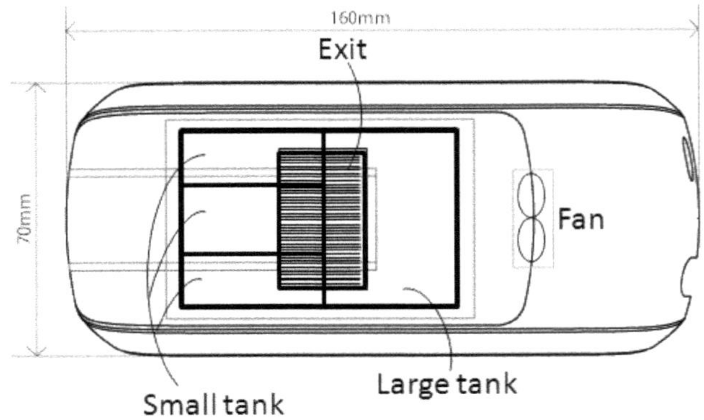

Figure 2-B. Overhead view of olfactory display

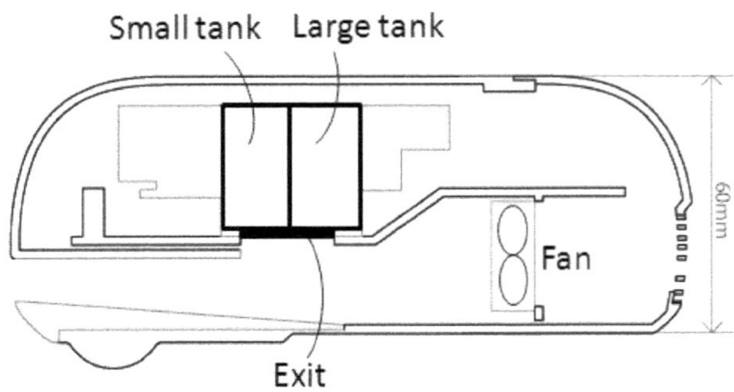

Figure 2-C. Sectional view of olfactory display

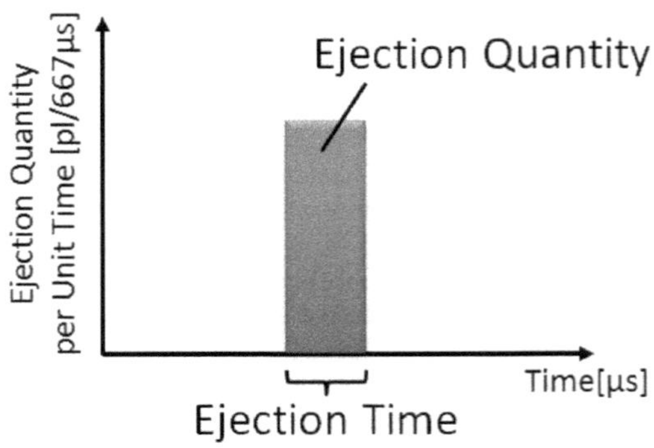

Figure 3. Pulse ejection

the videos by using closed-captioned data because smell videos can be applied to TV with no change in the current TV broadcast. Thus, we implement the system on the viewer end for the case of smell TV. Since the odor information will be conveyed via closed caption to a TV, it is required to extract the information from the caption data, as well as to emit odors from the olfactory display. The data are processed differently according to the viewers' situation. When the program has been recorded and is being watched after its original airtime, odor information is extracted by text analysis. On the other hand, when the program is watched as it airs, the data are instead obtained by image processing because it is encrypted by broadcast regulations and we cannot acquire it on the air.

We implemented this system using two laptop computers. One was connected to the TV and used for acquisition of the odor information from the closed-captioned data, and the other was connected to the wearable olfactory display and used for emitting the odors. The two laptops communicated via Bluetooth. Since the optimal TV viewing distance would differ according to the screen size [21], we implemented separately the processing of captions and the ejecting odors.

4.2.1 Smell Caption

In our system, the closed-captioned data containing the odor information is needed. It is represented as strings since the information can be easily inserted into the data. We call these strings "smell captions," and they are defined as follows.

&& [Number 1] [Number 2] [string (optional)] &&

"&&" bookends the smell caption. Since "&&" is rarely used in everyday text, smell captions are easy to pick out from the normal closed-captioned data. The [Number 1] field indicates the kind of odor. In this study, four kinds of odors can be used with the olfactory display, and we choose the familiar smells to our daily life. If an olfactory display can treat more kinds of odors, the numbers used in this field will be increased. The [Number 2] field indicates the odor intensity from three levels, where 1 is the recognition threshold, and 2 and 3 are increased stepwise logarithmically [16]. Table 1 outlines this system. After the two numbers, an optional string can be inserted, allowing a smell caption producer to add any desired comments. Since these comments are not used when the odors are emitted in viewer end, they are not indispensable. But here, the name of the odor indicating the smell caption is inserted as the comment because viewers can understand the mean of the smell caption when they watch the program while displaying the closed caption. When multiple odors are set to emit at one time, the captions are concatenated as follows: "&&13BANANA&&31MINT&&"

In our system, we use the SRT file format, one of the most popular softsub formats [18], for closed-captioned data. This format is chosen because it is text-based, easily editable, and contains accessory information such as the timestamp in addition to the caption itself. An example file containing the smell captions is shown in Figure 4. One caption data consists of four parts. The first line is a running number of the captions in the file. The second line is the time when the caption appears and disappears on the screen. The third or fourth line is the caption itself. The next blank line is a delimiter line. These four parts compose one caption as an entity. In this way, the data file is coincided with the videos by the timestamp, so the new infrastructure of synchronization is not needed.

Table 1. Smell caption number system

	Number 1 (Kind of Odor)	Number 2 (Odor Intensity)
1	Banana	Level 1 (Weak)
2	Rose	Level 2 (Medium)
3	Mint	Level 3 (Strong)
4	Lavender	

```
1
00:00:55,000 --> 00:00:58,333
Peeling a banana
&&11BANANA&&

2                                 — Running number
00:00:58,333 --> 00:01:00,000     — Display time
Peeling a banana                  — Caption
&&12BANANA&&                      — Smell caption

3                                 — Running number
00:01:00,000 --> 00:01:01,666     — Display time
&&12BANANA&&                      — Smell caption

4
00:01:01,666 --> 00:01:05,000
&&13BANANA&&
```

Figure 4. Example SRT file containing smell captions

4.2.2 Retrieving the Closed-captioned Data

4.2.2.1 Text Analysis Method

When viewers watch a recorded smell TV program, the closed-captioned data are acquired by text analysis. The timestamp and the caption contents are retrieved from the program in advance. The transport format and protocol for the digital television standard is based on the MPEG-2 system specification defined by the Advanced Television Systems Committee [1]. The MPEG-2 system standard defines various tables that provide information to transport services with multiplexing. One such table is the program map table (PMT), a collection of the sections taken in the MPEG-2 compression transport stream (TS). The closed-captioned data can be acquired by referring to the PMT [3]. MPEG-2 TS analysis software has been developed recently, so that closed-captioned data can be easily handled. The timestamp and the contents of the closed captions are saved as an SRT file. When the recorded TV program is played back, the file is read, and the closed caption, by referring to the timestamp and text value, is displayed in time with the video.

4.2.2.2 Image Processing Method

When viewers watch a smell TV program live, the closed-captioned data is acquired by image processing because we cannot access the encrypted caption data. The system captures the TV images and converts them to texts by using an optical character recognition (OCR) program, here, the Microsoft Office Document Imaging software. The software captures the images every 0.1 sec

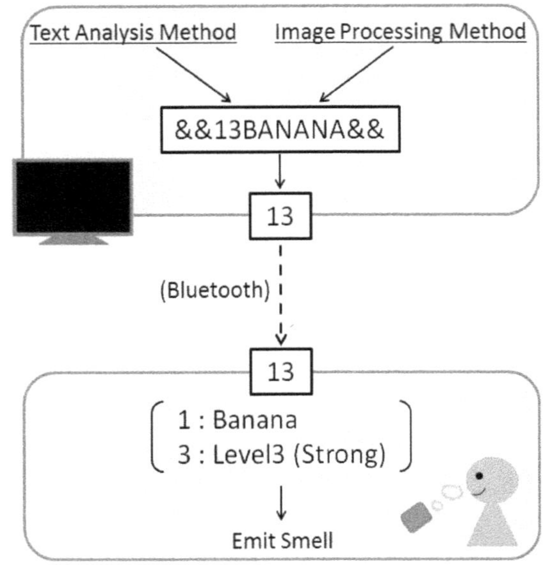

Figure 5. Odorant emission flowchart

and recognizes the closed-captioned data when any characters or numbers are displayed.

4.2.3 Odor Emission

After the closed-captioned data is acquired by text analysis or image processing, the smell captions bookended with "&&" are retrieved from it. After, the two key numbers in the smell captions are extracted. As mentioned earlier, one number indicates the kind of odor, and the other odor intensity. These numbers are sent together to the laptop PC that connects to the olfactory display. The olfactory display emits the odor according to the system previously outlined in Table 1. For example, if a smell caption "&&13BANANA&&" is retrieved, the number "13" would be sent to the olfactory display, which would emit a strong banana smell as summarized in Figure 5.

4.3 Authoring Tool of Smell Video

To enjoy smell videos in daily life, people would need to get smell video on TV or to set odors to their own videos. Most people, also TV producers, have probably not create smell effects for videos. We therefore designed an authoring tool to add and synchronize odors to videos, allowing people to easily create smell effects. Since they must be encoded as closed-captioned data using our system described above, our tool has functions for automatically converting and saving the smell effects to smell captions. It can also be used to make conventional captions. The tool interface is shown in Figure 6. The user watch the video in the upper half of the display and set the smell effects in the lower half. In Figure 6, the banana video [4] is used, and it is shown in the upper part.

The tool allows for setting the kinds of odors, the timing, and the odor intensity, to ensure the appropriateness of the smell effects for the presented scene. The kinds of odors are selected with the smell buttons located under the graph. The number of the smell buttons is based on the olfactory display, so it may be possible to increase the buttons if more kinds of odors will be used. When the video is stopped or paused, the emit button at the bottom can be clicked for the user to sample the odor selected by the smell button. When the video is playing, the emit button cannot be clicked. The timing and odor intensity are set using the graph, wherein time is the horizontal axis and intensity the vertical, which scrolls with the video playing in the top display. The red

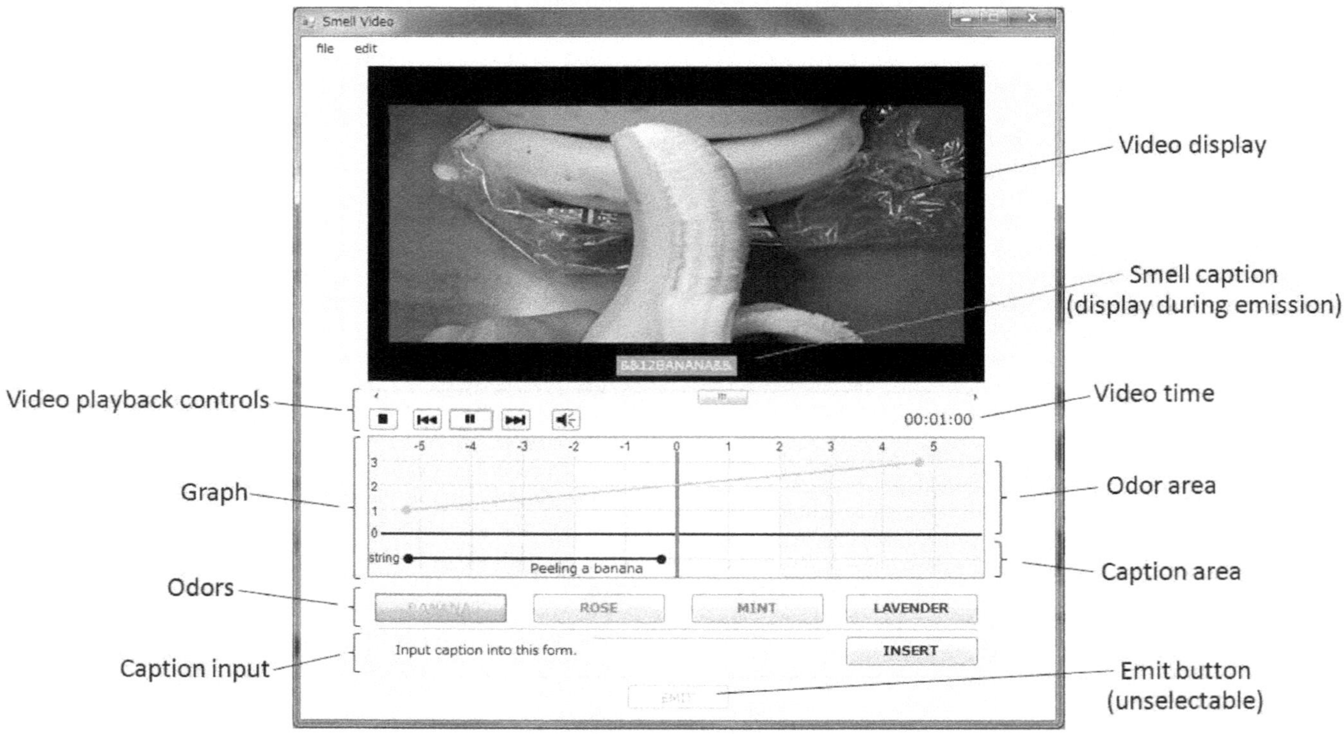

Figure 6. Application screen of adding smell into video

vertical line at X = 0 indicates the current position of the video. The section above the black line at Y = 0 is the odor-setting area, and the section below the line, where "string" is written to the left, is for setting captions. The user clicks the coordinates in the graph for the start and end point of each smell effect, resulting in a colored line as in Figure 6. The line color varies with each odor and corresponds to the color of each smell button. By drawing diagonal lines on the graph, the user can easily set shifts of odor intensity, allowing for fade-ins and fade-outs. This graphing system allows for timing and odor intensity to be set together. To make ordinary captions, the user inputs the strings in the form below the smell buttons, press the insert button, and set its duration time in the caption area. Then, the captions appear on the graph as a black line. If the black line is hovered over with the mouse, the corresponding caption will appear, as in Figure 6. This setup allows the user to create and check the smell effects set to the video with one application software.

When an odor is set to become stronger or weaker gradually, it is emitted so as to cause a sense of perspective [16]. When multiple odors are emitted at the same time, the odors are emitted such that the user feels stronger scents are closer and weaker scents are further away [10]. These patterns of emission are adopted to make the user smell effectively with the scene like this. The odors are emitted every 0.5 sec for the setting duration time in the manner of pulse ejection in order that the user can perceive them certainly. One emission of pulse is for 0.1sec. While the olfactory display is emitting the odor, the relevant smell caption is displayed at the bottom of the video screen. The smell effect information set with the tool is converted to the smell captions and saved as an SRT closed-captioned data file. Figure 4, mentioned earlier, is the captions which are converted in this way from the data set shown in Figure 6.

5. EVALUATION

5.1 Assessment of the System for Viewers

In the system for viewers, the closed-captioned data file, including smell captions, is needed. However, we cannot insert our captions into the existing caption data used in the current TV broadcasts. Therefore, we first acquired closed-captioned data from two TV programs, a one-hour news program and a one-hour variety show, and appended smell captions into these files. Each program had about 500 normal captions, and we inserted 150 smell captions to them respectively. We then demonstrated the text analysis method and measured the detection accuracy of the image processing method. As long as we wrote the program appropriately, the text analysis worked properly. Hence we verified the feasibility of our system with the image processing method. Since we were unable to get smell video from the current TV infrastructure, we used the popular video-sharing site, YouTube. The video and the caption data were uploaded to YouTube, allowing the Internet and YouTube to play the roles of TV broadcast and TV respectively. We found that the image processing system implemented here could recognize and convert real-time closed-captioned data as long as the video was viewed as a full-screen display and advertisements were eliminated. We played the videos with the updated captions in this way, and attempted to capture the smell captions by the OCR software. We counted the number of false smell caption detections, and the results are shown in Table 2. There were no false detections of the smell captions. Thus, the image processing method is a practical approach and is readily accepted. Both in the news program and the variety program, the smell captions were detected correctly, indicating that OCR accuracy was not dependent on the contents of the programs or the vocabulary used. It would thus appear that this method can be used and detect smell captions in other TV programs.

We also measured the time it took to emit odors from displaying smell captions in the image processing method. It had the OCR processing and the Bluetooth connection before odor emission, so we measured each time. The results are shown in Table 3. It took about 1.0 sec to emit odors in both programs. Thus, the image processing method could put into practical use because there are rarely scenes changed every one second. To synchronize the odor emission time with the caption display time strictly, it is only necessary to set the caption time ahead by 1.0 sec. In Table 3, most of the time to emit odors was spent in OCR processing, not Bluetooth connection. In the text analysis method, OCR processing is not need and it has only Bluetooth connection, so that there is less time lag. As just described, the accuracy of the image processing method and the time lag was confirmed. We also executed the text analysis method and verified its viability. We therefore believe that the system for viewers that we propose is practical for smell TV.

Table 2. Number of false smell caption detection

	News Program	Variety Show
False Detection	0 / 150	0 / 150

Table 3. Time lag of image processing method [sec]

	OCR Processing	Bluetooth Connection
News Program	0.93 ± 0.23	0.06 ± 0.03
Variety Show	0.82 ± 0.08	0.03 ± 0.04

5.2 Producer Usability

We evaluated the usability of our smell video authoring tool. 16 subjects (11 men and 5 women) participated to it. They were graduate or undergraduate students who were majoring in information engineering and used to typing at a keyboard, and nobody has created smell effects to videos. We asked them to add odors to videos and make closed-captioned data files containing smell captions as SRT files. Each participant used two approaches; the one was by using our tool (TOOL), and the other was typing the captions manually by using a video player and text editor (TYPING). If our authoring tool was not constructed, it would be necessary to type the smell captions manually when smell videos using closed captions were produced. We therefore compared TOOL with TYPING. Different videos were used for each approach. That is, first the half of the participants used a certain video by TOOL, and the other half used it by TYPING. Then, another video was used in the other way. We reduced the influence of the order of these methods in this way. Before the experiment, participants were briefed on how to use our tool and SRT file formatting. In this experiment, we used the videos which were about 80 sec long and had four scenes. We provided the participants with instructions and asked them to add odors to all four scenes of a video. Most scenes had specific instructions as to kinds of odors and odor intensity. In addition, there were also instructions regarding duration time of odor emission, change of intensity, and multiple odors to be emitted simultaneously. The instructions are shown in Table 4 for a video which had scenes of rose garden, cooking banana, a banana tart with mint, and lavender farm. We evaluated the time it took to add the smell effects to the video and create the closed-captioned data. In addition, we calculated the percentage of the captions which were made correctly as instructed (match rate), along five categories: timing, the kind of odor, odor intensity, SRT file format, and the smell caption string. At the end of the experiment, we asked the subjects to answer some questionnaires about our authoring tool.

Table 4. Sample instructions

Scene	Kind of Odor	Intensity Level
Rose Garden	Rose	2
Cutting and Mashing a Banana	Banana	Cutting : 2 Mashing : 3
Banana Tart	Banana and Mint	Banana : 3 Mint : 1
Lavender Farm	At Subject's Discretion	

The results are shown in Table 5. The average time of the TOOL was 402 sec, which was shorter than the time of TYPING. This time, we used an approximately 80 second-long video and the subjects could create the smell captions within 10 minutes using either method. The difference in time between the groups was about 2 minutes. The longer the video is, the more pronounced this time difference will become; for instance, if the video is 1 hour-long, the difference between the two methods will be expected to be about 1.5 hours. Thus, we believe that our application is an efficient tool for producing smell videos. In regard to the match rate, the average of TOOL was 93.8%, which was relatively high, indicating that most participants could add odors and make captions as instructed when using the tool. The standard deviation of TOOL was not very high, indicating that the rate did not vary much between individuals. The results by the nonparametric Wilcoxon signed-ranks test showed that there were significant differences between TOOL and TYPING in both the measured time ($z = -2.95$, $p < 0.05$) and the match rate ($z = -2.67$, $p < 0.05$). For this result, our authoring tool will enable users who are not experts in odor or caption to create smell effects quickly and properly.

Table 5. Comparison of smell caption production methods

	TOOL	TYPING
Time [sec]	402 ± 143	532 ± 159
Match Rate [%]	93.8 ± 9.3	77.5 ± 17.1

Table 6. Questionnaire about our authoring tool

Questionnaire	Average (5-point Scale)
Easy to Use	3.87
Intuitive Operation	4.33
Imagine the Real Smell Video on TV	4.00
Get Sensation of Designing Odor	4.47

The subjects rated the authoring tool on a five-point scale (5: Strongly Agree - 1: Strongly Disagree). Table 6 shows the questionnaire items and the results. All questionnaire items have over half of points. It seems that they could use our tool easily and intuitively. In respect of smell design, our tool received a high evaluation. They also could add odors to videos with the image of smell TV. Therefore, our authoring tool is user-intuitive and useful to create smell effects for videos.

6. CONCLUSION

In recent years, the potential of human five senses in particular to olfaction in information and communication technology has drawn attention, and some videos that make use of smell effects, like smell films, have been attempted in theaters. However, these smell videos have not been widely prevalent. One of the reasons is odor lingering and mixing. If viewers smell the mixed odors, they will be unpleasant. In addition, people have not been able to enjoy smell videos on TV at home. Since there is no current infrastructure for the broadcast of odor information, and it is difficult to synchronize odor with video, smell TV has not yet been realized. People also have not added odors to their videos and produced smell videos.

Therefore, we proposed a system of smell video to enjoy at home, dealing with the problems of odor mixing, realization of smell TV, and smell video production. Our system used closed caption to synchronize videos with odors in view of the current TV broadcast. Odor information is inserted into the preexisting closed-captioned data and sent to viewers' home TVs, where it is read and the odors are emitted from the viewer's olfactory display. Producers of smell videos will need to add smell effects to videos. So that the odors match the scenes, producers must set the kind of smell, the timing, and the odor intensity of the smell effects, and then make closed captions to contain these data. For viewers, the data are acquired and the odors are presented in time with their video's scenes. With the implemented system in this study, the method of data acquisition depends on the way viewers watch the program. When they watch it from a recording, text analysis is used, and when they watch it on the air, the data are acquired by image processing. We tested the use and accuracy of these systems of both viewers and producers, and found it promising. Our proposed system will make smell videos to become a commonplace in the near future, and people will be able to enjoy videos with odors in a daily life. In addition, it would make a contribution to developing the field of olfactory interaction.

7. ACKNOWLEDGMENTS

This research was supported in part by a Grants-in-Aid for Scientific Research (C), 2014, No.26330229 from the Ministry of Education, Culture, Sports, Science and Technology in Japan, and Takasago International Corporation.

8. REFERENCES

[1] ATSC Digital Television Standard, Part 1 - Digital Television System. *The Advanced Television Systems Committee*. http://www.atsc.org/cms/standards/a53/A53-Part-1-2013.pdf.

[2] Choh, N., Wyszynsky, B., Takushima, H., Nitikarn, N., Kinoshita, M., and Nakamoto, T. 2008. Demonstration of interactive teleolfaction with movie. In *Proceedings of the 2008 International Conference on Advances in Computer Entertainment Technology* (Yokohama, Japan, December 03

- 05, 2008). ACE '08. ACM, New York, NY, 395. DOI = http://doi.acm.org/10.1145/1501750.1501844.

[3] Digital Video Service Multiplex and Transport System Standard for Cable Television. *Society of Cable Telecommunications Engineers*. ANSI/SCTE 54 2009. http://www.scte.org/documents/pdf/Standards/ANSI_SCTE %2054%202009.pdf.

[4] Foods Channel. *YouTube*. https://www.youtube.com/watch?v=lTJsn8ZIp20

[5] Ghinea, G. and Ademoye, O. 2012. User perception of media content association in olfaction-enhanced multimedia. *ACM Ttans. Multim. Comput.* 8, 4, Article 52 (Nov. 2012), 19 pages. DOI = http://doi.acm.org/10.1145/2379790.2379794.

[6] Kadowaki, A., Sato, J., Bannai, Y., and Okada, K. 2007. Presentation Technique of Scent to Avoid Olfactory Adaptation, In *Proceedings of the 17th International Conference on Artificial Reality and Telexistence* (Esbjerg, Denmark, November 28 - 30, 2007). ICAT '07. IEEE, Washington, DC, 97-104. DOI = http://doi.ieeecomputersociety.org/10.1109/ICAT.2007.8.

[7] Kaye, J. 2004. Making Scents: aromatic output for HCI. *Magazine interactions*. 11, 1 (January + February 2004), 48-61. DOI= http://doi.acm.org/10.1145/962342.964333.

[8] Lipton, B.C.D. Making Smell-o-Vision A Reality. *The Harvard Crimson*. http://www.thecrimson.com/article/2007/12/7/making-smell-o-vision-a-reality-in-1971/.

[9] Matsukura, H., Yoneda, T., and Ishida, H. 2012. Smelling screen: Technique to present a virtual odor source at an arbitrary position on a screen. In *Proceedings of the 2012 Virtual Reality Short Papers and Posters* (Costa Mesa, USA, March 04 - 08, 2012). VR '12. IEEE, Washington, DC, 127-128. DOI = http://doi.ieeecomputersociety.org/10.1109/VR.2012.6180915.

[10] Noguchi, D., Ohtsu, K., Bannai, Y., and Okada, K. 2009. Scent Presentation Expressing Two Smells of Different Intensity Simultaneously. In *Proceedings of the 15th Joint virtual reality Eurographics conference on Virtual Environments* (Lyon, France, December 07 - 09, 2009). JVRC '09. ACM, New York, NY, 53-60. DOI = http://doi.acm.org/10.2312/EGVE/JVRC09/053-060.

[11] Ohtsu, K., Sato, J., Bannai, Y., and Okada, K. 2009. Scent Presentation Technique of Pulse Ejection Synchronized with Breathing. In *Proceedings of the 9th Annual International Symposium on Applications and the Internet* (Seattle, USA, July 20 - 24, 2009). SAINT '09. IEEE, Washington, DC, 125-128. DOI = http://doi.ieeecomputersociety.org/10.1109/SAINT.2009.28.

[12] Pornpanomchai, C., Threekhunprapa, A., Pongrasamiroj, K., and Sukklay, P. 2009. SUBSMELL: Multimedia with a Simple Olfactory Display. In *Proceedings of the 3rd Pacific Rim Symposium on Advances in Image and Video Technology* (Tokyo, Japan, January 13 - 16, 2009). PSIVT '09. Springer-Verlag, Berlin, Heidelberg, 462-472. DOI = http://doi.acm.org/ 10.1007/978-3-540-92957-4_40.

[13] Tomono, A., Koyori, K., and Otake, S. 2011. Effect of Smell Presentation on Individuals with Regard to Eye Catching and Memory. *Electron. Commun. JPN*. 94, 3 (Mar. 2011), 9-19.

[14] Tomono, K., Katsuyama, H., and Tomono, A. 2011. A Scent-Emitting Video Display System. In *Proceedings of the 1st International Symposium on Virtual Reality Innovation* (Singapore, March 19 - 20, 2011). ISVRI '11. IEEE, Washington, DC, 335-336. DOI = http://doi.ieeecomputersociety.org/10.1109/ISVRI.2011.5759666.

[15] Ray Shih and Pieter Blignaut. 2011. The influence of gender and internet experience on the acceptability of smell as interaction modality. In *Proceedings of the South African Institute of Computer Scientists and Information Technologists Conference on Knowledge, Innovation and Leadership in a Diverse, Multidisciplinary Environment* (Cape Town, South Africa, October 03 - 05, 2011). SAICSIT '11. ACM, New York, NY, 205-214. DOI = http://doi.acm.org/10.1145/2072221.2072245.

[16] Sato, J., Ohtsu, K., Bannai, Y., and Okada, K. 2008. Pulse Ejection Technique of Scent to Create Dynamic Perspective. In *Proceedings of the 18th International Conference on Artificial Reality and Telexistence* (Yokohama, Japan, December 01 - 03, 2008). ICAT '08. The Virtual Reality Society of Japan (VRSJ), Tokyo, Japan, 167-174.

[17] Spy Kids Smells Like 4D. *IGN Entertainment*. http://www.ign.com/articles/2011/06/24/spy-kids-smells-like-4d.

[18] SRT Subtitles. *Matroska*. http://matroska.org/technical/specs/subtitles/srt.html.

[19] The Sporadic History of Aromatic Cinema. *AnOther*. http://www.anothermag.com/reader/view/4366/The_Sporadic_History_of_Aromatic_Cinema.

[20] Ward Philippa, Davies Barry J., and Kooijman Dion. 2003. Ambient Smell and the Retail Environment: Relating Olfaction Research to Consumer Behavior. *Journal of Business & Management*. 9, 3 (July. 2003), 289-302.

[21] Yeh, Y. and Lee, D. 2012. Characteristics of subtitle on preferred viewing distance and subjective preference of liquid crystal display high-definition television. In *Proceedings of the 5th International Congress on Image and Signal Processing* (Chongqing, China, October 16 - 18, 2012). CISP '12. IEEE, Washington, DC, 1734-1737. DOI = http://doi.ieeecomputersociety.org/10.1109/CISP.2012.6469783.

CrossMotion: Fusing Device and Image Motion for User Identification, Tracking and Device Association

Andrew D. Wilson and Hrvoje Benko
Microsoft Research
Redmond, WA 98052 USA
awilson@microsoft.com, benko@microsoft.com

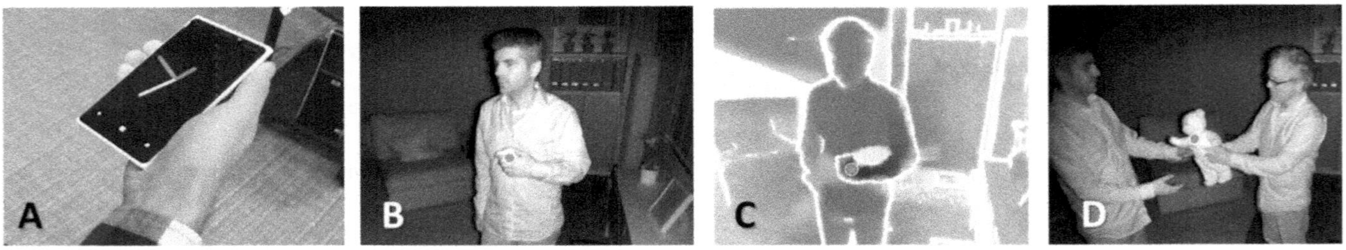

Figure 1. CrossMotion matches phone device acceleration with accelerations observed in the infrared and depth images of the Kinect v2 camera. (a): the phone's acceleration is calculated in the Earth's coordinate frame, shown by the axis; (b) CrossMotion finds the phone held by the user (red marker); (c) image and device acceleration match image (darker is better); (d) toys and other objects can be tracked by embedding or attaching the device (the device itself does not need to be directly visible to the camera).

ABSTRACT
Identifying and tracking people and mobile devices indoors has many applications, but is still a challenging problem. We introduce a cross-modal sensor fusion approach to track mobile devices and the users carrying them. The CrossMotion technique matches the acceleration of a mobile device, as measured by an onboard internal measurement unit, to similar acceleration observed in the infrared and depth images of a Microsoft Kinect v2 camera. This matching process is conceptually simple and avoids many of the difficulties typical of more common appearance-based approaches. In particular, CrossMotion does not require a model of the appearance of either the user or the device, nor in many cases a direct line of sight to the device. We demonstrate a real time implementation that can be applied to many ubiquitous computing scenarios. In our experiments, CrossMotion found the person's body 99% of the time, on average within 7cm of a reference device position.

Categories and Subject Descriptors
I.4.8 Image Processing and Computer Vision: Scene Analysis – *Sensor Fusion, Tracking*

Keywords
Sensor fusion; depth cameras; inertial measurement units

1. INTRODUCTION
Tracking a mobile device and its owner is useful for a number of ubiquitous computing scenarios that rely on identifying and tracking the device's owner to provide location-based services, such as connecting the smartphone with nearby infrastructure such as a wall display. In this paper we consider the problem of tracking a mobile device user with a video camera.

ICMI '14, November 12 - 16 2014, Istanbul, Turkey
Copyright 2014 ACM 978-1-4503-2885-2/14/11…$15.00
http://dx.doi.org/10.1145/2663204.2663270

Recognizing and tracking mobile devices from video is difficult for a number of reasons. Many smartphones are small, shiny, and dark, making them difficult to image clearly. It might be impossible to differentiate two devices of the same model. Handheld devices may be partially occluded by the hand, while those kept in a purse or clothes pocket can't be seen at all. Active markers such as infrared LEDs can assist in tracking and identification [16]. For example, Xbox One and Sony PS4 controllers use infrared and visible LEDs to assist in tracking and associating controllers with players. However, such active markers are rare, and require a line of sight.

We present a sensor fusion approach to locating and tracking a mobile device and its user in video. CrossMotion matches device acceleration with acceleration observed in the infrared and depth images of the Kinect camera (Figure 1). It uses the inertial sensors common to many mobile devices to find device acceleration. Device and image accelerations are compared in the 3D coordinate frame of the environment, thanks to the absolute orientation sensing capabilities common in today's smartphones, as well as the range sensing capability of commodity depth cameras.

Previous works ([4], [13], [15], [11]) explore the fusion of device sensors and visual features to find the user carrying the device. These rely on external means of determining candidate objects in the video. For example, ShakeID considers which of up to four tracked hands holds the device. Rather than compare the motion of a small number of candidate objects in the video, CrossMotion sensor fusion is performed *at every pixel in the video image* and requires no separate process to suggest candidate objects to track. The technique requires no knowledge of the appearance of the device or the user, thereby avoiding many of the difficulties of traditional appearance-based approaches, and allows for a wide range of camera placement options and applications. An interesting and powerful consequence of the technique is that the device user, and in many cases the device itself, may be reliably tracked even if the device is in the user's pocket (Figure 4), or embedded in another object (Figure 1d).

In this paper, we review related work, detail the CrossMotion algorithm, discuss our implementation, present the results of two evaluations of the algorithm's performance, and discuss considerations and limitations in applying the technique.

2. RELATED WORK

2.1 Device Association Using Sensor Fusion

"Sensor fusion" refers to the combination of multiple disparate sensors to obtain a more useful signal. Of particular relevance to the present work are fusion techniques that seek to associate two devices by finding correlation among sensor values taken from both. For example, when two mobile devices are held together and shaken, accelerometer readings from both devices will be highly correlated ([3], [7]). Detecting such correlation can cause application software to pair or connect the devices in some useful way. Similarly, when a unique event is observed to happen at the same time at both devices, various pairings may be established. Perhaps the simplest example is connecting two devices by pressing buttons on both devices simultaneously [10], but the same idea can be applied across a variety of sensors. For example, two devices that are physically bumped together will measure acceleration peaks at the same moment in time. Hinckley et al. [2] refers to these interactions as "synchronous gestures."

It can be particularly useful to establish correlations across very different modalities, since often such modalities complement each other. We mention just a few of these "cross-modal" approaches: a mobile phone may be located and paired with an interactive surface by correlating an acceleration peak in the device with the appearance of a touch contact [12], or when the surface detects the visible flashing of a phone at the precise moment it is triggered [18]. An object tagged with an RFID chip can be detected and located as it is placed on an interactive surface by correlating the appearance of a new surface contact with the appearance of an RFID tag [8].

2.2 Correlating Image and Device Motion

A small number of previous works investigate the idea of correlating mobile device inertial sensor readings with movement observed in a video camera.

Kawai et al. [4] propose correlating accelerometers worn at the waist with visual features to track young children in school. They consider tracking head-worn red LEDs, as well as tracking the position of motion blobs. For the accelerometer measurements, they consider integrating to obtain position for direct comparison with the visual tracking data, as well as deriving pedometer-like features. While the paper lacks specifics, the authors favor pedometer features in combination with markerless motion blob visual features.

Shigeta et al. [13] propose computing normalized cross-correlation between the motion trajectory of an object and device accelerometer readings to determine which of several tracked objects contains the device. Their approach requires a window of many samples to perform correlation and relies on an external process to find and track objects from monocular video. Plötz et al. [9] use a similar approach to synchronize inertial sensors and video cameras.

Teixeria et al. [15] propose identifying and tracking people across multiple existing security cameras by correlating mobile device accelerometer and magnetometer readings. They describe a hidden Markov model-based approach to find the best assignment of sensed devices to tracked people. As with Shigeta et al., they rely on an external process to generate tracked objects and use a large matching window, though they demonstrate how their approach can recover from some common tracking failures.

Most closely related to the present work is Rofouei et al.'s ShakeID system, which matches smartphone accelerometer values with the acceleration of up to four hands tracked by the Microsoft Kinect sensor [11]. The hand holding the phone is inferred by matching the device acceleration with acceleration of hand positions over a short window of time (1s). A Kalman filter is used to estimate the acceleration of each hand. The hand with the most similar pattern of acceleration is determined to be holding the device. This previous work further studies the correlation of contacts on a touch screen by the opposite hand. Ultimately touch contacts are associated with the held device by way of the Kinect tracked skeleton that is seen to be holding the device.

All of the above previous works require that a small number of candidate objects are first tracked. The subsequent correlation process involves determining which of these object's motion most closely matches that of the device. The step of generating candidate objects can be prone to failure. For example, ShakeID compares the motion of the tracked hands of the one or two users detected by the Kinect sensor skeletal tracking process. If the device is not held in the hand, or if the Kinect skeletal tracking fails, the device cannot be tracked. Furthermore, holding a mobile device can impact the hand tracking process to an extent that estimating hand acceleration robustly is difficult. Kinect skeletal tracking requires a fronto-parallel view of the users. Thus relying on Kinect skeletal tracking constrains where the camera may be placed. For example, skeletal tracking fails when the camera is mounted in the ceiling for an unobstructed top-down view of the room.

In comparison to previous work, CrossMotion avoids the difficulty of choosing candidate objects by matching low level motion features throughout the image. It may be used in many situations where skeletal tracking is noisy or fails outright and thus can be used in a wide variety of application scenarios. Whereas most of the related work performs matching over a significant window in time, CrossMotion uses a fully recursive formulation that relies on storing only the previous frame's results, not a buffer of motion history. In fact, the recursive nature of the computation allows it to be applied everywhere in the image in real time, avoiding the need to track discrete objects.

We argue that to correlate image and device motion for the purposes of locating the device or the user carrying it, the best approach is to match image motion directly, since as with "synchronous gestures" the pattern of image motion will provide the discriminative power to robustly detect the device or its user. Making fewer assumptions about the appearance of the device or user extends the range of applicability of the approach, and makes the technique less complex, more robust, and ultimately more useful.

We take some inspiration from models of visual search which feature a pre-attentive, massively parallel processing stage in which low level features are computed across the visual field, to be selected by further higher-level top-down processes [19]. For example, a pedestrian can detect interesting motion in the periphery, such as a car approaching a crosswalk, even on a windy day where the visual scene is full of motion.

Maki et al. [5] and Stein et al. [14] similarly propose matching trajectories of a set of features tracked using optical flow. Trajectory acceleration magnitude is compared to device acceleration magnitude to find the closest matching trajectory. These previous works require that the tracked points be periodically resampled to maintain even distribution throughout the image. Maki et al. demonstrates tracking 512 points, while our recursive approach uses optical flow rather differently, considering all pixel locations in the image without relying on a set of proposed features, effectively tracking a few hundred thousand points. Furthermore, these previous works compare acceleration *magnitude* which is invariant to orientation. CrossMotion instead uses the full 3D acceleration in a known coordinate frame, and thus avoids many simple scenarios that lead to false matches when using only acceleration magnitude (e.g., a motion to the left will have the same acceleration magnitude as a similar motion to the right).

3. CROSSMOTION ALGORITHM

The CrossMotion algorithm matches device (e.g., smartphone) acceleration with acceleration observed in the infrared and depth images of the Kinect camera (Figure 1). This matching process is performed at each pixel in the infrared image (Figure 1c). By virtue of the absolute orientation sensing available on the smartphone and the ability to determine the 3D position of an observed point in the Kinect color image, the match is performed in a common 3D coordinate frame (world reference frame).

In this paper, we present results using the Kinect for Windows v2 sensor, which includes a time of flight depth camera. Other depth sensors may also be used. For example, we have a CrossMotion implementation that uses the first Kinect for Windows sensor which is based on a structured light depth sensor.

The algorithm may be summarized as:

1. Find device acceleration: During runtime, mobile device acceleration is continually transmitted to a host PC (Figure 1a).
2. Find image motion: Simultaneously, dense optical flow is computed on the Kinect infrared image (Figure 2a). Each flow vector is converted to a 3D motion using the depth image, and transformed to the coordinate frame of the mobile device.
3. Estimate image acceleration: 3D acceleration is estimated by a Kalman filter at each point of the image, with the 3D flow at the point provided as input (Figure 2b).
4. Match device and image accelerations: The difference between image and device acceleration is computed at each pixel in the Kinect infrared image (Figure 2cd). Small values indicate the possible presence of the device at those pixel locations.

We next describe each of the above steps in detail.

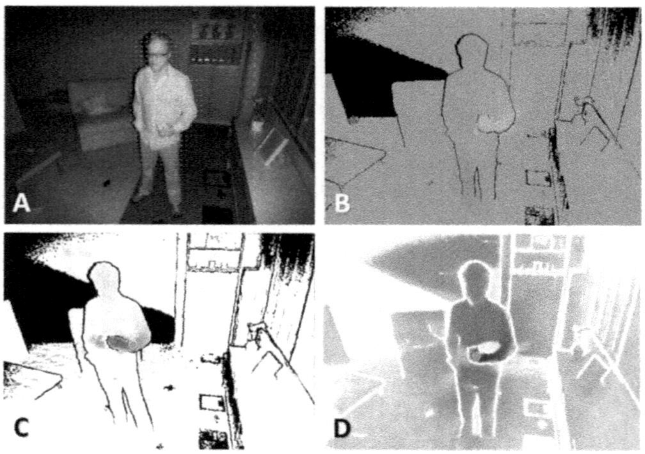

Figure 2. Stages of the CrossMotion algorithm: (a) dense optical flow is computed from the infrared image; (b) per-pixel acceleration estimates using Kalman filter; (c) instantaneous match image (darker is better) and (d) filtered match image.

3.1 Device Motion

Many mobile device APIs offer real time device orientation information. Today orientation is computed by combining information from the onboard accelerometers, gyroscopes and magnetometers. Because this orientation is with respect to magnetic north (as measured by the magnetometer) and gravity (as measured by the accelerometer, when the device is not moving), it is often considered an "absolute" orientation. In the work reported in this paper, the mobile device reports orientation in a standard "ENU" (east, north, up) coordinate system. While magnetic north is disturbed by the presence of metal and other magnetic fields present in indoor environments, in practice it tends to be constant in a given room. For our purposes it is only important that magnetic north not change dramatically as the device moves about the area imaged by the Kinect sensor.

Mobile device accelerometers report device acceleration in the 3D coordinate frame of the device. Having computed absolute orientation using the magnetometers, gyros and accelerometers, it is easy to transform the accelerometer outputs to the ENU coordinate frame and subtract acceleration due to gravity. Of course, the accuracy of this estimate of device acceleration in the ENU coordinate frame is only as good as that of the orientation estimate. While many smartphone SDKs include functions to report absolute orientation, for reasons explained later we implement our own algorithm.

Our prototype implementation of CrossMotion transmits this device acceleration (ENU coordinates, gravity removed) over WiFi to the host PC that performs sensor fusion.

3.2 Image Motion

The CrossMotion algorithm compares the 3D acceleration of the mobile device with 3D acceleration observed in video. Our approach to find acceleration in video is to first compute the velocity of movement at every pixel in the Kinect infrared image using a standard optical flow technique. This 2D image-space velocity is augmented with depth information and converted to velocity in real world 3D coordinates (meters per second). Acceleration is estimated at each point in the image using a Kalman filter. We next describe each of these steps in detail.

3.2.1 Finding 2D Velocity with Optical Flow

Rather than track the position of a discrete set of known objects in the scene, image motion is found by computing dense optical flow on the entire Kinect infrared image. Dense optical flow algorithms model the motion observed in a pair of images as a displacement u, v at each pixel. There are a variety of optical flow algorithms. Our prototype implementation uses the algorithm proposed by Brox et al. [1], which is known for its accuracy. While optical flow is typically used to compute the motion forward from time $t-1$ to the frame at time t, for reasons explained later CrossMotion computes flow from the current frame at time t to the frame at time $t-1$. The velocity u, v at each point x, y we denote as $u_{x,y}$ and $v_{x,y}$. We note that x, y are integer-valued, while u, v are real-valued.

3.2.2 Converting to 3D Motion

Depth cameras such as the Microsoft Kinect sensor report distance to the nearest surface at every point in its depth image. The Microsoft Kinect for Windows v2 SDK provides an API to compute the 3D position of a point in the depth camera in real world units (meters). We denote the 3D position corresponding to a 2D point x, y in the infrared image at time t as $\mathbf{z}_{x,y,t}$.

Rather than convert 2D velocities (as computed by optical flow) to 3D quantities directly, CrossMotion uses a Kalman filter-based technique that estimates velocity and acceleration at each pixel.

3.2.3 Estimating Acceleration

CrossMotion uses a Kalman filter to estimate acceleration of moving objects in the image. The Kalman filter incorporates our knowledge of sensor noise and is recursive (that is, it incorporates all previous observations). The technique thus allows much better estimates of acceleration compared to the approach of using finite differences. While it is beyond the scope of the paper to fully explain the Kalman filter (see [17] for a good introduction), we attempt to describe the basics of the technique by way of explaining the particular formulation used in CrossMotion.

The Kalman filter is closely related to the simpler "exponential" filter which computes a smoothed estimate x_t of a scalar z_t using the recursive relation:

$$x_t = x_{t-1} + \alpha(z_t - x_{t-1})$$

where the gain $\alpha \in (0,1)$ controls the degree to which the filter incorporates the "innovation" $z_t - x_{t-1}$. The smaller the gain, the less the filter follows the observation z_t, and the more the signal is smoothed. An improved version of the exponential filter is

$$x_t = x_t^* + \alpha(z_t - x_t^*)$$

where x_t^* is a prediction of x_t given x_{t-1} (for example, by assuming constant velocity). The Kalman filter is essentially this "improved" exponential filter, and moreover includes a principled means to set the value of the gain given our uncertainty in both the prediction x_t^* and observation z_t.

For our problem of estimating acceleration from image motion, we first consider the motion of a single object in 3D. The familiar equations of motion predict the object's position $\mathbf{x}_t^*$, velocity $\mathbf{v}_t^*$ and acceleration $\mathbf{a}_t^*$ from previous values, $\mathbf{x}_{t-1}$, $\mathbf{v}_{t-1}$, and $\mathbf{a}_{t-1}$:

$$\mathbf{x}_t^* = \mathbf{x}_{t-1} + \mathbf{v}_{t-1}\Delta t + \frac{1}{2}\mathbf{a}_{t-1}\Delta t^2$$

$$\mathbf{v}_t^* = \mathbf{v}_{t-1} + \mathbf{a}_{t-1}\Delta t$$

$$\mathbf{a}_t^* = \mathbf{a}_{t-1}$$

Given observation $\mathbf{z}_t$ of the 3D position of a tracked object, we correct the predictions of position, velocity and acceleration with

$$\mathbf{x}_t = \mathbf{x}_t^* + \mathbf{k}_x * (\mathbf{z}_t - \mathbf{x}_t^*)$$

$$\mathbf{v}_t = \mathbf{v}_t^* + \mathbf{k}_v * (\mathbf{z}_t - \mathbf{x}_t^*)$$

$$\mathbf{a}_t = \mathbf{a}_t^* + \mathbf{k}_a * (\mathbf{z}_t - \mathbf{x}_t^*)$$

where $*$ denotes element-wise multiplication. Kalman gains $\mathbf{k}_x$, $\mathbf{k}_v$, $\mathbf{k}_a$ relate the innovation, or error in the prediction of position, to changes in each of our estimates of position, velocity and acceleration. Kalman gain is computed as described in [17], and is related to our uncertainty in our predictive model $\mathbf{x}_t^*$ and observations $\mathbf{z}_t$. In particular, it is crucial to assign a high uncertainty to our estimate of acceleration $\mathbf{a}_t$ to reflect our belief that acceleration of the object varies over time (indeed, this is the quantity we wish to estimate). Similarly, our uncertainty in $\mathbf{z}_t$ is related to the noise of our sensor.

Finally, we note that the usual formulation of Kalman gain is time-varying. However, if the uncertainty of our predictive model and observations is constant, Kalman gain converges to a constant value [17], as presented above. This leads to a simplified implementation of the update equations, and further underscores the relationship between the Kalman filter and the simpler exponential filter.

3.2.4 Incorporating Flow

CrossMotion maintains a Kalman filter of the form described above to estimate 3D acceleration at each pixel location in the image. We denote our estimated position, velocity and acceleration at each pixel location x, y as $\mathbf{x}_{x,y,t}$, $\mathbf{v}_{x,y,t}$ and $\mathbf{a}_{x,y,t}$ respectively.

Optical flow information is used in two ways: first, the flow at a point in the image is a measurement of the velocity of the object under that point. It thus acts as input to our estimate of acceleration using the Kalman filter. Second, we can use flow to propagate motion estimates spatially, along patches of the image whose motion is being estimated. In this way the Kalman filter can use many observations to accurately estimate the acceleration of a given patch of an object as it moves about the image.

Flow quantities $u_{x,y}$ and $v_{x,y}$ (which we abbreviate as u and v) are incorporated by predicting $\mathbf{x}_{x,y,t}^*$, $\mathbf{v}_{x,y,t}^*$, and $\mathbf{a}_{x,y,t}^*$ from $\mathbf{x}_{x+u,y+v,t-1}$, $\mathbf{v}_{x+u,y+v,t-1}$, and $\mathbf{a}_{x+u,y+v,t-1}$ using the equations of motion as above. In practice, $\mathbf{x}_{x,y,t}$, $\mathbf{v}_{x,y,t}$ and $\mathbf{a}_{x,y,t}$ are stored as a 2D array the same dimension as the Kinect infrared image, but because $x+u$ and $y+v$ are real valued, quantities $\mathbf{x}_{x+u,y+v,t-1}$, $\mathbf{v}_{x+u,y+v,t-1}$, and $\mathbf{a}_{x+u,y+v,t-1}$ are best computed by bilinear interpolation on the 2D array. Finally, observation $\mathbf{z}_{x,y,t}$ is simply the 3D world coordinate position at image coordinates x, y. In this process, the Kalman filter at x, y updates motion estimates found at $x+u, y+v$ in the previous time step, and motion estimates follow along or "track" the objects whose motion is being estimated.

This interpolation finally motivates computing optical flow in reverse fashion, from time t to time $t-1$: $u_{x,y}$ and $v_{x,y}$ are defined for all integer values x, y. Computing flow in the usual fashion from time $t-1$ to time t might leave some pixels without "predecessors" from the previous frame, even if previous motion estimates are distributed across multiple pixels using bilinear interpolation. Computing flow from time t to time $t-1$ avoids this problem.

3.3 Sensor Fusion

3.3.1 Common Coordinate System

In the following, we describe a one-time calibration procedure which obtains the camera's orientation with respect to the ENU coordinate frame of the mobile device. Motion observed in the camera may then be transformed to ENU coordinates and compared to device accelerations directly.

While there are many ways to compute the relative orientation of the Kinect camera to the coordinate system used by our mobile device, we adopt a straightforward semi-automatic procedure that is easy to implement and gives good results. First the mobile device is placed display-side down on a plane that is easily observed by the Kinect camera, such as a wall or desk. Viewing the color video stream of the camera, the user clicks on three or more points on the plane.

The 3D unit normal $\mathbf{n}_k$ of the plane in Kinect coordinates is computed by first calculating the 3D position of each clicked point and fitting a plane by a least-squares procedure. The same normal $\mathbf{n}_w$ in ENU coordinates is computed by rotating the unit vector $\mathbf{z}$ (out of the display of the device) by the device orientation. Similarly, gravity unit vector $\mathbf{g}_k$ in camera coordinates is taken from the 3-axis accelerometer built in to the Kinect sensor. Gravity $\mathbf{g}_w$ in the ENU coordinate frame is by definition $-\mathbf{z}$.

The 3×3 rotation matrix $\mathrm{M}_{\text{kinect}\rightarrow\text{world}}$ that brings a 3D camera point to the ENU coordinate frame is calculated by matching the normals $\mathbf{n}_k$ and $\mathbf{n}_w$, as well as gravity vectors $\mathbf{g}_k$ and $\mathbf{g}_w$, and forming orthonormal bases K and W by successive cross products:

$$\mathbf{k}_1 = \mathbf{n}_k, \mathbf{k}_2 = \frac{\mathbf{n}_k \times \mathbf{g}_k}{\|\mathbf{n}_k \times \mathbf{g}_k\|}, \mathbf{k}_3 = \mathbf{n}_k \times \mathbf{k}_2, \mathrm{K} = \begin{bmatrix} \mathbf{k}_1 \\ \mathbf{k}_2 \\ \mathbf{k}_3 \end{bmatrix}$$

$$\mathbf{w}_1 = \mathbf{n}_w, \mathbf{w}_2 = \frac{\mathbf{n}_w \times \mathbf{g}_w}{\|\mathbf{n}_w \times \mathbf{g}_w\|}, \mathbf{w}_3 = \mathbf{n}_w \times \mathbf{w}_2, \mathrm{W} = \begin{bmatrix} \mathbf{w}_1 \\ \mathbf{w}_2 \\ \mathbf{w}_3 \end{bmatrix}$$

$$\mathrm{M}_{\text{kinect}\rightarrow\text{world}} = \mathrm{K}^{-1}\mathrm{W}$$

While this procedure uses a mobile device to place the Kinect camera in ENU coordinates, we note that this calibration need only be performed once when the camera is mounted. An unfamiliar device will work with the system without further calibration as long it also reports orientation in ENU coordinates.

3.3.2 Matching

3D image accelerations are estimated at each pixel and transformed to the ENU coordinate system as described above. The acceleration observed at each pixel may be compared directly to the device acceleration $\mathbf{d}_t$:

$$r_{x,y,t} = \sqrt{\left\|\mathbf{a}_{x,y,t} - \mathbf{d}_t\right\|^2}$$

Regions of the image that move with the device will give small values of $r_{x,y,t}$. In particular, the hope is that pixels that lie on the device will give the smallest values (Figure 2c). If we assume that the device is present in the scene, it may suffice to locate its position in the image by finding x^*, y^* that minimizes $r_{x,y,t}$. However, other objects that momentarily move with the device, such as those rigidly attached (e.g., the hand holding the device and the arm) may also match well.

In practice, locating the device by computing the instantaneous minimum over $r_{x,y,t}$ will fail to find the device when it is momentarily still or moving with constant velocity. In these cases device acceleration may be near zero and so matches many parts of the scene that are not moving, such as the background. We address this by smoothing $r_{x,y,t}$ with an exponential filter to obtain $s_{x,y,t}$. This smoothed value is "tracked" using optical flow and bilinear interpolation, in the same manner as the Kalman motion estimates (Figure 2d). Small values over the smoothed value $s_{x,y,t}$ will pick out objects that match device acceleration over the recent past (depending on smoothing parameter α) and "remember" the moments when some non-zero device acceleration uniquely identified it in the image. In the case where the device stops moving, the small values $s_{x,y,t}$ will stay with the device for some time, hopefully until the device moves again.

Our current implementation takes a further optional step to avoid the problem of matching static backgrounds by adding a small penalty to pixel locations that exhibit little motion.

An important consideration in performing the above matching process is that the latency of the Kinect sensor is much greater than that of the mobile device, including WiFi communications. Without accounting for this difference, the measure of similarity $r_{x,y,t}$ will be inaccurate. CrossMotion accounts for the relative latency of the Kinect sensor by artificially lagging the mobile device readings by some small number of frames. In our prototype implementation this lag is tuned empirically to five frames, approximately 80ms.

Figure 3 shows a typical trace of device acceleration and image acceleration at x^*, y^*. Considering that these values are computed in very different ways, they track each other surprisingly well.

In some applications it may not be appropriate to assume that the device is in the scene. For example, the user holding the device may leave the camera's field of view. In this case the minimum value over $s_{x,y,t}$ can be checked against a threshold to reject matches of poor quality. We denote the minimum value at x^*, y^* as s^*.

4. IMPLEMENTATION

Our prototype implementation of CrossMotion uses a Microsoft Kinect for Windows v2 sensor and a Nokia Lumia 920 running Windows Phone 8. Device acceleration and orientation information is transmitted to a host PC over WiFi at a rate of approximately 50Hz. The Kinect camera is configured using the Microsoft Kinect for Windows v2 Developer Preview SDK to acquire infrared and depth images at resolution 512×424 at 30Hz. CrossMotion uses the Brox optical flow API in OpenCV 2.4.7. This optical flow implementation uses the GPU to achieve real time performance, and is written in Nvidia's CUDA GPU programming language. Our host PC runs Windows and includes an Nvidia GeForce GTX 660Ti graphics card hosting CUDA 5.5.

All image processing runs at 30Hz. Optical flow calculations are performed on the full resolution infrared image. Per-pixel Kalman filter updates and sensor fusion matching is implemented in CUDA. Optical flow parameters (e.g., smoothness) and Kalman filter parameters (sensor noise and process noise) are derived empirically.

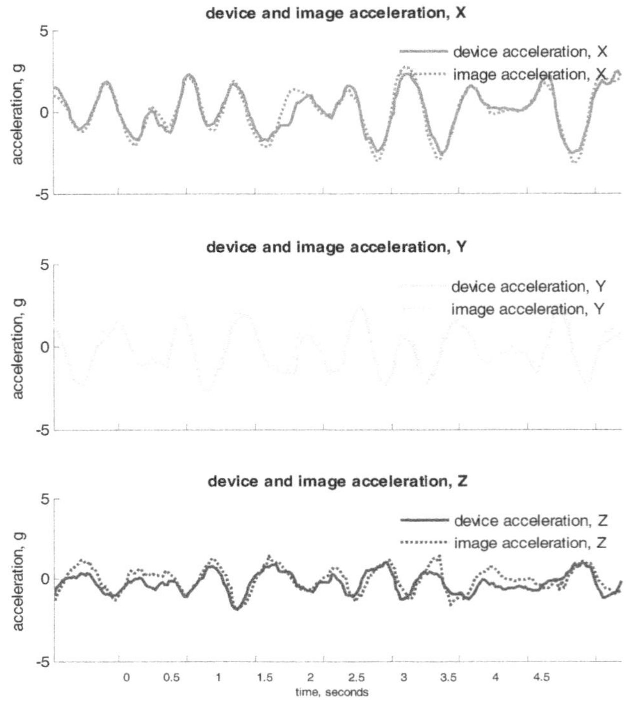

Figure 3. Device acceleration compared to image acceleration at the point x^*, y^* in each of the coordinate axes. The device was held in by the user and moved back and forth. Note how device and image acceleration track each other closely.

4.1.1 Computing Orientation

Today's mobile devices combine gyros, accelerometers and magnetometers to compute absolute orientation. Gyros measure angular velocity and are used to provide fast, accurate updates to orientation, while the noisier magnetometers and accelerometers are used to take observations of magnetic north and gravity. The absolute orientation information in the observations of magnetic north and gravity is applied to gradually remove the inevitable drift encountered when using gyros alone. Accelerometers measure the direction of gravity only when the device is motionless. Thus, if the device is undergoing significant motion, the orientation estimate may be distorted for some time. We find that when using the built-in Windows Phone 8 API for orientation, orientation estimates are disrupted by vigorous motion, and several seconds are required to recover. Because CrossMotion relies on accurate orientation information to transform accelerometer outputs to the ENU coordinate frame, when using the built-in API vigorous motion causes CrossMotion fusion to fail for a few seconds.

Our own implementation of an algorithm to compute absolute orientation allows us to make trade-offs that differ from the built-in implementation. Our implementation opts for near instantaneous drift correction when the device is deemed motionless, and otherwise performs updates to the orientation estimate using the gyro running at 250Hz.

5. EVALUATION

CrossMotion may be useful in applications where the user interacts with a large display using speech and gesture, or with a phone application that is connected with the display. In these settings it may be valuable to know the identity of the user, their location in front of the display, and possibly the location of the device.

To evaluate CrossMotion's performance we considered two particular modes of use that may be useful in interacting with large displays by mobile device: gesturing towards the display while holding the device in the hand, and wearing the device in a pocket while moving about in front of the display.

5.1 Experiment 1: Gesturing with the Device

In our first experiment, we tested CrossMotion's ability to track the mobile device as the user gestures in a front display, holding the device in the moving hand. This configuration approximates how a user might interact with a remote display application by gesturing with the device. As we are interested to see if CrossMotion performance is impacted by increasing distance from the camera, we varied the participants' distance to the display. In a second set of trials we introduced a distractor user (one of the experimenters) which did their best to mimic the motion of the participant. This was repeated for each distance condition, giving a 2×2 design with distance and the presence of a distractor as experimental conditions. For the purposes of this study we take as ground truth the output of the Kinect SDK body tracking, which includes the 3D position of the hands, hip and middle of the spine.

5.1.1 Procedure

We solicited five adult participants (one female, four male) from the authors' institution. All were right-handed and were familiar with using smartphones.

Participants were instructed to stand on a marked spot on the floor 1.5m from the display (near condition) or 2.5m from the display (far condition), and were directed to attend to the display, a 24" LCD. The Kinect camera was mounted above the display, about 180 cm above the floor, to observe the area in front of the display. An experimenter instructed the participant to hold the device in their right hand, orienting it so that it is approximately vertical, with the smartphone's screen facing them.

The experimenter explained the following set of trials, repeated for each distance condition: a letter was shown on the display for four seconds. During that time, the participant was instructed to "draw" the letter with the device by moving the device in the space in front of their body, and to finish approximately in four seconds. This duration was conveyed by a progress bar animation which finished at the end of four seconds. At the end of four seconds the screen was blanked. After a three second pause, during which time the participant was instructed to return to a comfortable center position in front of their body, another letter was presented. After a few practice trials, the participant performed the same task for each of the unistroke letters in the alphabet (17 letters, e.g., B, C, D, etc.). We note the letter stimulus was employed to merely cause the user to exhibit a variety of gestures, not to test letter recognition. Participants were told that the order of strokes in performing the letter gestures was unimportant.

This set of trials was repeated but with the introduction of a distractor user (one of the experimenters) who did their best to mimic the precise motion of the participant. This distractor stood next to the participant and performed the same letter in the same stroke order, and at the same pace. This second set of trials was included to test the performance of CrossMotion in the presence other people, as well as give an initial indication of how easy it is to "spoof" a user's motion.

During every CrossMotion frame, including pauses, software logged the 3D position corresponding with the algorithm's best match as well as the right hand joint position returned by the Kinect SDK body tracker. Software also logged whether the position of CrossMotion's solution x^*, y^* lies on the participant's body as determined by the Kinect SDK's "body index" image.

5.1.2 Results

Across all trials, of the 76,296 video frames (about 41 min), 1,629 frames (2.1%) occurred when the WiFi connection from the mobile device dropped temporarily. Of the rest, 98.9% correctly placed x^*, y^* on the participant's body. Taking the right hand position as ground truth, average error in 3D was 6.9cm (s.d. = 11.6cm). Position error in the "near" condition was 6.5cm (s.d. = 8.7cm), while error in the "far" condition was 7.4cm (s.d. = 14cm). The increase in error in the "far" condition may be attributed to one participant in that condition. We suspect that in that trial the magnetometer had fallen out of calibration. In any case, there is no reason to suspect that the difference in near and far is statistically significant. CrossMotion never placed its solution on the distractor user, thus the distractor condition had no effect on the results, and we do not report them separately.

5.2 Experiment 2: Wearing the Device

In the second experiment, we tested CrossMotion's ability to reliably pick out the person carrying the phone; i.e., does x^*, y^* lie on the user's body. We are also interested to see if CrossMotion can further locate the device on the person. In many circumstances we might not expect to be able to locate the device, since, as noted earlier, CrossMotion does not track the device, but instead finds regions of the image which are consistent the motion of the device. Thus parts of the user's body which are rigidly attached to the device may match as well as locations on the device itself.

We consider two locations of the device on the body: hanging from a lanyard hung around the user's neck, and placed in the right front pocket of a jacket. These positions were selected because they both have good analogues in Kinect's body tracking outputs: the lanyard position matches well with the "middle spine" position, while the jacket pocket corresponds well with the "right hip" position. We used the same participants as in the first experiment.

5.2.1 Procedure

The placement of camera and display was the same as in the first experiment. In the "middle spine" condition, the phone was placed in a wearable lanyard-style badge holder, of the kind sometimes used at conferences. In the "right hip" condition, the phone was placed in the right front pocket of a light fleece jacket. In both conditions, the participant was instructed to move to any one of four markers on the floor when the remote display indicated, but to do so in way that they continually faced the remote display. Two of the markers were the same used in the first experiment, while two more were located at distance of 2m from the display, but at a distance of 0.5m on either side of the line connecting the first two points. The four markers thus formed a diamond shape. The participant moved a total of 34 times in a session (4 seconds between each move).

Software logged the same information as in the first experiment, except rather than logging the right hand position returned by the Kinect SDK, the right hip and middle spine positions were logged.

5.2.2 *Results*

Across all trials, of the 43,060 video frames (about 24 min) analyzed, 1,352 frames (3.1%) occurred when the WiFi connection from the mobile device dropped temporarily. These frames can be considered invalid. Of the rest, 99.0% correctly placed x^*, y^* on the participant's body. Considering "middle spine" and "right hip" positions together, average error in 3D was 20.5cm (s.d. = 14.3cm). Position error in the "middle spine" condition was 17.1cm (s.d. = 7.8cm), while error in the "right hip" condition was 23.9cm (s.d. = 20.7cm). The results suggest a trend of larger error for the right hip, which is consistent with informal observation of the system in observation. In part this may be explained by the inherent lack of agreement between our choice of ground truth (Kinect SDK tracked body points) and the actual position of the device. In fact, if we examine the average error as a 3D vector quantity we see that much of the error is in the z coordinate, consistent with the fact that the device is worn outside the body, while the body skeleton reported by Kinect typically lies inside the body.

Comparing average error in position across both experiments, we note that error in the second experiment is greater than that of the first. This is unsurprising, since (as discussed in the next section) a smaller moving object more precisely indicates position than a large rigid moving object. In fact, we are pleasantly surprised at how well the device is tracked when it is worn.

5.3 Discussion

While CrossMotion does not require an appearance model of the device, in order to detect and track the user it requires that the camera have a line of sight to some part of the user that moves with the device. Contrast this with other vision-based approaches that require observing the device directly. Our example sequences demonstrate that the technique will often track the person holding the device if the device is in the user's shirt pocket or pants pocket (Figure 4). In these cases CrossMotion finds objects that move precisely with the device. This behavior may be appropriate for applications that require tracking at the level of the user. In those cases placing the point x^*, y^* anywhere on the user would be a positive match.

Furthermore, our examples show that CrossMotion often finds the position of the device itself, even if it is not directly in view. This ability requires that the device motion is unique against the background of the rest of the motion in scene, at least periodically. While our initial experiments are promising examples of where this is often true, it will require more work to show that this works generally since it depends on the surrounding context of motion. For example, the ability to localize the device on the user's leg when it is in their pants pocket depends in part on the leg's occasionally moving differently than the torso. Conversely, when holding the device it is not uncommon for it to find some part of the arm holding the device (however, we are surprised by the system's ability to find the phone in the user's shirt pocket, since it would seem that any point on the torso should match equally as well).

By the same token, because it matches device motion to image motion, CrossMotion cannot initially detect the mobile device if it does not move. If the device is being held by its user, it is likely that even a slight motion of the user is enough to establish reliable tracking, but if the device is lying on a desk, CrossMotion will not be able to detect it against a static background.

Our initial experiments show that a simple threshold on the value of s^* is not enough to reliably determine if the smartphone is in the view of the camera or off camera. By inspecting some test sequences, it seems that this is primarily because during moments when the user is not moving, static parts of the physical environment imaged by the camera can sometimes give good matches. In our own experiments we have been reluctant to add application-specific heuristics to the basic localization algorithm to address this problem. Partly, this is to investigate the power of the simplest version of the algorithm. However, we note that there are a number of pre-processing steps that would be reasonable to incorporate in a production version of CrossMotion. For example, the static background could be modeled and removed from consideration. Similarly, in many applications it may be possible to use the "body index" segmentation made available by the Kinect SDK. This coarse segmentation assigns each pixel of the depth map to one of up to six people or the background, and could be used as a mask or given some hysteresis at the level of the user.

An interesting question is whether it is possible for one mobile device user to "spoof" another mobile device user by mimicking their motion simultaneously. While our first experiment suggests that it is very difficult to do, in theory it is possible. In such cases it should be possible to at least detect that two devices appear to match the same image motion, or themselves, and block further action. Another approach is to use CrossMotion's results to bootstrap further vision-based analysis to achieve a two-factor authorization. For example, device or user identity and location within the image could seed a targeted face recognition process.

Finally, we note that the CrossMotion fusion described in this paper assumes that the device motion and corresponding image motion consists only of translation, and not rotation. Consider, for example, spinning the mobile device in place. In this case CrossMotion may not find the device, since the device accelerometers will give very low values, while there may be extensive motion observed about the device. In practice this rarely is an issue, as the rotation of the device and user is often accompanied by significant translation. We envision extending the model to more completely model device motion by including angular velocity as reported by device gyros and observed by rotation in the optical flow field about the device. Including angular velocity may improve the precision and robustness of the matching process.

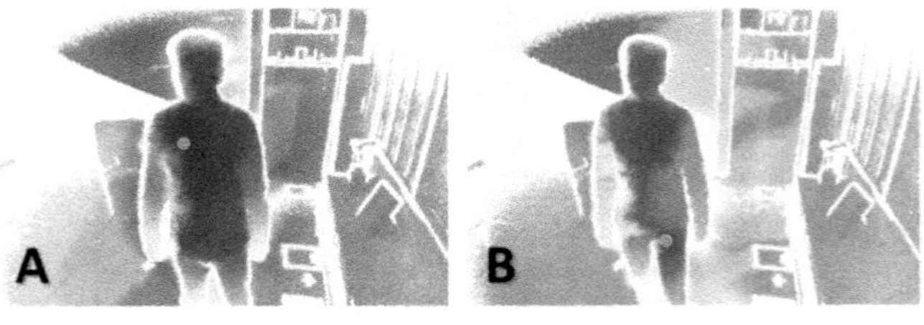

Figure 4. Image of $s_{x,y,t}$ for phone located in (a) shirt pocket and (b) pants pocket. Darker pixels indicate better match.

6. APPLICATIONS

Because it makes few assumptions about the appearance of the mobile device or the user carrying it, CrossMotion can be used in a wide variety of application settings.

Robust indoor person tracking is useful in providing location-based services to individuals. Way-finding and delivering targeted advertising are two often-cited example applications. CrossMotion can be used in many indoor person tracking applications where a computer vision-based approach would be acceptable, and where users are likely carrying a mobile device such as a smartphone or tablet. Computer vision-based approaches to person tracking are attractive because they can yield fine-grained position information but they typically either rely on visible markers (as in [16]) or complex models of the user's appearance. Other approaches require the user to carry new devices and therefore are unlikely to be adopted outside of critical applications. As an example way-finding application, consider providing directions to a visitor as they approach key hallway intersections, or when they leave an elevator. A CrossMotion-equipped depth camera could be installed at these locations to direct the visitor.

CrossMotion's ability to track and identify users by way of their mobile device makes it particularly appropriate for various device association problems. For example, a connection between a mobile device user and a wall display could be automatically established as the user approaches the display. Knowing the precise position with respect to the display can be used in number of ways. For example, when there are multiple simultaneous users, the wall display can render each user's own set of virtual objects nearby. Users can "flick" objects from their device onto the display. Fine-grained person tracking and device association can also be used to detect when users bring their devices near to each other, which can used for a variety of applications [6].

CrossMotion may be useful in various settings where it is valuable to track objects of interest as they move about the environment, particularly when it is undesirable to attach visual markers to those objects. For example, young children wearing small wrist worn sensor packages could be tracked in school [4], a child's stuffed animal could be tracked throughout the house, while real animals could be tracked to study their patterns of movement. The Xbox One Skype app performs an automatic digital pan and zoom to capture the active participants in the room, based on simple image motion processing techniques. CrossMotion might be used to limit this selection to particular users. Similarly, given a future long-range depth camera, a calibrated pan/tilt/zoom camera might follow a particular soccer player on the field.

7. CONCLUSION

We introduce CrossMotion, a cross-modal sensor fusion technique to detect and track mobile devices and the people carrying them. Because it matches inertial device motion with motion observed in video, it makes very few assumptions about the appearance of either the device or the user. This paper details a real time implementation of the technique based on estimating image acceleration from optical flow. Our initial experiments with the technique demonstrate its ability to find the user reliably (99% of the time). In many cases it can find the device itself even when it is not in direct view of the camera. While there are a number of considerations in applying the technique, we believe it is a unique and potentially useful option in many ubiquitous computing scenarios.

8. REFERENCES

[1] Brox, T., Bruhn, A., Papenberg, N., and Weikert, J. High accuracy optical flow estimation based on a theory for warping. In *Proc. 8th European Conference on Computer Vision,* vol. 4. 2004. 25-36.

[2] Hinckley, K., Ramos, G., Guimbretiere, F., Baudisch, P., and Smith, M. Synchronous gestures for multiple persons and computers. In *Proc. UIST 2003*. 149-158.

[3] Holmquist, L.E., Mattern, F., Schiele, B., Alahuhta, P., Beigl, M., and Gellersen, H. Smart-Its friends: A technique for users to easily establish connections between smart artefacts. In *Proc. Ubicomp 2001*. 116-122.

[4] Kawai, J., Shintani, K., Haga, H., and Kaneda, S. Identification and positioning based on motion sensors and a video camera. In *Proc. 4th IASTED Int. Conf. on Web-Based Education,* 2005.

[5] Maki, Y., Kagami, S., and Hashimoto, K. Accelerometer detection in camera view based on feature point tracking. In *Proc. IEEE/SICE Int'l Symp. On System Integration*. 2010. 448-453.

[6] Marquardt, N., Hinckley, K., and Greenberg, S. Cross-device interaction via micro-mobility and F-formations. In *Proc. UIST 2012*. 13-22.

[7] Mayrhofer, R., and Gellersen, H. Shake well before use: intuitive and secure pairing of mobile devices. *IEEE Transactions on Mobile Computing*, 8(6). 2009. 792-806.

[8] Olwal, A., and Wilson, A.D. SurfaceFusion: Unobtrusive tracking of everyday objects in tangible interfaces. In *Proc. Graphics Interface 2008*. 235-242.

[9] Plötz, T., Chen, C., Hammerla, N. Y., and Abowd, G.A. Automatic synchronization of wearable sensors and video-cameras for ground truth annotation- a practical approach. In *Proc. 16th Int. Symp. on Wearable Computers,* 2012.

[10] Rekimoto, J., Ayatsuka, Y., and Kohno, M. SyncTap: An interaction technique for mobile networking. In *Proc. Mobile CHI 2003*. 104-115.

[11] Rofouei, M., Wilson, A.D., and Brush, A.J. Your phone or mine?: Fusing body, touch, and device sensing for multi-user device-display interaction. In *Proc. ACM SIGCHI*. 2012. 1915-1918.

[12] Schmidt, D., Chehimi, F., Rukzio, E., and Gellersen, H. PhoneTouch: A technique for direct phone interaction on surfaces. In *Proc. UIST 2010*. 13-16.

[13] Shigeta, O., Kagami, S., and Hashimoto, K. Identifying a moving object with an accelerometer in a camera view. In *Proc. Int. Conf. Intelligent Robots and Systems,* 2008.

[14] Stein, S., and McKenna, S.J. Accelerometer localization in the view of a stationary camera. In *Proc. Ninth Conference on Computer and Robot Vision,* 2012. 109-116.

[15] Teixeira, T., Jung, D., and Savvides, A. Tasking networked CCTV cameras and mobile phones to identify and localize multiple people. In *Proc. Ubicomp,* 2010. 213-222.

[16] Want, R., Hopper, A., Falcão, V., and Gibbons, J. The active badge system. *ACM Transactions on Information Systems,* 10(1), 1992. 91-102.

[17] Welch, G., and Bishop, G. An introduction to the Kalman filter. Technical Report TR 95-041. University of North Carolina at Chapel Hill Dept. of Computer Science. 1995.

[18] Wilson, A.D., and Sarin, R. BlueTable: connecting wireless mobile devices on interactive surfaces using vision-based handshaking. In *Proc. Graphics Interface 2007*. 119-1.

[19] Wolfe, J.M. Guided search 2.0: a revised model of visual search. *Psychonomic Bulletin & Review 1, 2* (1994), 202-238.

Statistical Analysis of Personality and Identity in Chats Using a Keylogging Platform

Giorgio Roffo[1]
giorgio.roffo@univr.it

Cinzia Giorgetta[2]
cinzia.giorgetta@loa.istc.cnr.it

Roberta Ferrario[2]
roberta.ferrario@loa.istc.cnr.it

Walter Riviera[1]
walter.riviera@univr.it

Marco Cristani[1]
marco.cristani@univr.it

[1] Department of Computer Science, University of Verona, Strada le Grazie 15, 37134 Verona, Italy
[2] ISTC–CNR, via alla Cascata 56/C, I-38123 Povo (Trento), Italy

ABSTRACT

Interacting via text chats can be considered as a hybrid type of communication, in which textual information delivery follows turn-taking dynamics, resembling spoken interactions. An interesting research question is whether personality can be observed in chats, similarly as happening in face-to-face exchanges. After an encouraging preliminary work on Skype, in this study we have set up our own chat service in which key-logging functionalities have been activated, so that the timings of each key pressing can be measured. Using this framework, we organized semi-structured chats between 50 subjects, whose personality traits have been analyzed through psychometric tests, and a single operator, for a total of 16 hours of conversation. On this data, we have observed that some personality traits are linked with the way we are chatting (measured by stylometric cues), by means of statistically significant correlations and regression studies. Finally, we have assessed that some of the stylometric cues are very discriminative for the recognition of a user in a identification scenario. These facts taken together could underlie that some personality traits drive us in chatting in a particular fashion, which turns out to be very recognizable.

Keywords

chat analysis, personality, authorship attribution

Categories and Subject Descriptors

H.5.3 [**Group and Organization Interfaces**]: Synchronous interaction

1. INTRODUCTION

Text chatting is probably one of the most typical communication phenomena of the last 20 years, characterized by a massive worldwide diffusion[1]. The peculiarity of text chats stands in the fact that they show both aspects of literary text and of spoken conversation, due to the turn-taking dynamics that characterize text delivery. Therefore, it is interesting to investigate which aspects of these two communication means are intertwined in chat exchanges. In particular, we will try to discover how personality comes into play in chats: in fact, though connections of personality traits both with speech [8, 6] and with text [12, 11, 4, 7]have been long studied, a computational analysis of the role of personality in chats is missing. At the same time, we are also interested in discovering whether the manifestation of very particular, that is, recognizable chatting styles may correspond to distinguishable personality profiles. If this is the case, we may single out personality traits that are the most evident via chat, and individuate new means for chats to bring about meaning in addition to literary content. While so far many studies have been published on the recognition of writing style in literary texts (commonly known as *authorship attribution*) [1, 16], when it comes to chats the research is still moving its early steps [15].

A first direction towards these goals has been presented in [14], where a corpus of spontaneous Skype conversations between 45 different couples have been recorded during a period of 3 months and analyzed. From the corpus a pool of "stylometric" chat features have been extracted, which have been shown to codify the chatting style of users [15], together with some personality traits (Barratt Impulsiveness Scale [10], Interpersonal Reactivity Index [5]). A first correlation study has been conducted, which highlighted some weak but significant links among stylistic features and personality cues.

In this paper, we move a step ahead, providing a more solid study on the subject, changing radically the analysis protocol. In this case, we build a chat service, embedded into the *Klimble* social network[2], with key logging capabilities; this in practice allows us to retain the timing of each single hit of a key, recording at the finest level the behavior of users while they chat. In the [14] paper, timing information was limited to the recording of each return key pressure, introducing some evident approximations and limitations in the information that could be gathered. Conversely, here a novel set of stylometric features can be extracted, capturing a set of cues so far impossible to get, as the number of

[1] `http://goo.gl/2NrKFG`

[2] `http://www.klimble.com/`

ICMI'14, November 12–16, 2014, Istanbul, Turkey.

http://dx.doi.org/10.1145/2663204.2663272.

backspace hits, the speed of digitation of words, and so on; in particular, we design 11 novel features that are much more fine-grained than in the previous work. Take speed as an instance: if the style of an individual is characterized by slow turns, this may be caused by long pauses between a word and the other, or by the fact that the individual often erases what he/she has just written. On this chatting platform, we collect a new dataset in Italian containing data of 50 different subjects, collected within a two months period. All subjects (18-27 years old university students) are asked to chat with an operator barely known by them[3], for an average duration of 20 minutes. The operator performs semi-structured conversations, in order to reach a certain degree of homogeneity in the verbal content of the conversations and highlighting possible differences in the non-verbal behavior. To get information on some psychological traits of the subjects, we have used three well-known self-administered questionnaires: 1) the Barratt Impulsiveness Scale [10], focused on 3 different impulsiveness factors (attentional, motor and non-planning impulsiveness) [10], 2) BIS-BAS [2], decoding human motivations to behavioral inhibition (BIS) and activation (BAS), and 3) PANAS [17], analyzing positive and negative affectivity traits. Contrarily to the Big Five [13], these traits have shown to be more effective in capturing basic personality aspects [3]. In this study we have abandoned the Interpersonal Reactivity Index because, differently from the previous study, chats were all performed with the same (not well-acquainted with the subjects) operator, posing the same questions to everyone, and therefore features investigated by the IRI [5] , such as those related to the ability to take into account other's perspective or empathic concerns were not so relevant here.

The first analysis was aimed at investigating the relation between stylometric cues and personality traits. To this sake, correlations have been calculated, showing that 6 psychological factors correlate with 10 out of 28 total stylometric features, in a statistically significant way (*p-value* < 0.05); for example, our data show that subjects with higher positive affectivity tend to use to write slowly and to use a smaller number of long words. In addition, we perform regression on the personality traits using the features, showing that it is possible to generate predictions which correlate significantly with the original score for 4 personality traits, namely non planning impulsiveness, BIS punishment avoidance, negative affectivity and anxious personality.

The second analysis is aimed at verifying how discriminative is the chatting style of a person when compared to that of other subjects. To this aim, a detailed study is conducted analyzing the contribute of each stylometric feature in terms of recognition capability. Highly discriminative features have been found, some of them correlating with personality traits. Connecting these two analyses allows to hypothesize that possibly some personality traits lead people to chat in a particular style, which makes them very recognizable. For example, in the example above, the use of short words is a discriminative characteristic in chats, and is significantly correlated with higher non planning impulsiveness, highlighting that people who score higher in this factor of impulsiveness use also a greater number of short words, that is, the more subjects are impulsive, the shorter the time they stop on each single word while writing.

The rest of the paper is organized as follows: in Sec. 2 we present the literature review, focusing on the computational approaches of chat analysis and on the psychological theories on the relation between interaction and personality. In Sec. 3 we present our dataset, detailing also the performed psychological questionnaires. Our novel stylometric features are presented in Sec. 4. The results of correlation between personality traits and stylometric features are reported in Sec. 5, while the results on the prediction of the personality traits given the stylometric features are reported in Sec. 6. Results on identity recognition are presented in Sec. 7, and the discussion on how discriminative features are linked to personality traits is reported in Sec. 8. Finally, conclusions are drawn and future perspectives are envisaged in Sec. 9.

2. RELATED WORK

2.1 Computational Approaches

Most computational approaches on inferring personality traits from text depend strongly on a semantic analysis of the content: usually, psychologists individuate semantic features that are then validated through computational approaches. One of the first studies on the subject dates back to 1999 [12], while the most cited studies concerning the design of features are about the Linguistic Inquiry and Word Count (LIWC) features [11]: these include both syntactic (e.g. past tense verbs) and semantic cues (e.g. anger words, reference to family members), all validated by experts. Another important source of cues is the MRC Psycholinguistic database [4], containing statistics for over 150K words, and defininig features like "syllables per words" and "concreteness". A study that pools together all these features is [7], which is focused on finding relations with the Big Five personality traits, and where it is shown that MRC features are useful for models of emotional stability, while LIWC features are applicable to all traits. In this study, we neglect semantic analysis of the text, for privacy issues, and we deal with chat conversations corpora, which have never been considered before. Regarding the author recognition issue, the most related field is that of Authorship Attribution (AA), which introduced the term "stylometric feature". In this case, the related literature agrees essentially in considering the taxonomy of [1], which partitions features into five major groups: *lexical, syntactic, structural, content-specific and idiosyncratic*. The typical workflow of an AA approach is that of extracting from a set of training texts (related to some gallery subjects) a set of features, feeding them into discriminative classifiers, and proceeding with the testing on some unseen texts. The application of AA to chat conversations is quite recent, see [16] for a survey. Notably, the taxonomy of stylometric features has been enlarged in [15] with *turn-taking based* features, which explicitly account for the dynamics of the turns of text delivery in chats. The same paper also contains a summary table of the most important stylometric features.

2.2 Psychological Literature

On the other hand, the psychological literature has shown that people tend to use rapid judgements on personality traits as a guide during interaction. In conversation this occurs in a significant way. Indeed, several studies showed

[3]Such choice is motivated by the fact that we want on the one hand to prevent the style of the subjects to be influenced by that of different interlocutors and, on the other, to avoid styles that are peculiar to specific kinds of long term interactions.

that individuals tend to believe that speakers' speech characteristics are indicative of their personality traits [6]. Other researches have effectively demonstrated that speakers' voice type (loud-slow, loud-fast, soft-slow, soft-fast) is related with speakers' personality traits [8]. As shown by several studies, text analysis has proven to be a useful aid for measuring personality traits. For example, [12] showed correlation between lexical expressions and basic personality measures assessed by the Big Five questionnaire. Positive correlation between neuroticism and the use of emotional words with a negative valency, and between extroversion and emotional words with a positive valency were reported. Similar results were also found in [9]; however, in this study the content of the verbal material was not taken into consideration. A more recent study, [3], instead, analyzed to which degree basic elements of personality can be measured by using lexical analysis of verbal expression of autobiographical and personally relevant material. Two well-validated models of personality aimed at investigating, respectively, positive and negative affectivity traits (PANAS) and human motivations to behavioral inhibition (BIS) and activation (BAS) were used. Findings showed that individuals with high levels of positive affectivity and behavioral activation tended to express more positive emotions in their natural speech, whereas those with high levels of negative affectivity and behavioral inhibition tended to show more negative emotions.

3. THE DATASET

The data collection has been based on a public social network, where the text chatting interface has been equipped with keylogging functionalities. At the moment of the subscription, users have been informed that text chatting would have triggered a key logging application, but that the produced keylogs would have been kept private. The data collection has been realized on this platform by setting up a campaign of chats; the subscribers meeting certain requirements have been invited to participate to an experiment on personality, involving a text chat session plus the filling of three personality questionnaires. The explanation of the experiment was given in general terms, and the involvement of timings was not specified. The selected subjects should be in the age interval of 18-30 years, and be Master or PhD students. The chats were conducted by a single operator, not having friendship ties with the subjects. The chats were at least 20 minutes long, and the generic arguments suggested by the operator were "holidays" and "friends". The visual interface employed in the dialogs mirrors common instant-messaging platforms like Facebook and Skype. Thanks to the implementation of the chat software, the key logging mechanism allows to get the timings of each button hit with a precision of milliseconds, synchronized with the timing of the other participant.

A total of 50 subjects participated to the experiment, with an average age of 24 years, standard deviation $\rho = 1.5$. At the end of the text chat, the participants were asked to fill the following three well-known self-administered questionnaires, aimed at evaluating psychological factors:

1. The Barratt Impulsiveness Scale, version 11 (BIS-11) [10], to measure three categories of impulsiveness, and specifically the "attentional impulsiveness", indicating a lack of attention and cognitive instability, the "motor impulsiveness", indicating a lack of control in motor behavior, and the "non-planning impulsiveness", indicating a deficit in planning their own behavior. The test for these traits is composed by the same items (30), answered on a 4-points scale, ranging from "never" to "always". Combining opportunely the answers allows to get scores for the three traits, whose range is (8,32), (11,44), (11,44), respectively, where a high score indicates a strong lack in the related kind of impulsiveness.
2. The Behavioral Inhibition and the Behavioral Activation Scales (BIS/BAS; [2]) were used to analyze participants' likelihood of approaching rewards (BAS) or avoiding punishments (BIS) when making a choice. There are 20 items, answered on a 5-points scale, from "very true for me" to "very false for me". The diverse combinations of the answers give the scores for BIS (min = 7, max = 13) and BAS (min = 13, max = 65), where a high score indicates compulsive will in approaching rewards, and strong will in avoiding punishment, respectively.
3. The Positive Affect and Negative Affect Scales (PANAS [17]) were used in order to analyze positive (PA) and negative (NA) affectivity. There are 20 items in total, inquiring "to which extent subjects feel this way" (indicated by each affective word) and answered on a 5-point scale, from "very slightly or not at all" to "extremely". Even in this case, combining opportunely the answers provides the scores for PA (min = 10, max = 50) and NA (min = 10, max = 50), where high scores indicate higher positive (for PA) and negative (for NA) experienced affectivity, lower scores indicate instead lower positive (for PA) and negative (for NA) experienced affectivity.

In total the tests provide a quantitative indication for 7 personality traits, whose cumulative statistics over the 50 subjects are reported in Fig. 1.

Notice that, differently from the mainstream in existing literature, we do not use the Big Five to test personality traits. Big Five are focused on complex personality traits (for example agreeableness and openness to experience): here we are interested in more basic measures, such as the affectivity (positive or negative), behavioral motivations (that is, tendency to behavioral inhibition or activation) and impulsiveness traits, as we are more concerned with possible interrelations between traits and cues rather than on the traits themselves. This is similar in spirit to [12, 2], where personality traits are correlated with text writing style [12] and natural speech [2] respectively.

4. STYLOMETRIC FEATURES

In the design of stylometric features we follow the idea of [15, 14], that is, of using the turn length, and not simply the entire conversation, as fundamental unity for computing stylometric statistics. The big limitation of such works was that timings were calculated by considering the duration of each turn, as given by the Skype APIs; this introduced some approximations, like the ones needed for evaluating the writing speed (number of characters/turn duration) and limited the design of the features (for example, it was not possible to calculate the effective speed in writing words, excluding the spaces).

All these limitations have been overcome with our framework. Since our system has been designed to work on social

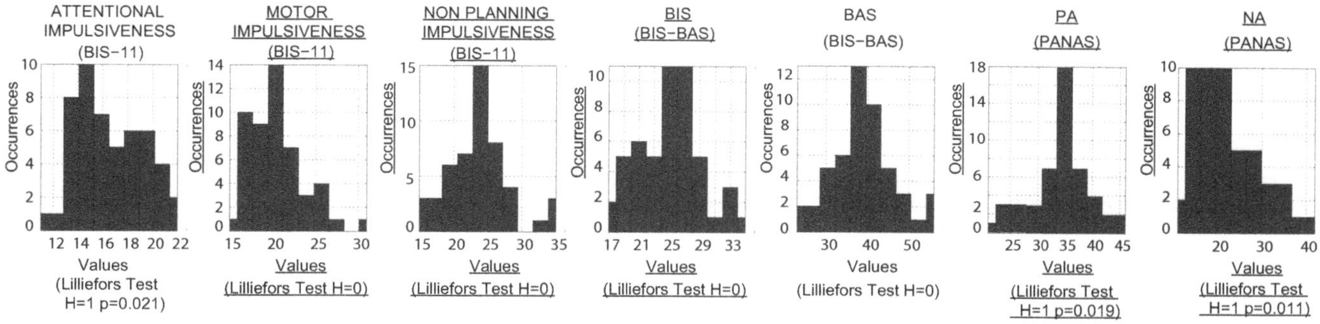

Figure 1: Traits distribution. On the bottom, the output of the Lilliefors test for distribution normality (H=0 indicates data normally distributed). Underlined, those personality traits which correlate with at least one stylometric feature.

networks, we have paid much attention to privacy issues: the idea is to neglect the content of the conversation, accounting only for the way it is performed. Our features follow this guideline, avoiding any kind of natural language processing, while other features, as length of words, punctuation, emoticons etc. are preserved and analyzed.

For each person involved in a conversation, we analyze his/her stream of turns (suppose T), ignoring the content of the input from the other subject. This means that we assume that the chat style (as modeled by our features) is independent from the interlocutor (hereafter called *operator*) – who in this case was the same for all participants, and was barely known by the subjects analyzed.

From each turn, a stylometric feature is extracted, generating a number; therefore, with T turns we obtain T feature values. Depending on the kind of feature and task to perform (measuring correlations or doing person identification), an histogram or the mean/median is computed, and the resulting measure becomes a part of the signature which characterizes a given individual. In the following, the list of the features together with their explanation is presented.

For convenience, and whereas possible, we have kept the name of the features proposed in the literature, with the substantial difference that in this case the feature extraction was performed using a key-logging framework, ensuring a more precise and capillary temporization. Specifically, all the *turn-taking features* are brand new. How features have been treated to calculate correlations with personality traits or similarities for the sake of recognition will be discussed in the following. In the list below, the numbers in parenthesis indicate the feature ID.

Lexical Features.

(1) **Number of words (#W)**: number of words per turn. With "word" we intend a string of *characters* (see below);

(2) **Number of chars (#C)**: number of characters per turn. With "character", we intend every normal key on the QWERTY keyboard, ignoring special keys like the SPACE, CTRL, etc.;

(3) **Number of uppercase chars (#Uppercase)**: number of uppercase characters in a turn;

(4) **Number of uppercase chars / number of chars (#Uppercase/#C)**: usually, entire words written in capital letters indicate a strong emotional message. This feature accounts for such communicative tendency;

(5) **Mean word length**: average length of the words in a turn;

(6-7) **1(2)-order length transitions (1oLT,2oLT)**: these features resemble the n-grams of [16]; the strong difference here is in the fact that we consider solely the length of the words, and not their content. See [15] for further details.

Syntactic Features.

(8) **Number of ? and ! marks (#?!)**: we keep the "?" and the "!" marks in the same feature, since taken separately their relevance is very low;

(9) **Number of suspension points (#...)**;

(10) **Number of generic marks (#Marks)**: a high number of generic marks (",.:*;) usually indicates a more accurate writing style;

(11,12,13) **Number of *positive*, *negative* and *uncategorized* emoticons (# Emo+, # Emo-, # Emo=**, respectively**)**: features related to emoticons aim at individuating a particular mood expressed in a turn. In particular, 101 diverse emoticons have been divided in three classes, portraying positive emotions (happiness, love, intimacy, etc. – 20 emot.), negative emotions (fear, anger, etc. – 19 emot.) and other emoticons (portraying actions, objects etc. – 62 emot.);

(14) **Number of emoticons (#Emo)**: Number of emoticons in a turn, independently from their type;

(15-16) **Number of emoticons / number of words (chars) (#Emo/#W, #Emo/#C**, respectively**)**: it considers how often pictorial symbols are used in a sentence considering the number of words (chars) typed;

(17) **Number of deletions (#Back)**; it models the number of hits of the backspace key during a turn.

Turn-taking Features.

For these novel features, the temporization of the key hits is crucial. In the following, we indicate with t_n the instant when the $n-$th hit of the button b_n occurs during a turn.

(18) **Turn time**: We indicate with T the length of the period in which a turn is kept (before pressing the "return" key);

(19) **Typing time**: thanks to the exact timings of key presses, this feature approximates the time spent in writing words, as the pauses and the time spent in deciding what to say and in reading what the other has written is not included in the counting. A word is assumed to be a string of consecutive alphanumeric characters, which is anticipated and followed by a blank space. Formally, let us define I_k, the interval of time spent in writing the $k-$th word; we have

$$I_k = t_n - t_m \quad (1)$$

such that $n > m$, b_{m-1}, b_{n+1} are space keys and b_m, $b_{m+1}, \ldots, b_n$ are not space keys. In these cases,

$$\text{Typing time} = \sum_k^K I_k \quad (2)$$

assuming to have K words in the turn under analysis. Calculating this feature is different than simply computing the time spent in a turn, as it allows for instance to distinguish a person who is very fast in typing words but uses long pauses between a word and another (he/she thinks a lot what to write) from an individual whose typing speed is slower, but knows what to say and takes fewer and shorter breaks while writing a sentence;

(20) **Mean typing time**: it divides the total typing time in a conversation of a subject by the number of turns;

(21) **Mean writing speed**: it measures the typing time divided by the number $\#C$ of written chars in a turn;

(22) **Deviation writing speed**; the standard deviation of the timings required for typing a character. Assuming $\tilde{t}_n = t_n - t_{n-1}$ and t_n is the time when a char button is hit, we have

$$\text{Dev.writ.speed} = \frac{1}{\#C - 1} \sum_{n=1}^{\#C} (\tilde{t}_n - \text{Mean writ.sp.})^2 \quad (3)$$

(23) **Silence time** (ST): the time spent in pressing the space bar, which is collected by summing all those intervals of the form

$$S_k = t_n - t_m \quad (4)$$

such that $n > m$, b_m, b_n are not space keys and b_m, $b_{m+1}, \ldots, b_n$ are space keys. Therefore

$$\text{Silence time} = \sum_k^K S_k \quad (5)$$

This feature models the pauses that are taken between a word and another, which could be thought as the counterpart of the silence in spoken interactions;

(24) **Speech ratio**: the ratio between the time spent typing words and typing spaces. It gives an idea of the balance between being inactive (because one is waiting for the other's reply, or because he/she is thinking what to write) and being actively typing;

(25-26) **Imitation per word, per char (#W imit, #C imit)**: ratio between number of chars -or words- in the current turn and number of chars -or words- in the previous turn of the interlocutor; this feature models the tendency of a subject to imitate the conversation style of the interlocutor (at least for what concerns the length of the turns);

(27) **Answer time**: this feature is the time spent to answer a question presented in the previous turn of the interlocutor. We assume the presence of a question whenever there is a question mark;

(28) **Typing time length** n **(Typing time n)**> it models the average time needed for writing a word of a given length L ($L = 1, \ldots, 15$), where the averaging operation here is built on the entire conversation, and not solely on a single turn.

Since these features are collected for each turn (except the Typing time n, 1oLT and 2oLT features), and assuming there are T turns in a conversation, we end up with T numbers for each feature.

These features are subsequently used for two applications: correlation with psychological traits and user recognition. Depending on the task at hand, the feature values are treated differently, as discussed in the following.

5. CORRELATIONS TRAITS-FEATURES

In order to inquire whether a connection holds between psychological traits and features, we consider the cues extracted from the chat of each single subject and the scores of his/her questionnaires. In particular, for each feature we calculate the mean or the median number over all the turns of the conversation, obtaining one value per feature, per user. As notable exception, for the 1oLT and 2oLT we keep the maximum values contained within. The reason is simple (take as example the 1oLT): having a high entry at the position i, j of the matrix means that a word of i characters, followed immediately by a word of j characters have been written many times by a subject; this indicates a certain stylistic pattern that, if high, indicates a sort of blueprint for that user.

For the estimation of the correlation, we calculate the Pearson correlation coefficient (where both the distribution of features values and traits are normal), the Spearman coefficient otherwise. The test for normality is the Lilliefors test. Results are shown in Table 1, showing 17 significant correlations (p-value< 0.05). Note that Attentional Impulsiveness and BAS did not show any correlation.

Our findings suggest that subjects who scored higher in motor and non-planning impulsiveness used shorter words (low *mean word length*), indicating that they were taking less time to provide their answer. Moreover, subjects who referred higher deficit in planning their own behavior (non-planning impulsiveness) tended to imitate to a larger extent what the other interlocutor did (high *imitation rate*) and used a lower number of emoticons in relation to the used words/chars, as suggesting that they were, again, available neither to loose time in chatting nor in thinking about what and how to write.

Relatively to traits involved in human motivation to act and write in a way rather than in another, our findings are also of interest. Specifically, subjects with higher levels of behavioral inhibition (that is, punishment avoidance) showed a lower tendency to imitate the other interlocutor's style in chatting. This result is not clearly intuitive as, usually, in order to avoid punishment, people tend to be accommodating and in this framework one would expect them

	Motor impulsiveness	Non planning impulsiveness	BIS punishment avoidance	PA Positive affectivity	NA Negative affectivity
#Emo (n14) *[66.4%]*	/	/	-0.31	/	/
#Emo/#W (n15) *[60.7%]*	/	-0.28	-0.29	/	-0.30
#Emo/#C (n16) *[61.0%]*	/	-0.28	-0.29	/	-0.31
#Emo+ (n11) *[/]*	/	/	/	/	/
#W (n1) *[60.4%]*	/	/	/	-0.29	/
Mean word length (5) *[63.5%]*	-0.41	-0.38	/	+0.38	/
Mean writing speed (20) *[65.9%]*	/	/	/	-0.36	/
1oLT (n6) *[69.9%]*	/	/	/	-0.34	/
#C imit (n26) *[57.1%]*	/	+0.36	-0.29	/	-0.31
#W imit (n25) *[55.9%]*	/	+0.30	/	/	/

Table 1: Correlations between stylometric features. In brackets, the ID of the features. In squared brackets the nAUC score, witnessing how effective the feature is in distinguishing people (the higher the more effective, see Sec. 7). Numerical values in the table indicate statistically significant correlations (*p-value*< 0.05). Attentional Impulsiveness and BAS did not show any correlation, so they are not reported here.

to imitate the interlocutor's style. Nonetheless, it has to be noticed that the specific task did not imply any punishment, therefore subjects could feel free to write sponta-neously, without imitating the interlocutor. Interestingly, they used a lower number of emoticons, not only in absolute terms, but also relatively to the number of words or chars used in writing (low #Emo/#W and #Emo/#C). Also the latter chatting style can be the manifestation of a tendency to avoid to show emotions, be they positive or negative, and might be driven by a behavior of punishment avoidance, represented by high scores in BIS scale.

The same negative correlation with the number of emoticons used has been found in connection with higher levels of negative affectivity, showing again a higher tendency to avoid to express emotions while chatting. These findings seem to be related to those found by [3], where subjects with behavioral inhibition and negative affectivity tended to show more negative emotions in their natural speech. Also, subjects with higher negative affectivity showed a lower tendency to imitate the interlocutor's chatting style. Subjects with higher positive affectivity showed a higher tendency to use long words and to write slowly, to use a smaller number of words, and to have a higher tendency to change their chatting style (low *1oLT*). These findings, taken together, seem to suggest that positive affectivity leads to emphasize the specific words used, preferring the length rather than the quantity of words, writing them slowly, and feeling free to change their chatting style.

It is worth noting that the 28x7 correlation tests cannot be taken together and compared with the number of significant correlation values, since they refer to highly different cues and diverse personality markers; instead, the 17 correlations found are meaningful, since they concentrate on few stylometric features (10), which represent few distinct aspects of chatting. Even if the correlations are somewhat weak, they resemble numerical results obtained by analogue studies on personality and writing style, see [12] as an example.

6. PREDICTION BY REGRESSION

To assess the reliability of the correlations, we investigate how well an automatic system can predict the personality traits of a person given a portion of his/her chat. To this sake, for each trait we select all the features which show significant correlations with it, and we train a separate multivariate Epsilon Support Vector Regressor (ϵ-SVR) with RBF kernel, in a Leave One Out sense (learning on N-1 people, testing on the Nth one, for all the people). We use ϵ-SVRs after having tried linear regression, which gave worst performances. As for the parameter selection, we set a single ϵ-SVR parameterization, which work reasonably well on all the traits, that is $C = 220$, $\gamma = 1.6$, $\epsilon = 1$. As evaluation metrics we use the standard R^2 measure and we also perform correlation between the predicted values and the original ones, to show if, apart from bias, there is some regularity in the prediction of the regressor. The results are shown in Table 2. As visible, we obtain significant correlations with 3 out of 5 traits, even if the R2 score is very weak. Anyway, our aim is not to promote a product which performs such kind of prediction, but only to assess the influence of personality traits in the way a chat is performed.

7. PERSON RECOGNITION BY STYLE

Here the aim is to analyze to which extent stylometric features can distinguish a person among many others. For every subject we collect one conversation and extract the related features. Then, a similarity score is calculated between each subject and all the others, first by accounting for each single feature separately, then using all the features together. In the former case, the similarity score is obtained by taking the T values of the feature, organizing them into an 8-bin histogram, where the range of the quantization values had been fixed by considering the whole dataset. The match between any two histograms is calculated using the Bhattacharyya distance. This process is applied to all kinds of features, except for the 1oLT and 2oLT features, where the diffusion distance [15] is employed, and for the Typing time n, where Euclidean distance is adopted.

The turns of each subject are split into *probe* and *gallery* set, so that the probe samples can be given as test and the recognizer can evaluate the matches with the gallery elements. Probe and gallery set contain snaps of 10 turns of conversation each in order to avoid biases due to quantitatively different available material. Whenever possible, we have selected different turns (maintaining their chronological order) in order to generate different probe/gallery partitions. For each feature the re-identification has been repeated 30 times, varying probe and gallery partitions.

	Motor impulsiveness	Non planning impulsiveness	BIS punishment avoidance	PA Positive affectivity	NA Negative affectivity
ρ	**0.31**	**0.43**	0.23	-0.16	**0.44**
p	**0.03**	**0.001**	0.09	0.27	**0.002**
R^2	**0.09**	**0.06**	<0	<0	**0.15**

Table 2: Regression results: for each trait, we report the Pearson correlation coefficient ρ calculated between the predicted and the original personality traits, its associated p-value and the R^2 metrics.

Then, for each subject we extract a particular feature from the probe set and calculate the distance with the gallery of the corresponding feature for all subjects. If we take N subjects, we obtain a $N \times N$ distance matrix. At this point we have ranked the N distances for each probe element in ascending order and thus we have computed the *Cumulative Match Characteristic* (CMC) curve, i.e., the expectation of finding the correct match in the top n positions of the ranking. The CMC has been recognized as an effective performance measure for authorship attribution [15], and we have then used it to evaluate the task of *identity recognition*, i.e. the ability to discover the identity of a subject among a set of N other subjects. In particular, the value of the CMC curve at position 1 is the probability that the probe ID signature of a subject is closer to the gallery ID signature of the same subject than to any other gallery ID signature; the value of the CMC curve at position n is the probability of finding the correct match in the first n ranked positions.

Given the CMC curve for each feature (obtained by averaging on 30 trials), the normalized Area Under Curve (nAUC) is calculated as a measure of accuracy. The results are shown in Fig. 2, where the features are listed in decreasing order of accuracy. The cues which correlate with at least one personality trait are portrayed in red. We have not reported the features producing an nAUC lower than 0.52.

As visible, all the CMC curves related to the different features are similar in expressivity, but not strongly effective; the probability of guessing the right people with only one attempt (corresponding to analyzing the performance of the CMC curve at rank 1) is below the 10%. Anyway, if we combine all features, mediating the related distances computed among the probe and the gallery subject, we obtain a much more informative curve (see Fig. 2, *All features*). In this case, getting the correct guess after the first attempt is around the 30%, and with the 80% of probability we can individuate the correct subject among the first 10 ranked subjects.

8. LINKING PERSONALITY TO RECOGNIZABILITY: DISCUSSION

Looking jointly at Fig. 2 and Table 1, one can immediately notice that positive affectivity is the trait which is most strongly related with the style of a person (it correlates with 4 stylometric features), making it recognizable with the highest probability (if we use only its correlated features, with the approach detailed in Sec. 7, we obtain 72.1% of nAUC). This result is intuitive, since positive affectivity may favor the tendency of writing following a well defined structure (the 1oLT feature, capturing the fact that short words follow short words, short words follow long words etc.) and of using few long words, slowly written.

A second important personality trait is the non planning impulsiveness (how much a person refers higher deficit in planning his/her own behavior), whose 5 correlated features, if combined, give 69.4% of nAUC. The same nAUC score is given by the 4 features correlated with the punishment avoidance (people with higher levels of behavioral inhibition). Negative affectivity has 3 correlated features (65.9% nAUC). The less indicative trait, among the ones which correlate, is the motor impulsiveness, with only one feature (63.5% nAUC).

These findings are very interesting as, congruently with the aim of this study, they clearly suggest that specific psychological factors related with impulsivity and involved in human interaction can be predictive of peculiar writing styles people use in writing chat texts.

9. CONCLUSIONS

The analysis of the relations between personality and writing style has been an hot topic in both computational linguistics and psychology fields; recently, the topic has been renowned with the massive diffusion of the chats, where textual artifacts and elements of the spoken interaction coexist. In this scenario, our long term goal is to evaluate whether the influence of personality on chatting style is stronger than in standard text, and in which measure this is manifested by non verbal signals, that is, aspects that go beyond the semantics of the content. This way, algorithms that recognize personality profiles of the speakers may be employed in a privacy respectful manner, facilitating the conversation with diverse chatting layouts, or encouraging contacts between "compatible" subjects. At the same time, we are interested in discovering whether the manifestation of a very particular chatting style, that is, very recognizable, may correspond to having also a distinguishable personality profile. In this way we may understand which are the personality traits that are more evident via chat, and in which measure chats can be considered a transparent means of communication. This study goes in this direction, showing that positive affectivity is connected with the usage few long words, slowly written by following a particular rhythm and this turns out to be the most recognizable trait, followed by non planning impulsiveness, behavioral inhibition, negative affectivity and planning impulsiveness.

10. ACKNOWLEDGMENTS

C. Giorgetta and R. Ferrario are supported by the VisCoSo project grant, financed by the Autonomous Province of Trento through the "Team 2011" funding programme.

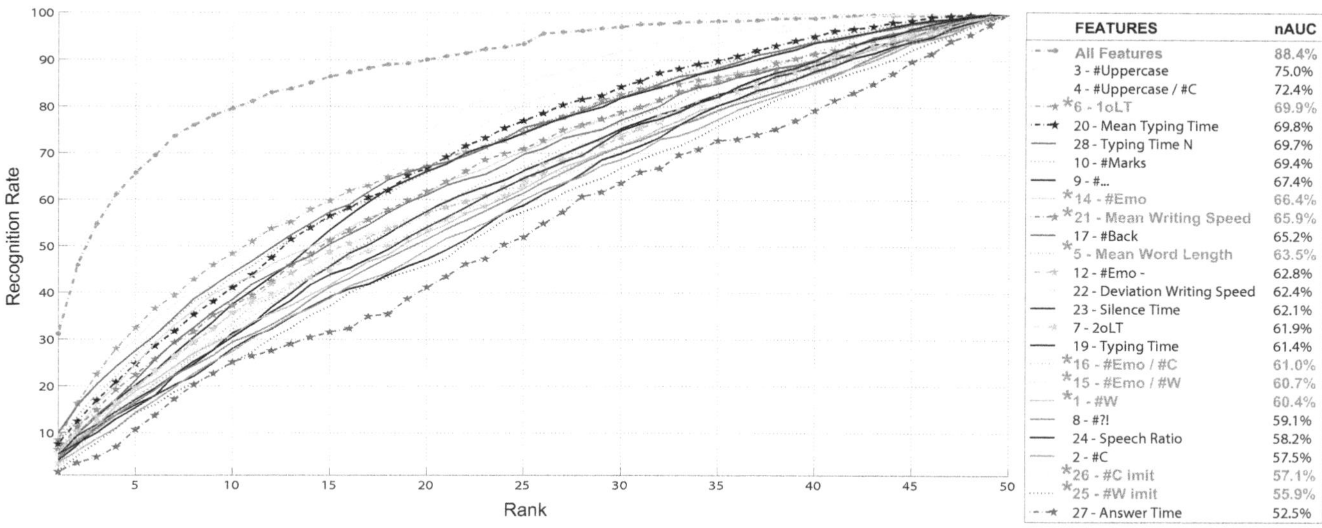

Figure 2: CMC curves for each feature. After each feature, their ID and the value of the correspondent nAUC. With an asterisk, in red, we specify those features which correlate at least with a personality trait. The *All features* CMC indicates the performance of averaging the distance of all the features and calculating the ranking.

11. REFERENCES

[1] A. Abbasi and H. Chen. Writeprints: A stylometric approach to identity-level identification and similarity detection in cyberspace. *ACM Transactions on Information Systems*, 26(2):1–29, 2008.

[2] C. Carver and T. White. Behavioral Inhibition, Behavioral Activation, and Affective Responses to Impending Reward and Punishment: The BIS/BAS Scales. *Journal of Personality and Social Psychology*, 67:319–333, 1994.

[3] A. S. Cohen, K. S. Minor, L. E. Baillie, and A. M. Dahir. Clarifying the Linguistic Signature: Measuring Personality from Natural Speech. *Journal of Personality Assessment*, 90(6):559–563, 2008.

[4] M. Coltheart. The MRC Psycholinguistic database. *The Quarterly Journal of Experimental Psychology*, 33(4):497–505, 1981.

[5] M. H. Davis. Measuring Individual Differences in Empathy: Evidence for a Multidimensional Approach. *Journal of Personality and Social Psychology*, 44(1):113–126, 1983.

[6] R. Hassin and Y. Trope. Facing faces: Studies on the Cognitive Aspects of Physiognomy . *Journal of Personality and Social Psychology*, 78:837–852, 2000.

[7] F. Mairesse, M. A. Walker, M. R. Mehl, and R. K. Moore. Using Linguistic Cues for the Automatic Recognition of Personality in Conversation and Text. *Journal of Artificial Intelligence Research*, 30:457–500, 2007.

[8] N. Markel, J. Phillis, R. Vargas, and K. Howard. Personality Traits Associated with Voice Types. *Journal of Psycholinguistic Results*, 1:249–255, 1972.

[9] M. R. Mehl, S. D. Gosling, and J. W. Pennebaker. Personality in Its Natural Habitat: Manifestations and Implicit Folk Theories of Personality in Daily Life. *Journal of Personality and Social Psychology*, 90(5):862–877, 2006.

[10] J. H. Patton, M. S. Stanford, and E. S. Barratt. Factor structure of the barratt impulsiveness scale. *Journal of Clinical Psychology*, 51:768–774, 1995.

[11] J. W. Pennebaker, M. E. Francis, and R. J. Booth. Linguistic Inquiry and Word Count: LIWC 2001. *Mahway: Lawrence Erlbaum Associates*, 71:2001, 2001.

[12] J. W. Pennebaker and L. A. King. Linguistic Styles: Language Use as an Individual Difference. *Journal of Personality and Social Psychology*, 77(6):1296, 1999.

[13] B. Rammstedt and O. P. John. Measuring Personality in One Minute or Less: A 10-item Short Version of the Big Five Inventory in English and German. *in Journal of Research in Personality*, 41:203–212, 2007.

[14] G. Roffo, C. Giorgetta, R. Ferrario, and M. Cristani. Just The Way You Chat: Linking Personality, Style and Recognizability in Chats. In *5th International Workshop on Human Behaviour Understanding (associated to ECCV)*, 2014.

[15] G. Roffo, C. Segalin, V. Murino, and M. Cristani. Reading Between the Turns: Statistical Modeling for Identity Recognition and Verification in Chats. In *IEEE International Conference on Advanced Video and Signal-Based Surveillance (AVSS 2013)*, 2013.

[16] E. Stamatatos. A Survey of Modern Authorship Attribution Methods. *Journal of the American Society for Information Science and Technology*, 60(3):538–556, 2009.

[17] D. Watson, L. Clark, and A. Tellegen. Development and Validation of Brief Measures of Positive and Negative Affect: The PANAS Scales. *Journal of Personality and Social Psychology*, 54:1063–1070, 1988.

Understanding Users' Perceived Difficulty of Multi-Touch Gesture Articulation

Yosra Rekik
Inria Lille & LIFL, University of Lille 1, France
yosra.rekik@inria.fr

Radu-Daniel Vatavu
University Stefan cel Mare of Suceava, Romania
vatavu@eed.usv.ro

Laurent Grisoni
Inria Lille & LIFL, University of Lille 1, France
laurent.grisoni@lifl.fr

ABSTRACT

We show that users are consistent in their assessments of the articulation difficulty of multi-touch gestures, even under the many degrees of freedom afforded by multi-touch input, such as (1) various number of fingers touching the surface, (2) various number of strokes that structure the gesture shape, and (3) single-handed and bimanual input. To understand more about perceived difficulty, we characterize gesture articulations captured under these conditions with geometric and kinematic descriptors computed on a dataset of 7,200 samples of 30 distinct gesture types collected from 18 participants. We correlate the values of the objective descriptors with users' subjective assessments of articulation difficulty and report path length, production time, and gesture size as the highest correlators (max Pearson's r=.95). We also report new findings about multi-touch gesture input, *e.g.,* gestures produced with more fingers are larger in size and take more time to produce than single-touch gestures; bimanual articulations are not only faster than single-handed input, but they are also longer in path length, present more strokes, and result in gesture shapes that are deformed horizontally by 35% in average. We use our findings to outline a number of 14 guidelines to assist multi-touch gesture set design, recognizer development, and inform gesture-to-function mappings through the prism of the user-perceived difficulty of gesture articulation.

Categories and Subject Descriptors

H.5.2. [**Information Interfaces and Presentation**]: Information Interfaces and Presentation

Keywords

Multi-touch, articulation difficulty, ease of execution, user study, gesture articulation, number of fingers, number of strokes, number of hands, gesture structure, gesture geometry, gesture kinematics.

1. INTRODUCTION

Designing gesture sets can prove a challenging task because of users' different preferences in terms of articulation patterns [2,15, 16] and gesture-to-function mappings [22]. The current practice of gesture interface design has outlined several guidelines to assist practitioners in this regard, according to which gesture shortcuts should be unambiguously recognized [10], fast to articulate [3], ergonomically easy to execute [11,22], easy to learn and recall [3,12, 13], and well fit to application functions [13,22]. However, these guidelines are not straightforward to apply because of the little understanding of the factors acting behind them, *e.g.,* what causes articulation difficulty and what triggers gesture recall? There is also a lack of methodology and models to reliably estimate these factors *a priori*, which makes practitioners resort to involving users in time-consuming studies to identify good gesture designs [5,11,12,22] .

In this context, we argue that the user-perceived difficulty of gesture articulation is an important factor for gesture set design that has been little explored so far and, consequently, is little understood. While it is not straightforward to precisely define the notion of *gesture articulation difficulty*, we believe it captures many facets of gesture production, such as *ergonomic difficulty* to physically articulate the gesture path and *cognitive difficulty* required to learn and recall the geometry of the gesture shape and, conceivably, the specifics of its articulation (*e.g.,* the number of fingers to employ and the gesture stroke structure). Although the notion of gesture articulation difficulty has been mentioned as design criteria by many works [11,13,22], it has only been examined thoroughly for unistrokes [20]. However, opposed to unistrokes, multi-touch gestures present considerably more degrees of freedom afforded during articulation, such as employing various number of fingers, different stroke count and ordering, and single-handed and bimanual input [15]. In this work, we examine users' perceived difficulty of multi-touch gesture articulation for symbolic gesture types [3,15,19–21], such as those from Figure 1, and we provide the community the first understanding of this phenomenon as well as its potential implications in terms of gesture set design, multi-touch recognizer development, and gesture-to-function mappings.

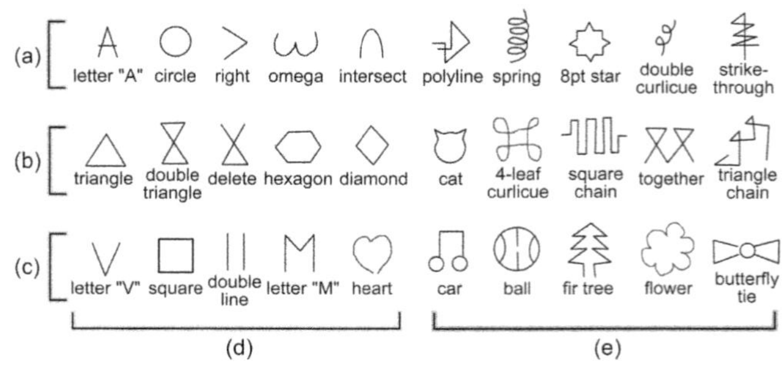

Figure 1: The set of 30 gestures used for our experiment addressing the effect of the number of (a) fingers, (b) strokes, and (c) hands on perceived difficulty. The left 15 gestures (d) were designed to be familiar and the right 15 gestures (e) unfamiliar to our participants.

ICMI '14, November 12 - 16 2014, Istanbul, Turkey.

ACM 978-1-4503-2885-2/14/11 $15.00.
http://dx.doi.org/10.1145/2663204.2663273

Our contributions are as follows: (1) we conduct the first investigation of the user-perceived difficulty of multi-touch gesture articulation, and deliver results in terms of gesture *difficulty ratings* and *rankings*; in doing so, we examine the effect of finger count, stroke count, and single-handed and bimanual articulation conditions on perceived articulation difficulty; (2) we report correlation results between users' subjective assessments of difficulty and objective gesture descriptors to enable a better understanding of the phenomena involved in the perception of articulation difficulty; as a practical result, we report gesture path length and production time as the highest correlators with users' perceived difficulty of gesture articulation; (3) we report novel findings on multi-touch gestures articulated under different conditions, *e.g.*, bimanual articulations result in gesture shapes horizontally stretched by 35% than their single-handed counterparts; (4) finally, we use our large body of results to compile a set of 14 guidelines for multi-touch gesture set design and mapping gestures to functions by considering the ergonomics of multi-touch input through the prism of the user-perceived difficulty of gesture articulation. We hope our results will prove useful to designers and practitioners interested in maximizing the ease of execution of their multi-touch gesture set designs.

2. EXPERIMENT

We employ the methodology of Vatavu et al. [20] to collect users' self-reported difficulty assessments and apply it for multi-touch gestures. We use the methodology for a series of three experimental tasks designed to collect multi-touch gestures articulated under various conditions in terms of (1) number of fingers, (2) number of strokes, and (3) single-handed and bimanual input.

2.1 Participants

Eighteen (18) participants (four females) volunteered to take part in our experiment involving acquisition of multi-touch gestures. Participants' ages varied between 22 and 35 years (mean age 27.4, SD=3.4 years). All participants, except one, were right-handed. Fourteen participants were regular users of smart phones and tablet devices with multi-touch screens, but none had previous experience with large-screen interactive tabletops.

2.2 Apparatus

Multi-touch gestures were collected on a 32 inch (81 cm) 3M™ multi-touch display (model C3266PW) that was set to work at a screen resolution of 1920×1080 pixels. The display supports detection of up to 40 simultaneous touches. The device was positioned horizontally on a table and connected to a computer running Windows and our custom data acquisition software. Participants entered gestures in an area of 1140×950 pixels (42×35 cm).

2.3 Procedure

We controlled the following conditions for multi-touch gesture articulation: (1) number of fingers, (2) number of strokes, and (3) number of hands and their sequential and synchronous use during articulation. In order to keep the overall duration of the data collection procedure manageable for our participants [1], the effect of each condition was tested as an individual experimental task.

Task #1: Effect of number of fingers. Each trial began by presenting participants with the gesture to articulate and the number of fingers to use during articulation: one (1F), two (2F), and three or more fingers (3+F). For the 3+F condition, participants were instructed to use their preferred number of fingers, as long as there were at least three fingers employed. Participants were instructed to enter gestures at normal speed, using their preferred hand, fingers, and number of strokes. The number of fingers was a fixed constraint during the entire articulation, but participants were allowed to use their prefered fingers. The order of trials was randomized. Each gesture type was articulated with five repetitions, with a total of 10 gestures × 3 finger conditions × 5 repetitions = 150 articulations produced by each participant. Our software application randomly presented the 150 articulations to our participants. This task took in average 30 minutes to complete.

Task #2: Effect of number of strokes. Each trial began by presenting participants with the gesture to articulate and the number of strokes to use: one (1S), two (2S), and three or more strokes (3+S). In the 3+S condition, participants were instructed to use their preferred number of strokes, as long as there were at least three strokes. Participants articulated gestures at normal speed and using their preferred hand, with 10 gestures × 3 stroke conditions × 5 repetitions = 150 articulations per participant. The 150 articulations were randomly presented to our participants. The task took in average 30 minutes.

Task #3: Effect of number of hands. Each trial began by presenting participants with the gesture to articulate and the number of hands to use during articulation. In the single-handed condition, all gesture strokes had to be entered one after the other. We also refer to this condition as sequential articulation (SEQ). For the bimanual condition, participants were instructed to articulate strokes in parallel (*i.e.*, synchronous articulation, SYNC). The number of hands was a fixed constraint that had to be fulfilled during the entire articulation, but participants were given freedom with respect to the number of strokes and number of fingers to employ. Each gesture was executed for five times in each condition, with a total number of 10 gestures × 2 hand conditions × 5 repetitions = 100 articulations produced by each participant. The 100 articulations were randomly presented to our participants. This task took around 20 minutes to complete.

To minimize the influence of each experimental task over the others, task order was counter-balanced across participants.

Perceived articulation difficulty was collected after each experimental task using absolute RATING and relative RANKING measurements, similar to the methodology of Vatavu et al. [20]. RATING was collected using a 5-point Likert scale (see Table 1), which was presented to participants as a table with five columns, one column for each RATING value. Participants were asked to draw each gesture in the appropriate difficulty column, after having articulated it one more time on the multi-touch surface in order to re-enact the articulation experience and, consequently, perceived difficulty. Participants were allowed to change the ratings of previously rated gestures at any time as they moved along with the rating process until they were confident of the final classification of gesture types into difficulty classes. After rating each gesture under each condition, participants were asked to provide an ordered list of combined gesture types and articulation conditions in increasing order of perceived difficulty, which represents our RANKING measurement.

2.4 Gesture set

We employed 30 gesture types for our experiment, with 10 gestures per task (see Figure 1). All gestures for the stroke task were carefully chosen so that they could be articulated both as single and multi-strokes. All gestures selected for the number of hands task expose a symmetry axis, as it has been observed previously that only symmetric gestures can be conveniently parallelized during articulation [15]. In addition, half of the gesture shapes were selected to appear *familiar* to our participants, where we defined the *familiarity* of a shape as previous, frequent practice articulating that specific shape during everyday handwriting (*e.g.*, familiarity

1. Which was of approximately one hour and 20 minutes per participant.

Likert RATING (1–5)	Explanation provided to participants
1. very easy to execute	I executed these gestures immediately and effortlessly with absolutely no need to pay attention.
2. easy to execute	I executed these gestures easily, almost without paying attention.
3. moderate difficulty	I occasionally paid attention during execution.
4. difficult to execute	I paid special attention with each execution.
5. very difficult to execute	I had to concentrate for each execution. There were times when I did not get the right shape from the first attempt.

Table 1: Likert questions employed to elicit absolute articulation difficulty of multi-touch gestures (*i.e.*, RATINGs), similar to [20].

occurs for example for letters and simple geometric shapes). The remaining half of the gesture set was designed to be *unfamiliar* to our participants, which enabled us to collect their subjective perceptions of articulation difficulty on the first encounter with a new geometric shape (*e.g.,* the "four curlicue" or the "stroke-through" gestures of Figure 1). This approach at gesture set design follows the methodology of Vatavu et al. [20] as well as current observations from the gesture literature according to which shape familiarity and practice affect human performance when articulating gestures (*e.g.,* smaller production times can be observed with gesture practice [6,18,20]). Please also note that the familiarity of a gesture is more related to practice than to the complexity of its geometrical shape [20]. For instance, a gesture can be considered familiar and, consequently, rated "easy to perform" by users although it is geometrically complex, and the opposite is also true (e.g., see letter 'g' and discussion from [20]). In this work, we investigate symbolic multi-touch gestures instead of standard gestures traditionally used for multi-touch interaction (*e.g.,* pan, zoom, rotate, etc.), because symbols are more versatile to generalize for other applications.

2.5 Design

Our experiment was a within-participants design with four independent variables:

1. FINGER-COUNT, ordinal with 3 values corresponding to using one (1F), two (2F), and three or more fingers (3+F).
2. STROKE-COUNT, ordinal with 3 values corresponding to producing one (1S), two (2S), and three or more strokes (3+S).
3. SYNCHRONICITY, nominal with 2 values: one hand sequential input (SEQ) and bimanual synchronous input (SYNC).
4. GESTURE, nominal with 10 values per task, and 30 values for the entire experiment (see Figure 1).

The dependent variables were participants' absolute RATING and relative RANKING of perceived articulation difficulty, which were collected during a post-experiment questionnaire:

1. RATING, ordinal variable, measures the absolute difficulty of articulating a multi-touch gesture into five levels, and was presented in the form of a Likert scale (see Table 1).
2. RANKING, ordinal variable, measures the relative difficulty of articulating multi-touch gestures. RANKING takes values in the set $\{1,2,\dots 30\}$ for the first two tasks (corresponding to 10 gesture types $\times$ 3 conditions), and in the set $\{1,2,\dots 20\}$ for the third task (*i.e.*, 10 gestures $\times$ 2 conditions).

3. RESULTS #1: PERCEIVED DIFFICULTY

We are interested in this section in the level of agreement between participants in terms of their perceived difficulty of multi-touch gestures articulated under various conditions. To this end, we report and analyze 144 individual ratings of absolute difficulty and 54 rankings of relative difficulty collected from 18 participants.

3.1 Assumption of gesture familiarity

Half of the gestures (15 gestures) were specifically selected to look familiar to participants (see our definition of familiarity in the previous section), while the other half were new gestures, specifically designed for our experimental tasks. In order to validate our initial assumptions about gesture familiarity, we asked participants to report at the end of each task which gestures looked familiar to them. In total, we counted 43 deviations from our gesture set assumed familiarity out of 540 total answers, which represents an error rate of less than 8%. Gestures such as "ball", "butterfly-tie", "four curlicue", and "square chain" were classified as familiar by some participants, although they witnessed no previous practice with these shapes. Under these circumstances, we can safely consider the assumptions of familiarity met for our gesture set.

3.2 Effect of finger count on difficulty

Figure 2 illustrates participants' responses of the perceived difficulty of multi-touch gestures articulated with one (1F), two (2F), and three or more fingers (3+F). Overall, we found a high degree of agreement between participants' responses, as reflected by Kendall's coefficient of concordance [2] (W=.77, $\chi^2(29)$=403.340, $p<.001$ for RATING, and W=.82, $\chi^2(29)$=428.748, $p<.001$ for RANKING). The level of agreement between participants also stayed high (*i.e.,* above .80 for RATING and above .85 for RANKING, $p<.001$) when we ran the analysis for each value of the finger count condition individually (*i.e.,* one, two, and three or more fingers). These findings indicate that the articulation difficulty of multi-touch gestures is perceived by people in a consistent manner, which justifies further investigation of the self-reported difficulty assessments.

We found a significant effect of the number of employed fingers on perceived articulation difficulty measured as both RATING ($\chi^2(2)$=23.130, $p<.001$) and RANKING ($\chi^2(2)$=21.778, $p<.001$), with more fingers causing an increase in the perceived difficulty of gesture articulation (see Figure 2, inner graphs). Post-hoc Wilcoxon signed-rank tests (Bonferroni corrected at p=.01/2=.005) confirmed a significant difference between two and three or more fingers with a medium to large effect (r=.51), and a nonsignificant difference between one and two fingers conditions.

Familiar gestures were rated as less difficult to execute (median RATING=1 corresponding to "very easy to execute") than unfamiliar gestures (median RATING=3 or "moderate difficulty"). These differences were significant, as confirmed by Wilcoxon signed-rank tests ($z_{(N=18)}=-3.782$, $p<.001$, $r=-.63$). The fifteen familiar gestures were among the first sixteen gestures in ascending order of RATING and RANKING (Figure 2), with 13/15=87% of familiar gestures being rated as "very easy to execute" (RATING=1). At the same time, 10/15=67% of the unfamiliar gesture articulations were rated from "moderate" to "very difficult to execute". We also found participants less consistent when rating familiar than unfamiliar gestures (W=.28 versus .65 for RATING and W=.56 versus .72 for RANKING, all $p<.001$), which suggests that people develop different preferences with practice for articulating gestures in terms of preferred number of fingers.

3.3 Effect of stroke count on difficulty

Figure 3 illustrates participants' RATING and RANKING assessments of the self-perceived difficulty when articulating multi-touch gestures with one (1S), two (2S), and three or more strokes (3+S). This time, we found a lower degree of consensus between partici-

2. Kendall's coefficient of concordance is a normalization of the statistic of the Friedman test used to asses continuity of judgement among multiple individuals. W takes values in [0..1], where 0 denotes no agreement at all and 1 perfect agreement [9].

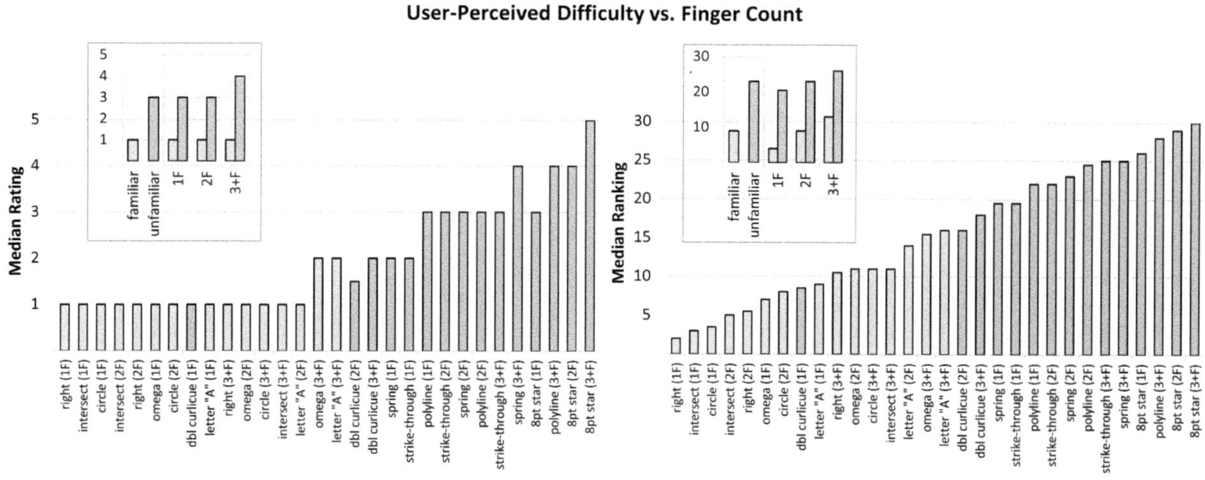

Figure 2: Median values for the user-perceived difficulty of articulating multi-touch gestures measured as absolute RATING (left) and relative RANKING (right) function of the number of employed fingers: one (1F), two (2F), and three or more fingers (3+F). NOTE: In both graphs, gestures are ordered by ascending RANKING values; higher numerical values show larger articulation difficulty.

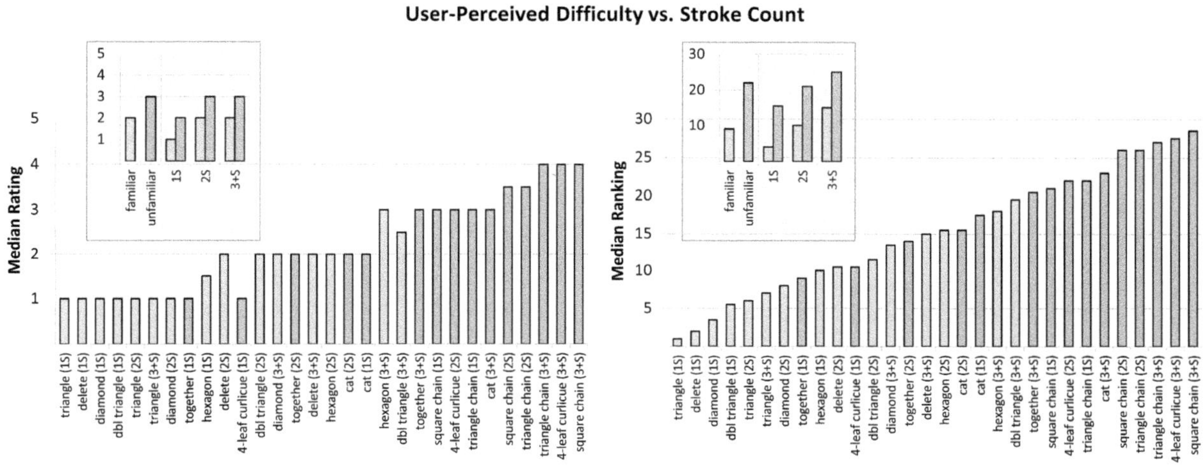

Figure 3: Median values for the user-perceived difficulty of articulating multi-touch gestures measured as absolute RATING (left) and relative RANKING (right) function of the number of gesture strokes employed during articulation: one (1S), two (2S), and three or more strokes (3+S). NOTE: In both graphs, gestures are ordered by ascending RANKING values; higher numerical values show larger articulation difficulty.

pants' assessments of articulation difficulty, as opposed to the finger count task. However, Kendall's coefficients stayed above .50, which shows large Cohen effect sizes[3] (W=.58, $\chi^2(29)$=308.816, p<.001 for RATING and W=.71, $\chi^2(29)$=369.095, p<.001 for RANKING). When calculating agreement for each stroke condition, Kendall's W coefficients stayed above .50 for RATING and above .60 for RANKING (p<.001). The lower degree of consensus compared to the previous finger count task suggests that STROKE-COUNT is a factor with a stronger influence on the self-perceived difficulty of articulated gestures than FINGER-COUNT.

We found a significant effect of the number of strokes on perceived difficulty for both RATING ($\chi^2(2) = 23.049$, $p < .001$) and RANKING measures ($\chi^2(2) = 32.444$, $p < .001$), with more strokes causing an increase in the self-perceived difficulty of gesture articulation (see Figure 3, inner graphs). In average, gestures articulated with one stroke were perceived as "very easy" and "easy to execute" (median RATING = 1.5), two-stroke gestures as "easy to execute" (median RATING = 2), and gestures articulated with three or more strokes having "moderate difficulty" (RATING = 3). Post-hoc Wilcoxon signed-rank tests confirmed significant differences (at p=.01/2=.005) between the 1S and 2S conditions, as well as between 2S and 3+S with medium to large effect sizes (r>.50).

As in the previous experimental task, familiar gestures were rated less difficult to execute (median RATING=2 corresponding to "easy to execute") than unfamiliar gestures (median RATING=3, "moderate difficulty"). These differences were significant, as confirmed by Wilcoxon signed-rank tests ($z_{(N=18)}=-3.535$, p<.001, $r = -.60$). The fifteen familiar gestures were among the first twenty gestures in ascending order of RATING and RANKING (Figure 3), with 14/15=93% of familiar gestures being rated as "very easy" and "easy to execute" (RATING values 1 and 2). At the same time, 10/15=67% of the unfamiliar gesture articulations were rated from "moderate" (RATING=3) to "difficult to execute" (RATING=4). Again, we found participants less consistent when rating familiar than unfamiliar gestures (W=.40 versus .51 for RATING and W=.61 versus .57 for RANKING, all p<.001).

3. Kendall's W coefficient is related to the average of $\binom{n}{2}$ Spearman rank correlation coefficients between pairs of the n rankings [9] (p. 276). Therefore, we use Cohen's suggested limits of .10, .30, and .50 for interpreting the magnitude of the effect size [8].

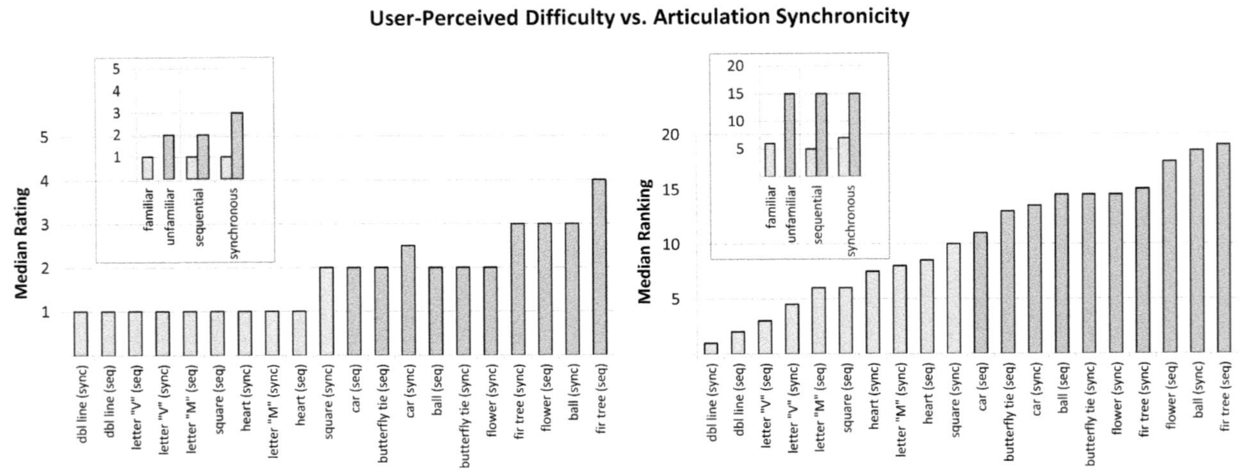

Figure 4: Median values for the user-perceived difficulty of articulating multi-touch gestures measured as absolute RATING (left) and relative RANKING (right) for sequential and bimanual synchronous input. NOTE: In both graphs, gestures are ordered by ascending RANKING values; higher numerical values show larger articulation difficulty.

3.4 Effect of synchronicity on difficulty

Figure 4 illustrates participants' assessments of difficulty in terms of RATING and RANKING for multi-touch gestures articulated with strokes in sequential order (*i.e.,* one stroke at a time) and synchronously (*i.e.,* strokes articulated in parallel). The degree of consensus between participants, when asked to rate and rank the difficulty of gestures articulated under sequential and bimanual conditions, stayed above .59 (W=.59, $\chi^2(19)$=201.477, p<.001 for RATING and W=.75, $\chi^2(19)$=257.921, p<.001 for RANKING). We found a higher degree of consensus among participants when rating gestures articulated with strokes in sequential order than in parallel (W=.73 versus .53 for RATING and W=.86 versus .70 for RANKING, all p<.001). However, there was no significant effect of articulation type on self-perceived difficulty for either RATING ($z_{(N=18)}$=−1.363, *n.s.*) or RANKING ($z_{(N=18)}$=−1.244, *n.s.*).

As in the other experimental tasks, familiar gestures were rated less difficult to execute (median RATING=1, "very easy to execute") than unfamiliar gestures (median RATING=2, "easy to execute"). These differences were significant, as confirmed by Wilcoxon signed-rank tests ($z_{(N=18)}$=−3.680, p<.001, r=−.61). The ten familiar gestures were the first in ascending order of RATING and RANKING (Figure 4), with 9/10=90% of familiar gestures rated "very easy". Again, our participants showed less agreement when rating familiar than unfamiliar gestures (W=.26 versus .37 for RATING and W=.61 versus .39 for RANKING, p<.001), which suggests again that people develop with practice different articulation preferences, this time in terms of bimanual input.

4. RESULTS #2: GESTURE ARTICULATION AND PERCEIVED DIFFICULTY

In this section, we accompany the results on participants' self-reported assessments of gesture articulation difficulty with a quantitative analysis comprising geometric and kinematic gesture descriptors that we apply to our dataset composed of 7,200 multi-touch gesture samples of 30 distinct gesture types collected from 18 participants under various articulation conditions.

4.1 Gesture descriptors

We selected several gesture descriptors commonly employed in the gesture recognition and analysis literature [1,2,4,17,20,21] in order to characterize the articulation of gesture types belonging to different difficulty classes. In order not to overload our discussion with extensive numerical data, we limit our analysis to a subset of eleven representative descriptors that we believe adequate to characterize gesture articulations in terms of gesture structure, geometry and visual appearance, and kinematics [4]. We characterize the structure of a multi-touch gesture by its number of points and number of strokes; gesture geometry is characterized by path length, bounding box size, and total absolute turning angle; and production time and speed are used to report the kinematics of multi-touch gesture articulation. As these descriptors are common and frequently used, we save paper space and do not define them here again. Instead, we refer the interested reader to previous works in which they are properly defined [1,2,4,17,20,21]. We are also interested in capturing subtle details specific only to multi-touch input. To this end, we proposed variations for computing some of the most used gesture features, and we denote these variations as *actual* number of strokes, *actual* path length, and *actual* total absolute turning angle. The term *actual* placed in front of a descriptor means the descriptor is computed using data points from all fingers touching the surface. For example, the *actual* path length is defined as the cumulative length produced by all fingers touching the surface, whereas (simple) path length produces a value independent of finger count (reflective of the path length irrespective of how it was articulated).

We computed Pearson correlations between all gesture descriptors and participants' self-perceived articulation difficulty reported as absolute RATING and relative RANKING measures. Table 2 shows the correlation values for each experimental condition. The largest value in each column is highlighted as there are all the other values not significantly different from it. In the following, we discuss specific findings for each gesture descriptor category.

4.2 Gesture structure and difficulty

We characterize the structure of a multi-touch gesture by its number of points, number of strokes, and *actual* number of produced strokes, where the latter includes the effect of employing multiple fingers and also covers unintentional finger slips.

Clearly, more fingers touching the surface will generate more points sampled by the device for the gesture path, with an expected and uninteresting linear relationship between the number of employed fingers and the number of sampled points (Figure 5a). Simi-

4. See Blagojevic et al. [4] for a comprehensive set of gesture features.

	Finger count		Stroke count		Hand count	
	RATING	RANK	RATING	RANK	RATING	RANK
A. Gesture structure						
Number of points	**.89****	.84**	.74**	.79**	.88**	.92**
Number of strokes	.65**	.59*	.60**	.55**	*n.s.*	.49*
Actual num. strokes	.71**	.61**	.60**	.55**	*n.s.*	.49*
B. Gesture geometry						
Path length	.83**	**.88****	.71**	.76**	.86**	**.95****
Actual path length	.73**	.73**	.71**	.76**	.86**	**.95****
Size	.79**	.80**	.73**	.79**	.68**	.59*
Aspect ratio	*n.s.*	*n.s.*	*n.s.*	*n.s.*	*n.s.*	*n.s.*
Total abs. angle	.65**	.68**	.51*	.58**	.74**	.82**
Actual abs. angle	.53**	.64**	.51*	.58**	.74**	.82**
C. Gesture kinematics						
Production time	.88**	.85**	**.90****	**.91****	**.90****	.91**
Average speed	-.81**	-.83**	-.69**	-.73**	-.53*	-.60*

NOTE: Pearson correlation coefficients are reported at p=.005 (**) and p=.05 (*) significance levels. N=30 for the finger and stroke count experimental tasks and N=20 for the synchronicity task. The largest coefficient in each column is highlighted. Coefficients not significantly different at p=.05 than the maximum value in each column, as indicated by the t statistic for dependent Pearson's r's [7], are also highlighted.

Table 2: Pearson correlations between gesture descriptors and median RATING and RANKING values for each experimental task.

larly, more fingers will produce more strokes, which we measured as the *actual* number of strokes (Figure 5c). Interestingly however, we found a significant effect of FINGER-COUNT on the (simple) number of strokes ($\chi^2(2)$=127.96, p<.001) (Figure 5b). We correlate this finding with comments from participants that felt three fingers or more required more effort. Also interesting, significantly more points and strokes (≈1.5 times more) were produced when participants articulated strokes synchronously instead of sequentially, as revealed by Wilcoxon signed-rank tests ($z_{(N=900)}$=23.56, p<.001, effect size r=.56 for the number of points descriptor and $z_{(N=900)}$=22.87, p<.001, r=.54 for the number of strokes).

We found significantly more points produced for unfamiliar gestures (two times more) than for familiar ones under all experimental conditions (p<.001, r=−.61). This finding confirms the fact that people tend to be more confident when articulating familiar gestures, which makes them faster [6,18], as deduced from the number of points sampled by the touch sensitive surface. Results also show people more careful when synchronizing bimanual movements involved in the articulation of multi-touch gestures (Figure 5a).

The number of points had one of the strongest Pearson correlation with both RATING and RANKING measures (average r=.84 and .85 respectively, p<.005, see Table 2).

4.3 Gesture geometry and difficulty

We characterize gesture geometry in terms of path length (and corresponding *actual* path length), size of the bounding box area, total absolute turning angle (and the correspondent *actual* form), and aspect ratio measurements (Figures 5d–5i on the next page).

Overall, we found a significant effect of FINGER-COUNT on all gesture geometry descriptors. While this finding was expected for the *actual* descriptors due to the way they were defined to capture the effect of more fingers touching the surface, the finding is particularly interesting for the other descriptors. Specifically, participants produced gestures significantly longer in path length by 10–25% ($\chi^2(2)$=902.11, p<.001) and larger in area size by 10–29% ($\chi^2(2)$=494.18, p<.001) when more fingers were in touch with the surface (Figures 5d–5f). Another interesting effect was found for total absolute turning angle (Figures 5g–5i), with more fingers causing a decrease in gesture path smoothness ($\chi^2(2)$=559.74, p<.001). Friedman tests revealed a significant effect of STROKE-COUNT on path length ($\chi^2(2)$=17.84, p<.001), gesture size ($\chi^2(2)$ = 19.10, p<.001), and the *actual* total absolute tuning angle ($\chi^2(2)$ = 1058.45, p<.001). Unlike gestures articulated with more fingers, gestures with more strokes presented smoother paths. Participants produced gestures that were longer yet smaller in area size during bimanual articulations when compared to sequential ones ($z_{(N=900)}$=17.06, p<.001, r=.40 for path length and $z_{(N=900)}$=−17.04, p<.001, r=−.40 for area size respectively). We also found an interesting effect of SYNCHRONICITY on the aspect ratios of gesture articulations: participants deformed gesture shapes more for bimanual articulations than for sequential ones ($z_{(N=900)}$=−21.54, p<.001, r=−.51) by producing gestures narrower by 35% in average when two hands were used.

Familiar gestures were significantly shorter (≈1.8 times shorter) than unfamiliar gestures under all experimental conditions, as shown by Wilcoxon signed-rank tests (all p<.001, r=−.61), and they were also smaller in area size (p<.001, effect sizes between −.60 and −.44). We found a significant effect of FAMILIARITY on the turning angle measures with familiar gestures presenting smoother paths (p<.001, effect sizes between −.61 and −.55).

Out of all geometric descriptors, path length presented the highest correlation with RATING and RANKING (average Pearson r=.80 and .86 respectively, p<.005, see Table 2).

4.4 Gesture kinematics and difficulty

We use production time and average speed to describe the kinematic dimension of multi-touch gesture articulation (Figures 5j, 5k).

We found significant effects of FINGER-COUNT on both production time ($\chi^2(2)$=900.05, p<.001) and average articulation speed ($\chi^2(2)$=111.72, p<.001), with more fingers touching the surface causing larger articulation times and smaller speeds. More strokes had a similar effect causing longer production times ($\chi^2(2)$=953.71, p<.001) and smaller execution speeds ($\chi^2(2)$=934.22, p<.001). Synchronous bimanual articulations were faster by 33% than sequential ones ($z_{(N=900)}$=−19.66, p<.001, r=−.46). A Wilcoxon signed-rank test revealed a corresponding significant effect of SYNCHRONICITY on average speed as well ($z_{(N=900)}$=23.86, p<.001, medium to large effect size r=.56).

We reconfirm that familiar gestures are produced faster than unfamiliar ones [6,18,20], a finding that appeared under all experimental conditions for both production time (all p<.001, r=−.60) and average speed (all p<.001, effect sizes r between .22 and .57).

Out of all kinematic descriptors, production time presented the highest correlation with RATING and RANKING (average Pearson coefficients r=.89 and .89 respectively, p<.005, see Table 2).

5. DISCUSSION & DESIGN GUIDELINES

We found participants highly consistent when assessing the difficulty of articulating multi-touch gestures under various FINGER-COUNT, STROKE-COUNT, and SYNCHRONICITY conditions, as indicated by Kendall's W coefficients of concordance between .58 and .82. At the same time, we found less consensus between participants' ratings for familiar and unfamiliar gestures (average W=.31 and .51 respectively), which suggests that people develop different preferences *with practice* for articulating multi-touch gestures.

Overall, more fingers and more strokes were significantly related to more perceived difficulty during gesture articulation. More fingers touching the surface caused longer path lengths, larger gesture

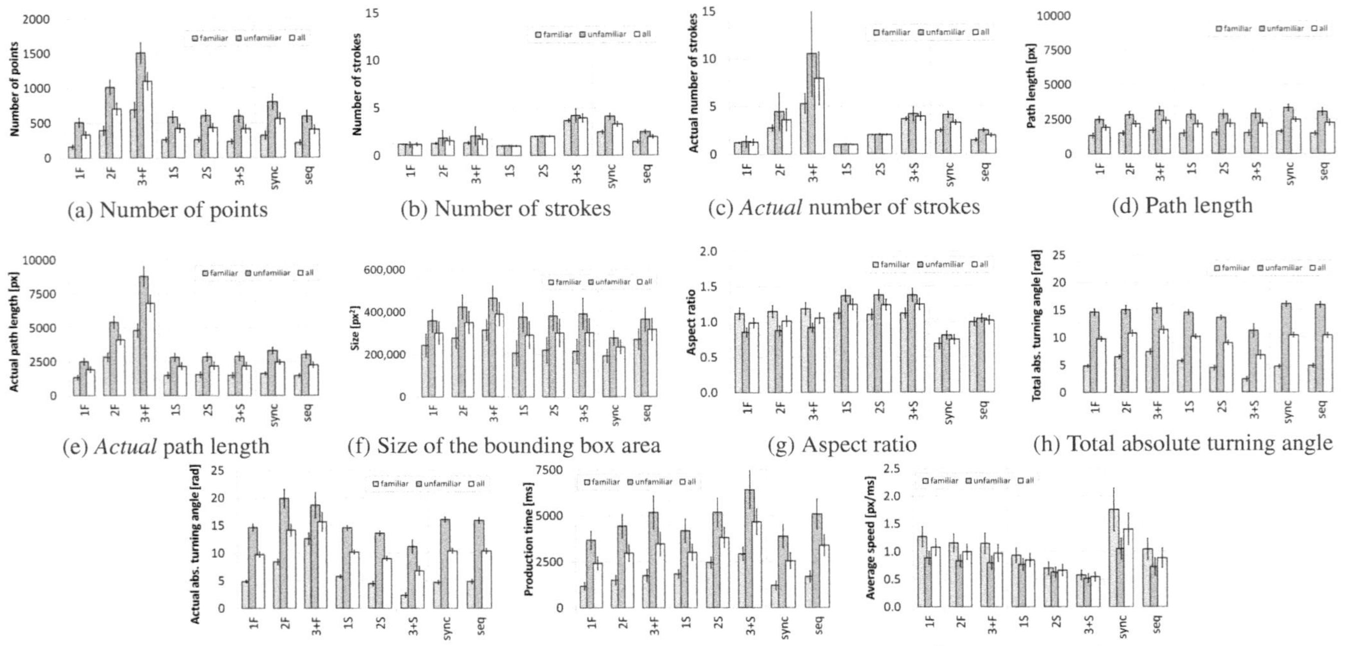

(a) Number of points (b) Number of strokes (c) *Actual* number of strokes (d) Path length (e) *Actual* path length (f) Size of the bounding box area (g) Aspect ratio (h) Total absolute turning angle (i) *Actual* total abs. turning angle (j) Production time (k) Average speed

Figure 5: Descriptors for gestures articulated with different number of fingers, strokes, and hands.

sizes, longer production times, but also more strokes being produced, which all suggest more effort to articulate gestures. Articulating gestures with more strokes resulted in longer production times, which is explained by the transition times required to move fingers in air between consecutive strokes. Bimanual input resulted in more strokes, longer path lengths, and faster executions when compared to sequential input, and, interestingly, caused horizontal deformations in gesture shape by 35% in average. Familiar gestures were produced faster, with less strokes, and were shorter, smaller, and smoother than unfamiliar shapes. These results on multi-touch input add to the body of knowledge on gesture articulation difficulty by complementing the findings of Vatavu et al. that investigated unistrokes [20]. Informed by our findings, we are able to outline a number of 14 guidelines for designing multi-touch gesture interfaces that address (1) gesture ergonomics, (2) gesture recognizer development, and (3) principles of gesture set design. Note that some of these guidelines are common-sense, however we deliberately chose to state them explicitly, because they followed naturally from our study. Finally, our set of guidelines are in agreement with other recommendations available in the gesture literature [2,14,22], while they also open new opportunities for user interface practitioners to design easy-to-produce gestures from the users' perspective.

❶ Multi-touch gesture ergonomics guidelines.

(a) Single-touch unistrokes should be preferred to multi-finger gestures whenever possible (see also [2,14], p. 92 and p. 1133), as they are generally perceived easier to articulate. (Single-touch unistrokes are also produced faster than all other articulations.)

(b) Two-finger gestures should be equally exploited, as they were perceived not more difficult to produce than single-finger articulations (as long as the choice of employed fingers is left to the user to decide). This guideline was suggested by our participants and later confirmed by our gesture descriptor analysis.

(c) Where possible, privilege bimanual over sequential articulations, as they are faster and are perceived no more difficult to produce than sequential articulations. Note however that different users may produce different patterns during bimanual articulation. Also, avoid synchronous input for shapes that do not present easily identifiable axes of symmetry. For instance, we observed that our participants preferred gestures for which the geometrical shape presented a vertical axis of symmetry.

(d) Design for flexible input by allowing users to employ their preferred choice for the number of strokes that structure a multi-stroke gesture. Otherwise, before designing the multi-stroke structure of a gesture shape, observe how users naturally decompose that shape into strokes. Our participants decomposed gestures into lines and curves with similar shape and orientation to maximize parallelization during bimanual input. We also observed that our participants decomposed directional gestures into multiple line segments whenever there was a direction change.

(e) Prefer familiar to unfamiliar shapes (also see [2], p. 92), as they are produced faster, smoother and are perceived less difficult to articulate under all tested conditions (*i.e.,* number of fingers, number of strokes and single-handed and bimanual input).

(f) Gesture shapes with complex geometries (i.e., mixtures of lines and curves) should be designed so that (1) they are easy to articulate such that learning and memorization are facilitated (a recommendation suggested by our participants during their first trials) and (2) encourage bimanual (and, therefore, faster) articulations. Design such gesture shapes with an easily identifiable axis of symmetry to guide users during bimanual input (in this regard, also see our guideline (c) above).

(g) Design articulation patterns (*i.e.,* ways to produce gestures) that connect to users' previous gesture practice whenever possible, *e.g.,* our participants preferred to use one finger sequential strokes for letters and numbers as these symbols have always been produced with one contact point in pen writing.

(h) Use objective gesture descriptors to inform gesture design be privileging shapes perceived by users less difficult to articulate. As informed by the results of our correlation analysis, gestures that take longer to produce, are longer in path length and larger in size were also perceived as more difficult to articulate (see Table 2).

❷ Multi-touch gesture recognizers guidelines.

(i) Design flexible recognizers (*e.g.*, [16]) that are invariant to users' preferred articulation patterns, especially when these patterns are likely to be perceived equally difficult to articulate, such as employing one or two fingers.

(j) Train gesture recognizers with different articulation patterns in terms of finger count, stroke count, and single and bimanual input. Equivalently, this guideline suggests training recognizers in *articulation-independent* scenarios, which is a step further beyond the current practice of employing *user-dependent* and *user-independent* training procedures.

(k) Detect whether two hands are touching the surface simultaneously and make use of this knowledge to increase the tolerance of shape recognizers to horizontal deformations, as we found users horizontally stretching their gesture shapes by 35% during bimanual synchronous input.

(l) More fingers touching the surface produce longer path lengths, larger sizes, and larger production times. Consequently, employ with caution recognizers that rely on geometric and kinematic gesture descriptors, such as [17] (p. 335).

❸ Strategies to map gestures to functions.

(m) Exploit the number of fingers as parameter to increase the expressiveness of gesture input (also see [22], p. 1091). For example, assign multi-finger gestures to more complex tasks to intuitively match users' perceptions of articulation difficulty with task complexity. Or, associate the number of fingers with different parameter values by following a proportional mapping, *e.g.*, more fingers employed cause the brush to paint thicker for a drawing application. For instance, our participants felt that they were drawing a thicker stroke when touching the surface with more fingers during single-handed input. Another example is to use more fingers to scroll faster when browsing a document. As the most simple scenario, privilege designs employing one and two finger gestures, as we found them being perceived as equally difficult to articulate.

(n) Use thoughtfully the number of strokes as parameter for gesture input, as we found our participants often expressing= dissatisfaction when entering multiple strokes. When suitable, connect the number of strokes to the complexity of the task to execute, as we found that gestures with more strokes were perceived more difficult to articulate.

5.1 Gesture dataset availability

As a service to the community interested in replicating our results or in conducting further investigations on multi-touch difficulty, we make available our set of 7,200 samples of 30 gesture types from 18 users annotated with RATING and RANKING data. [5]

6. CONCLUSION

We reported the first investigation of users' perceived difficulty during the articulation of multi-touch gestures. By employing correlation analysis, we reported significant high correlations between the subjective perception of difficulty and commonly-employed descriptors that characterize gesture articulation. We hope that our results on the perception of articulation difficulty together with new findings on multi-touch input and our set of guidelines will prove useful to gesture interface designers, assisting them toward improved gesture set designs and gesture-to-function mappings that consider users' perceived difficulty of gesture articulation.

5. The dataset can be downloaded for free at `https://sites.google.com/site/yosrarekikresearch/projects/gesturedifficulty`.

7. ACKNOWLEDGEMENTS

This paper was partially funded by the Europeen Commission project "NUBOMEDIA - An elastic Platform as a Service (PaaS) cloud for interactive social media", ref. FP7-ICT-2013.1.6 GA-610576 and ERDF funds and equipex IRDIVE, ANR-11-EQPX-0023.

8. REFERENCES

[1] Anthony, L., Brown, Q., Nias, J., and Tate, B. Examining the need for visual feedback during gesture interaction on mobile touchscreen devices for kids. IDC'13 (2013), 157–164.

[2] Anthony, L., Vatavu, R.-D., and Wobbrock, J. O. Understanding the consistency of users' pen and finger stroke gesture articulation. GI'13 (2013), 87–94.

[3] Appert, C., and Zhai, S. Using strokes as command shortcuts: cognitive benefits and toolkit support. CHI'09, ACM (2009), 2289–2298.

[4] Blagojevic, R., Chang, S. H.-H., and Plimmer, B. The power of automatic feature selection: Rubine on steroids. SBIM'10, Eurographics Association (2010), 79–86.

[5] Buchanan, S., Floyd, B., Holderness, W., and LaViola, J. J. Towards user-defined multi-touch gestures for 3D objects. ITS'13, ACM (2013), 231–240.

[6] Cao, X., and Zhai, S. Modeling human performance of pen stroke gestures. CHI'07, ACM (2007), 1495–1504.

[7] Chen, P., and Popovich, P. *Correlation: Parametric and nonparametric measure*. Thousand Oaks, CA: Sage, 2002.

[8] Cohen, J. A power primer. *Psychological Bulletin 112*, 1 (1992), 155–159.

[9] Kendall, M., and Babington Smith, B. The problem of m rankings. *The Annals of Math. Stat. 10*, 3 (1939), 275–287.

[10] Long, Jr., A. C., Landay, J. A., and Rowe, L. A. Implications for a gesture design tool. CHI '99, ACM (1999), 40–47.

[11] Morris, M. R., Wobbrock, J. O., and Wilson, A. D. Understanding users' preferences for surface gestures. GI'10, Canadian Inf. Proc. Soc. (2010), 261–268.

[12] Nacenta, M. A., Kamber, Y., Qiang, Y., and Kristensson, P. O. Memorability of pre-designed and user-defined gesture sets. CHI'13, ACM (2013), 1099–1108.

[13] Nielsen, M., Störring, M., Moeslund, T., and Granum, E. A procedure for developing intuitive and ergonomic gesture interfaces for HCI. GW'03, Springer (2004), 409–420.

[14] Oh, U., and Findlater, L. The challenges and potential of end-user gesture customization. CHI '13 (2013), 1129–1138.

[15] Rekik, Y., Grisoni, L., and Roussel, N. Towards many gestures to one command: A user study for tabletops. INTERACT '13, Springer-Verlag (2013), 246–263.

[16] Rekik, Y., Vatavu, R.-D., and Grisoni, L. Match-up & conquer: A two-step technique for recognizing unconstrained bimanual and multi-finger touch input. AVI'14, ACM (2014), 201–208.

[17] Rubine, D. Specifying gestures by example. *SIGGRAPH Comput. Graph. 25*, 4 (July 1991), 329–337.

[18] Vatavu, R.-D., Anthony, L., and Wobbrock, J. O. Relative accuracy measures for stroke gestures. ICMI '13, ACM (2013), 279–286.

[19] Vatavu, R.-D., Anthony, L., and Wobbrock, J. O. Gesture heatmaps: Understanding gesture performance with colorful visualizations. ICMI '14, ACM (2014).

[20] Vatavu, R.-D., Vogel, D., Casiez, G., and Grisoni, L. Estimating the perceived difficulty of pen gestures. INTERACT'11, Springer-Verlag (2011), 89–106.

[21] Willems, D., Niels, R., van Gerven, M., and Vuurpijl, L. Iconic and multi-stroke gesture recognition. *Pattern Recognition 42*, 12 (2009), 3303–3312.

[22] Wobbrock, J. O., Morris, M. R., and Wilson, A. D. User-defined gestures for surface computing. CHI'09, ACM (2009), 1083–1092.

A Multimodal Context-based Approach for Distress Assessment

Sayan Ghosh*, Moitreya Chatterjee* and Louis-Philippe Morency
Institute for Creative Technologies, University of Southern California
12015 E. Waterfront Drive, Playa Vista, CA
{sghosh, mchatterjee, morency} @ ict.usc.edu

ABSTRACT

The increasing prevalence of psychological distress disorders, such as depression and post-traumatic stress, necessitates a serious effort to create new tools and technologies to help with their diagnosis and treatment. In recent years, new computational approaches were proposed to objectively analyze patient non-verbal behaviors over the duration of the entire interaction between the patient and the clinician. In this paper, we go beyond non-verbal behaviors and propose a tri-modal approach which integrates verbal behaviors with acoustic and visual behaviors to analyze psychological distress during the course of the dyadic semi-structured interviews. Our approach exploits the advantages of the dyadic nature of these interactions to contextualize the participant responses based on the affective components (intimacy and polarity levels) of the questions. We validate our approach using one of the largest corpus of semi-structured interviews for distress assessment which consists of 154 multimodal dyadic interactions. Our results show significant improvement on distress prediction performance when integrating verbal behaviors with acoustic and visual behaviors. In addition, our analysis shows that contextualizing the responses improves the prediction performance, most significantly with positive and intimate questions.

Categories and Subject Descriptors

G.3 [**Mathematics of Computing**]: Probability and Statistics-dimensionality reduction; I.5.4 [**Computing Methodologies**]: Pattern Recognition-applications; J.3 [**Computer Applications**]: Life and Medical Sciences - health

General Terms

Human Factors, Experimentation, Algorithms

Keywords

Audiovisual Analysis, Distress, Nonverbal Indicators, Psychological Behaviors, Decision Support Technology, Depression, Post-traumatic Stress

---

*- indicates equal contribution.

ICMI'14, November 12–16, 2014, Istanbul, Turkey
Copyright 2014 ACM 978-1-4503-2885-2/14/11…$15.00
http://dx.doi.org/10.1145/2663204.2663274

1. INTRODUCTION

The prevalence of psychological distress disorders, of the likes of, depression and post-traumatic stress in our society demands a serious effort to create new tools and technologies to help with their diagnosis and cure. This process typically involves a face-to-face dyadic interaction between a clinician and the patient. Recent works in the field have proposed new computational approaches to objectively analyze patient nonverbal behaviors over the duration of the whole session [1, 2, 3]. These techniques have the potential to aid clinicians with their decision for diagnosis or treatment, by giving them a summary of the patient behaviors (i.e., distress indicators) which can be compared with those of the previous sessions of the same person or with a reference population.

Recent approaches in this direction have mostly focused on acoustic, visual and paralinguistic cues for automatically identifying distress indicators [1, 2, 3], ignoring the verbal aspect of the patient responses. Moreover these analyses are performed in a holistic fashion by summarizing the observed cues over the whole interaction. In other words, the responses of the patient are analyzed independent of the context of the questions asked by the interviewers. This discounts the essential information about the affective nature of each stimuli (i.e., questions asked by the clinician/interviewer), which potentially influences the patient's response.

In this paper, we go beyond nonverbal behaviors and propose a tri-modal approach which integrates verbal behaviors with acoustic and visual modalities to analyze psychological distress indicators during dyadic interviews. Our approach takes advantages of the dyadic, semi-structured nature of these interactions to contextualize the participant responses based on the affective components of the questions. In other words, we explore the role of prior knowledge about the affective nature of the stimuli, an individual is subjected to, in predicting psychological distress. Specifically we address this challenge by categorizing the questions asked based on their intimacy and polarity levels. We conduct experiments on a large corpus of 154 semi-structured dyadic interview interactions between a virtual interviewer and a participant.

In the following section, we discuss prior related work in the field of psychology and automatic computational approaches. In Section 3, we present our research hypotheses. Section 4 describes the dataset and the multimodal features, along with our multimodal fusion approach and our experimental methodology. We present the experimental results, along with the feature analysis in Section 5, and conclude the paper with a discussion of future work in Section 6.

2. RELATED WORK

Several researchers in the field of psychology have explored the relationship between both verbal and non-verbal behavior in individuals with general psychological distress and depression. Ellgring has examined the relationship between psychological states and behavior, and its consequences for clinical diagnosis [4]. He investigates the role of non-verbal behavior in depression such as latency in response, motor retardation and lack of emotional variability. Kirsch compared the facial affective behavior of patients suffering from post-traumatic stress disorder with those of healthy subjects, and observed that expressions of joy appear less often in traumatized patients [7]. Fairbanks reported averted eye-gaze, more fidgeting and self-grooming in depressed subjects [8]. Perez and Riggio claim that depressed patients frequently display flattened or negative affect, including less emotional expressivity, heightened anger and gaze aversion [24]. Hall et al. reports shortened speech and lengthened duration of pauses amongst depressed individuals, during verbal interactions [6].

Previous studies have also focused on the automated assessment of psychological disorders. Cohn et al. detected depression by measuring facial actions using AAM (Active Appearance Modeling) and manual FACS (Facial Action Coding System) coding, and prosody using pitch extraction [5]. Stratou et al. explored the role of gender in assessing psychological conditions from recorded video interactions, based on nonverbal behaviors such as affect, expression and motor variability [9]. Valstar et al. suggested looking at both the acoustic and the visual modalities simultaneously [25]. DeVault et al. used paralinguistic cues to investigate the correlation between conversational features and psychological disorders [3]. They conducted their analysis using aggregate dialogue-level features like onset time, filled pauses and speaking rate. Yu et al. proposed a multimodal HCRF (Hidden Conditional Random Field) model to consider commonalities among adjacency pairs of questions to infer psychological states of participants in semi-structured interviews [2].

To our knowledge, this work is the first to propose a context-based computational analysis of psychological distress which integrates verbal behaviors with acoustic and visual. This analysis and integration is performed by taking into account the context of the interviewer questions, obtained by considering the varying degrees of intimacy and polarity of the questions asked.

3. RESEARCH HYPOTHESES

In this section we present the central research hypotheses that we seek to verify through our experiments.

Verbal Behavior: As shown in the previous section, researchers have shown a relationship between para-linguistic cues and psychological distress. For example, research findings report paralinguistic cues such as reduced speech, slow speech, delay in delivery [3, 6]. Inspired by these results and the work of Rude et al who observed, the use of more valenced words amongst people with psychological distress [10], we propose the following hypothesis:

Hypothesis 1a (H1a): Verbal behaviors can be used to predict general distress in individuals.

Integrating verbal and nonverbal information has been shown to improve predictive performance in many social interaction settings. For example, research findings suggested that integrating descriptors of para-verbal behavior with those of non-verbal behavior improve predictability of depressed individuals [2]. This leads us to hypothesize:

Hypothesis 1b (H1b): Integrating markers of verbal behavior with their nonverbal counterparts helps improve the prediction of general distress.

Nature of Stimuli: In the field of psychology, a landmark revelation has been that depressive disorders are manifested by differences in emotional reactivity, such as positive attenuation and negative potentiation. [11, 12]. Thus the affective nature of the stimuli (positive or negative) the participant is subjected to might constitute vital information in terms of predicting psychological distress in humans. We thus propose the following hypothesis:

Hypothesis 2 (H2): Taking into consideration the nature of the affective stimuli favorably influences the task of predicting general distress.

4. EXPERIMENTS

4.1 Dataset

The dataset used in our experiments is an extension of the Virtual Human Distress Assessment Corpus introduced in [26]. It consists of 154 semi-structured interviews between a human participant and a virtual human, an animated human character. Each interaction lasted about 10 minutes on an average. The virtual interviewer, Ellie is controlled in a Wizard of Oz (WoZ) scenario and not only asks questions to the participant, but also provides responses and back-channels, sometimes prompting the participant to expand on a previous answer. This setting requires a human operator sitting behind the wall and deciding on the next spoken utterance of Ellie. The questions asked by Ellie are initially designed to create a rapport with the participant, such as questions about Los Angeles. Subsequent questions are more personal in nature, such as "*Who's someone that has been a positive influence in your life*?" Following this, Ellie switches to questions whose replies may be suggestive of psychological disorders, such as "*How easy is it for you to get a good night's sleep?*"

The participants for the study were recruited via Craigslist and consisted of 183 participants, with 99 males and 84 females. However, due to the errors in logging the data pertaining to certain participants had to be removed. Hence our experimental dataset consists of 154 participants.

Distress Measure Questionnaires are provided to the participants, and the PHQ-9 [16] and PCL-C [15] severity scores are computed by an expert coder based on the questionnaire responses. The severity scores for PHQ-9 gives a measure of depression while that of PCL-C gives a measure of PTSD. In our dataset, about 30% of the participants had a high PCL-C score, while 21% of the participants had high PHQ-9 scores.

It has been observed that the PHQ-9 and PCLC-C scores exhibit significant positive correlation, due to high comorbidity between PTSD and depression [17]. Since we are interested in studying psychological distress in general and developing a decision support tool for healthcare providers, we compute the corresponding z-normalized scores and average them to obtain a measure of general psychological distress, which we refer to as Distress Measure (DM) score. This score is used for computing the ground-truth labels. The ground-truth labels are obtained by using the median of this DM score as a threshold. Whichever subjects score above the median are considered as positive samples while the rest as negative.

4.2 Question Context

During the course of this semi-structured virtual human interview, the participant is asked a series of questions. They are obtained from a question-bank which was used in [27]. To properly quantify the context around each response of the participant, we propose to analyze two aspects of the interviewer questions: intimacy and polarity. We represent the intimacy level on a scale from 1 (not intimate) to 3 (strongly intimate). The polarity aspect of each question is judged on a Likert Scale defined between -2 (strongly negative) up to +2 (strongly positive), where 0 represents neutral. One big advantage of analyzing interactions with a virtual interviewer is that all questions are asked the same way and the list of questions is well-defined.

The questions were rated by two expert coders for their polarity and intimacy. The ratings were averaged out to determine the intimacy and polarity levels of each question. The inter-coder agreement as measured by Krippendorff's α was 0.86 [14]. This is indicative of a high degree of inter-coder agreement. Each question is either a main question or a follow-up. For the purposes of our experiment all follow-up questions were merged with the main ones. For example, follow-up questions such as "*Can you tell me more*?" are grouped with the previous question, using the same intimacy and polarity label, as noted above.

We propose to categorize the questions in three major groups:

- **Intimate-Positive** This group includes all questions with strong intimacy level (larger than or equal to 1.5) and a positive average polarity score (larger than or equal to 1.5). On an average during the course of each interaction, there were about 3 intimate-positive questions.
- **Intimate-Negative** This group captures intimate questions (larger than or equal to 1.5) with negative polarity scores (less than or equal to -1.5). There were about 7 intimate-negative questions that were asked, during an interaction.
- **Non-intimate** This group represents questions that are not polarized (polarity levels between -0.5 and 0.5) and have low intimacy levels (less than or equal to 0.5). During the course of an interaction, such questions numbered around 11 on an average.

4.3 Multimodal Features

We present in this sub-section the verbal, visual and acoustic features used in our experiments.

Verbal features The textual features have been extracted from transcripts of the participants' conversations with the virtual human. The LIWC (Linguistic Inquiry and Word Count) is a text-analysis program which takes in text as its input, and scans each word in it, finally calculating the normalized term-frequency of the words in each LIWC category [18]. The core of the program is the LIWC dictionary, where each LIWC category (80 in total) is defined based on the social and physiological meaning of words. Words are associated with each category, on the assumption that the categories themselves are linked to social, affective and cognitive processes. They include not only *function* words (such as pronouns, prepositions, articles, auxiliary verbs and conjunctions), but also *emotion* words, which are indicative of positive and negative sentiments. LIWC includes a hierarchical categorization of words such as:

1. Social processes which includes concepts about social partners such as family, friends or, more generally, humans.

2. Affective processes which qualify the emotional state such as anxiety, anger or sadness.

3. Cognitive processes which characterize aspects related to thoughts such as insight, causation and inhibition.

4. Perceptual processes pertaining to the basic senses such as seeing, hearing and feeling.

5. Linguistic processes, which include pronouns like *I, you, we* and assent/negation words such as *yes, OK, no*.

6. Personal concerns relating to issues such as achievements, activities done in leisure, domestic and financial matters.

7. Biological processes which are described by words related to body, health, and sexuality.

These LIWC features have been widely used in the cognitive analysis and study of affect from text and have been applied to different domains, such as prediction of the tie strength in social media [19], and detection of flirtation from speed dates [20].

Visual Features We use visual features obtained from the GAVAM Head Tracker [21], since it has been shown from previous studies [4] that motor variability could be a potential indicator of general distress. GAVAM measures the head rotation in three directions (the pitch, yaw and tilt), along with their means and standard deviations. Five GAVAM features were used in the experiments, corresponding to the mean and standard deviation of pitch and yaw, along with the standard deviation of total rotation in all directions. We also use the CERT (Computer Expression Recognition Toolbox) to measure the Action Units (AUs), which are suggestive of non-verbal expressions [22]. For example, AU 12 corresponds to lip-corner stretching, which is indicative of smiles, and AU 4 corresponds to lowering of eyebrows, suggestive of frowns. CERT also measures the six basic prototypical emotions and expression neutrality such as *Anger*, *Fear*, *Joy*, *Surprise*, *Sadness*, *Contempt*, *Disgust* and expression *neutrality*, which indicates lack of emotions. We use a total of 15 features from CERT, corresponding to six expression based features and nine AU-based features which have been shown to be promising for depression recognition [1].

Acoustic Features For the acoustic modality, we have used 14 acoustic features which have shown promising results in previous studies on psychological disorder analysis. Specifically we use (1) features derived from the glottal source signal obtained by inverse amplitude filtering, such as Normalized Amplitude Quotient (NAQ), Quasi-open Quotient (QOQ) and OQ-NN, a parameter for estimating the open quotient using Mel-frequency cepstral features, and a neural network; (2) H1H2, which is the difference in amplitude (in the spectrum) between harmonics H1 and H2 with low difference for tense voices and high difference for breathy voices; (3) VUV, which is an indicator of whether vocal fold vibration is present and is a measure of the deviation of that vibration (4) Peak slope based features, which identify glottal closure instances from glottal pulses with different closure properties; (5) spectral stationarity for a characterization of prosody range; (6) fundamental frequency for voiced regions of the speech signal; (7) Energy of the speech signal (8) Maxima Dispersion Quotient (MDQ) useful for discriminating breathy and

Table 1. Classification performances of unimodal and multimodal classifiers

Experimental Condition		Precision	Recall	F1-Scores	Accuracy
Unimodal	Text	0.675	0.605	0.6380	63.02%
	Audio	0.622	0.593	0.6071	58.63%
	Video	0.607	0.628	0.6171	58.00%
Audio, Video	Late	0.635	0.628	0.6315	60.50%
	Early	0.642	0.605	0.6227	60.50%
Text, Audio, Video	Late	**0.705**	0.648	**0.6751**	**66.40%**
	Early	0.700	**0.651**	0.6746	66.14%
Majority Baseline		-	-	-	53.86%

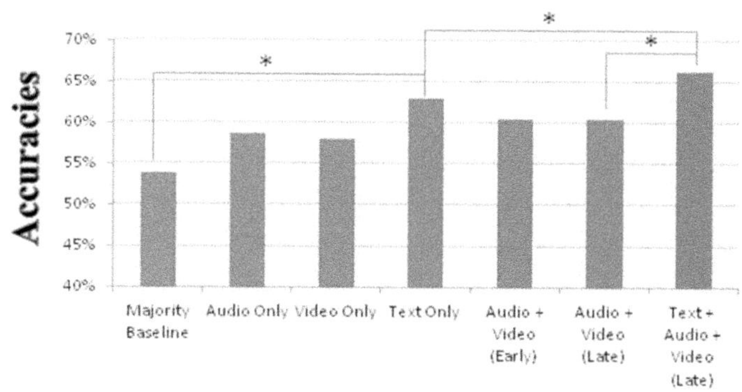

Figure 1: Classification accuracies for implemented models. * indicates statistically significant accuracies with p-value less than or equal to 0.05.

tense voices. The interested reader is referred to [17] for a detailed description of the features.

4.4 Prediction Models

In this subsection, we describe the classification models which we use for the automatic assessment of general distress, including an early and a late fusion scheme for combining information from verbal and non-verbal cues. We wish to explore the effect of verbal and non-verbal cues as well as contextual information, thus we have chosen a simple maximum entropy (binary logistic regression) classifier as a basic building block for the models. This ensures that an improvement in the reported classification performances can be attributed to the feature sets, and not to the presence of more sophisticated prediction models.

Majority Baseline As a baseline model, we include a conventional approach where all samples are assigned to the majority label, i.e. with distress. For our experiments, a majority baseline classifier is accurate 53.86% of the time.

Unimodal Classifiers (Verbal, Acoustic or Visual) We used a maximum entropy classifier for each of the individual modalities. The classifier is regularized using an L_2 norm based penalty term, which is validated automatically.

Verbal + Acoustic + Visual (Early Fusion) To fuse information from multiple modalities, such as verbal, acoustic and visual, we use an early fusion scheme where the features from these modalities are stacked together and provided as an input to the classifier (maximum entropy model).

Verbal + Acoustic + Visual (Late Fusion) We employ a probabilistic late-fusion approach to perform a fusion of the features obtained from multiple modalities. For this, we design a two-layered hierarchical model for this task. The first layer consists of three separate maximum entropy classifiers, each trained on the individual modalities. The output probabilities from these classifiers are fused to train a new classifier in the second layer. The classifier in the second layer is trained using a stacked generalization approach [13] and the Expectation-Maximization (EM) algorithm is used to learn the optimal convex weights for combining each of the modalities in the second layer.

Acoustic + Visual (Early and late fusion) As a way to compare with prior work which focused only on nonverbal behaviors, we included two classifiers (early and late fusion) with only the acoustic and visual features.

4.5 Methodology

All our experiments follow the Leave-One-Person-Out testing scheme to confirm generalization across participants. Automatic validation of the regularization parameter was performed using a hold-out validation set for each fold. The distress labels were defined by using the median of the distress measure over all participants, as discussed in the Section 4.1. The choice of median as a threshold assured a balanced distribution of the dataset between distressed and non-distressed labels. The experiments have been conducted using scikit-learn [23], a popular open source Python toolbox for machine learning.

We performed automatic feature selection to help with interpretation and performance. Our original set of multimodal features contained 80 verbal features from LIWC, 14 acoustic features from the audio modality, and 20 visual features from the video. We employ the Welch's unpaired t-test to select features with a p-value threshold of 0.10, where the two populations correspond to distressed and non-distressed labels. The t-test takes into account the assumption that the two populations have unequal variances and are normally distributed. A different set of feature was automatically selected for the 4 conditions: No-Context scenario (i.e. computing a single set of features for all the questions asked), Intimate-Positive, Intimate-Negative and Non-Intimate (discussed in Section 4.1), with 23, 13, 17 and 20 selected features respectively.

All predictive models were evaluated with the same standard metrics: precision, recall and F-score, which is the harmonic average of the first two metrics.

5. RESULTS AND DISCUSSION

Our experiments were designed to test our research hypotheses described in Section 3. We first analyzed the effect of verbal behaviors on the task of distress prediction and then studied the role of different context (i.e., affective stimuli).

5.1 Verbal Behaviors and Multimodal Fusion

Our first set of experiments focuses on the efficacy of using verbal behaviors for the prediction of general distress, without any contextual information. Figure 1 and Table 1 show our results comparing unimodal classifiers with a classifier trained by fusing features obtained from the acoustic and visual modalities (acoustic

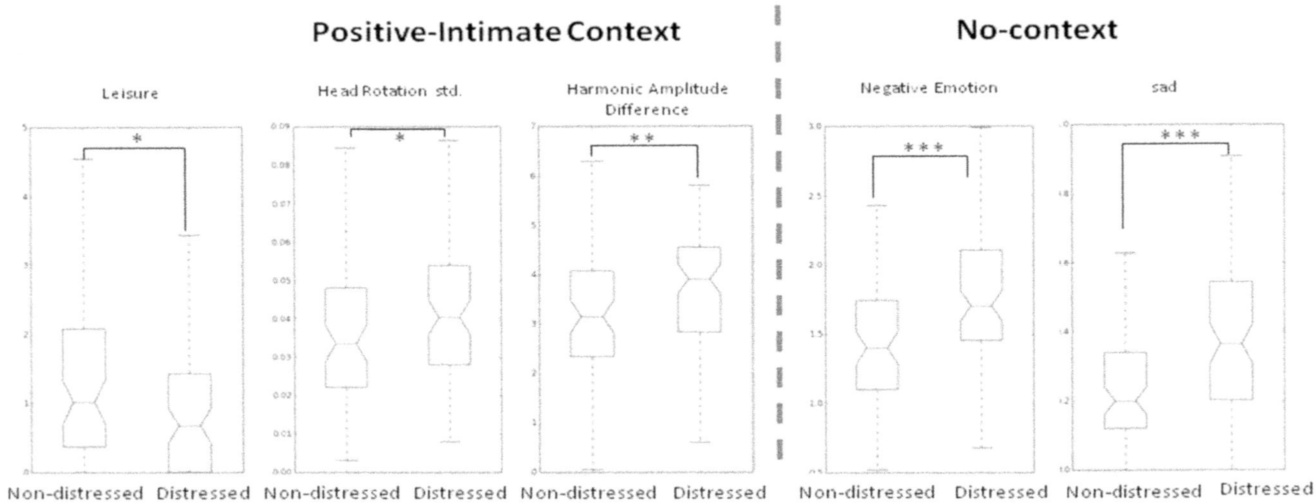

Figure 2: This figure shows the boxplots of some of the statistically significant features for no-context scenario and positive-intimate context. *, ** and ** indicates statistically significant features with p-value <= 0.05, p-value <= 0.01 and p-value <= 0.001 respectively

+ visual). This is followed up by a similar comparison but now with a classifier obtained by fusing the verbal, acoustic and visual modalities (verbal+acoustic+visual), we explore both early and late fusion settings as described in Section 4.3.

Focusing first on Table 1, we observe that the unimodal classifier trained only using verbal features performs marginally significantly better than the majority baseline classifier (see Figure 2), with a t-test statistical result of p=0.05. The direct increase from the majority baseline is 11%.

Here it is worthwhile to point out that other approaches based on multimodal fusion of acoustic and visual features achieved F-scores of 0.664 [2] and 0.88 [1] using more state-of-the-art classifiers such as HCRF or SVM. However the objective of this paper is to explore the discriminative power of the multimodal feature descriptors and hence it is by design that we choose a simpler MaxEnt (Maximum Entropy) model. We also hypothesize that a lower accuracy compared to [1] is also because they used a different dataset (substantially smaller) for a different prediction task, focusing only on predicting depression.

To understand why an improvement in performance is obtained by combining features from the three modalities, we analyze the selected features. Table 2 highlights the most predictable of these selected features for all three modalities, as measured by their p-values, while Figure 2 shows boxplot visualizations for some of them. An analysis of these selected features shows multiple emotionally salient high-level descriptors of verbal behavior to be significant. The significance of descriptors such as *anxiety* and *anger,* which show negative valence, is in concurrence with the findings of [10]. Even verbal markers of positive sentiment such as *assent* or *leisure* are strong predictors. This may be explained by the phenomenon of positive potentiation amongst depressed individuals [11]. Based on these first results, we can confirm hypothesis H1a.

Table 2. A list of the most predictive features under No-Context Condition

Features		p-Values
Text	*Sad*	0.001
	Health	0.001
	negative emotion	0.001
	Anxiety	0.004
	Anger	0.020
	Leisure	0.026
	Negate	0.034
	Hear	0.076
	I	0.085
	assent	0.090
Video	Head Motion std	0.092
	Facial Expression_Neutral	0.085
	Facial Expression_Anger	0.059
Audio	Harmonic Amplitude Diff.	0.012
	Vocal fold vibration deviation	0.022

Furthermore, we also observe from Table 1 and Figure 1 that integrating markers of verbal behaviors with their non-verbal counterparts (visual and acoustic) leads to a statistically significant improvement in the prediction performance, with a p-value=0.04. This result suggests multimodal complementarity when descriptors from the audio (voicing and deviations in amplitude of harmonics) and video (standard deviation of head motion, facial expression of anger) modalities are coupled with their verbal counterparts. This leads to a more accurate prediction over a bimodal late-fusion. Table 2 shows a partial list of selected acoustic and visual features. For example, the visual modality contains negative facial expression which can be complemented with verbal concepts such as anger, negate and sad. This improvement in prediction performance validates our hypothesis H1b.

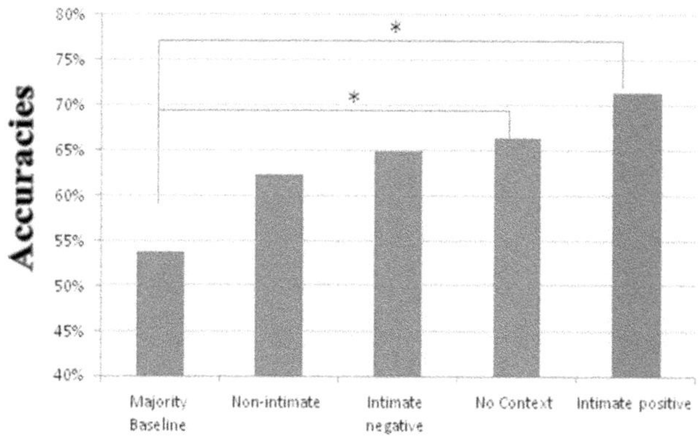

Figure 3: Classification accuracies for various contexts. * indicates statistically significant accuracies with p-value less than or equal to 0.05. All classifiers were trained using tri-modal features with the late-fusion setting.

5.2 Role of Question Context

We designed our second set of experiments to examine the role of the prior knowledge about the affective (positive or negative) nature of stimuli in predicting human psychological distress. As described in Section 4.2, we categorized the interviewer questions in three groups: *Non-Intimate*, *Intimate Positive* or *Intimate Negative*. In the following experiments, we analyze the predictive power of classifiers trained and tested only using the responses to the corresponding specific affective stimuli.

Table 3 and Figure 3 summarize the performances obtained when prior knowledge about the nature of questions asked is known. The results reveal the superiority of the *Intimate Positive* context over the others. This follows from the trend of potentiation of behavioral traits (both verbal and non-verbal) corresponding to positive stimuli amongst distressed individuals as reported in [11]. A relatively lower performance of the other contexts may be explained by a similarity of behavioral traits among individuals of both the distressed and the healthy populace during these scenarios.

Table 4 shows a list of most predictive features for the Intimate-Positive context, as measured by p-value. It is interesting to note that behavioral markers corresponding to both positive and negative affective state of an individual are significant in this context. The positive ones include leisure, achievement in the verbal modality and head nodding (corresponding to the standard deviation of head motion) in the visual modality are particularly interesting since the distressed individuals express a suppressed response on these parameters. The behavioral markers corresponding to the negative affective state of the individual are expressed by the use of words marking negation and the use of sexually abusive words in the verbal modality and facial expression of anger in the visual modality, for instance, hint at a prolonged continuation of a negative affective state of individuals with distress as opposed to ones without it.

Thus our experiments reveal that during the course of the entire interaction between the participant and the interviewer, it is the intimate and positive group of questions that are the most informative. This is in concurrence with our hypothesis H2.

Table 3. Performances of context-based classifiers

Experimental Condition	Precision	Recall	F1-Scores	Accuracy
Intimate Positive	**0.7468**	**0.7108**	**0.7285**	**71.42%**
Non-Intimate	0.6712	0.5903	0.6282	62.33%
Intimate Negative	0.7042	0.6024	0.6451	64.93%

Table 4. A list of most predictive features extracted from the Intimate-positive context

Features		p-Values
Text	*achieve*	0.001
	sexual	0.019
	negate	0.020
	leisure	0.034
	cause	0.069
	you	0.079
Video	Head Motion std	0.035
	Facial Expression_Anger	0.051
	Facial Expression_Joy	0.096
Audio	Harmonic Amplitude Diff.	0.009

It is interesting to note, that the optimal distribution of convex weights (i.e. the weights sum to unity) amongst the three modalities in all scenarios (i.e. intimate-positive, intimate-negative, neutral and non-intimate, no-context) showcases a dominance of the text modality over the others. This is also manifested by the unimodal accuracies reflected in Table 1, which shows the supremacy of the text modality over the others.

6. CONCLUSION AND FUTURE WORK

This paper presented an approach for predicting human psychological distress which integrates verbal, acoustic and visual behaviors. Our results on a large scale dataset of about 160 interactions emphasizes the importance of including verbal behaviors with previously studied acoustic and visual modalities. Our results further highlight the predictive power of using the nature of interview questions, specifically in terms of their intimacy and polarity levels of questions. As future work, we plan to extend this work to include other verbal descriptors such as language model based representations (e.g., unigrams and bigrams) and syntactic information (e.g., part-of-speech tags). Building on top of our significant results with a simple multimodal classifier (maximum entropy model), we are also planning to explore more complex multimodal fusion approaches.

ACKNOWLEDGEMENT

The authors wish to acknowledge Giota Stratou, Prof. Stefan Scherer and Prof. Jonathan Gratch for their insightful suggestions to improve this paper. Sayan Ghosh also acknowledges the USC Viterbi Graduate School Fellowship for funding his graduate studies. The effort here is supported by DARPA under contract W911NF-04-D-0005 and the U.S. Army. Any opinion, content or information presented does not necessarily reflect the position or the policy of the United States Government, and no official endorsement should be inferred.

REFERENCES

[1] Scherer S., Stratou G., and Morency, L.P.. 2013. Audiovisual behavior descriptors for depression assessment. In *Proceedings of the 15th ACM International Conference on Multimodal Interaction* (ICMI '13). ACM, New York, NY, USA, 135-140. DOI=10.1145/2522848.2522886

[2] Yu Z., Scherer S., Devault D., Gratch J., Stratou G., Morency L.P., and Cassell J., 2013. Multimodal Prediction of Psychological Disorder: Learning Verbal and Nonverbal Commonality in Adjacency Pairs, *Workshop on Semantics and Pragmatics of Dialogue (SEMDIAL).*

[3] DeVault, D., Georgila, K., Artstein, R., Morbini, F., Traum, D. 2013. Verbal indicators of psychological distress in interactive dialogue with a virtual human. *Proceedings of SigDial 2013.*

[4] Ellgring, H. 1986.. Nonverbal expression of psychological states in psychiatric patients. *European archives of psychiatry and neurological sciences*, *236*(1), 31-34.

[5] Cohn, J. F., Kruez, T. S., Matthews, I., Yang, Y., Nguyen, M. H., Padilla, M. T, and De la Torre, F. 2009, Detecting depression from facial actions and vocal prosody. In *Affective Computing and Intelligent Interaction and Workshops, 2009. ACII 2009. 3rd International Conference on* (pp. 1-7). IEEE.

[6] Hall, J. A., Harrigan, J. A., and Rosenthal, R. 1996. Nonverbal behavior in clinician—patient interaction. *Applied and Preventive Psychology*, *4*(1), 21-37.

[7] Kirsch, A., and Brunnhuber, S. 2007. Facial expression and experience of emotions in psychodynamic interviews with patients with ptsd in comparison to healthy subjects. *Psychopathology*, *40*(5), 296-302.

[8] Fairbanks, L. A., McGuire, M. T., and Harris, C. J. 1982. Nonverbal interaction of patients and therapists during psychiatric interviews. *Journal of abnormal psychology*, *91*(2), 109.

[9] Stratou, G., Scherer, S., Gratch, J., and Morency, L. P. 2013. Automatic Nonverbal Behavior Indicators of Depression and PTSD: Exploring Gender Differences. In *Affective Computing and Intelligent Interaction (ACII), 2013 Humaine Association Conference on* (pp. 147-152). IEEE.

[10] Rude, S., Gortner, E. M., & Pennebaker, J. (2004). Language use of depressed and depression-vulnerable college students. *Cognition & Emotion*, *18*(8), 1121-1133.

[11] Bylsma, L. M., Morris, B. H., and Rottenberg, J. 2008. A meta-analysis of emotional reactivity in major depressive disorder. *Clinical psychology review*,*28*(4), 676-691.

[12] Rottenberg, J., Gross, J. J., and Gotlib, I. H. 2005. Emotion context insensitivity in major depressive disorder. *Journal of abnormal psychology*, *114*(4), 627.

[13] Wolpert, D. H. 1992. Stacked generalization. *Neural networks*, *5*(2), 241-259.

[14] Hayes, A. F., and Krippendorff, K. 2007. Answering the call for a standard reliability measure for coding data. *Communication methods and measures*,*1*(1), 77-89.

[15] Blanchard, E. B., Jones-Alexander, J., Buckley, T. C., and Forneris, C. A. 1996. Psychometric properties of the PTSD Checklist (PCL). *Behaviour research and therapy*, *34*(8), 669-673.

[16] Kroenke, K., Spitzer, R. L., and Williams, J. B. 2001. The Phq-9. *Journal of general internal medicine*, *16*(9), 606-613.

[17] Scherer, S., Stratou, G., Mahmoud, M., Boberg, J., Gratch, J., Rizzo, A., and Morency, L. P. 2013. Automatic behavior descriptors for psychological disorder analysis. In *Automatic Face and Gesture Recognition (FG), 2013 10th IEEE International Conference and Workshops on* (pp. 1-8). IEEE.

[18] Tausczik, Y. R., and Pennebaker, J. W. 2010. The psychological meaning of words: LIWC and computerized text analysis methods. *Journal of Language and Social Psychology*, *29*(1), 24-54.

[19] Gilbert, E., and Karahalios, K. 2009. Predicting tie strength with social media. In *Proceedings of the SIGCHI Conference on Human Factors in Computing Systems.* ACM.

[20] Ranganath, R., Jurafsky, D., and McFarland, D. 2009. It's not you, it's me: detecting flirting and its misperception in speed-dates. In *Proceedings of the 2009 Conference on Empirical Methods in Natural Language Processing: Volume 1-Volume 1* (pp. 334-342). Association for Computational Linguistics.

[21] Morency, L., Whitehill, J., and Movellan, J. 2008. Generalized adaptive view-based appearance model: Integrated framework for monocular head pose estimation. In *Automatic Face & Gesture Recognition, 2008. FG'08. 8th IEEE International Conference on* (pp. 1-8). IEEE.

[22] Bartlett, M., Littlewort, G., Wu, T., and Movellan, J. 2008. Computer expression recognition toolbox. In *Automatic Face & Gesture Recognition, 2008. FG'08. 8th IEEE International Conference on* (pp. 1-2). IEEE.

[23] Pedregosa, F., Varoquaux, G., Gramfort, A., Michel, V., Thirion, B., Grisel, O. and Duchesnay, E. 2011. Scikit-learn: Machine learning in Python. *The Journal of Machine Learning Research*, *12*, 2825-2830.

[24] Perez, J. E., and Riggio, R. E. (2003). Nonverbal social skills and psychopathology. *Nonverbal behavior in clinical settings*, 17-44.

[25] Valstar, M., Schuller, B., Smith, K., Eyben, F., Jiang, B., Bilakhia, S., Schnieder, S., Cowie, R., and Pantic, M. 2013. AVEC 2013 – The Continuous Audio/Visual Emotion and Depression Recognition Challenge. In *Proceedings of the 21st ACM International conference onMultimedia 2013* (MM '13).

[26] Gratch, J., Artstein, R., Lucas, G., Stratou, G., Scherer, S., Nazarian, A., Wood, R., Boberg, J., DeVault, D., Marsella, S., Traum, D., Rizzo, A., and Morency, L.-P. 2014. The Distress Analysis Interview Corpus of Human and Computer Interviews. In *Proceedings of Language Resources and Evaluation Conference, 2014.*

[27] DeVault, D., Artstein, R., Benn, G., Dey, T., Fast, E., Gainer, A., Georgilla, K., Gratch, J., Hartholt, A., Lhommet, M., Lucas, G., Marsella, S., Morbini, F., Nazarian, A., Scherer, S., Stratou, G., Suri, A., Traum, D., Wood, R., Xu, Y., Rizzo, A., and Morency, L.-P. 2014. SimSensei Kiosk: A Virtual Human Interviewer for Healthcare Decision Support. In *Proceedings of Autonomous Agents and Multiagent Systems*, 2014.

Exploring a Model of Gaze for Grounding in Multimodal HRI

Gregor Mehlmann
Human Centered Multimedia
Augsburg University, Germany
mehlmann@hcm-lab.de

Kathrin Janowski
Human Centered Multimedia
Augsburg University, Germany
janowski@hcm-lab.de

Markus Häring
Human Centered Multimedia
Augsburg University, Germany
haering@hcm-lab.de

Tobias Baur
Human Centered Multimedia
Augsburg University, Germany
baur@hcm-lab.de

Patrick Gebhard
German Research Center for
Artificial Intelligence
patrick.gebhard@dfki.de

Elisabeth André
Human Centered Multimedia
Augsburg University, Germany
andre@hcm-lab.de

ABSTRACT

Grounding is an important process that underlies all human interaction. Hence, it is crucial for building social robots that are expected to collaborate effectively with humans. Gaze behavior plays versatile roles in establishing, maintaining and repairing the common ground. Integrating all these roles in a computational dialog model is a complex task since gaze is generally combined with multiple parallel information modalities and involved in multiple processes for the generation and recognition of behavior. Going beyond related work, we present a modeling approach focusing on these multi-modal, parallel and bi-directional aspects of gaze that need to be considered for grounding and their interleaving with the dialog and task management. We illustrate and discuss the different roles of gaze as well as advantages and drawbacks of our modeling approach based on a first user study with a technically sophisticated shared workspace application with a social humanoid robot.

Categories and Subject Descriptors

H.5.2 [**Information Interfaces and Presentation**]: User Interfaces; D.2.11 [**Software Engineering**]: Software Architectures

General Terms

Algorithms, Languages, Design

Keywords

Human-Robot Interaction; Multi-Modal Fusion; Dialog Modeling

1. INTRODUCTION

The participants of a human interaction constantly establish, maintain and repair the *common ground*, which Herbert Clark defines as "the set of knowledge, beliefs and suppositions that the participants believe they share" [7]. Disruptions of this common ground mainly arise from misunderstandings, ambiguous utterances, missing attention or whenever one of the participants presumes sensory, perceptive or cognitive abilities that the other cannot serve with.

ICMI '14 November 12 - 16 2014, Istanbul, Turkey
Copyright 2014 ACM 978-1-4503-2885-2/14/11...$15.00.
http://dx.doi.org/10.1145/2663204.2663275.

Humans seek to ensure the grounding of their information states with the *least collaborative effort* [9, 7, 8]. To achieve this, they usually exploit multiple parallel information modalities. Among those, gaze and its interplay with the other modalities plays versatile important roles for grounding. Rendering account of and serving these roles is essential for social humanoid robots that interact naturally with humans in collaborative shared workspaces, as in the application that we describe and investigate in this paper.

Figure 1: Our shared workspace setting with the NAO[1] robot.

Figure 1 shows the scenario of our application, a collaborative game between a human user (Fig. 1 ①) and the humanoid *NAO*[1] robot *Nali* (Fig. 1 ②) on a shared workspace realized with a *Microsoft*[2] surface table (Fig. 1 ③). The user wears *SMI* eye tracking glasses[3] and a microphone for speech recognition. The puzzle pieces have distinguishable features such as a shape, size, color and position. They are marked on both sides, to track their position and to recognize the pieces the user is looking at via marker tracking on the video of the glasses. The robot is supposed to facilitate a sorting task by instructing the user to move puzzle pieces into certain puzzle slots. Both interaction partners may use any combination of gaze, pointing gestures and speech to multi-modally refer to the objects, to regulate the speaker and listener roles and to draw the other participant's attention to the objects or even themselves.

Resembling human interaction, both partners exploit a variety of gaze mechanisms during this collaboration. Thereby, gaze is com-

[1] http://www.aldebaran-robotics.com/
[2] http://www.microsoft.com/
[3] http://www.smivision.com/

bined with multiple parallel information modalities and involved in a variety of parallel and bi-directional processes for the generation and recognition of multi-modal behavior. Gaze cues are aligned with verbal contributions to ground the speaker and listener roles [22, 15, 10, 28] in a fluent conversation. Both partners use gaze to continually give and elicit feedback signals [35, 5] and to follow and direct the other's attention to objects in the environment or to themselves [3, 1, 19]. Finally, disruptions of the common ground caused by ambiguous verbal referring expressions are disambiguated by considering the partner's gaze [23, 24, 30].

Embedding all these parallel and bi-directional roles of gaze and synchronizing them with each other and the task management in a uniform dialog model is a complex task. Previous research on dialog models in HRI considered these roles of gaze mainly in isolation. We present a modeling approach focusing on the multi-modal, parallel and bi-directional aspects of gaze and validate it in our shared workspace application. We evaluate our approach in an experimental study, discuss the results in detail and formulate recommendations for future efforts in this research area.

2. RELATED WORK

During the past years, a number of researchers studied several roles of gaze as conversational coordination mechanism that only represent individual aspects of the grounding process in HRI .

Most of this research studied the roles of gaze for *joint attention*, the "ability to follow the direction of the gaze and gestures of others in order to share a common point of reference" and the "use of gestures and eye contact to direct others' attention to objects, to events, and to themselves" [19]. Huang and Thomaz found that a robot that continually ensures the user's joint attention is perceived as more natural [14] while Staudte and Crocker found that exploiting the speaker's focus of visual attention via gaze-following has a positive influence on utterance comprehension to anticipate, ground, and disambiguate spoken references [30]. Mutlu *et al.* investigated the importance of joint attention for collaborative settings in which human and robot are performing joint actions [21] on a shared workspace. Mutlu *et al.* also studied gaze mechanisms that are used for the regulation of the dialog structure and for grounding different speaker and listener roles [20] in human-robot dialog.

Rich *et al.* studied computational models of recognizing and generating *engagement* [25, 13], a process "by which two (or more) participants establish, maintain and end their perceived connection during interactions they jointly undertake" [29]. This work captures the role of directed gaze and mutual gaze for the connectivity status of interaction partners but not the role of gaze for the disambiguation of speech or the use of gaze for eliciting feedback.

Other related research focuses on generic modeling languages for multi-modal fusion or dialog logic for multi-modal user interfaces [16], embodied conversational agents [6, 32] and human-robot interaction [31] but does not focus on grounding or similar concepts or sub-concepts, such as joint attention or engagement.

The related efforts either studied individual roles of gaze for grounding in human-robot interaction in isolation or presented a generic modeling approach without focusing on grounding at all. The work in this paper draws on valuable ideas from this related work but goes beyond it because it combines those individual aspects of grounding in a novel uniform modeling approach.

3. GROUNDING IN HRI

In this section we systematically review the roles of gaze that contribute to grounding in human-robot interaction and illustrate them based on our representative application shown in Figure 1.

3.1 Disambiguating Speech

Humans distribute information across different modalities, depending on the effort and the expressive power of each channel and rely on their partners' ability to combine this information in order to resolve ambiguities [23, 24]. Isolated verbal referring expressions can be ambiguous and thus cause a disruption of the common ground. In this case, a listener usually tries to combine the speaker's verbal statement with his gestures and eye gaze into an unambiguous interpretation before asking for a clarification. Referential gaze in speech typically precedes the corresponding linguistic reference by approximately 800-1000 milliseconds and people look at what they hear after about 200 milliseconds [18, 12].

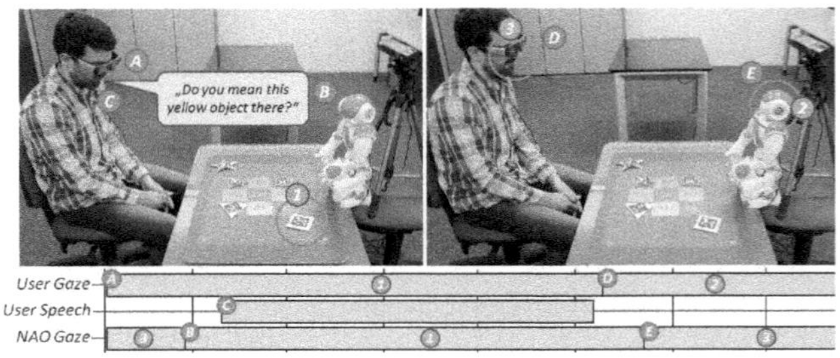

Figure 2: Producing an object reference with speech and gaze.

In our application, the robot is able to combine an ambiguous verbal referring expression with the user's eye gaze during this time window. For example, in Figure 2 the user starts looking (Fig. 2 Ⓐ) at an object (Fig. 2 ①) and the robot follows the user's gaze (Fig. 2 Ⓑ). The user asks the clarification question *"do you mean this yellow object there?"* (Fig. 2 Ⓒ) and afterwards looks (Fig. 2 Ⓓ) to the robot (Fig. 2 ②) in order to yield the floor. Although there are several objects on the table that match the verbal referring expression, the robot infers that the user referred to the large yellow triangle by considering the user's gaze direction at the right time.

3.2 Joint Visual Attention

During collaborative activities, humans seek to direct their partners' attention to objects in the environment or to themselves [8]. Beside verbal references and pointing gestures they often use gaze and a combination of these modalities to reach that goal [9, 4, 26]. They also follow their partners' gaze to share their point of reference [19] which usually results in directed gaze and joint attention to an object [15]. In this way they signal their partners that they are engaged in the joint activity and able to identify the referred objects. When the partners pay attention to each other they perform mutual gaze [1]. Both gaze mechanisms for joint attention are essential for maintaining the common ground.

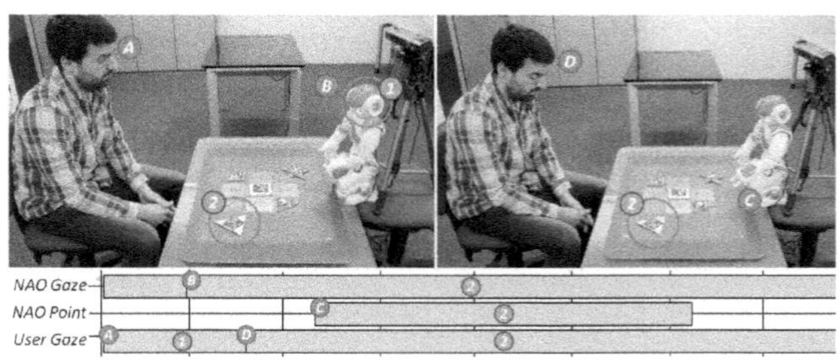

Figure 3: Drawing the user's attention to an object using gaze.

The robot in our application is able to draw the user's attention to an object which is relevant for the next step in the task or to itself whenever it starts an instruction or clarification. Figure 3 shows such a situation in which the user is looking (Fig. 3 Ⓐ) at the robot (Fig. 3 ①) expecting an instruction. The robot starts looking (Fig. 3 Ⓑ) at an object (Fig. 3 ②) and points to it (Fig. 3 Ⓒ) a few moments later. The user immediately follows the robot's gaze (Fig.3 Ⓓ) which leads to directed gaze and attention to the object.

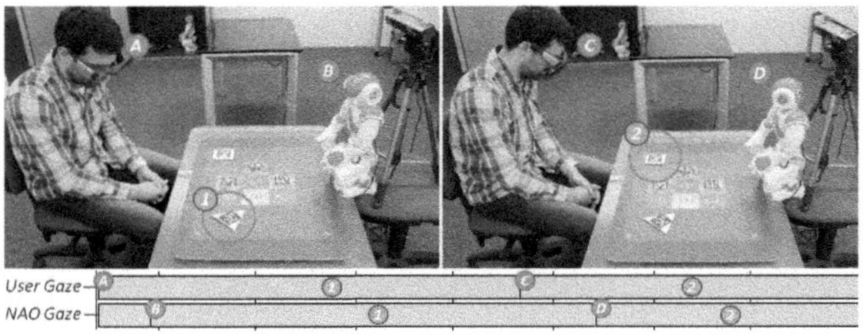

Figure 4: Following the user's gaze to focus to the same objects.

Analogous to the direction of attention, the robot can also pay constant attention to the user's gaze shifts and manipulations of the objects on the workspace. It is able to follow the user's gaze and to focus on the objects that the user looks or points to while it answers with mutual gaze whenever the user looks at the robot. In Figure 4 the user looks (Fig. 4 Ⓐ) at an object (Fig. 4 ①) and a few moments later the robot follows the user's gaze by looking (Fig. 4 Ⓑ) at the same object. Next, the user moves his gaze (Fig. 4 Ⓒ) to another object (Fig. 4 ②) and again the robot follows the user's gaze (Fig. 4 Ⓓ) to the second object for joint attention.

3.3 Regulating Turn-Taking

A fluent conversation requires successful regulation mechanisms for grounding the speaker and listener roles [15, 10]. Thereby, gaze direction serves as a key signal in managing or inhibiting the exchanges of these roles. Speakers usually look away from their addressees to indicate that they want to keep the floor and look at one of their partners to pass the floor [22]. The exchange of turns can be delayed if a contribution does not end with gaze at a partner [15].

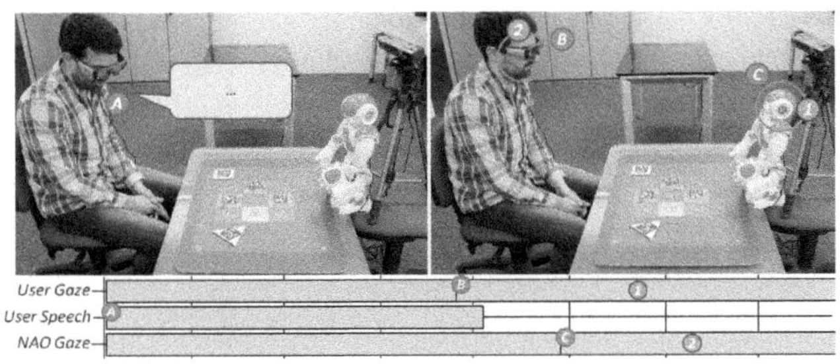

Figure 5: Passing the floor to the robot after the contribution.

In our application, the robot avoids mutual gaze while giving an instruction or clarification and looks to the human partner to pass the floor when finishing its turn. In return, it is able to detect the user's end of speech and whenever the user looks to the robot via a marker on its chest. Both events in close temporal alignment are the signal for the robot that the user wants to pass the floor. Such a situation is shown in Figure 5 in which the user is asking a question (Fig. 5 Ⓐ) and afterwards looks (Fig. 5 Ⓑ) at the robot (Fig. 5 ①) to yield the turn. The robot (Fig. 5 Ⓒ) then answers with mutual gaze (Fig. 5 ②) to signal that it is going to take the turn now.

The interaction partners continually produce back-channel signals to let the partner know that they are still engaged and understand what has been said and done [35] to ground their information states. This feedback is provided by the listener via nonverbal cues such as head nods or short verbal statements while the partner is speaking or performing an activity. In return, speakers occasionally perform a short glance of mutual gaze to the listener with the aim to elicit feedback cues at specific points in time [15, 5]. Although the gaze cues for feedback eliciting and turn-yielding might look very similar at first sight, it is very important not to confuse these signals and to handle them differently in the dialog model.

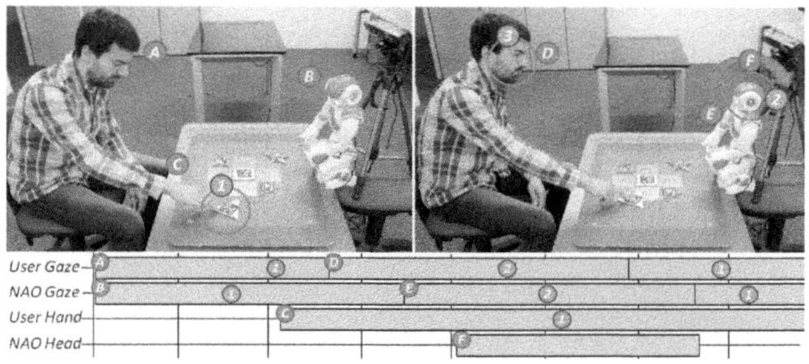

Figure 6: The user elicits a head nod feedback from the robot.

In this work we are not further investigating the role of feedback eliciting for grounding but of turn-regulating gaze signals. Therefore, in our application, the robot is able to recognize the user's behavior pattern that are supposed to elicit feedback, to distinguish them from turn-yielding cues and to react with an adequate feedback signal. Figure 6 shows such a situation in which both the user (Fig. 6 Ⓐ) and the robot (Fig. 6 Ⓑ) look at an object (Fig. 6 ①) before a few moments later the user starts moving the object (Fig. 6 Ⓒ) and looking at the robot (Fig. 6 Ⓓ) nearly simultaneously. The robot reacts to this behavior pattern with mutual gaze (Fig. 6 Ⓔ) and a feedback signal in form of a head nod (Fig. 6 Ⓕ).

4. REALIZATION

The dialog flow and interaction logic in our application are modeled with a *Sceneflow* [11, 17]. This is a hierarchical and concurrent state chart which is used to control and synchronize multiple parallel processes modeling the robot's behavior and input processing on different abstraction levels. This model decomposition divides the responsibilities in the model so that each process resembles a single role of gaze, a fusion process or a dialog phase. The robot's context knowledge and user inputs are represented as feature structures in a *Prolog* [34] fact base. The fact base defines domain specific logic predicates that are called from within the Sceneflow. This logic is used for multi-modal fusion, knowledge reasoning and for the exchange of information between parallel processes. This highly modular modeling approach makes already modeled state chart components and predicates easily reusable and adaptable.

4.1 Input Processing

The movement of puzzle pieces and other touch events are directly forwarded from the surface table to the fact base. All other user input events are first processed and interpreted by the *SSI* framework [33]. The resulting interpretations are then asserted as events to the fact base. They carry modality-independent features, such as timestamps and confidence values, and modality-specific semantic information, such as gaze distributions and dialog acts.

For gaze recognition we rely on Algorithm 1 that reduces the influence of recognition errors that arise whenever the user blinks,

Algorithm 1 Compute Fixation Events from Input Streams

1: **procedure** TRANSFORM($Video\ v,\ Point\ g,\ List\ l$)
2: $\quad \Delta_{max} \leftarrow \sqrt{v_w^2 + v_h^2}$
3: $\quad$ **if** $g_x \geq 0 \land g_x \leq v_w \land g_y \geq 0 \land g_y \leq v_h$ **then**
4: $\quad\quad$ **for all** $m \in l$ **do**
5: $\quad\quad\quad$ **if** $visible(m)$ **then**
6: $\quad\quad\quad\quad \Delta_m \leftarrow \sqrt{(g_x - m_x)^2 + (g_y - m_y)^2}$
7: $\quad\quad\quad$ **else**
8: $\quad\quad\quad\quad \Delta_m \leftarrow min(\delta \cdot \Delta_m, \Delta_{max})$
9: $\quad\quad\quad$ **end if**
10: $\quad\quad\quad \Phi_m^* \leftarrow (1 - (\Delta_m / \Delta_{max}))^{\phi}$
11: $\quad\quad\quad \Phi_m \leftarrow \sigma \cdot \Phi_m + (1 - \sigma)\Phi_m^*$
12: $\quad\quad$ **end for**
13: $\quad$ **end if**
14: **end procedure**

rolls his eyes or is shortly distracted. In each frame we compute the distances of all recognized markers on the puzzle pieces and the robot's chest to the user's gaze position (Alg. 1 ⑥). Then we compute a fixation confidence for each marker based on this distance and the respective confidences in the past few frames (Alg. 1 ⑪). We assume the user is looking at the environment if all confidences are below a certain threshold. Every couple of frames we produce an event carrying this fixation confidence distribution and assert it to the fact base where it is processed by the logic.

```
type:  event, # This feature structure is an event
sent:  ssiv2, # The sender is the SSI framework
mode:  eyegaze, # A marker probability distribution
dist:  121, # The event has started 121 ms ago
life:  43, # The event's total lifetime is 43 ms
time:  62946, # The VSM framework arrival time
conf:  1.0, # The event's confidence value is 1.0
data:  ① [[type: marker,   ], ..., [type: marker, ]]
          [name: 1,        ]       [name: 9,      ]
          [conf: 0.88      ]       [conf: 0.001   ]
```

Figure 7: A gaze distribution event as a feature structure.

Figure 7 shows the representation of a gaze distribution event containing the confidence values for all markers (Fig. 7 ①). Within our interaction model these events are then used to realize gaze following, recognize when the user yields the turn and elicits feedback and for the disambiguation of speech. For this reason, they are hold in the fact base for some seconds so that they can be combined with the user's speech input that usually needs longer to be interpreted.

The user's speech is processed by a semantic parser plug-in of SSI which is based on the *Microsoft®* speech platform[4]. Utterances are translated into abstract dialog acts with communicative functions from the *information seeking* category of the *DiAML* classification scheme[5]. *Set questions* ask for a decision between a number of puzzle pieces, *choice questions* prompt a decision between a list of candidates, while *propositional questions* seek confirmation for exactly one proposed puzzle piece. Figure 8 shows the representation of the choice (Fig. 8 ①) question *"the green triangle or the yellow object there?"* with the included location referent (Fig. 8 ④). Our robot can resolve unimodal referring expressions such as *"the green triangle"* (Fig. 8 ②) using an algorithm similar to that described by Ros *et al.* [27]. It determines a set of puzzle pieces on the table that match the list of features from the user's verbal description and computes the optimal set of discriminating features to correct the user with an unambiguous answer.

```
type:  event,
...,   # General event properties, i.e. timestamp, modality, etc.
data:  [type:      dialog # A dialog act feature structure
        category:  seeking # Information seeking category
        function:  choice ① # Choice question function
        contents:  [② [type: description # The 1st object
                       data: [color: green # is green and
                              shape: triangle # a triangle]],
                    ③ [type: description # The 2nd object
                       data: [color:    yellow # is yellow
                              location: reference ④]]]]
```

Figure 8: A choice question dialog act as a feature structure.

```
1   fuseWithGaze(SpeechEvent, FusedAct) :-
2     // Get The Speech Act Of The Speech Event
3     getSpeechAct(SpeechEvent, SpeechAct),
4     // Get The Speech Act's Object Description
5     getDescription(SpeechAct, Description),
6     // Get The Gaze Fixation During The Speech
7     getBestFixation(SpeechEvent, GazeFixation),
8     // Update The Object Description With Gaze
9     has(Description,           ,              ),
10    set(Description,           , GazeFixation).
11    // Update The Object Description Of The Speech
12    // Act And Return The Fused Multi-Modal Action
13    update(SpeechAct, Description, FusedAct).
14
15  fuseWithGaze(SpeechEvent, SpeechAct) :-
16    getSpeechAct(SpeechEvent, SpeechAct).
```

Figure 9: The predicate combining user's speech and gaze.

If the utterance contains location referents such as *"there"* or *"here"* (Fig. 8 ③), then we additionally consider the user's referential gaze to resolve this multi-modal referring expression using the logic predicates shown in Figures 9 and 10. We determine the focused object based on the gaze events during a time window relative to the user's utterance (Fig. 9 ③-⑦ and Fig. 10 ①-⑨) and add the reference to the object description (Fig. 9 ⑨-⑬).

```
1   getBestFixation(SpeechEvent, GazeFixation) :-
2     // Get The Time Interval Of The SpeechEvent
3     start(SpeechEvent, Start),
4     end(SpeechEvent, End),
5     // Infer All Gaze Events In The Time Window
6     findall(EyeGaze, (during(EyeGaze, SpeechEvent),
7       mode(EyeGaze,             )), GazeEventList),
8     // Compute The Object With The Most Fixations
9     fixationMajority(GazeEventList, GazeFixation).
```

Figure 10: Predicate inferring eye gaze aligned to speech.

4.2 Interaction Modeling

Figure 11 shows an overview of our application's interaction model consisting of three parallel state charts that are exchanging information via the fact base. The first state chart (Fig. 11 Ⓐ) is used for monitoring the system time and for retracting outdated events that are not needed any more. The second state chart (Fig. 11 Ⓑ) is processing touch, speech and gaze distribution events in three parallel processes. They are updating the fact base positions

[4]http://msdn.microsoft.com/library/hh361572.aspx

[5]http://semantic-annotation.uvt.nl

of objects that have been moved on the surface table and produce higher-level events carrying the user's last speech act and discrete fixation change events from the continuous gaze distribution events. These events are consumed by the processes in a third state chart (Fig. 11 ©) that is modeling higher-level event processing. It enfolds a process for the multi-modal fusion of gaze and speech as well as processes for the detection of turn-taking and feedback eliciting signals. A last state chart (Fig. 11 Ⓓ) is modeling the dialog flow in two separate states for the user's and the robot's turn.

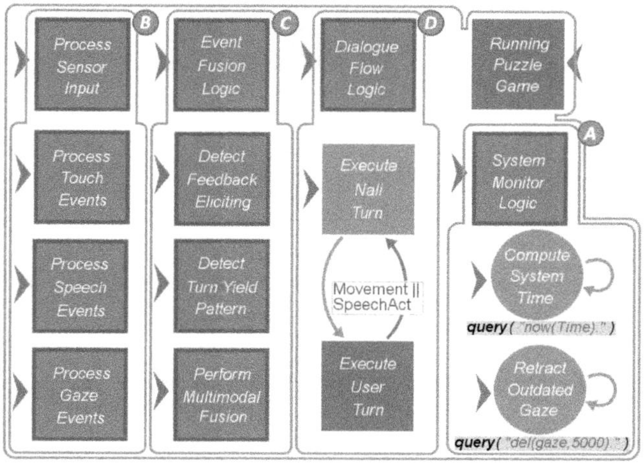

Figure 11: The high-level view of the application's sceneflow.

Figure 12 shows these processes modeling the dialog flow in more detail. When the user has the turn, the robot either follows the user's gaze fixations and object placements or performs feedback while waiting for a turn-yielding event from the process detecting the relevant behavior pattern. When the user finishes his turn by moving an object to a field or speaking an utterance and looking to the robot, then these processes are immediately interrupted and the turn is assigned to the robot. The robot then checks the type of the user's contribution and performs an adequate reaction, such as answering a question or giving the next instruction.

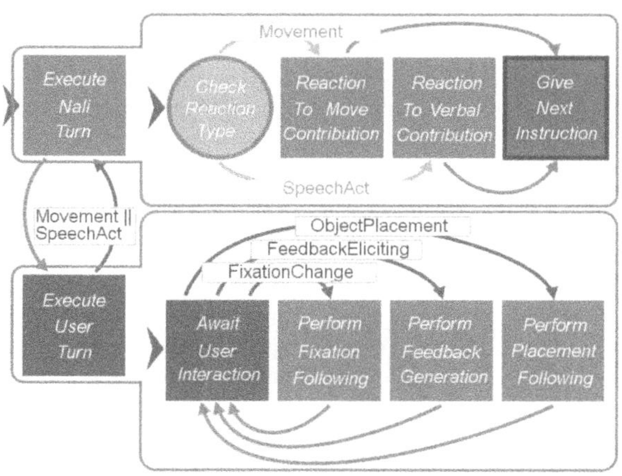

Figure 12: The sceneflow modeling the dialog flow logic.

The robot's verbal and nonverbal behavior is specified in a multimodal *Scenescript*, resembling a movie script with dialog utterances and stage directions for gestures, postures, and facial expressions. Individual *Scenes* from this script are executed from the nodes in the Sceneflow and then scheduled on the robot to generate the behavior. Figure 13 shows an example of such a script and the corresponding scheduling. It shows that nonverbal behavior can be executed either in parallel with speech or sequentially. This specification method allows us to generate the robot's gaze behavior for directing and following the user's gaze and yielding the speaker role. In addition, is allows us to easily align the robot's gaze and other nonverbal behavior such as feedback cues and pointing gestures with its speech in a very intuitive but also effective way.

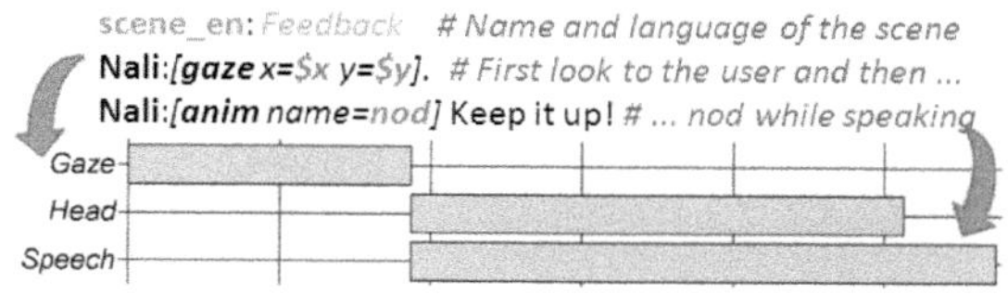

Figure 13: A feedback scene and the corresponding schedule.

5. EVALUATION

We evaluated our application and the underlying computational dialog model in order to answer two questions. First, we wanted to validate our modeling approach as described in Section 4 and check to what extent our computational model covers the aspects of gaze for grounding presented in Section 3. Second, we wanted to find out how the different roles of gaze influence the subjective perception and the efficiency of the interaction in our application. Thereby, we were interested in the effect of two independent variables that were manipulated in a $2x2$ within-subjects design:

- *Referential gaze* with the levels O^+ and O^-: In condition O^+, the robot always looked at the puzzle pieces it was referencing during the instructions and was able to disambiguate the user's ambiguous clarification requests by considering the user's referential gaze. In condition O^-, the robot did not look at any particular puzzle piece on the shared workspace to facilitate object grounding during instructions. Furthermore, it was not able to resolve the user's multi-modal references by considering the user's referential gaze during the user's clarification requests.
- *Social gaze* with the levels U^+ and U^-: In condition U^+, the robot tried to establish mutual gaze with the user, reacted to turn-yielding gaze cues and followed the user's gaze or hand movements to signal attentiveness. It reacted to speech acts and placement attempts after the user looked at it in order to pass the floor, or after a maximum delay of 3.1 seconds [25]. In condition U^-, the robot did not react to the user's gaze for turn-taking or attention following. Instead, it simulated ideal gaze behavior by looking at the shared workspace for 70% of the time and at the user otherwise as suggested by the literature [2]. It waited for 1 second before taking the turn and answering a question [25].

Accordingly, we implemented four variations of the dialog model and conducted a within-subjects experiment with each subject participating in all four conditions in a randomized order. A total of 13 subjects, 3 female and 10 male, in age from 19 to 34 years ($M = 26.4$, $SD = 4.41$) participated in the experiment. Most of them were students or researchers in Computer Science and Multimedia. For each participant and condition, we recorded the speech and gaze fixation events, the raw input streams from which they were derived and the video and audio from an external camera which captured the whole scene and synchronized these data streams prior to the annotation. In total, we collected 3 hours and 8 minutes of material per channel. Afterwards, multivariate analysis of variance (*MANOVA*) and univariate analysis of variance (*ANOVA*) tests were conducted to assess differences on mean user scores across the two categories of referential and social gaze.

5.1 Objective Measures

In order to measure the efficiency of the human-robot dialog, the system automatically logged the duration as well as the number of placement attempts and clarification questions that the users asked. Results of a *Two-Way Repeated Measure MANOVA* revealed no significant multivariate effect of referential gaze or social gaze on the three dependent variables we investigated as objective measurements. However, we observed a univariate effect for referential gaze on all three dependent variables. Overall, the efficiency was significantly improved by adding gaze for disambiguation. The participants asked fewer clarification questions ($F = 11.636$, $p = 0.005$), the dialog was shorter ($F = 11.128$, $p = 0.006$) and less placement attempts were made ($F = 9.794$, $p = 0.009$) by the users when referential gaze was recognized by the robot.

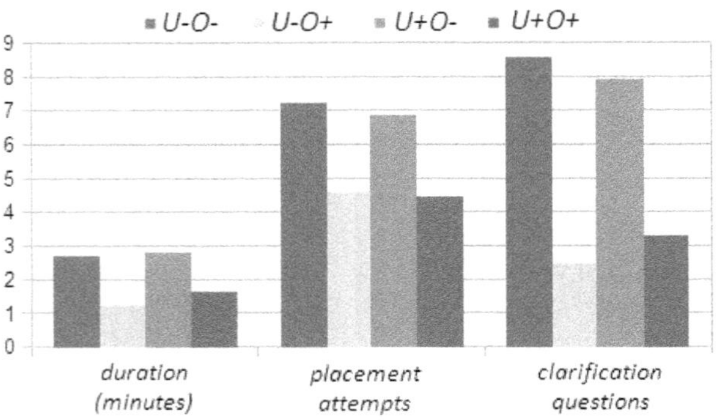

Figure 14: Results of the objective task performance measures.

As shown in Figure 14, the O^+ conditions took only about half of the time that was used in the O^- conditions. The number of placement attempts was reduced by about one third and the number of clarification questions even by two thirds.

5.2 Subjective Measures

After each condition the subjects filled in a questionnaire, rating several aspects of their interaction experience and the robot's behavior in the condition on 7-point Likert scales. Depending on the question, these ranged either from 1 for *never* to 7 for *always* or from 1 for *complete disagreement* to 7 for *full agreement*. As shown in Figure 15, their answers confirmed the trend that had already been observed for the objective measures, demonstrating again an advantage of the O^+ conditions over the O^- conditions.

Results of a *Two-Way Repeated Measure MANOVA* revealed that there were no significant multivariate effects for referential or social gaze on the set of dependent variables. Apart from two exceptions, all univariate effects for referential gaze were, however, significant and showed that referential gaze was associated with positive user ratings of the robot. Participants stated that the robot appeared more natural ($F = 8.348$, $p = 0.014$), more interested ($F = 13.5$, $p = 0.003$) and more understanding ($F = 14.990$, $p = 0.002$). They also thought that the dialog with the robot was more fluent ($F = 8.794$, $p = 0.012$). Furthermore, they believed more often that the robot was following their hand movements ($F = 6,464$, $p = 0.026$) as well as their gaze movements ($F = 14.495$, $p < 0.002$) and that it was more often trying to establish eye contact with them ($F = 27.307$, $p < 0.0005$).

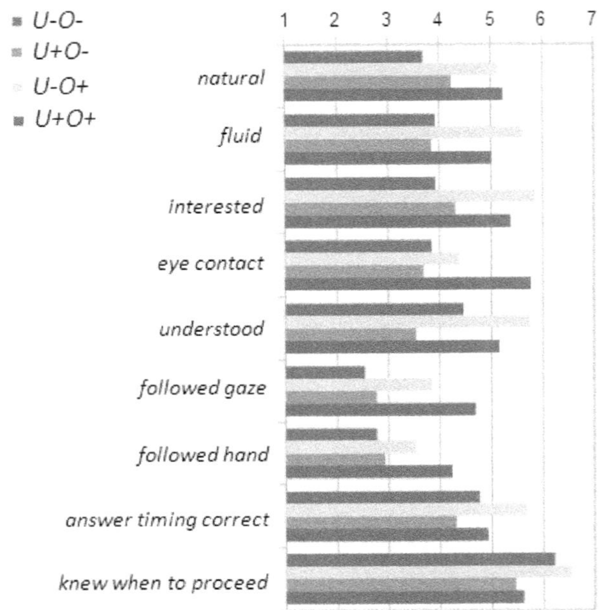

Figure 15: Results of the subjective questionnaire ratings.

Unfortunately, we obtained two significant univariate effects for social gaze that reflected some synchronization issues between the user and the robot. In both cases, U^- scored significantly better than U^+. For U^+, participants stated that they thought less often that the robot responded to their questions at the right point in time ($F = 7.870$, $p = 0.016$). They also said that they knew less often when they were supposed to continue ($F = 4.697$, $p = 0.051$).

There was also a significant interaction effect between referential and social gaze for "The robot tried to establish eye contact with me." ($F = 6.936$, $p = 0.022$). The use of referential gaze had a positive effect on the rating of this item. The additional use of social gaze then led to a further increase of this improvement.

6. DISCUSSION

Our evaluation revealed that the robot's dialog behavior was rated better when it made use of referential gaze and considered the user's referential gaze. In line with the subjective assessments, the objective measurements demonstrated that task performance was improved by referential gaze as well. The users indeed noticed that the robot was following their gaze towards the focused objects and also believed that the robot understood them better when it was able to disambiguate speech with gaze. The results of both subjective and objective measures confirmed our expectations that the gaze mechanisms for speech disambiguation and joint visual attention, realized with our modeling approach as described in Section 4, had a positive influence on user experience and performance.

However, our expectations for the effect of social gaze were disappointed. The key difference between the conditions with and without social gaze, and also the main difference in the users' assessment of those conditions, lied in the robot's turn-taking behavior, or more precisely in the robot's reaction to the users' gaze signals for yielding the turn. We had hoped that responding to the user's turn-regulating gaze cues in the U^+ conditions would improve the interaction compared to the idealized turn-taking in the U^- conditions. However, the opposite was the case, as the conditions without social gaze were often perceived as equal to or even better than their counterparts. Although the robot was not adapting to any gaze cues the user employed for turn-taking, the timing of the robot's responses was considered to be more appropriate.

6.1 Corpus Analysis

In order to explain the results of our experiment, we analyzed our video recordings of the three conditions U^-O^+, U^+O^- and U^+O^+ for all thirteen participants. We annotated the robot's and users' speech behavior as well as the users' gaze behavior which accompanied a total of 209 clarification requests during 2 hours and 14 minutes of video corpus. This analysis revealed that the users yielded their turn using mutual gaze after 78% of the questions. For this purpose, they looked at the robot shortly before (60%) or after (18%) they finished speaking. For about 20% of the questions, they did not look towards the robot at all. While this observation is mainly in line with previous studies and our own expectations, we found that 83% of the questions which were not accompanied by a turn-yielding gaze at the robot contained location referents which required additional information to be resolved. For example, referential gaze had to be considered to disambiguate questions such as *"This one here?"* or *"Do you mean the one over there?"*.

In contrast to that, for the great majority of unambiguous questions, the users gazed towards the robot as a turn-yielding signal as we had expected. A second interesting observation was that those users who made use of pointing gestures tended to employ gaze for the purpose of turn-regulation more frequently. Obviously, the issues with social gaze were not caused by technical limitations of the modeling approach. Rather they can be ascribed to some misconceptions included in the robot's behavior model. These issues could be resolved by giving up specific assumptions regarding the use of gaze cues for turn-regulation that did not hold for all users.

6.2 Interpretation

A reason for the minor role of social gaze might be the emphasis on the task-oriented nature of the dialog. The users knew that they were supposed to collaboratively solve a task as opposed to engaging in a purely social interaction. They were also aware that the robot was able to disambiguate verbal utterances by considering their gaze behavior. Therefore, the users might have devoted a lot of their attention to the production of non-ambiguous references using both speech and gaze, thus focusing on the functional aspect of gaze rather than making use of gaze for turn-regulation. The effect might have been reinforced by the structure of the dialog that did not require sophisticated turn-taking behaviors. An interesting topic for a follow-up experiment would be to investigate the effect of social gaze during interactions with a much more social component, such as discussing photos displayed on the surface table.

Another factor to consider is the robot's inability to detect pointing gestures. To fill the role of pointing gestures, some users might have relied more heavily on gaze behaviors. As described in [25], a common pattern for directing a listener's gaze is to start looking at the target object, pointing at it shortly afterwards and then looking back up to monitor the partner's behavior while continuing the gesture. In the absence of gesture recognition, the gaze fixation becomes the only modality capable of maintaining the focus this way. Thus, it appears plausible that gaze was employed in a similar manner as gestures. Four users indeed tried placing their finger on the object or picking the object up and then displayed the regular gaze behavior, looking at the robot near the end of their utterance. Consequently, it might be worthwhile to explore the effect of gesture recognition on the user's gaze behavior. Our generic modeling approach would easily allow for the addition of a gestural input device. This extension would enable us to investigate the interplay of gaze and gestures in both social and task-oriented types of dialogs.

6.3 Technical Issues

The evaluation also revealed some technical issues with our current implementation that we would like to share at this point.

6.3.1 Eye-Tracking Approach

Our eye tracking solution worked well with most of the participants, but we also observed some effects which might cause problems in the long run. For instance, identifying the user's gaze target using *ARTK*$^+$ markers only works if they are clearly recognizable in the input video. It will be hard to prevent them from being occluded when we are going to add pointing gestures. In the current study, two participants already made the markers unreadable by placing their fingers on the puzzle pieces during a pointing gesture.

Another problem is the limited field of view of the *SMI* glasses. If participants move only their eyes rather than their head, they are able to look at a target outside these boundaries which can not be detected by the system. For 21 of the 209 annotated turns, it was impossible to detect the turn-yielding gaze because the marker on the robot's chest was partially or even fully outside the video image. This might depend on individual preferences since it only happened with 4 of the 13 participants, but also on other factors, such as the distance between the referent and the partner's face.

6.3.2 Speech Understanding

To avoid recognition problems, we had limited the grammar to questions that could be answered with "yes" or "no" and gave the participants example sentences that were understood by our speech recognition. However, about 44% of the users' questions were still not covered by our grammar. For example, our system was able to understand phrasings like *"Do you mean the red one?"*, but not *"Is the color red?"*. About half of these utterances were still matched with the correct attributes, allowing the interaction to continue without any problems. The others, however, were either ignored or interpreted as referring to a wrong object. The former led to additional delays because the users spent several seconds waiting for a reaction, whereas the latter led to answers which appeared to be inappropriate. Both might have interfered with the effect of the robot's gaze behavior. To counter these problems, we are going to expand our grammar based on the utterances we collected in our experiment. We are also thinking of adding a feedback signal when an utterance is being processed, such as the flashing ear LEDs described by Huang and Thomaz [14], so that users can repeat or rephrase an utterance which was not understood by the robot.

7. CONCLUSION

In this paper, we reviewed the roles of gaze that are essential for grounding in collaborative and situated human-robot interaction. Going beyond previous work on computational models of human-robot dialog that covers only certain subsets of these roles, we illustrated a modeling approach which copes with all of them. Our approach combines the flexibility and re-usability of hierarchical and concurrent state charts with the expressiveness and declarative nature of logic programming. We evaluated and discussed our approach based on our collaborative shared workspace scenario.

In line with previous studies, the evaluation confirms that adding gaze tracking to enable crucial task-oriented functions of gaze, specifically gaze following to referenced objects and the disambiguation of spoken referring expressions, improves the interaction with a robot by making it more natural, pleasant and efficient.

However, we made very interesting and unexpected observations for the role of gaze as turn-yielding signal. Our findings suggest that it depends on the combination of modalities used and whether the dialog is task-oriented or social. Gaze is preferably used as a turn-yielding cue for most of the unimodal questions and for most of those multi-modal questions in which the user decides to use a pointing gesture rather than gaze for disambiguating speech. In those utterances which require referential gaze for disambiguation, this functional aspect of gaze has priority over the use as a turn-yielding signal. In future work, we will use our modeling approach to investigate whether these behavior patterns are grounded in the task-oriented nature of our scenario and if they can still be observed in dialogs with a more pronounced social component.

Acknowledgements

The work described in this paper was partly supported by the Free State of Bavaria, in the form of a doctoral scholarship through the Innovationsfonds.

8. REFERENCES

[1] M. Argyle and M. Cook. *Gaze and Mutual Gaze*. Cambridge University Press, 1976.

[2] M. Argyle and J. Graham. The central europe experiment: Looking at persons and looking at objects. *Environmental psychology and nonverbal behavior*, 1(1):6–16, 1976.

[3] M. Argyle, R. Ingham, F. Alkema, and M. McCallin. The different functions of gaze. *Semiotica*, 7:19–32, 1973.

[4] A. Bangerter. Using pointing and describing to achieve joint focus of attention in dialogue. *Psychological Science*, 15:415–419, 2004.

[5] J. Bavelas, L. Coates, and T. Johnson. Listener responses as a collaborative process: The role of gaze. *Communication*, 52:566–580, 2002.

[6] J. Brusk, T. Lager, A. Hjalmarsson, and P. Wik. Deal: Dialogue management in scxml for believable game characters. In *Proceedings of Future Play '07*, pages 137–144. ACM, New York, NY, 2007.

[7] H. Clark. *Using Language*. Cambridge University Press, May 1996.

[8] H. H. Clark. Coordinating with each other in a material world. *Discourse Studies*, 1:507–525, 2005.

[9] H. H. Clark and D. Wilkes-Gibbs. Referring as a collaborative process. *Cognition*, 22:1–39, 1986.

[10] S. Duncan. Some signals and rules for taking speaking turns in conversations. *Personality and Social Psychology*, 23:283–292, 1972.

[11] P. Gebhard, G. Mehlmann, and M. Kipp. Visual scenemaker: A tool for authoring interactive virtual characters. *Journal on Multimodal User Interfaces*, 6:3–11, 2012.

[12] Z. Griffin and K. Bock. What the eyes say about speaking. *Psychological Science*, 11:274–279, 2000.

[13] A. Holroyd, C. Rich, C. Sidner, and B. Ponsler. Generating connection events for human-robot collaboration. In *RO-MAN*, pages 241–246, 2011.

[14] C.-M. Huang and A. Thomaz. Effects of responding to, initiating and ensuring joint attention in human-robot interaction. In *RO-MAN*, pages 65–71, 2011.

[15] A. Kendon. Some functions of gaze-direction in social interaction. *Acta Psychologica*, 26:22–63, 1967.

[16] D. Lalanne, L. Nigay, P. Palanque, P. Robinson, J. Vanderdonckt, and J. F. Ladry. Fusion engines for multimodal input: A survey. In *Proceedings of ICMI' 09*, pages 153–160. ACM, New York, NY, USA, 2009.

[17] G. U. Mehlmann and E. André. Modeling multimodal integration with event logic charts. In *ICMI*, pages 125–132, 2012.

[18] A. Meyer, A. Sleiderink, and W. Levelt. Viewing and naming objects: eye movements during noun phrase production. *Cognition*, 66:25–33, 1998.

[19] P. Mundy and L. Newell. Attention, joint attention, and social cognition. *Current Directions in Psychological Science*, 16:269–274, 2007.

[20] B. Mutlu, T. Kanda, J. Forlizzi, J. Hodgins, and H. Ishiguro. Conversational gaze mechanisms for humanlike robots. *ACM Trans. Interact. Intell. Syst.*, 1(2):12:1–12:33, Jan. 2012.

[21] B. Mutlu, A. Terrell, and C.-M. Huang. Coordination mechanisms in human-robot collaboration. In *Workshop on Collaborative Manipulation at ACM/IEEE HRI*, 2013.

[22] G. Nielsen. *Studies in Self Confrontation*. Munksgaard, Copenhagen, 1962.

[23] S. Oviatt. Advances in robust multimodal interface design. *IEEE Comput. Graph. Appl.*, 23(5):62–68, September 2003.

[24] S. Oviatt. *The Human-Computer Interaction Handbook*, chapter Multimodal Interfaces, pages 413–432. Mahwah, NJ: Lawrence Erlbaum and Associates, 2008.

[25] C. Rich, B. Ponsler, A. Holroyd, and C. Sidner. Recognizing engagement in human-robot interaction. In *HRI*, pages 375–382, 2010.

[26] D. C. Richardson and R. Dale. Looking to understand - the coupling between speakers' and listeners' eye movements and its relationship to discourse comprehension. *Cognitive Science*, 29:1045–1060, 2005.

[27] R. Ros, S. Lemaignan, E. Sisbot, R. Alami, J. Steinwender, K. Hamann, and F. Warneken. Which one? grounding the referent based on efficient human-robot interaction. In *RO-MAN, 2010 IEEE*, pages 570–575, 2010.

[28] H. Sacks, E. Schlegloff, and G. Jefferson. A simplest systematics for the organization of turn-taking. *Language*, 50:696–735, 1974.

[29] C. L. Sidner, C. Lee, C. D. Kidd, N. Lesh, and C. Rich. Explorations in engagement for humans and robots. *Artificial Intelligence*, 166(1-2):140–164, 2005.

[30] M. Staudte and M. W. Crocker. Investigating joint attention mechanisms through spoken human-robot interaction. *Cognition*, 120:268–291, 2011.

[31] R. Stiefelhagen, H. K. Ekenel, C. Fugen, P. Gieselmann, H. Holzapfel, F. Kraft, K. Nickel, M. Voit, and A. Waibel. Enabling multimodal human–robot interaction for the karlsruhe humanoid robot. *Robotics, IEEE Transactions on*, 23(5):840–851, 2007.

[32] D. Traum, A. Leuski, A. Roque, S. Gandhe, D. DeVault, J. Gerten, S. Robinson, and B. Martinovski. Natural language dialogue architectures for tactical questioning characters. In *Army Science Conference*, 2008.

[33] J. Wagner, F. Lingenfelser, T. Baur, I. Damian, F. Kistler, and E. André. The social signal interpretation (ssi) framework: Multimodal signal processing and recognition in real-time. In *Proceedings of the ACM International Conference on Multimedia*, pages 831–834, New York, NY, USA, 2013.

[34] J. Wielemaker, T. Schrijvers, M. Triska, and T. Lager. SWI-Prolog. *Theory and Practice of Logic Programming*, 12(1-2):67–96, 2012.

[35] V. H. Yngve. On getting a word in edgewise. In *Regional Meeting of the Chicago Linguistic Society*, pages 657–677, 1970.

Predicting Learning and Engagement in Tutorial Dialogue: A Personality-Based Model

Alexandria Katarina Vail, Joseph F. Grafsgaard, Joseph B. Wiggins,
James C. Lester, Kristy Elizabeth Boyer
Department of Computer Science
North Carolina State University, Raleigh, North Carolina, USA
{akvail, jfgrafsg, jbwiggi3, lester, keboyer}@ncsu.edu

ABSTRACT

A variety of studies have established that users with different personality profiles exhibit different patterns of behavior when interacting with a system. Although patterns of behavior have been successfully used to predict cognitive and affective outcomes of an interaction, little work has been done to identify the variations in these patterns based on user personality profile. In this paper, we model sequences of facial expressions, postural shifts, hand-to-face gestures, system interaction events, and textual dialogue messages of a user interacting with a human tutor in a computer-mediated tutorial session. We use these models to predict the user's learning gain, frustration, and engagement at the end of the session. In particular, we examine the behavior of users based on their Extraversion trait score of a Big Five Factor personality survey. The analysis reveals a variety of personality-specific sequences of behavior that are significantly indicative of cognitive and affective outcomes. These results could impact user experience design of future interactive systems.

Categories and Subject Descriptors

H.1.2 [**User/Machine Systems**]: Human factors, Human information processing; H.5.2 [**User Interfaces**]: Natural language; J.4 [**Social and Behavioral Sciences**]: Psychology

General Terms

Experimentation, Human Factors

Keywords

Personality; Tutorial Dialogue; Engagement; Frustration; Learning

1. INTRODUCTION

Multimodal learning analytics is a growing research area that focuses on multiple communication modalities, including speech, writing, posture, gesture, and facial expressions [28]. In the field of learning analytics, the goal is to predict student learning and learning-related outcomes in a reliable and effective manner. Multimodal learning analytics expands upon this mission by supporting a richly featured view of the learning process, allowing for a deeper understanding of how students communicate, collaborate, and grow to understand material while learning. In particular, multimodal learning analytics have the potential to help create systems that are more reliable and more adaptive than prior work. This paper explores multimodal analytics for supporting one of the most effective modes of human learning: tutorial dialogue [7, 10].

One promising direction for creating more personalized tutoring environments is to investigate the affective channel, a key component of natural 'human' interaction [13, 26]. Understanding this affective channel and its implications for goal-oriented interactions is a promising direction for improvement in effective systems that aim to harness some of the power of human communication. In particular, the study of nonverbal displays of affect, such as facial expression, posture, and gesture is receiving increasing attention [8]. Examining these features holds great promise for capturing a rich picture of the learning interactions.

Another important direction for developing adaptive systems is to incorporate and adapt based upon incoming user traits. While incoming traits such as knowledge level have long been considered central, it has been suggested by some studies that users of different personalities may react more favorably to different system behaviors [27, 30]. Prior work has also demonstrated that this benefit may extend to the context of learning [31]. Some studies have suggested that extraverted or introverted tendencies of the user are particularly sensitive to system behavior, a critical concern when designing tutorial systems [5].

We hypothesize that the cognitive and affective outcomes of user interactions can be better predicted when incorporating incoming student traits. We utilize a widely validated personality questionnaire, the Big Five Factor Inventory, to determine the personality profile of each student [11]. We then split the students into 'introverts' and 'extraverts', and build predictive models of three cognitive and affective outcomes of the interaction: learning gain, frustration, and engagement. The results suggest that predictive models built on classes of student personality are more effective than those that are not. In particular, we discover that extraverts benefit significantly from some tutorial dialogue moves, whereas introverts may not be. These results could benefit the design of the next generation of adaptive learning environments.

ICMI'14, November 12–16, 2014, Istanbul, Turkey.

http://dx.doi.org/10.1145/2663204.2663276.

2. RELATED WORK

Most studies to date have examined the use of verbal and nonverbal behaviors to predict user personality, particularly in conversational video. One line of investigation has examined YouTube video blogs with the goal of automatically predicting blogger *personality impression* on the Big Five Factor personality scale. Unlike the present analysis, personality impressions involve an external observer completing the survey, rather than the user completing the survey himself. Several conversational video blogs were downloaded from YouTube and characterized with the Computer Expression Recognition Toolbox (CERT) universal facial expressions of emotion: 'anger', 'joy', 'contempt', 'disgust', 'surprise', 'sad', 'fear', and 'neutral'. Significant success has been found in this domain when attempting to predict personality impressions of Extraversion, Conscientiousness, and Openness, in particular [5]. In an expanded follow-up survey, the Extraversion trait was found to be most accurately predicted by facial indicators of emotion among all five traits [4].

A further study on the same corpus of YouTube video blogs examined verbal content cues for indicators of personality. The analysis revealed that the content of student utterances can significantly improve the accuracy of prediction algorithms for user scores on the Big Five Factor personality traits in general [6]. However, the improvement in Extraversion prediction was not statistically significant; the authors suggest that a user's Extraversion trait would be best predicted using audiovisual activity and facial emotion cues, rather than dialogue content.

A similar analysis examined group meetings, in which three or four persons were asked to debate preparation for a hypothetical situation. Audio and video were captured from all members of the group. It was revealed that Extraversion was the best predicted trait in this domain as well, producing a prediction algorithm with a 75% accuracy. The selected features suggest that users scoring high in Extraversion exhibited more energy in their nonverbal movements than those that score lower [2]. A subsequent cross-domain analysis attempted to apply the previous YouTube video blog model to the group meeting corpus, and discovered that Extraversion impressions could still be predicted with 70% accuracy [1]. This result suggests that the audiovisual cues indicative of of Extraversion could be generalizable across domains.

Although these studies have suggested promising directions for the prediction of Extraversion in users, it is important to question whether similar reflections of personality can be discovered in the educational domain. Some studies have examined groups of students working through a set of problems in mathematics, attempting to predict incoming student traits with a rich multimodal dataset containing digital paper notes, audio recordings, multi-angle video recordings, and writing patterns of the students. These studies attempted to identify two student traits in particular: social dominance (the 'leader' quality) and domain knowledge (the 'expert' quality). A preliminary study revealed a variety of nonverbal cues specific to these types of students, including the energy level of the user's voice and the ratio between time spent writing and time spent speaking [28]. This study was followed by an analysis of the same corpus with the goal of predicting solution correctness in advance of the actual submission. It was discovered that the 'leader' and 'expert' rank-order of the students had a significant impact on the solution correctness prediction algorithm [25]. This finding suggests that user personality traits are pertinent to the prediction of student learning.

In contrast to these prior studies, which attempted to use expressed affect and learning to predict personality traits, the present analysis takes into account a student's Extraversion score before attempting to predict learning and affective outcomes. Prior work has discovered key differences in dialogue progression between tutoring sessions with extraverts and those with introverts [31]. We hypothesize that this difference extends to nonverbal behaviors as indicators of mental state. That is, we hypothesize that students of differing Extraversion tendencies will exhibit different behaviors to indicate the same cognitive and affective states, and we attempt to model these differences through models that predict learning.

3. DATA COLLECTION

The corpus examined in this analysis consists of computer-mediated human-human interactions during tutorial sessions in introductory computer science (specifically, programming in Java) [23, 17]. Each tutoring session consisted of an interaction between one tutor and one student collaborating to create a text-based adventure game during a series of six lessons. Participants were university students in the United States (average age 18.5 years, s = 1.5 years) who participated voluntarily in exchange for course credit in an introductory engineering course. No previous computer science knowledge was assumed or required. Tutors were primarily graduate students with prior experience in tutoring or teaching Java programming.

Students and tutors interacted through a web-based interface for introductory programming in Java, shown in Figure 1.The interface consists of four panes: the task objective description, the student's Java source code, the compilation and execution output, and the textual dialogue messages between the tutor and the student. The student could write, compile, and execute source code, as well as send textual dialogue messages to the remote tutor. The interface was synchronized in real time between the tutor and the student; however, the tutor's interactions with the system were limited to sending textual messages to the student and displaying the next task when the student completed the current objective.

Figure 1: The web-based interface for introductory Java programming.

The data were collected during the Fall 2011 and Spring 2012 academic semesters. During this time frame, $N = 67$ student-tutor pairs completed the entire set of six lessons over four weeks, each lesson constrained to forty minutes. Data recorded from the interactions consisted of database logs, webcam video, Kinect depth video, and skin conductance readings. This study examines the database logs, webcam video, and Kinect depth video from the first lesson only. This first lesson covered the development of a text-based adventure, introducing simple concepts such as conditionals and variables.

Prior to each tutorial session, students were administered a content-based pretest. After the completion of the session, students completed a posttest (identical to the pretest) and a post-session survey. The post-session survey included the User Engagement Survey [24] and the NASA-TLX workload survey [18], which included an item for Frustration Level. We focused on Frustration level in particular, as prior work has shown that Frustration has a significant impact on learning [3]. These are the cognitive and affective outcomes we aim to predict in the present analysis (see Section 5).

3.1 Personality Profile Measurement

Prior to the first tutoring session, students completed a pre-survey constructed to measure incoming student characteristics. Included in this survey was a questionnaire developed for identification of five personality traits [12, 19]. This model of personality includes items to identify extraversion vs. intraversion [11]. The overall questionnaire included 44 items created to place an individual on a scale for five different factors of personality: Openness, Conscientiousness, Extraversion, Agreeableness, and Neuroticism [11], but the analysis detailed in this paper focused only on the items pertaining to the Extraversion trait, identified in Table 1. According to this model, the Extraversion score measures a person's assertiveness, activity, gregariousness, positive emotions, excitement-seeking nature, and warmth [19].

I see myself as someone who ...
... is talkative.
... is reserved.*
... is full of energy.
... generates a lot of enthusiasm.
... tends to be quiet.*
... has an assertive personality.
... is sometimes shy, inhibited.*
... is outgoing, sociable.

Table 1: Items of the Big Five Inventory used to identify a person's Extraversion score. Asterisks (*) represent items negatively associated with extraversion.

The possible Extraversion score on the questionnaire ranges from -10 (highly introverted) to 25 (highly extraverted). The mean Extraversion score of the students in this corpus was 6.40 ($s = 6.42$). The distribution of scores was largely normally distributed. Students were binned into two groups: the 'introverts', who scored below or equal to the median extraversion score of 7, and the 'extraverts', who scored above the median score. These groups contained 34 students and 33 students, respectively. We split on the median score of our student sample rather than a larger population median because personality ranges greatly by sample, and no large study to date has examined university students to establish personality norms.

4. MULTIMODAL CORPUS

Data from the Kinect depth camera, computer webcam, and database logs were combined to form the multimodal corpus examined in this analysis. The features generated from each data stream are detailed in the following subsections.

4.1 Gestural and Postural Features

The Kinect depth camera video was used to discover posture and gesture of the student during the tutorial session. Previously-developed tracking algorithms were employed to identify these features; prior evaluations of these algorithms determined an accuracy of 92.4% in posture tracking and 92.6% in gesture tracking [13]. Gestures consisted of one- or two-hand-to-face gestures (ONEHTF and TWOHTF, respectively). With regards to posture, the average student distance from the workstation was denoted the 'mid' postural position; distances at one or more standard deviations closer or farther from 'mid' were considered 'near' or 'far', respectively. The events MOVEFORWARD and MOVEBACK were extracted from student movements between these postural zones.

4.2 Facial Expression Features

Identification of facial expressions was performed by a state-of-the-art facial expression recognition tool, the Computer Expression Recognition Toolbox (CERT) [21]. Providing frame-by-frame tracking of a wide variety of facial action units by locating faces in each frame, CERT identifies facial features for the nearest face and calculates weights for each facial action unit using support vector machines [20]. This analysis was applied to the webcam video collected during the first tutoring session.

Five action units were selected for inclusion in the present study, based on a validation of adjusted CERT output against manual FACS annotations in prior work on tutorial dialogue [14]. The adjustment to the CERT output consisted subtracting the average value from each measurement, as a baseline, to adjust for systematic tracking error. Furthermore, although CERT considers any positive output value an action unit, it was empirically determined that a higher threshold results in a reduction of false positives; thus, an an action unit was recorded when the baseline-adjusted CERT output was equal to or greater than $\lambda = 0.25$. One of five possible events was recorded when a facial action unit was triggered: AU1 (Inner Brow Raise), AU2 (Outer Brow Raise), AU4 (Brow Lowering), AU7 (Lid Tightener), and AU14 (Mouth Dimpling).

4.3 Task Event Features

As students progressed through each task, the system logged dialogue messages, typing status, and task progress to the database. Tutorial dialogue occurred at any time during the session; no turn-taking was enforced (see Subsection 4.4 for details). When the student began writing code, the system logged a typing event (CODING). After the student finished coding, he could attempt to compile the code (COMPILESTART), which would either be successful (COMPILESUC-

CESS) or encounter an error (COMPILEERROR). A student could also run the code (RUNPROGRAM). Finally, when the student stopped interacting with the system for over three seconds (a manually-determined window), a pause was registered (TASKPAUSE).

4.4 Dialogue Features

All student and tutor messages in the corpus were tagged with a previously-developed dialogue act annotation scheme [32]. This annotation scheme represents a refinement of previous dialogue act tagsets developed for task-oriented tutoring [17], with an emphasis on the decomposition of frequent tags, in order to capture more fine-grained interactions in the dialogue. The tags included in this annotation scheme are listed in Table 2.

We utilize an automated decision tree-based classifier trained on a manually tagged subset of the corpus [31]. This classifier achieved an accuracy of 80.11% (Cohen's kappa of 0.786) on a held-out test set tagged manually. The present analysis makes use of these automatically-tagged dialogue utterances. Each tutor message was recorded as one event, the sending of the dialogue message (e.g., POSFEEDBACK (Tutor)), but each student message was recorded with timestamp for the start of typing the message, e.g., TYPINGACK, and the sending of the message, e.g., ACKNOWLEDGE (Student). This additional logging is so that multimodal features co-occurring with the formulation of a message can be identified.

5. ANALYSIS

The goal of the present analysis is to identify differences in student behavior between extraverts and introverts and to determine whether these differences are predictive of tutoring outcomes. In particular, we examine the conditional probabilities of any set of two events occurring in sequence (i.e., the probabilities $Pr(X_t|X_{t-1})$) within a three-second interval during each tutorial session. We had initially performed an exploratory analysis of isolated unigrams, but none were significant. Each row of the data set to be modeled represents the conditional probability features summarizing a single student's tutorial session.

Initially, all variables were standardized (centered at the mean and scaled to a unit standard deviation) to enable comparison between variables. Feature selection was then performed using the model averaging feature of the JMP statistical software (constructing all models of one or two features, and computing the average coefficient magnitude of each variable across all models) [29]. The top 10% of features were selected using the average coefficient magnitude estimate from models with one or two predictive variables. The predictive models described in the following sections were constructed with the goal of maximizing the leave-one-out cross-validated R^2 value (the coefficient of determination), while enforcing a strict $p < 0.05$ cut-off for significance of included variables. Separate models were built for extraverted and introverted students for each dependent variable: learning gain, frustration, and engagement. These models are described in the following subsections.

5.1 Predicting Learning Gain

Normalized learning gain was computed using pretest and posttest scores, as in Equation 1. This equation measures how much a student learned relative to how much she could have learned, based on her pretest score [22].

$$norm\_gain = \begin{cases} \frac{post-pre}{1-pre} & post > pre \\ \frac{post-pre}{pre} & post \leq pre \end{cases} \quad (1)$$

Using the feature selection approach described above, the predictive model for learning gain in extraverts contains three features. The more likely an inner brow raise (AU1) was followed by positive feedback from the tutor (POSFEEDBACK (Tutor)), or the more frequently a student moved forward (MOVEFORWARD) after an outer brow raise (AU2), the higher the student's learning gain at the end of the session. The former result may emerge from parallel reactions to a successful event: the student expresses a nonverbal indicator of joy, and the tutor congratulates the student on his work. A negative correlation with learning gain was observed when positive tutor feedback (POSFEEDBACK (Tutor)) was more frequently followed by an outer brow raise (AU2). This sequence may result from a student disbelieving the positive feedback, perhaps because he does not understand the material as well as the tutor perceived. The cross-validated model effect size (the measure of variance explained by the model) was $r = 0.6183$. The model is shown in Table 3, and selected features are illustrated in Figure 2a.

Students Tending Toward Extraversion

Normalized Learning Gain =	R^2	p
−0.5012 * POSFEEDBACK (Tutor) → AU2	0.1952	0.003
0.3574 * AU1 → POSFEEDBACK (Tutor)	0.1053	0.007
0.2877 * AU2 → MOVEFORWARD	0.0818	0.024
−0.0420 (Intercept)		1.000
Leave-One-Out Cross-Validated $R^2 = 0.3823$		

Table 3: Predictive model for standardized normalized learning gain in students scoring above the median in Extraversion.

The predictive model for learning gain in introverts contains five features, the largest model built in this analysis. Two features were purely postural: a movement backward through two postural 'zones' (MOVEBACK → MOVEBACK) and a forward movement followed by a movement backward (MOVEFOWARD → MOVEBACK). Both of these features were negatively correlated with learning gain. Qualitative examination of the video corpus revealed that these sequences were frequently activated by a student shifting in his seat, which suggests discomfort, particularly in introverts, as extraverts are naturally more restless [2]. The more frequently that the composition of an acknowledgement (TYPINGACK) was followed by eyelid tightening (AU7), or the more likely that eyelid tightening (AU7) was followed by a two-hands-to-face gesture (TWOHTF), the lower the predicted learning gain. Since student acknowledgements are usually given following a tutor explanation or information turn, the former may indicate that the student is skeptical of the information that the tutor provided; introverts are more likely to simply acknowledge than question the information and engage in deeper dialogue [19]. Finally, a mouth dimpling (AU14) frequently followed by an outer brow raise was negatively associated with learning gain. The cross-validated model effect size was $r = 0.7593$. The model is shown in Table 4, and selected features are illustrated in Figure 2b.

Dialogue Acts			
Acknowledge (ACK)	*Okay.*	Greeting (GRE)	*Have a good day!*
Extra Domain Answer (AEX)	*I'm doing well.*	Information (I)	*Variable names must be one word.*
Ready Answer (AR)	*Yes, I'm ready.*	Observation (O)	*See, we have an error.*
WH-Question Answer (AWH)	*Line 9.*	Extra Domain Other (OEX)	*Calculus is difficult.*
Yes/No Answer (AYN)	*No, sir.*	Confirmation Question (QC)	*It's line 6, right?*
Correction (CO)	**explanation*	Direction Question (QD)	*What do I do next?*
Directive (D)	*Test your program.*	Evaluative Question (QE)	*Does that make sense?*
Explanation (E)	*Your code stops on line 2.*	Extra Domain Question (QEX)	*How are you today?*
Negative Feedback (FN)	*No, that's incorrect.*	Factual Question (QF)	*What line is it waiting on?*
Elaborated Negative Feedback (FNE)	*That's not the right syntax.*	Information Question (QI)	*Why does that happen?*
Not Understanding Feedback (FNU)	*I don't know why that works...*	Open Question (QO)	*How can you fix it?*
Other Feedback (FO)	*That's an okay implementation.*	Probing Question (QP)	*Do you think that looks correct?*
Elaborated Other Feedback (FOE)	*That's alright, but you need to fix line 9.*	Question Prompt (QQ)	*Any questions?*
Positive Feedback (FP)	*Very good!*	Ready Question (QR)	*Ready to move on?*
Elaborated Positive Feedback (FPE)	*That's a very good approach.*	Reassurance (R)	*We have plenty of time left.*
Understanding Feedback (FU)	*Oh, that makes sense!*		

Table 2: Dialogue act tags.

Students Tending Toward Introversion

Normalized Learning Gain =	R^2	p
−0.8210 * MoveBack → MoveBack	0.0896	0.001
−0.4717 * AU14 → AU2	0.3051	0.009
−0.4212 * AU7 → TwoHTF	0.0840	0.017
−0.3912 * MoveForward → MoveBack	0.0430	0.033
−0.4159 * TypingAck → AU7	0.0548	0.047
−0.2116 (Intercept)		1.000
Leave-One-Out Cross-Validated $R^2 = 0.5765$		

Table 4: Predictive model for standardized normalized learning gain in students scoring below the median in Extraversion.

5.2 Predicting Frustration Level

The Frustration Level scale of the NASA-TLX workload survey consists of a student's self-report of how insecure, discouraged, irritated, or annoyed she felt during the session [18]. Interestingly, no statistically significant predictive model could be built for Frustration Level in students scoring below the median in Extraversion.

The predictive model of frustration for extraverts was composed of four features. A higher likelihood that a movement backward (MoveBack) was followed by an inner brow raise (AU1) or mouth dimpling (AU14) was correlated with lower frustration in the student. Mouth dimpling (AU14) has been correlated with learning gain in a prior study on the same corpus [15]. A mouth dimpling (AU14) following a backward movement (MoveBack) suggests a confident student, relaxing in her seat while working through the task. Extraverts tend to express more energy in postural movement [2], so an exaggerated motion such as this may be more likely to be observed with an extravert. Similarly, if a student was more likely to mouth dimple (AU14) after eyelid tightening (AU7), the less likely that she was frustrated. Interestingly, the final feature, a hand-to-face gesture (OneHTF) following a successful compilation (CompileSuccess), was negatively correlated with frustration in this analysis, and has been correlated with higher engagement in a prior study on the same corpus [16]. This suggests that when extraverts are more engaged with the system, they are less frustrated; this agrees with the fact that extraverts are more likely to enjoy engagement [19]. The cross-validated model effect size was $r = 0.8044$. The model is shown in Table 5, and selected features are illustrated in Figure 3.

5.3 Predicting Engagement

Each student's engagement score was computed as the sum of the Focused Attention (perception of time passing), the Felt Involvement (perception of being involved in the task), and the Endurability (perception of the experience as worthwhile) sub-scales of the User Engagement Survey administered at the end of each session [24].

The predictive model for engagement in extraverts contains four features. This model is more reliant on dialogue features than any other model in the analysis. The more likely a brow lowering (AU4) was followed by an inner brow raise (AU1) or a pause in task activity (TaskPause), the

AU1 → PosFdbk (Tutor) | AU2 → MoveFwd | PosFdbk (Tutor) → AU2

(a) Features included in the predictive model for normalized learning gain in extraverts.

AU7 → TwoHTF | AU14 → AU2 | TypingAck → AU7

(b) Features included in the predictive model for normalized learning gain in introverts.

Figure 2: Selected features of the predictive models built on student learning gain.

Students Tending Toward Extraversion

Frustration Level =	R^2	p
−0.6437 * MoveBack → AU1	0.1528	< 0.001
−0.6346 * AU7 → AU14	0.2417	< 0.001
−0.3698 * CompileSuccess → OneHTF	0.1597	0.003
−0.4220 * MoveBack → AU14	0.0928	0.004
0.1203 (Intercept)		1.000
Leave-One-Out Cross-Validated $R^2 = 0.6470$		

Table 5: Predictive model for standardized Frustration Level in students scoring above the median in Extraversion.

AU7 → AU14 | C. Success → OneHTF | MoveBack → AU14

Figure 3: Features included in the predictive model for Frustration Level in extraverts.

lower the perceived engagement by the student. An inner brow raise (AU1) more frequently followed by an explanation from the tutor (Explanation (Tutor)) was similarly negatively correlated with engagement. It is possible that this may have been an unnecessary tutor intervention; the student encountered difficulty in the task, but the tutor stepped in to explain the problem before the student could work through the problem herself. This would agree with the interpretation of an inner brow raise (AU1) as an indicator of surprise or anxiety. The only feature positively associated with engagement in extraverts was the likelihood of an inner brow raise (AU1) after an information turn from the tutor (Information (Tutor)). Considering that an information turn is usually unprompted extra information, this may indicate that the student was surprised by the new tutor move; as before mentioned, inner brow raise (AU1) has been previously associated with surprise. The cross-validated model effect size was $r = 0.6630$. The model is shown in Table 6, and selected features are illustrated in Figure 4a.

The predictive model for engagement in introverts contains four features. Brow lowering (AU4) was prominently featured in this model; if it is likely to follow an eyelid tightening (AU7), it suggests less engagement, but if it is likely to follow the typing of an acknowledgement (TypingAck), it suggests more engagement. Recall that eyelid tightening (AU7) also featured prominently in the learning gain model for introverts, negatively in both cases. This may suggest that a student does not understand the material, and is therefore becoming less engaged with the system. Both of these interpretations align with the prototypical definition of introverts, who are less likely to seek extra discussion for additional information [19]. In the case of the other feature, as before mentioned, student acknowledgements frequently followed tutor explanation or information turns, so brow lowering (AU4) may be a nonverbal sign that the student is considering the information that the tutor provided and is in the process of internalizing the new material; brow lowering (AU4) has been previously associated with student struggle. The other two features involved task actions. The more likely an unsuccessful compilation (CompileError) follows a mouth dimpling (AU14), the lower the predicted engagement of the student. The more likely a student pauses (TaskPause) after moving forward (MoveForward), the higher the predicted engagement. The cross-validated model effect size was $r = 0.7572$. The model is shown in Table 7, and selected features are illustrated in Figure 4b.

6. DISCUSSION

Understanding how multimodal displays are associated with personality and the outcomes of tutorial dialogue holds great promise for understanding and enhancing the user experience with adaptive learning environments. We have presented predictive models of learning, engagement, and frustration that selected features from among a variety of dialogue, task, and multimodal data streams. The results show that predictive models for extraverts tend to rely on dialogue, particularly from the tutor, more often than the predictive models for introverts. Although extraverts by definition engage in increased conversation compared to introverts [19], it is interesting to note that dialogue has a meaningful impact on tutorial outcomes as well. In particular, student engagement and learning gain were discovered to be positively or negatively affected by certain dialogue moves on the part of the tutor. Frustration, however, was more often associated with posture; half of the selected features involved a movement backward in the seat. This movement was always predictive of a decrease in frustration. It is possible that this movement is part of the realization of a 'power pose', in which a person alters his posture in order to ap-

Students Tending Toward Extraversion

Engagement =	R^2	p
-0.5166 * AU4 → TaskPause	0.2196	< 0.001
0.2976 * Information (Tutor) → AU1	0.0925	0.017
-0.3976 * AU1 → Explanation (Tutor)	0.0420	0.008
-0.2904 * AU4 → AU1	0.0855	0.019
-0.2592 (Intercept)		1.000
Leave-One-Out Cross-Validated $R^2 = 0.4396$		

Table 6: Predictive model for standardized engagement in students scoring above the median in Extraversion.

Students Tending Toward Introversion

Engagement =	R^2	p
-0.6217 * AU7 → AU4	0.1302	< 0.001
-0.3999 * AU14 → CompileError	0.2285	0.005
0.3356 * MoveForward → TaskPause	0.1383	0.004
0.3246 * TypingAck → AU4	0.0764	0.020
0.3434 (Intercept)		1.000
Leave-One-Out Cross-Validated $R^2 = 0.5734$		

Table 7: Predictive model for standardized engagement in students scoring below the median in Extraversion.

AU1 → Explain (Tutor) | AU4 → AU1 | Info (Tutor) → AU1

(a) Features included in the predictive model for engagement in extraverts.

AU7 → AU4 | AU14 → C. Error | TypingAck → AU4

(b) Features included in the predictive model for engagement in introverts.

Figure 4: Selected features of the predictive models built on student engagement.

pear more dominant [9]; however, further advanced postural tracking methods would be necessary to perceive this level of nuanced movement.

Introverts, on the other hand, may indicate their own internal state more often with postural movement. Both of the predictive models built for introverts included features involving postural shifts. Learning gain was negatively associated with backward postural movement, perhaps indicating discomfort or anxiety in introverts. In the predictive model for engagement, however, a forward movement was correlated with increased engagement. Previous studies have discovered that extraverts shift in their seat more often [2]. Considering that introverts are naturally more reserved individuals [19], the fact that postural movement appears as significant in the predictive models for introverted students suggests that the movement of introverts may be more meaningful than that of extraverts.

7. CONCLUSION

The field of multimodal learning analytics is the focus of growing interest in recent years. Rich multimodal analysis of natural language and behavioral communication holds the potential to inspire great strides in developing truly adaptive, context-sensitive learning systems. Whereas prior work has examined methods for automatically identifying incoming user personality traits, the present analysis has expanded upon this line of study by taking the next step of identifying differences in behavior that contribute to the outcomes of the interaction. In this study, the outcomes considered were student learning gain at the end of the tutorial session, self-reported frustration at the end of the session, and student response to a User Engagement Survey. The results identified a variety of personality-specific behaviors that may contribute or detract from each of these goals; for example, we find that extraverts are more sensitive to tutor dialogue than introverts, and the models highlight the importance of detecting posture, particularly for introverts. There are several promising directions for future work. First, we must consider how tutors, whether human or automated, should respond to student multimodal behaviors. We should also continue to build rich models of how tutor or system events are responded to by the student, either verbally or nonverbally, in order to develop more personalized student models. The study presented in this paper has provided evidence that students of differing personalities may indicate the same mental states with different interaction patterns. Harnessing these differences to inform intelligent agents and user models will be crucial to the development of the next generation of truly adaptive systems.

Acknowledgements

The authors wish to thank the members of the LearnDialogue group at North Carolina State University for their helpful input. This work is supported in part by the Department of Computer Science at North Carolina State University and the National Science Foundation through Grants DRL-1007962 and IIS-1409639, and the STARS Alliance, CNS-1042468. Any opinions, findings, conclusions, or recommendations expressed in this report are those of the participants, and do not necessarily represent the official views, opinions, or policy of the National Science Foundation.

8. REFERENCES

[1] O. Aran and D. Gatica-Perez. Cross-domain personality prediction: from video blogs to small group meetings. In *Proceedings of the 15th ACM on International Conference on Multimodal Interaction*, pages 127–130, Sydney, Australia, 2013. ACM.

[2] O. Aran and D. Gatica-Perez. One of a Kind: Inferring Personality Impressions in Meetings. In *Proceedings of the*

15th ACM on International Conference on Multimodal Interaction, pages 11–18, Sydney, Australia, 2013. ACM.

[3] R. S. J. d. Baker, S. K. D'Mello, M. T. Rodrigo, and A. C. Graesser. Better to Be Frustrated Than Bored: The Incidence, Persistence, and Impact of Learners' Cognitive-affective States During Interactions with Three Different Computer-based Learning Environments. *Int. J. Hum.-Comput. Stud.*, 68(4):223–241, Apr. 2010.

[4] J.-I. Biel and D. Gatica-Perez. The YouTube Lens: Crowdsourced Personality Impressions and Audiovisual Analysis of Vlogs. *IEEE Transactions on Multimedia*, 15(1):41–55, Jan. 2013.

[5] J.-I. Biel, L. Teijeiro-Mosquera, and D. Gatica-Perez. FaceTube: Predicting Personality from Facial Expressions of Emotion in Online Conversational Video. In *Proceedings of the 14th ACM International Conference on Multimodal Interaction*, pages 53–56, Santa Monica, California, USA, 2012. ACM.

[6] J.-I. Biel, V. Tsiminaki, J. Dines, and D. Gatica-Perez. Hi YouTube!: Personality Impressions and Verbal Content in Social Video. In *Proceedings of the 15th ACM on International Conference on Multimodal Interaction*, pages 119–126, Sydney, Australia, 2013. ACM.

[7] B. S. Bloom. The 2 Sigma Problem: The Search for Methods of Group Instruction as Effective as One-to-One Tutoring. *Educational Researcher*, 13(6):4–16, 1984.

[8] R. A. Calvo and S. K. D'Mello. Affect Detection: An Interdisciplinary Review of Models, Methods, and Their Applications. *IEEE Transactions on Affective Computing*, 1(1):18–37, 2010.

[9] D. R. Carney, A. J. Cuddy, and A. J. Yap. Power Posing: Brief Nonverbal Displays Affect Neuroendocrine Levels and Risk Tolerance. *Psychological Science*, 21(10):1363–1368, Oct. 2010.

[10] P. A. Cohen, J. A. Kulik, and C.-L. C. Kulik. Educational Outcomes of Tutoring: A Meta-analysis of Findings. *American Educational Research Journal*, 19(2):237–248, 1982.

[11] L. R. Goldberg. The structure of phenotypic personality traits. *American Psychologist*, 48(1):26–34, 1993.

[12] S. D. Gosling, P. J. Rentfrow, and W. B. Swann. A very brief measure of the Big-Five personality domains. *Journal of Research in Personality*, 37(6):504–528, Dec. 2003.

[13] J. F. Grafsgaard, R. M. Fulton, K. E. Boyer, E. N. Wiebe, and J. C. Lester. Multimodal Analysis of the Implicit Affective Channel in Computer-Mediated Textual Communication. In *Proceedings of the ACM International Conference on Multimodal Interaction (ICMI)*, pages 145–152, Santa Monica, California, USA, 2012. ACM.

[14] J. F. Grafsgaard, J. B. Wiggins, K. E. Boyer, E. N. Wiebe, and J. C. Lester. Automatically Recognizing Facial Expression: Predicting Engagement and Frustration. In *Proceedings of the International Conference on Educational Data Mining (EDM)*, pages 43–50, Memphis, Tennessee, USA, 2013.

[15] J. F. Grafsgaard, J. B. Wiggins, K. E. Boyer, E. N. Wiebe, and J. C. Lester. Automatically Recognizing Facial Indicators of Frustration: A Learning-Centric Analysis. In *Proceedings of the International Conference on Affective Computing and Intelligent Interaction (ACII)*, pages 159–165, Geneva, Switzerland, 2013.

[16] J. F. Grafsgaard, J. B. Wiggins, K. E. Boyer, E. N. Wiebe, and J. C. Lester. Predicting Learning and Affect from Multimodal Data Streams in Task-Oriented Tutorial Dialogue. In *To appear in Proceedings of the 7th International Conference on Educational Data Mining*, London, United Kingdom, 2014.

[17] E. Y. Ha, J. F. Grafsgaard, C. M. Mitchell, K. E. Boyer, and J. C. Lester. Combining Verbal and Nonverbal Features to Overcome the 'Information Gap'in Task-Oriented Dialogue. Number July, pages 247–256, 2012.

[18] S. G. Hart and L. E. Staveland. Development of NASA-TLX (Task Load Index): Results of empirical and theoretical research. *Advances in Psychology*, 52:139–183, 1988.

[19] O. P. John and S. Srivastava. The Big Five trait taxonomy: History, measurement, and theoretical perspectives. *Handbook of Personality: Theory and Research*, 2:102–138, 1999.

[20] M. R. Lepper and M. Woolverton. The wisdom of practice: Lessons learned from the study of highly effective tutors. *Improving Academic Achievement: Impact of Psychological Factors on Education*, pages 135–158, 2002.

[21] G. Littlewort, J. Whitehill, T. Wu, I. Fasel, M. Frank, J. Movellan, and M. Bartlett. The computer expression recognition toolbox (CERT). In *Automatic Face Gesture Recognition and Workshops (FG 2011), 2011 IEEE International Conference on*, pages 298–305, Mar. 2011.

[22] J. D. Marx and K. Cummings. Normalized change. *American Journal of Physics*, 75(1):87, 2007.

[23] C. M. Mitchell, E. Y. Ha, K. E. Boyer, and J. C. Lester. Learner characteristics and dialogue: recognising effective and student-adaptive tutorial strategies. *International Journal of Learning Technology (IJLT)*, 8(4):382–403, 2013.

[24] H. L. O'Brien and E. G. Toms. The development and evaluation of a survey to measure user engagement. *Journal of the American Society for Information Science and Technology*, 61(1):50–69, 2010.

[25] S. Oviatt and A. Cohen. Written and Multimodal Representations As Predictors of Expertise and Problem-solving Success in Mathematics. In *Proceedings of the 15th ACM on International Conference on Multimodal Interaction*, pages 599–606, Sydney, Australia, 2013. ACM.

[26] M. Pantic, A. Pentland, A. Nijholt, and T. S. Huang. Human Computing and Machine Understanding of Human Behavior: A Survey. In *Artifical Intelligence for Human Computing*, pages 47–71. Springer Berlin Heidelberg, New York, New York, USA, 2007.

[27] B. Reeves and C. Nass. *The Media Equation: How People Treat Computers, Television, and New Media*. Cambridge University Press, 1997.

[28] S. Scherer, N. Weibel, L.-P. Morency, and S. Oviatt. Multimodal Prediction of Expertise and Leadership in Learning Groups. In *Proceedings of the 1st International Workshop on Multimodal Learning Analytics*, pages 1–8, Santa Monica, California, USA, 2012. ACM Press.

[29] M. R. Symonds and A. Moussalli. A brief guide to model selection, multimodel inference and model averaging in behavioural ecology using Akaike's information criterion. *Behavioral Ecology and Sociobiology*, 65(1):13–21, Aug. 2010.

[30] A. Tapus and M. J. Mataric. Socially Assistive Robots: The Link between Personality, Empathy, Physiological Signals, and Task Performance. In *AAAI Spring Symposium: Emotion, Personality, and Social Behavior*, pages 133–140, 2008.

[31] A. K. Vail and K. E. Boyer. Adapting to Personality Over Time: Examining the Effectiveness of Dialogue Policy Progressions in Task-Oriented Interaction. In *To appear in Proceedings of the 15th Annual SIGDIAL Meeting on Discourse and Dialogue*, Philadelphia, Pennsylvania, USA, 2014.

[32] A. K. Vail and K. E. Boyer. Identifying Effective Moves in Tutorial Dialogue: On the Refinement of Speech Act Annotation Schemes. In *Proceedings of the 12th International Conference on Intelligent Tutoring Systems*, Honolulu, Hawaii, USA, 2014.

Eye Gaze for Spoken Language Understanding in Multi-Modal Conversational Interactions

Dilek Hakkani-Tür
Microsoft
Mountain View, CA, USA
dilek@ieee.org

Malcolm Slaney
Microsoft
Mountain View, CA, USA
malcolm@ieee.org

Asli Celikyilmaz
Microsoft
Mountain View, CA, USA
asli@ieee.org

Larry Heck
Microsoft
Mountain View, CA, USA
larry.heck@ieee.org

ABSTRACT

When humans converse with each other, they naturally amalgamate information from multiple modalities (i.e., speech, gestures, speech prosody, facial expressions, and eye gaze). This paper focuses on eye gaze and its combination with speech. We develop a model that resolves references to visual (screen) elements in a conversational web browsing system. The system detects eye gaze, recognizes speech, and then interprets the user's browsing intent (e.g., click on a specific element) through a combination of spoken language understanding and eye gaze tracking. We experiment with multi-turn interactions collected in a wizard-of-Oz scenario where users are asked to perform several web-browsing tasks. We compare several gaze features and evaluate their effectiveness when combined with speech-based lexical features. The resulting multi-modal system not only increases user intent (turn) accuracy by 17%, but also resolves the referring expression ambiguity commonly observed in dialog systems with a 10% increase in F-measure.

Categories and Subject Descriptors

I.2.7 [**Natural Language Processing**]: Language Parsing and Understanding—*speech and gaze understanding*

Keywords

spoken language understanding, reference resolution, eye gaze

1. INTRODUCTION

Humans naturally use information from multiple modalities when interacting with each other, motivating the integration of these signals when interpreting user requests to a conversational-interaction system. In this work, we focus on the use of two modalities for spoken language understanding: voice and eye gaze. Users see information on a display and use their voice to control a conversational interaction, such as finding information about a topic or performing a transaction.

In such systems, there are two types of conversational turns: generic and referential. A referential turn refers to an item on display, while a generic turn does not. First we must detect that the user has a generic request, independent of the display contents. For example, the first turn of an interaction (such as a user asking *show me movies nearby*) is usually not referring to an item on display. In the second type of user turn the user's utterance refer to an item on display—understanding involves resolution of that item. In this paper, we focus on this second step. We wish to identify an item to which the user is referring in a spoken utterance, using the location of their eye gaze on a display.

In our previous work on using multi-modal information for spoken-language understanding, we integrated hand-pointing gestures with spoken utterances for click intent detection [7]. Furthermore, in simulated experiments, we analyzed the accuracy of click intent detection with respect to the distance between the targeted item and the pointing position. We also performed a detailed analysis of lexical features for this task for a variety of display designs, interaction domains and user devices [2]. Other related studies include work by Misu *et al.* [9], who proposed an in-car spoken dialog system that integrates multi-modal inputs of speech, geo-location, gaze (as estimated from face direction) and dialog history to answer drivers' queries about their surroundings. Due to the in-car nature of the dialog application, what the user sees changes over time. Cooke *et al.* [3] also investigated integration of eye gaze with spoken utterances, with a focus on dynamic model-based adaptation methods for noise-robust automatic speech recognition (ASR). For evaluation, they use a dataset recorded for a 'put that there' task [1], where the user tells a receiver to position a colored shape on a displayed map. Along similar lines to our work, Prasov and Chai [10] studied contribution of eye gaze for reference resolution. Their work targets situated understanding, where users refer to objects in context, and eye gaze compensates for the lack of domain modeling. Similarly, Kennington *et al.* [8] looked into interpolation of lexical, eye gaze and pointing models for this task, where the semantic space is predefined as the set of puzzle-pieces. A special feature of their modeling framework is incremental understanding, allowing for understanding of user's input incrementally during each user turn.

ICMI'14, November 12–16, 2014, Istanbul, Turkey.
Copyright 2014 ACM 978-1-4503-2885-2/14/11 ...$15.00.
http://dx.doi.org/10.1145/2663204.2663277 .

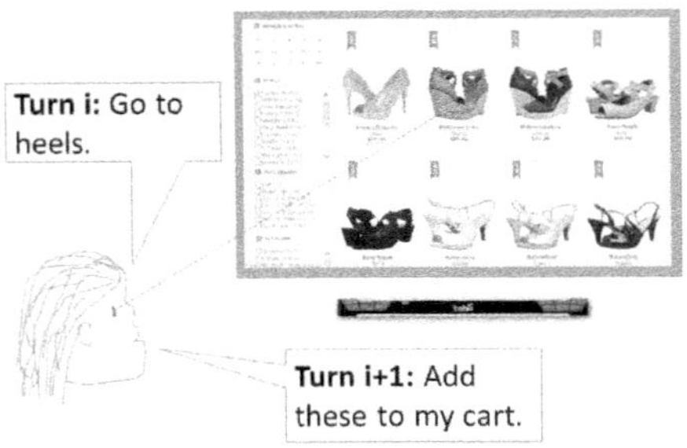

Figure 1: Setting for gaze supported interactions with a conversational system.

Symbol	Desctiption
t	turn id
$s(t)$	sentence at turn t
$l_k(t)$	candidate link k at turn t
$L(t)$	set of links at turn t
$d[\cdot]$	distance between two points on the display
$P_{start(t)}$	fixation point at the beginning of the utterance
$P_{end(t)}$	fixation point at the end of the utterance
$md[\cdot]$	closest fixation point during the utterance
$f(t)$	features extracted at turn t
$\hat{l}(t)$	predicted link at turn t

Table 1: The notation used in the paper.

In this work, to simulate various forms of visual displays and conversational interaction tasks, we chose a conversational search and browse task that allows users to navigate web pages that include various forms of hyperlinks, buttons, text boxes, etc. Figures 1 and 2 show the system setting, user utterances and system actions in a sample interaction. In such a conversational system, users may explicitly refer to items on web pages (i.e., user utterance includes the full or partial text of a link) or make implicit referrals (i.e., *select* or use position of items on the page, *select the top one*). Lexical features that measure the textual similarity between user utterances and displayed items are expected to be useful for resolving explicit referrals, but are not satisfactory for the implicit referrals. Gaze features help resolve both cases, especially with erroneous ASR, where user utterances are not always correctly recognized.

In the following sections, we first describe our approach for modeling the resolution of referring expressions using spoken utterances and user's eye gaze. Then, in Section 3, we describe the experimental setup and the data collection. In the experiments section, we first analyze the collected data in terms of different types of referrals. We then present experiments where we analyze the contribution of lexical and eye gaze features. Results from the experiments where we use both types of features show that both modalities are useful for resolution of referring expressions, and their contribution is complementary.

2. MODELING FOR RESOLUTION OF REFERRING EXPRESSIONS

We frame the resolution of referring expressions as a binary classification problem, where all links on the page displayed to the user $l_k(t) \in L(t)$ $(k = 1, ..., |L(t)|)$, paired with user's utterance $s(t)$ at turn t, and their eye gaze fixation points form the examples to be classified. We consider examples that include the link targeted by the user as positive examples, and all the rest of the candidates are negative examples.

User: I wanna shop for women's shoes at <website>.com
System: [opens up <website>.com, women's shoes page]
User: Go to heels
System: [follows "heels" link]
User: Add these shoes to my cart

Figure 2: An example multi-modal conversational interaction, with a transcription of user utterances, system actions and display contents.

We then extract a set of features that compute lexical similarity between the text associated with each candidate link, $l_k(t)$, and the user utterance, $s(t)$ (referred to as lexical features). These features include:

- cosine similarity between term vectors of $l_k(t)$ and $s(t)$,
- number of characters in the longest common subsequence of $l_k(t)$ and $s(t)$, and
- a binary feature that indicates if the link text was included in user's utterance or not, and if so, the length of the link text.

To provide robustness to possible errors in tokenization and ASR, we compute similarity features both at the word and character levels.

To capture the information from user's eye gaze, we first compute fixation points where a user's eye gaze lands, and the start and end time of that fixation. Our eyes process information during short fixation times when the eye is not moving. The eyes reorient during quick ballistic movements known as saccades, but we are not processing information during these times. We need to identify the fixation points to know what has been read. We use an algorithm by Salvucci [4] to identify each fixation point from our eye-gaze data. For each recorded eye-gaze location, we look for a set of points extending over at least 100ms that are clustered together. A cluster is defined by a Manhattan distance of less than 40 pixels. Thus with an average sampling rate of 30Hz, we need at least three points in close proximity to determine that there is a fixation point. In this work, we use the centroid of this cluster as the fixation point, and we suggest that the subject is referring to items in close proximity to this point.

We then extract eye gaze features that represent distance $d[\cdot]$ from the surrounding box of candidate link, $l_k(t)$, to:

- the fixation point at the beginning of the utterance $start(t)$, $P_{start(t)}$: $d[P_{start(t)}, l_k(t)]$
- the fixation point at the end of the utterance $end(t)$, $P_{end(t)}$: $d[P_{end(t)}, l_k(t)]$
- closest eye gaze fixation point during the utterance, $md[start(t), end(t)]$:
  $md[start(t), end(t)] = min_{x \in (start(t), end(t))} d[P_x, l_k(t)]$
- closest eye gaze fixation point during the 2 second window before the start of the user's utterance,
  $md[start(t) - 2, start(t)]$

Figure 3 depicts the computation of the distance. Note that, during the saccades, the distance to any candidate link is set to a large number.

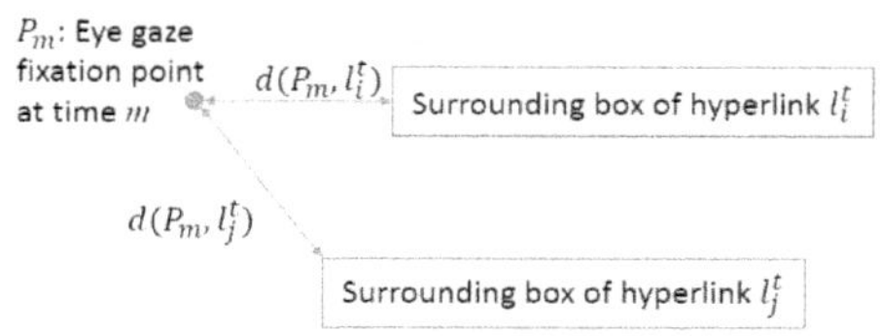

Figure 3: Computation of distance between hyperlinks displayed at turn t and eye gaze fixation points.

During runtime, at each turn t, we parse the displayed pages for the set of candidate links $L(t)$ and select the candidate $l_k(t)$ that has the highest probability of being the positive class example given the user's utterance and the associated set of features $f(t)$:

$$\hat{l}(t) = argmax_{l_k(t) \in L(t)} P(positive|l_k(t), f(t))$$

In experiments, we compare the contribution of each type of feature, as well as their combination. Furthermore, to see the effect of the quality of speech transcription, we experiment with clean (i.e. manual) and noisy (i.e., automatic) speech transcription conditions.

3. DATA COLLECTION AND EXPERIMENT SET UP

We collected real-time eye-gaze data using a Tobii REX. Users were seated at slightly more than arm's distance from a 24-inch display. We used the standard Tobii calibration process. This system provides eye-gaze information at approximately 30 Hz.

Before each session, subjects were presented a task description and asked to perform the task naturally, using multiple modalities. The tasks included browsing for information, such as finding a nearby restaurant, as well as transactions, such as buying flight tickets. The wizard heard the spoken utterances of the subjects and was shown the same display contents as the subject. However, on wizard's display, the area where the user's eye gaze was pointing to (as captured by Tobii) was shaded with a circle. The wizard took actions to satisfy the user's request, such as clicking on a link, or filling in web forms.

At each turn, we recorded the user's spoken utterances, the list of candidate links on display as well as the complete contents of the web page. We also recorded each wizard action, time synchronized with the user's actions.

4. EXPERIMENTS

4.1 Data Sets

In our experiments we collected data from 27 speakers, each performing 9 tasks. User turns included requests to follow links on display, system commands such as *scroll down*, utterances possibly not addressed to the machine (such as, *'oh'*, *'no'*), and form filling requests. The tasks result in an average of 12.2 user turns. The data set includes 2,965 turns, 581 of which aim to follow a link on the screen. There are in total 175,113 candidate links on the web pages visited by the users (an average of 301.4 per each click turn).

We use a state-of-the-art large vocabulary ASR system in our experiments [5]. The acoustic models incorporate the latest advances in context-dependent deep neural networks (DNN) for estimating senone likelihoods. The language model (LM) is a general-purpose backoff 4-gram model with a vocabulary of about 400K words. This generic LM (GLM) was trained on a wide variety of sources ranging from transcribed speech from deployed ASR applications, such as voice search, to text from a diverse set of web resources. The GLM was not tailored or adapted to the tasks of our study.

As described earlier, users can refer to items on display in several different ways. Table 2 shows the types of utterances observed in our data set and their relative frequencies.

4.2 Results

We performed 27-fold classification experiments, where we take out the data set of one user at each fold, to use it as the test set, and use all the remaining examples as the training set. We use icsiboost [6] for classification. Table 3 shows the turn accuracy and F-measure results from these experiments. Turn accuracy refers to the percentage of turns where only a single link was returned by the classifier and that was the link targeted by the user. For many examples, two or more links were assigned the same probability by the classifier, but only one was the one targeted by the user. These cases are considered as system errors for turn accuracy. However, reducing the set of candidates from many examples to a few, where the system can ask a clarification question to the user (instead of asking the user to repeat the request) may result in a better conversational interaction experience. Hence, we also report F-measure results, macro-averaged over turns in this table.

As seen in Table 3, lexical features result in higher turn accuracy and F-measure than gaze features alone. This could be explained by the fact that majority of utterances in our data set include exact match or explicit referrals, which can easily be resolved, especially since usually (but not always) there is a single link with the matching text. Also, many pages are densely populated with links, and many links are in close proximity to user's eye-gaze fixations. Hence, while the set of candidates may be reduced by gaze features, it may be difficult to identify the correct one. However, the gaze features are also useful, and the combination of the two types of features results in the best performance in terms of both measures. The turn accuracy (and F-measure) of 42.7% (55.6%) with just lexical features improves to 59.7% (65.6%) when we include gaze features in the experiments.

When erroneous ASR transcriptions are used instead of the clean/manual transcriptions, as will be the case with a real application, the performance with lexical features degrades significantly: turn accuracy drops from 42.7% to 32.9%, while performance with gaze features stays the same. The ASR word error rate on this data set is 44.8%. The performance numbers with the combined set of features is again better than the performance with individual set of features.

4.3 Discussions and Future Work

Our study shows significant connections between gaze features and the variables characterizing the lexical overlap with the targeted link. It is interesting to observe that the target focused gaze indicates the presence of the targeted link nearby. Nevertheless, we observed data and framework related issues that may have interfered with the model's accuracy and that we should investigate more as a follow-up study. These can be summarized as:

- **Text normalization issues**: We observe such issues when the text normalization becomes complex, for in-

Referral Type	Example User Utterance	Example Text Associated with Link/Image/Button	Relative Frequency
Exact Match	*how to register a vessel*	*how to register a vessel*	35.3%
Explicit	*go to sneakers and athletic shoes*	*sneakers and athletic shoes*	34.1%
Explicit Partial	*that to my cart*	*add to cart*	9.6%
Implicit, Position	*select the second one*	*yumeya sushi*	3.9%
Implicit	*select this*	*how to register a vessel*	8.6%
Multiple	*click on yumeya that's number two*	*yumeya sushi*	1.0%
Other	*find vendors*	*search* or no text associated with link	7.5%

Table 2: Examples from conversational interactions.

Experiment	MANUAL		ASR	
	TA	F	TA	F
Only Lexical Features	42.7%	55.6%	32.9%	43.2%
Only Gaze Features	18.6%	25.6%	18.6%	25.6%
All Features	59.7%	65.6%	51.8%	56.3%

Table 3: Turn accuracy (TA) and F-measure with manual and ASR transcriptions.

stance, the link text shows '*7:00 pm*', but the user speaks '*seven o'clock*'. In the future, we plan to use better text normalization as a preprocessing step to interpret the relation between the utterance and link text.

- **Display related issues**: The display screen in our framework is a typical web page, which may introduce additional ambiguities to our model. Specifically, when users refer to an item on a web page they would think that the item is a clickable object, when it is actually not.

The main conclusion we glean from our experiments is that we observe the best performance when we include both types of features. We think that it would be beneficial had we integrated the features from the two modalities, such as, adding a linking binary feature to indicate the closest link candidate with matching text. In a follow-up study, we plan to investigate such features.

Other avenues that we can investigate include:

- joint modeling of automatic detection of referrals to displayed items and resolution of referring expressions.
- improving ASR by using displayed page contents [7] and eye-gaze focused language models [11],
- extending the set of lexical features by using extended set of ASR hypotheses (such as, n-best lists and word lattices) and matching between phone sequences.

5. CONCLUSIONS

We presented a framework that exploits gaze features for spoken language understanding in human-machine dialog systems. Our model interprets the user's intent in a conversational browsing scenario (e.g., clicking on a link) using a combination of gaze and voice. We introduced several new gaze features and evaluated their efficiency together with the lexical features. The features were extracted from the user's eye-gaze pattern, spoken utterances, and the text displayed on the screen. The resulting multi-modal system not only increases user intent (turn) accuracy by 17%, but also resolves referring expression ambiguity commonly observed in dialog systems with a 10% increase in F-measure.

Acknowledgments: Authors would like to thank Rahul Rajen, Gokhan Tur, Zhaleh Feizollahi, and Ruhi Sarikaya for discussions and help with the data collection.

6. REFERENCES

[1] R. A. Bolt. "put-that-there": Voice and gesture at the graphics interface. volume 14. ACM, 1980.

[2] A. Celikyilmaz, Z. Feizollahi, D. Hakkani-Tür, and R. Sarikaya. Resolving referring expressions in conversational dialogs for natural user interfaces. In *Proceedings of EMNLP*, 2014.

[3] N. Cooke, A. Shen, and M. Russell. Exploiting a 'gaze-lombard effect' to improve asr performance in acoustically noisy settings. In *Proceedings of IEEE International Conference onAcoustics, Speech and Signal Processing (ICASSP)*, 2014.

[4] J. H. D. D. Salvucci. Identifying fixations and saccades in eye-tracking protocols. In *Eye Tracking Researchand Application*, pages 71–79, 2000.

[5] L. Deng, J. Li, J.-T. Huang, K. Yao, D. Yu, F. Seide, M. Seltzer, G. Zweig, X. He, and J. Williams. Recent advances in deep learning for speech research at microsoft. In *Proceedings of IEEE International Conference onAcoustics, Speech and Signal Processing (ICASSP)*, 2013.

[6] B. Favre, D. Hakkani-Tür, and S. Cuendet. Icsiboost. http://code.google.come/p/icsiboost, 2007.

[7] L. Heck, D. Hakkani-Tür, M. Chinthakunta, G. Tur, R. Iyer, P. Parthasarathy, L. Stifelman, A. Fidler, and E. Shriberg. Multimodal conversational search and browse. In *Proceedings of IEEE Workshop on Speech, Language and Audio in Multimedia*, 2013.

[8] C. Kennington, S. Kousidis, and D. Schlangen. Interpreting situated dialogue utterances: an update model that uses speech, gaze, and gesture information. In *Proceedings of SIGDial*, 2013.

[9] T. Misu, A. Raux, I. Lane, J. Devassy, and R. Gupta. Situated multi-modal dialog system in vehicles. In *Proceedings of the 6th ACM workshop on Eye gaze in intelligent human machine interaction*, pages 25–28, 2013.

[10] Z. Prasov and J. Y. Chai. What's in a gaze?: the role of eye-gaze in reference resolution in multimodal conversational interfaces. In *ACM Proceedings of the 13th international conference on Intelligent user interfaces*, pages 20–29, 2008.

[11] M. Slaney, R. Rajen, A. Stolcke, and P. Parthasarathy. Gaze enhanced speech recognition. In *Proceedings of IEEE International Conference onAcoustics, Speech and Signal Processing (ICASSP)*, 2014.

SoundFLEX: Designing Audio to Guide Interactions with Shape-Retaining Deformable Interfaces

Koray Tahiroğlu,
Department of Media
Aalto University, School of Arts, Design and Architecture
PO 16500 00076 Aalto Finland
koray.tahiroglu@aalto.fi

Thomas Svedström
Department of Media
Aalto University, School of Arts, Design and Architecture
PO 16500 00076 Aalto Finland
thomas.svedstrom@aalto.fi

Valtteri Wikström
Department of Media
Aalto University, School of Arts, Design and Architecture
PO 16500 00076 Aalto Finland
valtteri.wikstrom@aalto.fi

Simon Overstall
Department of Media
Aalto University, School of Arts, Design and Architecture
PO 16500 00076 Aalto Finland
simon.overstall@aalto.fi

Johan Kildal
Nokia Research Center
PO Box 407, FI-00045
Nokia Group, Finland
johan.kildal@nokia.com

Teemu Ahmaniemi
Nokia Research Center
PO Box 407, FI-00045
Nokia Group, Finland
teemu.ahmaniemi@nokia.com

ABSTRACT

Shape-retaining freely-deformable interfaces can take innumerable distinct shapes, and creating specific target configurations can be a challenge. In this paper, we investigate how audio can guide a user in this process, through the use of either musical or metaphoric sounds. In a formative user study, we found that sound encouraged action possibilities and made the affordances of the interface perceivable. We also found that adding audio as a modality along with vision and touch, made a positive contribution to guiding users' interactions with the interface.

Categories and Subject Descriptors

H.5.2 [**Information interfaces and presentation**]: UIs - Input devices and strategies, Auditory feedback.

General Terms

Theory and Exploration

Keywords

Multimodal interaction; deformable interfaces; shape-retaining interfaces; audio feedback; sonic interaction; sound design

1. INTRODUCTION

Deformable user interfaces (DUIs) represent a growing area of research in Human Computer Interaction (HCI), as we show in the literature review below. Among them, shape-retaining DUIs (i.e., interfaces made of materials that present plastic mechanical deformation behaviors), have received particularly little attention. Increased tangible affordances of these interfaces provide a strong sense of physical engagement with digital artifacts and offer unique design challenges. The interaction with DUIs employs physical manipulations that users are able to perform, within a set of pre-designed interaction patterns (e.g., bend, twist, squeeze...). Many design solutions with DUIs provide enhanced tangibility cues of the deforming material, and they often go accompanied by visualizations on a flexible display. However, an auditory display that is well integrated with input actions has not been well studied yet. Therefore current design solutions with DUIs do not ensure a model for users to engage fully with real-world physical interactions. Real physical interactions are multimodal by their own nature, as "we touch and feel, listen and hear, look and see at the same time" [5].

ICMI '14 November 12 - 16 2014, Istanbul, Turkey
Copyright 2014 ACM 978-1-4503-2885-2/14/11 ...$15.00
http://dx.doi.org/10.1145/2663204.2663278.

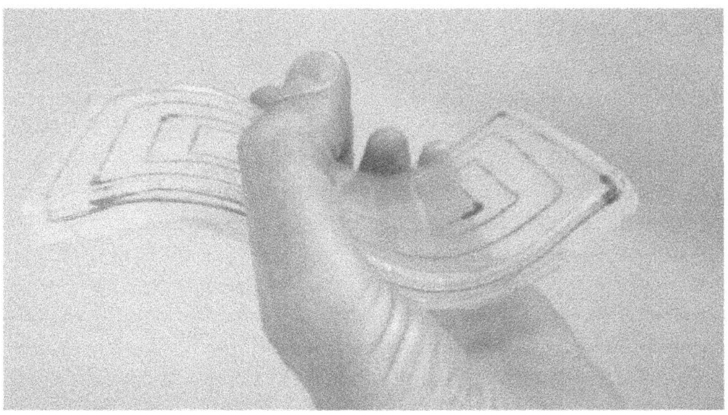

Figure 1: Prototype implementation of the research.

Such multimodality has been largely neglected in previous designs of deformable interactions, falling short of providing physically-engaging interactions (and resulting user experiences - UXs) in the long run. We believe that designing interactions for such interfaces should start with integrating the design well within the multimodal nature of human perception and actions. As a result, interactions would offer basic perceptual and conceptual structures that could be easily understood. When a shape-retaining, freely-deformable device can take such a large number of different shapes, molding it into just a small subset of shapes can be a challenge. A multimodal interaction design could encourage users to discover input deformation affordances, and guide them towards specific target shapes. In this endeavor, audio may have a valuable role to play, along with vision and touch.

In this paper, we report the current status of our research on shape-retaining, freely-deformable handheld interfaces and the role that digital audio can play in the guidance along the interaction cycle, and in the resulting UX. We first present an overview of related work in the context of deformable and organic UIs (including methods of deformation, materials and form factors, and their shape-function structures), and also relevant work on interactive sound synthesis. Following this, we introduce our prototype implementation of a shape-retaining, freely deformable handheld interface (see Fig. 1), including a summary description of the iterative prototype and sound design process that led to its current state. We then describe two alternative sound design implementations; Metaphoric and Musical sound designs. With this functional hardware setup and sound design, we report on a formative user study that we conducted. Within the overarching research goal of understanding the role of audio in interactions with deformable interfaces, our intentions with the user study were threefold:

- to gain insight into user expectations and experience in manipulating a shape-retaining deformable device,
- to collect the participant's opinions of our designed sounds,
- to understand how the audio feedback guided the participants in forming particular shapes.

We discuss our quantitative and qualitative findings in relation to an analysis of the user-test data collected and in the final section we present our conclusion and future work.

2. RELATED WORK

There has been research on physically deformable interfaces for almost two decades. Among the early work is a deformable cubical interface [20] that was designed for 3-D modeling. The device was made of an electrically conductive elastic material. The user interacted with the device by squeezing, and the deformation was mapped to control the shape of a corresponding virtual object on a screen. A few years later, the initial idea for organic UIs (OUI) was presented in [10]. The work included three hand-held prototypes of manipulative UIs based on real life metaphors such as book page turning. While the previous work had focused on creating new controllers for existing artifacts, here the idea was to make the artifact itself a controller. This idea determined the direction of organic UIs.

Gummi [23] could be considered the forerunner of the modern OUI's. Gummi was a foldable mobile size device, in which the controller and the artifact were inseparable, as was suggested in [10]. Gummi consisted of bend-sensors and a touchpad for 2D position control. The device was bendable upwards and downwards and the amount of bending was measured. Gummi was evaluated for example in a map application, in which bending was mapped to zooming. Gummi inspired new bendable interfaces. A smartphone named PaperPhone [17] contained a flexible e-ink screen and a bend sensor. Nokia Kinetic Device [14] was a smartphone prototype exploring bending and twisting as interaction method. A more recent approach are the malleable and shape changing and retaining devices. MorePhone [9] has shape memory and it incorporates actuators in order to transform into a certain shape. For example an incoming call causes the screen to bend. Similarly, ShapePhone [8] is a malleable prototype that can be deformed to physically represent different devices e.g. a watch, phone or remote controller.

To our knowledge, there is no work that considers sound as a design element in organic UIs. However, sound as an emerging design material engenders various opportunities in interaction. First of all, it is an efficient feedback channel, which is able to draw attention from one task to another [13, 15]. It has also been used to convey information in order to reduce visual load or when vision is occupied. Furthermore, sound has been used to provide cross-modal feedback [2] or to enhance and alter the perceived physicality of a rigid surface [18]. Moreover, the capabilities of sonification for teaching gestures and providing feedback in learning process has been studied [1, 21].

Sonification has been recently applied into new research areas. Briefly, it is the process of presenting information with sound [11]. Classic (symbolic) sonification examples are earcons and auditory icons [16]. More recent methods such as the parameter mapping sonification (PMS), the model-based sonification (MBS) [11], and auditory scene segmentation [4] present more dynamic uses of sound. Furthermore, Sonic Interaction Design (SID), an emerging research field, examines the use and role of sound as the primary information channel and it takes place at the intersection of interaction design, ubiquitous computing and interactive arts [22].

3. PROTOTYPE IMPLEMENTATION

We designed and implemented the prototype of a shape-retaining, freely-deformable interface that was audio reactive. This means that the user not only felt in her hands the material deforming (passive tactile feedback of the real material), but she also heard a closely-coupled digital audio expression of that same deformation.

3.1 Prototype and Audio Design Story

We can summarize our design story by briefly describing four prototypes we developed before arriving at the current implementation. Our first experiments with deformable interfaces involved insulating and conductive dough made according to the Squishy Circuits recipe [12]. In our early tests we explored the resistive properties of the dough by inserting two electrodes and measuring the variable resistance caused by deformations (see Fig. 2a). This measurement controlled the playback rate of a short looping drum sample in sound synthesis module. The audio mapping was designed in relation to perceivable actions; a longer stretch of dough between the electrodes resulted in a slower and lower pitched loop. This approach had problems, because the electrodes were displaced during the deformation, and it would have required several electrodes to be in contact with the dough for multidimensional measurements. Despite these limitations, we felt encouraged to take our first tests further.

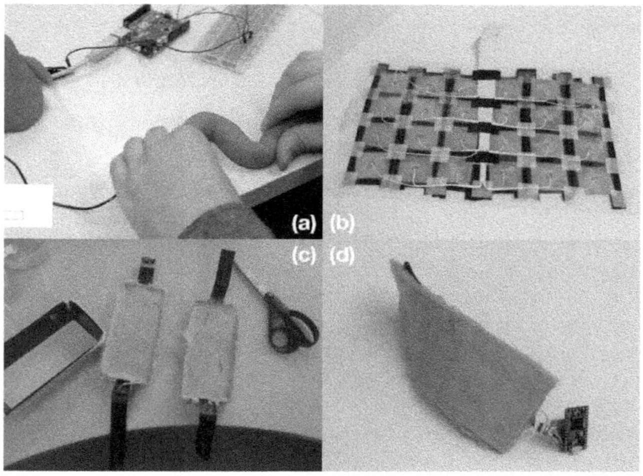

Figure 2: Early prototypes; (a) conductive dough with electrodes, (b) tabletop capacitive sensor, (c) molding silicon material and (d) with embedded microcontroller.

Next we explored the capacitive properties of the dough. Using a custom-made tabletop capacitive sensor we measured the deformations of the dough wirelessly (see Fig. 2b). The capacitive sensor allowed for sensing the dough in two dimensions, for detecting the separation and combination of pieces of dough, and for the dough to act as a touch sensor. In this prototype, different shapes and degrees of touch altered sound synthesis parameters generating different timbres as the dough was shaped. The detection of discrete shapes, such as disc, stick and angled shape, triggered an envelope giving a sharp change in the audio parameters. These experiments inspired us to explore the possibilities of using audio to guide the user into moulding the deformable interface into distinct shapes. This prototype was not developed further because the sensing paradigm did not afford mobile use and required continuous touch-connection with the dough for successful sensing.

Our third prototype was more limited in deformability than dough, but afforded more accurate sensing and mobility. Based on the Quimo material by Maas et al [19] we produced a silicon material with built-in metal mesh that was both deformable and retained its shape when deformed (see Fig. 2c). Custom-made sensors and a microcontroller were embedded in the prototype making the device capable of standalone sensor data processing (see Fig. 2d). We were able to distinguish the deformation of the device in three different shapes: a flat shape representing a phone, a bent shape representing a wristwatch and a folded shape representing a media player. It was at this point that we introduced the concept of action and validation sounds in our sound design strategy. A continuous audio feedback, giving the impression of a pressure change in the material, informed the user of how close they were to any functional shape. Each functional shape triggered an iconic sound sample, breaking the feedback sound and informing the user that the target shape had been reached. We found this sound design strategy fruitful, but also found that users were disoriented by the sharp change in audio parameters, when the iconic sample was played. This hardware prototype was bulky, fragile and the sensors only functioned in a single dimension, making the sensing of certain shapes non-exclusive.

For the fourth version the prototype was improved by introducing a proprietary sensor, Shapetape by Measurand Inc (Fredericton, Canada). This sensor technology reduced the weight and greatly improved the sensing accuracy, although the mobility was limited by a hardwired connection to the main processing unit. We demonstrated the prototype to visitors at ACM CHI'13. This served as a non-formal user study aiding the development of current prototype [25].

3.2 Current Prototype

The current prototype has a new silicone based model, shape detection software and an alternative sound design. The model, software and sound design improves the shape detection robustness and the physical durability. As we investigated shapes that were afforded by the new prototype, we came upon three target shapes; fold, bend and twist. While the deformable behavior of the prototype may suffice for very simple form transitions, the development of design ideas with a "function follows form" manner is of the utmost importance to designing the interaction in this project [25].

3.2.1 The physical prototype

The prototype was made out of dense, transparent, silicone material as it is shown in Fig. 1. The physical dimensions are 16.2x8.5x1cm. In order to provide shape-retaining capabilities, there are five metal wires in the shape of a rectangle inside the model. Furthermore, there is a rail that penetrates the whole model. The sensor (ShapeTape) is inserted into this rail.

3.2.2 Shape detection software

The shape detection software is based on a machine learning toolkit for Max/MSP. The toolkit, created by Benjamin D. Smith [24], uses Adaptive Resonance Theory (ART). We taught the system the three target shapes (fold, bend and twist) and implemented further shape detection logic. The system measures the completeness or the distance to each of the target shapes and reports it as a floating-point number that ranges from zero to one. The shape is deducted by using these three values. A fold occurs when one of the ends is pointing up or down. The shape is determined to be a bend if both ends are bowed in the same direction. A twist occurs as the two edges are rotated around the horizontal axis in opposite directions. In addition to the shape information, the system measures energy density i.e. the amount of force that is applied to the prototype.

3.2.3 Auditory Feedback Design

The auditory feedback guides the deformation process towards the three target shapes. Sounds are divided into two categories: action and validation sounds. Action sounds are designed to inform the user how closely the current shape resembles the predefined target shapes. Audio parameters are controlled by the shape distance and energy density values. The three action sounds are simultaneously audible, and the action sound of the shape that most closely resembles the current shape, is the most prominent. This is illustrated in Fig. 3. "All at once" design aimed to present all the possible shapes together. Validation sounds are played when the shape completely resembles a target shape. Validation sounds also interrupt all other sounds. For example (see

Fig. 4), if the user is folding one end, all the action sounds are audible, but the fold related action sound is altering towards a resolution. As the user follows the fold action sound and reaches a complete fold shape, all the action sounds are interrupted, the fold validation sound is played.

Based on these guidelines, we created two sound designs - metaphorical and musical. The idea of the metaphoric sound design was to use sounds that have equivalents in the real world. The musical sound design consists of sounds that are in 12-tone scale.

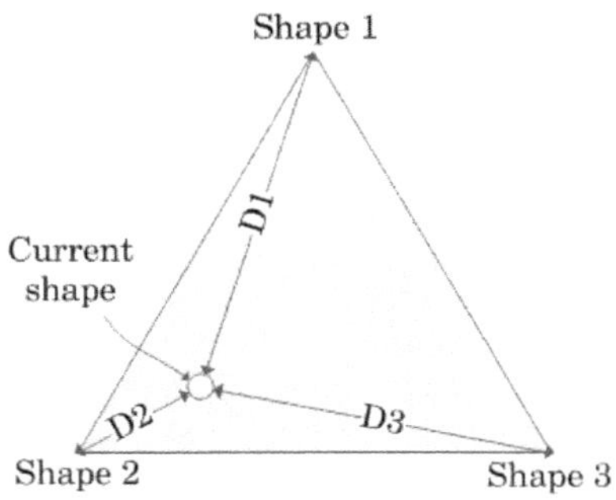

Figure 3: Auditory feedback design. The system measures distance to the three target shapes. User will hear all the three shapes at the same time and the shape that resembles the device most closely has the most emphasis.

3.2.4 Metaphoric Sound Design

As we perform an action on a physical object, there is a natural connection between the sound and action. However, the prototype is essentially silent when it is deformed and there are no natural mappings between the sound and action. Thus, we created a set of artificial sounds that have real-life equivalents. The three action sounds were cracking, bubbles and a rubber twang. The sound synthesis methods are modifications of the examples presented in [7] with some additional parameters and elements to emphasize the deformation and sound relation. These three action sounds are chosen because of the designed characteristics of their audio parameters; the sounds have distinct timbres and they are distinguishable when played simultaneously.

The three sounds were connected with the three target shapes (fold, bend and twist). The cracking sound was coupled with folding. The sound was designed to resemble more the cracking of a rubbery material than rigid. The cracking sound becomes more intense and tight as the device is folded. The amount of applied force made the cracking effect sharper. The validation sound for fold is a loud bang created by manipulating a door-closing sample. The bubbles were coupled with bending. When bent, the prototype resembles an U-shape pipe. The sound progression of the bubbles towards a bend creates an enclosing cavity- bubbles flow in the pipe freely in the first place and as the shape approaches a bend, the flow is disturbed and certain formant frequencies become more pronounced. The bend validation sound was a rapid and enhanced swoosh sound that indicates the "pipe" is now closed. Finally, rubber twang was coupled with the twisting. Twisting required the most force and the physical act creates feeling of tension. Similarly, in order to produce a twang sound, the rubber band must be tightened. Three sound samples with rising pitch were used to sonificate the twisting. The samples were played when certain distance thresholds were exceeded. The validation sound was a loud twang with a wavering tail.

3.2.5 Musical Sound Design

With the musical sound design we aimed to consider the subjective experience of users with sounds in 12-tone scale. Thus, we explored more abstract concepts, some associated with music. These concepts include: consonance and dissonance, harmonicity and inharmonicity, rich and dull timbres, and slow and fast tempi. In this context consonance refers to when two pitches are agreeable with each other, smooth sounding, whereas dissonance is when the pitches clash and there is interference between their frequencies. Consonance is at a maximum when two pitch are in unison, or the same Harmonicity and inharmonicity is a similar idea applied to the frequency components inside a sound. When these components clash the sound is inharmonic, such as a bell, when the components are compatible with each other the sound is harmonic, like a flute. Rich timbres have lots of energy in many of their frequency components making for a complex sound such as the crash of a cymbal, while dull timbres are are simple like a pure sine tone.

Sound synthesized with frequency modulation (FM) based techniques accept parameters correlated with these concepts. An FM synthesis function was implemented in Pure Data. In FM synthesis the frequency of a carrier oscillator is modulated by another oscillator. At above audio rates modulation products become audible as new components of the spectrum of the carrier. In musical sound design each of the three action sounds were created by a FM synthesizer. Each synthesizer produced a distinct timbre by using different parameters. The action sounds became louder as they approached their target shapes. The fold related synthesizer changed from a dull, slow sound to a richer, quicker one. For twist the sound varied only in its tempo from slow to quick. The validation sounds for the musical design are bells like sounds generated from vibraphone samples. The bell is played once for fold, twice for bend, and three times for twist.

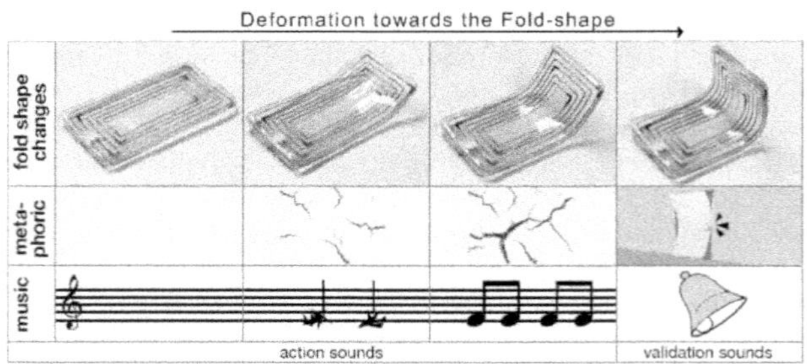

Figure 4: Action and validation sounds in both sound design for the shape fold.

4. EVALUATION

In relation to our design strategies, we were interested in using two sound designs as different viewpoints from which to understand how audio influences the interaction with current prototype of shape-retaining deformable interface. To this end we conducted a user test study and we used a number of techniques to collect information from the participants, including a "think-aloud method", interviews, surveys and sensor data collection, which provided a rich data set.

4.1 User Study: Audio Guided Deformations

The participants were volunteers who responded to a call sent to our institution. There were seventeen participants. The age range of the participants was 22 to 51. Eleven out of the seventeen subjects were male. The subjects were primarily students, staff and faculty with some amount of art, design or music background. We specifically asked about each participant's background with regard to sound design, and music as it was relevant to the area of investigation.

4.2 Methods

The tests were conducted with the participant and two researchers, one who primarily operated the test and one who primarily interacted with the participant. The participants were seated at a table with the prototype device and a loudspeaker, which played the audio. Each session was audio and video recorded. In addition, the two researchers present took notes. The participants were informed of the nature, scope and structure of the study at the outset.

For each participant the user test was conducted in three stages; first stage did not include audio feedback, the second and third stages included the two sound designs on a randomized order. Each stage began with an exploratory "think-aloud" phase, in which the participants interacted with the prototype device. As necessary they were encouraged by asking questions and an engaging conversational demeanor. The first stage with no audio feedback contained only the exploratory phase. Following that stage, the participants were asked to perform a deformation task. The participants were motivated by pretending that prototype device was a real device with real deformable functions and briefly shown images of the three target shapes. The participants then were asked to form those shapes from memory and with the audio guidance. The use of images to communicate the target shapes was intended to be more effective than verbal communication and less influential than demonstration. The participants were encouraged to "think-aloud".

After the deformation task, the participants filled out NASA-TLX and a short survey of our own. The latter survey consisted of nine attributes (satisfying, instantaneous, intuitive, precise, consistent, direct, responsive, engaging, fluent) that were evaluated on a 5-step Likert-scale. These attributes were a mixture of what we have used in our previous research, and the interaction attributes that were introduced in [6]. Furthermore, there were three questions examining the role audio played in the interaction for that participant referring to the perception of change in the sound and how this relation was understood. These questions were "Did you hear the sound change as you manipulated the device?" (perceivable), "Was the change in sound connected to the manipulations?" (coupled) and "Did the changes in the sounds suggest you were getting closer or farther to the shapes?" (guidance).

Finally the participants were interviewed to elicit responses to specific concepts and to ensure all areas of interest were addressed. The interviewing researcher chose from a list of questions that covered topics such as the participant's musical or sound design background, their evaluations of the sounds they were hearing, the perceived connection between the sound and their actions, their thoughts on the three shapes they were asked to form and the actual object itself, and their ideas for possible application areas. We also recorded sensor data and the analysis of data. The analysis data was related to energy density levels, shape values, and output from the machine learning functions.

5. RESULTS

5.1 Quantitative Analysis

The quantitative data gathered from the user study were obtained from the survey, NASA TLX paper and pen version and the recorded sensor data.

5.1.1 Sensor Data

The sensor activity levels for each sound condition are shown in Fig. 5. The central line denotes the mean activity level for each participant and the lighter colored area the standard deviation. The empty parts, i.e. the parts where the participant was being instructed or was talking, were removed and the data was smoothed with an interpolating function. A two-sample t-test was applied to examine whether the sound has an impact on the exploration phase duration. We found that the exploration phase was significantly longer with the two sound designs ($p = 7 * 10^{-6}$ metaphoric, $p = 2 * 10^{-6}$ musical). There was no statistically significant difference in length between the musical and metaphorical sound designs ($p = 0.98$).

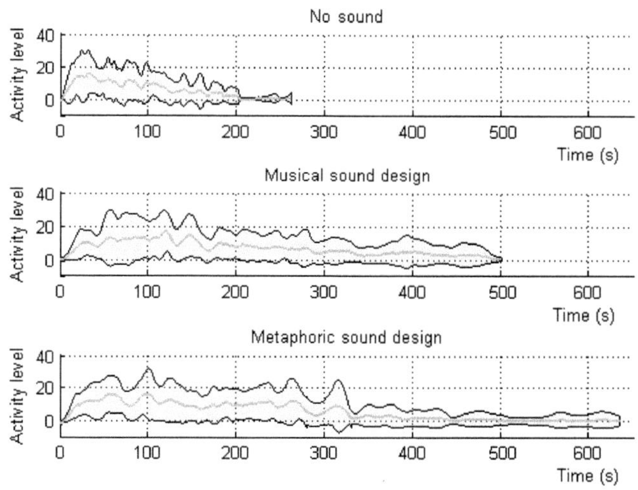

Figure 5: Activity levels for the three sound conditions measured from the sensor. The central line denotes the mean value and lighter area the standard deviation for all subjects.

5.1.2 Surveys

The two surveys did not show significant differences between the two sound designs. Wilcoxon signed-rank test was applied to each attribute, but the null hypothesis of equal medians could not be rejected at 95% confidence level for any attribute. However, on our survey, the mean ratings were above neutral on all attributes except "precise" for both sound designs. As for the action and sound coupling related attributes, the subjects were able to tell the connection between the action and sound ($M = 4.3$, $SD = 0.9$

metaphoric; $M = 4.1$, $SD = 1.1$ musical), but the attribute regarding the sound guidance produced a lower rating and a large variance ($M = 3.2$, $SD = 1.4$ metaphoric; $M = 3.4$, $SD = 1.4$). Interestingly, the two sound designs produced an identical mean NASA TLX score of 32.2 ($SD = 12.9019$ metaphoric and $SD = 11.6364$ musical).

5.2 Qualitative Analysis

In addition to the quantitative data, the data we collected from the participants with the "think-aloud method" and interviews provided a hybrid structure for us in terms of analysis to apply a qualitative analytic method. The thematic analysis method has been introduced in the field of psychology, and focuses on identifying patterns and themes within data [3]. This method allowed us to establish a thematic framework, informed by the responses.

Using this method we familiarized ourselves with the responses and certain themes emerged: expectations with the behavior of the device, latency, sounds depicting the actions, lack of consistency in sensor input, flexibility in device interaction, surprised sounds, etc. Combining these themes into groups based on how they are linked to participant's interaction allowed us to identify high-level themes: *From Inactive to Live!*, *Coupling Offers Meaning* and *Flavored Expressivity*. After clarifying the scope of these emerging high-level themes, we went back to the survey's open-ended questions, interview and "think-aloud" results and studied related data within the framework of the main themes. This process allowed us to organize responses in accordance with the thematic subjects, drawing out a potential narrative that was not guided or formed by the design of our questions.

5.2.1 From Inactive to Live!

From Inactive to Live reflects the range of comments and general terms participants used to identify their interaction with our prototype when they explored it with no audio rather than with either of the audio designs. Inactive, useless and ordinary was often articulated in the responses about their interaction with no audio features.

" *Initial impression for me is it's just a mysterious random object. [It] doesn't make any sense.*" (#2)

" *it seems to have no capabilities at all.*" (#0)

" *I would say, in the first place, it doesn't look like it is useful at all.*" (#15)

After either of the sound designs was activated users spent more time exploring the device. This finding is also consistent with the energy level activities we extracted from the raw sensor data. They used much stronger and evocative language to describe their emotional responses. The responses were both negative and positive, but more intense comparison to the previous no-audio session.

" *That's nice because it makes me kind of willing to explore a bit more. It's kind of more, I would say like more an embodied experience.*" (#12)

" *(laughs) I'm bending it and I was a little surprised by the sound. Uh, and it sounds like water falling of some sort. (laughs again) It's a lot of fun*" (#1)

While there were a number of responses that limit the current use of the device to toy, instrument, phone or tablet, it is also mentioned that when audio was activated it helped participants to see alternative potential for the device.

" *But having these special attributes, bending and making sounds, I guess it could be something else. I'd have to think. Definitely once you can do these things it can be more than just an e-book reader or a tablet.* (#9)

" *It's certainly much more, uh, satisfying. There's more to explore and I do feel that I'm almost, like, exploring a 3-dimensional space in a way with it, with the sounds* (#13)

5.2.2 Coupling Offers Meaning

The theme Coupling Offers Meaning was found in those responses that reflect the meaning that was expected to arise throughout the interaction. While the audio encouraged exploration and gave the participant an ability to manipulate the design, this process also allowed participants to establish meaning with the interface.

" *I think the sound in this case somehow tries to communicate, like, texture because this material is just same texture".* (#3)

1mm " *The second set (metaphoric) I like quite a lot. I felt like it was very well connected with the object. The flexibility was suggested through those sounds*" (#9)

This meaning increased the user's engagement with the device. Increased engagement led to further exploration of the interaction and enrichment of the meanings.

" *It's a little more dramatic, a little more foley (foley is a movie term for manually produced sound effects). You start creating a story out of it*" (#5)

" *It's as if, uh, as if I'm manipulating some kind of a balloon and it explodes.*" (#9)

Often users indicated awareness of the connection between sound and action with direct descriptions of cause & effect.

" *Tempo changes if I bend something really sharply.*" (#6)

" *It's more like, ah, it's adapting to the different stages of the bending.*" (#2)

Users recognized sounds as signifiers and understood sound and action were coupled clearly.

" *It sounds a bit like "ding!" I succeeded in finding the shape*" (#7)

" *It would seem that 'twang' is the point of 'twist'* (#13)

" *it's kind of a very clear indicator of now you are in another level* " (#12)

Critical comments showed comprehension of the coupling, even though they indicated it could be better.

" *I wasn't sure about what the sound? I mean it was, I mean kind of informative as a sound. I felt there was something going on, but I didn't, I didn't, kind of connect it to anything, like specific.*" (#11)

5.2.3 Flavored Expressivity

We were interested in what could be learned from the differences and commonalities in participant's responses and the theme Flavored Expressivity emerged from participant responses that described the sounds in objective manners. Many users were critical of the musical design, finding the sounds unpleasant and the interaction slow and confusing.

" The second one [music] was, all over, somehow just annoying sounds " (#10)

" In the first case [music] no [the sound didn't encourage action]. It's more intimidating, actually. I was, in the first case I was even, uh trying to make it stop. But sometimes I just touching and it would start again " (#7)

In general users were more positive of the metaphorical design preferring the sounds and the responsiveness.

" It feels like I'm manipulating something liquid. Yeah, and it gives me a sense of space so it feels like it's something real. It doesn't feel very synthetic." (#1)

" And I feel it really reacts very, like really instantly this uh <vocalizes creaking sound> to what I'm doing. So if I take it like that, but then I just release it a bit I hear it immediately. So that's, that's nice." (#7)

Also, some users were critical of both designs for having multiple sounds at once, wanting to control just one sound at a time.

" That is a bit tricky because during the entire manipulation of the object I wasn't sure how to produce one, single, sound, which I think is the only part which is a bit confusing about it." (#8)

" It's quite difficult to isolate one sound." (#13)

6. DISCUSSION

We can take the high-level themes that we have identified throughout the thematic analysis as a sort of spectrum. At first, when participants explored the prototype with no audio features, they felt that the interaction was limited, disappointing and the prototype itself was useless and there was nothing interesting with it. Some participants continued exploring the prototype despite these limitations, but just for a very short time as a random rubbery object. Others did not deform the prototype until prompted; device deformation was not perceived as a particularly interesting affordance. After exploring the device with its audio features, the participants described more distinct interactions with extended meanings. Sound was communicating something to them and prompted participants to action. Participant responses indicate that both of the sound designs encouraged them to perform further actions to form the three particular shapes.

We believe that this is due to the tight coupling that occurred between audio and participants' actions, which highlighted the affordance of device deformation to interact with the system. It can be noted here that the interaction capabilities of sound and the direct response to user's actions were well integrated within the design of the interaction. Participant responses show that coupling of sounds and actions progressively established meaning of that interaction. We must fully recognize in the process of designing interaction for deformable interfaces that there are alternative couplings open to us.

In reviewing the participant comments we also gained insight into the participant's opinions of our designed sounds. We found a large number of negative responses to the musical sound design, though this was not reflected in the quantitative data. The participants quite frequently invoked the word 'annoying' in reference to the musical design, sometimes quite emphatically. Looking closer we could see that there were two different sources for this annoyance. Some participants described the musical design as sounding 'ringing', 'sharp', or 'high pitched'. These could be non-expert terms describing the timbre of the inharmonic, highly modulated synthesized sounds present in the design. While this effect could be attenuated by adjusting the synthesis parameters it is important to note that not all participants disliked the design. At least one participant expressed a preference for the sounds of the musical design over the metaphorical one. This points to the importance of allowing for different aesthetic choices when evaluating musical design. The other source of annoyance seemed to be related to how quickly the musical design can respond to the participant's actions. The synthesized tones finish playing after being triggered so sound events of a relatively long duration mean it takes a relatively long time for the sound to respond. Participants made comments such as "*there is too much delay*" or that "*the response was slow*" and described the sound as 'overlapping'. Having multiple sounds at the same time to imply multiple possible shapes did not seem effective either. No participants communicated any kind of awareness of this condition, some participants were critical of hearing many sounds at once.

Participants' comments also demonstrate how the sound emulated their experience from the real world. The responses helped us to identify user expectations and experience in manipulating a shape-retaining deformable device. The sonic responses directly associated with materials, textures and metaphors were used by participants to identify their experience. The Metaphoric sound design was appreciated for these qualities. More interesting was the affirmation of one of the sounds for actually depicting the action that the users were enacting. The sound usually referred to as the 'creaking' sound was commented on quite often.

In the quantitative evaluation of the user test study, the two sound designs were assessed almost identically in the two surveys. There was a positive reaction to both. The survey results show that the prototype was most of all perceived as engaging and responsive, but not very precise. The participants were clearly aware of the connection between action and sound, and the coupling of the sound and shape, but the guidance aspect produced more mixed results.

7. CONCLUSION

In this paper we have presented our techniques and design strategies applied to the prototype that aimed to investigate the role of audio feedback in deformable and shape-retaining interfaces. Our user-test study suggests that sound encouraged interacting and both the metaphoric and the musical designs guided the participants in forming particular shapes. We, therefore propose using sound to encourage user actions in interaction in order to open up new possibilities to explore the design challenges and specific affordances of deformable, shape-retaining UIs.

In our study, all the actions we observed as the participants were exploring the device with its audio features can be seen from the perspective that the user was fully engaged and found what they needed for the interaction. Facilitating such interaction gives the user an ability to find connections between their actions and the feedback of the system. Our solution addresses interaction as a dynamic whole with each feedback channel possessing an identity of its own. Audio feedback plays an important role in HCI and the way it facilitates interaction in an eye-free manner provides more degrees of freedom to UIs. We can conclude that audio feedback can increase the feeling of control and encourage interaction, especially when it is designed with digital audio applied to operational aspects of its interaction principles. We will proceed with our implementation, looking further into the role of audio in interaction efficiency and emotional acceptance in interaction design.

8. ACKNOWLEDGMENTS

This research was a part of New Interaction Solutions project funded by the Finnish Funding Agency for Technology and Innovation TEKES and steered by Nokia Research Center and the Aalto Starting Grant.

9. REFERENCES

[1] T. H. Andersen and S. Zhai. "writing with music": Exploring the use of auditory feedback in gesture interfaces. *ACM Transactions on Applied Perception (TAP)*, 7(3):17, 2010.

[2] C. Asakawa, H. Takagi, S. Ino, and T. Ifukube. Auditory and tactile interfaces for representing the visual effects on the web. In *Proceedings of the fifth international ACM conference on Assistive technologies*, pages 65–72. ACM (2002).

[3] V. Braun and V. Clarke. Using thematic analysis in psychology. *Qualitative research in psychology*, 3(2):77–101, 2006.

[4] C. Cullen. The sonic representation of mathematical data. *Doctoral Thesis*, Dublin Institute of Technology (2006).

[5] J. Dewey. *Art As Experience*. New York: Perigee Trade, 2005.

[6] S. Diefenbach, E. Lenz, and M. Hassenzahl. An interaction vocabulary. describing the how of interaction. In *CHI'13 Extended Abstracts on Human Factors in Computing Systems*, pages 607–612. ACM (2013).

[7] A. Farnell. *Designing sound*. MIT Press Cambridge, 2010.

[8] S. Follmer, D. Leithinger, A. Olwal, N. Cheng, and H. Ishii. Jamming user interfaces: programmable particle stiffness and sensing for malleable and shape-changing devices. In *Proceedings of the 25th annual ACM symposium on User interface software and technology*, pages 519–528. ACM (2012).

[9] D. T. Gallant, A. G. Seniuk, and R. Vertegaal. Towards more paper-like input: flexible input devices for foldable interaction styles. In *Proceedings of the 21st annual ACM symposium on User interface software and technology*, pages 283–286. ACM (2008).

[10] B. L. Harrison, K. P. Fishkin, A. Gujar, C. Mochon, and R. Want. Squeeze me, hold me, tilt me! an exploration of manipulative user interfaces. In *Proceedings of the SIGCHI conference on Human factors in computing systems*, pages 17–24. ACM Press/Addison-Wesley Publishing Co. (1998).

[11] T. Hermann, A. Hunt, and J. G. Neuhoff. *The Sonification Handbook*. Logos Verlag, 2011.

[12] S. Johnson and A. P. Thomas. Squishy circuits: a tangible medium for electronics education. In *CHI'10 Extended Abstracts on Human Factors in Computing Systems*, pages 4099–4104. ACM (2010).

[13] M. Karjalainen. *Kommunikaatioakustiikka (Communication Acoustics, textbook)*. Helsinki University of Technology, 2008.

[14] J. Kildal, S. Paasovaara, and V. Aaltonen. Kinetic device: designing interactions with a deformable mobile interface. In *CHI'12 Extended Abstracts on Human Factors in Computing Systems*, pages 1871–1876. ACM (2012).

[15] P. Kortum. *HCI Beyond the GUI: Design for Haptic, Speech, Olfactory, and Other Nontraditional Interfaces*. Morgan Kaufmann Series in Interactive Technologies. Morgan Kaufmann, 2008.

[16] G. Kramer. *Auditory display: Sonification, audification, and auditory interfaces*. Addison-Wesley Reading, MA, 1994.

[17] B. Lahey, A. Girouard, W. Burleson, and R. Vertegaal. Paperphone: understanding the use of bend gestures in mobile devices with flexible electronic paper displays. In *Proceedings of the SIGCHI Conference on Human Factors in Computing Systems*, pages 1303–1312. ACM (2011).

[18] C.-H. Lai, M. Niinimäki, K. Tahiroğlu, J. Kildal, and T. Ahmaniemi. Perceived physicality in audio-enhanced force input. In *Proceedings of the 13th international conference on multimodal interfaces*, pages 287–294. ACM (2011).

[19] E. T. Maas, M. R. Marner, R. T. Smith, and B. H. Thomas. Quimo: A deformable material to support freeform modeling in spatial augmented reality environments. In *3D User Interfaces (3DUI), 2011 IEEE Symposium on*, pages 111–112. IEEE (2011).

[20] T. Murakami and N. Nakajima. Direct and intuitive input device for 3-d shape deformation. In *Proceedings of the SIGCHI Conference on Human Factors in Computing Systems*, pages 465–470. ACM (1994).

[21] U. Oh, S. K. Kane, and L. Findlater. Follow that sound: using sonification and corrective verbal feedback to teach touchscreen gestures. In *Proceedings of the 15th International ACM SIGACCESS Conference on Computers and Accessibility*, page 13. ACM (2013).

[22] D. Rocchesso, S. Serafin, F. Behrendt, N. Bernardini, R. Bresin, G. Eckel, K. Franinovic, T. Hermann, S. Pauletto, and P. Susini. Sonic interaction design: sound, information and experience. In *CHI'08 Extended Abstracts on Human Factors in Computing Systems*, pages 3969–3972. ACM (2008).

[23] C. Schwesig, I. Poupyrev, and E. Mori. Gummi: a bendable computer. In *Proceedings of the SIGCHI conference on Human factors in computing systems*, pages 263–270. ACM (2004).

[24] B. D. Smith and G. E. Garnett. Unsupervised play: Machine learning toolkit for max. In *Proceedings of NIME*. (2012).

[25] V. Wikström, S. Overstall, K. Tahiroğlu, J. Kildal, and T. Ahmaniemi. Marsui: malleable audio-reactive shape-retaining user interface. In *CHI Extended Abstracts on Human Factors in Computing Systems*. ACM (2013).

Investigating Intrusiveness of Workload Adaptation

Felix Putze
Cognitive Systems Lab
Karlsruhe Institute of Technology
Karlsruhe, Germany
felix.putze@kit.edu

Tanja Schultz
Cognitive Systems Lab
Karlsruhe Institute of Technology
Karlsruhe, Germany
tanja.schultz@kit.edu

ABSTRACT

In this paper, we investigate how an automatic task assistant which can detect and react to a user's workload level is able to support the user in a complex, dynamic task. In a user study, we design a dispatcher scenario with low and high workload conditions and compare the effect of four support strategies with different levels of intrusiveness using objective and subjective metrics. We see that a more intrusive strategy results in higher efficiency and effectiveness, but is also less accepted by the participants. We also show that the benefit of supportive behavior depends on the user's workload level, i.e. adaptation to its changes are necessary. We describe and evaluate a Brain Computer Interface that is able to provide the necessary user state detection.

Keywords

Workload adaptive assistance; Brain Computer Interface; User Study; Intrusiveness

Categories and Subject Descriptors

H.5.2 [**Information Interfaces and Presentation (e.g. HCI)**]: User Interfaces

1. INTRODUCTION

Since the beginning of the century, researchers in Human-Computer Interaction (HCI) systematically strive to design natural and intuitive user interfaces. One important aspect to achieve this goal is the design of adaptive interfaces which can react appropriately to the user's affective or cognitive state. Doing so requires two components: A recognizer which is able to detect the manifestation of a certain user state and an interaction manager with an adaptation strategy to react to the detected state. An important category of user state recognizers are passive Brain Computer Interfaces (BCIs) which use Electroencephalography (EEG) to determine the mental state of a user, for example the mental workload of a user [14]. A workload BCI offers potential benefits for HCI, especially in professional environments where specialists have to operate complex,

ICMI'14, November 12–16, 2014, Istanbul, Turkey.

ACM 978-1-4503-2885-2/14/11 ...$15.00.

dynamic and demanding user interfaces under time pressure. Adaptive interfaces in such scenarios have a huge potential of supporting a user when their mental workload rises, for example caused by the difficulty or number of tasks or due to external distractions. If not enough cognitive resources are available to satisfy all those demands, performance will drop and mistakes will occur, potentially with dire consequences. An adaptive interface is able to remedy those consequences by simplifying the interface or by simplifying the task by providing support in form of (partial) automation when high workload is detected. In this paper, we describe a study which compares different strategies designed to support a user in a complex, interactive task in high workload situations. A main contribution of this work is that we do not only look at the objective benefits of supporting the user but also at usability side effects of adaptive automation, namely the level of intrusiveness of a support strategy.

2. RELATED WORK

The general feasibility of workload BCIs has already been documented in the literature. For example, Lei et al. [15] used EEG to assess driver's workload. They used a simulated driving task and a secondary n-back memory task. They showed significant effects of task difficulty and multitasking in power spectrum, e.g. power attenuation in the α-band with increased working memory load. Murata et al. [16] recognized different workload levels in a continuous matching task where workload was controlled by levels of task difficulty. They used wavelets to estimate spectograms of each block for workload classification. Berka et al. [2] used simulated combat scenarios with five levels of difficulty assigned. EEG band power features were used to classify workload levels on epochs of one second length. Dijksterhuis et al. [5] recorded data from 34 participants in a driving simulator. They used stages of different driving demand levels to induce different levels of workload. Common Spatial Patterns (CSPs) were applied to generate person-specific spatial EEG filters for feature extraction. Wang et al. [17] controlled workload using different levels of difficulty of the Multi-Attribute Task battery. The authors concentrated on cross-person classification with a hierarchical Bayesian model trained on data from multiple participants. They achieved a recognition accuracy of 80% for person-independent classification on a corpus of eight participants.

Workload BCIs have been used in the literature for the development of workload adaptive user interfaces. For example, Wilson et al. [18] evaluated workload recognition for the Multi-Attribute Task Battery. In high workload condition, two of the subtasks were turned off and the authors showed that this adaptation improved the performance for the remaining tasks drastically. Kohlmorgen et al. [13] showed that a real-time detection of workload can be successfully used to manage distractions while driving in real driving situations by suppressing certain tasks during high workload. Chen et al. [3] employed a similar adaptation mechanism to reduce distraction by cell phone notifications in high workload situations. In [19], participants controlled a remotely piloted aircraft in scenarios with variable difficulty levels. The authors successfully evaluated an adaptation mechanism which reduced task speed and memory load when high workload is detected. Christensen et al. [4] used a similar scenario. Their presented system providds support in the form of target highlighting. They showed significant improvements compared to the non-adaptive baseline, but only after the user trained with the system for two days. Bailey et al. [1] compared the effect of adaptive automation versus adaptable automation for two different tasks. The authors saw that performance increases and subjectively perceived workload decreased for the adaptive system which does not require user-initiated intervention. They also observed that for the adaptable case, users hesitate to manually activate automation even in situations in which they would benefit from doing so.

The studies on workload adaptive systems cited above all concentrate on objective performance metrics to document the success of adaption. However, less attention has been payed to subjective criteria of usability, namely user satisfaction. This is surprising because meta-studies [7, 11] indicated that objective and subjective usability criteria are only weakly correlated and sometimes even contradictory. One example of a more thorough usability evaluation of an adaptive interface (but outside the context of workload adaptation) was given by Gajos et al. [8]. They explored different adaptation strategies to promote functionality which was frequently or recently used in the past. They investigated both the perceived benefits as well as the perceived costs (e.g. caused by sub-optimal choices of the system or its unpredictability) and showed that even slightly different strategies are located at different spots in the benefit-cost space. They also show that there is no general relationship between perceived benefit and user satisfaction.

In the present paper, we try to close the gap on subjective evaluation of adaptive interfaces. For this purpose, we focus on multiple usability aspects of adaptive automation, as acceptance of a support strategy is a critical factor for its success. In [10], Heger et al. documented that adaptive switching between different behavior styles based on the workload estimate of a BCI improved both effectiveness and user satisfaction. In that study, the design of the supportive behavior was straight-forward as it transformed the presentation style of the system and did not interfere with the task directly. In cases where explicit support of the user is desired, the designer of an adaptive strategy has to chose between several possible behaviors. We believe that one of the major factors which determines the acceptance of supportive behavior is its level of intrusiveness; a highly intrusive support might be able to provide more substantial help, but risks be rejected by its users. In the present work, we conduct a user study to investigate this trade-off to determine how a workload-adaptive system can optimally support the user. To our best knowledge, this is the first evaluation of workload adaptive interfaces which addresses side effects of adaptation like intrusiveness.

3. METHODOLOGY

The goal of the presented study is to systematically investigate support strategies with different levels of intrusiveness. We do so for a scenario which realistically reflects the demands of a complex task: A constant stream of inputs which require the user's attention, planning and decision making under time pressure and multitasking. Those are requirements typical for a profession like emergency call agent, air traffic controller or dispatcher.

3.1 Task Design

More concretely, the participants of the study are told to work as a dispatcher in a factory, allocating workers with different skills to different upcoming requests. Requests appear randomly in a list. Each request has a title (e.g. 'mechanical defect in factory 2') and a skill requirement. Each request is also assigned a timeout, which is unknown to the user, after which it disappears and is marked as failed. Each worker has a primary skill and a secondary skill. The user is instructed to assign workers which match the required skill with their primary or at least secondary skill. Only if neither is possible, an unskilled worker is still better than letting the request go unaddressed. The quality of the assignment also depends on the time elapsed since the arrival of the request (shorter is better). When the worker is assigned, the request is removed from the list and the worker is disabled and unavailable for a period of time. As the number of workers is limited, this creates situations in which the user has to decide whether to wait for the return of a worker or to perform a sub-optimal assignment immediately. Each run of the task lasts for 3.5 minutes and has total of 30 requests. We call this primary task the *Dispatcher Task* (**DT**). It requires constant visual attention, quick decision making and planning, as assigning one worker may take away crucial options to handle other tasks satisfactorily. The frequent occurrence of new tasks maintains a constant workload level over the course of one run.

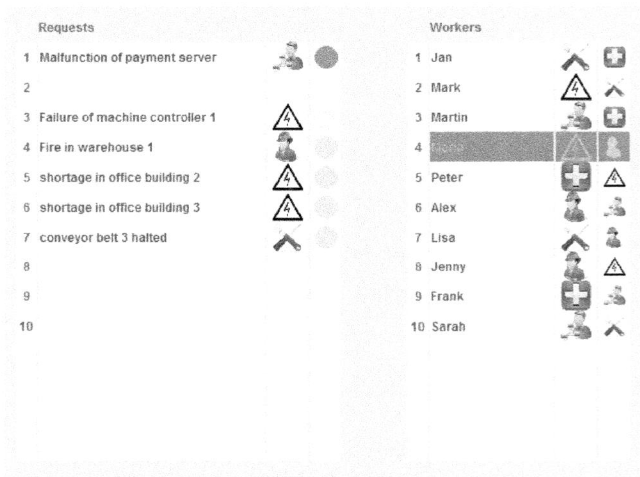

Figure 1: User Interface of the Dispatcher Task with list of requests on the left (with skill requirement and timer) and list of workers on the right (with primary and secondary skill). Workers marked in grey were already assigned and are not available.

In some configurations of the experiment, the participant is also handling an additional secondary task. This is a classification task which asks the user to sort out important messages from a constant flow of e-mails: The participant was asked to classify each message as either "spam" not "not spam" based on the occurrence of certain target words in subject line of the message. Entries which are not dealt with in a certain time window are discarded and scored as failures. This task runs in a second window on the same screen and requires the user to constantly divide their attention between the two tasks, making well-planned distribution of workers in the **DT** much more difficult. We call this secondary task the *Mail Task* (**MT**). We also refer to the configurations without **MT** as *low workload condition* and the configurations with **MT** as *high workload* *condition*. We will justify this naming scheme later by comparing subjective workload ratings.

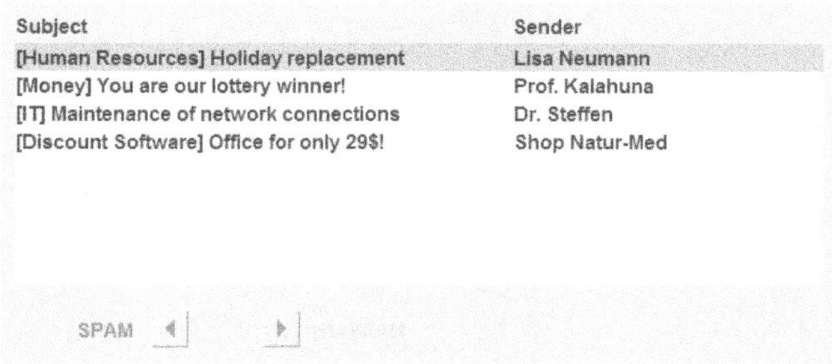

Figure 2: User Interface of the Mail Task, consisting of a list of e-mail headers which need to be classified as "spam" (red) or "no spam" (green).

3.2 Support Strategies

To relieve the participant in the high workload condition, we provide a virtual assistant which is able to intervene in the **DT** (e.g. by assigning workers to requests) and which can give advice and information to the user via synthesized speech. The behavior of the assistant is controlled by a *support strategy*.

We implement several support strategies. Those support strategies were designed to shift some of the decisions of the **DT** from the user to the system, thus reducing the number of required mental operations in a given time. The strategies differ mainly in their level of intrusiveness. More intrusive strategies are potentially more effective as they remove more decisions, but they also might reduce the level of control. Also note that the system is not omniscient concerning task timeouts and task requirements. More precisely, the system will perform optimal assignments only with a probability of 70%. If no such worker was selected (or none was available), the system selected a (random) worker with fitting secondary skill with a probability of 50%. If no such worker was selected (or none was available), it selected a (random) worker with no fitting skill. This procedure simulates the fact that in a typical use case in a professional environment, the user is an expert whose knowledge is difficult to reproduce automatically. It is instead approximated with an error prone heuristic. Therefore, the user will usually generate better results if no assistant is present and if they can fully concentrate on the task.

All support strategies are activated as soon as the number of present tasks passes a fixed threshold. The three (non-trivial) support strategies with decreasing level of intrusiveness are as follows: The `ACT` strategy, when activated, selects the oldest available task and assigns a worker to it. The strategy is constrained in that it may not act while the user has selected items to avoid interference with the user's decisions. The automatic assignment is then reported to user via speech synthesis with a statement that names the quality of skill match and the name of the removed task. This feedback is potentially useful as it informs them of the intervention and the resulting change in the task state. It also helps the user to judge whether dedicating more attention to the Dispatcher Task may improve assignment quality. However, ignoring the system statements does not influence the course of the task. The `OPT-OUT` strategy allows the user to exert more influence on the intervention of the system. Instead of directly executing an assignment, the system proposes it to the user by verbalizing it and by simultaneously marking it in a special color in the graphical interface. Again, those proposals are guaranteed to not interfere with a partial selection of the user. While the proposal is pending, the user can operate the task in the usual way. After five seconds, the proposal is executed (if still valid). The user has the ability to suppress this execution by pressing a button. In that case, the proposal is discarded and potentially replaced by a new one. The `OPT-IN` strategy further reduces the intrusiveness of the system. It generates and presents assignment proposals to the user in the same fashion as `OPT-OUT` does. The central difference is that for `OPT-IN`, the system requires a key press to accept and execute such a proposal. If not accepted within a certain period of time, the proposal is discarded and potentially replaced by a new one. For comparison, we call the 'support strategy' which does nothing and remains silent throughout a session `NONE`.

We made the design choice to use synthesized speech as output modality for all support strategies, as the visual load of both **DT** and **MT** is already high and because the participant can process verbalized information regardless of his focus of visual attention. While the strategies were mainly designed to support the user in a high workload situation, the system is not directly aware of the presence of a secondary task. If adaptive behavior is desired, we need to provide an external workload recognition.

3.3 Workload BCI

To provide adaptive behavior, the system has to recognize the user's workload level. The setup of the workload BCI mainly follows [10]: Classification is performed on windows of EEG data of 2s duration with an overlap of 1.5s. For preprocessing, the influence of ocular artifacts is reduced by performing Independent Component Analysis and automatically removing components containing artifact patterns. Frequency-based features (power of 28 frequency bins from 4 Hz to 45 Hz) are calculated for each electrode and then concatenated into a feature vector of 896 dimensions. A classifier based on Linear Discriminant Analysis is trained person-dependently on the binary classification task of separating low and high workload conditions. Temporal integration of the results of ten subsequent windows is performed to improve recognition stability. In contrast to [10], we perform an offline workload classification in this study, as we focus on the evaluation of the different support strategies.

3.4 Experimental Setup

The experimental setup is as follows: First, the participants were introduced to the Dispatcher Task with written and oral instructions. Following that, they performed several training runs of the task to familiarize with the keyboard layout and the task flow. Then, the order of the four support strategies was determined randomly and a block of four runs in that order was executed. Immediately before a run, the corresponding strategy was explained and demonstrated. After each run, the participant filled out a questionnaire on the user experience in that session (see Table 1). The questionnaire covered several aspects of user satisfaction which we deemed relevant for assessing the quality of a task. It included statements on subjective task performance, quality aspects of the system behavior, attribution of success and intrusiveness. The questionnaire used a five point Likert scale. Subjective workload was estimated using the NASA TLX questionnaire [9]. After the first block, the Mail Task was introduced and demonstrated. The participants performed a training run of the high workload condition. Again, the order of the four support strategies was determined and the participants performed a second block of four runs with subsequent questionnaires. In total, a participant performed eight runs plus two training runs, each with a duration of 3.5 minutes. This lead to a total recording time of 35 minutes for each participant. With this setup, we recorded a total of 16 participants. Participants were all university students or staff members. Mean age of participants was 22.1 ($\sigma = 3.6$); Five of the participants were female. Participants were paid 15 Euro for their participation in the study. 12 of those sessions were performed with EEG recordings for the analysis of a BCI for the classification of mental workload. EEG was recorded using a 32 channel BrainVision actiCap with active electrodes, sampled at 500 Hz and referenced at Pz.

Item	Text
Q1	I had no problems with handling the task.
Q2	I am content with my performance.
Q3	I pressed keys randomly.
Q4	I was in control of the task.
Q5	The assistant supported me.
Q6	I could work relaxedly.
Q7	I listened carefully to the assistant.
Q8	The assistant helped in a timely fashion.
Q9	I felt patronized by the assistant.
Q10	The assistant distracted me from the task.
Q11	I felt I was not up to the task.
Q12	The assistant allowed accurate task execution.
Q13	The assistant behaved intrusive.
Q14	The assistant allowed fast task execution.
Q15	I wanted to succeed without support.
Q16	Task success was on me.
Q17	It was pleasant to work with the assistant.
Q18	I had to work against the assistant.
Q19	I would chose to work with the assistant.

Table 1: Items of the user satisfaction questionnaire for the DT.

4. EVALUATION

For evaluation, we looked at three research questions: First, do the support strategies lead to an improved task performance and is there a difference in the extend how they do so? Second, how are different support strategies assessed subjectively by the participants? Third, do benefit and subjective rating of support strategies change with the workload condition? If this is the case, we can make a strong point for the application of adaptive system behavior, i.e. switching between support strategies, depending on the detected workload level.

4.1 Objective Performance Metrics

Before analysis, we filter the data corpus by sorting our participants which are *high performers*, who are able to handle the Dispatcher Task with a success rate of 100% even in the presence of the Mail Task and their Mail Task success rate is also $> 95\%$. For those participants, no assistance of any type can improve their performance and this will also influence their subjective assessment of the support strategies. Of the 16 participants, five fit the definition of a high performer. For the analysis of task performance and user satisfaction, we exclude those participants to avoid ceiling effects. From exploratory sessions, we estimated that high performers exhibit the same effects as outlined below for a higher task difficulty.

We employ three different performance metrics for the **DT** and one performance metric for the **MT**: For both, we measure success rate (*SR*) as the relative number of items that was handled before they expired. For the **DT**, we additionally evaluate reaction time (*RT*) as the time it took to deal with an item (only regarding items which were eventually dealt with at all) and assignment quality (*AQ*) as the average match between assigned worker skill and request requirements (assignment quality of 2 means a primary skill match, assignment quality of 1 is a secondary skill match and assignment quality of 0 is no match).

		DT *SR* [%]	**DT** *RT* [s]	**DT** *AQ* [Quality]	**MT** *SR* [%]
DT only	NONE	0.91	7.18	1.64	-
	OPT-IN	0.86	7.65	1.52	-
	OPT-OUT	0.93	7.04	1.63	-
	ACT	0.99	5.15	1.67	-
DT+MT	NONE	0.79	8.95	1.39	0.93
	OPT-IN	0.88	8.35	1.47	0.92
	OPT-OUT	0.87	8.30	1.48	0.95
	ACT	0.99	5.61	1.67	0.96

Table 2: Average performance metrics for Dispatcher and Mail Task.

Table 2 summarizes averaged performance metrics for all eight runs. We first note that, unsurprisingly, the mail task has a strong impact on the performance in the Dispatcher Task: The average success rate drops significantly[1] by 13.2% ($t = 3.23$, $p = 0.004$) between the low workload condition and the high workload condition for theNONE strategy; the average skill match drops significantly by 15.2% ($t = 3.13$, $p = 0.005$) and the average reaction time rises significantly by 24.7% ($t = 2.38$, $p = 0.02$). Furthermore, the raw subjective workload index (unweighted sum of all TLX items) rises significantly by more than 30% ($t = 3.97$, $p = 0.001$).

In the low workload condition, performance is not influenced much by the employed strategies. There is a maximum improvement in *SR* of 8.2% for ACT compared to NONE, but also a decrease of 5.5% for OPT-IN compared to NONE. We see the same pattern for *AQ*. For *RT*, only ACT provides a substantial reduction compared to NONE. This is understandable as ACT is the only strategy where multiple assignments can be processed truly in parallel. Overall, the benefit of all support strategies is small. In the high workload condition, the gain of employing a support strategy is more substantial: *SR* now improves by 24.9% for ACT compared to NONE and overall, all strategies yield significantly higher *SR* than NONE ($t = 3.13$, $p = 0.005$ for ACT, $t = 3.24$, $p = 0.004$ for OPT-IN and $t = 2.11$, $p = 0.03$ for OPT-OUT). While in the low workload condition, there is no notable difference in *AQ*, in the high workload condition, there is an improvement in *AQ* of more than 20% for ACT compared to NONE ($t = 3.06$, $p = 0.006$). This means that under high workload, it is not only possible to handle more items, but the performed assignments are also better. This is an interesting result as the assistant is programmed to perform sub-optimally compared to an expert user. Also for OPT-IN and OPT-OUT, we see small improvements in *AQ* between 5% and 6%. *RT* is again only influenced positively by the ACT strategy. Overall, we see substantial improvements for the ACT strategy and positive effects for all three strategies. ACT increases all performance metrics to or above the levels of the low workload condition with the NONE strategy. Differences in task performance are also reflected in subjective workload assessment, measured by the TLX questionnaire. For example, the important item 'mental demand' drops significantly from 15.8 to 13.8 between NONE and ACT in the high workload condition ($t = 2.11$, $p = 0.03$) and there is

[1]For all differences reported as 'significant' in this section, this refers to a paired, one-sided t-test with $\alpha = 0.05$. Tests were family-wise error-corrected for multiple testing using the Bonferroni-Holm method. We report the t-value and the resulting p-value for each test.

a similar trend for the other TLX items. On the other hand, the OPT-IN strategy basically shows no difference in those dimensions compared to ACT. For the low workload condition, OPT-IN and OPT-OUT even increase the subjective workload index as they impose additional decisions on the user.

Id	Loading Items (Correlation)	Interpretation
F1	Q8 (0.87), Q12 (0.78), Q14 (0.76)	objective benefit of assistant
F2	Q9 (0.88), Q13 (0.93), Q18 (0.61)	intrusiveness of assistant
F3	Q2 (0.96), Q4 (0.65), Q6 (0.50)	task control
F4	Q10 (0.73), Q15 (0.69), Q16 (0.51), Q18 (0.52)	desired independence
F5	Q1 (0.92), Q3 (-0.60), Q7 (0.56)	overload

Table 3: Result of the factor analysis for user satisfaction questionnaire items.

4.2 User Satisfaction Metrics

Next, we analyze the answers for the questionnaires to evaluate how participants judge the different supporting strategies. A general summary of this judgment is given by the overall acceptance (Q19) of the strategies. Compared between runs with and without **MT**, acceptance for all three strategies improves for the high workload condition. This is explained by participants reporting that they are less ambitious to handle the task completely on their own in the high workload condition compared to the low workload condition (agreement to Q15 drops by 30.1% averaged across all strategies). This result is highly relevant for the application of adaptive user interfaces as it shows that a supportive behavior must not simply be activated all the time to be helpful, but must adapt to the user's workload level. The ranking of the strategies derived from acceptance: OPT-IN is significantly preferred to OPT-OUT ($t = -2.72$, $p = 0.006$) which is preferred to ACT (although the difference is less pronounced and therefore not significant: $t = -1.02$, $p = 0.16$). This means the order of preference is reversed compared to the order derived from performance improvement. Such discrepancy between objective performance metrics and subjective user satisfaction is long known in usability research [7]. To our knowledge, our study documents such relationship between objective and subjective usability metrics for the first time in the context of adaptive automation. When taking a more detailed look at the items of the questionnaire, we see that those cover different aspects of the interaction. To group those items, we perform an explorative factor analysis with Varimax rotation on all items except Q19. We extracted five factors, which in total explain more than 70% of the variance in the data. The resulting factors are summarized in Table 3. We see that the items of the questionnaire are grouped together in an interpretable way, representing objective benefit of the assistant, its intrusiveness, the amount of control exerted by the participant, the desired level of independence and the level of experienced overload. This result shows that there are actually different independent aspects of user satisfaction covered by the questionnaire. To discern the effect of workload conditions on the different factors and to analyze the influence of the factors on overall acceptance, we need to investigate them separately.

Table 4 presents the item scores for the different strategies, averaged across the items loading on the corresponding factors. We see significant differences between strategies for F1, F2 and F3. In contrast, differences for F4 and F5 are not significant. This means that participants perceive the objective benefits (F1) of ACT compared to OPT-OUT ($t = -1.76$, $p = 0.047$) and of OPT-OUT compared to OPT-IN ($p = 0.09$). On the other hand, they also evaluate ACT as much more intrusive (F2) compared to OPT-OUT ($t = 4.47$, $p = 0.0007$) which is perceived as slightly more intrusive than OPT-IN (however not significantly: $t = 0.68$, $p = 0.25$). This indicates that participants perceive task execution by the system itself as more intrusive, not the mode of presentation. Furthermore, participants also felt more strongly that they lost control over the task (F3) from OPT-IN to OPT-OUT ($t = 3.66$, $p = 0.001$) and from OPT-OUT to ACT ($t = 3.31$, $p = 0.002$). F4, i.e. the desire for independence from the assistant, on the other hand does not vary with strategy and seems to be a more stable personality trait. Experienced overload (F5) also does not change with the strategy. This is in line with the observation that none of the six workload dimensions of the NASA TLX correlates significantly with acceptance ($r \leq 0.19$ for all dimensions).

As the overall acceptance item Q19 was excluded from factor analysis, we can now predict this item from the resulting factors. For this purpose, we estimate a linear regression model with Q19 as dependent variable and F1, ..., F5 as independent variables. In the result, the overall model achieves an r^2 of 0.51. Looking at individual factors, F2 and F4 are significant predictors of Q19 ($p = 0.0001$ and $p = 0.04$, respectively) and most strongly influence the overall acceptance of the system, while the influence of the objective benefits of the assistant (i.e. F1) is not significant. Of those influential factors, F2 varies strongly between OPT-IN and the other two strategies, and is slightly more positive for OPT-OUT compared to ACT, but not significantly. This explains the observed preference pattern reflected by Q19, which behaves analogously. The fact that F4 ("'desired independence") is also a predictor of acceptance indicates that not only situational workload plays a role for strategy acceptance, but also the user's personality.

	F1	F2	F3	F4	F5
OPT-IN	2.80	3.53	3.92	2.83	2.78
OPT-OUT	3.01	2.94	3.17	2.83	2.52
ACT	3.41	2.82	2.41	2.92	2.88

Table 4: Scores for the different support strategies summarized for the factors from Table 3

4.3 Workload BCI Evaluation

We finally evaluate the recognition accuracy of the workload recognizer. We assign to all data from the low workload conditions of one participant the label LOW and assign to all data from the high workload condition the label HIGH. For this binary classification problem, we perform the analysis offline in a person-dependent 16-fold cross-validation. Overall, we see a recognition accuracy of 75.8%, with an standard deviation of 16.8%. If we exclude one participant for which technical problems compromised data quality of some electrodes, recognition accuracy improves to 79.3% with a standard deviation of 12.1%. This indicates that the system is able to reliably differentiate between the different workload levels, with similar accuracy as reported in related work (see first Section). Given that the training material is very heterogeneous, this is a satisfying result. [10] showed that a recognition accuracy in a similar range already allows adaptive automation with substantial improvements in task performance and user satisfaction compared to non-adaptive systems.

In a seminal work, Fairclough [6] dealt with fundamental issues of physiological computing. Following this work, it is important to reflect about the "specificity of the psychophysiological inference" and the "psychophysiological validity" of the workload recognizer. Concerning specificity, the investigated workload recognizer is limited by the fact that it is trained on only one combination of primary and secondary task. However, when we studied related works (see first Section), we saw that frequency-based EEG features react specifically to high workload levels for a variety of different task selections. We can therefore conclude that despite a limit evaluation data set, the learned ability for class discrimination is specific to workload. One limitation of the present workload evaluation regarding psychophysiological validity is the fact that the order of the workload conditions is fixed (in contrast to the order of the support strategies). This can potentially bias the workload classifier towards learning temporal effects instead of workload differences. However, Jarvis et al. [12] showed that the employed workload classifier was robust against such ordering effects. As the classification setup in [12] was similar to the present one, we are optimistic that this robustness also transfers to the workload classification in the present work. Note that this ordering limitation will not substantially influence the relative behavioral results of the study. In general, participants improve their skills on both **DT** and **MT**, i.e. switching the order of workload conditions would only emphasize the benefit of the support strategies which we showed in the evaluation.

5. DISCUSSION

There are three main points we conclude from this user study: First, it is technically possible to estimate the workload level of a user in the employed scenario. Second, supporting behavior is helpful to the user and generally accepted, but only in the high workload condition. This shows the importance of adaptive user interfaces which turn on assisting behavior only when required. Third, and most importantly, the level of intrusiveness is a major determinant of how well a specific support strategy is perceived. The objectively most successful support strategy was ranked low compared to a more acceptable, less intrusive alternative. The results give no easy indication on what strategy is optimal in the given scenario. A designer will have to decide whether an additional performance gain is worth the cost of discontented users. This decision will for example be driven by the costs of mistakes during the main task. A reliable workload classifier can help to only activate such intrusive support when necessary to reduce the negative effect on user satisfaction to a minimum. Although the employed main task was presented with a cover story of a dispatching scenario, it is abstract in nature so we expect results can be transferred to any task with the same main properties, i.e. 1) heterogeneous but frequent inflow of requests, 2) distraction by a secondary task and 3) the property that work can be freely and independently distributed between human operator and machine. Examples of such tasks are air traffic control or crisis management.

Besides the rather small sample size (as five participants had been excluded as high performer) which limits the power of statistical analysis, one limitation of this study is the fact that workload recognition is performed offline. We argue that previous research indicates that online workload recognition is feasible at performance levels which are sufficient to provide significant usability improvements. Still, an analysis with an online workload recognizer for selection of supporting behavior would introduce realistic errors. Another limitation is that the strategies we investigated in this work are limited to local decisions, i.e. each request is treated independently. This is helpful as it maximizes the flexibility of the system and allows immediate switching between different behaviors. As the inflow of future tasks cannot be predicted by the system or the user, this flexibility is needed. Still, in slightly different scenarios, long-term variants of the presented strategies (which would store the user's decision on desired support over a certain period of time) could provide a more efficient and less intrusive behavior.

6. REFERENCES

[1] Bailey, N. R., Scerbo, M. W., Freeman, F. G., Mikulka, P. J., and Scott, L. A. Comparison of a brain-based adaptive system and a manual adaptable system for invoking automation. *Human Factors: The Journal of the Human Factors and Ergonomics Society 48*, 4 (2006), 693–709.

[2] Berka, C., Levendowski, D. J., Ramsey, C. K., Davis, G., Lumicao, M. N., Stanney, K., Reeves, L., Regli, S. H., Tremoulet, P. D., and Stibler, K. Evaluation of an EEG workload model in an aegis simulation environment. In *Defense and Security*, vol. 5797 (2005), 90–99.

[3] Chen, D., and Vertegaal, R. Using mental load for managing interruptions in physiologically attentive user interfaces. In *Extended Abstracts on Human Factors in Computing Systems* (USA, 2004), 1513–1516.

[4] Christensen, J. C., and Estepp, J. R. Coadaptive aiding and automation enhance operator performance. *Human Factors: The Journal of the Human Factors and Ergonomics Society* (2013), 0018720813476883.

[5] Dijksterhuis, C., Waard, D. d., and Mulder, B. L. J. M. Classifying visuomotor workload in a driving simulator using subject specific spatial brain patterns. *Frontiers in Neuroprosthetics 7* (2013).

[6] Fairclough, S. H. Fundamentals of physiological computing. *Interacting with Computers 21*, 1–2 (2009), 133–145.

[7] Frøkjær, E., Hertzum, M., and Hornbæk, K. Measuring usability: are effectiveness, efficiency, and satisfaction really correlated? In *Proceedings of the Conference on Human Factors in Computing Systems* (New York, USA, 2000).

[8] Gajos, K. Z., Czerwinski, M., Tan, D. S., and Weld, D. S. Exploring the design space for adaptive graphical user interfaces. In *Proceedings of the Working Conference on Advanced Visual Interfaces* (New York, USA, 2006).

[9] Hart, S. G., and Staveland, L. E. Development of NASA-TLX (task load index): Results of empirical and theoretical research. In *Advances in Psychology*, vol. 52 of *Human Mental Workload*. North-Holland, 1988, 139–183.

[10] Heger, D., Putze, F., and Schultz, T. An EEG adaptive information system for an empathic robot. *International Journal of Social Robotics 3*, 4 (2011), 415–425.

[11] Hornb\a ek, K., and Law, E. L.-C. Meta-analysis of correlations among usability measures. In *Proceedings of the SIGCHI Conference on Human Factors in Computing Systems*, CHI '07, ACM (New York, NY, USA, 2007), 617–626.

[12] Jarvis, J., Putze, F., Heger, D., and Schultz, T. Multimodal person independent recognition of workload related biosignal patterns. In *Proceedings of the 13th International Conference on Multimodal Interfaces*, ICMI '11, ACM (New York, NY, USA, 2011), 205–208.

[13] Kohlmorgen, J., Dornhege, G., Braun, M., Blankertz, B., Müller, K.-R., Curio, G., Hagemann, K., Bruns, A., Schrauf, M., and Kincses, W. Improving human performance in a real operating environment through real-time mental workload detection. In *Toward Brain-Computer Interfacing*. 2007, 409–422.

[14] Kothe, C., and Makeig, S. Estimation of task workload from EEG data: New and current tools and perspectives. In *Proceedings of the Engineering in Medicine and Biology Society* (2011), 6547–6551.

[15] Lei, S., and Rötting, M. Influence of task combination on EEG spectrum modulation for driver workload estimation. *Human Factors 53*, 2 (2011), 168–179.

[16] Murata, A. An attempt to evaluate mental workload using wavelet transform of EEG. *Human Factors 47*, 3 (2005), 498–508.

[17] Wang, Z., Hope, R. M., Wang, Z., Ji, Q., and Gray, W. D. Cross-subject workload classification with a hierarchical bayes model. *NeuroImage 59*, 1 (2012), 64–69.

[18] Wilson, G. F., Lambert, J. D., and Russell, C. A. Performance enhancement with real-time physiologically controlled adaptive aiding. *Proc. of the Human Factors and Ergonomics Society Annual Meeting 44*, 13 (2000), 61–64.

[19] Wilson, G. F., and Russell, C. A. Performance enhancement in an uninhabited air vehicle task using psychophysiologically determined adaptive aiding. *Human Factors 49*, 6 (2007), 1005–1018.

Smart Multimodal Interaction Through Big Data

Tosun, Cafer
SAP SE
Berlin, Germany
cafer.tosun@sap.com

ABSTRACT

Smart phones and mobile technologies have changed software usage dramatically. Ease of use and simplicity has made software accessible to a huge number of users. In addition, technological advancements in multimodal interaction are opening new frontiers in software. Users are interacting with software systems through multiple channels such as gestures and speech. Touch screens, cameras, sensors, and wearable devices are enablers of this interaction.

The user expectation is that the interaction with business software also becomes as simple as the interaction with consumer software. In particular, through the usage of mobile devices, consumer and business software is coming closer together.

Moreover, life is becoming more and more connected. We can observe this increasing connectivity in multiple categories:

1. Connected Processes: creating networks of businesses and new processes.
2. Connected People: through social media.
3. Connected Devices: as part of the Internet of Things; enabling smart homes, connected cars, M2M and Industry 4.0.

Also, these categories are becoming connected with each other and eventually turning into a world of "connected everything". In such a connected world, we need new ways of smart and contextual interactions. The connectivity leads to a huge increase in data. Such big data is opening new possibilities and opportunities, which can be used to enhance smart multimodal interaction. In-memory technologies such as SAP HANA can increase context sensitivity and make multimodal interaction smarter. It also provides instant contextual information to increase the ease of use.

Sensor rich machines, from aircrafts to manufacturing robots, collect vast amount of data, enabling real-time machine health monitoring. Using big data and applying data mining techniques enables predicting machine failure before it happens, notifying the technicians and starting the ordering process for the necessary parts ahead of time. During this process, user experience can be enhanced and technician's work can be simplified with the use of mobile and wearable devices. Looking at the machine with an intelligent goggle, a technician can get a report on the machine health, create work orders and initiate the maintenance process. A tablet with an animated 3D model of the broken machine will then support the technician throughout the repair process.

Not only business software and industries, but also the entire society is affected by this trend. Schools and education will utilize multimodal capabilities, turning schools into smart schools. Virtual classrooms using augmented reality are going to revolutionize education. In addition to enhancing the learning process, it will also catalyze sharing of ideas.

In the field of sports, real-time data streams coming from wearable sensors and cameras are being used for performance-enhancing insights for players and coaches on the playfield. In healthcare, air quality of the cities can be monitored in real-time and provide recommendations for joggers on their mobile devices to help them pick their running routes to reduce exposure to air pollution.

Next generation software systems and applications will have to enable smart, seamless and contextual multimodal interaction capabilities. New tools, technologies and solutions will be required to increase the ease of use and to build the user experience of the future.

ICMI '14, Nov 12-16 2014, Istanbul, Turkey
ACM 978-1-4503-2885-2/14/11.
http://dx.doi.org/10.1145/2663204.2669985

Categories and Subject Descriptors

H.1.2 [User/Machine Systems]: Human information processing

General Terms

Performance, Design, Human Factors.

Keywords

User experience, Internet of things, Connected Living, Human-Computer Interaction, User-centered software, Augmented reality, SAP HANA, Interactive Software, Smart City

BIO

Cafer Tosun is Senior Vice President for Strategic Innovations at SAP. In his role he is responsible for the global strategic innovation programs at SAP. He heads all public research relationship with governments, strategic partners and universities. At the same time Cafer Tosun is the responsible executive Managing Director in charge of SAP Innovation Center in Turkey. Prior to his role he served as the Managing Director of SAP's first Innovation Center and was responsible for the joint projects with the Hasso Plattner Institute for Software Systems Engineering in Potsdam.

Cafer Tosun has been with SAP since 1993. In that time, he has held various development, consulting and management positions. He has worked 8 years in Silicon Valley in California. He studied computer science and is a certified project manager from Stanford University.

In 2012, Cafer Tosun has been appointed into the MIT Technology Advisory Board. He is Co-Chair of the Networked European Software and Services Initiative (NESSI). He is an executive board member of the Connected Living Organization and the CEO of the German Turkish Advanced Research Center (GT-ARC) for ICT.

Natural Communication about Uncertainties in Situated Interaction

Tomislav Pejsa*
University of Wisconsin-Madison
1210 West Dayton Street
Madison, WI, 53706
tpejsa@cs.wisc.edu

Dan Bohus
Microsoft Research
One Microsoft Way
Redmond, WA, 98052
dbohus@microsoft.com

Michael F. Cohen
Microsoft Research
One Microsoft Way
Redmond, WA, 98052
mcohen@microsoft.com

Chit W. Saw
Microsoft Research
One Microsoft Way
Redmond, WA, 98052
nick.saw@microsoft.com

James Mahoney
Black Lobster Digital Arts
30 Bucket Ln
Yarmouth, ME 04096
james@BlackLobsterDigitalArts.com

Eric Horvitz
Microsoft Research
One Microsoft Way
Redmond, WA 98052
horvitz@microsoft.com

ABSTRACT
Physically situated, multimodal interactive systems must often grapple with uncertainties about properties of the world, people, and their intentions and actions. We present methods for estimating and communicating about different uncertainties in situated interaction, leveraging the affordances of an embodied conversational agent. The approach harnesses a representation that captures both the magnitude and the sources of uncertainty, and a set of policies that select and coordinate the production of nonverbal and verbal behaviors to communicate the system's uncertainties to conversational participants. The methods are designed to enlist participants' help in a natural manner to resolve uncertainties arising during interactions. We report on a preliminary implementation of the proposed methods in a deployed system and illustrate the functionality with a trace from a sample interaction.

Categories and Subject Descriptors
H.1.2 **[Models and Principles]:** User/Machine System – *Human Information Processing*; H.5.2 **[Information Interfaces and Presentation]**: Multimedia Information Systems – *Audio input/outputs;* User Interfaces – *Natural Language*

General Terms
Algorithms; Human Factors

ICMI '14, November 12–16, 2014, Istanbul, Turkey.

http://dx.doi.org/10.1145/2663204.2663249

* Research conducted during an internship at Microsoft Research

Keywords
Embodied conversational agents; situated interaction; multiparty; uncertainty; grounding

1. INTRODUCTION
Physically situated, multimodal interactive systems often rely on probabilistic inferences drawn from multiple streams of noisy perceptual data. Multiple uncertainties come to the fore during interactions. For example, dialog systems reason about uncertainties that arise in recognizing natural language via measures of recognition confidence and may employ clarification strategies such as explicit or implicit confirmations to keep a conversation on track. Robots or virtual agents that interact with users in physically situated settings grapple with uncertainties extending well beyond speech. These systems use probabilistic models to continually make state inferences based on streaming evidence from multiple sensors such as cameras, microphones, and proximity sensors. They must reason about people engaging with the system as well as those in the periphery, considering their physical position, orientation, and motion, focus of attention, interaction roles, intentions, and relationships. Beyond reasoning about the presence and contents of speech, these systems must monitor engagement (understanding who is involved in the interaction, when participants are joining or leaving, *etc.*) and turn-taking (understanding who is talking to whom, who has the conversational floor, to whom they are releasing the floor, *etc.*) Uncertainties arise in each of these processes and managing communication becomes particularly challenging.

Physically situated conversational agents may have at their disposal the affordances of a virtual or physical embodiment, with the ability to communicate via facial expressions, posture, and gaze. Just as in human-human interaction, these nonverbal affordances can be leveraged and coordinated with verbal grounding acts, so as to communicate about and help to resolve uncertainties.

We present a methodology for reasoning and communicating about the multiple uncertainties that arise in multiparty situated dialog. We use entropy as a measure of uncertainty about inferred beliefs and consider the magnitude and the sources of each uncertainty. We introduce a set of policies to schedule and coordinate the production of verbal utterances and nonverbal behaviors that reflect the system's uncertainties. The affordances of embodiment (facial expressions, posture, and eye gaze) are leveraged to signal the inferred underlying causes of confusion and to direct signals to the users who are best positioned to assist with resolving the uncertainties. We have implemented the methodology in the context of a deployed, physically situated automated assistant.

We begin with a review of related work, followed by a description of the various types of inferences and associated uncertainties considered by a physically situated system. In Section 4, we describe the proposed approach and each of its components. In Section 5, we illustrate the approach with an analysis of a trace from a multiparty interaction with the implemented system. Finally, in Section 6 we summarize and present directions for future work.

2. RELATED WORK

In previous research in psycholinguistics, models of grounding [1] have been proposed to explain how participants establish and maintain mutual understanding over the course of the conversation. Participants coordinate their actions as they present utterances to each other, and they produce evidence of understanding in return. This evidence can come in multiple forms, *e.g.*, continued attention, a relevant next contribution, or an acknowledgement, such as a head nod or short verbal utterance (*"Uh-huh"*, *"Yeah"*, *etc.*). The latter acts are also referred to as feedback or backchannel responses [2]. Grounding is achieved if the provided evidence satisfies the grounding criterion [3], defined as follows: "The contributor [of the utterance] and the partners mutually believe that the partners have understood what the contributor meant to a criterion sufficient for the current purpose." If the grounding criterion is not satisfied, the contributing participant can initiate a repair, for example, by repeating or restating their previous utterance.

Computational models of grounding have also been proposed and have found practical implementation in human-computer interaction [4]. Such models include Traum's *grounding acts* model [5], which represents the grounding process as a series of communicative actions that serve specific functions, such as providing acknowledgment of understanding or requesting repair. An adaptation of the model has been proposed [6] within a framework for multiparty interaction with embodied agents, which considers conversation as a multilayer process requiring inferences about engagement, turn-taking, and utterance contents of multiple actors. Paek and Horvitz [7,8] explicitly model spoken dialog as decision-making under uncertainty. Their system uses Bayesian models to represent and infer uncertainty about the contents and targets of spoken utterances, requesting clarifications when uncertainty is high or when the expected value of seeking clarification is positive. Nakano et al. [9] propose an approach to multimodal, embodied grounding, which takes into account nonverbal grounding acts produced by users. Their system monitors users' gaze and head nods for evidence of understanding.

In addition to making inferences about the users' grounding acts, embodied agents need to produce coordinated verbal and nonverbal acts in response. Poggi and Pelachaud [10] propose a representation of communicative acts that decouples propositional content from performative aspects, mapping them to verbal utterances and nonverbal behaviors, respectively. Marsi et al. [11] model the agent's head motions and facial expressions to convey uncertainty about the information the agent is conveying through speech. Other work has focused on providing incremental embodied feedback to ongoing user utterances [12, 13], using verbal confirmations and clarification requests, as well as nonverbal cues such as head nods and facial expressions, to indicate the system's degree of understanding. The DeepListener system [8] uses verbal clarification requests paired with smooth shifting of the color of a glowing lens graphic to provide incremental feedback about the system's confidence and readiness to accept utterances.

Our work is related to the aforementioned efforts and aims to construct an integrative solution that enables embodied communication under uncertainty in situated, multiparty contexts. Like Traum and Rickel [6] and Paek and Horvitz [7, 8], we model conversation as action that happens at multiple levels, each supported by a different set of communicative competencies. The latter work also focuses on representations and handling of uncertainty. The main difference is that we focus on a broader range of communicative competencies, and construct an implementation that operates in the more complex context of a deployed multiparty, situated interactive system.

3. UNCERTAINTIES AND INTERACTION

Developing systems that are capable of engaging in interaction in physically situated settings leveraging multiple streams of sensory evidence hinges on a minimal set of communicative competencies, such as the ability to manage engagement and turn-taking and to recognize and understand speech. These competencies rely in turn on lower-level perceptual processes like vision and auditory scene analyses, and often involve probabilistic inferences. Inaccuracies in inferences can lead to failures at one or more levels of analysis, and ultimately to the breakdown of interaction.

Table 1 enumerates layered competencies for situated dialog and highlight key uncertainties encountered at each level. For concreteness, we shall focus on examples from the *Assistant* project. The Assistant is an embodied conversational agent that make continuous inferences about the presence and availability of its owner, and interacts with visitors on the handling of various administrative tasks, such as setting up meetings or relaying messages. The system is deployed outside its owner's office, and displays an animated, expressive head. A typical interaction might start with the Assistant looking up, making eye contact and saying, *"Hi, are you here to see [owner]?"*

Perception. Communicative competencies are anchored in a *perceptual layer*, which enables the system to sense its surrounding environment through the use of cameras, microphones, and other sensors. The visual channel often carries large amounts of information, and vision algorithms can be used to detect and track people in the environment, as well as their orientation, body pose, and gaze direction or visual focus of attention. Audio data, captured via microphone arrays, can be processed to infer the content and directional source of speech. Beyond sensing the physical environment, we also include in this category the processes that enable the system to access domain-specific information relevant for the task at hand. For instance, the Assistant has access to its owner's calendar and computing activities, as well as to inferences from predictive models about the expected cost of interruption of the owner, the probability distribution over time until the system's owner will return to his office or read email, and the likelihood of the owner attending particular meeting. Across all of these different channels, perception involves the use of probabilistic models, which produce beliefs over hidden world state variables, such as the location of a participant in the scene, their focus of attention, and the directions sounds are coming from. As these inferences underpin many of the higher-level communicative abilities, uncertainty and inaccuracies often propagate to the higher levels, where they can lead to interaction breakdowns.

Table 1: Uncertainties at various levels of processing modeled in the current implementation

Level	Uncertainty type	State variable	Potential uncertainty sources	Instances
Intention Recognition	Concept	Domain specific relevant intentions and information	UserIdentity, SpeechInputPresent, SpeechInputTarget, SpeechInputContents, SpeechInputSource	Per-concept
	UserIdentity	The identity (e.g. name) of a user	-	Per-user
Speech Understanding	SpeechInputTarget	Target of a spoken utterance	-	Per-input
	SpeechInputSource	Source of a spoken utterance	-	Per-input
	SpeechInputContents	Contents of a spoken utterance	-	Per-input
	SpeechInputPresent	Whether or not a spoken utterance was produced since the last system floor release	FloorReleaseDidAnyUserTake	1
Turn taking	FloorReleaseTarget	Target of the last user floor release	-	1
	FloorReleaseDidAnyUserTake	Indicates whether any user took floor since the last system floor release	FloorReleaseDidUserTake	1
	FloorReleaseDidUserTake	Indicates whether a given user took the floor since the last system floor release	-	Per-user
Engagement	Engagement	Whether a given user intends to be engaged with the system	FaceTracking	Per-user
Perception	FaceTracking	Whether a user is present at the location specified by the face tracker	-	Per-user

Engagement. A base-level challenge with interaction that must be resolved is that of initiating, maintaining, and terminating a connection with one or more participants in the conversation. We refer to this process as *engagement* [14]. In human-human interaction, engagement is a mixed-initiative process that involves verbal and nonverbal signals, including facial expressions, proximity, and body posture. In multimodal interaction, inferences about engagement intentions and actions are made with models that leverage lower-level perceptual and sensory evidence [15], such as a participant's location or focus of attention. Uncertainties may arise about whether a participant is still maintaining or terminating an interaction, or whether someone is initiating a new engagement. Inaccurate inferences may lead to incorrect initiations of engagement with people passing by, or to abrupt, early terminations of engagement while participants expect the interaction to continue.

Turn taking. Once engaged in an interaction, the system must coordinate with other participants on the production of verbal outputs throughout the conversation in a process known as *turn taking*. Like engagement, turn taking involves nonverbal signals and cues [16, 17, 18]. Managing multiparty turn taking is challenging and hinges on accurate tracking of several variables, including who is currently speaking or expected to speak, the sources and targets of utterances, and the floor control actions performed by the participants. The Assistant uses a turn-taking model [19] that relies on tracking which participant has the conversational floor, and the floor actions produced by each engaged participant, *e.g.* holding, taking, or releasing the floor. In this context, uncertainties can arise about which participant took the floor and to whom a floor release action is targeted towards. Making good turn-taking decisions, such as whether now is a good time for the system to start an utterance, depends on the probabilities inferred about who is likely to next start talking and when they will start [20] and inaccurate inferences about these variables may lead to interaction breakdowns. For instance, if the system misrecognizes a release of the floor by one participant to another as a release to the system, it may start talking at an inopportune moment, leading to a potential floor battle. On the other hand, if the system is not able to correctly recognize that a participant has taken the floor and has provided a response, it may pause for an unusually long time while waiting for the participant's turn, creating an awkward gap in the conversation.

Language understanding. Typically, automatic speech recognition and natural language understanding systems analyze the audio signal and produce an n-best list of hypotheses, which captures the belief over the contents of the utterance. In multiparty settings, systems must additionally identify the source and target of each utterance. Such an understanding of intentions and roles in a conversation is important in understanding contributions and in guiding plans for interaction. Left unchecked, uncertainty in speech recognition often leads to misunderstandings and can throw an interaction off track.

Intention understanding. At the next level, the contents of the decoded utterances must be placed in context and used in conjunction with the discourse history and other perceptual evidence to continuously track beliefs over the high-level user goals and intentions, as well as other world state information that are relevant to the task at hand. For instance, if the identity of a user is important for a given task, a physically situated system may update its belief over the identity by integrating probabilistic evidence from multiple decoded utterances across a clarification dialog about identity, *e.g.*, "*Sorry, did you say you're John?*", with evidence that is streaming continuously from a face recognizer. Inaccurate inferences at lower levels may lead to incorrect understanding at the intention level, *e.g.*, the system might incorrectly infer the user's identity on the basis of inaccurate facial recognition and speech recognition results.

In summary, uncertainties arise at many levels of the system, ranging from perceptual uncertainty (visual and auditory), to uncertainty about the state of the conversation (engagement and turn taking), to the higher-level uncertainty about intentions. We next discuss how we incorporate communications about important uncertainties into the interactions through nonverbal expressions and verbal utterances.

4. METHODOLOGY

We now describe methods that can provide interactive systems with capabilities to communicate about key uncertainties arising during an interactive session. Our goal is to give systems the ability to enhance interactive sessions by sharing uncertainties and enlisting the help of participants to resolve them—all in a natural manner. Key components of such capabilities include: (1) *uncertainty state estimation*—assessing and diagnosing relevant uncertainties in the system, (2) *uncertainty communication policy*—selecting and coordinating verbal and nonverbal behaviors that communicate one or more uncertainties, with a goal of enhancing interaction by sharing or working to reduce uncertainty, and (3) *uncertainty behavior execution*—rendering these behaviors.

Complex interactive systems often use layered inferences per considerations of modularity and tractability. As such, key variables typically depend on inferences made about other variables, as well as attributes observed in streams of perceptual information. For instance, inferences for engagement intention may leverage inferences about lower-level variables, such as tracking confidence, estimated visual-focus of attention, proximity, and motion. In light of such dependencies, multiple steps can be taken to resolve the degree of uncertainty about one or more variables deemed to be important in the success of an interaction. In the general case, plans for sharing the uncertainty for a target variable can be guided by computing the *expected value of information* over all influencing variables and seeking to identify observations or states that would best resolve the uncertainty. Beyond information value, plans for sharing and coordinating about uncertainties must also consider the constraints of available gestures and perceived naturalness of interaction. The general problem of computing policies for identifying and communicating about key uncertainties is a complex decision-theoretic challenge. Below, we describe key representation elements and an initial framework and implementation that we have developed. The implementation uses handcrafted heuristics for identifying and communicating about key sources of uncertainty arising during interactions.

4.1 Uncertainty State Estimation

We assume as a starting point an existing system that tracks the world state ($\boldsymbol{S}$) via probabilistic inference models, *i.e.*, for each *world state variable* $X_i \in \boldsymbol{S}$ (or *variable* in short), an inference model computes the *belief* over X_i, *i.e.*, $p(X_i)$. Variables may represent any relevant properties of an individual user (*e.g.*, engagement intention, floor action, goals and domain specific intentions), of an utterance (*e.g.*, its source, target, or contents), of a floor action, etc. The belief captures the system's probabilistic estimate for the variable's possible values.

We measure the uncertainty in the inferred belief of a variable X_i by computing the entropy $H(X_i)$, defined as:

$$H(X_i) = \sum_j -p(X_i = x_j^i) \log_b \left(p(X_i = x_j^i)\right)$$

We consider influences among X_i and other variables used in the estimation of X_i in considering plans for communicating about and resolving potential failures in understanding. We use a recursive *uncertainty state representation* that captures not just the magnitude of the uncertainty (entropy), but also contributing influences or sources of error.

Specifically, we define an *uncertainty state* u_i as a tuple consisting of the *world state variable* X_i, its *uncertainty score* $H(X_i)$, and a set of *uncertainty sources* U_i, which are other uncertainty states:

$$u_i = (X_i, H(X_i), U_i)$$

In the current implementation of the framework, we identify uncertainty sources based on heuristic rules, informed by the structure of inferences in the system. For instance, at the highest level of the communicative stack (Intention level in Table 1), our system reasons about *concepts*, state variables which capture domain-specific information such as user goals and intentions, *e.g.*, *IsPersonOnCalendar*, *IsLookingForOwner*, etc. The system's belief over concepts is typically updated based on speech recognition results. As a consequence, a low-confidence recognition result can give rise to uncertainty over the concept. In such a case, the lower level *SpeechInputContents* uncertainty would be assigned as a source of the *Concept* uncertainty. However, speech recognition confidence is not the only potential source leading to concept uncertainties. In Section 5 we present in more detail an example where concept uncertainty arises based on uncertainty about which user spoke the utterance (*SpeechInputSource* uncertainty). The set of uncertainty states implemented so far, together with their corresponding state variables and their potential sources are shown in Table 1.

4.2 Policies for Communicating Uncertainties

At any given time, based on its assessment of the uncertainties present, the Assistant must decide which uncertainties to communicate to the users and how to communicate them. The actions are guided by the *uncertainty communication policy*. Given the state of the art with perception and recognition, uncertainties generally abound in situated systems, to a much larger degree than in human-human interaction. For instance, the Assistant will be confused much more often than a human would be about where a person is, whether they are still engaged, and who is speaking to whom. Thus, it may not be useful and could even appear unnatural if all uncertainties that arose were communicated. The uncertainty communication policy judiciously selects among *multiple* uncertainty states that may exist at any given time, and coordinates the production of corresponding communicative behaviors *across time*. This must be done in a manner that focuses the effort on the uncertainties that are most critical to the task at hand, while working to keep the interaction natural and useful. In the most general sense, the policy must take into account not only the instantaneous joint uncertainty state over all variables, but the history and dynamics of the uncertainty state.

In an effort to alleviate challenges with coordination between verbal and nonverbal behaviors for communicating uncertainty, we structured the uncertainty communication policy into two sub-policies: (1) a *speaking policy* selects and triggers verbal dialog acts, whose production may be accompanied by synchronized nonverbal gestures, and (2) a *listening policy* selects and triggers nonverbal gestures that communicate uncertainty when the agent is not speaking. We now describe each of these components.

4.2.1 Speaking Policy

The task of a *speaking policy* is to trigger verbal dialog acts that alert users about uncertainty and attempt to resolve grounding failures. Given the current world state and joint uncertainty state, every time the system is about to take a turn, the speaking policy may decide to produce a dialog act, *i.e.* a set of verbal utterances, coupled with nonverbal behaviors, that communicates and attempts to resolve a given uncertainty. This is a two-step process. In the first step, a dialog act is constructed, specifying the *semantic content* that is being communicated (a semantic representation of the prompt, including the domain-specific information communicated or requested), a set of *addressees* (users at whom the act will be addressed), and an *uncertainty communication action* that captures the uncertainty states being communicated and the set of *resolving users*, *i.e.*, users expected to be involved in the resolution of these uncertainties. In a second step, the dialog act is mapped into a lexical form (prompt) accompanied by nonverbal behaviors, which are then rendered via the embodied agent.

In the most general case, speaking policies produce dialog acts that aim to clarify uncertainties over concepts, so the uncertainty communication action will typically reflect a *Concept* uncertainty state. As previously described, the *Concept* uncertainty state may in turn point to other uncertainties as its sources. This representation of uncertainty sources enables the speaking policy to

Figure 1. Nonverbal expressions of uncertainty.

construct a more refined rendering of the dialog act that communicates not just general uncertainty about a concept, but also indicates the suspected sources of this uncertainty. For instance, if the source of the *Concept* uncertainty is low recognition confidence, *i.e.*, *SpeechInputContents* uncertainty, the policy may trigger a dialog act requesting a confirmation or clarification. Another example, discussed in Section 5, has *SpeechInputSource* uncertainty attached as source of the *Concept* uncertainty. In this case, the speaking policy can trigger a dialog act that points to the problem ("*Sorry, I can't tell who is speaking...*") and asks for a clarification ("*Which one of you said they were John?*")

The set of resolving users specified as part of the uncertainty communication action is usually the same as the set of addressees; the system communicates the uncertainty to people who are expected to assist with its resolution. There are counter-examples, however. Sometimes concepts are not elicited from the users, but may be updated from external knowledge sources, *e.g.*, information about the owner's whereabouts and expected return time. When such information is uncertain, the uncertainty communication action does not specify any resolving users. As such, the produced verbal utterance and nonverbal behavior communicate the uncertainty in a way that does not explicitly solicit external help, for instance by producing a confused expression accompanied by a gaze avert (see example from Section 5.)

4.2.2 Listening Policy

The listening policy enables the system to communicate about uncertainty nonverbally, during listening periods, without committing to verbal dialog acts. This is in accordance with the principle of least joint effort in grounding [1], which states that partners in a conversation expend the minimal effort required to achieve mutual ground.

In general, the listening policy maps the various uncertainty states to certain nonverbal behaviors. For example, partial hypotheses generated by the speech recognizer during a user utterance may already indicate uncertainty about speech contents, as the utterance is in progress. Based on this, the listening policy can trigger a corresponding nonverbal expression of straining to hear, in an attempt to convey the uncertainty and also potentially shape future user behavior – in this case, speak more clearly. Similarly, a *FaceTracking* uncertainty is mapped to a straining to see expression, and so on. The set of expressions we have currently implemented is described in the next section.

When multiple uncertainties occur simultaneously, the listening policy must select which one to attend to. The prioritization is done based on two criteria. First, the system considers it more important to communicate uncertainty about things said or done by users who are currently involved in the interaction. The listening policy therefore prioritizes uncertainties pertaining to engaged users over ones pertaining to bystanders. Second, it is more critical to resolve uncertainties about communicative processes that are more fundamental to supporting the interaction. The listening policy therefore prioritizes uncertainties on the lower levels in the communicative stack (Table 1).

The listening policy also considers history when deciding whether it communicates about a particular uncertainty state. Specifically, we prevent excessive nonverbal feedback about the same communicative problem by using a simple principle: only one nonverbal communicative behavior is produced per listening stage for each uncertainty state.

4.3 Behaviors

Policies coordinate the production of verbal utterances and nonverbal behaviors to signal uncertainty. Nonverbal behaviors are constructed by coordinating facial expression changes, postural shifts, and eye gaze. In this section we provide a brief overview of the behaviors supported in our current implementation and explain the coordination mechanisms.

4.3.1 Facial Expressions and Posture

To support the production of nonverbal behaviors, we have developed a set of six predefined facial *expressions: StrainToHear, StrainToSee, StrainToPerceive, Bewildered, Confused, Understood.* These expressions were authored by a professional 3D artist, who was guided by his intuitions about human motion and prior literature on nonverbal expressions of uncertainty [21, 22].

Each expression includes both facial movements and posture changes. The expressions are parameterized by a continuous *intensity* score in the 0-1 interval. At the lower level, the animation procedure for each expression constructs a set of animation curves that smoothly animate the agent's facial expression and posture at the specified intensity. The construction of these curves involves a certain degree of randomization, so facial actions and posture shift directions are not always the same, even when the expression is triggered with the same intensity. Figure 1 shows the peak points of the six predefined expressions, applied at intensity 0.7.

The performance of nonverbal behaviors is carried out via a sequence of expression intensity updates. For listening policies, these updates are set to happen at predefined times. For example, when the listening policy executes the behavior for communicating *Engagement* uncertainty towards an engaged participant, the behavior first applies the *Bewildered* expression at intensity 0.15, then after 2.0 seconds it increases the intensity of the expression to 0.3. For speaking policies, expression changes are synchronized with verbal utterances via tags embedded into the prompts that can specify starting points, duration and intensities for expressions.

4.3.2 Eye Gaze

Apart from facial expressions and posture changes, the nonverbal uncertainty communication behaviors also control eye gaze. This is a particularly important affordance in multiparty interaction, as it enables the agent to unambiguously indicate addressees of communicative acts [23]. In the implementation, the agent relies on gaze to communicate uncertainty towards or to solicit help from specific participants.

Addressees for communicative acts about uncertainty are generally chosen on the basis of utility; the system conveys uncertainty to participants who are most likely to assist with resolution. In practice, this can mean gazing towards participants who are believed to be "responsible" for uncertainty in the first place. For example, when there is *SpeechInputContents* uncertainty about an utterance, the non-verbal feedback produced by the listening policy is accompanied by gaze towards the user who is the source of the utterance. In other cases, uncertainty signals are addressed at multiple parties; an example is the dialog act about *SpeechInputSource* uncertainty presented in Section 5. On the other hand, informing acts that communicate a *Concept* uncertainty not arising from the communicative process are accompanied by averted gaze (see example in Section 5), as the agent does not expect users' help in its resolution.

5. EXAMPLE

We implemented the methodology described above within a previously developed infrastructure for physically situated, spoken language interaction used to construct the Assistant [24]. We demonstrate the operation of the implementation with a sample interaction with the Assistant. In the scenario, two people arrive for a meeting with Zack, the Assistant's owner. The Assistant knows about the meeting from Zack's calendar, but only one person is expected to arrive for that meeting. In addition, Zack himself is not there at the moment. Both of these facts coupled with ambiguity in verbal interactions lead to various forms of uncertainty within this short interaction. This scenario was constructed to illustrate the various functional aspects of the proposed methodology. A trace of the interaction with relevant key frames is shown in Figure 2 and a video is available at http://1drv.ms/1uwhfrm.

At the beginning of the interaction, two participants enter in the space in front of the Assistant, as they approach Zack's office. They do not directly engage with the Assistant, rather they peer into the office (located to the left). During this time (segment A) the engagement inference model indicates that the probability that the participants are trying to engage is in the middle range, which leads to an increase in the uncertainty scores about engagement for both users – see *Engagement* scores, Figure 2.A. As the Assistant has not yet engaged in a conversation, the listening policies, based on the high uncertainty state, activate and trigger a *Bewildered* expression (Figure 2.A.1), which persists for a few seconds (Figure 2.A.2). Several seconds later, as participants turn their attention and orient towards the system, uncertainty about engagement intention dissipates, and the system begins the interaction (Figure 2.A.3).

Later in the dialog (segment B), the Assistant tries to determine if one of the participants is the person expected for the 2 o'clock meeting (captured by the concept *IsPersonOnCalendar*), by asking: "*Is one of you John?*" The left participant responds "*Yes*". As the utterance is being produced, information from the sound source localizer is used to infer which participant is speaking. As the participants are close together, there is high uncertainty about the utterance source (Figure 2.B, *SpeechInputSource* score, pink graph). Throughout the production of the utterance, the system is listening; the listening policy activates (Figure 2.B.1) and responds to the *SpeechInputSource* uncertainty by triggering the *Bewildered* expression at a low intensity. Once the utterance finishes, while its contents are correctly understood, because the utterance source is uncertain a *Concept* uncertainty state for *IsPersonOnCalendar* is constructed that points to the lower level *SpeechInputSource* uncertainty state as its source. The speaking policy constructs an appropriate grounding act that both points to the source of the problem "*Sorry, I can't tell who is speaking when you stand so close together*", and requests a clarification "*Which one of you said they're John?*" The production of this verbal utterance is coupled with a nonverbal *Bewildered* expression which temporally extends and increases the intensity of the *Bewildered* expression already started by the listening policy (Figure 2.B.2). Furthermore, since this grounding act is directed towards both participants, the Assistant's gaze shifts between them throughout the production of these utterances (see System Gaze in Figure 2.B).

Informed by the agent about the speech source inference issue, participants move apart and the left participant responds "*I did.*" (Figure 2.B.3) The utterance is recognized with fairly low confidence, but sufficient for current purposes. This time there is little *SpeechInputSource* uncertainty, and the Assistant considers the *IsPersonOnCalendar* concept grounded. The speaking policy first triggers a verbal grounding act that presents evidence of understanding, and then continues the interaction. The understanding act is rendered by saying "*Right!*" coordinated with a nonverbal *Understood* behavior, rendered as a head-nod and confident smile (Figure 2.B.4).

Next, the Assistant tries to determine whether the participant on the right will be joining the meeting (Segment C). At this point the participants move slightly back and start speaking softly to each other. As time elapses and the Assistant does not receive an utterance, the floor inference model leads to increased uncertainty in the system about whether any of the participants took the floor (see *FloorDidAnyUserTake* score, Figure 2.C.1). The listening policy responds by beginning a *Bewildered* expression at low intensity (Figure 2.C.1). Simultaneously, uncertainty about *Engagement* also increases. With both uncertainties present, the engagement issue takes precedence–as it is on a lower level of the communicative stack–and the corresponding policy continues the existing *Bewildered* expression at low intensity (Figure 2.C.2).

Eventually, after enough time has elapsed with no contribution detected from the users, the system decides to take the turn. The speaking policy checks the *Engagement* uncertainty for each user and, seeing that it is high for both, plans a dialog act that communicates the system's uncertainty: the Assistant produces a filled pause "*So…*" (Figure 2.C.3.) Note that, at the moment that the Assistant takes the turn, the *FloorDidAnyUserTake* uncertainty collapses, as now the system has the floor. As the participants start turning back towards the system, the *Engagement* uncertainty for the right participant is reduced (*Engagement* score, dark red graph), which triggers the next system contribution. The *UserJoiningMeeting* is still not grounded, and in this case the speaking policy produces a clarification request for that concept, accompanied again by an extension of the *Bewildered* expression.

After the participant on the right responds, the Assistant informs the participants that the owner might be running late (segment D). The dialog act (Figure 2.D.1) presents the concept *OwnerShortReturn*, which is ungrounded and has a high *Concept* uncertainty score (Figure 2.D, *Concept* score, green plot). The verbal utterance reflects the agent's uncertainty (*"I think Zack is running a little late."*) and is coordinated with the production of a nonverbal *Confused* expression (Figure 2.D.2). The dialog act is targeted at both participants, but the system does not solicit help from either of them to resolve the *Concept* uncertainty. For that reason the *Confused* expression is accompanied with a coordinated gaze aversion gesture, where the Assistant's gaze is directed upwards, away from the participants (indicated by the gray region on System Gaze track in Figure 2.D)

6. CONCLUSION

We discussed key uncertainties that can arise in physically situated interactive systems, explored methods for endowing a system with the ability to reflect about and share its uncertainties with people, and characterized the general challenge of identifying and resolving key uncertainties. We described a specific implementation based on

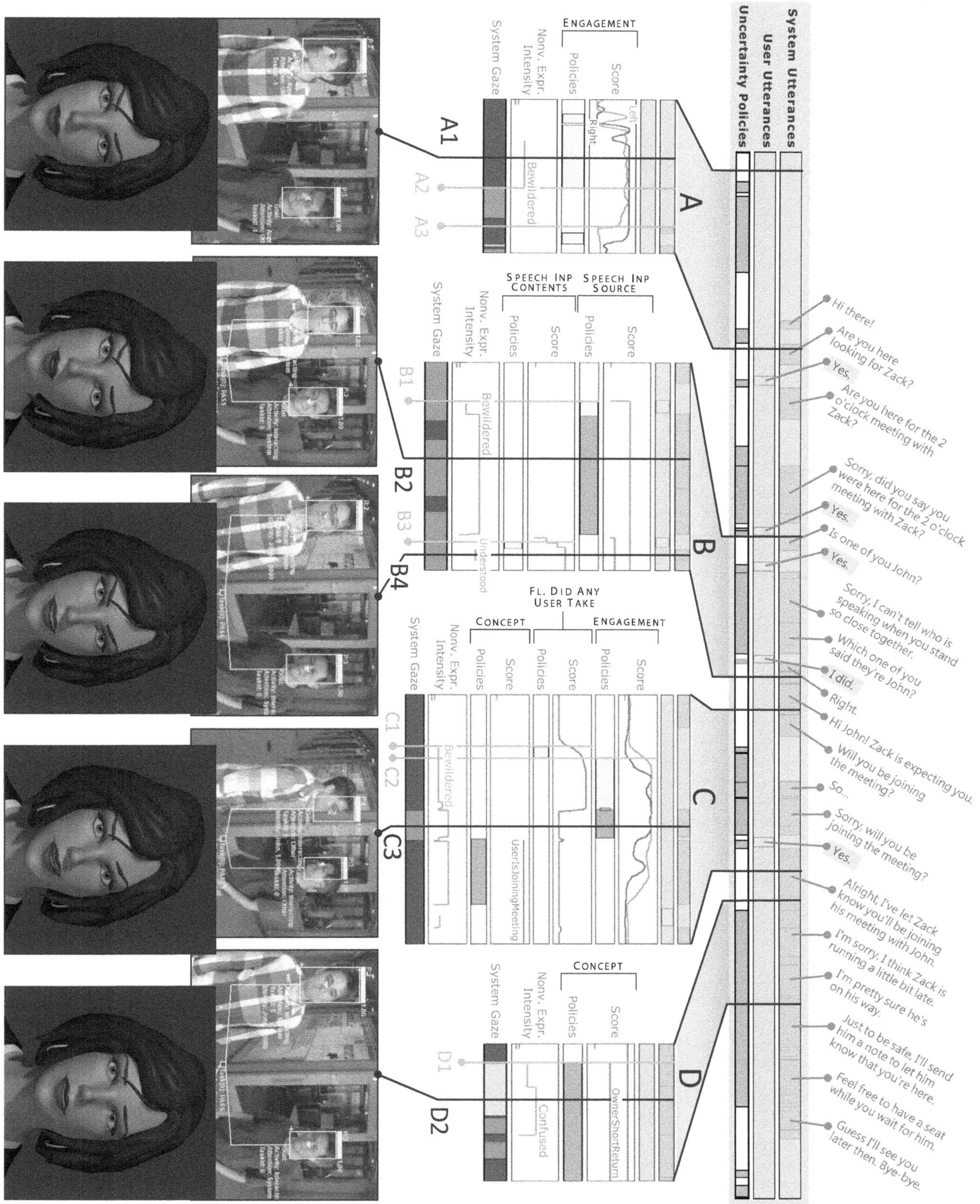

Figure 2. Trace of a demo interaction. (Top) System and user utterances, uncertainty policy activities. (Middle) Interaction segments, highlighting uncertainty scores (color-coded by the object of uncertainty; *purple* – right user; *blue* – left user; *green* – both users or concept), policy execution (*light yellow* – listening; *dark yellow* – speaking), nonverbal expression intensity, and system gaze (*purple* – right user; *blue* – left user; *grey* – averted gaze). (Bottom) System view and agent. In system view images, red dot is the agent's gaze target, yellow arrows indicate the participants' attention direction, while yellow lines show engagement.

a representation that captures both the magnitude and sources of uncertainty. We presented policies to coordinate the production of verbal utterances and nonverbal behaviors to communicate the system's uncertainties to the conversational participants and to enlist their help in resolving them. We illustrated the functionality of the proposed approach with a trace from an example interaction.

The described implementation, while still preliminary, provides a foundation for future developments and experimentation. Extensions to the approach include introducing uncertainty states for other inferences in the system, developing more sophisticated blame-assignment models to identify and communicate uncertainty sources, building robust, utility-driven policies that take into account the dynamics of uncertainty over time, and explicitly computing expected costs of persisting or resolving uncertainties when deciding whether to communicate about them. Finally, we have found that even subtle changes in the rendering of nonverbal expressions can have significant influence on the meaning seen in the signals by people, so we wish to further explore the rich lexicon of nonverbal uncertainty behaviors and their link to utterances.

The motivation for the work reported here lies in the hypothesis that, using the affordances of embodiment and communicating about uncertainty not only explicitly, but via the broader nonverbal channel, can lead to increased naturalness and efficiency in interaction. We expect that, in communicating its internal states of uncertainty, an agent may better convey to users its limitations, and implicitly shape their behavior so as to optimize interactions over time. We expect that such capabilities may have significant influence on user empathy and on the overall perceptions of the system. User studies will be required to test these hypotheses.

Finally, we note that uncertainty is only one factor in the successful grounding during the volley of contributions in conversational dialog. Other aspects include signaling about expectation and surprise, as well as expressing confidence and eureka following the resolution of key uncertainties, e.g., the *Understood* expression used in the example. We plan to continue work to understand and integrate other signals that may be useful in the engagement and overall grounding of communication and collaboration. We believe that the capability to express such rich internal states verbally and nonverbally, in stream with the evolving situation, will come to serve a central role in human-computer interaction.

ACKNOWLEDGMENTS

We thank Anne Loomis Thompson for her contributions to the project.

7. REFERENCES

[1] Clark, H. H., and Brennan, S. A. 1991. Grounding in Communication, *Perspectives on Socially Shared Cognition*. 127-149, Washington, DC.

[2] Yngve, V. 1970. On Getting a Word in Edgewise, *Proc. CLS 6*, 567-577.

[3] Clark, H. H., and Schaefer, E. F. 1989. Contributing to Discourse, *Cognitive Science*, 13, 259-294.

[4] Traum, D. R. 1999. Computational Models of Grounding in Collaborative Systems, *Proc. AAAI Fall Symposium on Psychological Models of Communication*, 124-131.

[5] Traum, D. R. A Computational Theory of Grounding in Natural Language Conversation. Ph.D. Thesis, Computer Science Dept., U. Rochester, December 1994.

[6] Traum, D. R., and Rickel, J. 2002. Embodied Agents for Multi-Party Dialogue in Immersive Virtual Worlds, *Proc, AAMAS'02*, 766-773.

[7] Paek, T., and Horvitz, E. 2000. Conversation as Action under Uncertainty, *Proc. UAI'00*, 455-464.

[8] Paek, T., and Horvitz, E. 2000. DeepListener: Harnessing Expected Utility to Guide Clarification Dialog in Spoken Language Systems, *Proc. ICLSP'00*, Beijing.

[9] Nakano, Y. I., Reinstein, G., Stocky, T., and Cassell, J. 2003. Towards a Model of Face-to-Face Grounding, *Proc. ACL'03*, 1, 553-561.

[10] Poggi, I., and Pelachaud, C. 2000. Performative Facial Expressions in Animated Faces, *Embodied Conversational Agents*, 155-188, Cambridge, MA.

[11] Marsi, E., and Rooden, F. 2007. Expressing Uncertainty with a Talking Head in a Multimodal Question-Answering System, *Proc. MOG'07*, 105-116, Enschede, The Netherlands.

[12] Kopp, S., Allwood, J., Grammer, K., Ahlsen, E., and Stocksmeier, T. 2008. Modeling Embodied Feedback with Virtual Humans, *Lecture Notes in Computer Science*, 4930, 18-37.

[13] Kopp, S., Stocksmeier, T., and Gibbon, D. 2007. Incremental Multimodal Feedback for Conversational Agents, *Lecture Notes in Computer Science*, 4722, 139-146.

[14] Sidner, C. L., Kidd, C. D., Lee, C., and Lesh, N. 2004. Where to Look: A Study of Human-Robot Engagement, *Proc. IUI'04*, 78-84.

[15] Bohus, D., and Horvitz, E. 2009. Learning to Predict Engagement with a Spoken Dialog System in the Open-World, *Proc. SIGdial'09*, London, UK.

[16] Duncan, S. 1972. Some Signals and Rules for Taking Speaking Turns in Conversation, *Journal of Personality and Social Psychology*, 23, 283-292.

[17] Sacks, H., Schegloff. E., and Jefferson, G. 1974. A Simplest Systematics for the Organization of Turn-taking in Conversation, *Language*, 50, 696-735.

[18] Wiemann, J., and Knapp, M., 1975. Turn-taking in Conversation, *Journal of Communication*, 25, 75-92.

[19] Bohus, D., and Horvitz, E., 2010. Facilitating Multiparty Dialog with Gaze, Gesture and Speech, in *Proc. ICMI'10*, Beijing, China.

[20] Bohus, D., and Horvitz, E., 2011. Decisions about Turns in Multiparty Conversation: From Perception to Action, in *Proc. of ICMI'11*, Alicante, Spain.

[21] http://center-for-nonverbal-studies.org/uncert.htm

[22] Stone, M., and Oh, I. 2008. Modeling Facial Expression of Uncertainty in Conversational Animation, *Lecture Notes in Computer Science 4930*, 57-76.

[23] Vertegaal, R., Slagter, R., Veer, G., and Nijholt, A. 2001. Eye Gaze Patterns in Conversations: There is More to Conversational Agents than Meets the Eyes, *Proc. CHI'01*, 301-308, Seattle, WA.

[24] Bohus, D., and Horvitz, E. 2009. Dialog in the Open World: Platform and Applications, *Proc. ICMI'09*, Boston, MA.

The SWELL Knowledge Work Dataset for Stress and User Modeling Research

Saskia Koldijk
ICIS, Radboud University
& TNO, The Netherlands.
s.koldijk@cs.ru.nl

Maya Sappelli
ICIS, Radboud University
& TNO, The Netherlands.
m.sappelli@cs.ru.nl

Suzan Verberne
ICIS, Radboud University, The Netherlands.
s.verberne@cs.ru.nl

Mark A. Neerincx
II, Delft University of Technology
& TNO, The Netherlands.
mark.neerincx@tno.nl

Wessel Kraaij
ICIS, Radboud University
& TNO, The Netherlands.
wessel.kraaij@tno.nl

ABSTRACT

This paper describes the new multimodal SWELL knowledge work (SWELL-KW) dataset for research on stress and user modeling. The dataset was collected in an experiment, in which 25 people performed typical knowledge work (writing reports, making presentations, reading e-mail, searching for information). We manipulated their working conditions with the stressors: email interruptions and time pressure. A varied set of data was recorded: computer logging, facial expression from camera recordings, body postures from a Kinect 3D sensor and heart rate (variability) and skin conductance from body sensors. The dataset made available not only contains raw data, but also preprocessed data and extracted features. The participants' subjective experience on task load, mental effort, emotion and perceived stress was assessed with validated questionnaires as a ground truth. The resulting dataset on working behavior and affect is a valuable contribution to several research fields, such as work psychology, user modeling and context aware systems.

Categories and Subject Descriptors

E.0 [**Data**]: General; H.1.2 [**Models and Principles**]: User/Machine Systems—*Human factors, Human information processing*; J.4 [**Social and Behavioral Sciences**]: Psychology

General Terms

Human Factors, Experimentation, Measurement

Keywords

Dataset; stress; mental state; facial expressions; body postures; computer interaction; physiology

ICMI '14, November 12 - 16 2014, Istanbul, Turkey

ACM 978-1-4503-2885-2/14/11 ...$15.00.
http://dx.doi.org/10.1145/2663204.2663257.

1. INTRODUCTION

Nowadays most work involves computer usage and information processing. People that use and produce information as their main task are called knowledge workers. They typically experience all sorts of demands during their work days, such as several tasks that need to be finished before a deadline (high workload, temporal demand). For this they need to combine different information sources, for example from the internet (requiring mental effort). Incoming emails may be an important source of distraction during a task (potentially causing frustration). In case people feel they cannot handle the demands posed upon them, they can experience stress [3]. Stress is a broad concept referring to psychological and biological processes during emotional and cognitive demanding situations. We follow a pragmatic approach and define stress in terms of: (1) the task load, which poses demands on the worker, (2) the mental effort, which the worker needs to handle a task and (3) the emotional response to a task. In this paper, we focus on short term effects of stressors that can be measured within a 3 hour work session.

Stress is a well-known experience in our connected environments. Ruff [16] speaks of 'hurry sickness' as "the belief that one must constantly rush to keep pace with time" and 'plugged in compulsion' as "the strong need to check mail and the internet to stay in touch". Mark, Gudith and Klocke [13] investigated the cost of interruptions and came to the conclusion that "after only 20 minutes of interrupted performance people reported significantly higher stress, frustration, workload, effort and pressure". Stress from time to time with enough room for recovery is no problem [2]. However, when stress builds up this can be a danger to well-being, in the worst case resulting in burn-out.

In our project SWELL (Smart Reasoning for Well-being at Home and at Work)[1] we aim to develop ICT tools that help knowledge workers to cope with stress and gain more well-being at work [8]. We want to interpret recordings in the office real-time in terms of stress and the context in which it appears. Based upon this information, we aim to develop coaching software that can help knowledge workers to gain a more healthy work style. Moreover, we want to develop smart information support tools that assist the knowledge worker in handling the large amount of (incom-

[1] `http://www.swell-project.net`

ing) information he has to work with. In this way, we extend traditional approaches (e.g. questionnaires or department wide interventions, [11, 12]) by empowering individual users to self-manage their own well-being.

To be able to develop the ICT tools we envision, research communities like work psychology, user modeling and context aware systems are in need of a good dataset. This dataset should ideally have the following characteristics: Data should be recorded in a realistic office setting. Stressors should be manipulated in a systematic way and subjective experience should be assessed with validated questionnaires, to be able to investigate the effects of stressors. A multimodal set of sensors from different research fields should be used, to enable multidisciplinary research. The focus should lie on sensors that are readily available in office settings, to make the to be developed system usable outside the lab. To our knowledge no such dataset existed.

In this paper we present a newly collected rich dataset which has these characteristics. Our dataset overcomes three drawbacks that are typically observed in related work:

- Instead of a rather artificial task, participants perform natural office work with systematically manipulated stressors.
- Instead of expensive and/or obtrusive equipment, we decided to combine a variety of sensors that can easily be deployed in real-world office settings.
- Instead of only collecting data for our own use, we will make the anonymized dataset available for access by the scientific community, for benchmarking of techniques and algorithms. We will not only provide raw data, but also data in preprocessed and interpreted form.

With our new dataset, we aim to bring research on psychology and computer science together. With this dataset, research questions from several fields can be answered, for example:

- Work psychology: What effect do stressors like time pressure have on the working behavior of knowledge workers? What is the effect of an incoming email? What effect do stressors have on subjective experience of task load, mental effort, emotion or perceived stress? What is the relation between what people mean when they feel 'stressed' and the concepts of arousal, mental effort and valence? Do we see effects of stressors in physiological sensor data?
- User modeling: Can we estimate the mental state or emotion of knowledge workers from unobtrusive sensor data? Do knowledge workers show particular affective expressions during computer work? Are there typical facial expressions or postures that are indicative of mental effort, high workload or stress?
- Context aware systems: Can we automatically determine the task or topic someone is working on? Is there a relation between stress and the context in which it occurs? Can we filter irrelevant emails? Can we make information retrieval more context aware?

In this paper we mainly focus on work stress and user modeling. For more details about the data regarding context recognition and information support, we refer to [17].

This paper is structured as follows. We first present some related work (Section 2). We then outline our experimental setup in which the dataset was collected (Section 3). We describe the dataset in detail in Section 4. Some example analyses are presented in Section 5. We finish with a Discussion and Conclusion (Section 6 and 7).

2. RELATED WORK

In this section we present some related research on work psychology and user modeling, in which sensor data is used to estimate stress, mental or affective states. We specifically address the type of sensors used, the context in which data has been collected and the kind of inferences that have been made. This gives a theoretical framework for research on our collected dataset.

In work psychology, questionnaires are commonly used to get insight in the general working experiences (e.g. [20]). Advances in sensing, as well as the quantified self movement make it possible to extend such an approach with on-site measurements.

Work in the area of affective computing investigates the possibility of inferring stress and emotion from sensor data. Most often, physiological sensors are used and data are collected in experimental environments. In research by Riera et al. [15], for example, electroencephalography (EEG) and facial electromyography (EMG) data were collected. The authors show that EEG and EMG can be used for monitoring emotion (valence and arousal) and stress. Although its great potential, we think deploying EEG in a daily office setting is not yet realistic. Other common measurements in stress research are pupil diameter and electrocardiogram (ECG). Mokhayeri, Akbarzadeh-T and Toosizadeh [14], for example, collected such data in context of the Stroop color-word (SCW) test. They state that pupil diameter and ECG have great potential for stress detection. However, the question that arises is: can we also make an estimate of affective and mental states outside the lab? We see some potential for ECG measurements, with the rise of wearable sensors, which are becoming more and more integrated into devices as watches and bracelets. But, besides measuring the physiological stress response directly, we also see great potential in measuring outward characteristics, such as facial expressions, postures or computer interactions as indicators for the user's state.

In related work, facial expressions are widely used for inferring emotions. The data are often recorded while emotions are induced in participants. The publicly available multimodal dataset described by Soleymani et al. [18], for example, was collected in context of watching emotion inducing video clips and consists of: face videos, audio signals, eye gaze data and physiological signals (EEG, ECG, GSR, respiration amplitude, skin temperature). Although this dataset is very interesting, emotions in a daily computer work context are probably less intense than the valence or arousal experienced during watching a movie clip. An interesting question is whether people show facial emotions during computer work, and whether their facial expressions are indicative of mental states. Preliminary results by Dinges et al. [4] suggest that high and low stressor situations could be discriminated based on facial activity in mouth and eyebrow regions.

Regarding postures, Kapoor and Picard [7] present research in which posture data was collected together with facial expressions and computer information while children solved an educational computer puzzle. Sensors in the chair were used to extract posture features (like leaning back, sitting upright) and activity level (low, medium, high). Posture information yielded the highest unimodal accuracy (80%) for estimating interest (vs. uninterest). Performance was further improved by adding facial expression and computer information. We conclude that posture information and movement are an interesting source for estimating the users' mental state. We see potential for posture measurements in the office, as with the Kinect recently an affordable 3D camera with skeleton detection has entered the market.

Finally, in some research, stress or emotions are estimated from computer interaction data. Vizer, Zhou and Sears [19], for example, investigated the effect of stress on typing patterns. Participants first performed a mentally or physically stressful task (e.g. remembering digits or exercising) and were then asked to write an email. Results indicate that stress can produce changes in typing patterns. This makes computer logging a valuable sensor for user state modeling. We think not only typing patterns, but also more general computer behavior might be indicative of mental states, like the amount of window switching, number of typos or time spent browsing.

Besides inferring stress or particular mental or affective states, the context in which they appear can be interesting. Computer interactions give rich insight in the user's current working behavior. Research by Koldijk et al. [10] shows that it is possible to infer the task someone is working on from computer interaction data. Moreover, one could add analysis of contents worked on.

To conclude, research from various related fields shows the potential of using sensors for estimating stress, mental and affective states and the context in which they appear. In each field, a particular setup of sensors is used. We decided to combine several of these in our unique dataset: computer interactions, video for facial expressions, Kinect 3D for postures and body sensors for heart rate and skin conductance.

3. DATA COLLECTION CONTEXT

In this section we present the experimental setup that was used to collect data.

3.1 Design

In our experiment we manipulated the conditions under which our participants worked:

- Neutral: the participant was allowed to work on the tasks as long as he/she needed. After a maximum of 45 minutes the participant was asked to stop and told that enough data of 'normal working' was collected.
- Stressor 'Time pressure': the time to finish all tasks was 2/3 of the time the participant needed in the neutral condition (and maximally 30 minutes).
- Stressor 'Interruptions': 8 emails were sent to the participant during the task. Some were relevant to one of the tasks, others were irrelevant. Some emails required a reply, others did not. Examples are: "Could you look up when Einstein was born?" or "I found this website with lots of nice pictures for presentations.".

All participants worked under all 3 conditions. The neutral condition was always the first condition, in order to collect an uninfluenced baseline of normal working. The order of the two stressor conditions was counterbalanced, see Figure 1. The within-subject design included relaxation breaks to start each condition in a well-rested state.

Order		Block1	Q		Block2	Q		Block3	Q
A	Relax	Neutral		Relax	Stressor interruptions		Relax	Stressor time pressure	
B		Neutral			Stressor time pressure			Stressor interruptions	

Figure 1: Design. For 13 participants order A was used, for 12 participants order B.

3.2 Tasks

The participants performed knowledge worker tasks on a desktop computer in a controlled lab setting. We asked them to write reports and make presentations on predefined topics (in English). We selected 6 topics on which people with various backgrounds could work:

- 3 opinion topics: Experience and opinion about 'stress at work', 'healthy living' and 'privacy on the internet'.
- 3 information topics: 'describe 5 Tourist attractions in Perth (West Australia)', 'plan a coast to coast road-trip in the USA' and 'write about the life of Napoleon'.

Some detail on what to include in the report was also given. Participants' were allowed to look for information on the internet and use documents that we previously stored on the computer. This setting is typical for knowledge work as available information can be combined with the worker's own input in a coherent way, with the purpose of generating a new information product. During the task the email program Outlook was running and participants were told to make use of information from incoming emails and reply when necessary. In this way, a realistic office work scenario was created.

We wanted to ensure that the participants worked on the tasks seriously. Therefore we told them that it was important to finish all required tasks for receiving the full subject fee. Moreover we told them that they would have to give one of the prepared presentations. After the experiment, we debriefed all participants and informed them that they did not need to give a presentation and would get the full subject fee.

3.3 Procedure

To be able to record stress responses as a result of our experimental manipulations, we instructed the participants to not smoke or drink caffeine 3 hours prior to the experiment, as these are possible confounders. Before the experiment started, the experiment and recordings were explained and all participants signed a consent form to confirm that the recorded data may be used for research purposes. Body sensors were applied and while the experimenter checked the recordings, the participant read the experiment instructions and filled in a general questionnaire.

The experiment was divided into three blocks for the different stressor conditions, each taking approximately one hour. Each of the experimental blocks started with a relaxation phase of about 8 minutes (which is typical for stress research) in which a nature film clip was shown. Then the participants received instructions on the tasks to work on. In each block the participants were provided with 2 of the 6 topics, which were randomly selected from the list, in such a way that always an opinion topic was combined with an information topic. The participants were instructed to write 2 reports, one on each topic, and make 1 presentation on one of the topics (participants could choose the topic). To prevent learning effects, the participants were provided with different topics in every block. In both stressor conditions, participants were provided a count-down clock for showing them the remaining time.

After completion of the tasks, the participants were asked to fill in a questionnaire about the current block. This procedure of relaxation, tasks execution and questionnaire was then repeated for block 2 and 3 (see Figure 1). Between the conditions the subjects were allowed a short break and the total experiment took about 3 hours. After the experiment the participants were debriefed.

3.4 Apparatus

Participants performed their tasks on a computer (Dell Latitude E6400) with Windows 7 Professional with a 17 inch screen and mouse and keyboard (see Figure 2). Office 2010 was installed, which the participants used for email (Outlook), report writing (Word) and making presentations (Powerpoint). As a browser, Internet Explorer was used with Google as default search engine. The start page of Internet Explorer was www.google.nl.

Figure 2: Experimental set-up.

3.5 Subjective Ratings

To collect a ground truth of the subjective experience after each block, we used a combination of validated questionnaires. Task load (in terms of mental demand, physical demand, temporal demand, effort, performance and frustration) was determined with the 'NASA-Task Load Index' [6]. Mental effort was assessed with the 'Rating Scale Mental Effort' [21]. Emotion response (in terms of valence, arousal and dominance) was determined with the 'Self-Assessment-Manikin Scale' [1]. Moreover, we asked participants to report their perceived stress on a visual analog scale from 'not stressed' to 'very stressed' (10 point scale).

Furthermore, we asked the participant's to fill in the 'Internal Control Index' questionnaire [5]. People with an internal locus of control tend to praise or blame themselves, whereas people with an external locus tend to praise or blame external factors. This might be of influence on participants' stress perception or behavior. Moreover, participants were asked to rate their interest in the topics, as well as how difficult they found it to write a report or make a presentation on a topic on a 7-point Likert scale (from 'not interesting / difficult' to 'very interesting / difficult').

3.6 Sensors

Computer logging. Computer interactions were logged with the key-logging application uLog (version 3.2.5, by Noldus Information Technology), which ran as a background application on the users' computer.

Video. Video recordings of the participants face and upper body were made with a high-resolution USB camera (iDS uEye UI-1490RE, 1152x768) which was positioned below the participants' monitor. The AVI files from the USB camera were further analyzed using the facial expression analysis software FaceReader (version 5.0.7 RC 4.5 (Beta)). An additional webcam (Philips SPC 900NC, SVGA resolution) was placed above the participants' monitor.

Kinect 3D. The participants body posture was recorded with a Kinect (for Windows, model 1517) depth camera. The camera was placed in front of the participants at a distance of about 2 meters, such that their whole body, including their legs under the desk were visible (see Figure 2). Besides 3D depth video, Kinect also recorded normal RGB video. Recordings were made with Kinect Studio (v1.7.0), which resulted in xed-files. From the recorded Kinect data the depth image and information on the skeletal model were extracted using the Windows Kinect SDK (v1.7). We smoothened the data with several predefined filters.

Body sensors. ECG was recorded using a Mobi device (TMSI) with self-adhesive electrodes. The electrodes were placed across the heart, one below the participants right collar-bone, the other left below the chest, with a grounding electrode below the left collar-bone. Some preprocessing was programed into the recording software Portilab2. To record skin conductance, Mobi was used with finger electrodes. These were fixed with Velcro tape around the lower part of the thumb and ring finger of the participant's non-dominant hand. Recording frequency was 2048 Hz. All signals (ECG and skin conductance, raw and preprocessed) were stored together in S00-files.

Additional Lab Recordings. The lab's ceiling camera and microphones were used for making records of the lab during the whole experiment, as well as a screen capture of the participant's screen. The video files are encoded in AVI-format with a codec specific to the labs recording software (GeoVision's CCS5). Audio is encoded in separate wav-files.

3.7 Participants

25 students participated in our experiment, of which 8 were female and 17 male. The average age was 25 (standard deviation 3.25). Most participants were native Dutch. They were interns from TNO and students from Delft University of Technology who were approached by advertising. Since these interns and students are experienced in handling (large amounts of) information for their courses, and often use computers as their most important tool, they are assumed to be representative of knowledge workers. Additionally, they are experienced with the knowledge worker tasks we have chosen: writing reports and preparing presen-

tations. The participants received a standard subject fee for their participation in the experiment.

To assess whether the participants worked on the tasks seriously, we checked the quality of the written reports and presentations. As the quality was satisfactory, none of the subjects needed to be excluded from the corpus. Of the participants, 2 were left handed and 8 wore glasses (which could be of concern for the software analyzing facial expressions). Results of our pre-questionnaire showed that none of the participants indicated to have a heart disease or take medicine which could have influenced their heart rate. About half the participants indicated that they were physically active before the experiment as they came by bike. 4 participants indicated that they had experienced stress prior to the experiment. None of the participants smoked, drank caffeine or alcohol 3 hours prior to the experiment. The participants scored on average 3.67 on on the internal control index (scale from 1 to 5, with higher scores indicating more internal control; stdv = 0.29).

4. DATASET

In this section we present the public SWELL-KW dataset in more detail. We collected data from the following sensors: computer logging, video, Kinect 3D and body sensors. Handling this data requires expertise in different fields. We preprocessed this data to get an aggregation of computer interactions, extraction of facial expressions, postures, heart rates and skin conductance levels. We finally aggregated this data into features per minute. For an overview of all available data see Table 1. We now fist describe the available fully preprocessed and aggregated feature data. Then we describe the available raw data and preprocessing.

4.1 The Feature Data

The feature dataset contains our completely preprocessed data, aggregated per minute, for all 25 participants. It contains the following features: 12 computer interaction features, 40 facial expression features, 88 body posture features and 3 physiology features as listed in the right column of Table 1. The feature dataset is annotated with the conditions under which the data was collected. Per participant three times 6 minutes relaxation data are included, ca. 45 minutes of working under normal conditions, ca. 45 minutes working with email interruptions and ca. 30 minutes working under time pressure.

Moreover, we provide the scores on our questionnaire items as ground truth for the subjective experience in each condition, see Table 3. As 25 participants each rated 3 conditions, this yields 75 ratings in total.

4.2 The Raw Data and Preprocessing

Besides the completely preprocessed and aggregated data, we also provide some raw data and files resulting from our preprocessing, as listed in the middle column of Table 1.

Computer logging. The computer logging software recorded detailed timestamped information in XML format about each computer event. Examples of computer events are mouse clicks, mouse scrolls and application changes. Moreover we parsed the files and printed them in a more intelligible timestamped table format, which will also be made available. Finally, we computed several relevant mouse, keyboard and application characteristics per minute (listed in Table 2), which are contained in the feature dataset.

Table 2: Computer interaction features (aggregated per minute).

Type	Feature	Description
Mouse	MouseActivity	Number of all MouseEvents
	LeftClicks	Number of left clicks
	MouseWheel	Number of mouse wheel scrolling
Keyboard	KeyStrokes	Number of all KeyEvents
	ShortcutKeys	Number of shortcut keys (Ctrl+ c/x/v/z/s/a; Shift+Tab)
	DirectionKeys	Number of direction keys (arrow left/right/up/down)
	Characters	Number of characters (a-z)
	CharactersRatio	#characters devided by #keyStrokes
	ErrorKeys	Number of error keys (Backspace, Delete, Ctrl+Z)
	ErrorKeyRatio	#errorKeys devided by (#characters + #spaces)
Applications	AppChanges	Number of application changes
	TabfocusChange	Number of tab focus changes

Facial expressions from video. We do not include the fully recorded videos in our dataset to keep our participants anonymous. Instead, we provide data files with the analysis of facial activation. These were extracted from the video per timeframe using the software FaceReader. The characteristics that are included in the dataset are: quality, estimates on the orientation of the head, some global features of the face like looking direction and the amount of activation in several facial action units. Moreover, FaceReader provides an estimate of the subjects emotion, which is also available in our dataset. We parsed these files to get a more intelligible timestamped table format, which will also be made available. Besides data per video frame, we also calculated averages per minute for all characteristics (see Table 1), which are contained in the feature dataset.

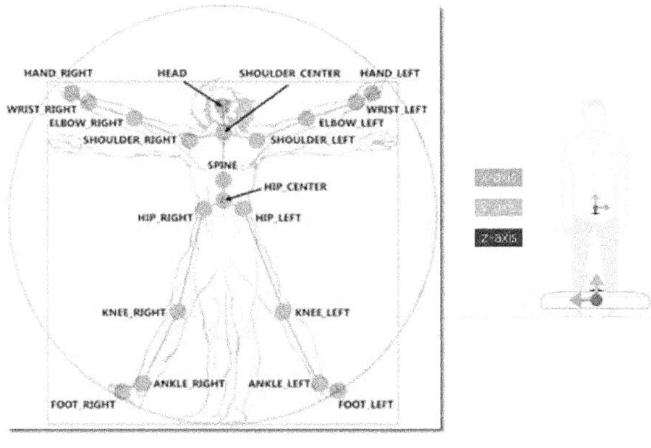

Figure 3: Kinect joints and Kinect orientation from Kinect SDK. Images from: http://msdn.microsoft.com

[2]http://www.noldus.com/human-behavior-research/products/ulog

[3]http://www.noldus.com/human-behavior-research/products/facereader

[4]http://www.tmsi.com/en/products/mobi.html

Table 1: Our dataset contains data from 25 participants (3 hours each). The listed raw and preprocessed sensor data, as well as a feature dataset (aggregated per minute) will be made available.

Type	Available raw and preprocessed data	Available features (#features)
Computer interactions	uLog output[2] (i.e. xml-logs of all computer events) Parsed data (i.e. txt-file with timestamped data)	Mouse (3) Keyboard (7) Applications (2) (for details see Table 2)
Facial expressions	FaceReader output[3] (i.e. txt-logs with facial information and emotions) Parsed data (i.e. txt-file with timestamped data)	Head orientation (3) Facial movements (10) Action Units (19) Emotion (8)
Body postures	Joint coordinates extracted with Kinect SDK (i.e. txt-file with timestamped data) Angles of the upper body (i.e. txt-file with timestamped data)	Distance (1) Joint angles (10) Bone orientations (3x11)) (as well as stdv of the above for amount of movement (44))
Physiology	Data from Mobi[4] (i.e. S00-files with raw and filtered signals)	Heart rate (variability) (2) Skin conductance (1)

Body postures from Kinect 3D sensor. We do not include the recorded 3D Kinect files in our dataset to keep our participants anonymous. Instead, we provide data files with analysis of the participant's body posture per time-frame. These were extracted from the 3D Kinect recordings using the Kinect SDK. By fitting the Kinect skeletal model (see Figure 3, left), we got coordinates of all body joints per frame. This data will be made available. We further used these joint coordinates to determine joint angles between bones of the upper body, for example the angle between the upper and lower arm. Moreover, we determined bone orientations of the upper body relative to the x, y and z axis (see Figure 3, right), for example the angle between the left shoulder and the up pointing y axis.[5] This information on angles per frame will be made available. From the depth image the average distance of the user was also determined. Finally, we determined average angles per minute, which are contained in the feature dataset. We also calculated standard deviations for each minute, to determine features that indicate the amount of movement and changes in joint angles. These are also contained in the feature dataset.

Physiology from body sensors. We provide raw and preprocessed ECG data. The raw ECG signal was filtered as described in the TMSI[6] manual: First a high pass filter (8Hz) was applied to filter out large fluctuations in the signal. A 15ms second delay was added, together with a delta filter to let the low frequency parts of the signal disappear. To be independent of the direction of the QRS complex (due to morphology of the ECG), we took the absolute signal. Finally, a moving window averager (0.1sec) was added to get the envelope of the signal. This yielded a filtered signal with clear peaks. The raw and preprocessed ECG data will be made available.

We also calculated the heart rate and heart rate variability. Therefore, we processed the filtered data further in Matlab. First of all we applied a peak detection algorithm to the filtered signal. To determine the heart rate, the found peaks were counted per 1 minute time-frame. Then we calculated the distance between the found peaks (R-R). To determine the heart rate variability we took the root mean square of all these peak distances (RMSSD). Due to some remaining noise in the signal, the peak finding algorithm sometimes failed to accurately detect peaks. Therefore we excluded all 1-minute time frames in which more than one peak distance appeared unusual. We defined an unusual peak distance as a distance larger than 1.2 seconds where probably a peak was missed (or otherwise the HR would be below 50bpm) or a distance smaller than 0.5 seconds where probably an extra peak was detected (or otherwise the HR would be over 120bpm). The resulting heart rate and heart rate variability are contained in the feature dataset.

Moreover, we provide raw skin conductance data. We also calculated the average skin conductance level by averaging the raw signal per minute, which is contained in the feature dataset.

5. EXAMPLE ANALYSES

In this section we present some research that was done based on our dataset, as an example of its use.

Work stress. To find relations between the measured concepts, we performed a correlation analysis on the questionnaire data. We found that perceived stress is moderately related to high task load in terms of mental demand, temporal demand and frustration. Moreover, stress is related to emotion in terms of negative valence and high arousal. For more details on these results, see [9].

To investigate the effect of our stressors on the participants' subjective experience, we compared the questionnaire ratings of the neutral baseline condition with the time pressure and email interruption conditions (see Table 3). Under the stressor time pressure, participants experienced significantly higher temporal demand and higher arousal. The stressor email interruptions yielded reports of more mental effort, more positive valence and more dominance. We found that perceived stress did not differ significantly between the stressor and neutral conditions. Stress might be a too complex concept to measure in a short-termed work task. For more details on our results, see [9]. These analyses show the potential of using the dataset for research on the effect of

[5]We use a projection to the plane to distill only variance in one direction.

[6]`http://www.tmsi.com`

Table 3: Subjective experience data (one rating per block). Average values for the Neutral, Interruption and Time pressure condition can be found in the last 3 columns.

Type	Feature	Description	N	I	T
TaskLoad (NASA-TLX)	MentalDemand (0: low - 10: high)	How much mental and perceptual activity was required (e.g. thinking, deciding, calculating, remembering, looking, searching, etc.)?	4.9	5.4	4.9
	PhysicalDemand (0: low - 10: high)	How much physical activity was required (e.g. pushing, pulling, turning, controlling, activating, etc.)?	1.9	2.3	2.7
	TemporalDemand (0: low - 10: high)	How much time pressure did you feel due to the rate or pace at which the task or task elements occurred?	5.7	5.9	7.1
	Effort (0: low - 10: high)	How hard did you have to work (mentally and physically) to accomplish your level of performance?	5.2	5.9	6.1
	Performance (0: poor - 10: good)	How successful do you think you were in accomplishing the goals of the task set by the experimenter (or yourself)?	4.8	6.1	6.0
	Frustration (0: low - 10: high)	How insecure, discouraged, irritated, stressed and annoyed versus secure, gratified, content, relaxed and complacent did you feel during the task?	3.5	3.6	3.5
Mental Effort (RSME)	MentalEffort (0: no - 10: extreme effort)	How high was the mental effort for the tasks you just finished?	5.5	6.5	6.3
Emotion (SAM)	Valence (1 - 9)	How do you feel at this moment? (unhappy - happy)	4.8	5.7	5.3
	Arousal (1 - 9)	How do you feel at this moment? (calm - excited)	3.3	3.9	4.6
	Dominance (1 - 9)	How do you feel at this moment? (submissive - dominant)	5.2	6.2	5.9
Stress (VAS)	Stress (0: not - 10: very stressed)	How stressed do you feel?	2.9	3.2	3.8

work stressors on experience and behavior.

User modeling. We are aiming to develop algorithms that can estimate the level of workload and stress that a knowledge worker is experiencing from sensor data, in order to unobtrusively model their mental state. To investigate whether the stressors affected the participants' behavior, we compared computer interactions and facial expressions in the two stressor conditions with the neutral baseline condition. Under time pressure we see significantly more key strokes than in the neutral condition, and under interruptions we see more application changes and left clicks. So both stressors create typical behavioral patterns.

Explorative correlation analysis on questionnaire and facial expression data showed that moderate correlations were found for mental effort with several facial features. When working in a condition with higher mental effort, participants looked more disgusted and sad and they showed more activation in the facial action units LidTightener, UpperLipRaiser, BrowLowerer and CheekRaiser. So mental effort might be estimated based upon video information. For more details on our results, see [9]. These analyses show the potential of using the dataset for research on user modeling.

Context recognition and Information support. The tasks of writing reports and preparing presentations enabled us to use the dataset in the fields of context recognition and search behavior as well. For this purpose, the raw events were aggregated in event blocks, which were labeled for their task content. Details can be found in [17], where also some initial analyses of the search behavior in the data are described.

6. DISCUSSION

To our knowledge, our dataset is the first in which a set of unobtrusive sensors from different research fields was used to collect data in a realistic office context, while stressors were manipulated.

In collecting and preprocessing the data, we encountered a number of challenges. First, simulating a realistic work setting and inducing stress was challenging. We do think that we succeeded in simulating a realistic work setting. Some participants noted afterwards, that although they knew that the emails were fake, they felt responsible to reply. We also think we were able to manipulate the working conditions with stressors: the questionnaire data showed that participants' experience of task load, mental effort and emotion changed in the stressor conditions. Due to our experimental design of always starting with the neutral baseline condition, subjects might have experienced order or fatigue effects. We do, however, think that the relaxation phases helped participants to start each condition in a well-rested state. We did not find significant effects of our working conditions on perceived stress. Real-world stress might be complex, involving worries or thing outside work and stress building up over days. Therefore, a limitation of this dataset is that only short term effects of stressors can be investigated. For longitudinal research on temporal (stress) patterns over days or weeks, we are currently recording the presented sensor suite in a real-world office.

A second challenge was synchronization of all data. Different sensors were recorded via different computers. We synced computer clocks, and most sensors made exact starting timestamps upon hitting the record button. Nevertheless, we cannot guarantee second-precise synchronization among modalities (especially the uEye camera start times may be somewhat unprecise).

Finally, using different sorts of sensors requires multidisciplinary expertise, like knowledge (and software) for processing physiological, image or Kinect data. Our contribution is to provide a dataset that not only contains raw data, but also preprocessed and aggregated data, which makes it easier for other researchers to use the data.

The strength of this dataset is its richness in terms of modalities and its size in terms of the amount of data per participant. Although limited in size of participants (25), initial experiments have shown that the dataset has sufficient power to detect significant differences. With the presented new dataset, automatic inference of a rich set of context information of a user in the office can be studied. It can be used to develop context aware systems to support knowledge workers during their work. Moreover, it provides ample resources for stress and work style related studies.

7. CONCLUSION

We identified the need of a rich dataset and its desired characteristics. In this paper we described how we collected such a new dataset that overcomes drawbacks common in related work: We used a realistic office setting while stressors were manipulated systematically. We used a varied set of sensors: computer logging, video, Kinect 3D and body sensors. We preprocessed the data and extracted features per minute. The resulting dataset SWELL-KW will be shared with the scientific community. We presented a selection of research questions that could be answered with this dataset. As demonstrated, analyses of the data can yield insights in the effects of stressors at work, or on the relation between subjective ratings and the sensor data. The presented new affective and behavioral dataset is a valuable contribution to research fields like work psychology, user modeling and context aware systems.

More information on the dataset and its access can be found at `http://persistent-identifier.nl/?identifier=urn:nbn:nl:ui:13-kwrv-3e`

8. ACKNOWLEDGEMENTS

This publication was supported by the Dutch national program COMMIT (project P7 SWELL).

9. REFERENCES

[1] M. M. Bradley and P. J. Lang. Measuring emotion: the self-assessment manikin and the semantic differential. *Journal of behavior therapy and experimental psychiatry*, 25(1):49–59, 1994.

[2] E. Demerouti, A. B. Bakker, S. A. Geurts, and T. W. Taris. Daily recovery from work-related effort during non-work time. *Research in Occupational Stress and Well-being*, 7:85–123, 2009.

[3] E. Demerouti, A. B. Bakker, F. Nachreiner, and W. B. Schaufeli. The job demands-resources model of burnout. *Journal of Applied psychology*, 86(3):499, 2001.

[4] D. F. Dinges, R. L. Rider, J. Dorrian, E. L. McGlinchey, N. L. Rogers, Z. Cizman, S. K. Goldenstein, C. Vogler, S. Venkataraman, and D. N. Metaxas. Optical computer recognition of facial expressions associated with stress induced by performance demands. *Aviation, space, and environmental medicine*, 76(Supplement 1):B172–B182, 2005.

[5] P. C. Duttweiler. The internal control index: A newly developed measure of locus of control. *Educational and Psychological Measurement*, 44(2):209–221, 1984.

[6] S. G. Hart and L. E. Staveland. Development of nasa-tlx (task load index): Results of empirical and theoretical research. *Advances in psychology*, 52:139–183, 1988.

[7] A. Kapoor and R. W. Picard. Multimodal affect recognition in learning environments. In *Proceedings of the 13th annual ACM international conference on Multimedia*, pages 677–682. ACM, 2005.

[8] S. Koldijk. Automatic recognition of context and stress to support knowledge workers. In *Proceedings of the 30th European Conference on Cognitive Ergonomics*, pages D20–D23. ACM, 2012.

[9] S. Koldijk, M. Sappelli, M. Neerincx, and W. Kraaij. Unobtrusive monitoring of knowledge workers for stress self-regulation. In *User Modeling, Adaptation, and Personalization*, pages 335–337. Springer, 2013.

[10] S. Koldijk, M. van Staalduinen, M. Neerincx, and W. Kraaij. Real-time task recognition based on knowledge workers' computer activities. In *Proceedings of the 30th European Conference on Cognitive Ergonomics*, pages 152–159. ACM, 2012.

[11] L. Koppes, E. d. Vroome, G. Mars, B. Janssen, M. Zwieten, and S. v. d. Bossche. Nationale enquete arbeidsomstandigheden 2012: Methodologie en globale resultaten, 2012.

[12] K. Kraan, S. Dhondt, I. Houtman, R. Nelemans, and E. d. Vroome. Handleiding nova-weba: Hernieuwde versie., 2000.

[13] G. Mark, D. Gudith, and U. Klocke. The cost of interrupted work: more speed and stress. In *Proceedings of the SIGCHI conference on Human Factors in Computing Systems*, pages 107–110. ACM, 2008.

[14] F. Mokhayeri, M.-R. Akbarzadeh-T, and S. Toosizadeh. Mental stress detection using physiological signals based on soft computing techniques. In *Biomedical Engineering (ICBME), 2011 18th Iranian Conference of*, pages 232–237. IEEE, 2011.

[15] A. Riera, A. Soria-Frisch, A. Albajes-Eizagirre, P. Cipresso, C. Grau, S. Dunne, G. Ruffini, and S. aStarlab Barcelona. Electro-physiological data fusion for stress detection. *Studies in health technology and informatics*, 181:228–32, 2012.

[16] J. Ruff. Information overload: Causes, symptoms and solutions. *Harvard Graduate School of Education*, pages 1–13, 2002.

[17] M. Sappelli, S. Verberne, S. Koldijk, and W. Kraaij. Collecting a dataset of information behaviour in context. In *Proceedings of the 4th Workshop on Context-awareness in Retrieval and Recommendation*, 2014.

[18] M. Soleymani, J. Lichtenauer, T. Pun, and M. Pantic. A multimodal database for affect recognition and implicit tagging. *Affective Computing, IEEE Transactions on*, 3(1):42–55, 2012.

[19] L. M. Vizer, L. Zhou, and A. Sears. Automated stress detection using keystroke and linguistic features: An exploratory study. *International Journal of Human-Computer Studies*, 67(10):870–886, 2009.

[20] D. Zapf. Stress-oriented analysis of computerized office work. *The European Work and Organizational Psychologist*, 3(2):85–100, 1993.

[21] F. Zijlstra and L. van Doorn. The construction of a scale to measure subjective effort. Technical report, Delft University of Technology, 1985.

Rhythmic Body Movements of Laughter

Radoslaw Niewiadomski
DIBRIS, University of Genoa
Viale Causa 13
Genoa, Italy
radek@infomus.org

Maurizio Mancini
DIBRIS, University of Genoa
Viale Causa 13
Genoa, Italy
maurizio.mancini@unige.it

Yu Ding
CNRS - Telecom ParisTech
37-39, rue Dareau
Paris, France
yu.ding@telecom.paristech.fr

Catherine Pelachaud
CNRS - Telecom ParisTech
37-39, rue Dareau
Paris, France
catherine.pelchaud@telecom.paristech.fr

Gualtiero Volpe
DIBRIS, University of Genoa
Viale Causa 13
Genoa, Italy
gualtiero.volpe@unige.it

ABSTRACT

In this paper we focus on three aspects of multimodal expressions of laughter. First, we propose a procedural method to synthesize rhythmic body movements of laughter based on spectral analysis of laughter episodes. For this purpose, we analyze laughter body motions from motion capture data and we reconstruct them with appropriate harmonics. Then we reduce the parameter space to two dimensions. These are the inputs of the actual model to generate a continuum of laughs rhythmic body movements.
In the paper, we also propose a method to integrate rhythmic body movements generated by our model with other synthetized expressive cues of laughter such as facial expressions and additional body movements. Finally, we present a real-time human-virtual character interaction scenario where virtual character applies our model to answer to human's laugh in real-time.

Categories and Subject Descriptors

H.1.2 [**Information Interfaces and Presentation**]: User/ Machine Systems—*Human factors*; I.3.8 [**Computing Methodologies**]: Computer Graphics—*Applications*; H.5.1 [**Information Interfaces and Presentation**]: Information Interfaces and Presentation—*Artificial, augmented, and virtual realities*

General Terms

Human Factors

Keywords

laughter; nonverbal behaviors; realtime interaction; virtual character

ICMI '14 November 12 - 16 2014, Istanbul, Turkey

ACM 978-1-4503-2885-2/14/11...$15.00.
http://dx.doi.org/10.1145/2663204.2663240

1. INTRODUCTION

During laughter, the whole body (head, torso, shoulders, face) is involved [11, 22]. Body movements are important markers allowing distinguishing laughter from smiling (besides facial and vocal expressions). The presence of body movements influences the perceived intensity of laughter [6]. Some body movements, but not all, are due to the respiration phases [22]. Despite the important role of body movements, most of the laughter synthesis algorithms for virtual characters (VCs) are limited to facial animation [5, 17].

In this paper, we propose a model of *rhythmic body movements* (RBM) based on spectral analysis of laughter episodes. We describe a multimodal synchronization schema to integrate all facial and body movements of laughter including RBM. We also present a human-virtual character (H-VC) interaction scenario where laughter is triggered: the VC's rhythmic laughter behaviors are generated in real-time and in link with human's laughter.

The bodily expressive patterns of laughter are complex. According to Ruch and Ekman [22], a laughter episode is usually composed of several repetitive laugh pulses that are caused by forced exhalation. The maximum number of these pulses is between 9 and 12 depending on volume of the lungs. Long laughter episodes include additional inhalations that can result in a higher number of pulses. Several attempts to measure laughter pulses frequency (e.g., [19] in audio modality, [2] in respiration) converge to similar results: laughter pulses have the frequency between 4 and 6 Hz. The body movements observed during laughter can be of two types [22]. Most of laughter body movements are associated with the respiratory patterns of laughter [22]. Examples of such movements are the backward movements of head and trunk that appear to ease the forced exhalations, or the upward movements of torso that are related to the inhalation phase. Laughter pulses generate also visible vibrations of the shoulders and of the trunk. Since these movements are related to respiration phases, one expects they are repetitive and have a fixed rhythm. The movements related to respiration can be accompanied by other body movements such as sideways rocking, which are, however, of different origin [22].

In the first part of the paper, we focus on a significant subset of laughter body movements, the rhythmic body movements. We use Fast Fourier Transform (FFT) to build a

RBM model. Using computer vision algorithms we extract the position of upper-body points from several laugh episodes. We conduct spectral analysis on this data. We associate the prevalent harmonics resulting from this analysis to different types of laughter movements (e.g., shake shoulders). Next we conduct statistical analysis on the harmonics' parameters (i.e., amplitude, frequency). Finally, to allow a human animator an easy control over VC's RBMs, we introduce two high-level normalized variables: *intensity* and *velocity* and we provide a mapping between these two variables and the harmonics' parameters needed to synthesize RBM. Our model allows us to control VC laughter rhythmic body movements via high-level commands like: "shake shoulders with $intensity = X$ and $velocity = Y$".

The rhythmic body movements are just one element of laughter expressive pattern. Other body and face movements have important role in laughter [22] and need to be included. We present how RBMs can be synchronized with facial and other body animations [8]. To generate a multimodal laughter animation, our model takes as input the phonetic transcription of laughter [27]. We end the paper by presenting a scenario of H-VC realtime interaction.

The paper is organized as follows. The next section presents a survey of works on visual laughter synthesis, laughter based interactive systems, and nonverbal synchronization of movements in general. Section 3 is dedicated to the analysis and synthesis of the rhythmic body movements of laughter. Section 4 focuses on multimodal synchronization and Section 5 presents an interactive scenario. We conclude our paper in Section 6.

2. STATE OF THE ART

2.1 Visual Laughter Synthesis

Few models of laughter animations were proposed recently [5, 17] but they are restricted to facial displays. The major exception is by Di Lorenzo et al. [7], who proposed an audio driven model of upper body animation during laughter.

The model defines the relationship between lungs pressure and laughter phase that can be derived from the amplitude of the audio signal. It applies an anatomically-inspired and physics-based model of human torso that is a combination of rigid and deformable components. The model is able to produce realistic animations but it is computationally expensive.

In other works, algorithms based on FFT were applied to animate VCs. Unuma et al. [25] used Fourier decomposition of motion capture data to model emotional walks, whereas Troje [24] successfully modeled walks with the first two components of Fourier series. More recently, Tilmanne and Dutoit [23] extended this approach by applying Fourier decomposition to angular representation of various style walking sequences. In a perceptive study they showed that various walking styles can be successfully modeled with the first two components.

2.2 Nonverbal Behavior Mirroring

Several virtual character systems were build that synchronize certain nonverbal behaviors. Bailenson and Yee [1] studied the Chameleon Effect in the interaction with virtual characters. In their study, a VC that mimics head nods of the human interaction partner is shown to increase perceived effectiveness. Prepin and Pelachaud [18] presented a dynamic coupling model based on the concept of an oscillator able to synchronize different nonverbal behaviors of virtual characters or of a human and a virtual character. In their model the interactants' movements become synchronized to communicate reciprocal understanding of the verbal content. Riek et al. [21] studied how a robot mimicking the human head nodding influences human perception of interaction. No effect of mimicry was observed.

2.3 Laughter Based Interactive Systems

Urbain et al. [28] developed a system able (i) to detect human laugh and (ii) to answer it by displaying virtual character pre-synthetized laugher responses. The system contains a database of pre-synthetized laugher episodes extracted from real human audio recordings that are directly replayed, and the corresponding facial animations obtained by retargeting the motion capture data. The choice of the VC's response from the database is done algorithmically and it is based on the real-time analysis of acoustic similarities with the input laughter. Fukushima et al. [9] studied laughter contagion in human-robot interaction. They used simple toy robots that play pre-registered laughter sounds when the system detects the initial human laughter. The evaluation study showed that robots' laughter was contagious and increased human laughing. Niewiadomski et al. [14] proposed an interactive TV watching scenario in which a human participant and a virtual agent watch together funny content. The agent is able to detect human laughs and can laugh in response to the detected behavior by using synthetized facial expressions and audio. Such laughter response is generated by taking into the consideration the duration and the intensity of the human laugh.

Figure 1: A frame from MMLI recordings [15]. On the left: a participant is wearing green markers. On the right: another participant is wearing a motion capture suit and green markers.

2.4 Beyond the State of the Art

Existing works may produce even very realistic animations of laughter (see Section 2.1). In this work our main aim, however, is not to improve the realism of laughter animation but to build a simple and computationally cheap method for laughter synthesis, which can be used and controlled in realtime in H-VC interaction. Importantly, we propose a procedural approach in which the synthetized body movements can be easily controlled manually by a human animator (by using a high level language such as BML, see Section 3.3) or by a machine (e.g. see Section 5).

Secondly, unlike the existing interactive realtime systems (see Section 2.3) which do not analyze human body movements when generating VC laughter, we focus on body movements of both a human and a VC. However, we do not use the copy-synthesis method to reconstruct the whole nonverbal behavior of the human as it might be perceived to be awkward or even as mockery. Inspired by previous works on H-VC interaction (see Section 2.3), in which only some dynamic characteristics of movement are considered, we propose to tune one aspect only: laughter rhythm. Thirdly, although spectral analysis was previously used in procedural synthesis of nonverbal behaviors e.g., walk (see Section 2.1), applying this method to analyze and synthetize body movements of laughter is a novel approach.

3. MODEL OF RHYTHMIC BODY MOVEMENTS OF LAUGHTER

3.1 Data Analysis

Two types of movements are involved in laughter RBM: *torso leaning* and *shoulder vibration*. The first one is rather slow and it may have different directions: linear, e.g., front/back and left/right, or circular. The shoulder movement is much faster and it is always repetitive. It is also symmetric - both shoulders are involved and move synchronously [22, 11].

The freely accessible MMLI corpus[1][15] was used to analyze laughter body movements as it is, to our knowledge, the largest freely accessible corpus dedicated to full-body expressions of laughter. Participants wear mocap sensors, and two green markers (lightweight polystyrene balls) on shoulders. Data consists of synchronized 3D coordinates streams, 3 audio streams, and 6 video streams (640x480, 30fps).

Despite the variety of sensors used in the MMLI corpus, in our analysis only RGB video streams are used. In particular, the inertial motion capture sensors used in MMLI were not placed on participant's shoulders so the resulting data could not capture shoulder vibration.

Thirty-five episodes ($N = 35$) from five participants (2 males) containing both types of RBMs have been chosen for analysis. They contain spontaneous laughter that is either induced (watching videos task) or interactive (social games task). During all episodes participants were standing. Additional selection criteria required that (i) the green markers had to be well visible during the whole segment and (ii) that the person is not walking. An example of a video frame taken from the MMLI corpus is displayed in Figure 1. The mean duration of an episode is $2.87s$ ($\sigma = 2.22$, $min = 1.4s$, $max = 13.43s$).

- color tracking is performed by the EyesWeb XMI platform[2]: we isolate the green component of the input RGB 30 fps video stream and we apply a threshold on it; we determine the barycenter of the 2 largest pixel groups corresponding to the green markers; since shoulder movements are usually symmetric, for each episode we consider only one marker (left or right shoulder) and only its vertical coordinate $y_i(t)$;
- since the values of $y_i(t)$ are not comparable across different videos (i.e., different cameras configurations were used to record the participants), we normalize $y_i(t)$ by the participant's head height: e.g., normalized $||y_i(t)||$ is equal to 2 if the marker vertical position is equal to two times the head height, where coordinate $||y_i(t)|| = 0$ corresponds to the top image border;

[1]http://www.infomus.org/people/mmli/

[2]http://www.eyesweb.infomus.org

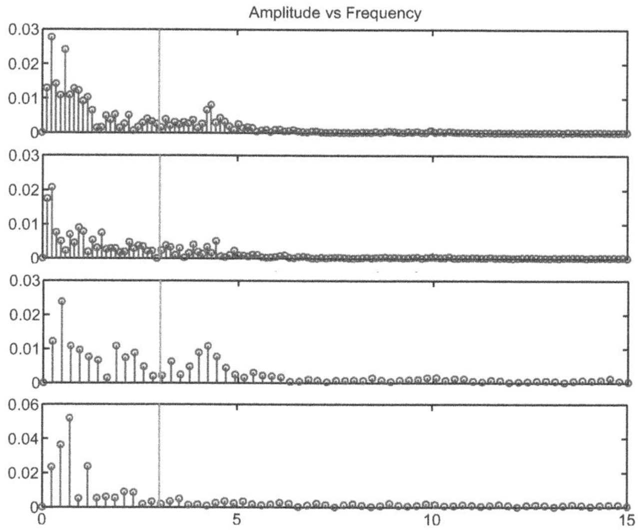

Figure 2: Examples of spectrum analysis for four different episodes

- FFT is applied to $||y_i(t)||$, that is, it is applied to the green marker's vertical coordinate for the entire episode i.

We observe that two frequency intervals can be identified in the resulting frequency spectra for each episode (see Figure 2). The first one - around $0.5 - 1.5Hz$ - contains the fundamental frequency. However, relatively strong peaks can be identified also around $3.5 - 6Hz$. Following the literature (see Section 1) we assume that: slower components, that is, frequencies around $0.5 - 1.5Hz$, correspond to torso forward/backward leaning whereas faster components, that is, frequencies around $3.5 - 6Hz$, correspond to shoulder vibration.

3.2 Signal Reconstruction with Estimation of Error

We process the input signal $s_i = ||y_i(t)||$ in 2 steps: (i) filtering and (ii) error computation. By performing low and high pass filtering we extract torso and shoulder movements. Then, we reconstruct the input signal to estimate the reconstruction error and validate the process.

3.2.1 Filtering

We apply two filters to $s_i = ||y_i(t)||$: the first one (low pass) allows us to extract only the torso leaning component; the second one (high pass) allows us to extract only the shoulder vibration component. Starting from the literature on laughter (see Section 1) we define a threshold at $Th = 3Hz$: the first filter allows one to isolate only frequencies in the interval $I_1 = [0, 3)Hz$; the second one allows one to isolate only frequencies in the interval $I_2 = [3, 15]Hz$.

Next, in each frequency interval I_1, I_2, we find the harmonics exhibiting the two highest local maxima of amplitude and we sort them in frequency ascending order. More precisely, for I_1, we define a matrix L of size $N \times 6$ (where $N = 35$ is the number of laughter episodes). Let $L_{i,\_}$ be the i-th row of matrix L, $L_{i,\_}$ contains the 6 torso leaning parameters of episode i, that is, $L_{i,\_} = [a_{1,i}, f_{1,i}, \phi_{1,i}, a_{2,i}, f_{2,i}, \phi_{2,i}]$,

components	mean	σ	min	max
all	0.16	0.18	< 0.01	0.72
2	0.21	0.20	0.05	0.77
4	**0.18**	**0.15**	**0.05**	**0.54**
6	0.18	0.16	0.04	0.57

Table 1: Signal reconstruction error computed on 26 signals

where $a_{j,i}$ means amplitude, $f_{j,i}$ - frequency, $\phi_{j,i}$ - phase of $\{j,i\}$-harmonics, and $f_{1,i} < f_{2,i}$, $f_{1,i}, f_{2,i} \in [0,3)Hz$. Similarly, for I_2, we define a matrix V of size $N \times 6$ such that the i-th row $V_{i,\_}$ of V contains the 6 shoulder vibration parameters of episode i, that is, $V_{i,\_} = [A_{1,i}, F_{1,i}, \Phi_{1,i}, A_{2,i}, F_{2,i}, \Phi_{2,i}]$, where $F_{1,i} < F_{2,i}$ and $F_{1,i}, F_{2,i} \in [3,15]Hz$. Also, we indicate with $L_{\_,j}$ and $V_{\_,j}$, the j-th columns of matrices L and V, respectively. For example, $L_{\_,2}$ (resp. $V_{\_,2}$) of L (resp. V) is a column vector that contains the lower frequencies, among the above selected ones, in $[0,3)Hz$ (resp. $[3,15]Hz$); while $L_{\_,5}$ (resp. $V_{\_,5}$) is a column vector that contains the higher frequencies, among the above selected ones, in $[0,3)Hz$ (resp. $[3,15]Hz$).

3.2.2 *Error Computation*

For each laughter episode i we reconstruct the original signal using the harmonics described by matrices L and V. We use 4 harmonics: $\{(a_{k,i}, f_{k,i}, \phi_{k,i}) | k \in \{1,2\}\} \in L$ and $\{(A_{k,i}, F_{k,i}, \Phi_{k,i}) | k \in \{1,2\}\} \in V$. Thus the reconstructed signal r_i is:

$$r_i = \sum_{k=1..2} (a_{k,i} cos(2\pi f_{k,i} t + \phi_{k,i}) + A_{k,i} cos(2\pi F_{k,i} t + \Phi_{k,i})) \quad (1)$$

Then we compute the reconstruction error for episode i as the normalized maximum difference between the original signal s_i and r_i:

$$E_i = \frac{\max(|s_i - r_i|)}{\max(s_i) - \min(s_i)} \quad (2)$$

The mean error E, computed according to the above equation on 26 episodes, is $E = 0.18$ (see Table 1).[3] We finally check how the reconstruction mean error depends on the number of harmonics. We compare 4 harmonics reconstruction error with the following additional cases: (i) reconstruction performed on the entire FFT spectrum; (ii) reconstruction performed on 2 harmonics, the prevalent one in $[0,3)Hz$ and the prevalent one in $[3,15]Hz$; (iii) reconstruction performed on 6 harmonics, 3 in $[0,3)Hz$ and 3 in $[3,15]Hz$ selected in a similar way as for L and V. The corresponding computed errors are reported in Table 1. It can be seen that the signal reconstructed with the use of four harmonics provides satisfactory results (see Figure 3). Adding more harmonics does not reduce significantly the mean error. Thus, it is a good compromise between the accuracy and the number of parameters needed to describe the signal.

[3]Remaining 9 episodes had only one local maximum of amplitudes in one of two considered ranges and, thus, they have been discarded.

3.3 Model of Rhythmic Movements in Laughter

To generate RBMs with our model one needs to specify the type of the movement (i.e., torso leaning, shoulders vibration), the desired duration of the movement t, and two additional variables that describe the movement: intensity $INT \in [0,1]$ and velocity $VEL \in [0,1]$ (see Section 3.3.2 for details). For a frame to be displayed at time t, the model outputs two values: torso leaning $l(t)$ and shoulder vibration $v(t)$. Accordingly to results presented in Section 3.1 and 3.2 each of these body movements is modeled using two harmonics:

$$\begin{aligned} l(t) &= a_1 cos(2\pi f_1 t + \phi_1) + a_2 cos(2\pi f_2 t + \phi_2) \\ v(t) &= A_1 cos(2\pi F_1 t + \Phi_1) + A_2 cos(2\pi F_2 t + \Phi_2) \end{aligned} \quad (3)$$

Thus, body movements in our model can be fully controlled within 12 parameters. However, controlling the animation generation with such a high number of parameters would be not intuitive for a human. Thus in the next step we reduce the dimensionality of the body animation control space and we map the parameters of Equation 3 onto high-level input variables. For this purpose, we use the values of matrices V and L and a mapping for input parameters: high values of the intensity variable INT correspond to strong movements (i.e., movement with high amplitude) whereas high values of the velocity variable VEL correspond to high frequencies. Next, for each column of V and L we compute its mean and standard deviation. Shoulder animation $v(t)$ is finally computed using Equation 3 where:

$$\begin{aligned} A_1 &= \overline{V}_{\_,1} + \sigma_{V_{\_,1}}(2\,INT - 1) \\ A_2 &= \overline{V}_{\_,4} + \sigma_{V_{\_,4}}(2\,INT - 1) \\ F_1 &= \overline{V}_{\_,2} + \sigma_{V_{\_,2}}(2\,VEL - 1) \\ F_2 &= \overline{V}_{\_,5} + \sigma_{V_{\_,5}}(2\,VEL - 1) \\ \Phi_2 &= \Phi_1 + C \\ C &= \frac{\sum_{i=1..N}(|V_{i,3} - V_{i,6}|)|)}{N} \end{aligned} \quad (4)$$

where Φ_1 is a random value in $[0,\pi]$, $\overline{V}_{\_,i}$ is the mean value of the elements of the i-th column of matrix V and $\sigma_{V_{\_,i}}$ is the standard deviation of the elements of the i-th column. For example, $\overline{V}_{\_,4}$ is the mean of the amplitudes of the higher frequencies among the selected ones. Thus, the values A_i, F_i of synthetized RBM are in the range of the values $a_{k,i}$, $f_{k,i}$ observed in the real data. If the amplitudes and frequencies in matrices V do not vary a lot then amplitudes and frequencies of the synthesized movements do not vary a lot either, independently of the values of INT and VEL. If the amplitudes and frequencies in matrices V vary a lot then the values of the variables INT and VEL provided by a human animator influence strongly the final animations (i.e., generated RBMs vary a lot depending on INT and VEL).

Torso leaning $l(t)$ is computed using a similar set of equations defined on L.

3.3.1 *Virtual Character Animation*

The duration $t = [t_1, t_2]$ is the third input to our model. As shoulders, during vibration, firstly move up (and then down), we find a time t_{min} that corresponds to the minimum value of $v(t)$ on the time interval $[t_1, t_1 + Period]$, where $Period$ is the actual period of $v(t)$. Next the animation $v(t)$ is computed on the interval $VI = [t_{min}, t_{min} + t_2 - t_1]$. This ensures that the shoulders movement will always start from

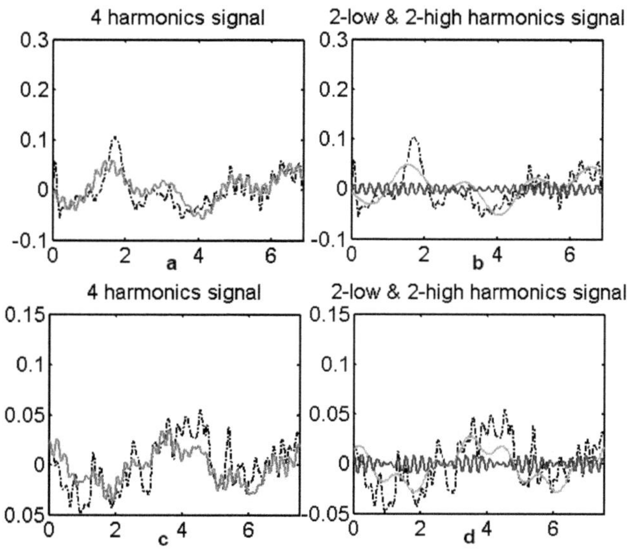

Figure 3: Reconstruction of two first signals from Figure 2. The original signal is dotted; the red curve shows signal reconstructed using 4 components (2 above and 2 below 3Hz), the green curve shows the sum of the two prevalent harmonics below 3 Hz, while the blue curve shows the sum of the two prevalent harmonics above 3 Hz.

the neutral (lowest) position.

Torso leaning can be performed in both directions (forward, backward). To ensure that torso animation starts from the neutral position, it is computed from time $t_0 > t_{min}$, where $l(t_0) < 0.001$. Next the animation $l(t)$ is computed on the interval $LI = [t_0, t_{min} + t_2 - t_1]$ while $l(t) = 0$ for $t \in [t_{min}, t_0]$. This ensures that torso movement is still synchronized with shoulders movement, but it does not need to start from the first frame of the animation.

At the end of the animation, additional frames may be added to allow shoulders and torso to come back to the neutral position. In the last step, the values of $v(t)$ and $l(t)$ computed on the intervals VI and LI are applied to joints of the VC skeleton but starting from the original time t_1.

3.3.2 Controlling Behaviors with BML Language

BML[4] is an XML-based language used to control behaviors of VCs. Shoulder movements are not encompassed in version 1.0 of the BML standard. In order to control such movements, we propose to extend it. In particular, to control RBMs we add the tag *shoulder* with the lexeme "shake" as well as the lexeme "leaning" to the repository of *pose* tag. Both tags have all obligatory BML's attributes such as *id*, *start*, and *end* as well as two additional attributes, *intensity* and *velocity*, taking values in $[0, 1]$ (see Table 2). For example, to generate a two seconds shoulder vibration one may use the following command:

<shoulder id="s1" start="1.0" end="3.0" lexeme="shake" side="both" intensity="1" velocity="1">.

The full description of the new tags is out of the scope of this paper.

[4]http://www.mindmakers.org/projects/bml-1-0

Attribute	Type	Required	Default
lexeme	UP|FRONT|BACK|SHAKE	Yes	-
intensity	float $\in [0..1]$	Not	1
velocity	float $\in [0..1]$	Not	0.5
Side	LEFT|RIGHT|BOTH	Not	BOTH

Table 2: Attributes of the shoulder tag

4. INTEGRATION: MULTIMODAL LAUGHTER SYNTHESIS

In this section we briefly introduce our laughter expressions model for torso movement and facial expression. Next, we describe how to generate the complete multimodal expression of laughter by combining rhythmic body movements, facial expressions, additional body movements and by synchronizing them with laugh sound.

4.1 Contextual Gaussian Model and PD Controller Laughter Synthesis

To model laughter animation, we rely on our previous work [8]: lip and jaw animations are modeled with a Contextual Gaussian Model (CGM) while head, eyebrow, eyelid and cheek animations are generated by concatenating segmented motions. Finally torso animations are synthesized with a proportional-derivation (PD) controller.

Animations were developed on the data of the freely available AVLC dataset [28] that contains facial motion capture data synchronized with audio. Fourteen pseudo-phonemes have been defined (see [27] for their detailed description). Phonetic transcription of audio stream with these 14 pseudo-phonemes was extracted [27]. Then we divided motion capture data of facial motions for the laugh episodes in AVLC into segments where each segment has a duration of one pseudo-phoneme. All segments were labelled by their corresponding pseudo-phoneme and clustered into 14 sub-datasets corresponding to the 14 pseudo-phonemes.

The input I to the laughter animation model consists of the phonetic transcription of the laughter to be generated. It contains the following information:

- pseudo-phonemes sequence as well as their respective duration, which can be extracted automatically from a laughter audio file (e.g., [27]),
- prosodic features of laughter. We consider two features, pitch and energy, at each frame. These features are extracted using PRAAT [3].

The animations of different parts of the body are generated with different methods: lip and jaw animations are modeled with a Contextual Gaussian Model (CGM). The output animation is described using 23 animation parameters: 22 parameters for the lip movements and 1 for the jaw motion.

A CGM is a Gaussian distribution whose mean vector depends on a set of contextual variable(s). In our case, contextual variables are the values of pitch and energy at each frame. When such CGM with a parameterized mean vector is used to model lip and jaw motions, the mean of the CGM obeys the following equation:

$$\hat{\mu}(\theta) = W^{\mu}\theta + \bar{\mu} \quad (5)$$

where W^{μ} is a 23×2 matrix and $\bar{\mu}$ is an offset vector. The mean μ is a 23-dimension vector containing values of all 23 animation parameters per frame. θ stands for a 2-dimension vector containing values of the pitch and energy (contextual variables) at a given frame. Each of the 14 pseudo-phonemes has its own CGM model. Each sub-dataset is used to build the CGM model, which is learned through Maximum Likelihood Estimation (MLE). So, each laughter pseudo-phoneme of the input I is used to select one from 14 CGMs; the values of pitch and energy are applied to the selected CGM to determine lip shape and jaw motion.

Head, eyebrow, eyelid, and cheek animations are determined by selecting and concatenating existing (captured) motion segments, which are scaled to the pseudo-phonemes duration specified in the input I. The synthetized animation is obtained by concatenating the segments that correspond to the input pseudo-phonemes sequence. Each sub-dataset for a given pseudo-phoneme contains many examples of motion segment. The choice of the motion segment from a sub-dataset depends on the sum of two criteria: *duration cost* and *continuity cost*. Duration cost is computed as the difference between expected (target) duration and the candidate segment duration; continuity cost is the distance between the end position of the previously selected segment and the beginning position of the candidate segment. The candidate with the least sum of the two costs is selected as output. Finally, the outputted motion is obtained by concatenating and interpolating the selected samples between two successive segments.

To overcome the unnatural effect of a moving head attached to a rigid body, the third part of our model generates additional torso movements. Thus we compute the torso movement from the head movement. The torso animations are generated by PD controllers. The input to the PD controllers are the three rotation angles of the head. Three PD controllers are independently built to control the three torso rotations (pitch, yaw, and roll). The output of the PD controllers depends on the input at the current frame and the output at the previous frame. Consequently, the torso rotations follow the head rotation, and the head rotations depends on the currently considered pseudo-phoneme. For example, when the head moves down (pitch rotation) then the torso leans forward (pitch rotation). In the PD controllers, the parameters, which define the relation between the head and the torso rotations, are manually defined.

4.2 Synchronization between Modalities

The model presented above is controlled by the phonetic transcription I (list of phonemes and their durations). The same input I is used to synchronize all the modalities: 1) to generate appropriate facial expressions with CGMs and torso movements by concatenation of motion segments, 2) to control (indirectly) the additional body movements (computed from head movement done at item 1), 3) to compute the rhythm of laughter and to control the model of rhythmic body movements, 4) to synchronize with real or synthesized sounds of laughter.

The synchronization procedure is presented in Figure 4. The animation can be synchronized with real or synthesized sounds of laughter. When using natural (real) laughter audio, we need to extract automatically the sequences of pseudo-phonemes. We use Urbain et al.'s laughter segmentation tool [27]. The topic of generating laughter audio synthesis is beyond the scope of this paper. We only mention that there exist several techniques for that, e.g., [26]. The

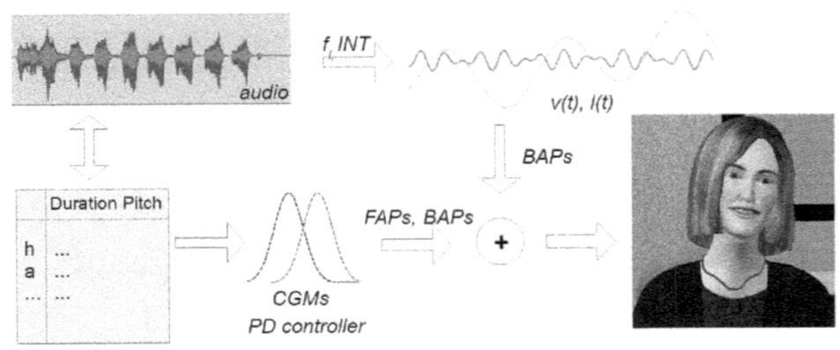

Figure 4: Synchronization procedure

animations generated with the model presented in Section 4.1 take as input the pseudo-phoneme lists and compute the animation based on the duration of each pseudo-phoneme.

Rhythmic body movements can also be synchronized with the whole animation. In the case of multiple modalities to be synchronized the values INT and VEL (see Section 3.3) are not controlled anymore by a human but they are computed from audio, and then applied to Equation 4. Both audio bursts and shoulder movements are caused by repetitive forced exhalations and display similar ranges of frequencies (see Section 1). Thus, we assume that to generate synchronized audio-visual laughter it is sufficient to align the main frequency of the shoulder movements F_1 with the mean frequency of the laughter bursts in the audio sample; this latter can be obtained from the phonetic transcription: $F_1 = \overline{|pho|}$. Using it and reversed Equation 4 one can compute the value of VEL and thus F_2. The laughter intensity of the audio sample can be estimated in real-time, we use a method proposed in [14]. Once we have the value of INT, we compute the remaining parameters of Equation 4, namely A_1, and A_2. Finally we know the value of $v(t)$.

Figure 5 shows an example of the synchronized multimodal animation. We used a freely available MPEG-4 compatible virtual character called Greta[5] [13].

5. INTERACTION SCENARIO: REAL-TIME ADAPTATION OF LAUGHTER RHYTHM

The approach presented in Section 3 has one important advantage: it can be applied during real-time H-VC interaction. In this section we propose how, using our models, a VC tunes the rhythm of its laughter to the nonverbal behavior of a human interacting with it. The ability to perform such an adaptation could contribute to, for example, increase entitativity or affiliation between the human and the VC [10]. We describe here the concept of such real-time interaction, leaving the system implementation and evaluation for future work.

Several interactive H-VC systems considering laughter for the VC side have been proposed, as discussed in Section 2.3. While in these works the VC is able to respond to the user by producing laughs, none of them takes into account human's laughter body movements. Our concept of interaction described below could be integrated within any of these systems.

At least two solutions can be proposed to map human nonverbal behavior onto the animation of a VC: (i) a low-level mapping in which the RBM parameters of the human

[5] http://perso.telecom-paristech.fr/~pelachau/Greta/

Figure 5: Example of animations created with the model

behavior are directly copied to VC's RBM, (ii) a high-level mapping in which more generic characteristics of human expressivity during laughter are captured and mapped onto the VC's RBM parameters. In this interaction scenario we focus on the second solution. Instead of directly copying the harmonics of rhythmic laughter movements, we measure higher-level expressive qualities of human nonverbal behavior during laughter and we propose a mapping of these values onto the laughter RBM harmonics from Equation 4. The idea of mapping human's expressive features to VC's expressive features without copying the movement itself is not novel [4, 20], however, to our knowledge, no previous work focused on body movements of laughter.

The EyesWeb XMI platform is used to analyze the expressive qualities of nonverbal behaviors in laughter. It is equipped with several algorithms to analyze expressive qualities of movement, such as quantity of motion or smoothness. Human data is captured and processed in real-time using EyesWeb XMI and the human's silhouette is automatically extracted from the depth map captured by a Microsoft Kinect sensor. From the silhouette, three expressive features are computed - Quantity of Motion, Contraction Index, and Smoothness Index - which have been widely discussed in literature, see for example [16]. Such features are then mapped onto the VC's RBM parameters $\{(a_k, f_k, \phi_k)|k \in \{1,2\}\}$ and $\{(A_k, F_k, \Phi_k)|k \in \{1,2\}\}$.

In particular, we propose the following mapping:

- Quantity of Motion, that is, the detected amount of human's body movement, is mapped onto the VEL variable (which determines the frequency of shoulder and torso pulses, see Equation 4);
- Contraction Index, that is, the detected amount of horizontal and vertical human's body contraction, is mapped onto the INT variable (which determines the amplitude of shoulder and torso movement, see Eq. 4);
- Smoothness Index, that is, the amount of continuity in human's body movement, is mapped onto the $C = \Phi_2 - \Phi_1$ (that determines the distance between the phases of the 2 harmonics of the generated movement, see Equation 4).

Consequently: (i) the more the human produces body movements during laughter, the more frequent are the VC's RBMs movements, (ii) the larger are the human's movements during laughter, the stronger are the RBM pulses; (iii) the smoother are the movements, the smoother are the trajectories of the VC's RBM movements.

The problem of the detection of human laughter is out of the scope of this paper. There exist several algorithms working in real-time for that, e.g., [12, 14].

6. CONCLUSION AND FUTURE WORK

In this paper we studied and modeled the rhythmic body movements of laughter. The spectral analysis of expressive body movements confirms the findings in literature about the rhythmic movements of laughter. We also showed that only 4 harmonics can effectively reconstruct RBMs. Our RBM model combines the ease of controlling an animation obtained by procedural approach with the accuracy and naturalness of animation based on experimental data. Our model is based on real data analysis but it allows a human to control the animation via a small set of parameters. Importantly, our approach is computationally light and it can be applied to any virtual character. It enables to map human movements to virtual characters in real-time. We believe that it could be easily extended to other rhythmic movements performed while, e.g., coughing or crying. In this paper we also showed how rhythmic animations can be synchronized with the other synthetized expressive cues of laughter such as facial expressions and other body movements. Finally we have also discussed an interactive application integrating our RBM model.

Several limitations and future works should be considered. Our current RBM model is based on a relatively small dataset. Anatomical differences as well as stances (e.g., sitting) may strongly influence movements in laughter. We plan to analyze more data of different gender and stances. Regarding the synthesis part, we are going to extend our model by considering other movement types, such as arm throwing, and knees bending. To validate our model we will perform a perceptive study. The study will provide feedback on the pertinence of our animation model of multimodal laughter. Participants will be asked to evaluate different stimuli of the virtual agent laughing. Three conditions will be compared; they will all use the same audio episode synchronized with facial animation, only the RBM movements will vary between conditions as follow: 1) animations with RBM movements generated with our model, which are synchronized with audio the episode, 2) RBM movements of frequency and amplitude beyond the intervals specified in Equation 4 of our model, 3) animations without RBM movements (the facial animation is still synchronized with audio). The believability, realism and naturalness of the animations will be compared.

7. ACKNOWLEDGEMENTS

The research leading to these results has received funding from the EU 7th Framework Programme under grant agreement n 270780 ILHAIRE. The authors would like to thank Jérôme Urbain (University of Mons) for providing the phonetic transcription of the audio samples used for synthesis.

8. REFERENCES

[1] J. N. Bailenson and N. Yee. Digital chameleons: Automatic assimilation of nonverbal gestures in immersive virtual environments. *Psychological Science*, 16(10):814–819, 2005.

[2] S. Block, M. Lemeignan, and N. Aguilera. Specific respiratory patterns distinguish among human basic emotions. *International Journal of Psychophysiology*, 11(2):141–154, 1991.

[3] P. Boersma and D. Weeninck. PRAAT, a system for doing phonetics by computer. *Glot International*, 5(9/10):341–345, 2001.

[4] G. Castellano, M. Mancini, C. Peters, and P. McOwan. Expressive copying behavior for social agents: A perceptual analysis. *Systems, Man and Cybernetics, Part A: Systems and Humans, IEEE Transactions on*, 42(3):776–783, May 2012.

[5] D. Cosker and J. Edge. Laughing, crying, sneezing and yawning: Automatic voice driven animation of non-speech articulations. In *Proc. of Computer Animation and Social Agents*, pages 21–24, 2009.

[6] C. Darwin. *The expression of emotion in man and animal.* John Murray, London, 1872.

[7] P. C. DiLorenzo, V. B. Zordan, and B. L. Sanders. Laughing out loud: control for modeling anatomically inspired laughter using audio. *ACM Transactions on Graphics (TOG)*, 27(5):125, 2008.

[8] Y. Ding, K. Prepin, J. Huang, C. Pelachaud, and T. Artières. Laughter animation synthesis. In *Proceedings of the 2014 International Conference on Autonomous Agents and Multi-agent Systems*, AAMAS '14, pages 773–780, 2014.

[9] S. Fukushima, Y. Hashimoto, T. Nozawa, and H. Kajimoto. Laugh enhancer using laugh track synchronized with the user's laugh motion. In *CHI '10 Extended Abstracts on Human Factors in Computing Systems*, CHI EA '10, pages 3613–3618, New York, NY, USA, 2010. ACM.

[10] D. Lakens and M. Stel. If they move in sync, they must feel in sync: Movement synchrony leads to attributions of rapport and entitativity. *Social Cognition*, 29(1):1–14, 2011.

[11] M. Mancini, J. Hofmann, T. Platt, G. Volpe, G. Varni, D. Glowinski, W. Ruch, and A. Camurri. Towards automated full body detection of laughter driven by human expert annotation. In *Proceedings of Affective Interaction in Natural Environments (AFFINE) Workshop*, pages 757–762, Geneva, Switzerland, 2013.

[12] M. Mancini, G. Varni, D. Glowinski, and G. Volpe. Computing and evaluating the body laughter index. *Human Behavior Understanding*, pages 90–98, 2012.

[13] R. Niewiadomski, E. Bevacqua, Q. A. Le, M. Obaid, J. Looser, and C. Pelachaud. Cross-media agent platform. In *Web3D ACM Conference*, pages 11–19, Paris, France, 2011.

[14] R. Niewiadomski, J. Hofmann, J. Urbain, T. Platt, J. Wagner, B. Piot, H. Cakmak, S. Pammi, T. Baur, S. Dupont, M. Geist, F. Lingenfelser, G. McKeown, O. Pietquin, and W. Ruch. Laugh-aware virtual agent and its impact on user amusement. AAMAS '13, pages 619–626, 2013.

[15] R. Niewiadomski, M. Mancini, T. Baur, G. Varni, H. Griffin, and M. Aung. MMLI: Multimodal multiperson corpus of laughter in interaction. In A. Salah, H. Hung, O. Aran, and H. Gunes, editors, *Human Behavior Understanding*, volume 8212 of *LNCS*, pages 184–195. Springer, 2013.

[16] R. Niewiadomski, M. Mancini, and S. Piana. Human and virtual agent expressive gesture quality analysis and synthesis. In M. Rojc and N. Campbell, editors, *Coverbal Synchrony in Human-Machine Interaction*, pages 269–292. CRC Press, 2013.

[17] R. Niewiadomski and C. Pelachaud. Towards multimodal expression of laughter. In *Proceedings of IVA'12*, pages 231–244. Springer-Verlag Berlin, Heidelberg, 2012.

[18] K. Prepin and C. Pelachaud. Effect of time delays on agents' interaction dynamics. In *The 10th International Conference on Autonomous Agents and Multiagent Systems - Volume 3*, AAMAS '11, pages 1055–1062, 2011.

[19] R. R. Provine and Y. L. Yong. Laughter: A stereotyped human vocalization. *Ethology*, 89(2):115–124, 1991.

[20] R. Pugliese and K. Lehtonen. A framework for motion based bodily enaction with virtual characters. In *Intelligent Virtual Agents*, volume 6895 of *LNCS*, pages 162–168. Springer Berlin Heidelberg, 2011.

[21] L. D. Riek, P. C. Paul, and P. Robinson. When my robot smiles at me: Enabling human-robot rapport via real-time head gesture mimicry. *Journal on Multimodal User Interfaces*, 3(1-2):99–108, 2010.

[22] W. Ruch and P. Ekman. The expressive pattern of laughter. In A. Kaszniak, editor, *Emotion, qualia and consciousness*, pages 426–443. World Scientific Publishers, Tokyo, 2001.

[23] J. Tilmanne and T. Dutoit. Stylistic walk synthesis based on Fourier decomposition. In *Proceedings of the INTETAIN*, Mons, Belgium, 2013.

[24] N. Troje. The little difference: Fourier based synthesis of gender-specific biological motion. In R. Würtz and M. Lappe, editors, *Dynamic perception*, pages 115–120. Berlin: AKA Verlag, 2002.

[25] M. Unuma, K. Anjyo, and R. Takeuchi. Fourier principles for emotion-based human figure animation. In *Proceedings of SIGGRAPH 1995*, pages 91–96, 1995.

[26] J. Urbain, H. Cakmak, A. Charlier, M. Denti, T. Dutoit, and S. Dupont. Arousal-driven synthesis of laughter. *Selected Topics in Signal Processing, IEEE Journal of*, 8(2):273–284, April 2014.

[27] J. Urbain, H. Cakmak, and T. Dutoit. Automatic phonetic transcription of laughter and its application to laughter synthesis. In *Proceedings of ACII '13*, pages 153–158, 2013.

[28] J. Urbain, R. Niewiadomski, E. Bevacqua, T. Dutoit, A. Moinet, C. Pelachaud, B. Picart, J. Tilmanne, and J. Wagner. AVLaughterCycle: Enabling a virtual agent to join in laughing with a conversational partner using a similarity-driven audiovisual laughter animation. *Journal on Multimodal User Interfaces*, 4(1):47–58, 2010. Special Issue: eNTERFACE'09.

Automatic Blinking Detection towards Stress Discovery

Alvaro Marcos-Ramiro
University of Alcala
Spain
amarcos@depeca.uah.es

Daniel Pizarro-Perez
University of Clermont-Ferrand
France
dani.pizarro@gmail.com

Marta Marron-Romera
University of Alcala
Spain
marta@depeca.uah.es

Daniel Gatica-Perez
Idiap Research Institute and
EPFL
Switzerland
gatica@idiap.ch

ABSTRACT

We present a robust method to automatically detect blinks in video sequences of conversations, aimed to discovering stress. Psychological studies have shown a relationship between blink frequency and dopamine levels, which in turn are affected by stress. Task performance correlates through an inverted U shape to both dopamine and stress levels. This shows the importance of automatic blink detection as a way of reducing human coding burden. We use an off-the-shelf face tracker in order to extract the eye region. Then, we perform per-pixel classification of the extracted eye images to later identify blinks through their dynamics. We evaluate the performance of our system with a job interview database with annotations of psychological variables, and show statistically significant correlation between perceived stress resistance and the automatically detected blink patterns.

Categories and Subject Descriptors

J.4 [**Computer Applications**]: Social and behavioral sciences; G.3 [**Mathematics and Computing**]: Miscellaneous; D.2.8 [**Image Processing and Computer Vision**]: Metrics—*Scene analysis*

General Terms

Blink detection; stress discovery; random forests

1. INTRODUCTION

Psychological studies have shown that nonverbal communication encodes information relative to the internal state of a person [7], and that humans unconsciously perceive nonverbal cues in order to form impressions of others. In situations like job interviews its importance is highlighted, as the interaction time is limited [4].

ICMI'14, November 12–16, 2014, Istanbul, Turkey.

ACM 978-1-4503-2885-2/14/11 ...$15.00.
http://dx.doi.org/10.1145/2663204.2663239.

In this work, we focus on the effect of involuntary blinks, and present a new method for their automatic detection in videos of conversations. Involuntary blinking has shown to be related with dopamine levels, which can be used as a proxy for stress discovery [1, 6]. Given that task performance has been shown to be correlated to both dopamine and stress levels through an inverted U shape [2], blinking detection can provide insights about stress in a non-intrusive fashion. Blink frequency and consistency along time are particularly revealing [6].

Traditionally, in psychological studies there has been the need for an annotator, which manually codes events in videos. Experimental video data to label can often be in tens (or even hundreds) of hours long, resulting in a very tedious task to endure. To address this problem, we build a real time, automatic blink detector from videos through computer vision and machine learning techniques, which is our first contribution. We first track and extract the eye region from frontal videos with an off-the-shelf face tracker [16]. Then, we normalize the color appearance of this region of interest, and we employ a non-linear Random Forest classifier in order to segment the different parts of the eye. Finally, we analyze the dynamics of the segmented eyes and evaluate the performance with a 11.5 hour real job interview corpus that has annotations, amongst other attributes, of stress resistance and personality [11, 12]. In addition, as our second contribution we show the viability of our approach by demonstrating significant correlation between the automatically discovered blink patterns and the perceived resistance to stress of job candidates.

The rest of the paper is structured as follows: in Section 2 the previous works are reviewed, in Section 3 we present our method, in Section 4 the used data is described, in Section 5 the results are presented and discussed, and finally we provide conclusions in Section 6.

2. PREVIOUS WORK

Given the psychology background presented in the previous section, and that blinking can be used to design human-machine interfaces in situations of reduced mobility, some works in the literature address the problem of blinking detection by means of computer vision.

Existing systems can be grouped into active sensing, in which special illumination or intrusive systems are used; and passive sensing, in which color images are used. Active sensing like infrared illumination [15] might cause damage to the retina or be intrusive. We focus on passive methods.

In passive methods, previous approaches include skin color models [8], template matching [5], generalized projection functions [17], or eye detection using Haar-like features [9].

To our knowledge, the most similar work to ours is [14], in which blink detection is also motivated towards inferring higher level psychological constructs. Hidden Markov Models and Support Vector Machines are used to estimate the likelihood of an open or close eye, given its dynamics. This method is more computationally complex than ours, as it involves the use of Histogram of Oriented Gradients, Gabor filters, and optical flow.

3. METHOD

Our automatic blink detection system consists of a three step process. First, the face is tracked and an eye region of interest is extracted. Then, using the eye region of interest as input to a classifier, the different parts of the eye are segmented. Finally, the variation of openness of the eye lid is measured to later detect blinks. The process is described with more detail as follows.

3.1 Face tracking and eye region extraction

We obtain and track a series of face points with an off-the-shelf method [16], from which we extract the eye region image $\mathbf{I}_e$. We first use the interocular line as reference (see Figure 1, in green), since it is the only face measure that is not affected by face deformations associated with changes of expression. Then, we obtain the head tilt angle and compensate for it, in order to have a stable region of interest (see Figure 1). We use the normalized V channel after converting the eye region into the HSV color space, and scale $\mathbf{I}_e$ to 147×51 pixels (as it is the average region of interest size) to provide consistency across different subjects and face poses.

Figure 1: Eye region extraction. Left: face tracking in an image taken from the BioID Face Database. Right: extracted eye region of interest.

3.2 Eye segmentation

Similar to [13], we use an offset sampling idea and a Random Forest classifier in order to associate every pixel of $\mathbf{I}_e$ with an eye part label: iris and pupil, sclera (white part), eyelids, and background (i.e. non-eye regions). An example can be seen in Figure 2. Random Forests have shown real time performance and very good generalization capabilities.

A set $\mathcal{U}$ of pixel offset features is built: $\mathcal{U} = \{\vec{u_{\delta i}}\}_{i=1}^{n_\delta} = \{(u_{\delta i}, v_{\delta i})\}_{i=1}^{n_\delta}$. For a given pixel $\vec{u}$, the feature response is computed with feature parameters $\vec{u_{\delta i}}$ that describe a number of n_δ 2D pixel offsets $(u_{\delta i}, v_{\delta i})$. In [13], features are normalized with the distance to the camera in order to make them depth-invariant. We use contrast values instead, thus defining local contrast differences as per-pixel features.

Let $L(\vec{u}, \vec{u_{\delta i}}, \mathbf{I}^1)$ be a lookup function that returns the feature associated with pixel $\vec{u}$, given a single-channel image $\mathbf{I}^1$ and an offset $\vec{u_{\delta i}}$ (that is, $\mathbf{I}_e(\vec{u} + \vec{u_{\delta i}})$). A feature f_e for a given pixel $\vec{u}$ is then expressed as:

$$f_e(\vec{u}|\vec{u_{\delta i}}) = L(\vec{u}, \vec{u_{\delta i}}, \mathbf{I}_e)\frac{1}{\mathbf{I}_e(\vec{u})}. \quad (1)$$

This feature encodes local appearance as contrast differences within a spatial window. It provides a rich description of the several eye parts, given the high contrast between the iris/pupil and sclera.

3.2.1 *Training the classifier*

A subset of data from the real job interview dataset is annotated in order to serve as a training set. For classification, annotations consist in a number of manually-labeled pixels in the image, in which the nature of each label corresponds to a given eye part. We compute the previously introduced per-pixel offset features for each labeled pixel in the training subset. We then train a Random Forest with the extracted features and the associated eye part labels. Given an unseen image $\mathbf{I}_e$, the classifier outputs the per-pixel predicted eye part and an associated confidence score (see Figure 2).

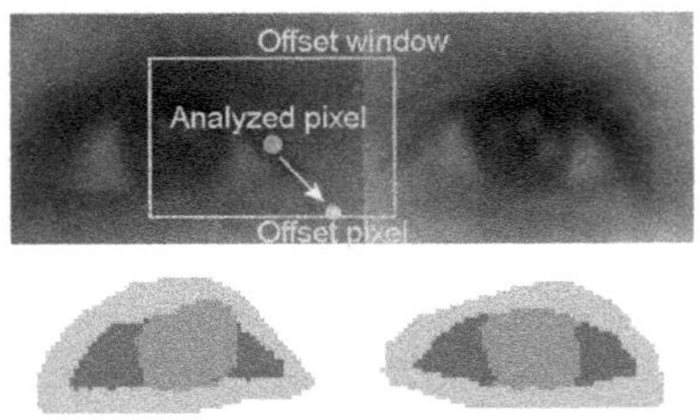

Figure 2: Classification features. Top: offset feature example. Bottom: manually annotated labels used to train the classifier: iris and pupil (red), sclera (blue), eyelids (green), and background (white). Best viewed in color.

3.3 Blinking dynamics

Blinking is defined as a quick closing and opening of the eyes. Therefore, we assume that the accumulated variation of openness of the eye along short periods of time peaks during blinking. We define an eye openness measure $e_{o,t}$ at time t as the number of pixels classified as pupil/iris and sclera, since they constitute the visible parts of the eye when it is open. The differential feature $e_{k,t}$ is therefore defined as the difference of openness between two time instants: $e_{k,t} = e_{o,t} - e_{o,t-1}$. Finally, we accumulate $e_{k,t}$ along a three-frame time window, in order to obtain the short-term accumulated feature $e_{a,t}$.

Since images $\mathbf{I}_e$ are normalized to the same size, a global threshold can be used to segment the $e_{a,t}$ signal, and works well in practice. Blinks are detected in instants in which the threshold is exceeded, resulting into the b_t signal. It is set to 1 during blinking, and 0 otherwise. See Figure 3 for an example, in which an empirically-set threshold of 0.1 is used.

4. DATA

We employed the data used in [11, 12]. An intelligent room and a set of experiments to record information of 60 participants in a real, for a sales-like job interviews were designed.

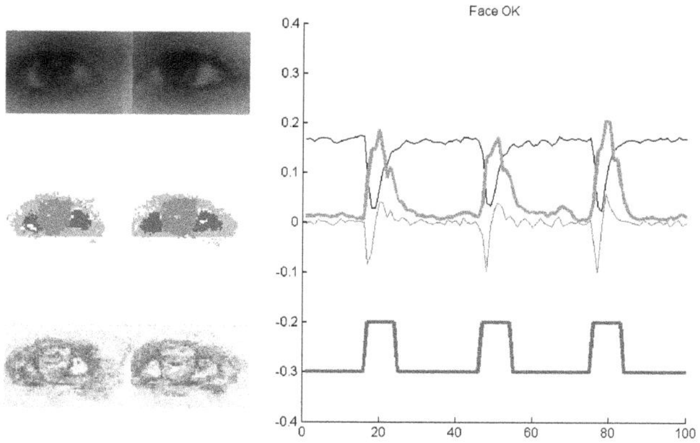

Figure 3: Blinking dynamics. Left: eye region of interest and classification results. Right: eye movement dynamics (thin black line: $e_{o,t}$; thin blue line: $e_{k,t}$; red line: accumulated variation of openness $e_{a,t}$; thick blue line: blink detection signal b_t). Best viewed in color.

An open position was advertised local universities using multiple communication channels. The average participant age was 24 years. Before starting the interview, applicants filled in a consent form. They then completed a questionnaire to assess their Big-Five personality scores [7], encoded with a 1-5 scale.

The interviews are dyadic, with the recruiter facing the job applicant. The protagonists were seated at both sides of a table. A total of 11.5 hours were recorded in 720p resolution. For the interview itself a structured design was used, where the sequence of instructions and questions remained constant across interviews in order to ensure that comparisons could be made between job candidates. The job applicants were asked to answer four behavioral questions related to past experiences in situations that require specific social skills, including resistance to stress, intelligence, and communication skills, in a five-point scale. Human resources experts annotated the perceived attributes of the participants while looking at audio only, at video only, and at both.

5. RESULTS

5.1 Experiments and measures

We define two experiments to assess the performance of our proposal: **experiment #1** is designed to evaluate the performance of the blink detection system. Blink events in multiple sequences containing different subjects from the real job interview corpus are manually labeled, and used as groundtruth to be compared with the automatic detections. Subjects are different to those used during training. In total, 330 seconds of video (five and a half minutes) and 10 subjects with different skin tones are employed for testing, containing 133 blinking events. The Random Forest classifier is trained with a disjoint subset of 32 eye images from 11 different subjects. As performance measure, we chose global accuracy and the F_1 score, which is defined as the harmonic mean between precision and recall:

$$F_1 = 2 \cdot \frac{precision \cdot recall}{precision + recall}. \quad (2)$$

F_1 is a strict measure that takes into account class balance. This is specially relevant in our case since blink events constitute very little proportion of the total video length. We define correct detections as blinking events that are detected within a four frame window of the blinking events contained in the groundtruth, as we accumulate the eye energy signal $e_{a,t}$ over a three-frame window, resulting in a slight delay in the detection. Performance results can be seen in Section 5.2.

In **experiment #2**, we assess the validity of our method to extract measures related to stress signals. We extract a series of features from the automatically extracted blink information, which we then correlate with the job candidates data obtained from the questionnaire data described in Section 4. The features that we extract are: (1) Shannon's entropy of the whole blinking event signal b_t; (2) entropy, mean, and standard deviation of the time lapses between blinking events; (3) entropy, mean, and standard deviation of the accumulated signal $e_{a,t}$.

Since the literature has shown that the regularity of blinking patterns is a proxy for stress discovery, we hypothesized that extra information can be extracted from the entropy of the signals.

5.2 Results and discussion

When evaluating our system with **experiment #1**, we obtain a F_1 value of 93.65% for event-based detection. We get 5 false positives (3.76%) and 11 undetected blinks (8.27%), out of the total 133 events. Upon visual inspection, the errors come from two sources: face tracking misplacements and eye part classification malfunctions due to a high rotation angle between the face and the camera. The latter could be corrected by using similar time moments during the training phase of the per-pixel classifier, while the former can only be addressed by discarding the mis-tracked periods through outlier detection. Nevertheless, the obtained F_1 value remains highly satisfactory, specially given the complexity of the task (high appearance variance across different subjects, face rotations, looking down to the table, or the distance from the face to the camera). In Figures 4 and 5, quantitative and qualitative results can be seen.

After conducting **experiment #2**, we present a series of statistically significant ($p < 0.05$) correlations, see Table 1. To obtain the correlation coefficients, we discarded lost tracking periods for the face, and used data for the 60 participants.

Table 1: Perceived attributes and modulus of the correlation coefficient obtained with our features (60 subjects).

Attribute	Corr	Feature
Stress resistance (audio)	0.27	Entropy of $e_{a,t}$
Openness to experience	0.31	Entropy of blink time lapses
Agreeableness	0.26	Standard deviation of $e_{a,t}$
Agreeableness	0.27	Mean of blink time lapses
Intelligence	0.28	Entropy of b_t
Communication skills	0.29	Entropy of $e_{a,t}$
Conscientiousness	0.33	Mean of $e_{a,t}$

The significant correlation between perceived stress resistance from annotating only with the audio channel validates our hypothesis, while also highlighting the multimodal nature of the stress perception (which is consistent with previous works [10]). Regarding correlation with other variables, interestingly, the highest correlation coefficient is obtained

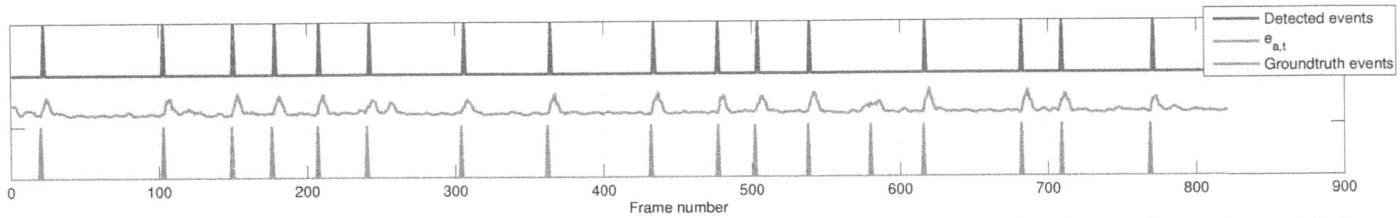

Figure 4: Blink extraction for one of the test sequences. The accumulated eye movement signal is used to estimate blink events.

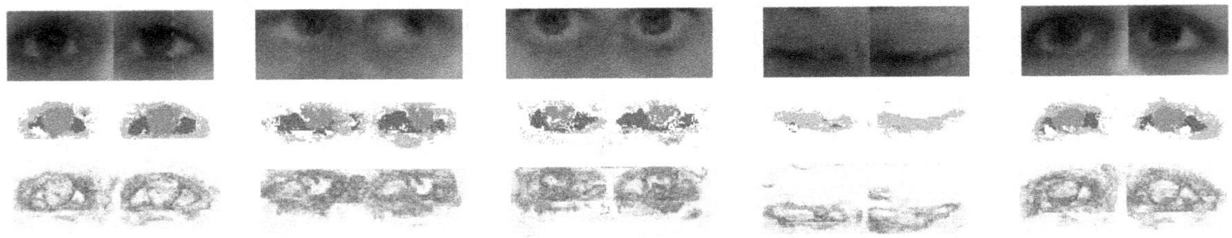

Figure 5: Qualitative results. Top row: eye region of interest. Central row: eye segmentation. Bottom row: classification confidence.

for conscientiousness. This goes in line with the literature on deception detection from blinking [14], given the known relationship between deception and conscientiousness levels [3].

The results also show that by processing directly the signal $e_{a,t}$, we are able to extract more information than just by using the binary blink events. This allows for a higher granularity in the intensity and duration of the eye blinks. As future work, we plan to approach the problem as a classification or regression task, in order to quantify the stress levels. In addition, blinking detection on subjects wearing glasses should be explored, given the problems that their use arise, such as reflexions and occlussions.

6. CONCLUSIONS

We have presented an automatic blink detection system towards stress discovery by using a computer vision approach. We first obtain track the face with an off-the-self method in order to extract the eye region of interest. Then, we employ a Random Forest classifier to segment the eyes into their different parts. Finally, we analyze the dynamics of the blinking thanks to their energy signal. We evaluated our computer vision approach with a challenging dataset, showing high performance in an unconstrained conversational setting. Then, we found moderate, yet significant correlation between blink detections and expert human annotations. This result provides a starting point to further investigate the connections of stress, amongst other attributes, with automatic blink discovery.

7. ACKNOWLEDGMENTS

This research was funded by SNSF UBImpressed project, the Spanish Ministry of Science and Innovation under project VISNU (ref. TIN2009-08984) and the University of Alcala FPI internship program.

8. REFERENCES

[1] C. Adler, I. Elman, N. Weisenfeld, L. Kestler, D. Pickar, and A. Breier. Effects of acute metabolic stress on striatal dopamine release in healthy volunteers. *Neuropsychopharmacology*, 22, 2000.

[2] P. L. Broadhurst. Emotionality and the yerkes-dodson law. *Journal of Experimental Psychology*, 54, 1957.

[3] R. B. Cattell. *The Scientific Analysis of Personality.* Penguin, London, 1965.

[4] J. Curhan and A. Pentland. Thin slices of negotiation: Predicting outcomes from conversational dynamics within the first five minutes. *Journal of Applied Psychology*, 2007.

[5] M. S. Devi and P. R. Bajaj. Driver fatigue detection based on eye tracking. In *International Conference on Emerging Trends in Engineering and Technology*, 2008.

[6] C. Karson. Spontaneous eye-blink rates and dopaminergic systems. *Brain*, 106, 1983.

[7] M. Knapp and J. Hall. *Nonverbal Communication in Human Interaction.* 2009.

[8] A. Krolak and P. Strumillo. Fatigue monitoring by means of eye blink analysis in image sequences. In *ICSES*, 2006.

[9] A. Krolak and P. Strumillo. Eye-blink detection system for human-computer interaction. *Universal Access in the Information Society*, 11, 2012.

[10] H. Lu, D. Frauendorfer, M. Rabbi, M. S. Mast, G. T. Chittaranjan, A. T. Campbell, D. Gatica-Perez, and T. Choudhury. Stresssense: Detecting stress in unconstrained acoustic environments using smartphones. In *ACM Ubiquitous Computing*, 2012.

[11] L. Nguyen, A. Marcos, M. Marron, and D. Gatica. Multimodal analysis of body communication cues in employment interviews. In *ACM International Conference on Multimodal Interaction (ICMI)*, 2013.

[12] L. S. Nguyen, D. Frauendorfer, M. Schmid Mast, and D. Gatica-Perez. Hire me: Computational inference of hirability in employment interviews based on nonverbal behavior. *IEEE Transactions on Multimedia*, 2014.

[13] J. Shotton, T. Sharp, A. Kipman, A. W. Fitzgibbon, M. Finocchio, A. Blake, M. Cook, and R. Moore. Real-time human pose recognition in parts from single depth images. In *IEEE CVPR*, 2011.

[14] Y. Sun, S. Zafeiriou, and M. Pantic. A hybrid system for on-line blink detection. In *Hawaii International Conference on System Sciences*, 2013.

[15] P. Thoumie, J. R. Charlier, M. Alecki, D. D. Erceville, A. Heurtin, J. F. Mathe, G. Nadeau, and L. Wiart. Clinical and functional evaluation of a gaze controlled system for the severely handicapped. *Spinal Cord*, 36, 1998.

[16] X. Xiong and F. De la Torre. Supervised descent method and its applications to face alignment. In *IEEE CVPR*, 2013.

[17] Z.-H. Zhou and X. Geng. Projection functions for eye detection. *Pattern Recognition*, 37, 2004.

Mid-air Authentication Gestures: An Exploration of Authentication Based on Palm and Finger Motions

Ilhan Aslan+, Andreas Uhl*, Alexander Meschtscherjakov+ and Manfred Tscheligi+
University of Salzburg, Salzburg, Austria
name.lastname@sbg.ac.at+
uhl@cosy.sbg.ac.at*

ABSTRACT

Authentication based on touch-less mid-air gestures would benefit a multitude of ubicomp applications, which are used in clean environments (e.g., medical environments or clean rooms). In order to explore the potential of mid-air gestures for novel authentication approaches, we performed a series of studies and design experiments. First, we collected data from more then 200 users during a three-day science event organised within a shopping mall. This data was used to investigate capabilities of the Leap Motion sensor and to formulate an initial design problem. The design problem, as well as the design of mid-air gestures for authentication purposes, were iterated in subsequent design activities. In a final study with 13 participants, we evaluated two mid-air gestures for authentication purposes in different situations, including different body positions. Our results highlight a need for different mid-air gestures for differing situations and carefully chosen constraints for mid-air gestures.

Keywords

mid-air gestures; authentication; Leap Motion sensor; design;

Categories and Subject Descriptors

H.5.2. [**Information Interfaces and Presentation**]: User Inter- faces - Interaction styles;

1. INTRODUCTION

There is a need for authentication in a world pervaded with more and more digital technologies. We authenticate ourselves by entering a PIN when we want to pay with our credit card. We get access to our mobile phones by connecting points on our smartphones. We type in passwords for authentication on websites. We use iris scanners for authentication in high-security areas. Thus, different interaction modalities are used for authentication in different contexts. The different modalities are often dependent on various factors, such as the degree of security and the availability of technology, as well as environmental factors like background noise or the physical position of interactive elements.

ICMI '14, November 12 - 16 2014, Istanbul, Turkey

http://dx.doi.org/10.1145/2663204.2663246 .

Another requirement for the right choice of authentication modalities is the "cleanness" of the interaction context (e.g., aseptic environments). Examples for such environments are well known from the medical domain. In such domains, keyboards or touch screens are not always the best choice for authentication. Users often wear gloves and must not contaminate themselves or the environment. In cooperations with an industrial partner from the semiconductor domain, we recognised that there is also a need for a clean and ideally touch-less way of interaction in the industrial domain, especially in the clean room.

A clean room in the semiconductor context is often a noisy and large environment, where workers need to wear special clothes including rubber gloves and a mask in order to minimise dust, which could cause defects in the production process of integrated circuits (see Fig. 1). Workers in clean rooms are mobile and need to authenticate themselves repeatedly during their daily activities on different workstations and in different situation. This is often realised via text-based passwords. Most workstations in the clean room are desktop computers, which are either used in a standard setting (i.e., seated with monitor, keyboard, and mouse positioned on a desk) or in a setting where the workers have to interact with the system while standing with the monitor and keyboard attached to the wall.

Figure 1: Clean room in a semiconductor factory. Operators are wearing suits and rubber gloves in order to reduce dust circulation.

While keyboards and mice provide an effective and well known way of interaction, they are also considered in-proper for clean rooms, since they attract dust. Therefore, more and more touch interfaces are integrated in clean rooms.

However, even touch interfaces pose an issue in clean rooms, since dust is attracted by touch screens and contaminate operators' gloves when they touch the screens. Following this argument, the interaction in the clean room should be touch-less whenever possible. Apart from using well-known biometric approaches such as face-, iris-, or voice-detection, we propose to use mid-air gestures for a touch-less authentication purposes.

Recently, touch-less interaction has vastly improved that off-the-shelf devices, such as the Leap Motion[1], sensor can be purchased for low costs. These sensors can recognise hand biometry and hand gestures and allow touch-less and gesture based interaction. Moreover, mid-air gestures are a promising modality for interaction in clean rooms and hand biometry information gleaned from mid-air gestures may even provide a clean way for authentication.

In order to explore the potential of mid-air gesture for authentication, we performed a series of studies. Hereby, we were motivated by related work in touch and gesture-based authentication [4, 26] , which has shown that gesture-based authentication can be an alternative to text-based passwords. Therefore, we aim to address the following research question in this paper, can authentication based on mid-air gestures and the Leap Motion controller be used in situation relevant for clean rooms?

In the following section, we first provide some background in gesture-based authentication. Then, we present our exploration of mid-air authentication gestures, which started with a field study and a series of subsequent design experiments based on inspirations gained from visits to actual clean rooms. The design experiments were conducted to specify the design problem and to infer design considerations for authentication gestures. Afterwards, we present a study with 13 participants, which shows authentication accuracy rates for two gestures performed in different situation and an overview of the user experience of the mid-air gestures based authentication method. We conclude that with recognition rates for single gestures around 89% that mid-air based authentication gestures are already an alternative for authentication based on touch gestures. Considering that 3D controllers are compared to touch sensitive screens in their infancy, there is great promise in mid-air gesture based authentication.

2. BACKGROUND

With systems and services becoming increasingly mobile and ubiquitous, novel approaches for authentication need to be easy to use in different situations. For mobile devices, which are used on the go, motion and shape-based approaches (e.g., password patterns used by Android-based mobile phones) have been introduced as alternatives to text-based password schemes (e.g., PIN-authentication). These approaches make use of the pictorial superiority effect [18] and the human motor memory [28] to reduce the cognitive burden of memorizing passwords.

While shape-based authentication approaches are easy to memorise and use, security aspects have been criticised due to the fact that they are easy to spy on (e.g., [3]). In order to improve the security of shape-based authentication approaches on mobile phones related work has investigated the use of an additional implicit authentication layer. Based on a series of user studies, DeLuca et al. [4] were able to show that inter-personal differences in drawing the same shape could be used to improve the security of shape-based authentication on mobile phones.

Inter-personal differences have also been exploited by Sae-Bae et al. [26] in a gesture-based authentication approach for multi-touch devices, which is based on a study with iPads. They developed a comprehensive set of five finger gestures based on hand ergonomics and were able to show that there are behavioural traits in gestures, which can be used to improve shape-based authentication on touch screens. On one hand, these inter-personal differences in human gestures can be disturbing when designing user interfaces due to the introduced inter-personal variability (variances among different users might get interpreted as distinct "commands"). On the other hand, they can be exploited for designing personalised user interfaces (the same gesture is interpreted differently when conducted by different users). In any case, these inter-personal differences are essential for gesture-based authentication.

In recent work the Leap Motion device has been used for recognising handwriting in the air [30] as well as for sign language recognition [21].

However, the capabilities of these sensors for authentication purposes have not yet been investigated in depth, including the influence of context on performing a mid-air authentication gesture.

Human (hand) gesture recognition [17, 14] has already been explored in many applications like sign language recognition [20], device [19] and software control [25], augmented reality application [23] and authentication [1, 7, 10]. We may distinguish *instrumented sytems*, which use trackable markers mounted to the fingers (e.g., infrared targets [23]) and *non-instrumented systems* relying on vision techniques only. Different types of sensors can also be used ranging from classical vision using still-image or video cameras [13, 22, 12, 31, 19, 7] to various depth imaging techniques [2, 32]. Research in mid-air based interaction has increased since sensors, such as Microsoft's Kinect device, have been on the market. Applications involving the Kinect include static hand gesture recognition [11, 24], dynamic hand/arm gesture recognition [33], software control [25], surgeons assistance [15], and authentication [29]. Other sensors employed for (hand) gesture recognition include (smartphone integrated) accelerators [9, 10, 16], virtual reality interfaces like Cyber Glove [20], and specific biometric devices (e.g. a Smart Pen [1]).

With respect to hand gesture-based authentication, few techniques have been proposed. Arm movements are captured for this purpose by (smartphone integrated) accelerators [9, 10, 16]. Mid-air handwriting recognition for authentication is conducted with different sensors (Kinect [29], Bio Smart Pen [1]); sign language recognition for identifying user-specific pass-codes is suggested in [12].

Independent from gesture recognition techniques, the obvious benefit of mid-air hand gestures is that humans already use their hands and fingers in different situations to manipulate real world objects. In the past, interaction design evolved through making use of human skills to improve interaction with the digital world [5]. Therefore, it can be assumed that mid-air gestures have the potential to improve interaction with ubiquitous systems, allowing users to interact more "naturally" with the digital world in different situations. A particular challenge for ubicomp application in

[1]http://www.leapmotion.com

clean rooms is that users need to perform a log-in action in different situations.

Although a multitude of authentication techniques exist, techniques for ubicomp application that use biometric information are favoured. Biometric information is always at hand and available anytime and anywhere. With off the-shelf-3D controllers that can track detailed movements of fingers, the usage of fine-grained mid-air hand gestures for authentication seems to become possible.

3. EXPLORATION OF MID-AIR GESTURES FOR AUTHENTICATION

The Leap Motion controller is a camera-based 3D controller, which uses depth and RGB cameras similar to Microsoft's Kinect device to recognise "body" movement. However, this 3D controller is a light, small sized device with a short range (approximately 1 inch to 2 feet above the device). Its software has been developed for a particular use; i.e., recognising palm and finger movements in detail. Being a small and lightweight 3D controller, it is flexible and can be attached to various surfaces (e.g., walls or desks). In fact, the device is already being embedded in laptops (i.e., the HP envy Leap Motion). Due to the device dimension, it could also be worn on the body (e.g., like a wrist watch).

Being a vision based tracking system, the Leap Motion sensor faces some obvious limitations, such as being able to recognise fingers only if they are in the field of vision. For example, hand rotations along the lower arm are difficult to recognise by the device if the device is used in a seated posture with the device placed on a desk. Based on our initial explorations, we also realised that the hands of some people are recognised better than others. To get an idea about how well the sensor tracks hand movements, we collected data in a field study, where we logged data from more then 200 people.

3.1 Field study

At a science event in November 2014, a few departments of University (blinded) presented their research to the public in a large shopping mall. Everyone could attend this event and engage with demonstrators, prototypes, and design artefacts. At this event, we presented different gesture based interfaces, which made use of the Leap Motion sensor. In one display, visitors could use a capacitive pen in combination with a Leap Motion sensor to create artful drawings. Visitors had to perform a specific mid-air gesture before they could start drawing.

By rotating their palm clockwise by 70 degrees, they could clean the canvas (screen of an iPad device). We logged hand movement data associated with this initial gesture. On a monitor that was positioned in front of the users, this initial gesture was presented as part of a promotional video for the booth. The 3D controller could either be positioned on the desk next to the iPad or worn on the wrist (e.g., as it is done by the participant in Figure 2). To allow users to wear the 3D controller on their wrist, we build an adjustable velcro wristband. Figure 2 presents the final setup, which was used at the field study. As also presented in Figure 2, many of the booth visitors were teenagers and the situation was crowded. We collected data from more then 200 visitors, 195 of those have agreed to fill in a post-hoc questionnaire providing demographic data. Inspection of the data we collected showed that only in 12% of the time 5 fingers were recognised (in 25% of the time 4 fingers, in 37% 3 fingers, in 53% 2 fingers and in 75% 1 finger was recognised) Even though the palm was recognised in 25 %, no fingers were recognised.

Figure 2: Setup at the science event. A participant has the 3D controller attached to his right wrist and is performing mid-air gestures with his left hand to interact with information presented at the iPad.

Further inspections of the data showed that the Leap Motion SDK only provides finger IDs depending on the order in which fingers are recognised for each frame, thus no semantic information is provided, such as if a recognised finger matches to a thumb or an index finger, etc. Furthermore, the same finger ID is mapped to semantically different fingers of the hand over the period of performing a gesture (see Figure 3). For authentication gestures, it is necessary to map fingers to their respective movement paths otherwise biometric informations is lost. Furthermore, five fingers should be recognised to get maximal data from the hand geometry. The main reason that not all fingers were recognised was that fingers were not clearly separated during gestures. Since gestures are not performed in exactly the same space (e.g., at the same distance to the sensor), it is also necessary to transfer gesture data to a canonical form. This is needed in order to recognise the same gesture even if it is performed with a slightly different orientation and at a different space. Taking these design constraints into account, we decided to design specific authentication gestures.

3.2 Designing authentication gestures

Inspired by the set of categories for five-finger touch gestures, which were reported by Sae-Bae et al. [26], we defined a five finger mid-air gesture for authentication (see Figure 3). We chose a complex gesture including circular finger and palm movements as well as finger closing and finger opening movements (all movements accruing in three dimensional space) to capture maximal biometric information and to study the boundaries of what is feasible.

We presented a video recording of this gesture and asked several people from our own department to replicate this authentication gesture. We used the data for further exploration. Figure 3 also presents the data, which was captured by the Leap Motion device. Even though we asked users to separate their fingers in the beginning of the gesture to ensure that all five fingers were recognised in the beginning, exploration of the captured data showed that for some users the sensor failed to recognise all five fingers in the beginning.

3.2.1 Normalising hand gesture data

Recognising five fingers in the beginning is important since we use the initial state of the hand to match movement sequence to individual fingers. Individual fingers are recognised by computing the distance between fingers. If the fingers are spread, the thumb has the highest distance to the other fingers. The index finger is nearest to the thumb, etc.

Once individual fingers are matched, the gesture data can be normalised based on the position of the palm, the index finger and the pinky by performing transformations; i.e., moving the palm to the origin, rotating the index finger twice, so that it's tip is on an the z-axis and on the x-plane. Afterwards, the pinky is rotate also on the x-plane.

In earlier attempts, we used the thumb instead of the palm. However, since the thumb is the most flexible finger it caused higher intra-personal difference (the same persons positioned their thumbs differently in the beginning of a gesture), which is undesirable for an authentication approach.

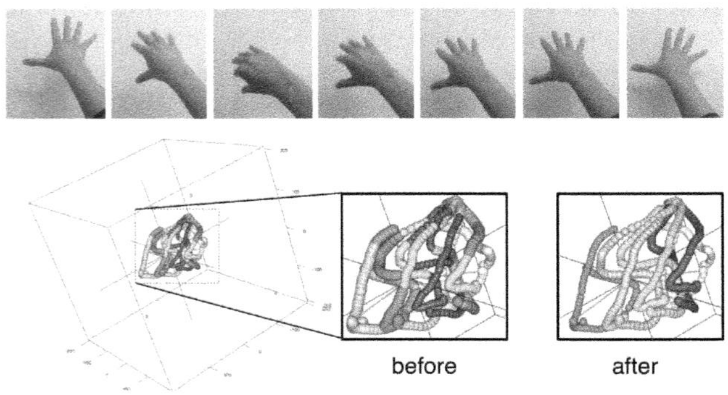

Figure 3: On the upper half a gestures is presented. On the lower half data representing the gesture before and after performing a matching algorithm is presented. The algorithm matches individual fingers to movement paths.

After matching captured data to individual fingers and normalising the gestures using the camera coordinate system, we needed to match individual fingers to the movement paths. This was a challenge since not all fingers were recognised during performing the gesture. Figure 3 visualises captured data before and after performing the matching algorithm.

3.2.2 Design workshop

In order to reflect on results gained and to discuss the design of authentication gestures in general with interdisciplinary professionals, we conducted a design workshop with six participants with backgrounds in computer science, game design, sociology, and psychology. We did this to obtain qualitative and critical feedback to the authentication gesture we designed so far and create new ideas for gestures taking into account restrictions of the Leap Motion sensor and naturalness of performing the gestures for authentication purposes.

In the workshop, we first presented our idea of using mid-air gestures for authentication. Then, we demonstrated the Leap Motion controller, what restrictions it has, and how it could also be worn on the wrist or attached to a wall. Three of the 6 participants have already visited clean rooms and knew the context well. We asked participants to walk around and perform mid-air gestures in situation relevant for the clean room to build empathy for the topic; i.e., seated with imagining the sensor on the desk and standing in front of a whiteboard with a sensor sketched on the whiteboard. Participants could also explore the capabilities of a Leap Motion sensor during the workshop. The workshop took an hour and several ideas were generated on top of our previous results.

The following main issues were raised in the workshop. Without visual feedback, it is difficult to memorise a gestures even if the gesture was chosen by a user themselves. Gestures should be short, simple and easy to repeat. Due to hand and body ergonomics, different contexts might need different gestures which needs to be explored. Shoulder, upper arm, and elbow muscle behaviour could also be used for the authentication.

Based on the insights gained and suggestions for authentication gestures, we refined two gestures and designed visual feedback for those gestures.

- Gesture 1 was an "upward" movement of the hand, with the hand slightly close and and opens. It makes use of finger movement behaviour.
- Gesture 2 is an "upward" movement, with the hand rotating anti-clockwise. It makes use of shoulder, upper arm, and elbow movement and, consequently, associated muscle behaviour.

For both gestures, the start and the end positions have been chosen to be different to allow an improved matching of individual fingers to movement paths. As visual feedback, we created an animation of an hand icon. We chose a very simple and abstract presentation, so that it could be presented on different kinds of small sized displays. Furthermore, presenting an abstract visualisation would allow users to define themselves how exactly the gestures should be performed. The key purpose of visual feedback was twofold: first, to provide feedback on the recognition quality (e.g., hand icon turns green if all five fingers are recognised) and, second, to guide and also remind the user of "what" and "how" to perform the gesture. Once the user is ready and five fingers are recognised, the hand icon was animated slowly to allow the user to "mirror" the gesture. We chose as duration for the animation two seconds based on our own experience.

4. USER STUDY

In order to investigate how the designed gestures would be perceived by users and to explore intra and inter-personal variabilities in performing mid-air authentication gestures, we conducted a user study. Moreover, we investigated their authentication strength in three different contexts

The three contexts were chosen based on prior observations during visits to actual clean rooms. There are two main situation in which workers authenticate themselves on workstations; i.e., seated with monitor, keyboard, and mouse positioned on a desk or standing with the monitor and keyboard attached to the wall. Depending on the physical setting, keyboards are even vertically attached to a wall with the mouse being placed on a small piece which is also attached to the wall. The third context, which we studied, includes a concept for a wearable 3D controller. Authentication on a wearable and mobile interfaces is a future alternative to the currently existing contexts. Using a small sized 3D controller as a wearable on a workers wrist is a realistic alternative for an interface in clean rooms, since workers already have special clothes that they need to wear during their work. In addition, there is a trend for wearable devices outside the clean room context (i.e., smart watches), which might inspire the future interface landscape in clean rooms.

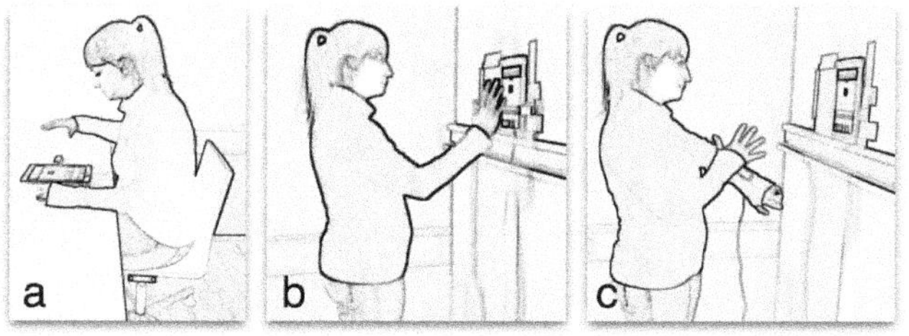

Figure 4: The three conditions in which mid-air gestures for authentication were studied a) 3D controller is positioned on the desk. b) 3D controller is positioned on the wall. c) 3D controller is worn on wrist.

4.1 Study setup

Figure 4 presents the three different physical setups we asked participants to perform mid-air authentication gestures. The visual guidance was presented on a second generation iPad which we positioned in each physical setting in a way that participants could easily perceive the visual feedback. For the study we recruited thirteen right handed participants (7f, 6m) between 26 and 41 years of age. All participants completed the study within 20 minutes.

Participants were asked perform each of the two gestures in 3 different conditions for 10 times in counter balanced order. The rate in which data was collected was between 50 and 55 per second. In sum, we collected data from 260 gestures and, for each gesture, we had between 100 and 110 frames. Participants were also told that the visualisation provides them guidance but that they can define for themselves how to perform the gesture specifically. After completing the tasks, participants were interviewed with the goal to get qualitative feedback on performing the gestures in die different conditions.

4.2 Analysis and results

In order to analyse the hand data, we normalised the data as we described it in the previous section and used dynamic time warping (DTW); i.e., the implementation for R by Toni Giorgino [8]. We chose to use DTW, since it has been already used in related work to compute dissimilarities between gestures for authentication purposes ([4, 26] in a very similar manner with similar sets of data from gestures).

DTW compares two gesture based on time series (e.g., a series of x, y and z coordinates of fingertip positions over the period of a gesture), which can be of different lengths and produces a distance (i.e., Euclidean distance) value between 0 and a positive value. The value is higher for gestures that are less similar to each other. Data from each gesture is formatted in way that it can be used as a parameter for DTW: $Gesture(t) = [palm_1, thumb_1, indexFinger_1, ringFinger_1, pinky_1, ..., palm_n, thumb_n, indexFinger_n, ringFinger_n, pinky_n]$ where n is the number of frames (i.e., a number between 100 and 110). Hereby, $palm_i$ (for example) is the vector of x,y and z co-ordinates of the ith record of the palm position; $palm_i = [x, y, z]$

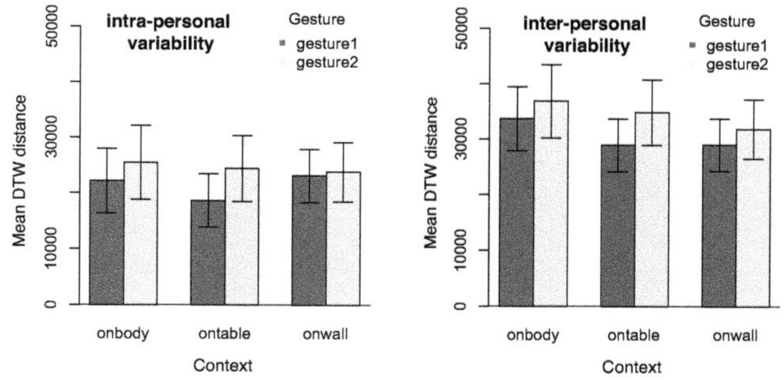

Figure 5: Mean values and intra-personal variability in performing the two gestures are presented on the left (for each condition). Similar values for Inter-personal variability are presented on the right. Y-axis denotes the DTW distance, a value presenting the dissimilarity between two gestures. Error bars denote the standard deviation.

We computed the mean DTW distance and the associated standard deviation (see Figure 5) for each participant, each condition, and each gesture . Based on these values, we computed the intra-personal and inter-personal variability of participants of our study. The difference between intra-personal and inter-personal variability, which is apparent in all conditions, is promising and indicates that mid-air gesture could be used for authentication. Interestingly, the differences seems to be highest for the "onbody" condition. This might be due to the fact that users not only have inter-personal differences in performed gestures but also differences regarding their body posture when having the sensor on their wrist.

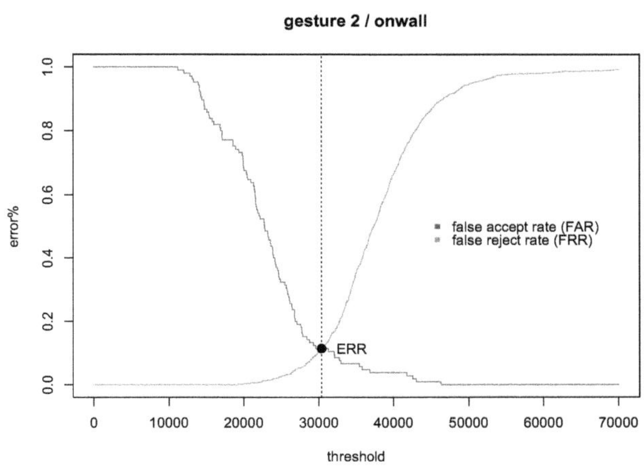

Figure 6: For the condition in which participants were asked to perform gesture 2 with the 3D control attached to the wall FAR and FRR are plotted for a range of thresholds. The Equal Error Rate (EER) is identified and thresholds for dissimilarity score is derived.

4.2.1 *Analysis of biometric data*

Similar to how Sae-Bae et al. [26] analysed authentication

Table 1: Equal error rates and derived thresholds

Gesture	context	EER	Threshold
1	ontable	0.0973	25926
1	onwall	0.1196	27678
1	onbody	0.1025	29669
2	ontable	0.1322	25926
2	onwall	0.1144	30365
2	onbody	0.1365	32224

gestures based on multi-touch data, we analysed the biometric data in mid-air gestures using Equal Error Rate (EER) to measure accuracy. The EER denotes the rate where False Acceptance Rate (FAR) and False Rejection Rate (FRR) are equal. FAR is compute by dividing the number of incorrectly verified forgery cases by the number of forgery cases. FRR is compute by dividing the number of rejected genuine cases by the number of genuine cases. Since we collected 10 samples (i.e., gestures) from each participant in each context, we used the first five samples to chose a template. The sample with minimum sum distance to the other four samples was taken as the template. The last five samples were used to test for genuine cases.

In order to calculate EER, all thresholds were used to compute FAR and FRR values. FAR and FRR were plotted for all thresholds to identify the ERR (see Figure 6). Table 1 presents the EER values and derived thresholds for both gestures and all three contexts. Overall, the two mid-air gestures achieved EER of 11.71% (as an averaged value between the two gestures). Gesture 2 achieved over all threse context ERR of 12.77 % and gesture 1, EER of 10.65101 %. Figure 7 presents corresponding accuracy rates in percentage.

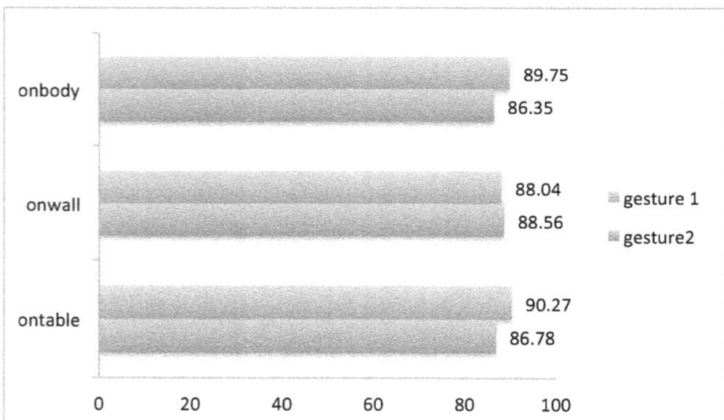

Figure 7: Overview of gesture accuracy (number of authenciatnion gestures that have been correctly accepted or rejected in %) for different contexts.

4.2.2 Analysis of user experience

In addition to measuring the authentication strength of mid-air gestures, we were also interested in exploring how users would perceive mid-air gestures as a modality for authentication. In order to get initial insights we used a semantic differential questionnaire. Participants were asked to answer the questions at the end of the study. Figure 8 provides an overview.

Afterwards, participants were briefly interviewed. Regarding the specific gestures, there was no overall response

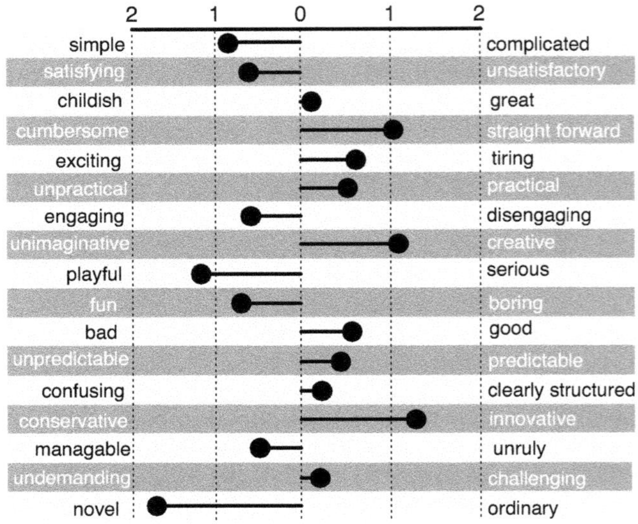

Figure 8: Overview of self-reported items, which participants were asked to provide in order to describe how mid-air gestures for authentication purposes were perceived overall.

on which gesture was easier or better for the purpose of authentication. Half of the participants preferred gesture 2, since rotating their palm did not include fine grade finger movements and was less exhausting. The other half preferred gesture 1, since they did not have to move their elbows and shoulders. However, both gestures were perceived as easy to perform.

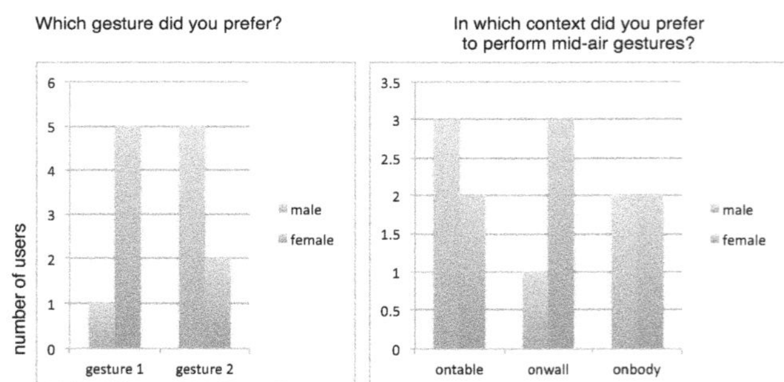

Figure 9: Overview of user preferences regarding mid-air gesture and context in which mid-air gestures were performed.

Interestingly, female participants preferred gesture 1 and male participants gesture 2 (see Figure 9). Participants were also asked to state in which context they felt most comfortable performing mid-air gestures. Our results show no obvious preference for one specific context. However, participants mentioned that they think having the sensor on the arm is, on the one hand practical while, on the other, it is mentally more demanding since they need to coordinate both arms.

The items of the questionnaire (see Figure 8) were inspired by various user experience questionnaires related to the attractiveness of a system or emotions associated with interactive systems, etc. The purpose of the questionnaire was to get an initial impression of how users perceived performing mid-air authentication gestures. Users choose mainly positive attributes to describe their experience, which motivates us to follow this line of research in our future work.

5. DISCUSSION

The accuracy rates, which we have observed in our study are very promising, considering that accuracy rates in multi-touch gestures [26] have been reported to be between 81-93% depending on the individual gestures. We observed accuracy rates between 86-91% for two different kinds of mid-air authentication gestures in different contexts. Sae-Bae et al. [26] suggest that two gestures, which are performed in sequence could improve accuracy rates for touch gestures up to 97%. Furthermore, they report accuracy rates of 97% for gestures, which were user defined. Through allowing users to define their own gestures accuracy rates for mid-air gestures could also be increased, making the technique scalable. However, due to the restrictions of the Leap Motion controller and the fact that users are not yet familiar using mid-air gestures, one would need to provide an easy way to assist in generating authentication gestures. Based on our experience, we would suggest a simple application, which visualises a user's hand gestures while they try out different gestures, providing feedback on how well the gesture would suit for authentication (e.g., how well fingers were recognised over the duration of the gesture).

In comparison to related work, we chose to use only one template (i.e., gesture) as a reference from each user for each context. We did this since we wanted the computation to be fast, so that the algorithm could be implemented and used in a real system in near future. However, it is not unusual to use more then one template; i.e., to use a set of templates and take the best match as the result. Using a set of templates would improve the accuracy rate.

Furthermore, we are aware that DTW produces more false positives due to the fact that the algorithm tries to match two time series (with different lengths). In our future work, we will explore other implementations (e.g., a python based implementation) of the DTW algorithm, which on the one hand might compute dissimilarity scores faster, allowing more than one template to be used as a reference. On the other hand we would investigate implementations [6] to improve the fact that DTW tends to produce false positives.

DTW is not claimed to be a better or worse choice than other possible approaches (e.g., machine learning). However, if there is potential in mid-air authentication gestures, then there is a high chance that DTW will show it [4, 26].

In figure 5 we presented the intra- and inter-personal variability, which seemed to suggest that differences are higher for the "onbody" context. However, the computation of authentication accuracy rates shows no visible difference between contexts. This could be due to possible outliers, and their influence based on the sample size of the user study. Based on our observations during the study, there was no good reason to take out samples from the analyses. However, since participants had to coordinate both hands in the "onbody" context, there might be a greater chance for outliers compared to contexts in which the sensors was physically attached to a still surface. We used the camera coordinate system for the normalization process, which could be an additional explanation for the slightly lower performance of gesture 2 when the sensor is worn on the body.

The rational for using the Leap Motion sensor is that it was a low cost solution, which potentially could be purchased in large numbers and integrated in a clean room environment in near future. Furthermore, it provided an easy way to use palm and finger motions without expertise in vision based recognition systems. Compared to the data provided by the leap motion, sensors using a skeleton-based gesture recognition would include considerably more complexity. Since, we used the Leap Motion controller, our results are specific for this 3D controller. However, with future improved 3D controllers, we expect improvements in usability as well as user experience of mid-air authentication gestures.

In sum, our investigations have shown that authentication based on mid-air gestures and the Leap Motion controller can be used in different contexts relevant for clean rooms.

Interaction based on mid-air gestures has the potential to replace existing interaction modalities in clean rooms, whenever possible. In practice, we expect to see interaction concepts for clean rooms, where mid-air gestures will be used in combination with other modalities. Based on our results, we could imagine to combine touch and touch-less gestures also for authentication purposes. Fusing existing interaction modalities in clean rooms with mid-air gestures would also introduce additional benefits, which are typical for multi-modal interfaces (e.g., naturalness of interaction, or improved performance).

6. CONCLUSION

We argued that clean rooms have particular constraints on interaction modalities and require clean and ideally touch-less ways to interact with workstations, which are distributed in the clean room depending on available space. Throughout the paper we put emphasis on reflective design activities [27] trying to explore mid-air authentication gestures. We used the Leap Motion controller to restrict but also focus our design activities. Based on visits to clean rooms we decided to study mid-air authentication gestures in two situation including body and 3D controller positions (i.e., seated with the 3D controller placed on the desk and standing with the 3D controller attached to a wall). Furthermore, we included a third context, which we thought has future relevance (i.e. using a 3D controller attached on the wrist). We were able to design two authentication gestures, which not only were perceived as easy to perform and suitable for all relevant situations, but also provided hand biometry information which could be used for a clean way of authentication.

7. ACKNOWLEDGMENTS

The financial support by the Austrian Federal Ministry of Science, Research and Economy and the National Foundation for Research, Technology and Development is gratefully acknowledged (Christian Doppler Laboratory for "Contextual Interfaces").

8. REFERENCES

[1] M. Bashir, G. Scharfenberg, and J. Kempf. Person authentication by handwriting in air using a biometric smart pen device. In *Proc. of BIOSIG 2011*, 2011.

[2] F. Colecal, T. Martinetz, and E. Barth. Gesture interfaces with depth sensors. In M. Grzegorzek et al.,

editors, *Time-of-Flight and Depth Imaging*, volume 8200 of *Springer Lecuture Notes on Computer Science*, pages 207–227. 2013.

[3] A. De Luca, M. Denzel, and H. Hussmann. Look into my eyes!: Can you guess my password? In *Proc. of the 5th Symposium on Usable Privacy and Security*, pages 7:1–7:12, New York, NY, USA, 2009. ACM.

[4] A. De Luca, A. Hang, F. Brudy, C. Lindner, and H. Hussmann. Touch me once and i know it's you!: Implicit authentication based on touch screen patterns. In *Proc. of CHI '12*, pages 987–996, New York, NY, USA, 2012. ACM.

[5] P. Dourish. *Where the Action is: The Foundations of Embodied Interaction*. A Bradford book. Bradford Books, 2004.

[6] H. Feng and C. C. Wah. Online signature verification using a new extreme points warping technique. *Pattern Recogn. Lett.*, 24(16):2943–2951, Dec. 2003.

[7] S. Fong, Y. Zhuang, I. Fister, and I. F. Jr. A biometric authentication model using hand gesture images. *Biomedical Engineering Online*, 12(111), 2013.

[8] T. Giorgino. Computing and visualizing dynamic time warping alignments in r: The dtw package. *Journal of Statistical Software*, 31(7):1–24, 8 2009.

[9] J. Guerra-Casanova, C. Sanchez-Avila, G. Bailador, and A. de Santos Sierra. Authentication in mobile devices through hand gesture recognition. *International Journal on Information Security*, 11(2):65–83, 2012.

[10] J. Guna, E. Stojmenova, A. Lugmayr, I. Humar, and M. Pogacnik. User identification approach based on simple gestures. In *Proc. of SAME*, pages 39–48, 2012.

[11] M. Hamissi and K. Faez. Real-time hand gesture recognition based on the depth map for human robot interaction. *International Journal of Electrical and Computer Engineering (IJECE)*, 3(6):770–778, 2013.

[12] K. Karthik, K. Varalakshmi, and S. Ravi. A file authentication system using hand gesture passcodes. *International Journal of Emerging Technologies in Computational and Applied Sciences (IJETCAS)*, 13(174):394–401, 2013.

[13] W. Kasprzak, A. Wilkowski, and K. Czapnik. Hand gesture recognition based on free£form contours and probabilistic inference. *International Journal of Applied Mathematics and Computational Sciences*, 22(2):437–448, 2012.

[14] S. Kavanagh. Facilitating natural user interfaces through freehand gesture recognition. In *Proc. of CHI '12*, New York, NY, USA, 2012. ACM.

[15] K. Kosic, B. Arzensek, A. Kuhar, and M. Vogrincic. Towards new user interfaces based on gesture and sound identification. In *Proc. of SQAMIA*, pages 45–53, 2013.

[16] J. Liu, Z. Wang, L. Zhong, et al. uWave: Accelerometer-based personalized gesture recognition and its applications. In *Proc. of PerCom'09*, 2009.

[17] S. Mitra and T. Acharya. Gesture recognition: A survey. *IEEE Transactions on Systems, Man, and Cybernetics - PartC: Applications and Reviews*, 37(3):311–324, 2007.

[18] D. L. Nelson, V. S. Reed, and J. R. Walling. Pictorial superiority effect. *Journal of Experimental Psychology: Human Learning and Memory*, 2(5), 1976.

[19] O. Nieto and D. Sasha. Hand gesture recognition in mobile devices: Enhancing the musical experience. In *Proc. of CMMR'13*, 2013.

[20] F. Parvini and C. Shahabi. An algorithmic approach for static and dynamic gesture recognition utilising mechanical and biomechanical characteristics. *International Journal on Bioinformatics Research and Applications*, 3(1):4–23, 2012.

[21] L. Potter, J. Araullo, and L. Carter. The leap motion controller: a view on sign language. In *Proc. of OzHCI'13*, pages 175–178, 2013.

[22] A. Ramamoorthy, N. Vaswani, S. Chaudhury, and S. Banerjee. Recognition of dynamic hand gestures. *Pattern Recognition*, 36:2069–2081, 2003.

[23] S. Reifinger, F. Wallhoff, M. Ablassmeier, T. Poitschke, and G. Rigoll. Static and dynamic hand-gesture recognition for augmented reality applications. In J. Jacko, editor, *Proc. of HCII 2007*, volume 4552 of *Springer Lecture Notes on Computer Science*, pages 728–737, 2007.

[24] Z. Ren, J. Yuan, and Z. Zong. Robust hand gesture recognition based on finger- earth mover£s distance with a commodity depth camera. In *Proc. of ACM Multimedia 2011*, pages 1093–1096, 2011.

[25] K. Sabir, C. Stolte, B. Tabor, and S. O'Donoghue. The molecular control toolkit: Controlling 3d molecular graphics via gesture and voice. In *Proc. of the IEEE Symposium on Biological Data Visualisation 2013*, pages 49–56, 2013.

[26] N. Sae-Bae, K. Ahmed, K. Isbister, and N. Memon. Biometric-rich gestures: A novel approach to authentication on multi-touch devices. In *Proc. of CHI '12*, pages 977–986, New York, NY, USA, 2012. ACM.

[27] D. A. Schön. Designing as reflective conversation with the materials of a design situation. *Knowledge-Based Systems*, 5(1):3–14, 1992.

[28] R. Shadmehr and T. Brashers-Krug. Functional stages in the formation of human long term motor memory. *Journal of Neuroscience*, 17(1):409–419, Jan. 1997.

[29] J. Tian, C. Qu, W. Xu, and S. Wang. Kinwrite: Handwriting-based authentication using kinect. In *Proc. of the 20th Annual Network & Distributed System Security Symposium*, 2013.

[30] S. Vikram, L. Li, and S. Russel. Writing and sketching in the air, recognizing and controlling on the fly. In *Extended Abstracts on Human Factors in Computing Systems CHI EA '13*, pages 1179–1184, 2013.

[31] Y. Yao and C.-T. Li. Real-time hand gesture recognition for uncontrolled environments using adaptive SURF tracking and hidden conditional random fields. In *Proc. of ISVC'13*, Springer, pages 542–551, 2013.

[32] M. Ye et al. A survey on human motion analysis from depth data. In *Time-of-Flight and Depth Imaging. Sensors, Algorithms, and Applications*, volume 8200 of *Springer*, pages 149–187. 2013.

[33] Y. Yin and R. Davis. Gesture Spotting and Recognition Using Salience Detection and Concatenated Hidden Markov Models. In *Proc. of ICMI'13*, pages 489–494, 2013.

Automatic Detection of Naturalistic Hand-over-Face Gesture Descriptors

Marwa Mahmoud, Tadas Baltrušaitis and Peter Robinson
University of Cambridge, Computer Laboratory, UK
{marwa.mahmoud, tadas.baltrusaitis, peter.robinson}@cl.cam.ac.uk

ABSTRACT

One of the main factors that limit the accuracy of facial analysis systems is hand occlusion. As the face becomes occluded, facial features are either lost, corrupted or erroneously detected. Hand-over-face occlusions are considered not only very common but also very challenging to handle. Moreover, there is empirical evidence that some of these hand-over-face gestures serve as cues for recognition of cognitive mental states. In this paper, we detect hand-over-face occlusions and classify hand-over-face gesture descriptors in videos of natural expressions using multi-modal fusion of different state-of-the-art spatial and spatio-temporal features. We show experimentally that we can successfully detect face occlusions with an accuracy of 83%. We also demonstrate that we can classify gesture descriptors (*hand shape*, *hand action* and *facial region occluded*) significantly higher than a naïve baseline. To our knowledge, this work is the first attempt to automatically detect and classify hand-over-face gestures in natural expressions.

Categories and Subject Descriptors

I.2.10 [**Vision and Scene Understanding**]: Video analysis

Keywords

Hand-over-face occlusions; Hand cues; Facial landmarks; Histograms of oriented gradient; Space-time interest points

1. INTRODUCTION

Over the past few years, there has been an increased interest in machine understanding and recognition of people's affective and cognitive mental states, especially based on facial expression analysis. One of the major factors that limits the accuracy of facial analysis systems is hand occlusion. People often hold their hands near their faces as a gesture in natural conversation. As many facial analysis systems are based on geometric or appearance based facial features, such features are either lost, corrupted or erroneously detected during occlusion. This results in an incorrect analysis of the person's facial expression. Although face touches are very common, they are under researched, mostly because segmenting of the hand on the face is very challenging, as face and hand usually have similar colour and texture. Detection of hand-over-face occlusion can significantly improve facial landmark detection and facial expression inference systems.

Moreover, hand-over-face occlusions are not just noise that needs to be removed. Recent studies show that body movements and gestures are significant visual cues that complement facial expressions [8] and they can be utilised in automatic detection of human internal states [2, 4]. Specifically, hand-over-face gestures can serve as an additional valuable channel for multi-modal affect inference [22]. These studies emphasise the need not only for an occlusion detection system, but also for a way to describe the gesture in terms of a set of quantitative descriptors that can be automatically detected. Moreover, automatic detection of these gesture descriptors can provide tools for experimental psychologists who study gesture - especially face touches - to automatically quantify and detect these gestures, instead of the common practice of manual coding. To date, there is no available automatic detection system that serves these purposes.

In this paper, we present an analysis of hand-over-face gestures in a naturalistic video corpus of complex mental states. We define three hand-over-face gesture descriptors, namely *hand shape*, *hand action* and *facial region occluded* and propose a methodology for automatic detection of face occlusions in videos of natural expressions.

We treat the problem as two separate tasks: detection of hand occlusion; and classification of hand gesture descriptors. The main contributions of this paper are:

1. Proposing a mutli-modal fusion approach to detect hand-over-face gestures in videos of natural expressions, based on state-of-the-art spatial and spatio-temporal appearance features.
2. Proposing the first approach to automatically code and classify hand-over-face gesture descriptors, namely *hand shape*, *hand action* and *facial region occluded.*
3. Demonstrating that multi-modal fusion of spatial and spatio-temporal features outperforms single modalities in all of our classification tasks.

We start by discussing the related work in Section 2. We present the details of gesture coding and dataset used in Section 3. We then present our proposed approach (illustrated

ICMI'14, November 12–16, 2014, Istanbul, Turkey

ACM 978-1-4503-2885-2/14/11 $15.00.
http://dx.doi.org/10.1145/2663204.2663258.

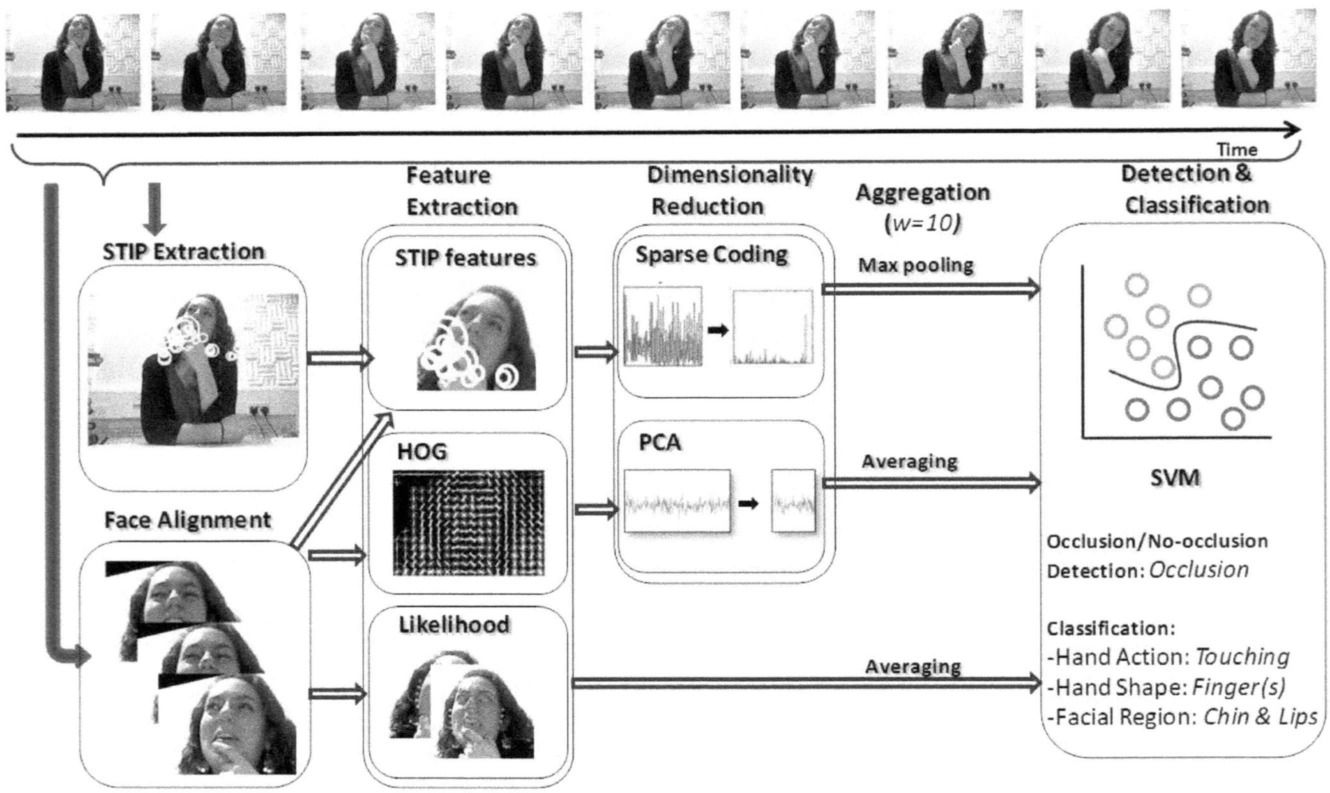

Figure 1: Overview Diagram shows the main steps in our approach.

in Figure 1), starting by the feature extraction in Section 4 followed by the experimental evaluation in Section 5. Conclusions and future directions are presented in Section 6.

2. RELATED WORK

There have been several previous attempts to detect and deal with occlusion in face area. Two such examples come from work done by Yu et al. [30] and Burgos-Artizzu et al. [3]. In both pieces of work the authors concentrated on building a facial landmark detector that is robust to various occlusions. They achieved this by explicitly recognising occluded landmarks of the face and using that information to detect the visible landmarks more robustly. Both pieces of work concentrated on facial occlusion in general and not specifically on hand-over-face occlusion. Furthermore, the authors were interested in detecting occluded facial landmarks, which are not necessarily semantically meaningful. Both of the approaches lead to better landmark alignment in the presence of occlusion. Another notable example is the work done by Hotta [15], that proposes a method for more robust face detection in presence of partial occlusion by using SVM with local kernels. However, none of the above mentioned authors distinguish between types of occlusion and make no special analysis of hand-over-face occlusions.

There have been a few attempts [26, 21] to detect the hand when it occludes the face. Gonzalez et al. [12] use colour and edge information to track and segment the hand during hand over face occlusion in sign language. Grafsgaard et al. [13] use depth images to detect two hand-to-face gestures (one hand touching face and two hands touching face) in a computer-mediated tutoring environment. In contrast to previous work, our work presents a more detailed and different classification of hand-over-face gesture descriptors.

3. CODING OF HAND-OVER-FACE GESTURES

Serving as a first step in automatic classification, we coded hand-over-face gestures using a set of descriptors. In this section, we describe the choice of the dataset, the coding schema, the labelling, annotation assessment and how we generate the ground truth labels that are used in our machine learning experiments.

3.1 Dataset

The first challenge was to find a corpus of videos of natural expressions. Since most of the work on affect analysis focuses on the face, most of the publicly available natural datasets also focus on faces with limited or no occlusion. Since we are interested in the temporal aspect of the hand gesture as well, still photograph corpora did not satisfy our criteria. The publicly available Cam3D [20] has natural expressions and does not restrict the video collection to faces. It includes upper body videos that have hand-over-face occlusions in around 25% of the videos. The expressions in Cam3D are elicited as part of an emotion elicitation experiment, which implies that the hand gestures expressed are most likely to be part of expression of emotion. We are interested in detecting such potentially informative gestures.

In Cam3D, segmentation is event-based, so each video segment contains a single action. The dataset has 192 video segments that contain hand-over face occlusions. These videos come from 9 participants with mean duration of the video being 6 seconds. We used all of the occluded videos. For balance, we also randomly selected another 173 video segments from the Cam3D dataset that do not contain face occlusions. The chosen no-occlusion videos were selected containing the same 9 participants while keeping the number of samples per each participant as balanced as possible. This led to a set of 365 videos in total.

3.2 Labelling

In order to proceed to automatic detection, we needed to code the hand-over-face occlusions present in the dataset. The goal was to code hand gestures in terms of certain descriptors that can describe the gesture. Inspired by the coding schema provided by Mahmoud et al. [22], we coded the gestures in terms of *hand shape*, *hand action* and *facial region occluded*.

Labelling was carried out using Elan video annotation tool [19]. Two expert coders (researchers in our research group) were instructed to label the videos given the following instructions :

- Hand Action: coded as one label for the whole video according to the action observed in the majority of the frames. Labels are: 1) **Touching** - If the hand is static while touching the face. 2) **Stroking/tapping** - repetitive motion of the hand on the face. 3) **Sliding** - any other hand motion that is not repetitive.
- Hand Shape: coded as one label per frame. It describes the shape of the hand on the face in a specific frame. Labels are mutually exclusive, i.e. one label is permitted per frame. Labels are: 1)**Fingers** or any separate fingers. 2) **OpenHand(s)** or palm(s). 3) **ClosedHand(s)** or a fist shape. 4)**HandsTogether** - tangled hands.
- Facial Region Occluded: coded as one - or multiple - labels per frame (labels are not mutually exclusive). It describes the face area covered - or partially covered - by the hand during occlusion. Labels are: 1) **Forehead**. 2)**Eye(s)**. 3)**Nose**. 4)**Cheek(s)**. 5)**Lips**. 6)**Chin**. 7)**Hair/ear**.

3.3 Coding assessment & refinement

To assess the coding schema and gain confidence in the labels obtained, we calculated inter-rater agreement between the two expert annotators using time-slice Krippendorff's alpha [16], which is widely used for this type of coding assessment because of its independence of the number of assessors and its robustness against imperfect data [14]. We got a Krippendorff's alpha coefficient of 0.92 for *hand action*, 0.67 for *hand shape* and an average alpha coefficient of 0.56 for *facial region occluded* (forehead 0.69, eye(s) 0.27, Nose 0.45, cheeks 0.65, lips 0.73, chin 0.83, hair/ear 0.25). All the classes had moderate agreement or above except for the facial regions: eyes, nose and hair/ear. When we explored the reason of the disagreement in these categories, this was mostly because of the very few samples available of these categories in the dataset, for example: eyes, forehead and hair/ear regions had only 25, 100 and 10 frame samples respectively, i.e. less than 0.2% of the total number of frames in total. We decided to exclude these categories (mostly upper face area) in the machine learning step, as it was unfair

Figure 2: Sample frames from videos in the dataset Cam3D showing examples of face touches present in the dataset [20]. Note the challenging - close to natural - recording settings like inconsistent lighting conditions and strong head rotations.

to try to automatically learn and classify these categories when the human annotators failed to agree.

Due to the nature of our unbalanced dataset, some labels had very few samples. In the classification stage, we decided to aggregate some of the groups together. The nose region was combined with the cheek region as one descriptor of the middle face region. For the *hand action* descriptor, we combined sliding, stroking and tapping in one group representing non-static hand gesture, i.e. any type of motion.

4. FEATURE EXTRACTION

The first building block of our approach is feature extraction. We chose features that can effectively represent hand gesture descriptors that we want to detect. Therefore, we extract spatial features, namely: Histograms of Oriented Gradients (HOG) and facial landmark alignment likelihood. Moreover, having the detection of hand action in mind, we also extract Space Time Interest Points (STIP) that combine spatial and temporal information. For HOG and STIP features, dimensionality reduction of features is then applied to obtain a more compact feature representation.

4.1 Space Time Features

Local space-time features [17, 18, 9] have become popular motion descriptors for action recognition [24]. Recently, they have been used by Song et al. [27] to encode facial and body microexpressions for emotion detection. They were particularly successful in learning the emotion valence dimension as they are sensitive to global motion in the video. Our methodology for space time interest points feature extraction and representation is based on the approach proposed by Song et al. [27].

Space Time Interest Points (STIP) capture salient visual patterns in a space-time image volume by extending the local spatial image descriptor to the space-time domain. Obtaining local space-time features is a two step process: spatio-temporal interest point (STIP) detection followed by feature extraction. Wang et al. [28] reports that using the Harris3D interest point detector followed by a combination of the Histograms of Oriented Gradient (HOG) and the Histogram of Optical Flow (HOF) feature descriptors provide good performance. Thus, we use the Harris3D detector with HOG/HOF feature descriptors to extract local sparse-time features. As we are interested in the face area, we use the face alignment input to crop the STIP features and discard any extracted points outside the face region.

The STIP box in the overview diagram in Figure 1 shows how the hand motion is captured by the space-time features (denoted by the yellow circles in the diagram).

The local space-time features extracted are dense as they capture micro-expressions. Since we are interested in more semantic feature representation, we use sparse coding to represent them so that only few salient features are recovered, i.e. features that appear most frequently in the data. Thus, we learn a codebook of features and use it to encode the extracted features in a sparse manner.

The goal of sparse coding is to obtain a compact representation of an input signal using an over-complete codebook, i.e. the number of codebook entries is larger than the dimension of input signal so that only a small number of codebook entries are used to represent the input signal. Given an input signal $\mathbf{x} \in \mathbb{R}^{\mathbf{N}}$ and over-complete codebook $\mathbf{D} \in \mathbb{R}^{\mathbb{N}\times\mathbb{K}}$, $\mathbf{K} \gg \mathbf{N}$, we find a sparse signal $\alpha \in \mathbb{R}^{\mathbf{K}}$ that minimises the reconstruction error,

$$\min_{\alpha\in\mathbb{R}^{\mathbf{K}}} \frac{1}{2}||\mathbf{x} - \mathbf{D}\alpha||_2^2 + \lambda||\alpha||_1, \quad (1)$$

where the first term in this equation measures reconstruction error and the second term is the L_1 regularisation that encourages the sparsity of vector α. λ controls the relative importance of the two terms so that we have α containing few non-zero linear coefficients compared to the codebook $\mathbf{D}$, which leads to the best approximation of $\mathbf{x}$.

In our work, we learn the codebook $\mathbf{D}$ from our data, i.e. the extracted space-time features $\{\mathbf{x}_1, \mathbf{x}_2, ..., \mathbf{x}_M\}$

$$\min_{\mathbf{D}} \frac{1}{M}\sum_{i=1}^{M} \min_{\alpha_i} \frac{1}{2}||\mathbf{x}_i - \mathbf{D}\alpha_i||_2^2 + \lambda||\alpha_i||_1. \quad (2)$$

The optimisation problem is convex in $\mathbf{D}$ with $\mathbf{A} = [\alpha_1, \alpha_2, ..., \alpha_M]$ fixed and in $\mathbf{A}$ with $\mathbf{D}$ fixed, but not in both at the same time [23]. Thus, it can be solved using online learning [23] by alternating the two convex optimisation problems. Once the codebook is learned, we can use it to encode each space-time feature $\mathbf{x}$ into α by solving Equation 2.

From each frame we obtain different number of local space-time features (and corresponding sparse codes). These features need to be aggregated to obtain a vector of a fixed dimension to be suitable for our classification step. Averaging or max pooling are typical ways of doing this. In our work, we use max pooling as it provides better representation that is invariant to image transformations and noise [29, 27]. The max-pooling operation is defined as:

$$\mathbf{z} = [\max_{i=1...M_v} |\alpha_{i,1}|, \max_{i=1...M_v} |\alpha_{i,2}|, ..., \max_{i=1...M_v} |\alpha_{i,\mathbf{K}}|], \quad (3)$$

where M_v is the number of sparse codes associated with a given space-time volume v.

To obtain a more compact representation of the features and to speed up processing time, we aggregate the space time features (and their corresponding sparse codes) over a window w=10 frames. This step is explained in Section 5.1.

4.2 Facial Landmark Detection - Likelihood

Facial landmark detection plays a large role in face analysis systems. In our case it is important to know where the face is in order to compute HOG appearance features around the facial region and to remove irrelevant STIP features.

Figure 3: An example of patch expert responses in presence of occlusion. Green shows high likelihood values, while red means low likelihoods.

We employ a Constrained Local Neural Field (CLNF) [1] facial landmark detector and tracker to allow us to analyse the facial region for hand over face gestures. CLNF is an instance of a Constrained Local Model (CLM) [6], that uses more advanced patch experts and optimisation function. We use the publicly available CLNF implementation [1].

The CLM model we use can be described by parameters $\mathbf{p} = [s, \mathbf{R}, \mathbf{p}, \mathbf{t}]$ that can be varied to acquire various instances of the model: the scale factor s; object rotation $\mathbf{R}$ (first two rows of a 3D rotation matrix); 2D translation $\mathbf{t}$; a vector describing non-rigid variation of shape $\mathbf{p}$. The point distribution model (PDM) is:

$$\mathbf{x}_i = s \cdot \mathbf{R}(\overline{\mathbf{x}}_i + \mathbf{\Phi}_i\mathbf{p}) + \mathbf{t}. \quad (4)$$

Here $\mathbf{x}_i = (x, y)$ denotes the 2D location of the ith feature point in an image, $\overline{\mathbf{x}}_i = (X, Y, Z)$ is the mean value of the ith element of the PDM in the 3D reference frame, and the vector $\mathbf{\Phi}_i$ is the ith eigenvector obtained from the training set that describes the linear variations of non-rigid shape of this feature point, and the vector $\mathbf{\Psi}_i$ is the ith eigenvector that describes the linear variations of non-rigid shape.

In CLM (and CLNF) we estimate the maximum *a posteriori* probability (MAP) of the face model parameters $\mathbf{p}$:

$$p(\mathbf{p}|\{l_i=1\}_{i=1}^{n}, \mathcal{I}) \propto p(\mathbf{p}) \prod_{i=1}^{n} p(l_i=1|\mathbf{x}_i, \mathcal{I}), \quad (5)$$

where $l_i \in \{1, -1\}$ is a discrete random variable indicating if the ith feature point is aligned or misaligned, $p(\mathbf{p})$ is the prior probability of the model parameters $\mathbf{p}$, and $\prod_{i=1}^{n} p(l_i = 1|\mathbf{x}_i, \mathcal{I})$ is the joint probability of the feature points $\mathbf{x}$ being aligned at a particular point $\mathbf{x}_i$, given an intensity image $\mathcal{I}$ (see Section 4.2.1).

We employ a common two step CLM fitting strategy [6, 25]; performing an exhaustive local search around the current estimate of feature points leading to a response map around every feature point, and then iteratively updating the model parameters to maximise Equation 5 until a convergence metric is reached. For fitting we use Non Uniform Regularised Landmark Mean-Shift [1].

As CLNF is a local optimisation approach it relies on initial face detection. However, few face detectors are suitable for the task in the presence of occlusion. In our work we used a Deformable Parts Model (DPM) based Zhu and Ramanan [31] face detector to initialise landmark detection and tracking. The subsequent frames were initialised using the previous frames estimate, only requiring to run the DPM detector multiple times in a video: to initialise; to reinitialise when tracking fails. It would have been possible to use the DPM to detect landmarks in every video frame, however it is not as accurate as dedicated landmark detectors such as CLNF [1], and is too slow to be used for video analysis.

4.2.1 Likelihood

In CLM patch experts are used to calculate $p(l_i = 1|\mathbf{x}_i, \mathcal{I})$, which is the probability of a feature being aligned at point $\mathbf{x}_i$ (Equation 4). As a probabilistic patch expert we use a Continuous Conditional Neural Field regressor [1], which given a local $n \times n$ image patch centered around current landmark estimate predicts the alignment likelihood.

The likelihood response from the patch expert will be low when it is either not aligned or the landmark is occluded, as they are trained on non-occluded examples of particular landmarks. This makes them useful as predictors of hand-over-face gesture descriptors. An example of patch expert responses in presence of occlusion can be seen in Figure 3.

4.3 HOG

Histograms of Oriented Gradients (HOG) [7] are a popular feature for describing appearance that has been successfully used for pedestrian detection [7], and facial landmark detection [31] amongst others.

HOG descriptor counts the number of oriented gradient occurrences in a dense grid of uniformly spaced cells. These occurrences are represented as a histogram for each cell normalised in a larger block area. HOG features capture both appearance and shape information making them suitable for a number of computer vision tasks.

5. EXPERIMENTAL EVALUATION

For our classification tasks, we used the labelled subset of Cam3D described in Section 3.1 to evaluate our approach. It has a total of 365 videos of $\sim$ 2190 seconds, which contains $\sim$ 65700 frames ($\sim$ 6570 data samples - one data sample per processing window $w = 10$).

5.1 Methodology

As a pre-processing step, we performed face alignment on all of our videos. Face detection was done using Zhu and Ramanan's [31] face detector followed by refinement and tracking using CLNF landmark detector [1]. After landmark detection, the face was normalised using a similarity transform to account for scaling and in-plane rotation. This led to a 160×120 pixel image - as seen in Figure 1. The output of the facial landmark detection stage was passed to the three feature extraction sub-systems.

The face detector did not manage to initialise in the first frame in all of the videos. To cope with this, we performed backwards tracking alongside forwards tracking from initial detection, leading to more robust landmark detection.

Even with these advanced tracking techniques, our analysis excluded 16 videos, as face detection on them was unsuccessful. Those videos included either extreme head rotation or extreme hand occlusion covering most of the face area that continued throughout the video, thus preventing the tracker from finding a non-occluded frame to recover (Figure 4 shows some examples).

Space time features were extracted at the original video frame rate (30 frames per second) using the implementation provided by Laptev *et al.* [18]. We removed the features not in the facial region by using the results from the landmark detector. For sparse coding, we used the implementation provided by Mairal et al. [23] to learn a codebook

Figure 4: Sample frames from videos that were badly tracked. Note the extreme occlusion and/or head rotations.

of size 750 for each training set. The size of the codebook was obtained by trying out different sizes (200, 500, 750) and cross validating across all the videos to obtain the best parameter that produced the minimum data reconstruction error. A user-independent cross validation was utilised for this task. Space time features were aggregated using max pooling across a window $w = 10$ frames.

For our task, we extracted HOG features from a similarity normalised 160×120 pixel image of a face. We used 8×8 pixel cells with 18 gradient orientations and block size of 2×2 cells. This led to a 9576 dimensional HOG descriptor. We reduced its dimensionality using Principal Component Analysis and keeping 90% of explained variance, leading to 1035 dimensions vector per frame. We aggregated the HOG features in a temporal manner by taking the mean value in a window $w = 10$ frames.

As a final feature, we used the landmark alignment likelihoods for each of the 68 landmarks. This was aggregated over a 10 frame window as well by taking its mean.

For classification, our experiments consisted of uni-modal and multi-modal early fusion of extracted features. We used a linear SVM classifier using Liblinear [10] library. We also evaluated an RBF kernel SVM classifier to check if this leads to any improvement in performance [5].

The optimal parameters for the SVM were automatically obtained using a leave-one-out cross validation, by holding all videos of one participant out for testing at each iteration. To ensure that our results are generalizable, all experiments were performed in a user-independent approach, as none of the participants in the test set are used for validation or training (both in the classifiers and the dimensionality reduction techniques).

To obtain the ground truth for each classification task, we aggregated the annotations provided by experts (As described in Section 3) for every window $w = 10$ frames. We obtained the ground truth by taking the majority vote across the window of size $w = 10$ frames from the two annotators and assigning the value of the most common label. In case of a tie (disagreement between the labellers) the window w was discarded from further analysis – as this implied that these frames were ambiguous. The total number of frames discarded at this step were less than 10% of the total number of frames in all of the categories.

Besides speeding up the computation time of our approach, the choice of the aggregation window size stemmed from our interest in coding and detecting hand gestures that are semantically higher than frame-level micro-expressions. In other words, we did not expect a change in hand gesture in less than one third of a second.

For all our experiments, we compared our approach performance with chance baseline and a naïve majority vote classifier baseline and evaluated the statistical significance using a Related Samples Friedman's ANOVA, with a fol-

Hand occlusion detection performance	Majority vote baseline	Uni-modal classification - Linear SVM			Multi-modal classification	
		Likelihood	HOG	STIP	**Linear SVM**	Non-linear SVM
F1 score	0.69	0.66	0.82	0.68	**0.83**	0.80
Accuracy	0.56	0.67	0.83	0.56	**0.83**	0.80

Table 1: Hand detection classification results comparing uni-modal and multi-modal feature fusion. Multi-modal fusion of features using a linear SVM classifier had the best detection rate (shown in bold), significantly higher than a naïve baseline.

low up post-hoc tests with a Bonferroni correction to p values [11]. This was chosen as we wanted to perform pair-wise comparisons and the data distribution cannot be assumed to follow a normal distribution.

5.2 Hand Occlusion Detection

The first task in our experiments was hand-over-face occlusion detection. The face was considered to be occluded if one or many facial regions are labelled as occluded. For this task, we used a binary classifier to detect if the face is occluded or not. We trained a linear SVM classifier using single modalities and feature-level fusion. Table 1 shows the classification results (accuracy and F1 score) of uni-modal features and multi-modal fusion. We found that the best performance is obtained from the multi-modal linear classifier (Accuracy 0.83, F1 score 0.83), which is higher than a naïve majority vote classifier (Accuracy 0.56, F1 score 0.69) or chance (Accuracy 0.5). To check the significance of the improved results, statistical tests showed that our classifier yielded significant improvement over chance ($p = 0.001$).

We also tested the muti-modal fusion in a non-linear SVM, which did not produce better results (Accuracy 0.80, F1 score 0.80). This may be because using a complex kernel has little - if any- impact on the classification performance if we are fusing different features of different representations.

If we look at single modality results, we notice that the feature that had the highest uni-modal classification results is HOG, which indicates that appearance features can differentiate well between occluded and non-occluded faces, even in the challenging conditions of hand occlusion.

5.3 Classification of Hand-over-Face gesture descriptors

After occlusion detection, the second task was to classify hand-over-face gesture descriptors (*hand shape*, *hand action* and *facial region occluded*). We treated each descriptor as a separate classification task. *Hand shape* and *facial region occluded* classifications were performed per window w, while *hand action* classification was done per video.

Facial region occluded descriptor's values are not mutually exclusive, i.e. we can have occlusion in more than one face region at any window w. That is why we used three binary classifiers, one for each face region. In each experiment, we used a linear SVM classifier using single features then fused the features in a multi-modal classifier. Table 2 shows the classification results using these different approaches, highlighting the best obtained result for each classification task.

Taking a closer look at the data distribution of different descriptors' values, we found that the data was mostly unbalanced. This is expected for this type of problems because we are analysing gestures in natural expressions with high variance in individual differences so we do not expect to see all the descriptors' values appearing with the same frequency in all the occlusion videos. This was particularly extreme in the chin region as we had hand covering chin in 92% of the occlusion videos. This is not a surprise as the hand would cover the chin in most of the face occlusion gestures as it comes from below the face. To remove the unbalanced effect for the chin classifier, we added more negative samples that were randomly selected from Cam3D dataset to the pool of videos used for chin training and classification. Different distribution of the descriptors' values among different participants also presented a challenge in the classification. Since our experiments are user-independent, unbalanced distribution of cues presented a challenge to the classifiers.

5.3.1 Facial region occluded

Table 2 shows the classification results for *facial region occluded* descriptor using the uni-modal and multi-modal classification approaches, highlighting the approach that has the best performance for each task. For chin occlusion detection, multi-modal fusion of features in a non-linear SVM classifier had the best performance (Accuracy 0.87, F1 score 0.84), just slightly higher than mutli-modal linear classification (Accuracy 0.85, F1 score 0.83). For lips occlusion detection, multi-modal linear SVM classifier had the best performance (Accuracy 0.90, F1 score 0.94). For middle face area occlusion detection (cheeks and nose), multi-modal linear SVM classifier had the best performance (Accuracy 0.78, F1 score 0.86). This confirms that multi-modal fusion of the feature performed better in all the *facial region occluded* classification tasks. Our detection results proved to be statistically significantly higher than a naïve chance baseline for the chin, lips and middle face areas (with p=0.003, p=0.001 and p=0.014 respectively).

5.3.2 Hand Shape

Classification of *hand shape* was implemented as a 4 class classification problem (one against all), as shape descriptor's values are mutually exclusive per processing window w. The classifier categorised the hand shape as one of four classes: fingers, open hand, closed hand and hands together (tangled). As shown in Table 3, Multi-modal fusion of features outperforms single modalities with an accuracy of 0.36 that is significantly higher than the majority vote classification baseline (Accuracy 0.14) ($p = 0.001$) and chance baseline (Accuracy 0.25).

5.3.3 Hand Action

For Hand action, the data was labelled as one label per video, describing the hand action as static or dynamic in the majority of the video frames. Therefore, we aggregated the features to obtain one feature set per video. Space time features (STIP) were aggregated using max pooling in the same way described in Section 4.1, this allowed us to capture the salient features in the sparse codes. For HOG and likelihood features, we calculated means and standard deviations to capture the changes in the features across the video.

Facial region		Majority vote baseline	Uni-modal classification - Linear SVM			Multi-modal classification	
			Likelihood	HOG	STIP	Linear SVM	Non-linear SVM
Chin	F1 score	0.68	0.84	0.68	0.68	0.83	**0.84**
	Accuracy	0.56	0.69	0.85	0.56	0.85	**0.87**
Lips	F1 score	0.78	0.88	0.92	0.90	**0.94**	0.93
	Accuracy	0.56	0.82	0.88	0.83	**0.90**	0.89
Middle face area (cheek/nose)	F1 score	0.73	0.86	0.85	0.87	**0.86**	0.86
	Accuracy	0.61	0.77	0.76	0.77	**0.78**	0.77

Table 2: Classification results of *facial region occluded* descriptor comparing uni-modal and multi-modal feature fusion. Occlusion of each face area is treated as a separate binary classification problem. Multi-modal fusion of features outperforms single modalities in all the classification tasks.

Hand shape classification results	Majority vote baseline	Uni-modal classification - Linear SVM			**Multi-modal classification**	
		Likelihood	HOG	STIP	**Linear SVM**	**Non-linear SVM**
Accuracy	0.14	0.31	0.35	0.19	**0.36**	**0.36**

Table 3: Classification results of *hand shape* descriptor comparing uni-modal and multi-modal feature fusion as a 4 class classification problem. The four classes are: fingers, closed hand, open hand and hands together. Multi-modal fusion of features outperforms single modalities with an accuracy that is significantly higher than the majority vote baseline.

We used a binary classification approach to categorise the hand action as dynamic or static. As shown in Table 4, SVM linear classification did not perform well on this descriptor, with classification accuracies swinging around the majority vote baseline accuracy, which is 0.7 (which is already high due to unbalanced data distribution). Multi-modal classification using a non-linear SVM classifier achieved the highest results (Accuracy 0.76, F1 score 0.83) which is higher than the majority vote and significantly higher than chance (p=0.007) . Unbalanced dataset and initial video segmentation criteria in Cam3D dataset can explain the low increase of the classification results of this descriptor compared to a naïve majority vote classifier, for example: some video segments have one part of the video with hand motion and the rest without motion, which indeed introduced confusion factor to the classifier. Re-segmenting the videos into shorter segments based on the hand motion would improve the classification accuracy, but we leave this part to future work.

5.4 Discussion

Figure 5 summarises our classification results for hand detection and classification obtained for for the six classification tasks. The results display mostly binary classifiers except for hand shape where we employed a 4 class classifier, hence the lower classification values. Our multi-modal fusion approach showed a statistically significant improvement over a naive classifier for all of our classification experiments.

For the challenging nature and novelty of the gesture classification task, we consider these results satisfactory, considering the nature of the unbalanced dataset we are dealing with (few training samples for some categories). Unbalanced distribution of the descriptors' values among different participants presented a challenge in the classification as well. Since our experiments are user-independent, unbalanced distribution of cues presented a challenge to the classifiers.

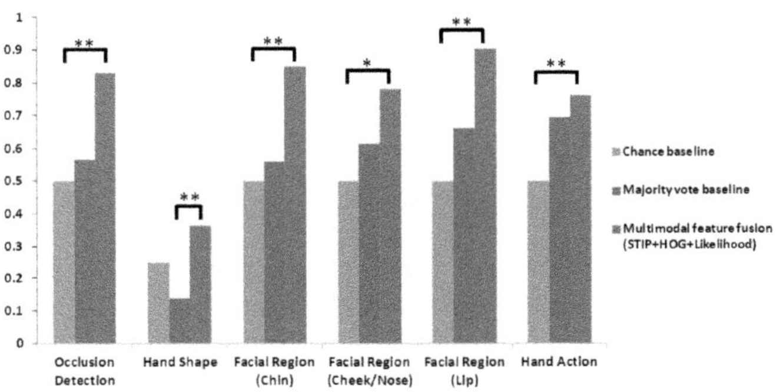

Figure 5: Classification results summary for all the classification tasks. All are binary classifiers except for (hand shape) where we employ a 4 class classifier, hence the lower classification values. Our multimodal fusion approach showed statistically significant improvement over naive classifier baselines for all of our hand detection and classification tasks. (* $p<0.05$, $p<0.01$)**

6. CONCLUSION AND FUTURE WORK

In this paper, we presented the first automatic approach to tackle the challenging problem of detection and classification of hand-over-face gestures. We treat the problem as two tasks: hand occlusion detection, then classification of hand gesture cues, namely - *hand shape*, *hand action* and *facial region occluded* . We extract a set of spatial and spatio-temporal features (Histograms of Oriented Gradients (HOG), facial landmark detection likelihood, and space-time interest points (STIP) features). We use feature-specific dimensionality reduction techniques and aggregation over a window of frames to obtain a compact representation of our features. Using a muti-modal classifier of the three features, we can detect hand-over-face occlusions and classify *hand shape*, *hand action* and *facial region occluded* significantly better than the majority vote and chance baselines. We also demonstrate that mutli-modal fusion of the features proved to outperform single modality classification results.

We believe that adding more temporal features and improving the segmentation of the videos would improve the *hand action* detection results but we are leaving this to fu-

Hand action classification	Majority vote	Uni-modal - Linear SVM			Uni-modal - non-Linear SVM			**Multi-modal classification**	
		Likelihood	HOG	STIP	Likelihood	HOG	STIP	Linear SVM	**Non-linear SVM**
F1 score	0.81	0.81	0.81	0.81	0.80	0.82	0.81	0.80	**0.83**
Accuracy	0.70	0.70	0.70	0.70	0.70	0.73	0.70	0.67	**0.76**

Table 4: Classification results of *hand action* descriptor comparing uni-modal and multi-modal feature fusion. Classification performance remained very close to the majority vote baseline, with the multi-modal fusion of features using a non-linear SVM classifier having the best results. Note that the unbalanced dataset and initial video segmentation criteria in Cam3D dataset influenced the performance of classifying this descriptor.

ture work. Future work also includes testing our multimodal features using more complex classifiers that incorporate temporal features. The coding schema can also be improved to include more hand articulations.

7. ACKNOWLEDGMENT

The research leading to these results has received funding from the European Community's Seventh Framework Programme (FP7/2007-2013) under grant agreement number 289021.

8. REFERENCES

[1] T. Baltrušaitis, P. Robinson, and L.-P. Morency. Constrained local neural fields for robust facial landmark detection in the wild. In *ICCV Workshops, 300 Faces in-the-Wild Challenge*. 2013.

[2] D. Bernhardt and P. Robinson. Detecting affect from non-stylised body motions. In *ACII*. 2007.

[3] X. P. Burgos-Artizzu, P. Perona, and P. Dollar. Robust face landmark estimation under occlusion. In *International Conference on Computer Vision*, 2013.

[4] G. Castellano, S. D. Villalba, and A. Camurri. Recognising human emotions from body movement and gesture dynamics. In *ACII*. 2007.

[5] C.-C. Chang and C.-J. Lin. Libsvm: a library for support vector machines. *ACM Transactions on Intelligent Systems and Technology*, 2011.

[6] D. Cristinacce and T. Cootes. Feature detection and tracking with constrained local models. In *BMVC*, 2006.

[7] N. Dalal and B. Triggs. Histograms of oriented gradients for human detection. In *CVPR*, 2005.

[8] B. de Gelder. Why bodies? twelve reasons for including bodily expressions in affective neuroscience. *Phil. Trans. of the Royal Society B*, 2009.

[9] P. Dollár, V. Rabaud, G. Cottrell, and S. Belongie. Behavior recognition via sparse spatio-temporal features. In *Visual Surveillance and Performance Evaluation of Tracking and Surveillance*, 2005.

[10] R.-E. Fan, K.-W. Chang, C.-J. Hsieh, X.-R. Wang, and C.-J. Lin. LIBLINEAR: A library for large linear classification. *JMLR*, 9, 2008.

[11] A. Field. *Discovering statistics using IBM SPSS statistics*. Sage, 2013.

[12] M. Gonzalez, C. Collet, and R. Dubot. Head tracking and hand segmentation during hand over face occlusion in sign language. In *Trends and Topics in Computer Vision*, pages 234–243. Springer, 2012.

[13] J. F. Grafsgaard, R. M. Fulton, K. E. Boyer, E. N. Wiebe, and J. C. Lester. Multimodal analysis of the implicit affective channel in computer-mediated textual communication. In *ICMI*, 2012.

[14] A. F. Hayes and K. Krippendorff. Answering the call for a standard reliability measure for coding data. *Communication methods and measures*, 2007.

[15] K. Hotta. A robust face detector under partial occlusion. In *ICIP*, 2004.

[16] K. Krippendorff. *Content analysis: An introduction to its methodology*. Sage, 2004.

[17] I. Laptev. On space-time interest points. *International Journal of Computer Vision*, 64(2-3):107–123, 2005.

[18] I. Laptev, M. Marszalek, C. Schmid, and B. Rozenfeld. Learning realistic human actions from movies. In *CVPR*, 2008.

[19] H. Lausberg and H. Sloetjes. Coding gestural behavior with the NEUROGES-ELAN system. *Behavior research methods*, 2009.

[20] M. Mahmoud, T. Baltrušaitis, P. Robinson, and L. D. Riek. 3D corpus of spontaneous complex mental states. In *ACII*. 2011.

[21] M. Mahmoud, R. El-Kaliouby, and A. Goneid. Towards communicative face occlusions: machine detection of hand-over-face gestures. In *Image Analysis and Recognition*, pages 481–490. Springer, 2009.

[22] M. Mahmoud and P. Robinson. Interpreting hand-over-face gestures. In *ACII*. 2011.

[23] J. Mairal, F. Bach, J. Ponce, and G. Sapiro. Online learning for matrix factorization and sparse coding. *The Journal of Machine Learning Research*, 2010.

[24] R. Poppe. A survey on vision-based human action recognition. *IVC*, 2010.

[25] J. Saragih, S. Lucey, and J. Cohn. Deformable Model Fitting by Regularized Landmark Mean-Shift. *IJCV*, 2011.

[26] P. Smith, N. da Vitoria Lobo, and M. Shah. Resolving hand over face occlusion. *IVC*, 2007.

[27] Y. Song, L.-P. Morency, and R. Davis. Learning a sparse codebook of facial and body microexpressions for emotion recognition. In *ICMI*, 2013.

[28] H. Wang, M. M. Ullah, A. Klaser, I. Laptev, C. Schmid, et al. Evaluation of local spatio-temporal features for action recognition. In *BMVC*, 2009.

[29] J. Yang, K. Yu, Y. Gong, and T. Huang. Linear spatial pyramid matching using sparse coding for image classification. In *CVPR*, 2009.

[30] X. Yu, F. Yang, J. Huang, and D. N. Metaxas. Explicit Occlusion Detection based Deformable Fitting for Facial Landmark Localization. In *FG*, 2013.

[31] X. Zhu and D. Ramanan. Face detection, pose estimation, and landmark localization in the wild. In *CVPR*, 2012.

Capturing Upper Body Motion in Conversation: an Appearance Quasi-Invariant Approach

Alvaro Marcos-Ramiro
University of Alcala
Spain
amarcos@depeca.uah.es

Daniel Pizarro-Perez
University of Clermont-Ferrand
France
dani.pizarro@gmail.com

Marta Marron-Romera
University of Alcala
Spain
marta@depeca.uah.es

Daniel Gatica-Perez
Idiap Research Institute and
EPFL
Switzerland
gatica@idiap.ch

ABSTRACT

We address the problem of body communication retrieval and measuring in seated conversations by means of markerless motion capture. In psychological studies, the use of automatic methods is key to reduce the subjectivity present in manual behavioral coding used to extract these cues. These studies usually involve hundreds of subjects with different clothing, non-acted poses, or different distances to the camera in uncalibrated, RGB-only video. However, range cameras are not yet common in psychology research, especially in existing recordings. Therefore, it becomes highly relevant to develop a fast method that is able to work in these conditions. Given the known relationship between depth and motion estimates, we propose to robustly integrate highly appearance-invariant image motion features in a machine learning approach, complemented with an effective tracking scheme. We evaluate the method's performance with existing databases and a database of upper body poses displayed in job interviews that we make public, showing that in our scenario it is comparable to that of Kinect without using a range camera, and state-of-the-art w.r.t. the HumanEva and ChaLearn 2011 evaluation datasets.

Categories and Subject Descriptors

J.4 [**Computer Applications**]: Social and behavioral sciences; G.3 [**Mathematics and Computing**]: Miscellaneous; D.2.8 [**Image Processing and Computer Vision**]: Metrics—*Scene analysis*

General Terms

Monocular motion capture; optical flow; social computing; job interviews

ICMI'14, November 12–16, 2014, Istanbul, Turkey.

ACM 978-1-4503-2885-2/14/11 ...$15.00.
http://dx.doi.org/10.1145/2663204.2663267.

1. INTRODUCTION

Nonverbal communication can influence how we are socially perceived, therefore this subject has been intensively analyzed in social psychology and cognitive science [14]. In these domains, however, there has traditionally been the need for an interpreter. That is, a person that emits a judgment on the perceived traits of the analyzed subject, or that codes specific behaviors from hours of video recordings. This judgment always carries a degree of subjectivity, which can lead to inconsistencies across different evaluations.

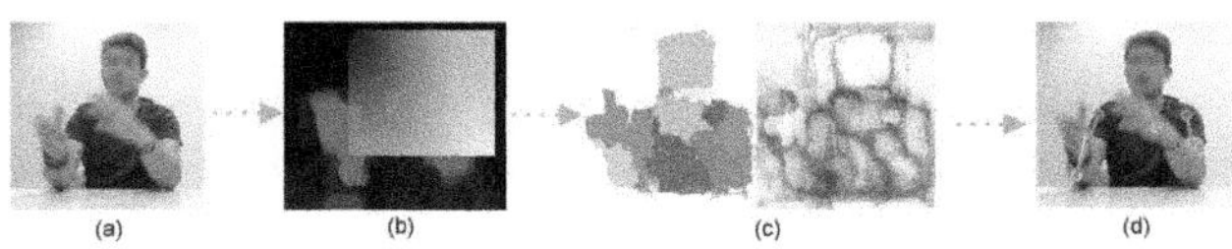

Figure 1: Data flow overview. (a) Original image. (b) Proposed 4-channel image. (c) Body part classification and confidence scores. (d) Obtained pose. Please view in PDF.

Markerless motion capture from monocular images is a good solution to this problem (as markers placed in the body can alter the behavior), but remains a challenge in computer vision. This is a consequence of many factors, such as the high-dimensionality of the data, camera projection distortions, appearance variability (*e.g.* clothing, skin, hair...) or external and self-occlusions. In the last few years range cameras have appeared in the mass market, largely solving the depth perception and color appearance problems. Other difficulties remain, however, such as clothing, the many different contexts in which the same body part can appear, and the high dimensionality of the articulated motion. The work in [25] presented a solution to human pose estimation with a machine learning approach: a classifier was trained with a very large database from simple offset features capturing depth differences between near pixels. Invariance to clothing, body types, and part appearances was therefore learned. This resulted in a very robust solution with previously unseen performance levels, assuming that depth is available.

In psychological studies, however, there is still a clear need for processing and analyzing in RGB-only images: most of the historical material and even newer studies [34] use traditional video, as psychology tends to be a discipline in which technological changes take time to be widely adopted. In

RGB images, the approach of [25] is not directly transferable: simple color differences as features would depend on the background and person appearance. In motion capture, several techniques have been proposed in order to get invariant features from RGB images. HOG-based Body Part Detectors (BPDs) in particular are able to obtain a rough estimate of the pose, later refined with a number of different solutions such as global coherence [30] or symmetry analysis [21]. However, the output of BPDs is often very noisy, with several parts interfering with one another. BPDs are also sensitive to changes in the background.

In this paper, we present a robust method to extract the body pose from sequences of seated conversations, applicable to RGB video data. Our main contributions therefore are: (1) our method provides a high degree of appearance and scale invariance while using only an uncalibrated RGB camera. To this end, we obtain a depth estimate through image motion, given the relationship between both [32]. The scale and spatial context problem is tackled with a single human body detector [9][7], thus avoiding the clutter of using many part detectors. To overcome the lack of information when there is no movement present, we integrate a Kanade-Lucas-Tomasi (KLT) tracker [29]. (2) We evaluate the method's performance with two existing databases and a database of upper body poses displayed in job interviews that we make public, showing that in our scenario it is comparable to that of [25] without using a range camera, and state-of-the-art in the HumanEva [26] and ChaLearn 2011 [1] datasets, used for motion capture system evaluation.

2. RELATED WORK

As explained, given all the challenges that recovering human pose generates, the single camera approach is considered the most elusive. The literature of monocular motion capture can be organized in many ways, but given the latest developments in the field, we classify it into methods that make use of BPDs and those who use other techniques.

Non BPD-based methods: The first BPD-based methods [8] were largely appearance-dependent, leaving the need for more robust solutions with alternative approaches. In [28], biological motion analysis is performed with graphs and motion capture data in order to infer and detect human movements. Using a similar idea, [15] applies optical flow in constrained situations to recover the position of the body limbs. In [12], a strong body model prior and a tracking method are coupled with optical flow recognition for biological motion perception and 3D lifting. The work in [2] also uses strong motion priors to get 3D from 2D images by mapping silhouette descriptors to body pose configurations. Doing so, no explicit body model is required. Instead of a strong motion prior, [3] uses a detailed upper body mesh model coupled with contours and optical flow to recover the pose. Finally, in [24] a range camera is used, and optical flow distinguishes the limbs in moments where depth fails to output reliable geodesic extrema.

BPD-based methods: A number of HOG-based methods have arisen, solving long-standing problems like automatic initialization. In [30] the co-occurrence relations and spatial tree-structured relationships between part detectors are modeled to improve global coherence. Coherence can also be improved with HOG co-dependent body-part Random Forests regressors [6], whereas [21] relies on symmetry analysis. In [11], HOG detectors are improved with skin color, contours, and contextual cues. In [27], 2D and 3D inference are simultaneously done with a generative Bayesian framework and discriminative HOG-based BPDs. In [33], 3D poses are retrieved in unconstrained videos through BPDs, action classification, and pose regression with spatiotemporal features. Finally, in [22] global and local pose cues are included and a convex objective and joint training for mode selection and pose estimation is used to improve the state-of-art performance-to-computing time ratio.

Closest techniques to ours: In [4], upper body motion capture is performed for language sign classification in long videos. Arm detections are used in order to disambiguate difficult hand detections. The torso shape is also inferred from a series of heuristics. However, this method assumes that the hands are generally visible, and the clothing is not problematic. In [23], optical flow and color are used to detect hands, with body part detectors being one of the image features, while [10] relies on optical flow and a precise 2D silhouette body model. In [35] a hand detector is trained with optical flow to then interpolate between correct guesses. However, they use image contours, which are prone to errors in certain situations. In [16] a hand detector is also used, but includes appearance-dependent features such as skin color. To conclude, in [13] multiple body part detectors are trained with Random Forests and per-pixel HOG features, which still inherits some of the appearance-dependence problems that edges entail.

In summary, the current tendencies for monocular RGB motion capture can be grouped into using multiple BPDs (where problems like overlap, interference, or background-appearance dependency arise), the use of strong motion models, strong body models, appearance-relying methods with a torso detector. In contrast, in the present work we combine a single torso detector with largely appearance-invariant features, while improving the best performance-to-computing time ratio of the state-of-the-art.

3. OVERVIEW

An overview of our method can be seen in Figure 2. Given two input consecutive frames $\mathbf{I}_{t-1}$ and $\mathbf{I}_t$, we compute the dense optical flow $\mathbf{I}_{OF}$ [5] and the subject torso bounding box $\vec{b} = [\vec{u_o}, b_w, b_h]$, where $\vec{u_o}$ is the top left pixel of the bounding box, b_w is its width and b_h is its height. We define a 4-channel (4-C) image as $\mathbf{I}_C = [\mathbf{I}_{OF}, \mathbf{I}_{bw}, \mathbf{I}_{bh}]$, where $\mathbf{I}_{bw}$ and $\mathbf{I}_{bh}$ images derived from the torso detection, that aim to give spatial context (see Section 4.1 for details). We then extract per-pixel offset features $\vec{u_\delta}$ from $\mathbf{I}_C$ from a training set (the only prior used) in a similar fashion to [25]. In order to predict the body part classification label image $\mathbf{I}_L$, a Random Forest classifier is used. The label image $\mathbf{I}_L$ and its associated confidence scores $\mathbf{I}_L'$ are used to train a Random Forest regressor that outputs the final body configuration.

4. OBSERVATION SYSTEM

4.1 Largely appearance-invariant features

As explained in Section 3, we aim to extract a series of features from the image that encode as much information as possible while maintaining a high appearance-invariance: they should be robust to clothing and skin color. Thanks to recent advances, dense optical flow and upper body detectors are good candidates. Therefore, we compose a 4-C image

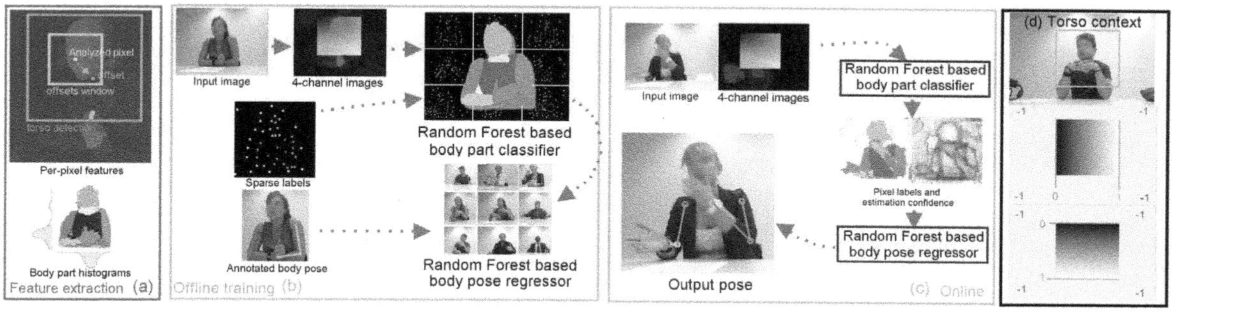

Figure 2: Pipeline of our proposal: (a) Image feature extraction, from the original RGB data and set of body part labels. (b) Offline training of the body part classifier and pose regressor, from sparsely labeled data. (c) Online usage: once the 4-C features have been computed, they are fed into the classifier. In turn, its output is used as input for the regressor, which estimates the body joints configuration. (d) Torso context: horizontal (center) and vertical (bottom) context images $\mathbf{I}_{bw}$ and $\mathbf{I}_{bh}$. Best viewed in PDF.

that merges the information that those low-level features provide. These channels are:

Optical flow modulus $\mathbf{I}_{OF,\rho}$: as mentioned in the introduction, depth and motion in an image are closely related. Therefore, the magnitude of the optical flow vector is a strong cue for positioning the body pose.

Optical flow orientation $\mathbf{I}_{OF,\phi}$: we hypothesize that in certain situations, such as when the hands move close to each other, the optical flow orientation is a useful cue in order to differentiate them.

Torso vertical context $\mathbf{I}_{bh}$: We use the torso detector output to place and estimate the size of the person in the image, adding contextual information. Given the bounding box $\vec{b}$, we encode relative height in the image $\mathbf{I}_{bh}$ (see Figure 2d). In $\mathbf{I}_{bh}$ pixels range from 0 to 1, from the bottom to the top within the bounding box, and are set to -1 outside the bounding box.

Torso horizontal context $\mathbf{I}_{bw}$: Analogous to $\mathbf{I}_{bh}$, while providing horizontal information.

4.2 Body part classification

At this point, highly appearance-invariant images $\mathbf{I}_C$ are obtained. Similar to [25], we use an offset sampling idea and a Random Forest classifier in order to associate every pixel with a body part label. A set $\mathcal{U}$ of pixel offset features is built: $\mathcal{U} = \{\vec{u_{\delta i}}\}_{i=1}^{n_\delta} = \{(u_{\delta i}, v_{\delta i})\}_{i=1}^{n_\delta}$. For a given pixel $\vec{u}$, the feature response is computed with feature parameters $\vec{u_{\delta i}}$ that describe a number of n_δ 2D pixel offsets $(u_{\delta i}, v_{\delta i})$. In [25], features are normalized with the distance to the camera in order to make them depth-invariant. In our case however it is not possible, as we use RGB only images. As a proxy for size of the person, we use the height of the torso bounding box b_h. We then extract the per-pixel features from each channel in a different way.

Optical flow modulus: both the offset distance and optical flow value are normalized with b_h, since motions that take place far from the camera result in a lower optical flow modulus value. Let $L(\vec{u}, \vec{u_{\delta i}}, \mathbf{I}^1)$ be a lookup function that returns the feature associated with pixel $\vec{u}$, given a single-channel image $\mathbf{I}^1$ and an offset $\vec{u_{\delta i}}$. An optical flow modulus feature becomes:

$$f_{OF,\rho}(\vec{u}|\vec{u_{\delta i}}) = L(\vec{u}, \frac{\vec{u_{\delta i}}}{b_h}, \mathbf{I}_{OF,\rho})\frac{1}{b_h} - \mathbf{I}_{OF,\rho}(\vec{u})\frac{1}{b_h} \quad (1)$$

It encodes the speed difference between pixel $\vec{u}$ and its associated offset $\vec{u_{\delta i}}$, after normalizing the offset distance and image speed with the torso size b_h.

Optical flow direction: in order to better differentiate parts of the body moving with similar speed modulus, but with different orientations, we also take the optical flow direction into account. For each pixel, we compute the direction similarity in relation to its offset features:

$$f_{OF,\phi}(\vec{u}|\vec{u_{\delta i}}) = L(\vec{u}, \frac{\vec{u_{\delta i}}}{b_h}, \mathbf{I}_{OF,\phi}) - \mathbf{I}_{OF,\phi}(\vec{u}) \quad (2)$$

Therefore, given the optical flow angle for pixel $\vec{u}$, the angle difference respective to the offset is computed. The discontinuity between 0 and 360 degrees is addressed so that the angle difference is less than or equal to 180 degrees.

Position relative to the torso: the feature is obtained in an identical way to that of the optical flow direction:

$$f_{bh}(\vec{u}|\vec{u_{\delta i}}) = L(\vec{u}, \frac{\vec{u_{\delta i}}}{b_h}, \mathbf{I}_{bh}) - \mathbf{I}_{bh}(\vec{u}) \quad (3)$$

$$f_{bw}(\vec{u}|\vec{u_{\delta i}}) = L(\vec{u}, \frac{\vec{u_{\delta i}}}{b_h}, \mathbf{I}_{bw}) - \mathbf{I}_{bw}(\vec{u}) \quad (4)$$

where equations $f_{bh}(\vec{u}|\vec{u_{\delta i}})$ and $f_{bw}(\vec{u}|\vec{u_{\delta i}})$ correspond to the vertical and horizontal context, respectively. With this approximation, each feature gives an idea of where the pixel is positioned in relation to the main portion of the torso.

The feature vector for classification $\mathcal{X}_{tr,class}$ is formed by concatenating all the features, providing information about the speed, direction, and position relative to the torso of every pixel of the image, hence forming a rich representation of human motion. We demonstrate its capabilities in the results section.

4.2.1 *Training the forest for classification*

A subset of data from the real job interview dataset is annotated in order to serve as a training set (see Section 7). For classification, annotations consist of a number of manually-labeled pixels in the image, in which the nature of each label corresponds to a given body part. We then compute the previously introduced per-pixel offset features for each labeled pixel in the training subset. As our method depends on the amount of movement in the image, we discard the pixels with low flow modulus. We then train a Random Forest (of depth 20) with the extracted pixel offset features and the associated body part labels. Given an unseen 4-

C image, the classifier outputs the per-pixel predicted body part and an associated confidence score (see Figure 2).

4.3 Body pose regression

The next step is to obtain the final body configuration $\mathcal{P}_o$ (defined as the pixel position in the image for every joint) from the output of the body part classifier: $\mathcal{P}_o = \Omega(\mathbf{I}_L, \mathbf{I}_L^{'}, \beta)$, where Ω is the regression model with β parameters. Therefore, we use a Random Forest regressor that takes information extracted from an image of densely classified body parts $\mathbf{I}_L$ and classification scores $\mathbf{I}_L^{'}$, resulting in the regression training set $\mathcal{X}_{tr,reg}$, through a process described below.

4.3.1 *Obtain images $\mathbf{I}_L$ and $\mathbf{I}_L^{'}$ to train the regressor*

In order to train the classifier, sparse labels are used. This responds to two reasons. First, to reduce annotation time: it can be reduced to less than half of the time required for dense labeling. Second, to force the classifier to generalize: as during training only a few ($\sim$100) pixels per image are labeled, the trained forest is shown later the same training images, obtaining the classification output for every pixel in the image. In this process, the provided classification scores $\mathbf{I}_L^{'}$ picture more realistically the confidence that the classifier will have in unseen images. This property is important when training the body pose regressor, as it is forced to learn from the mistakes that the body part classifier makes.

4.3.2 *Body part histograms from $\mathbf{I}_L$ and $\mathbf{I}_L^{'}$*

In order to capture more explicitly the characteristics of the predicted body parts placement in the image, we propose the use of vertical and horizontal per-class histograms of $\mathbf{I}_L$ and $\mathbf{I}_L^{'}$. We build three sets of histograms. The first one, $\mathcal{M}_l$, measures the frequency in which each body part appears in the vertical and horizontal axis of the image, and it is defined as $\mathcal{M}_l = [\vec{ml,_v}, \vec{ml,_h}]$, where $\vec{ml,_v}$ and $\vec{ml,_h}$ are the vertical and horizontal histograms. The second one, $\mathcal{M}_l^{'}$ adds the scores $\mathbf{I}_L^{'}$ in the pixels of the image that belong to the relevant body part, along the vertical and horizontal axis of the image, and it is defined as $\mathcal{M}_l^{'} = [\vec{m}_{l,v}^{'}, \vec{m}_{l,h}^{'}]$. The third one, $\mathcal{M}_l^{''}$, is the product of the previous two:

$$\mathcal{M}_l^{''} = [\vec{ml,_v}\vec{m}_{l,v}^{'}, \vec{ml,_h}\vec{m}_{l,h}^{'}] \quad (5)$$

This results in the body part frequency histogram $\mathcal{M}_l$ to be weighted with its associated confidence scores $\mathcal{M}_l^{'}$. The effect can be seen in Figure 3: the resulting histogram $\mathcal{M}_l^{''}$ shows better where the most confident predictions are located in the image, for a given body part. In order to reduce the dimensionality of the histograms, the images $\mathbf{I}_L$ and $\mathbf{I}_L^{'}$ are down-sampled to a resolution of 128x96 pixels. Therefore, a given vertical histogram becomes 96-dimensional, and a horizontal histogram becomes 128-dimensional. Since there are 10 different body parts classes, 10 different set of histograms $\mathcal{M}_l^{''}$ are obtained (one for each body part). This results in a 2240-dimensional feature vector $\mathcal{X}_{tr,reg}$ for regression $\mathcal{X}_{tr,reg} = \{\mathcal{M}_{l,i}^{''}\}_{i=1}^{n_j}$, where n_j is the number of body parts (classes). For each feature vector $\mathcal{X}_{tr,reg}$ there is an associated annotated body pose, consisting in the pixel position of 6 joints: shoulders, elbows and wrists. It is therefore 12-dimensional. Both the feature vector and the labels are used to train the regression model Ω.

As a summary, in order to obtain the body pose from a unseen pair of $\mathbf{I}_t$, $\mathbf{I}_{t-1}$ images, the associated 4-C image $\mathbf{I}_C$ is first composed, and then input into the body part classifier. The resulting densely-labeled image and confidence scores ($\mathbf{I}_L^{'}$ and $\mathbf{I}_L$) are fed into the body pose regressor, which outputs the predicted final pose configuration $\mathcal{P}_o$ as pixel positions of every joint.

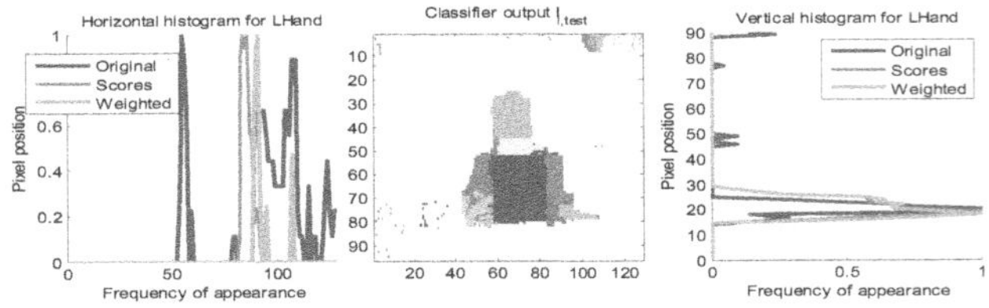

Figure 3: Body part histogram example. Left and right: $\vec{ml,_v}$ and $\vec{ml,_h}$ for the left hand. Center: classifier output. The confidence weighting helps to maintain the detection peak in the right position. Best viewed in color.

5. TRACKING

In order to reliably obtain the body pose in every situation, we propose a tracking method where hands are tracked using the KLT framework when the body part classifier is not reliable. We then impose temporal smoothness to avoid sudden changes in the pose.

Tracking the hands. The main drawback of our proposal is the need for movement in the image, as the classifier needs optical flow measurements in order to classify different body parts. We extend the pose retrieval framework by adding a KLT tracker, based on image features. KLT trackers work better with slow motion, as motion blur and quick appearance changes become a problem when obtaining good features to track. On the other hand, it has shown to be very reliable when small motions are present. Since our pose detection method is most confident when movement is present, the KLT functions in a natural, complementary way with the pose regressor.

Taking this into account, a detection followed by tracking framework is proposed to obtain the body pose along a whole video. As finding the hands' position removes a high degree of uncertainty in the pose [17], we employ this approach only in them. When the scores image $\mathbf{I}_L^{'}$ falls under a manually set threshold for a hand region, the detection is deemed unreliable, and the last reliable detection is used to initialize a KLT tracker, that takes control of the hand position until a new reliable detection is found, usually when the hand starts to move again. An example can be seen in Figure 4. Since both hands are considered separately, two KLT trackers are used, one for each hand.

Stabilizing the body pose. At this point, a body pose configuration $\mathcal{P}_o$ is available. Given that the ultimate goal of our method is to serve as information to later analyze nonverbal communication, a further post-processing step is needed. When a subject stands still, ideally the output pose would remain perfectly still too. However, as the system involves a high degree of tracking by detection, $\mathcal{P}_o$ slightly fluctuates along time.

In order to compensate this effect, a simple yet effective approach is followed. If the joints stay within some radius for a certain period then they are frozen in that position. Especifically, for each body joint a small pixel radius κ_m is defined. If the predicted body joint falls under the radius longer than a small pre-defined time t_m, then the joint is defined as the center of the static circle that is configured with κ_m. The timing parameter t_m is necessary in order to avoid the discretization of continuous movements, as they would evolve in κ_m steps otherwise.

6. DATASETS

6.1 Upper body pose interview database

We construct a case-relevant database (that we make public) from a set of one-shot, non-consecutive color and depth images extracted from a series of real job interview videos (kindly shared by [19, 20]), containing 34 different subjects (8 male, 26 female), as Figure 7 shows. The interviewee is sitting in front of a table, and a Kinect device is pointing frontally at him/her, therefore only the upper-body is visible. As the images have been extracted from real job interviews, the appearance, clothing, or movement of the participants are not restricted or acted in any way. We selected 1420 frames with a resolution of 640x480 both for RGB and depth, in which the subject is moving at least a part of the body. As shown by previous works with Random Forests, a large amount of training data is required, therefore we distributed the frames as 1100 for training and 320 for testing. Even if the amount of data is significatively lower that one of [25], given the similarity of the underlying methods, it still allows comparison in generalization capabilities. In addition, as only the upper-body is considered, the degrees of freedom of the body configuration is much lower. The data will be made publicly available with blurred faces due to privacy reasons.

6.1.1 *Annotation*

Test images ground-truth is obtained by manually labeling every pixel of the testing images with 10 labels: right and left hands, right and left forearms, right and left arms, head, torso, neck and background (see Figure 2). For the training images, manual sparse labeling has been followed. That is, we only label a few (around 100) pixels per image, in the parts that carry less uncertainty. For example, if there is a self-occlusion, only the pixels in which the different parts of the body are clearly distinguished are labeled. Manual sparse labeling carries two main advantages: first, the labeling time is greatly reduced; secondly, it allows us to choose the parts of the image that better represent each part. With the aid of a purpose-built script, labeling takes an average of only 25 seconds per image, with a speed close to 5 pixels per second. In contrast, dense labeling would take almost 1 minute per frame.

As seen in Figure 2, if enough data has been sparsely labeled, it is possible to get an approximate dense labeling by using the method in [25] on the sparse labels, which can be manually corrected later. Also, we effectively double the amount of training data by mirroring each image, both during classification and regression. Finally, the groundtruth for the regression task is obtained by annotating the joint positions of the wrist, elbow and shoulder position in every image.

6.2 Additional datasets

In order to validate our methods, show generalization of performance, and allow for comparisons, we test our proposal in two publicly-available datasets. We choose the subsets of experiments that are most relevant to our scenario: similar upper body movements to those that are found in conversations.

ChaLearn 2011 contains 437 non-consecutive, 320×240 color and depth frames, in which body joints have been manually annotated. The environment is uncontrolled, and different backgrounds, high variance of poses, clothing, positioning and lighting appear. In some of the frames, there is no movement at all.

HumanEva-I contains 7 calibrated video sequences (4 grayscale and 3 color) that are synchronized with 3D body poses obtained from a motion capture system. The database videos contain 4 subjects (S1-S4) performing a 6 common actions (e.g. walking, jogging, gesturing, etc.). The dataset contains training, validation and testing sets. We chose sequences 'gestures' and 'box' sequences of S1 and S3 for evaluation.

7. RESULTS

We evaluate the effects of different parameters in our system's performance, and compare it with the current state-of-the-art. For the one-shot-detection part of the approach, we define two experiments: one for classification and one for regression. For classification, we compare the output of our method to annotations of every body part. The result is given in per-pixel accuracy for each class. For regression, we compare the output pose that we get with manual annotations of the database we used, measuring joint detection rate. A joint is defined as detected if the predicted point falls within a given distance threshold.

7.1 Classification

The performance is evaluated in our job interview database. We train both our algorithm and [25] with the same number of images. As our method depends on the amount of movement in the image, we discard the pixels that fall below a motion threshold. This results in fewer but reliable data points. In total, more than 110k pixels were used for depth training, and 88k for optical flow training. The same classifier parameters were used in both cases: 75 trees, an offset window of 250 pixels and 700 features. We generate 320x240 classified images in order to have a reasonable resolution while maintaining a competitive processing time. The results can be seen in Figure 4 for the different cases.

Using depth, a **67.7%** accuracy is achieved for the pixels associated with the person, which is consistent with the previous findings of [25], when taking into account the much lower training information. Over the whole image, the accuracy is **92.3%**. Using optical flow and torso detections, the accuracy for the person is **63%**, and **87.7%** for the whole image. This shows that our method can achieve similar results to depth when there is body movement. An interesting finding is that our method outperforms [25] in hand detection. As the reviewed literature shows, hand position is a very good proxy in order to infer the rest of the body pose. The usefulness of optical flow in hand and arm detection is confirmed, as when combining depth and optical flow modulus, the body accuracy increases to **70%**, with the whole image at **92.2%**.

Sensitivity to parameters results can be seen in Figure 5. When considering offset window size before scale normalization, it is found that a size of 200x200 improves the body-related detections, but introduces more background noise than 250x250 sizes, making the regression system more prone

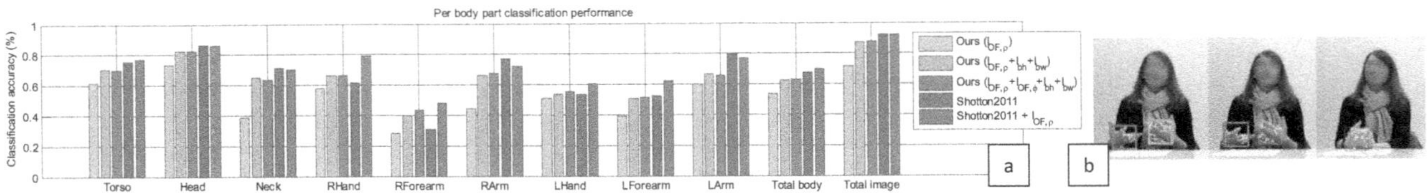

Figure 4: Left: **Results of our method versus [25]**, when trained with the same number of images: Reported as classification rates for every body segment. Performance is asymmetrical as the camera is slightly off-center. Right: **Integration with the KLT tracker example**. Reliable detections are represented with a thick box. The good features to track are shown as white crosses.

to errors. Surprisingly, using a very low number of offset features did not cause big performance drops. Already with 150 pixel offset features, very competitive results are obtained, as a result of the rich contextual information that the torso detector provides. As for the number of trees used, it is found that after 5 trees, there is only a slight performance increase to be found. Finally, when considering the amount of training data, competitive results can already be obtained with 300 training images (effectively 600, since they are mirrored). This highlights the generalization capabilities of the proposed features.

7.2 Regression

Performance is measured with two different datasets: our upper-body interview dataset, and ChaLearn 2011, which is non-conversational, but allows to show generalization of performance. Rates of correct detected parts can be found in Figures 5. We found 40 pixels to be the limit of a reliable guess while using 640x480 images.

Job interview dataset. Our method performs similarly to [25], and outperforms [9] and [22]. The latter work had been trained with their FLIC database, and is considered as the best method in terms of performance to processing time ratio. Wrists are the hardest body part to detect, and our method achieves close to **20%** higher performance than [22]. When compared against [25], our method is less than **10%** behind. Using the classification weights scores, accuracy is improved by almost **5%** for the hands. In Figure 7 some qualitative results can be found.

ChaLearn 2011 We perform leave-one-out after dividing the data in 10 arbitrary groups. As it can be seen in Figure 5, the trends shown in our job interview dataset are reproduced when there is enough movement available. The gap to [25] appears larger due to several factors: (a) less training data: only 57% of the total labeled points are used in our approach as we only use points that contain movement information in order to train the forest. This also gives an idea of the little movement information present in the dataset. As Figure 7 top right shows, in the left hand there is a higher amount of movement, greatly reducing the gap with [25]. (b) Some subjects move out of frame (the head or one arm is not visible), making it a hurdle for the torso detection to be correctly placed, and reducing the accuracy of shoulders and elbows. (c) In some cases the subject casts shadows in the background wall, producing spurious optical flow detections. Despite this, we found that in some instances the context provided by the torso detector is able to filter errors out. In any case, our method performs clearly better than the RGB-only baselines, and given the challenging conditions, remarkably close to [25] when there is movement present. Also, it shows that our system performs well with different body scales.

7.3 Tracking

In order to evaluate the tracking proposal, we define three experiments. The **experiment #1** evaluates hand positioning, as it is a very good proxy for the global pose [17]. During two minutes of video from 4 subjects, the hand position was manually annotated. The **experiment #2** follows the same approach, but containing a very challenging 30 second sequence (see column 3 of Figure 7 left), as she has no sleeves (therefore a lot of skin exposed, which produce appearance-dependence situations when using a skin segmentation scheme), moves her hair which is a similar color to that of the skin, and displays a series of unusual movements (such as the shoulders being closer to the camera than the hands at some points). Finally, the **experiment #3** uses the HumanEva I database.

The baseline for the experiments #1 and #2 is a state-of-the-art hand detection measure [31]. Hand saliency is defined as $\mathbf{I}_{H,t} = \mathbf{I}_{S,t} \cdot \mathbf{I}_{F,t} \cdot (\kappa_1 \mathbf{I}_{OF,\rho,t} + \kappa_2 \mathbf{I}_{D,t})$, where $\mathbf{I}_{S,t}$ is the skin segmentation, $\mathbf{I}_{F,t}$ is the face region subtraction, $\mathbf{I}_{D,t}$ is the distance to the camera, and κ_1 and κ_2 are manually set constants. For comparison purposes between RGB-only methods, we use the same saliency measure without the addition of $\mathbf{I}_{D,t}$, denoted as $\mathbf{I}'_{H,t}$. We apply a best path tracking scheme to the local maxima of $\mathbf{I}_{H,t}$ and $\mathbf{I}'_{H,t}$.

The results of our tracking method applied for hand position can be seen in Figure 6. In experiment #1, the hand detection rate is **78.6%**, marginally higher than the baseline obtained with $\mathbf{I}_{H,t}$ (**78.2%**), even though no depth information is used in our approach. When compared to the performance of $\mathbf{I}'_{H,t}$, our framework shows a clear increase of performance. In the challenging experiment #2, we found that our approach significantly increases the performance gap with respect to the $\mathbf{I}_{H,t}$ baseline, which uses depth, obtaining a detection rate of **66%**, compared to **31%**. This clearly shows that our method does not simply label body parts that move the fastest as hands, but rather takes the actual shape of the body part movements into account in the learning process. It also carries the extra advantage of being able to explicitly distinguish between right and left hands.

As Figure 6 shows, we obtain state-of-the-art performance in HumanEva I (in [18] an average of 12.6 pixel error is reported). The largest errors occur when the performed pose substantially differs to those contained in the training set. Given the very few data samples that HumanEva I makes available for training (we use an average of 46 sparsely labeled frames per sequence), and the fact that our method requires large training sets [25], we find the performance very encouraging overall. See Figure 7 for qualitative results.

7.4 Computing time

Computing time is key in psychological studies, given the large amount of data. In [22], there appears an analysis

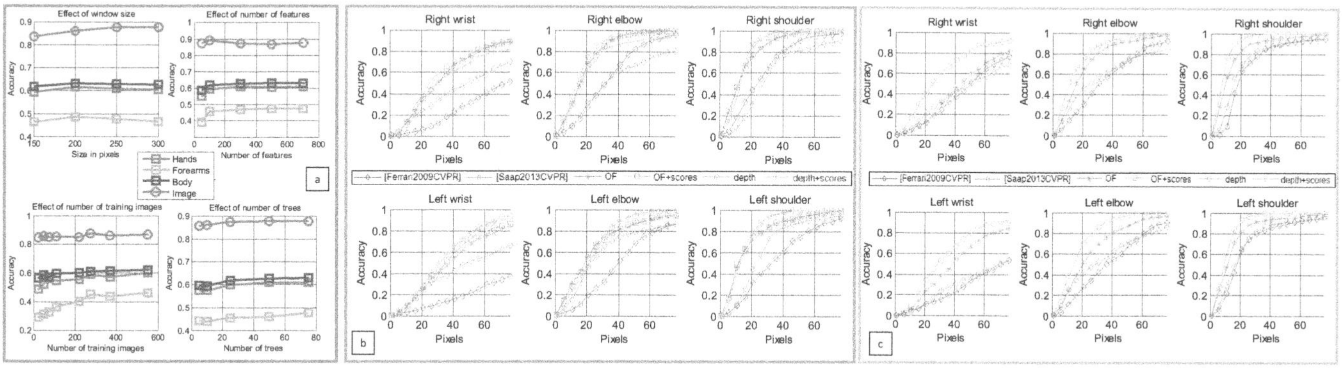

Figure 5: a: Parameter sensitivity of the classifier. b: Accuracy of the regressor in our job database, compared against [9] (blue) and [22] (magenta). c: Results in ChaLearn2011, compared against [9] (blue) and [22] (magenta). Best viewed in PDF in high zoom.

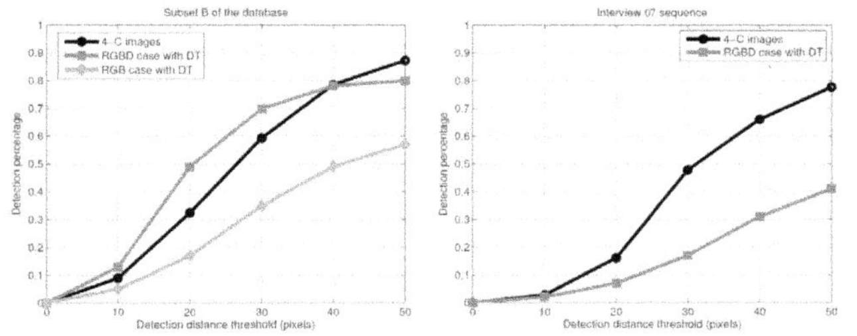

Subject	Action	Error (pixels)
S1	Gestures	5.0
S1	Box	13.2
S3	Gestures	11.3
S3	Box	21.3

Figure 6: Tracking results. Left graph: first experiment. Right graph, using a specially challenging sequence. Table: Average error in HumanEva. Best viewed in color.

of the state-of-the-art performance versus computing time, with their work being the best placed. Using the code they provide, our database is computed on a laptop with an Intel i7 processor in an average of 5.18 secs per frame (standard deviation 0.16 secs).

In our case, assuming that pre-computed optical flow is available (it can be comfortably processed in real time with modern GPUs), the average processing time from input features to body pose is **1.59 secs** per frame (standard deviation 0.11 secs), using the same hardware. Our per-pixel feature retrieval implemented in Matlab takes most of the running time. Since regression needs the output of the classifier with a resolution of 128x96 pixels in order to build the histograms, we obtain features for every fifth pixel of the 4-C composed image. If only classification results are needed, we obtain comparable processing times to [22] by using a resolution of 320x240 for I_l, recording a mean of 5.05 secs and (standard deviation 0.14 secs). This offset feature-based approach is implemented on an XBox 360 in [25] at 200 fps. Finally, an average of an extra **0.027 secs** per frame is required in order to track the hands with the KLT approach.

Limitations: Our method requires a static camera and static background, but optical flow based methods in the literature have shown to overcome that problem by tracking background features. As the torso bounding box misplacements are one of the main sources of error, our approach can highly benefit from an elaborated torso bounding box tracking technique.

8. CONCLUSIONS

We proposed a fast, largely appearance-invariant method for upper body monocular motion capture of people engaged in conversation, which integrates detection and tracking. Detection was achieved through optical flow and body detectors, providing a proxy for depth information, visual context, and scale. This information was used to classify body parts in the image with a Random Forests classifier. The classification output and per-pixel confidence was later used to build per body part image histograms, and were fed to a regressor in order to infer the body pose. The integration of a KLT tracker allowed to follow the body pose when there are no reliable detections, thus resulting in a complementary framework.

We evaluated our method with three different datasets, showing very close performance to that of the best depth-based method, while using only monocular information. We also clearly outperform the state-of-the art in the ratio accuracy to processing time. Our method is therefore attractive to process video data in typical psychology lab studies, where depth data is not yet available. Our database of static upper-body poses in interviews will be made public, providing a reliable benchmark for real-world performance.

9. ACKNOWLEDGMENTS

This research was funded by SNSF SONVB and UBImpressed projects, the Spanish Ministry of Economy and Competitiveness under project SPACES-UAH (TIN2013-47630-C2-1-R) and the University of Alcala FPI program.

10. REFERENCES

[1] Chalearn gesture dataset (cgd2011), chalearn, california, 2011. copyright (c) chalearn - 2011. http://gesture.chalearn.org/data.

[2] A. Agarwal and B. Triggs. Recovering 3d human pose from monocular images. *IEEE PAMI*, 28(1), 2006.

[3] T. Brox, B. Rosenhahn, and D. Cremers. Contours, optic flow, and prior knowledge: cues for capturing 3D human motion in videos. In *Human Motion - Understanding, Modeling, Capture, and Animation*. 2007.

[4] P. Buehler, M. Everingham, D. P. Huttenlocher, and A. Zisserman. Upper body detection and tracking in extended signing sequences. *IJCV*, 95(2), 2011.

[5] A. Chambolle and T. Pock. A first-order primal-dual algorithm for convex problems withÂăapplications to imaging. *JMIV*, 2011.

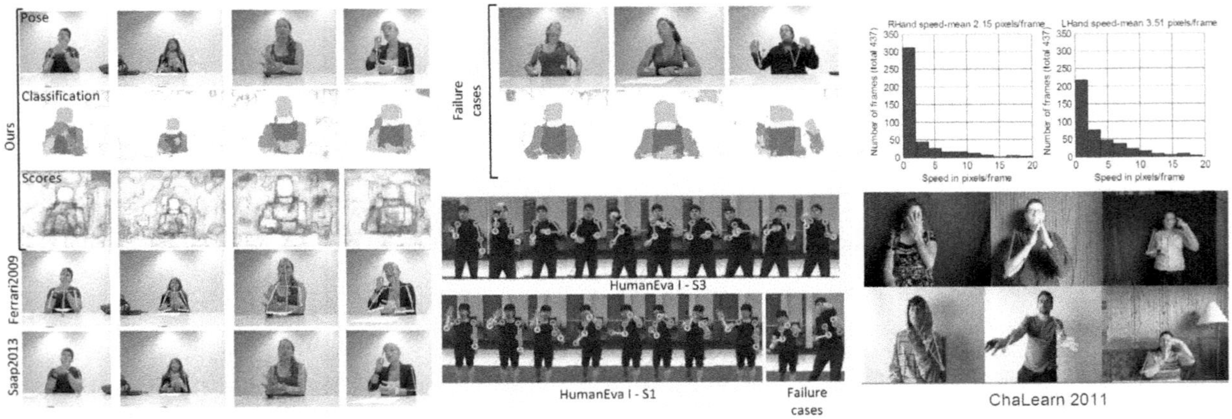

Figure 7: Qualitative results. Left: comparison with the baselines [9] and [22]. Top center: failure cases. From left to right: untrained pose, not enough movement information, torso detection failure. Bottom center: HumanEva I results for S1 and S3. Failure cases, from left to right: untrained pose, torso detection failure. Top right: speed histograms for each hand. Bottom right: examples of obtained poses in ChaLearn 2011. Best viewed in PDF in high zoom.

[6] M. Dantone, J. Gall, C. Leistner, , and L. V. Gool. Human pose estimation using body parts dependent joint regressors. In *IEEE CVPR*, 2013.

[7] P. Dollar, R. Appel, and W. Kienzle. Crosstalk cascades for frame-rate pedestrian detection. In *IEEE ECCV*, 2012.

[8] P. Felzenszwalb and D. Huttenlocher. Efficient matching of pictorial structures. In *IEEE CVPR*, 2000.

[9] V. Ferrari, M. Marin-Jimenez, and A. Zisserman. Pose search: Retrieving people using their pose. In *IEEE CVPR*, 2009.

[10] K. Fragkiadaki, H. Hu, and J. Shi. Pose from flow and flow from pose. In *IEEE CVPR*, 2013.

[11] G. Gkioxari, P. Arbelaez, L. Bourdev, and J. Malik. Articulated pose estimation using discriminative armlet classifiers. In *IEEE CVPR*, 2013.

[12] N. R. Howe. Flow lookup and biological motion perception. In *International Conference on Image Processing (ICIP)*, 2005.

[13] V. Kazemi, M. Burenius, H. Azizpour, and J. Sullivan. Multi-view body part recognition with random forests. In *British Machine Vision Conference (BMVC)*, 2013.

[14] M. Knapp and J. Hall. *Nonverbal Communication in Human Interaction.* 2009.

[15] D. Kulic, D. Lee, and Y. Nakamura. Whole body motion primitive segmentation from monocular video. In *IEEE ICRA*, 2009.

[16] A. Marcos-Ramiro, D. Pizarro-Perez, M. Marron-Romera, L. Nguyen, and D. Gatica-Perez. Body communicative cue extraction for conversational analysis. In *IEEE FG*, 2013.

[17] E. Marinoiu, D. Papava, and C. Sminchisescu. Pictorial Human Spaces. How Well do Humans Perceive a 3D Articulated Pose? In *IEEE ICCV*, 2013.

[18] V. Morariu, D. Harwood, and L. Davis. Tracking people's hands and feet using mixed network and/or search. *Pattern Analysis and Machine Intelligence, IEEE Transactions on*, 35, 2013.

[19] L. Nguyen, A. Marcos, M. Marron, and D. Gatica-Perez. Multimodal analysis of body communication cues in employment interviews. In *ACM ICMI*, 2013.

[20] L. S. Nguyen, D. Frauendorfer, M. Schmid Mast, and D. Gatica-Perez. Hire me: Computational inference of hirability in employment interviews based on nonverbal behavior. *IEEE Transactions on Multimedia*, 2014.

[21] V. Ramakrishna, T. Kanade, and Y. Sheikh. Tracking human pose by tracking symmetric parts. In *IEEE CVPR*, 2013.

[22] B. Sapp and B. Taskar. Modec: Multimodal decomposable models for human pose estimation. In *IEEE CVPR*, 2013.

[23] B. Sapp, D. Weiss, and B. Taskar. Parsing human motion with stretchable models. In *IEEE CVPR*, 2011.

[24] L. A. Schwarz, A. Mkhitaryan, D. Mateus, and N. Navab. Estimating human 3d pose from time-of-flight images based on geodesic distances and optical flow. In *IEEE FG*, 2011.

[25] J. Shotton, T. Sharp, A. Kipman, A. W. Fitzgibbon, M. Finocchio, A. Blake, M. Cook, and R. Moore. Real-time human pose recognition in parts from single depth images. In *IEEE CVPR*, 2011.

[26] L. Sigal, A. Balan, and M. Black. Humaneva: Synchronized video and motion capture dataset and baseline algorithm for evaluation of articulated human motion. *IJCV*, 87(1), 2010.

[27] E. Simo-Serra, A. Quattoni, C. Torras, and F. Moreno-Noguer. A joint model for 2d and 3d pose estimation from a single image. In *IEEE CVPR*, 2013.

[28] Y. Song, L. Goncalves, and P. Perona. Learning probabilistic structure for human motion detection. In *IEEE CVPR*, 2001.

[29] C. Tomasi and T. Kanade. Detection and tracking of point features. *IJCV*, 1991.

[30] Y. Yang and D. Ramanan. Articulated pose estimation with flexible mixtures-of-parts. In *IEEE CVPR*, 2011.

[31] Y. Yin and R. Davis. Gesture spotting and recognition using salience detection and concatenated hidden markov models. In *ACM ICMI*, 2013.

[32] A. Yoonessi and C. L. Baker. Contribution of motion parallax to segmentation and depth perception. *Journal of Vision*, 11, 2011.

[33] T.-H. Yu, T.-K. Kim, and R. Cipolla. Unconstrained monocular 3d human pose estimation by action detection and cross-modality regression forest. In *IEEE CVPR*, 2013.

[34] X. Yu, S. Zhang, Y. Yu, N. Dunbar, M. Jensen, J. Burgoon, and D. Metaxas. Automated analysis of interactional synchrony using robust facial tracking and expression recognition. In *FG Workshops*, 2013.

[35] S. Zuffi, J. Romero, C. Schmid, and M. J. Black. Estimating human pose with flowing puppets. In *IEEE ICCV*, 2013.

User-Independent Gaze Estimation by Exploiting Similarity Measures in the Eye Pair Appearance Eigenspace

Nanxiang Li and Carlos Busso
Multimodal Signal Processing (MSP) Laboratory
University of Texas at Dallas
800 W Campbell Rd, Richardson, TX 75080
nxl056000@utdallas.edu, busso@utdallas.edu

ABSTRACT

The design of gaze-based computer interfaces has been an active research area for over 40 years. One challenge of using gaze detectors is the repetitive calibration process required to adjust the parameters of the systems, and the constrained conditions imposed on the user for robust gaze estimation. We envision user-independent gaze detectors that do not require calibration, or any cooperation from the user. Toward this goal, we investigate an appearance-based approach, where we estimate the eigenspace for the gaze using *principal component analysis* (PCA). The projections are used as features of regression models that estimate the screen's coordinates. As expected, the performance of the approach decreases when the models are trained without data from the target user (i.e., user-independent condition). This study proposes an appealing training approach to bridge the gap in performance between user-dependent and user-independent conditions. Using the projections onto the eigenspace, the scheme identifies samples in training set that are similar to the testing images. We build the sample covariance matrix and the regression models only with these samples. We consider either similar frames or data from subjects with similar eye appearance. The promising results suggest that the proposed training approach is a feasible and convenient scheme for gaze-based multimodal interfaces.

Categories and Subject Descriptors

H.5 [**Information Interfaces and Presentation**]: Miscellaneous

Keywords

User-independent gaze estimation; similar subject measurement; eigenspace analysis; computer user interface

1. INTRODUCTION

Gaze indicates visual awareness, thus, it is important for understanding human intention and attention. The study of gaze has drawn attentions from many research fields including *human-computer interaction* (HCI), market analysis, social behavior, and driver distraction [5, 8, 10]. For HCI, using gaze as an input modality has unique advantages over other modalities: for the users, gaze is a natural and fast way to indicate their interest and intentions; for the computers, being aware of the gaze allows more effective interventions. However, two limitations of employing gaze as input are the repetitive and tedious calibration process, and the constrained conditions imposed on the user to achieve accurate estimation. User and setting specific parameters are usually calibrated by asking the users to look at several reference points [3]. Although the number of reference points can be reduced by employing more light sources or cameras [12, 6], the process still need to be conducted whenever the setting changes. Using head mount devices addresses some of the problems, but it is an intrusive alternative that requires initial calibration. We envision user-independent gaze detectors that do no require calibration or any cooperation from the user. Appearance-based models are appealing approaches for this purpose.

Many studies proposed appearance-based models for gaze estimation. However, most of them focus on user-dependent conditions that require calibration. Baluja and Pomerleau [1] use a neural network to estimate gaze position using the eye image. Tan et al. [11] used local linear interpolation among sparse appearance samples to approximate the gaze. Few studies have considered appearance-based gaze estimation models under user-independent conditions. Shiele and Waibel [9] study user-independent gaze estimation with neural network, where they estimated coarse gaze directions based on head pose without considering the iris position. Rikert and Jones [7] used morphable models to estimate user-independent gaze, where the main challenge is the initial match between the model parameters and the image.

We recently proposed an appearance-based gaze estimation approach that consists in building an eigenspace for patches displaying both eyes [4]. The projections onto the eigenspace are used to train a regression model to predict the target screen coordinates. We implemented the approach operating under user-dependent (i.e., training and testing on the same subject) and user-independent (i.e., training and testing on different subjects) conditions. The results reveal a drop in accuracy for the user-independent condition. Building upon this approach, this study proposes a training scheme to reduce the gap in performance between user-dependent and user-independent gaze estimation.

ICMI'14, November 12–16, 2014, Istanbul, Turkey.

http://dx.doi.org/10.1145/2663204.2663250.

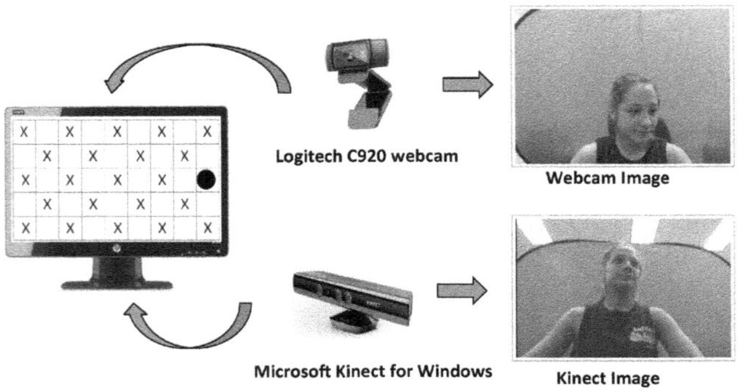

Figure 1: The data collection includes a 22-inch HP monitor, a Logitech C920 webcam and a Microsoft Kinect for Windows. A green screen is placed behind the subject to provide uniform background.

One factor affecting the performance of the appearance-based gaze approach in user-independent mode is that the eigenspace created from the sample covariance matrix does not offer a good representation for the target user. Starting from the premise that *not all data is good data*, we propose to identify a reduced set of frames from the training database that have similar appearance to the samples from the target user. We build the eigenspace and the regression models using this reduced set. This approach offers many advantages (1) it uses data from subjects in the training set with similar eye appearance improving the orthogonal basis to represent the target user; (2) it uses samples where the user is looking to similar screen locations; (3) it uses samples where the user's head position is similar to the target frame. We evaluate the performance of the proposed approach under different conditions (with/without head movement, various user-computer distance). The proposed training scheme improves the performance of the user-independent system, showing that it is a feasible and convenient approach to facilitate gaze-based multimodal interfaces.

2. MSP-GAZE DATABASE

The MSP-GAZE corpus was collected to study appearance-based gaze estimation methods [4]. It considers various factors that affect gaze estimation in HCI: individual appearance differences, head movement, inter-session variability, and distance between user and screen. The data was collected in a laboratory environment using a standard 22-inch HP monitor, a commercial webcam (Logitech C920) placed on top of the monitor and a Microsoft Kinect sensor for Windows placed below the monitor (Fig. 1).

The database includes data from 46 subjects whose average age was 22.7 (min 19, max 35). The corpus is balanced in terms of gender. It also includes a diverse ethnic representation of the students from University of Texas at Dallas (Caucasian, Asian, Indian, and Hispanic populations). We recorded each subject in two different days separated with an average interval of five days. During each of these two sessions, we collected 12 training recordings and 2 testing recordings. The different recordings include the following configuration: with and without head movement; and four user-screen distances (user defined, near 0.4m, medium 0.5m and far 0.6m). The user is asked to click on a randomly generated point displayed on predefined regions. During the training recordings, one of the four predefined user-screen distances is used and the random points are projected in selected regions (See Fig. 1). During the testing recordings, the users selected the distance from the screen and the points are randomly placed on the monitor without any constraint. For each subject, we have about 90 minutes of data over the two sessions. We simultaneously recorded the videos, the location of the target points, the position of the mouse cursor, and the mouse click actions. The details of the corpus are given in Li and Busso [4].

Table 1: Average correlation using appearance-based gaze estimation under user-dependent and user-independent conditions (W: with head motion; W/O: without head motion).

User-Screen Distance	User-Dependent W/O	User-Dependent W	User-Independent W/O	User-Independent W
Far	0.89	0.91	0.84	0.79
Medium	0.90	0.92	0.88	0.82
Near	0.89	0.83	0.89	0.84
User-Defined	0.93	0.92	0.85	0.79
Average	0.91	0.90	0.86	0.80

This study relies on data from 24 subjects that has been preprocessed (data cleaning and eye pair extraction). They comprise a gender and ethnic balanced dataset (3×2 gender $\times$ 4 ethnic background). We extracted patches with both eyes, following the approach proposed in our previous work [4] (see Fig. 2). Considering both eyes reduces eye detection errors, and improves robustness against head motion. The eye pair image extraction is done automatically using the Viola-Jones object detection framework. We use the implementation provided by the *open computer vision library* (OpenCV) with the eye-pair detector developed by Castrillón et al. [2]. For each point displayed on the screen, we extract the eye pair images from three frames (< 0.14s) after the user clicks on the target points. For each of the 14 recordings per session, we consider 92 points resulting in 276 eye pair images (92 points $\times$ 3 frames).

3. APPEARANCE-BASED GAZE MODEL

In our previous study, we focused on the webcam videos and investigated an appearance-based approach that builds an orthonormal basis of the extracted eye pair images [4]. By resizing all extracted eye pair images to 100 x 25 pixels, a covariance matrix is built and the PCA is implemented. The projections onto the PCA basis are used to train a linear regression model which predicts the gaze location (screen's coordinates). Two linear regression models are built separately to estimate the gaze position in the horizontal (x) and vertical (y) coordinates. This approach was evaluated for both user-dependent (training and testing on the same subject) and user-independent (training and testing on different subjects) conditions. We re-implement the evaluation for the 24 subjects considered in this study. The evaluation considers the top 100 principal components, which capture over 90% of the variance [4]. For the user-dependent condition, we train and test the model with recordings from the same subjects. For the user-independent condition, we use a *leave-one-subject-out* (LOSO) cross-validation approach, where in each fold we train with data from 23 subjects and and test with data from the remaining subject. The evaluation considers matched training/testing settings in terms of user-screen distances and head movement conditions. We calculate the correlations between the estimated and the actual gaze positions in the horizontal (ρ_x) and vertical (ρ_y) directions, and report the average correlation ρ between the two:

$$\rho = \frac{\rho_x + \rho_y}{2} \tag{1}$$

Table 1 lists the results which show that the average correlation ρ decreases approximately 0.1 from the user-dependent to the user-independent conditions when head movement is allowed. While these results are competitive given that the approach does not require any calibration, this gap can be reduced by implementing better training schemes.

3.1 Proposed Approach: Finding Similar Data

Appearance-based models are sensitive to variation in the patch images. Therefore, the differences between subjects in the training set affect the orthogonal basis to represent the target subject. Following this direction, we propose to build the eigenspace and the regression models using only patches that are similar to the eye appearance from the target subject. The approach offers various advantages. It improves the orthogonal basis to appropriately represent the eigenspace of the target subject. Since similar images most likely share the same gaze direction, it considers training images spanning the target gaze directions. It also increases the robustness against head motion, since the selected frames will tend to have similar head poses.

The orthogonal basis corresponds to the eigenvectors belonging to the larger eigenvalues of the covariance matrix Σ. If all N training samples are used, Σ_{All} is calculated with Equation 2, where Φ_i is the mean removed images concatenated as a vectors. If we reduced the training images to a set $\mathcal{S}$ including only similar images, we can build a target user-specific covariance matrix $\Sigma_{\mathcal{S}}$ with Equation 3. The key problem consists in selecting the set $\mathcal{S}$ (i.e., finding similar images to the target user).

$$\Sigma_{All} = \frac{1}{N}\sum_{i=1}^{N} \Phi_i \Phi_i^T \tag{2}$$

$$\Sigma_{\mathcal{S}} = \frac{1}{|\mathcal{S}|}\sum_{i \in \mathcal{S}} \Phi_i \Phi_i^T \tag{3}$$

We propose the following steps to achieve this goal. First, we estimate Σ_{All} following Equation 2. Then, we project each training image into the first 100 principal components. The testing images are also projected into this 100D space. Finally, we estimate the Euclidean distance between the projections of the training and testing images. Figures 2(a) and 2(c) show two images in the testing set. Figures 2(b) and 2(d) gives the closest images in the training set, respectively. The figures show that the testing and training images have similar head pose and gaze direction. The ground truth gaze positions associated with Figures 2(a) and 2(b) are the screen's coordinates (68, 160), and (75, 99), respectively. For Figures 2(c) and 2(d), the screen's coordinates are (1600, 967) and (1526, 931).

This study considers two criteria to select $\mathcal{S}$: similar subjects and similar frames. For similar subjects, the goal is to find subjects that have similar appearance to the target user. After projecting all the testing images into the eigenspace of Σ_{All}, we select the most similar frame in the training set for each of the target images. From this selected training frames, we can associate the identity of the selected training subjects. By ranking in descending order the training subjects according to the number of selected images belonging

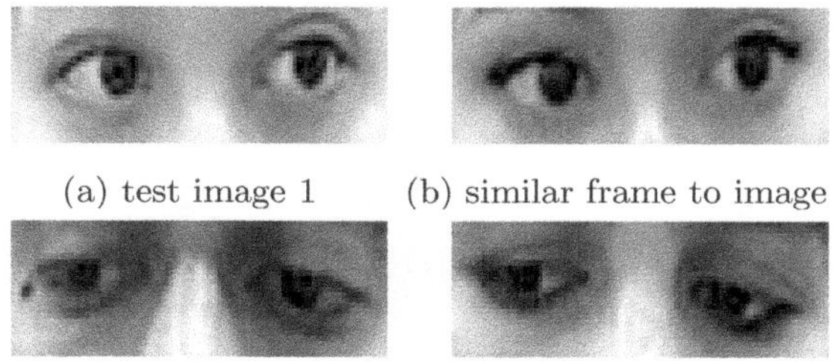

(a) test image 1 (b) similar frame to image 1

(c) test image 2 (d) similar frame to image 2

Figure 2: Two testing images and their closer patches in the training set, as measured by the Euclidean distance in the projected eigenspace.

to them, we define $\mathcal{S}$ as the set with the data from the top n subjects in the list. This approach guarantees a balanced distribution of the training samples over the screen's coordinates. For similar frames, we search for the top n images in the training set that are similar to each of the testing images. We define $\mathcal{S}$ as the set including these selected images.

3.2 Experimental Evaluation

By using the reduced set $\mathcal{S}$, we estimate a new eigenspace from $\Sigma_{\mathcal{S}}$ using Equation 3. We train separate linear regression models for the horizontal (x) and vertical (y) coordinates, where the projections onto this new basis are the independent variables, and the corresponding ground truth gaze positions are the dependent variables. The output of these regression models are limited to be within the screen size. Following the approach presented in our previous work, we report the average correlation ρ defined in Equation 1 to evaluate the proposed solution. The evaluation also uses LOSO cross-validation scheme with matched training/testing conditions (head motion and user-screen distance).

Figure 3(a) shows the average correlation ρ across user-screen distances when $\mathcal{S}$ includes images from the top n similar subjects. We evaluate n =1, 2, 3, 5, 7, and 9. The straight lines in the figures correspond to the performance for user-dependent (solid line), and user-independent (dash line) conditions using Σ_{All} (Table 1). When we consider more than 5 subjects, the performance increases compared with the results in user-independent conditions considering all the training subjects. The best ρ is achieved when n = 12 (ρ=0.87) without head movement, and n = 5 (ρ=0.82) with head movement. Although these results are still worse than the ones achieved under user-dependent conditions, we expect improvements when the pool of subjects in the training set increases (i.e., finding better matches).

Figure 3(b) shows the result when $\mathcal{S}$ includes the top n images that are closer to each testing set. We evaluate n = 30, 100, 300, 500 and 1000. Even with n = 30, we observe better performance than the results for user-independent condition, which demonstrate the potential of this training approach.

Table 2 reports the experimental results for 7-similar subjects and 100-similar frame across different conditions. Both approaches have similar performance across conditions. For the user-defined distance with head movement recordings, using similar frames is slight better than using similar subjects. Both cases are better than the ones for the user-independent condition using all training data (Table 1).

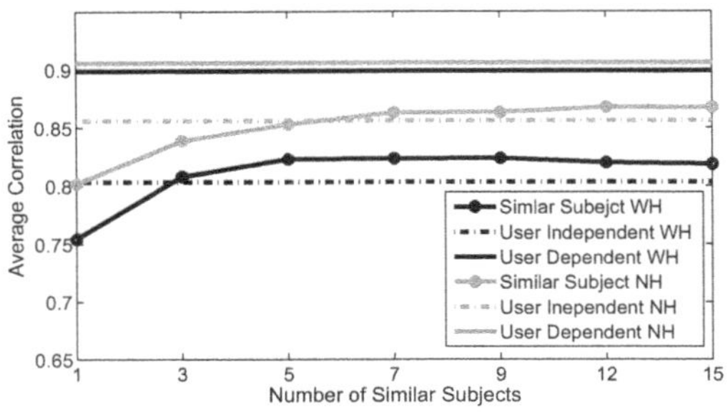

(a) Similar subject approach

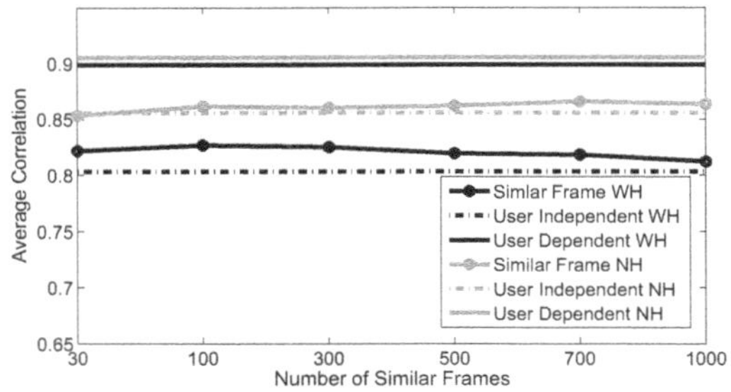

(b) similar frame approach

Figure 3: Evaluation of the training scheme implemented with similar *subjects* and similar *frames*. (WH: with head motion; NH: without head motion)

4. CONCLUSIONS AND DISCUSSION

This paper proposed a training scheme to improve an appearance-based, user-independent gaze estimator. The proposed approach identifies similar data samples in the training set and uses this reduced set to build the eye appearance eigenspace, and the regression models to estimate the screen's coordinates. The proposed approach eliminates the requirement for tedious calibration, which is required for most gaze estimation systems. The results demonstrate the robustness against the user's head motion. The promising experimental results show the effectiveness of the proposed approach, reducing the gap between user-dependent, and user-independent gaze estimation accuracy.

One limitation of the approach is that it requires testing samples to define the set $\mathcal{S}$. One possible solution is to start the gaze estimation with user-independent models. As more test samples become available, we can create/update the set $\mathcal{S}$ and estimate $\Sigma_{\mathcal{S}}$. This approach can be implemented for real-time applications. The results presented in this study focus on the case when test samples are available, toward understanding the benefits of the proposed approach compared to the speaker independent mode.

Our future work considers extensions of the proposed training approach to improve the performance of user-independent gaze estimation. This study only considered 24 subjects from the corpus to have a balanced dataset in terms of gender and ethnic background. We will reestimate the system by including all the subjects. By increasing the training set, we expect that the selected samples will be more similar to the testing images. Another direction for user-independent gaze estimation is to take advantage of the test images and perform on-line calibration. We can incorporate this idea by adapting the covariance matrix to the target subject.

Table 2: User-independent gaze estimation results. The reduced set $\mathcal{S}$ includes images from either the top 7 similar *subjects*, or the top 100 similar *frames*. (W: with head motion; W/O: without head motion).

		W/O		W	
	Distance	ρ_x	ρ_y	ρ_x	ρ_y
Subjects	Far	0.90	0.79	0.88	0 .72
	Medium	0.93	0.82	0.90	0.74
	Near	0.93	0.87	0.93	0.78
	User-Defined	0.91	0.78	0.88	0.74
Frames	Far	0.90	0.81	0.88	0.72
	Medium	0.92	0.80	0.90	0.74
	Near	0.93	0.82	0.93	0.77
	User-Defined	0.92	0.81	0.90	0.76

5. ACKNOWLEDGMENTS

This work was funded by NSF (IIS 1217104) and Samsung.

6. REFERENCES

[1] S. Baluja and D. Pomerleau. Non-intrusive gaze tracking using artificial neural networks. Technical Report CMU-CS-94-102, Carnegie Mellon University, Pittsburgh, PA, USA, January 1994.

[2] M. Castrillón, O. Déniz, C. Guerra, and M. Hernández. ENCARA2: Real-time detection of multiple faces at different resolutions in video streams. *Journal of Visual Communication and Image Representation*, 18(2):130–140, April 2007.

[3] D. Hansen and Q. Ji. In the eye of the beholder: A survey of models for eyes and gaze. *IEEE Transactions on Pattern Analysis and Machine Intelligence*, 32(3):478–500, March 478-500.

[4] N. Li and C. Busso. Evaluating the robustness of an appearance-based gaze estimation method for multimodal interfaces. In *International conference on multimodal interaction (ICMI 2013)*, pages 91–98, Sydney, Australia, December 2013.

[5] Y. Matsumotot, T. Ino, and T. Ogsawara. Development of intelligent wheelchair system with face and gaze based interface. In *Robot and Human Interactive Communication, 2001. Proceedings. 10th IEEE International Workshop on*, pages 262–267. IEEE, 2001.

[6] T. Nagamatsu, J. Kamahara, T. Iko, and N. Tanaka. One-point calibration gaze tracking based on eyeball kinematics using stereo cameras. In *Symposium on Eye tracking research & applications*, pages 95–98, Santa Barbara, CA, USA, March 2008.

[7] T. Rikert and M. J. Jones. Gaze estimation using morphable models. In *IEEE International Conference on Automatic Face and Gesture Recognition (FG 1998)*, pages 436–441, Nara, Japan, April 1998.

[8] D. Salvucci and J. Anderson. Intelligent gaze-added interfaces. In *SIGCHI conference on Human Factors in Computing Systems (CHI 2000)*, pages 273–280, The Hague, The Netherlands, April 2000.

[9] B. Schiele and A. Waibel. Gaze tracking based on face-color. In *International Workshop on Automatic Face-and Gesture-Recognition*, pages 344–349, Zurich, Switzerland, June 1995.

[10] H. Skovsgaard, J. Mateo, and J. Hansen. Evaluating gaze-based interface tools to facilitate point-and-select tasks with small targets. *Behaviour & Information Technology*, 30(6):821–831, 2011.

[11] K. Tan, D. Kriegman, and N. Ahuja. Appearance-based eye gaze estimatio. In *IEEE Workshop on Applications of Computer Vision (WACV 2002)*, pages 191–195, Orlando, FL, USA, December 2002.

[12] A. Villanueva and R. Cabeza. A novel gaze estimation system with one calibration point. *IEEE Transactions on Systems, Man, and Cybernetics, Part B: Cybernetics*, 38(4):1123–1138, August 2008.

Exploring Multimodality for Translator-Computer Interaction

Julián Zapata
School of Translation and Interpretation
University of Ottawa
jzapa026@uottawa.ca

ABSTRACT

Multimodal interaction has the potential to become one of the most efficient, cost-effective and ergonomic working strategies for translation professionals, in the near future. This paper describes our doctoral research project on multimodality in translator-computer interaction (TCI). The specific objective of this project is to observe and analyze the translator experience (TX) with off-the-shelf voice-and-touch-enabled multimodal interfaces, as compared to the interaction with traditional keyboard-and-mouse graphical user interfaces. Overall, this project aims to collect user-centered data and provide recommendations for better-grounded translation tool design. Thus, the study will make an original contribution to the advancement of knowledge in the fields of TCI and human-computer interaction in general.

Author Keywords

Multimodal interaction; translator-computer interaction; translation technology; translation dictation; voice recognition

INTRODUCTION

The present paper describes our research project on multimodality in translator-computer interaction (TCI). The project is carried out within the framework of a doctorate in translation studies.

TCI is the field of study that investigates the interaction of translators with computers. The notion of TCI was coined by Sharon O'Brien in 2012 [20] and represents a logical extension of human-computer interaction. Although the notion of TCI remains relatively new, the interaction of translators with machines is far from being a recent phenomenon. "Already with the introduction of the electronic typewriter [...] and the use of dictaphones, translation became a computer-interactive task" [20]. Over the past decades, a significant number of developments in natural language processing have taken place, leading to the emergence of an array of computer aids for translators. These applications, known as computer-aided translation tools [3], continually modify the way human translators interact with machines to obtain and produce information. This being said, computer-aided translation tools marketed today have rarely been designed with the end user – in this case, the translator – in mind. O'Brien [20] states that "[t]echnology created without consideration for the task or end users removes those end users from the equation [...]. [Now,] [c]an translators make their jobs more human through [human-computer interaction]? Can we allow the machine to take over the boring, repetitive tasks and free ourselves up for the harder, subtler and more complex problems? And what are those problems that machines cannot solve, but human translators can? These are some of the large questions facing us."

Today, with the introduction of tablets, smartphones and touchscreen computers, the nature of the interaction between humans and technologies is radically changing. Recent efforts in human-computer interaction have focused attention on the end users, in search of more effective, efficient and ergonomic applications. These new developments are centered largely on finding alternatives to traditional keyboard-and-mouse input, which is the basis for interaction with graphical user interfaces or WIMP (windows, icons, menus and pointer) interfaces, such as (traditional) desktop computers. Emerging input modes include voice, touch, gaze, manual gestures, and even head and full-body movements [17, 22]. These input modes, as stand-alone or in combination, often provide a better user experience in several applications or, in other words, a more natural interaction with the technology.

Our doctoral research introduces multimodal interaction to translation, considering the unparalleled robustness of commercially available voice- and touch-enabled multimodal interfaces, such as tablets and touchscreen computers, and their anticipated and documented advantages in other domains and areas of application. Specifically, the objective of our doctoral project is to observe and analyze the translator experience (TX) with off-the-shelf multimodal interfaces, in order to provide recommendations for designing and developing the user interface of a multimodal

ICMI '14, November 12 - 16 2014, Istanbul, Turkey
Copyright 2014 ACM 978-1-4503-2885-2/14/11 $15.00
http://dx.doi.org/10.1145/2663204.2666280.

interactive translation dictation tool, which is our ultimate research goal.

The notion of TX is introduced in this research. Based on ISO's definition of user experience [14], TX can be defined as *a translator's perceptions and responses resulting from the use or anticipated use of a product, system or service.*

BACKGROUND AND MOTIVATIONS

Translation has existed for millennia. Archeological evidence (tools, cave paintings, carvings, etc.) suggests that early humans, who made their appearance hundreds of thousands of years ago, had the type of intellect that could support language [21]. Now, (oral) translation activity is believed to date back to the development of humans' ability to produce speech and use language. Consequently, written translation very likely emerged in parallel with alphabets, writing systems and writing tools. The Rosetta stone, displayed at the British Museum in London, is one of the oldest standing artifacts that account for translation activity in ancient times [5]. Throughout history, translators, as well as writers of any kind, have adopted different tools according to ongoing developments in science and technology: from stone-engraving tools, to papyrus and ink pens, to typewriters and – most recently – personal computers.

Yet the physical act of writing is not very popular among certain translators and writers in general: many wish that their hands moved at the speed of their thoughts. In fact, either by preference or because of health issues, some writers and translators have opted for dictation (i.e., the oral production of their texts into a voice recorder – also known as a dictaphone – for later transcription, or even directly to a secretary or professional transcriptionist, who transcribes the words as they are being dictated).

Translation dictation was a very popular – and indeed effective – working technique in the 1960s and 1970s [9], but started to fade away as professional translators' workstations experienced the massive influx of typewriters and personal computers. However, the tremendous improvements in natural language processing, particularly in voice recognition (VR) technology, provide today an excellent opportunity to bring back translation dictation to the profession, this time in a new form, using emerging technologies and applications.

For over three decades, a great number of empirical studies in user interface design and development have strived to demonstrate the efficiency of voice input versus keyboard-and-mouse input. Although it was implicit in the earliest of these works that VR systems were expected to completely replace – rather than enhance – other input modes, it was soon proposed that, for many tasks, voice input achieved better performance in combination with other input modes [23]. Shneiderman [26] affirms that VR is "the bicycle of user interface design: it is great fun to use and has an important role, but it can carry only a light load." Among other challenges, stand-alone VR systems require a great amount of computational power, and users are often uncertain about whether or not a particular input will be accepted by the machine [15]. The combination of voice with other input modes is therefore often thought as more useful and even preferable for many applications. Thus, in recent years, multimodal interaction has increasingly become a hot topic in human-computer interaction research.

What characterizes multimodal interfaces is their ability to process two or more combined user input modes (such as voice, stylus, touch, gaze and gestures) in parallel and in a coordinated manner [22]. As far as the translation sector is concerned, multimodal interfaces, and particularly voice-enabled interfaces, offer great potential for translation students and professionals, since VR "has the potential to be a better interface than the keyboard for tasks for which full natural language communication is useful" [15]. This is precisely the case in translation practice, which is nonetheless currently characterized by the extended use of keyboard-and-mouse interfaces.

This being said, over the past two decades, certain researchers, trainers and professionals have demonstrated an interest in using VR technology in translation [1, 4, 6, 7, 8, 10, 11, 18, 19, 24, 25]. However, none of today's off-the-shelf stand-alone VR systems was developed specifically for translation purposes. This project explores multimodality, and particularly the combination of voice, touch and stylus input, in the prospect of designing an interactive translation dictation tool. Interactive translation dictation – a notion first introduced in our Master's thesis [28] – is defined here as a translation technique that involves mainly voice interaction with a multimodal interface equipped with VR technology throughout the entire translation process, namely during preparation, production and revision.

To sum up the current state of affairs, VR technology offers considerable potential for translation students and professionals, but it will need to be used differently and integrated more efficiently. One possible way to do this is by enabling multimodal interaction. In a recent study by Mesa-Lao [19], student translators surveyed reported that they would welcome the integration of voice input as one of the possible input modes for performing translation tasks. Indeed, 80% of respondents stated that they would definitely consider adopting VR in combination with non-speech input modes in their daily work as translators. VR is thus a complement rather than a substitute for non-speech input methods. The paper concludes that further studies still need to be conducted in order to build up new knowledge about the way in which VR technology can be adapted to translation tasks. Our research on interactive translation dictation is thus a promising avenue, since it promotes the use of VR technology in a multimodal environment. Indeed, according to some of the findings of our earlier study [28], and the literature review and empirical experiments conducted so far in our PhD, multimodal interfaces are expected to provide a better quality-in-use [2, 13] than monomodal, stand-alone VR systems, or traditional input devices, such as the keyboard and mouse.

RESEARCH QUESTION AND HYPOTHESIS STATEMENT

This research project is motivated by an underlying research question and hypothesis, which stem from our preliminary investigations, observations and pilot experiments.

The research question which will be used as the basis of our usability study is formulated as follows:

> *Does the physical prototype of a multimodal interactive translation dictation interface consistently provide various translators with a better quality-in-use than a traditional keyboard-and-mouse interface, when preparing, producing and revising a translation?*

Our hypothesis is formulated as follows:

> *Based on the combined analysis of objective and subjective usability measures, the prototypical multimodal environment consistently provides various translators with a better quality-in-use than the keyboard-and-mouse environment, throughout the entire translation process.*

A Note on Quality-In-Use and Usability Measures

Studying and improving the quality-in-use of interactive systems has been a key element of human-computer interaction research. Quality-in-use is "the extent to which a product satisfies stated and implied needs when used under stated conditions" [2]. Although thoroughly measuring usability and quality-in-use has been considered a highly challenging task, it is possible for researchers to operationalize the usability construct to find aspects of usability that can actually be measured and analysed. Traditionally, usability measures have reported on three aspects: (1) effectiveness (measures of the quality of or the satisfaction with the outcomes of the interaction); (2) efficiency (measures of the interaction process); and/or (3) user satisfaction (measures of users' attitudes and experience). Now, it has been proposed that for usability studies to succeed, a better assessment of the correlations between these three aspects needs to be done, and a better understanding of the correlations between objective and subjective measures needs to be achieved [13]. In studying the usability of the physical prototype of an interactive translation dictation interface, we will adapt to the working model proposed by Hornbæk [13], which includes objective measures such as expert assessment of outcome, task times, usability patterns and physiological usability; and subjective measures such as users' perception of outcome, subjectively experienced time and perception of task difficulty.

A Note on Physical Prototyping

Prototyping is a vital part of the design and development process of any application or product. To arrive at usable user interface designs, designers commonly build prototypes (i.e., approximations of a product). A prototype embodies a design hypothesis and enables a designer to test it [12]. Given the scope and limitations of a doctoral project in translation studies, we will use the physical prototyping technique. Applied early in the design process, physical prototyping utilizes and combines all kinds of existing tools and materials.

In sum, we are not intending to *build* a system as part of our doctorate, but rather to collect quantitative and qualitative data from a sample of professional English-French translators using different off-the-shelf devices and software, in order to inform the design and the development of an eventual tool.

METHODOLOGY OVERVIEW

A crucial step in usability study design is determining the type of research to be carried out; the sources of data; and the data collection tools and techniques to be used. Considering the scope and limitations of a doctoral project (in the humanities) and the various challenges inherent to the research methods and tools commonly used in translation process research, our study includes active observation of users with video recording, screen recording, input logging and semi-structured interviews.

In order to observe and analyze the TX in a multimodal environment, a physical prototype of an interactive translation dictation tool will be built. This prototype will consist of two commercial multimodal interfaces, with which users will interact through – and only through – voice, touch and stylus: a 10" Android tablet and a 27" Windows touchscreen computer, as shown in Figure 1:

Figure 1. Experimental multimodal setup

The tablet will be equipped with a cloud-based VR system, integrated in a fast-typing virtual keyboard app (Swype, by Nuance). Experimental participants will use this interface to do searches online (e.g., by using Google [voice] search) and access various online computer-aided translation tools, such as terminology databases, dictionaries and corpora, while preparing and/or revising their translation. The touchscreen computer will be equipped with a text-processing application (Microsoft Word 2013), a state-of-the-art VR system (Dragon NaturallySpeaking 13, by Nuance) and Windows 8's virtual keyboard. Participants will use this device to read/prepare the source text and to dictate and/or type the target text and make corrections or changes to it. Figure 2 illustrates the combined use of voice, touch and stylus input throughout the translation process in a multimodal interactive translation dictation environment:

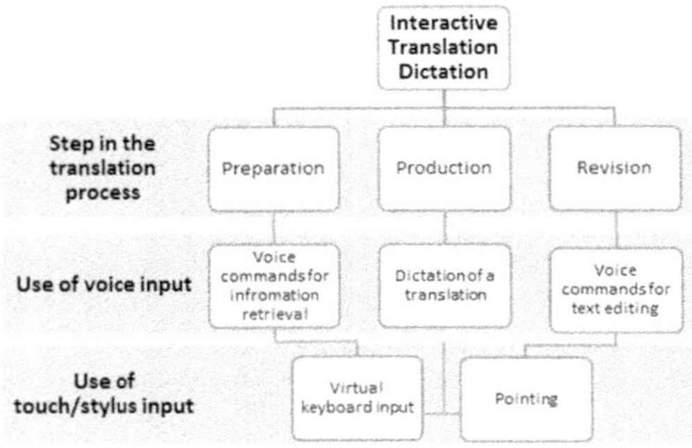

Figure 2. Uses of voice, stylus and/or touch input at different stages of the interactive translation dictation process

Lastly, a control group will be recruited. Control participants will translate the same text using conventional input modes (i.e., a keyboard and a mouse on a desktop computer) and will be instructed to translate the text "as they would normally do" at work.

Once the analysis phase begins, all digital video, audio, screen recordings and input log data collected during the experiments will be used to measure usability and to compare results. Video recordings will allow us to time individual tasks and to observe the participants' interaction with the different interfaces, tools and devices, and their body and facial reactions. Input log data and screen recordings will allow us to have a closer look at the interaction with the different input devices and the various information sources used throughout the translation process, and to conduct a detailed response time and error analysis. Lastly, audio recordings will allow us to study the participants' answers to interview questions and transcribe them accurately for our doctoral dissertation and subsequent publications. In sum, our PhD experiment will allow us to investigate whether the combined use of voice, stylus and touch puts forward a better quality-in-use for the bulk of experimental participants than conventional input modes, and where the speed bumps and frustrations lie in this interaction. In light of such an analysis, we will be able to provide recommendations for interactive translation dictation tool design in order to build, in collaboration with a team of developers, a functional prototype in the near future (at the post-doctoral level).

EXPECTED CONTRIBUTIONS

This project will make an original contribution to the body of knowledge in the fields of translation studies and human-computer interaction. In recent years, there has been an increased awareness in translation of the importance of technologies and the role they play in translation research, teaching and practice. More than ever before, translation researchers, trainers and professionals are aware of the need to improve existing tools and create new tools to cope with the evolution of technology and the ever-changing professional needs of translators. On the one hand, current computer-aided translation tools often lead users to frustration [16, 27], and full integration of these tools in the translation industry has not yet been achieved. On the other hand, dictation has often been an ideal strategy in any writing activity, and has historically proved effective and ergonomic in translation. Likewise, VR technologies have increasingly achieved higher performance and maturity levels in several major languages, to the point of becoming attractive, efficient and ergonomic in certain professional domains and even, to a certain degree, in professional translation, since it "quite simply makes life much more comfortable because you are not physically tied to your keyboard or screen" [1].

In light of this, it seems more than appropriate to consider an optimal integration of VR technology to the translator's toolbox (i.e., the adaptation of this technology to the array of tasks that translators perform at work). Considering the demonstrated success of translation dictation as a translation technique and the potential of combining emerging input modes such as voice, touch and stylus, this doctoral study conceives and tests new ways of using these emerging technologies in translation to provide a basis for better-grounded TCI research and, specifically, for the design and development of multimodal interfaces.

CONCLUSION

No one denies that translators, and humans in general, are increasingly dependent on computer tools. Thus, at the age of translation technology, mobile computing and ubiquitous information, research on multimodal interaction will become increasingly important in TCI. Usability studies like ours that explore multimodality will play a crucial role in the design and development of new tools that are user-friendly and adapted to translators' needs and to the changing reality of the translation industry, reflecting the continuous transformations in the relationship between humans and machines.

ACKNOWLEDGMENTS

This project is funded by the *Fonds québécois de la recherche – société et culture (FQRSC)* under grant 31791. I gratefully acknowledge the continuous support of my research advisor, Professor Jean Quirion.

REFERENCES

[1] Benis, Michael. "Softly Spoken or Hard of Hearing?" *Language International* 14.3 (2002), 26-29.

[2] Bevan, Nigel. "Measuring Usability as Quality of Use." *Software Quality Journal* 4 (1995), 115-150.

[3] Bowker, Lynne. *Computer-Aided Translation Technology: A Practical Introduction*. Ottawa: University of Ottawa Press, 2002.

[4] Brousseau, Julie et al. "French Speech Recognition in an Automatic Dictation System for Translators: The TransTalk Project." *Proc. Eurospeech'95*, 1995.

[5] Budge, E. A. Wallis. *The Rosetta Stone*. New York: Dover, 1989.

[6] Désilets, Alain et al. "Evaluating Productivity Gains of Hybrid ASR-MT Systems for Translation Dictation." *Proc. IWSLT'08*. 2008. 158-165.

[7] Dragsted, Barbara, Inge Gorm Hansen, and Henrik Selsøe Sørensen. "Experts Exposed." *Copenhaguen Studies in Language* 38 (2009), 293-317.

[8] Dymetman, Marc et al. "Towards an Automatic Dictation System for Translators: The TransTalk Project." *Fourth European Conference on Speech Communication and Technology*. Citeseer, 1994.

[9] Gingold, Kurt. "The Use of Dictation Equipment in Translation." *La traduction, une profession. Actes du VIIIe congrès mondial de la Fédération internationale des traducteurs*. Ed. Paul A. Horguelin. Ottawa: Conseil des traducteurs et interprètes du Canada, 1978, 444-448.

[10] Gouadec, Daniel. *Profession : Traducteur*. Paris: La maison du dictionnaire, 2002.

[11] Gouadec, Daniel. *Translation as a Profession*. Amsterdam: John Benjamins, 2007.

[12] Hartmann, Björn et al. "Reflective Physical Prototyping through Integrated Design, Test, and Analysis." *Proc. UIST'06*, 2006.

[13] Hornbæk, Kasper. "Current practice in measuring usability: Challenges to usability studies and research. International." *Journal of Human-Computer Studies* 64.2 (2006), 79-102.

[14] ISO DIS 9241-210:2008. *Ergonomics of Human System Interaction - Part 210: Human-Centred Design for Interactive Systems (formerly Known as 13407)*. International Organization for Standarization (ISO), Switzerland, 2008.

[15] Jurafsky, Daniel, and James H. Martin. *Speech and Language Processing: An Introduction to Natural Language Processing, Computational Linguistics, and Speech Recognition*. 2nd ed. Upper Saddle River, New Jersey: Pearson Prentice Hall, 2009.

[16] LeBlanc, Matthieu. "Translators on Translation Memory (TM). Results of an Ethnographic Study in Three Translation Services and Agencies." *The International Journal for Translation & Interpreting Research* 5.2 (2013), 1-13.

[17] Lee, Bongshin et al. "Beyond Mouse and Keyboard: Expanding Design Considerations for Information Visualization Interactions." *IEEE Transactions on Visualization and Computer Graphics* 18.12 (2012), 2689-2698.

[18] Mees, Inger M. et al. "Sound Effects in Translation." *Target* 25.1 (2013), 140-154.

[19] Mesa-Lao, Bartolomé. "Speech-Enabled Computer-Aided Translation: A Satisfaction Survey with Post-Editor Trainees." *Workshop on Humans and Computer-Assisted Translation*, 2014, 99-103.

[20] O'Brien, Sharon. "Translation as Human–computer Interaction." *Translation Spaces* 1.1 (2012), 101-122.

[21] O'Grady, William. "Language: A Preview." *An Introduction to Contemporary Linguistic Analysis*. Ed. William O'Grady and John Archibald. 5th ed. Toronto: Pearson Education Canada, 2004.

[22] Oviatt, Sharon. "Multimodal Interfaces." *The Human-Computer Interaction Handbook: Fundamentals, Evolving Technologies and Emerging Applications*. Ed. Julie A. Jacko. 3rd ed. New York: Lawrence Erlbaum Associates, 2012, 415-429.

[23] Pausch, Randy, and James H. Leatherby. "An Empirical Study: Adding Voice Input to a Graphical Editor." *Journal of the American Voice Input/Output Sociery* 9.2 (1991), 55-66.

[24] Reddy, Aarthi, and Richard C. Rose. "Integration of Statistical Models for Dictation of Document Translations in a Machine Aided Human Translation Task." *IEEE Transactions on Audio, Speech and Language Processing* 18.8 (2010), 1-11.

[25] Seaman, Lee. "Voice Recognition for Translators, Or Why I Started Talking To My Computer." *JLD Times. Newsletter of the Japanese Language Division of the American Translators Association,* 2002, 6-8.

[26] Shneiderman, Ben. *Designing the User Interface: Strategies for Effective Human-Computer Interaction*. 3rd ed. Reading, Massachusetts: Addison-Wesley, 1998.

[27] Taravella, Anne-Marie. "L'homme et la machine, duo productif… et positif ?" *L'Actualité langagière* 10.2 (2013).

[28] Zapata, Julián. "Traduction dictée interactive : intégrer la reconnaissance vocale à l'enseignement et à la pratique de la traduction professionnelle." University of Ottawa, 2012.

Towards Social Touch Intelligence: Developing a Robust System for Automatic Touch Recognition

Merel M. Jung
University of Twente
P.O. Box 217, 7500 AE, Enschede, The Netherlands
m.m.jung@utwente.nl

ABSTRACT

Touch behavior is of great importance during social interaction. Automatic recognition of social touch is necessary to transfer the touch modality from interpersonal interaction to other areas such as Human-Robot Interaction (HRI). This paper describes a PhD research program on the automatic detection, classification and interpretation of touch in social interaction between humans and artifacts. Progress thus far includes the recording of a Corpus of Social Touch (CoST) consisting of pressure sensor data of 14 different touch gestures and first classification results. Classification of these 14 gestures resulted in an overall accuracy of 53% using Bayesian classifiers. Further work includes the enhancement of the gesture recognition, building an embodied system for real-time classification and testing this system in a possible application scenario.

Keywords

Social touch; Touch gesture recognition; Touch corpus; Touch sensing; Human-Robot Interaction (HRI)

Categories and Subject Descriptors

H.5.2 [**User Interfaces**]: Haptic I/O; I.5.2 [**PATTERN RECOGNITION**]: Design Methodology—*Classifier design and evaluation*

1. INTRODUCTION

Researchers have investigated how to make robots or robotic devices sensitive to human touch in order to simulate interpersonal touch [1, 2, 3, 5, 6, 7, 8, 9, 10, 11, 13]. The human sense of touch consists of various physiological inputs: receptors in the skin register pressure, pain and temperature, while receptors in the muscles, tendons and joints register body motion [4]. However, just equipping a robot or interface with touch sensors to mimic the human somatosensory system is not enough. Automatic recognition of social touch is necessary to transfer the tactile modality from interpersonal interaction to areas such as Human-Robot Interaction (HRI) and remote communication [4, 5]. One of the envisioned applications for touch sensitive HRI is robot therapy, were a robot can be used to provide the known health benefits of a real animal companion without problems regarding hygiene and allergies [3, 11].

Initial attempts have been made to recognize different sets of touch gestures performed on specific interfaces (e.g. [5, 6, 7]). However, most sets were small and recognition rates depend on the degree of similarity between the touch gestures. In order to engage in touch interaction with a robot or an interface reliable recognition of a wide range of social touch gestures is needed [2, 5]. Therefore, the goal of this research is to work towards a robust touch gesture recognition system for real-time touch interaction.

The remainder of the paper is organized as follows: the next section discusses related work on the sensing and recognition of social touch; followed by an outline of the research program describing the current state of the research as well as future work; the paper ends with the conclusion in the last section.

ICMI'14, November 12–16, 2014, Istanbul, Turkey.

ACM 978-1-4503-2885-2/14/11 ...$15.00.
http://dx.doi.org/10.1145/2663204.2666281

2. RELATED WORK

2.1 Sensing touch

The first step towards intelligent touch interaction is sensing touch. Naya et al. used sheets of pressure sensitive ink to cover a robot [8], while Silvera-Tawil et al. developed an artificial skin based on the principle of Electrical Impedance Tomography to measure pressure [9, 10]. Cooney et al. covered a mock-up of a humanoid robot with two types of photo-interrupter sensors to detecting perpendicular movement (i.e. towards and from the body surface) such as patting and lateral movement (i.e. parallel to the body surface) such as stroking [2]. A robot head was covered by a hard plastic hemisphere by Kim et al. [5]. Underneath the hemisphere, charge-transfer touch sensors measured the proximity to the robot's head and an accelerometer measured the force of the touch based on the head's vibrations.

Besides humanoid robots, touch sensitive animal robots were developed such as *The Huggable*, a teddy bear which is equipped with thermistors, electric field sensors and Quantum Tunneling Composite sensors [11]. Follow-up work on the touch sensing capabilities of the teddy bear led to the development of *The Sensate Bear* platform which used capacitive sensors to register proximity and contact area as well as to distinguish between humans and objects [6]. *Hap-*

tic Creature is a lap animal which is covered with force sensing resistors to measure pressure [1, 13]. Further research on different sensing techniques for the *Haptic Creature* led to a zoomorphic creature covered with a layer of piezoresistive fabric, to measure pressure, underneath an outer layer of conductive fur to measure disruptions of the fur (e.g. stroking) [3].

Aside from HRI, the sensing and recognition of touch can also be used for other types of interfaces such as *Emoballoon* which is a balloon interface containing a barometric pressure sensor and a microphone to register touch [7].

2.2 Touch gesture recognition

Recognition of social touch gestures is still in its infancy. Automatic classification on several sets of touch gestures, ranging from 4 to 20 different touch gestures, performed on the above mentioned robots, robot skins and interfaces yielded mixed results. For example, recognition varied per gesture [6, 11] and location [1]. Reported accuracies were mostly > 70% however, direct comparison between studies based on these accuracies is difficult because of differences in gesture sets, sensors, and classification protocols. Some of the reported accuracies were the result of a best-case scenario intended to be a proof of concept [1, 8], while other studies focused on the location of the touch rather than the touch gesture, such as distinguishing between a head-pat and a foot-rub [6] or a handshake and a back-pat [2]. Although, it could be argued that some touch gestures will be more suitable for particular body locations. Also, as expected, within-subjects results outperformed between-subjects classification [3, 7, 9]. Some studies have even taken the first steps towards real-time classification [1, 5, 6].

Development of an artificial skin to provide new and current robot systems with a sense of touch is beneficial but comes with additional design requirements such as flexibility and stretchability to cover curved surfaces and moving joints [9, 10]. In the short term, the use of a fully embodied robot covered with individual sensors has the advantage of providing information about body location which can be used to recognize touch [2, 6]. However, this can lead to inadequate sensor density on curved body parts [1]. Furthermore, Silvera-Tawil et al. showed that comparable accuracies can be achieved using partial embodiment in the form of an arm covered with artificial skin [9, 10].

In summary, from the literature it becomes apparent that there is still a lot of ground to cover. More research is needed on how these touch gestures can be recognized and interpreted into a social context. A robust system for touch recognition should recognize several different touch gestures, work in real-time and be generalizable across users. Also, a central problem is the unavailability of a touch gesture data set for research and benchmarking. In the next section a research program is outlined to address the need for available touch data, to enhance classification by exploring features and methods and to build and test a real-time touch gesture recognition system.

3. THE RESEARCH PROGRAM

The research program can be divided into four parts from data recordings to application scenarios:

Table 1: Touch dictionary adapted from Yohanan et al., 2012.

Gesture label	Gesture definition
Grab	Grasp or seize the arm suddenly and roughly.
Hit	Deliver a forcible blow to the arm with either a closed fist or the side or back of your hand.
Massage	Rub or knead the arm with your hands.
Pat	Gently and quickly touch the arm with the flat of your hand.
Pinch	Tightly and sharply grip the arm between your fingers and thumb.
Poke	Jab or prod the arm with your finger.
Press	Exert a steady force on the arm with your flattened fingers or hand.
Rub	Move your hand repeatedly back and forth on the arm with firm pressure.
Scratch	Rub the arm with your fingernails.
Slap	Quickly and sharply strike the arm with your open hand.
Squeeze	Firmly press the arm between your fingers or both hands.
Stroke	Move your hand with gentle pressure over arm, often repeatedly.
Tap	Strike the arm with a quick light blow or blows using one or more fingers.
Tickle	Touch the arm with light finger movements.

3.1 CoST: Corpus of Social Touch (finished)

To address the need for social touch data sets we recorded a corpus consisting of pressure sensor data from 31 participants, each performing 6 repetitions of 3 variations (normal, gentle and rough) of 14 different touch gestures. After segmentation and filtering of unrecorded instances, the data collection contained 7805 touch gesture instances. This data set is publicly available[1].

3.1.1 Touch gestures

CoST consists of 14 different touch gestures performed on a sensor grid wrapped around a mannequin arm. The touch gestures (see Table 1) included in the data collection were chosen from a touch dictionary composed from literature on human-human and human-animal interaction by [13]. The list of gestures was adapted to suit interaction with an artificial human arm. Instructions on which gesture to perform were given by showing participants the name of the gesture and not the definition from [13]. Instead, they were shown an example video before the start of the data collection in which each gesture was demonstrated. During the data collection, 14 different touch gestures were performed 6 times in 3 variations, resulting in 252 gesture instances per participant. The order of gestures was pseudo-randomized into three blocks using the following rule: each instruction was given two times per block but the same instruction was not given twice in succession. A single fixed list of gestures was constructed using this criterion. This list and the reversed order of the list were used as instructions in a counterbalanced design. After each touch gesture, the participant had to press a key to see the next gesture. The keystrokes were used for segmentation afterwards.

[1]Data available on request, contact *m.m.jung@utwente.nl*

Figure 1: Set-up showing the pressure sensor (the black fabric) wrapped around the mannequin arm.

3.1.2 Setup

Touch gestures were performed on an 8×8 piezoresistive touch sensor grid (from *plug-and-wear*[2]) which was connected to a Teensy 3.0 microcontroller board (by *PJRC*[3]). After A/D conversion, the pressure values of the 64 channels range from 0 to 1023 (i.e., 10 bits). Sensor data was sampled at 135 Hz. The sensor was attached to the forearm of a full size rigid mannequin arm consisting of the left hand and the arm up to the shoulder (see Figure 1). The mannequin arm was fastened to the table to prevent it from slipping. Video recordings were made during the data collection as verification of the sensor data and the instructions given. Instructions were displayed to the participants on a PC monitor.

3.1.3 Participants

A total of 32 people volunteered to participate in the data collection. Data of one participant was omitted due to technical difficulties. The remaining participants, 24 male and 7 female, all studied or worked at the University of Twente in The Netherlands. The age of the participants ranged from 21 to 62 years ($M = 34, SD = 12$) and 29 were right-handed.

3.2 Automatic gesture recognition (in progress)

3.2.1 Feature extraction

From the sensor data, 28 features were extracted for every gesture instance based on the literature:

- *Mean pressure* was calculated by taking the mean pressure of all channels averaged over time (1).
- *Maximum pressure* is the maximum channel value of the gesture (2).
- *Pressure variability* indicates the differences in pressure applied during the gesture. The variability over time was calculated as the mean absolute pressure differences summed over all channels (3).

[2]www.plugandwear.com
[3]www.pjrc.com

- *Mean pressure per column* of the 8×8 sensor grid was calculated over time, resulting in eight feature values (4-11).
- *Mean pressure per row* of the 8×8 sensor grid was calculated over time, again resulting in eight feature values (12-19).
- *Contact area* was calculated per frame as the percentage of sensor area (i.e. the number of channels divided by the total numbers of channels) that exceed 50% of the maximum pressure. The size of the contact area indicates whether the whole hand is used for a touch gesture, as is expected for grab, or for example only one finger, as is expected for a poke. Two features were calculated: the mean of the contact area over time (20) and the contact area of the frame with the maximum overall pressure (i.e. the highest summed pressure over all channels) (21).
- *Peak count* is the number of positive crossings of the threshold, which indicates whether a touch gesture consist of continuous touch contact as is expected for squeeze or consecutive moments of touch contact alternated by non-contact which can be expected for a pat. Two ways to calculate the threshold were used, resulting in two features: one threshold is defined as 50% of the frame with the maximum summed pressure (22), the other is defined as the mean of the summed pressure over time (23).
- *Displacement* indicates whether the area of contact is static during a gesture or whether the hand moves across the contact area (i.e. dynamic). Center of mass is used to calculate the movement on the contact surface in both the x-axis and the y-axis. Four features were calculated, both the mean over time and the summed absolute difference of the center of mass on the x-axis (24-25) and the y-axis (26-27).
- *Duration* is the time used to perform the gesture (i.e. duration of contact with the sensor) which is measured in frames at 135 fps (28).

3.2.2 Classification

The features from the previous section were used for classification using MATLAB® (release 2013b). Classification of the touch gestures from the total dataset was based on the gesture's class, hereby disregarding the variant. Touch gesture instances were also classified within each variant, splitting the data into 3 subsets: normal, gentle, and rough. Rough gesture variants were expected to have a more favorable signal-to-noise ratio compared to the softer variants. The baseline of classifying a sample into the correct class based on random guessing is $1/14 \approx 7\%$. Classification results were evaluated using leave-one-subject-out cross-validation.

First, Gaussian Bayesian classifiers were used as baseline performance for touch gesture recognition. The mean and covariance for each class were calculated from the training data. The parameters for the multivariate normal distribution were used to calculate the posterior probability of the test sample belonging to the given class. Samples were assigned to the class with the maximum posterior probability. Between participants the correct rate over all classes

Table 2: Confusion matrix of leave-one-subject-out cross-validation using Bayesian classifiers [Overall accuracy = 53%]. *Legend* – classification of touch gesture instances into a class: $\geq 10\%$, $\geq 50\%$.

		Actual class													
		grab 1	hit 2	mass 3	pat 4	pinc 5	poke 6	pres 7	rub 8	scra 9	slap 10	sque 11	stro 12	tap 13	tick 14
Predicted class	1	401	0	6	0	6	0	52	3	5	0	206	1	0	0
	2	0	296	0	56	1	13	1	1	1	117	0	3	65	2
	3	3	1	344	1	10	3	2	52	25	1	17	4	2	19
	4	5	16	1	122	4	3	4	14	35	29	1	25	59	15
	5	3	9	40	7	358	48	39	13	11	2	78	5	5	7
	6	0	31	0	23	75	418	46	0	10	10	6	1	68	12
	7	40	18	3	27	46	21	363	30	10	13	47	6	12	1
	8	3	2	47	7	0	1	5	179	72	0	0	57	3	44
	9	2	0	7	16	0	1	2	56	203	0	0	23	5	71
	10	2	114	0	70	3	6	1	1	1	300	0	10	60	0
	11	97	4	18	2	43	1	25	4	1	1	201	1	4	0
	12	1	0	44	18	1	1	9	159	53	2	0	368	10	40
	13	0	63	1	192	7	35	9	6	21	75	0	12	253	40
	14	1	4	46	16	4	7	0	39	110	8	1	40	12	306
	sum	558	558	557	557	558	558	558	557	558	558	557	556	558	557

for the combined variants ranged from 26% to 74% ($M = 53\%, SD = 11\%$). The summed results of the 31-fold cross-validation of all gesture variations are displayed in the confusion matrix in Table 2.

Second, the more complex Support Vector Machines (SVMs) were used as comparison. We treated the classification of touch gestures as a multi-class problem using the one-vs.-all approach using the linear kernel. No convergence was reached for the combined data set within the maximum number of iterations at the default parameter setting ($C = 1$) therefore the value was lowered to $C = 0.5$. Using this approach, models were trained for every touch gesture versus all other gestures. A test sample was classified for all models as either belonging to the gesture class or the other class. In the case that a test sample was classified as belonging to only one gesture class the test sample was assigned to that respective class, while in case of multiple classes or no class outcome, the example was classified as the most likely class based on the distance to the hyperplane. Between participants the correct rate over all classes for all combined variants ranged from 22% to 63% ($M = 46\%, SD = 9\%$).

Overall accuracies and standard deviations of leave-one-subject-out cross-validation for both classifiers for both the whole dataset and the variant subsets are displayed in Table 3. The Bayesian classifiers outperformed the SVMs on every data(sub)set. Gentle variations were the most difficult to distinguish which could be explained by a higher signal-to-noise ratio in the sensor data.

The most frequent confusion of touch gestures was between: grab and squeeze; hit, pat, slap and tap; rub and stroke; scratch and tickle. Confusion between grab and squeeze can be explained by the similarity in contact area (i.e. usage of the whole hand) and the duration of the gesture. Furthermore, it can be argued that a grab is part of the squeeze gesture. Hit, pat, slap and tap show similarities in duration and contact area, although higher pressure can be expected for hit and slap compared to pat and tap. Both stroke and rub are prolonged gestures in which a back and forth and movement is expected, although higher pressure levels can be expected for rub. Scratch and tickle are both characterized by a frequent change of direction and long duration, although for tickle, pressure levels are expected to be lower and more variability in direction is expected compared to the back and forth movement of scratch.

Table 3: Overall accuracies of leave-one-subject-out cross-validation using Bayesian classifiers and SVMs. Standard deviations in parenthesis.

		Classifier	
		Bayes	SVM
Variation	Normal	.56 (.11)	.48 (.10)
	Gentle	.47 (.11)	.42 (.10)
	Rough	.54 (.12)	.53 (.11)
	All	.53 (.11)	.46 (.09)

The inclusion of touch gesture variants could have increased the difficulty of differentiating between gesture classes because pressure is one of the main characteristics on which the classification was based. Instructions to perform the touch gestures in gentle, normal and rough variations, could have encouraged subjects to use pressure levels to differentiate between gesture variants (e.g. gentle pat vs. rough pat) rather than between gesture classes (e.g. pat vs. slap). However, in natural settings force differences in touch gestures can be expected between subjects based on personal characteristics such as physical strength but also within subjects based on the social context.

3.2.3 *Improving touch gesture recognition*

Further work includes an analysis on the distinctiveness of the current feature set as well as the use of dimension reduction methods such as principle component analysis. Moreover, features which describe the temporal aspect of the gesture will also be taken into consideration. Furthermore, other classification methods such as neural networks, classification trees and hidden Markov models will be explored. Another option is to classify based on sequence distance by comparing the touch gesture intensity of two touch gesture instances using dynamic time warping to overcome the problem of different gesture duration [12].

3.3 Real-time gesture recognition (future work)

Real-time classification is needed for natural touch interaction to provide real-time response to touch input. The continuous data stream from the touch sensor(s) can be processed using a sliding window based approach [5]. Software for the gesture recognition system will be developed by a scientific programmer.

Depending on the application, embodiment of the gesture recognition system is needed. Recognition of touch gestures on a full body has the advantage of providing additional information about the touch interaction [2, 6]. However, relying too much on body location can make the recognition of touch gestures less robust against gestures that are not body location specific [6]. Moreover, it could be desirable to combine the sensing of pressure with other sensing techniques such as electric field sensing to detect proximity and soft touches [11]. Complexity rises with the expansion of the system from one touch sensor grid on an arm to a fully embodied system, possibly including multiple sensor types. Challenges lie in both the scalability of touch recognition on different body parts and the technical implementation (e.g. sampling rate and sensor fusion).

3.4 Exploration of application scenarios (future work)

Possible application scenarios for social touch interaction will be explored and can be used as a proof of concept for the real-time touch gesture recognition system. In this situation social touch behavior needs to be interpreted based on the classification and the social context. Interpretation could be in the form of a binary classification as either a positive or a negative reward [5] or other abstract meanings such as appreciation or sympathy [2]. Furthermore, to complete the interaction cycle, the embodied system should be able to react to touch in a meaningful way for example in form of visual cues, sound, speech or touch.

4. CONCLUSION

This paper describes a PhD project working towards reliable understanding of social touch to make computers behave socially intelligent. More knowledge is required about the characterizing features that distinguish between touch gestures and how to interpret the use of these gestures in a social context. Thus far, my contributions are a Corpus of Social Touch (CoST) to address the lack of available touch data sets and the insights from a first exploration into the recognition of these social touch gestures. CoST consists of the pressure sensor data of 14 different touch gestures performed in three variations: normal, gentle and rough. Classification of all the touch gesture variants showed that 14 gesture classes could be classified with an overall accuracy of 53% using a Bayesian classifier, which is more than 7 times higher than the accuracy achieved by random guessing ($1/14 \approx 7\%$). Further work includes the enhancement of the touch gesture recognition by exploring other features and classification methods, building a real-time embodied system and testing this system in an application scenario.

5. ACKNOWLEDGMENTS

This publication was supported by the Dutch national program COMMIT. The author would like to thank Dirk Heylen and Mannes Poel for their contributions to this work.

6. REFERENCES

[1] J. Chang, K. MacLean, and S. Yohanan. Gesture recognition in the haptic creature. In *Proceedings of the International Conference EuroHaptics, (Amsterdam, The Netherlands)*, pages 385–391, 2010.

[2] M. D. Cooney, S. Nishio, and H. Ishiguro. Recognizing affection for a touch-based interaction with a humanoid robot. In *Proceedings of the International Conference on Intelligent Robots and Systems (IROS), (Vilamoura, Portugal)*, pages 1420–1427, 2012.

[3] A. Flagg and K. MacLean. Affective touch gesture recognition for a furry zoomorphic machine. In *Proceedings of the International Conference on Tangible, Embedded and Embodied Interaction (TEI), (Barcelona, Spain)*, pages 25–32, 2013.

[4] A. Gallace and C. Spence. The science of interpersonal touch: an overview. *Neuroscience & Biobehavioral Reviews*, 34(2):246–259, 2010.

[5] Y.-M. Kim, S.-Y. Koo, J. G. Lim, and D.-S. Kwon. A robust online touch pattern recognition for dynamic human-robot interaction. *Transactions on Consumer Electronics*, 56(3):1979–1987, 2010.

[6] H. Knight, R. Toscano, W. D. Stiehl, A. Chang, Y. Wang, and C. Breazeal. Real-time social touch gesture recognition for sensate robots. In *Proceedings of the International Conference on Intelligent Robots and Systems (IROS), (St. Louis, MO)*, pages 3715–3720, 2009.

[7] K. Nakajima, Y. Itoh, Y. Hayashi, K. Ikeda, K. Fujita, and T. Onoye. Emoballoon a balloon-shaped interface recognizing social touch interactions. In *Proceedings of Advances in Computer Entertainment (ACE), (Boekelo, The Netherlands)*, pages 182–197, 2013.

[8] F. Naya, J. Yamato, and K. Shinozawa. Recognizing human touching behaviors using a haptic interface for a pet-robot. In *Proceedings of the International Conference on Systems, Man, and Cybernetics (SMC), (Tokyo, Japan)*, volume 2, pages 1030–1034, 1999.

[9] D. Silvera-Tawil, D. Rye, and M. Velonaki. Touch modality interpretation for an eit-based sensitive skin. In *Proceedings of the International Conference on Robotics and Automation (ICRA), (Shanghai, China)*, pages 3770–3776, 2011.

[10] D. Silvera-Tawil, D. Rye, and M. Velonaki. Interpretation of the modality of touch on an artificial arm covered with an eit-based sensitive skin. *The International Journal of Robotics Research*, 31(13):1627–1641, 2012.

[11] W. D. Stiehl, J. Lieberman, C. Breazeal, L. Basel, L. Lalla, and M. Wolf. Design of a therapeutic robotic companion for relational, affective touch. In *Proceedings of International Workshop on Robot and Human Interactive Communication (ROMAN), (Nashville, TN)*, pages 408–415, 2005.

[12] Z. Xing, J. Pei, and E. Keogh. A brief survey on sequence classification. *SIGKDD Explorations Newsletter*, 12(1):40–48, 2010.

[13] S. Yohanan and K. E. MacLean. The role of affective touch in human-robot interaction: Human intent and expectations in touching the haptic creature. *International Journal of Social Robotics*, 4(2):163–180, 2012.

Facial Expression Analysis for Estimating Pain in Clinical Settings

Karan Sikka
University of California San Diego
9450 Gilman Drive, La Jolla, California, USA
ksikka@ucsd.edu

ABSTRACT

Pain assessment is vital for effective pain management in clinical settings. It is generally obtained via patient's self-report or observer's assessment. Both of these approaches suffer from several drawbacks such as unavailability of self-report, idiosyncratic use and observer bias. This work aims at developing automated machine learning based approaches for estimating pain in clinical settings. We propose to use facial expression information to accomplish current goals since previous studies have demonstrated consistency between facial behavior and experienced pain. Moreover, with recent advances in computer vision it is possible to design algorithms for identifying spontaneous expressions such as pain in more naturalistic conditions.

Our focus is towards designing robust computer vision models for estimating pain in videos containing patient's facial behavior. In this regard we discuss different research problem, technical approaches and challenges that needs to be addressed. In this work we particularly highlight the problem of predicting self-report measures of pain intensity since this problem is not only more challenging but also received less attention. We also discuss our efforts towards collecting an in-situ pediatric pain dataset for validating these approaches. We conclude the paper by presenting some results on both UNBC Mc-Master Pain dataset and pediatric pain dataset.

Keywords

machine learning; pediatric pain; machine learning; regression; facial action coding system; expression analysis

Categories and Subject Descriptors

H.5.1 [**Information Interfaces and Presentation (e.g. HCI)**]: Multimedia Information Systems; I.4.9 [**Image Processing and Vision Applications**]: Applications; G.1.1 [**Numerical Analysis**]: Probability and Analysis

ICMI'14, November 12-16, Istanbul, Turkey.

ACM 978-1-4503-2885-2/14/11$15.00
http://dx.doi.org/10.1145/2663204.2666282

1. INTRODUCTION

Pain is an unpleasant yet necessary signal that warns us of actual or impending bodily damage, and allows an individual to take action [8]. In clinical settings, this action could translate to patient diagnosis, medications or even a surgical procedure. Thus measurement of pain is imperative for effective treatment. Despite its significance, clinical pain is often misunderstood and underestimated, which makes its management difficult [8, 21, 24, 7]. It was also highlighted in a recent survey that pain management in children demands more attention due to lack of evidence based studies and also since ineffective pain management in children can lead to long-term undesirable effects [7].

Estimates of pain intensity are commonly obtained in clinical settings via self-report and behavioral measures [25, 22, 23]. The self-report measure allows an individual to verbally communicate the amount of experienced pain and suffers from several drawbacks such as subjective bias and patient idiosyncrasies. Moreover, it cannot be employed by verbally impaired patients. On the other hand, observational measures are based on inspecting non-verbal clues (such as the face, body or voice of an individual) related to pain for reporting pain intensity. Such measures are disrupted by the presence of observer's bias, considerable demands on clinicians time, and the influence of factors such as likability of patient [10], underestimation of pain [17]. Since pain is inherently a subjective and internal experience, self-report measures are preferred over others and considered the gold-standard for conveying pain intensity [23, 28, 6].

The field of facial expression analysis has recently seen significant progress due to advancements in machine vision. Several studies have shown that facial behavior can be used as a modality for predicting internal states such as mood, confusion, [13, 3]. Case studies on understanding pain have also established relationship between facial behavior and experienced pain. In particular the Facial Action Coding System (FACS) has been shown to provide objective indicators of facial expressions that are correlated with self-report measures of pain [17, 6]. Other works have also explored approaches for facial expression analysis that do not require FACS coding. These methods employed discriminative features such as Local Binary Patterns (LBP), Bag of Words (BoW), Active Appearance Model (AAM), for representing facial behavior [20, 16, 27].

Our work is focused towards developing an automated system for predicting pain. We propose to use facial expression information to objectify the process of both detecting and measuring pain intensity in clinical settings. Since pain is a complex signal such a system should be able to capture both the appearance variation and temporal dynamics of pain expression. This system will be evaluated on the task of predicting both postoperative ongoing pain and experimentally induced acute pain. Since appropriate datasets are required to validate computer vision algorithms for prediction pain, we are also collecting an in-the wild clinical dataset that could be used to validate the posed research question. Such automated methods for measuring pain intensity could be used to aid clinical staff in long-term patient monitoring. Moreover, machine observers could be used to alert clinicians to instances of pain and thus free up resources for more efficient allocation of clinical attention. Such systems are also useful in cases where verbal self-report ratings are not available.

2. RELATED WORK

Over the years there have been significant research efforts towards automatic facial expression analysis (AFEA). This progress has been fueled by improvements in fields such as computer vision and by the availability of research datasets such as Extended Cohn-Kanade (CK+) and UNBC Pain dataset [14, 15]. Initially the field focused on analyzing posed facial expressions, obtained under controlled laboratory settings, where subjects were instructed to perform certain expressions. The AFEA research is now shifting towards spontaneous expressions that differ from posed facial expression in a number of ways and are inherently challenging owing to head-motion, low-intensity expressions and temporal variations [3]. Since pain expression is spontaneous in nature, designing algorithms to recognize and quantify pain expression is a step forward in the research on AFEA.

A significant contribution towards research on spontaneous pain expression was the public release of UNBC-McMaster Pain dataset [15]. This dataset contains video sequences of subjects experiencing shoulder pain. They were asked to perform a series of active and passive movements of their affected and unaffected shoulders while being videotaped with a front-facing camera. Each sequence was annotated with several labels: (1) patient self-report, and (2) expert observers rating referred to as Observer Pain Index (OPI). The dataset also included FACS code for certain AUs for each frame. The first computer vision work on this dataset was to design a system to predict pain/no-pain for each sequence [2] and use the binarized observer ratings observers ratings (OPI) as the ground-truth. Their approach began by first extracting AAM based features from each frame. The AAM features from each video were then clustered and a video was represented by these cluster centers. This was followed by assigning the label of the video to each clustered frame and using the data was used to train a Support Vector Machine (SVM). During prediction the SVM classifier was used to assign a score to each test-frame. A video was classified as pain if the average score of its member frames was above a threshold. Lucey et al. [16] showed improvement on this work by compressing the AAM-based features using a Discrete Cosine Transform (DCT) instead of clustering them. Sikka et al. [20] later proposed multiple segment representation in combination with weakly supervised learning to address the inherent drawbacks in these approaches. Weakly supervised learning addressed the problem of label-level ambiguity introduced by assigning each frame the label of the sequence. Multiple segment representation was used to add temporal information in the decision process and also to handle the ambiguity in the location and duration of pain signal in a sequence. Their work showed significant improvement in performance over previous approaches.

Another problem addressed via this dataset involves continuous per-frame pain intensity estimation. The ground-truth employed for this task is the Prkachin and Solomon pain intensity index (PSPI) that combines intensities of four pain-related AUs and returns a pain intensity score between $0 - 16$. Kaltwang et al. [9] trained multiple regression models using relevance vector machines for shape and appearance based features. The outputs from these models were later combined to obtain a continuous estimate of pain intensity. Later Rudovic et al. [18] proposed a model based on Conditional Ordinal Random Fields to incorporate the ordinal nature of pain intensities and their temporal dynamics.

These studies focused on either predicting binary observer's ratings or anatomically defined pain intensity ratings such as PSPI. None of these studies targeted the problem of predicting self-report measures of pain intensity. This could be because alternate pain ratings seem to be more objective and have less subjective bias relative to self-report ratings. Moreover designing accurate machine learning based approaches for making continuous estimates of self-report measures, in clinical settings, requires a massive amount of data, which might be difficult to obtain. As discussed in the Introduction Section, however, self-report ratings are considered to be the primary source of information in clinics; this work places a special attention to the problem of predicting self-report measures.

2.1 METHODOLOGY

In this section we have discussed the data collection procedure, proposed approach and related technical challenges.

2.2 Data Collection

Data are being collected in collaboration with Rady ChildrenâĂŹs Hospital, San Diego, California. The participants for this study were children, aged between 5 and 18, who had undergone an appendectomy within the past 24 hours. The participants were selected without any history of medication in past six months and without any mental disorder.

Videos of study participants are recorded while they lay in an upright position on the hospital bed. Although care is taken to obtain the face video in frontal position, we observe significant out-of-plane head rotations. In order to collect pain behavior at different intensities, we record video samples at different times after the surgery. Samples for both ongoing pain (five minute rest period) and experimentally induced acute pain are collected. At the end of each pain period, the children are asked to provide pain ratings by pointing out a number between $0 - 10$ on the Numerical Rating Scale. Several studies have validated the use of NRS for recording children's self-report measures of pain intensity. We also obtain observer or proxy ratings from parents and nurses using the NRS. Both of them are asked to look at the participant and point out to a number on the NRS that corresponds to maximum severity of pain experienced by the children. Children's ratings were not available to the proxy participants.

We shall refer to this dataset as pediatric pain dataset. The data is currently being collected and a manuscript highlighting the data-collection procedure, population demographics and statistics will be released soon. As mentioned earlier collecting relevant data is one of the major challenges involved in this project. The data should not only adhere to certain guidelines but also represent the variability in input-output space for learning accurate models.

2.3 Automatic Facial Expression Analysis

AFEA approaches can be categorized into static, space-time and sequential approaches. A very similar taxonomy was also employed for classifying human action recognition in videos [1]. Static approaches work by first extracting static features such as LBP or Gabor in individual images (or video frames). This is followed by either a temporal pooling strategy or feature extraction from the apex frame in order to obtain a vector representation. Finally a ML classifier such as SVM is used for the AFEA task. Although these approaches happen to be the starting point for any AFEA system, they are not suited for spontaneous expressions since they fail to incorporate temporal information into the decision process. On the other hand, space-time approaches extract features by treating a video as a XYT volume, such as LBPTOP or spatio-temporal gabor [26]. Although these approaches perform better than static approaches, they still do not explicitly encode temporal information leading to performance loss. Moreover, as mentioned by Sikka et al. [20], such approaches are known to work well with uniform actions that span the entire video (CK dataset). However, their performance falls down when actions have high intra-class variations and are localized in the video (UNBC Mc-Master Pain dataset). Sequential methods model a video as a sequence of observations and employ dynamic models such as Hidden Markov Models for modeling both appearance and transitions space of a video or expression class [5]. These methods suffer from drawbacks such as over-fitting due to many parameters and poor generalization performance on unseen test data as the model is limited by underlying probabilistic assumptions. In this work we briefly discuss an approach for predicting self-report pain intensity measures using AFEA.

We propose to employ FACS-based image attributes for predicting self-report measures of pain. To meet the requirements of an automated system, the FACS code are computed using the Computer Expression Recognition Toolbox (CERT) [12]. CERT is a software tool that codes each frame in a video with respect to a set of continuous dimensions that describe facial actions from the FACS and also returns other parameters such as probabilities of 6 basic emotions and 3D pose information. CERT works by first detecting a frontal face in a video and warping it to a canonical frame. The registered face is then convolved with a gabor filter bank to obtain image features. These features, along with labeled data, are then used to train separate SVMs for each AU. During run-time these pre-trained models are used to report activations for different AUs in a face containing image. The CERT output for a segment containing facial expression will be a time-series for different AUs. Since training a ML model requires a vector representation for each sample, an approach is required to summarize the time-series into a compact vector representation. A static approach to accomplish this is to summarize the time-series using naive statistics, such as mean, maximum and minimum, followed by feature concatenation [11]. It is also possible to use space-time approaches, such as "bag of temporal features" as used by Bartlett et al. [4], for obtaining a vector representation. Since our system is expected to predict continuous outputs, we need to train an appropriate regression model. The regression model should be (1) robust to noisy self-report labels, and (2) robust to over-fitting since the available data is not sufficient to handle complexities in input and output space. This requirement could be made possible in any regression model by adding a penalty factor over learned weights and obtaining a sparse solution such as Relevance Vector Machines [9], $\epsilon-$SVM [19], regression based feature selection via AdaBoost.RT [19].

3. EXPERIMENTAL ANALYSIS

In this section we discuss the experimental analysis performed on both the pediatric pain dataset and UNBC Mc-Master Pain dataset.

3.1 Pediatric Pain Dataset

In order to substantiate the viability of the proposed method, we conducted some basic statistical analyses on a subset of the dataset. These analyses were used to test two specific hypotheses: (1) do AU measurements differ between pain and no-pain periods, and (2) are AU intensities and self-report measures correlated. These experiments were conducted on a subset containing 40 children, aged between 5-15 (mean age: 12 years), with their facial expressions recorded in clinical pain (within 24 hours of surgery) and no-pain (after clinical resolution) situations. This analysis was performed on the video segments corresponding to the 5 minute ongoing pain (or rest) period. These video segments were passed as input through CERT and activation for AUs related to pain were extracted (AUs $4, 6, 7, 9, 10, 25, 43$). The time-series for each AU was consolidated into a single number using the mean statistic. The pain ratings provided by children on NRS scale were used as the self-report ratings. We found in our results that the mean difference between pain and no-pain periods is statistically significant for AU4, AU 7, AU9, AU25 and AU45. The AUs that had significant correlation with self-report measures were AU4 (r=0.22), AU9 (r=0.47), AU25 (r=0.3) and AU45 (r=0.39). The testes are conducted at 5% significance level.

3.2 Self-Report Predictions on UNBC Mc-Master Pain Dataset

We designed a self-report pain intensity prediction task on this dataset (200 videos and 25 subjects), which assessed the ability of a system to predict pain intensity. Since our approach is based on FACS coding, the feature representation for this dataset was also constructed over FACS. This dataset is provided with manual FACS codes for several pain related AU (AU$4, 6, 7, 9, 10, 12, 20, 25, 26, 43$). The time-series for each AU was summarized using mean statistic and finally a video was represented by vector containing the mean measurement for different AUs. This feature representation was employed to train a regression model (SVM with rbf kernel) using self-report ratings on VAS scale as the ground-truth. The experiments were conducted in a leave-one-subject-out cross validation format by partitioning the data into subsets (called folds) that contain data from only one subject. The data from one fold were held for testing and the model is trained on the remaining folds, and the process was repeated for all folds. The first performance metric used for evaluation in this work was Mean Absolute Error (MAE), which is the mean difference between the predictions and the true labels. The second metric calculated the Pearson correlation coefficient between the predictions and the true labels. Instead of calculating metrics separately for each fold, we calculated them by concatenating the predictions from different folds into a single vector, as was done by Ashraf et al. [2].

The results for self-report prediction experiments on the UNBC Mc-Master Pain dataset are show in Figure 1 as a plot between true labels (X-axis) and prediction along with standard error (Y-axis). The plot reveals that (1) there is a positive correlation between the true labels and the predictions, (2) the trend between the true and the predicted labels is non-linear, and (3) local regions of constant predictions can be observed on Y-axis. Since the number of training samples is less for self-report ratings with higher intensity, the prediction error seems to increase with higher intensities. The MAE is 2.28 and the Pearson correlation coefficient is 0.51. The chance prediction in this experiment corresponds to predicting 5 (mean value of self-report intensities) in all cases. The MAE for chance classification is 3.05 and the correlation coefficient is undefined owing to zero variance in the predictions. This shows that the SVM-based regression is performing better than chance classification. It is also interesting to note that the correlation between Observers' ratings (OPI) and self-report is 0.66, which is higher than the correlation obtained using our model predictions. However it should be noted that these ratings were performed by expert observers and the correlation in case of inexperienced observers are known to be reduced [17].

3.3 Pain Detection on UNBC Mc-Master Pain Dataset

We would also like to highlight our recent work on automatic pain recognition in videos [20]. This approach tackled the joint problem of, (1) classifying the expression in a video as pain/no-pain, and (2) detecting pain in each video frame. The problem was challenging since the algorithm was trained with limited ground-truth that informed about only the absence or presence of pain in the video without any information about its location. Our approach consisted of using a latent model (called multiple instance learning) for learning visual patterns related to pain. This was combined with a novel method of representing each video as bags of multiple segments (or sub-sequences) in order to address temporal information. Rigorous experiments demonstrated that our method obtained state-of-the-art results on the task of pain classification compared to previous approaches. Moreover it was also able to achieve promising results on the task of pain localization compared to algorithms trained using complete ground-truth.

4. DISCUSSION

The results on the pediatric pain dataset highlight that certain AUs show a statistically significant difference between their measurements at pain and no-pain events and also have significant correlation with the self-report measures. We are hopeful that more data will allow us to perform more thorough analyses and yield interesting insights into the problem of predicting self-reports in pediatric pain. It is also evident from the results on the UNBC Mc-Master Pain dataset that machine learning models built over FACS coding are capable of predicting self-report measures of pain intensity. Moreover there are various way for extending the naive system presented in this paper and improving performance. Lastly our previous work on pain detection showed that the problem of estimating pain can benefit by using high-level machine learning approaches that can effectively encode the underlying assumptions in a problem.

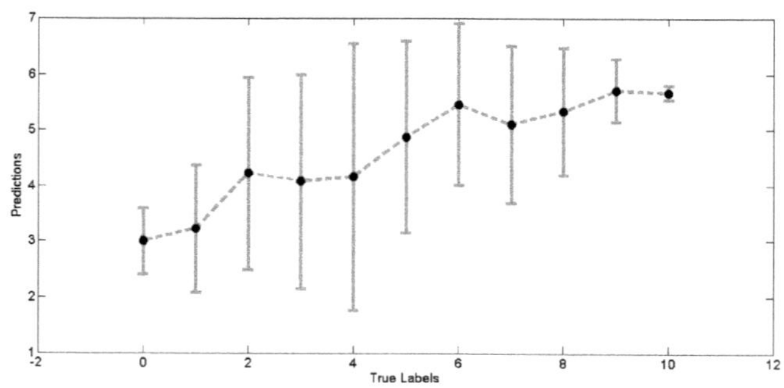

Figure 1: Plot between true labels and predictions for the task concerning prediction of self-report measures on the UNBC Mc-Master Pain dataset.

4.1 Progress and Future Work

We wish to explore multiple research avenues for the problem of estimating pain using AFEA. Firstly we are in the process of preparing a detailed manuscript for presenting our initial findings on the pediatric pain dataset. With this work we wish to explore interesting questions pertaining to AFEA for pain expression such as: (1) which action units contribute towards predicting self-report measures in pediatric population, (2) difference in facial behavior during ongoing and acute pain, (3) is it possible to design an automatic system that can perform equivalent or better than human observers such as parents and nurses, (4) possibility of using multiple source of pain intensity groundtruth such as self-reports and observer ratings, and (5) is it possible to predict time since surgery using facial expression information. In addition this work also requires working with robust regression models that can handle noisy labels and variations in data. As a future plan we plan to combine visual information along with Electrodermal activity (EDA) for predicting pain.

As an extension of our previous work on detecting pain using multiple instance learning, we are also investigating the application of various latent models for improving expression recognition in video in natural environments. This involves choosing apt underlying assumptions for a particular problem and also making the inference and learning procedures tractable. We believe that the analysis of the underlying patterns discovered by models involving latent variables will be of significant interest. We are also interested in discovering novel machine learning methods for modeling the temporal dynamics in a video. This would require either modifying previous algorithms to include temporal information as done by Sikka et al [20] or using robust sequential models [5]. The student is in the process of presenting his thesis proposal to a committee.

5. ACKNOWLEDGMENTS

This work would like to thank Dr. Marian Bartlett (University of Calfornia San Diego), Dr. Jeannie Huang (Rady's Children Hospital and Univeristy of California San Diego) and Dr. Ken Craig (The University of British Columbia) for leading the project. We would also like to acknowledge contributions from other members of the team- Alex Ahmed, Damaris Diaz and Laura Terrones. This PhD work is supported by NIH grant NIH R01NR013500. Any opinions, findings, conclusions or recommendations expressed in this material are those of the author(s) and do not necessarily reflect the views of the National Science Foundation.

6. REFERENCES

[1] Aggarwal, J., and Ryoo, M. S. Human activity analysis: A review. *ACM Computing Surveys (CSUR) 43*, 3 (2011), 16.

[2] Ashraf, A. B., Lucey, S., Cohn, J. F., Chen, T., Ambadar, Z., Prkachin, K. M., and Solomon, P. E. The painful face–pain expression recognition using active appearance models. *Image and vision computing 27*, 12 (2009), 1788–1796.

[3] Bartlett, M. S., Littlewort, G. C., Frank, M. G., Lainscsek, C., Fasel, I., and Movellan, J. Recognizing facial expression: machine learning and application to spontaneous behavior. In *Computer Vision and Pattern Recognition, 2005. CVPR 2005. IEEE Computer Society Conference on*, vol. 2, IEEE (2005), 568–573.

[4] Bartlett, M. S., Littlewort, G. C., Frank, M. G., and Lee, K. Automatic decoding of facial movements reveals deceptive pain expressions. *Current Biology 24*, 7 (2014), 738–743.

[5] Cohen, I., Sebe, N., Garg, A., Chen, L. S., and Huang, T. S. Facial expression recognition from video sequences: temporal and static modeling. *Computer Vision and Image Understanding 91*, 1 (2003), 160–187.

[6] Craig, K. D. The facial expression of pain better than a thousand words? *APS Journal 1*, 3 (1992), 153–162.

[7] Howard, R. F. Current status of pain management in children. *Jama 290*, 18 (2003), 2464–2469.

[8] Huguet, A., Stinson, J. N., and McGrath, P. J. Measurement of self-reported pain intensity in children and adolescents. *Journal of psychosomatic research 68*, 4 (2010), 329–336.

[9] Kaltwang, S., Rudovic, O., and Pantic, M. Continuous pain intensity estimation from facial expressions. In *Advances in Visual Computing*. Springer, 2012, 368–377.

[10] Kaseweter, K. A., Drwecki, B. B., and Prkachin, K. M. Racial differences in pain treatment and empathy in a canadian sample. *Pain*

Research & Management: The Journal of the Canadian Pain Society 17, 6 (2012), 381.

[11] Littlewort, G. C., Bartlett, M. S., Fasel, I., Susskind, J., and Movellan, J. Dynamics of facial expression extracted automatically from video. *Image and Vision Computing 24*, 6 (2006), 615–625.

[12] Littlewort, G. C., Whitehill, J., Wu, T., Fasel, I., Frank, M., Movellan, J., and Bartlett, M. The computer expression recognition toolbox (cert). In *Automatic Face & Gesture Recognition and Workshops (FG 2011), 2011 IEEE International Conference on*, IEEE (2011), 298–305.

[13] Littlewort, G. C., Whitehill, J., Wu, T.-F., Butko, N., Ruvolo, P., Movellan, J., and Bartlett, M. The motion in emotionâĂŤa cert based approach to the fera emotion challenge. In *Automatic Face & Gesture Recognition and Workshops (FG 2011), 2011 IEEE International Conference on*, IEEE (2011), 897–902.

[14] Lucey, P., Cohn, J. F., Kanade, T., Saragih, J., Ambadar, Z., and Matthews, I. The extended cohn-kanade dataset (ck+): A complete dataset for action unit and emotion-specified expression. In *Computer Vision and Pattern Recognition Workshops (CVPRW), 2010 IEEE Computer Society Conference on*, IEEE (2010), 94–101.

[15] Lucey, P., Cohn, J. F., Prkachin, K. M., Solomon, P. E., and Matthews, I. Painful data: The unbc-mcmaster shoulder pain expression archive database. In *Automatic Face & Gesture Recognition and Workshops (FG 2011), 2011 IEEE International Conference on*, IEEE (2011), 57–64.

[16] Lucey, P., Howlett, J., Cohn, J. F., Lucey, S., Sridharan, S., and Ambadar, Z. Improving pain recognition through better utilisation of temporal information. In *AVSP* (2008), 167–172.

[17] Prkachin, K. M., Berzins, S., and Mercer, S. R. Encoding and decoding of pain expressions: a judgement study. *Pain 58*, 2 (1994), 253–259.

[18] Rudovic, O., Pavlovic, V., and Pantic, M. Automatic pain intensity estimation with heteroscedastic conditional ordinal random fields. In *Advances in Visual Computing*. Springer, 2013, 234–243.

[19] Savran, A., Sankur, B., and Taha Bilge, M. Regression-based intensity estimation of facial action units. *Image and Vision Computing 30*, 10 (2012), 774–784.

[20] Sikka, K., Dhall, A., and Bartlett, M. Weakly supervised pain localization using multiple instance learning. In *Automatic Face and Gesture Recognition (FG), 2013 10th IEEE International Conference and Workshops on*, IEEE (2013), 1–8.

[21] Solomon, P. Congruence between health professionalsâĂŹ and patientsâĂŹ pain ratings: a review of the literature. *Scandinavian Journal of Caring Sciences 15*, 2 (2001), 174–180.

[22] Stinson, J. N., Kavanagh, T., Yamada, J., Gill, N., and Stevens, B. Systematic review of the psychometric properties, interpretability and feasibility of self-report pain intensity measures for use in clinical trials in children and adolescents. *Pain 125*, 1 (2006), 143–157.

[23] Tomlinson, D., von Baeyer, C. L., Stinson, J. N., and Sung, L. A systematic review of faces scales for the self-report of pain intensity in children. *Pediatrics* (2010), peds–2010.

[24] Turk, D. C., and Melzack, R. *Handbook of pain assessment*. Guilford Press, 2011.

[25] von Baeyer, C. L., and Spagrud, L. J. Systematic review of observational (behavioral) measures of pain for children and adolescents aged 3 to 18 years. *Pain 127*, 1 (2007), 140–150.

[26] Wu, T., Bartlett, M. S., and Movellan, J. R. Facial expression recognition using gabor motion energy filters. In *Computer Vision and Pattern Recognition Workshops (CVPRW), 2010 IEEE Computer Society Conference on*, IEEE (2010), 42–47.

[27] Zhao, G., and Pietikainen, M. Dynamic texture recognition using local binary patterns with an application to facial expressions. *Pattern Analysis and Machine Intelligence, IEEE Transactions on 29*, 6 (2007), 915–928.

[28] Zhou, H., Roberts, P., and Horgan, L. Association between self-report pain ratings of child and parent, child and nurse and parent and nurse dyads: meta-analysis. *Journal of Ddvanced Nursing 63*, 4 (2008), 334–342.

Realizing Robust Human-Robot Interaction under Real Environments with Noises

Takaaki Sugiyama
Osaka University
Osaka, Japan
sugiyama@ei.sanken.osaka-u.ac.jp

ABSTRACT

A human speaker considers her interlocutor's situation when she determines to begin speaking in human-human interaction. We assume this tendency is also applicable to human-robot interaction when a human treats a humanoid robot as a social being and behaves as a cooperative user. As a part of this social norm, we have built a model of predicting when a user is likely to begin speaking to a humanoid robot. This proposed model can be used to prevent a robot from generating erroneous reactions by ignoring input noises. In my Ph.D. thesis, we will realize robust human-robot interaction under real environments with noises. To achieve this, we began constructing a robot dialogue system using multiple modalities, such as audio and visual, and the robot's posture information. We plan to: 1) construct a robot dialogue system, 2) develop systems using social norms, such as an input sound classifier, controlling user's untimely utterances, and estimating user's degree of urgency, and 3) extend it from a one-to-one dialogue system to a multi-party one.

Categories and Subject Descriptors

I.2.m. [**Artificial Intelligence**]: Miscellaneous

General Terms

Experimentation

Keywords

human-robot interaction; spoken dialogue systems;

1. INTRODUCTION

A human speaker considers her interlocutor's situation when she determines to begin speaking in human-human interaction. For example, if her interlocutor is speaking and/or looks busy, she refrains from beginning speaking. We call this the *social norm*. We assume this social norm is also applicable to human-robot interaction when a human treats a humanoid robot as a social being and behaves as a cooperative user.

ICMI'14, Novemver 12 - 16, 2014, Istanbul, Turkry.

ACM 978-1-4503-2885-2/14/11...$15.00.

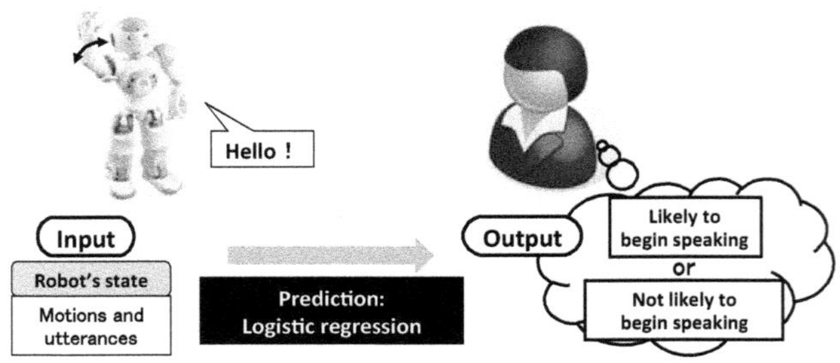

Figure 1: Overview of prediction model that how user is likely to begin speaking to humanoid robot

As a part of this social norm, we have tackled the problem of predicting when a user is likely to begin speaking to a humanoid robot [11]. An overview of the proposed method is shown in Figure. 1. We cast the problem as a binary machine learning task with the input consisting of features describing the robot's state, such as its postures, motions, and utterances, and the output indicating whether the user is "likely to begin speaking" or "not likely to begin speaking".

The goal of my Ph.D. thesis is to realize robust human-robot interaction under real environments with noises. As a result of my studies, a robot can know when a user is likely to begin speaking. In my future work, we need to show that this is useful for realistic speech interaction. To achieve this, we began constructing a robot dialogue system using multiple modalities, such as audio and visual, and the robot's posture information. Specifically, we are planning to proceed as shown in Figure 2.

Firstly, we are planning to develop an input sound classifier for realizing noise-robust speech interaction by using visual and audio information in addition to our model that predicts when a human will start speaking to a humanoid robot. To realize noise-robust human-robot interaction, it is essential to prevent the robot from recognizing noises as interlocutor's utterances by accident. Thus we verify that the social norm is useful for realizing noise-robust interaction.

Secondly, we are planning to use our proposed model to control user's untimely utterances. In particular, we actively generate the robot's action by using the model in addition to the passive usage. For example, when it is very noisy, the robot can generate an action so that the user does not want to speak. Therefore we show that the social norm can be used actively.

Thirdly, we are planning to use our proposed model to estimate a user's degree of urgency in human-robot interaction. For example, if a user begins speaking simultaneously when the robot is speak-

Goal: Robust human-robot interaction

1. Construct robot dialogue system
2. Develop systems using social norm

   Passive

   (i) Input sound classifier

   Active

   (ii) Controlling user's utterances

   (iii) Estimating user's degree of urgency
3. Extend to multi-party dialogue system

Figure 2: Research plan

Figure 3: Robot is introducing laboratory to user while user is looking at screen

ing, the robot can deduce that the user is in a hurry. We thus show that the model can be used to estimate this degree.

Finally, we are planning to extend our dialogue system from one-to-one to multi-party. Thus, we will realize a human-robot multi-party dialogue in a daily environment.

2. NOISE-ROBUST SPOKEN INTERACTION

It is not possible for a conventional method used audio features only[4, 14] to distinguish between human voices and sounds similar to a human voice, such as the voice on radio and the singing voice on TV. By using this method, it is possible to distinguish between human voices and sounds that are different from the user's utterances, such as the electronic sounds of mobile phones and coughing. For example, Lee et al. [7] proposed a method to distinguish human voices from noises by using a Gaussian mixture model (GMM) based on acoustic features.

Now, we suppose the robot turns towards the user in the situation of Figure 3 and 4. Figure 3 shows that the robot is introducing the laboratory to the user. Figure 4 shows successful and failed examples, in which we assume an ambulance runs around there. In this case, the ambulance is giving a warning to pedestrians. In the failed example, the robot responded incorrectly to the warning from the ambulance. In the case of using an input sound classifier by using audio information only, the output may be classified as "human voice" because part of this warning is actually a recording of a human voice.

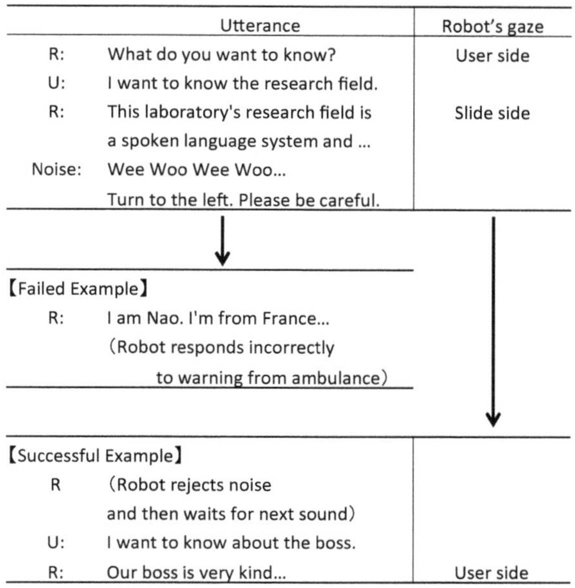

Figure 4: Successful and failed examples when ambulance is moving near a human-robot interaction

On the other hand, by using our proposed model, the robot can know when a cooperative user is likely to begin speaking. For example, when the robot turns on the TV and talks to the user, as shown in Figure 3, the user feels "not likely to begin speaking". If the robot estimates audio information received when the user is unlikely to begin speaking as probably not speech, the robot can ignore this noise, and then wait for the next sound.

3. PREDICTING MODEL OF HOW THE USER IS LIKELY TO BEGIN SPEAKING TO HUMANOID ROBOT

3.1 Formalization

Our model predicts whether a user is likely to begin speaking to the robot or not as its target label [11]. We show the system's overview in Figure 1. This is the output of our model in the classification phase and is used as the teaching signal in the training phase. As the prediction model, we use logistic regression,

$$P(y|x_1, x_2, ..., x_n) = \frac{1}{1 + \exp(-f(\boldsymbol{x}))} \tag{1}$$

$$f(\boldsymbol{x}) = a_0 + a_1x_1 + a_2x_2 + ... + a_nx_n$$

where $y \in \{0, 1\}$ is the objective variable, a_n are coefficients, and $P(y|x_1, x_2, ..., x_n)$ is the conditional probability that y takes 1 for an input feature vector $(x_1, x_2, ..., x_n)$. In the training phase, we assign '1' to "likely to begin speaking" and '0' to "not likely to begin speaking".

In the classification phase, whether the user is likely to begin speaking or not is classified every 0.1 seconds for its input features. The threshold is set to 0.5 as the default. That is, the model outputs "likely to begin speaking" when $P \geq 0.5$ and "not likely to begin speaking" otherwise.

Our prediction target corresponds to the transition relevance place (TRP) in human-human conversations [8]. It indicates places where

Table 1: Input features obtained from robot behaviors

x_1	Speech interval [second]	Elapsed time from the end of robot utterance
x_2	Utterance pattern (0 or 1)	Whether the robot's utterance is interrogative
x_3	Prosody (0 or 1)	Whether the robot's utterance ends with rising intonation
x_4	Motion (head) [degree]	Angle difference from previous frame
x_5	Motion (left arm) [degree]	Angle difference from previous frame
x_6	Motion (right arm) [degree]	Angle difference from previous frame
x_7	Motion (legs) [degree]	Sum of angle differences of legs from previous frame
x_8	Head direction (horizontal) [degree]	Angle position from the front
x_9	Head direction (vertical) [degree]	Angle position from the front

the addressee is likely to begin speaking, i.e., when he or she will take a turn to speak. Several studies analyzing human conversations have also revealed that non-verbal behaviors are useful cues for turn-taking [2, 3].

These findings have been introduced into human-machine interaction. Skantze et al. monitored users' attention by tracking their head movements [9], while Vertegaal et al. constructed a conversational system that uses eye movements to estimate to which agent the user is listening or speaking [12]. We use multi-modal information provided not by the human user but rather by the humanoid robot. Because robot behaviors are controllable by the system developer, one of our ambitious applications of the prediction model is to control user's utterances as well as to ignore noises. For example, when the robot cannot correctly accept input sounds, e.g., during calibration, it can produce situations in which the user is not likely to begin speaking.

The input features consist of the nine listed in Table 1. x_1 to x_3 represent the robot's utterance, x_4 to x_7 represent the robot's motion, and x_8 and x_9 represent the robot's head direction. x_2 and x_3 are invoked when robot utterances satisfying the conditions end until the start of the following utterance. These features are obtained every 0.1 seconds; therefore, the prediction is performed every 0.1 seconds. Our model focuses on the robot's appearance from the user's viewpoint and thus uses no information obtained from users. This is because we want to model how a cooperative user feels (i.e., the robot makes her feel) from the robot's status. In my Ph.D. thesis, we will verify that our model can be used in conjunction with existing approaches that focus on input sounds to distinguish user utterances with noises. Furthermore, the results of our study [10] have indicated that the robot's utterance was the most dominant for the prediction. The robot's motion and head direction were less effective but were still helpful when used together with other features.

3.2 Data Collection

We collected annotated data for machine learning. Our aim is to build the prediction model independent of the specific participants. To this end, we collected a data set to which 25 human participants in general public gave labels. The participants watched the entire sequences of the robot's behaviors because we felt their decisions would be affected by the preceding robot behaviors. We asked the participants to give labels via a GUI displayed at every time frame while they watched the behavior sequences of a humanoid robot. We used two sequences of robot behaviors, hereafter called sequence X and sequence Y. The content of the two sequences are self-introductions by the robot. Sequences X and Y are 150.0 and 259.3 seconds long, respectively. Sequence Y contains more varied combinations of robot actions than sequence X. Each collected data was used as the training and evaluation data later.

3.3 Training Data

We used the data from the data collection by using sequence Y. For the training data, we use the parts to which 21 or more participants commonly gave the same labels, indicating whether they would be likely to begin speaking. The numbers of frames for which 21 of them gave the same labels would be likely and not likely to begin speaking were 259 and 1,123, respectively. We gave weight to the cases of "likely to begin speaking" based on the ratio of the two labels (4.34).

3.4 Evaluation

We evaluated the performance of our model. The performance was measured in terms of the macro-average F1, which is the arithmetic average of the two F-values for the two labels "Likely to begin speaking" and "Not likely to begin speaking". The macro-average F1 is a famous measure in the text categorization community [13]. The F-value is the harmonic mean of the precision and recall rates. The numbers between the two labels are imbalance, so we use this measure to equivalently evaluate the prediction performance of the two labels.

To make the evaluation data, we used the parts to which most the participants commonly gave the same labels. Specifically, we set this condition as 18 or more participants gave the same labels, by which the macro-average F1 was the highest. 18 or more participants gave the same labels for 1,362 frames. The numbers of frames at which they were likely and not likely to begin speaking were 135 and 1,227, respectively. The macro-average F1 was 84.3%.

4. BUILDING ROBOT DIALOGUE SYSTEM

As a result of the previous section, a robot can know when a user is likely to begin speaking during a conversation. Next, we have to construct a robot dialogue system to show that our model can be used for noise-robust speech interaction. The overview of the robot dialogue system is shown in Figure 5. We have already implemented almost modules of this system except the module concerned with vision.

4.1 Processing flow

In this section, we introduce the processing flow of this system. In the case of a normally spoken dialogue system, the system's input is audio only. Because our target is human-robot interaction, we should also consider vision and the robot's posture information. Therefore, this system's input is audio and visual, and its posture information. These information is obtained from the robot's microphone and camera, and Application Programming Interface (API).

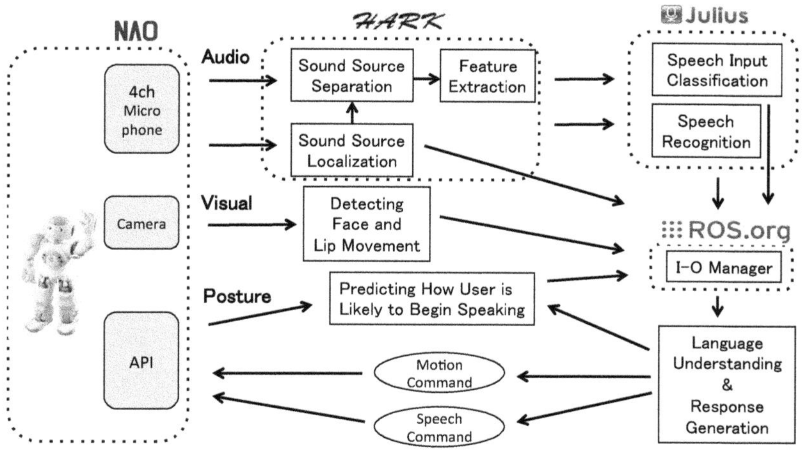

Figure 5: Overview of spoken dialogue system for humanoid robot

We used a humanoid robot, Nao, made by Aldebaran Robotics[1]. In this system, we run main processes, such as speech recognition and sound source localization, and separation, by using an external computer. Because the robot's CPU does not have enough computational power to perform computationally intensive processes. We used Julius as the speech recognition decoder software[2].

This information is sent to an I-O manager and then sent to a language understanding and response generation module. The language understanding and response generation module sends commands of speech and motion to the robot's API, NAOqi[3]. Finally, for the robot's response, its voice sound file, which is placed in the Nao in advance, is played from the robot's speaker. We used VoiceText as the text-to-speech (TTS) engine[4]. Similarly, the robot moves by sending commands from the language understanding and response generation module to the API.

4.2 Advantages

This system has the following two advantages.

1. Using multiple modalities as input
2. Synchronization

Using multiple modalities as input: Under real environments with noises, the interpretation of sounds which obtained from the robot's head-mounted microphones is much more difficult than the interpretation of sounds obtained a headset or directional microphone[6]. Therefore, to ignore these sounds, we use not only audio information but also visual and posture information as input. To realize robust speech interaction, it is essential that the robot can interpret these information comprehensively.

Audio information is obtained via the robot's four head-mounted microphones. We use these for sound source localization, sound source separation, speech recognition, and distinguishing between human voices and ambiguous noises. We have made a Gaussian mixture model (GMM) using HTK[5] for classifying speech input on the basis of features of speech signals. Therefore, we use this model for distinguishing between human voices and ambiguous noises.

[1]http://www.aldebaran-robotics.com/
[2]http://julius.sourceforge.jp/en_index.php?q=index-en.html
[3]https://community.aldebaran-robotics.com/doc/1-14/dev/naoqi/index.html
[4]http://voicetext.jp/
[5]http://htk.eng.cam.ac.uk/

Next, visual information is obtained via a robot's head-mounted camera. We use these to obtain the interlocutor's position by face detection results and lip movement using intraface[6]. Several other studies have also used visual information to detect a user's face and lip movement [1]. By using this method, it is possible to recognize whether or not a user's mouth is moving regardless of the acoustic environment. Thus, a sound can be regarded as noise if the user's mouth is not moving at the time.

Finally, the robot's posture information is obtained via API and the dialogue manager. We use this for predicting how a user is likely to begin speaking to a humanoid robot.

Synchronization: Processing delay is often a problem when transferring large amounts of data from a robot to an external computer, especially if the multi-modal function is used. For example, if there is a delay to the input of the visual information at one time t, this input may be transferred at the same timing as the next audio signal at another time $t + 1$. To prevent this, we use Robot Operating System (ROS)[7] as an I-O control. ROS has the function that it manages each input and output of modules for each time series. I avoid the processing delay by managing the information needed to generate the response of the robot via ROS in advance. Furthermore, it is easy for ROS to add the new module to the dialogue system because ROS manages each module in parallel.

5. RESEARCH PLAN

We will realize robust human-robot speech interaction by using the robot dialogue system. In the future, we are planning to proceed as shown in Figure 2.

5.1 Input Sound Classifier

We are planning to demonstrate that the robot dialogue system can realize robust human-robot interaction under real environments with noises. We are trying to robustly detect human utterances by using visual and audio, and the robot's posture information. In particular, we will develop the input sound classifier by using these information. We will verify that this system can be used to prevent the robot from generating erroneous reactions by ignoring input noises.

[6]http://www.humansensing.cs.cmu.edu/intraface/
[7]http://www.ros.org/wiki/

5.2 Controlling User's Untimely Utterances

Next, we are planning to add a function, which can be used to produce situations in which the user is likely to begin speaking, to the robot dialogue system. By using this function, the robot can control the timing when the user is likely to begin speaking. For example, when it is very noisy, it is difficult for the robot to recognize user's utterances. In this situation, in order to control user's utterances in this timing it can produce situations in which the user is not likely to begin speaking. This corresponds to the active usage while the previous section is concerned with the passive one.

5.3 Estimating User's Degree of Urgency

In addition, we are planning to develop the system that estimates the user's degree of urgency in human-robot interaction. Komatani et al. showed that the user's degree of urgency could be estimated from the information obtained during a conversation, such as the frequency of barge-in[8] [5]. In addition to this method, if the robot can estimate how the user is likely to begin speaking, we can divide the barge-in in accordance with the situation. If a user talks to the robot immediately when the user begins feeling that he or she is "likely to begin speaking", the robot can predict that the user is in a hurry. Conversely, if a user talks to the robot after enough time has elapsed from when the robot finishes talking, the robot can predict that the user is not in a hurry.

5.4 Expanding to Multi-party Dialogue System

Finally, we are planning to extend such interactions from one-to-one dialogue to multi-party one. In these studies described above, we assume one-to-one interactions. On the other hand, in the case of a more realistic situation when an embodied robot is placed in daily environments, the robot may need to talk to two or more users simultaneously. We will thus realize a human-robot multi-party dialogue in daily environments.

6. CONCLUSION

To realize speech interaction with a humanoid robot, it is necessary to avoid incorrect actions to environmental noises. The goal of my Ph.D. thesis is to realize robust human-robot interaction under real environments with noises. To achieve this, we began developing a robot dialogue system using multiple modalities, such as audio and visual, and the robot's posture information.

We are planning to proceed as follows. First, we will use our proposed model to distinguish between human voice and unnecessary noises by using multiple modalities. That is, we will investigate whether the social norm is useful for realizing noise-robust speech interaction. Secondly, we are planning to tackle controlling user's untimely utterances by actively generating the robot's action. Thirdly, we will use it to estimate the user's degree of urgency in human-robot interaction. Finally, we are planning to expand these systems to multi-party dialogue systems.

7. ACKNOWLEDGEMENTS

I would like to express my deepest appreciation to my supervisor, Professor Kazunori Komatani for providing me helpful comments on previous versions of this document.

[8]The user begins speaking simultaneously when the robot is speaking.

8. REFERENCES

[1] C. Bregler and Y. Konig. Eigenlips for robust speech recognition. *International Computer Science Institute*, 2:669–672, 1994.

[2] S. Duncan. Some signals and rules for taking speaking turns in conversations. *Journal of Personality and Social Psychology*, 23:283–292, 1972.

[3] A. Kendon. Some functions of gaze direction in social interaction. *Acta Psychol*, 26:22–63, 1967.

[4] W. Kim and H. Ko. Noise variance estimation for Kalman filtering of noisy speech. *IEICE Transactions on Information and Systems*, E84-D(1):155–160, 2001.

[5] K. Komatani, S. Ueno, T. Kawahara, and H. G. Okuno. User modeling in spoken dialogue systems to generate flexible guidance. *User Modeling and User-Adapted Interaction*, 15(1):169–183, 2005.

[6] I. Kruijff-KorbayovÃą, H. CuayÃąhuitl, B. Kiefer, M. SchrÃűder, P. Cosi, G. Paci, G. Sommavilla, F. Tesser, H. Sahli, G. Athanasopoulos, W. Wang, V. Enescu, and W. Verhelst. Spoken language processing in a conversational system for child-robot interaction. In *Proc. of the INTERSPEECH Workshop on Child-Computer Interaction*, pages 132–134, 2012.

[7] A. Lee, K. Nakamura, R. Nisimura, H. Saruwatari, and K. Shikano. Noise robust real world spoken dialogue system using GMM based rejection of unintended inputs. In *Proc. Interspeech*, pages 173–176, 2004.

[8] H. Sacks, E. A. Schegloff, and G. Jefferson. A simplest systematics for the organization of turn-taking for conversation. *Language*, 50(4):696–735, 1974.

[9] G. Skantze and J. Gustafson. Attention and interaction control in a human-human-computer dialogue setting. In *Proc. SIGDIAL 2009 Conference*, pages 310–313, 2009.

[10] T. Sugiyama, K. Komatani, and S. Sato. Predicting when people will speak to a humanoid robot. In *Proc. International Workshop on Spoken Dialog Systems*, 2012.

[11] T. Sugiyama, K. Komatani, and S. Sato. Evaluating model that predicts when people will speak to a humanoid robot and handling variations of individuals and instructions. In *Proc. International Workshop on Spoken Dialog Systems*, pages 62–72, 2014.

[12] R. Vertegaal, R. Slagter, G. C. van der Veer, and A. Nijholt. Eye gaze patterns in conversations: there is more to conversational agents than meets the eyes. In *Proc. SIGCHI conference on Human factors in computing systems*, pages 301–308, 2001.

[13] Y. Yang. An evaluation of statistical approaches to text categorization. *Information Retrieval*, 1:69–90, 1999.

[14] S. Yoon and C. D. Yoo. Speech enhancement based on speech/noise-dominant decision. *IEICE Transactions on Information and Systems*, E85-D(4):744–750, 2002.

Speaker- and Corpus-Independent Methods for Affect Classification in Computational Paralinguistics

Heysem Kaya*
Department of Computer Engineering
Boğaziçi University
34342, İstanbul, Turkey
heysem@boun.edu.tr

ABSTRACT

The analysis of spoken emotions is of increasing interest in human computer interaction, in order to drive the machine communication into a humane manner. It has manifold applications ranging from intelligent tutoring systems to affect sensitive robots, from smart call centers to patient telemonitoring. In general the study of computational paralinguistics, which covers the analysis of speaker states and traits, faces with real life challenges of inter-speaker and inter-corpus variability. In this paper, a brief summary of the progress and future directions of my PhD study titled *Adaptive Mixture Models for Speech Emotion Recognition* that targets these challenges are given. An automatic mixture model selection method for Mixture of Factor Analyzers is proposed for modeling high dimensional data. To provide the mentioned statistical method a compact set of potent features, novel feature selection methods based on Canonical Correlation Analysis are introduced.

Categories and Subject Descriptors

G.3 [**Mathematics of Computing**]: Probability and Statistics–Correlation and regression analysis; I.5.4 [**Computing Methodologies**]: Pattern Recognition-Signal processing

General Terms

Human-Computer Interaction

Keywords

canonical correlation analysis; factor analysis; local fisher discriminant analysis; mixture modeling; mixture of factor analyzers; speech emotion recognition audio-visual fusion; feature extraction; depression recognition

*Author acknowledges support from Turkish Scientific and Technological Research Council (TÜBİTAK) and Turkish Higher Education Council (YÖK).

ICMI '14, November 12 - 16 2014, Istanbul, Turkey.

http://dx.doi.org/10.1145/2663204.2666284.

1. INTRODUCTION

A fundamental aspect of human communication is non-verbal. In order the computing machinery to advance, not only the commands but also the traits (e.g. cultural background, personality) and the states (e.g. sleepiness, emotions) of the interacting individual should be taken into account. Moreover, the computer based systems can also be employed to detect and monitor the level of a long term illness, such as depression, which is inherently related to emotions.

The study of computational paralinguistics, which evolves into a branch of science by itself, deals with automatic analysis of speaker's states and traits rather than the spoken content [20]. Apart from the acoustics, other modalities, such as video and text are also shown to enhance prediction. However, the study of computational paralinguistics has many challenges to face. One major challenge in the field that must be elaborately handled for a real-life application in the wild is handling the large variability stemming from e. g. speakers, acoustic recording conditions, spoken content, used language, culture etc [23]. Performance improvements due to local modeling is already shown in the field (c. f. [21]). In this regard, my research problem is finding efficient and flexible speaker- and corpus-independent methods for affect classification in computational paralinguistics.

In multivariate statistics and pattern recognition, mixture models are intended to cope with large variability [1]. Let $\boldsymbol{x}$ denote a random variable in $\mathbb{R}^d$, a mixture model represents the distribution of $\boldsymbol{x}$ as a mixture of K component distributions:

$$p(\boldsymbol{x}) = \sum_{k=1}^{K} p\left(\boldsymbol{x}|\mathcal{G}_k\right) p\left(\mathcal{G}_k\right), \quad (1)$$

where $\mathcal{G}_k$ correspond to components, and $p\left(\mathcal{G}_k\right)$ are the prior probabilities of the components. The likelihood term, expressed by $p\left(\boldsymbol{x}|\mathcal{G}_k\right)$, can be modeled by any distribution. The most commonly employed mixture model in pattern recognition and speech signal processing is the Gaussian Mixture Model:

$$p\left(\boldsymbol{x}|\mathcal{G}_k\right) \sim \mathcal{N}(\boldsymbol{\mu}_k, \boldsymbol{\Sigma}_k), \quad (2)$$

where $\boldsymbol{\mu}_k$ and $\boldsymbol{\Sigma}_k$ denote the mean and covariance of the kth component distribution, respectively. However, GMMs suffer the curse of dimensionality heavily, therefore are either used with a small set of features with full covariance or with only diagonal covariance, which neglects important feature correlations that are very useful in speech processing. It is possible to keep a low number of parameters for the model without sacrificing correlation information by adopting a factor analysis approach. Factor Analysis (FA) is a latent variable model, which assumes the observed variables are linear projections of a small number of independent factors $\boldsymbol{z}$ with additive Gaussian noise:

$$\boldsymbol{x} = \boldsymbol{\Lambda z} + \boldsymbol{u}, \boldsymbol{z} \sim \mathcal{N}(0, \boldsymbol{I}), \boldsymbol{u} \sim \mathcal{N}(0, \boldsymbol{\Psi}), \quad (3)$$

where $\boldsymbol{\Lambda}$ is a $d \times p$ *factor loading matrix* and $\boldsymbol{\Psi}$ is a diagonal uniquenesses matrix representing the common sensor noise. Subsequently, the covariance matrix in eq. 2 is expressed as $\boldsymbol{\Sigma}_k = \boldsymbol{\Lambda}_k \boldsymbol{\Lambda}_k^T + \boldsymbol{\Psi}$, effectively reducing the number of parameters from $O(d^2)$ to $O(dp)$, with $p << d$. If each Gaussian component is expressed in the latent factor space, the result is a mixture of factor analyzers (MoFA). Both for FA and MoFA Expectation-Maximization (EM) algorithm [3] based methods exist to infer model parameters [7]. Hyper-parameters (the number of components and local dimensionalities), however should be given to EM algorithm. Though there are also Bayesian methods to infer hyper-parameters of MoFA [8] especially resorting to Markov Chain Monte Carlo methods, the drawback of learning efficiency makes them impractical for computational paralinguistics. Therefore, one major objective of this thesis study was to develop an efficient and robust model selection algorithm for MoFA.

To address this latter issue, a fast and parsimonious model selection algorithm called *Adaptive Mixture of Factor Analyzers* (AMoFA) [13] is proposed. AMoFA is capable of adapting a mixture model to data by selecting an appropriate number of components and factors per component. Instead of relying on a validation set, AMoFA uses a Minimum Message Length (MML) based criterion to control model complexity, and is also capable of removing factors and components when necessary. The efficacy of AMoFA algorithm is evaluated in clustering, manifold learning as well as class conditional modeling (classification).

Despite its efficiency and accuracy in modeling high dimensional data, AMoFA also requires a compact set of relevant features. For this purpose, a set of already existing feature selection methods were investigated and novel discriminative projection based feature selection methods were proposed with successful application to acoustic depression recognition and physical load prediction [11, 16].

In short, three intended contributions of this study are developing an automatic mixture model selection method, finding highly potent features for acoustic emotion recognition and applying adaptive mixture models to the field. The remainder of this paper is organized as follows. In the next section background on processing of speech for computational paralinguistics, and two statistical methods is given. In Section 3, proposed methods are briefly introduced with sample results. In Section 4, further contributions related to the thesis study are presented. Finally, Section 5 provides an outlook of past and ongoing work.

2. BACKGROUND

2.1 Paralinguistic Speech Processing

The state-of-the-art speaker Computational Paralinguistics applications are built using suprasegmental features obtained from functionals (e.g. moments, extremes) operating on frame-level Low Level Descriptors (LLD) e.g. F0, MFCC, jitter, shimmer [20]. Brute-force extraction of high-dimensional potent features is commonly encountered in competitive baseline feature sets of the most recent Computational Paralinguistics challenges [22, 28, 21].

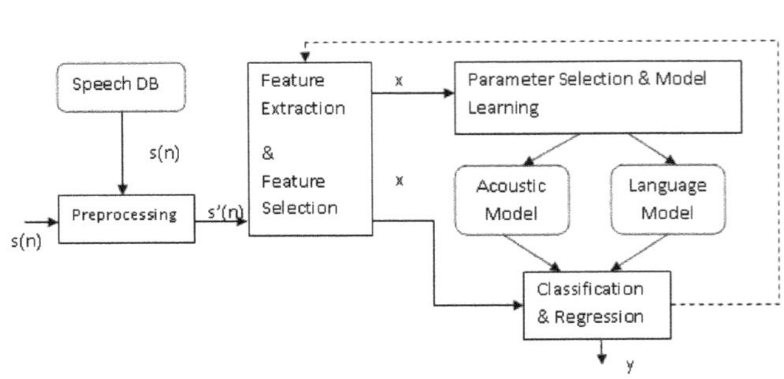

Figure 1: Speaker State and Trait Recognition Pipeline. Adapted from [20]

Similar to speech processing in general, the signal is pre-processed and LLDs are extracted. After suprasegmental feature extraction by means of functionals, selection and model learning is carried out. Apart from acoustic and linguistic ones, when available models from visual modality are combined to enhance prediction. The pipeline is summarized in Figure 1.

In the state-of-the-art system, feature extraction part is not a bottleneck since brute-forcing yields an over-complete set. However, this approach requires an elaborate task-relevant pruning of features, and subsequently modeling them in a robust manner. As stated earlier, these bottlenecks comprise the research sub-problems of this thesis.

2.2 Mixture of Factor Analyzers

Despite their widespread use, GMMs have a major drawback: they require covariances to be non-singular. It is also known that posterior mode of a Gaussian resides in singular values of covariance [26]. In this respect, being capable of simultaneous local dimensionality reduction and mixture model fitting, MoFA not only extends Mixture of Probabilistic Principal Component Analyzers (MPPCA) [25], but also overcomes the drawbacks of GMMs, especially with regards to high dimensional data. Therefore, Ghahramani and Hinton refer to MoFA as "a reduced dimensionality mixture of Gaussians" [7]. Apart from clustering tasks to find the structure of the data, MoFA models can be employed in supervised tasks for 1) class-conditional modeling and 2) training local models with component specific factors. In my study, I try to benefit from the latter advantage of MoFA for supervised tasks.

The EM algorithm is used to find maximum likelihood solutions to latent variable models [3], and it can be used for training a MoFA [7]. However, it does not address the model selection problem, and requires the number of components and factors per component to be fixed beforehand. The AMoFA Algorithm proposed to tackle this model selection issue is presented in Section 3.1. AMoFA utilizes fast component selection measures for splitting and factor addition from Incremental Mixture of Factor Analyzers (IMoFA) [19]; and extends it with a Bayesian related MML criterion. Incorporation of the MML criterion eliminates the need for a validation set used to tune the model complexity against the generalization performance.

3. PROPOSED METHODS

3.1 Adaptive Mixture of Factor Analyzers

Salah and Alpaydın [19] introduced an incremental MoFA algorithm (IMoFA) which starts with a single component - single factor model and increments the number of factors and components using fast heuristic measures until a convergence criterion is met. The algorithm allows components to have as many factors as necessary. While the outer loop controls the incremental model evolution, the MoFA fitting with given initialized model parameters is done by the regular EM for MoFA. This algorithm uses a validation set to stop model adaptation as well as to avoid over-fitting.

AMoFA [13] extends the IMoFA algorithm with a generalized version of a Bayesian related MML criterion proposed in [5]. This approach overcomes the requirement of a validation set, adding capability of component annihilation.

The Generalized Message Length Criterion.

To allow local factor analyzers to have independent latent dimensionality, the MML criterion in [5] is generalized accordingly to reflect the individual code length of components:

$$\mathcal{L}(\boldsymbol{\theta}, \mathcal{X}) = \sum_{k:\pi_k>0} \frac{C_k}{2}\log(\frac{N\pi_k}{12}) + \frac{K_{nz}}{2}\log\frac{N}{12} + \sum_{k:\pi_k>0} \frac{(C_k+1)}{2} - \log p(\mathcal{X}|\boldsymbol{\theta}), \quad (4)$$

where we use individual parameter cost C_k instead of a global C. The criterion given in eq. (4) lacks code length for K_{nz}. We use here Rissanen's *universal prior for integers* [18]:

$$w^*(k) = c^{-1}2^{-log^* k}, \quad (5)$$

which gives the (ideal) code length

$$L^*(k) = log\ 1/w^*(k) = log^*(k) + log\ c, \quad (6)$$

where c is the normalizing sum $\sum_{k>0} 2^{-log^*(k)}$ that is tightly approximated as $c = 2.865064$ [18]. It is straightforward to write a recursive algorithm for $log^*(k) = logk + loglogk + ...$ term in eq. (6). We finally obtain $L^*(K_{nz})$, the cost to encode the number of components, and similarly $\sum_{k:\pi_k>0} L^*(p_k)$, the cost to encode the local dimensionalities $\{p_k\}$ and add them to eq. (4) to obtain a message length criterion:

$$\mathcal{L}(\boldsymbol{\theta}, \mathcal{X}) = \sum_{k:\pi_k>0} \frac{C_k}{2}\log(\frac{N\pi_k}{12}) + \frac{K_{nz}}{2}\log\frac{N}{12} + \sum_{k:\pi_k>0} \frac{(C_k+1)}{2} - \log p(\mathcal{X}|\boldsymbol{\theta}) + L^*(K_{nz}) + \sum_{k:\pi_k>0} L^*(p_k) \quad (7)$$

The idea in AMoFA is as follows. Given a dataset AMoFA first fits a 1-component, 1-factor model, where the factor is initialized from the principal component of the data. At each step, it adds more components and factors to the mixture, running EM iterations between additions of new parameters. During the M-step of EM, the adopted MML criterion requires weak components to be annihilated if necessary (based on support). Apart from this automatic annihilation, when the incremental progress no longer improves the MML criterion, downsizing component annihilation starts and continues until a single component is left. At each adaptive step after EM convergence, the algorithm logs the model and finally outputs the one giving the minimum message length.

Component Annihilation.

In a Bayesian view, the message length criterion (eq. (7)) adopted from Figueiredo and Jain [5] corresponds to assuming a flat prior on component parameters $\boldsymbol{\theta}_k$, and a Dirichlet prior on mixture proportions π_k:

$$p(\pi_1, \cdots, \pi_K) \propto exp\{\sum_{k=1}^{K_{nz}} -\frac{C_k}{2}log\pi_k\} = \prod_{k=1}^{K_{nz}} \pi_k^{-C_k/2}. \quad (8)$$

Thus, in order to minimize the adopted cost in eq. (7), the M-step of EM is changed for π_k :

$$\hat{\pi}_k^{new} = \frac{max\{0, (\sum_{i=1}^{N} h_{ik}) - \frac{C_k}{2}\}}{\sum_{j=1}^{K_{nz}} max\{0, (\sum_{i=1}^{N} h_{ij}) - \frac{C_k}{2}\}}, \quad (9)$$

which means that all components having a soft count (N_k) smaller than half the number of local parameters C_k will be annihilated. This threshold enables the algorithm to get rid of components that do not justify their existence. In the special case of AMoFA, the number of parameters per component are defined as:

$$C_k = d * (p_k + 2) + L^*(p_k), \quad (10)$$

where d is the original dataset dimensionality, p_k is the local latent dimensionality of component k, and $L^*(p_k)$ is the code length for p_k. The additive constant 2 inside the bracket accounts for the parameter cost of mean $\boldsymbol{\mu}_k$ and local diagonal uniquenesses matrix $\boldsymbol{\Psi}_k$. Finally, the localized annihilation condition to check at the M step of EM is simply $N_k < T_k = C_k/2$.

Clustering and classification performance of AMoFA is evaluated on a variety of synthetic and real life datasets [13]. It is observed that it provides on par with or better clustering performance than the renowned Unsupervised Learning of Finite Mixture Models [5], where the latter deteriorates totally in high dimensional class-conditional modeling. In high-dimensional classification, MoFA variants (i. e. IMoFA and AMoFA) are found statistically significantly better than GMM modeling in all experimented datasets. Output of AMoFA on Geva's face dataset [6], which is used as a benchmark in automatic mixture model selection can be seen in Figure 2.

As an application to computational paralinguistics, while AMoFA can be used in classification via class-conditional modeling, it also can be applied for locally linear, globally non-linear feature (local factor) extraction.

3.2 Discriminative Projection Based Filters

In the preliminary work on discriminative projection based feature filters, we used Canonical Correlation Analysis for predicting depression severity level [11]. Recently, the approach is extended incorporating Local Fisher Discriminant Analysis (LFDA) [24] in multi-view setting, where the views are formed based on Low Level Descriptors (LLD) [16].

The main idea behind the CCA based filter in [11] is as follows. When all features on one view are subjected to CCA against the labels on the other view, the absolute value of the

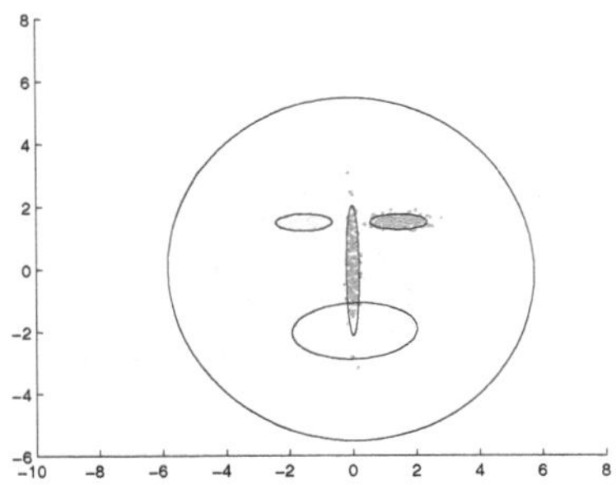

Figure 2: A sample AMoFA output for Geva's face data. Class labels are indicated with colors and found clusters are shown with 2-std contour plots. We see all the clusters (facial regions) are found correctly. AMoFA obtains 98% correct clustering on this benchmark problem out of 100 runs with randomly generated datasets.

projection matrix W can be used to rank the features. The application to regression is straightforward since the resulting matrix is $n \times 1$, therefore a vector. It can be applied in the same way to 2-class classification where the classes can be denoted with 0 and 1 in the target vector. For $K > 2$ classes, we can use the canonical correlation value (r^i) to weight the corresponding projection column (eigenvector W^i). In short, the Sample versus Labels CCA Filter (SLCCA-Filter) algorithm, which inputs the dataset $X \in \mathbb{R}^{n \times d}$ and label matrix $T \in \{0,1\}^{n \times (K)}$; and outputs feature ranking R is given as:

$$[W, V, r] = CCA(X, T), \quad (11)$$

$$H = \sum_{i=1}^{m} abs(W^i) r^i, \quad (12)$$

$$R = \text{sort(H,'descend')}, \quad (13)$$

where $m = min(rank(X), rank(Y))$, and the 1-of-C coded label matrix T is defined as

$$T_{i,k} = \begin{cases} 1 & \text{if } y_i = k, \\ 0 & \text{if } y_i \neq k. \end{cases} \quad (14)$$

Since K classes have $K-1$ degrees of freedom, the rank of matrix T is $K-1$. Therefore it is possible to remove any of the columns from 1-of-C coded matrix. The filter can be applied to LFDA in a similar manner, where instead of the canonical correlation value square root of the corresponding eigenvalue λ^i is used.

In the first application to AVEC 2013 Depression Sub-challenge (DSC), SLCCA-Filter reached 9.44 RMSE on test set using only 17% of the baseline features improving the challenge audio baseline (14.12 RMSE) 30%, relative [11]. Recently, SLCCA-Filter in LLD-based multi-view setting is applied on INTERSPEECH 2014 Physical Load sub-challenge, improving the test set baseline Unweighted Average Recall (UAR) from 71.9% to 75.35% [16].

4. AUDIO-VISUAL FUSION FOR DEPRESSION AND AFFECT PREDICTION

In this section, supportive studies about multimodal depression/affect prediction using recent challenge corpora are presented.

Motivated from the previous successful audio-visual fusion applications, we carried out feature and decision level fusion on AVEC 2013 DSC [15]. At feature level, we fused SLCCA-Filter selected acoustic features from [11] with AVEC 2013 baseline visual features [28] using CCA. The fusion was carried out for each of 4×4 facial regions, separately. A second level CCA between ranked audio-visual covariates from each region and the target labels is applied to obtain a single covariate as feature for regression.

Challenge test set results with audio only, video only and audio-visual modalities are compared. The best performance is obtained using audio-visual decision fusion (9.44 RMSE), which is followed by video only (9.72 RMSE) and audio only system (9.78 RMSE), respectively. The CCA based audio-visual fusion gives 10.81 RMSE, ranking behind audio only system. Important to note that all the results obtained are better than challenge baselines (14.12 RMSE for audio and 13.61 RMSE for video) and best three performances compare favorably to systems reported at AVEC 2013 challenge workshop [2, 17].

A CCA ensemble is employed for regression in AVEC 2014 challenge [27] outperforming the test set baselines using frame level prediction [12]. The Pearson's correlation between the predictions and the ground truth test set affect labels is increased from 0.1966 to 0.3932 [12].

For emotion recognition in the wild 2014 challenge [4], we employ modality specific Extreme Learning Machines [14]. Extreme Learning Machine (ELM) was introduced as a fast alternative training method for Single Layer Feedforward Networks (SLFNs) [9, 10]. To the best of our knowledge our study was the first to use ELM in multimodal emotion recognition. Challenge test set audio and video baseline accuracies are 26.2% and 34.4%, respectively. By combining modality specific ELMs and focusing on inner facial regions, we reach a test set accuracy of 44.23%.

5. DISCUSSION AND OUTLOOK

Regarding inter-speaker variability, all studies are carried out in a speaker independent setting as this is the expected research outcome in the field. In previous works using popular emotional corpora, 20-25% (absolute) decrease of UAR is observed shifting from speaker dependent to independent setting. Similarly, UAR performance degrades to almost chance level when cross-corpus evaluation is carried out [23], where the authors consider the effect of various preprocessing techniques such as corpus and speaker normalization.

AMoFA is proposed to provide flexibility and robustness for statistical modeling of large acoustic variability. However, finding a small but very relevant set of features that can be effectively used in AMoFA is still an open problem as the features differ across corpora. Moreover, our preliminary studies have shown that proposed CCA based filter methods learn better from continuous labels than class labels. Thus, an investigation and improvement of other feature selection methods (e. g. based on mutual information) for cross-corpus evaluation is necessary.

We verify the performance boost due to multimodal fusion on two recent emotion related challenge corpora. Ongoing works include validating the proposed filter methods on commonly used acoustic emotional corpora. Application of AMoFA to cross-corpus acoustic emotion recognition constitutes the nearest future work.

6. REFERENCES

[1] C. M. Bishop. *Pattern Recognition and Machine Learning*. Information Science and Statistics. Springer, 2006.

[2] N. Cummins, J. Joshi, A. Dhall, V. Sethu, R. Goecke, and J. Epps. Diagnosis of depression by behavioural signals: a multimodal approach. In *Proc. of the 3rd ACM Intl. Workshop on Audio/Visual Emotion Challenge*, AVEC '13, pages 11–20, 2013.

[3] A. P. Dempster, N. M. Laird, and D. B. Rubin. Maximum likelihood from incomplete data via the em algorithm. *Journal of the Royal Statistical Society, Series B*, 39(1):1–38, 1977.

[4] A. Dhall, R. Goecke, J. Joshi, K. Sikka, and T. Gedeon. Emotion recognition in the wild challenge 2014: Baseline, data and protocol. In *Proc. of the 16th ACM Intl. Conf. on Multimodal Interaction (ICMI 2014)*. ACM, 2014.

[5] M. A. T. Figueiredo and A. K. Jain. Unsupervised Learning of Finite Mixture Models. *IEEE Trans. PAMI*, 24(3):381–396, 2002.

[6] A. B. Geva. Hierarchical unsupervised fuzzy clustering. *IEEE Trans. Fuzzy Systems*, 7(6):723–733, 1999.

[7] Z. Ghahramani and G. E. Hinton. The em algorithm for mixtures of factor analyzers. Technical Report CRG-TR-96-1, University of Toronto, 1997.

[8] D. Gorur. *Nonparametric Bayesian Discrete Latent Variable Models for Unsupervised Learning*. Ph.D. Thesis, Technical University of Berlin, 2007.

[9] G.-B. Huang, Q.-Y. Zhu, and C.-K. Siew. Extreme learning machine: a new learning scheme of feedforward neural networks. In *Neural Networks, 2004. Proceedings. 2004 IEEE International Joint Conference on*, volume 2, pages 985–990. IEEE, 2004.

[10] G.-B. Huang, Q.-Y. Zhu, and C.-K. Siew. Extreme learning machine: theory and applications. *Neurocomputing*, 70(1):489–501, 2006.

[11] H. Kaya, F. Eyben, A. A. Salah, and B. W. Schuller. CCA Based Feature Selection with Application to Continuous Depression Recognition from Acoustic Speech Features. In *Proc. IEEE Intl. Conference on Acoustics, Speech, and Signal Processing (ICASSP 2014)*, pages 3757–3761, Florence, Italy, 2014. IEEE.

[12] H. Kaya, F. Çilli, and A. A. Salah. Ensemble CCA for Continuous Emotion Prediction. In *Proc. 4th ACM International Workshop on Audio/Visual Emotion Challenge*, Orlando, Florida, USA, Nov 2014. ACM.

[13] H. Kaya and A. A. Salah. Adaptive Mixture of Factor Analyzers (submitted).

[14] H. Kaya and A. A. Salah. Combining Modality-Specific Extreme Learning Machines for Emotion Recognition in the Wild. In *Proc. of the 16th ACM Intl. Conf. on Multimodal Interaction (ICMI 2014)*, Istanbul, Turkey, 2014. ACM.

[15] H. Kaya and A. A. Salah. Eyes Whisper Depression: A CCA based Multimodal Approach. In *Proc. ACM Multimedia 2014*, Orlando, Florida, USA, Nov 2014. ACM.

[16] H. Kaya, T. Özkaptan, A. A. Salah, and S. F. Gürgen. Canonical Correlation Analysis and Local Fisher Discriminant Analysis based Multi-View Acoustic Feature Reduction for Physical Load Prediction. In *Proc. INTERSPEECH 2014*, Singapore, Sep 2014. ISCA.

[17] H. Meng, D. Huang, H. Wang, H. Yang, M. AI-Shuraifi, and Y. Wang. Depression recognition based on dynamic facial and vocal expression features using partial least square regression. In *Proc. of the 3rd ACM Intl. Workshop on Audio/Visual Emotion Challenge*, AVEC '13, pages 21–30, 2013.

[18] J. Rissanen. *Information and complexity in statistical modeling*. Information Science and Statistics. Springer, Dordrecht, 2007.

[19] A. A. Salah and E. Alpaydın. Incremental mixtures of factor analysers. In *Proc. of the Pattern Recognition, 17th Intl. Conference on (ICPR '04) Volume 1*, pages 276–279, 2004.

[20] B. Schuller. Voice and Speech Analysis in Search of States and Traits. In A. A. Salah and T. Gevers, editors, *Computer Analysis of Human Behavior*, chapter 9, pages 227–253. Springer London, 2011.

[21] B. Schuller, S. Steidl, A. Batliner, J. Epps, F. Eyben, F. Ringeval, E. Marchi, and Y. Zhang. The INTERSPEECH 2014 Computational Paralinguistics Challenge: Cognitive & Physical Load. In *Proc. INTERSPEECH 2014*, Singapore, Sep 2014. ISCA.

[22] B. Schuller, S. Steidl, A. Batliner, A. Vinciarelli, K. Scherer, F. Ringeval, M. Chetouani, F. Weninger, F. Eyben, E. Marchi, M. Mortillaro, H. Salamin, A. Polychroniou, F. Valente, and S. Kim. The INTERSPEECH 2013 Computational Paralinguistics Challenge: Social Signals, Conflict, Emotion, Autism. In *Proc. INTERSPEECH 2013*, pages 148–152, Lyon, France, August 2013. ISCA, ISCA.

[23] B. Schuller, B. Vlasenko, F. Eyben, M. Wollmer, A. Stuhlsatz, A. Wendemuth, and G. Rigoll. Cross-corpus acoustic emotion recognition: variances and strategies. *Affective Computing, IEEE Transactions on*, 1(2):119–131, 2010.

[24] M. Sugiyama. Local fisher discriminant analysis for supervised dimensionality reduction. In *Proc. of the 23rd Intl. Conference on Machine Learning*, ICML '06, pages 905–912, New York, NY, USA, 2006. ACM.

[25] M. E. Tipping and C. M. Bishop. Mixtures of probabilistic principal component analyzers. *Neural Comput.*, 11(2):443–482, Feb. 1999.

[26] N. Ueda, R. Nakano, Z. Ghahramani, and G. E. Hinton. Smem algorithm for mixture models. *Neural Computation*, 12(9):2109–2128, 2000.

[27] M. Valstar, B. Schuller, K. Smith, T. Almaev, F. Eyben, J. Krajewski, R. Cowie, and M. Pantic. AVEC 2014–3D Dimensional Affect and Depression Recognition Challenge. In *Proc. of the 4rd ACM Intl. Workshop on Audio/Visual Emotion Challenge*, AVEC '14, 2014.

[28] M. Valstar, B. Schuller, K. Smith, F. Eyben, B. Jiang, S. Bilakhia, S. Schnieder, R. Cowie, and M. Pantic. AVEC 2013–The Continuous Audio/Visual Emotion and Depression Recognition Challenge. In *Proc. of the 3rd ACM Intl. Workshop on Audio/Visual Emotion Challenge*, AVEC '13, pages 3–10, 2013.

The Impact of Changing Communication Practices

Ailbhe N. Finnerty
Fondazione Bruno Kessler
Via Sommarive, 18, Povo (TN), Italy
finnerty@fbk.eu

ABSTRACT

Due to advancements in communication technologies, how we interact with each other has changed significantly. An advantage is being able to keep in touch (family, friends) and collaborate (colleagues) with others over large distances. However, these technologies can remove behavioural cues, such as, changes in tone, gesturing and posture which can add depth and meaning to an interaction. In this paper two studies are presented which investigate changing communication practices in 1) the workplace and in 2) a loosely connected social group. The interactions of the participants were analysed by comparing synchronous (occurring in real time; e.g. face to face) and asynchronous (delayed; email, sms) patterns of communication. The findings showed a prevalence of asynchronous methods of communication in Study 1, which had an impact on affective states (positive and negative) and on self reported measures of productivity, creativity, while in Study 2 synchronous communication patterns affected stress.

Author Keywords

Communication; Technology; Stress; Social Networks; Organisational Psychology

ACM Classification Keywords

J.4 Psychology; **H.5.3** Asynchronous Interaction; CSCW

INTRODUCTION

Previous research to date has investigated the way we communicate and interact and how social media and technologies, the widespread availability of smartphones and wearable computing have changed and are continually changing our social interactions [15]. While there are considerable advantages of new advances in communication technology, what is necessary is an analysis of how they can affect issues such as satisfaction and productivity in the workplace, stress in everyday life [3]. This is necessary in order to be more aware of our practices and to maintain meaningful relationships, while still taking full advantage of the benefits of modern technology. In this paper two studies will be presented. They deal with communication and interaction in two different settings, within 1) an organisation and 2) a community based in the same location, using two different methods of data collections 1) Sociometric Badges and 2) Smartphones. The studies aim to explore the differences between communication types (face to face, emails, calls, sms etc.) to understand their impact on human behaviour.

ICMI '14, November 12 – 16, 2014, Istanbul, Turkey.
Copyright 2014 ACM 978-1-4503-2885-2/14/11...$15.00.
http://dx.doi.org/10.1145/2663204.2666285

RESEARCH QUESTIONS

In order to differentiate between types of communication that will be the focus of the studies in this paper we will refer to the differences as a) synchronous (immediate, happening in real time; e.g. face to face, calls) and b) asynchronous (delayed, when there is a gap between sending and receiving a message; e.g. email, sms) [24; 8].

The key research questions that will be addressed through this research are: **1)** What are the effects that technology has on relationships in a traditional workplace setting, where communication was more commonly face to face, but which is now changing due to the prevalent use of email? **2)** What effects does technology have on our social relationships, at work and at home, and how maintaining these relationships, such as, dealing with high volumes of communication, both synchronous and asynchronous, can have an impact on our mood?

The work will focus on the impact of communication practices on both the positive and negative affective states of the individual as well as self reports of stress, including "techno-stress" which is due to overuse or intrusiveness of technology [4]. Based on these research questions we form the following general hypotheses.

H1- There will be more asynchronous (email, sms) communication rather than synchronous (face to face, calls) reflecting the change in how we interact and communicate with each other (Study 1&2).

H2- There will be negative affect associated with asynchronous communication and positive affect associated with synchronous communication (Study 1&2).

STUDY 1: COMMUNICATION IN AN ORGANISATION

In this first study the Sociometric Badge Corpus [16] will be presented. The Corpus consists of data collected within an organisation and through various analyses will attempt to address the previously noted research questions.

RELATED LITERATURE

With constant new developments in communication technology, it has become important to examine the effects that these technologies (the virtual workplace, smart phones and ubiquitous computing), have on our everyday lives, in the workplace, at home and in society. Within organizations, in an increasing trend, more workers are situated remotely from a designated office space [6]. What is required is a method to improve communication within an organization, due to the changing nature of its structure. This is also necessary with the changes in how workers communicate and collaborate and the effectiveness of working in teams [21; 24]. With virtual communication certain issues can become misunderstood due to the lack of a context or shared working environment. Of course the major disadvantage of virtual teams is the lack of physical interaction, with its associated verbal and nonverbal cues, that accompany face-to-face communication. However, despite these drawbacks, virtual teams are quickly becoming more popular [12]. But studies have found that face to face communication is preferred even when electronic communication is available, as it develops a sense of community and allows small problems to be discussed and fixed rapidly [9; 6].

Studies show that using extensive digital networks in the workplace can increase productivity by 7%; however, cohesive face to face networks were found to have an increase of 30% [23]. In terms of group collaborations, email has been researched extensively and along with all its advantages, there are many disadvantages. High levels of emails can be stressful to try and manage. Due to this, emails are becoming less used and wiki's and blogs are becoming more commonplace for collaborating on group projects [13], and minimising email actually improved communication in collaborative work [22]. Furthermore, studies found that more information technology usage in the workplace can at times lead to productivity losses because of 'technology overload', when additional technological tools begin to crowd out an individuals' productivity, instead of enhancing it [14]. The suggestion from their findings was to tailor the use of technology to the individuals' specific needs [14]. Features of electronic communication can be used to informally discuss with a colleague, but while it is a quicker form of communication it also is much less rich than face to face contact [5].

The Sociometric Badge Corpus [16] collected data from fifty four (Female=6) employees of a research centre, over a six week period. The data collected by the sociometric badges [22] consisted of face to face interactions (infra-red) and social co-location (Bluetooth) as well as speech and activity features. Internal email and phone logs (without content) were also collected. Using Experiencing Sampling methods [7] the participants completed an online survey three times daily (11am, 2pm, 5pm), the questions were related to affective states, personality, interactions (e.g. I was continuously interacting with those around me etc.) and situations (e.g. I had a deadline, etc.).We also collected measures of self-perceived productivity and creativity as we were interested in whether the communication used by the participants affected how they worked.

Methodology

We used the Experience Sampling data as well as a subset of the total data collected as part of this study, this included;

Infra-Red (IR): The infra-red hits represented face to face interactions as both badges registered a hit at the same time if participants were less than one metre apart directly facing each other.

Email: Emails from participant to participant, with *only one* recipient were used for the study. This was done to consider each exchange (email - sent and received) as a one to one interaction.

Bluetooth (BT): The radio signal strength indicator (RSSI) of the BT, can be used as a coarse indicator of proximity between devices, hence people.

Infra-Red and Bluetooth Combined (IRBT): We combined IR hits and close BT hits (less than one metre distance apart) as a measure of close communication.

All data were normalised in order to compare them to each other.

Analysis of Variance in Communication Type

A measure of communication (IR and Email) in the 30 minutes prior to the survey was used. The data was calculated in this way to be able to compare the communication features to the Experience Sampling data, for which the questions related to the previous 30 minutes.

To try and answer our first research question and to test our first hypothesis we took the total number of normalised hits and emails, by aggregating the 30 minute segments, for both 'friends' and 'not friends' groups and ran a 2 (Communication; Email, IR) x2 (Relationship; Not Friends, Friends) Analysis of Variance (ANOVA) with the independent variable "relationship" and the dependent variable "communication", Bonferroni correction was applied to the analysis.

The analysis revealed a main effect of Relationship [$F(51,1)=67.65$, $p < .001$], that there were more interactions between 'friends' than 'not friends'. The analysis also revealed an interaction between Communication and Relationship [$F(51,1) = 10.67$, $p < .05$], with more communication between friends than colleagues, with a slightly greater value of face to face interaction than email for the friends group (3.0 vs. 2.17), while for colleagues it was found that there was a smaller proportion of face to face communication than email communication (0.13 vs. 0.77). While email was more prevalent, the analysis showed that our relationships impacted how we communicated.

Time Series Analysis of Communication and Affect

To further examine changes of communication and to compare it to *Affective States* the data was analysed as a Growth Model. A Growth Model was used in order to understand the relationship between the communication features and the self-reported variables for each time the survey was filled in by the participant. For this, features extracted from infra-red and emails were used, as well as Bluetooth (a measure of co-location).

IR The results found that interacting with more people face to face (t=2.78) was related to higher *Positive Affect* especially when your task was freely chosen (t=2.109), but also that higher number of face to face interactions with 'friends' (t's=-5.32; -4.65) was negatively related to self reported measures of *Productivity* and *Creativity*.

BT The same trend was found when considering co-location with others through BT signals, that being co located with 'friends' (t=2.93) was related to higher reports of *Positive Affect* but that higher number of interactions, with more people in the canteen (t's=-4.99;-3.95) and when having coffee (t's=-6.11;-3.1) were found to negatively impact the reported levels of *Productivity* are *Creativity*. However for the BT features it was found that more time interacting (t=2.532) and being co located with 'friends' (t=4.411) had a positive effect on *Productivity* but not Creativity, whereas being surrounded by more people (t=3.919) regardless of relationship led to higher reports of *Creativity* (p's<.05).

IRBT The features used for this analysis did not show any differences to the IR and BT results from when they were analysed separately.

EMAIL Average email length was the only feature to have any impact on task status, if what you were doing was *Interesting* (t=1.99) or if there was a Deadline (t=-1.98).

Discussion

From the first analyses evidence was found to support our first hypothesis that there would be more asynchronous than synchronous communication between the participants. By analysing the data as a time series we found partial support for our second hypothesis as over the course of the study different patterns emerged where the communication impacted the *Affective States* and self reported measure of the participant's *Productivity* and *Creativity*. Interacting with 'friends' face to face had an impact on *Positive Affective* state but a negative effect on self reported *Productivity* and *Creativity* especially during lunch or coffee breaks. Co location just with friends found higher levels of self reported *Productivity* only, while being co located with more people in general was found to have a greater impact on self reported *Creativity*. Email was found to have minimal impact on the self-reported variables of *Affective* states, leaving us unable to draw conclusions as to the impact of asynchronous communication on states and other self-reported measures.
Further analysis on Personality states and whether they can impact our communication patterns are currently being done.

STUDY 2: COMMUNICATION AND STRESS

In this second study the Telecom Database will be presented along with preliminary results of the analysis.

RELATED LITERATURE

While communication practices can impact the productivity of a working team or affect the outcomes of project meetings [21; 23], we need to look beyond this and examine how our behaviours and interactions affect us and those around us. A study investigating the impact of mobile technologies in public spaces found that the mere presence of a phone can reduce social signals, such as smiling, an important nonverbal cue to instigate interactions. This makes us less likely to interact with others, as phone use in social spaces constitutes a negative disturbance to proximate others [2].

We have created a communication culture which has primed us to receive a quick message, to which we are expected to provide just as rapid a response [25]. Even when we have the chance to speak with each other face to face, we prefer to text, and as a result being more connected has made us more isolated [26]. An increased use of mobile phones for the purpose of relationship maintenance actually had the reverse effect on the closeness of individuals, as the increased dependence on mobile phones led to feelings of entrapment, guilt and pressure to respond [10]. The always on and always connected device has led to a dependency especially from younger generations, the device encourages partners to be in constant contact, leading to hyper coordination [18; 19] and it becomes more about quantity than quality [17]. We are increasing the number of 'friends' we have and as a consequence the quality of our interactions is lessened. Dunbar's number [11] states that the ideal number of individuals with whom we can maintain meaningful relationships with is approximately 150, suggesting that we cannot possibly maintain meaningful relationships with all our 'friends' and 'followers' through social networks in today's society. The problem that researchers consider now is that the increasing use of the internet and social networking sites to connect with others is pulling us away from friends and are distancing us from each other [20].

The data used for the second study was collected through a collaboration with Telecom Italia SKIL Lab. Call and sms logs were recorded over a five week period for seventy participants (Female= 33). The logs were collected using the funf platform [1] installed on their smartphones. The participants made up a community of users with young families based in the same city, but not a closely connected community. As well as data collected from the smartphones we administered a short questionnaire collecting data on affective states, as well as categories of stressors (e.g., having a lot of housework/work, financial problems, interpersonal conflict etc.). Further measures on perceived levels of stress and quality of sleep were also collected.

For this study we are interested in the same research questions previously outlined, using the same hypotheses, with one additional hypothesis concerning stress.

H3- There will be more stress associated with maintaining larger communication networks, such as, high number of contacts (one SD above the group mean) and larger volume of calls (synchronous) and sms (asynchronous).

Methodology

A number of communication features from the raw data were calculated. To be able to compare our findings to the previous dataset we considered calls as a measure of synchronous and sms a measure of asynchronous communication. Data concerning affective states, perceived stress and sleep quality, were recorded once daily. As done in the previous study the call and sms data were normalised to be able to directly compare them to each other.

Results

Through a number of paired sample t-tests, we compared the two different communication types and found that there were far more calls (.204) than sms (.182) [t(2149)=9.09, p<.001] within this community. We also found that that there were more unique contacts for calls (6.83) than sms (4,25), [t(2149)=38.36, p<.001], which did not lend support to our first hypothesis.

To address our second hypothesis a series of Spearman correlations was run on the data. It was found that *Negative Affect* was correlated with a higher number of contacts for calls *rs*(.054), p<.05 and *Positive Affect* was negatively correlated with incoming *rs*(-.081) and total calls *rs*(-.073) (p's < .001). When we added our *Stress* variable to the analysis, we found that it was significantly correlated with higher numbers of incoming calls *rs*(.056) p < .05 and higher number of total contacts *rs*(.076), p<.001.

Discussion

From this analysis we found that because there was more overall synchronous communication (calls) that our first hypothesis was not supported. Because of this we also did not find support for our second hypothesis which expected that asynchronous communication would be related to negative affective state. However from some initial correlations we found that higher levels of communication in total (calls) were related to higher levels of *Negative Affective* states whereas lower levels of calls, due to the negative correlations were related to *Positive Affective* states. We added a further analysis on self reported levels of *Stress* in this study and found that a higher number of incoming calls and total number of contacts was correlated with higher reported measures of stress which supports our third hypothesis.

Further data collection is planned which will focus on stress due to the overuse of technology, 'Techno-stress' [4]. Data will be collected on running apps, social network and communication online via smartphones (e.g., Skype, viber, whatsapp etc).

CONCLUSIONS

The studies presented here show some support for our hypotheses presented in this paper. However more work is required for a clearer interpretation of the findings from the analyses. In an organisation we found that there was more asynchronous communication and that patterns of interacting and communication had an impact on our Positive Affective states and in a less clear manner our Productivity and Creativity, where it seems that being close to our friends leads to increases in Productivity and by being co located with others, not friends, leads us to feel more Creative. Our second study found that through smartphone use there was more synchronous communication, which did not support our first hypothesis, but that the communication features did support our third hypothesis, that a higher volume of overall communication and managing a large network of contacts was related to higher levels of self reported stress. Further analysis is planned for both these studies to continue to examine our research questions in more depth.

FUTURE DIRECTIONS

The majority of the work that has been the focus of my PhD has dealt with attempting to understand our communication with others, and the effect that it can have on the individual. The studies which are detailed in this paper have examined communication using sensors (Sociometric Badge) or logs of interactions (smartphones), as well as information about the context and affective states of the participant collected through daily written surveys. While the methods used for these studies have allowed us to collect large amounts of data from hundreds of participants, understanding how we communicate (synchronously or asynchronously) and how it can affect the way that we feel (Study 1 and 2), work (Study 1) or experience stress (Study 2), are not always evident from the data which has been collected. This can be due to many reasons, such as, missing or sparse data (due to malfunctioning devices and uncontrolled data collection settings), unbalanced demographics (skewed distributions of gender, age), and other interruptions to the process, which can affect how reliable the data is to interpret.

The planned future work to complete my PhD thesis is to re-concentrate my research efforts on the affect that interactions and communication have on the individual. I plan to examine this issue with respect to the principles of Organisational Psychology, while using methodologies from both Psychology and Social Computing. The aim is to focus particularly on stress which is experienced in the workplace, and how to develop coping strategies to deal with these experiences to lessen their affect on our health and overall wellbeing. The specific situations which will be examined are job interviews and various job positions in the hospitality industry (reception, catering, housekeeping etc.).

The overall aim of the proposed study is to learn how to convey a positive and successful first impression and how to maintain this impression in a working environment, where you are exposed to a variety of interactions daily, some of which may be stressful or unpleasant. This is an issue that is particularly important for the hospitality industry, an area where making a good first impression can impact job performance. This aim will be extended to a field study with the goal of improving the participants' performance in dealing with customers and, in particular, these stressful situations by maintaining a good impression.

RESEARCH CONTRIBUTIONS

The work presented in this paper offers a contribution to social computing, organisational psychology and ubiquitous computing domains. By combining methodologies we have two rich datasets which allow us to address our research questions using more advanced analysis techniques to gain a better understanding of social interactions and behaviours.

REFERENCES

1. Aharony, N., Pan, W., Ip, C., Khayal, I., & Pentland, A. (2011). Social fMRI: Investigating and shaping social mechanisms in the real world. *Pervasive and Mobile Computing*, *7*(6), 643-659.
2. Banjo, O., Hu, Y., & Sundar, S. (2008). Cell phone usage and social interaction with proximate others: Ringing in a theoretical model. *Open Communication Journal*, *2*, 127135.
3. Böhmer, M., Hecht, B., Schöning, J., Krüger, A., & Bauer, G. (2011, August). Falling asleep with Angry Birds, Facebook and Kindle: a large scale study on mobile application usage. In *Proc of the 13th International Conference on Human Computer Interaction with Mobile Devices and Services* (pp. 47-56). ACM.
4. Brod, C. (1984). *Technostress: The human cost of the computer revolution* (Vol. 13, p. 242). Reading, MA: Addison-Wesley.
5. Cameron, A. F. & Webster, J. (2005). Unintended consequences of emerging communication technologies: Instant Messaging in the workplace. Computers in Human Behaviour, 21, 85-103.
6. Cascio, W. F. (2000). Managing a virtual workplace. Academy of Management Executive, 14, 81–90.
7. Csikszentmihalyi, M., & Larson, R. (1987). Validity and reliability of the experience-sampling method. *The Journal of nervous and mental disease*, *175*(9), 526-536.
8. Dennis, A. R., Fuller, R. M., & Valacich, J. S. (2008). Media, tasks, and communication processes: A theory of media synchronicity. *MIS quarterly*, *32*(3), 575-600.
9. Ean, L. C. (2010). Face-to-face Versus Computer-mediated Communication: Exploring Employees' Preference of Effective Employee Communication Channel. International journal for the advancement of science & arts, 1, 28-38.
10. Hall, J. A., & Baym, N. K. (2012). Calling and texting (too much): Mobile maintenance expectations,(over) dependence, entrapment, and friendship satisfaction. *New media & society*, *14*(2), 316-331.
11. Hill, R. A., & Dunbar, R. I. (2003). Social network size in humans. *Human nature*, *14*(1), 5372.
12. Ishii, H., Kobayashi, M. & Arita, K. (1994). "Iterative Design of Seamless Collaboration Media" *Communications of the ACM (CACM), Special Issue on Internet Technology, ACM, 37*, 83-97.
13. Johri, A. (2011). Look Ma, No Email! Blogs and IRC as Primary and Preferred Communication Tools in a Distributed Firm, March 19–23, Hangzhou, China, ACM, 2011.
14. Karr-Wisniewski, P., & Lu, Y. (2010). When more is too much: Operationalizing technology overload and exploring its impact on knowledge worker productivity. *Computers in Human Behavior*, *26*(5), 1061-1072.
15. Kraut, R., Patterson, M., Lundmark, V., Kiesler, S., Mukophadhyay, T., & Scherlis, W. (1998). Internet paradox: A social technology that reduces social involvement and psychological well-being? *American psychologist*, *53*(9), 1017.
16. Lepri, B., Staiano, J., Rigato, G., Kalimeri, K., Finnerty, A., Pianesi, F., & Pentland, A. (2012, September). The sociometric badges corpus: A multilevel behavioral dataset for social behavior in complex organizations. In *Privacy, Security, Risk and Trust (PASSAT), 2012 International Conference on Social Computing (SocialCom)* (pp. 623-628). IEEE.
17. Licoppe, C. (2008). The mobile phone's ring. In: Katz JE (ed.) Handbook of Mobile Communication Studies. Cambridge, MA: MIT, 139–152.
18. Ling, R. (2004) The Mobile Connection: The Cell Phone's Impact on Society. San Francisco, CA: Elsevier.
19. Ling, R., and Ytrri, B. (2002) Hypercoordination via mobile phones in Norway. In: Katz JE and Aakhus M (eds) Perpetual Contact: Mobile Communication, Private Talk, Public Performance. Cambridge, MA: Cambridge University Press, 139–169.
20. Marche, S. (2012). Is Facebook making us lonely. *The Atlantic*, *309*(4), 60-69.
21. Olguín, D. O., Waber, B. N., Kim, T., Mohan, A., Ara, K., & Pentland, A. (2009). Sensible organizations: Technology and methodology for automatically measuring organizational behavior. *Systems, Man, and Cybernetics, Part B: Cybernetics, IEEE Transactions on*, *39*(1), 43-55.
22. Olguín, D. O., Gloor, P. A., & Pentland, A. (2009, April). Wearable sensors for pervasive healthcare management. In *Pervasive Computing Technologies for Healthcare, 2009. PervasiveHealth 2009. 3rd International Conference on* (pp. 1-4). IEEE.
23. Pentland, A. (2009) How Social Networks Network Best. Harvard Business Review, February, 37.
24. Shirani, A. I., Tafti, M. H., & Affisco, J. F. (1999). Task and technology fit: a comparison of two technologies for synchronous and asynchronous group communication. *Information & Management*, *36*(3), 139-150.
25. Turkle, S. (2007). Can You Hear Me Now? Thanks to technology, people have never been more connected-or more alienated. *Forbes*, *179*(10), 176.
26. Turkle, S., (2011). Alone Together: Why we expect more from Technology and Less from Each Other. New York: BasicBooks

Multi-Resident Human Behaviour Identification in Ambient Assisted Living Environments

Hande Alemdar
Boğaziçi University
Department of Computer Engineering Istanbul, Turkey
hande.alemdar@boun.edu.tr

ABSTRACT

Multimodal interactions in ambient assisted living environments require human behaviour to be recognized and monitored automatically. The complex nature of human behaviour makes it extremely difficult to infer and adapt to, especially in multi-resident environments. This proposed research aims to contribute to the multimodal interaction community by (i) providing publicly available, naturalistic, rich and annotated datasets for human behaviour modeling, (ii) introducing evaluation methods of several inference methods from a behaviour monitoring perspective, (iii) developing novel methods for recognizing individual behaviour in multi-resident smart environments without assuming any person identification, (iv) proposing methods for mitigating the scalability issues by using transfer, active, and semi-supervised learning techniques. The proposed studies will address both practical and methodological aspects of human behaviour recognition in smart interactive environments.

Categories and Subject Descriptors

I.5.2 [**Design Methodology**]: Pattern analysis

Keywords

Ambient Assisted Living; Human Behaviour Monitoring; Smart Homes; Machine Learning

1. INTRODUCTION

Recognizing human behaviour in an automated manner is essential in many ambient intelligence applications such as smart homes, health monitoring and assistance applications, emergency services, and transportation assistance services [18]. It is foreseen that in the near future, smart environments that interact with the people according to their specialized needs will be become a part of daily life. Since the global increase in the ratio of the elderly population is already prominent, the aging in place gained importance. It is possible to reduce the economic effects of global aging by enabling the elderly to stay active and healthy for longer years in their own homes where living independently is more natural and comfortable [15].

In order to promote a healthier life style in smart living environments, continuous monitoring of the natural everyday behaviour is essential. We can identify the behaviour that needs to be changed with continuous monitoring, then we can design persuasive interfaces to induce the change in that behaviour and we can monitor and confirm the change in that behaviour. Therefore, automated monitoring of human daily activities in smart environments is of significant importance. There has been a significant research effort on the subject already [1]. Several machine learning methods are used for inferring human behaviour using the data collected from the smart environments but those methods require annotated datasets to be trained on. Recording and annotating such datasets are costly since they require time and human effort. The datasets recorded in real world conditions rather than laboratory settings are even more difficult to obtain and also more valuable since they reflect the natural human behaviour.

Moreover, the performance of newly developed inference methods for more accurate behaviour recognition are evaluated using metrics widely used in machine learning domain such as accuracy, precision, recall and F-measure. Although these metrics are solid, they may fail to reveal the actual performance in terms of behaviour understanding. Human behaviour is characterized by frequency and duration of several activities. In order to evaluate the performance in terms of behaviour recognition, we need to define metrics that are suitable for modelling human behaviour. Also, my study focuses on making smart houses smart enough to provide long term health monitoring for not only people who live alone but also with a spouse or a flat mate. In that respect, we need to recognize behaviour individually in multi-resident environments without assuming any person identification which generally requires the use of wearable technology that can be obtrusive.

Finally, the human behaviour recognition methods in smart interactive environments depend on both the environment and the people, therefore the models and the parameters are subject to change across different environments and different people. In order to deploy these systems on a large scale, we need to relearn the parameters for each setting. Moreover, even for the same setting, they are subject to change over the course of the time. This change can stem from a variety of reasons such as the changes in the behaviour of the people, changes in the environment or changes in the sensor behaviours. Learning the parameters for every different setting from scratch is not feasible since it requires large amount of annotated data which is hard to obtain. Instead, diffusing the previously obtained knowledge across different settings would be more desirable.

ICMI'14, November 12–16, 2014, Istanbul, Turkey.

ACM 978-1-4503-2885-2/14/11 ...$15.00.
http://dx.doi.org/10.1145/2663204.2666286.

My research aims at addressing the above mentioned issues by collecting publicly available benchmark datasets, improving the ways of evaluating different approaches and models, handling multi-resident environments in an unobtrusive manner and by using active, transfer and semi-supervised learning for large scale deployments.

2. RELATED WORK

Activity recognition systems proposed so far in the literature generally make use of wireless sensors. The sensors used can be both ambient [20] or wearable [4]. Ambient sensors include wireless sensors that can measure several properties of the environment such as humidity, temperature, light and sound levels. They can also determine whether there is a motion in the environment or certain objects are being used by using passive infrared sensors or RFID sensors [5]. Ambient sensors are generally used for in-home settings. Wearable sensors can also be used for outdoors as well as indoor settings [8].

The research efforts on indoor settings mainly focus on two different fields. In the first group, there are studies where hundreds of sensors and sensor equipped home appliances are deployed in smart laboratory houses [13, 12]. Those studies generally focus on human interactions with the future smart environments and do not necessarily have a healthcare focus. The second group of studies focus on human activity detection for health status monitoring [7, 9].

Although proposed systems employ various sensing modalities and try to recognize different types of activities in different settings, the common point in all types of systems is that they all use machine learning for recognizing the activities. Probabilistic models are used often and they work well for activity recognition. Especially, hidden Markov models (HMM) are widely used to model the human activity recognition since they are well suited for sequential nature of human activities [11, 6].

3. RESEARCH PLAN

I have four studies in my research plan. Study 1, collecting and disseminating ARAS (Activity Recognition with Ambient Sensing) datasets, and Study 2, behavioural performance evaluation methods, have already been completed. Study 3 is currently in progress. For Study 4, I have preliminary experiment results for active and semi-supervised learning. I will extend the preliminary studies with larger set of experiments using different learning strategies.

3.1 Study 1: Collecting ARAS Datasets

ARAS (Activity Recognition with Ambient Sensing) human activity recognition datasets are collected from two real houses with multiple residents during two months. The datasets contain the ground truth labels for several activities. Each house was equipped with 20 binary sensors of different types that communicate wirelessly using a low power communication protocol called ZigBee, which enables the sensors to have longer battery lifetimes. A full month of information which contains the sensor data and the activity labels for both residents was gathered from each house, each with two residents, resulting in a total of two months data.

Regarding the activity labelling for ground-truth collection purposes, overall, we could manage to obtain from 60 to 100 activity labels for each day. More than 20 different activities were captured, including every day activities, like sleeping, brushing teeth, watching TV, toileting, preparing a meal and eating. Rare activities that are not performed every day, such as hanging out laundry, having a guest, doing cleaning and having a nap, are also captured. These rare activities might have great significance in an application inferring the health status or wellbeing of the residents. Therefore, we gathered information about such activities, unlike most of the previous studies. The total number of activity occurrences in House A and House B is 2177 and 1023, respectively. The total number of sensor readings is around 26 million. Further details about the datasets and preliminary results on activity recognition preformance using HMM can be found in [2].

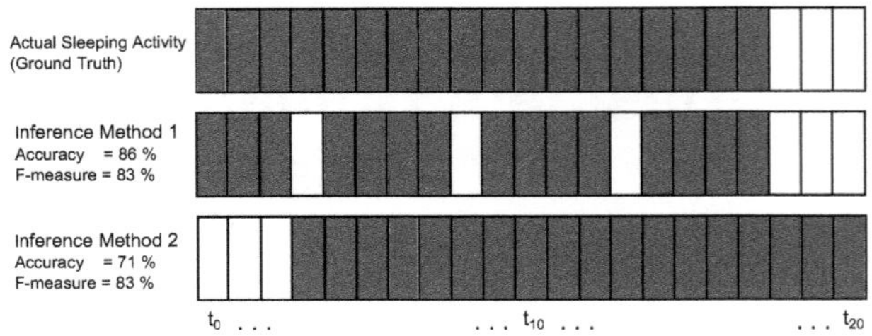

Figure 1: Two example of inference output sequence for sleeping activity with the same F-measure performance according to time-slice based evaluation

3.2 Study 2: Behavioural Performance Evaluation

In this study, I address the challenges in the evaluation of different approaches for the purposes of human behaviour understanding through a well-being assessment perspective. The metrics used in the performance evaluation of newly developed algorithms are directly taken from the machine learning domain. Consider the scenario in Fig. 1 and assume that inference method 1 and 2 are being proposed in order to identify sleeping behaviour and their time-slice level outcome is being compared to the ground truth sleeping activity. From a machine learning perspective, both methods have the same F-measure performance of 83% and the first method have higher accuracy than the second method. From a behaviour monitoring perspective, the output of the first method indicates that the person may have a sleeping disorder whereas the output of the second method identifies the normal sleeping behaviour correctly with a shift in start the time. Human behaviour analysis requires analysis of daily activities in terms of timing, duration and frequency. Given the high variations in these attributes for different activities, the general purpose metrics fail to accurately reflect the actual performance. I proposed an evaluation method considering three different types of activities, i.e. duration sensitive, frequency sensitive, and both duration and frequency sensitive activities.

Duration sensitive activities are the ones that only the total duration of the activity is important in terms of medical assessment, rather than the number of times the activities are performed. Activities such as watching tv, reading a book, leaving the house, cleaning the house, studying and talking on the phone can be categorized in this group. For the duration sensitive activities, merging and fragmentation errors can be neglected as long as they do not result in overfill and underfill. Frequency sensitive activities, on the other hand, are the ones only the number of occurrences matters in terms of medical assessment. Having a snack or drink, brushing teeth, taking medicine are the candidate activities for this category. The important error types for this activity category are the fragmentation and merging errors since they can lead to wrong interpretations about the frequency of the activity. Timing errors such as overfill and underfill can be ignored since they do not change the frequency output.

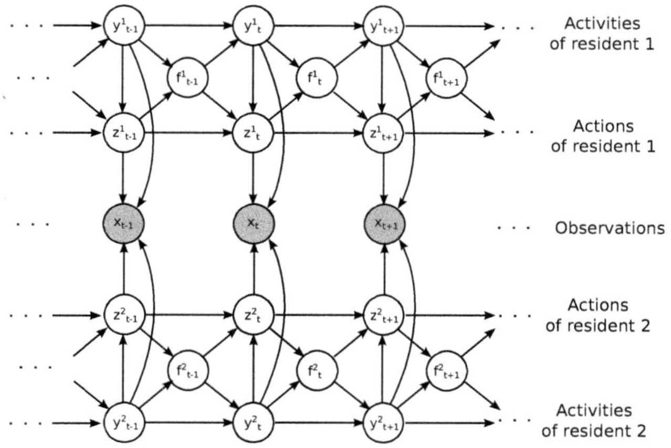

Figure 2: Hierarchical Factorial Hidden Markov Model for Activity Recognition for Multiple Residents

3.3 Study 3: Multi-resident Behaviour Monitoring

In order to identify the individual activities for multiple users, I will use factorial hidden Markov models (FHHMM) which are generally used for identifying multiple chains of hidden states. In my case, there are two chains of states belonging to each resident. Moreover, the hierarchical hidden Markov models are suitable for modelling complex human activities by separating them into several sub-states, i.e. actions. Consider for example the cooking activity. It contains several sub-states such as taking the vegetables and ingredients from the fridge, preparation of the ingredients, cooking them on the stove etc. By modelling these sub-states as actions in one layer and then the whole actions as the activity of cooking will enable us to have a more realistic and better model. By merging these two models, I will use a factorial hierarchical hidden Markov model as depicted in Figure 2 in order to recognize the individual behaviour in multi-resident environments. To the best of our knowledge, there are not any applications of this specific model to any other domain although there exist studies on changing FHHMM into a Bayesian Network in order to be able to perform efficient inference [10].

3.4 Study 4: Scalable Learning Strategies

In order to deploy automatic human behaviour recognition systems on a large scale, we make use of several machine learning techniques. Using these techniques requires a set of model parameters, denoted by θ, to be learned. The parameters can be learned using the training data set $\mathcal{D}$. Formally, we define

- $x = \{x_1, x_2, ...x_T\}$ as the set of data points (i.e. data collected from the sensors)
- $y = \{y_1, y_2, .., y_T\}$ as the set of true labels (i.e. activity performed by the user)
- $l = \{l_1, l_2, .., l_Q\}$ as the set of all possible labels (i.e. complete set of recognized activities)

The training data set $\mathcal{D} = \{x_i, y_i \mid x_i \in x, \quad y_i \in (l \cup \emptyset), \quad 1 \leq i \leq T\}$ where $y_i = \emptyset$ means that we do not have the true label for time slice i. Typically we have more time slices where $y_i = \emptyset$ than $y_j \in l$, i.e. times slices with the true activity labels. We can obtain the true label for a given data point by asking a human annotator called *the oracle*. This process is called the annotation. Therefore, we define $f_{oracle}(\cdot, l)$ as the annotation function. The oracle can either be the actor himself or someone else.

Algorithm 1 Human Activity Recognition

input: $\mathcal{D}$

$\theta_0 = f_{init}()$ {Transfer Learning}

$\mathcal{D}_0 = \mathcal{D}$
$i = 0$
repeat
  $x_i = f_{select}(\mathcal{D}_i, \theta_i)$ {Active Learning}
  $y_i = f_{oracle}(x_i, l)$
  Update $\mathcal{D}_i$ into $\mathcal{D}_{i+1}$ using y_i
  $\theta_{i+1} = f_{learn}(\mathcal{D}_{i+1}, \theta_i)$ {Semi-supervised Learning}
  $i = i + 1$
until convergence

output: θ

The algorithm for scalable human behaviour recognition is given in Algorithm 1. The algorithm starts with a set of parameters θ. We define $f_{init}()$ function for initializing the parameters that have been learned from an earlier setting using transfer learning. If transfer learning is not used, the initial set of parameters can be randomly initialized. After initialization of the parameters, the algorithm goes into an iterative stage in which it continually selects the most informative data points using active learning with function $f_{select}(\mathcal{D}, \theta)$, obtains the labels from oracle and updates the model parameters. Finally, we need to relearn the model parameters at each iteration of the algorithm. This is handled by semi-supervised learning function $f_{learn}(\mathcal{D}, \theta)$.

3.4.1 Semi-Supervised Learning

Using both the labeled and unlabeled data in parameter learning task is called the semi-supervised learning [21]. In its simplest form, the learning process uses its own predictions to teach itself, called the self-training [14]. The main idea in self-training is to first train a classifier only on labeled data. Then, this classifier is used to predict the labels for the unlabeled data. A subset of the unlabeled data, together with their predicted labels, are then selected to be included in the labeled data.

More sophisticated type of semi-supervised learning algorithms use generative probabilistic models. In generative models, one common criterion for finding the best parameters is the maximum likelihood estimate (MLE). Given training data $\mathcal{D}$, the MLE parameters are the ones under which the data likelihood $p(\mathcal{D}|\theta)$ is the largest.

$$\hat{\theta} = \arg\max_{\theta} p(\mathcal{D}|\theta) = \arg\max_{\theta} logp(\mathcal{D}|\theta) \quad (1)$$

In order to benefit from semi-supervised learning, some assumptions are needed. Making the right assumptions or detecting wrong assumptions are not trivial in many cases. Therefore, "which semi-supervised model should we use?" is an open research question.

3.4.2 Active Learning

Active learning is a technique for selecting the most informative data points for annotation and it has been generally used in part of speech tagging problems in natural language processing [19]. Active learning is different from classical learning framework. In Figure 3(a), the classical learning framework is depicted. In classical learning, given the data set $\mathcal{D}$, the model parameters denoted by θ, can be learned using $f_{learn}(\mathcal{D}, \theta)$ function (i.e. semi-supervised learning) as we described in the previous section. On the other hand, as depicted in Figure 3(b), the active learning algorithm iteratively learns new parameters using semi-supervised learning and elects the most informative data points according to the current model parameters and obtain their labels.

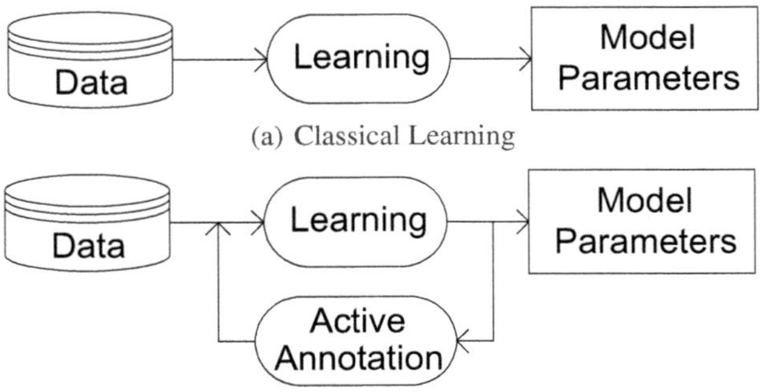

(a) Classical Learning

(b) Active Learning

Figure 3: Learning Frameworks

The iterations continue until convergence. At each iteration, the most informative data points are selected by $f_{select}(\mathcal{D}, \theta)$ method according to some informativeness measure. Although, the general framework for active learning is the same, there are two approaches for selection.

1. **Pool-based Approach** The learner selects the instances among the the whole or a part of training data set $\mathcal{D}$ according to some "informativeness measure" defined by the selection function. After the selection of all the points to be queried in that iteration, we consult the oracle to obtain true labels with the function $y = f_{oracle}(x, l)$.

2. **Sequential Approach** resembles to the pool-based approach but instead of bulk processing, it decides whether or not to ask the label at each instance. The question is "ask or not" rather than "which ones to ask". In a sequential setting, we decide whether to obtain y_i for each x_i, $1 \leq i \leq N$. The selection function is called with the arguments $f_{select}(\mathcal{D}, \theta)$ where $\mathcal{D} = x_i$ contains a single element. Also, the selection function may return an empty result. When the result is empty, it is certain that the result of $f_{oracle}(y, l)$ with $y = \{\}$ will be empty. This implies that we choose not to ask the true label to the oracle. In that case, we continue the algorithm with the following observation without calling the f_{oracle} function.

In [3], we performed some preliminary studies on active learning using a pool based approach for selection. We used three different measures of uncertainty for selecting the most informative data points and evaluated their performance by using three different real world data sets. Experiments showed that all three proposed uncertainty measure method works well for the activity recognition system. We showed through experiments on real world data sets that, by using the active learning instead of random selection, the required number of data points is reduced by 66% to 80% for different houses.

3.4.3 *Transfer Learning*

Traditional machine learning algorithms make predictions on the future data using probabilistic models that are trained on previously collected labeled or unlabeled training data. Transfer learning, in contrast, allows the domains, tasks, and distributions used in training and testing to be different. Transfer learning is the ability of a system to recognize and apply knowledge and skills learned in previous tasks to novel tasks. In this definition, transfer learning aims to extract the knowledge from one or more source tasks and applies the knowledge to a target task [16]. In activity recognition context, this translates to using the model parameters learned in a different setting in a new one. Transfer learning can improve learning in three measures

- The initial performance in the target envrionment: By using only the transferred knowledge, initial performance obtained in the target house can be higher compared to the initial performance of starting from scratch.

- The amount of time it takes to fully learn the new set of parameters: The amount of time needed to achieve the same level of performance is less when using the transferred knowledge.

- Final performance: The highest achievable performance in the new home compared to the final level that can be achieved without transfer can be higher.

In transfer learning, there are two components, a domain and a task. The *domain* consists of two components: a feature space $\mathcal{X}$ and a marginal probability distribution $P(X)$. In general, if two domains are different, then they may have different feature spaces or different marginal probability distributions. The *task* is composed of a label space $\mathcal{Y}$ and a predictive function $f(.)$ which is not observed but can be learned from the training data. In my case, there is a single task, which is classifying the activities. On the other hand, every different house's data that have been obtained from an earlier setting correspond to different domains. These are also called the source domains, and the feature space and marginal probability distribution for the target house is called the target domain. This specific type of transfer learning is called the transductive transfer learning. In transductive transfer learning, the source and target tasks are the same, while the source and target domains are different. In this situation, no labeled data in the target domain are available while a lot of labeled data in the source domain are available. In addition, according to different situations between the source and target domains, we can further categorize the transductive transfer learning setting into two cases.

1. The feature spaces between the source and target domains are different

2. The feature spaces between domains are the same but the marginal probability distributions of the input data are different

The former case corresponds to differences in the layout of houses and the sensor settings and the latter case corresponds to the differences in the behaviour of the residents in each house. My research will mainly focus on these two problems.

4. CONCLUSION AND FUTURE WORK

My research focuses on human behaviour recognition in ambient assisted living environments where multimodal interaction is essential. This research will contribute to the community in several aspects. To begin with, we provide two rich human behaviour datasets that have been collected from two real smart homes under naturalistic settings. The real-world setting rather than a laboratory setting is important in developing naturalistic interfaces for real human behaviour. Since annotated datasets are extremely hard to obtain, the collected datasets are made public for community to benefit.

Secondly, the evaluation of different methods on provided benchmark data sets from a behaviour monitoring perspective rather than a machine learning perspective is important for revealing the actual application level performance which is directly related with the interaction of the system with the users. For this purpose, we propose using specialized evaluation mechanisms that reflects the activity level performance rather than time-slice level performance.

Thirdly, interaction in multi-resident environments requires identification of individual behaviour for each resident. I propose using factorial hierarchical hidden Markov model for this case. In order to eliminate the training problems with limited annotated datasets, I will consider using variational learning and mean field approximations. Furthermore, I will also use simpler models such as influence models and compare the performances [17].

Finally, I aim developing novel learning methods that will enable ambient assisted living systems to be automatically adapt to new settings, hence paving the way to world wide deployment. To this end, the next steps of my studies will focus on accurate modelling and differentiating everday human activities in multi-resident smart environments. I will also use advanced methods like nonparametric Bayesian models and unsupervised learning techniques.

5. ACKNOWLEDGMENTS

I would like to thank my advisor, Prof Cem Ersoy, for his guidance and Boğaziçi University Research Fund for the grant number 8684.

6. REFERENCES

[1] H. Alemdar and C. Ersoy. Wireless sensor networks for healthcare: A survey. *Computer Networks*, 54(15):2688 – 2710, 2010.

[2] H. Alemdar, H. Ertan, O. D. Incel, and C. Ersoy. ARAS Human Activity Datasets in Multiple Homes with Multiple Residents. In *7th International Conference on Pervasive Computing Technologies for Healthcare*, pages 232 – 235, Venice, Italy, May 2013.

[3] H. Alemdar, T. van Kasteren, and C. Ersoy. Using active learning to allow activity recognition on a large scale. In *International Joint Conference on Ambient Intelligence (AmI'11)*, Amsterdam, November 2011.

[4] K. Altun, B. Barshan, and O. Tunc. Comparative study on classifying human activities with miniature inertial and magnetic sensors. *Pattern Recognition*, 43:3605–3620, 2010.

[5] M. Buettner, R. Prasad, M. Philipose, and D. Wetherall. Recognizing daily activities with RFID-based sensors. In *Proceedings of the 11th international conference on Ubiquitous computing*, pages 51–60. ACM, 2009.

[6] B. Cheng, Y. Tsai, G. Liao, and E. Byeon. HMM machine learning and inference for Activities of Daily Living recognition. *The Journal of Supercomputing*, 54:29–42, 2010.

[7] D. J. Cook. Learning setting-generalized activity models for smart spaces. *IEEE Intelligent Systems*, 27(1):32–38, 2012.

[8] R. R. Fletcher, K. Dobson, M. S. Goodwin, H. Eydgahi, O. Wilder-Smith, D. Fernholz, Y. Kuboyama, E. B. Hedman, M.-Z. Poh, and R. W. Picard. iCalm: wearable sensor and network architecture for wirelessly communicating and logging autonomic activity. *IEEE transactions on information technology in biomedicine*, 14(2):215–23, Mar. 2010.

[9] M. Gallissot, J. Caelen, N. Bonnefond, B. Meillon, and S. Pons. Using the multicom domus dataset. Research Report RR-LIG-020, LIG, Grenoble, France, 2011.

[10] S. Gelly, N. Bredeche, and M. Sebag. From factorial and hierarchical hmm to bayesian network: A representation change algorithm. In *Proceedings of the 6th International Conference on Abstraction, Reformulation and Approximation*, pages 107–120, 2005.

[11] J. He, H. Li, and J. Tan. Real-time daily activity classification with wireless sensor networks using Hidden Markov Model. In *International Conference of the IEEE Engineering in Medicine and Biology Society*, volume 2007, pages 3192–5, Jan. 2007.

[12] S. S. Intille, K. Larson, J. S. Beaudin, J. Nawyn, E. M. Tapia, and P. Kaushik. A living laboratory for the design and evaluation of ubiquitous computing technologies. In *In Extended Abstracts of the 2005 Conference on Human Factors in Computing Systems*, pages 1941–1944. ACM Press, 2005.

[13] J. A. Kientz, S. N. Patel, B. Jones, E. Price, E. D. Mynatt, and G. D. Abowd. The Georgia Tech Aware Home. In *HI '08 Extended Abstracts on Human Factors in Computing Systems*, 2008.

[14] B. Longstaff, S. Reddy, and D. Estrin. Improving activity classification for health applications on mobile devices using active and semi-supervised learning. In *4th International Conference on Pervasive Computing Technologies for Healthcare (PervasiveHealth)*, pages 1–7. IEEE, 2010.

[15] National Institute on Aging. Why population aging matters: A global perspective, March 2007.

[16] S. J. Pan and Q. Yang. A Survey on Transfer Learning. *IEEE Transactions on Knowledge and Data Engineering*, 22(10):1345–1359, Oct. 2010.

[17] W. Pan, W. Dong, M. Cebrian, T. Kim, J. Fowler, and A. Pentland. Modeling dynamical influence in human interaction: Using data to make better inferences about influence within social systems. *IEEE Signal Processing Magazine*, 29(2):77–86, March 2012.

[18] A. A. Salah, T. Gevers, N. Sebe, and A. Vinciarelli. Challenges of Human Behavior Understanding. In *Proceedings of the First International Conference on Human Behavior Understanding*, HBU'10, pages 1–12, Berlin, Heidelberg, 2010. Springer-Verlag.

[19] B. Settles and M. Craven. An analysis of active learning strategies for sequence labeling tasks. In *Proceedings of the Conference on Empirical Methods in Natural Language Processing - EMNLP '08*, page 1070, Morristown, NJ, USA, 2008. Association for Computational Linguistics.

[20] T. L. M. van Kasteren, A. Noulas, G. Englebienne, and B. J. A. Kröse. Accurate activity recognition in a home setting. In *Proceedings of the 10th international conference on Ubiquitous computing - UbiComp '08*, page 1, Seoul, South Korea, 2008. ACM Press.

[21] X. Zhu and A. B. Goldberg. *Introduction to Semi-Supervised Learning*. Synthesis Lectures on Artificial Intelligence and Machine Learning. Morgan & Claypool, 2009.

Gaze-Based Proactive User Interface for Pen-Based Systems

Çağla Çığ
Koç University
Istanbul, Turkey
ccig@ku.edu.tr

ABSTRACT

In typical human-computer interaction, users convey their intentions through traditional input devices (e.g. keyboards, mice, joysticks) coupled with standard graphical user interface elements. Recently, pen-based interaction has emerged as a more intuitive alternative to these traditional means. However, existing pen-based systems are limited by the fact that they rely heavily on auxiliary mode switching mechanisms during interaction (e.g. hard or soft modifier keys, buttons, menus). In this paper, I describe the roadmap for my PhD research which aims at using eye gaze movements that naturally occur during pen-based interaction to reduce dependency on explicit mode selection mechanisms in pen-based systems.

Author Keywords: Sketch-based interaction; multimodal interaction; predictive interfaces; gaze-based interfaces; feature representation; multimodal databases

ACM Classification Keywords
H.1.2 **[Models and Principles]**: User/Machine Systems – *Human information processing;* H.5.2 **[Information Interfaces and Presentation]**: *Input devices and strategies, Interaction styles, User-centered design*

INTRODUCTION

People commonly prefer pen and paper for brainstorming, for exchanging ideas with others, or simply for taking notes. Due to this tendency, pen-based user interfaces promise a more intuitive and accessible alternative to traditional graphical user interfaces. Via pen-based interfaces, users can virtually *produce* and *manipulate* various kinds of free-form sketches (e.g. flowcharts, family trees, and electrical circuit diagrams). Some examples to frequently employed virtual manipulation tasks are dragging, maximizing, or minimizing individual sketch parts or scrolling the whole sketch canvas. During a typical interaction scenario, users repeatedly alternate between sketching and these manipulation tasks. However, prior to sketching or performing a manipulation task, users need to specify the intended mode of interaction via various auxiliary mode switching mechanisms (e.g. multi-finger gestures, context/pop-up menus, and external buttons). For example, in pen-enabled smart phones, users are forced to put the pen aside and switch to multi-finger gestures for many tasks (e.g. spread/pinch for zoom in/out and swipe to navigate back/forward). These gestures require the simultaneous use of 2, 3, or even 4 fingers [1] (Figure 1). The necessity of switching between pen and multi-touch input goes against the goal of seamless interaction in pen-based devices.

ICMI '14, November 12 - 16, 2014, Istanbul, Turkey.

http://dx.doi.org/10.1145/2663204.2666287

In this paper, I describe my PhD research plan and progress which is centered around a novel multimodal approach to alleviate dependence on explicit mode switching in pen-based systems. The first part of my PhD research explores whether gaze movements that naturally accompany pen-based user interaction can be used to infer a user's task-related intentions and goals. Based on our preliminary results indicating a connection between gaze movements and pen-based interaction tasks, for the second part of my PhD research, we envision a proactive system capable of actively monitoring user's eye gaze and pen input to detect the intention to switch modes in an online setting, and act accordingly.

Figure 1. Switching between pen and multi-touch input for object manipulation (e.g. image resizing) in pen-enabled smart phones.

RESEARCH OVERVIEW

Our overall approach to gaze-based proactive user interfaces for pen-based systems consists of two parts: offline part where we build our gaze-based virtual task prediction system and online part where we integrate our prediction system to build a proactive user interface. Both parts entail interpreting pen and eye gaze input within a machine learning framework.

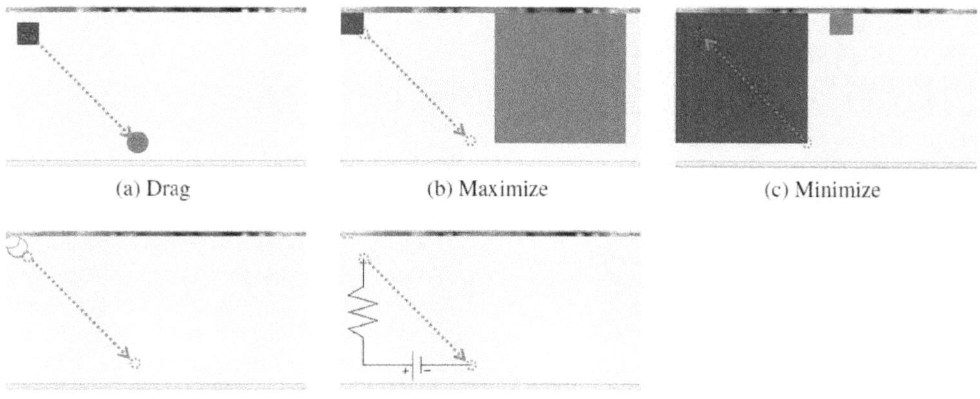

(a) Drag (b) Maximize (c) Minimize (d) Scroll (e) Free-Form Drawing

Figure 2. Pen-based virtual interaction tasks included in our research. Starting and ending regions of desired pen motion in each task are visualized with dotted circles. In the rest of the article, the center points of these regions will be referred to as *anchor points*. Direction of the desired pen motion in each task is visualized with a dotted arrow connecting the starting and ending regions. It is important to note that the dotted visualizations only serve as a reference within this paper and they are not shown to the user during data collection.

This primarily requires large amounts of data for training classifiers. Therefore, initially we have collected sketch and gaze data during a number of pen-based interaction tasks and built a multimodal database. Detailed description and discussion of each part can be found in the following sections.

Multimodal Data Collection (Completed)

We have collected data in a controlled setup where the users were asked to carry out a number of frequently employed pen-based virtual interaction tasks (Figure 2). To create a database composed of synchronized sketch and gaze data, we used a tablet and a Tobii X120 stand-alone eye tracker for the sketch and gaze modalities, respectively. Multimodal data was collected across three different scales to test our system in terms of scale-invariance. The scale variable determines the length of the path connecting the two anchor points present in each task (Figure 2). In light of facts about human vision, lengths of the paths were set to 21 cm, 10.5 cm, and 5.25 cm for the *large*, *medium*, and *small* scales, respectively. We refer to each run of a certain task at a certain scale as *a task instance*. Our multimodal database consists of 1500 task instances collected from 10 participants (6 males, 4 females) over 10 randomized repeats of 5 tasks across 3 scales. This carefully compiled database is the first of its kind, and we believe it will serve as a reference database for future research on the topic.

Offline Part (Ongoing)

Briefly, our task prediction system will be built as follows: We will extract novel gaze-based features from our multimodal database and train a task prediction model using supervised machine learning techniques. These steps will be executed only once. Then, our system will be ready for online prediction.

Novel Gaze-Based Feature Representation

Our system will utilize only two kinds of features for gaze-based task prediction: *Instantaneous Distance Between Sketch and Gaze Positions* and *Within-Cluster Variance of Gaze Positions*. The strength of these features stems from the fact that they eliminate the need for possibly subject- and interface-specific preprocessing steps common in gaze-based systems. Some examples of these common error-prone preprocessing steps include segmentation of gaze data into fixations and saccades and manual specification of regions of interest.

Feature 1: Instantaneous Distance Between Sketch and Gaze Positions

Hand-eye coordination behavior inherent in virtual interaction tasks changes over the course of a task instance as a function of changes in user sub-tasks [2, 3, 4, 5]. The multiple steps of each task can be thought of as consecutive sub-tasks and each sub-task entails a different type of hand-eye coordination behavior. The rationale behind the first feature of our novel gaze-based feature representation is based on this observation and attempts to capture the goal-dependent dynamic aspects of human hand-eye coordination behavior through the evolution of the distance between instantaneous gaze and sketch positions calculated over a task instance.

Consider the task in Figure 2a. In a typical instance of this task, the user is instructed to drag a source object (the blue square) onto a target object (the green circle). The sub-tasks of this task are 1) positioning the pen on the source object, 2) determining the position of the target object and 3) dragging the source object towards the target object. We argue that the dynamic aspects of human hand-eye coordination behavior are reflected in the distance values between instantaneous gaze and sketch positions calculated over time. Figure 3 and Figure 4 generated from the same sample task instance support our argument. Figure 3 gives a visualization of the user's sketch data along with a number of sketch and gaze data samples. Sketch and gaze data points collected at identical time instances are connected with dotted lines. The length of a connection line denotes the value of the sketch-gaze distance feature for the corresponding instance. Figure 4 demonstrates how the value of this feature changes over time. In this figure, the sketch-gaze distance feature is plotted for the same user and same task, over three different scales. Peaks of the plots could conceivably mark the second sub-task during which the user, after having positioned the pen on the source object, is now gazing at the target object. Note that sketch-gaze distance feature expresses similar characteristics across different scales; thus our approach and our novel feature can be generalized and applied to data collected across different scales.

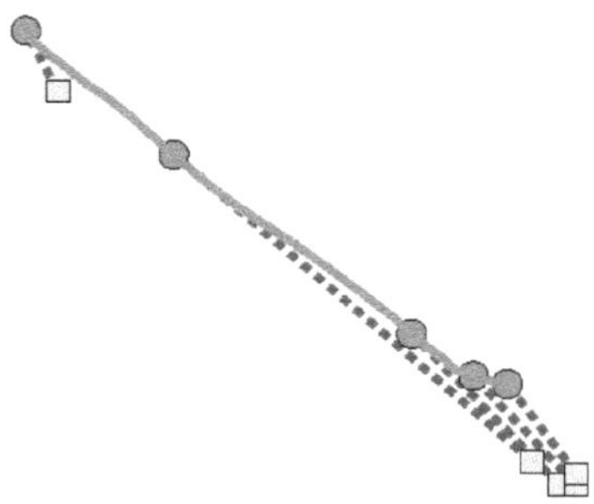

Figure 3. Visualization of the user's sketch data (solid line) along with a number of sketch (circles) and gaze (squares) data samples. Dotted lines connect the instantaneous sketch and gaze sample pairs.

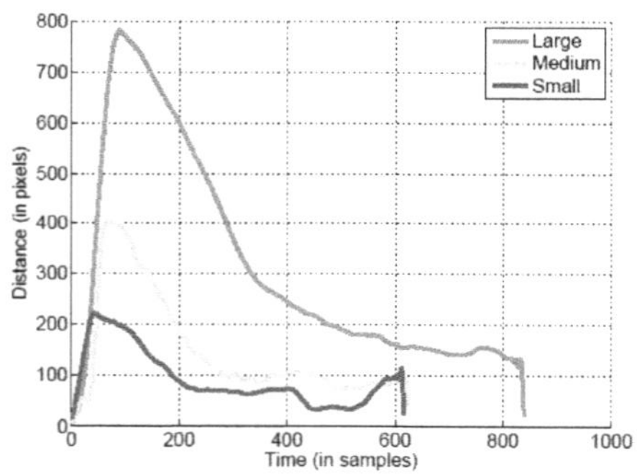

Figure 4. Visualization of the changes in the value of sketch-gaze distance feature as a function of time.

Inspection of the sketch-gaze distance curves for the *drag* task reveals that the rapid rise and gradual decline behavior is typical of all instances of the *drag* task. Similarly, the distance curves for the other tasks also display task-specific characteristic rise and fall behaviors. We will compute distinct sketch-gaze distance curves for each virtual interaction task using sketch-gaze distance curves of all task instances.

Feature 2: Within-Cluster Variance of Gaze Positions

Humans employ two different modes of voluntary gaze shifting mechanism to orient the visual axis. These modes are referred to as saccadic and smooth pursuit eye movements. It is widely accepted that "saccades are primarily directed toward stationary targets whereas smooth pursuit is elicited to track moving targets" [6]. Typical virtual interaction tasks contain both stationary and moving targets. A user's attention can be dominantly directed towards targets of either type depending on the intended task.

Our experiments show that in a typical *drag* task, saccades are more common and the user's attention is drawn from one stationary target which is the initial position of the object currently being dragged to the other stationary target which is the intended position of the object (Figure 5a). Conversely during *free-form drawing* (Figure 5b), smooth pursuit is more common and the user's attention is drawn to the moving target (the newly appearing ink). In saccades, gaze points accumulate around the stationary targets whereas in smooth pursuit, gaze points scatter along the pursuit path. The second feature of our novel gaze-based feature representation is based on these observations, and hence attempts to quantify how the data is structured in terms of saccades and fixations.

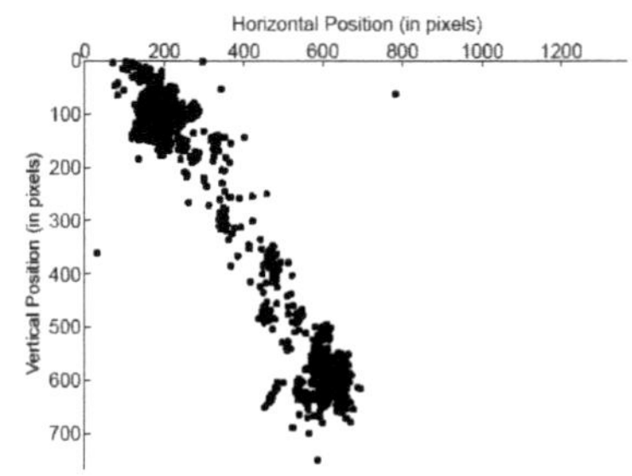

(a) Gaze data for the *drag* task. Saccadic eye movements result in gaze point clusters with low within-cluster variance.

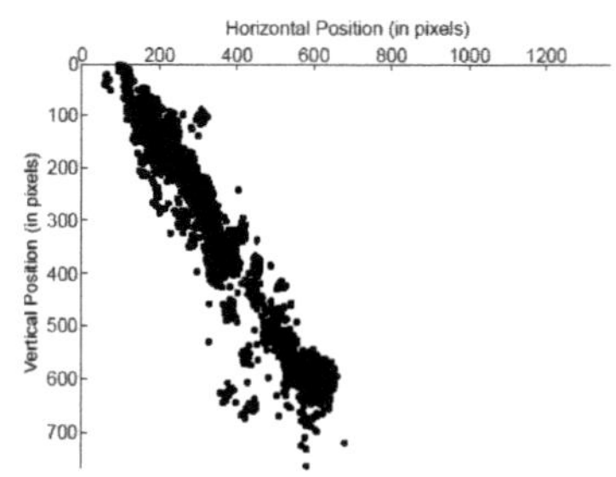

(b) Gaze data for the *free-form drawing* task. Smooth pursuit eye movements result in gaze point clusters with high within-cluster variance.

Figure 5. Gaze data corresponding to 10 repeated task instances of a user.

Intention Prediction and Evaluation

We plan to conduct comprehensive tests to evaluate the effectiveness of the features introduced above in predicting virtual interaction tasks. During evaluation, we will focus on several aspects, including the prediction accuracy and scale-invariance. In addition, we will run feature selection tests to evaluate the relevance and redundancy of the features introduced above.

Practical usage of our prediction system may involve a range of display devices and user interfaces with varying sizes and constraints. Robustness of a feature representation to scale variances is important if we want our prediction system to work equally accurately despite these variances. Therefore, we plan to conduct *scale-invariance tests* to evaluate the robustness of our feature representation to such variances in scale.

We will also compare the prediction power of our novel gaze-based feature representation to that of commonly utilized and well-established sketch-based feature representations in the literature, namely IDM Features [7] and Zernike Moments [8]. Lastly, we will explore whether gaze-based and sketch-based feature representations can be combined via classifier-level or fusion-level fusion methods to increase prediction accuracy.

Online Part (Ongoing)

In the light of preliminary results indicating a connection between gaze movements and pen-based interaction tasks, the second part of our research explores the feasibility of using our prediction system to build a proactive user interface. When the user performs a pen action (demarcated by a pen-down and a pen-up event), the planned proactive user interface will actively detect and switch to the currently intended mode of interaction based on user's synchronized pen trajectory and eye gaze information during pen-based interaction. Intention predictions will be carried out by the previously trained model and the features extracted from the corresponding sketch-gaze data of the user.

The biggest challenge we face here is concerned with providing feedback. In line with the feedback principle of design [9], while the user is performing a pen action, the user interface must provide immediate and appropriate visual feedback about the effects of user's actions and do this without causing any changes in user's natural eye gaze behavior. However, the effects of user's actions depend on user's task-related intentions and goals, which are not known to the interface until the action is completed. Therefore, the interface must provide feedback about user's intentions, from the start to the end of a pen action, without knowing user's intentions. To this end, we propose a proactive user interface approach where effects of all possible actions are visualized simultaneously for the duration of an action. Variety of possible actions at any instant depends on the context and these context-dependent action rules will be defined in the later phases of our research. When the action is finalized, irrelevant effects disappear and only the effects of the predicted action remain visible.

To realize this approach, we introduce a practical application scenario that involves frequent use of all five tasks currently distinguishable by our task prediction system. This scenario that we refer to as *The Categorical Tree Application* is a type of diagramming application that can be used for mind mapping purposes (Figure 6). The application interface consists of rectangles with arbitrary dimensions. These rectangles represent conceptual categories, sub-categories, and sample objects presumably created quickly by the user at the beginning of the mind mapping process. The user's task at this point is to organize the mind map by dragging and resizing rectangles, connecting them as appropriate, and scrolling the application interface if necessary. The user is free to perform these sub-tasks naturally in any desired order, and without any constraints. More importantly, the user does not have to make a specific gesture or locate the correct button to repeatedly switch the interaction mode in-between these sub-tasks.

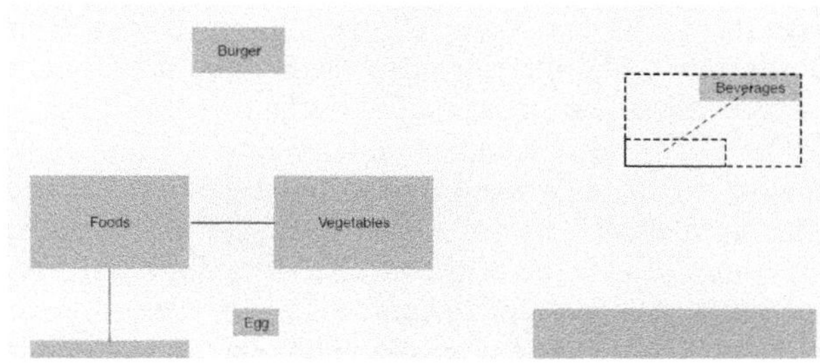

(a) The interface during the pen action on *Beverages* category. Effects of all possible actions (i.e. *drag* and *maximize*) are visualized simultaneously with dotted lines.

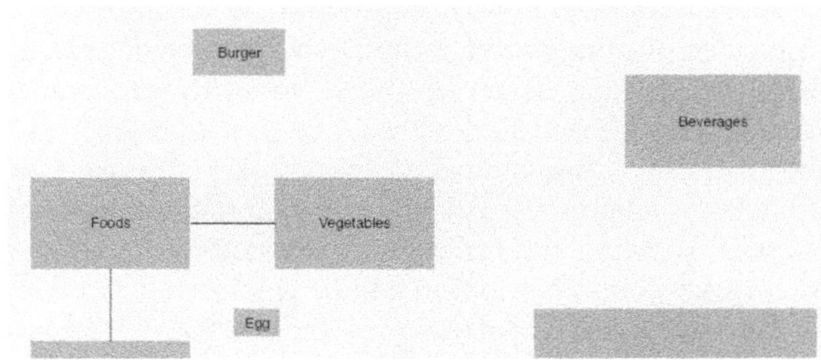

(b) The interface at the end of the pen action visualizing only the effects of the predicted action (i.e. *maximize*).

Figure 6. The Categorical Tree Application. The user is able to issue a *maximize* command without going into the trouble of switching modes beforehand.

CONTRIBUTIONS AND FUTURE WORK

We have proposed a novel multimodal approach to alleviate dependence on explicit mode switching in pen-based systems. This approach initially entails building a gaze-based virtual task prediction system that infers intended user actions by monitoring and analyzing eye gaze movements that users naturally exhibit during pen-based user interaction. Our prediction system will open the way for more natural user interface paradigms where the role of the computer in supporting interaction is to "interpret user actions and [do] what it deems appropriate" [10]. It is widely accepted that intelligent mode selection mechanisms that provide low cost access to different interface operations will dominate new user interface paradigms [11].

Our first contribution is a carefully compiled multimodal dataset that consists of eye gaze and pen input collected from participants completing various virtual interaction tasks. Our second contribution is a novel gaze-based feature representation, which is rooted in our understanding of human perception and gaze behavior. Our feature representation is neither subject- nor interface-specific, and is expected to perform better than common, well-established sketch recognition feature representations in the literature. Our third contribution is expected to be a novel gaze-based task prediction system based on this feature representation that can generalize to variations in task type and scale.

Further experiments will be required to evaluate the usability aspects of our proactive user interface, and compare it to the state of the art mode switching mechanisms in the literature. However, there are a number of major issues we need to address beforehand. First, we need to find a way to handle prediction errors. Although our intention prediction system is expected to be fairly accurate (with a success rate of more than 80%), inaccurate predictions will still be possible. Therefore, further research is required to investigate approaches for detecting and recovering from system errors. Otherwise, users might confuse system errors with user-induced errors and diverge from natural gaze behavior in an effort to avoid them. In turn, this divergence will conceivably reduce the quality of the user's experience with the interface as well as the accuracy of our prediction system that assumes natural user behavior. Second issue we need to address concerns visualization. We envision a proactive user interface where effects of all possible actions are visualized simultaneously until a pen action is finalized and a prediction is made. However, showing the effects of irrelevant actions for the entire duration of a pen action can be cumbersome and lead to a heavily cluttered interface as the number of possible actions increases. In consequence, several questions remain to be addressed with respect to visualization of user's task-related intentions and goals: Can we benefit from eager recognition techniques to avoid waiting until the end of a pen action to make a prediction? Can we use increasing levels of transparency to indicate decreasing likelihoods of a pen action being the intended pen action, i.e. highly probable actions become more emphasized as unlikely actions fade out? Formal user studies will be needed to obtain definitive answers to such questions. Lastly, this research was concerned with pen-based systems; however, the results should be applicable also to other kinds of pointer-based systems that accept stylus, finger, or mouse input. However, more experiments will be needed to verify whether our task prediction system or a similar system inspired by our current findings generalizes well to such systems.

ACKNOWLEDGMENTS

The author would like to thank Dr. T. Metin Sezgin for his invaluable guidance and feedback. The author appreciates the assistance of Eren Sezener regarding the design of the Categorical Tree Application. Financial supports from TÜBİTAK (The Scientific and Technological Research Council of Turkey) under grant number 110E175 and TÜBA (Turkish Academy of Sciences) are gratefully acknowledged.

REFERENCES

1. Samsung Galaxy Note 2 [Online image]. Retrieved September 3, 2014, from http://www.cnet.com/products/samsung-galaxy-note-2/2.
2. Hayhoe, M. and Ballard, D. Eye movements in natural behavior. *Trends in Cognitive Sciences 9*, 4 (2005), 188-194.
3. Fathi, A., Li, Y. and Rehg, J.M. Learning to recognize daily actions using gaze. In *Proc. ECCV 2012*, Springer-Verlag (2012), 314-327.
4. Johansson, R.S., Westling, G., Bäckström, A. and Flanagan, J. R. Eye-hand coordination in object manipulation. *The Journal of Neuroscience 21*, 17 (2001), 6917-6932.
5. Ballard, D.H., Hayhoe, M.M., Li, F., Whitehead, S.D., Frisby, J.P., Taylor, J.G. and Fisher, R.B. Hand-eye coordination during sequential tasks [and discussion]. *Philosophical Transactions: Biological Sciences 337*, 1281 (1992), 331-339.
6. Orban de Xivry, J.-J. and Lefèvre, P. Saccades and pursuit: two outcomes of a single sensorimotor process. *The Journal of Physiology 584*, 1 (2007), 11-23.
7. Ouyang, T.Y. and Davis, R. A visual approach to sketched symbol recognition. In *Proc. IJCAI 2009*, Morgan Kaufmann Publishers Inc. (2009), 1463-1468.
8. Khotanzad, A. and Hong, Y.H. Invariant image recognition by zernike moments. *IEEE Transactions on Pattern Analysis and Machine Intelligence 12*, 5 (1990), 489-497.
9. Norman, D.A. *The design of everyday things.* Basic Books, 2002.
10. Nielsen, J. Noncommand user interfaces. *Communications of the ACM 36*, 4 (1993), 83-99.
11. Negulescu, M., Ruiz, J. and Lank, E. Exploring usability and learnability of mode inferencing in pen/tablet interfaces. In *Proc. SBIM 2010*, Eurographics Association (2010), 87-94.

Appearance Based User-Independent Gaze Estimation

Nanxiang Li
Multimodal Signal Processing (MSP) Laboratory
University of Texas at Dallas
800 W Campbell Rd
Richardson, TX 75080
nxl056000@utdallas.edu

ABSTRACT

An ideal gaze user interface should be able to accurately estimates the user's gaze direction in a non-intrusive setting. Most studies on gaze estimation focus on the accuracy of the estimation results, imposing important constraints on the user such as no head movement, intrusive head mount setting and repetitive calibration process. Due to these limitations, most graphic user interfaces (GUIs) are reluctant to include gaze as an input modality. We envision user-independent gaze detectors for user computer interaction that do not impose any constraints on the users. We believe the appearance of the eye pairs, which implicitly reveals head pose, provides conclusive information on the gaze direction. More importantly, the relative appearance changes in the eye pairs due to the different gaze direction should be consistent among different human subjects. We collected a multimodal corpus (MSP-GAZE) to study and evaluate user independent, appearance based gaze estimation approaches. This corpus considers important factors that affect the appearance based gaze estimation: the individual difference, the head movement, and the distance between the user and the interface's screen. Using this database, our initial study focused on the eye pair appearance eigenspace approach, where the projections into the eye appearance eigenspace basis are used to build regression models to estimate the gaze position. We compare the results between user dependent (training and testing on the same subject) and user independent (testing subject is not included in the training data) models. As expected, due to the individual differences between subjects, the performance decreases when the models are trained without data from the target user. The study aims to reduce the gap between user dependent and user independent conditions.

Categories and Subject Descriptors

H.5 [**Information Interfaces and Presentation**]: Miscellaneous

ICMI'14, November 12–16, 2014, Istanbul, Turkey.

http://dx.doi.org/10.1145/2663204.2666288.

Keywords

User-independent gaze estimation; eigenspace analysis; tensor analysis; domain adaptation

1. INTRODUCTION

Gaze is a fast and natural way to identify the vision attention of the user. Accurate gaze estimation enable human computer interfaces to have targeted and effective interactions[1, 4]. Gaze estimation has drawn attention from many different research communities [7, 11, 13]. An ideal gaze tracking system should be accurate and easy to use. Although accurate wearable eye tracking devices with flexible setting do exist, they come with high cost. Common gaze tracking system requires tedious calibration process or imposes constraints on the users. These constraints are required to estimate parameters related to the subject, data acquisition equipments and system settings. The calibration process usually involves letting the users to look at several reference points while calculating the relative eye movement [5]. Additional constraints, such as limited or no head movement, or wearing a head mount device, are added to ensure the reliability of the calibrated parameters. Without these constraints, calibration process has to be re-estimated whenever the parameter changes (head pose, user position).

Most current gaze estimation approaches focus on feature based methods, where the goal is to extract eye pupil and glint (bright reflection of the active light from the eye). Although good results have been achieved in this direction, this method involves the calibration process and requires both camera and active light source. An alternative direction is the appearance based method where the explicit pupil and iris features estimation is not required. This approach is ideal for the gaze estimation system that we envision, since it can be built with normal webcam. Many appearance-based gaze estimation studies focus on user-dependent conditions that require calibration. Baluja and Pomerleau [2] trained a neural network with the eye images and achieved 1.5° angular error gaze estimation. Tan et al. [14] proposed a local linear interpolation approach in a sparse eye image sample space, which had less than 0.5° angular error in their dataset.

In this proposal, we aim to develop an appearance based user independent gaze approach which eliminates the calibration process. Few studies have addressed user independent gaze estimation. Shiele and Waibel [12] relied on head pose to estimate a coarse gaze direction using neural network. Their result shows 12° angular error on average for the test data. Rikert and Jones [10] considered morphable models to estimate user-independent gaze, and achieved better results. Overall, due to the individual difference, a gap between the user dependent and user independent results is observed. The proposed study aims to reduce this gap. A multimodal corpus (MSP-GAZE) is collected to understand various factors that affect the performance of appearance-based gaze estimation approaches, and to develop robust user independent gaze estimation system.

The primary contributions of this proposal include:

- We collect a novel multimodal corpus (MSP-GAZE) to study and evaluate appearance based gaze estimation methods.
- We study the effect of different factors (individual differences, head movement, distance between the user and the interface's screen) on the appearance based gaze estimation approaches.
- We evaluate different model adaptation strategy to improve the performance of user independent gaze estimation, where no calibration is required. The result of this study can lead to a convenient and practical gaze estimation system for human computer interaction.

2. PRELIMINARY RESULTS

This section summarizes the preliminary results including the description of the MSP-GAZE database, the difference between user dependent and independent gaze estimation results, and our initial attempt to improve the performance of the user independent model by using similarity measures in the eye pair appearance eigenspace.

2.1 MSP-GAZE Database

The MSP-GAZE database is collected in a laboratory setting where sufficient and steady illumination condition is guaranteed. The data collection process involves letting the participants look at and click at randomly projected points displayed on a monitor, and having their glancing behavior and mouse movement recorded. The system includes a regular 22-inch HP monitor, a commercial webcam (Logitich C920) and a Microsoft Kinect sensor. Fig. 1 illustrates the data collection setting and samples of the collected video frames. As shown in the figure, the webcam is placed on top of the monitor and the Kinect sensor is placed below the monitor. Both devices are aligned with the center of the monitor. The webcam and Kinect sensor capture the subject glance behavior from different perspective relative to the field of interest. By comparing the captured data, we can 1) understand and evaluate the effect of camera position; 2) build a robust gaze estimation model using both devices since both the webcam and the Kinect sensor have their own limited view, especially for the vertical gaze position prediction. In addition, the Kinect sensor provides depth estimation which can be used to estimated the user head pose and the distance between the user and the monitor.

A total of 46 students from different disciplines at the University of Texas at Dallas participated in the data collection. The average age of the participants is 22.7 (min 19, max 35). They are balanced between genders. Moreover, they are balanced between a diverse ethnic group including Caucasian, Asian, Indian, and Hispanic. The diverse ethnic

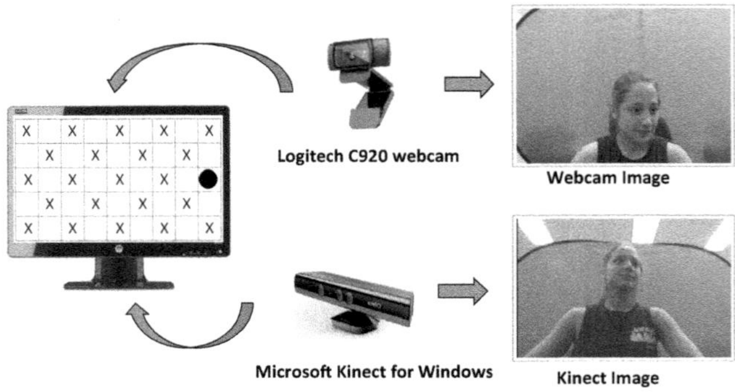

Figure 1: The data collection includes a 22-inch HP monitor, a Logitech C920 webcam and a Microsoft Kinect for Windows. A green screen is placed behind the subject to provide uniform background.

Table 1: Recordings conditions for each session.

Recording	Head Movement	Distance	Pattern
1	Yes	User-defined	Testing
2	Yes	User-defined	Training
3	Yes	Near	Training
4-5	Yes	Medium	Training
6-7	Yes	Far	Training
8	No	User-defined	Testing
9	No	User-defined	Training
10	No	Near	Training
11-12	No	Medium	Training
13-14	No	Far	Training

representation introduces a variety of facial appearances, allowing us to evaluate the effect of individual differences on the appearance model. To simplify the eye detection process and focus on the gaze estimation modeling, we did not consider the cases where the participant wears glasses.

Each subject participated in 2 data collection sessions, each at different days following the same process. The purpose of collecting data from the same subject on different days is to evaluate the consistency of the appearance model across time. The average interval between the sessions is five days.

Each data collection session consists of 14 recordings with different conditions list in Table 1. The first two recordings are collected under no constrains where the subjects decide the user-monitor distance ("User-defined"). The goal is to mimic the normal user computer interaction for each individual. Recordings 3 to 7 uses predefined user-monitor distance where "Near" is 0.4 meter, "Medium" is 0.5 meters and "Far" is 0.6 meters. Recordings 8 to 14 further add the no head movement constraint, where the subjects are required to fix their head pose. Since head movement and user monitor distance affect the appearance model, the constrained data recordings allow us to evaluate the effect of these factors.

The data collection considered two random point projection schemes, which results in "Training" (recordings 3-7 and 9-14) and "Testing" (recordings 1 and 8) recordings. The "Training" projection pattern emphasizes the coverage of the monitor screen (as mush as possible) such that a full mapping between the eye appearance and different ground truth gaze position can be established. We achieve this by dividing the screen into a 5 by 9 grid and projecting points randomly inside the 23 highlighted grids (marked with 'X' in Fig. 1). As shown in the figure, the 23 grid span the whole screen area vertically and horizontally. In addition, we design the projection process in a way that each of the 23 grids is visited 4 times, generating 92 total random points in each "Training" recording. For the "Testing" projection pattern, the purpose is to evaluate the gaze estimation performance thus does not consider any constraints. Points are randomly projected over the whole screen. A detailed description can be found in Li and Busso [6]. Notice that similar point projection patterns have been used in previous studies [8, 9, 14].

2.2 Appearance-Based PCA Approach

We considered the eye pair image to build the appearance model since it implicitly models the head pose. Also, detecting eye pair is more robust than single eye detection. We use the implementation of Viola-Jones objection detection in the *open computer vision library* (OpenCV) to automatically extract the eye pairs from the collected video frames [3]. We only consider the video frames when the user clicks on the projected point (3 frames before and after the mouse click) during which the mapping between the eye appearance and the projected point is accurate.

Using these extracted eye pair images, we build an orthonormal basis of the eye pair appearance. The orthogonal basis corresponds to the eigenvectors of the covariance matrix Σ estimated from the training images. The projections onto the PCA basis are regarded as a compact representation of the eye appearance, thus can be used to train a regression model to predict the gaze position (screen's coordinates). Two linear regression models are separately built to estimate the gaze position in the horizontal (x) and vertical (y) coordinates.

Under matched training/testing settings (user-screen distances and head movement), we evaluate the performance using the correlation between the ground truth and the prediction (ρ_x, ρ_y), as well as the average between the two (ρ).

This evaluation was done for both user-dependent (training and testing on the same subject) and user independent (training and testing on different subjects) conditions. For the user independent result, we use a *leave-one-subject-out* (LOSO) cross-validation approach, where in each fold we train with data from all subjects , with the exception of the test subject. Table 2 lists the results. It shows that the proposed approach is not affected much by the subject's head motion. The evaluations with and without head movements provide similar gaze estimation performance. We also notice that the distance between the user and the computer monitor has little affect on the accuracy of the system. In addition, we evaluate the consistency of the subject dependent model across time, where the data in one session is trained and tested on another session. We observed similar performance between the two. Overall, the consistent results under different conditions show promising potential for human computer interaction applications.

A better measurement of the gaze estimation performance is the angular error θ_{error}. Accurate estimation of θ_{error} requires accurate measurement of the distance between the eyes and monitor. As the future work, we will use the Kinect depth image to estimate the user to the monitor distance d_{u-mc}. Using this information, along with the fact that the users' eye center is aligned with the monitor center, we can estimate the angular error θ_{error} by the following equation:

$$\theta_{error} = \cos^{-1}(\frac{d_{u-tp}^2 + d_{u-pp}^2 - d_{error}^2}{2d_{u-tp}d_{u-pp}}) \quad (1)$$

where d_{u-tp} and d_{u-pp} stand for the distance between the user eye center to the true gaze point and the predicted gaze point, respectively. d_{error} stands for the distance between the true gaze point and the predicted gaze point. This calculation is based on the *Law of Cosine*, where the triangle is formed by the user eye center, the true gaze position and the predicted gaze position. Notice that d_{u-tp} and d_{u-pp} can be estimated by the *Pythagorean theorem*, as shown in the following equations,

$$d_{u-tp} = \sqrt{d_{u-mc}^2 + d_{mc-tp}^2} \quad (2)$$

$$d_{u-pp} = \sqrt{d_{u-mc}^2 + d_{mc-pp}^2} \quad (3)$$

where d_{mc-tp} and d_{mc-pp} stand for the distance between the monitor center to the true gaze point and the predicted gaze point.

2.3 Similarity Measures in the Eye Pair Appearance Eigenspace

Due to individual difference between the users, usually the appearance based gaze estimation approach does not consider user independent case. This effect is clearly shown in Table 2 where the results of user independent models is worse than the user dependent models. In our case, the differences between subjects affects the eye pair image covariance matrix Σ, from which we derive the orthogonal basis representation of the test subject eye appearance. One way to reduce this difference is to predict the test subject gaze using a subset of training samples $\mathcal{S}$ that have similar eye appearance as the test subject. Following this direction, we propose to find similar training data to the test subject eye appearance, and build the target subject image covariance matrix $\Sigma_{\mathcal{S}}$ using the selected data samples $\mathcal{S}$.

We first estimate the covariance matrix using all the training data, which we referred to as Σ_{All}. For any test subject eye appearance, we search for similar training eye appearance images in the eigenspace defined by Σ_{All}. Specifically, we use the projection of the images to the top 30 eigenvectors of Σ_{All} as a compact representation in a 30 dimension space, and calculate the Euclidean distance between the projected 30D coordinates to measure the similarity between images. Fig. 2 shows the nearest neighbor training sample of two given test images. Although the difference between the selected training sample and test subject exists, they both show similar gaze directions. In fact, the ground truth gaze positions associated with the selected training samples and the test image are very close, with (68, 160) for Fig. 2(a) and (75, 99) for Fig. 2(b), (1600, 967) for Fig. 2(c) and (1526, 931) for Fig. 2(d).

Based on the similar training sample search scheme, we consider two ways to define $\mathcal{S}$: similar n frames and similar n subjects. The similar n frames method considers n nearest neighbors of the given test image in the eigenspace of Σ_{All}, while the similar n subjects method considers all training samples from the n subjects that have the closest average distance to the test image in the eigenspace of Σ_{All}.

Table 2: **Appearance based PCA gaze estimation results.**

	User Dependent						User Independent					
	Without head motion			With head motion			Without head motion			With head motion		
Distance	ρ_x	ρ_y	ρ	ρ_x	ρ_y	ρ	ρ_x	ρ_y	ρ	ρ_x	ρ_y	ρ
Near	0.90	0.85	0.87	0.91	0.84	0.87	0.85	0.76	0.81	0.87	0.75	0.81
Medium	0.89	0.84	0.87	0.91	0.83	0.87	0.86	0.75	0.81	0.85	0.74	0.79
Far	0.88	0.83	0.86	0.90	0.83	0.87	0.85	0.68	0.77	0.85	0.73	0.79
User-Defined	0.89	0.82	0.86	0.88	0.82	0.85	0.85	0.78	0.82	0.86	0.70	0.78

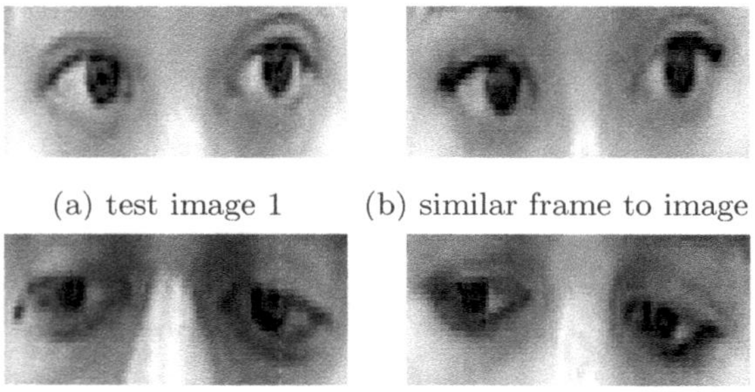

(a) test image 1 (b) similar frame to image 1

(c) test image 2 (d) similar frame to image 2

Figure 2: Two testing images and their closer patches in the training set, as measured by the Euclidean distance in the projected eigenspace.

Table 3: User-independent gaze estimation results. The reduced set $\mathcal{S}$ includes images from either the top 7 similar *subjects*, or the top 100 similar *frames*. (W: with head motion; W/O: without head motion).

		W/O		W	
	Distance	ρ_x	ρ_y	ρ_x	ρ_y
Subjects	Far	0.90	0.79	0.88	0 .72
	Medium	0.93	0.82	0.90	0.74
	Near	0.93	0.87	0.93	0.78
	User-Defined	0.91	0.78	0.88	0.74
Frames	Far	0.90	0.81	0.88	0.72
	Medium	0.92	0.80	0.90	0.74
	Near	0.93	0.82	0.93	0.77
	User-Defined	0.92	0.81	0.90	0.76

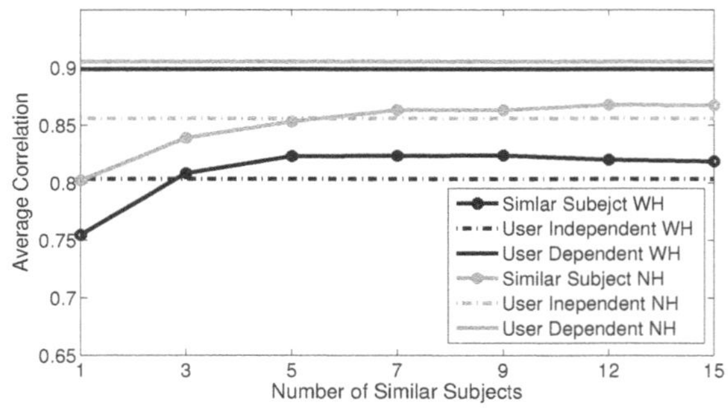

(a) Similar subject approach

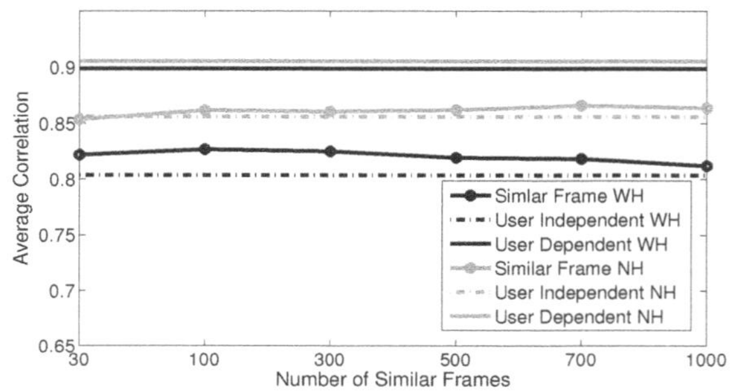

(b) similar frame approach

Figure 3: Evaluation of the training scheme implemented with similar *subjects* and similar *frames*.

We evaluate the proposed approach with different n values for both the similar n frames (n =30, 100, 300, 500, 700, 1000) and similar n subjects (n =1, 3, 5, 7, 9, 12, 15). The average correlation $\rho = \frac{\rho_x+\rho_y}{2}$ across different settings is shown in Figure 3. In the figure, we also highlight the performance of user dependent and independent models with straight lines. The goal of the proposed study is to achieve performance close to the dotted straight line (user dependent model). We observe that both similar search models can achieve better result than the user independent model. The best performance is achieved when n = 100 for similar n frames and n =7 for the similar n subjects, respectively.

Between the similar n frames and similar n subjects methods, it appears that the n similar frames scheme has better performance. One interesting result about the n similar frames approach is that it achieve better performance in terms of angular error when the subjects were free to move their head. This finding suggests that the selected training images have similar head pose as the test subject, improving the accuracy of the gaze detection system. (see Fig. 2).

Table 3 shows the correlation (ρ_x, ρ_y) results where the best performance is achieved with 100 similar frames and with 7 similar subjects. As observed before, similar frame approach performs slightly better than the similar subject approach, especially when the setting is with head movement. Although the results are still lower than the ones observed for user-dependent case, we observe an improved performance using the proposed method, compared with the results for use-independent case. We expect further improvement when more subjects are involved in the training set (i.e., finding better matches leading to better gaze estimation).

3. PROPOSED RESEARCH PLAN

We consider the following three directions to reduce the gap between the user dependent and independent models:

- **Incoorperate multimodal dataset**

  The MSP-GAZE corpus contains data collected from both a webcam and Kinect sensor. Although the study

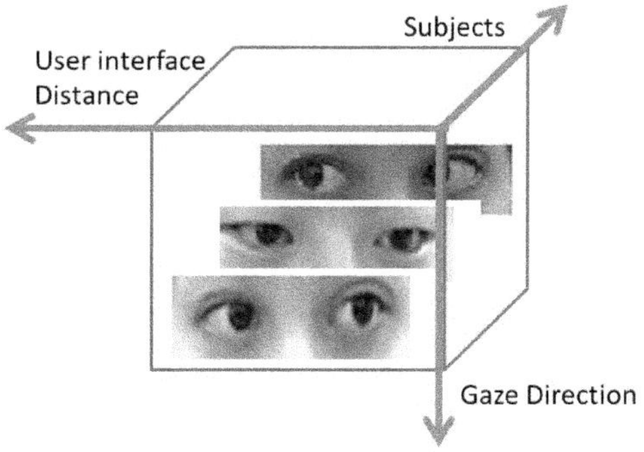

Figure 4: Tensor decomposition of the gaze data.

so far only considered the webcam images, the Kinect sensor provides additional RGB image and depth information. The RGB image is captured from a different angle and can be used to improve the robustness of the captured eye pair appearance. We believe it will be helpful for the vertical gaze estimation since the Kinect sensor is placed below the screen, see Figure 1. The depth information can be used to estimate the head pose, and distance between the monitor and the participant.

In addition, We can also include the mouse click and mouse movement information to refine and update the gaze prediction result. For the human computer interaction, mouse click provide useful information about the visual interest of the user.

- **Tensor analysis**

  The MSP-GAZE corpus include various factors: gaze direction, individual difference, head movement, and distance between the user and the interface's screen. Since most of these factors are labeled (the last two parameters can be estimated from the kinect depth data), we can apply tensor analysis to decompose the database into the multiple subspaces, each corresponding to a particular factor. Figure 4 illustrate the idea. The subspace learnt by the training data have better representation than the PCA approach, thus it can improve the user independent gaze estimation.

- **Domain adaptation**

  General machine learning approaches assume same underlying distribution between the training and testing data. In our case, it may not be true due to individual difference. To be specific, the PCA of Σ_{All} and Σ_{Target} may not represent similar variation factors in the dataset. Domain adaptation approaches consider both shared or no shared support between source and target data, and aims to use the unlabeled data from the target domain to help learning. The idea of user-independent gaze estimation is very much in line with this concept. In particular, it belongs to the learning under covariance shift problems, where the goal is to adapt the covariance Σ_{All} to be as close as possible to Σ_{Target}. Our initial approach tries to estimate Σ_{Target} with Σ_S where training data are selected based on the similarity to the target data. We believe different domain adaptation approaches can be considered for this problem. Since it requires unlabeled test data, this approach is suitable for online user-independent gaze estimation.

4. REFERENCES

[1] G. Anders. Pilot's attention allocation during approach and landing- eye-and head-tracking research in an a 330 full flight simulator. *Focusing Attention on Aviation Safety*, 2001.

[2] S. Baluja and D. Pomerleau. Non-intrusive gaze tracking using artificial neural networks. Technical Report CMU-CS-94-102, Carnegie Mellon University, Pittsburgh, PA, USA, January 1994.

[3] M. Castrillón, O. Déniz, C. Guerra, and M. Hernández. ENCARA2: Real-time detection of multiple faces at different resolutions in video streams. *Journal of Visual Communication and Image Representation*, 18(2):130–140, April 2007.

[4] C. Ghaoui. *Encyclopaedia of Human Computer Interaction*. ITPro collection. Idea Group Reference, 2006.

[5] D. Hansen and Q. Ji. In the eye of the beholder: A survey of models for eyes and gaze. *IEEE Transactions on Pattern Analysis and Machine Intelligence*, 32(3):478–500, March 478-500.

[6] N. Li and C. Busso. Evaluating the robustness of an appearance-based gaze estimation method for multimodal interfaces. In *International conference on multimodal interaction (ICMI 2013)*, pages 91–98, Sydney, Australia, December 2013.

[7] Y. Matsumotot, T. Ino, and T. Ogsawara. Development of intelligent wheelchair system with face and gaze based interface. In *IEEE International Workshop on Robot and Human Interactive Communication*, pages 262–267, Bordeaux and Paris, France, September 2001.

[8] Y. Ono, T. Okabe, and Y. Sato. Gaze estimation from low resolution images. In *Advances in Image and Video Technology*, pages 178–188. Springer, 2006.

[9] T. Proscevičius, V. Raudonis, A. Kairys, A. Lipnickas, and R. Simutis. Autoassociative gaze tracking system based on artificial intelligence. *Electronics and Electrical Engineering.-Kaunas: Technologija*, (5):101, 2010.

[10] T. Rikert and M. J. Jones. Gaze estimation using morphable models. In *IEEE International Conference on Automatic Face and Gesture Recognition (FG 1998)*, pages 436–441, Nara, Japan, April 1998.

[11] D. Salvucci and J. Anderson. Intelligent gaze-added interfaces. In *SIGCHI conference on Human Factors in Computing Systems (CHI 2000)*, pages 273–280, The Hague, The Netherlands, April 2000.

[12] B. Schiele and A. Waibel. Gaze tracking based on face-color. In *International Workshop on Automatic Face-and Gesture-Recognition*, pages 344–349, Zurich, Switzerland, June 1995.

[13] H. Skovsgaard, J. Mateo, and J. Hansen. Evaluating gaze-based interface tools to facilitate point-and-select tasks with small targets. *Behaviour & Information Technology*, 30(6):821–831, 2011.

[14] K. Tan, D. Kriegman, and N. Ahuja. Appearance-based eye gaze estimatio. In *IEEE Workshop on Applications of Computer Vision (WACV 2002)*, pages 191–195, Orlando, FL, USA, December 2002.

Affective Analysis of Abstract Paintings Using Statistical Analysis and Art Theory

Andreza Sartori
DISI, University of Trento, Italy - Telecom Italia - SKIL, Trento, Italy
Via Sommarive, 18 38123 Povo
andreza.sartori@disi.unitn.it

ABSTRACT

A novel approach to the emotion classification of abstract paintings is proposed. Based on a user study, we employ computer vision techniques to understand what makes an abstract artwork emotional. Our aim is to identify and quantify which are the emotional regions of abstract paintings, as well as the role of each feature (colour, shapes and texture) on the human emotional response. In addition, we investigate the link between the detected emotional content and the way people look at abstract paintings by using eye-tracking recordings. A bottom-up saliency model was applied to compare with eye-tracking in order to predict the emotional salient regions of abstract paintings. In future, we aim to extract metadata associated to the paintings (e.g., title, keywords, textual description, etc.) in order to correlate it with the emotional responses of the paintings. This research opens opportunity to understand why a specific painting is perceived as emotional on global and local scales.

Categories and Subject Descriptors

J.5 [**Computer Applications**]: Arts and Humanities - fine arts; I.2 [**Artificial Intelligence**]: Vision and Scene Understanding; H.3.1 [**Information Search and Retrieval**]: Content Analysis and Indexing

General Terms

Algorithms, Experimentation, Theory, Human-Computer Interaction

Keywords

Visual Art; Abstract Paintings; Emotion Recognition; Eye tracking; Metadata.

1. INTRODUCTION

The growing number of digitalized images has raised the request for automated tools to support efficient search of images. Several studies are trying to address this problem with the use of textural indexing and Content-Based Image Retrieval Systems (CBIR), in which CBIR is mostly based on low-level features such as colours, textures and shapes [17]. However, when humans query images often use complex and emotional aspects to describe them. This gap between the human perception and emotion of images and the interpretation computed by the machine, is one of the main challenges of computer vision and multimedia community [15].

The study of emotions conveyed by images and artworks has been an active topic not only in psychology and visual art research, but also from a computational point of view. Moreover, there is an increase of interest on understanding the link between the emotional responses by humans and the low-level features in images [15]. These low-level features, i.e., colour, shape, texture, are particularly used by artists on abstract paintings to depict emotion.

Since a painting can be considered as a combination between the emotions the artist meant to depict and the emotional interpretation from the viewer, we believe that a computational approach on emotion recognition of abstract paintings can lead to a new perspective in art theory. Moreover, such an approach can enrich computer vision techniques by understanding emotional patterns and structures of images.

However, some challenges come into question: what makes an abstract artwork to be perceived as emotional by the viewer? How a machine can learn which are the low-level features that can explain the emotional responses conveyed by a painting? Why people prefer to look at some specific regions of paintings? Can computer predict the emotional regions of the abstract paintings?

In my PhD thesis, I aim to incorporate the extended studies of art theory and psychology to computer vision techniques in order to automatically recognize and classify the emotions conveyed in abstract paintings. Our approach, based on empirical studies, presents a significant contribution to identify and quantify emotional valence regions of abstract paintings. Moreover, we employ an in-deep analysis of the effects of texture on emotional responses. An analysis of colour combination and metadata associated to the painting is being conducted. In addition, we present a study of the viewer's eye movements while looking at paintings, which shows the regions where people prefer to look. We also applied a computational model of attention to predict attention on the abstract paintings. This study offers a useful addition not only to the psychological and art theory point of view, but also for computer vision and human-computer interaction.

ICMI '14, November 12 - 16 2014, Istanbul, Turkey

http://dx.doi.org/10.1145/2663204.2666289.

2. RELATED WORK

Emotion can be defined as the physiologic and psychological effect caused by human mind and behaviour in a determined context [1]. During the past century philosophers and psychologists proposed theories of emotions which still today continue to support the research in this area. Currently, two of the most popular psychological approaches to classify emotions are used: discrete and dimensional. The discrete approach categorizes emotion in six basic emotional groups: happiness, sadness, anger, fear, surprise and disgust [2]. In the dimensional approach, emotions are categorized along arousal and valence dimensions [20]. Arousal delimitate the intensity of emotion, and valence measures the positive and negative emotions. The current works on emotional categorization of artworks and images points out as advantages of using the dimensional approach the disambiguation of the emotional states and the consistency with the way the brain processes emotion [13, 12, 15, 19]. This work applies the dimensional approach of emotion. We use positive and negative valence to quantify the emotional message evoked by the paintings.

Several works had observed that emotions are directly associated with human attention, perception and memory. The growing need for intelligent tools for image retrieval and the advance of technology to detect physiological human signals, developed the interest on the computer vision and multimedia community in detecting emotional information [8]. The emotional categorization of images is considered a significant support to bridge the *semantic gap* between the high level emotions from humans and the low-level features computed by the machine[22] as well as allows for improvements in human-computer interaction [21].

Many psychological approaches attempts to understand the human perception, in order to interpret the art appreciation and the emotional responses conveyed in paintings. Leder et al.[13] conducted an empirical analysis of how art is appreciated based on the level of expertise in art of the participants, the different classes of artworks (Abstract, Modern and Classic), the measure of emotion (valence and arousal) and the artwork comprehension. Their results showed that emotion is the strongest predictor of art appreciation, independently of styles of art and the expertise of people.

Recently, there is an increase of interest of computer vision and multimedia research on the automatic emotion recognition of artworks. The main reason relies on that artworks are specifically composed to convey emotions. Yanulevskaya et al. [28] proposed an approach based on assessment of local image statistics, which applied supervised learning of emotion categories using Support Vector Machines to provide an emotion categorization system of paintings. The work of Machajdik and Hanbury [17] combined concepts of psychology and art theory with low-level features to categorize emotionally images. Lu, et al. [15] investigate through statistical analysis how shapes are related to emotions in natural images. The works of [28], [17], and [15] conducted experiments to measure the performance of their methods on the International Affective Picture System (IAPS). The IAPS is an image collection annotated and categorized based on semantic and psychological concepts [9].

A recent work [30] applied multiple kernel learning framework for affective classification of digital abstract art images. These studies concentrate on detecting emotions evoked by artworks as a whole. In our work we apply computer vision techniques to identify the emotional parts of abstract paintings.

3. PROPOSED METHODOLOGY

Most of the aforementioned related work identifies emotional features in standard datasets of semantically rich images. In this research we investigate the emotional responses evoked in abstract artworks. When the artist composes an abstract artwork, he uses lines, shapes, colour and texture to depict emotion. These artworks are composed by forms that are detached from the natural and historical context, which mean these paintings have no semantic content. We use computer vision techniques to analyse the same features (colour, shapes and texture) used by the artist, in order to understand the emotions depicted in abstract artworks. To validate our findings and to understand which the most emotional regions of the paintings are, we investigate the interaction between the viewer and the paintings by applying an eye-tracking study [29].

This research concentrates on abstract paintings in order to learn how low-level features evoke emotions and how they influence the emotional responses of paintings. In addition, we used the state-of-the-art of computer vision techniques which are effective on extracting the exact features used by the artist to convey emotion. We do not concentrate on figurative paintings as it would be necessary to apply different approaches and different studies of emotions as humans would be influenced by the semantic content.

3.1 Emotion Recognition of Professional and Amateur Abstract Paintings

To analyse how abstract artworks affect emotionally people, we conducted a set of experiments with two datasets of abstract paintings. The first dataset is composed by a collection of 500 professional abstract artworks from the electronic archive of Museum of Modern and Contemporary Art of Trento and Rovereto (MART) [29]. The second dataset is an amateur collection of 500 abstract paintings from deviantArt, an online social network dedicated to user-generated art.

As a first study, 100 people was recruited and were asked to rate in 1-7 Likert scale the paintings of MART dataset in positive and negative emotions. In this Absolute Scale of annotation, the score 1 meant highly negative and the score 7 highly positive. In a second study a Relative Scale annotation was applied, in which people were asked to choose the more positive paintings out of two. This experiment was conducted for both MART dataset and for deviantArt dataset. In this study it was applied the True Skill ranking system [4] in order to optimally rank the paintings from the most positive to the most negative. In addition, a third study was conducted to analyse the emotional responses, positive and negative, invoked by MART dataset with no hue value.

These studies allow us to set a ground truth of which abstract painting conveys which emotion. For Absolute Scale Annotation an average for each painting over all scores is computed. The paintings with average score equal or lower than 4 was considered as negative and the average score higher than 4 was defined as positive. For Relative Scale Annotation, as each painting was compared 15 times, the True Skill score of the painting chosen 8 times as the more positive was considered as threshold.

3.2 Colour and Texture: Feature Extraction

In order to train a classifier to distinguish paintings between positive and negative emotions, we apply a standard Bag-of-Visual-Words classification framework. Our approach is based on colour LAB visual words and texture SIFT visual words.

The LAB colour space is a 3 dimension space where L represent the lightness and a and b the colour-opponent dimensions of an image. We use LAB colour space as it corresponds closely to the human brain-eye system. To map LAB descriptors to visual words, we quantize the colour space into 343 different colours by dividing uniformly each colour into 7 different levels.

The SIFT descriptor, Scale-Invariant Feature Transform, describes the local distribution of contours, edges and textures within images [14]. We take local patches of 16-by-16 pixels sampled at every single pixel. From these patches we extract grey-scale SIFT descriptors and two colour variants, RGB-SIFT and RGI-SIFT as recommended by van de Sande *et al.* [24]. To create a visual vocabulary we quantize 250,000 randomly selected SIFT descriptors into 4096 clusters using a hierarchical implementation of k-means clustering [26].

For both annotation approaches, Absolute and Relative Scale, we train a Support Vector Machine with a Histogram Intersection Kernel for supervised learning of [18]. We tested our model using a two-fold cross-validation repeated 1,000 times. To analyse the contribution of each type of visual words we separately evaluate the accuracy of the system based on LAB visual words and on SIFT visual words. Then we combine both systems by averaging their classification scores.

Overall, the proposed method performs significantly better than chance level for both professional (MART) and Amateur (deviantArt) datasets of abstract paintings. Our results on MART dataset shows that for both Absolute and Relative Scale annotation, LAB visual words are more effective for emotional classification of abstract paintings compared to SIFT visual words. The combination of LAB and SIFT visual words raises the accuracy for both Absolute Scale (0.764) and Relative Scale (0.772). For deviantArt dataset, the combination of LAB and SIFT raises the accuracy to 0.770. These results indicates that both colour-based LAB visual words and texture-based SIFT visual words are relevant features for emotion recognition in both professional and amateur abstract paintings. Moreover, we observe that both absolute and relative scale annotation methods can provide a reliable ground-truth for a positive/negative emotion recognition task in abstract paintings.

3.2.1 Backprojection

In this research we also apply the backprojection technique of [23] to visualize the positive and negative contribution that comes from each pixel in the painting. With this method we could analyse the regions which convey the most relevant information in the classification task. Figure 1, reports the results for the four highly positive and highly negative paintings. The results shows that dark colours such as black, dark blue and dark green have mostly negative emotional response, while light colours, such as red, yellow, and light blue often evoke positive emotions. Moreover, we observed that positive emotions often come from straight lines and smooth curves. In contrast, chaotic textured regions often evoke negative emotions.

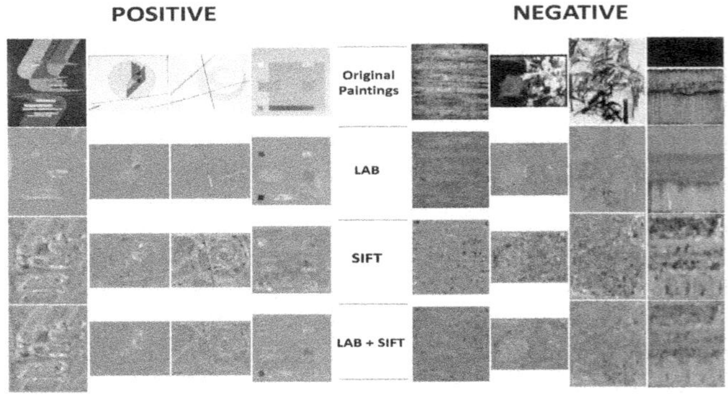

Figure 1: Visualisations of pixel-wise contribution to the classification for highly positive(column 1-4) and highly negative paintings(column 6-9). The original paintings are shown in the first row. The second row displays the contribution of LAB Visual Words, followed by the the contribution of SIFT visual words in row 3. The combination of LAB and SIFT Visual words are displayed in row 4. Yellow colour corresponds to the positive emotional evidence and blue colour corresponds to the negative emotional evidence.(Courtesy of MART photographic archive, Rovereto)

3.3 The Contribution of Colour and Texture

With the previous analysis we observed the importance to look into each feature (colour and textures) and make an indeep study of how these features affect emotionally people on abstract painting. Indeed, we are investigating which are the specific aspects of each feature, in order to understand the emotional interaction between the human and the painting and why abstract paintings convey emotion.

3.3.1 The Role of Textures

To investigate the role of textures on positive and negative emotions on abstract paintings, we use a study from the psychophysics literature that looked into the contribution of texture. In [16], they used synthetic and parameterized textures created with Perlin noise to conduct a user study. With this study they distribute texture in four emotional scales: warmness-coldness, masculinity-femininity, heaviness-lightness, and hardness-softness perception. Then they created a model that maps the Perlin parameters of the image to the feeling it induces.

In this analysis, we derive these parameters for MART dataset by an inverse-Perlin parametrization, and use the psychophysical model proposed in [16] to characterize texture. We did not computed warmness-coldness as it depends on colour. To obtain this parametrization, we derive MR8 texture feature descriptors of [25], and train a classifier that maps these features to the respective Perlin parameters. With this analysis we could observe that the effect of texture is more influential in the hard-soft scale, followed by masculine-feminine, and then heavy-light. The paintings with geometrical composition and pure lines are ranked as soft, and the paintings with complex lines and granular patterns are ranked as hard. We observed a similar pattern in the masculine-feminine distribution, in which dark and chaotic paintings seem to be more masculine, while light and plain designs more feminine.

Moreover we contrasted the results of the annotation conducted with MART dataset in coloured and non-coloured versions. We could observe that there was a small but positive correlation between the emotional responses of subjects (correlation coefficient: 0.3674), even though it was applied the same annotation approach, but with different group of subjects. Our analysis shows that people reacted differently when annotate emotionally greyscale versions of the abstract paintings. In addition, these results suggest that texture by itself has a smaller contribution for the positive and negative emotional valence of coloured paintings compared to the contribution of colour.

3.3.2 The Role of Colours

The precedent work shows that the contribution of colour is more prominent to emotional response than texture. For this reason we aim to analyse the colour combinations of abstract paintings. This study is based on Itten's theory of colour expression, according to which it is observed that it is difficult to define the expressive properties of a colour without relating it to other colours [6]. Indeed, in the theory of colour expression Itten observed two-colour combinations. A study on Itten's theory and an empirical research about emotions in colour combinations are being conducted. The aim of this study is to understand how the combination, amount, position and distance between colours influence the emotion in abstract paintings.

3.4 Visual Attention and Emotional Content

While people are evaluating emotionally the paintings, different regions of the painting may influence the subject in different ways. To identify the most influential regions and the interaction between the viewer and the painting we apply an eye-tracking study. As we have previously identified the emotional parts (positive or negative) conveyed by the abstract paintings, we investigated the correlation between the emotional content and the way people look at paintings.

We recorded eye movements while 9 observers looked at 110 abstract paintings to understand if people prefer to focus at the positive or negative parts of the paintings. The 110 selected paintings were composed by positive, negative, and neutral contribution to the classification (at least 25% of its pixels). We compared the averaged pixel-wise contributions to the classifier from fixated and non-fixated locations. We considered Positive Attention Bias when the average contribution of fixated locations on positive visual words (the combination of LAB and SIFT visual Words) is higher than the non-fixated locations. The opposite situation we called Negative Attention Bias. The attention bias is considered neutral when the average of fixated and non-fixated regions does not differ significantly. Our results showed that there was a positive attention bias when people look at abstract paintings. An eye-tracking analysis of the same paintings in grayscale is planned to do as future work.

In addition, we applied a computational model of attention that can simulate the subject gaze behaviour. The human attention is driven by a bottom-up and top-down principles. Bottom-up is guided by low level properties of the visual stimulus, and top-down is dependant of cognitive factors, such as context, knowledge and tasks [7]. As abstract artworks have low semantic content, and most of the computational models of attention are bottom-up, we expected that the visual attention of abstract painting will be mostly a bottom-up process. To validate our hypothesis, we have compared the predictions of a prominent computational saliency model, implemented by Dirk and Koch [27], with the eye-tracking results obtained on the MART dataset [29].

We use the Fixation Analysis Software of Le Meur [10] to compare predictions of the computational model of attention with the eye fixation data of MART dataset. The Area Under the Curve (AUC) measure, computed from the ROC curve, provides the degree of similarity of fixation points and saliency maps. The AUC value equal to 1.00 indicates a perfect performance, while the AUC equal to 0.50 denotes a random performance. The average AUC between eye-fixation ground truth and simulations of the computational model of attention were 0.93 for coloured paintings and 0.94 for grayscale paintings. With these results we could observe that bottom-up computational model is effective to find the salient locations of abstract paintings. Moreover, the little difference in salient locations for coloured and grayscale paintings can implies that while colour is the dominant feature to evoke emotions, texture dominates in driving the attention of the subject.

3.5 The Contribution of Metadata

Psychological studies observed that titles and description influences the perception of paintings. Some of these works showed that people describe paintings differently after they read the title [3]. Also, they postulate that title and description of paintings can improve the understanding [11] and the aesthetic evaluation [5]. For this reason we believe that the metadata associated with paintings (e.g., title, keywords, description, etc.) are a fundamental characteristic of the emotional interaction between the viewer and the painting.

We plan to extract the correspondent metadata of the paintings and apply Sentiment Analysis to investigate the correlation of positive and negative emotions between the titles, descriptions and abstract paintings. Moreover we plan to do an eye-gaze study to understand the changes on the interactions between the viewer and the painting, as well as how this content influences people emotions while they are looking at abstract paintings.

4. CONCLUSIONS AND FUTURE WORK

This research aims to understand of what makes an abstract artwork emotional. We made an in-deep analysis of the effects of colour and texture in the positive and negative emotions evoked in abstract artworks. This analysis allows us to develop effective methods to predict emotional valence (positive and negative) of paintings with no semantic content. We conducted 2 different user studies, Absolute and Relative Scale annotation, in two distinct collections of abstract paintings, professional and amateur. The professional collection is from MART Museum and the amateur set is from deviantArt social network. We applied advanced computer vision techniques to classify the emotional valence of these abstract paintings. By training a Bag-of-Visual-Words system and by backprojecting the classification evidence, we could visualize which parts of the paintings conveyed positive and negative emotions. With the correlation of the localized emotional evidence with eye movements we could understand where people prefer to look. Our results show that there is a positive attention bias when people look at abstract paintings. Moreover, we investigated the saliency distribution of these paintings, in which shows that computational models of bottom-up attention are effective to predict emotional valence in abstract paintings. The study of preferential biases can be a useful tool to improve interaction between the viewer and the image, in which it can be applied in studies of aesthetics and interestingness of images.

In order to understand the specific characteristics of each feature (colour, texture and shapes), as future steps we plan to investigate each feature separately. We also aim to study the effect of metadata in the emotional responses on abstract paintings by applying Sentiment Analysis approach. Moreover, we plan to apply an eye-gaze study to understand how the metadata content influences the emotional responses. The emotional categorization of paintings can be a powerful support not only to art researches and museum curators, but also can improve the image retrieval and the human-computer interaction, by bridging the semantic gap.

5. ACKNOWLEDGMENTS

I would like to thank my advisor Nicu Sebe for his support in every stage of my PhD.

6. REFERENCES

[1] R. de Sousa. Emotion. In E. N. Zalta, editor, *The Stanford Encyclopedia of Philosophy*. 2012.

[2] P. Ekman. Facial expression and emotion. *American Psychologist*, 48(4):384–392, 1993.

[3] M. B. Franklin, R. C. Becklen, and C. L. Doyle. The influence of titles on how paintings are seen. *Leonardo*, 26, No. 2:103–108, 1993.

[4] R. Herbrich and T. Graepel. Trueskill(tm): A bayesian skill rating system. *no. MSR-TR-2006-80*, 2006.

[5] E. Hristova, S. Georgieva, and M. Grinberg. Top-down influences on eye-movements during painting perception: the effect of task and titles. In *COST 2102*, pages 104–115, 2011.

[6] J. Itten. *The Art of Color: The Subjective Experience and Objective Rationale of Color*. Wiley, 1974.

[7] L. Itti and C. Koch. A saliency-based search mechanism for overt and covert shifts of visual attention. *Vision Research*, 40:1489–1506, 2000.

[8] D. Joshi, R. Datta, E. A. Fedorovskaya, Q.-T. Luong, J. Z. Wang, J. Li, and J. Luo. Aesthetics and emotions in images. *IEEE Signal Process. Mag.*, 28(5):94–115, 2011.

[9] P. J. Lang, M. M. Bradley, and B. N. Cuthbert. International affective picture system (iaps): Affective ratings of pictures and instruction manual. Technical report, University of Florida, 2008.

[10] O. Le Meur and T. Baccino. Methods for comparing scanpaths and saliency maps: strengths and weaknesses. *Behavior Research Methods*, 45(1):251–266, 2012.

[11] H. Leder, C.-C. Carbon, and A.-L. Ripsas. Entitling art: Influence of title information on understanding and appreciation of paintings. *Acta psychologica*, 121(2):176–98, 2006.

[12] H. Leder, G. Gerger, D. Brieber, and N. Schwarz. What makes an art expert? emotion and evaluation in art appreciation. *Emotion & Cognition.*, 28(6):1137–1147, 2014.

[13] H. Leder, G. Gerger, S. G. Dressler, and A. Schabmann. How art is appreciated. *Psychology of Aesthetics, Creativity, and the Arts.*, Vol 6(1), 2012.

[14] D. G. Lowe. Distinctive image features from scale-invariant keypoints. *IJCV*, 60(2):91–110, 2004.

[15] X. Lu, P. Suryanarayan, R. Adams Jr, J. Newman, and J. Wang. On shape and the computability of emotions. In *ACM Multimedia*, 2012.

[16] M. P. Lucassen, T. Gevers, and A. Gijsenij. Texture affects color emotion. *Color Research & Application*, 36(6):426–436, 2011.

[17] J. Machajdik and A. Hanbury. Affective image classification using features inspired by psychology and art theory. In *ACM Multimedia*, pages 83–92, 2010.

[18] S. Maji, A. C. Berg, and J. Malik. Classification using intersection kernel support vector machines is efficient. In *CVPR*, 2008.

[19] E. Pihko, A. Virtanen, V. Saarinen, S. Pannasch, L. Hirvenkari, T. Tossavainen, A. Haapala, and R. Hari. Experiencing art: The influence of expertise and painting abstraction level. *Front Hum Neurosci*, 5, 2011.

[20] J. Russell. A circumplex model of affect. *J. of personality and social psychology*, 39(6):1161–1178, 1980.

[21] N. Sebe, I. Cohen, and T. S. Huang. Multimodal emotion recognition. *Handbook of Pattern Recognition and Computer Vision*, pages 387–410, 2005.

[22] A. W. M. Smeulders, M. Worring, S. Santini, A. Gupta, and R. Jain. Content-based image retrieval at the end of the early years. *PAMI*, 22(12):1349–1380, 2000.

[23] J. R. R. Uijlings, A. W. M. Smeulders, and R. J. H. Scha. The Visual Extent of an Object. *IJCV*, 2012.

[24] K. E. A. van de Sande, T. Gevers, and C. G. M. Snoek. Evaluating color descriptors for object and scene recognition. *IEEE Transactions on Pattern Analysis and Machine Intelligence*, 32(9), 2010.

[25] M. Varma and A. Zisserman. A statistical approach to texture classification from single images. *International Journal of Computer Vision*, 62(1-2):61–81, 2005.

[26] A. Vedaldi and B. Fulkerson. VLFeat – an open and portable library of computer vision algorithms. In *ACM Multimedia*, 2010.

[27] D. Walther and C. Koch. Modeling attention to salient proto-objects. *Neural Networks*, 19:1395–1407, 2006.

[28] V. Yanulevskaya, J. V. Gemert, K. Roth, A. Herbold, N. Sebe, and J. Geusebroek. Emotional valence categorization using holistic image features. In *ICIP*, pages 101–104, 2008.

[29] V. Yanulevskaya, J. Uijlings, E. Bruni, A. Sartori, E. Zamboni, F. Bacci, D. Melcher, and N. Sebe. In the eye of the beholder: employing statistical analysis and eye tracking for analyzing abstract paintings. In *ACM Multimedia*, 2012.

[30] H. Zhang, Z. Yang, M. Gönen, M. Koskela, J. Laaksonen, T. Honkela, and E. Oja. Affective abstract image classification and retrieval using multiple kernel learning. In *Neural Information Processing*, volume 8228 of *Lecture Notes in Computer Science*, pages 166–175. 2013.

The Secret Language of Our Body - Affect and Personality Recognition Using Physiological Signals

Julia Wache
Department of Information Engineering and Computer Science (DISI)
University of Trento, Italy
Julia.Wache@disi.unitn.it

ABSTRACT

We present a novel framework for decoding individuals' emotional state and personality traits based on physiological responses to affective movie clips. During watching 36 video clips we used measures of Electrocardiogram (ECG), Galvanic Skin Response (GSR), facial-Electroencephalogram (EEG) and facial emotional responses to decode i) the emotional state of participants and ii) their Big Five personality traits extending previous work that had connected either *explicit* (user ratings) with some *implicit* (physiological) affective responses or one of them with selected personality traits.

We make the first dataset comprising both affective and personality information publicly available for further research and we further explore different methods and implementations for automated emotion and personality detection for future applications.

Author Keywords

Pattern recognition; Bio-signals; Affective Computing; Emotions; Personality

Categories and Subject Descriptors

H.1.2 [User/Machine Systems]: Human information processing; I.5.2 [Pattern Recognition Design Methodology]: Pattern analysis

INTRODUCTION

With technology developing fast, research constantly aims at improving the interactive working processes of humans and computers in order to facilitate the working experience and improve the interaction with users. One important factor for human behavior is emotion. External cues from the environment as well as internal states and the personality influence emotions that can have a substantial effect on the person's experience and the following actions. A system adapting to user's emotions and personality might enhance the user experience therefore we are interested in analyzing this relationship.

In order to reach the first goal – automated emotion recognition – the emotions need to be detected first. Emotions are psychological phenomena but they also have physiological concomitants that can be measured and analyzed (e.g. [15]). The challenge is to accurately detect physiological changes caused by affective responses and understand the correlations between physiological signals and the emotions of users. Hence it is important to i) choose a method that reliably induces similar specific emotions in people and ii) to select adequate physiological reactions that correlate with those emotions. Multimedia contents such as movies intend to do exactly that, evoke specific emotions in viewers to stimulate a certain emotional experience. In fact, often the emotional experience stimulated is the aspect people value most when selecting and watching a video.

Understanding the affective content of media has been identified as crucial towards enhancing applications such as personalized media recommendation. Affective media tagging has evoked considerable interest among multimedia researchers lately. Varied methodologies have been adopted for characterizing affective media including analysis of the content [5], or the behavior of users viewing emotional content in terms of facial expressions [6] and physiological responses such as brain activity, heart beat rate and skin conductance [2,10,11,16] but so far the influence of personality differences on emotion perception has not been examined by prior affect recognition works. Our work is one of the first to predict personality dimensions through multimodal fusion of users' physiological responses to affective stimuli.

We constructed a database with measurements of 36 users viewing affective movie clips while being monitored by portable sensors measuring heart rate, skin conductance, single-dry EEG activity and facial expression. The measurements were done with commercially available sensors that are portable and should be easy to ignore in order not to influence the spontaneous emotional responses by disturbing them with the set up. As stimuli we used movie clips, as movies are inherently intended to evoke emotions, and certain movie genres such as *thriller*, *comedy* or *horror* are expressly defined by the emotions they evoke.

We use the physiological data not only to be correlated to both emotional reactions and personality traits but we also attempt to train classifiers to predict them.

To our knowledge this work is the first to have the following research contributions:

1. We attempt personality profiling based on implicit user responses to affective multimedia. Personality assessment has traditionally been achieved through the use of questionnaires [12] or by analyzing users' behavior in videos and social media [17]. The methodology we propose could enable simultaneous and automated characterization of affect and personality.
2. We attempt prediction of *all* the big-five factors while using movie stimuli for eliciting emotions.

ICMI '14, November 12 - 16 2014, Istanbul, Turkey

ACM 978-1-4503-2885-2/14/11...$15.00 .
http://dx.doi.org/10.1145/2663204.2666290

3. We focus on the personality-affect relationship, to predict personality traits from users' physiological responses.

RELATED WORK

In this section, we review relevant literature about affect and personality to give an overview of the state of the art in the related fields.

Implicit Affect Decoding

Decoding emotion by monitoring user behavior via their facial expressions [6] or spontaneous physiological responses [10] has gained in popularity. While facial expressions might be controlled willingly implicit user responses like changes in heart rate, skin conductance level, blood pressure and facial EMG measurements are not easy to influence. They are used in the seminal work described in [15] to show that emotional responses to negative and neutral valence stimuli are different. Lisetti and Nasoz [11] review the technologies for capturing physiological signals that are associated with emotions using wearable devices.

Recently, user-centric characterization of emotions in audio-visual stimuli such as music and movie clips has been studied. A maximum 84% recognition accuracy on six basic emotions is achieved in [11] using GSR, heart rate and temperature signals. Abadi et al. [1] compiled a 18 subjects' dataset with Magneto-encephalogram (MEG), Electrooculogram (EOG), Electromyogram (EMG) and ECG responses for 40 music and 36 movie clips, and observed that emotion elicitation (measured on the Arousal-Valence dimensions), and affect prediction, was better for movie clips as compared to music video clips.

Affective Responses to Multimedia content

Different aspects of multimedia content can be indicators of the emotions they induce, e.g. the dominant color or the pace of a movie, which is influenced by the shot length [3]. Although aspects of videos might hint at emotional content it is not sufficient in order to (automatically) detect which kind of emotions they will provoke. Emotions need to be taken into account.

A new way of searching multimedia material could be to employ physiological responses that depend on emotions. Zeng et al. [19] investigated how to advance affect sensing technology. In order to measure which kind of emotions are evoked by the presented content it is necessary to understand which physiological effects reflect which emotions. To correlate them, visceral reactions to stimuli (e.g. visual) are measured and are correlated to subjective valence and arousal ratings. In order to facilitate research on this topic Soleymani et al. [16] created the MAHNOB-HCI multimodal database presenting emotional video clips to participants. Koelstra et al. [10] published the DEAP dataset presenting music video clips, collecting rating on arousal, valence, liking, and dominance During the experiments they recorded peripheral physiological signals and EEG of adult users to correlate them with specific emotions.

Creating affective datasets is an important contribution to emotion recognition and implicit tagging research. Data is especially valuable if many modalities are recorded simultaneously with a high synchronization, high number of participants and many trials, increasing the accuracy of results [16] and the usability for further analyses. However, none of the currently available data sets includes personality data of the subjects.

Personality and the Relation to Affect Perception

The Big-Five or the five-factor model describes human personality in terms of five dimensions: Extraversion (sociable vs. reserved), Agreeableness (compassionate vs. dispassionate and suspicious), Conscientiousness (dutiful vs. easy-going), Neuroticism or emotional stability (nervous vs. confident), and Openness or Creativity (curious vs. cautious) [12]. The traditional method to measure these personality dimensions has been through the use of questionnaires or self-reports. One of the first works on automated personality estimation was done by Argamon et al. [4], who used lexical cues from informal texts for recognizing Extraversion and Neuroticism.

When examining the relationship between personality and emotion perception using explicit or implicit user responses, mostly the relationship of Neuroticism and Extroversion with arousal and valence perception are studied so far e.g. in [13]. Personality effects on brain activation related to valence and arousal in [7] shows based on functional magnetic resonance imaging (fMRI) that in response to neutral and positive images the level of Neuroticism negatively correlated with positive valence, and positively correlated with arousal.

Analysis of related literature on affect recognition and personality analysis reveals three unique aspects of this work: (1) None of the (user-centric) affect recognition studies has considered the influence of personality differences on emotional perception. (2) While personality has been typically assessed by using questionnaires, we present a framework for decoding both affect and personality traits from physiological signals. (3) We strive to demonstrate *recognition* not only of Extraversion and Neuroticism, like often in previous literature, but of all big-five traits from user responses to emotionally homogeneous stimuli.

PROBLEM STATEMENT

In the state of the art we have seen that emotions are correlated to physiological responses but it is not yet very clear how personality affects this relationship. Affect recognition is important when interacting with intelligent systems, e.g. to adapt the next interactions between systems, users and their affective states. So far it is not possible to automatically employ information about current emotional states and personality while interacting with computer systems.

Consequently, the problem we want to contribute to is:

How can we automatically detect emotions in users and employ them to improve interactions with intelligent systems such as information retrieval? How does personality affect emotional responses?

Therefore the following research questions arise:

How can we correlate physiological data to emotions and personality traits? Can we estimate those from physiological signals? Which are the most useful ones?

In the next step we want to find out whether we can use the results for applications to increase user experience.

We expect the contributions of our research to include the following aspects:

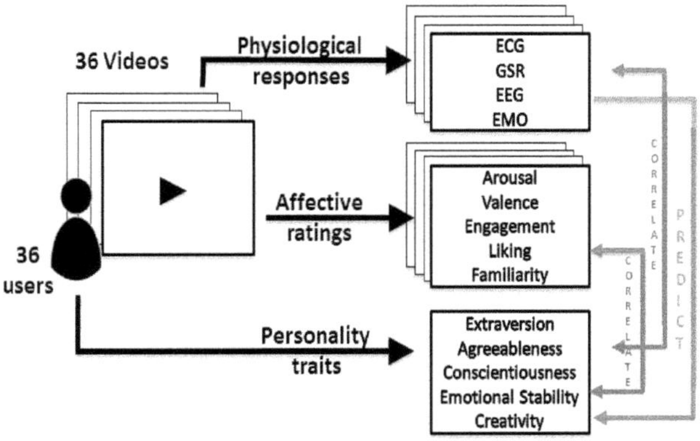

Figure 1: Overview of the experimental setting; 36 participants watch 36 movie clips and rate each along five dimensions. Additionally they perform one personality test to determinate five traits that are correlated to both ratings and physiological signals.

1. We publish a rich database recorded in response to affective multimedia content with the objective of emotion recognition. This will be a helpful contribution to the Affective Computing community as, to our knowledge, none of those databases includes measurements of personality traits of the participants.
2. We try to identify and understand the correlations between specific emotional dimensions as well as traits with corresponding physiological effects and how (with which sensors) to capture them best.
3. We apply machine-learning approaches to develop algorithms to predict emotions and investigate where to implement them in innovative applications to solve real life problems, people encounter in their daily activities.

AFFECTIVE MULTIMEDIA ANALYSIS AND RETRIEVAL OF PHYSIOLOGICAL DATA

Physiological changes are correlated to the emotions that provoke them. To study the personality-affect relationship, we performed a study where users' physiological responses were recorded as they viewed affective movie clips. They gave direct emotional feedback after each clip and provided personality measures for the big-five dimensions. An overview is given in Figure 1.

Stimuli, Subjects and Personality Scores

We chose the 36 Hollywood movie clips used by Abadi et al [2] as stimuli for our study. The clips were between 51s and 128s long (μ =80, σ =20), and were uniformly distributed according to the valence and arousal dimension (9 clips per quadrant). 36 people (12 female, mean age = 29.2) participated in our study. Although none of them was native English speaking they all understood English well and could follow the dialogues easily. All subjects completed the big-five marker scale (BFMS) questionnaire [14] from which scores along the five personality dimensions were computed.

Experimental Set-up and Procedure

One PC with two monitors was used, one for video clip presentation at 1024 × 768 pixel resolution with 60 Hz screen refresh rate. It was placed roughly one meter in front of the user. The other monitor allowed the experimenter to check the recorded sensor data. Physiological sensors (GSR, ECG and facial-EEG) were positioned on the body as demonstrated in Figure 2(a). Also, a webcam was placed in front of the subject to record facial responses.

Each participant performed the experiment in a session lasting about 90 minutes. After two practice trials, movie clips were randomly shown in two blocks of 18 trials, with a short break in between to avoid fatigue. In each trial, a fixation cross was displayed for four seconds with a short break in between to avoid fatigue. In each trial, a fixation cross was displayed for four seconds before the clip presentation began. After viewing each clip, subjects reported their emotional state by rating the clip for reported their emotional state by rating the clip for arousal, valence, engagement, liking, and familiarity (see Figure 2(b)).

The mean arousal-valence (AV) user ratings for the 36 movie clips are presented in Figure 2(c). Different colors are used to denote the HAHV (high arousal-high valence), HALV (high arousal- low valence), LALV (low arousal-low valence) and LAHV (low arousal-high valence) stimuli as per ground-truth (GT) ratings provided in [2].

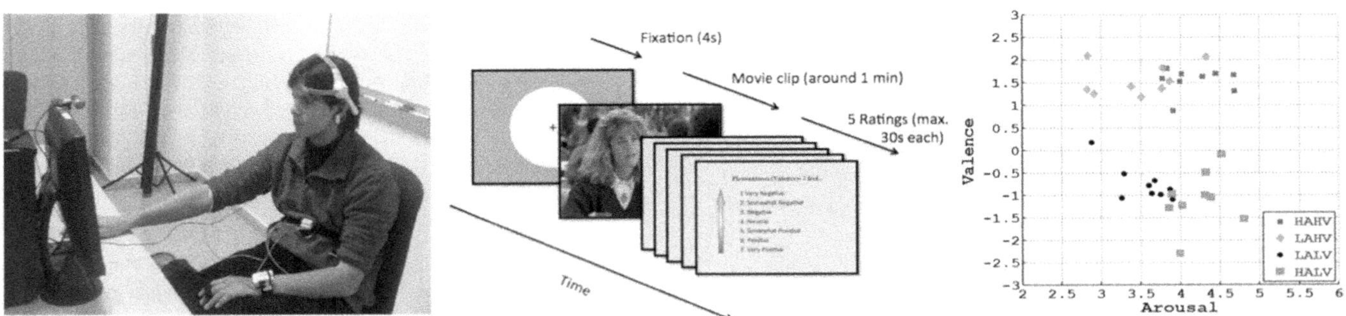

Figure 2: Participant with sensors (EEG, ECG and GSR visible) during the experiment; (b) Sequence of each trial; (c) Mean Arousal-Valence (AV) ratings for the 36 movie clips used in the experiment

Modality	Extracted features
ECG	Inter beat interval (IBI), heart rate (HR), heart rate variability (HRV) over time, low frequency PSD (power spectral density), time interval between PRT peaks.
GSR	Average skin resistance, average rising time of the GSR signal
Facial EEG	Alpha, beta, gamma, delta and theta EEG power signal density (PSD), attention, meditation
Video analysis	Statistics over the movement of each of 12 motion units (MU)

Table 1: All modalities and derived features.

Feature Extraction

Descriptions of the physiological sensors and applications used and the extracted features are as follows (Table 1).

Galvanic Skin Response (GSR) measures transpiration rate of the skin, which is controlled by the sympathetic nervous system. Therefore GSR changes depending on how the person feels. We extracted 31 GSR features similar to [9,16].

Electroencephalography (EEG) measures small changes in the skull's electrical field produced by brain activities. The facial-EEG responses not only include frontal lobe activity in different frequency bands, but also the level of facial activation and eye-blink rate and strength.

With the *Electrocardiogram (ECG)* signal, we can detect PQRST heartbeats precisely and compute features derived from it as in [8] (for details see Table 1).

A *facial tracking module* [6] was used to detect facial expressions and the displacements of 12 facial interest points or motion units (MU) in each video frame (EMO).

Preliminary Results and Discussion

So far we did first analyses of the data acquired. First we investigated differences between valence and arousal perception for different personality traits. In the next step we attempted binary classification of each personality and emotion dimension using physiological features.

Personality hypotheses

We can support some hypotheses about connections between Personality and Emotionality suggested by literature. We found a significant difference in ratings for high-arousal videos between Emotional stable and more neurotic people ($t(34) = -1.9928$, $p < 0.05$) and a slightly significant difference for low-arousal videos ($t(34) = -1.322$, $p = 0.098$). Our analyses support the hypothesis that Neuroticism is associated with higher arousal [7,13].

We found a negative correlation between Openness and arousal as proposed in [18]. Between-group comparisons of arousal ratings provided by creative and conservative subjects were found to be marginally different for high arousal stimuli ($t(34) = -1.5767$, $p = 0.0621$). Quadrant-wise comparisons showed that conservative individuals experienced significantly higher arousal for HALV ($t(16) = -1.9834$, $p < 0.05$), so more open people are less aroused by HALV stimuli.

	V	A	Extr	Agree	Consc	ES	Crea
ECG	0.28	0.46	0.43	**0.37**	**0.31**	**0.50**	0.54
GSR	0.52	0.23	0.14	0.34	0.28	0.20	**0.91**
EMO	0.45	0.28	**0.59**	0.34	0.11	0.37	0.26
EEG	**0.61**	**0.66**	0.34	0.28	0.13	**0.50**	0.50
Ffus	**0.80**	0.52	0.43	**0.45**	0.14	0.15	0.59
W_{est}	0.67	0.71	**0.60**	0.37	**0.31**	0.63	**0.91**

Table 2: Emotion and Personality classification considering responses to all stimuli. Maximum F1-scores obtained using unimodal and multimodal methods are shown in bold.

Classification results

We then attempted binary classification of each emotion and personality dimension using physiological features. For emotion classification, the objective was to determine the valence and arousal label of each of the 36 clips assuming that the participant population is represented by a single subject whose responses are equal to the mean physiological responses of all users. For each personality dimension, the objective was to label each of the 36 subjects as 'high' or 'low' trait based on the mean physiological response for all stimuli and for homogeneous stimuli. The linear libSVM implementation was used, and a Leave-one-out cross-validation scheme was adopted.

For analysis we report the F1 score, a good measure of test accuracy as it considers both the precision and the recall (Table 2). Facial-EEG provides best prediction of arousal (F1=0,66), valence (F1=0,61) and the personality trait Emotional stability (F1=0,50), while GSR provides best prediction for Creativity (F1=0,91). Agreeableness (F1=0.37) and Conscientiousness (F1=31) are best predicted by ECG. Better than chance categorization is achieved only for three of the five personality traits. To enhance these results we analyzed also feature fusion. Better results are achieved when analyzing physiological signals for homogeneous videos, e.g. classification for agreeableness only on HAHV videos improves to F1= 0.84.

We are aware of the difficulties to conduct classification experiments with few subjects and will therefore continue to collect data. This will help to account for the heterogeneity between individuals and their physiological signals. We will continue experimenting with changing the videos, the feature selection and the classification approaches to identify optimal solutions for inducing homogeneous emotions, sensing physiological signals and ultimately predicting affect and personality.

RESEARCH OUTLINE AND CONTRIBUTION

Physiological data of emotional responses have been investigated before but not together with personality traits yet.

Our research outline includes the following aspects:

1. We collected and continue to collect physiological and psychological data from more people in emotional contexts such as watching video clips together with their personality data to analyze correlations.

a. We already created one database that contains emotion-correlated and personality data for future analyses. It will be published to be used also by other researchers.
b. We further analyze which methods and sensors compose the most effective and least invasive combination for emotion detection.
2. We plan to develop algorithms to predict emotions and personality traits that can then be implemented in different applications.
3. We will investigate how and in which contexts we can use the results to actually improve the user experience in real life settings, e.g. we plan to conduct an experiment on multimedia selection to test the usefulness of affect and personality recognition for recommender systems (e.g. to reduce stress, to relax or make people laugh).

We search for correlations and classifications for specific emotions, aspects of personality and the physiological reactions they cause. We then explore application possibilities for automated emotion and personality detection.

ACKNOWLEDGEMENT

I thank my advisor Nicu Sebe for constant support with my thesis. I also appreciate the help of my colleagues Mojtaba Khomami Abadi and Ramanathan Subramanian and all the participants of the experiments.

REFERENCES

1. Abadi, M.K., Kia, M., Subramanian, R., Avesani, P., and Sebe, N. Decoding Affect in Videos Employing the MEG Brain Signal. *2013 10th IEEE International Conference and Workshops on Automatic Face and Gesture Recognition (FG)*, (2013), 1–6.
2. Abadi, M.K., Kia, S.M., Subramanian, R., Avesani, P., and Sebe, N. User-centric Affective Video Tagging from MEG and Peripheral Physiological Responses. *2013 Humaine Association Conference on Affective Computing and Intelligent Interaction*, (2013), 582–587.
3. Adams, B., Dorai, C., and Venkatesh, S. Novel approach to determining tempo and dramatic story sections in motion pictures. *Image Processing, 2000. Proceedings. 2000 International Conference on Vol. 2, IEEE.*, (2000), 283–286.
4. Argamon, S., Dhawle, S., Koppel, M., and Pennbaker, J.W. Lexical predictors of personality type. *Interface and the Classification Society of North America*, (2005).
5. Hanjalic, A. and Xu, L.-Q. Affective video content representation and modeling. *IEEE Transactions on Multimedia 7*, 1 (2005), 143–154.
6. Joho, H., Staiano, J., Sebe, N., and Jose, J.M. Looking at the Viewer: Analysing Facial Activities to Detect Personal Highlights of Multimedia Contents. *Multimedia Tools and Applications 51*, 2 (2011), 505–523.
7. Kehoe, E.G., Toomey, J.M., Balsters, J.H., and Bokde, A.L.W. Personality modulates the effects of emotional arousal and valence on brain activation. *Social cognitive and affective neuroscience 7*, 7 (2012), 858–70.
8. Kim, J. and André, E. Emotion recognition based on physiological changes in music listening. *IEEE transactions on pattern analysis and machine intelligence 30*, 12 (2008), 2067–83.
9. Kim, K.H., Bang, S.W., and Kim, S.R. Emotion recognition system using short-term monitoring of physiological signals. *Medical & biological engineering & computing 42*, 3 (2004), 419–27.
10. Koelstra, S., Mühl, C., Soleymani, M., et al. DEAP: A Database for Emotion Analysis Using Physiological Signals. *IEEE Transactions on Affective Computing 3*, 1 (2012), 18–31.
11. Lisetti, C.L. and Nasoz, F. Using Noninvasive Wearable Computers to Recognize Human Emotions from Physiological Signals. *EURASIP Journal on Advances in Signal Processing 2004*, 11 (2004), 1672–1687.
12. McCrae, R.R. and John, O.P. An introduction to the five-factor model and its applications. *Journal of personality 60*, 2 (1992), 175–215.
13. Ng, W. Clarifying the relation between neuroticism and positive emotions. *Personality and Individual Differences 47*, 1 (2009), 69–72.
14. Perugini, M. and Blas, L. Di. Analyzing personality-related adjectives from an etic–emic perspective: The Big Five Marker Scales (BFMS) and the Italian AB5C taxonomy. *Big Five Assessment*, (2002), 281–304.
15. Sinha, R. Multivariate Response Patterning of Fear and Anger. *Cognition & Emotion 10*, 2 (1996), 173–198.
16. Soleymani, M., Lichtenauer, J., Pun, T., and Pantic, M. A Multimodal Database for Affect Recognition and Implicit Tagging. *IEEE Transactions on Affective Computing 3*, 1 (2012), 42–55.
17. Srivastava, R., Feng, J., Roy, S., Sim, T., and Yan, S. Don't Ask Me What I'm Like, Just Watch and Listen. *Proceedings of the 20th ACM international conference on Multimedia. ACM, 2012.*, (2012), 329–338.
18. Tok, S., Koyuncu, M., Dural, S., and Catikkas, F. Evaluation of International Affective Picture System (IAPS) ratings in an athlete population and its relations to personality. *Personality and Individual Differences 49*, 5 (2010), 461–466.
19. Zeng, Z., Pantic, M., Roisman, G.I., and Huang, T.S. A survey of affect recognition methods: audio, visual, and spontaneous expressions. *IEEE Transactions on pattern analysis and machine intelligence 31*, 1 (2009), 39–58.

Perceptions of Interpersonal Behavior are Influenced by Gender, Facial Expression Intensity, and Head Pose

Jeffrey M. Girard
University of Pittsburgh
4322 Sennott Square
Pittsburgh, PA 15260
jmg174@pitt.edu

ABSTRACT

Across multiple channels, nonverbal behavior communicates information about affective states and interpersonal intentions. Researchers interested in understanding how these nonverbal messages are transmitted and interpreted have examined the relationship between behavior and ratings of interpersonal motives using dimensions such as agency and communion. However, previous work has focused on images of posed behavior and it is unclear how well these results will generalize to more dynamic representations of real-world behavior. The current study proposes to extend the current literature by examining how gender, facial expression intensity, and head pose influence interpersonal ratings in videos of spontaneous nonverbal behavior.

Categories and Subject Descriptors

J.4 [**Computer Applications**]: Social and Behavioral Sciences—*Psychology*

General Terms

Experimentation, Measurement

Keywords

Multimodal fusion; FACS; pose; gender; agency; communion

1. INTRODUCTION

In 1872, Darwin [5] argued that nonverbal behavior is an important and reliable avenue of emotional communication. A century later, Ekman [7] presented empirical evidence to support these claims for facial expressions. Since then, decades of research have explored and debated the extent and reliability of the information that can be gleaned from the nonverbal channels of facial expression, body posture, gesture, gaze, and vocal prosody [9, 10]. Advances in the study of emotion, psychopathology, and social psychology were all made possible by this work [11]. A number of changes have also swept the field during this time.

ICMI '14 Istanbul, Turkey

http://dx.doi.org/10.1145/2663204.2667575.

First, dimensional models of affect have gained in popularity. Much of the seminal work in nonverbal research classified affective displays in terms of discrete categories such as "basic emotions" [8, 22]. However, many have challenged the utility of these categories and have instead advocated for the use of continuous and dimensional approaches that are more parsimonious and can capture affective subtleties, mixtures, and fluctuations over time [33].

Circumplex spaces formed by the intersection of multiple dimensions have been particularly popular. For instance, Russell's circumplex model of affect [32] captures the interaction of emotional valence and arousal, modeling discrete emotions with reference to only two parameters. Such models have been applied to nonverbal behavior [19].

Second, researchers have begun to measure and analyze multiple channels of nonverbal behavior. Many have also called for *multimodal fusion* or integration of these channels [28], although this is still a developing area of research [2]. Convergence among multiple channels would allow researchers to be more confident in their interpretations and divergence would be an interesting signal in its own right.

Finally, researchers have begun to appreciate the social functions of nonverbal behavior. In addition to revealing information about an individual's affective state, nonverbal behavior can also communicate behavioral intent, augment verbal messages, and even dissemble [9, 13]. These uses of nonverbal behavior are especially important for negotiating interpersonal interactions, which many argue to be where "the most important expressions of personality and psychopathology occur" [29, p. 142].

Similar to circumplex models of affect, the Interpersonal Circumplex (IPC) [25] is often used to parsimoniously explain interpersonal behavior, as well as the motives and appraisals underlying it. The IPC includes *agency* and *communion* as its primary dimensions. Agency captures self-assertion, power, and mastery while communion captures intimacy, warmth, and solidarity. When manifest in behavior, agency ranges from submit to dominate, while communion ranges from separate to affiliate. Figure 1 provides examples of specific behaviors at various points of the IPC. The closer two points (i.e., behaviors, motives, or traits) are in the IPC space, the more positively correlated they are; points orthogonal to one another are uncorrelated and those across the circumplex from one another are negatively correlated.

Three preliminary studies examined how nonverbal behavior influences perceptions of agency and communion. It is important to note that agency is also referred to as dominance and communion is also referred to as affiliation.

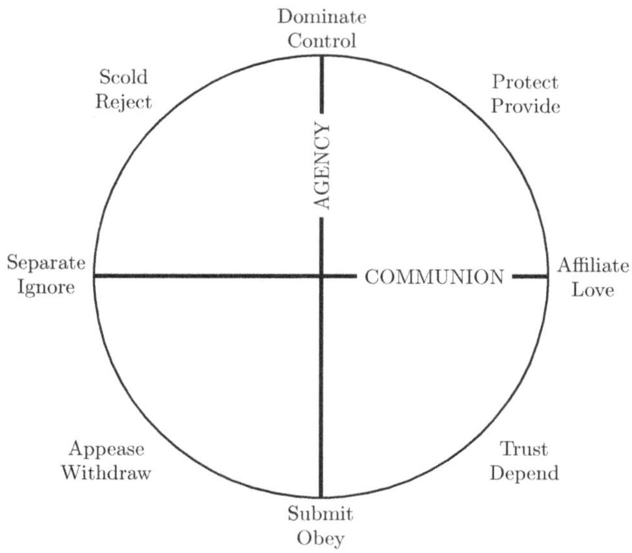

Figure 1: Interpersonal Circumplex (IPC) Model

Gifford [14] observed participants during an unstructured social interaction and found that high dominance ratings were related to increased leg movement and decreased object-manipulation. He also found that high affiliation ratings were related to increased gesturing, nodding, and orienting the head towards others, as well as decreased leg movement and arm-wrapping.

Knutson [24] had participants rate images of posed emotional facial expressions and found that displays of anger and disgust were rated as hostile and dominant, displays of fear and sadness were rated as friendly and submissive, and displays of happiness were rated as friendly and dominant.

Finally, Hess et al. [20] explored the influence of gender, ethnicity, and facial expression intensity on ratings of dominance and affiliation in posed emotion images. They found that displays of sadness and fear were rated as submissive; displays of anger and disgust were rated as hostile; and displays of happiness, fear, and sadness were rated as friendly. Low intensity facial expressions influenced affiliation ratings but not dominance ratings, meaning that "whereas a slight smile is a sign of affiliation, only a strong frown signals dominance" [p. 282]. Gender and ethnicity moderated the degree but not the sign of dominance and affiliation ratings.

While these studies provided interesting food for thought and have informed the interpretation of nonverbal behavior in future studies [18], there is still a lot to be learned about the relationship between nonverbal behavior and its perceived interpersonal meaning. There were also several important limitations to the previous studies.

First, two of the studies had participants rate stimuli depicting posed behavior, which is demonstrably different from spontaneous behavior [27]. Second, two of the studies had participants rate static images, a process which is not representative of how people view behavior in real-world interactions. Third, none of the studies examined multiple modalities of behavior simultaneously. However, in most social interactions, we have access to the information provided by facial expressions, body posture, gaze, gesture, and voice prosody. These channels often offer redundant information, but sometimes conflict with one another in ways that are critical to the behavior's meaning.

The current study proposes to extend the literature and address some of its limitations. Naive participants will rate dynamic videos of spontaneous nonverbal behavior in terms of agency and communion. These ratings will then be compared with automatic measures of facial expression intensity and head pose using a sophisticated statistical analysis that controls for both modalities at once and also examines the presence of gender effects. We would have also liked to include other modalities, but the recording setup precluded this possibility: only participants' heads were visible and participants rarely spoke.

Given the results of previous studies, we expect that gender, facial expression intensity, and head pose will all influence perceived interpersonal meaning. The hypotheses for facial expression intensity are informed by the connection between individual facial actions and emotion displays [10], whereas the hypotheses for head pose are determined by their impact on looking behavior (i.e., gaze).

Specifically, we propose the following six hypotheses: (1) females will be perceived with more communion and less agency than males, (2) the intensity of facial expressions related to happiness (AU 6 and AU 12) will be positively related to agency and communion, (3) the intensity of facial expressions related to disgust/contempt (AU 10 and AU 14) will be negatively related to communion and positively related to agency, (4) the intensity of facial expressions related to sadness (AU 17) will be positively related to communion and negatively related to agency, (5) head pitch will be positively related to agency and its absolute value will be negatively related to communion, and (6) the absolute value of head yaw will be negatively related to communion.

We also expect there to be interactions between modalities. For instance, previous research [1] has found that smiles are perceived as indicative of enjoyment or embarrassment depending in part upon the head orientation they are combined with. As such, we predict that smiles (AU 12), which are normally rated as dominant, will be rated as submissive when combined with negative head pitch.

2. METHODS

2.1 Materials

The current study proposes to analyze digital video of 36 individuals (50.0% female, 49.1% white, ages 18–29) from the BP4D-Spontaneous database [37]. These individuals were recruited from the departments of psychology and computer science and from the school of engineering at Binghamtom University. All individuals gave informed consent to the procedures and permissible uses of their data.

Individuals sat approximately 51 inches in front of a Di3D dynamic face capturing system [6] during a series of 8 emotion elicitation tasks. A subset of four tasks will be analyzed in the current study, including those designed to elicit happiness/amusement, sadness, embarrassment, and anger/upset. If these elicitations were successful, they should yield nonverbal behaviors in all four quadrants of the IPC model.

The 2D texture video data had a standard frame rate of 25 frames per second and a resolution of 1040×1392 pixels/frame. For the current study, a 540×720 pixel area centered around the individual's face was cropped from each frame and used for analysis (Figure 2).

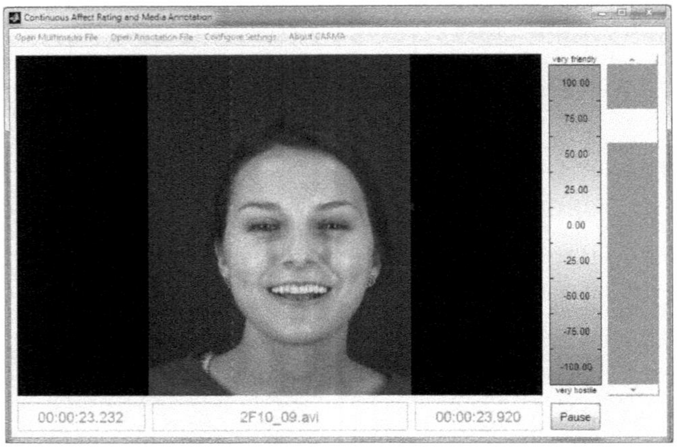

Figure 2: Screenshot of a stimulus video in CARMA

2.2 Participants

Participants will be recruited from the University of Pittsburgh undergraduate research pool. As such, this group will be largely composed of undergraduate students enrolled in introductory psychology courses. The main task of these participants will be to provide continuous ratings of the stimulus videos. Because the "effective reliability" of a group of raters increases as a function of both the number of raters and the mean reliability of each rater [31], we propose to use the average of 10 raters. With this many raters, they would only need to achieve a mean reliability of 50% to yield an effective reliability of 90%.

2.3 Continuous Ratings

Participants will rate the video clips on two interpersonal dimensions using CARMA [16], a software package developed by the author for media annotation and the collection of continuous ratings (Figure 2). While watching the video clips without sound, participants will use a computer mouse or keyboard to rate the clips in terms of their moment-by-moment changes along the interpersonal dimensions of agency and communion. In order to reduce cognitive load on the raters, each dimension will be rated separately.

2.4 Automated Measurement

In order to better understand the relationship between nonverbal behavior and its perceived meaning, several nonverbal channels were automatically measured. These channels include facial expression and head pose. Previous research has found that these two channels make important contributions to the perceived meaning of behavior [1].

2.4.1 *Facial Expression*

Facial expressions in the BP4D-Spontaneous database were measured using the Facial Action Coding System (FACS) [12], which is the current standard for facial measurement in the behavior sciences [11]. FACS is an anatomically-based system that decomposes facial expressions into component parts called action units (AU). Each AU represents the contraction of one or more facial muscles. Any facial expression can be represented by a single AU or by a combination of multiple AUs. In addition to providing rules for the changes in facial shape and appearance generated by each AU, the FACS manual also provides rules for coding the intensity (i.e., muscle contraction magnitude) for a given AU. In the current version of FACS, there are five ordinal intensity levels ranging from "trace" to "maximum" contraction.

Expert coders at the University of Pittsburgh manually annotated the presence and absence of 34 AUs in the BP4D-Spontaneous database. Frame-by-frame intensity was also annotated for five AUs (i.e., AUs 6, 10, 12, 14, and 17). These AUs were selected for intensity annotation due to their high rates of occurrence and because of their involvement in displays of affect and social signaling [10].

The intensity annotations for AU 12 were used in a previous study [15] to train a fully-automated smile intensity coding system. This system was composed of five steps. First, sixty-four facial landmark points were tracked in each frame using the LiveDriver^{TM} SDK from Image Metrics [21]. Second, a common space for comparison between frames was created by correcting out-of-plane rotation using a similarity transformation [35]. Third, appearance information was extracted around each facial landmark point using scale-invariant feature transform (SIFT) descriptors [26]. Fourth, the dimensionality of the SIFT features was reduced using Laplacian eigenmaps and spectral regression [3, 4]. Finally, smile intensity for each frame was estimated using trained multi-class support vector machines [36].

The current study proposes to extend this methodology to the other four AUs, yielding frame-by-frame intensity estimations for AU 6, AU 10, AU 12, AU 14, and AU 17.

2.4.2 *Head Pose*

Head pose was automatically measured in three spatial dimensions using the LiveDriver^{TM} SDK from Image Metrics [21]. For each video frame, head pose was measured in terms of pitch, yaw, and roll. Pitch corresponds to vertical motion such as nodding, yaw corresponds to horizontal motion such as shaking the head, and roll corresponds to lateral motion such as tipping the head sideways.

2.5 Statistical Analysis

The current study proposes to examine which nonverbal channels influence raters' perceptions of agency and communion. These factors include the intensity of various facial expressions and the degree of head rotation in three spatial dimensions. Other potentially moderating factors will also be added to the model, including gender of the individual.

The statistical relationship between these factors will be captured by hierarchical linear modeling (HLM) [30], which is a powerful analytical tool for modeling data with a "nested" or interdependent structure. In the current study, repeated observations are nested within individuals. By creating submodels (i.e., partitioning the variance and covariance) for each level, HLM accounts for the fact that observations from the same individual are likely to be more similar than observations from different individuals. HLM also accounts for the variance that is shared between predictor variables, allowing us to quantify the effect of one variable while controlling for the influence of all other variables.

The dependent variable for each HLM model is the average of all raters' scores for agency or communion during each second-long observation. On the first level of the model, second-by-second averages of automatically-measured AU intensity and head pose will be added as predictor variables. Within each individual, the model estimates the relationship between facial expression intensity and head pose with

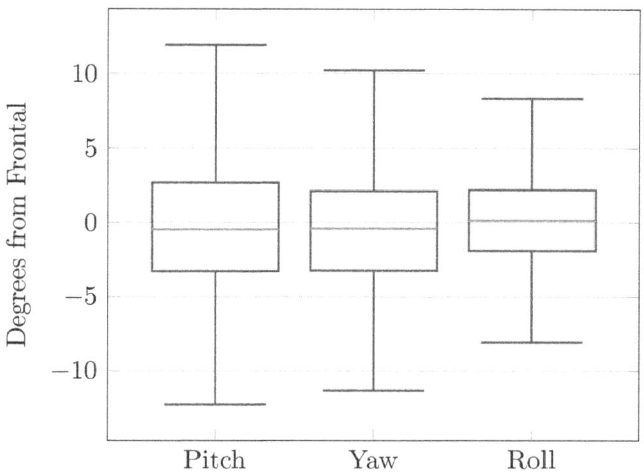

Figure 3: Box plot of head pose distributions

the raters' average score. On the second level of the model, the gender of the individual in the video clip will be dummy coded (and possibly other covariates will be added). Finally, random error terms will be added to account for differences between individuals.

3. RESULTS

3.1 Results to date

3.1.1 Facial expression

Manual intensity annotation has been completed. For all five AUs, the lower intensities (i.e., 1, 2, and 3) are much more common than the higher intensities (i.e., 4 and 5), which is consistent with findings that spontaneous expressions tend to be weak and ambiguous [27]. The intensity distribution for AU 17 is particularly skewed, with intensity levels higher than 1 or 2 being extremely rare.

Automated intensity estimation has been completed for AU 12. The inter-system reliability (i.e., intraclass correlation) for these estimations was 0.92, which can be considered very strong performance [34]. The facial landmark tracking, registration (i.e., pose correction), and feature extraction completed for AU 12 can also be applied to the other AUs.

3.1.2 Head pose

Automatic measurement of head pose has been completed. Figure 3 shows that the majority of frames were within 15 degrees of frontal for all dimensions. Head pitch showed the most variability, followed by yaw, and finally roll.

3.2 Remaining work and open questions

The remaining work includes collecting interpersonal ratings, completing the automatic AU intensity estimation for the remaining AUs, and formulating the HLM models. Because the first three steps of automatic intensity estimation are already complete, all that remains is to reduce the features and train the classifiers for the remaining four AUs.

A few questions also remain, which the author would appreciate feedback on from the doctoral consortium mentors. These include how much data to include from each video, which AUs to analyze, whether or not to consider AU combinations, and how to handle the autocorrelation of adjacent segments in the time series data.

Although five AUs have been manually annotated for intensity, a subset of these could be focused on or additional AUs could be added. Similarly, AUs can be analyzed individually or in specific combinations. What are the most important AUs and combinations to focus on for interpersonal behavior? Finally, individual observations (i.e., seconds) that are temporally close to one another are likely to be more similar than those that are more distant. How important is it to model this dependency within the HLM model, and what would be the best way to do so?

4. AUTHOR'S CONTRIBUTIONS

Over the past four years of graduate school, I have made a number of contributions to the fields of psychology and affective computing. Much of my work has focused on developing and validating methods for automatic facial expression analysis [17], including the collection of a spontaneous 3D facial expression database [37], methods for facial expression intensity estimation [15, 23], and software for the collection of continuous ratings [16]. I am also excited about applying these methods to the study of psychological phenomena and incorporating additional nonverbal modalities. Most recently, my collaborators and I used automated coding of facial expressions and head pose to test the behavioral hypotheses of three different theories of clinical depression [18]. Interpreting the results of this work was what first sparked my interest in the Interpersonal theory.

It is my belief that automated and multimodal measurement of nonverbal behavior will have a major influence on psychology and the behavior sciences in the near future. By continuing to develop my technical skills and clinical experience, I hope to contribute a unique and valuable perspective to this burgeoning endeavor.

Acknowledgments

This material is based on work supported by the National Science Foundation under grant CNS-1205195. The author thanks his advisor, Dr. Jeffrey F. Cohn, for his guidance.

References

[1] Z. Ambadar, J. F. Cohn, and L. I. Reed. All smiles are not created equal: Morphology and timing of smiles perceived as amused, polite, and embarrassed/nervous. *Journal of Nonverbal Behavior*, 33(1):17–34, 2009.

[2] P. K. Atrey, M. A. Hossain, A. El Saddik, and M. S. Kankanhalli. Multimodal fusion for multimedia analysis: a survey. *Multimedia Systems*, 16(6): 345–379, 2010.

[3] M. Belkin and P. Niyogi. Laplacian eigenmaps for dimensionality reduction and data representation. *Neural Computation*, 15(6):1373–1396, 2003.

[4] D. Cai, X. He, W. V. Zhang, and J. Han. Regularized locality preserving indexing via spectral regression. In *Conference on Information and Knowledge Management*, pages 741–750. ACM, 2007.

[5] C. Darwin. *The expression of emotions in man and animals.* Oxford University, New York, 3rd edition, 1872.

[6] Dimensional Imaging. URL http://www.di3d.com/.

[7] P. Ekman. Universals and cultural differences in facial expressions of emotion. In J. Cole, editor, *Nebraska Symposium on Motivation*, pages 207–282. University of Nebraska Press, Lincoln, 1972.

[8] P. Ekman. Basic emotions. In T. Dalagleish and M. Power, editors, *Handbook of cognition and emotion*, pages 45–60. John Wiley & Sons, UK, 1999.

[9] P. Ekman and W. V. Friesen. The repertoire of nonverbal behavior: Categories, origins, usage, and coding. *Semiotica*, 1:49–98, 1969.

[10] P. Ekman and D. Matsumoto. Facial expression analysis. *Scholarpedia*, 3, 2008.

[11] P. Ekman and E. L. Rosenberg. *What the face reveals: Basic and applied studies of spontaneous expression using the facial action coding system (FACS).* Oxford University Press, New York, NY, 2nd edition, 2005.

[12] P. Ekman, W. V. Friesen, and J. Hager. *Facial action coding system: A technique for the measurement of facial movement.* Research Nexus, Salt Lake City, UT, 2002.

[13] A. J. Fridlund. *Human facial expression: An evolutionary view.* Academic Press, 1994.

[14] R. Gifford. Mapping nonverbal behavior on the interpersonal circle. *Journal of Personality and Social Psychology*, 61(2):279–288, 1991.

[15] J. M. Girard. *Automatic detection and intensity estimation of spontaneous smiles.* Master's thesis, 2014.

[16] J. M. Girard. CARMA: Software for continuous affect rating and media annotation. *Journal of Open Research Software*, 2(1):e5, 2014.

[17] J. M. Girard and J. F. Cohn. Criteria and metrics for thresholded AU detection. In *Proceedings of the IEEE International Conference on Computer Vision Workshops*, pages 2191–2197. IEEE, 2011.

[18] J. M. Girard, J. F. Cohn, M. H. Mahoor, S. M. Mavadati, Z. Hammal, and D. P. Rosenwald. Nonverbal social withdrawal in depression: Evidence from manual and automatic analyses. *Image and Vision Computing*, 32(10):641–647, 2014.

[19] H. Gunes and B. Schuller. Categorical and dimensional affect analysis in continuous input: Current trends and future directions. *Image and Vision Computing*, 31(2):120–136, 2013.

[20] U. Hess, S. Blairy, and R. E. Kleck. The influence of facial emotion displays, gender, and ethnicity on judgments of dominance and affiliation. *Journal of Nonverbal Behavior*, 24(4):265–283, 2000.

[21] Image Metrics. URL http://image-metrics.com/.

[22] C. E. Izard. *Human emotions.* Plenum Press, New York, NY, 1977.

[23] L. A. Jeni, J. M. Girard, J. F. Cohn, and F. De la Torre. Continuous AU intensity estimation using localized, sparse facial feature space. In *Proceedings of the IEEE International Conference on Automated Face & Gesture Recognition Workshops*, pages 1–7. IEEE, 2013.

[24] B. Knutson. Facial expressions of emotion influence interpersonal trait inferences. *Journal of Nonverbal Behavior*, 20(3):165–182, 1996.

[25] T. Leary. *Interpersonal diagnosis of personality: A functional theory and methodology for personality evaluation.* Ronald Press, Oxford, England, 1957.

[26] D. G. Lowe. Object recognition from local scale-invariant features. *IEEE International Conference on Computer Vision*, pages 1150–1157, 1999.

[27] M. Motley and C. Camden. Facial expression of emotion: A comparison of posed expressions versus spontaneous expressions in an interpersonal communication setting. *Western Journal of Speech Communication*, 52(1):1–22, 1988.

[28] M. Paleari and C. Lisetti. Toward multimodal fusion of affective cues. In *Proceedings of the ACM International Workshop on Human-Centered Multimedia*, pages 99–108, 2006.

[29] A. Pincus and E. Ansell. Interpersonal theory of personality. In *Handbook of Psychology*, pages 209–229. 2003.

[30] S. W. Raudenbush and A. S. Bryk. *Hierarchical linear models: Applications and data analysis methods.* Sage, Thousand Oaks, CA, 2nd edition, 2002.

[31] R. Rosenthal. Conducting judgment studies. In K. R. Scherer and P. Ekman, editors, *Handbook of Methods in Nonverbal Behavior Research*, pages 287–365. Cambridge University Press, New York, NY, 1982.

[32] J. A. Russell. A circumplex model of affect. *Journal of Personality and Social Psychology*, 39(6):1161, 1980.

[33] J. A. Russell. Core affect and the psychological construction of emotion. *Psychological Review*, 110(1): 145–172, 2003.

[34] P. E. Shrout and J. L. Fleiss. Intraclass correlations: Uses in assessing rater reliability. *Psychological Bulletin*, 86(2):420, 1979.

[35] R. Szeliski. *Computer vision: Algorithms and applications.* Springer, London, 2011.

[36] V. Vapnik. *The nature of statistical learning theory.* Springer, New York, NY, 1995.

[37] X. Zhang, L. Yin, J. F. Cohn, S. Canavan, M. Reale, A. Horowitz, P. Liu, and J. M. Girard. BP4D-Spontaneous: a high-resolution spontaneous 3D dynamic facial expression database. *Image and Vision Computing*, 32(10):692–706.

Authoring Communicative Behaviors for Situated, Embodied Characters

Tomislav Pejsa
University of Wisconsin-Madison
1210 West Dayton Street
Madison, WI, 53706
tpejsa@cs.wisc.edu

ABSTRACT
Embodied conversational agents hold great potential as multimodal interfaces due to their ability to communicate naturally using speech and nonverbal cues. The goal of my research is to enable animators and designers to endow ECAs with interactive behaviors that are controllable, communicatively effective, as well as natural and aesthetically appealing; I focus in particular on spatially situated, communicative nonverbal behaviors such as gaze and deictic gestures. This goal requires addressing challenges in the space of animation authoring and editing, parametric control, behavior coordination and planning, and retargeting to different embodiment designs. My research will aim to provide animators and designers with techniques and tools needed to author natural, expressive, and controllable gaze and gesture movements that leverage empirical or learned models of human behavior, to apply such behaviors to characters with different designs and communicative styles, and to develop techniques and models for planning of coordinated behaviors that economically and correctly convey the range of diverse cues required for multimodal, user-machine interaction.

Categories and Subject Descriptors
H.1.2 [**Models and Principles**]: User/Machine Systems – *Human factors*; H.5.2 [**Information Interfaces and Presentation**]: User Interfaces – *Evaluation/methodology*, *User-centered design*; I.3.7 [**Computer Graphics**]: Three-Dimensional Graphics and Realism – *Animation*.

General Terms
Algorithms; Design; Experimentation; Human Factors

Keywords
Embodied conversational agents; animation; gaze; gestures; nonverbal communication; behavior coordination; behavior planning; multimodal interfaces; situated interaction

1. INTRODUCTION
A central objective in character animation is to enable characters to communicate, through the use of speech, gaze, gestures, posture, and other communicative cues, their intentions, emotions, and cognitive states. This communication must be natural, effective, economical, and reflecting the character's personality and style. In multimodal interaction, this objective becomes even more challenging, because the character's communicative behaviors must be synthesized interactively, in response to changing multimodal inputs (e.g., presence of a user and their utterance and actions). In this paper, I use the term "embodied conversational agent" (ECA) [4] to refer to such interactive, animated characters, even though the research I discuss is very much applicable to any kind of animated character operating in an interactive setting.

The ultimate goal of my research is to give designers and artists the ability to make their ECAs engage in natural, multimodal interaction with users. This entails a number of challenges. First, we need to construct computational models for synthesis of nonverbal cues. These models need to be parametrically controllable (so the designer or high-level automated module can specify what the cue should communicate) and communicatively effective (meaning users must be able to accurately interpret the semantic content of the communicative cue). In my work I focus on spatially situated behaviors, such as gaze, body orientation, and pointing gestures, due to their importance in physically situated interaction with multiple parties and key information embedded in a physical or virtual environment. While extensive research has been conducted on understanding, modeling, and implementing situated interaction with ECAs (for example, [2]), nonverbal behaviors that arise in such interaction and their computational synthesis and coordination have received less attention.

Furthermore, communication between people is a collaborative activity that involves tightly coordinated verbal and nonverbal actions, fulfilling a variety of communicative functions. To engage in smooth and meaningful interaction with users, ECAs must possess many communicative competencies, which all make use of the character's modalities to produce appropriate communicative cues. For example, an ECA might have a discourse model that produces gaze aversions at discourse and turn-taking boundaries, a grounding model that generates nonverbal feedback such as eye contact and head nods to signal understanding of the user's inputs, an affective model that uses the eyes and facial expressions to signal the agent's emotions, etc. A second challenge in animating ECAs is planning and coordinating a large number of visible behaviors, triggered by various high-level modules, such that all those signals get communicated correctly, in an economical and timely manner, and without any unnatural combinations of cues that might make the agent more difficult to understand. Researchers in the embodied interaction field have tackled this challenge by developing languages and systems for specifying and realizing coordinated behaviors, such as BML [7, 14]. My interest is in producing these coordinated behaviors automatically, under diverse inputs, and with artistic control over the output.

ICMI '14, November 12 – 16, 2014, Istanbul, Turkey.

http://dx.doi.org/10.1145/2663204.2667576.

Figure 1: Examples of characters of different designs that can fulfill the role of conversational agents.

Last but not the least, it is not enough for the ECA to be simply an AI construct with a graphical representation. Rather, it needs to be a *character*–it must have an appealing design, it must move and express itself in a way that is natural, lifelike, and appealing, it must have a personality and a particular communicative style characterized by idiosyncrasies that make the character memorable and likeable to the user (Figure 1). Artistic principles and techniques that animators use to create lifelike characters are extensively covered in animation literature, but many unsolved problems remain in supporting these techniques in the context of interactive character animation.

To address these challenges, I adopt a research approach that follows several key principles. First, I focus on developing models of communicative behaviors that are parametrically controllable, that achieve naturalness by making use of empirically-derived laws and human subjects' data (ranging from tagged videos of human interactions to motion capture data), and that are inherently retargetable to characters with different designs, including non-human or highly stylized characters.

Second, I aim to increase the artist's involvement in the process of producing the agent's behaviors. While traditionally animators have authored behaviors at a fairly low level, using keyframing tools to produce individual animation clips, my goal is to provide animators with tools and controls that enable them to specify higher-level aspects of behavior, such as frequency properties (e.g., eye blink rate), spatial and temporal coordination properties (e.g., specify how much the character's body will reorient as part of a gaze shift), properties of the environment (e.g., change the way the character is looking by moving the objects they are looking at), or joint patterns of behavior (e.g., specify that two character should engage in eye contact over some timespan).

Finally, I intend to bring these principles together in the context of interactive planning of coordinated behaviors, in order to improve the correctness, naturalness, and responsiveness of the agent's behavior in multimodal interaction. While behavior planning using learned models has been applied to the problem of conversational behavior generation [9, 12], most prior systems consider limited inputs (e.g., only speech signal properties) and perform motion synthesis at a fairly low level (kinematic properties of motion data). The key ideas behind my approach are to perform planning with respect to a broader range of inputs (e.g., semantic content, discourse and turn-taking structure, user's behavior, spatial locations of users and objects) and to facilitate greatest artistic control over synthesized motion by enabling planning with respect to higher-level properties of behaviors that capture their communicative meanings, while their kinematic realization is achieved through artist-authored constructs.

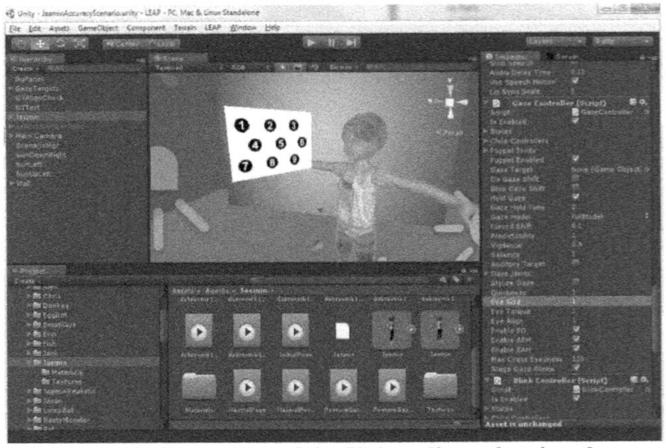

Figure 2: Screenshot of the Unity editor, showing the configuration of a behavior component in the embodied interaction framework.

2. RESEARCH OVERVIEW

In this section I give an overview of current and planned research projects that tie into my overall agenda. These include building a software framework for implementing ECAs and their behaviors, computational synthesis of gaze shifts, artist-directed synthesis and editing of situated gaze behavior, computational modeling of situated arm motion and its coordination with gaze, and planning of coordinated gaze and arm behaviors in the presence of multimodal inputs and multiple communicative goals.

2.1 Embodied Interaction Framework (ongoing)

As part of my efforts to enable authoring of communicative behaviors for animated characters, I am building an embodied interaction framework based on Unity game engine[1]. The framework is designed to enable rapid implementation of virtual agents and application scenarios involving virtual agents, which is achieved by harnessing the features of Unity game engine. The framework makes use of Unity's robust and programmable art pipeline to facilitate easy import of character models, animation clips, and other art assets. Unity's component-based architecture and modern scripting language (C#) afford rapid implementation of parametrically controllable behaviors, which can be attached to virtual agents in order to grant them new communicative capabilities; e.g., gaze shifts, eye blinks, and speech recognition are all implemented as Unity components. Along similar lines, the framework enables rapid prototyping of application logic and includes support for implementing and executing sequences of linear scenarios, which is particularly useful for implementing user studies. Finally, Unity provides a powerful and extensible GUI editor, which enables us to expose framework features as interactive graphical controls – a key capability to enable easy usage and rapid prototyping by designers and artists (Figure 2).

The framework is under continuous development. In particular, as my research progresses, I plan to incorporate new motion synthesis, editing, and planning techniques into the framework as I develop

[1] http://unity3d.com/

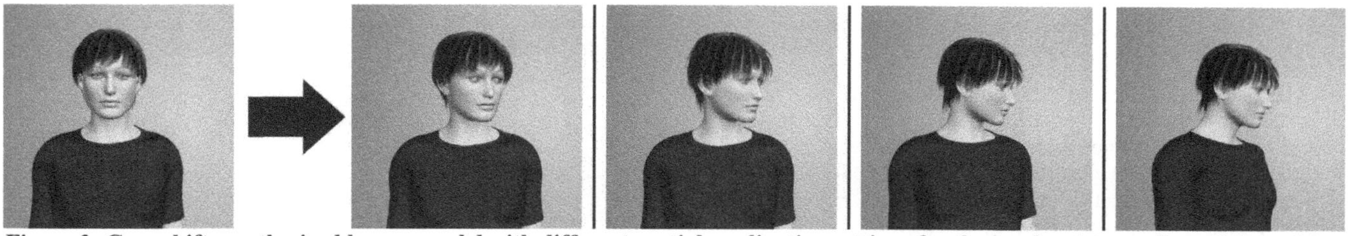

Figure 3: Gaze shifts synthesized by our model with different spatial cordination settings for the head and torso. From left to right: eye contact, sideways glance (minimal head alignment), sideways look (full head alignment), sideways turn (minimal torso alignment), sideways turn (full head alignment).

them, and I will also continuously add new agent behaviors into the current library.

2.2 Animating Gaze Shifts (completed)

Gaze is a nonverbal cue that fulfills many important functions in human communication [13]. People use gaze to signal their attention direction [6], ground verbal references and establish affiliation and rapport [1], facilitate conversational processes such as turn-taking [5], etc. The building blocks of human gaze behavior are *gaze shifts*, coordinated movements of the eyes, head, and upper body towards objects and information in the environment. It follows therefore that embodied agents require computational models for gaze shift synthesis to communicate naturally and effectively using gaze. Gaze is particularly important for situated interaction with the agent, due to its capability to signal and redirect attention towards people, objects, and information in space.

The foundation of my work involving gaze is the procedural, parametric model for gaze shift animation developed by Andrist and myself [10]. The model is informed by neurophysiological measurements of human gaze, enabling it to synthesize natural-looking gaze shift animations. The model also offers an intuitive parametrization that enables animators and designers to more easily author expressive gaze behaviors. It exposes control parameters for spatial and temporal coordination between eye, head, and torso movements in gaze shifts. For example, head and torso *alignment* parameters specify how much the head and torso will reorient towards the gaze target during the gaze shift (Figure 3). We have shown in studies with human participants [10] that, by adjusting these parameters, we can control the strength of attention cues conveyed by the agent's gaze and manipulate its social and cognitive effects in multimodal interaction; e.g., if the agent rotates its head and torso more towards an image in the environment, it is perceived as being more interested in that image.

In follow-up work, I have also extended this model with techniques for adaptation to stylized and non-human character designs [11]. The base model incorporates neurophysiological constraints of human gaze, such as eye size, movement velocity, and ocular motor range (OMR), so it cannot be used to animate the eyes of non-human or very stylized characters, as their abnormal anatomy would result in noticeable visual artifacts in the resulting animation. My proposed adaptation techniques modify gaze shift trajectories, poses, and velocity profiles in such a way that animation artifacts are eliminated, while communicative power afforded by eye, head, and torso coordination is retained. This enables us to apply expressive, humanlike gaze to embodiments of highly diverse designs (Figure 1).

2.3 Authoring Situated Gaze Behaviors (ongoing)

While my previous work focused on animating individual gaze shifts, little consideration was given to animating the character's overall gaze behavior, consisting of many gaze shifts. In order to situate a character in an environment and interaction context and make their behavior appear natural, we need to give them gaze behavior that matches that environment and context. This includes scanning and idle gaze, in which the character gazes at salient objects and people in the environment, as well as interplay of conversational gaze behaviors such as mutual gaze, gaze aversions, and deictic (referential) gaze, that occur when the character is engaged in conversation with another party.

Authoring such gaze behaviors is still an open problem. To tackle this problem, I consider first the non-interactive case, where we have a captured body motion, describing the character's behavior as part of some interaction, possibly involving one or more other parties, and an editable environment. In a traditional workflow, the character's gaze would need to be animated manually, since synchronous body motion and eye capture is still difficult to achieve. Even if that were not the case, manual editing would still be required to adapt the gaze behavior to changes in the spatial layout of the environment or interactional partners.

While a number of researchers have proposed automated methods for gaze synthesis with respect to properties of the environment and the interaction [8, 12], the approach I propose is to use properties of the body motion and environment to synthesize a best-guess gaze behavior, which can then be edited further by the animator. The key idea of my approach is to expose high-level communicative properties to the animator and enable editing of complex gaze behaviors over a large span of time using a small number of intuitive controls. Rather than edit animation curves controlling gaze direction, animators could edit frequency-domain properties such as gaze shift rate, likelihood of gazing at specific environmental features, and spatial layout of these features. The animator would also be able to edit interaction state properties that govern gaze behaviors of multiple characters simultaneously, such as conversational role (speaker vs. addressee) and the functional pattern of the characters' joint gaze behavior (e.g., mutual gaze, referential gaze towards shared reference, floor-holding gaze). Enabling gaze editing through high-level controls frees the animator of the burden of specifying precise timing, spatial direction, and kinematic profile of each individual gaze shift. These low-level properties could then be derived empirically, learned from human subjects' data, or manually specified by the artist only once, as part of the character's animation rig.

2.4 Coordinated Gaze and Arm Motion (planned)

After developing techniques for synthesis and editing of gaze behavior, the next phase in my research will be to investigate arm motion and its coordination with gaze. I am particularly interested in enabling ECAs to communicate using deictic and iconic gestures, due to the ability of such gestures to convey spatial concepts such as position, orientation, and direction, which are important in spatially situated interaction tasks.

This research thread will involve the following objectives. First, I will develop computational models of arm motion, using an approach analogous to the one used for the gaze shift model. I plan to make use of measurements of arm motion published in literature, data obtained using motion capture, and artistic intuitions of skilled animators, to derive parametrically controllable models for gesture animation, as well as investigate how these might be adapted to characters of different proportions and designs.

Second, I seek to understand how gaze and arm gestures coordinate in situated activities, as well as how they occur with respect to verbal references. This will require collection of human subjects' data in the form of annotated videos of human-human interactions.

Finally, I will develop models for planning of coordinated gaze and arm gestures in interactive, spatially situated tasks. The planning formulation must support a broad range of inputs that describe the meaning of the current communicative act (e.g., a request accompanied by a deictic reference towards some object), dialog state (e.g., discourse and turn-taking boundaries), and spatial layout of the situated interaction (locations of interaction partners and objects being referenced). Furthermore, in addition to producing natural and communicatively correct behavior for the given inputs, the planning formulation must also allow for artistic control, in order to improve the aesthetic appeal of the character's behavior and enrich it with idiosyncrasies reflecting its particular personality and style. For example, while the hand of a human might follow the shortest path in a pointing gesture, a cartoon character might instead point with a flourish, its hand following a dramatically exaggerated arc. I anticipate that this goal might be achieved by extending key ideas from the previous project. For instance, the notion of reusable, parametrized, functional patterns could be extended to incorporate arm gestures in addition to gaze; by giving animators the ability to manually author such patterns, we enable them to inject style and personality into the character's behavior. As a final outcome of this step, I envision a behavior planning approach that can produce such artist-directed behaviors in real-time, multimodal interaction, in combination with other nonverbal cues, without appearing unnatural or disrupting their communicative function.

3. EXPECTED CONTRIBUTIONS

The expected contributions from my research are as follows:

1. A set of parametric models for synthesis of nonverbal cues, informed by collected human subjects' data and prior research on human motion, exposing intuitive controls to designers and animators, and retargetable to a range of character designs. Current and planned nonverbal cues include building blocks of spatially situated behaviors, such as gaze shifts, deictic gestures, and iconic gestures.
2. Techniques for synthesis and editing of situated behaviors that allow enhanced artistic control through high-level communicative properties such as behavior frequency, spatial distribution, spatial layout, and communicative patterns.
3. Cohesive framework for planning coordinated nonverbal behaviors in situated, multimodal interaction that achieves the goals of behavior naturalness, communicative correctness and economy, and artistic control.
4. Software framework for embodied interaction based on Unity game engine, that provides animators and designers with tools needed to rapidly implement ECAs and endow them with natural behaviors for situated, multimodal interaction.

4. ACKNOWLEDGMENTS

This research has been supported by National Science Foundation awards 1017952 and 1208632. I would like to thank my advisors, Michael Gleicher and Bilge Mutlu, my colleagues in the Graphics Group and Human-Computer Interaction Group at the University of Wisconsin-Madison, as well as my mentors and colleagues at the Adaptive Systems and Interaction Group at Microsoft Research.

5. REFERENCES

[1] Andrist, S., Pejsa, T., Mutlu, B., and Gleicher, M. 2012. Designing effective gaze mechanisms for virtual agents, *Proc. CHI 2012*, 705-714.

[2] Bohus, D., and Horvitz, E. 2009. Dialog in the Open World: Platform and Applications. *Proc. of ICMI 2009*, 31-38.

[3] Cafaro, A., Gaito, R., and Vilhjalmsson, H. 2009. Animating Idle Gaze in Public Places. *Proc. IVA 2009*, 250-256.

[4] Cassell, J. 2000. More Than Just Another Pretty Face: Embodied Conversational Interface Agents, *Communications of the ACM*, 43, 70-78.

[5] Cassell, J., Torres, O.E., and Prevost, S. 1999. Turn Taking versus Discourse Structure. *Machine Conversations*, 511, 143-153.

[6] Frischen, A., Bayliss, A.P., and Tipper, S.P. 2007. Gaze Cueing of Attention: Visual Attention, Social Cognition, and Individual Differences. *Psychological Bulletin*, 133(4).

[7] Kopp, S., Krenn, B., Marsella, S., Marshall, A., Pelachaud, C., Pirker, H., Thórisson, K., and Vilhjalmsson, H. 2006. Towards a Common Framework for Multimodal Generation in ECAs: The Behavior Markup Language, *Proc. IVA 2006*, 205-217.

[8] Lee, S.P., Badler, J.B., and Badler, N.I. 2002. Eyes Alive. *ACM Transactions on Graphics*, 21, 637-644.

[9] Neff, M., Kipp, M., Albrecht, I., and Seidel, H.-P. 2008. Gesture Modeling and Animation Based on a Probabilistic Re-creation of Speaker Style, *ACM Transactions on Graphics*, 27(1), 5:1-5:24.

[10] Pejsa, T., Andrist, S., Gleicher, M., and Mutlu, B. 2014. Gaze and Attention Management for Embodied Conversational Agents, under review.

[11] Pejsa, T., Mutlu, B., and Gleicher, M. 2013. Stylized and Performative Gaze for Character Animation. *Computer Graphics Forum*, 32(2), 143-152.

[12] Pelachaud, C., and Bilvi, M. 2003. Modelling Gaze Behavior for Conversational Agents. *Proc. IVA 2003*, 93-100.

[13] Poggi, I., Pelachaud, C., and De Rosis, F. 2000. Eye Communication in a Conversational 3D Synthetic Agent. *AI Communications*, 13(3), 169-181.

[14] Thiebaux, M., Marsella, S., Marshall, A.N., and Kallmann, M. 2008. SmartBody: Behavior Realization for Embodied Conversational Agents. *Proc. AAMAS 2008*, 151-158.

Multimodal Analysis and Modeling of Nonverbal Behaviors during Tutoring

Joseph F. Grafsgaard
Department of Computer Science
North Carolina State University, Raleigh, NC, USA
jfgrafsg@ncsu.edu

ABSTRACT
Detecting learning-centered affective states is difficult, yet crucial for adapting most effectively to users. Within tutoring in particular, the combined context of student task actions and tutorial dialogue shape the student's affective experience. As we move toward detecting affect, we may also supplement the task and dialogue streams with rich sensor data. In studies of introductory computer programming tutoring, human tutors communicated with students through text-based interfaces. Manual and automated approaches were leveraged to annotate dialogue, task actions, facial movements, postural positions, and hand-to-face gestures. Prior investigations in this line of doctoral research identified associations between nonverbal behavior and learning-centered affect, such as engagement and frustration. Additionally, preliminary work used hidden Markov models to analyze sequences of affective tutorial interaction. Further work will address the sequential nature of the multimodal data. This line of research is expected to improve automated understanding of learning-centered affect, with particular insights into how affect unfolds from moment to moment during tutoring. This may result in systems that treat student affect not as transient states, but instead as interconnected links in a student's path toward learning.

Categories and Subject Descriptors
H.1.2 [**User/Machine Systems**]: Human factors; H.5.m [**Information Interfaces and Presentation (e.g., HCI)**]: Miscellaneous

General Terms
Human Factors

Keywords
Affect; multimodal; engagement; frustration; facial expression; gesture; posture; sequential analysis; tutorial dialogue

ICMI'14, November 12 - 16, 2014, Istanbul, Turkey
Copyright 2014 ACM 978-1-4503-2885-2/14/11…$15.00
http://dx.doi.org/10.1145/2663204.2667611

1. INTRODUCTION
Recent years have seen a growing recognition of the central role of affect and motivation in learning. In particular, learning-centered cognitive-affective states such as anxiety, confusion, engagement, and frustration may co-occur with positive or negative cycles of learning [17]. In the same way that highly effective human tutors pay attention to more factors than whether a student is simply correct or incorrect [13], automated approaches may be used to identify and understand students' nonverbal behaviors. Observed channels such as posture, gesture and facial expression provide key insights into students' affective and motivational states.

As students engage in computer-mediated task-oriented dialogue with a human tutor, their affective states are expressed through posture, gesture, and facial expression. Posture and gesture were tracked using novel algorithms on Kinect depth images [9]. This allowed for automated labeling of whether a student was shifting posture or contacting the lower face with a hand. Facial expression was recognized using an existing tool, the Computer Expression Recognition Toolbox (CERT) [14], which identified fine-grained facial movements at each frame of video. Prior analyses within this body of work have identified associations of nonverbal behavior and learning-centered affective states, such as anxiety, effortful concentration, engagement, and frustration [8–10].

Preliminary work used hidden Markov models (HMMs) to analyze sequences of affective tutorial interaction [8]. Descriptive HMMs were machine-learned from the combined context of facial expression, tutorial dialogue, and task progress in an unsupervised approach using the Baum-Welch algorithm. More recent work has produced a multimodal representation of nonverbal behavior related to affect during tutoring. These results will be extended with development of a framework for sequential analysis of affect, and comparison of multimodal affect sequences across students. This line of research is expected to improve automated understanding of learning-centered affect, with particular insights into how affect unfolds from moment to moment during tutoring. This may result in systems that treat student affect not as transient states, but instead as interconnected links in a student's path toward learning.

2. MULTIMODAL TUTORING CORPUS
The JavaTutor corpus consists of computer-mediated tutorial dialogue for introductory computer science collected during the 2011-2012 academic year. Students (N=67) and tutors interacted through a web-based interface that provided learning tasks, an interface for computer programming, and textual dialogue.

2.1 Study I: Initial Corpus

An initial corpus was collected during a tutorial dialogue study [3]. Students solved an introductory computer programming problem and engaged in computer-mediated textual dialogue with a human tutor. The corpus consists of 48 dialogues annotated with dialogue acts. Annotations also include information about student progress on the programming task [4]. The tutoring sessions ranged in duration from thirty minutes to over an hour. This corpus was used in preliminary investigations of facial expression and dialogue.

2.2 Study II: JavaTutor Corpus

The participants were university students in the United States, with average age of 18.5 years (*stdev*=1.5). The students voluntarily participated for course credit in an introductory engineering course, but no prior computer science knowledge was assumed or required. Recordings of the sessions included database logs, webcam video, skin conductance, and Kinect depth video. For logistical reasons, video and physiology were recorded only at the student workstations. The present analyses examine the database logs, webcam video, and Kinect depth video from the first lesson as a multimodal tutoring corpus. The JAVATUTOR interface is shown in Figure 1.

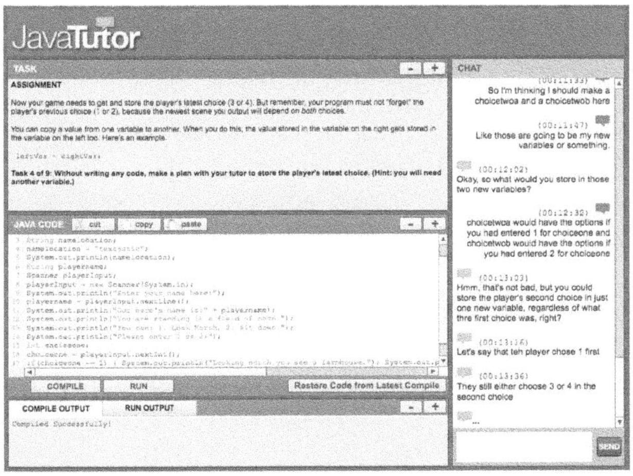

Figure 1. The JAVATUTOR interface

Before each session, students completed a content-based pretest. After each session, students answered a post-session survey and posttest (identical to the pretest). The post-session survey items included the User Engagement Survey (UES) [16] and the NASA-TLX workload survey [11], which included an item for Frustration Level.

2.3 Dialogue Acts

Student-tutor dialogue provides a rich source of data. Analyzing the dialogue transcripts can shed light on the effectiveness of tutoring strategies and participation of the student. Additionally, certain dialogue moves are related to student task progress and learning, as a tutor may need to provide more or less help.

The corpus was previously manually annotated using a fine-grained dialogue act annotation scheme [21]. A J48 decision tree classifier was constructed from these labels, producing an accuracy of 80.11% (Cohen's K = 0.79) on a held-out test set. This automatic dialogue act classifier [20] provided annotations of over 8,300 tutor and student messages across the corpus.

2.4 Nonverbal Behavior

We examined nonverbal behavior modalities as potential indicators of learning-centered cognitive-affective states across tutoring sessions. Recent advances in nonverbal behavior tracking were leveraged to recognize facial expression, hand-to-face gestures, and body posture. Due to human data collection error, the multimodal tutoring corpus includes nonverbal data for sixty-three of the sixty-seven students (N=63). The recording configuration is shown in Figure 2.

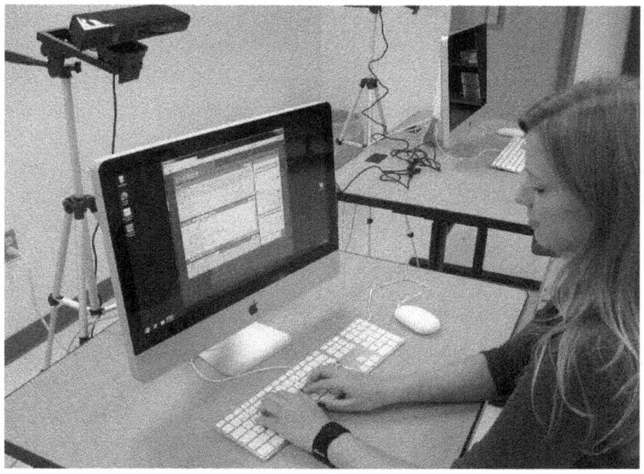

Figure 2. Student workstation with Kinect depth sensor, skin conductance bracelet, and computer with webcam

2.4.1 Facial Expression

The corpus includes facial expression annotations from the Computer Expression Recognition Toolbox (CERT) [14]. This tool recognizes fine-grained facial movements, or facial *action units (AUs)*, detailed in the Facial Action Coding System [7]. CERT finds faces in a video frame, locates facial features for the nearest face, and outputs weights for each tracked facial action unit using support vector machines.

Based on the results of a validation study of CERT output, we adopt the method of mean-centering the output of CERT [10]. The validation study showed that this adjustment to CERT output produced excellent aggregate agreement with manual FACS annotations on a subset of five action units, while unadjusted CERT output did not. Also in accordance with that study [10], we use a mean-centered output threshold of 0.25 for presence of a facial action unit. This higher threshold may reduce false positives compared to the default threshold of any positive value. Additionally, we examine the five action units that were previously validated: AU1 (Inner Brow Raiser), AU2 (Outer Brow Raiser), AU4 (Brow Lowerer), AU7 (Lid Tightener), and AU14 (Mouth Dimpler).

2.4.2 Posture

Postural features were created using depth image recordings from the Kinect sensor. A posture tracking algorithm identified distances of the head, upper torso, and lower torso. This posture tracking algorithm was previously found to be 92.4% accurate versus manual labels [9].

Head distances were then used to discretize postural distance (POSNEAR, POSMID, and POSFAR), based on workstation-specific median distances and standard deviation. One standard deviation closer or farther than the median (across subjects) was considered "near" or "far," respectively.

Additionally, postural movements were labeled based on acceleration of the head tracking point. The absolute sum of frame-to-frame acceleration was accumulated in a rolling one-second window at each frame. The average amount of acceleration in a one-second interval was computed across all students. If acceleration in the present interval was above average, it was marked as a postural movement, PosMove; otherwise, it was marked as NoMove.

2.4.3 Gesture
Hand-to-face gestures were also tracked in the Kinect depth sensor recordings. A gesture detection algorithm recognized one or two hands touching the lower face. This algorithm relies on surface propagation from the center of the head, with pixel distances from the center used to identify a round (i.e., normal head shape) or an oblong shape (i.e., surface extends beyond the head) formed by the surface pixels. The hand-to-face gesture detection algorithm was previously found to be 92.6% accurate compared to manual labels [9].

2.5 Multimodal Features
The automatically recognized dialogue acts and nonverbal behaviors were combined with task action features in order to form the multimodal tutoring corpus. As students worked on programming tasks, the database logged dialogue messages, typing, and task progress. Tutorial dialogue occurred at any time during the sessions, with student and tutor messages sent asynchronously (StudentMessage and TutorMessage, respectively). Each of these student and tutor messages has an associated dialogue act label, as described in Section 2.3. These dialogue events comprise the Dialogue data stream.

The Task data stream consists of student task actions. As a student completed the programming task, he or she would press a compile button to convert the Java program code into a format that is ready to run. These compile attempts may be successful (CompileSuccess) or fail due to an error in the program code (CompileError). The student would also run his or her program (RunProgram) in order to test the output and interact with it. The student may also be working on the program code (Coding), or have stopped coding (StopCoding) at each moment.

The Nonverbal data stream consists of student facial expression, hand-to-face gestures, and posture. Each of the nonverbal behaviors were tracked at all times, so they were combined in parallel (i.e., each interval records the presence or absence of facial expression, gesture, and posture).

These data streams were discretized into one-second intervals. The most recent event of a given type (Dialogue, Nonverbal, Task) was used as the current value at each interval. For instance, if a student had been coding but stopped after half a second into the current interval, the task action would be assigned to StopCoding. These one-second time intervals were used to calculate relative duration following a specific dialogue event or task action, or during a particular nonverbal behavioral display. Thus, each possible feature has a single numerical value (relative duration) for each student session. This enables corpus-wide analysis of multimodal events relevant to affect in tutoring.

3. MULTIMODAL FEATURE ANALYSIS
Recent analyses were conducted to identify multimodal nonverbal behaviors associated with tutorial outcomes. Linear regression models were built for each of the three tutoring outcomes (described in Section 2.2): engagement, frustration, and learning gain. The results identified multimodal events related to cognitive and affective tutorial outcomes. Excerpts of these results, shown in Sections 3.2 through 3.4, describe multimodal events significantly predictive of the respective tutorial outcomes.

3.1 Model Construction
Model averaging was used to identify the most generalizable features and to reduce the feature space [19]. This approach produces average coefficient estimates and standard error across a wide range of linear regression models. Ratios of absolute value of the coefficient estimate versus standard error were also computed. These ratios provided a tradeoff between predictive weight and numerical stability. The features were then sorted using the ratios and the top twenty were selected for use in model building. Predictive models were built using forward stepwise linear regression. Features were selected to optimize the leave-one-out cross-validated R^2 value of each model.

3.2 Engagement
A sequence of tutoring events related to engagement is shown in Figure 3. The left image shows the student coding the program. The middle shows when the student had stopped coding and read a yes/no answer from the tutor. In the right image, the student has returned to coding the program.

Coding | AYN-Tutor, PosNear, StopCoding | Coding

Figure 3. Sequence related to engagement

3.3 Frustration
A sequence of tutoring events related to frustration is shown in Figure 4. First, the student encounters a compile error. The tutor then directs the student on how to fix the problem. Second, the student reports her understanding of the directive and implements the solution. Third, the tutor tells the student to compile and she does so successfully.

CompileError | FU-Student, PosNear, Coding | CompileSuccess

Figure 4. Sequence related to frustration

3.4 Normalized Learning Gain

A sequence of events related to learning is shown in Figure 5. In the first image, the student is testing his program. Further in the session, the student has begun coding more of the program. In the second image, the student has stopped coding and displayed AU4 as the tutor asked an open-ended question. The third image shows the student at a farther postural distance after successfully compiling the program.

RUNPROGRAM QO-TUTOR, AU4, STOPCODING COMPILESUCCESS

Figure 5. Sequence related to normalized learning gain

4. CONTRIBUTIONS

This doctoral research project explores the fundamental human experience of emotion within the context of tutoring. Effective human tutors attend to a student's feelings and motivation in addition to cognitive performance [13]. Thus, a comprehensive approach to tutoring necessarily considers nonverbal expressions of emotion. Accordingly, this line of doctoral research investigates posture, gesture, and facial expression as indicators of student cognitive and affective states.

4.1 Prior Contributions

This work has added to the research literature in affective computing, educational data mining, intelligent tutoring systems, and multimodal interaction. Initial investigations examined individual modalities of nonverbal behavior related to affect during tutoring, with more recent work examining multimodal data.

Facial Expression Annotation: Facial expression was manually annotated to provide high quality information on facial expression and for comparison with automated techniques. Coders were trained in the standard research protocol for facial expression annotation (the Facial Action Coding System) and inter-rater agreement was assessed [8].

Multimodal Data Collection: A large human-human tutoring corpus was collected using a wide array of affect channels, including facial expression, posture, gesture, and skin conductance. This effort also involved synchronization of the data streams at millisecond precision (Section 2).

Automated Facial Expression Recognition: An automated facial expression recognition toolbox was validated against manual annotations and then applied to the large human-human tutoring corpus. The validation analysis presented a first-of-its-kind large-scale comparison of manual annotations and automated facial expression tracking output [10].

Novel Posture Tracking & Gesture Detection Algorithms: New techniques were developed to allow automated tracking of posture and gesture from Kinect depth recordings in the tutoring corpus. Accuracy of these algorithms was compared against manual labels [9].

Analyses of Nonverbal Behavior in Tutoring: The associations among nonverbal behavior, affect, and learning were explored through multiple analyses. These analyses provided insight into key affective states, such as confusion, engagement, and frustration, as well as tutoring phenomena including self-efficacy and learning [9, 10].

Multimodal Affect Representation and Feature Selection: Affective states may be represented in terms of behavioral data streams (e.g., posture, gesture, facial expression) or as labels of momentary affective states. With a large, automated dataset of nonverbal behavior, it is possible to consider a variety of representations. Low-level descriptors of nonverbal behaviors were merged with task events to provide synchronized multimodal events (Section 2.5).

4.2 Expected Contributions

Further work in this line of doctoral research will focus on the sequential nature of the multimodal data. A sequential analysis framework will be developed to investigate multimodal sequences related to student affect during tutoring.

A Framework for Sequential Analysis of Affect: Preliminary results in the author's prior work showed that hidden Markov models could identify frequently repeated sequences of student and tutor interaction, with corresponding student facial expressions [8]. These results will be extended by using sequential analysis across a wider set of nonverbal behavior in the automatically labeled corpus of posture, gesture, and facial expression.

Comparison of Multimodal Sequences: Sequential modeling will be used to examine student differences in cognitive and motivational characteristics, as well as task performance and affective tutoring outcomes. The proposed approach will contrast sequences of affective tutorial interaction specific to groups of students segmented by cognitive and affective tutorial outcomes and incoming characteristics.

5. FUTURE WORK

Work on sequential analysis in tutoring has addressed the issue of analyzing learning-centered affective states over time. The approaches used have evolved from direct analyses of conditional probabilities to more complex statistical and algorithmic techniques. Further work on this doctoral research will focus on developing a framework for sequential analysis of multimodal event sequences.

Initial work focused on identifying which learning-centered affective states were most likely to occur next given a particular affective state. This has been termed the *L* metric, which provides a value of how likely a transition from one affective state to another is, while correcting for the base probability of transitioning to that state. This has been used to examine student affect during intelligent tutoring, [5, 6] classroom observations [1, 2], and interactions with narrative-centered learning environments [15].

Motif discovery is an algorithmic approach to identify frequent subsequences in time series. This approach involves tabulation of events as symbols. Similar events are compared with a hamming distance threshold and added as a motif. This has been applied to interactions with the Wayang Outpost intelligent tutoring system, revealing sequences associated with frustration, on-task behavior, and gaming the system [18].

Differential sequence mining is a statistical approach that has been used to identify repeated subsequences in tutoring event time series. This approach considers time series across students, identifying the most frequent subsequences using pattern mining across the corpus (*sequence support*) and for each individual student (*instance support*). Statistical comparisons are used to identify the most significant differences in the sequences across two groups of students. This approach has identified sequences of tutorial interaction related to productive or unproductive work in the Betty's Brain tutoring system, but it has not been applied to analysis of affect [12].

The next step in this doctoral research project is to develop a framework for sequential analysis of multimodal data. Differential sequence mining is the ideal technique, as it enables readily interpretable comparisons between two student groups. Thus, sequential patterns of multimodal events may be found that distinguish between high and low levels of student cognitive-affective states, such as engagement or frustration. There are two technical hurdles to this approach: 1) the pattern mining algorithm must allow for multiple modalities, and 2) an instance support measure must be implemented.

The sequential analyses are expected to address two hypotheses:

H1: Multimodal sequences in the tutoring corpus are significantly associated with students' retrospective affect self-reports, both in terms of *engagement* and *frustration*.

H2: Multimodal sequences differ significantly across student groupings based on incoming characteristics, specifically *self-efficacy*.

ACKNOWLEDGEMENTS

This work is supported in part by the North Carolina State University Department of Computer Science along with the National Science Foundation through Grants DRL-1007962 and IIS-1409639. Any opinions, findings, conclusions, or recommendations expressed in this report are those of the participants, and do not necessarily represent the official views, opinions, or policy of the National Science Foundation. I would also like to express gratitude to my advisors, Kristy Elizabeth Boyer and James C. Lester, and colleagues in the Center for Educational Informatics for their support and feedback during my doctoral research.

REFERENCES

[1] Baker, R.S.J. d., D'Mello, S.K., Rodrigo, M.M.T. and Graesser, A.C. 2010. Better to Be Frustrated than Bored: The Incidence, Persistence, and Impact of Learners' Cognitive-Affective States during Interactions with Three Different Computer-Based Learning Environments. *International Journal of Human-Computer Studies*. 68, 4, 223–241.

[2] Baker, R.S.J. d., Rodrigo, M.M.T. and Xolocotzin, U.E. 2007. The Dynamics of Affective Transitions in Simulation Problem-Solving Environments. *Proceedings of the 2nd International Conference on Affective Computing and Intelligent Interaction*, 666–677.

[3] Boyer, K.E., Ha, E.Y., Wallis, M., Phillips, R., Vouk, M.A. and Lester, J.C. 2009. Discovering tutorial dialogue strategies with hidden Markov models. *Proceedings of the 14th International Conference on Artificial Intelligence in Education*, 141–148.

[4] Boyer, K.E., Phillips, R., Ingram, A., Ha, E.Y., Wallis, M., Vouk, M.A. and Lester, J.C. 2010. Characterizing the Effectiveness of Tutorial Dialogue with Hidden Markov Models. *Proceedings of the 10th International Conference on Intelligent Tutoring Systems*, 55–64.

[5] D'Mello, S.K. and Graesser, A.C. 2012. Dynamics of affective states during complex learning. *Learning and Instruction*. 22, 2, 145–157.

[6] D'Mello, S.K., Taylor, R.S. and Graesser, A.C. 2007. Monitoring Affective Trajectories during Complex Learning. *Proceedings of the 29th Annual Meeting of the Cognitive Science Society*, 203–208.

[7] Ekman, P., Friesen, W. V. and Hager, J.C. 2002. *Facial Action Coding System*. A Human Face.

[8] Grafsgaard, J.F., Boyer, K.E. and Lester, J.C. 2011. Predicting Facial Indicators of Confusion with Hidden Markov Models. *Proceedings of the 4th International Conference on Affective Computing and Intelligent Interaction*, 97–106.

[9] Grafsgaard, J.F., Fulton, R.M., Boyer, K.E., Wiebe, E.N. and Lester, J.C. 2012. Multimodal Analysis of the Implicit Affective Channel in Computer-Mediated Textual Communication. *Proceedings of the 14th ACM International Conference on Multimodal Interaction*, 145–152.

[10] Grafsgaard, J.F., Wiggins, J.B., Boyer, K.E., Wiebe, E.N. and Lester, J.C. 2013. Automatically Recognizing Facial Expression: Predicting Engagement and Frustration. *Proceedings of the 6th International Conference on Educational Data Mining*, 43–50.

[11] Hart, S.G. and Staveland, L.E. 1988. Development of NASA-TLX (Task Load Index): Results of Empirical and Theoretical Research. *Human Mental Workload*. P.A. Hancock and N. Meshkati, eds. Elsevier Science. 139–183.

[12] Kinnebrew, J.S., Loretz, K.M. and Biswas, G. 2013. A Contextualized, Differential Sequence Mining Method to Derive Students' Learning Behavior Patterns. *Journal of Educational Data Mining*. 5, 1, 190–219.

[13] Lepper, M.R. and Woolverton, M. 2002. The Wisdom of Practice: Lessons Learned from the Study of Highly Effective Tutors. *Improving Academic Achievement*. J. Aronson, ed. Elsevier. 135–158.

[14] Littlewort, G., Whitehill, J., Wu, T., Fasel, I., Frank, M., Movellan, J.R. and Bartlett, M.S. 2011. The Computer Expression Recognition Toolbox (CERT). *Proceedings of the IEEE International Conference on Automatic Face and Gesture Recognition*, 298–305.

[15] McQuiggan, S.W., Robison, J.L. and Lester, J.C. 2010. Affective Transitions in Narrative-Centered Learning Environments. *Educational Technology & Society*. 13, 1, 40–53.

[16] O'Brien, H.L. and Toms, E.G. 2010. The Development and Evaluation of a Survey to Measure User Engagement. *Journal of the American Society for Information Science and Technology*. 61, 1, 50–69.

[17] Pekrun, R. 2006. The Control-Value Theory of Achievement Emotions: Assumptions, Corollaries, and Implications for Educational Research and Practice. *Educational Psychology Review*. 18, 4, 315–341.

[18] Shanabrook, D.H., Cooper, D.G., Woolf, B.P. and Arroyo, I. 2010. Identifying High-Level Student Behavior Using Sequence-based Motif Discovery. *Proceedings of the 3rd International Conference on Educational Data Mining*, 191–200.

[19] Symonds, M.R.E. and Moussalli, A. 2010. A Brief Guide to Model Selection, Multimodel Inference and Model Averaging in Behavioural Ecology using Akaike's Information Criterion. *Behavioral Ecology and Sociobiology*. 65, 1, 13–21.

[20] Vail, A.K. and Boyer, K.E. 2014. Adapting to Personality Over Time: Examining the Effectiveness of Dialogue Policy Progressions in Task-Oriented Interaction. *Proceedings of the 15th Annual SIGDIAL Meeting on Discourse and Dialogue*, 41–50.

[21] Vail, A.K. and Boyer, K.E. 2014. Identifying Effective Moves in Tutoring: On the Refinement of Dialogue Act Annotation Schemes. *Proceedings of the 12th International Conference on Intelligent Tutoring Systems*, 199–209.

Computation of Emotions

Peter Robinson
University of Cambridge Computer Laboratory
15 JJ Thomson Avenue
Cambridge CB3 0FD England
pr@cl.cam.ac.uk

ABSTRACT

When people talk to each other, they express their feelings through facial expressions, tone of voice, body postures and gestures. They even do this when they are interacting with machines. These hidden signals are an important part of human communication, but most computer systems ignore them. Emotions need to be considered as an important mode of communication between people and interactive systems. Affective computing has enjoyed considerable success over the past 20 years, but many challenges remain.

Categories and Subject Descriptors

H.5 [**Information Systems**]: Information interfaces and presentation—*User interfaces*; I.3.6 [**Computing Methodologies**]: Computer Graphics—*Interaction techniques*.

Keywords

Affective computing, emotions, human-computer interaction.

1. INTRODUCTION

Charles Darwin published *The expression of the emotions in man and animals* in 1872, exploring the role of emotional expression in communication between humans. Over a century later, Rosalind Picard observed that effective communication between people and computers also requires emotional intelligence; computers must have the ability to recognize and express emotions.

The study of affective computing has blossomed subsequently. This paper presents a summary of some of the challenges involved in affective computing, and illustrates them with examples drawn from work in the Computer Laboratory at the University of Cambridge[1]; it is not intended as a comprehensive survey. We have also produced a video, *The Emotional Computer* [6], which gives a light-hearted account of some of the projects[2].

[1] `http://www.cl.cam.ac.uk/emotions/`
[2] `http://www.youtube.com/watch?v=whCJ4NLUSB8`

ICMI'14, November 12–16, 2014, Istanbul, Turkey.
ACM 978-1-4503-2885-2/14/11.
http://dx.doi.org/10.1145/2663204.2669638.

2. RECOGNISING EMOTIONS

Although Darwin concentrated on facial features to convey emotions in Expression, he also mentions vocal sounds, other sounds, body posture and gesture, and physiological responses as further indications of emotion. All of these channels have been considered as ways of automatic monitoring emotion in humans, although these sensors used for some are more invasive than for others. Signals that can be monitored non-invasively are of particular interest for pervasive computing.

2.1 Facial expressions

People routinely express their mental states through their facial expressions and this is one of the clearest channels for communication. Inference from facial expressions has been studied using a variety of techniques but mostly restricted to six basic emotions. Recognising complex, cognitive mental states is more difficult, but probably more useful as part of general interaction with computer systems. We have developed a fully automatic system requiring no human intervention which operates in real-time [4]. Our Facial Affect Inference System uses a multi-level representation of the video input, combined in a Bayesian inference framework operating at four levels: facial feature points, FACS action units (AUs), gestures composed of several AUs, and mental states.

An evaluation considered six conditions together covering a tenth of the range of mental states. For a mean false positive rate of 4.7%, the overall accuracy of the system is 77%. The system also generalises well to faces not included in the training data.

We have also considered inference of continuous measures of valence (from negative to positive) and arousal (from passive to active) [1].

2.2 Non-verbal aspects of speech

The voice provides another significant channel for the expression of emotions. Features such as the pitch, energy and tempo can reveal a lot about the mood of the speaker. There are no characteristic features that indicate particular mental states but it is possible to distinguish between using two emotions using a small number of features, with a different set of features may be required to distinguish those emotions from others. Our approach [8] has been to calculate a large collection of about 170 features for each utterance. A training phase uses data mining to identify the features that separate each pair of emotional conditions. The operational phase then uses these pair-wise comparisons as preferences in a voting scheme to give an overall ranking.

Evaluation separated nine conditions with an accuracy of 70%, increasing to 83% if multiple winners were considered. The approach also generalises well to speakers other than those used for training, and even to other languages.

2.3 Body posture and gesture

The third natural channel for expression of emotions includes body posture and gesture. However, characteristics indicating the movement being considered and who is doing it must be discounted before it is possible to analyse how it is being done. Movement involves an individual bias, so the analysis is harder than for facial expressions or voice [2].

Our approach breaks complex motions down into a system of isolated elements whose dynamic cues can be used to distinguish affects. As with speech, pair-wise comparisons are used on individual motion segments, and each segment is classified using a majority vote. A complete motion is then classified by a majority vote of its component segments.

The method was tested on a corpus of about 1200 motion samples, representing roughly equal numbers of four expressions of four different actions. The average recognition rate of 81% is comparable to the rates achieved by human observers of similar data.

3. EXPRESSING EMOTIONS

Humans routinely convey empathetic responses through involuntary facial mimicry, and this extends to human-robot interaction. An experiment showed that conversation between a participant and a robot is enhanced when the robot mimics the subject rather than moves randomly. This raises questions about the degree of human-likeness required in the appearance of robots that interact with humans. A further experiment investigated participants' empathy for robots shown in film clips, and the responses were directly correlated with human-likeness.

The technology has been tested using a high-fidelity robotic head which simulates movements disorders that might be encountered by trainee doctors [5], and we are currently looking at its use as an intervention for autism therapy.

4. APPLICATIONS

An early application of affective inference is monitoring cognitive load in command-and-control systems. Driving a car provides a good model for this, but it is difficult to construct repeatable experiments using real cars on real roads. Simulation allows controlled experiments, but fails to engage participants. Remote control of real vehicles retains control while enhancing emotional investment [3].

Autism Spectrum Conditions (ASCs) are neurodevelopmental conditions characterized by social communication difficulties and restricted and repetitive behaviour patterns. The European ASC-Inclusion project [7] aims to create and evaluate the effectiveness of an internet-based game platform, intended for children with ASCs and their carers. The platform combines several state-of-the art technologies in one comprehensive virtual world providing training through games, and including feedback from analysis of the player's gestures, facial and vocal expressions using a standard webcam and microphone. The game also includes text communication with peers and smart agents, animation, video and audio clips. One component of the game monitors the player's face while he or she is acting a particular emotion. Computer vision and machine learning are then used to infer the emotion depicted and report back, both assessing the player's performance and also suggesting changes to make it resemble a canonical performance more closely.

5. ACKNOWLEDGEMENTS

Many colleagues in the Computer Laboratory at the University of Cambridge have contributed to this work – notably Andra Adams, Shazia Afzal, Tadas Baltrušaitis, Ntombi Banda, Daniel Bernhardt, Ian Davies, Neil Dodgson, Yujian Gao, Vaiva Imbrasaitė, Rana el Kaliouby, Marwa Mahmoud, Tomas Pfister, Laurel Riek, Metin Sezgin and Tal Sobol Shikler. Simon Baron-Cohen and his colleagues in the Autism Research Centre have provided numerous technical insights. Kevin Hull produced and directed the *Emotional Computer* video. Parts of the work have been undertaken with support from the EPSRC, the European Commission, the Cambridge-MIT Institute, the Gates Cambridge Trust, Hanson Robotics, the Yousef Jameel Studentship, the Qualcomm Studentship, Thales Research & Technology, Toyota ITC, Vicon UK, the Neil Wiseman Fund and the University of Cambridge. ASC-Inclusion has received funding from the European Community's Seventh Framework Programme (FP7/2007-2013) under grant agreement number 289021.

6. REFERENCES

[1] T. Baltrušaitis, N. Banda, and P. Robinson. Dimensional affect recognition using continuous conditional random fields. In *IEEE Conference on Automatic Face and Gesture Recognition*, April 2013.

[2] D. Bernhardt and P. Robinson. Detecting affect from non-stylised body motions. In *Affective Computing and Intelligent Interaction*, pages 59–70, Lisbon, Portugal, 2007. Springer-Verlag.

[3] I. P. Davies and P. Robinson. Emotional investment in naturalistic data collection. In *Affective Computing and Intelligent Interaction*, Memphis, TN, Oct. 2011.

[4] R. el Kaliouby and P. Robinson. Real-time inference of complex mental states from facial expressions and head gestures. In *Computer Society Conference on Computer Vision and Pattern Recognition*, page 154, Washington, DC, 2004.

[5] L. D. Riek and P. Robinson. Synthesising head and facial movement disorders on android robots. In *International Symposium on Facial Analysis and Animation*, Edinburgh, Scotland, October 2010.

[6] P. Robinson, T. Baltrušaitis, I. P. Davies, T. J. Pfister, L. D. Riek, and K. Hull. The emotional computer. In *International Conference on Pervasive Computing*, San Francisco, CA, June 2011.

[7] B. W. Schuller, E. Marchi, S. Baron-Cohen, H. O'Reilly, P. Robinson, I. P. Davies, O. Golan, S. Fridenson, S. Tal, S. Newman, N. Meir-Goren, R. Shillo, A. Camurri, and S. Piana. ASC-Inclusion: Interactive emotion games for social inclusion of children with Autism Spectrum Conditions. In *Intelligent Digital Games for Empowerment and Inclusion*, May 2013.

[8] T. Sobol Shikler and P. Robinson. Classification of complex information: inference of co-occurring affective states from their expressions in speech. *IEEE Transactions on Pattern Analysis and Machine Intelligence*, 32(7):1284–1297, July 2010.

Non-Visual Navigation Using Combined Audio Music and Haptic Cues

Emily Fujimoto
University of California, Santa Barbara
efujimoto@cs.ucsb.edu

Matthew Turk
University of California, Santa Barbara
mturk@cs.ucsb.edu

ABSTRACT

While a great deal of work has been done exploring non-visual navigation interfaces using audio and haptic cues, little is known about the combination of the two. We investigate combining different state-of-the-art interfaces for communicating direction and distance information using vibrotactile and audio music cues, limiting ourselves to interfaces that are possible with current off-the-shelf smartphones. We use experimental logs, subjective task load questionnaires, and user comments to see how users' perceived performance, objective performance, and acceptance of the system varied for different combinations. Users' perceived performance did not differ much between the unimodal and multimodal interfaces, but a few users commented that the multimodal interfaces added some cognitive load. Objective performance showed that some multimodal combinations resulted in significantly less direction or distance error over some of the unimodal ones, especially the purely haptic interface. Based on these findings we propose a few design considerations for multimodal haptic/audio navigation interfaces.

Categories and Subject Descriptors

H.5.2 [**Information Interfaces and Presentation**]: User Interfaces—*auditory feedback, evaluation, haptic I/O*

Keywords

Non-visual navigation; spatial audio; vibrotactile feedback

1. INTRODUCTION

Many people today rely on navigation devices, especially their smartphones, to guide them from one place to another. While users can receive spoken instructions, most applications rely on visual information, such as maps or directions lists. However, walking while looking at one's phone, while common, is not safe (e.g. [9]). It also requires users to hold and actively interact with their phone, interrupting whatever else they are doing. Imagine instead an interface that could guide users without needing to be removed from their pocket, one that could integrate itself into another common activity, like listening to music. This would improve safety and require little additional effort from the user.

Audio and tactile cues are the two most commonly used visual replacements. In addition to verbal instructions, spatial audio has also been used for navigation. Usually this is done by making it appear as though there is a sound source on the target location. Vibration cues is another method for giving directions with haptics. However, in many instances this involves custom hardware with multiple vibrators that the user must acquire independently. Because of this, recent research has explored using off-the-shelf smartphones due to their ubiquitous nature. Unfortunately this significantly limits what can be manipulated as current phones only have one vibrating motor that can only be turned on or off; the vibration strength or roughness cannot be modified.

Although many audio and haptic alternatives have been explored, almost no alternatives using a combination of the two have been investigated without custom hardware. The benefit of using audio is that people already listen to music while walking, providing a behavior that could easily be adapted to suit navigational needs. It also requires no extra training to locate a sound source, unlike current methods of single vibrator navigation. However, modifying the user's music might decrease their enjoyment of it. There could also be confusion between between natural musical changes and manipulated ones meant to convey information. A vibrotactile interface does not have this problem and would not interfere with musical enjoyment, but it is not as natural as audio cues. A combination of these two modalities could create a navigational interface that is clearly understandable without detracting from the user's original activity. This paper explores how some combinations affect a user's performance, perceptions, and music listening experience.

2. RELATED WORK

As mentioned, one method of giving directions through audio cues is with spatial audio. For example, instead of saying "Go left," a virtual sound source could be placed to the user's left to indicate their target direction. Since it is not feasible to place speakers everywhere, this is accomplished through audio processing and headphones. One advantage of using spatial audio over spatial language is that spatial audio requires less mental effort to decode [7].

One of the early navigation studies by Holland et al. [5] used spatial audio to pan a tone right or left to indicate the target location. To help users find their goal, they added an extra "chase" tone that matched the pitch of the original

ICMI'14, November 12–16, 2014, Istanbul, Turkey.
Copyright 2014 ACM 978-1-4503-2885-2/14/11 ...$15.00.
http://dx.doi.org/10.1145/2663204.2663243.

tone until the user strayed off course, at which point its pitch would rise or fall. Distance was conveyed by how quickly the tone was repeated, using a geiger counter metaphor to increase the rate of the tone as the user got closer.

One advantage to using tones, like Holland et al. did, is that factors such as pitch and timbre can be used to convey information. However, it far more likely that people would prefer to listen to music rather than tones, so many later studies focus on manipulating music instead. While music could be modified like the tones were, Jones et al. [6] found that users disliked even a slight pitch alteration. This constrains the ways that information can be passed.

Since it would be annoying to pulse music like a geiger counter, distance is usually conveyed through volume, louder signifying closer. While this matches the idea of placing a musical source on the target, there are a couple of drawbacks. One is that, as seen in the work of Jones et al. [6], users can have trouble distinguishing gradual volume changes, resulting in heading in the wrong direction for some time before realizing that the sound is getting softer. In addition, the natural crescendos and decrescendos in the music can be confused with a change in distance information. Some have chosen to address this with further audio augmentation, such as adding a low-pass filter to muffle the music when the user is heading away from their target [3]. Liljedahl et al. [8], however, chose only to give distance information when approaching a turning point. Once at that point, they would pan the sound to one side, mimicking a turning gesture, to indicate where to head next. Furthermore, their use of notification tones rather than music avoided any confusion between natural changes and those they were manipulating.

Instead of using audio, some have experimented with using haptic cues for navigation. One advantage with haptics is that tactile senses, unlike auditory ones, are not generally used while navigating. One approach to conveying information has been to place multiple vibrating motors on the user's body, lending a spatial quality to the information. Information can then be conveyed by vibrating them in different patterns [2, 13]. However, this requires custom hardware, so subsequent work has focused on using only a single vibrating device such as cellphones. Since there are no longer spatial cues, this unfortunately means the user requires more training to learn the different signals.

To find the most intuitive interface Pielot et al. [10, 11] have tried conveying different types of information, including approaching or departing and a target direction expressed on either a discreet (left, right, straight ahead) or continuous scale. The final interface, Pocket Navigator, used a geiger counter metaphor for distance and a series of pulses for directions on a continuous scale. If the phone gave two short vibrations, the target was in front of the user. The longer the first vibration was in comparison to the second, the further to the left the target was, and vice versa for targets to the right. If the target was immediately behind the user, the phone would vibrate three times (Figure 1).

Rukzio, Hardy, and Rumelin [12] instead combined various vibration strengths, durations, patterns, and roughness to communicate direction and distance. Their interface, aptly named NaviRadar, would signal the current heading, wait as the imaginary radar "swept" the screen, and then signal again when it had reached the desired direction (Figure 2). Their final design used the vibration intensity for

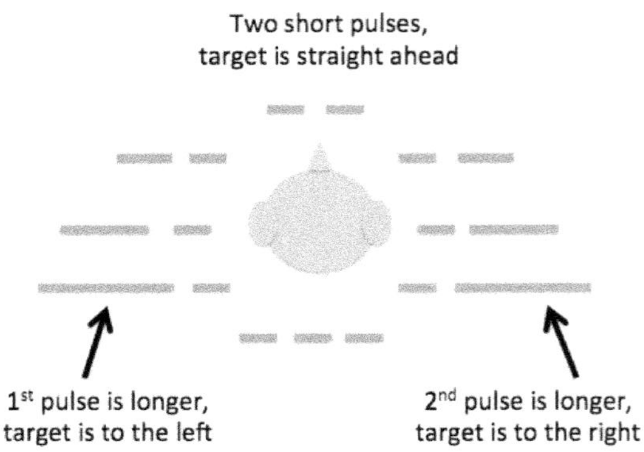

Figure 1: The vibration encodings to communicate different directions used by Pocket Navigator[11].

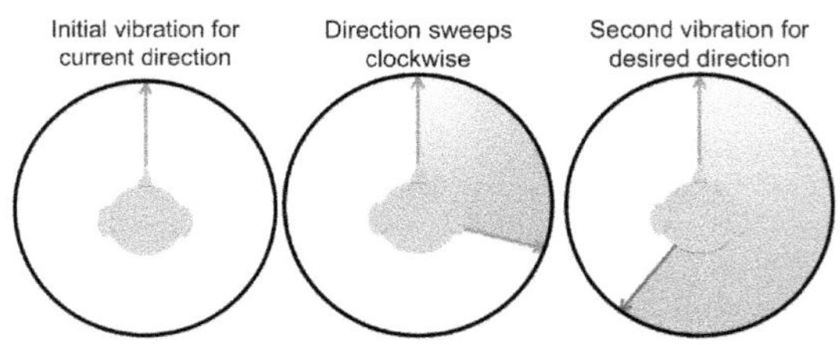

Figure 2: The direction interface used by NaviRadar[12]. The first vibration represents the direction the user is facing. Then an imaginary line sweeps around the user like radar to vibrate again, in a different pattern, in the desired direction.

distance and different rhythms (one vibration versus two) to distinguish the current direction from desired.

A great deal of work has been done with both audio and tactile navigation methods individually. However, the only interface that has combined both audio and single-motor vibrations is in the work of Hara et al. [4]. Since their focus was on the testing environment rather than the navigation technique, the interface was relatively simplistic; when the user began to stray off course, the device vibrated and played a chime at the same time, using different patterns to indicate how far off course the user was. To our knowledge, no one has attempted to combine more complicated unimodal interfaces. By joining these two modalities, we can start to find ways to leverage the benefits of each one.

3. EXPERIMENTAL METHODS

Users tested six interfaces in a simulated navigational task. For this task, users walked around a room while responding to periodic navigational cues. The room had two large projector screens taking up the majority of two adjacent walls. The area in front of the projectors was left open with a square outlined on the floor to circle the majority of the space as a rough guideline of where to walk. At the back of the room was a table and lamp for filling out forms and some chairs for resting (see Figure 3). To encourage awareness of their surroundings during the task, as is needed to safely navigate, users were also asked to note when a given target image appeared on one of the projector screens. Both screens displayed the same image at all times, and to make it easier to see the projected images, the overhead lights were

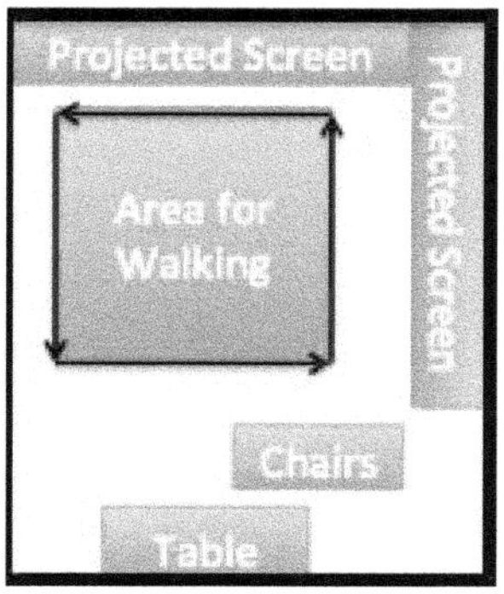

Figure 3: Experimental setup.

Table 1: Summary of direction and distance encodings to be tested.

	Haptic	Audio	
Direction	*DirHapVib* Vibration patterns 1	*DirAudSpatial* Stationary sound source 2	*DirAudSweeps* Moving sound source 3
Distance	*DistHapGeiger* Time between vibrations A	*DistAudVol* Music volume B	

turned off. However, the lamp at the back of the room was kept on to provide enough light to see their surroundings.

3.1 Interfaces

To test the effectiveness of combined audio/haptic interfaces, we chose to communicate very basic navigational information: direction and distance. Based on previous work we chose to communicate *direction* using three methods and *distance* with two, for six total interfaces. We limited ourselves to methods that could be implemented on off-the-shelf smartphones. This constrained haptic manipulation to turning the vibrator on and off. We also focused on interfaces that did not require the user actively to manipulate their device, meaning the user could receive directions with the phone still in their pocket. This keeps the user's hands free and able to perform other tasks.

We refer to the three direction methods as DirHapVib (1), DirAudSpatial (2), and DirAudSweeps (3). DirHapVib (1) is from Pocket Navigator, which uses two vibrations to indicate direction as described above. DirAudSpatial (2) is the method most commonly used for spatial audio navigation: make sound come from the target direction. DirAudSweeps (3) is from the work of Liljedahl et al. which also uses spatial audio. Instead of placing a stationary sound source, the interface places the target in front of the user and gradually "sweeps" around until it is at the target location before resetting and repeating. The two distance methods are DistHapGeiger (A) and DistAudVol (B). DistHapGeiger (A) users the geiger counter metaphor used by Pocket Navigator. DistAudioVol (B) relies on the metaphor of placing an audio beacon on a target, so the music is louder the closer the user is to the target (see Table 1 for a summary).

Direction information was limited to the 180 degrees in front of the user. We did this for two reasons. First, since most travel is walking forward with occasional turns, most of the cues are likely to fall in this range. The user rarely needs to turn more than 90 degrees unless they have made a mistake. Second, while front-back errors are common in spatial audio, there are a number of different ways in which one could try to compensate for this, including those previously mentioned. We did not want to further complicate the study, so we controlled for this factor by limiting the possible directions. Distance used a linear scale from 0.0 ("near") to 1.0 ("far"). We chose to communicate relative rather than absolute distance because the degree of precision appropriate for absolute distance varies based on context, and because absolute distance does not map well to our problem formulation of navigation as a background task. Labels such as near and far are more flexible and can easily be changed to percent completion if desired. By using relative distance, we believe that our results will be more generalizable to a variety of situations and contexts.

All music must have a volume level and some distribution of sound between the user's ears. All vibrations have some rhythm and interval. Because of this, for interfaces where a given direction or distance method was not being used, the manipulated variable was set to the middle or "straight ahead" value. For example, DirHapVib/DistAudVol (1B) had the audio balanced between both ears ("straight ahead") and the vibrations came at medium distance intervals.

We investigated which interface users prefer and perform best with. For this, we have the following hypotheses.

H1) Because humans do not need consciously to retrieve signal-meaning mappings, when comparing DirAudSpatial (2) and DirHapVib (1), DirAudSpatial (2) will
  a) require less effort
  b) take less time to identify
  c) be more accurate

H2a-c) Same as H1a-c but with DirAudSweeps (3) instead of DirAudSpatial (2).

H3) Since it provides a moving target, users will rate changes in direction as more easily perceived for DirAudSweeps (3) than DirAudSpatial (2).

H4) DirAudSweeps (3) will interfere more with the music listening experience than DirAudSpatial (2).

H5) Since many people already listen to music, making adoption of DirAudSpatial (2) and DistAudVol (B) require little added effort, when compared with DirHapVib (1) and DistHapGeiger (A), users will
  a) be more open to adopting interfaces using DirAudSpatial (2) and DistAudVol (B)
  b) prefer interfaces with DirAudSpatial (2) and DistAudVol (B)

H6) Since modified cues will not be confused with musical changes, interfaces using DistHapGeiger (A) as compared to DistAudVol (B) for distance will
  a) be easier to use
  b) take less time to identify

3.2 Study Design

To simulate actual navigation, we had users perform two tasks while walking around the test room: a distractor task and a navigation task. This distractor task measured situational awareness since one goal is for users to pay more attention to their surroundings than their navigation tool. For this, the user watched for a specific target image. When they saw their target, users then left-clicked a wireless mouse. All of the target images were cars of various shapes and colors

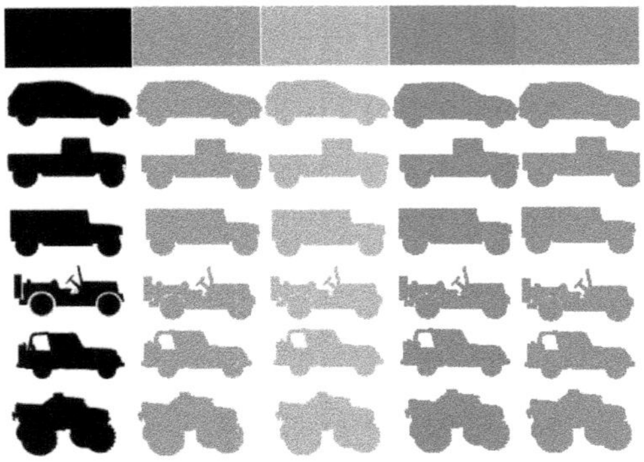

Figure 4: All possible targets for the distractor task. The first row is the "easy" condition where just a color, but not a specific shape, is the target.

(see Figure 4). To measure the effect of different levels of cognitive load on performance, users were randomly placed into one of two conditions. In the "easy" condition, the user's target was a single color, meaning they had to indicate when any car of the given color appeared. In the "hard" condition, the target was one specific car shape of a given color. The projector screen would remain blank for a random amount of time (2-12 seconds) before a car would appear in a random location for a random period of time (3-10 seconds) before disappearing. In both conditions, their target image would appear with a frequency of about 20%. When the user left-clicked to indicate that they had spotted their target image, the screen would flash green briefly to indicate that click had registered. Users also had the option to right-click to pause the task. To further distract the users and add to the realism of their task, we played ambient sounds similar to those that might be heard while walking along a street.

For the navigation task the user interpreted the music and/or vibration cues of a given interface and inputted the corresponding direction and distance into a smartphone. For a random period of time (10-20 seconds) the signal given was a neutral signal indicating that the target was directly ahead of the user and at a medium distance away. After that the direction and distance would randomly change, and the user could input the new information into the phone using the interface shown in Figure 5. When they entered an answer, the signal would return to neutral again and the process would repeat. To avoid situations where the user could not detect the change in stimulus, we added a small visual cue to the application. When the stimulus was neutral, the submit button was disabled. When the button became active, it was an indication that the user should enter information.

While direction randomly changing is realistic, random distance seems less so. Normally the distance would slowly decrease until it jumped far away when a new target had been acquired. However, most of the time users only need to affirm that they are on the correct path, meaning that it would be most important to have distance information right after reaching a target. This would tell the user how long they had before they needed to focus on navigation again, and this is consistent with randomly changing distances.

Since users did not need to interact with the device constantly for the navigation task, it was recommended that they spend most of their time looking for their visual targets and pause when they wanted to use the phone. We

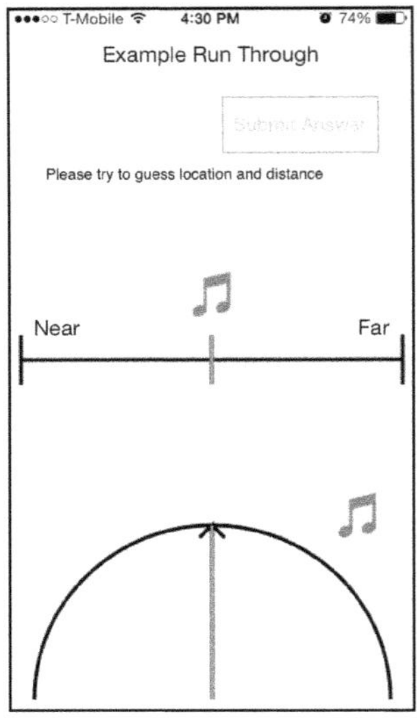

Figure 5: The application interface during the Trial phase. The user drags the red lines to indicate a distance and direction.

chose to allow users to do this because in practice, the user would not need to look at the device to enter information upon receiving a signal. Instead they would simply change where they were headed, which would require minimal visual attention and therefore not subtract from the user's awareness of their surroundings as much as needing to look at the phone screen. This is also similar to users finding a safe location where they can pause to interact with the device.

While the distractor task difficulty was between-subjects, the interface was varied within subjects, so each user tried all six interfaces. The order of interfaces was counterbalanced using a Latin square design. For each interface, the user went through four phases. The first was a *training phase* where the user could control the direction and distance information to become familiar with the feedback. When they felt comfortable, they moved on to the *quiz phase*. During this part, the user was asked to identify what direction and distance the interface had randomly chosen to communicate. They were then shown the correct answer. If they were within 20 degrees of the actual direction and 0.15 of the actual distance, which was measured on a scale from 0.0 to 1.0, their answer was deemed "correct." They continued to receive random directions and distances until either they had ten correct answers or five minutes had passed. After that, they moved on to the *trial phase*. For this, users were asked to walk in a circle around the test room while performing both the distractor and navigation tasks described above. While there was a box outlined on the floor to give users a rough guideline for where to walk, remaining on that path was not strictly enforced. Users continued to walk while performing their two tasks for the duration of two songs before moving on to the *final phase*, which is where the user filled out the NASA Task Load Index for the trial phase and was given the opportunity to comment on that interface.

3.3 Procedure

After filling out a demographic survey and listening to instructions about the task they would do, the users adjusted the volume of the device so they could still hear music at its softest but did not find the loudest volume painful. They then went through the four phases (detailed above) for each of the six interfaces. We recorded how accurately the user entered both distance and direction information, how long it took them to enter the information, how many of the distractor targets were found, missed, or incorrectly identified, and how long it took them to respond to the distractor task.

Once users had completed all the phases for each of the interfaces, they were finally given a post study questionnaire to fill out. The questionnaire had the following instructions. All ratings were on a 7-point Likert scale.

- Please rate each of the interfaces on how easy you found it to use.
- Please rate each of the interfaces on how much you think you'd use it for navigation if given the chance.
- Please rate each of the interfaces on how annoying you found them.
- Please rate each of the interfaces on how easily you could identify a change in distance or direction.
- Please rank each of the interfaces in order from your favorite (1) to least favorite (6).
- Why did you choose the interface that you did as your favorite?
- Why did you choose the interface that you did as your least favorite?
- For the interfaces using music, to what extent do you think using them would detract from your music listening experience?
- If you have any other comments that you'd like to add, write them here.

4. RESULTS

A total of 41 people (16 male, 25 female) age 18 to 24 ($\mu = 20.3, \sigma = 1.44$) were recruited for the study. The task took about an hour and a half to complete, and each participant was paid 10 dollars for their time. Most of the participants were familiar with smartphones (36/41).

A three-way ANOVA was run with difficulty, direction method, and distance method as the factors. Bonferroni corrected post-hoc pairwise comparisons were then done using a significance level of 0.05. Graphs with error bars show a 95% confidence interval.

4.1 Subjective

Three of the qualitative variables taken from the NASA TLX showed no significant difference between interfaces. These were physical demand, temporal demand, and effort. Unless otherwise noted, there were no significant interaction between factors or a significant effect on difficulty.

For conveying direction, when the DirAudSpatial (2) method was compared to the DirAudSweeps (3) method, it was rated significantly less annoying and easier to use. Furthermore, both the DirAudSpatial (2) and DirHapVib (1) methods were given a higher preference and rated more likely to be adopted than the DirAudSweeps (3) method (Figure 6).

For distance, DistAudVol (B) was rated significantly less annoying, easier to use, less frustrating, less mentally demanding, and more likely to be adopted compared to DistHapGeiger (A). In addition, DistAudVol (B) tended to receive higher preference in order of favorites (Figure 7).

For perceived performance, the distance method did not affect ratings while both difficulty and direction method did.

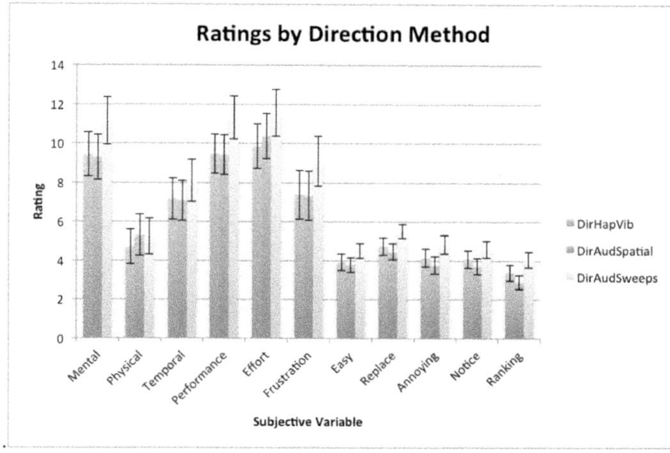

Figure 6: Summary of ratings for subjection questionnaire by direction method. The first 6 are from the NASA TLX with possible scores from 0.5 to 20.5. The last 4 are from the final questionnaire and range from 1 to 7. For all a lower score is preferable.

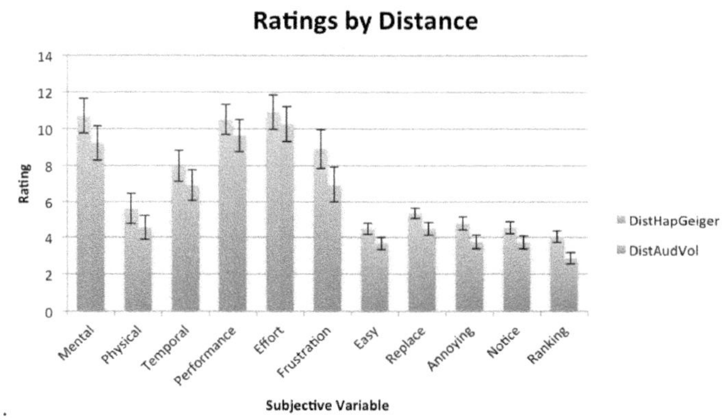

Figure 7: Summary of ratings for subjection questionnaire by distance method. The first 6 are from the NASA TLX with possible scores from 0.5 to 20.5. The last 4 are from the final questionnaire and range from 1 to 7. For all a lower score is preferable.

As would be expected, users in the hard condition thought they performed worse than those in the easy condition. Also, like many of the other variables, users thought they did better with both the DirAudSpatial (2) and DirHapVib (1) direction methods rather than DirAudSweeps (3).

The final qualitative variable was how easily users were able to notice a change in navigation information. Unlike previous variables, this one had interaction in all three of the main factors. Across both difficulties, users said they could recognize changes more easily when using DistAudVol (B) rather than DistHapGeiger (A). Direction, however, was only significant in the hard condition where DirAudSpatial (2) performed better than DirAudSweeps (3).

It is clear that the users did not like the DirAudSweeps (3) method; they rated it significantly worse than the other two direction methods on a number of factors. While there was no significant difference between DirAudSpatial (2) and DirHapVib (1), DirAudSpatial (2) performed significantly

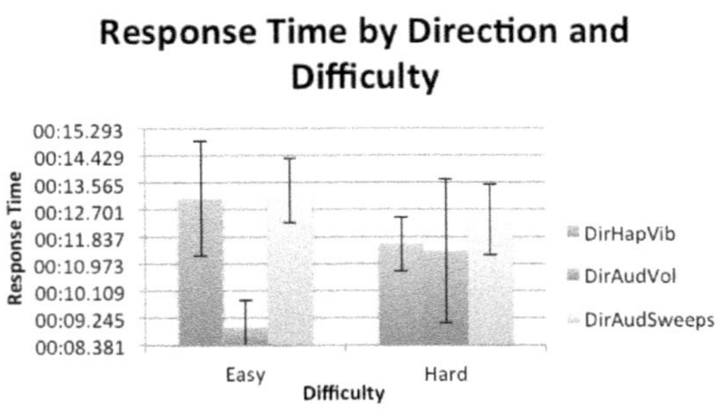

Figure 8: Time taken to decide upon a direction and distance, ignoring the distance method.

better than DirAudSweeps (3) on more factors than DirHapVib (1) did, suggesting that it might be a slightly better choice. Users also thought that DistAudVol (B) was better than DistHapGeiger (A). This information suggests that users preferred either the DirAudSpatial/DistAudVol (2B) or the DirHapVib/DistAudVol (1B) interface.

4.2 Objective

None of the data related to the distractor task showed any significant difference based on interface or difficulty. However, there were significant differences in the performance for the main task in the amount of time taken to input a user's answer and their direction and distance accuracy.

4.2.1 Response Time

For the amount of time taken to respond to the feedback, there was an interaction between the difficulty level of the distractor task and the method of conveying the direction. In the easy condition, users responded significantly faster with DirAudSpatial (2) than either DirHapVib (1) or DirAudSweeps (3). However this advantage disappeared when looking at the hard condition (Figure 8).

It makes sense that people would identify DirAudSpatial (2) cues faster since, unlike DirHapVib (1), the user does not consciously have to "decode" its meaning. However, this would not explain why DirAudSweeps (3) did not also perform well. Another explanation is that DirAudSpatial (2) is the only interface that does not have a minimum response time; for both DirHapVib (1) and DirAudSweeps (3) a certain amount of time must pass as the user waits to see either how long the vibration lasts or at what angle the audio beacon eventually stops. This requirement is not there for the DirAudSpatial (2) condition, but its advantage seems to disappear when the users are in the hard condition, suggesting that the added cognitive load of the distractor task masks any benefit gained by using this method.

4.2.2 Distance Error

For distance error, as might be expected, users in the hard condition had significantly higher error than those in the easy condition. Oddly enough, the direction method also significantly affected distance error. In particular, error went up significantly when DirAudSweeps (3) was used (Figure 9). If either distance or direction were haptic, there was also less error if the other dimension was DirAudSpatial (2) or DistAudVol (B) rather than also haptic (Figure 10).

One of the more interesting outcomes is the improvement interfaces with one of DirAudSpatial (2) or DistAudVol (B) combined with either DirHapVib (1) or DistHapGeiger (A)

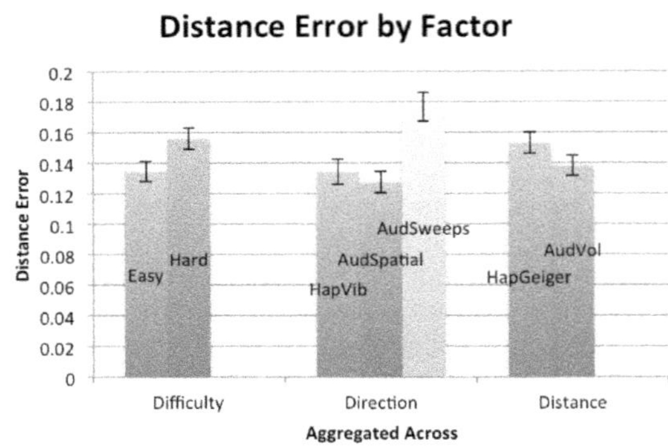

Figure 9: Distance error collapsed across the three main factors.

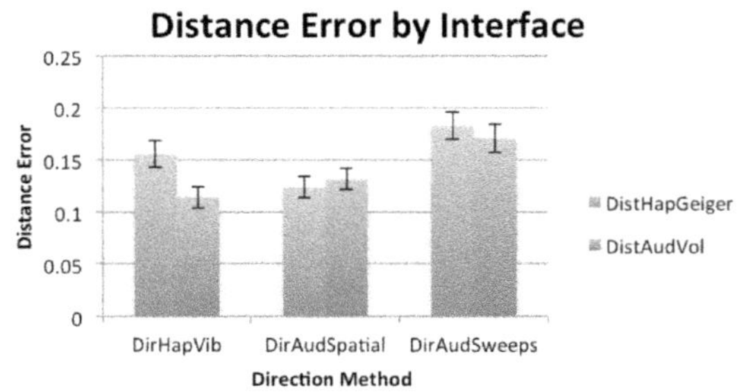

Figure 10: Distance error by interface ignoring difficulty.

had over a unimodal haptic interface. They also performed better than DirAudSpatial/DistAudVol (2B) but not significantly so. However, if it was just the cross modal nature that caused an improvement, one would expect DirAudSweeps/DistHapGeiger (3A) to also perform better since DirAudSweeps (3) also uses audio cues, which is not the case.

One explanation for why DirAudSweeps (3) so drastically decreases distance accuracy might be because humans are naturally inclined to notice changes and movement as a survival mechanism. Since the DirAudSweeps (3) method involves constant movement, it is possible that some amount of the users' attention was unconsciously diverted to monitor the change. Since DirAudSweeps (3) by itself does not convey any distance information, this would mean users' attention was being drawn to the direction over the distance information. This explanation could also help account for DirAudSweeps' (3) performance with directional error.

4.2.3 Direction Error

For directional error, surprisingly, DirAudSweeps (3) performed fairly well. In the hard condition, DirAudSweeps/DistAudVol (3B) performed significantly better than either DirAudSpatial/DistAudVol (2B) or DirHapVib/DistHapGeiger (1A). In the easy condition though, using DirHapVib/DistAudVol (1B) produced the least error, performing significantly better than all the other interfaces except for DirHapVib /DistHapGeiger (2A) (Figure 11).

Since attention to moving objects is often largely unconscious, it would make sense for users to do better with DirAudSweeps (3) in the hard condition, where more of their conscious attention would need to be focused on the distractor task. When that extra burden is not there, as in the easy condition, the added benefit of having more uncon-

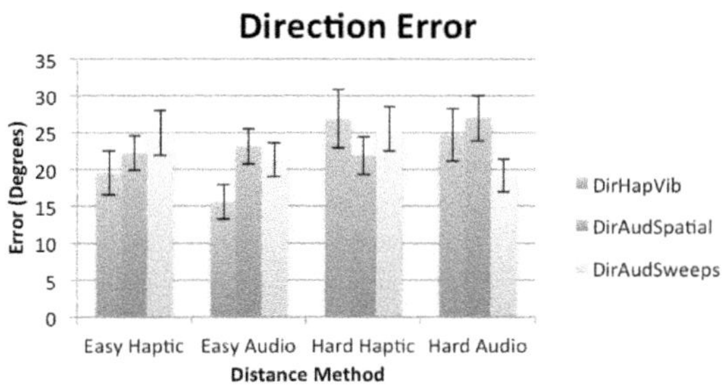

Figure 11: Direction error for all interfaces in both the easy and hard condition.

scious attention allocated to the DirAudSweeps (3) method might not make a noticeable difference as there are more attentional resources to devote to the navigation task.

Another explanation for why DirAudSweeps (3) would do better as compared to all the others is that in a way, DirAudSweeps (3) is a combination of information given in both DirAudSpatial (2) and DirHapVib (1) methods; the user still gets the spatial sound information from DirAudSpatial (2), but they also get timing information based on how long the audio beacon moves for before resetting. Timing information is what the DirHapVib (1) method is based off of since users must determine direction based on the amount of time the phone vibrates. However, if this was the main reason for DirAudSweeps' (3) performance, one would expect it to outperform DirHapVib (1) and DirAudSpatial (2) in both difficulty conditions instead of just the hard one, although it has comparable performance to all the other interfaces except for DirHapVib/DistAudVol (1B).

4.3 User Comments

While cross modal DirHapVib/DistAudVol (1B) and DirAudSpatial/DistHapGeiger (2A) interfaces did not perform worse than their unimodal DirHapVib/DistHapGeiger (1A) and DirAudSpatial/DistAudVol (2B) companions, and in fact sometimes had significantly better performance, a few users commented that they thought they were harder to use. User 15 thought that "*combining input from multiple sensory modalities in a task like this can be somewhat overwhelming*" while user 12 mentioned that he "*[h]ad to asses distance and direction in two separate trains of thought.*"

A few users also commented that they did not like waiting for vibration signals, especially for DistHapGeiger (A). This suggests that the haptic interfaces suffered for not being as instantaneous as DirAudSpatial (2) or DistAudVol (B). This means that haptic interfaces might benefit greatly if modern cell phones allowed for more control over the vibrating motor's behavior. This would allow applications to use channels of communication other than timing or patterns.

When asked to what extent they thought the musical interfaces would detract from their enjoyment of the music, 18 participants said they did not think it would affect it that much, 4 thought it would detract some but not a lot, 9 said that it would detract a lot, and 4 did not respond. The remaining 6 participants had mixed reactions. Of those 6, half broke the audio interfaces into their different types. All 3 mentioned that the DirAudSweeps (3) would detract a lot from the experience. The two that mentioned interfaces other than DirAudSweeps (3) both thought the DirAudVol (B) was ok, but had differing responses as to how detracting the DirAudSpatial (2) was. Of the other 3 with mixed reactions, two seemed to think that the interfaces' effect on the music would be ok if the primary goal was navigation but not if it was just for pleasure. The last one only thought it would be a problem if she were listening to new music.

At first, these responses seem discouraging; about 25% of the participants who responded thought audio manipulations would interfere a great deal with their musical enjoyment. However, the question did not separate out the different audio interfaces, meaning that this result may be skewed by DirAudSweeps (3), which likely does detract from the musical experience for most people. Since a great deal of research shows that negative experiences are more likely to be remembered and more likely to influence judgements [1], it is possible that these users based their answers largely on their reaction to DirAudSweeps (3) rather than all three audio interfaces as a whole. In light of this negativity bias, the results look fairly good as nearly 50% of responding participants reported that the audio interfaces would not detract much, if at all, from the overall experience.

5. DISCUSSION

While we did a lab study, we believe that the results can still tell us about performance in an outdoor navigation task. We included ambient noises such as might be heard while walking along a street as well as visual distractors. In addition, users actually walked about the room as they would have to when actually navigating. Furthermore, by using a lab study, we were able to test more interfaces without unduly increasing user fatigue.

H1: Audio Spatial vs Haptic Direction Subjectively users did not think DirAudSpatial (2) took less effort than DirHapVib (1), resulting in no evidence for hypothesis H1a. Users also were not more accurate with DirAudSpatial (2) and actually were worse in some interfaces in direct contradiction to hypothesis H1c. However, they were significantly faster, at least under low mental demand, supporting H1b.

H2: Audio Sweeps vs Haptic Direction When comparing DirAudSweeps (3) with DirHapVib (1), there was again no evidence that users thought it took less effort or less time to use (H2a and H2b). There is conflicting data in regards to the users' accuracy though with DirAudSweeps/DistAudVol (3B) doing better than DirHapVib /DistHapGeiger (1A) in the hard condition, but being outperformed by DirHapVib /DistAudVol (1B) in the easy condition, giving inconclusive evidence about H2c.

H3 and H4: Spatial vs Sweeps Audio Direction When comparing DirAudSweeps (3) and DirAudSpatial (2), surprisingly DirAudSpatial (2) was rated easier to notice in direct opposition to H3. However, there was support for H4 since users preferred DirAudSpatial (2) and rated it as less annoying, a point that was emphasized in some of the written comments, than DirAudSweeps (3).

H5 and H6: Audio vs Haptic While there was no significant difference in preference or likelihood of adoption for DirAudSpatial (2) compared to DirHapVib (1), users ranked DistAudVol (B) better than DistHapGeiger (A), giving mild support in favor of both H5a and H5b. DistAudVol (B) was also rated easier to use than DistHapGeiger (A) in direct contradiction to H6a, although a few users did specifically comment that they had trouble telling distance information from musical fade-outs despite being familiar with the music. There was no evidence either way as to if DirAudSpatial (2) and DistAudVol (B) or DirHapVib (1) and DistHapGeiger (A) took less time to identify, which was H5b.

Best Interface One remaining question is which interface is the best? While DirAudSweeps (3) does perform fairly well with directional error, its poor performance in nearly every other parameter outweighs its benefit, making it a bad choice. Furthermore, one user also commented that it made him feel physically ill. Of the remaining four interfaces, DirHapVib/DistHapGeiger (1A) is also not a particularly good choice; subjectively users preferred having DistAudVol (B), and it was either comparable or significantly worse for all objective measures. The last three interfaces are much closer to each other in preference, performing both significantly better and significantly worse on different parameters. However, DirAudSpatial/DistAudVol (2B) and DirHapVib/DistAudVol (1B) came out on top for more parameters; DirAudSpatial/DistAudVol (2B) was better in the subjective measures and response time in the easy condition, DirHapVib/DistAudVol (1B) was better in the subjective measures and direction error in the easy condition, and DirAudSpatial/DistHapGeiger (2A) was only better in the response time in the easy condition. This only leaves DirAudSpatial/DistAudVol (2B) and DirHapVib/DistAudVol (1B). The two of them seem to fall into an accuracy/time tradeoff under low cognitive load; DirAudSpatial (2) is faster to identify but DirHapVib (1) is more accurate. Under high cognitive load, their performance is about the same.

6. CONCLUSIONS

The data suggest a couple of design considerations. The first is that interfaces that convey information though temporal cues should aim to take up as little of the users' time as possible. Users seemed to respond well to DirHapVib(1), which communicated through temporal feedback in the relative lengths of vibration over a short time frame, but they responded poorly to DistHapGeiger(A), for which the pauses between signals were often significantly longer. This is supported by user comments about disliking needing to wait.

Another is that while a multimodal interface might benefit user performance, users might think it requires extra effort compared to a unimodal one. Some struggle with simultaneously interpreting data from two modalities, and must expend effort to mentally switch tracks as they concentrate on one modality and then the other. However, it is possible that this overhead is overshadowed by the overall effort of interpreting the data signals. This would explain the lack of significance in subjective effort, but more work would need to be done to determine to what extent this is true.

There are a number of directions future work could take. One would be to study how user preferences and performance change both over a longer period of time and when navigating a real environment. While we added a number of distractions similar to an outdoor environment, users might still respond differently simply by knowing that there are hazards that are not present in a controlled lab setting. Although these might not appear even with an outdoor experiment, as there is some expectation that the experimenter will be looking out for the subject, providing supervised safety that is not normally present. Another direction would involve testing out different distance scales. While we used a simple, linear scale, an exponential scale, for example, could emphasize when the user is particularly close to their target and might improve performance. This work provides a foundation for exploring these other areas while keeping a focus on creating a usable yet nonintrusive interface.

7. REFERENCES

[1] R. F. Baumeister, E. Bratslavsky, C. Finkenauer, and K. D. Vohs. Bad is stronger than good. *Review of General Psychology*, 5(4):323, 2001.

[2] S. Bosman, B. Groenendaal, J. Findlater, T. Visser, M. De Graaf, and P. Markopoulos. Gentleguide: An exploration of haptic output for indoors pedestrian guidance. *International Conference on Human Computer Interaction with Mobile Devices and Services*, 191(204):358–362, 2003.

[3] R. Etter and M. Specht. Melodious walkabout-implicit navigation with contextualized personal audio contents. *Third International Conference on Pervasive Computing*, 191(204), 2005.

[4] M. Hara, S. Shokur, A. Yamamoto, T. Higuchi, R. Gassert, and H. Bleuler. Virtual environment to evaluate multimodal feedback strategies for augmented navigation of the visually impaired. In *Engineering in Medicine and Biology Society*, pages 975–978, Aug 2010.

[5] S. Holland, D. R. Morse, and H. Gedenryd. Audiogps: Spatial audio navigation with a minimal attention interface. *Personal and Ubiquitous Computing*, 6(4):253–259, 2002.

[6] M. Jones, S. Jones, G. Bradley, N. Warren, D. Bainbridge, and G. Holmes. Ontrack: Dynamically adapting music playback to support navigation. *Personal and Ubiquitous Computing*, 12(7):513–525, 2008.

[7] R. L. Klatzky, J. R. Marston, N. A. Giudice, R. G. Golledge, and J. M. Loomis. Cognitive load of navigating without vision when guided by virtual sound versus spatial language. *Journal of Experimental Psychology: Applied*, 12(4):223–32, Dec. 2006.

[8] M. Liljedahl, S. Lindberg, K. Delsing, M. Polojärvi, T. Saloranta, and I. Alakärppä. Testing two tools for multimodal navigation. volume 2012, Jan. 2012.

[9] J. L. Nasar and D. Troyer. Pedestrian injuries due to mobile phone use in public places. *Accident Analysis & Prevention*, 57:91–95, 2013.

[10] M. Pielot, B. Poppinga, W. Heuten, and S. Boll. 6th senses for everyone!: The value of multimodal feedback in handheld navigation aids. In *International Conference on Multimodal Interfaces*, pages 65–72, 2011.

[11] M. Pielot, B. Poppinga, W. Heuten, and S. Boll. A tactile compass for eyes-free pedestrian navigation. In *Human-Computer Interaction, INTERACT 2011*, volume 6947, pages 640–656. 2011.

[12] S. Rümelin, E. Rukzio, and R. Hardy. Naviradar: A novel tactile information display for pedestrian navigation. In *Symposium on User Interface Software and Technology*, pages 293–302, 2011.

[13] K. Tsukada and M. Yasumura. Activebelt: Belt-type wearable tactile display for directional navigation. In *Ubiquitous Computing*, volume 3205, pages 384–399. 2004.

Tactile Feedback for Above-Device Gesture Interfaces: Adding Touch to Touchless Interactions

Euan Freeman, Stephen Brewster
Glasgow Interactive Systems Group
University of Glasgow
{first.last}@glasgow.ac.uk

Vuokko Lantz
Nokia Technologies
Espoo, Finland
vuokko.lantz@nokia.com

ABSTRACT

Above-device gesture interfaces let people interact in the space above mobile devices using hand and finger movements. For example, users could gesture over a mobile phone or wearable without having to use the touchscreen. We look at how above-device interfaces can also give feedback in the space over the device. Recent haptic and wearable technologies give new ways to provide tactile feedback while gesturing, letting touchless gesture interfaces give touch feedback. In this paper we take a first detailed look at how tactile feedback can be given during above-device interaction. We compare approaches for giving feedback (ultrasound haptics, wearables and direct feedback) and also look at feedback design. Our findings show that tactile feedback can enhance above-device gesture interfaces.

Categories and Subject Descriptors

H.5.2. [**User Interfaces**]: Interaction styles.

Keywords

Above-Device Interaction; Distal Tactile Feedback; Gestures; Tactile Feedback; Ultrasound Haptics; Wearables.

1. INTRODUCTION

Above-device gesture interfaces let people interact with mobile devices using mid-air hand gestures in the space above them. Users can gesture in a larger space above the device, overcoming issues with small touchscreen interaction and letting users interact more expressively; for example, users could provide more precise input on small wearables like smart-watches or could gesture imprecisely at their mobile phones while focusing on another task. Gestures also let users interact when touching a device would be inconvenient; for example, people could gesture over the display while cooking, to navigate a recipe without touching their tablet with messy hands.

Effective feedback is needed to help users overcome uncertainty about gesture performance and the complex sensing requirements of gesture interfaces. While visual feedback could be given about gestures, this takes already limited display space away from content. We think feedback should be given in the same space as users gesture, in this case the space above the device. We think that tactile feedback in particular could be given, helping users overcome uncertainty while gesturing. Providing tactile cues while users gesture in mid-air is a challenge: vibration from a distal device would go unnoticed and users receive no physical cues from touching something, like a touchscreen.

New haptic technologies and wearable devices can overcome this challenge, letting gesture interfaces provide tactile feedback remotely. Technologies such as ultrasound haptics [11] or air vortex generation [18] would let users experience tactile sensations in mid-air as they gesture. Users could also receive tactile feedback from a wearable device such as a smart-watch or item of jewellery. Future gesture interfaces could use wearables for tactile feedback, even combining or selecting from multiple accessories (e.g. rings and watches) for feedback.

In this paper we focus on tactile feedback for above-device interaction with mobile phones. Mobile phones are small devices which could benefit from tactile feedback when gesturing and recent phones, such as the Samsung Galaxy S4 and Google *Project Tango*[1], show an interest in giving phones sensors capable of detecting gestures away from the touchscreen. Our studies focus on selection gestures as selection is often used in above-device interfaces [5, 9, 1, 8, 19]. Selection gestures are also focused interactions, requiring high engagement from users, so will benefit from having another feedback modality.

We discuss the design and delivery of tactile feedback for above-device interfaces using two approaches: ultrasound haptics and wearable devices. We present the design of a gesture interface for mobile phones and discuss two experiments exploring different aspects of remote tactile feedback. Our findings show that tactile feedback can improve gesture interfaces and make it easier for users to gesture. Based on our findings, we present design recommendations for gesture interface designers to help them make the most of tactile feedback.

2. RELATED WORK

Researchers have developed a variety of ways of detecting mid-air gestures above or near devices, leading to a wide range of interaction techniques. Gesture interactions include simple hand movements over a device [13, 14], precise selection techniques based on finger movements [5, 9, 19] and more subtle gestures with wearable devices [1]. These interfaces give users feedback in a variety of ways. We now discuss some above-device interfaces with a focus on the feedback they provide.

[1] `http://www.google.com/atap/projecttango`

ICMI'14, November 12–16, 2014, Istanbul, Turkey.
Copyright 2014 ACM 978-1-4503-2885-2/14/11 ...$15.00.
http://dx.doi.org/10.1145/2663204.2663280.

2.1 Above-Device Interfaces

2.1.1 Visual Feedback

Most above-device gesture interfaces rely on visual feedback, although this is often just functional feedback showing the outcome of a gesture. In *HoverFlow* [13], for example, users could browse a colour palette with hand movements above a mobile device. Only functional visual feedback is given, when the colour palette updates in response to gestures. Interfaces with pointing gestures, such as *SideSight* [5] and *Abracadabra* [9], give continuous feedback about finger position using a cursor. Users see how their finger movements are tracked through updates in cursor position.

While functional feedback can help users interact, it provides little insight into how sensing works. Jones *et al.* [12] suggested that visualising sensor information could help guide users. Kratz *et al.* [13] proposed a technique for *HoverFlow* to show sensor readings, although users might not see this visual feedback as they gesture over the display. Niikura *et al.* [15] created a mid-air keyboard for mobile phones which showed a silhouette of users' fingertips as they typed, showing them how they were being tracked.

Visualising sensor information could be helpful as it gives users insight into how their gestures are being sensed. Users can then adapt their gestures to ease sensing and can gesture confidently knowing their movements are being recognised as intended. However, mobile devices have small displays. Designers must choose between emphasising visual content and sensor visualisations. Audio and tactile feedback can be used to present information non-visually, reducing the amount of visual content on display and making certain information more salient. These modalities may also be noticeable from a distance; visual feedback would be difficult to see when gesturing from an arm length away. Visual feedback may also be occluded as users gesture over the display.

2.1.2 Audio Feedback

Audio is mostly used in gesture interfaces to overcome a lack of visual feedback. *Nenya* [1], a wearable smart-ring, lets users make selections by rotating the ring around their finger. The name of the selected item is spoken as users make selections. A similar type of feedback is used in *Imaginary Phone* [8]; as users make selections by tapping on the palm of their hand, the name of the selected item is read aloud. These examples of functional feedback give no insight into how users are being sensed, however. Users only receive feedback *after* input. Continuous audio feedback would be needed during interaction to help users, although this could be socially unacceptable if it annoys other people nearby.

2.1.3 Tactile Feedback

Tactile feedback has been used by some above-device interfaces to acknowledge gestures, similar to how smartphones vibrate to acknowledge touch input. Niikura *et al.* [15] gave tactile feedback from their mid-air keyboard, using the vibration motor in a phone to deliver feedback to the hand holding the device. A limitation of this approach is that users had to be holding the phone to feel the vibrations. This is a problem because users would first have to pick up the device; one of the advantages of above-device gesture interaction is that it is touchless, letting users interact when touch input is unavailable or inconvenient.

This modality has also been used to give continuous sensor information during interaction. Users interacted with *AirTouch* [14] with hand movements over wrist-worn sensors. Each of its four sensors was paired with an actuator, giving spatial vibrotactile feedback to show which sensors detected input. Users did not perceive this, however, instead saying feedback only let them know when their hand was being detected. More work is needed to explore the design space of tactile feedback for above-device gesture interfaces, to see how more sophisticated feedback may help users gesture.

Giving tactile feedback in a gesture interface is challenging because users may not be touching the device they are interacting with. Vibration directly from a device (e.g. [15]) would only be noticed when holding it. We now discuss two alternatives for delivering tactile feedback in a gesture interface: non-contact feedback and distal feedback from wearables.

2.2 Non-Contact Tactile Feedback

Ultrasound haptics uses acoustic radiation pressure to create tactile sensations using sound. Iwamoto *et al.* [11] used an array of ultrasound transducers to focus sound upon a fixed point which could be felt as ultrasound reflected off skin. Later work [10] allowed the focal point to be moved in 3D space above the transducers. Carter *et al.* [6] built on this work and created an ultrasound tactile display which could produce many focal points of feedback at the same time. Wilson *et al.* [20] considered wearable ultrasound displays, finding ultrasound haptics from a smaller array to be effective.

Air pressure is an alternative to acoustic radiation pressure for creating non-contact tactile sensations. *AIREAL* [18] used air vortex generation to create mid-air tactile feedback which could be perceived several metres away. This approach creates feedback with a resolution of around 85mm, almost ten times lower than ultrasound haptics [20]. We think ultrasound haptics is more appropriate for above-device interfaces because of its high resolution. Precise tactile feedback can be created for subtle movements relative to small devices.

2.3 Distal Tactile Feedback

Gesture interfaces could alternatively use wearables to give distal tactile feedback. Some wearables already have vibrotactile actuators for giving notifications (e.g. *haptic wristwatch* [16])- we think these could also be used for feedback while gesturing. Distal tactile feedback has already been used with large interactive surfaces and can be as effective as direct feedback, even when given on the inactive arm [17].

2.4 Summary

Above-device interfaces mostly rely on visual feedback during interaction, giving users a combination of functional feedback and sensor information. Giving some of this information with other modalities, such as audio or tactile, can free up space for visual content on small displays and make feedback more noticeable when interacting from a distance. We have chosen to focus on tactile feedback as it is personal and may help users overcome the lack of tactile cues when gesturing. Tactile feedback directly from a device may not be noticed so novel ways of delivering tactile feedback from a distance are needed, as well as a better understanding of how to use this modality during gesture interaction.

3. GESTURE AND FEEDBACK DESIGN

Our research has three aims: (1) to evaluate ultrasound haptics and wearables for giving tactile cues during above-device interaction; (2) to understand what information users find useful when encoded tactually; and (3) to see how tactile feedback affects gesture performance. We chose to focus on above-device interaction with mobile phones as this is an emerging area of technology and well-designed tactile feedback can improve it.

In particular we focus on selection gestures. Selection is a continuous interaction, often requiring an active and focused engagement. Continuous interactions will benefit from multimodal feed-

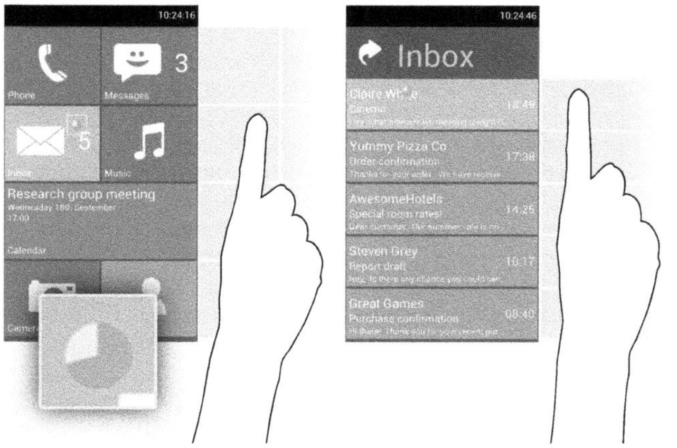

Figure 1: *Point*. A circular cursor (close-up shown in call-out on left) is mapped to finger position in the space beside the device. These images visualise how the space is divided between selection targets.

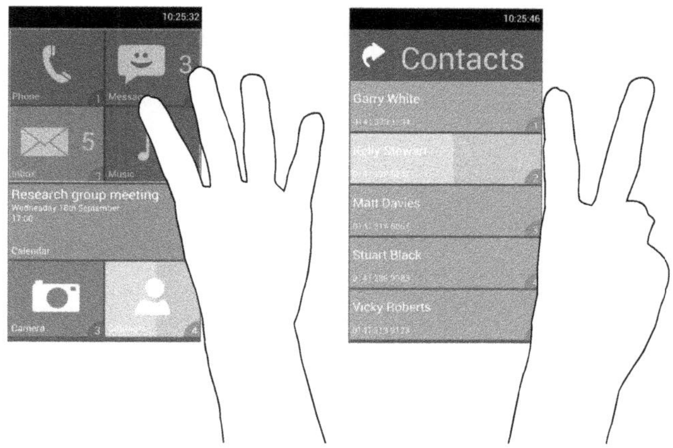

Figure 2: *Count*. Users can select from numbered targets by extending an appropriate number of fingers. The left image shows how palm position determines which group of targets is active.

back because users' movements are being sensed constantly so appropriate cues can keep them "in the loop" and help them gesture more effectively. Selection is also a common interaction in many above-device gesture interfaces [5, 9, 1, 8] so our work could help improve these interfaces. In this section of the paper we will discuss the design of two selection gestures, as well as the design of visual and tactile feedback given during interaction.

3.1 Selection Gesture Design

We chose two selection gestures, *Point* and *Count*, from an earlier gesture design study [7]. We were interested to see if tactile feedback could benefit both precise and imprecise gestures, so we choose a gesture requiring precise positional control (Point) and one which does not (Count). The Point gesture is used in a similar way to other around-device selection gestures (e.g. selection with *Abracadabra* [9]); users control an on-screen cursor which is mapped to their finger movements (Figure 1).

Users can make selections with Point by keeping the cursor over a target for 1000 ms. We chose this selection technique because it worked equally well for Point and Count, and because it let users see the effect of their actions, giving them a chance to correct their selection. We informally evaluated different dwell times and found that users were most comfortable with 1000 ms; shorter times were too fast for inexperienced users and longer times slowed the interaction too much. Rather than gesture above the display where occlusion may be a problem, we used the space beside the phone (as in other around-device interfaces [12]).

Our Count gesture is like the Finger-Count gesture described by Bailly *et al.* [2]. Users select from numbered targets by extending the required number of fingers; to select the second target, for example, the user extends two fingers (as in Figure 2, right). As with the Point gesture, a selection requires a dwell of 1000 ms. Users can navigate back through the user interface by swiping quickly from right to left with one or more fingers. An obvious limitation of Count is that users can only select from up to five targets. To allow a greater number of targets, we partition targets into groups of five or less. Depending on hand position relative to the device, users can select from within a group of targets. In Figure 2, for example, the hand is towards the bottom half of the screen on the left so the bottom three targets can be selected; the top four icons are darkened to show that they are inactive.

3.2 Feedback Design

3.2.1 Visual Feedback

As Point requires precise position control, we wanted to make the selection targets large in order to make them easier to select. Our user interface (shown in Figures 1 and 2) featured large buttons in grid and list layouts. For the Point gesture, a white circular cursor showed finger position. As the cursor entered a target the button was highlighted and the cursor filled radially to show dwell progress (see callout in Figure 1). We used the cursor to show dwell progress for Point as users were likely to focus on the cursor during interaction.

When using Count, each selection target had a number associated with it, drawn in the bottom corner of the button. When making selections, the selected button was highlighted, as was the number in the corner. The target background filled from left-to-right to show selection progress (Figure 2). We initially filled the target background for the Point gesture as well, but early prototyping revealed that this distracted users when focusing on the cursor position. When users were presented with multiple target groups, inactive groups were faded out to make the active group more visible (Figure 2).

3.2.2 Tactile Feedback

We created two types of tactile feedback for our selection gestures: *Continuous* and *Discrete*. Continuous feedback was a constant stimulus presented while the user interacted with the device. When targeting a button, users felt smooth vibrotactile feedback (a 175 Hz sine wave); when not over a button, users experienced a rougher sensation (a 175 Hz sine wave modulated with a 20 Hz sine wave, as in [4]). No feedback was given if a hand was not being tracked. The aim of Continuous feedback was to let users know their hand was being recognised by the device. Change in feedback aimed to let users know when they: (1) started making a selection (e.g. when moving over a button using Point, feedback felt smoother); (2) finished making a selection (e.g. after selection, feedback returned to feeling rough); and (3) were gesturing incorrectly, or were not being tracked (e.g. feedback stopped entirely when the hand was not recognised).

Discrete feedback used short Tactons [3], mapping feedback to the same user interface events that Continuous feedback identified.

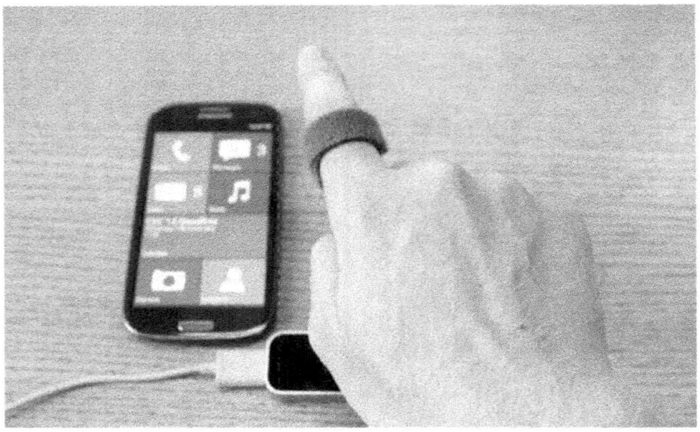

Figure 3: Sensor setup and vibrotactile ring prototype.

The selection start and selection complete Tactons were 150 ms and 300 ms duration smooth vibrotactile pulses, respectively (both 175 Hz sine waves). The tracking error Tacton was a 300 ms long rough vibrotactile pulse (a 175 Hz sine wave modulated with a 20 Hz sine wave).

We supported four types of tactile feedback (Figure 4): (1) ultrasound haptics; (2) distal feedback from a ring (worn on the pointing finger for Point); (3) distal feedback from a watch worn on the wrist of the gesturing hand; and (4) feedback directly from the phone (when held). Although direct feedback will be inappropriate in some situations, we included this to see if it made sense to users to feel feedback at their inactive hand. Watch and ring form factors were chosen for wearables as wearing objects on the wrist and finger is widely accepted and products already exist that can do this. Smart wearable accessories could give users options for how they get feedback; for some interactions it may make more sense to get feedback from a ring than a bracelet, for example.

3.3 Apparatus

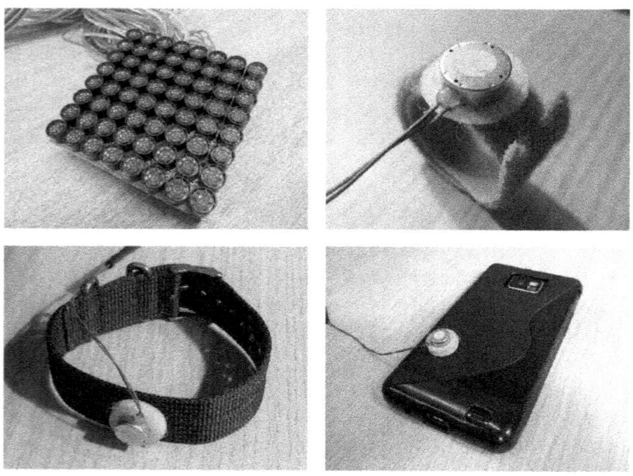

Figure 4: Hardware prototypes used to deliver tactile feedback: ultrasound array, ring, watch, mobile phone.

We used a Leap Motion sensor to track hands and fingers for input. The field of view is 150 degrees, offering a large space through which to track the hand. We created a gesture detector which ran on a desktop computer using Leap Motion's C# library. Information was sent to a mobile phone via a wireless network, allowing the phone to provide visual feedback during interaction (Figure 3).

A prototype ultrasound tactile display was used to provide non-contact tactile feedback. This device (Figure 4, top left) has sixty-four 40 kHz transducers arranged in an 8 x 8 grid. Each transducer has a diameter of 10 mm; at 80 x 80 mm, the device is slightly wider than a smartphone. Focal points could be created on a flat plane 100 mm above the display (a limitation of our experimental prototype; ideally feedback could be positioned anywhere in 3D space). As the human hand cannot detect vibration at ultrasound frequencies, ultrasound was modulated at 200 Hz to create a perceivable sensation (as explained by Carter *et al.* [6]). Modulation frequency was fixed in our prototype so we were unable to create different textures (e.g. to distinguish between targeting and not targeting a button for Continuous feedback). Instead, a focal point of constant feedback followed the user's fingertip for Continuous feedback. After prototype evaluation we decided to only use the ultrasound display for Continuous feedback; ultrasound haptics produces a subtle sensation which some users were unable to perceive in the short durations of the Tactons used by the Discrete feedback design.

Our wearable prototypes for distal feedback used a Precision Microdrives C10-100 Linear Resonant Actuator[2]. This actuator was chosen as its small size (10 mm diameter) and light weight meant it could be comfortably worn on the finger. We used an adhesive pad so that this actuator could be attached to a variety of prototype devices, including an adjustable velcro ring, a fabric watch strap and the rear of a mobile phone (shown in Figure 4; ring also in Figure 3). We attached an actuator to a phone (for direct feedback) for consistency, rather than use the rotational motor in the phone. Feedback was synthesised in real-time using Pure Data. Our tactile feedback designs (discussed previously) used 175 Hz sine waves as this is the optimal resonant frequency of the actuator.

4. STUDY 1

Our first study was a preliminary evaluation of our feedback designs and the ways we delivered feedback. We wanted to understand what users liked and disliked about ultrasound haptics and distal tactile feedback so that we can identify how best to use them in above-device gesture interfaces. We also wanted to evaluate our initial feedback designs to see how effective they are and to get insight into what types of information users find helpful when presented tactually.

We chose to use only the Point gesture in this study to minimise the number of study conditions. Using just Point also meant we could restrict gesturing to the space above the ultrasound array, making ultrasound feedback perceivable during input. We look at Count in our second study.

4.1 Design

We asked participants to complete selection tasks using our Point gesture. Each task required selecting a menu item from the third level of the user interface hierarchy, requiring three selections per task. Tasks were based on typical mobile phone operations: selecting an action to perform on a contact list entry or an inbox item. Task order was randomised.

Participants completed a block of 14 tasks for each of eight conditions, representing combinations of our feedback designs (*Continuous*, *Discrete*, *None*) and delivery methods (*Phone*, *Finger*, *Wrist*, *Ultrasound*). These conditions are: *None (N)*; *Phone-Continuous (PC)*; *Phone-Discrete (PD)*; *Finger-Continuous (FC)*; *Finger-Discrete*

[2] `http://www.precisionmicrodrives.com`

(FD); *Wrist-Continuous (WC)*; *Wrist-Discrete (WD)*; and *Ultrasound-Continuous (UC)*. There was no discrete ultrasound feedback as discussed previously. Participants experienced all conditions and condition order was balanced using a Latin square.

Sixteen people participated in this study (five female, three left-handed). Participants were recruited through mailing lists and social media websites, and were mostly undergraduate university students. Each participant was paid £6.

4.2 Procedure

Participants received a brief tutorial at the start of the study which demonstrated how to use the Point gesture. No tactile feedback was presented during the tutorial. After the tutorial, participants received a demonstration of the prototype feedback devices. We asked participants to hold the mobile phone in their non-dominant hand, beside the ultrasound array. As participants would have to hold the phone for conditions where feedback came directly from the device, this ensured that holding the phone was not a confounding factor for these conditions.

We interviewed participants at the end of the study to find out what they liked and disliked about tactile feedback while gesturing. During the interview we asked them to complete two card-sorting activities. The two sets of cards contained locations of tactile feedback (*Phone*, *Finger*, *Wrist*, *None*) and feedback designs (*Continuous*, *Discrete*, *None*). Participants were asked to sort the cards in order of preference. These activities gave us preference data and encouraged participants to focus on tactile feedback during the interview. When collecting location preferences, we asked participants to focus on the location of feedback rather than the device used: e.g. *Finger* could be vibrotactile or ultrasound feedback. We did this so we could better understand preference for location, rather than preference for a particular device.

4.3 Results

Table 1 shows median rankings for feedback locations and designs. Scores were assigned for each set of cards so that the highest ranked card received a score of 1 and the lowest ranked received a score of 4 (for location) or 3 (for design). Friedman's test found a significant difference in preference for location: $\chi^2(3) = 14.62$, $p = 0.002$. A *post hoc* Nemenyi test revealed significant differences between *None* and all other locations; no other pairwise differences were significant. There was no significant difference in ranks for tactile feedback design: $\chi^2(2) = 2.95$, $p = 0.23$.

Location				Design		
Phone	Finger	Wrist	None	Continuous	Discrete	None
1.75	2	2.5	4	1.5	2.5	2.0

Table 1: Median ranks for location and design (lower ranks are better).

4.4 Discussion

4.4.1 *Feedback Location*

All feedback locations were ranked significantly higher than None, although there were no other significant differences. We wanted to see if direct tactile feedback from the phone made sense to users, despite them gesturing with their other hand. Participants liked direct feedback because it was familiar; most who liked it said they were already used to their phone vibrating in response to touch input. Some participants suggested that direct feedback let them know when the phone was doing something, but other locations make more sense for gesture feedback. For example, interfaces could give feedback relating to hand movements to that hand or wrist.

Direct tactile feedback would be inappropriate in many gesture situations as users will not be holding the device they gesture at. In these situations, feedback from a ring or watch would let users experience tactile feedback. Participants gave feedback on the wrist and finger similar rankings. This shows the importance of supporting different wearable accessories and giving users choice of feedback location. In some situations it may even make sense to give feedback at several locations.

Participants liked tactile feedback on their finger because it was close to the point of interaction; fingertip position controlled the cursor so it made sense to receive feedback at this point. Ultrasound haptics was especially useful for this because feedback was given at the point of the finger tracked by the sensor. Although ultrasound feedback was not as noticeable as vibrotactile feedback on the finger, participants liked that they could experience it without having to wear anything.

Feedback on the wrist was further from the gesturing finger, yet people still found it helpful. We asked participants to wear the watch prototype on their dominant wrist, the opposite wrist from where most participants wore their own watch. Participants said they would be willing to wear their watch on the other wrist if it provided some purpose, such as feedback while gesturing. However, distal feedback from the opposite wrist may also be effective [17], letting users wear accessories on their preferred wrist.

4.4.2 *Feedback Design*

There were no significant differences in feedback design rankings. We noticed that participants who preferred *Continuous* feedback generally ranked *None* ahead of *Discrete*, and *vice versa*. People who liked *Continuous* feedback felt it made them aware of how the gesture interface was responding to their actions. The presence of continuous feedback assured them that they were being sensed and subtle changes in feedback reflected changes in interface state. *Discrete* feedback did not provide much insight into sensor state as feedback was only given in response to certain events. However, some participants preferred this because it was less obtrusive than constant vibration.

Ultrasound haptics was more acceptable for continuous feedback because it produced a more subtle sensation. Feedback could be given from a combination of ultrasound haptics and wearable devices, using ultrasound haptics for constant feedback while wearables give more concise feedback. Some participants suggested that a mixture of the feedback designs would be more appropriate, as they found that feedback all the time was too much, but discrete feedback did not tell them enough about the interaction.

We created new feedback designs which combined popular aspects of Continuous and Discrete feedback: continuous feedback was only provided during gestures; at all other times there was no feedback. We used a 175 Hz sine wave as before. This design aimed to make users aware of when the interface was tracking their gestures and making a selection, without being obtrusive. We used short Tactons to acknowledge when tracking started or stopped. Visual feedback let users know when their gestures were sensed, with tactile feedback complementing it and making some information more salient.

We also wanted to see if we could use vibrotactile feedback to encode information about selection progress. Some participants found subtle changes in Continuous feedback helpful for knowing when selection started, so we wondered if we could encode other information this way. Encoding information tactually could reinforce visual feedback and reduce the need for visual attention because the same information is given multimodally.

We created two more feedback designs which provided a dynamically changing stimulus during selection. Each used a different vibrotactile parameter to encode selection progress: amplitude and roughness. Amplitude increased from 0 to 100% so that as selection progress increased, stimulus from a 175 Hz sine wave became more intense. Amplitude increased exponentially as a linear increase proved more difficult to notice during pilot tests. For roughness we modulated a 175 Hz sine wave with another sine wave, whose frequency increased from 0 Hz to 75 Hz. As selection progressed, the tactile stimulus felt smoother. We considered using frequency as a dynamic feedback parameter as well, although the response range of the actuator limits frequency use.

5. STUDY 2

Our second study evaluated our refined tactile feedback designs and looked at the effects of tactile feedback on gesture performance. Two of our new feedback designs used vibrotactile parameters (amplitude and roughness) to communicate selection progress. Although this information was also given visually, we wanted to see if tactile presentation would benefit users. For this study we chose to deliver feedback to users' wrists as this location was widely accepted and may make more sense for the *Count* gesture. In this study we also compared a precise position-based gesture (*Point*) to a less precise gesture (*Count*), although our focus was on tactile feedback rather than gestures.

5.1 Design

There were two factors in this experiment: Feedback (*None*, *Constant*, *Amplitude* and *Roughness*) and Gesture (*Point* and *Count*), resulting in eight conditions. Participants experienced all conditions and condition order was balanced using a Latin square. As in the previous study, participants completed a block of 14 tasks for each condition. Our dependent variables in this study were selection time and estimated workload. Selection time was measured for each task from when users started gesturing to when they completed their final selection. We measured workload with NASA-TLX questionnaires after each block of tasks. Sixteen people participated in this study (six female, three left-handed, five participated in the previous study). Participants were recruited through mailing lists and social media websites and were paid £6.

5.2 Procedure

Experimental procedure was the same as the previous study. We placed the phone on a table in front of participants, with the Leap Motion positioned so that their dominant hand gestured beside the display. Unlike the last experiment, participants did not hold the phone. Participants completed eight blocks of tasks (one for each experiment condition).

We interviewed participants at the end of the experiment, using card-sorting activities to encourage discussion. We asked participants to sort two sets of cards: one for gestures (*Point* and *Count*) and the other for tactile feedback designs (*None*, *Constant* and *Dynamic*). We grouped *Amplitude* and *Roughness* under *Dynamic* feedback as we did not expect participants to identify each during the experiment. Also, we were more interested in what participants thought of using tactile feedback to encode other information.

5.3 Results

Mean selection time was 8529 ms (sd = 1729ms); see Figure 5 (all error bars show 95% CIs). This includes at least 3000 ms dwelling for each task and overheads for updating the UI. Performance was analysed using repeated-measures regression, with maximum likelihood estimation used to fit model parameters. Gesture was a significant predictor of selection time: $\chi^2(1) = 15.79$, $p < 0.001$. A *post hoc* Tukey comparison found that Point had significantly lower selection times than Count: $z = 5.19$, $p < 0.001$. Feedback design was not a significant predictor of selection time: $\chi^2(3) = 1.28$, $p = 0.73$.

Mean workload was 36.2 (sd = 17.5); see Figure 6. Workload was analysed using repeated-measures regression, with maximum likelihood used to fit model parameters. Gesture was a significant predictor of workload: $\chi^2(1) = 8.36$, $p = 0.004$. A *post hoc* Tukey comparison revealed that Point had a significantly lower estimated workload than Count ($z = 3.31$, $p < 0.001$). Tactile feedback was also a significant predictor of workload: $\chi^2(3) = 16.19$, $p = 0.001$. *Post hoc* Tukey tests revealed that tactile feedback using amplitude and roughness had significantly lower workload than no tactile feedback ($z = -3.58$, $p = 0.002$; and $z = -3.30$, $p = 0.006$). There was no significant difference between constant and no tactile feedback ($z = -1.20$, $p = 0.63$), amplitude and constant ($z = -2.38$, $p = 0.08$), roughness and constant ($z = -2.10$, $p = 0.15$), and roughness and amplitude ($z = 0.28$, $p = 0.99$).

We analysed card-sorting rankings as in the previous study. Table 2 shows median ranks for Feedback and Gesture. Friedman's test found a significant difference in preference for tactile feedback design: $\chi^2(2) = 11.44$, $p = 0.003$. A *post hoc* Nemenyi test revealed significant differences between no tactile feedback and all

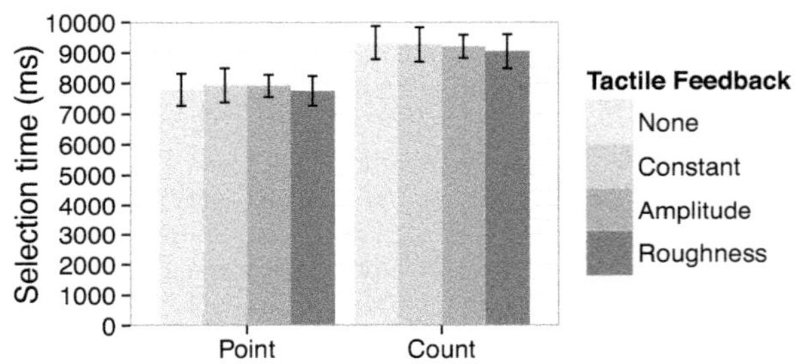

Figure 5: Mean selection times for each condition.

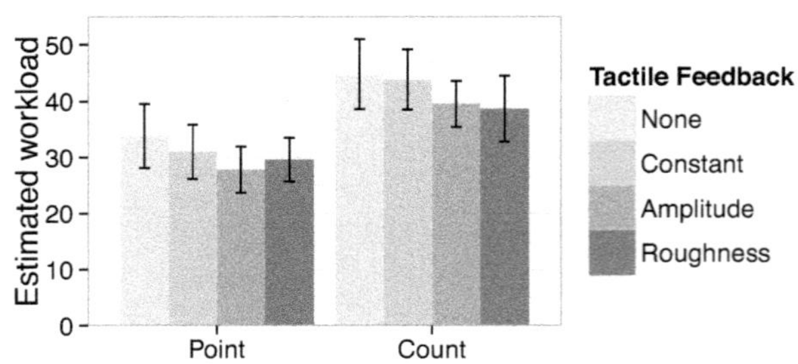

Figure 6: Mean estimated workloads for each condition.

Tactile Feedback			Gesture	
None	Constant	Dynamic	Point	Count
3	2	1	1	2

Table 2: Median ranks for feedback and gesture (lower ranks are better).

tactile feedback; there was no significant difference between constant and dynamic feedback. Wilcoxon's signed-rank test found users significantly preferred Point: $Z = 3.00$, $p = 0.004$.

5.4 Discussion

Tactile feedback had no significant effect on selection time. We think this may have been because selection was too easy for feedback to impact performance. However, dynamic tactile feedback did significantly lower task workload. Participants also ranked all tactile feedback significantly higher, in terms of preference, than no tactile feedback. These results suggest that tactile feedback is beneficial while gesturing. As in the previous study, we found a variety of reasons that users liked getting tactile feedback.

Some participants said dynamic tactile feedback made them more aware of how the interface was responding to their gestures. Subtle changes in dynamic feedback told users that something new was happening, for example a new gesture was starting to be recognised. Frequent changes in feedback also suggested sensors were having difficulty sensing gestures. One participant explained that unexpected changes in feedback told him something was wrong, for example a gesture was being misrecognised or he accidentally changed target with *Point*. Changes in amplitude were more noticeable than changes in roughness. As a result, most participants found amplitude a more useful way of encoding information.

Dynamic feedback also created familiar touch metaphors. One participant said changes in roughness were similar to what he would feel when moving over a physical button, crossing from a noticeable edge to a smooth surface. Another said increasing vibration strength was like pushing harder against a button. Even though we gave tactile feedback on the wrist, participants were able to associate these (unintended) aspects of feedback design with physical sensations.

We think our findings will apply to other above- and around-device interactions. Multimodal feedback improved users' awareness of interface state and made it easier to interact; we think giving tactile feedback will have similar benefits for other gestures near small devices.

6. DESIGN RECOMMENDATIONS

Based on our findings, we suggest above-device designers:

1. Give tactile feedback during above-device gesture input as this shows system attention, can improve user experience and can make interaction easier;

2. Use dynamic tactile feedback as subtle changes in feedback make users more aware of how the interface is responding to their actions. Constant feedback was also helpful although it gave less insight about continuous sensing;

3. Encode information multimodally as tactile feedback reinforces visual feedback and creates useful tactile cues. For example, we encoded selection progress tactually which created subtle cues to users about interface behaviour;

4. Give feedback about gestures close to the point of interest. For example, give feedback on a finger if tracking finger movement and users are wearing an appropriate accessory;

5. Give "familiar" feedback about generic interface events directly from the device, if held or worn while gestured at. For example, feedback not relating to gesture sensing;

6. Present important information in many ways, if possible. For example, show gesture acceptance using multiple accessories and directly from the device, if being held;

7. Use ultrasound haptics for more subtle types of tactile cue. For example, give continuous ultrasound feedback under the fingertip so users feel like they are touching something, but use more salient tactile displays for gesture feedback;

8. Let users choose their preferred tactile feedback accessories as feedback is effective at different locations. For example, some of our participants were not willing to wear rings but found watches and bracelets more acceptable;

7. CONCLUSIONS

In this paper we looked at how above-device gesture interfaces can give tactile feedback. Our first study was a preliminary look at how feedback may be designed and given from a gesture interface for mobile phones. We compared ultrasound haptics, distal tactile feedback from wearables and tactile feedback direct from a phone. Our second study evaluated refined feedback designs and investigated the effect of tactile feedback on gesture performance. We found that although tactile feedback did not affect interaction time for our interface, certain designs did make it easier for users to gesture. Users also showed strong preference for tactile feedback.

We recommend that above-interface designers, especially those creating interfaces for small devices like wearables or mobile phones, give tactile feedback. Tactile cues can improve gesture interfaces, making it easier for users to gesture by improving awareness of how the interface is responding to their gestures. As remote haptic technologies improve and wearable devices grow in popularity, gesture interfaces will have more options for giving tactile feedback. We contribute design recommendations based on our study findings. These recommendations will help others use tactile feedback effectively in above-device gesture interfaces.

8. ACKNOWLEDGEMENTS

This work was supported by Nokia Research Center, Finland. Tom Carter and Sriram Subramanian from University of Bristol very kindly provided hardware. We would also like to thank Graham Wilson for his helpful input.

9. REFERENCES

[1] Ashbrook, D., Baudisch, P., and White, S. Nenya: Subtle and Eyes-Free Mobile Input with a Magnetically-Tracked Finger Ring. In *Proc. CHI '11*, ACM, 2043–2046.

[2] Bailly, G., Muller, J., and Lecolinet, E. Design and evaluation of finger-count interaction: Combining multitouch gestures and menus. *Int. J. of Human Computer Studies 70*, 10 (2012), 673–689.

[3] Brewster, S., and Brown, L. M. Tactons: Structured Tactile Messages for Non-Visual Information Display. In *Proc. AUIC '04*, 15–23.

[4] Brown, L. M., Brewster, S., and Purchase, H. C. A First Investigation into the Effectiveness of Tactons. In *Proc. WHC '05*, IEEE, 167–176.

[5] Butler, A., Izadi, S., and Hodges, S. SideSight: Multi-âĂIJtouchâĂİ Interaction Around Small Devices. In *Proc. UIST '08*, ACM, 201–204.

[6] Carter, T., Seah, S. A., Long, B., Drinkwater, B., and Subramanian, S. UltraHaptics: Multi-Point Mid-Air Haptic Feedback for Touch Surfaces. In *Proc. UIST '13*, ACM, 505–514.

[7] Freeman, E., Brewster, S., and Lantz, V. Towards Usable and Acceptable Above-Device Interactions. In *Mobile HCI '14 Posters*, ACM, 459–464.

[8] Gustafson, S., Holz, C., and Baudish, P. Imaginary Phone: Learning Imaginary Interfaces by Transferring Spatial Memory from a Familiar Device. In *Proc. UIST '11*, ACM, 283–292.

[9] Harrison, C., and Hudson, S. E. Abracadabra: Wireless, High-Precision, and Unpowered Finger Input for Very Small Mobile Devices. In *Proc. UIST '09*, 121–124.

[10] Hoshi, T., Takahashi, M., Iwamoto, T., and Shinoda, H. Noncontact Tactile Display Based on Radiation Pressure of Airborne Ultrasound. *IEEE Trans. on Haptics 3*, 3 (2010), 155–165.

[11] Iwamoto, T., Tatezono, M., and Shinoda, H. Non-contact method for producing tactile sensation using airborne ultrasound. In *Proc. EuroHaptics '08*, 504–513.

[12] Jones, B., Sodhi, R., Forysth, D., Bailey, B., and Maciocci, G. Around Device Interaction for Multiscale Navigation. In *Proc. MobileHCI '12*, ACM, 83–92.

[13] Kratz, S., and Rohs, M. HoverFlow: Expanding the Design Space of Around-Device Interaction. In *Proc. MobileHCI '09*, ACM, Article 4.

[14] Lee, S. C., Li, B., and Starner, T. AirTouch: Synchronizing In-air Hand Gesture and On-body Tactile Feedback to Augment Mobile Gesture Interaction. In *Proc. ISWC '11*, IEEE, 3-10.

[15] Niikura, T., Watanabe, Y., Komuro, T., and Ishikawa, M. In-air Typing Interface: Realizing 3D operation for mobile devices. In *Proc. GCCE '12*, 223–227.

[16] Pasquero, J., Stobbe, S. J., and Stonehouse, N. A haptic wristwatch for eyes-free interactions. In *Proc. CHI '11*, ACM, 3257–3266.

[17] Richter, H., Loehmann, S., Weinhart, F., and Butz, A. Comparing Direct and Remote Tactile Feedback on Interactive Surfaces. In *Proc. EuroHaptics '12*, 301–313.

[18] Sodhi, R., Poupyrev, I., Glisson, M., and Israr, A. AIREAL: Interactive Tactile Experiences in Free Air. *Transactions on Graphics 32*, 4 (2013), Article 134.

[19] Wacharamanotham, C., Todi, K., Pye, M., and Borchers, J. Understanding Finger Input Above Desktop Devices. In *Proc. CHI '14*, ACM, 1083–1092.

[20] Wilson, G., Carter, T., Subramanian, S., and Brewster, S. Perception of Ultrasonic Haptic Feedback on the Hand: Localisation and Apparent Motion In *Proc. CHI '14* ACM, 1133–1142.

Once Upon a Crime: Towards Crime Prediction from Demographics and Mobile Data

Andrey Bogomolov
University of Trento,
Telecom Italia SKIL Lab
Via Sommarive, 5
I-38123 Povo - Trento, Italy
andrey.bogomolov@unitn.it

Bruno Lepri
Fondazione Bruno Kessler
Via Sommarive, 18
I-38123 Povo - Trento, Italy
lepri@fbk.eu

Jacopo Staiano
DISI, University of Trento
Via Sommarive, 5
I-38123 Povo - Trento, Italy
staiano@disi.unitn.it

Nuria Oliver
Telefonica Research
Torre Telefonica, Diagonal 00
Barcelona, Spain
nuriao@tid.es

Fabio Pianesi
Fondazione Bruno Kessler
Via Sommarive, 18
I-38123 Povo - Trento, Italy
pianesi@fbk.eu

Alex (Sandy) Pentland
MIT Media Lab
20 Ames Street
Cambridge, MA, USA
pentland@mit.edu

ABSTRACT

In this paper, we present a novel approach to predict crime in a geographic space from multiple data sources, in particular mobile phone and demographic data. The main contribution of the proposed approach lies in using aggregated and anonymized human behavioral data derived from mobile network activity to tackle the crime prediction problem. While previous research efforts have used either background historical knowledge or offenders' profiling, our findings support the hypothesis that aggregated human behavioral data captured from the mobile network infrastructure, in combination with basic demographic information, can be used to predict crime. In our experimental results with real crime data from London we obtain an accuracy of almost 70% when predicting whether a specific area in the city will be a crime hotspot or not. Moreover, we provide a discussion of the implications of our findings for data-driven crime analysis.

Categories and Subject Descriptors

I.5 [**Computing Methodologies**]: PATTERN RECOGNITION—*Models, Design Methodology, Implementation*; J.4 [**Computer Applications**]: SOCIAL AND BEHAVIORAL SCIENCES—*Sociology*

General Terms

Algorithms; Experimentation; Measurement; Theory

Keywords

crime prediction; urban computing; mobile sensing

ICMI'14, November 12 - 16 2014, Istanbul, Turkey.

http://dx.doi.org/10.1145/2663204.2663254.

1. INTRODUCTION

Crime, in all its facets, is a well-known social problem affecting the quality of life and the economic development of a society. Studies have shown that crime tends to be associated with slower economic growth at both the national level [24] and the local level, such as cities and metropolitan areas [12]. Crime-related information has always attracted the attention of criminal law and sociology scholars. Dating back to the beginning of the 20th century, studies have focused on the behavioral evolution of criminals and its relations with specific characteristics of the neighborhoods in which they grew up, lived, and acted. The study of the impact on behavioral development of factors like exposure to specific peer networks, neighborhood characteristics (*e.g.* presence/absence of recreational/educational facilities) and poverty indexes, has provided a wealth of knowledge from both individual and collective standpoints [44]. Existing works in the fields of criminology, sociology, psychology and economics tend to mainly explore relationships between criminal activity and socio-economic variables such as education [17], ethnicity [6], income level [26], and unemployment [19].

Several studies in criminology and sociology have provided evidence of significant concentrations of crime at micro levels of geography, regardless of the specific unit of analysis defined [7, 46]. It is important to note that such clustering of crime in small geographic areas (*e.g.* streets), commonly referred to as *hotspots*, does not necessarily align with trends that are occurring at a larger geographic level, such as communities. Research has shown, for example, that in what are generally seen as good parts of town there are often streets with strong crime concentrations, and in what are often defined as bad neighborhoods, many places are relatively free of crime [46].

In 2008, criminologist David Weisburd proposed to switch the popular people-centric paradigm of police practices to a place-centric one [45], thus focusing on geographical topology and micro-structures rather than on criminal profiling. In our paper, *crime prediction* is used in conjunction with a place-centric definition of the problem and with a data-driven approach: we specifically investigate the predictive power of aggregated and anonymized human behavioral data derived from a multimodal combination of mobile network activity and demographic information to determine whether a geographic area is likely to become a *scene of the crime* or not.

As the number of mobile phones actively in use worldwide approaches the 6.8 billion mark[1], they become a very valuable and unobtrusive source of human behavioral data: mobile phones can be seen as sensors of aggregated human activity [14, 23] and have been used to monitor citizens' mobility patterns and urban interactions [21, 48], to understand individual spending behaviors [33], to infer people's traits [13, 37] and states [3], to map and model the spreading of diseases such as malaria [47] and H1N1 flu [20], and to predict and understand socio-economic indicators of territories [15, 36, 34]. Recently, Zheng *et al.* proposed a multi-source approach, based on human mobility and geographical data, to infer noise pollution [49] and gas consumption [29] in large metropolitan areas.

In this paper, we use human behavioral data derived from a combination of mobile network activity and demography, together with open data related to crime events to predict crime *hotspots* in specific neighborhoods of a European metropolis: London. The main contributions of this work are:

1. The use of human behavioral data derived from anonymized and aggregated mobile network activity, combined with demographics, to predict crime hotspots in a European metropolis;

2. A comprehensive analysis of the predictive power of the proposed model and a comparison with a state-of-the-art approach based on official statistics;

3. A discussion of the theoretical and practical implications of our proposed approach.

This paper is structured as follows: section 2 describes relevant previous work in the area of data-driven crime prediction; the data used for our experiments are described in section 3; the definition of the research problem tackled in this work and detailed information on the methodology adopted is provided in 4; finally, we report our experimental results and provide a discussion thereof in sections 5 and 6, respectively.

2. RELATED WORK

Researchers have devoted attention to the study of criminal behavior dynamics both from a people- and place- centric perspective. The people-centric perspective has mostly been used for individual or collective criminal profiling. Wang *et al.* [42] proposed *Series Finder*, a machine learning approach to the problem of detecting specific patterns in crimes that are committed by the same offender or group of offenders. In [31], it is proposed a biased random walk model built upon empirical knowledge of criminal offenders behavior along with spatio-temporal crime information to take into account repeating patterns in historical crime data. Furthermore, Ratcliffe [28] investigated the spatio-temporal constraints underlying offenders' criminal behavior.

An example of a place-centric perspective is crime hotspot detection and analysis and the consequent derivation of useful insights. A novel application of quantitative tools from mathematics, physics and signal processing has been proposed by Toole *et al.* [39] to analyse spatial and temporal patterns in criminal offense records. The analyses they conducted on a dataset containing crime information from 1991 to 1999 for the city of Philadelphia, US, indicated the existence of multi-scale complex relationships both in space and time. Using demographic information statistics at community (town) level, Buczak and Gifford [9] applied fuzzy association rule mining in order to derive a finite (and consistent among US states) set of rules to be applied by crime analysts. Other common models are the ones proposed by Eck *et al.* [16] and by Chainey *et al.* [11] that rely on kernel density estimation from the criminal history record of a geographical area. Similarly, Mohler *et al.* [25] applied the self-exciting point process model (previously developed for earthquake prediction) as a model of crime. The major problem of all these approaches is that they relies on the prior occurrence of crimes in a particular area and thus cannot generalize to previously unobserved areas.

More recently, the proliferation of social media has sparked interest in using this kind of data to predict a variety of variables, including electoral outcomes [40] and market trends [4]. In this line, Wang *et al.* [43] proposed the usage of social media to predict criminal incidents. Their approach relies on a semantic analysis of tweets using natural language processing along with spatio-temporal information derived from neighborhood demographic data and the tweets metadata.

In this paper, we tackle the crime hotspot forecasting problem by leveraging mobile network activity as a source of human behavioral data. Our work hence complements the above-mentioned research efforts and contributes to advance the state-of-the-art in quantitative criminal studies.

3. DATASETS

The datasets we exploit in this paper were provided during a public competition - the Datathon for Social Good - organized by Telefónica Digital, The Open Data Institute and MIT during the Campus Party Europe 2013 at the O2 Arena in London in September 2013.

Participants were provided access to the following data, among others:

- Anonymized and aggregated human behavioral data computed from mobile network activity in the London Metropolitan Area. We shall refer to this data as the Smartsteps dataset, because it was derived from Telefonica Digital's Smartsteps product[2]. A sample visualization of the Smartsteps product can seen in Figure 3.1.;

- Geo-localised Open Data, a collection of openly available datasets with varying temporal granularity. This includes reported criminal cases, residential property sales, transportation, weather and London borough profiles related to homelessness, households, housing market, local government finance and societal wellbeing (a total of 68 metrics).

We turn now to describing the specific datasets that we used to predict crime hotspots.

[1]http://www.itu.int

[2]http://dynamicinsights.telefonica.com/488/smart-steps

3.1 Smartsteps Dataset

The Smartsteps dataset consists of a geographic division of the London Metropolitan Area into cells whose precise location (lat,long) and surface area is provided. Note that the actual shape of the cell was not provided. In total, there were 124119 cells. We shall refer to these cells as the Smartsteps cells.

For each of the Smartsteps cells, a variety of demographic variables were provided, computed every hour for a 3-week period, from December 9th to 15th, 2012 and from December 23rd, 2012 to January 5th, 2013.

In particular:

(1) *Footfall*, or the estimated number of people within each cell. This estimation is derived from the mobile network activity by aggregating every hour the total number of unique phonecalls in each cell tower, mapping the cell tower coverage areas to the Smartsteps cells, and extrapolating to the general population -by taking into account the market share of the network in each cell location; and

(2) an estimation of gender, age and home/work/visitor group splits.

That is, for each Smartsteps cell and for each hour, the dataset contains an estimation of how many people are in the cell, the percentage of these people who are at home, at work or just visiting the cell and their gender and age splits in the following brackets: 0-20 years, 21-30 years, 31-40 years, etc..., as shown in Table 1.

Table 1: SmartSteps data provided by the challenge organizers. All data refer to 1-hour intervals and to each Smartsteps cell.

Type	Data
Origin-based	total # people
	# residents
	# workers
	# visitors
Gender-based	# males
	# females
Age-based	# people aged up to 20
	# people aged 21 to 30
	# people aged 31 to 40
	# people aged 41 to 50
	# people aged 51 to 60
	# people aged over 60

Figure 3.1 shows a sample visualization of the information made available from the SmartSteps platform.

3.2 Criminal Cases Dataset

The criminal cases dataset includes the geo-location of all reported crimes in the UK but does not specify their exact date, just the month and year. The data provided in the public competition included the criminal cases for December 2012 and January 2013.

In detail, the crime dataset includes: the crime ID, the month and year when the crime was committed, its location (longitude, latitude, and address where the crime took place), the police department involved, the *lower layer super output area* code, the *lower layer super output area* name and its type out of 11 possible types (*e.g.* anti-social behavior, burglary, violent crime, shoplifting, etc.).

Lower Layer Super Output Areas (LSOAs) are small geographical areas defined by the United Kingdom Office for National Statistics following the 2001 census. Their aim here is to define areas, based on population levels, whose boundaries would not change over time. LSOAs are the smallest type of output areas used for official statistics, have a mean population of 1,500 and a minimum population threshold of 1,000.

The ground truth crime data used in our experiments corresponds to the crimes reported in January 2013 for each of the Smartsteps cells.

3.3 London Borough Profiles Dataset

The London borough profiles dataset is an official open dataset containing 68 different metrics about the population of a particular geographic area. The spatial granularity of the bourough profiles data is at the LSOA level.

In particular, the information in this dataset includes statistics about the population, households (census), demographics, migrant population, ethnicity, language, employment, NEET (Not in Education, Employment, and Training) people, earnings, volunteering, jobs density, business survival, house prices, new homes, greenspace, recycling, carbon emissions, cars, indices of multiple deprivation, children in out-of-work families, life expectancy, teenage conceptions, happiness levels, political control (*e.g.* proportion of seats won by Labour, LibDem and Conservatives), and election turnout.

4. METHODOLOGY

We cast the problem of crime hotspot forecasting as a binary classification task. For each Smartsteps cell, we predict whether that particular cell will be a crime hotspot or not in the next month. In this section we provide details of the experimental setup that we followed.

4.1 Data Preprocessing and Feature Extraction

Starting from the bulk of data described in Section 3, we performed the following preprocessing steps.

4.1.1 Referencing all geo-tagged data to the Smartsteps cells

As the SmartSteps cell IDs, the borough profiles and the crime event locations are not spatially linked in the provided datasets, we first geo-referenced each crime event by identifying the Smartsteps cell which is the closest to the location of the crime. We carried out a similar process for the borough profile dataset. As a result, each crime event and the borough profile information were linked to one of the Smartsteps cells.

4.1.2 Smartsteps features

Diversity and *regularity* have been shown to be important in the characterization of different facets of human behavior and, in particular, the concept of entropy has been applied to assess the predictability of mobility [35] and spending patterns [22, 33], the socio-economic characteristics of places and cities [15] and some individual traits such as personality [13]. Hence, for each Smartsteps variable (see Table 1) we computed the mathematical functions which characterize the distributions and information theoretic properties of such variables, *e.g.* mean, median, standard deviation, min and max values and Shannon entropy.

In order to be able to also account for temporal relationships inside the Smartsteps data, the same computations as above were repeated on sliding windows of variable length

Figure 1: Sample visualization of the high-level information provided by the Smartsteps platform. By combining aggregated and anonymized demographics and mobility data, fine-grained spatio-temporal dynamics can be exploited to derive valuable insights for the scenario of interest.

(1-hour, 4-hour and 1 day), producing *second-order features* that help reduce computational complexity and the feature space itself, while preserving useful data properties.

4.1.3 London borough profile features

No data preprocessing was needed for the London borough profiles. Hence, we used the original 68 London borough profile features.

4.1.4 Crime hotspots ground-truth data

The distribution of the criminal cases data is reported in Table 2.

Table 2: Number of crime hotspots in January.

Min.	Q1	**Median**	Mean	Q3	Max.
1	2	**5**	8.2	10	289

Given the high skewness of the distribution (skewness = 5.88, kurtosis = 72.5, mean = 8.2, median = 5; see Table 2) and based on previous research on urban crime patterns [2], we split the criminal dataset with respect to its median into two classes: a *low* crime (class '0') when the number of crimes in the given cell was less or equal to the median, and a *high* crime (class '1') when the number of crimes in a given cell was larger than the median.

Following the empirical distribution, the two resulting classes are approximately balanced (53.15% for the *high* crime class).

4.2 Feature Selection

We randomly split all data into training (80% of data) and testing (20% of data) sets. In order to accelerate the convergence of the models, we *normalized* each dimension of the feature vector [5].

As an initial step, we carried out a *Pearson correlation analysis* to visualize and better understand the relationship between variables in the feature space. We found quite a large subset of features with strong mutual correlations and another subset of uncorrelated features. There was room, therefore, for feature space reduction. We excluded using *principal component analysis* (PCA) because the transformation it is based on produces new variables that are difficult to interpret in terms of the original ones, which complicates the interpretation of the results.

We turned to a pipelined *variable selection* approach, based on *feature ranking* and *feature subset selection*, which was perfomed using only data from the training set.

The metric used for feature ranking was the mean decrease in the *Gini coefficient of inequality*. This choice was motivated because it outperformed other metrics, such as mutual information, information gain and chi-square statistic with an average improvement of approximately 28.5%, 19% and 9.2% respectively [32]. The Gini coefficient ranges between 0, expressing perfect equality (all dimensions have the same predictive power) and 1, expressing maximal inequality in predictive power. The feature with maximum mean decrease in Gini coefficient is expected to have the maximum influence in minimizing the out-of-the-bag error. It is known in the literature that minimizing the out-of-the-bag error results in maximizing common performance metrics used to evaluate models (*e.g.* accuracy, F1, AUC, etc...) [41].

In the subsequent text and tables this metric is presented as a percentage.

The feature selection process produced a reduced subset of 68 features (from an initial pool of about 6000 features), with a reduction in dimensionality of about 90 times with respect to the full feature space. The top 20 features selected by the model are included in Table 3.

4.3 Model Building

We trained a variety of classifiers on the training data following 5-fold cross validation strategy: logistic regression, support vector machines, neural networks, decision trees, and different implementations of ensembles of tree classifiers with different parameters.

The decision tree classifier based on the Breiman's Random Forest (RF) algorithm yielded the best performance when compared to all other classifiers. Hence, we report the performance results only for the the best model, based on this algorithm.

We took advantage of the well-known performance improvements that are obtained by growing an ensemble of trees and voting for the most frequent class. Random vectors were generated before the growth of each tree in the ensemble, and a random selection without replacement was performed [8].

The *consistency* of the random forest algorithm has been proven and the algorithm adapts to sparsity in the sense that the rate of *convergence* depends only on the number of strong features and not on the number of noisy or less relevant ones [1].

5. EXPERIMENTAL RESULTS

In this section we report the experimental results obtained by the Random Forest trained on different subsets of the selected features and always on the test set, which was not used during the training phase in any way.

The performance metrics used to evaluate our approach are: accuracy, F1, and AUC score. As can be seen on Table 4, the model achieves almost 70% accuracy when predicting whether a particular Smartsteps cell will be a crime hotspot in the following month or not. Table 4 includes all performance metrics obtained by our model.

A spatial visualisation of our results is reported on a map of the London metropolitan area in Figure 3 and compared with a similar visualisation of the ground truth labels in Figure 2. In the maps, green represents "low crime level" and red "high crime level".

Second order features, which we introduced to capture intertemporal dependencies for our problem, not only made the feature space more compact, but also yielded a significant improvement in model performance metrics.

In order to understand the value added by the Smartsteps data, we compared the performance of the Random Forest using all features with two different models trained with (i) only the subset of selected features derived from the borough profiles dataset (Borough Profiles) and (ii) only the subset of selected features derived from the Smartsteps dataset (Smartsteps).

Table 4 reports accuracy, F1, and the area under the ROC curve metrics for each of the models. In this Table, we also report the performance of (iii) a simple majority classifier, which always returns the majority class ("High Crime") as prediction (accuracy=53.15%).

As can be seen on Table 4, the borough-only model yields an accuracy of 62.18%, over 6% lower than the accuracy obtained with the Smartsteps model (68.37%). The Smartsteps+Borough model yields an increase in accuracy of over 7% when compared with the borough profiles model (69.54% vs 62.18% accuracy) while using the same number of variables.

6. DISCUSSION

The results discussed in the previous section show that usage of human behavioral data (at a daily and monthly scale) significantly improves prediction accuracy when compared to using rich statistical data about a borough's population (households census, demographics, migrant population, ethnicity, language, employment, etc...). The borough profiles data provides a fairly detailed view of the nature and living conditions of a particular area in a city, yet it is expensive and effort-consuming to collect. Hence, this type of data is typically updated with low frequency (*e.g.* every few years). Human behavioral data derived from mobile network activity and demographics, though less comprehensive than borough profiles, provides significantly finer temporal and spatial resolution.

Next, we focus on the most relevant predictors of crime level which show interesting associations. We first take a look at the top-20 variables in our model, which are sorted by their mean reduction in accuracy (see Table 3).

Table 4: Metrics Comparison

Model	Acc.,%	Acc. CI, 95%	F1,%	AUC
Baseline Majority Classifier	53.15	(0.53, 0.53)	0	0.50
Borough Profiles Model (BPM)	62.18	(0.61, 0.64)	57.52	0.58
Smartsteps	68.37	(0.67, 0.70)	65.43	0.63
Smartsteps + BPM	69.54	(0.68, 0.71)	67.23	0.64

The naming convention that we used for the features shown in Table 3 is: the original data source (*e.g.* "smartSteps") is followed by the temporal granularity T (*e.g.* "daily"), the semantics of the variable (*e.g.* "athome"), and its statistics at T (*e.g.* "mean"). Note that *second order* features where we computed statistics across multiple days appear *after* the first statistics. For example, feature 2 in the Table, "smartSteps.daily.athome.mean.sd", is generated by computing the standard deviation of the daily means of the percentage of people estimated to be at home.

As shown in the Table, the Smartsteps features have more predictive power than official statistics coming from borough profiles. No features listed in the top-20 are actually obtained using borough profiles. Moreover, Table 3 shows that higher-level features extracted over a sequence of days from variables encoding the daily dynamics (all features with the label smartSteps.daily.*) have more predictive power than features extracted on a monthly basis. For example, feature 2 in Table 3. This finding points out at the importance of capturing the temporal dynamics of a geographical area in order to predict its levels of crime.

Furthermore, features derived from the percentage of people in a certain cell who are at home (all features with *.athome.* in their label) both at a daily and monthly basis seem to be of extreme importance. In fact, 11 of the top 20 features are related to the *at home* variable.

It is also interesting to note the role played by diversity patterns captured by Shannon entropy features [30]. The entropy-based features (all features with *.entropy.* in their label) in fact seem useful for predicting the crime level of places (8 features out of the top 20 are entropy-based features). In our study, the Shannon entropy captures the predictable structure of a place in terms of the types of people that are in that area over the course of a day. A place with high entropy would have a lot of variety in the types of people visiting it on a daily basis, whereas a place with low entropy would be characterised by regular patterns over time. In this case, the daily diversity in patterns related to different age groups, different use (home vs work) and different genders seems a good predictor for the crime level in a given area. Interestingly, Eagle *et al.* [15] found that Shannon entropy used to capture the social and spatial diversity of communication ties within an individual's social network

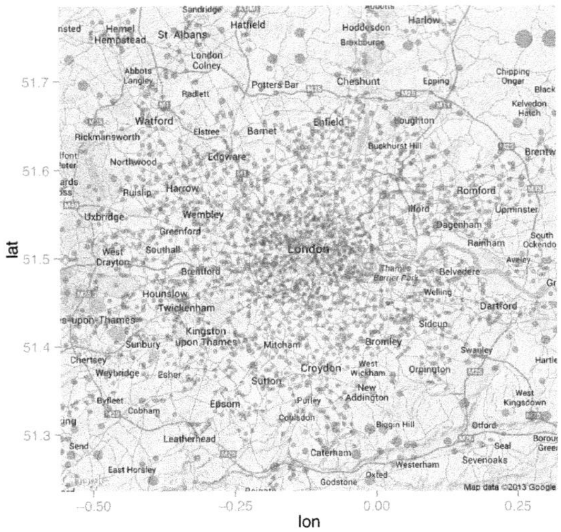

Figure 2: Ground Truth of Crime Hotspots

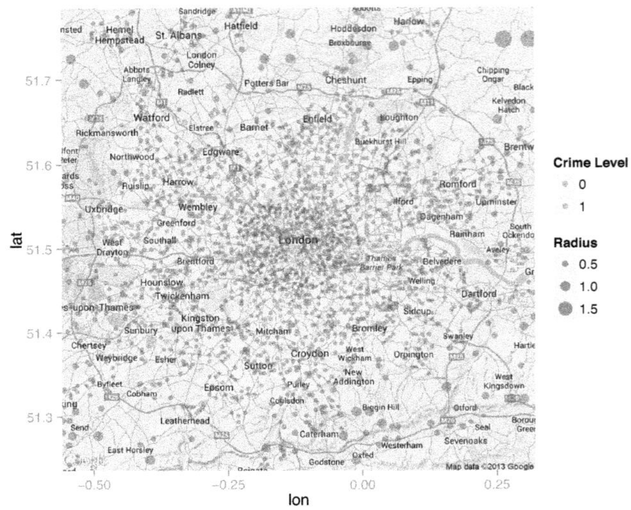

Figure 3: Predicted Crime Hotspots

Table 3: Top-20 Selected Features Ranked by Mean Decrease in Accuracy

Rank	Features	0	1	MeanDecreaseAccuracy	MeanDecreaseGini
1	smartSteps.daily.ageover60.entropy.empirical.entropy.empirical	4.48	5.43	9.02	18.75
2	smartSteps.daily.athome.mean.sd	3.20	7.60	8.91	27.13
3	smartSteps.daily.age020.sd.entropy.empirical	5.69	3.97	8.85	16.88
4	smartSteps.daily.age020.mean.entropy.empirical	3.09	5.88	8.85	17.26
5	smartSteps.daily.age020.mean.sd	4.50	5.27	8.65	16.03
6	smartSteps.daily.athome.min.entropy.empirical	6.39	2.32	8.61	15.99
7	smartSteps.daily.athome.sd.sd	3.22	8.58	8.60	45.82
8	smartSteps.daily.athome.sd.mean	3.35	5.83	8.57	24.93
9	smartSteps.daily.ageover60.entropy.empirical.sd	4.62	4.95	8.56	20.45
10	smartSteps.daily.athome.sd.median	5.41	5.04	8.50	26.48
11	smartSteps.daily.age3140.entropy.empirical.max	2.33	5.79	8.44	16.24
12	smartSteps.daily.age3140.min.sd	6.81	4.06	8.31	36.52
13	smartSteps.daily.athome.min.sd	4.36	6.85	8.29	34.26
14	smartSteps.daily.athome.sd.max	4.13	6.87	8.27	34.89
15	smartSteps.monthly.athome.max	3.92	5.42	8.26	29.86
16	smartSteps.monthly.athome.sd	4.43	4.17	8.21	39.70
17	smartSteps.daily.age5160.entropy.empirical.entropy.empirical	4.74	4.11	8.13	16.64
18	smartSteps.daily.age020.sd.sd	3.67	5.88	8.12	16.86
19	smartSteps.daily.athome.entropy.empirical.entropy.empirical	5.13	4.82	8.08	18.55
20	smartSteps.daily.athome.max.sd	2.83	6.29	8.07	26.85

was strongly and positively correlated with economic development.

As previously described, borough profile features (official statistics) have lower predictive power with respect to accuracy than features extracted from aggregated mobile network activity data. Six borough profile features were selected in the final feature vector, including the proportion of the working age population who claim out of work benefits, the largest migrant population, the proportion of overseas nationals entering the UK and the proportion of resident population born abroad –metrics based on 2011 Census Bureau data. The predictive power of some of these variables is in line with previous studies in sociology and criminology. For example, several studies show a positive association among unemployment rate and crime level of an area [27]. Still under debate is the positive association among number of immigrants and crime level [18]. However, our experimental results show that the static nature of these variables makes them less useful in predicting crime level's of a given area when compared with less detailed but daily information about the types of people present in a same area throughout the day.

7. IMPLICATIONS AND LIMITATIONS

We have outlined and tested a multimodal approach to automatically predict with almost 70% accuracy whether a given geographical area will have high or low crime levels in the next month. The proposed approach could have clear practical implications by informing police departments and city governments on how and where to invest their efforts and on how to react to criminal events with quicker response times. From a proactive perspective, the ability to predict the safety of a geographical area may provide information on explanatory variables that can be used to identify underlying causes of these crime occurrence areas and hence enable officers to intervene in very narrowly defined geographic areas.

The distinctive characteristic of our approach lies in the use of features computed from aggregated and anonymized mobile network activity data in combination with some demographic information. Previous research efforts in criminology have tackled similar problems using background historical knowledge about crime events in specific areas, criminals' profiling, or wide description of areas using socio-economic and demographic indicators. Our findings provide evidence that aggregated and anonymized data collected by the mobile infrastructure contains relevant information to describe a geographical area in order to predict its crime level.

The first advantage of our approach is its predictive ability. Our method predicts crime level using variables that capture the dynamics and characteristics of the demographics and nature of a place rather than only making extrapolations from previous crime histories. Operationally, this means that the proposed model could be used to predict new crime occurrence areas that are of similar nature to other well known occurrence areas. Even though the newly predicted areas may not have seen recent crimes, if they are similar enough to prior ones, they could be considered to be high-risk areas to monitor closely. This is an important advantage given that in some areas people are less inclined to report crimes [38]. Moreover, our approach provides new ways of describing geographical areas. Recently, some criminologists have started to use *risk terrain modeling* [10] to identify geographic features that contribute to crime risk, *e.g.* the presence of liquor stores, certain types of major stores, bars, etc. Our approach can identify novel risk-inducing or risk-reducing features of geographical areas. In particular, the features used in our approach are dynamic and related to human activities.

Our study has several limitations due to the constraints of the datasets used. First of all, we had access only to 3 weeks of Smartsteps data collected between December 2012 and the first week of January 2013. In addition, the crime data provided was aggregated on a monthly basis. Having access to crime events aggregated on a weekly, daily or hourly basis would enable us to validate our approach with finer times granularity, predicting crimes in the next week, day or even hour.

8. CONCLUSION

In this paper we have proposed a novel approach to predict crime hotspots from human behavioral data derived from mobile network activity, in combination with demographic information. Specifically, we have described a methodology to automatically predict with almost 70% of accuracy whether a given geographical area of a large European metropolis will have high or low crime levels in the next month. We have shown that our approach, while using a similar number of variables, significantly improves prediction accuracy (6%) when compared with using traditional, rich – yet expensive to collect – statistical data about a borough's population. Moreover, we have provided insights about the most predictive features (*e.g.* home-based and entropy-based features) and we have discussed the theoretical and practical implications of our methodology. Despite the limitations discussed above and the additional investigations needed to validate our approach and the robustness of our indicators, we believe that our findings open the door to exciting avenues of research in computational approaches to deal with a well-known social problem such as crime.

9. ACKNOWLEDGMENTS

Source data processing, reported data transformations and feature selection, which were derived from anonymised and aggregated mobile network dataset, provided by Telefónica Digital Limited were done only during the public competition – "Datathon for Social Good" organized by Telefónica, The Open Data Institute and the MIT during the Campus Party Europe 2013 at the O2 Arena in London during 2-7 September 2013, in full compliance with the competition rules and legal limitations imposed by the "Terms and Conditions" document.

The work of Andrey Bogomolov is partially supported by EIT ICT Labs Doctoral School grant and Telecom Italia Semantics and Knowledge Innovation Laboratory (SKIL) research grant T.

10. REFERENCES

[1] G. Biau. Analysis of a random forests model. *The Journal of Machine Learning Research*, 98888(1):1063–1095, 2012.

[2] S. L. Boggs. Urban crime patterns. *American Sociological Review*, 30(6):pp. 899–908, 1965.

[3] A. Bogomolov, B. Lepri, and F. Pianesi. Happiness recognition from mobile phone data. In *SocialCom 2013*, pages 790–795, 2013.

[4] J. Bollen, H. Mao, and X. Zeng. Twitter mood predicts the stock market. *Journal of Computational Science*, 2(1):1–8, 2011.

[5] G. E. P. Box and D. R. Cox. An Analysis of Transformations. *Journal of the Royal Statistical Society. Series B (Methodological)*, 26(2):211–252, 1964.

[6] J. Braithwaite. *Crime, Shame and Reintegration.* Ambridge: Cambridge University Press, 1989.

[7] P. L. Brantingham and P. J. Brantingham. A theoretical model of crime hot spot generation. *Studies on Crime & Crime Prevention*, 1999.

[8] L. Breiman. Bagging predictors. *Machine Learning*, 24(2):123–140, 1996.

[9] A. L. Buczak and C. M. Gifford. Fuzzy association rule mining for community crime pattern discovery. In *ACM SIGKDD Workshop on Intelligence and Security Informatics*, page 2. ACM, 2010.

[10] J. Caplan and L. Kennedy. *Risk terrain modeling manual: Theoretical framework and technical steps of spatial risk assessment for crime analysis.* Rutgers Center on Public Security, 2010.

[11] S. Chainey, L. Tompson, and S. Uhlig. The utility of hotspot mapping for predicting spatial patterns of crime. *Security Journal*, 21:4–28, 2008.

[12] J. Cullen and S. Levitt. Crime, urban flight, and the consequences for the cities. *Review of Economics and Statistics*, (81):159–169, 2009.

[13] Y.-A. de Montjoye, J. Quoidbach, F. Robic, and A. Pentland. Predicting personality using novel mobile phone-based metrics. In *Social Computing, Behavioral-Cultural Modeling and Prediction*, pages 48–55. Springer, 2013.

[14] W. Dong, B. Lepri, and A. Pentland. Modeling the co-evolution of behaviors and social relationships using mobile phone data. In *MUM 2011*, 2011.

[15] N. Eagle, M. Macy, and R. Claxton. Network diversity and economic development. *Science*, 328(5981):1029–1031, 2010.

[16] J. Eck, S. Chainey, J. Cameron, and R. Wilson. Mapping crime: understanding hotspots. *National Institute of Justice: Washington DC*, 2005.

[17] I. Ehrlich. On the relation between education and crime. 1975.

[18] L. Ellis, K. Beaver, and J. Wright. *Handbook of crime correlates*. Academic Press, 2009.

[19] R. B. Freeman. The economics of crime. *Handbook of labor economics*, 3:3529–3571, 1999.

[20] E. Frias-Martinez, G. Williamson, and V. Frias-Martinez. An agent-based model of epidemic spread using human mobility and social network information. In *Social Computing (SocialCom), 2011 International Conference on*, pages 57–64. IEEE, 2011.

[21] M. Gonzalez, C. Hidalgo, and L. Barabasi. Understanding individual mobility patterns. *Nature*, 453(7196):779–782, 2008.

[22] C. Krumme, A. Llorente, M. Cebrian, A. Pentland, and E. Moro. The predictability of consumer visitation patterns. *Scientific Reports*, (1645), 2013.

[23] J. Laurila, D. Gatica-Perez, I. Aad, J. Blom, O. Bornet, T. Do, O. Dousse, J. Eberle, and M. Miettinen. From big smartphone data to worldwide research: The mobile data challenge. *Pervasive and Mobile Computing*, 9:752–771, 2013.

[24] H. Mehlum, K. Moene, and R. Torvik. Crime induced poverty traps. *Journal of Development Economics*, (77):325–340, 2005.

[25] G. Mohler, M. Short, P. Brantingham, F. Schoenberg, and G. Tita. Self-exciting point process modeling of crime. *Journal of the American Statistical Association*, (106):100–108, 2011.

[26] E. B. Patterson. Poverty, income inequality, and community crime rates. *Criminology*, 29(4):755–776, 1991.

[27] S. Raphael and R. Winter-Ebmer. Identifying the effect of unemployment on crime. *Journal of Law and Economics*, 44(1), 2001.

[28] J. H. Ratcliffe. A temporal constraint theory to explain opportunity-based spatial offending patterns. *Journal of Research in Crime and Delinquency*, 43(3):261–291, 2006.

[29] J. Shang, T. W. Zheng, Y., and E. Chang. Inferring gas consumption and pollution emission of vehicles throughout a city. In *KDD 2014*, 2014.

[30] C. Shannon. A mathematical theory of communication. *Bell System Technical Journal*, 27:379–423, 623–656, July, October 1948.

[31] M. B. Short, M. R. D'Orsogna, V. B. Pasour, G. E. Tita, P. J. Brantingham, A. L. Bertozzi, and L. B. Chayes. A statistical model of criminal behavior. *Mathematical Models and Methods in Applied Sciences*, 18(supp01):1249–1267, 2008.

[32] S. R. Singh, H. A. Murthy, and T. A. Gonsalves. Feature selection for text classification based on gini coefficient of inequality. *Journal of Machine Learning Research-Proceedings Track*, 10:76–85, 2010.

[33] V. K. Singh, L. Freeman, B. Lepri, and A. S. Pentland. Predicting spending behavior using socio-mobile features. In *Social Computing (SocialCom), 2013 International Conference on*, pages 174–179. IEEE, 2013.

[34] C. Smith-Clarke, A. Mashhadi, and L. Capra. Poverty on the cheap: Estimating poverty maps using aggregated mobile communication networks. In *32nd ACM Conference on Human Factors in Computing Systems (CHI2014)*, 2014.

[35] C. Song, Z. Qu, N. Blumm, and A. Barabasi. Limits of predictability in human mobility. *Science*, (327):1018–1021, 2010.

[36] V. Soto, V. Frias-Martinez, J. Virseda, and E. Frias-Martinez. Prediction of socioeconomic levels using cell phone records. In *UMAP 2011*, pages 377–388, 2011.

[37] J. Staiano, B. Lepri, N. Aharony, F. Pianesi, N. Sebe, and A. Pentland. Friends don't lie - inferring personality traits from social network structure. In *ACM Ubicomp 2012*, pages 321–330, 2012.

[38] R. Tarling and K. Morris. Reporting crime to the police. *British Journal of Criminology*, (50):474–479, 2010.

[39] J. L. Toole, N. Eagle, and J. B. Plotkin. Spatiotemporal correlations in criminal offense records. *ACM Trans. Intell. Syst. Technol.*, 2(4):38:1–38:18, July 2011.

[40] A. Tumasjan, T. O. Sprenger, P. G. Sandner, and I. M. Welpe. Predicting elections with twitter: What 140 characters reveal about political sentiment. *ICWSM*, 10:178–185, 2010.

[41] E. Tuv, A. Borisov, G. Runger, and K. Torkkola. Feature selection with ensembles, artificial variables, and redundancy elimination. *The Journal of Machine Learning Research*, 10:1341–1366, 2009.

[42] T. Wang, C. Rudin, D. Wagner, and R. Sevieri. Learning to detect patterns of crime. In *Machine Learning and Knowledge Discovery in Databases*, pages 515–530. Springer, 2013.

[43] X. Wang, M. S. Gerber, and D. E. Brown. Automatic crime prediction using events extracted from twitter posts. In *Social Computing, Behavioral-Cultural Modeling and Prediction*, pages 231–238. Springer, 2012.

[44] S. K. Weinberg. Theories of criminality and problems of prediction. *The Journal of Criminal Law, Criminology, and Police Science*, 45(4):412–424, 1954.

[45] D. Weisburd. Place-based policing. *Ideas in American Policing*, 9:1–16, 2008.

[46] D. Weisburd and L. Green. Defining the street-level drug market. 1994.

[47] A. Wesolowski, N. Eagle, A. Tatem, D. Smith, R. Noor, and C. Buckee. Quantifying the impact of human mobility on malaria. *Science*, 338(6104):267–270, 2012.

[48] Y. Zheng, L. Capra, O. Wolfson, and H. Yang. Urban computing: concepts, methodologies, and applications. *ACM Transaction on Intelligent Systems and Technology*, 2014.

[49] Y. Zheng, T. Liu, Y. Wang, Y. Liu, Y. Zhu, and E. Chang. Diagnosing new york city's noises with ubiquitous data. In *ACM Ubicomp 2014*, 2014.

Impact of Coordinate Systems on 3D Manipulations in Mobile Augmented Reality

Philipp Tiefenbacher
Technische Universität München
philipp.tiefenbacher@tum.de

Daniel Merget
Technische Universität München
daniel.merget@tum.de

Steven Wichert
Technische Universität München
stevenwichert@gmail.com

Gerhard Rigoll
Technische Universität München
rigoll@tum.de

ABSTRACT

Mobile touch PCs allow interactions with virtual objects in augmented reality scenes. Manipulations of 3D objects are a common way of such interactions, which can be performed in three different coordinate systems: the camera-, object- and world coordinate systems. The camera coordinate system changes continuously in augmented reality as it depends on the mobile device's pose. The axis orientations of the world coordinate system are steady, whereas the axes of the object coordinates base on previous manipulations. The selection of a coordinate system therefore influences the 3D transformation's orientation independent from the used manipulation type.
In this paper, we evaluate the impact of the three possible coordinate systems on rotation and on translation of a 3D item in an augmented reality scenario. A study with 36 participants determines the best coordinates for translation and rotation.

Categories and Subject Descriptors

H.5.1 [**Information Interfaces and Presentation (e.g., HCI)**]: Multimedia Information Systems—*Artificial, augmented, and virtual realities*; H.5.2 [**Information Interfaces and Presentation (e.g., HCI)**]: User Interfaces—*Interaction styles*

Keywords

interaction; manipulation; augmented reality; mobile; coordinate systems; rotation; translation

1. INTRODUCTION

Mobile touch devices allow easy interaction with complete digital 2D content and mixed reality content. The difficulty of mixed reality content in comparison to pure digital 2D content lies in the extended interaction range of 3D space. The lack of dimension due to the 2D screen raises the question of intuitive manipulation methods. Two essential properties have to be determined for a manipulation in 3D: the axis and the type. In general, the manipulation type is chosen by a certain gesture, which affects the choice of axis, too. For instance, in camera coordinates, sliding a finger to the right should intuitively translate the object to the right.

ICMI '14 November 12 - 16 2014, Istanbul, Turkey

ACM 978-1-4503-2885-2/14/11...$15.00.
http://dx.doi.org/10.1145/2663204.2663234.

Henrysson et al. [4] analyze techniques for translation and rotation tasks on mobile devices. The main weakness in their study are the stationary subjects and the imprecise marker tracking. Different positions of the user reveal the specialties of the coordinate systems (CSs), that is why we investigate their influence in a mobile setup with precise tracking in a CAVE.
Multiple works of touch techniques for 3D object manipulation exist [5], though most works consider only stationary touch devices such as tabletops. We integrate a direct manipulation method, which is the primary input modality on smart devices.
We include three rigid body transformations of objects in 3D space: translation (3 DoF), rotation (3 DoF) and uniform scaling (1 DoF). Since the scaling is of a uniform kind, the coordinate axes are not adjusted separately. We investigate their influence only for translation and rotation.
In summary, the main contributions of this paper are:

- we evaluate the impact of coordinate systems on 3D transformations for a tracked mobile device;
- we identify the most suitable coordinate system for rotation and for translation.

In our setup, a change of the device's position alters the view to the 3D content on the mobile display due to active tracking. This is different from approaches with solid touch walls or tabletops. The camera position on stationary devices is fixed and can be manipulated only virtually [3].
Based on the body-centric design space from [17], our scenario can be described as a combination of mid-air gestures fixed in the world and on-device touch gestures relative to the body. The mid-air and on-device gestures control the device's position and the 3D manipulation, respectively.
The user needs to hold the device for the mid-air gestures. That is why the input technique is of a one-handed kind identical to the direct gestures of [16]. Works of interaction concepts on large stationary devices often include both hands. Two hands allow complex gestures, which change rotation and translation of the object simultaneously [15]. We separate rotation and translation because a single hand restricts the number and the ease of gestures. In addition, users in [7, 11] preferred that separation. A menu permits easy selection of rotation, translation and scaling such as in [12]. Obstacles in the real environment may prevent certain camera poses, which may lead to impossible manipulation tasks, when only a 2 DoF rotation or translation is included as in [12].

Consequently, we include two gestures for rotation and translation (one and two finger) in order to increase integration [9]. A virtual trackball [2] alters rotation on two axes. A two finger rotation around the object's center manipulates the remaining axis. One finger slides the object in the ground plane for the translation, whereas a two-finger slide moves the object in vertical direction of the selected CS.

Ohnishi et al. [13] proposes an alternative to transformations in standard CSs. Here, the 2D-3D mapping occurs in different virtual surfaces. However, the user has to know the correspondence of the input area and the 3D workspace. Martinet et al. [10] propose the Z-technique for the missing degree, which casts a ray into the 3D scene. The ray's direction depends on the touch position and the camera coordinates, thus this technique extends the standard CS with additional rays for interaction.

2. COORDINATE SYSTEMS

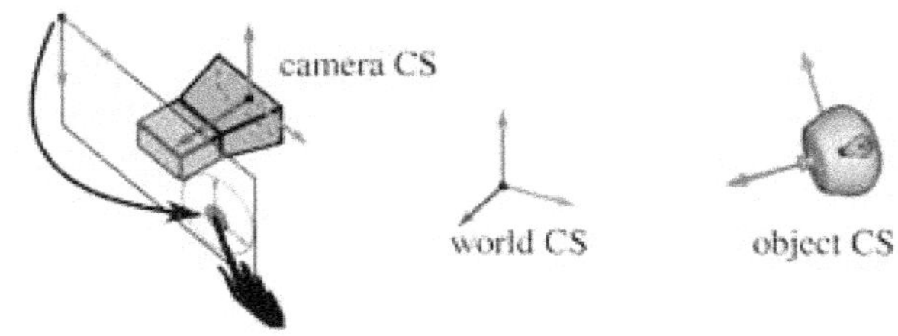

Figure 1: Illustration of the three CSs combined with the mobile device's screen. The direction of a finger move is mapped to one of these CSs, when performing a gesture. The mapping leads to object rotation or translation in the axes directions of the chosen CS. The arrow shows how screen and touch points are linked.

The axes of the camera CS depend on the tablet's current pose, also referred to as the user's view. The user's view is often used as a reference system for mobile AR manipulations [2, 10, 12]. A continuous tracking of the tablet's pose assures correct camera coordinates.

Each object in space has its specific 3D pose. The object CS contains this 3D pose. The object CS's characteristic is the axes' dependencies between translation and rotation. Consequently, a 3D item's rotation changes the axis for the translation also.

The world CS is the only static CS and represents the real world space. Figure 1 depicts all three CSs. Although the CSs are in 3D space, the touch screen of the mobile device is only 2D. Therefore, a mapping between the 3D scene to the 2D display is applied. Only two axes can be manipulated simultaneously on the 2D touch screen. The 3D $\mapsto$ 2D mapping recognizes these two manipulation axes by transforming all three axes with normalized length to the 2D screen. Then the shortest reproduced axis is ignored. The two remaining axes require an association with the horizontal and vertical screen's axis. Therefore, we calculate the absolute slope of the two mapped axes to the tablet PC's horizontal line. The axis with the smaller slope corresponds to the horizontal orientation, the other axis to the screen's vertical direction.

3. USER STUDY

The mobile device of the study is a 11.6" Windows 8 mobile PC. The user study is performed in a CAVE [14]. Lee et al. show in [8] that the completion times of the same task in MR and AR are not significantly different. This finding validates AR studies in our CAVE.

The virtual scene in the CAVE simulates an industrial line. Eight projectors display a realistic 3D scene on the four canvases (left, center, right, bottom). Figure 2 presents a participant during the experiment. Six infrared tracking cameras deliver precise tracking of the targets mounted on the mobile device and the glasses of the subject. The position of the user's head determines the rendered scene in the CAVE. The pose of the mobile device defines the scene on the mobile device's display in parallel. The scene on the tablet

Figure 2: The subject's head and the mobile device are tracked during the study. The mobile device includes additional machine parts, which are not shown in the CAVE.

PC includes the virtual industrial apparatus of the CAVE, but also AR elements which are rendered solely on the mobile device.

3.1 Scenario

Figure 2 presents the main task of the study. The subject steps into the role of an industrial plant fitter, who inserts three 3D machine parts (AR objects) at certain positions. Our goal is to determine differences in the coordinate systems. The objects, therefore, need to be rotated and translated on different axes to match the final pose. For that purpose, the final positions of the three machine parts differ spatially. The biggest distance of the three final poses is around one meter on every axis. For example, one part is close to the ground (0.3 m) and one at a height of 1.3 m.

Besides the manipulable AR parts, colored 3D shadows highlight their final poses in the AR scene. An AR object is fitted successfully as soon as the metrics of rotation, translation and scaling meet defined criteria which are estimated empirically. Thereafter, the subject proceeds by inserting the next AR item into the scene. As the mobile device is tracked during the whole process, the subject is able to move around the AR objects, which have defined positions in world coordinates. Three different AR objects need to be matched in total. The order and initial pose of the inserted 3D machine parts are constant throughout the study. The participants rank their experience in the NASA TLX questionnaire after each completion of the task.

3.2 Distance Metrics

Three different distance metrics are employed to quantify the quality of the AR objects' alignments:

- the rotation metric corresponds to the distance calculation $m_r = ||\mathbf{I} - \mathbf{R}_t \mathbf{R}_i^T||_F$ [6];
- the distance of the current AR object position $\mathbf{T}_i$ to the target $\mathbf{T}_t$ is defined as $m_t = ||\mathbf{T}_t - \mathbf{T}_i||_2^2$;
- the absolute difference characterizes the scaling metric $m_s = ||s_t - s_i||$.

$\mathbf{R}_t$ and $\mathbf{R}_i^T$ are the target and current rotation matrices, respectively. $\mathbf{I}$ is the identity matrix and $||\cdot||_F$ is the Frobenius norm. The rotation metric m_r is zero, when the rotations fit perfectly and $2\sqrt{2}$ in the worst case. We set the thresholds of a successful match to 0.25 for rotation, 0.08 m for translation and 0.15 for scaling.

3.3 Experimental Setup

36 subjects (7 females and 29 males) took part in the study. The average body height was 179.2 cm. The participants were aged between 19 and 34 with an average of 23.4. 35 of 36 subjects were accustomed to using touch devices on a regular basis. We split the 36 subjects into three groups. Each group performs its tests in one specific CS for translation. In this way, the comparison between the CSs for translation are obtained due to a between-subject design. Inside each group of 12 subjects, a within-subject design is applied. The within-subject design's main factor is the type of CS for rotation. The order of the CSs for rotation is altered based on the Latin Square design to reduce fatigue and learning effects.

4. RESULTS

The time necessary for the matching task is an evident metric, since the most user-friendly method leads to the fastest task accomplishment. For that reason, we recorded the manipulation times of each transformation type separately. We assume that the rotation times differ as we change the rotations' CSs. Hence, we first exhibit the pure rotation times. Then we compare the translation times between the test groups. Afterwards, we detail the complete manipulation times, which include the durations for rotation, translation and scaling. A subjective analysis of the different CSs is given with the R-TLX scores.
Henceforth, we use the following naming scheme. The capital letters define the kind of transformation. R for rotation and T for translation. The index states the used CS: c = camera, o = object and w = world, and we define the quantity $S = \{c, o, w\}$ with $x \in S$.

4.1 Rotation Time

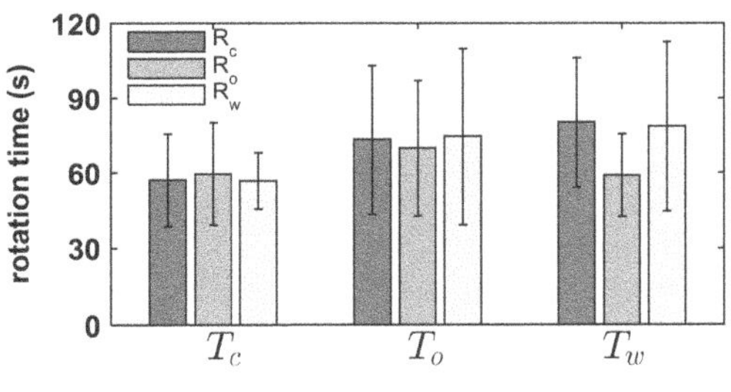

Figure 3: Mean and standard deviation of the rotation time (s).

Each group T_x is analyzed separately. Figure 3 shows the mean and standard deviation of the rotation times. First, the rotation times of the three groups are tested with the Shapiro-Wilk normality test at significance level of .05. The rotation times in T_c and T_o are not distributed normally, thus a Friedman test is applied, which leads to no significant differences. The times in T_w are distributed normally. Consequently, we perform an outlier detection based on [1], which results in the deletion of one entry. A 3x11 uni-variate ANOVA (analysis of variances) yields $F(3,30) = 3.92$, $p = .037 < .05$. Our repeated measure design requires a separate treatment of each subject besides the main factor. The subjects of T_w are significantly faster with R_o (M = 59.52 s, SD = 17.18 s) than with the two other CSs. The subjects of T_o are also fastest in R_o. In group T_c, R_o is the slowest method, however, this group is in average the fastest of all three groups.

4.2 Translation Time

Again, we perform a Shapiro-Wilk test, which finds that the translation times are not distributed normally. Hence, we deploy

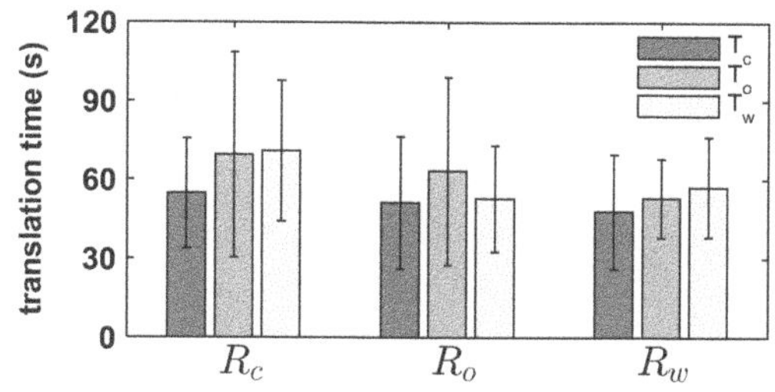

Figure 4: Mean and standard deviation of the transl. time (s).

the Friedman test. Here, an analysis of the translation times in the same rotation CS but in different T_x indicates no significant differences. Even though the results do not differ significantly, an inspection of Figure 4 indicates a general tendency between each T_x. The translation times in T_c have the lowest mean times independent from the CS for rotation R_x.
Conducting the manipulations in T_o yields the worst translation time in R_o. This seems reasonable, because an AR item's rotation leads to different directions of the axes for the translation. The translation times are highest in T_w, when rotating in R_c or R_w.

4.3 Manipulation Time

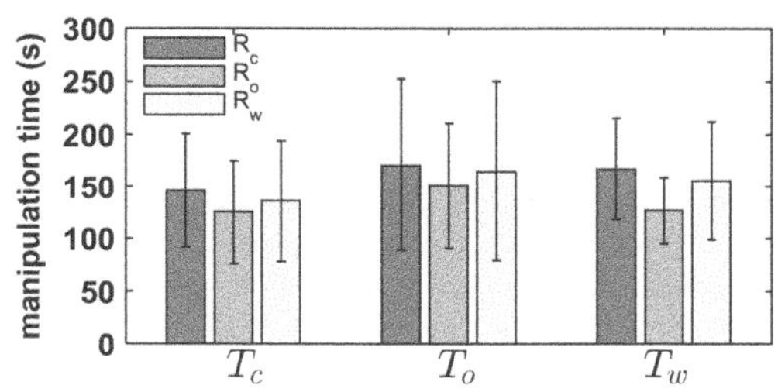

Figure 5: Mean and standard deviation of the manip. time (s).

Figure 5 comprises the complete manipulation times of the 36 subjects. Interestingly, the mean times of all three groups T_x are smallest when rotating the AR items in R_o. Furthermore, an analysis of the manipulation times in T_w shows no normal distribution regarding the Shapiro-Wilk test. A Friedman test results in significant variation of the manipulation time, $\mathscr{X}^2(2,22) = 6.5$, $p = .039 < .05$. Rotating an object in R_c needs the most time in each group T_x.
We compare the manipulation times obtained in the same R_x but in different CSs for translation. In this way, the fastest CS for translation can be determined. In every comparison, the group which positions the object in T_c is the fastest.

4.4 Questionnaires

The NASA-RTLX score indicates the subjective perceived strains, which are caused by mental, physical or temporal demands of the task. The physical workload remains the same throughout the study, because the device and the position of the AR items stays the same. Consequently, the differences in the mean RTLX of Figure 6 highlight mental and temporal demands mostly. The RTLX means are between 47.92 and 56.92 in a total range of 120. Performing the rotation in R_o leads to the smallest RTLX in groups T_c and T_w. In group T_o, R_o is not recommended as stated before. Here, R_w scores best. The scores of R_c and R_w are lowest in T_o, and R_o is lowest in T_w.

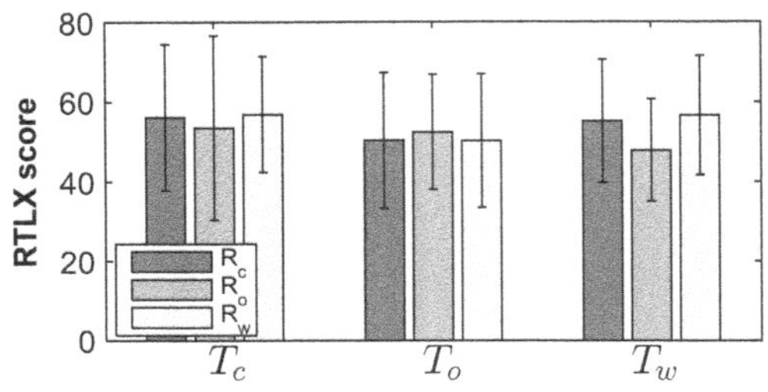

Figure 6: Mean and standard deviation of the raw TLX.

5. CONCLUSION & OUTLOOK

In this work, we detailed possible shortcomings of each CS and described a study for comparing the three possible CSs for translation and rotation separately. We conducted the study with 36 participants in a mixed reality setup, which enables repetitive user-studies since the environmental influences are reduced to a minimum. The participants had to match three different AR items at various spatial positions to ensure different camera poses.

The noticeable variances in the recorded data arise due to learning effects since none of our subjects experienced a mobile AR manipulation task before. Latin Square design, however, ensures similar influence of this effect between the methods.

First, we analyzed the recorded rotation times of the subjects. The findings suggest that the favorite CS for rotation is the object CS. Groups T_O and T_W accomplish the rotation fastest, when working in R_O. Additionally, the manipulation times are lowest in each group when using R_O. The different CSs for translation were split into three separate groups. Each group performed the task in a single CS for translation. We observed that T_C is the best one in regard to the translation time and the complete manipulation time.

It is interesting to note, that the subjects are faster with a static CS for rotation, but the user's view dependent CS is better for the translation. The use of R_O decouples the user's position from the rotation task. This way, the user can concentrate on the rotation task regardless of the position. We believe that this reduces the difficulty, because the user does not have to find the best position for matching the object. Instead the user can rely on the knowledge about the axis orientations.

This idea manifests further when considering the subjective RTLX results. Translation in T_O is the least straining CS, besides the combination $R_O T_O$ as discussed in Section 4.2.

Taken together, these finding suggest that it is easiest for the user to perform the transformation in the object CS. However, with slightly more effort in the camera CS, the users are faster at translating. Conducting the rotation in camera CS does not improve the manipulation time as it is the case for the translation.

We are of the opinion that the AR item's rotation requires more spatial imagination than a translation, which complicates the rotation task for some users. Our results are in good agreement with Henrysson et al. [4], who concluded that performing a translation based on the device's position is better than with the static keypad technique but the static keypad is better for a rotation task.

Consequently, we recommend the object CS for rotation and the camera CS for translation in a mobile AR scenario.

Further studies, which take other input concepts such as HOMER-S [12] into account, have to be undertaken to generalize our findings. Further work needs to be done to estimate the learning effects on the three CSs by conducting a study with multiple iterations in the same CS.

6. ACKNOWLEDGEMENTS

The research leading to these inventions has received funding from the European Union Seventh Framework Programm (FP7/2007-2013) under grant agreement n° 284573.

7. REFERENCES

[1] V. Barnett and T. Lewis. *Outliers in statistical data*, volume 3. Wiley New York, 1994.

[2] D. Fiorella, A. Sanna, and F. Lamberti. Multi-touch User Interface Evaluation for 3D Object Manipulation on Mobile Devices. *Multimodal User Interfaces*, 4(1):3–10, 2010.

[3] M. Hancock, T. ten Cate, and S. Carpendale. Sticky tools: full 6DOF force-based interaction for multi-touch tables. In *Proc. ITS*, pages 133–140. ACM, 2009.

[4] A. Henrysson, J. Marshall, and M. Billinghurst. Experiments in 3D interaction for mobile phone AR. In *Proc. GRAPHITE*, pages 187–194. ACM, 2007.

[5] U. Hinrichs and S. Carpendale. Gestures in the wild: studying multi-touch gesture sequences on interactive tabletop exhibits. In *Proc. CHI*, pages 3023–3032. ACM, 2011.

[6] D. Q. Huynh. Metrics for 3D Rotations: Comparison and Analysis. *Mathematical Imaging and Vision*, 35(2):155–164, 2009.

[7] K. Kin, T. Miller, B. Bollensdorff, T. DeRose, B. Hartmann, and M. Agrawala. Eden: a professional multitouch tool for constructing virtual organic environments. In *Proc. SIGCHI*, pages 1343–1352. ACM, 2011.

[8] C. Lee, G. A. Rincon, G. Meyer, T. Höllerer, and D. A. Bowman. The Effects of Visual Realism on Search Tasks in Mixed Reality Simulation. *Visualization and Computer Graphics*, 19(4):547–556, 2013.

[9] J. Liu, O. K.-C. Au, H. Fu, and C.-L. Tai. Two-Finger Gestures for 6DOF Manipulation of 3D Objects. *Computer Graphics Forum*, 31(7):2047–2055, 2012.

[10] A. Martinet, G. Casiez, and L. Grisoni. The design and evaluation of 3D positioning techniques for multi-touch displays. In *Proc. 3DUI*, pages 115–118. IEEE, 2010.

[11] A. Martinet, G. Casiez, and L. Grisoni. Integrality and separability of multitouch interaction techniques in 3d manipulation tasks. *Visualization and Computer Graphics*, 18(3):369–380, 2012.

[12] A. Mossel, B. Venditti, and H. Kaufmann. 3DTouch and HOMER-S: Intuitive Manipulation Techniques for One-Handed Handheld Augmented Reality. In *Proc. VRIC*, pages 12:1–12:10. ACM, 2013.

[13] T. Ohnishi, N. Katzakis, K. Kiyokawa, and H. Takemura. Virtual interaction surface: Decoupling of interaction and view dimensions for flexible indirect 3D interaction. In *Proc. 3DUI*, pages 113–116. IEEE, 2012.

[14] E. Ragan, C. Wilkes, D. A. Bowman, and T. Höllerer. Simulation of augmented reality systems in purely virtual environments. In *Proc. VR*, pages 287–288. IEEE, 2009.

[15] J. L. Reisman, P. L. Davidson, and J. Y. Han. A screen-space formulation for 2D and 3D direct manipulation. In *Proc. UIST*, pages 69–78. ACM, 2009.

[16] P. Tiefenbacher, A. Pflaum, and G. Rigoll. Touch Gestures for Improved 3D Object Manipulation in Mobile Augmented Reality. In *Proc. ISMAR*. IEEE, 2014.

[17] J. Wagner, M. Nancel, S. G. Gustafson, S. Huot, and W. E. Mackay. Body-centric Design Space for Multi-surface Interaction. In *Proc. CHI*, pages 1299–1308. ACM, 2013.

Digital Reading Support for The Blind by Multimodal Interaction

Yasmine N. El-Glaly
Faculty of Science, Port Said University, Egypt
College of Computers and Information Technology, Taif University, Saudi Arabia
yasmineg@vt.edu

Francis Quek
Texas A&M University
College Station, TX, USA
quek@tamu.edu

ABSTRACT

Slate-type devices allow Individuals with Blindness or Severe Visual Impairment (IBSVI) to read in place with the touch of their fingertip by audio-rendering the words they touch. Such technologies are helpful for spatial cognition while reading. However, users have to move their fingers slowly or they may lose place on screen. Also, IBSVI may wander between lines without realizing they did. In this paper, we address these two interaction problems by introducing dynamic speech-touch interaction model, and intelligent reading support system. With this model, the speed of the speech will dynamically change coping up with the user's finger speed. The proposed model is composed of: 1-Audio Dynamics Model, and 2- Off-line Speech Synthesis Technique. The intelligent reading support system predicts the direction of reading, corrects the reading word if the user drifts, and notifies the user using a sonic gutter to help her from straying off the reading line. We tested the new audio dynamics model, the sonic gutter, and the reading support model in two user studies. The participants' feedback helped us fine-tune the parameters of the two models. Finally, we ran an evaluation study where the reading support system is compared to other VoiceOver technologies. The results showed preponderance to the reading support system with its audio dynamics and intelligent reading support components.

Categories and Subject Descriptors

H.5.2 [**Information Interfaces and Presentation**]: User Interfaces—*interaction styles, auditory feedback*
; K.4.2 [**Computers and Society**]: Social Issues—*assistive technologies for persons with disabilities*

General Terms

Algorithms, Design, Human Factors, Standardization, Theory.

ICMI'14, November 12–16, 2014, Istanbul, Turkey.
Copyright 2014 ACM 978-1-4503-2885-2/14/11 ...$15.00.
http://dx.doi.org/10.1145/2663204.2663266.

Keywords

Audio rendering; multi-touch interaction; active reading; mobile development; assistive technology; blindness

1. INTRODUCTION

One of the most popular assistive technology paradigms currently is what we call in this paper "Read-What-You-Touch" systems (RWYT systems), such as Voice Over, and STAAR [7]. These systems support Individuals with Blindness or Severe Visual Impairment (IBSVI) to discover the on screen text by touch interaction. RWYT systems then render the touched text audibly. The main advantage of these systems is that IBSVI have the opportunity to keep place and locate themselves on the screen. Spatial location awareness give IBSVI the credit of using their spatial memory and spatial capabilities while accessing the screen. Spatial awareness is important because it increases comprehension by understanding the document's organizational structure [9]. However, reading word by word as in STAAR or Voice Over forces the user to be slow. If the user runs her finger quickly on the words or changes the accessing mode to read in bigger chunks of words, she will lose place, and the rendered audio will be liberated from the physical location of the text. Even if the settings of the RWYT system were changed to render words faster, still we have interaction problem because there is no relationship between the user's finger movement and the speed of the voice. In this paper we tackle the speech-touch interaction problem by introducing a dynamic speech-touch interaction model. We developed a new audio dynamics model to make the RWYT system more adaptable to the user's reading speed.

The second interaction problem we address in this paper, related to spatial reading systems, is line straying [7, 6]. When the user moves her finger along the horizontal lines of text to read, sometimes her finger strays towards the line above or the line below without her being able to notice. The reader system will audibly render the touched word leaving the IBSVI user confused hearing unrelated sequences of words. With the lack of visual access and a proper interaction feedback, the reading experience could be unsatisfactory for the IBSVI. In this paper, we propose an intelligent reading support system that is capable of predicting the intended word and render it instead of naively tended each touched word. The prediction model is coupled with a set of sonifications, we call it a sonic gutter. The system was tested in an evaluation study to assess its efficiency and effectiveness. The results show that the dynamic speech-touch interaction model and the intelligent reader support enhance the user's interaction experience without affecting the comprehensibility of the speech.

2. RELATED WORK

In this section, we review the main streams of reading technologies for IBSVI. We categorize them into 3 groups: digital Braille, audio books, and screen readers.

Transforming Braille to digital form has been done by refreshable Braille display [4, 10], and by display of virtual Braille dots [11]. However, most computer-based Braille translators cannot produce Grade 2 Braille transcription [17]. These high cost technologies solved the digitalization, portability and mobility problems of Braille books, however they eliminated the capability of Braille to provide spatial referencing because the size of the displays is relatively small. They consist of one-line display, where Braille text is generated in blocks of 20, 40, or 80 characters. While reading one line at a time is not passive as in listening to audible text, the information is represented in temporal sequential format. The reader cannot develop a mental map for the page she reads, and face text-locating problems [13].

Converting textbooks to audio books was the goal of various projects that aimed to offer a Braille alternative for IBSVI. Examples of these audio books are Talking Book [16] and DAISY books [1]. These popular audio readers are different from active reading. Audio readers cannot address the spatial bias we have identified. Audio format provides IBSVI with information in the form of linear stream with no spatial reference, which overloads IBSVI's working memory. Interviews with IBSVI who feel comfortable using audio and Braille, pointed out that audio is ideal for recreational reading, while Braille is mandatory for active reading [13]. Converting Braille to Audio for IBSVI is like converting print to audio for sighted population, leads to virtual illiteracy [13]. Auditory learners must read and write, in either print or Braille, to meet the competitive employment needs [5].

The screen reader is a part of the universal access technology of various computer systems, such as Windows Microsoft Narrator and Mac VoiceOver. There also exist popular commercial screen readers such as JAWS. This assistive technology is even extended to the touch tablets, such as the iOS VoiceOver for iPad, and the Ice Cream Sandwich Talk Back for Android tablets. These different types of screen readers have two main functions: reading the screen content, and navigating the screen. Screen readers have usability problems [14, 15], especially when the content of the screen is designed with the assumption that it will be visually read [3]. Browsing web pages by IBSVI, for example, using screen readers leads to more probing and takes longer than for sighted users [2]. Screen readers process pages sequentially, which leads to information overload [12]. The navigation function on desktop screens is achieved by keyboard shortcuts, which are typically different combinations of two keys. On touchscreens, IBSVI can navigate the screen by touch, or alternatively connect the touch device to a keyboard. Screen readers do not provide IBSVI with feedback regarding their location on the screen of both desktop and touch devices. In touch devices, the spatial awareness problem is reduced, however much more accuracy is needed in locating place because any unintended touch could lead to undesired interaction. Finally, screen readers are not built to support active reading, and they do not provide IBSVI with the needed mental model of the page.

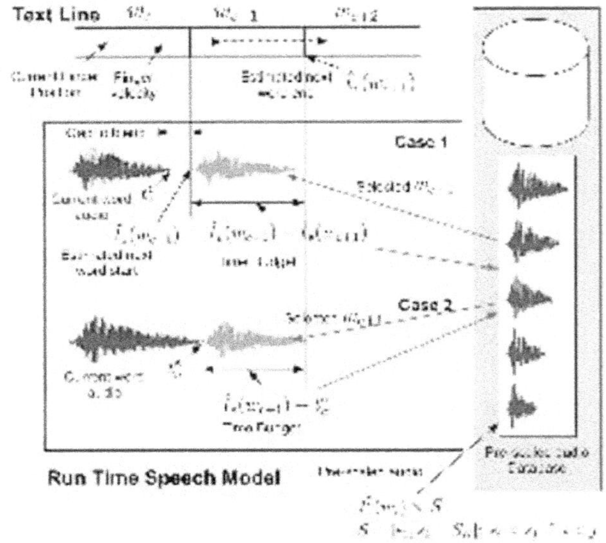

Figure 1: A graphical illustration to the audio model.

3. THE DYNAMIC SPEECH-TOUCH INTERACTION MODEL

In this section, we describe the details of the dynamic speech-touch interaction model, and the user study we conducted to test the model. The proposed model is composed of two parts: 1- Audio Dynamics Model, and 2- Off-line Speech Synthesis Technique.

3.1 Audio Dynamics Model

The touch interaction model should be synchronized with the TTS module. We developed a robust temporal model that predicts the future touched words and update this list dynamically according to the touch location and the speech machine timing. Figure 1 shows a graphical illustration to the audio model. We build a model that calculates the current speed of the user's finger. Also, the duration of the word at the normal speed $t^0(w_i)$ for word i is calculated. We apply a set of scales, S, to each word $t^0(w_i)$ where $S = [s_1, s_2, ...S_K]$ where S is monotonic (I.e. $s_i < s_j$ iff $i < j$). For now, we arbitrarily have $K = 3$ and $S = [0.5, 0.75, 1.0]$. Then we estimate the time the finger will enter the next words in the sequence of reading. The difference between the duration of the word to be spoken by the TTS at its 3 different speeds and the time left till the finger leaves the word is calculated, we call this: *time budget*. Assume the current word being articulated is w_c, and the end time of the audio snippet is t^e_c. If the estimated time for the finger to exit w_{c+1} is $\hat{t}_e(w_{c+1})$, then the time budget for w_{c+1} is $(\hat{t}_e(w_{c+1}) - \hat{t}_s(w_{c+1}))$. Assume that the estimated time the reading finger will arrive at w_{c+1} is $\hat{t}_s(w_{c+1}) > t^e_c$. Then, there would be a gap of $(\hat{t}_s(w_{c+1}) - t^e_c)$ before w_{c+1} is articulated.

Hence, we select s_j s.t. $(s_j * t^0(w_{c+1})$ is closest to the time budget $(\hat{t}_e(w_{c+1}) - \hat{t}_s(w_{c+1}))$. The word w_{c+1} will be rendered when the finger actually enters w_{c+1}. This will make w_{c+1} the new w_c and the process repeats. It is possible in our model for $\hat{t}_s(w_{c+1}) < t^e_c$, in which case there will be

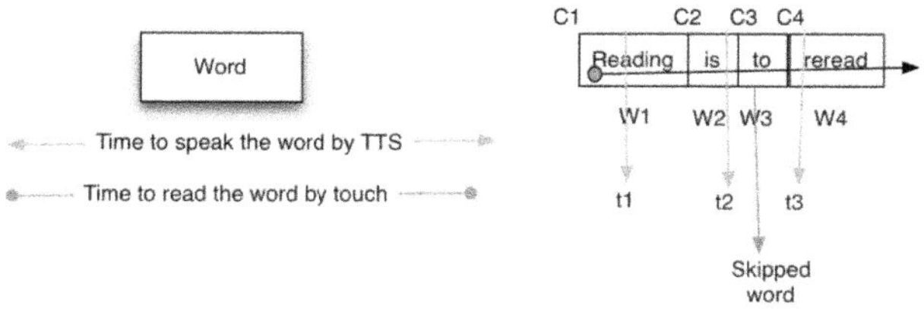

Figure 2: Left: Word temporal modeling. Right: Reading-Speech modeling.

no gap and the time budget for w_{c+1} will be reduced to $(\hat{t}_e(w_{c+1}) - t^e_c)$.

If the user's finger speed is within the limits of the word duration, the word will be rendered. If the user's finger would leave the location of the word before the fastest word could be spoken, the word will be skipped. To inform the user that she has skipped a word, a click sound will be played. Figure 2 illustrates an example where a user is reading while moving her finger with a varied speed. Clocks (C1,..,C4)) are the estimated times for entering/leaving the words. While she is moving from word to word, the time remaining to audibly render the word is calculated (t1, t2,..,etc.). When the user's finger enters W4 and the TTS has not yet started rendering W3, W3 will be skipped, and W4 will be synthesized. We believe that this audio model will solve the slow touch interaction problem and at the same time will keep the speech smooth and fluent. The preliminary results of the S and the K values showed acceptable inter-word gap.

3.2 Off-line Speech Synthesis Technique

We off-line synthesize whole sentence using Acapela TTS. Then using a speech processing software we segment the sentence back to individual words. The advantage of this technique is that the blending of words in sequence is automatically included by the TTS when the whole sentence is passed to the engine. Figure 3 shows an example of the audio signal of a sentence of 3 words generated by the TTS. The two black vertical lines in Figure 3 mark the end of the signal of one word and the beginning of the next one. Each segmented block is saved separately. For each word's audio signal, we generate three versions, each with a different speech rate as needed by the audio dynamics model. We create a database of audio files for the text, and a metadata file that contains the word index, its speed, and duration. The metadata is used by the audio dynamics model to play the right audio file upon touch. Table 1 shows an example for the word "Learning". The word is trimmed of the sentence and three versions of the word are generated, each has a different speed, and duration. As can be shown from the data in the table that the signal can be scaled down into a certain degree with keeping its articulation comprehensible. Further scaling down makes the articulated word very fast to be comprehensible. Each Audio Signal (AS) is associated with a code that is composed of three terms:

$$AS_{code} = p_i t_j x_n, i < i_{max}, j < k + 1, n < n_{max} \quad (1)$$

The first term (p_i) represents the page number where the text word (w_c) is located. The second term (t_j) reflects the word's speed (s_i). The last term (x_n) represents the index of the text word (w_c) within the page it is located. By embedding the positional and the scale information of each audio signal into its word representation, the *Text Renderer* module can directly handle its assigned tasks. The example given in Table1 shows a word in which its index is *150* in the *first* page of the rendered document.

Table 1: Example of the word "Learning" at S=0.5, 0.75, and 1.0.

S_i	S value	Duration	Signal	AS_{code}
1	1.0	0.357 sec.	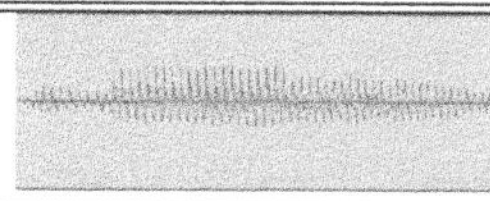	011150
2	0.75	0.285 sec.	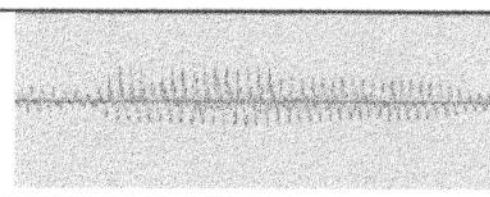	012150
3	0.5	0.238 sec.	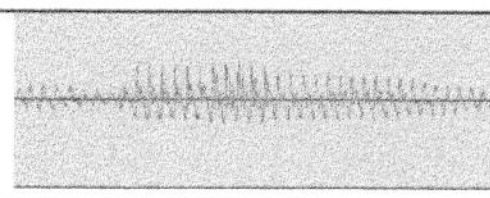	013150

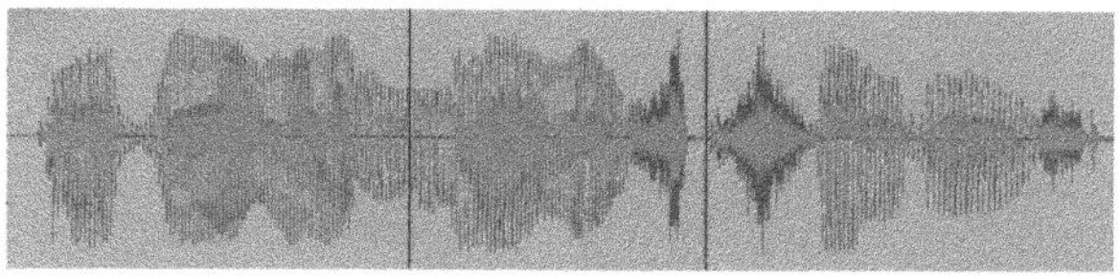

Figure 3: Audio signal of a sentence of 3 words.

3.3 User Study

We realized that using this model in reading could lead to reading one sentence with various speech rates, e.g. one word with normal speed, and the next word in faster speed, depending on the spatial occupation of the word, temporal period of the word articulation, and the finger's speed. We ran a user study to investigate if the users realize the variance in the speech rate, and how they might use it for controlling reading speed by their finger. The goals of the study are:

1. Test the effect of using the audio dynamics model on the comprehensibility of the speech.

2. Test whether the audio dynamics model enhances the speech-touch interaction.

3.3.1 Participants

The participants of this study are three IBSVI. They are 2 females and one male; their ages are 33, 66, and 71. They

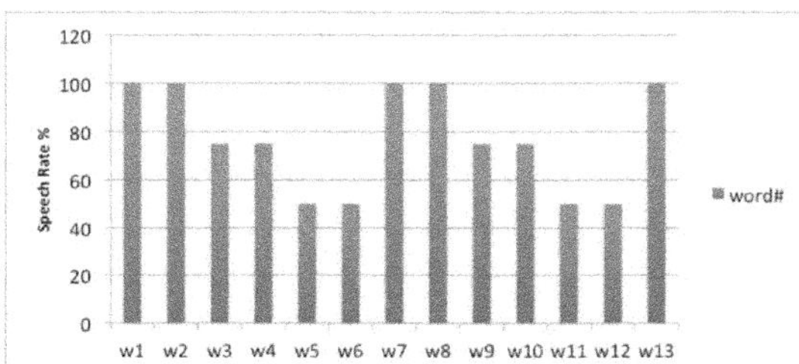

Figure 4: Synthesized variable speech rate sentence.

are all legally blind. The oldest one has no vision in his left eye, and 5% vision in his right eye. The youngest one has 10% vision in her eyes, and the last one's vision is 20/100. One of the participants uses iPhone with VoiceOver.

3.3.2 *Procedure*

The study consisted of two parts. For the first part, we pre-compiled 2 sentences consisting of 13 words, where each two words in sequence have different speech rate as illustrated in Figure 4. We played the audio file to each participant. Then the participant was asked a questionnaire about the speech and its clarity.

For the second part of the study, we prepared a passage of 3 lines of text. Each participant was asked to read the 3 lines with the audio dynamics model and the off-line speech synthesis technique implemented as described in the previous section. They were then asked whether the speech rate helped them to better interact with the system with respect to finger speed.

3.3.3 *Results and Discussion*

For the first part of the study, two participants find that the speech is clear and easy to comprehend. The third participant could not comprehend only one word from the 2 sentences. This word was articulated in 50% of its normal speed. For the second part of the study, all of the participants reported that the dynamic speech rate helped them to better interact with the system. The results we got from this study showed us that both the audio dynamics model and the off-line speech synthesis technique enhanced the user interaction with the system without decreasing the comprehensibility of the speech.

We found by observation that if a BSVI user slightly moved her finger to the line below or to the line above while reading horizontally, she cannot know that she had without an appropriate feedback. The authors in [7] described this interaction problem that IBSVI encountered while reading lines of text by finger touch. We address this problem by applying advanced statistical techniques that can predict the word meant to be touched and audibly render it. At the same time, an audio feedback is designed and activated whenever the user's finger deviates from the current horizontal line to provide information about place or location. We believe that helping IBSVI stay on the horizontal line while informing them with their location will eliminate the confusion that might occurred when their touch deviates and out of context words are heard.

4. INTELLIGENT READER

We developed an intelligent active reading support model that predicts the word the user wants to access, as shown in Figure 5. The green oval represents the current touched word (w_c). The next transition could be one of the following 6 states: 1-Next word in sequence: (w_{c+1}), 2- Possible stray below: (w_{below}), 3- Possible stray above: (w_{above}), 4- Close move: (w_{close}), 5- Far move: (w_{far}), and 6- Same word: (w_c).

The intelligent active reading support model estimates the intended word (w_i) based on the following three factors: 1- The number of previous in-sequence read words, or shortly length of history ($history_l$), 2- The distance (d_t) between the location of next word to current word (w_{c+1}) and the touched point (p_t), and 3-The angle (θ_t) between the current horizontal line and the touch point.

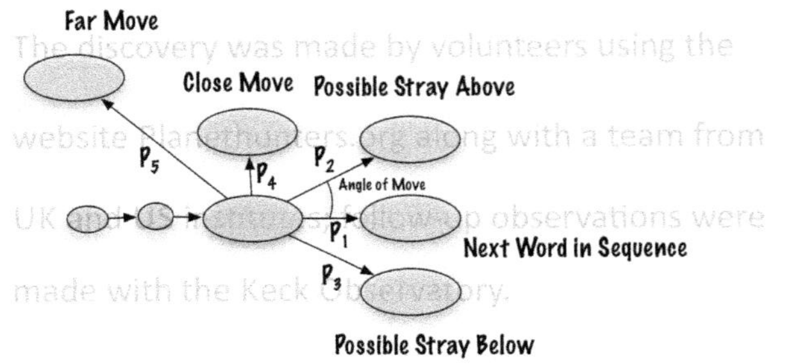

Figure 5: Intelligent reading support model to predict the intended word.

Table 2: Transition matrix of the reading support model.

Reading Mode	Condition	Intended word
Random	$W_c\vert\ history_l < history_{min}$	W_c; W_{c+1}; W_{above}; W_{below}; W_{close}; or W_{far}
Active	$W_c\vert history_l \geq history_{min}$ and $d_t < d_{max}$ and $\theta_t < \theta_{min}$	w_{c+1}

Our hypothesis is that the length of history is the most critical factor. If the current word is the initial state or the previous state is not its previous word; that means the user is in "random" reading mode. Consequently, the 6 states will have equal probability. While if the current word was preceded by a minimum length of history, and the d_t, and θ_t are below a threshold, that means the user is in active reading mode. Consequently, the first state ($wc + 1$) will be triggered. Table 2 summarizes the transitional behavior of the intelligent reading support model.

4.1 Intelligent Active Reading Support Model Parameters

In order to get an accurate prediction of w_i, we have to find approximate values for $history_{min}$, d_{min} , and θ_{max}. We conducted a parameters-searching session with five blindfolded participants to help us determine these three values. The participants' ages ranged from 25 to 67 with a mean of 39 (SD=16.92). Three participants were females and two were males. Each participant was familiarized with the system for 5-10 minutes. Then she was asked to read a passage of 8 lines using STAAR with different values of the model parameters as summarized in Table 3. A full factorial design

Table 3: Tested values of the reading support model parameters.

	Value 1	Value 2	Value 3	Value 4
θ_t	10°	30°	50°	70°
d_t	0.2 inch	0.4 inch	0.6 inch	0.8 inch
$history_l$	2	3	4	5

Table 4: **Conditions of the prediction model parameters study.**

	Cond. 1	Cond. 2	Cond. 3
θ_t	10°, 30°, 50°, 70°	Output θ of Cond.1	Output θ of Cond.1
d_t	0.8 inch	0.2, 0.4, 0.6 inch	Output d of Cond.2
$history_l$	2	2	3,4, 5

of testing these values will lead to 192 conditions. Alternatively, we applied a hierarchical study design (see Table 4), where we started the study with initial values for d_t and $history_l$. For the 1st condition we tested the 4 values of θ_t and keep d_t and $history_l$ constant. The value of θ that received the most positive results according to the participant was then used in the second condition of the study. In the second condition, four different values of d_t were tested, where the θ_t and $history_l$ are constant. Finally, in the 3rd condition we fix the θ_t and d_t values as elected from the previous two conditions. The value of $history_l$ was varied from 2 to 5. Each condition took 20 minutes.

During the task, the participant was asked to report every word she hears and she thinks it does not belong to the sentence. The researcher kept a log of these occurrences. We consider them failure of reading-support. The graph in Figure 6 shows that all participants had fewer drifting correction failures when θ was set to 30°. In condition 2, θ_t was set to 30°, and we changed the values of d_t. The frequencies of drifting correction failures are shown in Figure 7. The best results were observed with d_t =0.6 inches. Finally, we used these values in condition 3 where we varied the $history_l$. As illustrated in Figure 8, the highest drifting correction frequency occurred when $history_l$ was set to 2. The conclusion is that participants consider themselves engaged in active reading when they start reading horizontally at least 2 words in sequence. If the user's finger drifts with a distance that is at maximum 0.6 inches away from the end point of the previous read word, and with angle not more than 30°, the user expects a correction from the system to this drift. However, when the finger's movement is more twisted than that, it is highly likely that the user is not in the active reading mode, and so the system should read for her what she is really touching.

4.2 The Sonic Gutter

If the active reading support model detects drifting behavior in active reading mode and decides to play a word that is different than the physically touched word, a sonification will be played to alert the user that she is going off the line. We call this the sonic gutter. We used white static noise and pink static noise to sonify moving above the line or below the line, respectively. This audio feedback is played concurrently with the articulated word. Figure 9 shows an example of set of lines, where the second line is the current reading line. If the user starts drifting above or below the reading line, the sonic gutter will be activated. The above line, as well as the below line, sonic gutter is divided into two levels. The difference between the two levels is the frequency of the sound, where level 2 has higher frequency than level 1. The goal of having 2 levels of straying-alarm sonification is to provide the IBSVI with enough spatial in-

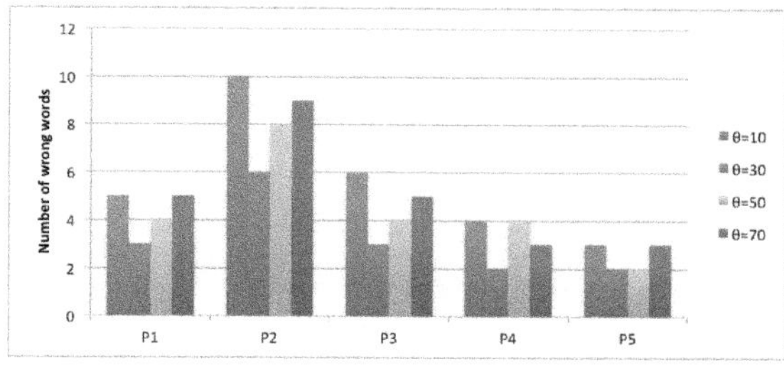

Figure 6: Frequencies of drifting-correction failures in condition 1.

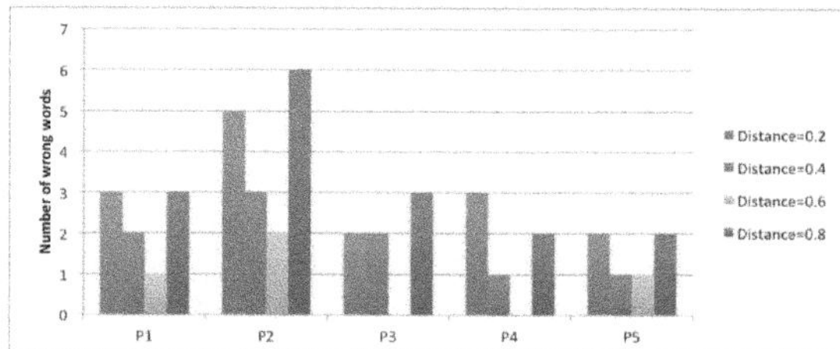

Figure 7: Frequencies of drifting-correction failures in condition 2.

formation about the distance she drifted, so that she may be enabled to develop an accurate mental model of the spatial relation between her physical touch and the text she is reading. The challenge was to find sonifications with the following characteristics:

1. Sonic gutter level 1 is audibly different from sonic gutter level 2, for both above the line and below the line.
2. Above line sonic gutter is audibly different from below line sonic gutter, for both levels.
3. All sonifications must be loud enough to be heard with the articulated word.
4. Articulated words must be clear enough to comprehend while the sonic gutter is played synchronously.

4.3 Intelligent Active Reading Support: Study

We conducted a usability study with three IBSVI. They are the same participants of the previous study. Their data are the same as reported in section 3.3, as the two studies were close in time. The session was divided into two parts, hearing session, and interaction session. The first part was a hearing session, where we played for them a set of sonifications to ask them whether they can audibly differentiate

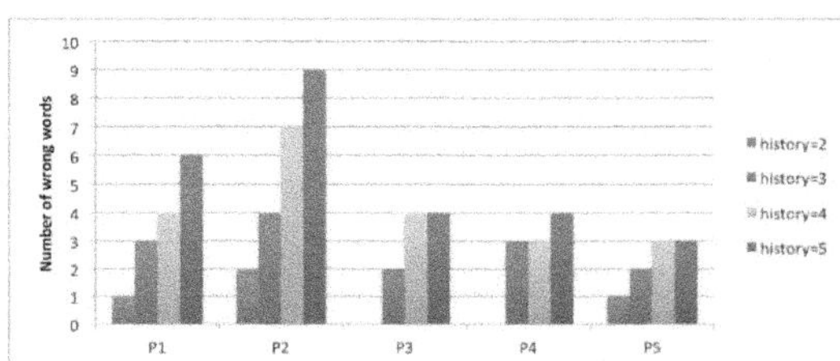

Figure 8: Frequencies of drifting-correction failures in condition 3.

Figure 9: Visual illustration for the sonic gutter.

between them or not. Then, we played a set of precompiled audio files. Each audio file consists of a whole synthesized sentence with one of the sonifications. The participants were asked if they could hear and comprehend the sentence despite the noise or not. Participants 1 and 2 were able to differentiate between all the sonifications, while participant 3 was not able to differentiate between the above line sonic gutter and the below line sonic gutter. Participants 1, 2, and 3 were able to hear and comprehend the sentences despite of the sonifications. However, participant 3 was not able to hear the above line sonic gutter level 1 that was combined with a sentence. Participant 3 is 71 years old, and that could be the reason behind his feedback. Based on the preliminary results, we recommend that future systems could have various sets of sonifications with adjustable settings e.g. pitch, volume, and frequency, so that the user can personalize the sonic interface according to her preferences.

In the second part of the study, we asked the 3 participants to read a passage of 4 lines with the reading support model and the sonic gutter. They were encouraged to try navigating in between the lines of the text to see the effect of the reading support model and the sonic gutter, and give us suggestions. The three participants found that the new features helped them stay on line. Moreover, they all found that the new features guided them back to the reading line when they drifted. One of the participants found that having that support and audio feedback from the system eliminated her need to the physical affordance of the tactile overlay [8]. She had a successful trial reading the text again without the overlay. This opens the question for the effect of tactile feedback compared with audio feedback and how much each component participates in supporting spatial reading for IBSVI.

5. EVALUATION OF THE ACTIVE READING SUPPORT SYSTEM

The goal of this study is to evaluate the efficiency and effectiveness of STAAR with the proposed Intelligent Active Reading support in re-finding information and spatial perception. We define efficiency as the mean time taken by the IBSVI to read a page. By effectiveness, we mean participants success of recalling and re-finding the information. Our operational definition of spatial perception is the ability to locate short sentences or phrases, and the ability to estimate the number of paragraphs in the page. STAAR system is unique with its features of enabling IBSVI to read spatially word-by-word at their own pace, and supporting IBSVI stay on line and finding next line. In order to evaluate STAAR, we decided to compare it to another reading tool that utilizes audio modality for information and does not elaborate the spatial information. The most advanced current technology that satisfies these conditions is the iOS VoiceOver. In general, the VoiceOver technology is based on the idea of announcing what the user touches, and wait for interaction. For reading, Apple has developed software called iBook, which is announced as fully compatible with VoiceOver. By default, iBook is set to read whole line once the user touches it. If the IBSVI wants to read word-by-word, she has to turn the rotor to the 'word' mode, then swipes in up-bottom direction to read word by word. If she wants to go back to a specific word, she has to swipe in the bottom-up direction until she reaches the word. Starting from iOS version 6.0, the VoiceOver sonifies empty spaces with a bonk sound. Hence, the only audio feedback provided by VoiceOver is the white space sonification. If we compare STAAR to iBook as is, we will have the problem of comparing reading whole line versus reading word-by-word. This difference has implications in both spatial perception, and information recalling and re-finding. To overcome this shortage in iBook, we tweaked the default mode to force it read only one word at a time upon touch, instead of reading the whole line at once. We call this: "word-by-word VoiceOver".

5.1 Method

We conducted a single factor within-subjects study. The independent variable is the system type, 4 levels, which are:

1. STAAR + overlay
2. Word-by-word VoiceOver
3. Word-by-word VoiceOver + overlay
4. iBook + VoiceOver

Per each condition, the participant was asked to read one page of text. We prepared 4 sets of reading materials. Each set is of equivalent length, layout, and content. All reading materials were at 8th grade level based on the Flesch-Kincaid Reading Ease scale. Two reading materials were arranged in two paragraphs, and the other two were arranged in 3 paragraphs. For conditions 1 and 4, the same overlay was used, which is the dense overlay. The order by which the conditions were presented to the participants was counterbalanced. The participants of this study are the three IBSVI whose data are reported in Section 3.3.

5.2 Procedure

Each participant was asked to read one page of text using the 4 systems: STAAR, word-by-word VoiceOver, word-by-word VoiceOver with the overlay, and iBook with VoiceOver. For each condition the following steps were followed:

1. Familiarization session with the tested system.
2. Read one page using the tested system.
3. Answer 4 questions about the reading material.
4. Answer a user experience questionnaire about the tested system.

Before starting each task, the participant was familiarized with the system by reading a separate passage. After reading the page of the task, the participant was asked 4 questions. Two questions were knowledge transfer questions, and the other 2 were for spatial perception assessment. The two spatial perception assessment questions were consistent among the 4 conditions. The first question was to locate a sentence

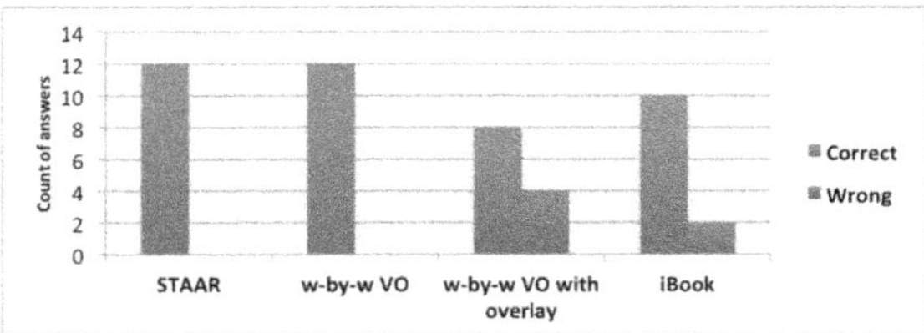

Figure 10: Knowledge transfer results.

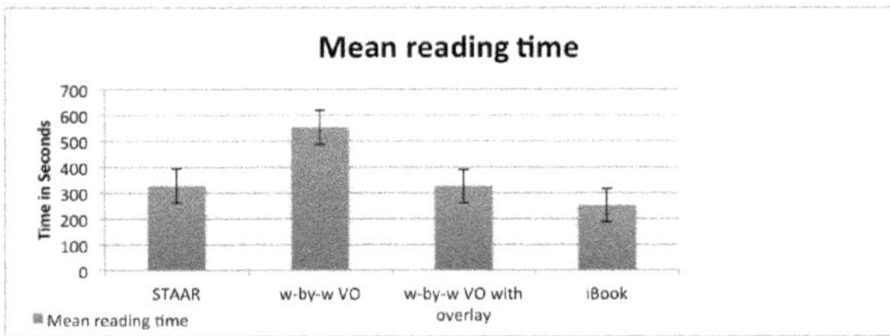

Figure 11: Mean of reading times by the four systems.

in the page. The sentence was chosen to be the first or the last sentence in a paragraph. The second question was to estimate the number of paragraphs in the reading page. In order to answer the 4 questions, the participants were allowed to re-access the page. After completing each task (reading and answering), participants were given a user experience questionnaire about the system they used. The questionnaire included rating questions and open-ended questions. Participants took a break between each 2 conditions. The 4 tasks were video recorded.

5.3 Results and Discussion

In this section, we analyze the data we collected from the reading tasks, and then we discuss the user experience questionnaires. By analyzing the knowledge transfer questions, we found that the participants were able to answer all the questions correctly in the case of STAAR, and word-by-word VoiceOver conditions, see Figure 10. In conditions word-by-word VoiceOver with overlay, and iBook, participants answered 4 and 2 questions wrong, respectively, although they re-read the page when tried to answer the questions. These preliminary results show us that STAAR and word-by-word with VoiceOver were more effective than word-by-word with VoiceOver and overlay, and iBook. To evaluate the efficiency of STAAR comparing to the other 3 systems, we measured

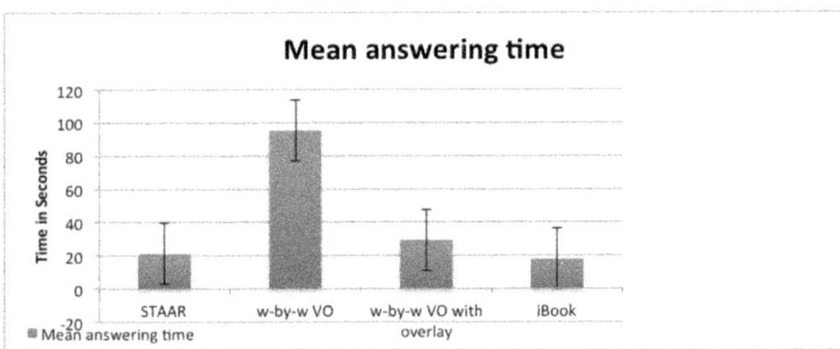

Figure 12: Mean of answering times by the four systems.

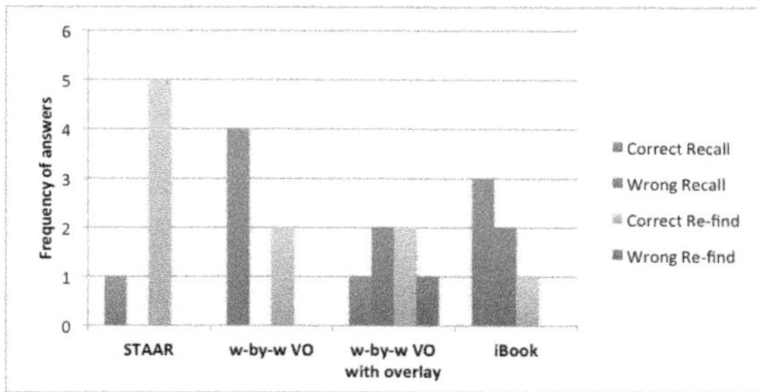

Figure 13: Strategies of answering: recalling and re-finding.

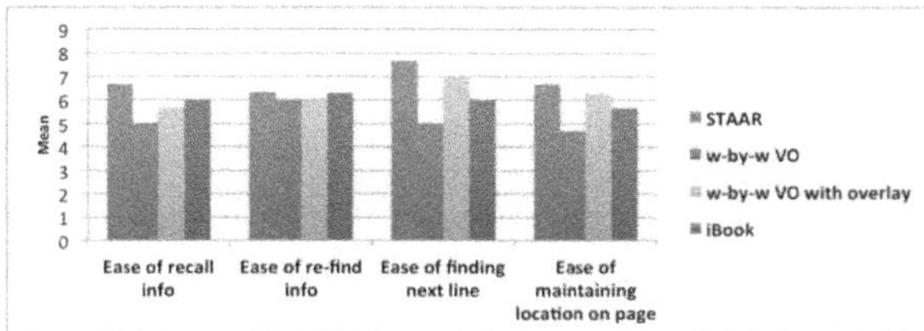

Figure 14: Mean user experience rating.

the time taken by participants to read the page, and the time they spent in answering the questions. Figure 12 shows the mean of the reading time, and Figure 11 shows the mean of the answering time for the 4 systems. The time is measured in seconds. We can see from the graph that the participants needed about double the time to read the same amount of text using word-by-word VoiceOver comparing to STAAR. When adding the overlay to the condition word-by-word VoiceOver, the reading time dropped by half. The number of lines in the page participants read with iBook was 17 lines, whereas the number of words they read with STAAR was 126 words. That means that reading a page with iBook needs at minimum17 touches, while with STAAR needs at minimum 126 touches. However, the difference in the mean reading time between the two systems was only 1 minute. What we observed during the study that in the word-by-word VoiceOver and the iBook conditions, the participants tend to repeat reading the same line several times and had difficulty finding the next line. That can explain why they were able to recall information with these conditions more than they did with STAAR, see Figure 13. The graph in Figure 13 shows both successful and failure trials of answering the knowledge transfer questions categorized by the answering strategy.

In the user experience questionnaire, the participants were asked to rate the ease of recalling information, and re-finding information on a scale from 1 to 10. They were also asked about how easy or difficult it was to find next line and maintain location on page. The graph in Figure 14 shows the mean of the participants' responses. Again, the results show that the word-by-word VoiceOver was the most difficult to find next line and to maintain location on page. Adding the overlay helped the participants according to their responses. STAAR received the highest scores in the participants' experience questionnaire with respect to ease of use and supporting spatial awareness. When answering the open-ended questions, the participants mentioned that for reading word-by-word, STAAR is much better than VoiceOver. One participant said she was lost without the sonifications. Also, one participant mentioned that the overlay helped a lot in the word-by-word VoiceOver with overlay condition. For the iBook, as it basically reads whole lines, the participants said that for active reading they may prefer to mix the two modes of reading word by word and reading whole lines in one system. In sum, these preliminary results with the 3 participants show us that STAAR is more effective than iBook in finding the correct answers, and more efficient in reading time than word-by-word VoiceOver. Additionally, the overlay was shown that it highly reduced the time needed for reading and re-finding when combined with VoiceOver compared to VoiceOver alone. But the overlay was not effective enough to support the participants finding the correct answers.

6. CONCLUSIONS

In this research, we proposed a multimodal reading support system that enables IBSVI to self-paced read in a spatial domain. This novel system enables IBSVI to read and make use of their spatial, auditory, and haptic capabilities. Our system integrates and fuses these two powerful modalities to achieve our research goals. Touch is the primary interaction mode in the presented multimodal system. The touch channel was used as a substitution for the vision channel to carry the functions of eye glancing in addition to focusing and reading. Complementarity between sonification and audible text, and spatial layout is the major organizational theme of the system's multimodal interaction. We addressed the speech-modeling problem. As the reader system responds to user's touch and reads word by word, the speech is generated word by word, and that causes choppiness to the speech. The audio dynamics model and the offline speech synthesis technique enhance the speech features and enabled IBSVI to better read at their own pace. We also increased the interaction robustness by embedding a supporting sonic gutter and intelligent reading support model into the system. We conducted a set of studies to test the sonic gutter and the intelligent active reading support. The studies helped us fine tune the parameters of the prediction model and confirmed the usefulness of the sonic gutter. The limited number of IBSVI participants in our studies does not allow us to generalize the results. However, the results indicate the system is promising as it can support continuous reading, correct drifting errors intelligently, and gives reading-specific support (i.e. reading not in the sense of deciphering isolated words as in a button label, but as expression of language).

7. ACKNOWLEDGMENTS

This research has been supported by the National Science Foundation under Grant No. IIS1117854. We thank our IBSVI participants for helping us gain the insights presented here.

8. REFERENCES

[1] *ANSI/NISO 2005. Specifications for the Digital Talking Book. ISBN: 1-880124-63-7. NISO.*

[2] J. P. Bigham, et. al. Webinsitu: a comparative analysis of blind and sighted browsing behavior. In *Proc. of the 9th international ACM SIGACCESS conf. on Computers and accessibility*, pages 51–58. ACM, 2007.

[3] Y. Borodin, J. P. Bigham, G. Dausch, and I. V. Ramakrishnan. More than meets the eye: a survey of screen-reader browsing strategies. In *International World Wide Web Conf.*, pages 1–10. ACM, 2010.

[4] C. Brown. Assistive technology computers and persons with disabilities. *Communications of the ACM*, 35(5):36–45, 1992.

[5] H. Deborah. Literacy leaps as blind students embrace technology. *English journal*, 90(2):52, 2000.

[6] G. S. Dhillon, Y. N. El-Glaly, W. H. Holbach, T. L. Smith-Jackson, and F. Quek. Use of participatory design to enhance accessibility of slate-type devices. In *Proceedings of the Human Factors and Ergonomics Society Annual Meeting*, volume 56, pages 1952–1956. SAGE Publications, 2012.

[7] Y. El-Glaly, F. Quek, T. Smith-Jackson, and G. Dhillon. Audible rendering of text documents controlled by multi-touch interaction. In *Proc. of the 14th ACM international conf. on Multimodal interaction*, pages 401–408. ACM, 2012.

[8] Y. N. Elglaly, F. Quek, T. Smith-Jackson, and G. Dhillon. Touch-screens are not tangible: Fusing tangible interaction with touch glass in readers for the blind. In *International Conference on Tangible, Embedded and Embodied Interaction*, 2013.

[9] J. D. E. Gabrieli and E. S. Norton. Reading abilities: Importance of visual-spatial attention. *Current Biology*, 22(9):R298–R299, 2012.

[10] P. C. Headley, V. E. Hribar, and D. T. Pawluk. Displaying braille and graphics on a mouse-like tactile display. In *Proc. of the 13th international ACM SIGACCESS conf. on Computers and accessibility*, pages 235–236. ACM, 2011.

[11] V. Lavesque, J. Pasquero, V. Hayward, and M. Legault. Display of virtual braille dots by lateral skin deformation: feasibility study. *ACM Trans. Appl. Percept.*, 2(2):132–149, 2005.

[12] J. Mahmud, Y. Borodin, D. Das, and I. V. Ramakrishnan. Combating information overload in non-visual web access using context. In *Proc. of the 12th international conf. on Intelligent user interfaces*, pages 341–344. ACM, 2007.

[13] S. Orlosky and D. Gilden. Simulating a full screen of braille. *Journal of Microcomputer Applications*, 15(1):47–56, 1992.

[14] P. Parente. Clique: a conversant, task-based audio display for gui applications. *SIGACCESS Access. Comput.*, (84):34–37, 2006.

[15] L. S. G. Piccolo,et al. Developing an accessible interaction model for touch screen mobile devices: preliminary results. In *Proc. of the 10th Brazilian Symposium on Human Factors in Computing Systems and the 5th Latin American Conf. on HCI*, pages 222–226, 2011.

[16] J. M. Taylor. Serving blind readers in a digital age. *American Libraries*, 35(11), 2004.

[17] R. Velazquez, et al. Making ebooks accessible to blind braille readers. In *IEEE International Workshop on Haptic Audio visual Environments and Games, 2008. HAVE 2008.*, pages 25–29, 2008.

Measuring Child Visual Attention using Markerless Head Tracking from Color and Depth Sensing Cameras

Jonathan Bidwell, Irfan A. Essa, Agata Rozga & Gregory D. Abowd
School of Interactive Computing & Center for Behavior Imaging
Georgia Institute of Technology, Atlanta, GA, USA

ABSTRACT
A child's failure to respond to his or her name being called is an early warning sign for autism and *response to name* is currently assessed as a part of standard autism screening and diagnostic tools. In this paper, we explore markerless child head tracking as an unobtrusive approach for automatically predicting child *response to name*. Head turns are used as a proxy for visual attention. We analyzed 50 recorded *response to name* sessions with the goal of predicting if children, ages 15 to 30 months, responded to name calls by turning to look at an examiner within a defined time interval. The child's head turn angles and hand annotated child name call intervals were extracted from each session. Human assisted tracking was employed using an overhead Kinect camera, and automated tracking was later employed using an additional forward facing camera as a proof-of-concept. We explore two distinct analytical approaches for predicting child responses, one relying on rule-based approached and another on random forest classification. In addition, we derive child response latency as a new measurement that could provide researchers and clinicians with finer grain quantitative information currently unavailable in the field due to human limitations. Finally we reflect on steps for adapting our system to work in less constrained natural settings.

CATEGORIES AND SUBJECT DESCRIPTORS
J.4 **[Computer Applications]**: social and behavioral sciences; I.4.8 **[Image Processing And Computer Vision]:** Scene Analysis; I.5.4 **[Pattern Recognition]**: Applications

GENERAL TERMS
Experimentation, Algorithms, Human Factors

KEYWORDS
Computational Behavioral Analysis; Autism Spectrum Disorder

ICMI '14, November 12 - 16 2014, Istanbul, Turkey
Copyright 2014 ACM 978-1-4503-2885-2/14/11…$15.00
.http://dx.doi.org/10.1145/2663204.2663235

INTRODUCTION
There is a long-standing interest in the autism research and clinical community in measuring children's tendency to attend to social stimuli, such as faces, voices, and gestures [10]. These multimodal stimuli require an understanding of speech, gestures and context for assessing child behaviors. The failure of a child to respond to a name call has received particular attention as a red flag for autism.

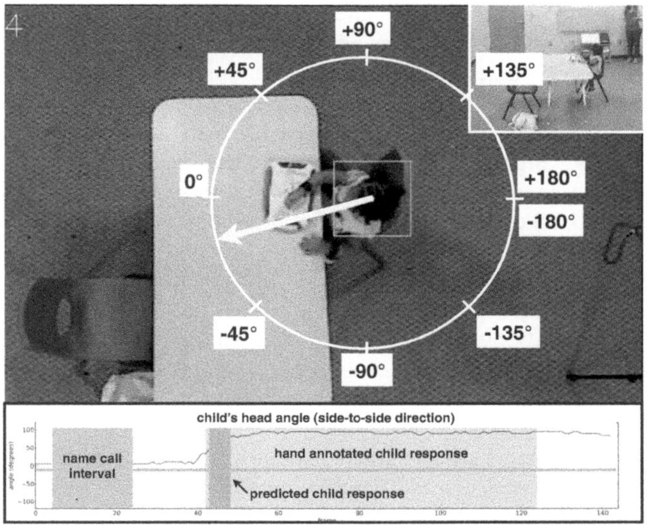

Figure 1: Markerless head pose estimation was employed for measuring a child's head angle at each frame. Head angles ranged between +/- 180 degrees with the child facing forward at zero degrees. The resulting head turn measurements were then used for predicting child *response to name*.

Response to name probes are now widely included in standard autism screening and diagnostic assessments, such as the M-CHAT [27] and ADOS [16] where a child's failure to respond to his or her name being called is considered an early warning sign for autism [1,14]. While these observations are conceptually simple to make—call a child's name and observe whether he or she responds—methods for capturing and quantifying these observations currently require direct human involvement. *Response to name* is typically annotated after-the-fact by researchers or made in-person by clinicians. These approaches can present logistical challenges for researchers seeking to conduct observations in a naturalistic settings and present cognitive bandwidth challenges for clinicians seeking to observe multiple child behaviors at the same time during in-person assessments.

In this work, we present initial steps towards an automated system for measuring a child's *response to name* through clinically standard inputs that include recorded audio and video feeds. Both human assisted and automated head tracking was performed to extract the left-right rotation of the child's head along the yaw axis as a marker for responding (see Figure 1). The system was evaluated on 50 sessions consisting of a standard response to name probe. Our goal was to predict whether the child responded to a name call by turning his/her head to face the examiner. Using automated tracking and a rule-based classifier, we predicted child response within a standard 3-second response time interval with a precision of 89.4% and recall of 80.4%. Using a learning-based approach, driven by a random-forest classifier, we obtained a precision of 76.9% and a recall of 83.3%. We further computed a *response to name* latency as the elapsed time between the call of the child's name and the onset of the predicted child response. These derived response latencies agreed closely with our ground truth annotations with an average absolute value error of 0.46 sec (and standard deviation (SD) of 0.35 sec) for the rule based classification approach, and 0.97 sec (SD = 1.22 sec) for the learning-based classification. These results highlight the potential for automating the measurement of children's orienting responses to social stimuli, a key factor in assessing developmental progress.

The research contributions of this work include:

1. Identifying that child head orientation can be used for predicting a child's response to a social stimulus (a call of their name) within defined time intervals.
2. Building a system that uses automated child head turn measurements and hand annotated name call intervals for reliably predicting *response to name* and measuring child response latency as a new fine-grained dimension of the response that may be beneficial to researchers.

RELATED WORK

The computer science community has long been interested in multimodal analysis for measuring human activities in natural environments [2,7,24]. Only recently has this work begun to focus on measuring child behaviors, and studying more nuanced behavioral phenomena such as social sharing and social bids for attention [5,26]. The ultimate context for our automated *response to name* measurement called for designing a system that would be both unobtrusive and unencumbering while requiring minimal instrumentation. We focused on head tracking as a primary indicator of child response for the four reasons, outlined below.

1. Head pose can serve as a proxy for attention. Human eye gaze has been correlated with visual focus of attention [8,9,11], and tends to agree with head direction. Kretch et al. instrumented infants with eye trackers and found that most infant eye gaze fixations occur within the middle of the child's field of view [15]. Stiefelhagen et al. performed a related study with four adults interacting at a meeting table, and found that eye gaze agreed 87% of the time with the direction of the subject's head [29].

2. Eye tracking solutions are limited for toddlers in room-sized environments. Traditional monitor-based eye tracking methods will not work in our use case where children may not be able to cooperate with calibration instructions, and responses must be measured in a 3D room-sized environment as opposed to a 2D screen. Head mounted eye trackers have been used to compare eye fixations between older neurotypical children and children with autism [5]; however these systems are cumbersome, require participants' active effort during calibration, and their form factor is not appropriate for young children [34,35]. Adult-worn video recording glasses and face tracking software have been used to infer eye contact by identifying when the child looks toward the camera; however, this approach requires the examiner to maintain the child within the camera's field of view at all times. More recently, a corneal-reflection based eye tracking technique has been proposed as an alternative for eye tracking in in 3D environments [23]. This system uses one or more cameras for tracking reflections on the user's cornea; however in our case such a system would require a prohibitive number of cameras as a child's eyes must need to remain visible throughout head turns [23,25].

3. Markerless motion capture has been applied for measuring head pose in room-sized environments. By contrast, methods based on ultrasonic [36], electromagnetic [37], or marker-based tracking [38,39] tend to be obtrusive and require instrumenting the child with special clothing. Markerless motion capture does not require instrumenting subjects [19] and has been successfully demonstrated in room-sized environments. Cutorian et al. [20] and Stiefelhagen [30] used 2D image based feature detection and tracking to estimate the head pose of people during meetings. In addition, many of the latest depth based methods for head tracking require placing cameras prohibitively close to the subject. Franelli et al. used a single Microsoft Kinect camera for tracking large head rotations up to +/- 90 degrees [13]; however due to the limited depth accuracy of the Kinect [17], subjects in the study had to sit within approximately 1 meter from a tripod-mounted camera. Maimone et al. addressed this by suspending multiple Kinects from the ceiling on long poles [18]. In our case, we aimed to position cameras as far away from the children as possible with the ultimate goal of measuring *response to name* in less constrained settings where the child may be moving around the room.

4. Head tracking beyond 90 degrees can be achieved from an overhead camera. Finally, we needed to track child head turns beyond 90 degrees. Most head pose estimation research assumes that images will contain easy to track facial features such as the eyes, nose and mouth, and assume side-to-side head rotation angles between +/- 90 degrees [21]. For example, Ba et al's system was trained on a dataset with head rotations ranging from -60 and 60 degrees [3]. Head tracking beyond this range presents an added challenge in that it introduces images (e.g., the back of someone's head) that contain fewer facial landmarks and thus have less detail for image segmentation and model fitting.. This problem has been addressed for similar situations through the introduction of priors such as a full body skeleton [6,28] or mapping an initial scan of the user's head in 2D or 3D to a lower dimensional representation for matching between frames [13,32]. In our case, the child's visual appearance can be difficult to anticipate in advance. While we could train a new model for each child, we felt this approach would present an unrealistic burden for researchers and clinicians hoping to use our system.

METHOD

Response to name administration (RTN)

Fifty *response to name* sessions were selected from the publically available Multimodal Dyadic Behavior Dataset (MMDB) [http://www.cbi.gatech.edu/mmdb]. The sessions contained 63 name calls and followed a similar protocol to *response to name* probe included in the ADOS [16], a standard diagnostic instrument for assessing autism (see Figure 2). The child sat at a table (either alone or in the parent's lap) and was given a small toy to occupy their attention. The examiner then positioned herself to the right and slightly behind the child, waited until the child's attention was on the toy, and called the child's name in a playful tone. If the child did not respond by turning his or her head and making eye contact with the examiner within 3 seconds, she called the child's name again, up to two more times. The examiner held a clipboard with a scoring sheet where she marked whether the child responded to the name call and if so, on which trial.

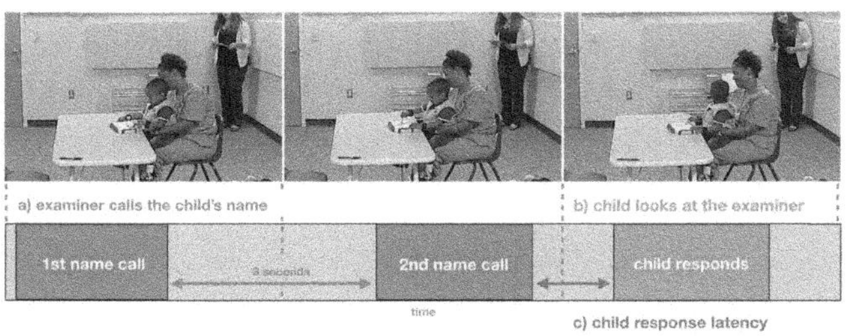

Figure 2: ***Response to name*** **administration and ground truth annotations. The examiner calls the child's name up to 3 times. In this example the examiner calls the child's name, but the child does not respond. The examiner waits three seconds and then calls the child's name again. This time the child responds by making eye contact.**

Hand annotated video observations

The audio and video recordings from the session were later reviewed by two research assistants, who used Elan annotation software [31] to mark frame-level onsets and offsets of each instance of the child's name being called, and any instances of the child responding by making eye contact with the examiner. If it was unclear from the video whether eye contact occurred, the research assistants consulted the examiner's scoring sheet. These annotations served as ground truth for training and evaluating our system (see Figure 2).

HEAD TRACKING

Human assisted tracking

Human assisted tracking was performed on all sessions in order to establish ground truth for child head turn measurements. This was accomplished via a graphical interface that allowed the user to monitor the output from a template tracker and then click and re-initialize the tracks as needed. The result was a set of "best case" head angle measurements that enabled us to evaluate the feasibility of using head turn measurements for classification of response to name, prior to addressing head tracking challenges such as head occlusions, child appearance variations, and out-of-plane head rotations.

Head pose estimation

The child's side-to-side head motion was measured from a forward facing camera (Canon Vixia) and the child's head position was measured using a ceiling-mounted kinect camera, centered and pointing directly down on the table. The Omron OKAO Vision Library [40] was used for tracking the child's head orientation within the forward facing camera's video feed, while Boston University (BU)'s Multi-Person Tracker was used for measuring the position of the child's head from the overhead camera [33]. These measurements were then used to first initialize and later update a Kanade–Lucas–Tomasi (KLT) template tracker from the overhead camera [4]. The template was updated with head orientation estimates from the front-facing camera every 80 frames. The resulting automated tracker was capable of measuring child head turns head turns that exceeded 90 degrees.

Automated tracking using template matching

Head tracking was performed using a template tracker. The template consisted of a pair of masked, overhead color and depth image of the child's head. The template's position and orientation were initialized as an oriented bounding box rectangle. Head position was defined as the first detected position from BU's Multi-Person Tracker [33] and head orientation was defined as the first head detection from Omron [40]. The child's head was segmented by excluding pixels greater than 10 cm above and 2 cm below the center pixel of the bounding box in the depth image. Hole filling was then performed by applying dilate and erode morphological operations and Gaussian smoothing. The resulting mask was then applied to the color and depth images for creating a template that excluded background pixels. This process was repeated for matching the template to the current tracked bounding box at each frame (see Figure **3**).

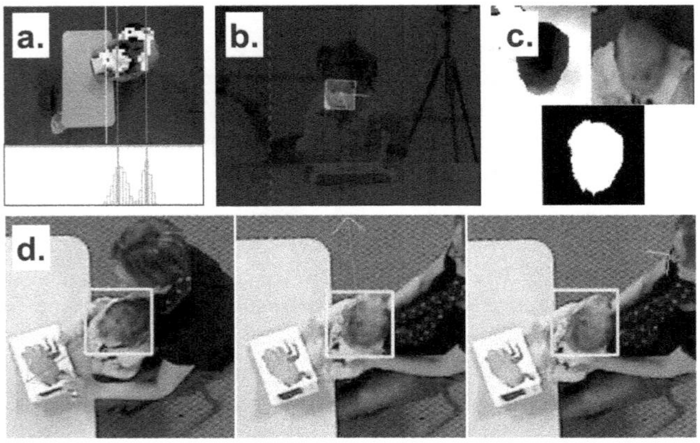

Figure 3: *Response to name* automated head tracking process. (a) Head position candidates are detected from the overhead camera and filtered using histogram binning. Head turns are measured from the overhead camera by tracking a segmented child head template between frames. (b) Head templates consist of an oriented bounding box where the position is automatically initialized from the overhead camera and the orientation is initialized from a front-facing camera using commercial head tracking software (c). Finally, (d) the template is segmented using the overhead camera depth image and tracked between frames using a KLT tracker (d).

This approach was chosen to address the following four challenges.

1. **Measuring large head rotations**. The Omron software provided side-to-side head rotation measurements [40]. While the software could detect side-to-side head turns between +/- 90 degrees; reliable measurements were limited to approximately +/- 30 degrees. In our case, we employed a template tracker to pick up where the Omron tracker left off and continued tracking the child head turns beyond this limited range.
2. **Robustness to occlusions**. The examiner and parents frequently occlude the child from the frontal camera. This results in missing data. The overhead KLT template tracker is more robust to these occlusions and provides greater tracking coverage.
3. **Robustness to appearance changes**. Hair and skin colors varied considerably between children. This appearance was also subject to out of plane rotations when viewed from the overhead camera. This led us to choose a template tracker for providing us with a more general model.

Head position filtering

The BU tracker was used for detecting candidate head positions, and this often resulted in multiple head position estimates per frame [33]. Head positions were filtered using histogram peak detection and binning as an additional step for isolating the child's head (see Figure **3**).

Head orientation updates

The orientation of the overhead-tracking template was periodically reset to the front facing head rotation angle every 80 frames as a value that worked well in practice.

BEHAVIOR CLASSIFICATION

Binary classifier evaluation

We employ two "*response to name*" classifiers (rule based and random-forest) on 50 sessions involving 63 individual name calls. Each classifier made predictions on a per response basis --- a separate binary decision (true or false) was made for each hand annotated child name call interval. In each case, the child's activity was analyzed on a within a time window that started at the offset of the name call interval and spanned for a maximum of 3 seconds (30 fps * 3 sec = 90 frames) or until the start of the next ground truth name call interval, whichever was shorter.

The resulting predictions were evaluated against our hand annotated ground truth observations as follows. Any prediction that fell within a window of +/- 3 seconds from the onset of the child's response, as determined by the ground truth annotation, was counted as a true positive. A failure to predict a ground-truth coded response that occurred within this window was counted as a false negative. The 3-second margin was selected based on a previously published study using an identical response to name administration protocol [22]. In cases where the child's name was called more than once, we also calculated true negatives (correct prediction of no response in the 3-second window following the offset of the ground-truth coded name call) and false positives (incorrect prediction of child response in the 3 second window following the offset of the ground-truth coded name call).

Child latency measure

Next, we also computed the latency for each response, defined as the elapsed time between the offset of the last name call and the onset of the child's response. The child response latency was computed for our ground truth and predicted responses as follows:

$$\begin{aligned}&\textit{ground truth latency}\\&= \textit{hand annotated child response onset}\\&- \textit{hand annotated name call offset}\end{aligned} \quad (4)$$

$$\begin{aligned}\textit{predicted latency} &= \textit{predicted child response onset}\\&- \textit{hand annotated name call offset}\end{aligned} \quad (5)$$

The error and absolute error between these latency measures was computed as follows:

$$\begin{aligned}&\textit{predicted latency error}\\&\qquad = \textit{ground truth latency}\\&\qquad - \textit{predicted latency}\end{aligned} \quad (6)$$

$$\begin{aligned}&\textit{absolute predicted latency error}\\&\qquad = |\textit{ground truth latency}\\&\qquad - \textit{predicted latency}|\end{aligned} \quad (7)$$

Negative values reflect predictions made ahead of our hand annotated child response intervals, and positive values reflect predictions that were made after the response.

Random-forest classification

Many aspects of the *response to name* task could not be known in advance. For example we observed that some children did a "double take" while responding rather than turning once, and thus realized we would need temporal features to encode such behaviors. The classifier was trained with features from our automated pipeline. Head tracking results were paired with our hand-annotated child response labels for creating a feature vector at each frame. Each vector contained the child's angle in degrees and the most recent elapsed time since the child's name was called in seconds.

The resulting feature vectors were then paired with our hand annotated ground truth labels. The child response label at each frame was appended for creating a set of positive or negative training examples. The random forest was then trained for predicting the child's response at each frame and evaluated using leave-one-out cross validation (see Table 2). The random forest classifier demarcated a positive response with a threshold of 15 consecutive "true" frames. This threshold was made on the assumption that children could not physically turn to make eye contact with the examiner in less than this time (15 frames / 30 fps = 0.5 seconds).

In general this approach enabled us to quickly evaluate the contribution of multiple features such as child position, head velocity and head acceleration. In our case, child head angle and the elapsed time since the name call were the two most discriminative features.

Rule-based classification

Next we evaluated the performance of a rule-based approach, which aims to capture the high-level structure of the interaction as opposed the temporal features as an additional benchmark. This approach established rules to find a set of thresholds and parameters that results in the best classifier performance. Specifically, the child was labeled as responding if s/he turned beyond a given head angle and remained beyond this angle for a minimum duration of time. We also added a median kernel width parameter to reduce noise in the head-tracking signal. Next we performed an exhaustive grid-search over these three variables to find the set of parameters yielding the highest precision rate.

The range for each grid-search value was informed by our understanding of the *response to name* protocol and the physical environment. For example, we knew the examiner always stood behind and to the right of the child while the child would always respond by turning to the right. Head turn responses would always be between 0 and 180 degrees. The duration of the child's response could be no less than 0.25 seconds as a limit on how fast children could turn and no longer than 3 seconds as the maximum time that the examiner would wait before calling the child's name again. The median kernel width ranged from 1-30 frames (see Figure **4**).

The rule-based classifier was trained using a grid-search were we first computed the average precision rate of the classifier using each combination of parameters over 10 trials with a random 50/50 training and test split and then chose set of parameters with the highest average precision value.

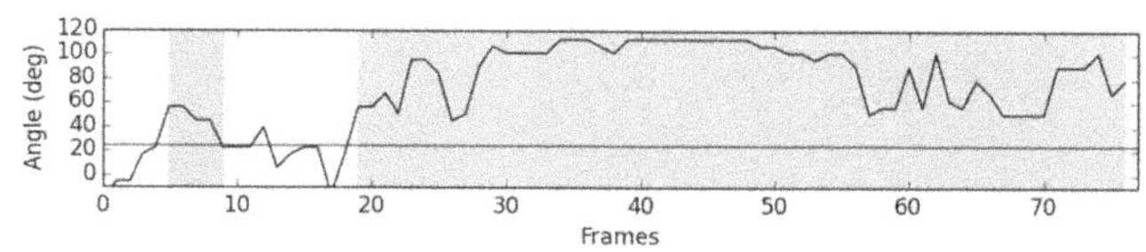

Figure 4: Rule based classification: The child is said to respond if his or her head angle (black line) exceeds a given head angle (blue line) for a minimum duration of time (15 frames). Intervals satisfying these criteria are shown in green.

RESULTS

The system was evaluated against human coding of the child's *response to name* from video. The 50 sessions contained a total of 63 name calls, with 48 instances of a response and 15 instances of a failure to respond. Only two children never responded to the call for their name.

Our first step was to examine the relationship between child head orientation and name call intervals for predicting *response to name*. Human assisted tracking measurements were used to evaluate the system's performance when tracking errors were minimized. These results indicated that predicting *response to name* from changes in head orientation was a tractable problem. The best set of grid-search parameters for the rule-based classifier were 27-degrees for the head turn threshold, 0.5-second minimum fixation duration and 15 frame median kernel width (see Table 1) with an average precision of 93.2%, a recall of 90.9%, an average latency error of -0.42 sec (SD = 0.55 sec), and an average absolute value latency error of 0.42 sec (SD = 0.55 sec). The random forest classifier had a precision of 93.3%, a recall of 87.5% an average latency error of 0.09 sec (SD = 0.68 sec), with an average absolute value latency error of 0.47 sec (SD = 0.53 sec).

Next, we evaluated the performance of the two classifiers using automatically generated head orientation measurements. The rule-based classifier had a precision of 89.4%, a recall of 80.4%, an average latency error of -0.27 sec (SD = 0.50 sec), and an average absolute value latency error of 0.46 seconds (SD = 0.35 sec). The random forest classifier had a precision of 76.9%, a recall of 83.3%, an average latency error of -0.04 sec (SD = 1.50 sec), and an average absolute value latency error of 0.97 sec (SD = 1.22 sec). The random forest performed better than the rule-based approach during three sessions where the child did a "double take" before turning to the examiner i.e., the children made eye contact on their second attempt after repositioning themselves to see around the parent. The performance of each classifier decreased with the automated tracking condition but remained reasonable for our application with precision and recall above 76% and predicted child response latency error within +/- 3 seconds. These results confirmed that automated *responses to name* predictions could accurately measure child latency within +/- 3 seconds of the child's actual response. The absolute value standard deviation latency error for both classifiers was less than 1 second.

Table 1 Rule-based classification results

a) Human assisted tracking		Actual	
		Child responded	Child did not respond
Predicted	Child responded	22	1.6
	Child did not respond	2.2	5.7
b) Automated tracking			
		Child responded	Child did not respond
Predicted	Child responded	19.4	2.3
	Child did not respond	4.7	6.2

Table 2 Random forest classification results

a) Human assisted tracking		Actual	
		Child responded	Child did not respond
Predicted	Child responded	42	3
	Child did not respond	6	12
b) Automated tracking			
		Child responded	Child did not respond
Predicted	Child responded	40	12
	Child did not respond	8	3

Binary classifier performance comparisons

The rule-based classifier had a consistent bias towards predicting earlier child responses for both head tracking conditions. The average rule-based latency error for human assisted tracking was -0.42 seconds and -0.27 seconds for automated tracking, respectively. This bias can be explained by how predictions are made. The rule-based head angle threshold did not account for the gradual turn of a child's head. Instead of predicting a response after the child had turned, that is, at the maximum of the plateau, our method would often make predictions earlier, at the moment the child initiated the head turn. This bias was not present with the random forest as the child's head turn was included in the negative training examples.

The random forest classifier was less accurate for predicting the onset of child responses and was more susceptible to false positives than the rule-based classifier (see Table 2). The absolute predicted response latency error distribution was also greater for the random forest at SD = 1.22 sec. as compared to SD = 0.35 sec. for the rule-based classifier. The rule-based classifier made predictions over multiple frames while random forest classifier made predictions on a per frame basis. These results suggest that longer duration temporal features may be needed for improving random forest classifier performance; however in practice these offsets were small and latency error remained well below our target application error margin of within +/- 3 seconds.

DISCUSSION

Head tracking was well suited for predicting *response to name* during our study for two reasons. First, the *response to name* probe elicited large head rotations by design. The examiner called the child's name from behind and to the left of the child. This prompted children to turn and face the examiner rather than glance to the side while responding. Measuring these head turns called for course-level tracking estimates.

Markerless head tracking provided us with sufficient accuracy for detecting the large angular sweep of the child's head turns responses without requiring more accurate techniques that would require instrumenting our cameras closer to the children [12]. Second, *response to name* was administered in a structured laboratory setting the position of the examiner and the child were both known in advance. This enabled us to apply a simple but effective rule-based classification approach for predicting children responses (see Table 1). Each classifier reliably predicted *response to name* using automated head tracking and hand annotated child name call intervals. Both classifiers agreed above 76% with the examiners' in-person observations and our latency error was well within our +/3 second cutoff window for in-person observations.

While at first glance our experimental setup may seem simplified and overly structured, we note that this type of test is standard practice in the psychology research community for supporting repeatable observations across participants. Our *response to name* probe was modeled on a standard diagnostic instrument for autism, which involves leaving the child occupied with a toy, moving behind and to the side, and calling the child's name up to three times [16]. Our setup has allowed us to demonstrate to our psychology collaborators that we can replicate their current practice with respect to *response to name* administration and scoring. The feedback that we received from our colleagues in the autism research community continues to emphasize the value of such objective measures as large, longitudinal datasets become increasingly common in the field.

In the future we seek to perform additional head tracking and speech processing for supporting automated *response to name* in a wider range of naturalistic social settings. Head tracking will be extended for including the examiner's position. The present system assumes that the examiner calls the child's name from a particular location in a particular room. The relative angle between the child's head position could be computed for enabling the examiner to move about the room. The more the child orients to the examiner's tracked position the smaller this angle would become. The resulting measure could support name calls in multiple locations. Speech processing is also planned for automatically identifying instances of *response to name* within longer less structured settings and labeling child name call intervals. In our early work we explored automated word spotting using commercial software. These efforts were unsuccessful due to child names being called with low phoneme counts and background noise. In the future we plan to develop speech diarisation software for addressing these shortcomings.

CONCLUSIONS

We presented a system for reliably predicting a child's *response to name*, given child head turn measurements with the long-term goal of deploying the system in a naturalistic setting. Moreover, we measured child response latency as a first step for providing a finer-grained measure of a child's response than administrators are currently able to capture. These measures may prove to be clinically meaningful for psychologists by providing a second source of information during clinical assessments and further serve researchers by reducing the need for scheduling observations, establishing inter-rater reliability between examiners, performing video annotation, establishing larger, more detailed datasets for contextualizing child behaviors.

Human assisted tracking was performed for establishing a set of "best-case" child head turn measurements, and we showed that we could reliably predict *response to name* and measure child response latency with precision and recall above 87% and measure child response latency with a maximum absolute average error of 0.47 seconds (SD=0.53 sec), respectively.

Next we implemented automated head tracking as a first step for supporting these predictions in more naturalistic environments, we showed that we could continue to reliably predict these measures with precision and recall above 76% and measure child response latency with a maximum absolute average error of 0.97 seconds (SD=1.22 sec) when using a random forest classifier.

The results of our work highlight the opportunities and challenges for *response to name* prediction in a naturalistic environment. The rule-based and random forest classifiers were evaluated for sessions where the examiner called the child's name from at a single, fixed position in the room. In the future, we plan to track the examiner's head position for evaluating our system with multiple name call locations.

ACKNOWLEDGMENTS

This paper is based upon work supported by the National science Foundation under Grant #1029679

REFERENCES

1. Adrien, J.L., Lenoir, P., Martineau, J., et al. Blind ratings of early symptoms of autism based upon family home movies. *Journal of the American Academy of Child & Adolescent Psychiatry 32*, 3 (1993), 617–626.
2. Ba, S.O., Hung, H., and Odobez, J. Visual activity context for focus of attention estimation in dynamic meetings. *IEEE International Conference on Multimedia and Expo, 2009. ICME 2009*, (2009), 1424–1427.
3. Ba, S.O. and Odobez, J.M. A Rao-Blackwellized mixed state particle filter for head pose tracking. *Proc. ACM-ICMI-MMMP*, (2005), 9–16.
4. Baker, S. and Matthews, I. Lucas-Kanade 20 Years On: A Unifying Framework. *International Journal of Computer Vision 56*, 3 (2004), 221–255.
5. Bal, E., Harden, E., Lamb, D., Hecke, A.V.V., Denver, J.W., and Porges, S.W. Emotion Recognition in Children with Autism Spectrum Disorders: Relations to Eye Gaze and Autonomic State. *Journal of Autism and Developmental Disorders 40*, 3 (2010), 358–370.
6. Ballan, L. and Cortelazzo, G.M. Marker-less motion capture of skinned models in a four camera set-up using optical flow and silhouettes. *3DPVT, Atlanta, GA, USA 37*, (2008).
7. Bernardin, K., Gehrig, T., and Stiefelhagen, R. Multi-level Particle Filter Fusion of Features and Cues for Audio-Visual Person Tracking. In R. Stiefelhagen, R. Bowers and J. Fiscus, eds., *Multimodal Technologies for Perception of Humans*. Springer Berlin Heidelberg, 2008, 70–81.
8. Conty, L. and Grèzes, J. Look at me, I'll remember you. *Human Brain Mapping 33*, 10 (2012), 2428–2440.
9. Von Cranach, M. The role of orienting behavior in human interaction. In *Behavior and Environment*. Springer, 1971, 217–237.
10. Devine, P.G. and Malpass, R.S. Orienting Strategies in Differential Face Recognition. *Personality and Social Psychology Bulletin 11*, 1 (1985), 33–40.
11. Emery, N.J. The eyes have it: the neuroethology, function and evolution of social gaze. *Neuroscience & Biobehavioral Reviews 24*, 6 (2000), 581–604.
12. Fanelli, G., Dantone, M., Gall, J., Fossati, A., and Gool, L. Random Forests for Real Time 3D Face

Analysis. *Int. J. Comput. Vision 101*, 3 (2013), 437–458.
13. Fanelli, G., Weise, T., Gall, J., and Gool, L.V. Real Time Head Pose Estimation from Consumer Depth Cameras. In R. Mester and M. Felsberg, eds., *Pattern Recognition*. Springer Berlin Heidelberg, 2011, 101–110.
14. Johnson, C.P. and Myers, S.M. Identification and Evaluation of Children With Autism Spectrum Disorders. *Pediatrics 120*, 5 (2007), 1183–1215.
15. Kretch, K.S., Franchak, J.M., and Adolph, K.E. Crawling and Walking Infants See the World Differently. *Child Development*, (2013), n/a–n/a.
16. Lord, C., Risi, S., Lambrecht, L., et al. The Autism Diagnostic Observation Schedule—Generic: A Standard Measure of Social and Communication Deficits Associated with the Spectrum of Autism. *Journal of Autism and Developmental Disorders 30*, 3 (2000), 205–223.
17. Maimone, A., Bidwell, J., Peng, K., and Fuchs, H. Enhanced personal autostereoscopic telepresence system using commodity depth cameras. *Computers & Graphics 36*, 7 (2012), 791–807.
18. Maimone, A. and Fuchs, H. Real-time volumetric 3D capture of room-sized scenes for telepresence. *3DTV-Conference: The True Vision - Capture, Transmission and Display of 3D Video (3DTV-CON), 2012*, (2012), 1–4.
19. Moeslund, T.B., Hilton, A., and Krüger, V. A survey of advances in vision-based human motion capture and analysis. *Computer Vision and Image Understanding 104*, 2–3 (2006), 90–126.
20. Murphy-Chutorian, E. and Trivedi, M.M. 3D tracking and dynamic analysis of human head movements and attentional targets. *Second ACM/IEEE International Conference on Distributed Smart Cameras, 2008. ICDSC 2008*, (2008), 1–8.
21. Murphy-Chutorian, E. and Trivedi, M.M. Head Pose Estimation in Computer Vision: A Survey. *IEEE Transactions on Pattern Analysis and Machine Intelligence 31*, 4 (2009), 607–626.
22. Nadig AS, Ozonoff S, Young GS, Rozga A, Sigman M, and Rogers SJ. A prospective study of response to name in infants at risk for autism. *Archives of Pediatrics & Adolescent Medicine 161*, 4 (2007), 378–383.
23. Nakazawa, A. and Nitschke, C. Point of Gaze Estimation through Corneal Surface Reflection in an Active Illumination Environment. In A. Fitzgibbon, S. Lazebnik, P. Perona, Y. Sato and C. Schmid, eds., *Computer Vision – ECCV 2012*. Springer Berlin Heidelberg, 2012, 159–172.
24. Nickel, K., Gehrig, T., Stiefelhagen, R., and McDonough, J. A Joint Particle Filter for Audio-visual Speaker Tracking. *Proceedings of the 7th International Conference on Multimodal Interfaces*, ACM (2005), 61–68.
25. Nishino, K. and Nayar, S.K. The world in an eye [eye image interpretation]. *Proceedings of the 2004 IEEE Computer Society Conference on Computer Vision and Pattern Recognition, 2004. CVPR 2004*, (2004), I-444–I-451 Vol.1.
26. Rehg, J.M., Abowd, G.D., Rozga, A., et al. Decoding Children's Social Behavior. *2013 IEEE Conference on Computer Vision and Pattern Recognition (CVPR)*, (2013), 3414–3421.
27. Robins, D.L., Fein, D., Barton, M.L., and Green, J.A. The Modified Checklist for Autism in Toddlers: An Initial Study Investigating the Early Detection of Autism and Pervasive Developmental Disorders. *Journal of Autism and Developmental Disorders 31*, 2 (2001), 131–144.
28. Shotton, J., Sharp, T., Kipman, A., et al. Real-time Human Pose Recognition in Parts from Single Depth Images. *Commun. ACM 56*, 1 (2013), 116–124.
29. Stiefelhagen, R. Tracking Focus of Attention in Meetings. *Proceedings of the 4th IEEE International Conference on Multimodal Interfaces*, IEEE Computer Society (2002), 273–.
30. Voit, M. and Stiefelhagen, R. 3D User-perspective, Voxel-based Estimation of Visual Focus of Attention in Dynamic Meeting Scenarios. *International Conference on Multimodal Interfaces and the Workshop on Machine Learning for Multimodal Interaction*, ACM (2010), 51:1–51:8.
31. Wittenburg, P., Brugman, H., Russel, A., Klassmann, A., and Sloetjes, H. Elan: a professional framework for multimodality research. *Proceedings of LREC*, (2006).
32. Xiong, X. and De La Torre, F. Supervised Descent Method and Its Applications to Face Alignment. *2013 IEEE Conference on Computer Vision and Pattern Recognition (CVPR)*, (2013), 532–539.
33. Zhang, J., Presti, L.L., and Sclaroff, S. Online Multi-person Tracking by Tracker Hierarchy. *2012 IEEE Ninth International Conference on Advanced Video and Signal-Based Surveillance (AVSS)*, (2012), 379–385.
34. FaceLab. 2014. http://www.seeingmachines.com/product/facelab/.
35. Mobile eye tracking - Tobii Glasses. 2014. http://www.tobii.com/en/eye-tracking-research/global/products/hardware/tobii-glasses-eye-tracker/.
36. Intersense. 2014. www.intersense.com.
37. Polhemus. 2014. http://www.polhemus.com/.
38. Vicon. 2014. http://www.vicon.com/.
39. PhaseSpace. 2014. http://www.phasespace.com/.
40. Omron. 2014. http://www.omron.com/r_d/coretech/vision/okao.html.

Bi-Modal Detection of Painful Reaching for Chronic Pain Rehabilitation Systems

Temitayo A. Olugbade[1], M. S. Hane Aung [1], Nadia Bianchi-Berthouze[1], Nicolai Marquardt[1], Amanda C. Williams[2],

[1]University College London, UCL Interaction Centre, Gower Street, London, WC1E 6BT
[2]University College London, Dept. Clinical Psychology, Torrington Place, London, WC1E 6BT
{temitayo.olugbade.13, m.aung, n.marquardt, amanda.williams, n.berthouze}@ucl.ac.uk

ABSTRACT

Physical activity is essential in chronic pain rehabilitation. However, anxiety due to pain or a perceived exacerbation of pain causes people to guard against beneficial exercise. Interactive rehabiliation technology sensitive to such behaviour could provide feedback to overcome such psychological barriers. To this end, we developed a Support Vector Machine framework with the feature level fusion of body motion and muscle activity descriptors to discriminate three levels of pain (none, low and high). All subjects underwent a forward reaching exercise which is typically feared among people with chronic back pain. The levels of pain were categorized from control subjects (no pain) and thresholded self reported levels from people with chronic pain. Salient features were identified using a backward feature selection process. Using feature sets from each modality separately led to high pain classification F1 scores of 0.63 and 0.69 for movement and muscle activity respectively. However using a combined bimodal feature set this increased to F1 = 0.8.

Categories and Subject Descriptors

H.1.2. Human Information Processing

General Terms

Algorithms, Experimentation, Human Factors.

Keywords: Emotion; Machine Learning; Motion Capture; Electromyography; Body Movement; Pain Rehabilitation Technology; Physical Rehabilitation.

1. INTRODUCTION

Interactive technology developed to motivate physical activity has been efficacious in the rehabilitation of chronic conditions [1]. However, for the specific case of chronic pain (CP), efficacy is more limited [2, 3]. One major reason is that rehabilitation technology is not designed to adapt to the emotional state of its user. The person's emotional state is important in CP because pain uniquely conveys threat [4], which generates fear, low confidence or catastrophic thinking leading to avoidance and self-protective behavior [5, 6]. In turn, this greatly reduces adherence to beneficial activity and leads to no progress or even negative effects. In CP rehabilitation, it is well understood that keeping active protects against weakening and stiffness, it inhibits the neurophysiological mechanisms underlying the spread of pain, increases confidence in physical ability, underpins achieving goals [7] and can improve quality of life [8]. Physiotherapists (and other healthcare staff) regularly educate and advise on activity and provide psychological support to encourage adherence. In Singh *et al.* [9], the authors discuss how physiotherapists make use of behavioral cues (such as guarding, avoidance, alteration of breathing or anxiety) from the patient to decide on the timeliness, amount and type of support to provide. This can vary from simple breathing prompts to partitioning the exercise to facilitate graded exposure, or simply providing information, reassurance or encouragement. However, limited human resource means there is a heavy reliance on self-management and self-rehabilitation where the psychological states are not observed and thus the aforementioned adherence issues occur [10].

Clearly, automated systems that have the capability to recognize such affective states are a potential solution. However, the development of recognition models to reliably detect pain expression or pain-related behavior remains a complex challenge. To date, the main expressive modality that has been researched is facial expression [11-16]. However, for the design of CP rehabilitation systems, expression from body movement is essential since many of the protective behaviors are manifest in whole-body motion [6]. To the best of our knowledge, automatic detection of pain-related expressions from body movement have barely been studied [17]; although in the wider context of generic affective states, there has been much recent work on automatic recognition from body movements and postures (for a review see [18]) and in sports-games [19]. In addition to outward expressions, another measure that reflects protective behavior is anomalous levels of muscle activity given a particular movement context. In a surface electromyographic (sEMG) study specific to chronic low back pain (CLBP), Watson *et al.* [20] showed that psychological factors influenced the prolonged use of lumbar paraspinal muscles during forward flexion exercises. Similarly, in a study by Van der Hulst *et al.* [21], the authors showed that there was an association between high sEMG levels and a guarded mechanism during walking. In Geisser *et al.* [22], the authors examined the relationship between lumbar flexion, dynamic sEMG and pain-related fear in people with CLBP. Correlations were found between pain-related fear and reduced lumbar flexion as well as increased sEMG during full flexion.

In this study, we develop and evaluate a recognition framework to automatically classify forward reaching motions (Fig. 1) in people without chronic pain, and people with chronic pain reporting low pain or high pain after the execution of the exercise. We used supervised machine learning with early fusion of features processed from whole body motion capture (MoCap) and sEMG data from the lumbar paraspinal and upper trapezius muscles. In Section 2, we describe the nature of the dataset we used and its

ICMI '14, Nov 12-16 2014, Istanbul, Turkey.
ACM 978-1-4503-2885-2/14/11.
http://dx.doi.org/10.1145/2663204.2663261

acquisition method. In Section 3, we describe the initial feature set identified as potentially descriptive of pain based on literature and initial inspection. In Section 4, we report the results of an ANOVA analysis of the features and we also report on the optimization and validation of three Support Vector Machine (SVM) frameworks using three initial feature sets: two frameworks were trained using unimodal features (MoCap and sEMG respectively) and the third using a combined bimodal feature set. We conclude in Section 5 by discussing how these findings inform current development of automatic CP rehabilitation technology.

Figure 1. Example of a forward phase of the reach exercise

2. DATASET DESCRIPTION

The data used in this study is a subset of the extensive multimodal database presented in [23], which contains a wider set of movements and sensing modalities and pain-related labeled behaviors. The subset considered here consists of 18 people with CLBP and 13 control subjects undergoing forward-reaching motions (Fig. 1), this yields 30 instances of reaching from the CLBP group and 19 instances from the control group. This exercise is part of rehabilitation routines in CLBP and is one that generates anxiety and fear possibly due to a perceived exacerbation of pain [9].

To capture movement the subjects wore a suit with Inertial Measuring Units (IMUs) (Animzaoo IGS-190). Each IMU was attached with a minimal amount of velcro-strapping to reduce invasiveness. Each IMU returned 3D Euler angle triplets in the BioVision Hierarchy format (BVH) at a sample rate of 60Hz. In conjunction, skeletal proportions were annotated from still photographs of each subject. Finally, 3D Cartesian positional triplets of 26 anatomical nodes over the whole body were calculated. Also, 4 wireless electromyographic (sEMG) sensors (BTS FREEEMG) were attached to the lumbar paraspinal muscles (hereafter, called lower-back muscles) and to the upper section of the trapezius muscles (hereafter, called upper-back muscles). Each pair of sensors was placed laterally equidistant to the spine and sampled at 1kHz. The recording procedure of the two sensing systems was automatically triggered for synchronization.

Each instance of a reached forward movement consisted of a forward reach with both hands while standing, then a retraction back to a standing pose (Fig. 1). After each instance, the CLBP participants were asked to report a level of pain defined as a value between 0 for no pain to 10 for extreme pain (mean 3.85, standard deviation 3.16). Within the CLBP group, instances were categorized as low pain if the self reported rating was < 5 and high pain if ≥ 5. This resulted in 15 instances in the low pain group and 15 in the high pain group. The 19 control instances are categorized as no pain. Overall, this is treated as a 3 category classification task for two main reasons. First, the control instances are not equivalent to CLBP instances with zero reported pain, control subjects will have no fear of pain exacerbation and no fear of performing the exercise and [5] are therefore a separate class. Secondly, self reporting is highly subjective and variable between subjects and a broad categorization is less dependent on the reported values compared to a regression task.

3. FEATURE EXTRACTION

In this section, we describe the feature set derived from MoCap and sEMG information. Due to the large amount of information that can be potentially processed from whole body MoCap and sEMG signals, we aimed to find a minimal feature set salient to the reaching forward movement.

Movement Features. With the rationale that pain intensity affects performance in physical exercise [24], we visually inspected the movement profiles of various body segments during each reaching instance. It was found that the vertical displacement of the forearm and the neck and flexion angles showed differences between the two pain level groups. We consider five features derived from these profiles as described in Table 1 (features 1 - 5). To account for differences in skeletal proportions, positional features were normalized accordingly.

Muscle Activity Characteristics. In concordance with [20] and [22], sEMG signal characteristics during a forward flexion movement shows typically high activity at the onset to apex phase followed by a significant decrease in activity during retraction. Fig. 2-left shows this expected sEMG profile with a drop in activation during retraction after the change point (indicated by a red spot). Fig 2-right shows an example of a lack of change in muscle activation due to poor execution or avoidance in performing the movement. Using the upper envelope of the rectified signal, we automatically extracted the change point, i.e. the approximate time at which the highly active onset to apex phase changes to the retraction phase with low activity. This was done by adapting the method in [25] using two equal-sized sliding windows (50-frame in width) with a 20-frame separation sliding across the whole signal. The twin-window location that optimizes the difference between the mean activities within the two windows was found. The middle frame value between the two windows normalized by the duration of the whole motion determines the feature *ChangePointTimeRatio*. Also the signed maximum difference in mean activity from the two windows normalized by the maximum activity of the whole motion yields the feature *ChangePointDifference*. These quantities were calculated for all four sEMG channels (see features 6 – 13 in Table 1). Pain-related waveforms with relatively high activity in the retraction phase gave lower differences or even negative values and occurred at irregular times.

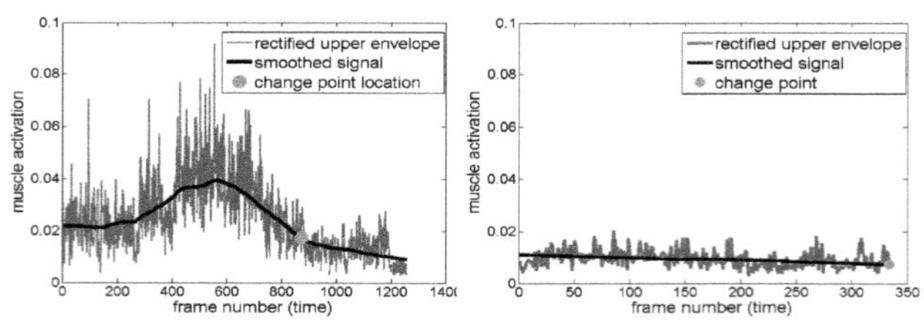

Figure 3. Lower back sEMG signals from a reaching motion with change point locations, normal pattern (left) with avoidance (right).

4. MODELLING AND RESULTS

An initial one-way analysis of variance (ANOVA) was carried out, using SPSS v.21, to test the statistical significance of each of the feature with the three levels of pain. We use the left arm only due to lateral symmetry thus avoiding the duplication of values and reducing feature dimensionality. The results showed that most of the features were statistically significant (see bold p- values in Table 1).

Table 1: Features and anatomical nodes (highlighted in yellow on the stick figure) used in the study. For clarity, TopNeck = 24, LowNeck = 12, Hip = 1, UpperRightLeg = 7, UpperLeftLeg = 2, LowerRightLeg = 8, LowerLeftLeg = 3, RightFoot = 9, LeftFoot = 4, UpperLeftArm=15, LowerLeftArm = 16.

	FEATURES	p-value	SVM model that includes the feature
MoCap	1. **Range-NeckBending$_i$** = Max(NeckBendingProfile$_i$) – Min (NeckBendingProfile$_i$)	**0.000**	M1
	2. **FlexionAngles$_i$** = Max (HipAnglesProfile$_i$) – Min (HipAnglesProfile$_i$)	**0.000**	M2,B1
	3. **LeftArmNumberOfPeaks$_i$** (ArmInclinationProfile$_i$)	0.782	M2
	4. **LeftArmMeanHeightPeaks$_i$** (ArmInclinationProfile$_i$)	0.229	M1,B2
	5. **LeftArmDistanceFirstLastPeaks$_i$** (ArmInclinationProfile$_i$)	**0.017**	B2
sEMG	6. **ChangePointDifference$_i$** at Right Lower Back Muscle	**0.023**	E1,E2
	7. **ChangePointDifference$_i$** at Left Lower Back Muscle	**0.013**	E2,B1,B2
	8. **ChangePointDifference$_i$** at Right Upper Back Muscle	**0.033**	E2,B1
	9. **ChangePointDifference$_i$** at Left Upper Back Muscle	**0.001**	E1,E2,B1
	10. **ChangePointTimeRatio$_i$** at Right Lower Back Muscle	**0.026**	E1,B1,B2
	11. **ChangePointTimeRatio$_i$** at Left Lower Back Muscle	**0.039**	E2,B1,B2
	12. **ChangePointTimeRatio$_i$** at Right Upper Back Muscle	0.884	E2,B2
	13. **ChangePointTimeRatio$_i$** at Left Upper Back Muscle	0.092	E2

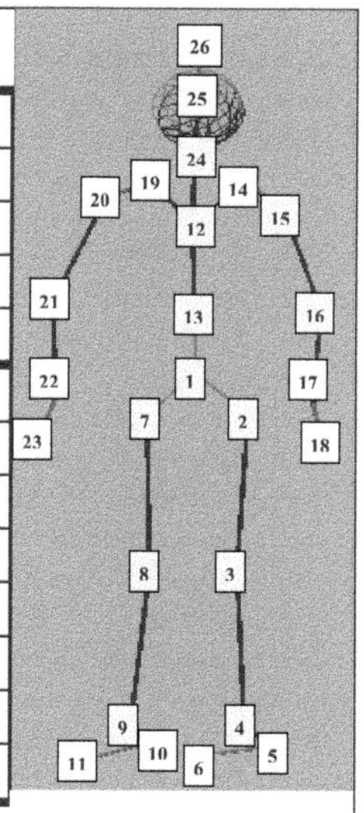

$NeckBendingProfile_i = \{(TopNeck_{it}(z) - LowNeck_{it}(z))/NeckLength_i;\ \forall t=1, \dots, T_i\}$
$SpineBendingProfile_i = \{(LowNeck_{it}(z) - Hip_{it}(z)) / PersonHeight_{it};\ \forall t=1, \dots, T_i\}$
$HipAnglesProfile_i = \{(3D\_Angle(LowNeck_{it}, Hip_{it}, LowerRightLeg_{it}) {}^*- (180 - LeftKneeAngle_{it})^*) + (3D\_Angle(LowNeck_{it}, Hip_{it}, LowerLeftLeg_{it}) {}^*- (180 - RightKneeAngle_{it})^*);\ \forall t=1, \dots, T_i\}$ *The calculations in between two asterisks are done only if the knee is bent forward*
$ArmInclinationProfile_i = \{Savitzky\text{-}Golay\ ((UpperArm_{it}(z) - LowerArm_{it}(z)) / LeftArmLength_{it})$, window size 50, order 1; $\forall t=1, \dots, T_i\}$

$NeckLength_i = 3D\_Distance\ (TopNeck_i, LowNeck_i)$
$LeftKneeAngle_{it} = 3D\_Angle(LeftUpperLeg_{it}, LeftLowerLeg_{it}, LeftFoot_{it})$
$RightKneeAngle_{it} = 3D\_Angle(RightUpperLeg_{it}, RightLowerLeg_{it}, RightFoot_{it})$
$LeftArmLength_i = 3D\_Distance\ (LeftUpperArm_i, LeftLowerArm_i)$
$PersonHeight_i$ = sum of the rigid segments from anatomical node 24 to anatomical node 4

$ChangePointDifference = (\max\{mean(EMGProfile(t-60, t-10)) - mean(EMGProfile(t+10, t+60))\ ;\ \forall t=60, \dots, T_i-60\}) / \max(EMGProfile(0, T_i))$
$ChangePointTimeRatio = (\operatorname{argmax}_t \{ mean(EMGProfile(t-60, t-10)) - mean(EMGProfile(t+10, t+60))\ ;\ \forall t=60, \dots, T_i-60\}) / T_i$

where: Exercise instance i with i=1, … N , N = number of total instances
Frame number t with t=1, …, T_i where T_i is the duration of the instance i;
[anatomical node] = its positional coordinates in the 3D space; [node](z) = its vertical coordinate. (See stick figure)

M1, E1 and B1are the SVM models for control vs. CLBP classification using MoCap features, sEMG features and a bimodal features respectively.
M2, E2 and B2 are the SVM models for high- vs. low-pain classification using MoCap features, sEMG features and a bimodal features respectively.

Table 2. Confusion Matrices showing number of instances.

	M1+ M2 models: Predicted using MoCap features only			
		Control	Low-Pain	High-Pain
Ground Truth	Control	13 (68.4%)	1 (5.3%)	5 (26.3%)
	Low-Pain	0 (0%)	11 (73.3%)	4 (26.7%)
	High-Pain	0 (0%)	4 (26.7%)	11 (73.3%)
	E1+ E2 models: Predicted using sEMG features only			
		Control	Low-Pain	High-Pain
Ground Truth	Control	19 (100%)	0 (0%)	0 (0%)
	Low-Pain	0 (0%)	13 (86.7%)	2 (13.3%)
	High-Pain	2 (13.3%)	4 (26.7%)	9 (60%)
	B1 + B2 models: Predicted using Bi-modal features			
		Control	Low-Pain	High-Pain
Ground Truth	Control	17 (89.4%)	1 (5.3%)	1 (5.3%)
	Low-Pain	0 (0%)	13 (86.7%)	2 (13.3%)
	High-Pain	0 (0%)	3 (20%)	12 (80%)

Next, we investigated the use of a hierarchically-structured SVM framework with two levels. This was done to create an overall three class model: no pain (control instances), low pain and high pain. The SVMs M1, E1 and B1 in level 1 of the hierarchy are trained to discriminate control instances from CLBP instances. If an instance is classed as belonging to the CLBP group, this invokes an SVM in level 2 referred to as M2, E2 or B2 trained to discriminate between high-pain and low-pain instances. We test 3 initial feature sets: MoCap only (M-models: features 1-5), sEMG only (E-models: 6-13) and bi-modal (B-models: 1-13).

For each initial set, we apply a backward feature selection process to prune indiscriminative features and reduce dimensionality. Subject dependent cross-validation (leave-one-subject-out) was applied to the SVM at each level of the hierarchy, which included an evaluation subject to test three different kernels (linear, polynomial and hyperbolic-tangent) as well as grid searching over a range of kernel parameters and the SVM regularisation parameter C. We obtain the following optimal models: MoCap only level 1 (M1) - hyperbolic-tangent kernel with coefficients 0.01 and -0.01, C = 0.01, MoCap only level 2 (M2) hyperbolic-tangent kernel with coefficients 10 and -10, C = 10; sEMG only level 1 (E1) - linear with C = 1, sEMG only level 1 (E2) - hyperbolic-tangent kernel with coefficients 1 and -1, C = 10; bi-modal level 1 (B1) quadratic kernel with C = 1, bi-modal level 2 (B2) -hyperbolic-tangent kernel with coefficients 1 and -1 and C =1. The third column in Table 1 shows which model utilized the described feature as a result of the backward selection. For the MoCap-only experiment, we obtain an overall F1 score of 0.63 with the high pain class as the positive class and an accuracy of 0.71. The sEMG-feature-based model gave a F1 score of 0.69 with an accuracy of 0.84. Using the bi-modal feature set, an F1 score of 0.80 and an accuracy of 0.86 were obtained. Table 2 shows the confusion matrices of the classified instances.

5. DISCUSSION

This study investigated the use of body movement and muscle activity features to detect perceived pain level in a typical exercise used in CLBP physical rehabilitation: reaching forward. The findings show good performance in separating healthy people from CLBP people using bi-modal data or with sEMG only. But to discriminate between low and high perceived pain levels, the use of bi-modal data yields the optimal performance. However, further optimization could include fusion at a decision level which could model the underlying distributions per modality in a better way. The ANOVA tests on each feature and the backward selections show lower back activity and forward flexion angle at the hip to be very important and to a lesser extent bending at the neck and upper back muscle activity. An understanding of important anatomical locations can inform the design of future wearable rehabilitation technology. Such outcomes are timely since unobtrusive low-cost MoCap systems are becoming more accurate and robust. Additionally, new smaller and wearable sEMG sensors make muscle activity measurement more affordable for home-based rehabilitation. In addition, it would be useful to extend this work to other typical exercises to understand the generalizability of the features. For CP rehabilitation, the robust recognition of painful motion can be used in personalized rehabilitation technology [26]. Being able to detect perceived pain would allow the tailoring of the rehabilitation technology to the psychological and physical skills of the patient as described in [9].

6. REFERENCES

[1] Lin, J., Mamykina, L., Lindtner, S., Delajoux G. and Strub H. 2006. Fish'n'Steps: Encouraging Physical Activity with an Interactive Computer Game, *UbiComp*, *LNCS* 4206 261-278.

[2] Schonauer, C., Pintaric, T., Kaufmann, H., Jansen, S. and Vollenbroek-Hutten M. 2011. Chronic pain rehabilitation with a serious game using multimodal input. *Proc. ICVR*, 1-8

[3] Cepeda, M., Carr, D., Lau, J., Alvarez, H. 2006. Music for pain relief. *Cochrane Database of Syst. Rev.* 2.

[4] Crombez, G., Eccleston, C., Van Damme, S., Vlaeyen, J., and Karoly, P. 2012. The fear avoidance model of chronic pain: the next generation. *Clin J Pain* 28, 475-483.

[5] Vlaeyen, J. and Linton, S. 2000. Fear-avoidance and its consequences in chronic musculoskeletal pain: a state of the art. *Pain* 85(3).

[6] Keefe, F. and Block, A. 1982. Development of an observation method for assessing pain behaviour in chronic low back pain patients. *Behaviour Therapy* 13(4), 363-375.

[7] Gatchel, R., Peng, Y., Peters, M. and Turk D. 2007. The biopsychosocial approach to chronic pain: scientific advances and future directions. *Psychol Bull* 133(4), 581–624

[8] Williams A. C. de. C., Eccleston, C, and Morley, S. 2012. Psychological therapies for the management of chronic pain (excluding headache) in adults. *Cochrane Database of Systematic Reviews*, Issue 11. Art. No.CD007407

[9] Singh, A., Klapper, A., Swann-Sternberg, T, *et al.* 2014. Motivating People with Chronic Pain to do Physical Activity: Opportunities for Technology Design, *ACM ,CHI' 2014.*

[10] Turk, D. and Okifuji, A. 2002. Psychological factors in chronic pain: evolution and revolution. *J Consult Clin. Psychol.* 70(3), 678–690.

[11] Romera-Paredes, B., Aung, M., Pontil, M., Watson, P., Williams, A CdeC, and Bianchi Berthouze, N. 2013. Transfer Learning to Account for Idiosyncrasy in Face and Body Expressions. *10th IEEE Int. Conf. Auto. Face & Gesture Rec.*

[12] Littlewort, G., Barlett, M., and Lee, K. 2009. Automatic coding of facial expressions displayed during posed and genuine pain. *Image Vision Comp* 27(12), 1797-1803.

[13] Niese, R., Al-Hamadi, A., Panning, A. *et al. 2009. Towa*rds Pain Recognition in Post Operative Phases using 3D based features from Video and Support Vector Machines. *Int J. Digital Content Tech. App.* 3(4).

[14] Rudovic, O., Pavlovic, V., and Pantic, M. 2013. Automatic Pain Intensity Estimation with Heteroscedastic Conditional Random Fields. *Adv. in Vis. Comp., Springer.* 8034, 234-243.

[15] Kaltwang, S., Rudovic, O., and Pantic, M. 2012. Continuous Pain Intensity Estimation from Facial Expressions. *Adv. in Vis.Comp., Springer, Heidelberg,* 7432, 368-377.

[16] Hammal, Z., and Cohn, J. F. 2012. Automatic detection of pain intensity. *14th Int. Conf. Multimodal Interaction*, 47-52.

[17] Aung, M., Romera-Paredes, B., *et al.* 2013. Getting rid of pain related behaviour to improve social and self perception: a technology based perspective. *14th Int. Workshop on Image. Anal. Multimedia Interactive Services.*1-4.

[18] Kleinsmith, A., and Bianchi-Berthouze, N. 2013. Affective Body Expression Perception and Recognition: A Survey. *IEEE Trans. on Affective Computing* 4(1), 15-33.

[19] Savva, N., Scarinzi, A., and Bianchi-Berthouze, N. 2012. Continuous Recognition of Player's Affective Body Expression as Dynamic Quality of Aesthetic Experience. *IEEE Trans. CIAIG 3*, 199–212.

[20] Watson, P., Booker, K., and Main, C. 1997. Evidence for the role of Psychological Factors in Abnormal Paraspinal Activity in Patients with Chronic Low Back Pain. *J. Musculoskelet. Pain* 5(4), 41-56.

[21] Van der Hulst, M., Vollenbroek-Hutton, M., Reitman, J. *et al.* 2010. Back Muscle Activation Patterns in Chronic Low Back Pain during Walking: A "Guarding" Hypothesis. *Clin J Pain* 26(1), 30-37

[22] Geisser, M., Haig, A., Wallbom, A., and Wiggert, E. 2004. Pain-related fear, lumbar flexion, and dynamic SEMG among persons with chronic musculoskeletal low back pain. *Clin J Pain.* 20(2), 61-69

[23] Aung, M.S.H., Kaltwang S., *et al.* 2014. Detecting Chronic Pain-Related Expressions and Behaviours from Multimodal Naturalistic Data. *IEEE Trans. on Affective Computing* (in submission).

[24] Rainville, J., Ahern, D., Phalen, L. et al. 1992. The Association of Pain with Physical Activities in Chronic Low Back Pain. *Spine 17*(9), 1060-1064.

[25] Marple-Horvat, D. E. and Gilbey, S. L. 1992. A method for automatic identification of periods of muscular activity from EMG recordings. *J Neurosci Mtds 42*(3), 163-167.

[26] Jensen, M., Turner, J., and Romano, J. 2001. Changes in beliefs, catastrophizing and coping are associated with improvement in multidisciplinary pain treatment. *J Cons Clin Psychol* 69(4), 655-662.

A World without Barriers: Connecting the World across Languages, Distances and Media

Prof. Dr. Alexander Waibel
Carnegie Mellon University, USA
Karlsruhe Institute of Technology, Germany

Abstract

As our world becomes increasingly interdependent and globalization brings people together more than ever, we quickly discover that it is no longer the absence of connectivity (the "digital divide") that separates us, but that new and different forms of alienation still keep us apart, including language, culture, distance and interfaces. Can technology provide solutions to bring us closer to our fellow humans?

In this talk, I will present multilingual and multimodal interface technology solutions that offer the best of both worlds: maintaining our cultural diversity and locale while providing for better communication, greater integration and collaboration.

We explore:

- Smart phone based speech translators for everyday travelers and humanitarian missions
- Simultaneous translation systems and services to translate academic lectures and political speeches in real time (at Universities, the European Parliament and broadcasting services)
- Multimodal language-transparent interfaces and smartrooms to improve joint and distributed communication and interaction.

We will first discuss the difficulties of language processing; review how the technology works today and what levels of performance are now possible. Key to today's systems is effective machine learning, without which scaling multilingual and multimodal systems to unlimited domains, modalities, accents, and more than 6,000 languages would be hopeless. Equally important are effective human-computer interfaces, so that language differences fade naturally into the background and communication and interaction become natural and engaging. I will present recent research results as well as examples from our field trials and deployments in educational, commercial, humanitarian and government settings.

ICMI'14, November 12–16, 2014, Istanbul, Turkey.
ACM 978-1-4503-2885-2/14/11.
http://dx.doi.org/10.1145/2663204.2666280.

Categories and Subject Descriptors

H.5.2 [**Information interfaces and presentation (e.g., HCI)**]: User Interfaces (D.2.2, H.1.2, I.3.6): Evaluation/methodology; Interaction styles (e.g., commands, menus, forms, direct manipulation); User-centered design; Natural language; Voice I/O

Keywords

Mulimodal Interfaces; Speech Translation; Human-Computer Interaction; Multilingual Systems, Computer Supported, Human-Human Interaction; Machine Learning.

BIO

Dr. Alexander Waibel is a Professor of Computer Science at Carnegie Mellon University, Pittsburgh and at the Karlsruhe Institute of Technology, Germany. He is the director of the International Center for Advanced Communication Technologies (interACT). The Center works in a network with eight of the world's top research institutions. The Center's mission is to develop multimodal and multilingual human communication technologies that improve human-human and human-machine communication. Prof. Waibel's team developed and demonstrated the first speech translation systems in Europe&USA (1990/1991 (ICASSP'91)), the world's first simultaneous lecture translation system (2005), and Jibbigo, the world's first commercial speech translator on a phone (2009 (www.jibbigo.com)).

Dr. Waibel was a founder and served as chairmen of C-STAR, the Consortium for Speech Translation Advanced Research in 1991. Since then he directed and coordinated many research programs in speech, translation, multimodal interfaces and machine learning in the US, Europe and Asia. He currently serves as director of EU-Bridge, a large scale European multi-site Integrated Project aimed at developing speech translation services for Europe. He also serves as co-director of IMMI, a joint venture between KIT, CNRS & RWTH and as principal investigator of US and European research programs on machine learning, language portability and performance. Following the acquisition of Jibbigo in 2013, he also served as

Director of Engineering at Facebook and established the FB Language Technology Group.

Dr. Waibel has received several awards for pioneering work on multilingual and multimodal communication technology. He has published extensively (>650 publications, >20,000 citations, h-index 73) in the field, and received/filed numerous patents.

During his career, Dr. Waibel founded and built 10 successful companies. The latest, Jibbigo, built and distributed the world's first speech-translator on a smart phone and was acquired and merged with Facebook in 2013. Since 2007, Dr. Waibel and his team deployed these technologies in humanitarian and disaster relief missions to improve communication between healthcare providers and patients in remote areas of the developing world.

Dr. Waibel received his BS, MS and PhD degrees at MIT and CMU, respectively.

Emotion Recognition In The Wild Challenge 2014: Baseline, Data and Protocol

Abhinav Dhall
Vision & Sensing Group
University of Canberra/
Australian National University
abhinav.dhall@anu.edu.au

Roland Goecke
Vision & Sensing Group
University of Canberra/
Australian National University
roland.goecke@ieee.org

Jyoti Joshi
Vision & Sensing Group
University of Canberra
jyoti.joshi@canberra.edu.au

Karan Sikka
Machine Perception Lab
Univesity of California
San Diego
karan.sikka@ucsd.edu

Tom Gedeon
Res. School of Computer
Science
Australian National University
tom.gedeon@anu.edu.au

ABSTRACT

The Second Emotion Recognition In The Wild Challenge (EmotiW) 2014 consists of an audio-video based emotion classification challenge, which mimics the real-world conditions. Traditionally, emotion recognition has been performed on data captured in constrained lab-controlled like environment. While this data was a good starting point, such lab controlled data poorly represents the environment and conditions faced in real-world situations. With the exponential increase in the number of video clips being uploaded online, it is worthwhile to explore the performance of emotion recognition methods that work 'in the wild'. The goal of this Grand Challenge is to carry forward the common platform defined during EmotiW 2013, for evaluation of emotion recognition methods in real-world conditions. The database in the 2014 challenge is the Acted Facial Expression In Wild (AFEW) 4.0, which has been collected from movies showing close-to-real-world conditions. The paper describes the data partitions, the baseline method and the experimental protocol.

Categories and Subject Descriptors

I.6.3 [**Pattern Recognition**]: Applications; H.2.8 [**Database Applications**]: Image Databases; I.4.m [**IMAGE PROCESSING AND COMPUTER VISION**]: Miscellaneous

General Terms

Experimentation, emotion recognition

ICMI '14, November 12 - 16 2014, Istanbul, Turkey
Copyright 2014 ACM 978-1-4503-2885-2/14/11 ...$15.00.
http://dx.doi.org/10.1145/2663204.2666275.

Keywords

Audio-video data corpus; Emotion recognition in the wild; EmotiW challenge.

1. INTRODUCTION

This paper describes the baseline, data and experimental protocol for the Second Emotion Recognition In The Wild Challenge (EmotiW) 2014. The recent advancement of social media has given users a platform to socially engage and interact with a larger population. Millions of images and videos are being uploaded every day by users on the web from different events and social gatherings. There is an increasing interest in designing systems capable of understanding human manifestations of emotional attributes and affective displays. Inferring the affective state of the users in images and videos, that are captured under real-world conditions, robust methods capable of performing facial expression analysis 'in the wild' are required. Here, the term **'in the wild'** signifies variability in environments/scenes and backgrounds, illumination conditions, head pose, occlusion *etc.* Automatic emotion analysis has made a significant progress over the last two decades. However, most of these frameworks have been restricted and evaluated on data collected in controlled laboratory settings with frontal faces, perfect illumination and posed expressions. To overcome this limitation, EmotiW 2014 provides a platform for researchers to create, extend and test their methods on a common 'in the wild' benchmarked data.

EmotiW 2014 follows the guidelines of the first EmotiW 2013 challenge and is based on the Acted Facial Expressions in the Wild (AFEW) database [ ]. Generally, face related databases have been collected in controlled environments (ambient lighting, simple and consistent background). However, for adapting emotion recognition approaches, that work well on controlled data, to real-world data, databases representing varied scenarios are required. Recently, few databases (e.g. AFEW [ ], GENKI [ ], Static Facial Expressions in the Wild [ ] and Happy People Images [ ] etc.), which represent real-world settings have been released.

There are several challenges to be tackled for emotion recognition 'in the wild'. Consider an illustrative example of categorization i.e. assigning an emotion label to a video clip of a subject(s) protesting at the Tahrir square in Egypt during the 2011 protests. In order to learn an automatic system for inferring the emotion label, labeled data containing video clips representing different emotions in diverse settings are required. A number of standard databases such as the Cohn-Kanade (CK) [ ], Multi-PIE [ ], FEEDTUM [ ] and RU-FACS [ ], exist and include both static and dynamic data of subjects displaying a fixed set of expressions. However, all of these databases contain samples with posed/spontaneous expressions under lab-controlled conditions. The field of facial expression recognition should ideally collect spontaneous data in uncontrolled settings to tackle challenges of real-world data. However, collecting spontaneous data in real-world conditions is a tedious task. Therefore, new methods which can speed up the process of creating databases representing real-world conditions are required.

Once the data is available, the next challenge is the detection of face and its constituent parts, followed by Head Pose Normalisation (HPN). It is obvious that a subject in an uncontrolled setting, such as the Tahrir square video clip example, may freely move his/her head leading of out-of-plane head movements. Such a setting gives rise to another challenge and adversely effects the performance of face and facial parts detections, that are required by HPN. It is also known that alignment in case of non-frontal faces is a non-trivial task and can further introduce noise/error during the feature extraction step. During spontaneous expressions, subjects also move their arms and hands as part of the non-verbal communication, leading to the problem of occlusion. Occlusion needs to be then detected and localised for finding accurate fiducial points. The problem becomes more severe with multiple subjects in the scene. Though EmotiW 2013 & 2014 deal with a single subject based emotion recognition, a future challenge for emotion recognition methods is to handle multiple subjects in a scene (e.g. [ ]).

From the audio modality perspective, one of the primary challenge is modeling background noise. In case of databases such as AFEW, background noise can be either music or sound, that may describe the context of the scene. Thus it needs to be investigated whether such background is correlated with the underlying emotion. Other related issues for speech modeling are (1) exploring approaches for dealing with variable length samples, (2) selecting robust features to describe the speech signal, among others. Emotion recognition in the wild is a problem involving multiple modalities and thus information cues can also be extracted from non-verbal body gesture and scenes. Thus exploring techniques for combining these multiple modalities for facial expression in the wild is a challenge in itself.

From choosing a classifier perspective, it needs to be investigated as on how beneficial are classifiers which explicitly handle the temporal nature of emotion as compared to regular classifiers? Papers in EmotiW 2013 used classification methods such as the Multiple Kernel Learning (MKL) [ ], deep learning [ ] etc. In a recent study [ ], authors compared the performance of graphical methods such as Conditional Random Field (CRF) with Support Vector Machine (SVM) on the AFEW data. They found that CRF out performed SVM based emotion recognition method.

2. EMOTIW 2013

In the first EmotiW challenge, a total of 27 teams registered for the challenge and 9 teams submitted test labels.

Attribute	Description
Length of sequences	300-5400 ms
No. of annotators	3
Emotion classes	Anger, Disgust, Fear, Happiness, Neutral, Sadness and Surprise
Total No. of clips	2577
Video format	AVI
Audio format	WAV

Table 1: Attributes of AFEW 4.0 database. EmotiW 2014 data is a subset of the AFEW 4.0 data.

Challenge	# of Samples	# of Subjects	Age Range	# of Movies
EmotiW 2013	1088	315	34.60	75
EmotiW 2014	1368	428	34.40	111

Table 2: Comparison of data and subject specifications in EmotiW 2013 and EmotiW 2014 challenges.

The database for the challenge was AFEW 3.0 [ ]. The data was divided into three sets: *Train*, *Val* and *Test*. [ ], proposed a deep learning based emotion recognition method and their system performed the best (41.02%) out of all participants. They used external data downloaded from Google along with the AFEW data. The second best performance is from the team of [ ]. They proposed a MKL based approach, where different modalities are fused as different kernels. They used AFEW data only for training the MKL classifier. The second runner up is from the team of [ ]. A method based on partial least square regression on Grassmannian manifolds was proposed. An early noisy aligned face removal is performed using PCA as a pre-processing step. Figure 1 compares the classification accuracy of EmotiW 2013 participants with the baseline and among each other. To validate the methods, a second on-site test was also conducted. A small test set was provided to the participants at the event.

Various important points regarding the problem of emotion recognition in challenging situations were discussed during the EmotiW 2013 event at Sydney. Labelling emotion on data from movie poses various challenges. We have updated the labelling process in EmotiW 2014 (w.r.t. to EmotiW 2013). We had noticed that a biase can be introduced in

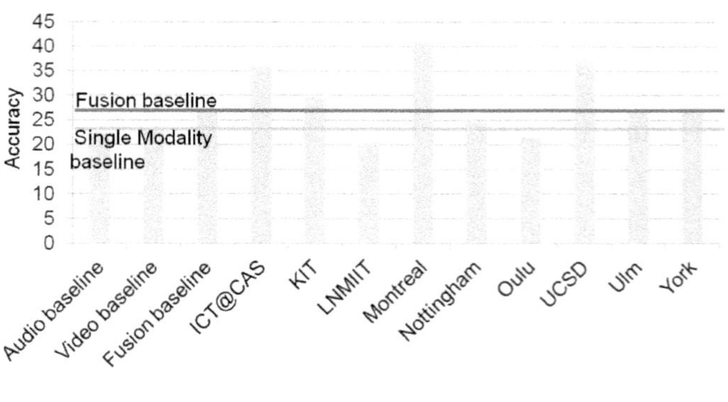

Figure 1: The graph compares the performance of participants of the first EmotiW 2013 challenge [ ].

Set	# of Subjects	Max Age	Avg. Age	Min. Age	# of Males	# of Females
Train	177	76	34.09	5	102	75
Val	136	70	35.12	10	78	58
Test	115	88	34.01	5	64	51

Table 3: Subjects attributes of subjects of the EmotiW 2014 data. Age is represented in years.

few of the video clip's labels in some cases, when the labeller knows about the movie (context or generally seen the movie before) and clips are played in sequence from the same movie. Therefore, this year, a sanity check has been added, wherein 3 labellers labelled all the samples in a random order. The new labels were compared with the semi-automatic process and among each other. The samples which had agreement were kept. Samples with no consensus were ignored. In emotion labelling, there are several other challenges such as ethnicity of labellers and type of emotion labelling (discrete/continous). In the current, AFEW 4.0, discrete emotion labelling is used as it is non-trivial to label using continuous labelling or action units in datasets such as the AFEW. Furthermore, it was discussed that some samples in the AFEW database may contain multiple expressions, for e.g. a short duration Neutral expression followed by a longer duration Happy expression (displayed by the same subject). In these cases the label is assigned to the dominating emotion. Even though there may be a secondary expression, which is exhibited by an actor, other cues such as audio, body language and context can help in disambiguating the sample's final emotion label. For AFEW 4.0, the labellers have removed samples which were ambiguous i.e. which had multiple expressions on actor's face and difficult to assign a single emotion label. Though, this issue also sparks an interesting question. Is this the right time to move to assigning multiple labels for to single sample? From the example above, this means assigning both Happy and Neutral to a sample, ranked by their dominance. From a machine learning perspective, weakly labelled learning approaches (which have recently found success in affect analysis task such as pain classification [ ]) can also be used for emotion recognition in such scenarios.

3. DATA

AFEW is developed using a semi-automatic process. Subtitle for Deaf & Hearing impaired (SDH) closed captions are parsed for presence of keywords related to emotion such as

Functionals
Arithmetic Mean
standard deviation
skewness, kurtosis
quartiles, quartile ranges
percentile 1%, 99%
percentile range
Position max./min
up-level time 75/90
linear regression coeff.
linear regression error(quadratic/absolute)

Table 4: Set of functionals applied to LLD.

Low Level Descriptors (LLD)	
Energy/Spectral LLD	PCM Loudness MFCC [0-14] log Mel Frequency Band [0-7] Line Spectral Pairs (LSP) frequency [0-7] F0 F0 Envelope
Voicing related LLD	Voicing Prob. Jitter Local Jitter consecutive frame pairs Shimmer Local

Table 5: Audio feature set - 38 (34 + 4) low-level descriptors.

'angry', 'cry', 'sad' etc. Short sequences which contain the keyword are selected by the labeller if it contains relevant data. The details of database collection are discussed in [ ]. For EmotiW 2014, the database is divided into three subsets: *Train* (578 samples), *Val* (383 samples) and *Test* (407 samples). EmotiW 2014 data is a subset of the AFEW 4.0 database. The current version, EmotiW 2014, available at http://cs.anu.edu.au/few contains two labelled sets. These are extended versions of the EmotiW 2013 [ ] sets are used for training and validation; for testing, new unseen data is used. Table 2 and 3 compare and describe the data statistics of EmotiW 2013 and 2014 data. The task in the challenge is to classify a sample (audio-video clip) into one of the seven emotion categories: *Anger*, *Disgust*, *Fear*, *Happiness*, *Neutral*, *Sadness* and *Surprise*. The labeled *Train* and *Val* sets were made available early in April and the new, unlabeled test set was made available in July 2014. There are no separate audio-only, video-only or audio-video challenges. Participants are free to use either modality or combinations. Participants are allowed to use their own features and classification methods. The labels of the testing set are not shared with the participants. Participants will need to adhere to the definition of *Train*, *Val* and *Test* sets. In their papers, they may report on results obtained on the *Train* and *Val* sets, but only the results on the *Test* set will be taken into account for the overall Grand Challenge results.

4. BASELINE

4.1 Visual Analysis

For face and fiducial points detection the Mixture of Parts (MoPs) framework [ ] is applied to the video frames. The Intraface tracker [ ] is used to track the fiducial points initialised using MoPs framework. The fiducial points are used to align the faces. Further, spatio-temporal features are extracted on the aligned faces.

4.1.1 Volume Local Binary Patterns

Local Binary Pattern - Three Orthogonal Planes (LBP-TOP) [ ] is a popular descriptor in computer vision. It considers patterns in three orthogonal planes: XY, XT and YT, and concatenates the pattern co-occurrences in these three directions. The local binary pattern (LBP-TOP) descriptor assigns binary labels to pixels by thresholding the neighborhood pixels with the central value. Therefore for a center pixel $\mathcal{O}_p$ of an orthogonal plane $\mathcal{O}$ and it's neighboring pixels N_i, a decimal value is assigned to it:

$$d = \sum_{\mathcal{O}}^{XY,XT,YT} \sum_{p} \sum_{i=1}^{k} 2^{i-1} I(\mathcal{O}_p, N_i) \quad (1)$$

LBP-TOP is computed block wise on the aligned faces of a video.

4.2 Audio Features

In this challenge, a set of audio features similar to the features employed in Audio Video Emotion Recognition Challenge 2011 [ ] motivated from the INTERSPEECH 2010 Paralinguistic challenge (1582 features) [ ] are used. The features are extracted using the open-source Emotion and Affect Recognition (openEAR) [ ] toolkit backend openSMILE [ ].

The feature set consists of 34 energy & spectral related low-level descriptors (LLD) × 21 functionals, 4 voicing related LLD × 19 functionals, 34 delta coefficients of energy & spectral LLD × 21 functionals, 4 delta coefficients of the voicing related LLD × 19 functionals and 2 voiced/unvoiced durational features. Table 4 and 5 describe the details of LLD features and functionals.

5. BASELINE EXPERIMENTS

For computing the baseline results, openly available libraries are used. Pre-trained face models available with the MoPS [ ] is applied for face detection and initialisation of the Intraface tracking libray [ ]. The fiducial points generated by Intraface are used for aligning the face and the face size is set to 128 × 128.

Post aligning LBP-TOP features are extracted from non-overlapping spatial 4×4 blocks. The LBP-TOP feature from each block are concatenated to create one feature vector. The concatenation is done left-to-right and top-to-bottom. Non-linear RBF kernel based SVM is learnt for emotion classification. The video only baseline system ($\mathbf{Val_{video}}$) achieves 33.15% classification accuracy on the *Val* set. The audio only baseline system is computed by extracting features using the OpenSmile toolkit. A linear SVM classifier is learnt. The audio only based system ($\mathbf{Val_{audio}}$)gives 26.10% classification accuracy on the *Val* set. A feature level fusion ($\mathbf{Val_{audio\text{-}video}}$) is performed, where the audio and video features are concatenated and a non-linear RBF kernel based SVM is learnt. The performance drops here and the classification accuracy is 28.19%. For 12 samples in the *Val* set, the face detection step failed. Therefore, for $\mathbf{Val_{audio\text{-}video}}$, wherever, face detection failed, audio only model was used.

On the *Test* set, the video only baseline system ($\mathbf{Test_{video}}$) accuracy is 33.66%; audio only based system ($\mathbf{Test_{audio}}$) classification accuracy is 26.78% and audio-video feature fusion ($\mathbf{Test_{audio\text{-}video}}$) is 24.57%. Table 8, Table 7 and Table 9 describe the classification accuracy of audio only, only and audio-video on the *Val* set. Table 11, Table 10 and Table 12 describe the classification accuracy of audio only, video only and audio-video on the *Test* set. The class-wise and overall accuracy are summarised in Table 6. The baseline performance are self-explanatory that emotion recognition in challenging conditions is a non-trivial problem. On investigating the reason for low performance of the baseline methods, several limitations were discovered. For video, there are several samples in the database for which the faces are poorly localised. The localisation error is further propagates in the fiducial point detection step. Furthermore, erroneous facial parts location lead to poor face alignment. Generally, if the face is non-frontal the fiducial parts detection quality can be poor. This leads to error in alignment and feature analysis. Recent, methods such as fiducial points free HPN [ ] can be one option for handling non-frontal faces in the wild. Also, features like LBP-TOP may miss the salient frames in some samples from databases such as the AFEW, as it is unknown, when an apex of the expression will occur. Therefore, methods such as the one based on multiple instance learning [ ] can be useful. For audio features, it is important for the method to know, if the speech in a scene belongs to the person of interest and not part of the background? Modelling background music score is challenging. The feature fusion performance on the *Val* and *Test* sets results in decrease in performance. This can be attributed to noise in the features and high dimensionality. Feature selection methods will be experimented with in future for increasing the performance of the audio-video analysis method.

	An	Di	Fe	Ha	Ne	Sa	Su
An	32	6	3	8	9	1	5
Di	7	10	3	4	9	2	5
Fe	15	4	7	8	5	4	3
Ha	4	3	9	36	5	6	0
Ne	4	5	4	11	12	13	4
Sa	5	7	6	10	19	10	4
Su	3	5	7	5	14	2	10

Table 7: Classification accuracy performance of $\mathbf{Val_{video}}$: the video system on the *Val* set. For 12 samples in the *Val* test the face detection step failed, these were regarded as failure cases and this was attributed to the final accuracy for the *Val* set.

	An	Di	Fe	Ha	Ne	Sa	Su
An	35	6	4	5	5	5	4
Di	11	1	1	8	13	3	3
Fe	12	5	9	9	5	2	4
Ha	12	6	6	23	9	4	3
Ne	12	7	4	17	22	1	0
Sa	2	14	12	12	10	7	4
Su	11	3	8	10	7	4	3

Table 8: Classification accuracy performance of $\mathbf{Val_{audio}}$: the audio system on the *Val* set.

6. CONCLUSION

The Second Emotion Recognition In The Wild Challenge 2014 provides a platform for researchers to benchmark and compete with their emotion recognition method on the Acted Facial Expressions In The Wild database. Emotion recognition in the wild is a challenging problem due to diversity in the scenes in the form of head pose, illumination, occlusion and background noise. This year's challenge carry forwards the platform started by the First Emotion Recognition In The Wild Challenge. The paper discusses the data partitions, baseline and experimental protocol. The performance of the baseline method is low, which speaks for the scope of work required in developing emotion recognition systems, which work well in the real-world conditions.

	Anger	Disgust	Fear	Happiness	Neutral	Sadness	Surprise	Overall
$\mathbf{Val}_{\mathbf{audio}}$	54.68	00.025	19.56	36.50	34.92	11.47	00.065	26.10
$\mathbf{Test}_{\mathbf{audio}}$	34.48	15.38	26.08	25.92	30.76	26.41	00.08	26.78
$\mathbf{Val}_{\mathbf{video}}$	50.00	25.00	15.21	57.14	34.92	16.39	21.73	33.15
$\mathbf{Test}_{\mathbf{video}}$	36.21	34.61	26.08	41.97	40.17	22.64	00.76	33.66
$\mathbf{Val}_{\mathbf{audio\text{-}video}}$	68.75	00.00	13.04	25.39	34.92	24.59	10.86	28.19
$\mathbf{Test}_{\mathbf{audio\text{-}video}}$	41.37	15.38	21.73	23.45	23.07	24.52	11.53	24.57

Table 6: Classification accuracy for *Val* and *Test* sets for *audio*, *video* and *audio-video* modalities.

	An	Di	Fe	Ha	Ne	Sa	Su
An	44	1	2	6	3	6	2
Di	11	0	2	8	9	9	1
Fe	15	3	6	6	6	7	3
Ha	16	4	4	16	12	7	4
Ne	7	10	2	9	22	7	6
Sa	8	8	7	13	5	15	5
Su	8	3	4	10	9	7	5

Table 9: Classification accuracy performance of $\mathbf{Val}_{\mathbf{audio\text{-}video}}$: the audio-video fusion system on the *Val* set.

	An	Di	Fe	Ha	Ne	Sa	Su
An	21	7	6	2	14	5	3
Di	2	9	1	3	5	5	1
Fe	8	5	12	5	9	5	2
Ha	5	5	4	34	8	22	3
Ne	9	14	11	10	47	22	4
Sa	9	7	4	7	10	12	4
Su	4	0	5	4	5	6	2

Table 10: Classification accuracy performance of $\mathbf{Test}_{\mathbf{video}}$: the video system on the *Test* set.

	An	Di	Fe	Ha	Ne	Sa	Su
An	20	6	7	7	7	4	7
Di	2	4	2	8	4	6	0
Fe	5	11	12	6	1	4	7
Ha	10	13	6	21	20	6	5
Ne	12	18	16	16	36	12	7
Sa	6	8	12	9	2	14	2
Su	6	1	6	6	2	3	2

Table 11: Classification accuracy performance of $\mathbf{Test}_{\mathbf{audio}}$: the audio system on the *Test* set.

	An	Di	Fe	Ha	Ne	Sa	Su
An	24	2	3	7	6	23	4
Di	5	4	2	7	4	3	1
Fe	9	0	10	7	2	7	11
Ha	16	5	7	19	15	13	6
Ne	13	14	8	29	27	15	11
Sa	13	2	6	12	3	13	4
Su	7	1	4	4	3	4	3

Table 12: Classification accuracy performance of $\mathbf{Test}_{\mathbf{audio\text{-}video}}$: the audio-video fusion system on the *Test* set.

APPENDIX

Movie Names: 21, About a boy, After the sunset, American, American History X, And Soon Came the Darkness, Aviator, Black Swan, Bridesmaids, Captivity, Carrie, Change Up, Chernobyl Diaries, Children of Men, Crying Game, December Boys, Deep Blue Sea, Descendants, Did You Hear About the Morgans?, Dumb and Dumberer: When Harry Met Lloyd, Elizabeth, Empire of the Sun, Evil Dead, Eyes Wide Shut, Extremely Loud & Incredibly Close, Feast, Four Weddings and a Funeral, Friends with Benefits, Frost/Nixon, Ghoshtship, Girl with a Pearl Earring, Gone In Sixty Seconds, Grudge, Grudge 2, Grudge 3, Hall Pass, Halloween, Halloween Resurrection, Hangover, Harry Potter and the Philosopher's Stone, Harry Potter and the Chamber of Secrets, Harry Potter and the Deathly Hallows Part 1, Harry Potter and the Deathly Hallows Part 2, Harry Potter and the Goblet of Fire, Harry Potter and the Half Blood Prince, Harry Potter and the Order Of Phoenix, Harry Potter and the Prisoners Of Azkaban, Harold & Kumar go to the White Castle, House of Wax, I Am Sam, It's Complicated, I Think I Love My Wife, Jaws 2, Jennifer's Body, Little Manhattan, Messengers, Mama, Mission Impossible 2, Miss March, My Left Foot, Nothing but the Truth, Notting Hill, One Flew Over the Cuckoo's Nest, Orange and Sunshine, Pretty in Pink, Pretty Woman, Remember Me, Runaway Bride, Quartet, Romeo Juliet, Saw 3D, Serendipity, Silver Lining Playbook, Solitary Man, Something Borrowed, Terms of Endearment, The American, The Aviator, The Caller, The Devil Wears Prada, The Girl with Dragon Tattoo, The Hangover, The Haunting of Molly Hartley, The Informant!, The King's Speech, The Pink Panther 2, The Ring 2, The Social Network, The Terminal, The Town, Valentine Day, Unstoppable, Uninvited, Valkyrie, Vanilla Sky, Woman In Black, Wrong Turn 3, You've Got Mail.

A. REFERENCES

[1] M. S. Bartlett, G. Littlewort, M. G. Frank, C. Lainscsek, I. R. Fasel, and J. R. Movellan. Automatic recognition of facial actions in spontaneous expressions. *Journal of Multimedia*, 1(6):22–35, 2006.

[2] A. Dhall, R. Goecke, J. Joshi, M. Wagner, and T. Gedeon. Emotion recognition in the wild challenge 2013. In *Proceedings of the ACM on International Conference on Multimodal Interaction (ICMI)*, pages 509–516, 2013.

[3] A. Dhall, R. Goecke, S. Lucey, and T. Gedeon. Acted Facial Expressions in the Wild Database. In *Technical Report*, 2011.

[4] A. Dhall, R. Goecke, S. Lucey, and T. Gedeon. Static Facial Expression Analysis In Tough Conditions:

Data, Evaluation Protocol And Benchmark. In *Proceedings of the IEEE International Conference on Computer Vision and Workshops BEFIT*, pages 2106–2112, 2011.

[5] A. Dhall, R. Goecke, S. Lucey, and T. Gedeon. Collecting large, richly annotated facial-expression databases from movies. *IEEE Multimedia*, 19(3):0034, 2012.

[6] A. Dhall, J. Joshi, I. Radwan, and R. Goecke. Finding Happiest Moments in a Social Context. In *Proceedings of the Asian Conference on Computer Vision (ACCV)*, pages 613–626, 2012.

[7] A. Dhall, K. Sikka, G. Littlewort, R. Goecke, and M. Bartlett. A Discriminative Parts Based Model Approach for Fiducial Points Free and Shape Constrained Head Pose Normalisation In The Wild. In *Proceedings of the IEEE Winter Conference on Applications of Computer Vision*, pages 1–8, 2014.

[8] F. Eyben, M. Wollmer, and B. Schuller. OpenearâĂŤintroducing the munich open-source emotion and affect recognition toolkit. In *Proceedings of the International Conference on Affective Computing and Intelligent Interaction (ACII)*, pages 1–6, 2009.

[9] F. Eyben, M. Wöllmer, and B. Schuller. Opensmile: the munich versatile and fast open-source audio feature extractor. In *Proceedings of the ACM International Conference on Multimedia (MM)*, pages 1459–1462, 2010.

[10] P. F. Felzenszwalb and D. P. Huttenlocher. Pictorial Structures for Object Recognition. *International Journal on Computer Vision*, 61(1):55–79, 2005.

[11] R. Gross, I. Matthews, J. F. Cohn, T. Kanade, and S. Baker. Multi-PIE. In *Proceedings of the IEEE International Conference on Automatic Face and Gesture Recognition (FG)*, pages 1–8, 2008.

[12] S. E. Kahou, C. Pal, X. Bouthillier, P. Froumenty, S. Jean, K. R. Konda, P. Vincent, A. Courville, and Y. Bengio. Combining modality specific deep neural networks for emotion recognition in video. In *Proceedings of the ACM on International Conference on Multimodal Interaction (ICMI)*, pages 543–550, 2013.

[13] T. Kanade, J. F. Cohn, and Y. Tian. Comprehensive database for facial expression analysis. In *Proceedings of the IEEE International Conference on Automatic Face and Gesture Recognition (FG)*, pages 46–53, 2000.

[14] M. Liu, R. Wang, Z. Huang, S. Shan, and X. Chen. Partial least squares regression on grassmannian manifold for emotion recognition. In *Proceedings of the ACM on International Conference on Multimodal Interaction (ICMI)*, pages 525–530, 2013.

[15] S. Nowee. *Facial Expression Recognition in the Wild: The Influence of Temporal Information.* PhD thesis, University of Amsterdam, 2014.

[16] B. Schuller, S. Steidl, A. Batliner, F. Burkhardt, L. Devillers, C. A. Müller, and S. S. Narayanan. The interspeech 2010 paralinguistic challenge. In *INTERSPEECH*, pages 2794–2797, 2010.

[17] B. Schuller, M. Valstar, F. Eyben, G. McKeown, R. Cowie, and M. Pantic. Avec 2011–the first international audio/visual emotion challenge. In *Proceedings of the International Conference on Affective Computing and Intelligent Interaction (ACII)*, pages 415–424, 2011.

[18] K. Sikka, A. Dhall, and M. Bartlett. Weakly supervised pain localization using multiple instance learning. *Proceedings of the IEEE International Conference and Workshops on Automatic Face and Gesture Recognition (FG)*, pages 1–8, 2013.

[19] K. Sikka, K. Dykstra, S. Sathyanarayana, G. Littlewort, and M. Bartlett. Multiple kernel learning for emotion recognition in the wild. In *Proceedings of the ACM on International Conference on Multimodal Interaction (ICMI)*, pages 517–524, 2013.

[20] F. Wallhoff. Facial expressions and emotion database, 2006. `http://www.mmk.ei.tum.de/~waf/fgnet/feedtum.html`.

[21] J. Whitehill, G. Littlewort, I. R. Fasel, M. S. Bartlett, and J. R. Movellan. Toward Practical Smile Detection. *IEEE Transaction on Pattern Analysis and Machine Intelligence*, 31(11):2106–2111, 2009.

[22] X. Xiong and F. De la Torre. Supervised descent method and its applications to face alignment. In *Proceedings of the IEEE Conference on Computer Vision and Pattern Recognition (CVPR)*, pages 532–539, 2013.

[23] G. Zhao and M. Pietikainen. Dynamic texture recognition using local binary patterns with an application to facial expressions. *IEEE Transaction on Pattern Analysis and Machine Intelligence*, 29(6):915–928, 2007.

[24] X. Zhu and D. Ramanan. Face detection, pose estimation, and landmark localization in the wild. In *Proceedings of the IEEE Conference on Computer Vision and Pattern Recognition (CVPR)*, pages 2879–2886, 2012.

Neural Networks for Emotion Recognition in the Wild

Michał Grosicki
Kielce University of Technology
al. Tysiąclecia Państwa Polskiego 7
Kielce, Poland
grosickimichal@gmail.com

ABSTRACT

In this paper we present neural networks based method for emotion recognition. Proposed model was developed as part of 2014 Emotion Recognition in the Wild Challenge. It is composed of modality specific neural networks, which where trained separately on audio and video data extracted from short video clips taken from various movies. Each network was trained on frame-level data, which in later stages were aggregated by simple averaging of predicted class distributions for each clip. In the next stage various techniques for combining modalities where investigated with the best being support vector machine with RBF kernel. Our method achieved accuracy of 37.84%, which is better than 33.7% obtained by the best baseline model provided by organisers.

Categories and Subject Descriptors

I.4.9 [**Image Processing and Computer Vision**]: Applications; I.5.4 [**Pattern Recognition**]: Applications—*computer vision, signal processing*; H.5.1 [**HCI**]: Multimedia Information Systems

General Terms

Machine Learning; Emotion Recognition

Keywords

Neural Networks; Multimodal; Dropout; Denoising Autoencoders

1. INTRODUCTION

Recognition and interpretation of emotions plays important role in communication between humans. Human beings use ability to recognize emotions in their everyday lives without any effort or conscious thought. It is used to pick up important, nonverbal clues about mood or intentions of the speaker. Unfortunately what comes natural to humans is extremely hard for machines. During last two decades much progress in the subject of emotion recognition from multimodal data has been made (for survey see [7]). The main caveat of all of these approaches is that they work on data sets which were collected in artificial, laboratory settings and are not really representative for the emotional states present in everyday life. This is the reason why those approaches don't work very well in real-world conditions. This motivated creation of Acted Facial Expression in th Wild (AFEW) data set [2, 3], which tries to provide researchers with consistent way of developing and testing of emotion recognition methods on real world-like data. This data set is especially challenging for emotion recognition methods because they have to deal with many factors of variation present in the video clips, such as in case of facial emotion recognition variability in scene lightning, different head poses or partial occlusions of the face. In case of audio-based recognition of emotion the main problems are variability in loudness of the speech, background noises like music or sound effects. All of this factors make emotion recognition extremely difficult.

Emotion recognition method that we propose in this paper is based on deep neural networks (for survey on deep learning techniques see [1]), which improved state of the art in many challenging problems during last few years (for example: [4, 6]). Indeed winners [5] of the last years challenge developed method that utilized several types of deep neural networks. While method proposed by us in this paper is not so sophisticated as theirs, it still outperforms baseline provided by challenge organisers. Our system is composed of two neural networks with two hidden layers each, trained on frames extracted from video and audio streams. Both networks were pre-trained using stacked denoising auto-encoders [9] and fine-tuned using stochastic gradient descent algorithm with dropout regularization [8]. After training finished, predictions returned by each modality specific network were separately aggregated across all frames for each given video clip. This new data set was used to train support vector machine responsible for fusion of the modalities.

The rest of this paper is organized as follows: in section 2 we describe training of models that are part of the method, aggregation techniques utilized by us are also briefly described; section 3 includes results for each stage of the method; finally section 4 contains our conclusions and final remarks.

2. EMOTION RECOGNITION MODELS

The following section describes neural network based models for emotion recognition from facial expressions and human speech. First two subsections describe methods for clas-

ICMI'14, November 12–16, 2014, Istanbul, Turkey.

ACM 978-1-4503-2885-2/14/11 ...$15.00.
http://dx.doi.org/10.1145/2663204.2666270.

sification of emotions from each modality separately. Last subsection describes fusion of the modalities.

2.1 Frame-level facial expression recognition

The first step of emotion recognition from facial expressions is preprocessing of each frame extracted from video files. For each frame detection and alignment of the faces is performed. For this we make use of extracted faces made available by organisers. Obtained faces are subsequently rescaled to 48x48 pixels. After face extraction, images are flattened to form vector with 2304 dimensions. This process produces data set with 32223 examples for train split and 19845 examples for validation split. The final step of preprocessing consists of standardizing the data by subtracting the mean and dividing by standard deviation computed on the train portion of the data set.

During the second step preprocessed data are fed as input of the stacked denoising auto-encoder (SDAE). This model is composed of hidden layers trained as denoising auto-encoders (DAE) [9], which learn to reconstruct clean data from noisy input. We utilize mini-batch stochastic gradient descent as training algorithm. Since the data is continuous first DAE is trained using Gaussian noise with some selected mean and standard deviation. This noise is applied to the randomly selected units in the input layer. Activation function used in hidden layer is logistic function $f(x) = 1/(1 + e^{-x})$. Consecutive DAEs are trained in the same way, but instead of Gaussian noise binomial noise is used. For better results we also utilize momentum term. Momentum coefficient β is set to some initial value which is scaled linearly over the course of α number of epochs until it reaches β_{max} value. During this pre-training procedure only train split of the data set is used.

After finished training, parameters of the obtained SDAE are used to initialize multilayer perceptron (MLP) network. As in SDAE model hidden layers use logistic activation function and output layer uses softmax activation function. Network is trained using dropout algorithm, but opposite to the[8] we do not halve the weights during testing. To futher avoid overfitting use early stopping during learning. As in training procedure of the DAE we use momentum term, as well as decreasing learning rate. Learning rate scaling schedule is given by (1), where η_0 is initial learning rate, τ is time-constant decay and t is the current iteration.

$$\eta_t = \frac{\eta_0 \tau}{\tau + t} \tag{1}$$

As can be seen proposed model requires setting of several hyper-parameters. In case of SDAE we need to choose: learning rates for each DAE, batch sizes, number of training epochs for each DAE, momentum coefficient, number of neurons in hidden layers, fraction of the input units to which noise is applied and in case of the first DAE mean and standard deviation of the Gaussian noise. In case of MLP there is even more hyper-parameters we need to set, namely: initial learning rate, time-constant decay, batch size, dropout rates in each layer, momentum, maximum number of training epochs, additional hidden layers sizes. Due to large number of hyper-parameters and time and hardware constraints only non-exhaustive manual search was performed. After learning with given set of hyper-parameters, performance on validation set was evaluated and network with best classification accuracy was kept. We refer to this model as *VNN*.

Table 1: Hyper-parameter for the VNN model

Hyper-parameter	SDAE	MLP
Learning rate η	$0.001, 0.1$	0.001
Time-constant decay τ	–	20
Number of hidden neurons	$1000, 500$	$1000, 500$
Momentum β	0.5	0.5
Maximum momentum β_{max}	0.9	0.9
Momentum scaling epochs	20	10
Dropout rate in visible layer	–	0.3
Dropout rate in hidden layers	–	0.5
Number of training epochs	100	500
Batch size	50	50
Gaussian noise mean	0	–
Gaussian noise standard deviation	1	–
Noise level	50%	–

Final hyper-parameters for this model are presented in Table 1.

2.2 Frame-level emotional speech recognition

For the purpose of the emotion recognition from speech we created model similar to the one used in emotion recognition from facial expressions. First from each video clip we extract its audio track and convert it to single channel with simultaneous subsampling to 16 kHz. After that we split each track into frames using 40 ms Hanning window with 20 ms overlap. Next we extract the following set of features using yaafe[1] library:

- amplitude modulation,
- auto correlation,
- complex domain onset detection,
- energy,
- envelope shape statistics,
- ten linear predictive coefficients,
- mel-frequency cepstral coefficients (40 filters) with first and second derivatives,
- octave band signal intensity (OBSI),
- logarithm of OBSI ratio between consecutive ration,
- perceptual sharpness,
- perceptual spread,
- spectral crest factor per band,
- spectral slop
- spectral variation,
- spectral decrease,
- spectral flatness,
- spectral rolloff,

[1]http://yaafe.sf.net — YAAFE: Yet Another Audio Feature Extractor

Table 2: Hyper-parameter for the ANN model

Hyper-parameter	SDAE	MLP
Learning rate η	$0.001, 0.1$	0.001
Time-constant decay τ	–	20
Number of hidden neurons	$500, 500$	$500, 500$
Momentum β	0.5	0.5
Maximum momentum β_{max}	0.9	0.9
Momentum scaling epochs	20	10
Dropout rate in visible layer	–	0.3
Dropout rate in hidden layers	–	0.5
Number of training epochs	100	1000
Batch size	50	50
Gaussian noise mean	0	–
Gaussian noise standard deviation	1	–
Noise level	50%	–

- spectral shape statistics,
- temporal shape statistics,
- zero-crossing rate.

After extraction of features for each frame, they are flattened which results in vector of 188 dimensions. The sizes of train and validation splits obtained during this process are 72447 and 44263 examples respectively. Finally the data is standardized by subtraction of the mean and division by standard deviation computed on the train portion of the data set.

Feature extraction learning process is similar to the one described in the previous subsection i.e. first we train stacked denoising auto-encoder, whose parameters are subsequently used for initialization of MLP network. This network is trained using dropout algorithm with early stopping, momentum and decreasing learning rate.

As was the case with the model for emotion recognition from facial expression we were not able to perform exhaustive hyper-parameters search. Using the same method as described earlier we arrived at the following settings presented in Table 2. We refer to this model as *ANN*.

2.3 Fusion of the modalities

After learning finished, we performed two final steps: per clip aggregation of frame-level predictions and fusion of representations for each modality in order to obtain final prediction.

2.3.1 Aggregation of frame-level predictions

For aggregation we considered three simple schemes: normalized prediction counts, smoothed normalized prediction counts and simple averaging of predicted probabilities across all frames for every clip. Each of these schemes was applied for each modality separately and obtained representations were concatenated to form single 14-dimensional vector.

First two aggregation techniques are very similar. In the case of the first one the process is as follows:

1. Get network prediction for a frame (i.e. single class number).
2. Increase counter in the new representation vector for this class.
3. When all frames of a clip are processed normalize counts so they sum up to one.

Normalization is necessary because number of frames between clips can vary significantly. One modification that we applied to this technique is add-one Laplacian smoothing, which yielded slightly better results on the validation set after fusion of the modalities.

The last scheme for aggregation is simple averaging of prediction probabilities, which yielded best results on validation set. We also tried to use averaged prediction probabilities for both modalities, thus obtaining 7-dimensional vector, but this scheme achieved inferior performance on validation set compared to the described techniques. It is important to note, that few clips in training and validation sets had zero detected faces, in such cases we used vector of uniform probabilities as their representations. Each aggregation scheme produced train and validation split of sizes 591 and 359 respectively.

2.3.2 Multimodal emotion classification

The last stage of our method is multimodal emotion classification using new representation obtained with described neural network models and aggregation techniques. We investigated two models for this task, the first one is dropout trained shallow neural network and second is support vector machine.

The first model we used for fusion of modalities was shallow neural network. Our first tries were with data aggregated using normalized prediction counts and smoothed normalized prediction counts. Smoothed version of data performed consistently better than their non-smooth counterparts. For this reason we decided to proceed with this aggregation scheme in our further experiments. As was the case with frame-level models we performed manual search for hyper-parameters, we were however able to investigate more hyper-parameters configurations due to much smaller model and data set size. Finally we arrived at the following hyper-parameters settings: initial learning rate — 3, time-constant decay — 1, initial momentum coefficient — 0.5 scaled linearly over the course of 10 epochs until it reached value of 0.9, batch size — 10, dropout rates 0.3 and 0.5 for input and hidden layer respectively, hidden layer's size — 150, maximum number of epochs was set to 5000, but learning stopped after about 1000 epochs. We refer to this model as *MMNN1*. Our second neural network based model was similar to the one described, but with few differences. Instead of smoothed normalized counts we utilized average prediction probabilities as input data, wider hidden layer consisting of 500 neurons and higher initial learning rate set to 4.5. This model achieved better results, than previous one. We refer to this model as *MMNN2*.

Another model we tested was support vector machine. We trained SVM models on data sets aggregated using techniques described previously. In case of SVM we were able to perform 5-fold cross-validation on the train set. We constructed grid of hyper-parameters composed of the settings presented in Table 3. As a result of this process, SVM with RBF kernel was chosen. After cross-validation finished, we performed additional manual search focusing solely on parameter C. We trained several models using the following set of values $\{0.01, 0.1, 1, 10, 100\}$ and evaluated each of them on validation set. Two SVM models were kept, one for each of the utilized aggregation techniques. Those models used

Table 3: Cross-validation hyper-parameters for SVM models

Hyper-parameter	Value
kernel type	linear, polynomial, RBF
C	$10^{-5}, 10^{-4}, 10^{-3}, 0.01, 0.1, 1, 10, 100$
γ	$10^{-7}, 10^{-6}, 10^{-5}, 10^{-4}, 10^{-3}, 10^{-2}, 0.1, 1, 10, 100, 10^{3}$
polynomial degree	$2, 3, 4, 5$
linear coefficient	$10^{-7}, 10^{-6}, 10^{-5}, 10^{-4}, 10^{-3}, 10^{-2}, 0.1, 1, 10, 100, 10^{3}$

Table 4: VNN's model confusion matrix computed on the validation set

	Anger	Disgust	Fear	Happy	Neutral	Sad	Surprise
Anger	**648**	294	248	474	424	705	423
Disgust	339	**384**	89	451	348	378	325
Fear	392	348	**154**	249	366	352	159
Happy	298	443	52	**1719**	366	352	159
Neutral	671	217	272	338	**1266**	753	97
Sad	394	442	347	700	375	**767**	262
Surprise	334	374	162	446	371	195	**248**

the same settings of hyper-parameters, namely RBF kernel with $\gamma = 1$ and $C = 1$. We refer to the model trained on smoothed normalized counts *SVM1*, and to the one trained on averaged prediction probabilities as *SVM2*. Additionally we retrained *SVM2* model on data from both train and validation sets. We refer to this model as *SVM3*.

Our complete emotion recognition method is presented in Figure 1.

3. RESULTS

In Tables 4 and 5 we present confusion matrices for VNN and ANN models computed on validation set. As can be seen both networks misclassify large part of extracted frames. Indeed classification accuracy is not very high. VNN model trained on human faces achieved 58.44% accuracy on training set and 26.13% on validation set. ANN achieved 28.12% and 26.19% accuracy on training and validation set respectively. Table 6 contains per-class accuracies for those two models. Here we observe that both models are complementary. For each emotion class one network significantly outperforms the other. It is especially visible in case of disgust and surprise classes, where ANN model was not able to learn to classify them correctly. While 15.97% and 11.97% accuracies obtained with VNN model are not impressive, they are better than near 0% achieved by ANN model. In general VNN model classifies happy, neutral and sad emotions with highest accuracy, while ANN achieves good accuracy for anger, neutral and fear.

Tables 7 and 8 contain confusion matrices for models, which used dropout-trained neural networks for fusion of the modalities, computed on train set . First matrix presents results obtained using smoothed normalized counts aggregation technique. This model achieved accuracy of 34.15%. MMNN1 model is able to classify anger, fear and happiness with good accuracy, however it achieves poor results for disgust and surprise. Results for MMNN2 are very similar to the ones obtained with MMNN1 model. This model was trained using averaged prediction probabilities and achieved slightly better accuracy of 34.40%. Per-class accuracies are also similar to those achieved by MMNN1 model with exception of surprise. In this case MMNN2 model performed much better, achieving accuracy of 23.08% compared to 7.69% achieved by MMNN1. MMNN2 model classifies with good accuracy anger, fear and happiness while achieving poor result for disgust.

In Tables 9 through 11 we present confusion matrices computed on test set, obtained with support vector machines used for fusion of the modalities. First of the models — SVM1 was trained with data aggregated using smoothed normalized counts scheme, while the other two utilized averaged prediction probabilities. Additionally SVM3 model is the only one trained on both train and validation sets. SVM-based models achieved 35.14%, 35.38% and 37.84% for SVM1, SVM2 and SVM3 respectively. All of them outperformed models based on neural networks. As was the case with MMNN1 and MMNN2 models best per-class classification results were obtained for anger, fear and happy emotions, and worst with disgust and surprise. Table 12 contains comparison of per-class and overall accuracies for all models.

Table 5: ANN's confusion matrix computed on the validation set

	Anger	Disgust	Fear	Happy	Neutral	Sad	Surprise
Anger	**3968**	12	367	587	2272	384	0
Disgust	1561	**10**	193	629	2710	161	2
Fear	1303	1	**1283**	407	1359	142	19
Happy	1937	2	653	**804**	3244	369	6
Neutral	1517	12	201	723	**4866**	497	9
Sad	1608	7	640	908	3490	**659**	4
Surprise	1298	1	449	674	2093	220	**2**

Table 6: VNN and ANN's accuracies computed on the validation set

	VNN	ANN
Anger	20.15%	52.28%
Disgust	15.97%	0.19%
Fear	8.53%	28.42%
Happy	50.72%	11.46%
Neutral	35.03%	62.19%
Sad	23.33%	9.00%
Surprise	11.64%	0.04%
Overall	26.13%	26.19%

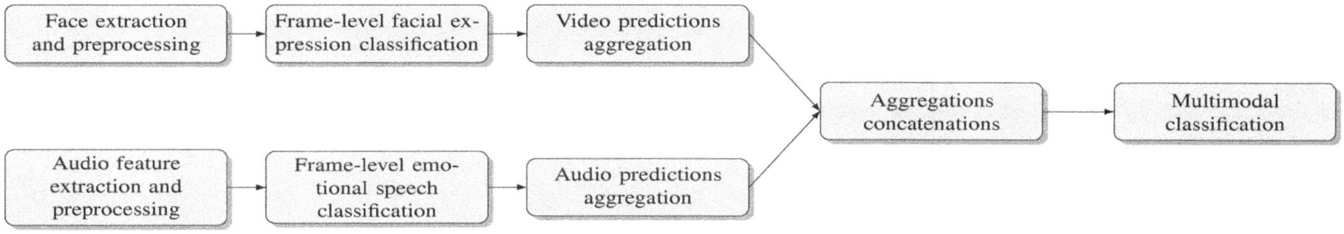

Figure 1: Block diagram of the proposed multimodal emotion recognition method.

Table 7: MMNN1's confusion matrix computed on the test set

	Anger	Disgust	Fear	Happy	Neutral	Sad	Surprise
Anger	**24**	2	9	3	6	11	3
Disgust	5	**2**	5	3	5	6	0
Fear	5	2	**24**	4	4	4	3
Happy	9	5	8	**38**	1	18	2
Neutral	13	6	29	6	**35**	20	8
Sad	9	5	12	7	4	**14**	2
Surprise	4	1	7	2	3	7	**2**

Table 8: MMNN2's confusion matrix computed on the test set

	Anger	Disgust	Fear	Happy	Neutral	Sad	Surprise
Anger	**31**	5	7	0	4	7	4
Disgust	9	**1**	3	5	4	2	2
Fear	11	2	**19**	4	3	3	4
Happy	15	11	3	**38**	4	9	1
Neutral	24	13	22	3	**34**	10	11
Sad	15	3	10	7	6	**11**	1
Surprise	6	2	4	1	3	4	**6**

Table 9: SVM1 model's confusion matrix computed on the test set

	Anger	Disgust	Fear	Happy	Neutral	Sad	Surprise
Anger	**22**	4	8	2	6	11	5
Disgust	5	**3**	3	5	5	3	2
Fear	6	3	**21**	4	4	4	4
Happy	8	12	3	**42**	4	10	2
Neutral	18	6	18	6	**40**	17	12
Sad	8	5	10	8	7	**11**	4
Surprise	4	1	6	1	4	6	**4**

Table 10: SVM2 model's confusion matrix computed on the test set

	Anger	Disgust	Fear	Happy	Neutral	Sad	Surprise
Anger	**28**	2	2	1	9	14	2
Disgust	6	**1**	3	5	6	5	0
Fear	14	1	**14**	4	5	5	3
Happy	10	5	3	**40**	8	14	1
Neutral	22	3	12	6	**46**	21	7
Sad	11	2	7	8	10	**13**	2
Surprise	6	0	6	1	4	7	**2**

Table 11: SVM3 model's confusion matrix computed on the test set

	Anger	Disgust	Fear	Happy	Neutral	Sad	Surprise
Anger	**27**	2	7	3	6	10	3
Disgust	5	**3**	3	5	3	4	3
Fear	5	2	**23**	4	4	4	4
Happy	8	4	6	**45**	4	12	2
Neutral	15	4	18	8	**40**	20	12
Sad	9	2	10	8	8	**12**	4
Surprise	4	1	5	1	4	7	**4**

Table 12: Accuracies computed on the test set for MMNN and SVM models

	MMNN1	MMNN2	SVM1	SVM2	SVM3
Anger	41.38%	53.45%	37.93%	48.28%	46.55%
Disgust	7.69%	3.85%	11.54%	3.85%	11.54%
Fear	52.17%	41.30%	45.65%	30.43%	50%
Happy	46.91%	46.91%	51.85%	49.38%	55.56%
Neutral	29.91%	29.06%	34.19%	39.32%	34.19%
Sad	26.42%	20.75%	20.75%	24.53%	22.64%
Surprise	7.69%	23.08%	15.38%	7.69%	15.38%
Overall	34.15%	34.40%	35.14%	35.38%	37.84%

4. CONCLUSIONS

In this paper we presented our submission to the 2014 Emotion Recognition in the Wild Challenge. Our method obtained satisfactory results, especially for classification of anger, fear, happy and neutral emotions. On the other hand poor accuracy was obtained for disgust and surprise. Modality specific neural networks trained by us complemented each other very well. We experimented with two emotion fusion schemes. The best one turned out to be the one based on support vector machines, which outperformed dropout-trained shallow neural network. We believe the cause of this is underfitting of the data by neural network. We tried to learn bigger network to remedy this, but the accuracy did not improve. Networks with wider hidden layer achieved slightly worse values of validation errors, while the training errors remained similar to the ones obtained with smaller network. We also tried to learn wider network without dropout. This resulted in severe overfitting. This results suggest that the problem lies not in the model, but representation used during learning. Representations obtained with SDAE, while being complementary and generally useful, are insufficient for the problem.

Our relatively simple method, in the best case, outperformed baseline provided by organisers by over 4 percent points, achieving accuracy of 37.84% on very challenging data set. This, as well as last year's winning submission, shows high usefulness of methods based on deep neural networks models in multimodal emotion recognition research.

Unfortunately level of accuracy obtained by our method, is not good enough for real world applications. There is still much space for improvement. Despite of our greatest efforts we were not able perform proper hyper-parameters search. We believe our method could improve with the use of extensive hyper-parameters search procedure. Furthermore we did not exploited temporal dependencies in data (aside from using overlap during windowing of audio data). We believe integrating temporal features in our method might be beneficial. Another path we consider as worth pursuing is inclusion of the additional modalities in the method, such as body pose. Those improvements will be focus of our future work.

5. REFERENCES

[1] Y. Bengio, A. Courville, and P. Vincent. Representation learning: A review and new perspectives. *IEEE Trans. Pattern Anal. Mach. Intell.*, 35(8):1798–1828, Aug. 2013.

[2] A. Dhall, R. Goecke, J. Joshi, M. Wagner, and T. Gedeon. Emotion recognition in the wild challenge 2014: Baseline, data and protocol. ACM International Conference on Multimodal Interaction, 2014.

[3] A. Dhall, R. Goecke, S. Lucey, and T. Gedeon. Collecting large, richly annotated facial-expression databases from movies. *MultiMedia, IEEE*, 19(3):34–41, July 2012.

[4] A. Graves, A. rahman Mohamed, and G. E. Hinton. Speech recognition with deep recurrent neural networks. In *ICASSP*, pages 6645–6649. IEEE, 2013.

[5] S. E. Kahou, C. Pal, X. Bouthillier, P. Froumenty, c. Gülçehre, R. Memisevic, P. Vincent, A. Courville, Y. Bengio, R. C. Ferrari, M. Mirza, S. Jean, P.-L. Carrier, Y. Dauphin, N. Boulanger-Lewandowski, A. Aggarwal, J. Zumer, P. Lamblin, J.-P. Raymond, G. Desjardins, R. Pascanu, D. Warde-Farley, A. Torabi, A. Sharma, E. Bengio, M. Côté, K. R. Konda, and Z. Wu. Combining modality specific deep neural networks for emotion recognition in video. In *Proceedings of the 15th ACM on International Conference on Multimodal Interaction*, ICMI '13, pages 543–550, New York, NY, USA, 2013. ACM.

[6] A. Krizhevsky, I. Sutskever, and G. E. Hinton. Imagenet classification with deep convolutional neural networks. In F. Pereira, C. Burges, L. Bottou, and K. Weinberger, editors, *Advances in Neural Information Processing Systems 25*, pages 1097–1105. Curran Associates, Inc., 2012.

[7] N. Sebe, I. Cohen, T. Gevers, and T. S. Huang. Multimodal approaches for emotion recognition: a survey, 2005.

[8] N. Srivastava, G. Hinton, A. Krizhevsky, I. Sutskever, and R. Salakhutdinov. Dropout: A simple way to prevent neural networks from overfitting. *Journal of Machine Learning Research*, 15:1929–1958, 2014.

[9] P. Vincent, H. Larochelle, I. Lajoie, Y. Bengio, and P.-A. Manzagol. Stacked denoising autoencoders: Learning useful representations in a deep network with a local denoising criterion. *J. Mach. Learn. Res.*, 11:3371–3408, Dec. 2010.

Emotion Recognition in the Wild: Incorporating Voice and Lip Activity in Multimodal Decision-Level Fusion

Fabien Ringeval, Shahin Amiriparian, Florian Eyben, Klaus Scherer* ,Björn Schuller † *
Machine Intelligence & Signal Processing Group
Technische Universität Müchen
Munich, Germany
fabien.ringeval@tum.de

ABSTRACT

In this paper, we investigate the relevance of using voice and lip activity to improve performance of audiovisual emotion recognition in unconstrained settings, as part of the 2014 Emotion Recognition in the Wild Challenge (EmotiW14). Indeed, the dataset provided by the organisers contains movie excerpts with highly challenging variability in terms of audiovisual content; e. g., speech and/or face of the subject expressing the emotion can be absent in the data. We therefore propose to tackle this issue by incorporating both voice and lip activity as additional features in a decision-level fusion. Results obtained on the blind test set show that the decision-level fusion can improve the best mono-modal approach, and that the addition of both voice and lip activity in the feature set leads to the best performance ($UAR = 35.27\%$), with an absolute improvement of 5.36% over the baseline.

Categories and Subject Descriptors

H.5.1 [**Information systems**]: Information systems applications—*Multimedia information systems*

Keywords

Emotion Recognition; Multimedia; Voice Activity Detection; Lip Activity Detection; Decision-Level fusion

1. INTRODUCTION

Automatic Emotion Recognition has become a major field of research in the last decade. Early research focused on theoretical definitions of emotion [5], and automatic recognition on prototypically, acted databases [4, 22]. Recently, more naturalistic data, e. g., [7, 16, 17], as well as other paralinguistic phenomena besides emotion, such as social signals and autism [20], physical and cognitive load [19], have been addressed. Emotion recognition on real-life data suffers from two issues: first, the variance of emotions expressed is very high in relation to the data available (sparseness), second, state-of-the-art methods are largely affected by additive and convolutive background noise [10]. While the second issue can be eased by multimodal approaches [7, 21] or noise robustness counter measures [10], the first issue remains.

To overcome the data-sparseness, larger and more realistic multimodal emotion datasets are required, such as the one collected for the SEMAINE project [16], or the RECOLA dataset [17]. An endless resource of acted, but realistic emotional portrayals seems to be available in TV series and movies. The first database building on this kind of data was introduced in [13]. It contains excerpts from the Vera am Mittag TV show. Recently, facial expressions from TV shows and movies were used for emotion analysis, namely the Static Facial Expressions in the Wild database (SFEW) [8] and the Acted Facial Expressions in the Wild (AFEW) database [9]. Last year, the first Emotion in the Wild (EmotiW 2013) challenge [7] provided an audiovisual dataset (AFEW + audio tracks) and a platform for researchers to create, extend, and validate their methods on real-world movie data.

The AFEW database contains video clips collected by searching closed caption keywords for emotion related content. The labels obtained in this way were validated by human annotators in order to cope with incorrect or unrelated captions [7]. For the second EmotiW challenge [6], an updated version of this database is used, namely version 4.0. The given training set has 578 video clips extracted from movies labelled with six emotional expressions (Angry, Disgust, Fear, Happy, Sad and Surprise) and a neutral state. In the development/validation set, 383 video samples with corresponding labels are contained. 407 video clips without labels are released as blind evaluation/test set.

This paper describes our submission to the 2nd EmotiW challenge (EmotiW 2014) and is organised as follows: In Section 2 we introduce our developed system composed of four components, voice and lip activity detection, feature extraction and multimodal classification. The results obtained on the development and the evaluation set are discussed in Section 3. Section 4 highlights the differences between our results and the baseline results of the challenge, summarises the paper and discusses the direction of future work.

*The author is affiliated with the Swiss Center for Affective Sciences at the University of Geneva, Geneva, Switzerland.

†The author is also affiliated with the Department of Computing, Machine Learning Group at the Imperial College London, London, UK.

ICMI'14, November 12–16, 2014, Istanbul, Turkey.

http://dx.doi.org/10.1145/2663204.2666271.

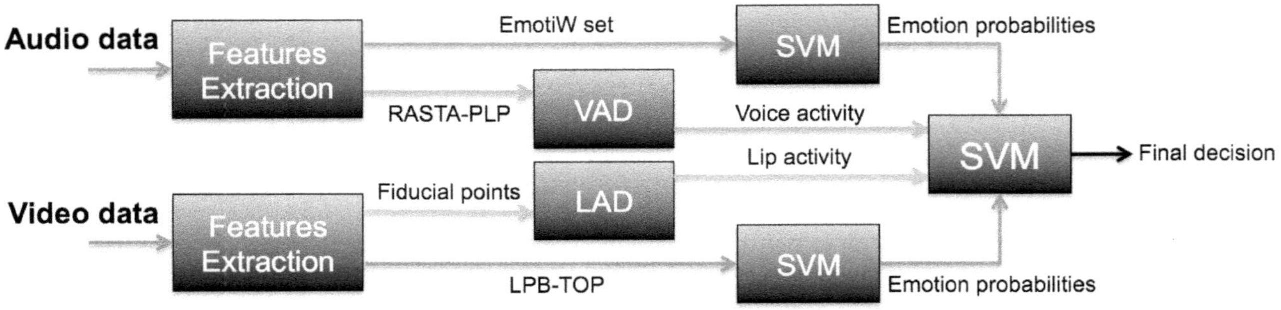

Figure 1: Flowchart of the emotion recognition system: mono-modal SVM based emotion recognition + decision-level fusion with both voice and lip activity as additional features.

2. SYSTEM

An overview of the system developed for the EmotiW 2014 challenge is shown in Fig. 1. Mono-modal emotion recognition is first performed separately on audio features and video features by using a supervised SVM learning. Outputs of these two systems (i. e., emotion probabilities) are then merged with the estimated mean voice and lip activity and a second SVM is used to predict the final emotion decision.

2.1 Voice Activity Detection

We used a voice activity detector to estimate the probability ρ_a of having speech in the audio instances of the dataset; we thus make the hypothesis that the emotion labelling procedure did not take into account the music content of the audiovisual excerpt, but only the spoken content for the audio modality. Because the probability of speech ρ_a was used for the emotion decision-level fusion, cf. Fig. 1, it was estimated only on the development and test dataset.

As the data provided for the EmotiW Challenge contain a high level of background noise and music, we employ our robust voice activity detector based on LSTM-RNN as introduced in [11], using topology $N1$. The input frontend to the neural network extracts RASTA-PLP [15] coefficients 1–18 and their first order delta regression coefficients. Our openSMILE toolkit [12] is used to extract the RASTA-RLP features. The output activation of the LSTM-RNN represents voice activity as values from approx. -1 to +1. This output was normalised into probabilities according to the minimum and maximum values observed on the validation set. Fig. 2 shows the histogram of the voice activity probability ρ_a estimated on all audio frames (frame rate is 10 ms) from both validation and test set. Frames for which the voice probability ρ_a is superior or equal to 0.5 can be interpreted as containing speech. Therefore, 38.48% of the overall audio frames doesn't contain speech.

2.2 Lip Activity Detection

Because speech can be present in the audiovisual instances while not being produced by the person seen in the video, we computed the lip activity from the video data[1]. We thus make the hypothesis that the emotion labelling was performed on the speech produced by the person seen in the video regarding the audio modality.

[1]In some rare cases (e. g., when depicting surprise), it is possible that the person seen in the movie doesn't talk while having the mouth open.

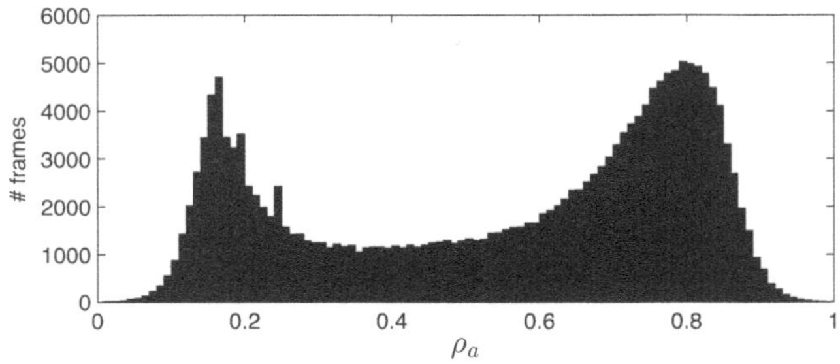

Figure 2: Histogram of voice activity ρ_a computed at the frame level (10 ms) on the development and test datasets; values of ρ_a that are superior or equal to 0.5 mean that speech is present in the corresponding frames.

The probability of lip activity ρ_l was estimated from the fiducial points provided by the organisers of the challenge, using a technique similar to the classic adaptive appearance model (AAM) methodology [1]. The fiducial points are estimated according to a given head pose, which the angle θ ranges from $-90°$ to $+90°$, with a step of 15°. The number of fiducial points modelling the face varies according to the head pose: there are 49 points for $\theta \in F : [-45°, +45°]$ and 39 points for $\theta \in NF$: $[-90°, -60°] \cup [+60°, +90°]$. Because it appeared that the alignment of the fiducial points on the face did not perform well with $\theta \in NF$, we only considered the frames where $\theta \in F$; Table 1 provides the association between the fiducial points and their corresponding region of the face; Fig. 3 shows the detected face and the fiducial points on a video frame of an instance labeled as happy in the training partition. As we noticed that errors in the detection of the fiducial points can appear with $\theta \in F$, we used the following list of checks:

1. the mean horizontal coordinate of the points modelling the nose has to be located in the middle of those computed on the points modelling the left and the right eye

2. the mean vertical coordinate of the points modelling the eyebrow has to be located above the mean vertical coordinate of the points modelling the corresponding eye, i. e., left and right, respectively

Table 1: Correspondances between the 49 detected fiducial points with the 7 modelled regions of the face when the absolute angle $|\theta|$ of the estimated head pose is inferior or equal to 45°

Indice of fiducial points	Face region
1–5	left eyebrow
6–10	right eyebrow
11–19	nose
20–25	left eye
26–31	right eye
32–43	outer mouth
44–49	inner mouth

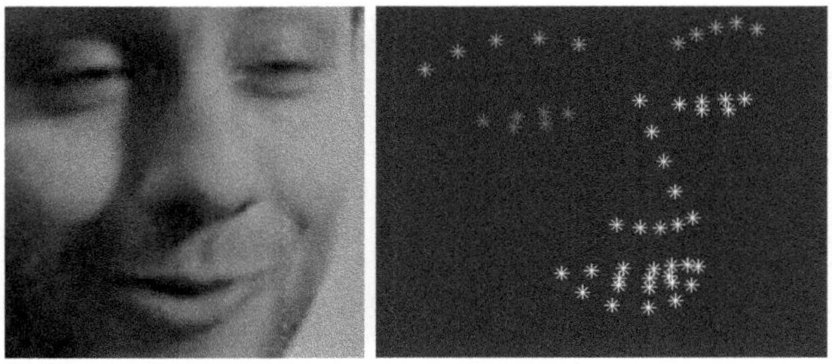

Figure 3: Detected face and fiducial points on a video frame of an instance labelled as happy (file: 000201320.avi, frame: 34; $\theta = 0°$, $\rho_l = 0.07$).

3. horizontal and vertical extremum of the points modelling the inner region of the mouth have to be bounded by the horizontal and vertical extremum of the points modelling the outer region of the mouth, respectively

On a total of 54.7 k frames available on the validation and test partitions, 4.94 % did not contain fiducial points (i. e., failure in the detection, e. g., not or partially visible face, too low level of luminosity), 5.07 % were obtained with a value of $|\theta| > 45°$ and 4.83 % were rejected by our check list.

To compute the probability of lip activity ρ_l, we first calculated the area A_{im} of the polygon formed by the points modelling the inner mouth region; the coordinates of the fiducial points were normalised in $[0, 1]$ to remove the influence of having various sizes of the face model over the instances. Because the area of the inner mouth region A_{im} depends on the angle of the head pose, we normalised this value with the maximum value observed on each head pose in absolute (accordingly), i. e., $|\theta| = [0°, 15°, 30°, 45°]$, to obtain the probability of lip activity ρ_l; the minimum value of A_{im} was always found to be equal to 0 for all angles $\theta \in F$ of head pose.

Fig. 4 shows the histogram of the lip activity probability ρ_l estimated on both validation and test set at the frame level (frame rate is 40 ms). This histogram shows that there is a high number of frames for which the probability of lip activity is close to 0, i. e., having the mouth closed; 22.07 % of the processed video frames present a value of $\rho_l < 0.1$. This percentage is lower than the one obtained on speech (38.48 % of frames doesn't contain speech), because there is the case where the mouth can be opened without producing sound.

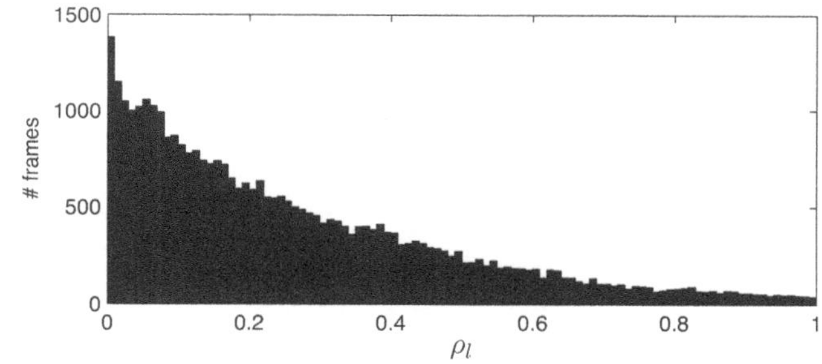

Figure 4: Histogram of the probability of lip activity ρ_l computed at the frame level (40 ms) on the development and test datasets; the lip activity ρ_l is computed by the area formed by the points modelling the inner region of the mouth, normalised by the maximum value observed on each head pose in absolute (accordingly), i. e., $|\theta| = [0°, 15°, 30°, 45°]$.

2.3 Features Extraction

We describe below the two feature sets we used for extracting information from the audio and video data, respectively.

2.3.1 Audio Features

In contrast to large scale brute-force feature sets, which have been successfully applied to many speech and music classification tasks, e. g., [20, 23], smaller, expert-knowledge based feature sets have shown high robustness for emotion recognition [3]. In this light, we assembled a small acoustic feature set for the EmotiW14 Challenge, using our openSMILE toolkit [12].

The set contains 102 parameters in total. The parameters are based on the following Low-Level Descriptors (LLD): Fundamental Frequency (F_0) represented on a logarithmic scale as well as on a linear scale, Loudness (computed as the sum of the intensities in 26 Mel-frequency scale auditory spectrum bands (20–8000 Hz)), Mel-Frequency Cepstral Coefficients (MFCC) 1–4, Jitter, Shimmer, Harmonics-to-Noise Ratio (HNR), Formants 1–3 (frequency, bandwidth and log of amplitude relative to F_0), spectral slopes and spectral flux. As functionals to summarise the descriptors over an analysis segment, mean and standard deviation are applied to all LLD, and to loudness and F_0 additionally the following functionals are applied: percentiles (20, 50, 80) and the range of percentiles 20–80, as well as the means and standard deviations of the slopes of rising and falling contour parts, and of the length of voiced and unvoiced segments. Further, the equivalent sound level (i. e., the average RMS energy converted to dB) is included.

2.3.2 Video Features

We used the feature set provided by the organisers as visual descriptors of the face contained in the video frames [7]. The system requires first to detect the face in the video frames; the MoPs framework was used for detection [26][2] and the Intraface tracker was employed for tracking [24][3]. Features of the face were then extracted with the Local Binary Pattern - Three Orthogonal Planes (LBP-TOP) method [25]. The set contains 2832 parameters in total.

[2] http://www.ics.uci.edu/~xzhu/face/

[3] http://www.humansensing.cs.cmu.edu/intraface/

Table 2: Matrix of confusion obtained on the 7 classes of the EmotiW14 dataset with a emotion perception test; training+validation+test datasets; last value in bold is the % UAR.

Partition	Angry	Disgust	Fear	Happy	Neutral	Sad	Surprise	% Recall
Angry	120	68	6	2	13	1	4	56.08
Disgust	3	49	0	5	37	27	11	37.12
Fear	4	5	101	0	21	5	23	63.52
Happy	1	3	1	217	21	2	7	86.11
Neutral	4	11	10	8	224	17	10	78.87
Sad	2	20	34	4	28	105	5	53.03
Surprise	1	8	17	5	22	4	72	55.81
% Precision	88.89	29.88	59.76	90.04	61.20	65.22	54.55	**61.51**

2.4 Machine Learning

Mono-modal emotion recognition of the 7 classes was performed by using a SVM classifier with the SMO training algorithm. For transparency and reproducibility, we used the implementation provided in the Weka data mining software [14] – version 3-6-10. Two types of features normalisation were used: either a normalisation between $[0-1]$ or a standardisation, i. e., subtracting the mean and dividing by the standard deviation. We used either a linear (the degree of exponent varied between 1 and 3 with a step of 1) or a gaussian kernel (the gamma coefficient varied on a logarithmic scale with 10 values between 10^{-5} and 0.5), and optimised the complexity parameter on a logarithmic scale (10 values between 10^{-3} and 1). The SVM was configured to provide as output the probability of each class by using logistic regression models. Performance was optimised on the validation set using the training set for learning the models, and the unweighted average recall (UAR), i. e., the mean value of the recall of each class in percentage, was used as metric; chance score is therefore equal to $1/7 = 14.29\,\%$.

For the multi-modal emotion recognition, we used as features the sets of probabilities obtained on the audio and video features, respectively. Additionally, we added the probability of voice and lip activity (the mean value was computed for each instance) to this feature vector. Finally, another SVM was used on this feature set, with the same set of parameters and configurations as used for mono-modal emotion recognition. Considering the limited number of instances available for each class on the validation partition (3 classes contain less than 50 instances, the other 4 classes contain less than 65 instances), we optimised the performance on this partition with a 2-fold cross validation.

3. RESULTS

We first present below the results obtained in a perception test of the full dataset; results obtained on the test partition were submitted as non-candidates for the challenge. The performance obtained by our system on the audio and video modalities are then described, followed by those obtained with the multi-modal fusion. A discussion of the results over each emotion class is provided at the end of this section.

3.1 Human perception test

We performed a perception test on all the audiovisual data provided for the EmotiW14 challenge to estimate the performance of human labelling in an emotion recognition task. One author of this paper labelled all instances of the corpus in a randomised order. Table 2 shows the confusion matrix obtained with this perception test; results obtained on the training, validation and test partitions were summed. The obtained performance ($\%UAR = 61.51$) is quite low and shows that the emotion classes contained in the EmotiW14 dataset are not easy to identify even for a human. In particular, 'Disgust' was the worst recognised emotion and the most confused, whereas 'Happy' was the best recognised emotion and the less confused. In comparison, the performance obtained by human labelling of audiovisual data on the GEMEP corpus - acted data from professional actors - is higher ($\%UAR = 76.00$) [2]; for comparison, we considered the 6 following classes: 'Joy (elation)', 'Hot anger (rage)', 'Panic fear', 'Sadness (depression)', 'Disgust' and 'Surprise', cf. Table 5 in [2]. This difference in accuracy of emotion perception is probably due to the fact that: (1) the audiovisual data present in the EmotiW14 dataset are highly compressed, which reduces the quality of the stimulus (2) the emotions portrayed in the GEMEP database are more prototypical than those used in EmotiW14, e. g., 'Angry' vs. 'Rage', 'Fear' vs. 'Panic fear', 'Sadness' vs. 'Depression' and (3) EmotiW14 contains an additional neutral case that is not present in GEMEP.

3.2 Audio features

Results obtained with the audio features (EmotiW set; 102 parameters, cf. section 2.3.1) on the validation partition are displayed in Fig. 5. The best performance ($\%UAR = 32.82$) is obtained with a gaussian kernel ($\gamma = 0.5$) and the lowest tested value of complexity, i. e., $C = 10^{-3}$, combined with a standardisation of the features. The absolute improvement over the baseline ($\%UAR = 23.74$) is 9.08 %; the baseline feature set includes 1582 parameters, which were proposed for the INTERSPEECH 2010 Paralinguistic challenge [18]. We can notice from Fig. 5 that performance decreases when the complexity parameter of the SVM increases, which let us suppose that there are many outliers in the audio data, since the system performs better when these outliers are not considered for computing the decision frontier. In the average, the RBF kernel performed better than the linear kernel, and the standardisation better than the normalisation (extremums are more sensitive to noise than mean and variance). Predictions on the test partition were submitted with the linear ($\%UAR = 32.16$) and the gaussian ($\%UAR = 31.61$) kernels, and we obtained again a better performance than the baseline ($\%UAR = 23.82$); absolute improvement with the linear kernel is 8.34%. Therefore, a smaller, expert-knowledge based acoustic feature set shows higher robustness for emotion recognition than a large scale brute-force feature set, as found in [3].

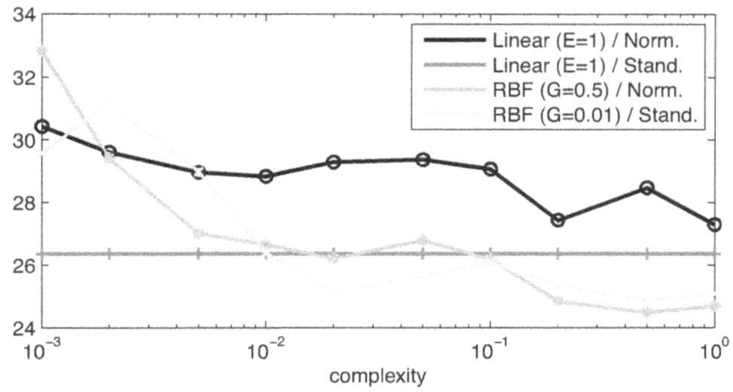

Figure 5: Emotion recognition performance on the EmotiW14 dataset (7 classes) with audio features (EmotiW set; 102 parameters) and SVM classifier, for different types of kernel (linear, RBF), normalisation procedures (norm: normalisation between $[0-1]$, stand.: standardisation to zero mean and unit variance) and values of complexity.

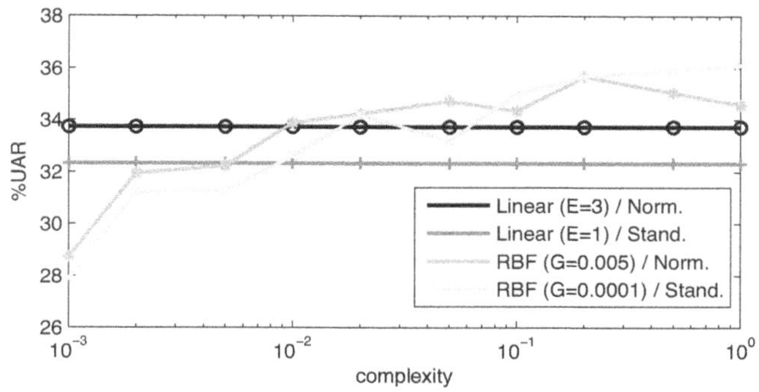

Figure 6: Emotion recognition performance on the EmotiW14 dataset (7 classes) with video features (baseline set; 2832 parameters) and SVM classifier, for different types of kernel (linear, RBF), normalisation procedures (norm: normalisation between $[0-1]$, stand.: standardisation to zero mean and unit variance) and values of complexity.

3.3 Video features

Results obtained with the video features (baseline set; 2832 parameters, cf. section 2.3.2) are displayed in Fig. 6. The best performance ($\% UAR = 36.13$) is obtained with a gaussian kernel ($\gamma = 10^{-4}$) and the highest tested value of complexity, i.e., $C = 1$, combined with a standardisation of the features. The absolute improvement obtained over the baseline ($\% UAR = 31.49$) is 4.64 %, which is smaller than the one achieved with audio features (9.08%), but we used as video data the baseline feature set and only tuned the parameters of the SVM and the normalisation technique. Whereas the performance doesn't vary over the different values of complexity for the linear kernel (same support vectors were probably obtained for the different values of complexity), the performance increased with the value of complexity with the gaussian kernel; the RBF based projection of the features helped to find a better discriminant space. Predictions on the test partition were submitted with the linear ($\% UAR = 29.07$) and the gaussian ($\% UAR = 32.33$) kernels, and we obtained a better performance than the baseline ($\% UAR = 29.91$) only with the RBF kernel; absolute improvement is 2.42 %. Video features thus did perform better than the audio features for the emotion recognition of the 7 classes of the EmotiW14 dataset, on both validation and test partitions. However, the difference in performance between audio and video features is rather small, especially on the test partition, which thus lets room for improvement by using a multi-modal approach.

3.4 Decision-level fusion

Predictions obtained with the audio and video features were learned by another SVM in order to perform a decision-level fusion. We used the same ensemble of machine learning settings for kernel and complexity as those employed for the mono-modal emotion recognition. Multi-modal predictions were performed separately regarding the type of kernel used for the audiovisual modalities, i.e., either linear or RBF kernel. Results obtained on the validation partition (2-fold cross validation) are depicted in Fig. 7. The best performance ($\% UAR = 37.78$) was obtained on the mono-modal predictions made with a linear kernel, with the following configuration: linear kernel (2nd order), normalisation of features in $[0-1]$ and with the lowest value of complexity, i.e., $C = 10^{-3}$. The absolute improvement over our best mono-modal approach ($\% UAR = 36.13$) is 1.65 %, and up to 12.41 % over the baseline ($\% UAR = 25.37$), which was obtained with a feature-level fusion – performance has dropped compared to the mono-modal baseline. Predictions on the test partition were submitted with the linear ($\% UAR = 30.46$) and the RBF ($\% UAR = 33.58$) based decision-level fusion. Whereas the linear kernel performed best on the validation partition for the decision-level fusion, the RBF kernel provided the best performance on the test partition. A small improvement can be observed compared to our best mono-modal result ($\% UAR = 32.33$). Therefore, a decision-level fusion appears more appropriate than a feature-level fusion, for the multi-modal emotion recognition of the EmotiW14 dataset, since we improved the performance whereas a drop was observed on the baseline.

The values of voice and lip activity (cf. section 2.1 and 2.2, respectively) were added to the feature vector used to perform the multi-modal decision-level fusion, i.e., emotion predictions obtained with the audio and video features. The goal is to provide the system some knowledge regarding the occurrence of speech in the audiovisual data, because some instances of the dataset doesn't contain speech, cf. Fig. 2 and 4. Results obtained on the validation partition (2-fold cross validation) are depicted in Fig. 8. The best performance ($\% UAR = 38.78$) was obtained on the mono-modal predictions made with a linear kernel, with the following configuration: RBF kernel ($\gamma = 5.10^{-3}$), normalisation of features in $[0-1]$ and with the complexity equal to $C = 0.2$. The absolute improvement over the previous approach, i.e., without adding the voice and lip activity, is quite small but still observable: 1.00 %. An improvement over the decision-level fusion was also observed on the test partition with the mono-modal predictions made with the RBF kernel: we obtained a performance of $\% UAR = 35.27$, for an absolute improvement of 1.69 %. These results show that the use of voice and lip activity as additional features helps to improve the multi-modal emotion recognition of the EmotiW14 dataset.

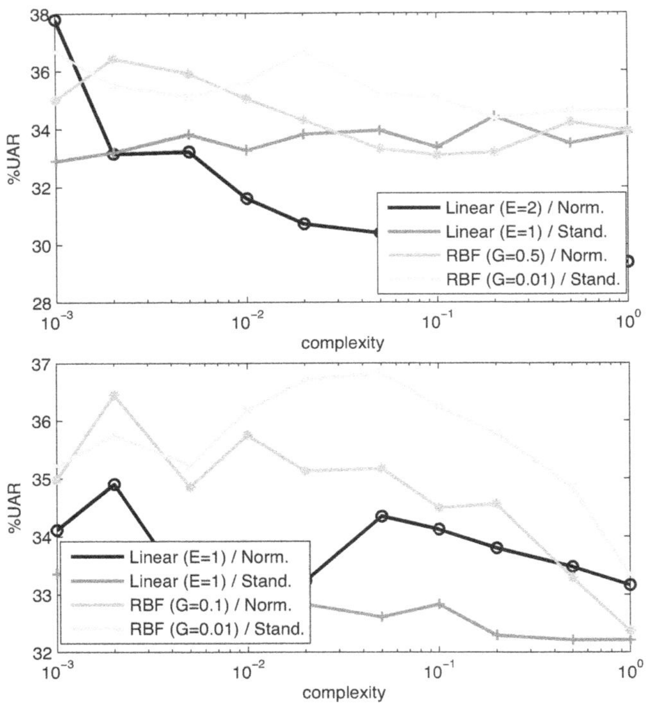

Figure 7: Emotion recognition performance on the EmotiW14 dataset (7 classes) with decision-level fusion of audio and video predictions (top: estimated with a linear kernel, bottom: estimated with a gaussian kernel), for different types of kernel (linear, RBF), normalisation procedures (norm: normalisation in [0 − 1], stand.: standardisation to zero mean and unit variance) and values of complexity.

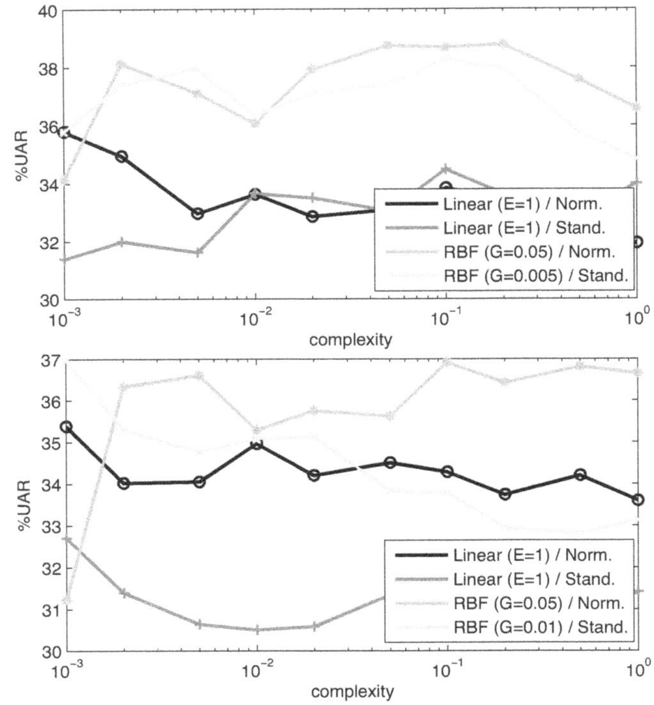

Figure 8: Emotion recognition performance on the EmotiW14 dataset (7 classes) with decision-level fusion of audio and video predictions (top: estimated with a linear kernel, bottom: estimated with a gaussian kernel) combined with voice and lip activity, for different types of kernel (linear, RBF), normalisation procedures (norm: normalisation in [0 − 1], stand.: standardisation to zero mean and unit variance) and values of complexity.

A summary of the best performance obtained on the automatic emotion recognition on the validation and test partitions of the EmotiW14 dataset for the different studied approaches, i. e., audio, video, decision-level fusion and with voice and lip activity, is given in Table 3.

3.5 Performance over the emotion classes

A detailed description of the automatic emotion recognition performance is given for each emotion class in Table 4; performance of human perception test and the baseline system are included as well. Interestingly, the automatic recognition system based on audio features performed better than human labelling for the emotion 'Angry' on the test partition; the multi-modal decision-level fusion with VAD and LAD also performed better on the validation partition. The audio modality provided the best performance on test for both 'Angry' and 'Neutral' classes, video modality performed best for 'Disgust' and 'Happy', whereas the multi-modal system, i. e., audio and video combined, performed best for 'Fear' and 'Sad'; performance was the same on 'Surprise' for both video and audiovisual based recognition systems. The analysis of the GEMEP corpus also shows that 'Fear', 'Sad' and 'Surprise' are best recognised with audio-visual data in comparison to mono-modal data, cf. Table 5 in [2].

4. CONCLUSIONS

We investigated the relevance of using voice and lip activity to improve performance of audiovisual emotion recognition in unconstrained settings, as part of the 2014 Emotion Recognition in the Wild Challenge (EmotiW14). A small, expert-knowledge based acoustic feature set (EmotiW: 102 parameters) was used for emotion recognition on audio data, and it showed higher robustness than the large scale brute-force feature set (INTERSPEECH 2010 Paralinguistic Challenge: 1582 parameters); the absolute improvement was equal to 9.08 % on the validation set and 8.34 % on the test set. Regarding video features, we used the baseline set (LBP-TOP method; 2832 parameters) proposed by the organisers. A tuning of the parameters of the SVM allowed to improve the baseline system with an absolute improvement of 4.64 % on the validation set and 2.42 % on the test set. Whereas the performance dropped with the multi-modal baseline system (feature-level fusion) compared to the mono-modal baseline system, our decision-level fusion achieved an absolute improvement of 1.65 % on the validation set and 1.25 % on the test set compared to our best mono-modal performance; a decision-level fusion appears thus more suitable than a feature-level fusion, for the multi-modal emotion recognition of the EmotiW14 dataset. Finally, the addition of both voice and lip activity as features in the multi-modal

Table 4: Emotion recognition performance (%*recall*) obtained on the 7 classes of the EmotiW14 dataset with perception test (human labelling), mono-modal and multi-modal (i. e., decision-level fusion) systems – best configurations of SVM are retained here; UAR: unweighted average recall; the baseline corresponds to the best system used by the organiser (i. e., using only video features); best automatic recognition performance obtained on the test set are in bold.

Partition	Angry	Disgust	Fear	Happy	Neutral	Sad	Surprise	%UAR
Perception test								
Validation	68.75	27.50	58.70	92.06	93.65	54.10	52.17	63.85
Test	46.55	46.15	78.26	91.35	64.96	62.26	65.39	64.99
Baseline								
Validation	50.00	25.00	15.22	57.14	34.92	16.39	21.74	31.49
Test	36.21	34.62	26.09	**41.98**	40.17	22.64	7.69	29.91
Audio								
Validation	57.81	12.50	43.48	30.16	65.08	16.39	4.35	32.82
Test	**60.35**	3.85	41.30	27.16	**64.10**	24.53	3.85	32.16
Video								
Validation	54.24	28.21	22.73	61.91	45.90	20.34	19.56	36.13
Test	37.93	**38.46**	23.91	35.80	42.74	32.08	**15.38**	32.33
Audio+Video								
Validation	60.93	12.50	34.78	55.56	39.68	26.23	34.78	37.78
Test	50.00	7.69	**52.17**	40.74	42.74	30.19	11.54	33.58
Audio+Video+VAD+LAD								
Validation	70.31	0.0	34.78	52.38	74.60	18.03	8.69	36.97
Test	53.45	7.69	50.00	40.74	41.88	**37.74**	**15.38**	**35.27**

Table 3: Performance on the automatic emotion recognition of the EmotiW14 dataset (7 classes) using different approaches: audio features, video features, audiovisual decision-level based fusion and audiovisual decision-level based fusion with voice (VAD) and lip (LAD) activity; baseline on audio was obtained with a linear kernel; baseline on video was obtained with a gaussian kernel; baseline on audio+video was obtained with a feature-level fusion (RBF kernel).

%UAR	Validation	Test
Audio		
Baseline	23.74	23.82
Linear kernel	30.42	**32.16**
Gaussian kernel	**32.82**	31.61
Video		
Baseline	31.49	29.91
Linear kernel	33.74	29.07
Gaussian kernel	**36.13**	**32.33**
Audio+Video		
Baseline	25.37	23.02
Linear kernel	**37.78**	30.46
Gaussian kernel	36.83	**33.58**
Audio+Video+VAD+LAD		
Linear kernel	**38.78**	31.13
Gaussian kernel	36.97	**35.27**

decision-level fusion allowed to obtain the best overall performance on both validation ($\%UAR = 38.78$) and test ($\%UAR = 35.27$) sets. Therefore, the add of knowledge of the occurrence of speech in the audiovisual data helps the system to know which modality to trust.

More complex machine learning algorithms than SVM, such as those exploiting non-linear dependencies (e. g., deep neural networks - DNN), could probably provide some additional improvement in the automatic emotion recognition of the highly challenging EmotiW14 dataset. However, we do not believe that recurrent based architectures, such as LSTM or BLSTM, would help further, because the duration of the instances is quite small (maximum duration is 5.4 s). Finally, some improvement could probably be obtained by tuning a bit more the feature sets. Regarding audio data, finely tuned features selection could be performed from a large brute-force feature set, whereas for video data, geometric based information could be added to the feature set, since the baseline set contains only appearance based information.

5. ACKNOWLEDGMENTS

This research was supported by an ERC Advanced Grant in the European Community's 7th Framework Programme under grant agreement 230331-PROPEREMO (Production and perception of emotion: an affective sciences approach) to Klaus Scherer, and by the National Center of Competence in Research (NCCR) Affective Sciences financed by the Swiss National Science Foundation (51NF40-104897) and hosted by the University of Geneva.

6. REFERENCES

[1] A. Abel, A. Hussain, Q. D. Nguyen, F. Ringeval, M. Chetouani, and M. Milgram. Maximising Audiovisual Correlation with Automatic Lip Tracking and Vowel Based Segmentations. *Biometric ID Management and Multimodal Communication, joint COST 2101 and 2102 International Conference, Madrid, Spain, September 16-18 2009, Lecture Notes in Computer Science*, 5707:65–72, 2009.

[2] T. Bänziger, M. Mortillaro, and K. Scherer. Introducing the Geneva Multimodal Expression Corpus for Experimental Research on Emotion Perception. *Emotion*, 12(5):1161–1179, 2012.

[3] D. Bone, C.-C. Lee, and S. S. Narayanan. Robust Unsupervised Arousal Rating: A Rule-Based Framework with Knowledge-Inspired Vocal Features. *IEEE Transactions on Affective Computing (TAC)*, 5(2):201–213, April-June 2014.

[4] F. Burkhardt, A. Paeschke, M. Rolfes, W. F. Sendlmeier, and B. Weiss. A Database of German Emotional Speech. In *Proc. of INTERSPEECH 2005*, pages 1517–1520, Lisbon, Portugal, 2005. ISCA.

[5] R. Cowie, E. Douglas-Cowie, N. Tsapatsoulis, G. Votsis, S. Kollias, W. Fellenz, and J. Taylor. Emotion Recognition in Human-Computer Interaction. *IEEE Signal Processing Magazine*, 18(1):32–80, January 2001.

[6] A. Dhall, R. Goecke, J. Joshi, K. Sikka, and T. Gedeon. Emotion Recognition in the Wild Challenge 2014: Baseline, Data and Protocol. In *Proc. of ICMI 2014*, Istanbul, Turkey, November 2014. ACM.

[7] A. Dhall, R. Goecke, J. Joshi, M. Wagner, and T. Gedeon. Emotion recognition in the wild challenge 2013. In *Proc. of ICMI 2013*, pages 509–516, Sydney, Australia, December 2013. ACM.

[8] A. Dhall, R. Goecke, S. Lucey, and T. Gedeon. Static Facial Expression Analysis in Tough Conditions: Data, Evaluation Protocol and Benchmark. In *Proc. of ICCV Workshops 2011*, pages 2106–2112, Barcelona, Spain, November 2011. IEEE.

[9] A. Dhall, R. Goecke, S. Lucey, and T. Gedeon. Collecting Large, Richly Annotated Facial-Expression Databases from Movies. *MultiMedia, IEEE*, 19(3):34–41, July-September 2012.

[10] F. Eyben, F. Weninger, and B. Schuller. Affect Recognition in Real-Life Acoustic Conditions – A New Perspective on Feature Selection. In *Proc. of INTERSPEECH 2013*, pages 2044–2048, Lyon, France, August 2013. ISCA.

[11] F. Eyben, F. Weninger, S. Squartini, and B. Schuller. Real-life Voice Activity Detection with LSTM Recurrent Neural Networks and an Application to Hollywood Movies. In *Proc. of ICASSP 2013*, pages 483–487, Vancouver, Canada, May 2013. IEEE.

[12] F. Eyben, M. Wöllmer, and B. Schuller. openSMILE – The Munich Versatile and Fast Open-Source Audio Feature Extractor. In *Proc. of ACM Multimedia 2010*, pages 1459–1462, Florence, Italy, 2010. ACM.

[13] M. Grimm, K. Kroschel, and S. Narayanan. The Vera am Mittag German audio-visual emotional speech database. In *Proc. of ICME 2008*, pages 865–868, Hannover, Germany, June 2008. IEEE.

[14] M. Hall, E. Frank, G. Holmes, B. Pfahringer, P. Reutemann, and I. H. Witten. The WEKA Data Mining Software: An Update. *ACM SIGKDD Explorations Newsletter*, 11(1):10–18, June 2009.

[15] H. Hermansky. Perceptual Linear Predictive (PLP) Analysis of Speech. *Journal of the Acoustical Society of America (JASA)*, 87(4):1738–1752, November 1990.

[16] G. McKeown, M. Valstar, R. Cowie, M. Pantic, and M. Schroder. The SEMAINE Database: Annotated Multimodal Records of Emotionally Colored Conversations between a Person and a Limited Agent. *IEEE Transactions on Affective Computing (TAC)*, 3(1):5–17, January-March 2012.

[17] F. Ringeval, A. S.onderegger, J. Sauer, and D. Lalanne. Introducing the RECOLA Multimodal Corpus of Remote Collaborative and Affective Interactions. In *Proc. of EmoSPACE 2013, held in conjunction with FG 2013*, Shanghai, China, April 2013. IEEE.

[18] B. Schuller, S. Steidl, A. Batliner, F. Burkhardt, L. Devillers, C. Müller, and S. Narayanan. The INTERSPEECH 2010 Paralinguistic Challenge. In *Proc. of INTERSPEECH 2010*, pages 2794–2797, Makuhari, Japan, 2010. ISCA.

[19] B. Schuller, S. Steidl, A. Batliner, J. Epps, F. Eyben, F. Ringeval, E. Marchi, and Y. Zhang. The INTERSPEECH 2014 Computational Paralinguistics Challenge: Cognitive & Physical Load. In *Proc. of INTERSPEECH 2014*, Singapore, Singapore, September 2014. ISCA.

[20] B. Schuller, S. Steidl, A. Batliner, A. Vinciarelli, K. Scherer, F. Ringeval, M. Chetouani, F. Weninger, F. Eyben, E. Marchi, M. Mortillaro, H. Salamin, A. Polychroniou, F. Valente, and S. Kim. The INTERSPEECH 2013 Computational Paralinguistics Challenge: Social Signals, Conflict, Emotion, Autism. In *Proc. of INTERSPEECH 2013*, pages 148–152, Lyon, France, August 2013. ISCA.

[21] B. Schuller, M. Valstar, R. Cowie, and M. Pantic. AVEC 2012: The Continuous Audio/Visual Emotion Challenge – An Introduction. In *Proc. of ICMI 2012*, pages 361–362, Santa Monica, CA, USA, October 2012. ACM.

[22] B. Schuller, B. Vlasenko, F. Eyben, G. Rigoll, and A. Wendemuth. Acoustic Emotion Recognition: A Benchmark Comparison of Performances. In *Proc. of ASRU 2009*, pages 552–557, Merano, Italy, December 2009. IEEE.

[23] F. Weninger, F. Eyben, B. W. Schuller, M. Mortillaro, and K. R. Scherer. On the Acoustics of Emotion in Audio: What Speech, Music and Sound have in Common. *Frontiers in Emotion Science*, 4(Article ID 292):1–12, May 2013.

[24] X. Xiong and F. De la Torre. Supervised Descent Method and its Applications to Face Alignment. In *Proc. of CVPR 2013*, pages 532–539, Portland, OR, USA, 2012. IEEE.

[25] G. Zhao and M. Pietikainen. Dynamic Texture Recognition Using Local Binary Patterns with an Application to Facial Expressions. *IEEE Transactions on Pattern Analysis and Machine Intelligence (PAMI)*, 29(6):915–928, June 2007.

[26] X. Zhu and D. Ramanan. Face Detection, Pose Estimation, and Landmark Localization in the Wild. In *Proc. of CVPR 2012*, pages 2879–2886, Providence, RI, USA, 2012. IEEE.

Combining Multimodal Features with Hierarchical Classifier Fusion for Emotion Recognition in the Wild

Bo Sun, Liandong Li, Tian Zuo, Ying Chen, Guoyan Zhou, Xuewen Wu
School of Information Science and Technology, Beijing Normal Univ., Beijing, China100875
tosunbo@bnu.edu.cn, bnulee@hotmail.com, tian.zuo21@gmail.com, chenying_1204@126.com, zgy996@163.com, xuewenwu@hotmail.com

ABSTRACT

Emotion recognition in the wild is a very challenging task. In this paper, we investigate a variety of different multimodal features from video and audio to evaluate their discriminative ability to human emotion analysis. For each clip, we extract SIFT, LBP-TOP, PHOG, LPQ-TOP and audio features. We train different classifiers for every kind of features on the dataset from EmotiW 2014 Challenge, and we propose a novel hierarchical classifier fusion method for all the extracted features. The final achievement we gained on the test set is 47.17% which is much better than the best baseline recognition rate of 33.7%.

Categories and Subject Descriptors

I.4.m[Image Processing and Computer Vision]: Miscellaneous; I.5.4 [Pattern Recognition]: Applications

General Terms

Algorithms; Performance; Experimentation

Keywords

Emotion Recognition; Feature Fusion; Support Vector Machine; Hierarchical Classifier; Multimodal

1. INTRODUCTION

Psychologists believe that facial expressions and verbal messages are sometimes used as the main channel of human communication [1]. In the recent years, automatic emotion recognition has received great attention. The development of technologies in emotion recognition is surprisingly fast, and many of them have already been used in our real life. At early stage researchers mostly focused on emotion analysis from single static facial images under ideal circumstance [2]. The result of recognition in the wild was poor certainly. As emotions turn into dynamic streaming, the research changes into emotion recognition through the video or image sequences. There are multiple methods for emotion recognition, which contain different kinds of features, such as Gabor [3], Local Binary Pattern Histogram (LBPH) [4], Histogram of Oriented Gradients (HoG) [5], and Active Appearance Models (AAM) [6], etc. Using single feature to recognize emotion is easy to implement, but the result is unsatisfactory.

The Emotion Recognition in the Wild Challenge and Workshop (EmotiW) 2014 grand Challenge consists of an audio-video based emotion classification challenge, which mimics real-world conditions [9]. Expression of face and people's speaking voice are mainly used in the recognition of emotion, so we choose to use the faces and speaking voice which extracted from the video for our experiments. Then we proposed a hierarchical classifier fusion framework which is decision-level fusion method to improve the result of emotion recognition. Our method is showed in Fig 1. Our classifier fused different classification results and gained promising recognition performance. In the experiments, we also tried feature-level fusion method through Multiple Kernel Learning [8] and got better result than single feature SVM classifier.

In this paper, we describe our work in the EmotiW 2014 challenge. The paper is organized as: Section 2 gives the features that we extracted (SIFT BoW, PHOG, LPQ-TOP, LBP-TOP and Audio features), we will detail the ideas of these algorithms and the experiment results of these single feature classification in Table 1, Section 3 introduces the classifiers that we have used in our work, Section 4 gives the entire experiments we have done, and the recognition rates of our experiments, then the finally conclusion is given in Section 5.

ICMI '14, November 12 – 16, 2014, Istanbul, Turkey
Copyright 2014 ACM 978-1-4503-2885-2/14/11...$15.00
http://dx.doi.org/10.1145/2663204.2666272

2. FEATURES

2.1 Bag of Multi-scale Dense SIFT features

Bag of Words (BoW) model based on multi-scale dense SIFT features (MDSF) [9] [11] is used to extract visual features, which has shown remarkable performance on object recognition [12] [13] and facial expression recognition [14]. The superiority of this approach lies in the combination of dense SIFT feature extraction, feature encoding using Locality-constrained Linear Coding [15] and spatial information fusion by multi-scale pooling over spatial pyramid [16].

2.1.1 Sampling Strategy and Features

First, we extracted multi-scale dense SIFT features with a stride of 2 pixels. In order to retain more spatial information at different scales, we employed 4 different scales in MDSF extraction, defined by setting the width of the SIFT spatial bins to 4, 8, 12 and 16 pixels. Empirical comparisons demonstrated that multi-scale SIFT features indeed lead to better performance than their single-scale counterpart.

2.1.2 Codebook Construction

The vocabulary for BoW is constructed by using approximate K-means clustering, which is based on calculating data-to-cluster distances using the Approximate Nearest Neighbor (ANN)

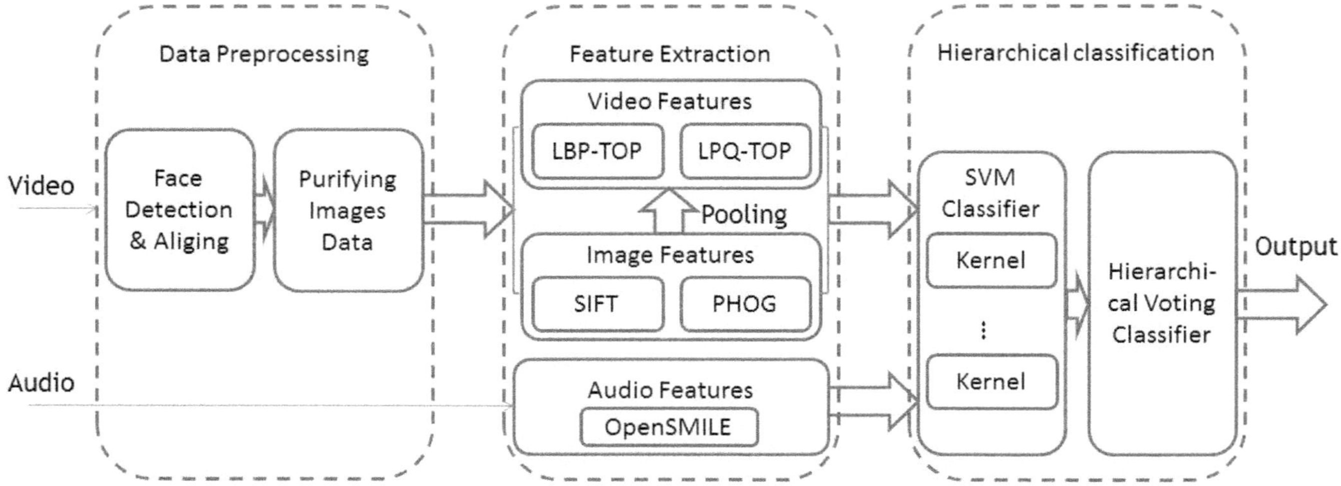

Figure 1: The proposed method for emotion recognition

algorithm. For clustering we used a feature subset extracted from 100 randomly selected images in train samples. The size of the dictionary was set based on empirical experiments to 800.

2.1.3 Encoding and Pooling

After the codebook of MDSF cluster centers was generated, Locality-constrained Linear Coding (LLC) [15] was used to encode MDSF features and pool them together. LLC projected each descriptor to a local linear subspace spanned by some codewords by solving an optimization problem. Then max pooling [17] is used to construct one single code each image or region, based on the maximization principle on each code dimension. LLC is known to be more robust to local spatial translations and captures more salient properties of visual patterns as compared to the original simple histogram spatial encoding. Most importantly, a linear kernel is sufficient to achieve good performance with LLC encoding, thus avoiding the computational expense of applying non-linear kernels [18], as is the case with spatial histogram based encoding [13] [16]. The parameter for LLC encoding, *knn*, the number of nearest visual words to be considered, was set to be 5.

The traditional Bag of Words model is robust to spatial translation, but sacrifices spatial layout information during the histogram computing process. To address this particular limitation, we have incorporated a particular extension of BoW called spatial pyramid matching (SPM) [16], that has shown significant success on a number of tasks [13] [19]. SPM implicitly incorporates spatial information into the feature representation through pooling histograms of different subdivisions of the image. For SPM each image was partitioned into $2^l \times 2^l$ segments at multiple scales l = 1, 2, 4, 8, 16.

The BoW representation was then computed within each of these segments using LLC, and all of these LLC codes were concatenated into a single feature vector of 272800 dimensions.

2.2 PHOG Features

Pyramid of Histograms of Orientation Gradients (PHOG) features have been used for object detection. PHOG features are frequently used to describe the represents local image shape and its spatial layout .The PHOG descriptor is based on two sources: 1) the image pyramid representation and 2) the Histograms of Orientation Gradients (HOG).

We use PHOG features to obtain the local shape information of the faces. The number of pyramids was set to 4 and the bin numbers was 9.We divide the face into 4 levels: 1×1, 2×2, 4×4, and 8×8 and calculated the histogram of orientation gradients of each level .The final PHOG vector is a weighted concatenation of histograms for all levels [21].

2.3 LBP-TOP Features

Local Binary Patterns from Three Orthogonal Planes (LBP-TOP) [23] are efficient representations of dynamic image texture which has been successfully applied to facial expression recognition. Dynamic texture is an extension of texture to the temporal domain. LBP-TOP is an extension of the LBP operator [24] which is widely used in ordinary texture analysis, generated by concatenating local binary patterns on three orthogonal planes (LBP-TOP): XY, XT and YT, considering only the co-occurrence statistics in these three directions. The XY plane provides the spatial texture information, while the XT and YT planes provide information about the space-time transitions.

The sequences of face images is divided into 4×4 blocks from which the LBP features are extracted and concatenated into an enhanced feature vector. All features extracted from each block volume are connected to one 2832 dimensions vector to represent the appearance and motion of the facial expression sequence.

2.4 LPQ-TOP Features

As a variant of LBP-TOP which is additionally robust to blur images, Local Phase Quantization from Three Orthogonal Planes (LPQ-TOP) [25] is based on binary encoding of the phase information of the local Fourier transform at low frequency points and is an extension to the LPQ operator used for spatial texture analysis.

The local Fourier transform is computed efficiently using 1-D convolutions for each dimension in a 3-D volume. The data achieved is compressed to a smaller dimension before a scalar quantization procedure. Finally, a histogram of all binary codewords from dynamic texture is formed. Like the LBP-TOP feature, we divided the Dynamic Volume into 16 blocks of volumes, then compute LPQ-TOP features on each block and concatenate them together.

2.5 Audio Features

The audio feature is computed by extracting features using the OpenSmile toolkit. OpenSmile, Speech & Music Interpretation by Large Space Extraction [26], is a fast and real-time audio features extraction utility for automatic speech, music and paralinguistic recognition research.

The 1582 dimensions audio feature is generated in three steps [27]: firstly, 38 low-level descriptors are extracted from the video with varying window type and size and smoothed by simple moving average low-pass filtering with a window length of three frames. Next, their first order regression coefficients are added. Then, 21 statistical functions are applied to each low-level feature stream in order to capture time-varying information in a fixed-length static feature vector for each instance in the database. Note that 16 zero-information features which is always zero are discarded. Finally, the two single features 'number of pitched segments' and turn duration are added.

Table 1: The accuracy of each feature with SVM classifier, gained from the Validation Set

Feature	Accuracy	Kernels & Parameters
SIFT BoW	42.32%	Linear, c 0.9
PHOG	31.27%	RBF, c 128, g 8
LBP-TOP	36.12%	RBF, c 1.2, g 2.8
LPQ-TOP	19.68%	RBF, c 2, g 8
Audio	26.68%	Linear, c 2

3. CLASSIFIER

3.1 SVM Classifier

Support vector machine (SVM) is supervised learning model with associated learning algorithms that analyze data and recognize patterns, used for classification and regression analysis. SVM constructs a hyperplane in a high or infinite dimensional space, which can be used for classification. Given a training set of N data points $\{x_k, y_k\}_{k=1}^{N}$, where $x_k \in \mathbb{R}^n$ is the kth input pattern and $y_k \in \mathbb{R}$ is the kth output pattern, the support vector method aims at constructing a classifier of the following form:

$$y(x) = sign[\sum_{k=1}^{n} a_k y_k k\psi(x, x_k) + b] \quad (1)$$

In multi-class classification, binary SVM classifiers are built to distinguish between (i) one of the labels and the rest (one-versus-all) or (ii) between every pair of classes (one-versus-one) [28]. Classification of new instances for the one-versus-all case is done by a winner-takes-all strategy, in which the classifier with the highest output function assigns the class. For the one-versus-one approach, classification is done by a max-wins voting strategy, in which every classifier assigns the instance to one of the two classes, then the vote for the assigned class is increased by one vote, and finally the class with the most votes determines the instance classification.

We used the LIBLINER and LIBSVM which both are popular open source machine learning libraries developed at the National Taiwan University. For each features listed above, we preformed the SVM classifier followed both one-vs-all (OVA) and one-vs-one (OVO) multi-class classifier strategy. For audio and BoW features, the linear kernel is used for classification. For the other features, we used grid search to find the suitable parameter C and G of the RBF kernels. The accuracies of those methods are showed in the Table. (Only the higher one between OVO and OVA is listed.)

3.2 Hierarchical Classifier Fusion

Observing the confusion matrix of each single feature SVM classifier, we found that those features show different results on each specific emotion. To take use of multiple features, we proposed a Hierarchical classifier to combine the results of each SVM classifier.

Firstly all the SVM classifiers with each feature make up the feature level classification. For the testing set of N data points $x_k \in \mathbb{R}^n$, the ith SVM outputs $\{x_k, y_k, \rho_k\}_{k=1}^{N}$ where $y_k \in \{1, 2, \ldots, 7\}$ is the predicted class label and ρ_k is the estimated accuracy of the predicted label y_k.

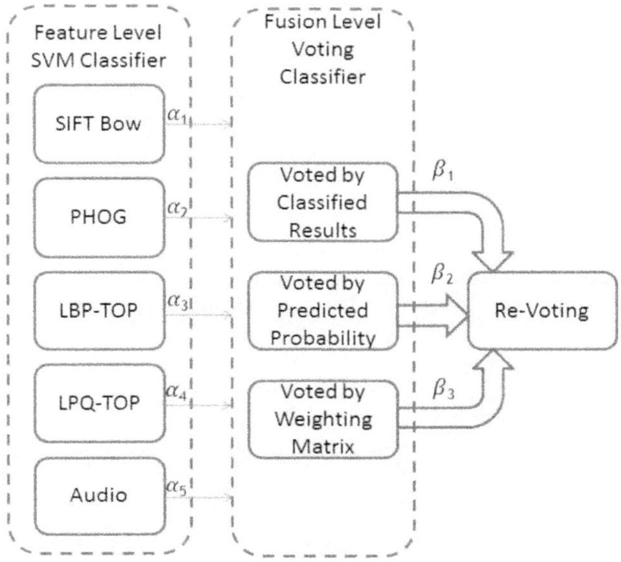

Figure 2: Levels of Hierarchical Classifier

On the second level, we use 3 different fusion methods of voting classification. 1) The first one is voted by classified results. We simply uses 5 parameters α_1, α_2, α_3, α_4, α_5, valued from 0.0 to 1.0, as the voting weights of each classifier. Each classifier classifies the date $x_k \in \mathbb{R}^n$ to one of the 7 emotions $y_k \in \{1, 2, \ldots, 7\}$, and the highest voted emotion is the result of this method. Then we tune the 5 voting weights to obtain the best results of validation set. 2) The second fusion classifier is same as the first one except that it is voted by estimated prediction probability generated by SVM classifier. Each feature level classifier votes with the estimated probability ρ_k as its weight to class y_k. 3) The last fusion classifier sets a 5×7 voting weight matrix M. For ith feature level classifier, its voting weight on the jth emotion is M(i, j). Since it's difficult to tune all those parameters, we uses the true positive rates of 7 emotions calculated from the validation set confusion matrix of classifier(i) as the default weight. Then we only need to tune the 1×7 weight parameters belong to the column of BoW feature classification on each emotion, since it has the highest single feature accuracy.

At last, we define β_1, β_2, β_3 as the weights of second level fusion classifiers, and re-vote for each data $x_k \in \mathbb{R}^n$. We can search the parameters to find the best results by grid search strategy. In practice, we also add the BoW classifier to the fusion level to obtain robust classification. Through the two-layer voting system, we can achieve better classification results.

4. EXPERIMENTS

4.1 Data Purification

In order to improve the effects of training, we try to obtain a better set of face images to train by a method of data purification. Principal Component Analysis projection has been applied to solve this problem.

Firstly, we get the original face images set:

$$X = \{x_1 x_2 \ldots x_n\}, x_i \in R^D.$$

Then, we use PCA projection learned on X to preserve a low energy: W.

The mean reconstruction error which can be used to distinguish images is:

$$MeanErr_t = \frac{1}{D}\left\| x_t - W^T W x_t \right\|^2 \quad (2)$$

The non-face or badly-aligned face images tend to have a large scale of MeanErr_t [22].

We set the threshold to 0.27 and get rid of the non-face or badly-aligned face images on EmotiW2014 training set like the ones in the following Fig 2. Trained with the purified data set, the accuracy of PHOG classifier had some improvement.

Figure 3: Samples with Largest Mean Reconstruction Error

4.2 BoW with SVM

Our first submission using only the Bag of Multi-scale dense SIFT features with SVM classifier has an overall classification accuracy of 44.72%.

	Angry	Disgust	Fear	Happy	Neutral	Sad	Surprise
Angry	79.31%	1.72%	1.72%	5.17%	5.17%	5.17%	1.72%
Disgust	7.69%	15.38%	7.69%	26.92%	26.92%	11.54%	3.85%
Fear	21.74%	8.70%	23.91%	8.70%	13.04%	17.39%	6.52%
Happy	7.41%	2.47%	7.41%	60.49%	7.41%	13.58%	1.23%
Neutral	14.53%	5.98%	8.55%	3.42%	52.14%	12.82%	2.56%
Sad	9.43%	13.21%	7.55%	15.09%	22.64%	16.98%	15.09%
Surprise	19.23%	0.00%	26.92%	7.69%	23.08%	15.38%	7.69%

Figure 4: Confusion Matrix of our first submission on the test set

Since each frame of the video produced a pyramid BoW feature vector, information from all frames of the video were combined using max pooling, accomplished by taking the maximum of the pyramid BoW feature vectors over all frames [20]. The BoW feature has a dimension of 272800, so we used the Linear SVM classifier with parameter C = 0.9.

4.3 Multimodal Features with Weighted Voting

Our second submission used the multimodal features with weighed voting and had an overall classification accuracy of 45.21%.

To take use of the multimodal features, we simply combined all of the feature level classifiers with a weighted voting. The parameters α_1, α_2, α_3, α_4 and $\alpha_5 = 1-\alpha_1-\alpha_2-\alpha_3-\alpha_4$, all valued from 0.0 to 1.0. Through the grid search method, we found that when α_1(BoW) = 0.375, α_2(PHOG) = 0.125, α_3(LBP) = 0.042, α_4(LPQ) = 0.083, α_5(Audio) = 0.375, the accuracy on the validation set has the best result of 43.40%. The result did not improved much but we noticed the confusion matrix was quite different from the first submission. So we intended to take some more voting strategies.

	Angry	Disgust	Fear	Happy	Neutral	Sad	Surprise
Angry	67.24%	0.00%	3.45%	8.62%	17.24%	3.45%	0.00%
Disgust	3.85%	7.69%	3.85%	53.85%	23.08%	7.69%	0.00%
Fear	21.74%	8.70%	19.57%	28.26%	17.39%	4.35%	0.00%
Happy	8.64%	0.00%	3.70%	62.96%	17.28%	6.17%	1.23%
Neutral	9.40%	1.71%	2.56%	16.24%	63.25%	5.98%	0.85%
Sad	16.98%	5.66%	5.66%	32.08%	20.75%	16.98%	1.89%
Surprise	15.38%	0.00%	15.38%	26.92%	26.92%	15.38%	0.00%

Figure 5: Confusion Matrix of our second submission

4.4 Multimodal Features with Hierarchical Classifier Fusion

Our third submission used the multimodal features with hierarchical classifier fusion and had an overall classification accuracy of 47.17%.

	Angry	Disgust	Fear	Happy	Neutral	Sad	Surprise
Angry	74.14%	0.00%	0.00%	3.45%	12.07%	8.62%	1.72%
Disgust	11.54%	19.23%	3.85%	26.92%	34.62%	3.85%	0.00%
Fear	23.91%	2.17%	17.39%	6.52%	23.91%	23.91%	2.17%
Happy	12.35%	3.70%	2.47%	59.26%	11.11%	11.11%	0.00%
Neutral	11.97%	3.42%	2.56%	4.27%	64.96%	12.82%	0.00%
Sad	11.32%	15.09%	1.89%	20.75%	28.30%	22.64%	0.00%
Surprise	15.38%	0.00%	11.54%	11.54%	38.46%	23.08%	0.00%

Figure 6: Confusion Matrix of our third submission

Table 2: The α and β weights of each classifier

	BoW	PHOG	LBP-TOP	LPQ-TOP	Audio	Accuracy	β weight
Voted by Results	0.375	0.125	0.042	0.083	0.375	43.40%	$\beta_1 = 0.3$
Voted by Probability	0.400	0.133	0.000	0.000	0.467	43.40%	$\beta_2 = 0.1$
	0.400	0.033	0.067	0.033	0.467	43.40%	$\beta_3 = 0.2$

With the tuned weights of feature level classifier, we obtained 43.40% on validation set with three fusion classifier. Notice that although the Audio feature performed not so well in SVM classification, it has a large scale of weight. We thought this showed that audio have some information which is complementary to the homogeneous video features. The voting Matrix fusion classifier had not got an impressive result, so we used the BoW classifier instead. After testing on the validation test, we got an accuracy of 45.55% with the weights $\beta_1 = 0.3$, $\beta_2 = 0.1$, $\beta_3 = 0.2$, β_4 (BoW) = 0.4.

4.5 BoW and Audio Features Fusion

In our fourth submission, we tried feature-level fusion MKL method with BoW and Audio features which have an overall classification accuracy of 47.17%. The audio linear kernel is L2-regularized L2-loss support vector classification (dual) with parameter c = 2. The weight of BoW kernel is 0.67, and 0.33 of audio kernel. We achieve better recognition result than single kernel SVM classifier

	Angry	Disgust	Fear	Happy	Neutral	Sad	Surprise
Angry	81.03%	0.00%	1.72%	1.72%	8.62%	5.17%	1.72%
Disgust	11.54%	19.23%	7.69%	23.08%	30.77%	7.69%	0.00%
Fear	26.09%	6.52%	23.91%	8.70%	17.39%	13.04%	4.35%
Happy	6.17%	3.70%	6.17%	61.73%	9.88%	11.11%	1.23%
Neutral	6.84%	2.56%	7.69%	5.98%	57.26%	12.82%	6.84%
Sad	9.43%	7.55%	7.55%	15.09%	28.30%	20.75%	11.32%
Surprise	26.92%	0.00%	15.38%	11.54%	26.92%	15.38%	3.85%

Figure 7: Confusion Matrix of our fourth submission

5. CONCLUSIONS

In this paper, we investigate different features and classifiers for multimodal human emotion recognition in the real world. For each features, we trained individual classifier which has different discriminative ability for emotions classification. We propose a novel hierarchical classifier fusion framework to utilize these feature characteristics which is decision-level fusion. The method is evaluated on EmotiW 2014 dataset and gain very promising achievement on the test set. At last we also implement a feature-level fusion method. In the future, we will try to integrate the feature-level fusion classifier into our hierarchical classifier framework to further improve the recognition performance. And we will conduct more experiments to compare our method with other existing methods to get more detailed performance analysis of our work.

6. ACKNOWLEDGEMENTS

This work is supported by the Fundamental Research Funds for the Central Universities of China (2012YBXS10).

7. REFERENCES

[1] M. Knapp and J. Hall, *Nonverbal communication in human interaction (Fourth Edition)*, Harcourt College Pub., 1996.

[2] Pantic, M., & Rothkrantz, L. J. M. (2000). Automatic analysis of facial expressions: The state of the art. *Pattern Analysis and Machine Intelligence, IEEE Transactions on, 22*(12), 1424-1445.

[3] Wu, T., Bartlett, M. S., & Movellan, J. R. (2010, June). Facial expression recognition using Gabor motion energy filters. In *Computer Vision and Pattern Recognition Workshops (CVPRW), 2010 IEEE Computer Society Conference on* (pp. 42-47). IEEE.

[4] Shan, C., Gong, S., & McOwan, P. W. (2009). Facial expression recognition based on local binary patterns: A comprehensive study. *Image and Vision Computing*, *27*(6), 803-816.

[5] Dalal, N., & Triggs, B. (2005, June). Histograms of oriented gradients for human detection. In *Computer Vision and Pattern Recognition, 2005. CVPR 2005. IEEE Computer Society Conference on* (Vol. 1, pp. 886-893). IEEE.

[6] Cootes, T. F., Edwards, G. J., & Taylor, C. J. (2001). Active appearance models. *IEEE Transactions on pattern analysis and machine intelligence,23*(6), 681-685.

[7] Suykens, J. A., & Vandewalle, J. (1999). Least squares support vector machine classifiers. *Neural processing letters*, *9*(3), 293-300.

[8] Gönen, M., & Alpaydın, E. (2011). Multiple kernel learning algorithms. *The Journal of Machine Learning Research*, *12*, 2211-2268.

[9] "The Second Emotion Recognition In The Wild Challenge and Workshop (EmotiW 2014)". http://cs.anu.edu.au/few/ChallengeDetails

[10] Lowe, D. G. (1999). Object recognition from local scale-invariant features. In *Computer vision, 1999. The proceedings of the seventh IEEE international conference on* (Vol. 2, pp. 1150-1157). Ieee.

[11] Vedaldi, A., & Fulkerson, B. (2010, October). VLFeat: An open and portable library of computer vision algorithms. In *Proceedings of the international conference on Multimedia* (pp. 1469-1472). ACM.

[12] Csurka, G., Dance, C., Fan, L., Willamowski, J., & Bray, C. (2004, May). Visual categorization with bags of keypoints. In *Workshop on statistical learning in computer vision, ECCV* (Vol. 1, No. 1-22, pp. 1-2).

[13] Zhang, J., Marszałek, M., Lazebnik, S., & Schmid, C. (2007). Local features and kernels for classification of texture and object categories: A comprehensive study. *International journal of computer vision*, *73*(2), 213-238.

[14] Sikka, K., Wu, T., Susskind, J., & Bartlett, M. (2012, January). Exploring bag of words architectures in the facial expression domain. In *Computer Vision–ECCV 2012.*

Workshops and Demonstrations (pp. 250-259). Springer Berlin Heidelberg.

[15] Wang, J., Yang, J., Yu, K., Lv, F., Huang, T., & Gong, Y. (2010, June). Locality-constrained linear coding for image classification. In *Computer Vision and Pattern Recognition (CVPR), 2010 IEEE Conference on* (pp. 3360-3367). IEEE.

[16] Lazebnik, S., Schmid, C., & Ponce, J. (2006). Beyond bags of features: Spatial pyramid matching for recognizing natural scene categories. In *Computer Vision and Pattern Recognition, 2006 IEEE Computer Society Conference on* (Vol. 2, pp. 2169-2178). IEEE.

[17] Yang, J., Yu, K., Gong, Y., & Huang, T. (2009, June). Linear spatial pyramid matching using sparse coding for image classification. In *Computer Vision and Pattern Recognition, 2009. CVPR 2009. IEEE Conference on* (pp. 1794-1801). IEEE.

[18] K. Chatfield, V. Lempitsky, A. Vedaldi, A. Zisserman. The devil is in the details: an evaluation of recent feature encoding methods. In *British Machine Vision Conference*, 2011.

[19] O.M. Parkhi, A. Vedaldi, A. Zisserman, C.V. Jawahar. Cats and dogs. In *IEEE Conference on Computer Vision and Pattern Recognition*, 2012

[20] Ojansivu, V., & Heikkilä, J. (2008). Blur insensitive texture classification using local phase quantization. In *Image and signal processing* (pp. 236-243). Springer Berlin Heidelberg.

[21] Bosch, A., Zisserman, A., & Munoz, X. (2007, July). Representing shape with a spatial pyramid kernel. In *Proceedings of the 6th ACM international conference on Image and video retrieval* (pp. 401-408). ACM.

[22] Liu, M., Wang, R., Huang, Z., Shan, S., & Chen, X. (2013, December). Partial least squares regression on grassmannian manifold for emotion recognition. In *Proceedings of the 15th ACM on International conference on multimodal interaction* (pp. 525-530). ACM.

[23] Zhao, G., & Pietikainen, M. (2007). Dynamic texture recognition using local binary patterns with an application to facial expressions. *Pattern Analysis and Machine Intelligence, IEEE Transactions on*, *29*(6), 915-928.

[24] Ojala, T., Pietikainen, M., & Maenpaa, T. (2002). Multiresolution gray-scale and rotation invariant texture classification with local binary patterns. *Pattern Analysis and Machine Intelligence, IEEE Transactions on*, *24*(7), 971-987.

[25] Päivärinta, J., Rahtu, E., & Heikkilä, J. (2011). Volume local phase quantization for blur-insensitive dynamic texture classification. In *Image Analysis* (pp. 360-369). Springer Berlin Heidelberg.

[26] Eyben, F., Wöllmer, M., & Schuller, B. (2010, October). Opensmile: the Munich versatile and fast open-source audio feature extractor. In *Proceedings of the international conference on Multimedia* (pp. 1459-1462). ACM.

[27] Wöllmer, M., Weninger, F., Eyben, F., & Schuller, B. (2011). Acoustic-Linguistic Recognition of Interest in Speech with Bottleneck-BLSTM Nets. In *INTERSPEECH* (pp. 77-80).

[28] Hsu, C. W., & Lin, C. J. (2002). A comparison of methods for multiclass support vector machines. *Neural Networks, IEEE Transactions on*, *13*(2), 415-425.

Combining Modality-Specific Extreme Learning Machines for Emotion Recognition in the Wild

Heysem Kaya*
Department of Computer Engineering
Boğaziçi University
34342, İstanbul, Turkey
heysem@boun.edu.tr

Albert Ali Salah
Department of Computer Engineering
Boğaziçi University
34342, İstanbul, Turkey
salah@boun.edu.tr

ABSTRACT

This paper presents our contribution to ACM ICMI 2014 Emotion Recognition in the Wild Challenge and Workshop. The proposed system utilizes Extreme Learning Machines (ELM) for modeling modality-specific features and combines the scores for final prediction. The state-of-the-art results in acoustic and visual emotion recognition are obtained either using deep Neural Networks (DNN) or Support Vector Machines (SVM). The ELM paradigm is proposed as a fast and accurate alternative to these two popular machine learning methods. Benefiting from fast learning advantage of ELM, we carry out extensive tests on the data using moderate computational resources. In the video modality, we test combination of regional visual features obtained from the inner face. In the audio modality, we carry out tests to enhance training via other emotional corpora. We further investigate the suitability of several recently proposed feature selection approaches to prune the acoustic features. In our study, the best results for both modalities are obtained with Kernel ELM compared to basic ELM. On the challenge test set, we obtain 37.84%, 39.07% and 44.23% classification accuracies for audio, video and multimodal fusion, respectively.

Categories and Subject Descriptors

I.5.4 [**Computing Methodologies**]: Pattern Recognition-Signal processing; I.4.7 [**Image Processing and Computer Vision**]: Feature Measurement

General Terms

Human-Computer Interaction

*Corresponding author

ICMI '14, November 12 - 16 2014, Istanbul, Turkey.

http://dx.doi.org/10.1145/2663204.2666273.

Keywords

Audio-visual emotion corpus; audio-visual fusion; feature extraction; emotion recognition in the wild; extreme learning machines

1. INTRODUCTION

Emotion recognition from video and audio is gaining increasing attention, especially because its outputs can be used in many related domains [5, 31]. In the last decade, a considerable amount of research efforts spent in the field was on on controlled, laboratory-condition data. In some of such corpora (e. g. Berlin Emotional Speech Database [3]) it was possible to obtain classification scores even better than human perception [31]. Now the field is moving on to less controlled conditions, including noisy audio-visual background, large variance in facial appearance and spoken content.

Audio-visual emotion related challenges have been instrumental in improving the state-of-the-art in this field, since the introduction of the INTERSPEECH 2009 Emotion Challenge [26]. The challenges provide a great opportunity for the researchers in the field and help advance the state-of-the-art by bringing together experts from different disciplines such as signal processing and psychology. Though in majority of challenges the central theme was emotion [26, 29, 28, 34, 7] other important real life problems such as depression [34, 33] and autism [28] are also targeted. One such challenge series is Emotion Recognition in The Wild (EmotiW) [7, 6] that provides out of laboratory data -Acted Facial Expression Wild (AFEW)- collected from videos that mimic real life [8].

Our contributions to EmotiW challenge are threefold. First, to the best of authors' knowledge, it is the first time ELM is applied in an audio-visual emotion recognition task. Second, we investigate feature/group selection in both modalities to enhance generalization of learned models. We further extract audio features using the most recent INTERSPEECH Computational Paralinguistic challenge baseline set [28] with openSMILE tool [10] and augment the AFEW dataset with four other publicly available emotional corpora: Berlin EMODB [3], Danish Emotion Database (DES) [9], eNTERFACE Database [22], and a Turkish Emotional Database (BUEMODB) that was introduced recently for public use [20]. To our surprise, we observe the best audio modality results using the baseline acoustic feature set, and that the additional corpora do not contribute significantly to emotion recognition in wild. However, using a semantically meaningful subset of facial regions, it was possible to obtain better recognition results than the full set, both in development and test set. We carry out score level fusion of modality-specific models, which boosts the performance of individual models.

The remainder of this paper is organized as follows. In the next section we provide background on ELM. Then in Section 3 we briefly introduce the corpus and baseline feature sets. In Section 4 we give experimental results, and in Section 5 conclude.

2. BACKGROUND: EXTREME LEARNING MACHINES

Extreme Learning Machine (ELM) was first introduced a decade earlier [15] as a fast alternative training method for Single Layer Feedforward Networks (SLFNs). The rigorous theory of the ELM paradigm is presented in 2006 by Huang et al. [16], where the authors compare the performance of ELM, SVM, and Back Propagation (BP) learning based SLFN in terms of training time and accuracy. The basic ELM paradigm has matured over the years to provide a unified framework for regression and classification; and is related to generalized SLFN class including Least Square SVM (LSSVM) [32, 14]. Due to fast and accurate results obtained via ELMs, the method is applied in many real life tasks ranging from gesture recognition to representational learning [13, 4]. In this section, we provide a brief introduction to the paradigm.

The argument of basic ELM introduced by Huang et al. is that the first layer (input layer) weights and biases of a neural network classifier do not depend on data and can be randomly generated; the second layer (output weights) can be effectively and efficiently solved via least squares [16]. It can be thought that the input layer carried out unsupervised feature mapping, then the activation function outputs (the output matrix) is subjected to a supervised learning procedure. Let $\mathbf{x} \in \mathbb{R}^d$ denote an input sample, $\mathbf{h}(\mathbf{x}) \in \mathbb{R}^p$ denote the hidden node output. Similarly, let $\mathbf{X} \in \mathbb{R}^{n \times d}$ denote the dataset and $\mathbf{H} \in \mathbb{R}^{n \times p}$ denote the hidden node output matrix. The hidden node activation via randomly generated mapping matrix $\mathbf{W}$ and bias vector $\mathbf{b}$ is defined as in regular SLFN:

$$H(l,t) = h_l(\mathbf{x^t}) = g(\mathbf{x^t}, \mathbf{w_l}, b_l), l = 1, ..., L, t = 1, ..., N, \tag{1}$$

where l and t index the hidden nodes and the feature vectors, respectively; and nonlinear activation function $g()$ can be any infinitely differentiable bounded function [16]. A common choice for $g()$ is sigmoid function:

$$g(\mathbf{x}, \mathbf{a}, b) = \frac{1}{1 + exp\left(-(\mathbf{a} \cdot \mathbf{x} + b)\right)}. \tag{2}$$

ELM proposes an unsupervised, even random generation of hidden node output matrix $\mathbf{H}$. The actual learning takes place in the second layer between $\mathbf{H}$ and the label matrix $\mathbf{T}$. $\mathbf{T}$ is composed of continuous annotations in case of regression therefore is a vector. In the case of K-class classification, $\mathbf{T}$ is represented in one vs. all coding

$$\mathbf{T}_{t,k} = \begin{cases} +1 & \text{if } y^t = k, \\ -1 & \text{if } y^t \neq k. \end{cases} \tag{3}$$

The second level weights β are learned by least squares solution to a set of linear equations $\mathbf{H}\beta = \mathbf{T}$. Proving first that random projections and nonlinear mapping with $L \leq N$ result in a full rank H, the output weights can be learned via

$$\beta = \mathbf{H}^\dagger \mathbf{T}, \tag{4}$$

where $\mathbf{H}^\dagger$ is the Moore-Penrose generalized inverse [25] that gives not only minimum L_2 norm solution to $||\mathbf{H}\beta - \mathbf{T}||$, but also minimizes the norm of projection $||\beta||$. The use of this special generalized inverse is motivated by Bartlett's theory stating that for networks approximating an arbitrarily small training error, the smaller the norm of weights is, the better the generalization capability of the network [2]. The universal approximation and classification capability of ELMs have been rigorously discussed in the literature (cf. [14]), and are beyond the scope of this paper. However, it is important to mention that ELM is related to Least Square SVMs via the following output weight learning formulation:

$$\beta = \mathbf{H}^T(\frac{\mathbf{I}}{C} + \mathbf{H}\mathbf{H}^T)^{-1}\mathbf{T}, \tag{5}$$

where $\mathbf{I}$ is $N \times N$ identity matrix, and C used to regularize the linear kernel $\mathbf{H}\mathbf{H}^T$ is indeed the complexity parameter of LSSVM [32]. The approach is extended to use any valid kernel. A popular choice for kernel function is Gaussian (RBF):

$$K(\mathbf{x_k}, \mathbf{x_l}) = \phi(\mathbf{x_k}) \cdot \phi(\mathbf{x_l}) = exp(-\frac{||\mathbf{x_k} - \mathbf{x_l}||}{\sigma^2}) \tag{6}$$

In both (basic and kernel) approaches, the prediction of $\mathbf{x}$ is given via $\hat{\mathbf{y}} = \mathbf{h}(\mathbf{x})\beta$. In case of multi-class classification the class with maximum score in $\hat{\mathbf{y}}$ is selected. In our study we utilize both basic and kernel version of ELM. Inspired by the success of SLFN based auto-encoders for feature enhancement and the relationship between Principal Component Analysis (PCA) and SLFNs [1], in this study we further consider the use of PCA instead of random generation of input weights.

We next briefly introduce the AFEW data [8] used for experimental validation.

3. THE CORPUS AND FEATURES

AFEW 4.0 introduces a total of 1 368 video clips collected from movies representing close-to-real-world conditions [8, 6]. The dataset is partitioned into training, development and test sets. The challenge participants are expected to develop their system using the first two sets and send their predictions for the test set, whose labels are sequestered. The organizers also provide baseline acoustic and visual features.

Table 1: Instance distribution per modality

#	Train	Val	Test	Total
Clips	578	383	407	1368
Video	567	371	407	1345
Audio	578	383	407	1368

The baseline video features consist of Local Binary Patterns from Three Orthogonal Planes (LBP-TOP) compacted via uniform LBP [23]. After face alignment and conversion to gray scale, LBP computation amounts to finding the sign of difference with respect to a central pixel in a neighborhood, transforming the binary pattern into an integer and finally converting the patterns into a histogram. Uniform LBP maps the patterns into 59 bins, observing that in a close neighborhood there the binary patterns differ by only two bits [23]. Since histogram representation does not keep the structural information, the face is divided into non overlapping $4 \times 4 = 16$ regions and an LBP histogram is computed per region. The TOP extension applies the relevant descriptor on XT, XT and YT planes independently and concatenates the resulting histograms. In total, we have $59 \times 3 = 177$ dimensional visual descriptors per region.

The baseline audio features are extracted via openSMILE tool [10] using INTERSPEECH 2010 Paralinguistic challenge baseline set [27]. The 1 582 dimensional feature set covers a range of popular Low Level Descriptors such as F0, MFCC [0-14], Line Spectral Pairs frequency [0-7] mapped to a fixed length feature vector by means of functionals such as arithmetic mean and extrema.

4. EXPERIMENTAL RESULTS

In our experiments we test the suitability of basic and kernel ELM to the problem of audiovisual emotion recognition. To probe the individual performance, we handle the video and audio separately, and then combine the decisions of best performing modality-specific ELMs. Though it is possible to utilize Deep Neural Networks and SVM as alternative classification approaches, the fast ELM training[1] gives us the ability to simulate a wide range of hypotheses with moderate system requirements. All our simulations are carried out using MATLAB 2014 on an Ubuntu 2012 Server operating system with a machine that has 16GB RAM and 8 CPU cores having 2.4GHz speed.

4.1 Comparison of Basic and Kernel ELM

As a preliminary system development step, we carried out tests using the full set of baseline features in both modalities to see which ELM type is better suited to the problem at hand. For basic ELM, we chose sigmoid activation function, since it provided the best among alternatives (sine, hard limit and Gaussian functions). Considering the dimensionality of video and audio features, we tested basic ELM with a set of hidden node numbers $2^{\{1,2,\ldots,9\}}$ both using random projection and PCA (ranked eigen vectors) for input weights. For Kernel ELM, we experimented on both Linear and RBF Kernels using a complexity parameter set $10^{\{-5,\ldots,5\}}$. The same set of hyper parameters was tested for scatter parameter σ of RBF kernel.

Table 2: Validation set classification accuracies of modality-specific ELMs with different kernels and input weight arrangement

Type	Basic ELM		Kernel ELM	
Modality	Random	PCA	Linear	RBF
Audio	27.94%	32.64%	35.77%	35.77%
Video	25.07%	37.74%	38.81%	39.35%

The best results from the preliminary experiments using EmotiW 2014 baseline features (without feature selection) are given in Table 2. We see that our conjecture of utilizing PCA for better input layer modeling holds on this dataset. Moreover, video modality features seem to better benefit from PCA than audio features. We also observe that Kernel ELM provides better performance in both modalities. We see that the best accuracy obtained in both kernel types are either the same (for audio) or very close. The challenge validation set baselines are 26.2% and 34.4% for audio and video, respectively. Though basic ELM with PCA modeling of input weights is found to outperform the challenge baselines, we decided to use Kernel ELM in the rest of our experiments.

[1] http://extreme-learning-machines.org/

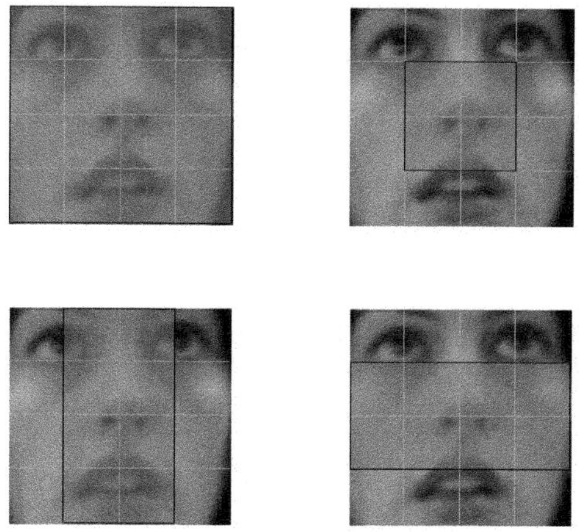

Figure 1: Illustration of facial regions tested in the study. Top-left: full face, top-right: inner face (regions 6, 7, 10 and 11), bottom-left: midface vertical, bottom-right: midface horizontal

4.2 Experiments with Visual Features

We proceed testing the hypothesis of improving performance using inner facial regions motivated by recent audiovisual studies on prediction of dimensional affect and depression level [19, 18]. Apart from reduced dimensionality for better modeling, the reason of focusing on the inner facial regions are (1) partial peripheral occlusion of face, (2) cluttered background in case the face is tilted and(3) the fact that the inner regions (e. g. eyes, and mouth) reflect actions. Some example facial group configurations are given in Figure 1.

Using the same experimental setting described in previous section for kernel hyper parameters, we issue ELM tests with Linear and RFB kernels on various facial region combinations. The best results for each region and kernel type are provided in Table 3. We see that even using features of a single facial region (e. g. region 11), it is possible to outperform the challenge baseline score. Moreover, using 2-by-2 inner facial regions or 2-by-4 vertical middle regions (midface vertical), we can obtain better performance than the full set of 16 regions. Our results indicate that for emotion related tasks, focusing on the inner face reduces the feature dimensionality while preserving discriminative information, and results in better classification rates. Note that we carry out group-wise feature selection, since individual selection of histogram features are not meaningful and sufficient for pattern recognition.

To keep the table uncluttered, the parameters yielding these results are not included, but reported here. The best RBF kernel results using at least four regions are obtained with scatter parameter $\sigma = 10^3$ and regularization parameter $\tau = 10$. On the other hand, best results with linear kernel are obtained with $\tau = 10^{-2}$. Both in video and audio modalities, we record the hyper parameters giving the best results to be later used in test set predictions.

Table 3: Accuracy comparison of facial regions using Linear and RBF. Region numbering startes from top-left of face to bottom-right, steps are first horizontal then vertical

Facial Regions (#)	RBF	Linear
Whole Face (16)	39.35%	38.81%
Midface Horizontal (8)	37.47%	39.08%
Midface Vertical (8)	38.89%	40.16%
Inner face (4)	39.89%	39.08%
Regions 6 and 7 (2)	36.39%	35.31%
Regions 10 and 11 (2)	37.47%	34.77%
Regions 6 and 11 (2)	37.74%	35.31%
Regions 6 and 10 (2)	36.12%	36.12%
Regions 7 and 10 (2)	36.12%	36.66%
Regions 7 and 11 (2)	37.74%	37.74%
Region 6 (1)	33.69%	34.23%
Region 7 (1)	33.15%	32.35%
Region 10 (1)	34.77%	33.96%
Region 11 (1)	36.66%	34.77%

4.3 Experiments with Acoustic Features

After the first probe into the full set of baseline acoustic features, we applied several feature selection methods. This was followed by extraction of a more recent and larger feature set that was used in INTERSPEECH 2013 via openSMILE tool.

Due to its popularity, we first used minimum Redundancy Maximum Relevance (mRMR) filter [24]. mRMR drives the feature selection in a set X, at step k maximizing the difference or ratio between relevance and redundancy terms [24]:

$$\max_{x_j \in X - S_{k-1}} \left[MI(x_j, t) - \frac{1}{k-1} \sum_{x_i \in S_{k-1}} MI(x_j, x_i) \right], \quad (7)$$

where $MI(x, y)$ is mutual information between random variables x and y. As suggested by the authors, we discretized the continuous acoustic features into bins based on z-scores such that the instances in the z-score range {(-∞,-2.5],(-2.5,-1.5],(-1.5,-0.5],(-0.5,0.5],(0.5,1.5],(1.5,2.5],(2.5,∞)} fall into bins {1,2,...,7}, respectively.

In addition to mRMR, we utilize a recently proposed multi-view feature filter based on Canonical Correlation Analysis (CCA) [21]. CCA is a statistical method that seeks to maximize the mutual correlation between two sets of variables by finding linear projections for each set [12, 11]. The method we used from [21] applies SLCCA-Filter [17] to LLD groups then augments the ranked k features from each group.

The main idea behind the SLCCA-Filter algorithm in [17] is as follows. When all features on one view are subjected to CCA against the labels on the other view, the absolute value of the projection matrix $\mathbf{V}$ can be used to rank the features. We extend the LLD based approach using mRMR and combine top $k = \{5, 10, 15, 20\}$ ranking features from each LLD group. For mRMR, the first 200 features are tested with steps of 10, each with the set of ELM hyper parameters discussed in previous sections. Together with regular mRMR, we test 3 feature selection approaches on baseline acoustic features.

The best validation set results of feature selection approaches utilized in the study are given in Table 4. We observe that the best LLD-based SLCCA-Filter outperforms the best performance obtained with LLD-based mRMR. However, no feature selection method performs better than the full set of features. The superior performance of the full set can be attributed to the ELM learning rule, which minimizes the norm of the projection, thus making use of all features without over-fitting. In a regular Neural Network, where the weights are learned via gradient descend based back-propagation, feature selection would help avoid over-fitting, therefore may yield better results than the full set. Another possible reason that a selected subset does not perform better than the full set is the fact that the paralinguistic information can be distributed over a wide range of features. This is the reason why state-of-the-art results in the field are obtained with very high dimensional supra-segmental acoustic features [31].

Table 4: Validation set performance comparison of acoustic feature selection methods

	RBF	Linear
All Baseline Feats	35.77%	35.77%
mRMR Ranked Feats	33.16%	34.46%
mRMR-LLD (k=10)	33.68%	32.38%
SLCCA-LLD (k=10)	35.51%	35.25%

We further included four other publicly available emotional corpora to AFEW 2014 training set (all with INTERSPEECH 2013 baseline feature set). The additional emotional corpora are Berlin EMODB [3], Danish Emotion Database (DES) [9], eNTERFACE Database [22], and a Turkish Emotional Database (BUEMODB) that was introduced recently for public use [20]. Class distribution and some basic information about the corpora are given in Table 5. Note that all corpora are acted, though two are recorded in studio. Here, we use only the instances belonging to seven classes of AFEW. Therefore we do not use boredom class instances.

Cross corpus evaluation results are given in Table 6. All corpora are individually normalized to range [-1,1]. Without corpus-wise normalization, the corpora are found to worsen the generalization of the learner. This finding is in accordance with cross corpus work of Schuller et al. [30]. On the first row, the best performance using INTERSPEECH 2013 feature set on AFEW 2014 is given. We see a performance decrease with respect to given baseline features. eNTERFACE and EMODB provide some performance increase with respect to INTERSPEECH 2013 baseline set, whereas BUEMODB and DES do not contribute at all. We see that even when all additional corpora are included, the performance is below the accuracy obtained via EmotiW 2014 challenge features. Therefore, we have not submitted test set predictions trained with multiple corpora.

Table 5: Class distribution of additional emotional corpora. Classes correspond to A(nger), B(oredom), D(isgust), F(ear), H(appiness), N(eutral), SA(dness), SU(rprise). All corpora are acted.

Corpus	Content	A	B	D	F	H	N	SA	SU	#All	Type
EMODB	German fixed	127	79	38	55	64	78	53	-	494	studio
DES	Danish fixed	85	-	-	-	86	85	84	79	419	normal
eNTERFACE	English fixed	200	-	189	189	205	-	195	182	1170	normal
BUEMODB	Turkish fixed	121	-	-	-	121	121	121	-	484	studio

Table 6: Best validation set performance of multi corpus training

Corpora	Accuracy
AFEW 4.0 IS13 Feats	33.42%
+ eNTERFACE	34.20%
+ EMODB	34.20%
+ BUEMODB	33.42%
+ DES	33.42%
+ ENTERFACE + EMODB	33.42%
+ All corpora	34.20%

4.4 Multimodal Fusion and Test Set Results

We finally test the best performing modality-specific systems using flat averaging combination scheme. Since ELM provides seven dimensional scores for each test set instance, we average the class-wise predictions to get a fused score. For one case, we test stacking Kernel ELM scores to basic ELM for fusion. However, it is found that ELM stacking does not improve performance. The best performing single modality systems give 37.84% (audio full baseline acoustic set) and 39.07% (video inner face) accuracy.

Validation and test set performances of multimodal decision fusion alternatives are provided in Table 7. We observe that using inner facial regions in audiovisual fusion provides better generalization than the full set of features. We see that multimodal fusion with midface features provides the highest validation set accuracy, but this does not yield close to validation set results observed in other fusion schemes. This might be attributed to over-fitting to validation set, however the hyper-parameters are not specifically optimized for this system. The most probable reason of the high discrepancy between validation and test set performances of systems using mid face vertical features is partial occlusion and registration errors. Thus, the higher generalization performance of inner facial features is not only due to the relevant information they contain, but also due to resilience to occlusion and environmental noise. Thus, we verify the robustness of audio-visual systems trained with inner facial regions, in line with recent studies on prediction of continuous depression and affect [18, 19].

Furthermore, from Table 7 we observe that the second best test set performance is obtained with the fusion of inner face based model predictions and the SLCCA-LLD reduced features. Though feature selection was not found to increase performance of the audio modality system in the validation set, we see that SLCCA-LLD reduced acoustic feature set provides a good generalization when combined with midface based video system. This test system gives the highest relative increase with respect to the validation set performance.

The test set confusion matrices for best performing audio, video and fusion systems are given in figures 2, 3 and 4,

Table 7: Decision fusion of modality-specific kernel ELMs. SFA: simple flat averaging, ELM: Stacking kernel ELM scores to second layer of basic ELM, AV-S1: Midface Vertical and Audio SLCCA-LLD (k=10), AV-S2: Midface Vertical and Audio All, AV-S3: Inner face and Audio All, AV-S4: Inner face and Audio All, AV-S5: Innerface and Audio SLCCA-LLD (k=10), AV-S6: Whole face and Audio All

System	Fusion	Val	Test
AV-S1	SFA	47.17%	38.33%
AV-S2	SFA	44.47%	38.08%
AV-S3	SFA	44.20%	44.23%
AV-S4	ELM	43.67%	40.29%
AV-S5	SFA	43.13%	43.98%
AV-S6	SFA	42.86%	43.00%

respectively. The diagonal elements indicate the recall of corresponding classes. On the overall, we observe that fusion system boosts the performance of single modality systems. However, since audio system does not recognize Disgust, Happiness and Surprise classes well (if not at all), the fusion system shows a lower recall in these classes compared to video only system. On the other hand, recall performance of audio based system outperforms video based system in the remaining four classes. These results imply that a confidence based fusion of modality-specific systems can advance the overall recognition. We also observe decreased recall in Sadness and Fear classes in the fused system compared to audio only system. It is known that acoustic features can provide good classification in arousal based discrimination but fail in valence classification. A multi level, hierarchical system is feasible for single modality applications. However, this requires a different multimodal system than score level fusion.

5. CONCLUSIONS AND OUTLOOK

In this study, we introduce ELMs for audiovisual emotion recognition in the wild. ELMs are beneficial in pattern recognition as they provide accurate results with several orders of magnitude faster training compared to SVMs and SLFNs. We test facial feature group selection as well as recently proposed acoustic feature selection approaches. We find that inclusion of other emotional corpora does not yield a significant boost. This may be attributed to the fact that the utilized corpora do not represent close-to-real-life conditions. We observe that even using a single facial region with ELM yields better results than challenge validation set baseline. Selecting inner facial regions that code action and less vulnerable to environmental occlusions is found to perform better in test set. We achieve the best validation and test set

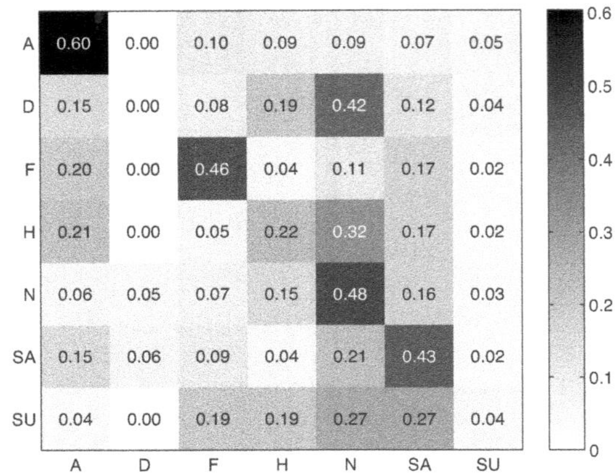

Figure 2: Test set confusion matrix of audio modality system. Classes correspond to A(nger), B(oredom), D(isgust), F(ear), H(appiness), N(eutral), SA(dness), SU(rprise).

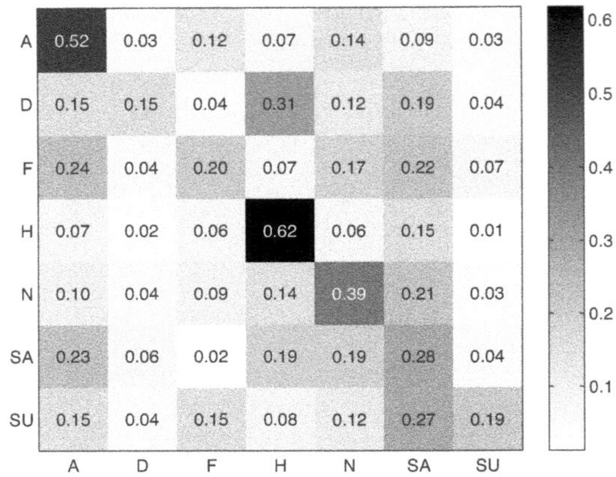

Figure 3: Test set confusion matrix of video modality system. Classes correspond to A(nger), B(oredom), D(isgust), F(ear), H(appiness), N(eutral), SA(dness), SU(rprise).

results with decision fusion of modality-specific ELM models. Using score level fusion of models trained on selected facial regions and full set of acoustic features, we reach a test set accuracy of 44.23%. Considering the confusion matrices of single modality systems, further study to combine the modality-specific scores based on classifier confidence would be beneficial.

6. REFERENCES

[1] E. Alpaydin. *Introduction to Machine Learning*. The MIT Press, 2nd edition, 2010.

[2] P. L. Bartlett. The sample complexity of pattern classification with neural networks: the size of the weights is more important than the size of the network. *Information Theory, IEEE Transactions on*, 44(2):525–536, 1998.

[3] F. Burkhardt, A. Paeschke, M. Rolfes, W. Sendlmeier, and B. Weiss. A database of german emotional speech. In *in Proc. of Interspeech*, pages 1517–1520, 2005.

[4] E. Cambria, G.-B. Huang, L. L. C. Kasun, H. Zhou, C.-M. Vong, J. Lin, J. Yin, Z. Cai, Q. Liu, K. Li, et al. Extreme learning machines. *IEEE Intelligent Systems*, 28(6):30–59, 2013.

[5] R. Cowie, N. Sussman, and A. Ben-Ze'ev. *In Petta, P. and Pelechaud, C. and Cowie, R. (eds) Emotion-Oriented Systems: The Humaine Handbook*, chapter Emotion: Concepts and Definitions, pages 9–32. Springer, 2011.

[6] A. Dhall, R. Goecke, J. Joshi, K. Sikka, and T. Gedeon. Emotion recognition in the wild challenge 2014: Baseline, data and protocol. In *Proc. of the 16th ACM Intl. Conf. on Multimodal Interaction (ICMI 2014)*. ACM, 2014.

[7] A. Dhall, R. Goecke, J. Joshi, M. Wagner, and T. Gedeon. Emotion recognition in the wild challenge 2013. In *Proc. of the 15th ACM Intl. Conf. on Multimodal Interaction (ICMI 2013)*, pages 509–516. ACM, 2013.

[8] A. Dhall, R. Goecke, S. Lucey, and T. Gedeon. Collecting large, richly annotated facial-expression databases from movies. *IEEE MultiMedia*, 19(3):34–41, July 2012.

[9] I. Engberg and A. Hansen. Documentation of the danish emotional speech database (des). Internal aau report, Center for Person Kommunikation, Denmark, 1996.

[10] F. Eyben, M. Wöllmer, and B. Schuller. Opensmile: the munich versatile and fast open-source audio feature extractor. In *Proc. of the intl. conf. on Multimedia*, pages 1459–1462. ACM, 2010.

[11] D. R. Hardoon, S. Szedmak, and J. Shawe-Taylor. Canonical correlation analysis: An overview with application to learning methods. *Neural Computation*, 16(12):2639–2664, 2004.

[12] H. Hotelling. Relations between two sets of variates. *Biometrika*, 28(3/4):321–377, 1936.

[13] G.-B. Huang, D. H. Wang, and Y. Lan. Extreme learning machines: a survey. *Intl. Journal of Machine Learning and Cybernetics*, 2(2):107–122, 2011.

[14] G.-B. Huang, H. Zhou, X. Ding, and R. Zhang. Extreme learning machine for regression and multiclass classification. *Systems, Man, and Cybernetics, Part B: Cybernetics, IEEE Transactions on*, 42(2):513–529, 2012.

[15] G.-B. Huang, Q.-Y. Zhu, and C.-K. Siew. Extreme learning machine: a new learning scheme of feedforward neural networks. In *Proc. IEEE Intl. Joint Conf. on Neural Networks*, volume 2, pages 985–990. IEEE, 2004.

[16] G.-B. Huang, Q.-Y. Zhu, and C.-K. Siew. Extreme learning machine: theory and applications. *Neurocomputing*, 70(1):489–501, 2006.

[17] H. Kaya, F. Eyben, A. A. Salah, and B. W. Schuller. CCA Based Feature Selection with Application to Continuous Depression Recognition from Acoustic Speech Features. In *Proc. IEEE Intl. Conf. on*

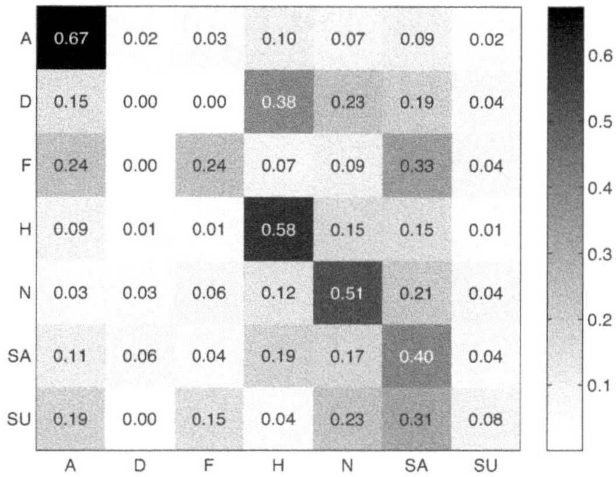

Figure 4: Test set confusion matrix of multimodal score fusion system. Classes correspond to A(nger), B(oredom), D(isgust), F(ear), H(appiness), N(eutral), SA(dness), SU(rprise).

Acoustics, Speech, and Signal Processing (ICASSP 2014), pages 3757–3761, 2014.

[18] H. Kaya, F. Çilli, and A. A. Salah. Ensemble cca for continuous emotion prediction. In *Proc. of the 4th ACM Intl. Workshop on Audio/Visual Emotion Challenge*, AVEC '14, 2014.

[19] H. Kaya and A. A. Salah. Eyes whisper depression: A cca based multimodal approach. In *Proc. of the 22nd Intl. Conf. on Multimedia*, ACM MM '14, Orlando, Florida, USA, 2014. ACM.

[20] H. Kaya, A. A. Salah, S. F. Gurgen, and H. Ekenel. Protocol and Baseline for Experiments on Bogazici University Turkish Emotional Speech Corpus. In *IEEE Signal Processing and Communications Applications Conf. (SIU), 2014 22nd*, pages 1698–1701, April 2014.

[21] H. Kaya, T. Özkaptan, A. A. Salah, and S. F. Gürgen. Canonical Correlation Analysis and Local Fisher Discriminant Analysis based Multi-View Acoustic Feature Reduction for Physical Load Prediction. In *Proc. INTERSPEECH*, Singapore, Sep 2014. ISCA, ISCA.

[22] O. Martin, I. Kotsia, B. Macq, and I. Pitas. The enterface '05 audio-visual emotion database. In *Proc. IEEE Workshop Multimedia Database Management.* IEEE, 2006.

[23] T. Ojala, M. Pietikainen, and T. Maenpaa. Multiresolution gray-scale and rotation invariant texture classification with local binary patterns. *Pattern Analysis and Machine Intelligence, IEEE Transactions on*, 24(7):971–987, 2002.

[24] H. Peng, F. Long, and C. Ding. Feature selection based on mutual information: Criteria of max-dependency, max-relevance, and min-redundancy. *IEEE Transactions on Pattern Analysis and Machine Intelligence*, 27(8):1226–1238, 2005.

[25] C. R. Rao and S. K. Mitra. *Generalized inverse of matrices and its applications*, volume 7. Wiley New York, 1971.

[26] B. Schuller, S. Steidl, and A. Batliner. The Interspeech 2009 Emotion Challenge. In *Proc. INTERSPEECH*, pages 312–315, Brighton, UK, September 2009. ISCA, ISCA.

[27] B. Schuller, S. Steidl, A. Batliner, F. Burkhardt, L. Devillers, C. A. Müller, and S. S. Narayanan. The interspeech 2010 paralinguistic challenge. In *Proc. INTERSPEECH*, pages 2794–2797, 2010.

[28] B. Schuller, S. Steidl, A. Batliner, A. Vinciarelli, K. Scherer, F. Ringeval, M. Chetouani, F. Weninger, F. Eyben, E. Marchi, M. Mortillaro, H. Salamin, A. Polychroniou, F. Valente, and S. Kim. The INTERSPEECH 2013 Computational Paralinguistics Challenge: Social Signals, Conflict, Emotion, Autism. In *Proc. INTERSPEECH*, pages 148–152, Lyon, France, August 2013. ISCA, ISCA.

[29] B. Schuller, M. Valstar, F. Eyben, R. Cowie, and M. Pantic. AVEC 2012 – The Continuous Audio/Visual Emotion Challenge. In L.-P. Morency, D. Bohus, H. K. Aghajan, J. Cassell, A. Nijholt, and J. Epps, editors, *Proc. of the 14th ACM Intl. Conf. on Multimodal Interaction, ICMI*, pages 449–456, Santa Monica, CA, October 2012. ACM.

[30] B. Schuller, B. Vlasenko, F. Eyben, M. Wollmer, A. Stuhlsatz, A. Wendemuth, and G. Rigoll. Cross-corpus acoustic emotion recognition: variances and strategies. *Affective Computing, IEEE Transactions on*, 1(2):119–131, 2010.

[31] B. Shuller. *In Salah, A. A. and Gevers, T. (eds) Computer Analysis of Human Behavior*, chapter Voice and Speech Analysis in Search of States and Traits, pages 227–253. Springer, 2011.

[32] J. A. Suykens and J. Vandewalle. Least squares support vector machine classifiers. *Neural processing letters*, 9(3):293–300, 1999.

[33] M. Valstar, B. Schuller, K. Smith, T. Almaev, F. Eyben, J. Krajewski, R. Cowie, and M. Pantic. AVEC 2014–3D Dimensional Affect and Depression Recognition Challenge. In *Proc. of the 4rd ACM Intl. Workshop on Audio/Visual Emotion Challenge*, AVEC '14, 2014.

[34] M. Valstar, B. Schuller, K. Smith, F. Eyben, B. Jiang, S. Bilakhia, S. Schnieder, R. Cowie, and M. Pantic. AVEC 2013–The Continuous Audio/Visual Emotion and Depression Recognition Challenge. In *Proc. of the 3rd ACM Intl. Workshop on Audio/Visual Emotion Challenge*, AVEC '13, pages 3–10, 2013.

Combining Multiple Kernel Methods on Riemannian Manifold for Emotion Recognition in the Wild

Mengyi Liu, Ruiping Wang, Shaoxin Li, Shiguang Shan, Zhiwu Huang, Xilin Chen
Key Lab of Intelligence Information Processing of Chinese Academy of Sciences (CAS),
Institute of Computing Technology, CAS, Beijing, 100190, China
{mengyi.liu, shaoxin.li, zhiwu.huang}@vipl.ict.ac.cn,
{wangruiping, sgshan, xlchen}@ict.ac.cn

ABSTRACT

In this paper, we present the method for our submission to the Emotion Recognition in the Wild Challenge (EmotiW 2014). The challenge is to automatically classify the emotions acted by human subjects in video clips under real-world environment. In our method, each video clip can be represented by three types of image set models (i.e. linear subspace, covariance matrix, and Gaussian distribution) respectively, which can all be viewed as points residing on some Riemannian manifolds. Then different Riemannian kernels are employed on these set models correspondingly for similarity/distance measurement. For classification, three types of classifiers, i.e. kernel SVM, logistic regression, and partial least squares, are investigated for comparisons. Finally, an optimal fusion of classifiers learned from different kernels and different modalities (video and audio) is conducted at the decision level for further boosting the performance. We perform an extensive evaluation on the challenge data (including validation set and blind test set), and evaluate the effects of different strategies in our pipeline. The final recognition accuracy achieved 50.4% on test set, with a significant gain of 16.7% above the challenge baseline 33.7%.

Categories and Subject Descriptors

I.5.4 [**Pattern Recognition**]: Applications—*computer vision, signal processing*; I.4.m [**Image Processing and Computer Vision**]: Miscellaneous

Keywords

Emotion Recognition; Riemannian Manifold; Multiple Kernels; EmotiW 2014 Challenge

1. INTRODUCTION

Automatic emotion recognition is a popular and challenging problem in the research fields of cognitive psychology, human-computer interaction, pattern recognition, and so on. Early stage research mostly focuses on the emotion databases collected in "lab-controlled" environment where human subjects posed particular emotions (e.g. angry, happy, and surprise). With recent advances in emotion recognition community, various spontanous or wild databases have been introduced for emotion recognition challenges, such as the Facial Expression Recognition & Analysis (FERA 2011) [33], Audio Video Emotion Challenges (AVEC 2011/2012/2013) [32], and Emotion Recognition in the Wild (EmotiW 2013) [8]. These challenges have provided common benchmarks for emotion recognition researchers.

Previous works on emotion recognition can be broadly categorized into two groups [39]: static image based methods [29, 42, 21] and video based methods [41, 38, 22]. The video based methods tend to utilize dynamic information extracted from image sequences for improving the performance. For instance, Zhao *et al.* [41] encoded spatial-temporal patterns in facial image sequences using LBP-TOP features. Liu *et al.* [22] modeled each emotion clip as a manifold of mid-level features for representing the local spatial-temporal variations on faces. As demonstrated in their experiments, various types of dynamic features are crucial for modeling emotion variations in the recognition task.

Generally, extracting dynamics from successive frames requires accurate image alignment to eliminate the rigid motion effect brought by camera or head pose. However, it is quite difficult especially when dealing with "wild data" due to the large variations caused by uncontrolled real-world environment. As a video clip can be simply regarded as an image set, it is natural to introduce the image-set-based classification methods [13, 35, 34, 20], which have been proved to be more robust to image misalignment. So in this paper, we propose to represent the emotion video clip using three kinds of image set models (i.e. linear subspace, covariance matrix, and Gaussian distribution) respectively, which can all be viewed as points residing on some Riemannian manifolds. Then different Riemanian kernels are employed on these set models correspondingly for similarity/distance measurement. For classification, three types of classifiers, kernel SVM, logistic regression, partial least squares, are investigated for comparisons. Finally, a score-level fusion of classifiers learned based on different kernel methods and different modalities (i.e. video and audio) is conducted to further improve the performance. An overview of the proposed method is illustrated in Figure 1. We will detail the whole procedure in the next section.

WOODSTOCK '97 El Paso, Texas USA
Copyright 2014 ACM 978-1-4503-2885-2/14/11 ...$15.00.
http://dx.doi.org/10.1145/2663204.2666274.

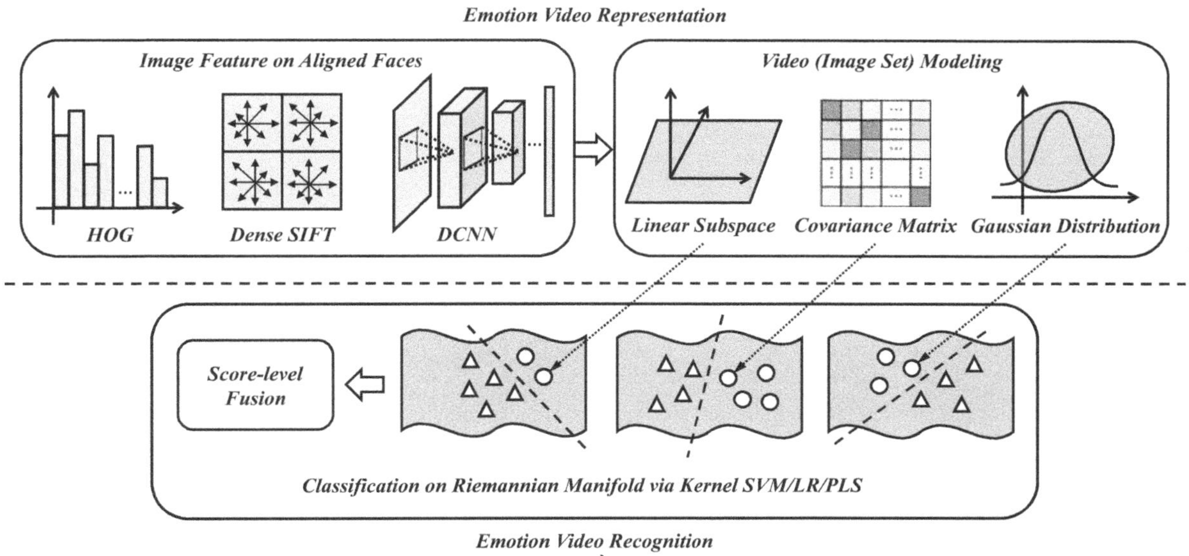

Figure 1: An overview of the proposed method. The whole procedure includes two stages: emotion video representation and recognition. In representation stage, different image features are first extracted from the coarsely aligned faces, then different image set models are employed on frame features respectively for representing each video clip. In recognition stage, classification on Riemannian manifold sapnned by the points (i.e. image sets) is performed using different types of classifiers by exploiting a group of Riemannian kernels. Finally a score-level fusion is conducted to combine the prediction results from different kernels.

2. THE PROPOSED METHOD

2.1 Image Feature

2.1.1 HOG

The Histogram of Oriented Gradients (HOG) [4] feature describes the local shape and appearance of objects by capturing the distribution information of intensity gradients or edge directions. The descriptor decomposes a local region into small squared cells, computes the histogram of different bins of oriented gradients in each cell, and normalizes the results using block-wise pattern (each block contains several cells). HOG is commonly used in computer vision problems, such as object detection and recognition. It has also been successfully used for facial expression analysis in [6, 30].

2.1.2 Dense SIFT

The Scale-Invariant Feature Transform (SIFT) [25] combines a feature detector and a feature descriptor. The detector extracts a number of interested points from an image in a way that is consistent with some variations of the illumination or viewpoint. The descriptor associates to the region around each interest point a signature which identifies its appearance compactly and robustly. For dense SIFT, it is equivalent to performing SIFT descriptor on a dense grid of locations on an image at a fixed scale and orientation. The obtained feature vectors characterizing appearance information are often used for categorization task.

2.1.3 Deep CNN Feature

Convolutional Neural Network (CNN) [19] is a type of feed-forward artificial neural network which is inspired from biology. The individual neurons are designed to simulate cells within visual cortex, which are sensitive to small subregions of input space, named receptive fields [15]. Thus the connections among neurons are tied in such a way that each output neuron only responds to a local region of input neurons. This mechanism is better suited to exploit the strong spatially local correlations presented in natural images. Currently, one of the most popular CNN architectures is the 9-layers deep model [17] designed for ImageNet ILSVRC-2012. There are four convolutional layers with their corresponding pooling layers, and finally followed by an output layer which is constructed according to category labels. As the experiments in some latest works [18, 12, 31] have shown, this architecture, even the pre-trained model via ImageNet data, can be well generalized to many other problems, without any further specific design but maintaining impressive performance.

2.2 Video (Image Set) Modeling

After extracting image features for each video frame, one video clip can be regarded as a set of feature vectors $F = [f_1, f_2, ..., f_n]$, where $f_i \in R^d$ denotes the i-th image with d-dimensional feature description. Based on the feature vector set, we exploit three types of image set models, linear subspace [13], covariance matrix [35], and Gaussian distribution [28, 1], for their desirable capability of capturing data variations to model emotion video.

2.2.1 Linear Subspace

The feature set $F = [f_1, f_2, ..., f_n]$ can be represented by a linear subspace $P \in R^{d\times r}$ via SVD as follows:

$$\sum_{i=1}^{n} f_i f_i^T = P\Lambda P^T, \tag{1}$$

where $P = [p_1, p_2, ..., p_r]$, p_j is the j-th leading eigenvector, r is the dimension of the subspace, and n is the number of frames in the video clip. All of the video samples can be modeled as a collection of linear subspaces [37, 13], which are also the data points on Grassmann manifold $Gr(r, d)$ (Grassmann manifold is a special case of Riemannian manifold [13]).

2.2.2 Covariance Matrix

We can also represent the image feature set with the $d \times d$ sample covariance matrix:

$$C = \frac{1}{n-1}\sum_{i=1}^{n}(f_i - \overline{f})(f_i - \overline{f})^T, \quad (2)$$

where $\overline{f}$ is the mean vector of the image features. As the raw second-order statistic of a set of samples, the covariance matrix makes no assumption about the data distribution, thus providing a natural representation by encoding the feature correlation information specific to each class [35]. It is also well known that the $d \times d$ nonsingular covariance matrices are Symmetric Positive Definite (SPD) matrices Sym_d^+ lying on a Riemannian manifold.

2.2.3 Gaussian Distribution

Suppose the feature vectors $f_1, f_2, ..., f_n$ follow a k-dimensional Gaussian distribution $\mathcal{N}(\mu, \Sigma)$, where μ and Σ are the data mean and covariance respectively:

$$\mu = E(f_i) = \frac{1}{n}\sum_{i=1}^{n} f_i, \quad (3)$$

$$\Sigma = E[(f_i - \mu)(f_i - \mu)^T] = \frac{1}{n-1}\sum_{i=1}^{n}(f_i - \mu)(f_i - \mu)^T. \quad (4)$$

The Gaussian jointly considers the first-order statistic mean and second-order statistic covariance in a single model. By embedding the space of Gaussians into a Lie group or regarding it as a product of Lie groups, we can measure the intrinsic distance between Gaussians on the underlying Riemannian manifold [20].

2.3 Riemannian Kernels

2.3.1 Kernels for Linear Subspace

As presented in Section 2.2.1, the video samples are modeled as a collection of linear subspaces which correspond to points lying on Grassmann manifold M (also in Riemannian space), denoted by $\mathcal{P} = \{P_i\}_{i=1}^N$, where N is the number of video samples. The similarity between two data points P_i and P_j can be measured via mapping the Grassmann manifold to Euclidean space using Mercer kernels [13]. One popularly used kernel [13, 14, 23] is the Projection kernel originated from the principle angles between two subspaces given by (see Figure 2):

$$\mathcal{K}_{i,j}^{Proj.-Poly.} = (\gamma \cdot ||P_i^T P_j||_F^2)^\alpha, \quad (5)$$

where $\mathcal{K}_{i,j}^{Proj.-Poly.}$ is an element in the kernel matrix. The corresponding mapping is $\Phi_{Proj.} = P_i P_i^T$. Then a form of

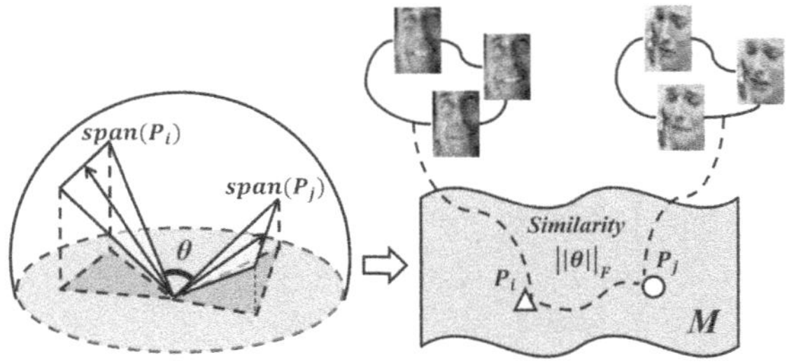

Figure 2: An illustration of principal angles of linear subspaces and their projection metric distances on Grassmann manifold M.

RBF kernel [34] can be generated using $\Phi_{Proj.}$ by:

$$\mathcal{K}_{i,j}^{Proj.-RBF} = exp(-\gamma||\Phi_{Proj.}(P_i) - \Phi_{Proj.}(P_j)||_F^2). \quad (6)$$

2.3.2 Kernels for Covariance Matrix

The $d \times d$ SPD matrices, i.e. non-singlular covariance matrices $\mathcal{C} = \{C_i\}_{i=1}^N$, can be formulated as data points on SPD Riemannian manifold [26]. A commonly used distance metric for SPD matrices is the Log-Euclidean Distance (LED) [2]. Based on LED, [35] proposed a Riemannian kernel that computes the inner-product in a vector space T obtained by mapping data points from the SPD manifold to the tangent space at the identity matrix I via ordinary matrix logarithm operator (see Figure 3).

$$\mathcal{K}_{i,j}^{LED-Poly.} = (\gamma \cdot trace[log(C_i) \cdot log(C_j)])^\alpha. \quad (7)$$

The mapping corresponding to $\mathcal{K}_{i,j}^{LED-Poly.}$ is given by $\Phi_{LED} = log(C_i)$. Similarly a form of RBF kernel [34] can be generated using Φ_{LED} by:

$$\mathcal{K}_{i,j}^{LED-RBF} = exp(-\gamma||\Phi_{LED}(C_i) - \Phi_{LED}(C_j)||_F^2). \quad (8)$$

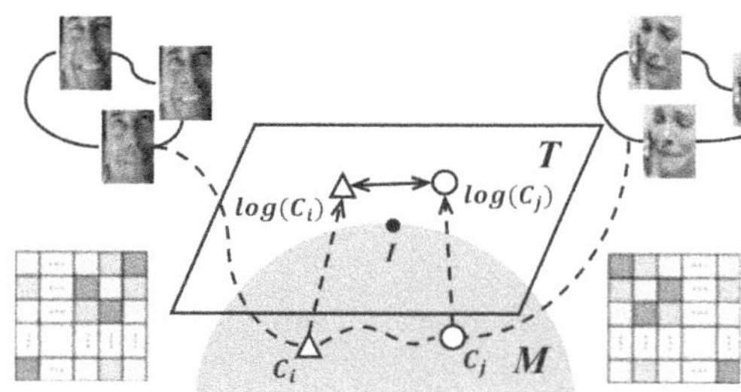

Figure 3: An illustration of mapping covariance matrices from the SPD Riemannian manifold M to the tangent space T (which is a vector space) at the point of identity matrix I on M.

2.3.3 Kernels for Gaussian Distribution

The space of d-dimensional multivariate Gaussians is a Riemannian manifold and can be embeded into the space of Symmetric Positive Definite (SPD) matrices [24], denoted as Sym_{d+1}^+. Thus A d-dimensional Gaussian $\mathcal{N}(\mu, \Sigma)$ is uniquely represented by a $(d+1) \times (d+1)$ SPD matrix G

as follows:

$$\mathcal{N}(\mu,\Sigma) \sim G = |\Sigma|^{-\frac{1}{d+1}} \begin{bmatrix} \Sigma + \mu\mu^T & \mu \\ \mu^T & 1 \end{bmatrix} \quad (9)$$

When obtaining the SPD matrices $\mathcal{G} = \{G_i\}_{i=1}^N$, we can calculate the corresponding Riemannian kernels similarly as in Section 2.3.2:

$$\mathcal{K}_{i,j}^{LED-Poly.} = (\gamma \cdot trace[log(G_i) \cdot log(G_j)])^{\alpha}. \quad (10)$$

$$\mathcal{K}_{i,j}^{LED-RBF} = exp(-\gamma||\Phi_{LED}(G_i) - \Phi_{LED}(G_j)||_F^2). \quad (11)$$

2.4 Classifiers

Based on the above six Riemannian kernels, traditional learning methods operating in vector space can be exploited to classify data points (i.e. image set models) on the Riemannian manifolds for emotion video recognition. In our framework, three types of classifiers are investigated as described below.

2.4.1 *Kernel SVM*

The Riemannian kernels enable the classifiers to operate in an extrinsic feature space without computing the coordinates of data in original space. An SVM classifier in the kernel space is given by

$$f(x) = \overrightarrow{w}^{*T}\Phi(x) + b^*, \quad (12)$$

where $\Phi(x)$ is the mapping (e.g. $\Phi_{Proj.}$ and Φ_{IP}) which generates the kernel function $k(\cdot,\cdot)$ by

$$\mathcal{K}_{i,j} = k(x_i, x_j) = \Phi(x_i)^T\Phi(x_j). \quad (13)$$

The weight vector $\overrightarrow{w}^*$ and bias b^* are given by

$$\begin{aligned} \overrightarrow{w}^*, b^* &= \underset{\overrightarrow{w},b,\eta}{argmin} \frac{1}{2}||\overrightarrow{w}||_2^2 + C\sum_i \eta_i. \\ s.t.\quad & y_i(\overrightarrow{w}^T\Phi(x_i) + b) \geq 1 - \eta_i, \eta_i \geq 0. \end{aligned} \quad (14)$$

For this work, we employ the LibSVM [3] implementation on our pre-calculated Riemannian kernel matrices for classification.

2.4.2 *Logistic Regression*

According to the Riemanian kernel matrices, the i-th row contains similarities between the i-th video (image set) and all videos in training set, which can be directly treated as a feature vector of this sample. For each sample in the training or test set, we calculate its similarities to all training samples thus obtain the training kernel matrix and test kernel matrix for feature representation. We employ an L2-regularized logistic regression on these features for classification by solving the objective function:

$$\min_{\overrightarrow{w}}(C\sum_i log(1 + exp(-y_i - \overrightarrow{w}^T x_i)) + \frac{1}{2}||\overrightarrow{w}||_2^2). \quad (15)$$

For this work, we employ the Liblinear [11] implementation for optimization.

2.4.3 *Partial Least Squares*

Similar to Section 2.4.2, we also apply the partial least square classifier [36] to the kernel matrices. We adapt it to a one-vs-all manner to especially deal with the difficult and confusion categories as in [23].

Suppose there are c categories of emotions, we design c one-vs-all PLS to predict each class simultaneously. For a single classifier, given feature variables X and 0-1 labels Y, the PLS decomposes them into

$$\begin{aligned} X &= U_x V_x^T + r_x \\ Y &= U_y V_y^T + r_y \end{aligned} \quad (16)$$

where U_x and U_y contain the extracted latent vectors, V_x and V_y represent the loadings, and r_x and r_y are residuals. PLS is to find weight vectors w_x and w_y that

$$[cov(u_x, u_y)]^2 = \max_{|w|=|v|=1} [cov(Xw_x, Yw_y)]^2, \quad (17)$$

where u_x and u_y are the column vectors of U_x and U_y respectively. $cov(u_x, u_y)$ is the covariance of samples. With the obtained latent vectors, the regression coefficients from X to Y are given by:

$$\begin{aligned} \beta &= W_x(V_x^T W_x)^{-1}U_x Y \\ &= X^T U_y (U_x^T X X^T U_x)^{-1} U_x^T Y, \end{aligned} \quad (18)$$

thus we can predict $\widehat{Y} = X\beta$ [27]. Applying the c one-vs-all PLS to each test sample, we can obtain c regression values respectively. The category corresponding to the maximum value is decided to be the recognition result.

2.4.4 *Fusion Scheme*

We learn each classifier on the six Riemannian kernels with different image features respectively. An equal-weighted linear fusion is conducted among the prediction scores obtained by the same type of classifiers. Besides the video modality, we also obtain prediction scores on audio features (extracted by OpenSMILE toolkit) [10]). A weighted term λ is introduced at decision level for video-audio fusion:

$$Score^{fusion} = (1-\lambda)Score^{video} + \lambda Score^{audio} \quad (19)$$

Similarly, The category corresponding to the maximum value of the score vector is decided to be the recognition result.

3. EXPERIMENTS

3.1 EmotiW 2014 Challenge

The Emotion Recognition in the Wild Challenge (EmotiW 2014) [7] consists of an audio-video based emotion classification task which mimics real-world conditions. The goal of this challenge is to extend and carry forward the new common platform for evaluation of emotion recognition methods in the wild defined in EmotiW 2013 [8]. The database in the 2014 challenge is the Acted Faical Expression in Wild (AFEW) [9] 4.0, which has been collected from movies showing close-to-real-world conditions. Three sets for training, validation, and testing are available for participants (The numbers of samples for each emotion category in the three sets are illustrated in Table 1). The task is to classify an audio-video clip into one of the seven emotion categories

Table 1: The numbers of samples for each emotion category in the training, validation and testing sets.

	An	Di	Fe	Ha	Ne	Sa	Su
Train	92	66	66	105	102	82	54
Val	59	39	44	63	61	59	46
Test	58	26	46	81	117	53	26

(i.e. angry, disgust, fear, happy, neutral, sad, and surprise). The labels of the testing set are unknown. Participants can learn their models on training set and optimize the parameters on validation set, then report the prediction results on testing set for evaluation.

3.2 Parameter Setting

We simply use the aligned face images provided by EmotiW 2014 organizers. All images are resized to 64×64 pixels. Three kinds of image features are employed on the aligned faces: HOG, Dense SIFT, and DCNN.

For HOG, we divide each image into $7\times7 = 49$ overlapping blocks with the size of 16×16 pixels (i.e. the strides are 8 pixels in both horizontal and vertical directions). The descriptor is applied by computing histograms of oriented gradient on 2×2 cells in each block, and the orientations are quantized into 9 bins, which results in $2 \times 2 \times 9 = 36$ dimensions for each block and $36 \times 49 = 1764$ dimensions for the whole image.

For Dense SIFT, we divide each image into 49 overlapping local regions as done for HOG. In each 16×16 pixels block, we apply the SIFT descriptor to the center point, and obtain a typical $4 \times 4 \times 8 = 128$ dimensions feature vector. For the whole image, we have $128 \times 49 = 6272$ dimensions feature.

For DCNN, we employ the Caffe [16] implementation, which is commonly used in several latest works [12, 31]. Two types of DCNN models are trained by feeding different training data: ImageNet ILSVRC-2012 [5] and Celebrity Faces in the Wild (CFW) [40]. The first one is for evaluating the generalization ability of the deep model and natural image data, so we exactly take use of the same parameters as that in [17], the 9216 nodes' values of the last convolutional layer are used for final image features. The second one is to explore the shared feature representations for both face identities and expressions. Over 150,000 face images from 1,520 people are used for training and the labels are their identities. The architecture is $3@237\times237 \rightarrow 96@57\times57 \rightarrow 96@28\times28 \rightarrow 256@28\times28 \rightarrow 384@14\times14 \rightarrow 256@14\times14 \rightarrow 256@7\times7 \rightarrow 4096 \rightarrow 1520$. Similar to the first model, the $256 \times 7 \times 7 = 12544$ nodes' values of the last convolutional layer are used for final image features.

3.3 Results Comparisons

The emotion recognition results on validation set based on different classifiers are illustrated in Figure 4. For each single classifier, the DCNN features have shown promising performance on the task, especially the features extracted by Caffe trained on CFW have achieved better results than the specific hand-crafted features.

We also demonstrate the results on validation set based on different features in Table 2. For each single feature, the results based on six Riemannian kernels and three classifiers are all listed respectively. As shown, PLS achieves the best performance for its one-vs-all manner which can especially deal with the difficult and confusion categories.

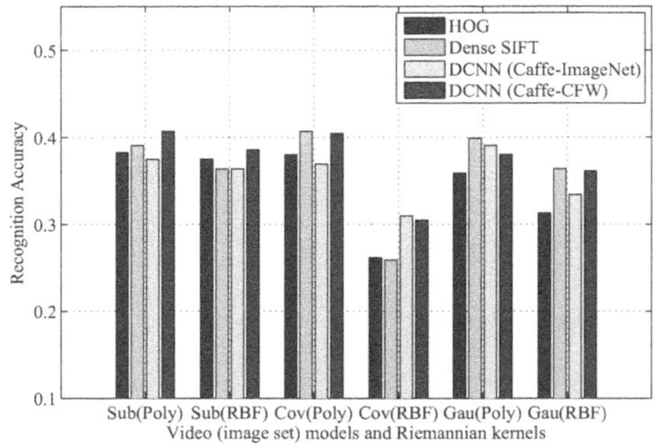

(a) Kernel SVM.

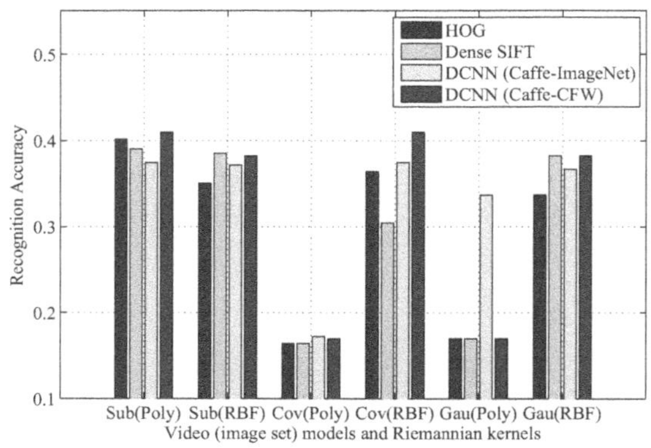

(b) Logistic Regression.

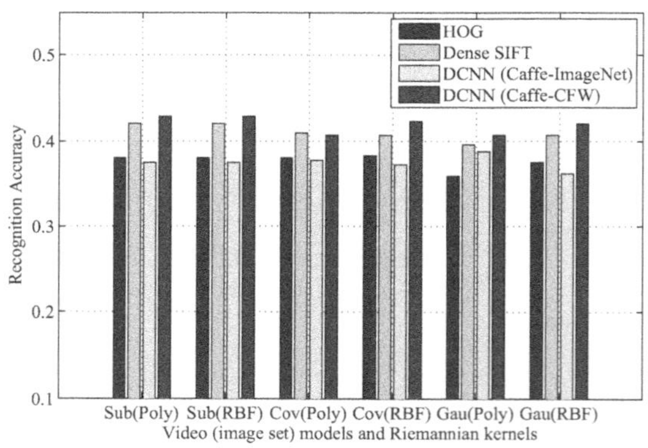

(c) Partial Least Squares.

Figure 4: Emotion recognition accuracy on validation set based on different classifiers.

The overall recognition results are obtained by one-vs-all PLS classifier using decision-level fusion over different kernels. As presented in Section 2.4.4, an equal-weighted linear fusion is conducted among the prediction scores based on the six Riemannian kernels with different features, and the weighted term for video-audio fusion is set as $\lambda = 0.3$ in the final submission. Different strategies of fusion and their corresponding results on validation and test sets are all listed in Table 3.

Table 2: **Emotion recognition accuracy on validation set based on different image features.**

(a) HOG

	Linear Subspace		Covariance Matrix		Gaussian Distribution	
	Proj.-Poly. Kernel	Proj.-RBF Kernel	LED-Poly. Kenrel	LED-RBF Kernel	LED-Poly. Kenrel	LED-RBF Kernel
Kernel SVM	38.27%	37.47%	38.01%	26.15%	35.85%	31.27%
Logistic Regression	40.16%	35.04%	16.44%	36.39%	16.98%	33.69%
Partial Least Squares	38.01%	38.01%	38.01%	38.27%	35.85%	37.47%

(b) Dense SIFT

	Linear Subspace		Covariance Matrix		Gaussian Distribution	
	Proj.-Poly. Kernel	Proj.-RBF Kernel	LED-Poly. Kenrel	LED-RBF Kernel	LED-Poly. Kenrel	LED-RBF Kernel
Kernel SVM	39.08%	36.39%	40.70%	25.88%	39.89%	36.39%
Logistic Regression	39.08%	38.54%	16.44%	30.46%	16.98%	38.27%
Partial Least Squares	42.05%	42.05%	40.97%	40.70%	39.62%	40.70%

(c) DCNN (Caffe-ImageNet)

	Linear Subspace		Covariance Matrix		Gaussian Distribution	
	Proj.-Poly. Kernel	Proj.-RBF Kernel	LED-Poly. Kenrel	LED-RBF Kernel	LED-Poly. Kenrel	LED-RBF Kernel
Kernel SVM	37.74%	36.39%	36.93%	31.00%	39.08%	33.42%
Logistic Regression	37.47%	37.20%	17.25%	37.47%	33.69%	36.66%
Partial Least Squares	37.47%	37.47%	37.74%	37.20%	38.81%	36.12%

(d) DCNN (Caffe-CFW)

	Linear Subspace		Covariance Matrix		Gaussian Distribution	
	Proj.-Poly. Kernel	Proj.-RBF Kernel	LED-Poly. Kenrel	LED-RBF Kernel	LED-Poly. Kenrel	LED-RBF Kernel
Kernel SVM	40.70%	38.54%	40.43%	30.46%	38.01%	36.12%
Logistic Regression	40.97%	38.27%	16.98%	40.97%	16.98%	38.27%
Partial Least Squares	42.86%	42.86%	40.70%	42.32%	40.70%	42.05%

The confusion matrix of the final submission method are shown in Figure 5. We can see that "angry", "happy" and "neutral" are much easier to be distinguished from other emotions, but it is still hard to do well on some difficult and confusion emotion categories such as "disgust", "fear", and "sad". Moreover, in contrast to the experience in emotion classification on lab-controlled data, in our experiments, "surprise" is hard to be recognized and easy to be confused with some other categories like "neutral" and "fear". The reason may lie in the following two aspects: first, few "surprise" data are provided for learning and testing compared to other categories (as shown in Table 1); second, the "surprise" emotion may not be acted exaggeratedly sometimes in the real-world condition, thus no typical appearance variations (e.g. mouth stretching, upper lip raising) are shown as that in lab-controlled data.

4. CONCLUSIONS

In this paper, we propose a method for video-based emotion recognition in real-world condition. Each emotion video clips is simply regarded as an image set and different kinds of image set models are used to represent the video clips as a collection of data points on Riemannian manifold. Then multiple Riemanian kernels are employed on these set models correspondingly for distance metrics. At last, a score-level fusion of classifiers learned based on different kernel methods and different modalities is conducted for final recognition results. The method is evaluated on EmotiW 2014 data and achieves promising results on both validation and unseen test data. In the future, we will try to deal with the few difficult categories and explore more effective fusion strategy to further improve the performance.

Table 3: Performance comparisons of different strategies on both validation and test set based on PLS.

Methods		Accuracy	
		Val	Test
Baseline (*provided by EmotiW organizers*)		34.4%	33.7%
Audio (*OpenSMILE Toolkit*)		30.73%	--
Video	HOG	38.01%	--
	Dense SIFT	43.94%	--
	DCNN (*Caffe-ImageNet*)	39.35%	--
	DCNN (*Caffe-CFW*)	43.40%	--
	HOG + Dense SIFT	44.47%	--
	HOG + Dense SIFT + DCNN (*Caffe-ImageNet*)	44.74%	--
	HOG + Dense SIFT + DCNN (*Caffe-CFW*)	45.28%	--
Audio + Video (*HOG+Dense SIFT*)		46.36%	46.68%
Audio+Video (*HOG + Dense SIFT + DCNN (Caffe-ImageNet)*)		46.90%	47.91%
Audio+Video (*HOG + Dense SIFT + DCNN (Caffe-CFW)*)		***48.52%***	***50.37%***

	Angry	Disgust	Fear	Happy	Neutral	Sad	Surprise
Angry	84.75%	3.39%	0.00%	1.69%	5.08%	5.08%	0.00%
Disgust	10.26%	17.95%	2.56%	28.21%	33.33%	5.13%	2.56%
Fear	27.27%	6.82%	27.27%	13.64%	11.36%	9.09%	4.55%
Happy	4.76%	0.00%	0.00%	82.54%	9.52%	3.17%	0.00%
Neutral	13.11%	0.00%	1.64%	8.20%	70.49%	6.56%	0.00%
Sad	13.56%	3.39%	6.78%	23.73%	28.81%	22.03%	1.69%
Surprise	17.39%	4.35%	28.26%	8.70%	32.61%	2.17%	6.52%

(a) Validation set

	Angry	Disgust	Fear	Happy	Neutral	Sad	Surprise
Angry	81.03%	3.45%	0.00%	5.17%	10.34%	0.00%	0.00%
Disgust	11.54%	3.85%	3.85%	34.62%	23.08%	15.38%	7.69%
Fear	26.09%	0.00%	23.91%	10.87%	19.57%	15.22%	4.35%
Happy	8.64%	0.00%	1.23%	64.20%	11.11%	14.81%	0.00%
Neutral	7.69%	1.71%	5.13%	9.40%	63.25%	11.97%	0.85%
Sad	11.32%	0.00%	3.77%	24.53%	24.53%	33.96%	1.89%
Surprise	11.54%	0.00%	19.23%	7.69%	34.62%	19.23%	7.69%

(b) Test set

Figure 5: Confusion matrix of the final submission method.

5. ACKNOWLEDGMENTS

The work is partially supported by Natural Science Foundation of China under contracts nos.61025010, 61222211, 61390511, 61379083.

6. REFERENCES

[1] O. Arandjelovic, G. Shakhnarovich, J. Fisher, R. Cipolla, and T. Darrell. Face recognition with image sets using manifold density divergence. In *CVPR*. IEEE, 2005.

[2] V. Arsigny, P. Fillard, X. Pennec, and N. Ayache. Geometric means in a novel vector space structure on symmetric positive-definite matrices. *SIAM journal on matrix analysis and applications*, 29(1):328–347, 2007.

[3] C.-C. Chang and C.-J. Lin. Libsvm: a library for support vector machines. *ACM Transactions on Intelligent Systems and Technology (TIST)*, 2(3):27, 2011.

[4] N. Dalal and B. Triggs. Histograms of oriented gradients for human detection. In *CVPR*. IEEE, 2005.

[5] J. Deng, W. Dong, R. Socher, L.-J. Li, K. Li, and L. Fei-Fei. Imagenet: A large-scale hierarchical image database. In *CVPR*. IEEE, 2009.

[6] A. Dhall, A. Asthana, R. Goecke, and T. Gedeon. Emotion recognition using phog and lpq features. In *FG*. IEEE, 2011.

[7] A. Dhall, R. Goecke, J. Joshi, K. Sikka, and T. Gedeon. Emotion recognition in the wild challenge 2014: Baseline, data and protocol. In *ACM ICMI*. ACM, 2014.

[8] A. Dhall, R. Goecke, J. Joshi, M. Wagner, and T. Gedeon. Emotion recognition in the wild challenge 2013. In *ACM ICMI*. ACM, 2013.

[9] A. Dhall, R. Goecke, S. Lucey, and T. Gedeon. Collecting large, richly annotated facial-expression databases from movies. *IEEE MultiMedia*, 2012.

[10] F. Eyben, M. Wöllmer, and B. Schuller. Opensmile: the munich versatile and fast open-source audio feature extractor. In *ACM MM*. ACM, 2010.

[11] R.-E. Fan, K.-W. Chang, C.-J. Hsieh, X.-R. Wang, and C.-J. Lin. Liblinear: A library for large linear classification. *The Journal of Machine Learning Research*, 9:1871–1874, 2008.

[12] R. Girshick, J. Donahue, T. Darrell, and J. Malik. Rich feature hierarchies for accurate object detection and semantic segmentation. *arXiv preprint arXiv:1311.2524*, 2013.

[13] J. Hamm and D. D. Lee. Grassmann discriminant analysis: a unifying view on subspace-based learning. In *ICML*. ACM, 2008.

[14] M. T. Harandi, C. Sanderson, S. Shirazi, and B. C. Lovell. Graph embedding discriminant analysis on grassmannian manifolds for improved image set matching. In *CVPR*. IEEE, 2011.

[15] D. H. Hubel and T. N. Wiesel. Receptive fields and functional architecture of monkey striate cortex. *The Journal of physiology*, 195(1):215–243, 1968.

[16] Y. Jia. Caffe: An open source convolutional architecture for fast feature embedding. *http://caffe. berkeleyvision. org*, 2013.

[17] A. Krizhevsky, I. Sutskever, and G. E. Hinton. Imagenet classification with deep convolutional neural networks. In *NIPS*, 2012.

[18] Z.-Z. Lan, L. Jiang, S.-I. Yu, S. Rawat, Y. Cai, C. Gao, S. Xu, H. Shen, X. Li, Y. Wang, et al. Cmu-informedia at trecvid 2013 multimedia event detection. In *TRECVID 2013 Workshop*, 2013.

[19] Y. LeCun, L. Bottou, Y. Bengio, and P. Haffner. Gradient-based learning applied to document recognition. *Proc. of IEEE*, 86(11):2278–2324, 1998.

[20] P. Li, Q. Wang, and L. Zhang. A novel earth mover's distance methodology for image matching with gaussian mixture models. In *ICCV*. IEEE, 2013.

[21] M. Liu, S. Li, S. Shan, and X. Chen. Au-aware deep networks for facial expression recognition. In *FG*. IEEE, 2013.

[22] M. Liu, S. Shan, R. Wang, and X. Chen. Learning expressionlets on spatio-temporal manifold for dynamic facial expression recognition. In *CVPR*, 2014.

[23] M. Liu, R. Wang, Z. Huang, S. Shan, and X. Chen. Partial least squares regression on grassmannian manifold for emotion recognition. In *ACM ICMI*. ACM, 2013.

[24] M. Lovrić, M. Min-Oo, and E. A. Ruh. Multivariate normal distributions parametrized as a riemannian symmetric space. *Journal of Multivariate Analysis*, 74(1):36–48, 2000.

[25] D. G. Lowe. Distinctive image features from scale-invariant keypoints. *International journal of computer vision*, 60(2):91–110, 2004.

[26] X. Pennec, P. Fillard, and N. Ayache. A riemannian framework for tensor computing. *International Journal of Computer Vision*, 66(1):41–66, 2006.

[27] R. Rosipal and N. Krämer. Overview and recent advances in partial least squares. In *Subspace, Latent Structure and Feature Selection*, pages 34–51. Springer, 2006.

[28] G. Shakhnarovich, J. W. Fisher, and T. Darrell. Face recognition from long-term observations. In *ECCV*. Springer, 2002.

[29] C. Shan, S. Gong, and P. W. McOwan. Facial expression recognition based on local binary patterns: A comprehensive study. *Image and Vision Computing*, 27(6):803–816, 2009.

[30] K. Sikka, K. Dykstra, S. Sathyanarayana, G. Littlewort, and M. Bartlett. Multiple kernel learning for emotion recognition in the wild. In *ACM ICMI*. ACM, 2013.

[31] K. Simonyan and A. Zisserman. Two-stream convolutional networks for action recognition in videos. *arXiv preprint arXiv:1406.2199*, 2014.

[32] M. Valstar, B. Schuller, K. Smith, F. Eyben, B. Jiang, S. Bilakhia, S. Schnieder, R. Cowie, and M. Pantic. Avec 2013: the continuous audio/visual emotion and depression recognition challenge. In *ACM Workshop on AVEC*. ACM, 2013.

[33] M. F. Valstar, B. Jiang, M. Mehu, M. Pantic, and K. Scherer. The first facial expression recognition and analysis challenge. In *FG*. IEEE, 2011.

[34] R. Vemulapalli, J. K. Pillai, and R. Chellappa. Kernel learning for extrinsic classification of manifold features. In *CVPR*. IEEE, 2013.

[35] R. Wang, H. Guo, L. S. Davis, and Q. Dai. Covariance discriminative learning: A natural and efficient approach to image set classification. In *CVPR*. IEEE, 2012.

[36] H. Wold. Partial least squares. *Encyclopedia of statistical sciences*, 1985.

[37] O. Yamaguchi, K. Fukui, and K.-i. Maeda. Face recognition using temporal image sequence. In *FG*. IEEE, 1998.

[38] P. Yang, Q. Liu, and D. N. Metaxas. Boosting coded dynamic features for facial action units and facial expression recognition. In *CVPR*. IEEE, 2007.

[39] Z. Zeng, M. Pantic, G. I. Roisman, and T. S. Huang. A survey of affect recognition methods: Audio, visual, and spontaneous expressions. *Pattern Analysis and Machine Intelligence, IEEE Transactions on*, 31(1):39–58, 2009.

[40] X. Zhang, L. Zhang, X.-J. Wang, and H.-Y. Shum. Finding celebrities in billions of web images. *Multimedia, IEEE Transactions on*, 14(4):995–1007, 2012.

[41] G. Zhao and M. Pietikainen. Dynamic texture recognition using local binary patterns with an application to facial expressions. *Pattern Analysis and Machine Intelligence, IEEE Transactions on*, 29(6):915–928, 2007.

[42] L. Zhong, Q. Liu, P. Yang, B. Liu, J. Huang, and D. N. Metaxas. Learning active facial patches for expression analysis. In *CVPR*. IEEE, 2012.

Enhanced Autocorrelation in Real World Emotion Recognition

Sascha Meudt
Institute of Neural Information Processing
University of Ulm
sascha.meudt@uni-ulm.de

Friedhelm Schwenker
Institute of Neural Information Processing
University of Ulm
friedhelm.schwenker@uni-ulm.de

ABSTRACT

Multimodal emotion recognition in real world environments is still a challenging task of affective computing research. Recognizing the affective or physiological state of an individual is difficult for humans as well as for computer systems, and thus finding suitable discriminative features is the most promising approach in multimodal emotion recognition. In the literature numerous features have been developed or adapted from related signal processing tasks. But still, classifying emotional states in real world scenarios is difficult and the performance of automatic classifiers is rather limited. This is mainly due to the fact that emotional states can not be distinguished by a well defined set of discriminating features. In this work we present an enhanced autocorrelation feature as a multi pitch detection feature and compare its performance to feature well known, and state-of-the-art in signal and speech processing. Results of the evaluation show that the enhanced autocorrelation outperform other state-of-the-art features in case of the challenge data set. The complexity of this benchmark data set lies in between real world data sets showing naturalistic emotional utterances, and the widely applied and well-understood acted emotional data sets.

Keywords

enhanced autocorrelation, audio features, emotion recognition, human computer interaction, affective computing

1. INTRODUCTION

Human affective state has been attracted researchers in medical, psychological and cognitive science since the mid 1960s [8, 24]. Because of the dramatically increasing computational power of modern information technology, numerous technical devices such as smart phones, tablets, laptops, personal computers and many more became more and more part of our daily life, and more even more important, the way we are using these computing devises has totally changed: Human-Computer interaction (HCI) in the 1980s and 1990s was dominated by keyboard and mouse interaction following a strict input-operation-output work flow. Recently, more and more options for multimodal interaction have been developed, e.g. control via speech or hand gestures, and in the future the analysis of the user's intentions or affective state will come into to focus of HCI research. Examples are the analysis of para-linguistic patterns or facial expressions, or more general, social signals of humans implicitly produced as a by-product when interacting or communicating to a computing device. This change in HCI caused computer scientists to focus on recognition of social signals, such as emotions, with the intention to use this information to alter subsequent actions in HCI scenarios. Humans express their emotions in many different ways and modalities, this makes automatic emotion recognition a very challenging task in computer science. In this emerging field, called *affective computing*, computers are seen as intelligent companions offering context sensitive advice and support to the human user, and techniques based on machine learning and pattern pattern recognition came more and more in the focus of research.

In the past, pattern recognition research in emotion recognition has been done mostly on recognizing acted, usually over-expressed, well defined emotional categories, and segmented data (isolated video clips, audio files) [33, 3], typical datasets consisted of audio [2], video [16] or audio-video recordings [1]. The classification of such data simple, and thus, the achieved classification results are accurate [9, 26]. However, such acted emotions do not appear in every day life HCI situations, thus the community changed their scope more towards non-acted scenarios and benchmark data [20, 25] containing more realistic emotional appearances. A famous benchmark data set is the data base introduced in AVEC Challenge [31], the EmoRec [36] and the Last-Minute data set [23] Unfortunately the ground truth is somewhat unclear and the data are very noisy in this datasets [15]. In case of the EmotiW challenge the ground truth is given by the storyboard of the movies the videos had been taken from. Hence, it is even for humans difficult to categorize the acted emotion without context.

Recognition systems thus have to deal with unreliable data containing various levels of expressiveness. In order to overcome those problems, different approaches are proposed [10, 19, 11]. Focus can, for example, be set on a single modality like video or speech signals and classification systems can thus be tailored on the special characteristics of those modalities. Advances in affective computing in recent

ICMI'14, November 12–16, 2014, Istanbul, Turkey
Copyright 2014 ACM 978-1-4503-2885-2/14/11 ...$15.00.
http://dx.doi.org/10.1145/2663204.2666276 .

years have come from better classifiers and fusion systems, but also from the adaptation and development of novel, discriminating features.

The EmotiW challenge [6, 4] in 2014 [5] again offers a challenging bimodal benchmark data set. EmotiW 2014 and 2013 are data sets derived from cinema movies and thus the complexity of the emotional utterances are in between acted and realistic emotions. For this reason the EmotiW database is an important benchmark to develop new features for emotion recognition.

Speech signals are appealing for emotion recognition because they are simple to process and their analyses present promising ways for future research [7, 27, 28, 29]. One of the main issues in designing an automatic emotion recognition system is the choice of the features that can represent the corresponding emotions. In recent years, several different feature types proved to be useful in the context of emotion recognition from speech: Nicholson et. al [21] used feature extraction based on pitch and linear predictive coding (LPC). In earlier work two feature types, comprising modulation spectrum (ModSpec) and relative spectral transform - perceptual linear prediction (RASTA-PLP) where used to recognize seven different emotions with an accuracy of approximately 79% on the Berlin database of emotional speech (EMO-DB [2]) [28, 22, 30, 32]. Other feature choices include the Mel Frequency Cepstral Coefficients (MFCC) as used in [17].

Developing powerful features which discriminate speech in their underling emotional categories in a good manor is still a hot topic in current research. In this paper we present the usage of the enhanced autocorrelation (EAC) feature in the field of emotion recognition. The feature was originally developed by Tolonen and Karjalainen [34] as multi pitch detector for music classification, to the best of our knowledge this feature has so far never been used in emotion estimation. In this paper we compare the performance of the EAC feature to a set of commonly applied features in emotion recognition from speech. The results show that EAC yields comparable and slightly better results on the AFEW 4.0 dataset. As many other features the EAC computation is based on an analysis in the frequency domain of the audio signal, hence resulting in a much higher output dimension which gives the classifier a better chance to discriminate the emotional classes.

In the following we give a short overview of the used common features followed by a detailed introduction of the EAC feature. Afterwards we compare the features based on the challenge dataset and present the results of our approach on the test dataset. A final conclusion and discussion is given in the closing section of the paper.

2. FEATURES

In the following 4 subsections we give a brief introduction on commonly used features in emotion recognition from speech. This is followed by a more detailed description of the EAC method. To the best of our knowledge EAC is used in the field of emotion recognition for the first time. Figure 1 gives an overview on the dimensions and shape of the utilized features. All features have in common that the audio signal is divided in overlapping windows, subsequently a Hamming window function $w(i) = 0.54 + 0.46 \cdot cos(\frac{2\pi i}{M})$, $i = -\frac{M}{2}, ..., \frac{M}{2} - 1$ with window size M and sample index i is applied to prevent edge effects. Finally in subsection 2.6 we propose a feature fusion method to reduce the number of instances to one per film sequence.

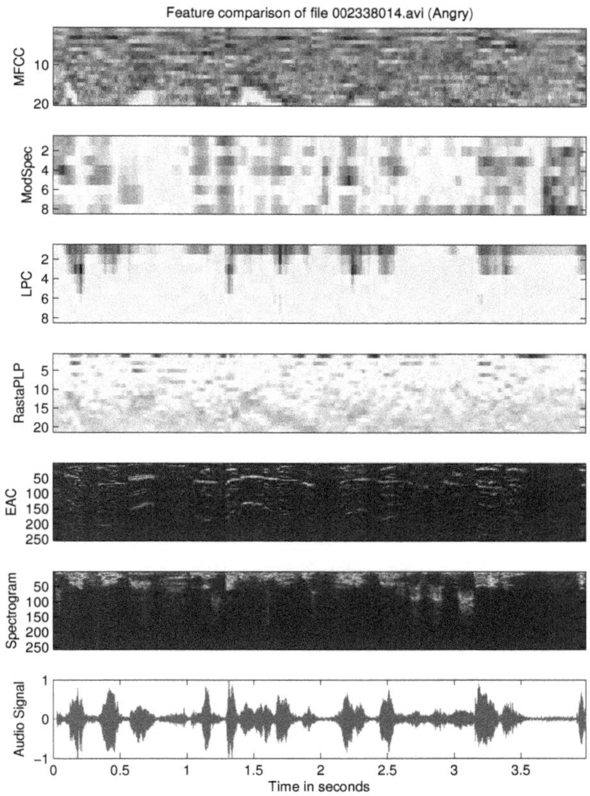

Figure 1: Shape comparison of all features on file 002338014.avi of class angry. From top to bottom: Mel Frequency Cepstral Coefficients, Modulation Spectrum, Linear Predictive Coding, Relative Spectral Perceptual Linear Predictive, Enhanced Autocorrelation, audio signal in frequency domain and audio signal in time domain.

2.1 Mel Frequency Cepstral Coefficients

The MFCC representation of a signal is motivated by the way how humans percept audio modulation in their ear. A filter bank with linear spaced filters in the lower frequencies and logarithmic scaled filters in the upper frequencies called MEL filter bank is used during feature extraction. MFCC are commonly used features in short term feature cases since their compact ability to represent the important information in speech processing applications while retaining most of the phonetical significant acoustics [18]

On each window a short-term fast Fourier transformation (FFT) is computed, and on the result the MEL filter bank of triangular filters is applied. The discrete cosine transformation (DCT) on each filter output yields the de-correlated cepstral coefficients of each window. A typical filter order is in the ranged from 8 and 24. In this work we extracted the coefficients on 40msec windows with an overlap of 20msec and a filter bank order of 20.

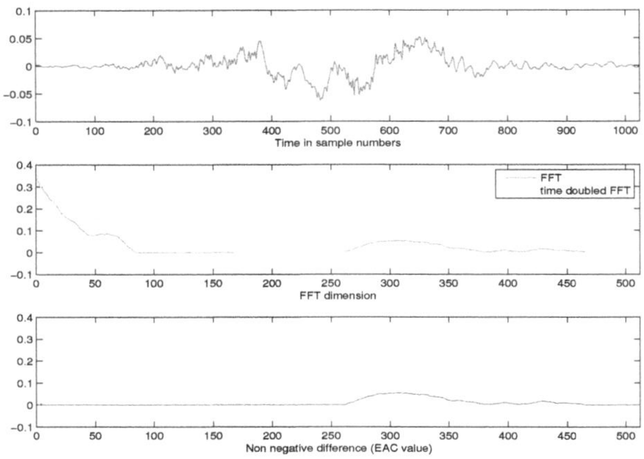

Figure 2: A window out of the audio signal (top) and corresponding EAC analysis (bottom) of film sequence 003042640.wav In the middle the zero clipped autocorrelation signal and their time doubled curve is shown.

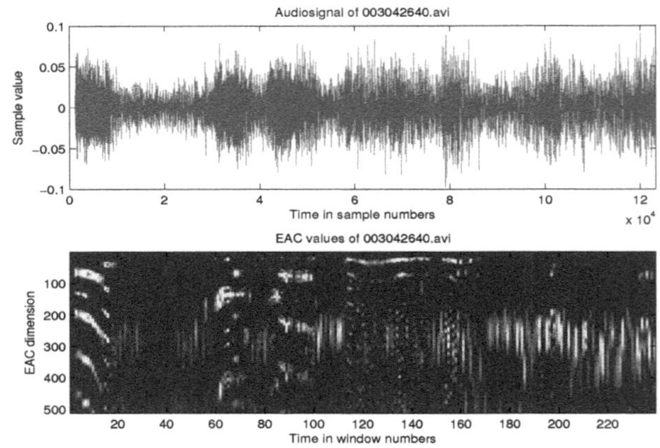

Figure 3: Audio signal and the corresponding EAC analysis of film sequence 003042640.wav. Falling multi pitch in the very beginning, a low frequent single pitch from window 120 to 160 and a very noisy and wide pitch in the end can be observed.

2.2 Modulation Spectrum

To reduce the influence of environmental noise Hermansky [12] introduced the Modulation Spectrum feature of speech to obtain the temporal dynamics of the speech segment. To gain the long term temporal modulations in the range from 2Hz to 16Hz window sizes of 200msec up to several seconds are applied. Due to the short audio segments of the EmotiW-challenge we fixed 200msec as the used window size. As for MFCC, firstly a FFT is computed on overlapping subwindows, and the MEL filter bank is applied too (we used 8 filters in this work). Instead of applying the DCT on each subwindow the response of all subwindows is aggregate and a FFT over the energy response per filter is calculated yielding the final feature vector. Strong rates of change of the vocal tract, holding important linguistic information are represented in the corresponding dimensions of the feature.

2.3 Linear Predictive Coding

Instead of analysing the signal by using FFT based approaches in LPC the speech sample $s(t)$ is approximated by linear combination of the past p samples [14]:

$$s(t) \approx a_1 s(t-1) + ... + a_p s(t-p), \quad (1)$$

where the coefficients $a_1, ..., a_p$ are assumed to be constant in a short signal segment. This results in a p dimensional vector corresponding to a curve fitting around the peaks of the short term log magnitude spectrum of a signal. As in the previous features the information is compressed, avoiding a transformation from time to frequency domain. In this work we use $p = 12$, extracted from 40msec windows with 20msec overlap.

2.4 Relative Spectral Perceptual Linear Predictive Coding

The perceptually and biologically motivations of *critical bands* and *equally loudness curve* build the basis of the perceptual linear prediction (PLP) [13]. The sound pressure (dB) that is required to perceive a sound of any frequency as loud as a reference sound of 1 kHz is approximated by:

$$E(w) = 1.151 \cdot \sqrt{\frac{(w^2 + 144 \cdot 10^4) \cdot w^2}{(w^2 + 16 \cdot 10^4) \cdot (w^2 + 961 \cdot 10^4)}} \quad (2)$$

As a result of this equation, frequencies below 1 kHz need higher sound pressure levels than the reference sound while sounds between 2 and 5 kHz need less pressure. As for MFCC filtering a critical band filtering is done (usual with about 21 filters), but in contrast to MFCC the filtering is linear in the Bark Scale and the filter shape is not triangular.

PLP is sensitive towards spectral changes caused by transmission channels caused by different microphones or telephone voice compression algorithms. Therefore after band filtering Hermansky suggested equal loudness conversion by transforming the spectrum to the logarithmic domain and applying a relative spectral (Rasta) filter processing followed by using exponential re-transformation. Finally, LPC coefficients are calculated similar to subsection 2.3 over the critical band energies.

In this work the features with filter order of 21, a window length of 25msec and an offset of 10msec have been applied.

2.5 Enhanced Auto Correlation

The EAC feature was originally introduced by Tolonen and Karjalainen [34] as multi pitch analyses in various different fields of audio signal processing. In our work we use a slightly modified version of their extraction process in order to extract the main harmonics of the vocal cord and the glottal source of the speech signal. Different emotional states could cause a variety of muscle tension in the vocal tract which influence the produced sound signal. Extracting the multi pitch harmonics based on the periodicity of the signal could therefore be a reliable feature containing a lot of emotional information independent of the underling spoken content. In addition the EAC feature is a very high dimensional feature in the field of audio processing which might help a classifier to distinguish between the distributions of the emotional classes.

Fusion type Feature type	instance wise Voting - Late Fusion	window average Early Fusion	window variance Early Fusion
MFCC	24.7 (2.44)	25.6 (1.56)	22.8 (2.06)
ModSpec	28.4 (1.71)	28.0 (3.86)	25.1 (1.95)
LPC	21.9 (0.80)	20.6 (2.18)	20.6 (3.23)
RastaPLP	22.8 (1.61)	19.9 (1.36)	29.1 (1.60)
EAC	**29.2** (1.13)	**30.7** (3.82)	**30.7** (2.80)

Table 1: Results for emotion recognition on the utilized features based on a 10-fold cross-validation on the unification of train and validation set (accuracy in percent, standard derivation in brackets).

As in most other feature extraction procedures we first divide the signal in overlapping Hamming windows. For each window containing the input signal S the autocorrelation function

$$acf(S) = \mathrm{Re}\left(\mathrm{iFFT}\left(|\mathrm{FFT}\left(\mathrm{Hamming}(S)\right)|^k\right)\right) \quad (3)$$

is applied in order to detect periodic signal parts. The parameter k allows the control of the periodicity detection with some non linear processing in the frequency domain. Peaks in the autocorrelation curve are an indicator for pitch periods. Normally, a lot of redundant information and noise is part of this curve. To improve the reliability of the detection the autocorrelation result is clipped at zero and all negative values are set to zero. In order to remove multiple peaks of the fundamental periods which are caused by the autocorrelation function the time doubled signal of the autocorrelation function is subtracted from the autocorrelation signal, and again all negative values are set to zero, yielding the final EAC feature vector.

Figure 2 shows a audio signal window applied with the Hamming function (upper part). In the middle plot the red curve shows the autocorrelation curve of the window clipped to zero and the time doubled curve in green. Finally in the bottom line the EAC curve is displayed, showing a wide single peak at 310. Keeping in mind that this procedure is repeated for every sliding window on the audio signal (Figure 3 top) the EAC result could be drawn as in Figure 3 bottom where the x-axis displays the time, the y-axis donates the dimensions of the feature and the color corresponds to the value at a given point (from blue = zero to red = one). One could see a falling multi pitch in the very beginning, a low frequent single pitch from window 120 to 160 and a very noisy and wide pitch in the end.

In the following the parameters of the EAC had been set to window size 1024 sample values (47msec) with a overlap of 512 samples resulting in 512 EAC dimensions per window. The parameter k was set to 1/3 designated by empirical experiences.

2.6 Per film feature representation

All above described features are derived from short time windows of a signal, resulting in a large number (200-300) of feature vectors per utterance or in case of the challenge film sequences. Keeping in mind that a typical EmotiW-challenge subset contains about 400 sequences the total number of instances presented to the classifier is above 100,000. In order to reduce the number of training instances we applied two different early fusion techniques which reduces the number of instances per film sequence to one per sequence. First we compute the average vector $x_\mu = \frac{1}{T}\sum_{t=1}^{T} x_t$ of all $t = 1, \ldots, T$ feature vectors per sequence. Computing the average loses the variety within a sequence, in order to reduce this disadvantage we second took the variance $x_{\sigma^2} = \frac{1}{T}\sum_{t=1}^{T}(x_t - x_\mu)^2$ of a vector sequence. In the following we build a separate classifier on the windowed sequence, sequence averages and variances.

3. RESULTS

The evaluation is divided in two parts. First the results according to the comparison of the features – ignoring the underling challenge – are presented. Second we choose the most promising features containing EAC and ModSpec and a fusion of all features to participate in the challenge. The other feature types are evaluated on the test set without taking them into account in the challenge.

3.1 Feature comparison

To compare the performance of the features we rearranged the train and validation set by combining them to a single dataset containing 962 film sequences. We extracted all features presented in section 2 in the windowed sequence, sequence average and variance option and applied a Support Vector Machine (SVM) with Gaussian kernel for each feature type. Each SVM was optimized according to their specific parameters C and γ based on unweighed accuracy measure. A 10-fold cross validation was applied. Table 1 gives an overview of the achieved results. In case of single frame based as well as sequence average and variance features the EAC outperforms all other features. The most common used MFCC feature performs only moderate on the EmotiW dataset, which is not very surprising based on our results of last years challenge participation[20]. On window instance based and sequence average vectors the ModSpec feature performs second best and third best on the variance of window based vectors.

3.2 Challenge Results

Based on the previous results we decided to use the ModSepc and EAC feature in all three (full, average and variance) options for the participation in the challenge. The six SVM‘s were trained and optimized on the train and validation set according to the challenge guidelines. Table 2 gives an overview of the results and endorses the dominance of the EAC feature family. Finally a fusion architecture was applied by summarizing the probabilistic outputs of the SVM classifiers which build an ensemble of the six members. The fusion architecture yield a overall accuracy of 40.1% which is gently higher than each single feature. As on the feature comparison results again the EAC features are better than the ModSpec feature.

Fusion type Feature type	instance wise Voting - Late Fusion	window average Early Fusion	window variance Early Fusion
MFCC	35.6	28.7	28.7
ModSpec	36.1	32.9	26.5
LPC	30.5	28.7	28.7
RastaPLP	35.6	20.4	28.7
EAC	**36.6**	**37.6**	**35.6**
Fusion of all	**40.1**		
Baseline	26.2		

Table 2: Results comparison for emotion recognition, trained on the train set according to the challenge guidelines. Classification Accuracy in percent

	Angry	Disgust	Fear	Happy	Neutral	Sad	Surprise	Accuracy
Angry	34	0	1	11	10	2	0	58.06
Disgust	4	0	0	4	17	1	0	0.0
Fear	14	0	13	4	11	4	0	28.3
Happy	9	1	1	19	43	8	0	23.5
Neutral	3	0	4	23	73	12	2	62.4
Sad	10	0	2	7	20	14	0	26.4
Surprise	8	0	1	7	8	2	0	0.00

Table 3: Confusion matrix of average EAC feature results on test set. Accuracy in percent, confusion matrix in absolute numbers.

In table 3 the confusion matrix is evinced, which shows a strong imbalance oft the classification accuracies along the different classes. *Neutral* and *angry* could be recognized very well while *disgust* and *surprise* couldn't be perceived at all. Compared to the last year results where we also had a imbalance of the classification accuracy towards the classes *angry*, *neutral* and *happiness* this imbalancing is not very surprising. May the poor results of *disgust*, *sadness* and *surprise* result from the lower train data amount and a priory probability in test data. In case of the challenge this result is a bit unsatisfying, while in the scope of affective computing were *neutral* and *angry* are very important classes it is a very promising result.

4. CONCLUSIONS

After our work in the field of feature selection in the last year we focused more on the development and usage of new or alternative features in the field of speech based emotion recognition on datasets which are recorded under mostly realistic and not strict controlled environments like the AFEW 4.0 dataset. In this work we presenter the EAC as a new feature and compared it to several state of the art features. All common features had been outperformed in all cases. The best result on the challenge dataset (40% accuracy) was archived by using a fusion combination of all features together an was slightly better than the best single feature (EAC average with 37% accuracy). In our opinion it is very important to search for new features which could discriminate speech towards emotions better than the existing ones which had mostly been developed for speech recognition, speaker identification or music classification. Based on better features the underlain classification problem could get much easier, which then result in higher classification accuracy based on single frame or short term signal analyses. May it is also suitable to analyse features towards their discrimination ability by using correlation dimension analyses [35]. Improving the basic input results could then finally improve results after a well designed multi modal fusion architecture dramatically.

5. REFERENCES

[1] T. Bänziger, H. Pirker, and K. Scherer. Gemep-geneva multimodal emotion portrayals: A corpus for the study of multimodal emotional expressions. In *Proceedings of LREC*, volume 6, pages 15–019, 2006.

[2] F. Burkhardt, A. Paeschke, M. Rolfes, W. F. Sendlmeier, and B. Weiss. A database of german emotional speech. In *Interspeech*, volume 5, pages 1517–1520, 2005.

[3] F. Dellaert, T. Polzin, and A. Waibel. Recognizing emotion in speech. In *Spoken Language, 1996. ICSLP 96. Proceedings., Fourth International Conference on*, volume 3, pages 1970–1973. IEEE, 1996.

[4] A. Dhall, R. Goecke, J. Joshi, M. Wagner, and T. Gedeon. Emotion recognition in the wild challenge. *ACM ICMI*, 2013.

[5] A. Dhall, R. Goecke, J. Joshi, M. Wagner, and T. Gedeon. Emotion recognition in the wild challenge 2014: Baseline, data and protocol. *ACM ICMI*, 2014.

[6] A. Dhall, R. Goecke, S. Lucey, and T. Gedeon. Collecting large, richly annotated facial-expression databases from movies. *IEEE Multimedia*, 19:34–41, 2012.

[7] N. Fragopanagos and J. Taylor. Emotion recognition in human-computer interaction. *Neural Networks*, 18:389–405, 2005.

[8] N. H. Frijda. Recognition of emotion. *Advances in experimental social psychology*, 4:167–223, 1969.

[9] M. Glodek, M. Schels, G. Palm, and F. Schwenker. Multi-modal fusion based on classifiers using reject

options and markov fusion networks. In *Proceedings of the International Conference on Pattern Recognition (ICPR)*, pages 1084–1088. IEEE, 2012.

[10] M. Glodek, S. Scherer, F. Schwenker, and G. Palm. Conditioned hidden markov model fusion for multimodal classification. In *INTERSPEECH*, pages 2269–2272, 2011.

[11] M. Glodek, S. Tschechne, G. Layher, M. Schels, T. Brosch, S. Scherer, M. Kächele, M. Schmidt, H. Neumann, G. Palm, et al. Multiple classifier systems for the classification of audio-visual emotional states. In *Affective Computing and Intelligent Interaction*, pages 359–368. Springer, 2011.

[12] H. Hermansky. The modulation spectrum in the automatic recognition of speech. In *Automatic Speech Recognition and Understanding, 1997. Proceedings., 1997 IEEE Workshop on*, pages 140–147. IEEE, 1997.

[13] H. Hermansky, N. Morgan, A. Bayya, and P. Kohn. Rasta-plp speech analysis technique. In *Acoustics, Speech, and Signal Processing, IEEE International Conference on*, volume 1, pages 121–124. IEEE, 1992.

[14] F. Itakura. Line spectrum representation of linear predictor coefficients of speech signals. *The Journal of the Acoustical Society of America*, 57(S1):S35–S35, 1975.

[15] M. Kächele, M. Glodek, D. Zharkov, S. Meudt, and F. Schwenker. Fusion of audio-visual features using hierarchical classifier systems for the recognition of affective states and the state of depression. In *Procóf ICPRAM*, pages 671–678, 2014.

[16] T. Kanade, J. F. Cohn, and Y. Tian. Comprehensive database for facial expression analysis. In *Automatic Face and Gesture Recognition, 2000. Proceedings. Fourth IEEE International Conference on*, pages 46–53. IEEE, 2000.

[17] C. M. Lee, S. Yildirim, M. Bulut, A. Kazemzadeh, C. Busso, Z. Deng, S. Lee, and S. S. Narayanan. Emotion recognition based on phoneme classes. In *Proceedings of ICSLP 04*, 2004.

[18] B. Logan et al. Mel frequency cepstral coefficients for music modeling. In *ISMIR*, 2000.

[19] S. Meudt and F. Schwenker. On instance selection in audio based emotion recognition. In *Artificial Neural Networks in Pattern Recognition*, pages 186–192. Springer, 2012.

[20] S. Meudt, D. Zharkov, M. Kächele, and F. Schwenker. Multi classifier systems and forward backward feature selection algorithms to classify emotional coloured speech. In *Proceedings of the 15th ACM on International conference on multimodal interaction*, pages 551–556. ACM, 2013.

[21] J. Nicholson, K. Takahashi, and R. Nakatsu. Emotion recognition in speech using neural networks. *Neural Computing and Applications*, 9:290–296, 2000.

[22] G. Palm and F. Schwenker. Sensor-fusion in neural networks. In E. Shahbazian, G. Rogova, and M. J. DeWeert, editors, *Harbour Protection Through Data Fusion Technologies*, pages 299–306. Springer, 2009.

[23] D. Rösner, J. Frommer, R. Friesen, M. Haase, J. Lange, and M. Otto. Last minute: a multimodal corpus of speech-based user-companion interactions. In *LREC*, pages 2559–2566, 2012.

[24] S. Schachter. The interaction of cognitive and physiological determinants of emotional state. *Advances in Experimental Social Psychology*, 1(Bd. 1):49–80, 1964.

[25] M. Schels, M. Glodek, S. Meudt, S. Scherer, M. Schmidt, G. Layher, S. Tschechne, T. Brosch, D. Hrabal, S. Walter, G. Palm, H. Neumann, H. Traue, and F. Schwenker. Multi-modal classifier-fusion for the recognition of emotions. In M. Rojc and N. Campbell, editors, *Coverbal synchrony in Human-Machine Interaction*, chapter 4. CRC Press, 2013.

[26] M. Schels, M. Kächele, M. Glodek, D. Hrabal, S. Walter, and F. Schwenker. Using unlabeled data to improve classification of emotional states in human computer interaction. *Journal on Multimodal User Interfaces*, 8(1):5–16, 2014.

[27] K. R. Scherer, T. Johnstone, and G. Klasmeyer. *Handbook of Affective Sciences - Vocal expression of emotion*, chapter 23, pages 433–456. Affective Science. Oxford University Press, 2003.

[28] S. Scherer, M. Oubbati, F. Schwenker, and G. Palm. Real-time emotion recognition from speech using echo state networks. In *Artificial Neural Networks in Pattern Recognition*, pages 205–216. Springer Berlin Heidelberg, 2008.

[29] S. Scherer, F. Schwenker, and G. Palm. Emotion recognition from speech using multi-classifier systems and rbf-ensembles. In *Speech, Audio, Image and Biomedical Signal Processing using Neural Networks*, pages 49–70. Springer Berlin Heidelberg, 2008.

[30] S. Scherer, F. Schwenker, and G. Palm. Classifier fusion for emotion recognition from speech. In W. Minker, M. Weber, H. Hagras, V. Callagan, and A. D. Kameas, editors, *Advanced Intelligent Environments*, pages 95–117. Springer, 2009.

[31] B. Schuller, M. Valstar, F. Eyben, G. McKeown, R. Cowie, and M. Pantic. Avec 2011–the first international audio/visual emotion challenge. In *Affective Computing and Intelligent Interaction*, pages 415–424. Springer, 2011.

[32] F. Schwenker, S. Scherer, M. Schmidt, M. Schels, and M. Glodek. Multiple classifier systems for the recognition of human emotions. In N. E. Gayar, J. Kittler, and F. Roli, editors, *Proceedings of the 9th International Workshop on Multiple Classifier Systems (MCS'10)*, LNCS 5997, pages 315–324. Springer, 2010.

[33] Y.-L. Tian, T. Kanade, and J. F. Cohn. Facial expression analysis. In *Handbook of face recognition*, pages 247–275. Springer, 2005.

[34] T. Tolonen and M. Karjalainen. A computationally efficient multipitch analysis model. *Speech and Audio Processing, IEEE Transactions on*, 8(6):708–716, 2000.

[35] C. Traina, A. Traina, L. Wu, and C. Faloutsos. Fast feature selection using fractal dimension. 2000.

[36] S. Walter, S. Scherer, M. Schels, M. Glodek, D. Hrabal, M. Schmidt, R. Böck, K. Limbrecht, H. C. Traue, and F. Schwenker. Multimodal emotion classification in naturalistic user behavior. In *Human-Computer Interaction. Towards Mobile and Intelligent Interaction Environments*, pages 603–611. Springer, 2011.

Emotion Recognition in the Wild with Feature Fusion and Multiple Kernel Learning

Junkai Chen[1], Zenghai Chen[1], Zheru Chi[1] and Hong Fu[1,2]
[1]Department of Electronic and Information Engineering, The Hong Kong Polytechnic University, Hong Kong
[2]Department of Computer Science, Chu Hai College of Higher Education, Hong Kong
Junkai.Chen@connect.polyu.hk, Zenghai.Chen@connect.polyu.hk,
chi.zheru@polyu.edu.hk, hongfu@chuhai.edu.hk

ABSTRACT
This paper presents our proposed approach for the second Emotion Recognition in The Wild Challenge. We propose a new feature descriptor called Histogram of Oriented Gradients from Three Orthogonal Planes (HOG_TOP) to represent facial expressions. We also explore the properties of visual features and audio features, and adopt Multiple Kernel Learning (MKL) to find an optimal feature fusion. An SVM with multiple kernels is trained for the facial expression classification. Experimental results demonstrate that our method achieves a promising performance. The overall classification accuracy on the validation set and test set are 40.21% and 45.21%, respectively.

Categories and Subject Descriptors
I.4.9 [**Image Processing and Computer Vision**]: Applications; I.5.4 [**Pattern Recognition**]: Applications.

General Terms
Algorithms; Performance; Experimentation

Keywords
Emotion Recognition; Feature Fusion; HOG_TOP; Multiple Kernel Learning; Support Vector Machine

1. INTRODUCTION
Facial expression analysis has been an active field of research for over two decades. In the early stage, most work focused on static images or posed facial expressions controlled under the lab. Researchers have made much progress on several popular public datasets, like JAFFE [1], CMU-PIE [2], MMI [3], and Multi-PIE [4]. The facial expressions in these datasets are lab-controlled. They are different from the facial expressions in the real world. Recently, more attention has been paid to emotion recognition in the wild. Compared with the lab-controlled expressions, expressions in the wild are more natural and spontaneous. They can truly reveal the emotions and intentions behind the expressions. To this end, the first step is to build a database of a reasonable size. This turns out to be a hard task, because expressions in the wild are transient and delicate. Some researchers find an alternative but useful way to collect facial expressions. They extract short video sequences from movies.

ICMI'14, Nov. 12–16, 2014, Istanbul, Turkey
Copyright 2014 ACM 978-1-4503-2885-2/14/11 ...$15.00.
http://dx.doi.org/10.1145/2663204.2666277

Although movies are shot in more or less controlled environments, they are close to real world environments, and the expressions are more realistic than the lab-controlled expressions [5]. AFEW [6] is such a dataset. With the AFEW dataset, researchers can evaluate their methods for emotion recognition in the real world. Dhall et al. organized the first Emotion Recognition in The Wild Challenge in 2013 with the AFEW database [7]. In 2014, they updated the AFEW dataset and organized the second Emotion Recognition in The Wild Challenge. This paper mainly presents the approach that we proposed for the Challenge 2014. We proposed a new feature descriptor called Histogram of Oriented Gradients from Three Orthogonal Planes (HOG_TOP) to represent the facial expressions. Multiple Kernel Learning (MKL) [8] is used to optimally combine the visual features and audio features.

The rest of the paper is organized as follows. Section 2 gives an overview of the related work. Our proposed emotion recognition approach is presented in Section 3. The description and discussion of the experiments are presented in Section 4. This paper is concluded in Section 5.

2. RELATED WORK
There has been a significant progress in automatic facial expression recognition because of the development of the computer vision and machine learning techniques. Two mainstream methods, geometry-based and appearance-based [9], are widely used for this purpose.

Geometry-based methods capture the shapes and configurations of the face and facial components like mouth, eyes, and brows etc. Facial expressions are caused by some facial muscle movements, which result in the deformations of the facial components. These deformations can be used to distinguish among different facial expressions. To this end, the facial fiducial points are extracted to form a vector to represent the shape or configuration of the face and facial components. The difficulty is to detect and locate the facial fiducial points precisely. Several algorithms have been proposed to solve this problem, such as Active Appearance Model (AAM) [10], [11], Constrained Local Models (CLM) [12], and Deformable Parts Model (DPM) [13].

Appearance-based methods, which represent the expressions with texture, are another primary method for facial expression recognition. Compared with geometry-based methods, appearance-based methods are easier to implement. It is not necessary to locate the facial landmarks. In general, appearance features are obtained by applying the hand-designed feature descriptors over the whole face. There are two widely accepted types of feature descriptors. One type is used for single and static images, such as Gabor filters [14], Local Binary Patterns (LBP)

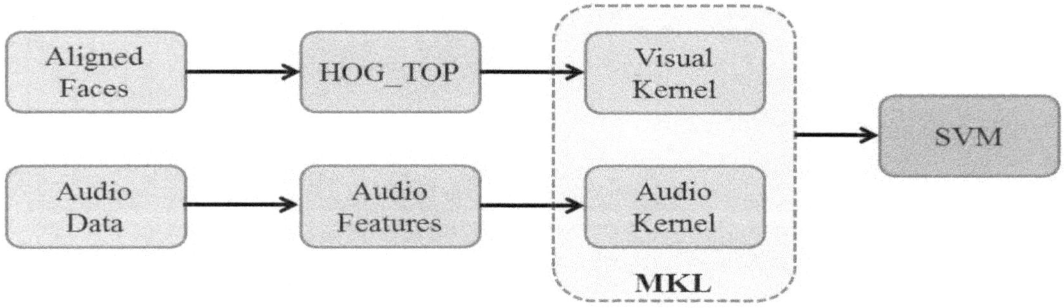

Figure 1: The flowchart of our proposed system.

[15], and Local Phase Quantization [16] etc. The other type of feature descriptor, such as LBP_TOP [17], LPQ_TOP [18], and PHOG [19] can represent the dynamic features of image sequences (videos).

Recently, some methods utilizing multimodal data including facial expressions, sound and scene for emotion analysis have achieved promising results. Kim et al. [20] proposed a suite of Deep Belief Network models, which explicitly captured complex non-linear feature interactions in multimodal data for emotion recognition. A study reported in [21] has shown that visual features coupled with audio features obtained better performance than using one-modal data alone. In [22], Karan et al. utilized different feature descriptors to represent multimodal data, and achieved a good accuracy for emotion recognition in the wild. Kahou et al. [23] combined modality specific deep neural networks for emotion recognition in the Wild and won the emotion recognition challenge in 2013.

Feature fusion and Multiple Kernel Learning (MKL) [24] have received increasing attention from the computer vision community with the development of multiple-modality emotion recognition. Psychological study in [25] showed that using multiple modalities was helpful for emotion analysis. Multiple modalities make use of both visual features and audio features. The point is to find an optimal way to integrate these modalities. MKL provides an effective manner to address this problem. MKL has been successfully applied for emotion and facial action unit recognition. For example, in [26], Zhang et al. applied the Multiple Kernel Learning (MKL) for facial expression recognition. They expanded the Hessian MKL algorithm into multiclass-SVM with the one-against-one rule. The proposed framework learned one kernel weight vector for each binary classifier. Zhang et al. [27] considered the underlying relations among action units and proposed a novel method, lp-norm multi-task multiple kernel learning (MTMKL) which collectively trained the classifiers for detecting the absence and presence of multiple action units.

3. THE PROPOSED APPROACH

This section describes in details the methods that we adopt for the emotion recognition in the Wild Challenge. The flowchart of our proposed approach is shown in Figure 1. We propose a new feature descriptor called HOG_TOP to represent the facial expressions. We also explore the properties of the HOG_TOP features and audio features and apply the Multiple Kernel Learning to find an optimal combination of the visual features and audio features. At last, an SVM with multi kernels is trained for emotion classification.

3.1 Histogram of Oriented Gradients from Three Orthogonal Planes

We propose a new feature descriptor called Histogram of Oriented Gradients from Three Orthogonal Planes (HOG_TOP) to represent the dynamic features of image sequences. HOG_TOP is an extension of the Histogram of Oriented Gradients (HOG) [28] which is used to deal with 2D spatial textures only. HOG_TOP expands to three dimensions and computes dynamic spatial-temporal textures.

Each position in a sequence has a 3-D (X-Y, X-T and Y-T) neighborhood which is shown in Figure 2. In order to obtain HOG_TOP, we first calculate the gradients along the X, Y and T directions with a 3×3 Sobel mask. Three gradient orientations are defined as

$$\theta_{XY} = \arctan(\frac{G_Y}{G_X})$$
$$\theta_{XT} = \arctan(\frac{G_T}{G_X}) \quad (1)$$
$$\theta_{YT} = \arctan(\frac{G_T}{G_Y})$$

where G_X, G_Y, and G_T are the gradients along the X, Y and T directions, respectively. These angles are quantized into K

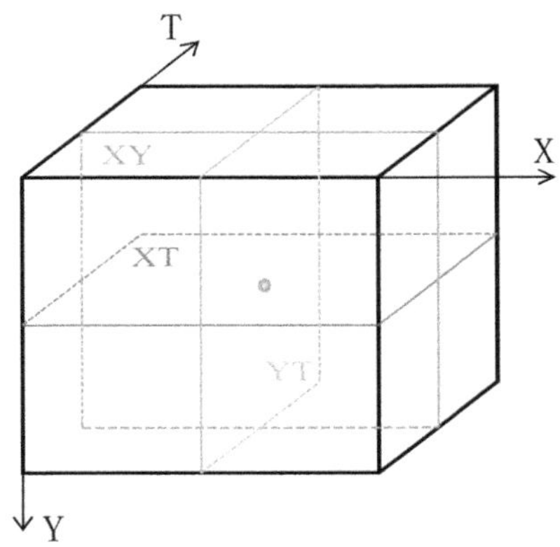

Figure 2: Three orthogonal neighborhoods of a point in an image sequence.

Figure 3: Some facial images from the dataset. The variation in illumination, pose and background increase the complexity of emotion analysis.

orientation bins with a range of $0° - 180°$ or $0° - 360°$. We obtain a histogram in each plane. The three histograms are concatenated to form a global description combing the spatial and temporal features.

3.2 Audio features

Another type of features employed in our study is extracted from the sound data provided. The organizers of the emotion recognition challenge have supplied the acoustic features. The features are extracted using the open-source Emotion Affect Recognition (openEAR) [29] toolkit backend OpenSMILE[30]. The features include energy/spectral Low Level Descriptors (LLD) and voicing related LLD. More details about the features are described in [31] and [32].

3.3 Feature Fusion and Multiple Kernel Learning for Classification

Once we have acquired different types of features, we need to find an optimal way to combine the features to improve the discriminatory ability of the classifier. Traditional Support Vector Machine (SVM) [33] only integrates the features directly and a single kernel is built for the combined features. Multiple Kernel Learning (MKL) [34] constructs a kernel for each feature type and finds an optimal linear combination for the kernels.

Given a training set with labeled samples:

$$D = \{(\mathbf{x}_i, y_i) \mid \mathbf{x}_i \in R^n, y_i \in \{-1,1\}\}_{i=1}^{N}$$

The dual formulation of the traditional single kernel SVM optimization problem is then given by

$$\max_{\alpha} \left[\sum_{i=1}^{N} \alpha_i - \frac{1}{2} \sum_{i=1}^{N} \sum_{j=1}^{N} \alpha_i \alpha_j y_i y_j k(\mathbf{x}_i, \mathbf{x}_j) \right] \quad (2)$$

subject to $\sum_{i=1}^{N} \alpha_i y_i = 0$, $0 \le \alpha_i \le C$.

MKL applies a linear combination of multiple kernels to substitute for the single kernel, which is defined in Eq. (3). In our study, we adopt the formulation proposed in [8] that the kernel is actually a convex combination of basis kernels:

$$K(\mathbf{x}_i, \mathbf{x}_j) = \sum_{m=1}^{M} \beta_m k_m(\mathbf{x}_i, \mathbf{x}_j) \quad (3)$$

with $\beta_m \ge 0$, $\sum_{m=1}^{M} \beta_m = 1$.

The basis kernels could be linear kernel, radial basis function (RBF) kernel and polynomial kernel etc. MKL learns the kernel weights β and α coefficients. We employ the SimpleMKL algorithm proposed in [8] to solve this problem.

4. EXPERIMENTS AND DISCUSSIONS

In order to evaluate our method, we conducted the experiments on the Acted Facial Expression in Wild (AFEW) 4.0 [6] , which has been collected from different movies showing close-to-real-world conditions. Some facial images extracted from the dataset are shown in Figure 3. From these images, we can see that the variation in illumination, pose and background contribute to the complexity of emotion analysis. For the emotion recognition challenge, the dataset is divided into three parts: training, validation and test. There are 578 video clips in the training set. The validation and test sets have 383 video clips and 407 video clips, respectively. The task is to classify a sample audio-video clip into one of the seven categories: Anger, Disgust, Fear, Happiness, Neutral, Sadness and Surprise.

Face extraction in the wild is a challenging problem. The variations in pose, illumination, and background could contribute to the complexity of the problem. The classic Viola-Jones face detector [35] is effective for front view faces. However, it is not robust to deal with the faces in the wild. Recently the researchers have paid attention to the deformable parts models. Zhu and Ramanan's model [13], which was based on a mixture of trees with a shared pool of parts, has been widely used for face detection in the wild. In their method, every facial landmark was modeled as a part and the global mixtures were used to capture topological changes in viewpoint. This model is able to estimate the pose of a face and detect the facial landmarks from the face. Face alignment can be done once the pose estimation and facial landmarks are obtained. The organizers of The Wild Challenge have adopted this model to extract faces and provided the aligned faces for this challenge.

As mentioned in the previous section, we extract the HOG_TOP features from aligned faces. The size of the aligned face is 128×128. We divide the face image into 8×8 non-overlap blocks and each block has a size of 16×16. We set the bin size to 9 and the orientation range to 0° – 180°. The final HOG_TOP feature is a 1×1728 vector. As for the acoustic features, we use the features supplied by the organizers. The audio feature is a 1×1584 vector.

We evaluate the performance of our method on the validation set first. Three feature combinations are explored: audio feature only, visual feature only, and the combined visual-audio features. The classification accuracy of the audio feature on the validation set is 32.89%. The visual feature achieves 35.77% accuracy on the validation set. The confusion matrixes of using individual feature sets are shown in Table 1 and Table 2, respectively.

From the experimental results, we can see that the emotions "angry", "happy" and "neutral" have a higher accuracy than the other emotions. And the accuracy of the emotion "surprise" is the lowest. Nearly all the predictions are incorrect, meaning that in this dataset, the emotion "surprise" is easy to be confused with the other emotions, in particular, with "neutral".

We further integrate the two features to achieve better performance on the validation set. We build a linear kernel for each feature set and apply the SimpleMKL algorithm to optimize the combination weights. Two kernels are used: one for the audio feature and the other for the visual feature. The best performance achieves when the kernel weights of the visual feature and audio feature are 0.73 and 0.27 respectively in our experiment. The overall classification accuracy is 40.21%, which is higher than the audio features and visual features applied alone. Table 3 shows the confusion matrix of using the combined visual-audio features on the validation set. From Table 3, we can see that the classification accuracy of emotion "angry", "happy" and "neutral" improves but the accuracy of emotion "surprise" is still the lowest.

Table 1: The confusion matrix showing performance of the audio feature on the validation set (%)

	AN	DI	FE	HA	NE	SA	SU
AN	64.06	3.13	4.69	12.50	10.94	1.56	3.13
DI	17.50	15.00	0.00	17.50	35.00	10.00	5.00
FE	32.61	2.17	26.09	13.04	15.22	2.17	8.70
HA	23.81	3.17	11.11	34.92	26.98	0.00	0.00
NE	7.94	9.52	6.35	14.29	57.14	3.17	1.59
SA	1.64	14.75	11.48	22.95	29.51	14.75	4.92
SU	17.39	8.70	13.04	17.39	34.78	8.70	0.00

Table 2: The confusion matrix showing the performance of the visual feature on the validation set (%)

	AN	DI	FE	HA	NE	SA	SU
AN	73.44	4.69	6.25	1.56	14.06	0.00	0.00
DI	22.50	22.50	7.50	12.50	32.50	2.50	0.00
FE	52.17	10.87	4.35	10.87	17.39	4.35	0.00
HA	4.76	6.35	7.94	60.32	19.05	1.59	0.00
NE	15.87	3.17	4.76	9.52	58.73	7.94	0.00
SA	31.15	13.11	0.00	8.20	42.62	4.92	0.00
SU	26.09	2.17	6.52	8.70	50.00	4.35	2.17

Table 3: The confusion matrix showing the performance of the audio-visual features on the validation set (%)

	AN	DI	FE	HA	NE	SA	SU
AN	76.56	6.25	1.56	1.56	10.94	3.13	0.00
DI	27.50	17.50	0.00	15.00	32.50	7.50	0.00
FE	39.13	8.70	15.22	15.22	19.57	2.17	0.00
HA	7.94	4.76	6.35	63.49	15.87	1.59	0.00
NE	9.52	7.94	0.00	7.94	69.84	4.76	0.00
SA	21.31	18.03	0.00	6.56	44.26	9.84	0.00
SU	21.74	4.35	6.52	15.22	50.00	0.00	2.17

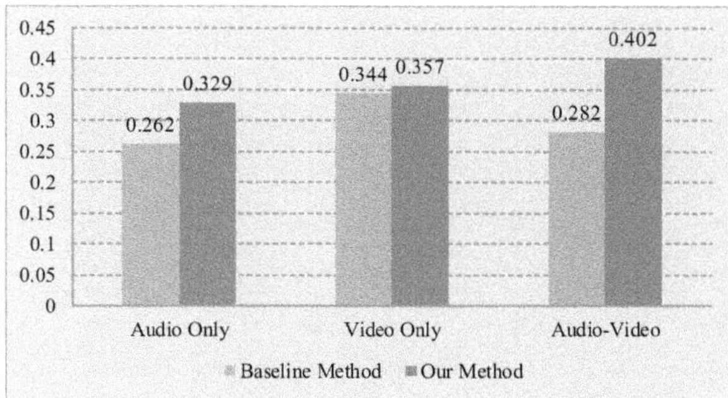

Figure 4: Experimental results on the validation set.

We also compare our results with the baseline method [36] on the validation set as shown in Figure 4. The baseline method applied the LBP_TOP [17] to extract the visual features from the aligned faces. A nonlinear SVM was learnt for the classification and the classification accuracy was 34.4%. The audio feature were obtained by using the OpenSmile toolkit [30] and a linear SVM was trained to perform the recognition. The accuracy was 26.2%. At last, a feature level fusion was performed, where the audio and video features were concatenated and a non-linear SVM was trained for the classification. It achieved an accuracy of 28.2%.

From Figure 4, we can see that, our method outperforms the baseline method. When the audio features apply alone, our classification accuracy is about 6% higher than the baseline method. And the classification accuracy of the visual features in our method is 4% higher than the baseline method. When the two futures are combined, our method is about 12% higher than the baseline method.

We also evaluated our method on the test set which includes 407 video clips without providing the ground-truth. We have to make the predictions for all the video clips and send the prediction labels to the organizers. The organizers then compared our predictions with the ground truth and calculate the overall classification accuracy. For the test set, we tried several different kinds of settings when we extracted the HOG_TOP features from aligned faces. The best performance on the test set is 45.21% when the block size is 8×8, the size of the faces is 64×64 and the number of the non-overlap blocks is 8×8. The confusion matrix is shown in Table 4. Experimental results on the test set are shown in Figure 5. For the baseline method on the test set, the video only achieves a classification accuracy of 33.7%; audio only achieves a classification accuracy of 26.8% and audio-video feature fusion can achieve an accuracy of 24.6%. We can see that our method is about 11% higher than the best performance of the baseline method.

Table 4: The confusion matrix showing the performance of the audio-visual features on the test set (%)

	AN	DI	FE	HA	NE	SA	SU
AN	68.97	5.17	6.90	3.45	6.90	8.62	0.00
DI	3.85	30.77	7.69	3.85	19.23	26.92	7.69
FE	13.04	8.70	41.30	4.35	6.52	17.39	8.70
HA	11.11	8.64	4.94	33.33	16.05	20.99	4.94
NE	5.13	12.82	4.27	4.27	52.14	13.68	7.69
SA	7.55	3.77	7.55	13.21	22.64	35.85	9.43
SU	7.69	7.69	11.54	3.85	15.38	15.38	38.46

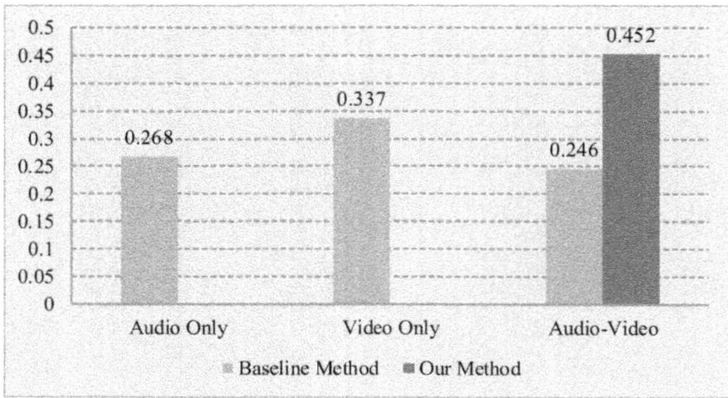

Figure 5: Experimental results on the test set.

5. CONCLUSION

Emotion recognition in the wild is a challenging problem. Many factors such as illumination, head pose and complex background increase the difficulty of this problem. In this paper, we propose an approach for emotion analysis in unconstrained near real-world conditions. We employ the multiple modalities including visual and acoustic information for emotion recognition. We propose a new feature descriptor called HOG_TOP to extract the dynamic visual features from video sequences. Multiple Kernel Learning (MKL) is used to find an optimal combination of the visual features and audio features. Our approach achieves a promising performance on both the validation set and test set. The overall classification accuracy on the validation set and test set are 40.21% and 45.21%, respectively, which are significantly better than the baseline methods.

6. ACKNOWLEDGMENT

This work was partially supported by a research grant from The Hong Kong Polytechnic University (Project Code: G-YL77).

7. REFERENCES

[1] M. Lyons, S. Akamatsu, M. Kamachi, and J. Gyoba, "Coding Facial Expressions with Gabor Wavelets," in Automatic Face and Gesture Recognition, Proceedings. Third IEEE International Conference on, 1998, pp. 200-205.

[2] T. Sim, S. Baker, and M. Bsat, "The CMU pose, illumination, and expression database," Pattern Analysis and Machine Intelligence, IEEE Transactions on, vol. 25, pp. 1615-1618, 2003.

[3] M. Pantic, M. Valstar, R. Rademaker, and L. Maat, "Web-based database for facial expression analysis," in Multimedia and Expo, 2005. ICME 2005. IEEE International Conference on, 2005.

[4] R. Gross, I. Matthews, J. Cohn, T. Kanade, and S. Baker, "Multi-pie," Image and Vision Computing, vol. 28, pp. 807-813, 2010.

[5] A. Dhall, R. Goecke, S. Lucey, and T. Gedeon, "Static Facial Expression Analysis In Tough Conditions," in Computer Vision Workshops (ICCV Workshops), 2011 IEEE International Conference on, 2011, pp. 2106-2112.

[6] A. Dhall, R. Goecke, S. Lucey, and T. Gedeon, "A semi-automatic method for collecting richly labelled large facial expression databases from movies," IEEE Multimedia, 2012.

[7] A. Dhall, R. Goecke, J. Joshi, M. Wagner, and T. Gedeon, "Emotion Recognition In The Wild Challenge 2013," in Proceedings of the 15th ACM on International conference on multimodal interaction, 2013, pp. 509-516.

[8] A. Rakotomamonjy, F. R. Bach, S. Canu, and Y. Grandvalet, "SimpleMKL," Journal of Machine Learning Research, vol. 9, pp. 2491-2521, 2008.

[9] S. Z. Li and A. K. Jain, Handbook of face recognition: springer, 2011.

[10] T. F. Cootes, G. J. Edwards, and C. J. Taylor, "Active appearance models," Pattern Analysis and Machine Intelligence, IEEE Transactions on, vol. 23, pp. 681-685, 2001.

[11] I. Matthews and S. Baker, "Active appearance models revisited," International Journal of Computer Vision, vol. 60, pp. 135-164, 2004.

[12] D. Cristinacce and T. F. Cootes, "Feature detection and tracking with constrained local models," in BMVC, 2006, pp. 929-938.

[13] X. Zhu and D. Ramanan, "Face detection, pose estimation and landmark localization in the wild," in Computer Vision and Pattern Recognition (CVPR), 2012 IEEE Conference on, 2012, pp. 2879-2886.

[14] H. G. Feichtinger and T. Strohmer, Gabor analysis and algorithms: Theory and applications: Springer, 1998.

[15] T. Ojala, M. Pietikainen, and T. Maenpaa, "Multiresolution gray-scale and rotation invariant texture classification with local binary patterns," Pattern Analysis and Machine Intelligence, IEEE Transactions on, vol. 24, pp. 971-987, 2002.

[16] V. Ojansivu and J. Heikkilä, "Blur insensitive texture classification using local phase quantization," in Image and Signal Processing, 2008, pp. 236-243.

[17] G. Zhao and M. Pietikainen, "Dynamic texture recognition using local binary patterns with an application to facial expressions," Pattern Analysis and Machine Intelligence, IEEE Transactions on, vol. 29, pp. 915-928, 2007.

[18] J. Päivärinta, E. Rahtu, and J. Heikkilä, "Volume local phase quantization for blur-insensitive dynamic texture classification," in Proceedings of the 17th Scandinavian conference on Image analysis, 2011, pp. 360-369.

[19] A. Dhall, A. Asthana, R. Goecke, and T. Gedeon, "Emotion recognition using PHOG and LPQ features," in Automatic Face & Gesture Recognition and Workshops IEEE International Conference on, 2011, pp. 878-883.

[20] Y. Kim, H. Lee, and E. M. Provost, "Deep learning for robust feature generation in audiovisual emotion recognition," in Acoustics, Speech and Signal Processing

(ICASSP), 2013 IEEE International Conference on, 2013, pp. 3687-3691.

[21] M. Liu, R. Wang, Z. Huang, S. Shan, and X. Chen, "Partial least squares regression on grassmannian manifold for emotion recognition," in Proceedings of the 15th ACM on International conference on multimodal interaction, 2013, pp. 525-530.

[22] K. Sikka, K. Dykstra, S. Sathyanarayana, G. Littlewort, and M. Bartlett, "Multiple kernel learning for emotion recognition in the wild," in Proceedings of the 15th ACM on International conference on multimodal interaction, 2013, pp. 517-524.

[23] S. E. Kanou, C. Pal, X. Bouthillier, P. Froumenty, Ç. Gülçehre, R. Memisevic, et al., "Combining modality specific deep neural networks for emotion recognition in video," in Proceedings of the 15th ACM on International conference on multimodal interaction, 2013, pp. 543-550.

[24] M. Gönen and E. Alpaydın, "Multiple Kernel Learning Algorithms," The Journal of Machine Learning Research, vol. 12, pp. 2211-2268, 2011.

[25] J. A. Russell, J. A. Bachorowski, and J. M. Fernandez-Dols, "Facial and vocal expressions of emotion," Annu Rev Psychol, vol. 54, pp. 329-349, 2003.

[26] X. Zhang, M. H. Mahoor, and R. M. Voyles, "Facial expression recognition using HessianMKL based multiclass-SVM," in Automatic Face and Gesture Recognition (FG), 2013 10th IEEE International Conference and Workshops on, 2013, pp. 1-6.

[27] X. Zhang, M. H. Mahoor, S. M. Mavadati, and J. F. Cohn, "A lp-norm MTMKL framework for simultaneous detection of multiple facial action units," in Applications of Computer Vision (WACV), 2014 IEEE Winter Conference on 2014, pp. 1104-1111.

[28] N. Dalal and B. Triggs, "Histograms of Oriented Gradients for Human Detection," in Computer Vision and Pattern Recognition, 2005. IEEE Conference on, 2005, pp. 886-893.

[29] F. Eyben, M. Wollmer, and B. Schuller, "OpenEAR — Introducing the munich open-source emotion and affect recognition toolkit," in Affective Computing and Intelligent Interaction and Workshops. ACII 2009. 3rd International Conference on, 2009, pp. 1-6.

[30] F. Eyben, M. Wöllmer, and B. Schuller, "Opensmile_ the munich versatile and fast open-source," in Proceedings of the international conference on Multimedia, 2010, pp. 1459-1462.

[31] B. Schuller, S. Steidl, A. Batliner, F. Burkhardt, L. Devillers, C. A. Müller, et al., "The INTERSPEECH 2010 paralinguistic challenge," in INTERSPEECH, 2010, pp. 2794-2797.

[32] B. Schuller, M. Valstar, F. Eyben, G. McKeown, R. Cowie, and M. Pantic, "Avec 2011–the first international audio/visual emotion challenge," in Affective Computing and Intelligent Interaction, ed: Springer, 2011, pp. 415-424.

[33] C. J. Burges, "A Tutorial on Support Vector Machines for Pattern Recognition," Data mining and knowledge discovery, vol. 2, pp. 121-167, 1998.

[34] G. R. Lanckriet, N. Cristianini, P. Bartlett, L. E. Ghaoui, and M. I. Jordan, "Learning the Kernel Matrix with Semi-Definite Programming," The Journal of Machine Learning Research, vol. 5, pp. 27-72, 2004.

[35] P. Viola and M. Jones, "Robust Real-Time Face Detection," International journal of computer vision, vol. 57, pp. 137-154, 2004.

[36] A. Dhall, R. Goecke, J. Joshi, K. Sikka, and T. Gedeon, "Emotion Recognition In The Wild Challenge 2014: Baseline, Data and Protocol," in ACM International Conference on Multimodal Interaction 2014., 2014.

Improved Spatiotemporal Local Monogenic Binary Pattern for Emotion Recognition in The Wild

Xiaohua Huang
Center for Machine Vision Research
Department of Computer Science and Engineering
University of Oulu, Finland
huang.xiaohua@ee.oulu.fi

Qiuhai He
Center for Machine Vision Research
Department of Computer Science and Engineering
University of Oulu, Finland
qiuhai.he@ee.oulu.fi

Xiaopeng Hong
Center for Machine Vision Research
Department of Computer Science and Engineering
University of Oulu, Finland
xhong@ee.oulu.fi

Guoying Zhao
Center for Machine Vision Research
Department of Computer Science and Engineering
University of Oulu, Finland
gyzhao@ee.oulu.fi

Matti Pietikänen
Center for Machine Vision Research
Department of Computer Science and Engineering
University of Oulu, Finland
mkp@ee.oulu.fi

ABSTRACT

Local binary pattern from three orthogonal planes (LBP-TOP) has been widely used in emotion recognition in the wild. However, it suffers from illumination and pose changes. This paper mainly focuses on the robustness of LBP-TOP to unconstrained environment. Recent proposed method, spatiotemporal local monogenic binary pattern (STL MBP) [14], was verified to work promisingly in different illumination conditions. Thus this paper proposes an improved spatiotemporal feature descriptor based on STLMBP. The improved descriptor uses not only magnitude and orientation, but also the phase information, which provide complementary information. In detail, the magnitude, orientation and phase images are obtained by using an effective monogenic filter, and multiple feature vectors are finally fused by multiple kernel learning. STLMBP and the proposed method are evaluated in the Acted Facial Expression in the Wild as part of the 2014 Emotion Recognition in the Wild Challenge. They achieve competitive results, with an accuracy gain of 6.35% and 7.65% above the challenge baseline (LBP-TOP) over video.

Categories and Subject Descriptors

I.4.9 [**Image Processing and Computer Vision**]: Applications; I.5.4 [**Pattern Recognition**]: Applications

ICMI '14, November 12 - 16 2014, Istanbul, Turkey
Copyright 2014 ACM 978-1-4503-2885-2/14/11 ...$15.00.
http://dx.doi.org/10.1145/2663204.2666278.

Keywords

Spatiotemporal feature; Monogenic signal analysis; Multiple Kernel Learning

1. INTRODUCTION

Facial expression recognition has become a valuable measurement for determining emotional state of a human being based on the facial images. The most common target is to recognize seven universal facial expressions, *i.e.* happiness, sadness, surprise, neutral, anger, fear and disgust, which are proposed by [9]. Early stage research mostly focused on the posed facial expression databases such as Cohn-Kanade (CK) database [19] and MMI database [25]. Unfortunately, these databases are collected under laboratory controlled environments. Such lab controlled data poorly represents the environment and conditions faced in the world situation. Though some attempts have been made to investigate the influence of sole environmental condition such as different illuminations or occlusions [13, 16], there is still no use facial expression recognition system in the wild, which contains numerous challenging environmental conditions. It is thus valuable to pursue the recognition under realistic image acquisition conditions.

The first Emotion Recognition in the Wild (EmotiW 2013) challenge [6] has recently provided a platform to create and verify their facial expression recognition systems. This challenge was based on an extended form of the Acted Facial Expression in the Wild (AFEW) database [7], in which short video clips have been annotated for different emotions. In this challenge, local binary pattern from three orthogonal planes [32] (LBP-TOP), which achieved promising performance in texture classification and posed facial expression, was implemented as the baseline. As far as we know, there are numerous facial expression recognition systems achieving more promising results than the baseline on this database [15, 18, 23]. Among them, the recent popular method, deep neural network [15], was the first time to be used in emotion recognition and won this competition. In their work, they

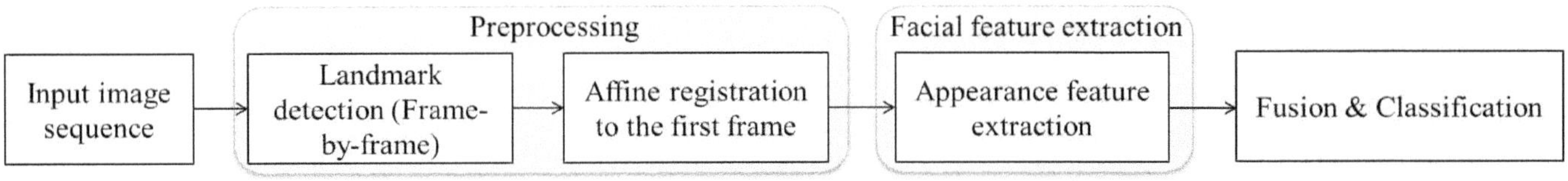

Figure 1: Procedure of the system for emotion recognition in the wild

combined multiple deep neural networks for video and audio features. On the other hand, some machine learning methods, *e.g.* multiple kernel learning (MKL) [23] and partial least square regression (PLSR) [18], were employed to distinguish different facial expressions. Some attempts were made to use other appearance-based features, *e.g.* Local Gabor binary pattern from three orthogonal planes (LGBP-TOP) [2], optical flow and Gabor [17]. In addition, the geometric features were only used in [17]. However, it is observed that the combination of optical flow, Gabor and geometric features work poorer than the baseline. One reason may be that optical flow and geometric features are sensitive to pose change and mis-alignment errors.

Now the second Emotion Recognition in the wild (EmotiW 2014) provides additional videos (567 videos samples for training, 371 for validation and 407 for test) compared with EmotiW 2013 (380, 396 and 312 for training, validation and test sets, respectively). The illumination variations and pose change are two critical problems to facial expression recognition. It is necessary to find out a robust feature representation for resisting them. In general, feature representation methods are categorized into appearance-based features and geometric-based ones. Certain studies [10, 28] demonstrate that appearance-based features are more robust to illumination variation and mis-alignment error than geometric features. In fact, the face detection, landmark localization and alignment procedure may fail due to the challenging conditions. It causes geometric feature not stable. Recalled from their work in EmotiW 2013, it is observed that appearance-based features are widely applied. The main reason is that they are robust to illumination variations and pose change.

Additionally, it is known that LBP-TOP [32] obtained promising results on facial expression recognition under controlled environment, while in the wild it poorly worked. One main reason is that the pixel-level information contains too much noise caused by illumination variation or pose change. There is still some space to increase the robustness of LBP-TOP in the wild. Thus we propose a novel facial expression recognition system based on face preprocessing procedure and appearance-based features, which is shown in Figure 1. In face preprocessing procedure, landmark detection is employed based on [33] and IntraFace. Each frame is aligned to the first frame. In facial feature extraction, we propose a two-layer architecture to describe the video sequences, which is based on spatiotemporal local monogenic binary pattern (STLMBP) [14]. In the first layer, an effective monogenic filter is presented to capture the lower-level features including magnitude, orientation and phase information. In the second layer, these lower-level features are further encoded by the respective methods, *e.g.*, the difference of sign (DoS) [21] or phase-quadrant encoding method (PQDC) [4]. The MKL method [22] is used to fuse multiple feature vector as output of the second layer. The main contributions of this work are to improve the method [14] by introducing the phase information and use the proposed method for the complex AFEW database, which are shown to promisingly outperform the challenge baseline results in EmotiW 2014.

The paper is organized as follows. Section 2 gives a brief overview of existing related work, followed by Section 3 that describes the proposed method in detail. Next, Section 4 summarizes the results, after which a conclusion is presented in Section 5.

2. RELATED WORK

This paper mainly focused on facial features for facial expressions. Various approaches have been proposed for facial feature representations [10, 28]. Two representative ones are local binary pattern (LBP) [21] and Gabor [20][30]. It is found that spatiotemporal LBP [32] and Gabor [2] have been widely used in EmotiW 2013, especially that LBP is also used as baseline algorithm in EmotiW 2014.

Some researchers have recently attempted to extract robust features on the lower-level still images, *e.g.*, Gabor images, rather than on the pixel-level [26, 27, 29, 30, 31]. In [31], the Gabor magnitude and LBP operator were used as the first and second layers, respectively. The first layer enhanced facial features, while the second layer used local structural information and histogram of sub-regions to describe the facial features. Some temporal extension of Gabor-based LBP are established in [1], which combined motion and appearance features extraction with a prior Gabor wavelet filtering. However, in [27], they suggested that the Gabor filter suffers from three limitations: (1) it is not optimal if the broad spectral information with maximal spatial localization need to be sought, (2) its maximum bandwidth is restricted to about one octave, and (3) the computational cost and the storage space are expensive due to many scales and orientations. An alternative method, called monogenic signal analysis [11], can avoid these limitations, because it is itself a compact representation of features with little information loss and does not use steerable filters to create multi-orientation features. The advantages of monogenic filters motivated some researchers to employ it as the first layer [27, 29]. They demonstrated that the monogenic binary pattern outperformed local Gabor binary pattern in face recognition.

Recent studies show that orientation information not only reduces the effect of specularity but also increases the stability to illumination variation [24]. The orientation has been developed as complement magnitude in monogenic binary pattern [27, 29]. Their works have been extended to temporal domain by [14]. In [14], they decomposed the orientation information into real and imaginary parts. They also demonstrated that orientation worked well in different illumination conditions. However, their works missed another important information, *i.e.*, phase information, which can

(a) (b)

Figure 3: Spatial domain representation of (a) $\mathcal{F}_1(u,v)$ and (b) $\mathcal{F}_2(u,v)$ of Riesz transform.

be output by monogenic filter. Further improvement to this work can be found in [26, 30]. They showed that the use of phase can provide complementary information for Gabor magnitude.

3. PROPOSED METHODOLOGY

3.1 Monogenic representation

The monogenic signal [11] generalizes the analytic signal to 2-D by the introduction of a Riesz filter $f(x,y)$, in which Fourier domain representation is $[\mathcal{F}_1(u,v), \mathcal{F}_2(u,v)]$. It can capture the phase, orientation and magnitude of an image in a rotation invariant way. The spatial visualization of Riesz transform is illustrated in Figure 3.

Given an image $I(x,y)$, the monogenic signal is represented as the convolution of 2-D signal with two Riesz filtered components $f(x,y) = g_s(\omega) * I(x,y) * [1, h_1(x,y), h_2(x,y)]$, where "*" is convolution operator, $h_i(x,y)$ is the spatial domain representation of $\mathcal{F}_i(u,v)$, and $g_s(\omega)$ is a Log-Gabor function on the linear frequency scale s. Here the Log-Gabor function has a transfer function of the form [12] as follows:

$$g_s(\omega) = \mathcal{F}^{-1}(G(\omega)) = \mathcal{F}^{-1}(\exp^{(-\log(\omega/\omega_c)^2)/2(\log(k/\omega_c)^2)}), \quad (1)$$

where $\omega_c \propto s$ is the filter's center frequency and s is number of wavelet scale of which a lower value will reveal more fine scale features while a larger value will highlight coarse features.

Therefore, the monogenic magnitude, phase and orientation of the signal can be formulated by:

$$A = \sqrt{h^2 + h_x^2 + h_y^2}, \quad (2)$$

$$\phi = \arctan(\sqrt{h_x^2 + h_y^2}/h), \quad (3)$$

$$\theta = \arctan(h_y/h_x), \quad (4)$$

where $h = g_s(\cdot) * I(\cdot)$, $h_x = h(\cdot) * h_1(\cdot)$, $h_y = h(\cdot) * h_2(\cdot)$, and the value ranges of phase and orientation are in $[0\ 2\pi]$ and $[0\ \pi]$, respectively.

3.2 Multiscale extension of monogenic

Since the log-Gabor filters are band-pass filters, multiscale monogenic representation is thus required to fully describe a signal. The direct concatenation of multi-scale representation for the sequences may cause high dimensionality and expensive computational time. Alternative, the sum of multi-scale representation can solve these limitations. Monogenic magnitude, phase and orientation (see in Eqs. 2, 3 and 4) can be re-written as:

$$\widetilde{A} = \sqrt{\widetilde{h}^2 + \widetilde{h}_x^2 + \widetilde{h}_y^2}, \quad (5)$$

$$\widetilde{\phi} = \arctan(\sqrt{\widetilde{h}_x^2 + \widetilde{h}_y^2}/\widetilde{h}), \quad (6)$$

$$\widetilde{\theta} = \arctan(\widetilde{h}_x/\widetilde{h}_y), \quad (7)$$

where $\widetilde{h} = \sum_{s=1}^{S} g_s(\cdot) * f(\cdot)$, $\widetilde{h}_x = \sum_{s=1}^{S} g_s(\cdot) * f(\cdot) * h_1(\cdot)$, $\widetilde{h}_y = \sum_{s=1}^{S} g_s(\cdot) * f(\cdot) * h_2(\cdot)$, and S is the number of scale in multi-scale log-Gabor filters.

3.3 Improved spatiotemporal local monogenic binary pattern

It is noted that each facial image can be represented by magnitude, phase and orientation of its monogenic signal. The magnitude and orientation have been utilized in [14], while the phase information is not still used. It is found that the phase information is useful to face recognition [26]. Motivated by their work, we attempt to exploit the information of phase for improving STLMBP. Next we will describe the formulation of spatiotemporal features.

Magnitude: In the monogenic representation of the image, the magnitude measures local structure energy, and the LBP operator can then be directly used to encode the variation of local energy. The histogram descriptor can thus be formulated as:

$$H_{mag}^{P,R} = \sum_{i=0}^{P-1} L((\widetilde{A}_{x_p,y_p} - \widetilde{A}_{x_c,y_c}) \geq 0)2^p, \quad (8)$$

where, $L(\widetilde{A}_{x_p,y_p} - \widetilde{A}_{x_c,y_c}) = \begin{cases} 1, \widetilde{A}_{x_p,y_p} - \widetilde{A}_{x_c,y_c} \geq 0 \\ 0, \widetilde{A}_{x_p,y_p} - \widetilde{A}_{x_c,y_c} < 0 \end{cases}$, and $\widetilde{A}_{x_c,y_c}$ is the monogenic magnitude value at the position (x_c,y_c), $\widetilde{A}_{x_p,y_p}$ is the magnitude value of P equally spaced pixels on a circle of radius R at this position.

Orientation: The orientation information $\widetilde{\theta}$ is decomposed into two subcomponents including real and imaginary pictures. The encoding measurement for real and imaginary parts can be defined as follows:

$$B(\widetilde{h}_i) = \begin{cases} 1, \widetilde{h}_i > 0 \\ 0, \widetilde{h}_i \leq 0 \end{cases}, \quad (9)$$

where, $i = x$ for real picture, and $i = y$ for imaginary picture. For a brief description, $\widetilde{h}_i$ is denoted as $\widetilde{h}$.

Then an alternative binary-compare function, local bit exclusive or operator (LXP), is exploited to calculate the correlation of the center and its neighbors. The histogram of real/imaginary can be formulated as follows:

$$H_{ori}^{P,R} = \sum_{p=0}^{P-1} (B(\widetilde{f}_{x_p,y_p}) \bigoplus B(\widetilde{f}_{x_c,y_c}))2^p, \quad (10)$$

where $B(\widetilde{f}_{x_p,y_p})$ is the PQDC value of P equally spaced pixels on a circle of radius R at the position (x_c,y_c), and $\bigoplus$ denotes the bit exclusive or operator. Furthermore, the uniform pattern in LBP, which contains at most two bitwise transitions from 0 to 1 or vice versa when the binary string

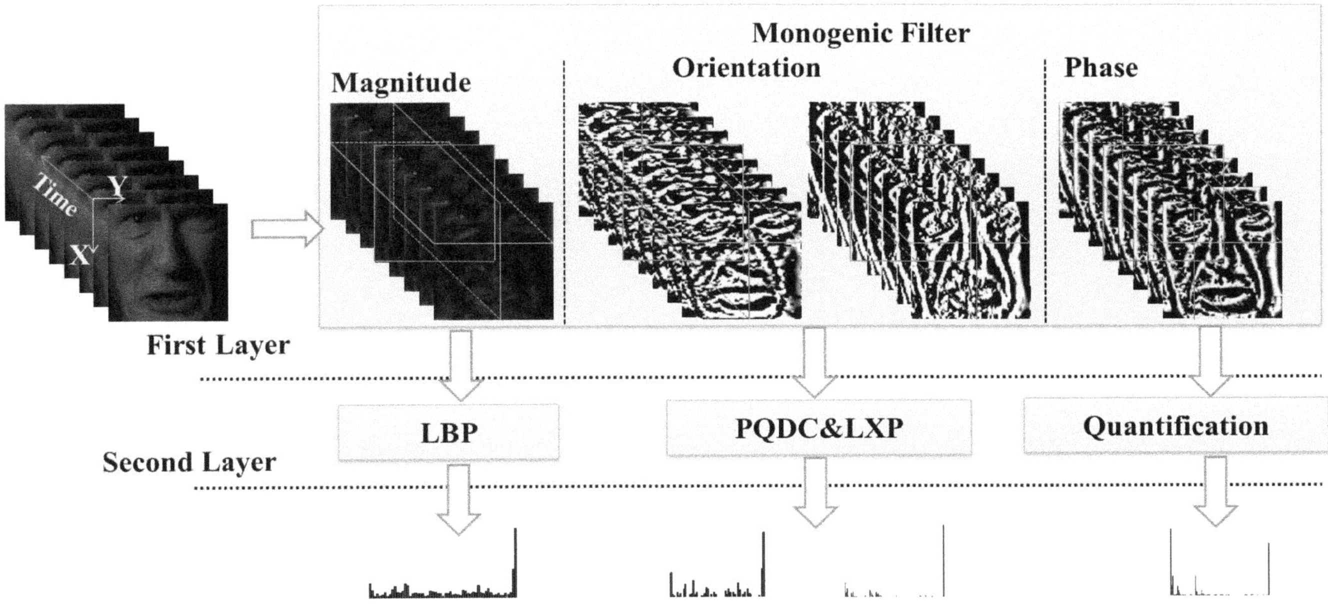

Figure 2: Overview of the proposed method in the emotion recognition in the wild

is considered circular, is used to preserve a simple rotation-invariant property and reduce the length of the feature vector.

Phase: Given the phase angle $\widetilde{\phi}(x, y)$ and its angles of neighbors $\widetilde{\phi}(x_p, y_p)$, it needs to exploit the operations of two phase angles according to the formulation of LBP. However, it is not reasonable to compare the difference of phase angles and use the unit function. Furthermore, the threshold method for the difference of phase angles is complicated and unstable since the threshold is empirically set. Instead, we rather quantify the phase angle by applying the quantification function:

$$q = mod(\lfloor \frac{\widetilde{\phi}(x, y)}{\frac{2\pi}{\varphi}} + 0.5 \rfloor, \varphi), \tag{11}$$

where *mod* is the modulo operation, and φ is the number of dominant orientation.

According to Eqn. 11, it is easy to get the dominant phase bins $q_{x,y}$ and q_{x_p,y_p} of (x, y) and (x_p, y_p), respectively. Then their operation is calculated as follows:

$$Q_p = \begin{cases} 0, q_{x,y} = q_{x_p,y_p} \\ 1, q_{x,y} \neq q_{x_p,y_p} \end{cases}. \tag{12}$$

The histogram of phase can be formulated as follows:

$$H^{P,R}_{phase} = \sum_{p=0}^{P-1} Q_p 2^p. \tag{13}$$

Extension to temporal domain: It is known that a video sequence can provide much more information than the static image. This induces another problem how to extend these methods to video sequences. Here we take the procedure producing the histogram of magnitude as an example. The procedure of all informations is illustrated in Figure 2. As shown in Figure 2, the magnitude images $\{\widetilde{A}_n\}_{n=1}^{N}$ extracted from N frames are orderly put into one cuboid. Furthermore, the features are extracted from three orthogonal planes (XY, XT and YT planes) for describing appearance and motions. For histogram of each plane, the uniform pattern is employed. Finally all histograms from three planes are concatenated into one feature vector. For other information, the similar procedure is implemented. One difference is the corresponding operators should be used.

In the implementation, the facial structure information is obtained by block-based method, which divided the facial image into several blocks. For each facial image, we divided all facial images into non-overlapping spatial 8×8 blocks.

3.4 Feature fusion and classification

Given multiple feature representation for each video, it is hoped to combine them in a way that increases the discriminatory power of the classifier. Two common methods for fusing multiple feature representations are feature-level, where a single classifier is trained using all features as input, and decision-level, where a classifier is trained for each feature separately and a decision rule combines the classifier outputs. We followed a feature fusion approach based on Multiple Kernel Learning (MKL) [8]. In our implementation, we used the UFO-MKL method as given in [22].

4. EXPERIMENTAL ANALYSIS

4.1 Data description and preprocess

The database provided by EmotiW 2014 [7] consists of short video clips extracted from popular movies. Each clip contains an actor expressing one of seven basic facial expressions: neutral (NE), happiness (HA), sadness (SA), disgust (DI), fear (FE), anger (AN), and surprise (SUR). The data is divided into three sets: *Train*, *Val* and *Test*, respectively containing 567, 371 and 407 video clips. *Train* and *Val* sets with facial expression labels are available for researchers, which are used to adjust the parameter and verify the facial expression model, while *Test* set contains unseen video

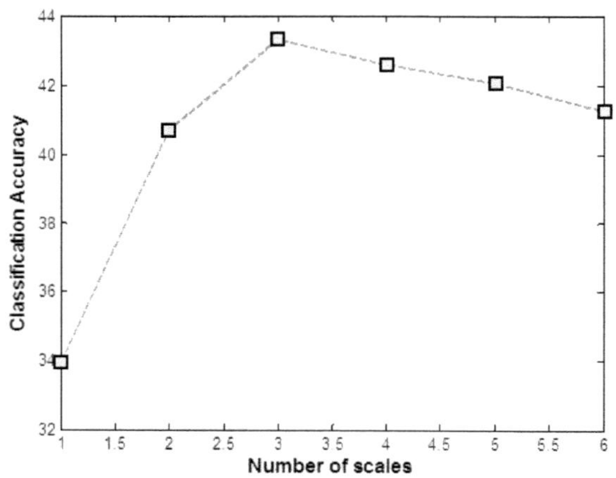

Figure 4: The recognition rate on validation set with different scale

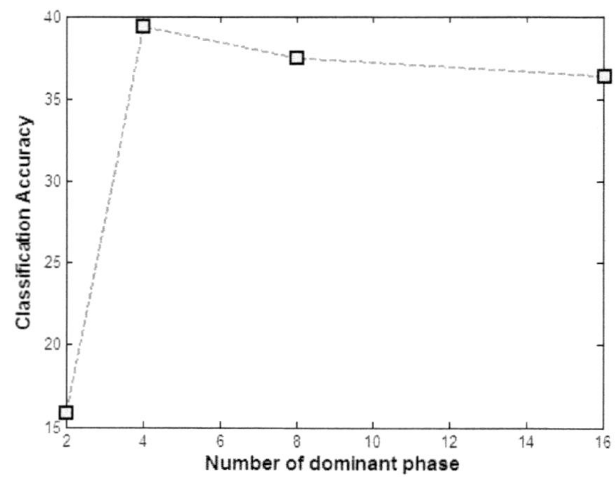

Figure 5: The recognition rate on validation set with different number of dominant orientation

clips. The goal of this dataset is to address the challenges in recognizing emotions in real-world conditions.

We simply use the aligned face images provided by EmotiW 2014 organizers. In their database, the face is localized using mixture of parts framework of [33] and tracking is performed using IntraFace Library. The fiducial points generated by IntraFace are used for aligning the face. The size of all face images is normalized into 128×128 pixels.

4.2 Experiment parameter

The proposed method has two important parameters, *i.e.* the number of scale and the number of dominant phase in Eqn. 11. We attempt to find out the best parameters for them on *Val* set.

Firstly, to evaluate the influence of scale in Section 3.2, we use STLMBP for obtaining the best parameter, since we expect less influence of another parameter. We tune the parameter s in range [1 6] and obtain difference results as shown in Figure 4. It is found that too many scales are not useless on predicting *Val* set. For *Test* set, we select the best parameter on validation set, *i.e.* $s = 3$ in Eqns. 5, 6 and 7.

Secondly, we only consider the phase information with three scales. Lib-SVM with Gaussian kernel [3] is used to classify the emotion on *Val* set. The number of dominant phase φ is tested in 2, 4, 8 and 16. We obtain the comparative results with different number as shown in Figure 5. It is found that when the number of dominant phase is 4, the feature descriptor achieves best. For *Test* set, we select $\varphi = 4$ for phase information in Eqn 11.

4.3 Result comparison

We demonstrate all of our results on the *Val* and *Test* sets, where the test results are evaluation feedbacks from EmotiW 2014 organizers) in Table 1. Firstly, we compare the performance of spatiotemporal features separately based on magnitude, real part, imaginary part and phase on *Val* set. Here we name them as STMBP, STRBP, STIBP and STPBP, respectively. It is found that all features except magnitude achieve better performance than the baseline on *Val* set (which adopted LBP-TOP features [32] for video and kernel SVM for classification) [5]. Furthermore, we also show the performance of STLMBP and improved STLMBP on *Val* and *Test* sets. STLMBP outperforms the baseline at the recognition rate of 6.35%. Improved STLMBP performs better than the STLMBP and baseline on both *Val* and *Test* sets.

The confusion matrix of final test results are shown in Table 2 and 3. We can see that "Happiness" and "Anger" are easy to be distinguished from other expressions, but it is still hard to do well on some difficult emotion classes such as "Disgust". One main reason is that the motion from "Happiness" and "Anger" is more obvious than other classes.

Table 1: The results of our methods on both *Val* and *Test* sets

Method	*Val*	*Test*
Video [5]	34.4%	33.7%
Audio [5]	26.2%	26.7%
Video+Audio [5]	28.2%	24.6%
STMBP	33.43%	-
STRBP	38.54%	-
STIBP	36.12%	-
STPBP	39.35%	-
STLMBP	43.13%	**40.05%**
Improved STLMBP	45.82%	**41.52%**

Table 2: Confusion matrix of classification on test data by using improved STLMBP

Expression	AN	DI	FE	HA	NE	SA	SUR
AN	37	4	4	3	3	4	3
DI	3	4	2	8	2	5	2
FE	14	0	8	4	11	5	4
HA	6	0	3	57	5	9	1
NE	12	5	6	19	45	18	12
SA	8	1	2	14	10	9	9
SUR	2	1	3	4	4	3	9

Table 3: Confusion matrix (%) on test data by using improved STLMBP

Expression	AN	DI	FE	HA	NE	SA	SUR
AN	**63.79**	6.90	6.90	5.17	5.17	6.90	5.17
DI	11.54	15.38	7.69	30.77	7.69	19.23	7.69
FE	30.43	0	17.39	8.70	23.91	10.87	8.70
HA	7.41	0	3.70	**70.37**	6.17	11.11	1.23
NE	10.26	4.27	5.13	16.24	38.46	15.38	10.26
SA	15.09	1.89	3.77	26.42	18.87	16.98	16.98
SUR	7.69	3.85	11.54	15.38	15.38	11.54	34.62

5. CONCLUSION

In this paper, we propose a new spatiotemporal feature descriptor for video-based emotion recognition in the real-world environment. For each video clip, magnitude, orientation and phase information are contained by using monogenic filter, and then they are encoded to represent the appearance-based features. In classification, multiple kernel learning is applied to fuse multiple feature vector and classify the video clip. The method is evaluated on EmotiW 2014 and shows promising results on unseen test data. In the future, we will try to explore the discriminative information from multiple feature vector to further improve the recognition performance.

6. ACKNOWLEDGMENTS

This work was sponsored by the Academy of Finland, Infotech Oulu and Nokia Foundation.

7. REFERENCES

[1] T. Almaev and M. Valstar. Local Gabor binary patterns from three orthogonal planes for automatic facial expression recognition. In *Humaine Association Conference on Affective Computing and Intelligent Interaction*, pages 356–361, 2013.

[2] T. Almaev, A. Yüce, A. Ghitulescu, and M. Valstar. Distribution-based interative parirwise classification of emotions in the wild using LGBP-TOP. In *ACM International Conference on Multimodal Interaction*, pages 535–541, 2013.

[3] C. Chang and C. Lin. Libsvm: a library for support vector machines. *ACM Transactions on Intelligent Systems and Technology*, 2(27):1–27, 2011.

[4] J. Daugman. High confidence visual recognition of persons by a test of statistical independence. *IEEE Transaction on Pattern Analysis and Machine Intelligence*, 15(11):1148–1161, 1993.

[5] A. Dhall, R. Goecke, J. Joshi, K. Sikka, and T. Gedeon. Emotion recognition in the wild challenge 2014: Baseline, data and protocol. In *ACM International Conference on Multimodal Interaction*, 2014.

[6] A. Dhall, R. Goecke, J. Joshi, M. Wagner, and T. Gedeon. Emotion recognition in the wild challenge (EmotiW) challenge and workshop summary. In *ACM International Conference on Multimodal Interaction*, pages 371–372, 2013.

[7] A. Dhall, R. Goecke, S. Lucey, and T. Gedeon. Collecting large, richly annotated facial-expression databases from movies. *IEEE Multimedia*, 19(3):34–41, 2012.

[8] A. Dileep and C. Sekhar. Representation and feature selection using multiple kernel learning. In *International Joint Conference on Neural Network*, pages 717–722, 2009.

[9] P. Ekman and W. Friesen. Facial action coding system: a technique for the measurement of facial movement. *Consulting Psychologists Press*, 1978.

[10] B. Fasel and J. Luettin. Automatic facial expression analysis: a survey. *Pattern Recognition*, 36:259–275, 2003.

[11] M. Felsberg and G. Sommer. The monogenic signal. *IEEE Transactions on Signal Processings*, 49(12):3136–3144, 2001.

[12] D. Field. Relations between the statistics of natural images and the response properties of cortical cells. *Journal of the Optical Society of America A*, 4(12):2379–2394, 1987.

[13] J. Hong and K. Song. Facial expression recognition under illumination variation. In *Advanced Robotics and Its Social Impacts*, pages 1–6, 2007.

[14] X. Huang, G. Zhao, W. Zheng, and M. Pietikäinen. Spatiotemporal local monogenic binary patterns for facial expression recognition. *IEEE Signal Processing Letters*, 19(5):243–246, May 2012.

[15] S. Kahou, C. Pal, X. Bouthillier, P. Froumenty, C. Gülcehre, R. Memisevic, P. Vincent, A. Courville, and Y. Bengio. Combining modality specific deep neural networks for emotion recognition in video. In *ACM International Conference on Multimodal Interaction*, pages 543–550, 2013.

[16] I. Kotsia, I. Buciu, and I. Pitas. An analysis of facial expression recognition under partial facial image occlusion. *Image and Vision Computing*, 26(7):1052–1067, 2008.

[17] T. krishna, A. Rai, S. Bansal, S. Khandelwal, S. Gupta, and D. Goyal. Emotion recognition using facial and audio features. In *International Conference on Language Resources and Evaluation*, pages 557–564, 2013.

[18] M. Liu, R. Wang, Z. Huang, S. Shan, and X. Chen. Partial least squares regression on grassmannian manifold for emotion recognition. In *ACM International Conference on Multimodal Interaction*, pages 525–530, 2013.

[19] P. Lucey, J. Cohn, T. Kanade, J. Saragih, and Z. Ambadar. The extended Cohn-Kanade dataset (CK+): A complete dataset for action unit and

emotion-specified expression. In *International Conference on Computer Vision and Pattern Recognition*, pages 94–101, 2010.

[20] M. Lyons, S. Akamatsu, M. Kamachi, and J. Gyoba. Coding facial expressions with Gabor wavelets. In *International Conference on Automatic Face and Gesture Recognition*, 1998.

[21] T. Ojala, M. Pietikäinen, and T. Mäenpää. Multiresolution gray-scale and rotation invariant texture classification with local binary pattern. *IEEE Transaction on Pattern Analysis and Machine Intelligence*, 24(7):971–987, 2002.

[22] F. Orabona and J. Luo. Ultra-fast optimization algorithm for sparse multiple kernel learning. In *International Conference on Machine Learning*, pages 1–8, 2011.

[23] K. Sikka, K. Dykstra, S. Sathyanarayana, G. Littlewort, and M. Bartlett. Multiple kernel learning for emotion recognition in the wild. In *ACM International Conference on Multimodal Interaction*, pages 517–523, 2013.

[24] G. Tzimiropoulos, S. Zafeiriou, and M. Pantic. Subspace learning from image gradient orientations. *IEEE Transaction on Pattern Analysis and Machine Intelligence*, 34(12):2454–2466, 2012.

[25] M. Valastar and M. Pantic. Induced disgust, happiness and surprise: an addition to the MMI facial expression database. In *International Conference on Language Resources and Evaluation*, pages 65–70, 2012.

[26] S. Xie, S. Shan, X. Chen, and J. Chen. Fusing local patterns of Gabor magnitude and phase for face recognition. *IEEE Transactions on Image Processing*, 19(5):1349–1361, January 2010.

[27] M. Yang, L. Zhang, L. Zhang, and D. Zhang. Monogenic binary pattern (MBP): A novel feature extraction and representation model for face recognition. In *International Conference on Pattern Recognition*, pages 2683–2690, 2010.

[28] Z. Zeng, M. Pantic, G. Roisman, and T. Huang. A survey of affect recognition methods: audio, visual and spontaneous expressions. *IEEE Transactions on Pattern Analysis and Machine Intelligence*, 33(1):39–58, 2009.

[29] L. Zhang, L. Zhang, Z. Guo, and D. Zhang. Monogenic-LBP: A new approach for rotation invariant texture classification. In *International Conference on Image Processing*, pages 2677–2680, 2010.

[30] W. Zhang, S. Shan, X. Chen, and W. Gao. Are Gabor phases really useless for face recognition. *Pattern Analysis and Application*, 12(3):301–307, 2009.

[31] W. Zhang, S. Shan, X. Chen, and W. Gao. Local Gabor binary pattern based on kullback-leilber divergence for partially occluded face recognition. *IEEE Signal Processing Letters*, 14(11):875–878, 2010.

[32] G. Zhao and M. Pietikäinen. Dynamic texture recognition using local binary pattern with application to facial expressions. *IEEE Transaction on Pattern Analysis and Machine Intelligence*, 29(6):915–928, 2007.

[33] X. Zhu and D. Ramanan. Face detection, pose estimation and landmark localization in the wild. In *Computer Vision and Pattern Recognition*, pages 1–8, 2012.

Emotion Recognition in Real-world Conditions with Acoustic and Visual Features

Maxim Sidorov
Institute of Communications Engineering
University of Ulm
Ulm, Germany
maxim.sidorov@uni-ulm.de

Wolfgang Minker
Institute of Communications Engineering
University of Ulm
Ulm, Germany
wolfgang.minker@uni-ulm.de

ABSTRACT

There is an enormous number of potential applications of the system which is capable to recognize human emotions. Such opportunity can be useful in various applications, e.g., improvement of Spoken Dialogue Systems (SDSs) or monitoring agents in call-centers. Therefore, the Emotion Recognition In The Wild Challenge 2014 (EmotiW 2014) is focused on estimating emotions in real-world situations. This study presents the results of multimodal emotion recognition based on support vector classifier. The described approach results in 41.77% of overall classification accuracy in the multimodal case. The obtained result is more than 17% higher than the baseline result for multimodal approach.

Categories and Subject Descriptors

I.6.3. [**Pattern Recognition**]: Applications; H.2.8 [**Database Applications**]: Image Databases; I.4.m [**Image processing and computer vision**]: Miscellaneous

Keywords

Audio-video data corpus, Facial expression, Feature-based fusion, Support vector machine.

1. INTRODUCTION

Automatic recognition of human emotions based on audio and visual cues is in the focus of research groups all over the world. While enabling machines to recognize human emotions may be useful in various applications, the recognition performance is still not satisfying. Meanwhile, computer systems are already deeply involved in recognizing, interpretation, or even synthesis of human emotions. For instance, Affective Computing [15] is one of the subject which deals with human affects.

Despite the fact that emotions have subjective nature, humans have a fine-tuned emotional model of people they know allowing for recognizing their emotional states more accurate. Furthermore, the basic emotions are shared between all people and cultures [17].

There is an increasing number of scientific papers, where the authors consider different ways of emotion recognition. Since the authors may use different corpora or performance metrics, these approaches are not always comparable. Therefore, such challenges as EmotiW, provide a general framework, by using that researches can objectively compare their achievements and set up state-of-the-art approaches. It was done during the first [21], the second [22], and the third [26] Audio/Visual Emotion recognition Challenges (AVEC), the first [8] Emotion Recognition in The Wild Challenges (EmotiW), the first international audio/visual mapping personality traits (MAPTRAITS) [5], and Computational Paralinguistics Challenge (ComParE) [20].

Each approach on multimodal emotion recognition addresses four key components: the audio and the video feature extraction procedure, the modelling algorithm and the fusion techniques. Scientific groups use the wide variety of approaches and their combinations.

For the audio part, all variety of Low-Level Descriptors (LLDs) and their functionals have been used for emotion recognition, based on their successful applications on such problems as automatic speech recognition, speaker and gender identification. LLDs of speech signals can be extracted using Praat software [3]. Several functionals-based feature sets have been specially developed for emotion recognition challenges. Thus, feature sets of 384 and 1,582 functionals have been proposed at the INTERSPEECH 2009 Emotion challenge [18] and at the INTERSPEECH 2010 Paralinguistic Challenge [19] correspondingly. The latest audio-based feature set consisting of 6,373 features has been suggested for the ComParE [20]. All of these features could be easily extracted, out of speech waveforms, using openSMILE software [10]. The authors in [16] used three different audio feature sets for affect recognition: 16 MFCCs with their delta and acceleration (48), energy and spectral features (34), 2,268 functionals which have been derived from LLDs. In [4] the authors have achieved reasonable results in emotion recognition by using the following set of audio-based features: the means, the standard deviations, the ranges, the maximum values, the minimum values and the medians of the pitch and the energy. Regarding the learning stage of emotion recognition using audio cues, the most common algorithms used are Multi Layer Perceptron (MLP) [24] and

ICMI'14, November 12–16, 2014, Istanbul, Turkey.

http://dx.doi.org/10.1145/2663204.2666279 .

Support Vector Machine (SVM) [12], as well as their combination [27].

Classical feature sets for the visual part, including Local Binary Patterns (LBP) [14, 1], Gabor [13], LPQ, PHOG [6] and their combination [25], have been successfully utilized for facial expression recognition and face detection. Recently suggested LPQ-TOP and LGBP-TOP[2] have also been successfully used for emotion recognition. Concerning the learning phase of visual-based emotion recognition, the most common method used is SVM for both classification and regression tasks.

Several fusion techniques may be utilized for merging the multimodal information. Thus, audio-visual affect recognition is based on three types of fusion methods: feature-level (also called early fusion), decision-level, and model-level [23, 28]. *Feature-level* fusion can be implemented by combining the features of different modalities into a single feature set. Feature-level fusion has the disadvantage of including the different kinds of modalities, which have different metric levels. Furthermore, high dimensionality of resulting feature set can become the other problem. In *decision-level* fusion, the multimodal data are treated independently and the single-modal hypothesises are combined at decision level, by using some criterion (weighted sum, product, etc.). Decision-level fusion overcomes the problems of the feature-level fusion, but it is based on the assumption that the data for different modalities are independent, that is not necessary true in reality. A Hidden Markov Model, in which different components are responsible for different data sources, can be an example of *model-level* fusion approach.

We present the multimodal emotion recognition system based on SVM trained by Sequential Minimal Optimization (SMO) algorithm [11], and feature-level fusion technique. We used baseline visual-based features with different sets of audio-features during audio-only and audio-visual experiments.

The rest of the paper is organized as follows: Section 2 describes EmotiW'14 corpus; Section 3 reviews the audio and video feature extraction methods; the proposed system is described in Section 4; Section 5 presents the experiments and results obtained for both the development and the test sets; finally, Section 6 presents the conclusions and future work.

2. CORPUS DESCRIPTION

The *AFEW* audio-visual emotion corpus [7] is used for the challenge. Highlighting the difference between acted and non-acted emotions, the authors of the challenge tried to collect close to real-world video extracts with human emotions. Thus, AFEW corpus consists of extracts from a number of Hollywood's moves. It is considered that professional actors are capable to express close to non-acted emotions in real-world environments (darkness, indoor, outdoor, background noise, etc.). The database comprises three subsets: train (578 fragments), validation (383), and test (407) partitions.

One of the following emotion primitives have been set by a human evaluator as a label for each extract: *angry*, *disgust*, *fear*, *happy*, *neutral*, *sad*, and *surprise*. The labelling of the corpus has been done in the following way. First, the subtitles of the corresponding movie are extracted and parsed by the recommender system, which searched for emotion-related keywords (happy, sad, etc.). Second, a human labeler annotates the recommended clips based on information available on the Internet.

Table 1: Results for emotion recognition with SVM-SMO. Performance is measured in accuracy values in per cents. The same visual-based features have been used for all of the experiments.

Audio Features	Audio	Visual	AV
Baseline	26.2	34.4	28.2
IS'13_ComParE	26.9	35.0	37.5
IS'09_emotion	25.6	–	40.7
emobase	26.4	–	**41.5**
emo_large	**28.7**	–	40.2
IS'12_speaker_trait_original	27.7	–	39.1
IS'12_speaker_trait	26.6	–	37.7

3. FEATURES

The organisers of the challenge have been realized multimodal audio-visual features in order to perform experiments [9]. A brief description of the suggested features are in the following Section.

3.1 Audio Features

The audio part of the recordings has been characterised by 1,582 dimensional feature vector similar to the features employed in Audio Video Emotion Recognition Challenge 2011 [21] motivated from the INTERSPEECH 2010 Paralinguistic challenge [19].

The following set of audio features has been selected to represent the challenge recordings: energy- and spectral-based LLDs (32 x 21 functionals), voicing LLDs (4 x 19 functionals), delta of energy/spectral features (34 x 21 functionals), delta of voicing features (4 x 19 functionals), and voiced/unvoiced duration features (2). The LLDs cover the state-of-the-art features in emotion recognition such as: loudness, MFCCs (1-16), jitter, shimmer, energy in different bands, probability of voicing, etc. Functionals features comprise the most descriptive functional dependences of LLDs: standard deviation, quartiles, linear regression slope and quadratic regression coefficient a with corresponding approximation errors, mean, maximum, minimum, etc.

3.2 Video Features

For the visual part, the face localisation using Mixture of Parts framework [29] and tracking using IntraFace library have been performed. First, the fiducial points generated by IntraFace have been utilized in order to align the faces. Second, the local appearance descriptor LBP-TOP has been extracted from non-overlapping spatial 4x4 blocks. Finally, the LBP-TOP features from each block are concatenated to form one feature vector.

4. EMOTION PREDICTION WITH MULTIMODAL FEATURES

To set up the baseline classification results, the organizers of the challenge used non-linear RBF kernel based SVN in case of visual cues only. Audio-based experiments have been conducted by applying a linear SVM classifier. A feature level fusion has been performed, where the audio and

Table 2: **Results for emotion recognition. Performance is measured in accuracy values in per cents.**

Approach	Development			Test		
	Audio	Visual	Audiovisual	Audio	Visual	Audiovisual
Baseline	26.2	34.4	28.2	26.7	33.7	24.6
SVN-SMO, baseline features	25.1	35.0	40.2	–	–	41.8

Table 3: Confusion matrix describing performance of the audio-visual system on the Test set.

	An	Di	Fe	Ha	Ne	Sa	Su
An	42	2	2	1	5	3	3
Di	3	4	3	7	3	3	3
Fe	14	2	12	4	4	4	6
Ha	9	10	2	40	10	7	3
Ne	7	17	14	12	49	11	7
Sa	8	7	2	9	4	16	7
Su	5	1	3	2	5	3	7

video features were concatenated and a non-linear RBF kernel based SVM has been learnt. The overall classification accuracy has been used for the performance evaluation. The baseline results are presented in Table 2.

By analysing the baseline results it can be concluded that the visual-based features are capable to catch more emotion-specific characteristics. Thus, the visual-based emotion classifier outperforms the audio-based for both development and test portions. Interesting that the accuracy of audio-visual system is significant lower than for the visual-only case. High-dimensional audio-visual features can become a key issue preventing SVM from obtaining higher classification accuracy. Thus, for test set the accuracy with hybrid audio-visual features was even lower than in case of the audio-based experiments.

To build our own emotion recognition system, firstly, we tried to use provided by the organizers baseline audio and visual features but with another classifier. The Support Vector Machine learned by the SMO algorithm has been deployed for solving the affect recognition tasks, based on its successful previous applications [5]. Then, another popular audio feature sets have been investigated and the results have been compared with the baseline (Table 1).

Firstly, audio and video features have been treated separately, then the feature-based fusion technique without further feature selection or reduction techniques has been utilized.

In order to rescale the attributes of different units and scales, the statistical normalization procedure (also called Z-transformation) has been applied as a preprocessing step.

To produce the affect hypothesises, the SVM instance has been trained with the training and the validation portions and evaluated with the testing set. The results of numerical evaluations are in the following Section.

5. EXPERIMENTAL RESULTS

Regarding the results, which have been achieved by using different audio-based features, the obtained performances, in terms of classification accuracy on the development set, are in Table 1. The feature sets as well as their titles are from openSMILE software. It should be noted that the same baseline visual-based features have been used for the experiments, therefore the repeated values are omitted in Table.

It turns out that *emo_large* is the optimal choice in case of audio-only modality. This features, comprising large set of 6,552 audio-based features (56 LLD, 56 delta, and their 39 functionals), result in 28.7% of accuracy (vs. 26.2% in case of baseline). However, this advantage dissipated in case of multimodality. Thus, the best option in case of audio-visual cues was *emobase* feature set. This set consists of 988 audio-based features (26 LLD, 26 delta, and their 19 functionals) and results in 41.5% (vs. 28.2 in case of baseline result).

The comparative results of the emotion recognition system application on the test portion are in Table 2. The results of emotion reignition with the single-modalities are quite similar to the baseline system's accuracy. Regarding the multimodal approach, it is obvious that the application of SVM trained by SMO results in significant higher performance values than the baseline and single-modality approaches. Thus, the multimodal approach with SMO-based SVM outperforms baseline results for both validating and testing.

The confusion matrix in Table 3 describes the classification results using the test set. By analysing the confusion matrix it seems that such emotion primitives as *Anger* (72.4% classification accuracy), *Happy* (49.4), *Neutral* (41.9), *Sad* (30.2) and partially *Surprise* (26.9) are much easy to recognise than *Disgust* (15.4) and *Fear* (26.1). Furthermore, recordings with *Anger* label have been frequently recognised by the system with label *Fear* and *Happy* instances as *Disgust*.

Nevertheless, it should be noted, that emotions themselves and their evaluations have subjective nature. Even for humans, it is not always evident to make a decision about an emotional label.

6. CONCLUSION

We have presented an audiovisual system for emotion recognition based on SVM trained by SMO algorithm. The modalities have been treated separately, as well as the merged features have been investigated. The described multimodal approach results in higher accuracy values than the results provided by the baseline system.

While an SVM already provides reasonable results for emotion recognition, we are still examining its general appropriateness. The usage of other—possibly more accurate—identifiers may improve the performance of the system. In addition, by applying feature selection techniques (principal component analysis, genetic algorithm-based feature selection, etc.) for these problems, further performance improvement could be achieved.

7. REFERENCES

[1] T. Ahonen, A. Hadid, and M. Pietikainen. Face description with local binary patterns: Application to face recognition. *Pattern Analysis and Machine Intelligence, IEEE Transactions on*, 28(12):2037–2041, 2006.

[2] T. R. Almaev and M. F. Valstar. Local gabor binary patterns from three orthogonal planes for automatic facial expression recognition. In *Affective Computing and Intelligent Interaction (ACII), 2013 Humaine Association Conference on*. IEEE, 2013.

[3] P. Boersma. Praat, a system for doing phonetics by computer. *Glot international*, 5(9/10):341–345, 2002.

[4] C. Busso, Z. Deng, S. Yildirim, M. Bulut, C. M. Lee, A. Kazemzadeh, S. Lee, U. Neumann, and S. Narayanan. Analysis of emotion recognition using facial expressions, speech and multimodal information. In *Proceedings of the 6th international conference on Multimodal interfaces*, pages 205–211. ACM, 2004.

[5] O. Celiktutan, F. Eyben, E. Sariyanidi, H. Gunes, and B. Schuller. Maptraits 2014: Introduction to the audio/visual mapping personality traits challenge. In *Proceedings of the 16th ACM on International conference on multimodal interaction*. ACM, 2014.

[6] A. Dhall, A. Asthana, R. Goecke, and T. Gedeon. Emotion recognition using phog and lpq features. In *Automatic Face & Gesture Recognition and Workshops (FG 2011), 2011 IEEE International Conference on*, pages 878–883. IEEE, 2011.

[7] A. Dhall et al. Collecting large, richly annotated facial-expression databases from movies. 2012.

[8] A. Dhall, R. Goecke, J. Joshi, M. Wagner, and T. Gedeon. Emotion recognition in the wild challenge 2013. In *Proceedings of the 15th ACM on International conference on multimodal interaction*, pages 509–516. ACM, 2013.

[9] A. Dhall, R. Goecke, J. Joshi, M. Wagner, and T. Gedeon. Emotion recognition in the wild challenge 2014. In *Proceedings of the 16th ACM on International conference on multimodal interaction*. ACM, 2014.

[10] F. Eyben, M. Wöllmer, and B. Schuller. Opensmile: the munich versatile and fast open-source audio feature extractor. In *Proceedings of the international conference on Multimedia*, pages 1459–1462. ACM, 2010.

[11] G. W. Flake and S. Lawrence. Efficient svm regression training with smo. *Machine Learning*, 46(1-3):271–290, 2002.

[12] Y.-L. Lin and G. Wei. Speech emotion recognition based on hmm and svm. In *Machine Learning and Cybernetics, 2005. Proceedings of 2005 International Conference on*, volume 8, pages 4898–4901. IEEE, 2005.

[13] C. Liu and H. Wechsler. Independent component analysis of gabor features for face recognition. *Neural Networks, IEEE Transactions on*, 14(4):919–928, 2003.

[14] T. Ojala, M. Pietikainen, and T. Maenpaa. Multiresolution gray-scale and rotation invariant texture classification with local binary patterns. *Pattern Analysis and Machine Intelligence, IEEE Transactions on*, 24(7):971–987, 2002.

[15] R. W. Picard. *Affective computing*. MIT press, 2000.

[16] E. Sánchez-Lozano, P. Lopez-Otero, L. Docio-Fernandez, E. Argones-Rúa, and J. L. Alba-Castro. Audiovisual three-level fusion for continuous estimation of russell's emotion circumplex. In *Proceedings of the 3rd ACM international workshop on Audio/visual emotion challenge*, pages 31–40. ACM, 2013.

[17] K. R. Scherer. Emotion. In *Sozialpsychologie*, pages 293–330. Springer, 1997.

[18] B. Schuller, S. Steidl, and A. Batliner. The interspeech 2009 emotion challenge. In *INTERSPEECH*, volume 2009, pages 312–315. Citeseer, 2009.

[19] B. Schuller, S. Steidl, A. Batliner, F. Burkhardt, L. Devillers, C. A. Müller, and S. S. Narayanan. The interspeech 2010 paralinguistic challenge. In *INTERSPEECH*, pages 2794–2797, 2010.

[20] B. Schuller, S. Steidl, A. Batliner, A. Vinciarelli, K. Scherer, F. Ringeval, M. Chetouani, F. Weninger, F. Eyben, E. Marchi, et al. The interspeech 2013 computational paralinguistics challenge: social signals, conflict, emotion, autism. 2013.

[21] B. Schuller, M. Valstar, F. Eyben, G. McKeown, R. Cowie, and M. Pantic. Avec 2011–the first international audio/visual emotion challenge. In *Affective Computing and Intelligent Interaction*, pages 415–424. Springer, 2011.

[22] B. Schuller, M. Valster, F. Eyben, R. Cowie, and M. Pantic. Avec 2012: the continuous audio/visual emotion challenge. In *Proceedings of the 14th ACM international conference on Multimodal interaction*, pages 449–456. ACM, 2012.

[23] N. Sebe, I. Cohen, and T. S. Huang. Multimodal emotion recognition. *Handbook of Pattern Recognition and Computer Vision*, 4:387–419, 2005.

[24] M. Sidorov, S. Ultes, and A. Schmitt. Emotions are a personal thing: Towards speaker-adaptive emotion recognition. In *IEEE International Conference on Acoustics, Speech, and Signal Processing (ICASSP)*, pages 4836–4840, May 2014.

[25] X. Tan and B. Triggs. Fusing gabor and lbp feature sets for kernel-based face recognition. In *Analysis and Modeling of Faces and Gestures*, pages 235–249. Springer, 2007.

[26] M. Valstar, B. Schuller, K. Smith, F. Eyben, B. Jiang, S. Bilakhia, S. Schnieder, R. Cowie, and M. Pantic. Avec 2013: the continuous audio/visual emotion and depression recognition challenge. In *Proceedings of the 3rd ACM international workshop on Audio/visual emotion challenge*, pages 3–10. ACM, 2013.

[27] C.-H. Wu and W.-B. Liang. Emotion recognition of affective speech based on multiple classifiers using acoustic-prosodic information and semantic labels. *Affective Computing, IEEE Transactions on*, 2(1):10–21, 2011.

[28] C. Xu, P. Du, Z. Feng, Z. Meng, T. Cao, and C. Dong. Multi-modal emotion recognition fusing video and audio. *Appl. Math*, 7(2):455–462, 2013.

[29] X. Zhu and D. Ramanan. Face detection, pose estimation, and landmark localization in the wild. In *Computer Vision and Pattern Recognition (CVPR), 2012 IEEE Conference on*, pages 2879–2886. IEEE, 2012.

ERM4HCI 2014 – The 2nd Workshop on Emotion Representation and Modelling in Human-Computer-Interaction-Systems

Kim Hartmann
Faculty of Electrical Engineering and Information Technology
Otto von Guericke University Magdeburg
Magdeburg, Germany
{kim.hartmann}@ovgu.de

Björn Schuller
Department of Computing
Imperial College London
London, UK
bjoern.schuller@imperial.ac.uk

Ronald Böck
Faculty of Electrical Engineering and Information Technology
Otto von Guericke University Magdeburg
Magdeburg, Germany
{ronald.boeck}@ovgu.de

ABSTRACT

In this paper the organisers present a brief overview of the second workshop on Emotion Representation and Modelling in Human-Computer-Interaction-Systems. The ERM4HCI 2014 workshop is again held in conjunction with the 16th ACM International Conference on Mulitmodal Interaction (ICMI 2014) taking place in Instanbul, Turkey. This year's ERM4HCI is focussed on the characteristics which are used to describe and further, to identify emotions. Moreover, the corresponding relations to personality and user state models are of interest. Especially, options towards a minimal set of characteristics will be discussed in the contex of multimodal affective Human-Computer Interaction.

Categories and Subject Descriptors

H.1.2 [**User/Machine Systems**]: Human factors, Human information processing; H.5 [**INFORMATION INTERFACES AND PRESENTATION**]: Multimedia Information Systems, User Interfaces

Keywords

Multimodality; Emotion Representation; Emotion Modelling; Human-Computer-Interaction; User Adaptation; Individualisation; Workshop; Summary

ICMI'14, November 12–16, 2014, Istanbul, Turkey
ACM 978-1-4503-2129-7/13/12.
http://dx.doi.org/10.1145/2522848.2535891

1. INTRODUCTION

[1]While developing user adaptable Human-Computer-Interaction (HCI), the role of emotions occurring during interaction gained in attention over the past years. Especially emotions, being widely accepted as essential to Human-Human-Interaction, became increasingly interesting for system designers of affective interfaces in order to provide natural, user-centred interaction. To adequately incorporate emotions in modern HCI systems, results from various and varying research disciplines must be combined.

Various difficulties in the emotion representation may arise, depending on the utilised modalities and the aim of the incorporate model. Therefore, this workshop concentrates on emotion representations, the characteristics used to describe and identify emotions and their relation to personality and user state models. Such relation can be age, gender, physical/cognitive load, etc. In this context we encourage a wide discussion about possible interdependencies of characteristics on an intra- and intermodality level. Interdependencies of characteristics may occur if two characteristics are influenced by the same physiological change in the observed user. Furthermore, other factors (technical, constructive, etc.) can cause interdependencies as well.

In a more broader sense, the workshop aims at identifying a minimal set of characteristics to represent and recognise emotions in multi-modal affective HCI. For this, some of the typical issues arising in multi-modal data processing for affective systems will be addressed. Such issues are, for instance, timing aspects, confidence metrics, discretisation issues and issues related to the translation between different emotion models.

Generally, the workshop offers a platform to discuss approaches for feature selection from a multimodal or physiological point of view. Moreover, theoretical papers contributing to the understanding of emotions in order to aid

[1]The text is taken in parts from the workshop's website including the call for paper (cf. [1]).

in the technical modelling of emotions for affective systems are intended. For this, the workshop provides a forum for discussions on the necessary prerequisites for consistent and interoperable emotion representations in multi-modal affective systems.
The main topics of the workshop are

- Personality models and the incorporation of emotion models
- Multimodal aspects of emotion recognition and representation
- Physiology of emotion representations and characteristics
- Feature selection for emotion recognition in HCI
- Interdependencies of emotion recognition features
- Minimal (multimodal) feature sets for affective HCI systems
- Approaches to the interoperability of emotion models
- Timing in multimodal emotion recognition scenarios
- Confidence metrics for emotion recognition/classification in HCI
- Consistent modelling of emotions in multimodal HCI systems
- Correlation of user states and emotion recognition features
- User state specific emotion modelling
- Domain specific emotion representations and interfaces
- Technical aspects of multimodal emotion recognition

2. ORGANISERS, PROGRAM COMMITTEE, AND REMARKS

2.1 Workshop Organisers

Kim Hartmann, Otto von Guericke University Magdeburg, Germany
Björn Schuller, Imperial College London, UK
Ronald Böck, Otto von Guericke University Magdeburg, Germany

2.2 Program Committee

Roman Bednarik, University Eastern Finland, Finland
Jonas Beskow, KTH Stockholm, Sweden
Nadia Bianchi-Berthouze, University College London, UK
Antonio Camurri, University Genova, Italy
Marc Cavazza, Teesside University, UK
Matthieu Courgeon, LIMSI-CNRS, France
Sidney D'Mello, University Notre Dame, USA
Hazim Kemal Ekenel, Istanbul Technical University, Turkey
Roland Göcke, University Canberra, Australia
Kristiina Jokinen, University of Helsinki, Finland
Daniel McDuff, MIT, USA
Gary McKeown, Queens University Belfast, UK
Dirk Reichardt, DHBW Stuttgart, Germany
Jianhua Tao, Chinese Academy of Sciences, China
Khiet Truong, University Twente, The Netherlands
Michel Valstar, University Nottingham, UK
Andreas Wendemuth, Otto von Guericke Magdeburg, Germany

2.3 Review Process

All accepted papers received at least two double-blind reviews.
For this, we would like to thank all PC members for their time and helpful contributions.

2.4 Acknowledgement

We acknowledge the continuous support and the fruitful discussion of *Klaus R. Scherer*, University of Geneva, Switzerland.

3. REFERENCES

[1] K. Hartmann, R. Böck, K. R. Scherer, and B. Schuller. Erm4hci website. *http://erm4hci.kognitivesysteme.de/*, September 08, 2014.

Gaze-in 2014: the 7th Workshop on Eye Gaze in Intelligent Human Machine Interaction

Hung-Hsuan Huang
Department of Information & Communication Science
Ritsumeikan University, Japan
huang@fc.ritsumei.ac.jp

Roman Bednarik
School of Computing
University of Eastern Finland
FI-80101, Joensuu, Finland
roman.bednarik@uef.fi

Kristiina Jokinen
Institute of Behavioural Sciences
University of Helsinki, Finland
FIN-00014 Helsinki, Finland
Kristiina.Jokinen@helsinki.fi

Yukiko Nakano
Dept. of Computer and Information Science
Seikei University, Japan
y.nakano@st.seikei.ac.jp

ABSTRACT

This paper presents a summary of the seventh workshop on Eye Gaze in Intelligent Human Machine Interaction. The Gaze-in 2014 workshop is a part of a series of workshops held around the topics related to gaze and multimodal interaction.

The workshop web-site can be found at http://hhhuang.homelinux.com/gaze_in/.

Categories and Subject Descriptors

H.1 [**Models AND PRINCIPLES**]: Eye Gaze, Speech Input, Reading, Sight Translation

General Terms

Design, Experimentation, Security, Human Factors, Theory

Keywords

Gaze, Interaction, Multimodality, Robotics

1. INTRODUCTION

Eye gaze is one of the most important aspects in understanding and modeling human-human communication, and it has great potential also in improving human-machine and robot interaction. In human face-to-face communication, eye gaze plays an important role in floor and turn management, grounding, and engagement in conversation. In human-computer interaction research, social gaze, gaze directed at an interaction partner, has been a subject of increased attention.

In the previous workshops we have discussed a wide range of issues for eye gaze involved in multimodal human-machine/robot/agent interaction; technologies for sensing human attentional behaviors, attentional behaviors in problem-solving and task-performing, multimodal communication, interpretation and generation. In addition to these topics, this workshop also focuses on eye gaze in multiparty interaction and real-world applications, especially on mobile platforms where remarkable progress has been achieved in recent years.

This year's workshop continues in these lines and explore the growing area of gaze in intelligent interaction research by bringing together researchers from domains of human sensing, multimodal processing, humanoid interfaces, intelligent user interfaces, and communication science. The participants exchange ideas to develop and improve methodologies for this research area with the long-term goal of establishing a strong interdisciplinary research community in "attention aware interactive systems."

2. THEMES

This workshop solicits papers that address the following topics:

- Technologies and methods for sensing and interpretation of human mental state by gaze in dyadic / multiparty interaction
  - Sensing, tracking, and interpreting attentional behaviors using bodily motions and multimodal and biometric signals in intelligent user interface
  - Utilizing gaze behaviors and other potential modalities to read human mind, estimation of personality and conversational attitude
- Eye gaze in multimodal generation and behavior production in conversational humanoids
  - Selecting appropriate eye-gaze behaviors for virtual agents and communication robots in the interaction with humans
  - Effective multimodal expressions by combining eye gaze and other modalities
- Technologies and methods for utilizing gaze behaviors in the real world
  - Applications utilizing gaze behaviors on mobile platforms

ICMI'14, November 12–16, 2014, Istanbul, Turkey.
ACM 978-1-4503-2885-2/14/11.
http://dx.doi.org/10.1145/2663204.2668316

- Utilizing gaze behaviors in navigation or other human-vehicle interaction applications

- Empirical studies of attentional behaviors
  - Attentional behaviors in dyads and multiparty face-to-face and remote conversations and collaboration
  - Implications of analysis of human attentional behaviors towards HCI design
- Evaluation and design issues for using eye gaze in multimodal interfaces
  - Evaluation methods for gaze-based multimodal interfaces
  - Designs of user studies to measure user experience and to identify the real impact of eye gaze in multimodal interfaces
- Any other new directions for gaze in multimodal interaction
  - Pervasive and ubiquitous interaction
  - Future scenarios

3. ORGANIZERS, PROGRAM COMMITTEE, AND PROGRAM

3.1 Workshop organizers

Hung-Hsuan Huang - Ritsumeikan University, Japan

Roman Bednarik - University of Eastern Finland, Finland

Kristiina Jokinen - University of Helsinki, Finland

Yukiko Nakano - Seikei University, Japan

3.2 Technical program committee

Andrew Duchowski (Clemson University, USA)

Ayse Kucukyilmaz (Imperial College London, UK)

Bert Oben (University of Leuven, Belgium)

Casey Kennington (Bielefeld University, Germany)

Catharine Oertel Genannt Bierbach (KTH-Royal Institute of Technology, Sweden)

Cristina Segalin (University of Verona, Italy)

Christian Nitschke (Kyoto University, Japan)

Enrique Sánchez-Lozano (University of Vigo, Spain)

Giorgio Roffo (University of Verona, Italy)

Hana Vrzakova (University of Eastern Finland, Finland)

Hendrik Buschmeier (Bielefeld University, Germany)

Ingo Siegert (Otto von Guericke University Magdeburg, Germany)

Jari Kangas (University of Tampere, Finland)

Lei Chen (Institution ETS, USA)

Ramanathan Subramanian (University of Trento, Italy)

Rudolph Triebel (TU Munich, Germany)

Samer Al Moubayed (Disney Research, USA)

Sean Andrist (University of Wisconsin, USA; Disney Research, USA)

Soroush Vosoughi (Massachusetts Institute of Technology, USA)

Xuan Guo (Rochester Institute of Technology, USA)

Yoshinori Kuno (Saitama University, Japan)

3.3 Submissions and paper review

The call for papers attracted eight submissions from Germany, Turkey, Japan, the United Kingdom, Poland, and the United States. These papers covers the following research topics: eye tracking in security and medical applications, eye gaze behavior analysis in grouped face-to-face communication and collaborative learning, and cognitive function in investigating musical sense and the conversation with virtual agents on mobile devices. Most of the papers were reviewed by three reviewers with some exceptions where there were only two reviewers.

3.4 Invited speaker

Gaze-in 2014 also featured a keynote talk by Dan Bohus (Microsoft Research, USA) titled: “Attention and Gaze in Situated Language Interaction.”

MAPTRAITS 2014: The First Audio/Visual Mapping Personality Traits Challenge – An Introduction

Perceived Personality and Social Dimensions

Oya Celiktutan
School of Electronic Eng. and Computer Science
Queen Mary University of London
E1 4NS London, UK
o.celiktutandikici@qmul.ac.uk

Florian Eyben
Machine Intelligence & Signal Processing
Technische Universität München
80290 München, DE
eyben@tum.de

Evangelos Sariyanidi
School of Electronic Eng. and Computer Science
Queen Mary University of London
E1 4NS London, UK
e.sariyanidi@qmul.ac.uk

Hatice Gunes
School of Electronic Eng. and Computer Science
Queen Mary University of London
E1 4NS London, UK
h.gunes@qmul.ac.uk

Björn Schuller*
Machine Intelligence & Signal Processing
Technische Universität München
80290 München, DE
schuller@tum.de

ABSTRACT

The Audio/Visual Mapping Personality Challenge and Workshop (MAPTRAITS) is a competition event that is organised to facilitate the development of signal processing and machine learning techniques for the automatic analysis of personality traits and social dimensions. MAPTRAITS includes two sub-challenges, the continuous space-time sub-challenge and the quantised space-time sub-challenge. The continuous sub-challenge evaluated how systems predict the variation of perceived personality traits and social dimensions in time, whereas the quantised challenge evaluated the ability of systems to predict the overall perceived traits and dimensions in shorter video clips. To analyse the effect of audio and visual modalities on personality perception, we compared systems under three different settings: visual-only, audio-only and audio-visual. With MAPTRAITS we aimed at improving the knowledge on the automatic analysis of personality traits and social dimensions by producing a benchmarking protocol and encouraging the participation of various research groups from different backgrounds.

*Dr. Schuller is also with Department of Computing, Imperial College London, SW7 2AZ London, UK.

ICMI'14, November 12–16, 2014, Istanbul, Turkey.
ACM 978-1-4503-2885-2/14/11.
http://dx.doi.org/10.1145/2663204.2668317.

Categories and Subject Descriptors

J.4 [**Social and Behavioural Sciences**]: Psychology, Sociology; H.1.2 [**Human/Machine Systems**]: Human Information Processing; I.5 [**Pattern Recognition**]: Applications—*Computer Vision, Signal Processing*

Keywords

Personality; Big Five Model; Attractiveness; Challenge

1. INTRODUCTION

Automatic assesment of people's personality is very important for multiple research domains, particularly those that are related to human-computer or human-robot interaction such as social robotics. Despite a growing interest on personality traits and their effects on human life, systems focusing on automatic analysis of personality traits have started to emerge only recently. Most systems focused on unimodal cues such as written texts, audio, speech, face and body gestures, with some tentative efforts on multimodal analysis. None of the proposed systems to date attempted to assess personality traits continuously in time and space along multiple trait dimensions at a given interaction time.

The MAPTRAITS Challenge aimed at advancing the state of the art in automatic analysis of personality traits and social dimensions by providing a benchmarking protocol that enables evaluation from multiple perspectives, and encouraging the participation of diverse research groups from different disciplines, in particular the audio and video analysis communities and those in the social sciences who study personality, traits, expressive and nonverbal behaviour.

We considered personality in terms of the Big Five model that consists of five traits, namely, extraversion, agreeableness, conscientiousness, neuroticism, openness. As for social dimensions, we considered four dimensions, namely, engagement, facial attractiveness, vocal attractiveness, and likability. Our benchmarking protocol was based on the well-known SEMAINE dataset, which consists of videos that involve a conversation between a person and an artificial agent [3]. In the scope of MAPTRAITS, we provided a ground truth for all afore-mentiond personality traits and social dimensions. The ground truth has been compiled by combining the annotations of multiple raters who annotated traits and dimensions based on their perception.

In summary, the task in MAPTRAITS was to correctly predict the perceived personality annotations for the audio-visual clips provided. We organised two sub-challenges, i.e. the continuous space-time sub-challenge and the quantised space-time sub-challenge. In continuous space-time challenge the task was to predict the perceived personal traits and social dimensions along with their temporal variation, whereas in the quantised space-time challenge the task was to predict the overall perceived traits and dimensions in shorter video clips. To analyse the effect of audio and visual modalities, we compared the results of each sub-challenge separately for audio and visual modalities, and also for the combination of the two modalities. MAPTRAITS 2014 is the first of an expected series of competitions. We hope that this first version will serve as a useful benchmarking protocol and will push the state of the art in the field by facilitating the development of novel approaches to unimodal/multimodal feature extraction/fusion and prediction.

2. THE MAPTRAITS PROTOCOL

2.1 Dataset

The dataset for quantised space-time challenge comprised 44 clips of 11 different subjects, each rated by 6 annotators along 9 dimensions (the five personality traits and four social dimensions). Videos were rated in a Likert scale ranging from 1 to 10. To promote multi-modal analysis, two sets of annotations were provided; one where annotators used only visual modality and one where annotators used both audio and visual modalities. For both sets of annotations, ground truth labels were generated by taking the average of the annotations per clip per dimension.

The continuous space-time sub-challenge dataset consisted of 30 clips of 10 subjects, each annotated by 21 raters in a scale that ranges from 0 to 100. Three sets of annotations were provided based on three different annotation settings, namely audio only, visual only and audio-visual. To produce the ground truth, we first aligned the annotations of multiple annotators using Dynamic Time Warping (DTW), then eliminated inconsistent annotations based on inter-rater agreement and finally computed the average of the remaining reliable annotations [1].

2.2 Metrics

To enable evaluation from multiple perspectives, we used a variety of evaluation metrics for each sub-challenge. For the quantised space-time challenge, we used the mean square error (MSE), Pearson's correlation coefficient (COR) and coefficient of determination (R^2) and unweighted average recall (UAR). For the continuous space-time challenge we used the MSE and COR metrics as well as the concordance correlation coefficient and cross correlation coefficient.

2.3 Baseline

We provided baseline results for both challenges in three settings: visual-only, audio-only and audio-visual. For the visual-only setting, we first aligned faces with the technique of Xiong and De La Torre [5], then computed the Quantised Local Zernike Moments (QLZMs) of aligned faces [4] and finally obtained predictions using ridge regression. For the audio-only setting, we extracted features such as energy, spectral, cepstral and voicing related low-level features using the openSMILE feature extractor [2] and obtained predictions using SVM (for quantised predictions) and SVR (for continuous predictions).

3. PARTICIPANTS AND RESULTS

For the quantised space-time challenge, the best baseline results in terms of MSE were obtained in audio-visual setting where the MSE of 9 dimensions varied from 0.61 to 3.20. For the continuous space-time sub-challenge, the best baseline results in terms of MSE were generally obtained in visual-only setting where MSE varied between 0.28 and 0.41.

Nine groups from six different countries registered for the MAPTRAITS Challenge. The results obtained by participating systems were not significantly higher than the baseline results, demonstrating the difficulty of the problem. MAPTRAITS 2014 was the first of an expected series of competitions that took the initiative for advancing the state of the art forward and produced a benchmarking protocol that can be used by future studies as well. We expect to see an increasing number of participants in the coming series of competitions with the hope of advancing the state of the art further in this challenging problem.

Acknowledgments

The work of Oya Celiktutan, Evangelos Sariyanidi and Hatice Gunes has been supported by the MAPTRAITS Project funded by the Engineering and Physical Sciences Research Council UK (EPSRC) (Grant Ref: EP/K017500/1).

4. REFERENCES

[1] O. Celiktutan and H. Gunes. Continuous prediction of perceived traits and social dimension in space and time. In *Proc. of IEEE Int. Conf. on Image Processing*, Paris, France, 2014.

[2] F. Eyben, F. Weninger, F. Gross, and B. Schuller. Recent developments in opensmile, the munich open-source multimedia feature extractor. In *Proceedings of the 21st ACM international conference on Multimedia*, pages 835–838. ACM, 2013.

[3] G. McKeown, M. Valstar, R. Cowie, M. Pantic, and M. Schroder. The semaine database: Annotated multimodal records of emotionally colored conversations between a person and a limited agent. *IEEE Trans. on Affective Computing*, 3(1):5–17, 2012.

[4] E. Sariyanidi, H. Gunes, M. Gökmen, and A. Cavallaro. Local Zernike moment representations for facial affect recognition. In *Proc. of British Machine Vision Conf.*, 2013.

[5] X. Xiong and F. De la Torre. Supervised descent method and its application to face alignment. In *Proc. of IEEE Conf. on Computer Vision and Pattern Recognition*, 2013.

MLA'14 – Third Multimodal Learning Analytics Workshop and Grand Challenges

Xavier Ochoa
Escuela Superior Politécnica del Litoral
Km. 30.5 Vía Perimetral
Guayaquil, Ecuador
xavier@cti.espol.edu.ec

Marcelo Worsley
Stanford University
520 Galvez Mall
Stanford, USA
mworsley@stanford.edu

Katherine Chiluiza
Escuela Superior Politécnica del Litoral
Km. 30.5 Vía Perimetral
Guayaquil, Ecuador
kchilui@espol.edu.ec

Saturnino Luz
Trinity College Dublin
College Green
Dublin, Ireland
Saturnino.Luz@cs.tcd.ie

ABSTRACT

This paper summarizes the third Multimodal Learning Analytics Workshop and Grand Challenges (MLA'14). This subfield of Learning Analytics focuses on the interpretation of the multimodal interactions that occurs in learning environments, both digital and physical. This is a hybrid event that includes presentations about methods and techniques to analyze and merge the different signals captured from these environments (workshop session) and more concrete results from the application of Multimodal Learning Analytics techniques to predict the performance of students while solving math problems or presenting in the classroom (challenges sessions). A total of eight articles will be presented in this event. The main conclusion from this event is that Multimodal Learning Analytics is a desirable research endeavour that could produce results that can be currently applied to improve the learning process.

Categories and Subject Descriptors

K.3.1 [**Computers in Education**]: Miscellaneous

Keywords

Learning analytics, educational data mining, multimodal interaction

1. INTRODUCTION

Learning Analytics is the "middle-space" where Educational Sciences, Computer Science, Learning Technologies and Data Science converge. The main goal of this new field of knowledge is to contribute to new empirical findings, theories, methods, and metrics for understanding how students learn and to use that knowledge to improve those students' learning.

One promising research line within Learning Analytics is Multimodal Learning Analytics, which emphasizes the analysis of natural rich modalities of communication during situated learning activities. This includes students' speech, writing, and nonverbal interaction (e.g., gestures, facial expressions, gaze, etc.). A primary objective of Multimodal Learning Analytics is to analyze coherent signal, activity, and lexical patterns to understand the learning process and to provide relevant feedback to participants and practitioners. The Third International Workshop on Multimodal Learning Analytics brings together researchers in multimodal interaction and systems, cognitive and learning sciences, educational technologies, and related areas to discuss the recent developments and future opportunities in this sub-field.

ICMI'14, November 12–16, 2014, Istanbul, Turkey.
ACM 978-1-4503-2885-2/14/11.
http://dx.doi.org/10.1145/2663204.2668318.

2. PROGRAM

Following the First International Workshop on Multimodal Learning Analytics in Santa Monica in 2012 and the ICMI Grand Challenge on Multimodal Learning Analytics in Sydney in 2013, this third workshop comprises a mixture of a workshop session and two data-driven grand challenge sessions.

2.1 Workshop Session

The workshop session focuses on the presentation of multimodal signal analysis techniques that could be applied in Multimodal Learning Analytics. Instead of requiring research results, that usually are presented at the Learning Analytics and Knowledge (LAK) or Multimodal Interaction (ICMI) conferences, this workshop challenges presenters to concentrate on benefits and shortcomings of different research and technical methods used for multimodal analysis of learning signals. This session includes four articles from diverse topics: theoretical and conceptual considerations for different forms of multimodal data fusion; voice analysis to determine the level of rapport in learning exercises; video analysis of live classrooms; and the role of multimodal analysis in the service of studying complex learning environments.

2.2 Challenge Sessions

Following the successful experience of the previous Multimodal Learning Analytics Grand Challenge in ICMI 2013, this year this event will provide two data sets with a wealth of research questions to be tackled by interested participants:

2.2.1 *Math Data Challenge*

The Math Data Corpus from the 2013 ICMI Multimodal Learning Analytics Grand Challenge was again made available for analysis. This corpus involves 12 sessions, with groups of three students collaborating while solving mathematics problems (i.e. geometry, algebra). Data were collected of participants' natural multimodal communication and activity patterns during these problem-solving sessions. The modalities collected include: speech, digital pen input, and video. In total, approximately 16 hours of multimodal data is available. Eighteen high-school students participated in this study. Each group of three students met for two sessions. The student groups varied in performance characteristics, with some low-to-moderate performers and others high-performing students. During the sessions, students were engaged in authentic problem solving and peer tutoring as they worked on 16 mathematics problems. The sixteen problems were uniformly distributed in terms of difficulty, with four of each type of question: easy, moderate, hard, and very hard difficulty levels. The data have been segmented by start and end time of each problem, scored for solution correctness, and also scored for which student solved the problem correctly.

This year, the dataset has been expanded with full manual and automatic transcripts of the students' speech. It also contains more than 10,000 annotations of the students' notes and diagrams. The main research questions considered include: 1) automatic prediction of which math problems will be solved correctly or incorrectly; 2) which student in a group is the dominant domain expert; and 3) identification of significant precursors of performance and learning. Predictors could be based on information from unimodal or multimodal signals, lexical/representational content, individual or group dynamics, or combined information sources. One article presented in this challenge provided a detailed exploration of how to use the digital pen information to predict the expertise in the group. This work reaches high levels of accuracy (83%) when i dentifying the expert student among the 3 participants.

2.2.2 *Presentation Quality Challenge*

This challenge includes a data corpus that involves 40 oral presentations of Spanish-speaking students in groups of 4 to 5 members. These participants are presenting projects on entrepreneurship ideas, literature reviews, research designs, software design, etc. Data were collected on presenters' natural multimodal communication in regular classroom settings. The following data is available: speech, facial expressions and physical movements in video, skeletal data gathered from Xbox Kinect for each individual, and slide presentation files. In total, approximately 10 hours of multimodal data is available for analysis of these presentations. In addition, individual and group grades (based on the quality of the slides) grading for individuals when doing their presentations is included as well as a group-grade related to the quality of the slides used when doing each presentation. This challenge seeks to solve the following questions: a) How multimodal techniques can help in evaluating presentation quality and presenter behaviors; and b) How good is a group presentation based on the individual presentations and the quality of the slides used in a presentation.

This session is composed of three articles. The first one explores the slide presentation files and the audio features to predict the grade obtained by each student. This work found that the models created from slide features were accurate up to 65%. The most relevant features for the slide-base models were: number of words, images, and tables, and the maximum font size. The audio-based models reach 69% accuracy, with pitch and filled pauses related features being the most significant. The second work makes use of all the provided modalities (audio, video, Kinect data and slide files) and suggests that multimodal cues can predict human scores on presentation tasks. Furthermore, this second paper shows that a scoring model comprising both verbal and visual features can outperform a unimodal model. The final article uses the video and Kinect information to predict human grading. The Machine-learning evaluations resulted in models that predicted human grading of eye contact and postures, and body language, with accuracies 61% and 68%, respectively. Furthermore, the results suggest that a set of body language features, such as arm movement and smoothness, are of high significance for predicting the level of development for presentation skills.

3. ORGANIZATION

Because this community is still in its infancy, the workshop and grand challenges chairs were selected from previous organizers and participants:

- Xavier Ochoa, ESPOL, Ecuador
- Marcelo Worsley, Stanford, USA
- Katherine Chiluiza, ESPOL, Ecuador
- Saturnino Luz, Trinity College Dublin, Ireland

4. CONCLUSIONS

The third Multimodal Learning Analytics Workshop and Grand Challenges (MLA'14) was organized to bring together experts in computer science, learning sciences, learning technologies and data science. It was envisioned that this expert meeting would be the space to initiate research in this nascent subfield of Learning Analytics. New challenges and insights will arise from the convergence of practitioners, academics and researchers, which in turn will create opportunities to collaborate and to create applications and tools to assist students, teachers and the community.

5. ACKNOWLEDGEMENTS

The organizers want to express their gratitude to Incaa Designs and Escuela Superior Politécnica del Litoral (ESPOL) for the access provided to their datasets. Without their help and work, this event would not be possible.

ICMI 2014 Workshop on Multimodal, Multi-Party, Real-World Human-Robot Interaction

Mary Ellen Foster
School of Mathematical and Computer Sciences
Heriot-Watt University
Edinburgh, UK
m.e.foster@hw.ac.uk

Manuel Giuliani
ICT&S Center
Universität Salzburg
Salzburg, Austria
manuel.giuliani@sbg.ac.at

Ronald Petrick
School of Informatics
University of Edinburgh
Edinburgh, UK
rpetrick@inf.ed.ac.uk

ABSTRACT

The Workshop on Multimodal, Multi-Party, Real-World Human-Robot Interaction will be held in Istanbul on 16 November 2014, co-located with the 16th International Conference on Multimodal Interaction (ICMI 2014). The workshop objective is to address the challenges that robots face when interacting with humans in real-world scenarios. The workshop brings together researchers from intention and activity recognition, person tracking, robust speech recognition and language processing, multimodal fusion, planning and decision making under uncertainty, and service robot design. The programme consists of two invited talks, three long paper talks, and seven late-breaking abstracts. Information on the workshop and pointers to workshop papers and slides can be found at `http://www.macs.hw.ac.uk/~mef3/icmi-2014-workshop-hri/`.

Categories and Subject Descriptors

I.2.9 [**Artificial Intelligence**]: Robotics

Keywords

Multimodal, multi-party, real-world interaction

1. INTRODUCTION

The development of robots capable of interacting with humans has made tremendous progress in the last decade, leading to an expectation that in the near future, robots will be increasingly deployed in public spaces, for example as receptionists, shop assistants, waiters, or bartenders. In these scenarios, robots must necessarily deal with situations that require interactions that are short and dynamic, potentially with multiple persons at once.

To support this form of interaction, robots typically require specific skills, including robust video and audio processing, fast reasoning and decision making mechanisms, and natural and safe output path planning algorithms. This physically embodied, dynamic, real-world context is the most challenging possible domain for multimodal interaction: for example, the state of the physical environment may change at any time; the input sensors must deal with noisy and uncertain input; while the robot platform must combine interactive social behaviour with physical task-based action.

This workshop brings together researchers from a range of relevant disciplines to explore the challenges and solutions for multimodal human-robot interaction from different perspectives. This workshop is the third in a series of meetings organised around this theme. Previous events in this series include the ICSR 2013 workshop on *Robots in public spaces: towards multi-party, short-term, dynamic human-robot interaction*, and the ICSR 2011 tutorial on *Joint action for social robotics: how to build a robot that works together with several humans*; details on the whole workshop series are available through `http://www.james-project.eu/`.

2. SCOPE

Contributions to the workshop were sought in all areas relevant to the overall goal of the workshop, including—but not limited to—the following topics:

- intention recognition
- activity recognition
- person tracking
- speech recognition in noisy environments
- robust spoken language processing
- audiovisual signal processing
- planning and decision making under uncertainty
- knowledge representation and reasoning
- multimodal fusion
- multimodal interaction management
- cognitive robotics
- natural language generation
- design of service robots / interaction systems in public spaces
- evaluation of robots in real-world contexts

These topics cover a wide range of research communities including multimodal interaction, dialogue systems, human-robot interaction, robotics, automated planning, computer vision, and signal processing. Due to the interdisciplinary nature of the workshop topic, relevant contributions from other fields were also welcome.

MMRWHRI'14, November 16, 2014, Istanbul, Turkey.
ACM 978-1-4503-0551-8/14/11.
http://dx.doi.org/10.1145/2666499.2666507 .

3. TALKS AND PAPERS

Overall, the workshop programme consists of two invited talks, three long papers, and seven late-breaking abstracts.

3.1 Invited talks

Two invited talks have been included in the workshop programme:

- **Daniel Gatica-Perez** from Idiap Research Institute, Martigny, Switzerland
- **Ryo Ishii** from NTT Communication Science Laboratories, Kanagawa, Japan.

3.2 Long Papers

Three six-page long papers have been accepted to the workshop:

- Birte Carlmeyer, David Schlangen, and Britta Wrede. *Towards Closed Feedback Loops in HRI: Integrating InproTK and PaMini.*
- Mohamed A. Sehili, Fan Yang, and Laurence Devillers. *Attention Detection in Elderly People-Robot Spoken Interaction.*
- Graham Wilcock and Kristiina Jokinen. *Advances in Wikipedia-based Interaction with Robots.*

3.3 Late-breaking abstracts

Seven two-page late-breaking abstracts have been accepted to the workshop:

- Suna Bensch and Thomas Hellström. *Towards Proactive Robot Behavior Based on Incremental Language Analysis.*
- Mary Ellen Foster, Mei Yii Lim, Amol Deshmukh, Srini Janarthanam, Helen Hastie and Ruth Aylett. *Affective Feedback for a Virtual Robot in a Real-World Treasure Hunt.*
- Manuel Giuliani, Thomas Marschall and Manfred Tscheligi. *Applying Topic Recognition to Spoken Language in Human-Robot Interaction Dialogues.*
- Hitoshi Nishimura, Yuko Ozasa, Yasuo Ariki and Mikio Nakano. *Selection of an Object Requested by Speech Based on Generic Object Recognition.*
- Yuhei Ogawa, Yuichiro Mori and Takahira Yamaguchi. *Applying Semantic Web Services to Multi-Robot Coordination.*
- Niels Schuette, John Kelleher and Brian Mac Namee. *Clarification Dialogues for Perception-based Errors in Situated Human-Computer Dialogues.*
- Andrés Trujillo-León and Fernando Vidal-Verdú. *Self-calibration of Attendance Device to Adapt to Different Users and Environments.*

In addition to the long papers and late-breaking abstracts—which will be published in the ACM Digital Library—additional late-breaking abstracts have been solicited from other workshop participants, which will be presented at the workshop and archived on the workshop website.

4. WORKSHOP FORMAT

The main objective of the workshop is to provide opportunities for participants to discuss their research and ideas related to the central theme of the workshop. As a result, the workshop included a mixture of invited talks and paper presentations (long and short), with ample time for questions and discussions. To break away from the typical format of other workshops, the late-breaking abstract papers will be presented as *Pecha Kucha*-style talks (see `http://www.pechakucha.org/` for more details on this format).

5. PROGRAMME COMMITTEE

The organisers are grateful to the Programme Committee for their help with reviewing submissions to the workshop.

- Mary Ellen Foster (Heriot-Watt University, Edinburgh, UK)
- Andre Gaschler (fortiss GmbH, Munich, Germany)
- Manuel Giuliani (University of Salzburg, Austria)
- Robin Hill (University of Edinburgh, UK)
- Simon Keizer (Heriot-Watt University, Edinburgh, UK)
- Sebastian Loth (University of Bielefeld, Germany)
- Kira Mourão (University of Edinburgh, UK)
- Ronald Petrick (University of Edinburgh, UK)
- Markos Sigalas (Foundation for Research and Technology - Hellas, Heraklion, Crete, Greece)
- Zhuoran Wang (Heriot-Watt University, Edinburgh, UK)

6. WORKSHOP ORGANISERS

Mary Ellen Foster is a Research Fellow in the Interaction Lab of the School of Mathematical and Computer Sciences at Heriot-Watt University in Edinburgh, Scotland. She received her PhD in Informatics from the University of Edinburgh, and has previously worked in the Robotics and Embedded Systems Group at the Technical University of Munich and in the School of Informatics at the University of Edinburgh. Her research interests include embodied communication, natural language generation, and multimodal dialogue systems; in particular, she is interested in designing, implementing, and evaluating practical artificial systems that support embodied interaction with human users

Manuel Giuliani is a senior scientist at ICT&S center, University of Salzburg. He received a Master of Arts in computational linguistics from Ludwig-Maximilian-University Munich, a Master of Science in computer science from Technische Universität München, and a PhD in computer science from Technische Universität München. His research interests include social robotics, human-robot interaction, natural language processing, multimodal fusion, multimodal output generation, and robot architectures.

Ronald Petrick is a Research Fellow in the School of Informatics at the University of Edinburgh. He received a Master of Mathematics degree in computer science from the University of Waterloo, and a PhD in computer science from the University of Toronto. His research interests include automated planning with incomplete information and sensing, cognitive robotics, knowledge representation and reasoning, and applications of planning to natural language dialogue, social robotics, and human-robot interaction.

An Outline of Opportunities for Multimodal Research

Dirk Heylen
University of Twente
Human Media Interaction
Enschede, The Netherlands
d.k.j.heylen@utwente.nl

Alessandro Vinciarelli
University of Glasgow
Sir A. Williams Bldg.
Glasgow, UK
Alessandro.Vinciarelli@glasgow.ac.uk

ABSTRACT

This paper summarizes the contributions to the Workshop "Roadmapping the Future of Multimodal Interaction Research including Business Opportunities and Challenges". We present major challenges and ideas for making progress in the field of social signal processing and related fields as presented by the contributors of the workshop.

Categories and Subject Descriptors

I.5.4 [**Pattern Recognition**]: Applications Signal Processing

Keywords

Social Signal Processing; Multimodal Interaction

Challenges In her paper, Elisabeth André presents a number of challenges that the community will need to address in order to achieve real impact and applications. The first of the major limitations of current research are that much of it is focussed on off-line processing of content instead of on-line analysis of humans interacting with a system). In as far as there is research on interaction it mostly remains in the laboratory and many real-life complications are thus ignored. Personalisation and adaptation to the situation is needed when moving into the real world. The use of the data that is currently offered by pervasive and mobile computing applications such as wearables may be very useful for this endeavor. André notes - as do many other contributors - that research into Social Signal Processing has made important progress through several challenges. Interesting though these may be, it should be noted that sometimes they are based on fabricated rather than real data. André proposes a challenge similar to the Loebner price but focussing on affective and social skills in which an integrative view on social skills is offered and also other modalities than the traditional ones are being investigated.

Approaches Alexandros Potamianos in his paper, presents an interesting perspective on the future of social signal processing. The overlapping fields of Affective Computing, Behavioural Computing and Social Signal Processing, he says, have made great progress on recognizing affect from low-level features from different modalities (audio, visual, text and multimodal). Also some progress has been made on the classification of personality, status, dominance, persuasion and rapport which are studied in SSP-type research. The current models classically use machine learning or reinforcement learning which need quite a bit of data and may not be the ideal methods to deal with personalisation and adaptation. Learning from few examples or generalizing across tasks remains a great challenge, for which we need to look to other methods.

The paper calls for another approach to social signal processing: less behaviouristic and more cognitively inspired one could say. This is an idea that also appears in other papers in different ways. In their paper "Statistical Pattern Recognition meets Formal Ontologies", Marco Cristani and Roberta Ferrario suggest to have the field move beyond "signal processing". Their approach is to incorporate semantics into the processing. They ilustrate their idea by using an ontology that captures the domain knowledge into the processing both during learning and inference.

Interesting Domains Rene Kaiser and Ferdinand Fuhrmann describe the potential of social signal processing techniques in control centers. Michel Valster introduces the term "Behaviomedics" in his paper. The domain is both challenging and rewarding. Valster's paper presents a list of studies that use social signal processing techniques to help diagnose, monitor and treat medical conditions or psychological disorders, in particular those that alter a person's social and affective signals. The paper presents studies in which automatic analysis or synthesis of affective social signals are used for mood and anxiety disorders, neuro-developmental disorders (such as adhd, autism) and pain. Also personality disorders or changes in behaviour due to paralysis, would be interesting cases to consider.

Interpersonal Zakia Hamal and Jeffrey Cohn raise the point that is relevant for social signal processing. Whereas it may be appear that emotion is something that belongs to the individual, in considering the case of social interaction it is important to look into what happens between people. The authors make clear that methods are required that model each person as both a cause and an effect of another's behavior.

Also the paper by Mohamed Chetouani looks at the case of interpersonal communication. The paper investigates metrics that can capture the dynamics of social interaction. The

ICMI'14, November 12–16, 2014, Istanbul, Turkey.

metrics are called Social Signatures. Investigating synchrony in parent-child interactions is one of the case studies presented in this paper. Not only does this tie in with the urge to look at dyads, it also considers a similar case study as the one presented in the paper by Hamal and Cohn. Furthermore, the goal of the study is to detect pathological cases (autism).

Interestingly, the paper also demonstrates two other trends in the field that appear in other papers. The first is the call for considering more modalities than the classical ones. Chetouani proposes an original contribution to use hormones in the process of identifying Social Signatures. Chetouani and his co-workers looked at the automatic extraction of behaviors with the goal to associate these behavioral dynamics with hormonal dynamics. Given the differences in the nature of the dynamics this poses interesting computational challenges. Another trend that this paper demonstrates is the search for new methodological approaches. In this case, the approach is not to use the physiological signals as features - as is usually done in emotion recognition - but to map the social signals into hormone changes, taking these as the "ground truth".

With the goal of detecting Social Signatures and the features that are relevant, one need not only consider the approach of analysing human-human interactions. Social agents and robots can be used to study Social Signatures with the agents and robots as controlled stimuli in interaction. Chetouani discusses a particular study they carried out in which distinctive social signatures were captured for different types of participants (children with ASD, TD children and healthy adults) interacting with a robot. In this case agents and robots are used for detecting metrics. Of course the goal of constructing social robots and other socially intelligent interactive systems is also a goal of social signal processing research. The paper by Albert Ali Salah and the paper by Steve Renals and co-authors[1] deals with such challenges and opportunities in the area of Conversational Interactive Systems.

Interactive Systems It is generally assumed that Socially Intelligent Interactive Systems need the skills to recognize and synthesize relevant social signals. The question whether the analytic skills should be modeled along the ways humans perform them was raised in the paper by Potamianos. It may be helpful in different ways. When building interactive systems such as social robots, it may however not always be useful to consider the "human-human" case as a guiding model. Salah notes that people may be prone to treat a humanoid robot in similar terms as a human in many ways, but not in all. The robot needs to understand the behaviour of humans and using cognitively inspired theories might help of course. However, humans interacting with robots behave differently from humans interacting with other humans. Similarly, the robot also needs to display social signals, but these can also be different from those used by humans. Humans, after all, are not the only species of a social animal. Also cats and other pets have particular interactive skills to engage with humans in a social way. So why not think of human-robot communication as yet another form of interspecies interaction?

[1] J. Carletta, H. Bourlard, P. Garner, A. Popescu-Belis, D. Klakow, A. Girenko, V. Petukhova, P. Wacker, A. Joscelyne, C. Kompis, S. Aliwell, W. Stevens and Y. Sabbah.

When looking at the future of social robotics, Salah points out that improving the analysis tools that can identify affective and social cues in humans may also need to look at the wider generative perspective. Social signals are not fixed but are generated and evolve within social interactions. They co-evolve in social, cultural contexts. To capture this dynamics is certainly an important challenge for the field. It might also require other approaches such as the ones proposed by Potamianos.

The goal of the Rockit project, as described in the paper by Renals et al. is to put down a roadmap to achieve the vision in which "human-human, human-machine, and human-environment communication are not hampered by differences in language capability, accessibility, or knowledge of the technology, and where security and privacy are built in". The paper presents their method to define the roadmap and it identifies the social, commercial and technological drivers. In their SWOT analysis, the authors point out that conversational interactive systems of the SIRI-kind are getting mainstream. It shows that speech recognition has reached an acceptable level to be integrated in querying systems. However, one of the weaknesses of current systems is that multimodality is still very limited: "Speech recognition makes errors in broad domains and realistic environments; unnatural-sounding speech synthesis, with very limited control of expression and emotion; dialogue systems operate in limited, simple domains; very few systems make use of multimodal, heterogeneous inputs."

Among the opportunities mentioned is the fact that more and more open data becomes available. However this is matched with the threat that much data is still proprietary and there are serious privacy issues in many cases. The issue of the availability of data, methods of collection and annotation is the topic of the paper by Maria Koustombogera and Harris Papageorgiou. They point out that there is a shortage of annotated data: it is costly to develop, standards are lacking and there are IPR and privacy restrictions. Challenges can help to alleviate some of these problems, making annotated data available for research. Related to this point, the paper by Francesca Bonin, Emer Gilmartin, Carl Vogel and Nick Campbell argues for the standardisation of annotation schemes. The paper argues for two more points: 1) the idea that not all social interactions are the same and 2) that "social signal' processing will need to be linked to content to improve applications.

Giuseppi Riccardi makes an overview of Mobile Virtual Agents currently available to deliver question-answering services and then moves on to discuss the possible application of this technology for personal healthcare applications on a smartphone. Riccardi lists a number of requirements that such systems should aim for such as spoken, multimodal and multisensorial understanding, understanding covert signals from wearable and mobile sensors, handle empathy and other emotions, and be context-aware. Social and communicative skills also need to be improved.

1. *ACKNOWLEDGMENTS

This publication was supported by the Dutch national program COMMIT.

UM3I 2014: International Workshop on Understanding and Modeling Multiparty, Multimodal Interactions

Samer Al Moubayed
Disney Research
Pittsburgh, USA
samer@disneyresearch.com

Dan Bohus
Microsoft Research
Redmond, WA, USA
dbohus@microsoft.com

Anna Esposito
Second University of Naples
Caserta, Italy
anna.esposito@unina2.it

Dirk Heylen
Twente University
Enschede, The Netherlands
d.k.j.heylen@utwente.nl

Maria Koutsombogera
Harris Papageorgiou
ILSP/ "Athena" R. C.
Athens, Greece
{mkouts,xaris}@ilsp.gr

Gabriel Skantze
KTH Royal Institute of Technology
Stockholm, Sweden
gabriel@speech.kth.se

ABSTRACT
In this paper, we present a brief summary of the international workshop on Modeling Multiparty, Multimodal Interactions. The UM3I 2014 workshop is held in conjunction with the ICMI 2014 conference. The workshop will highlight recent developments and adopted methodologies in the analysis and modeling of multiparty and multimodal interactions, the design and implementation principles of related human-machine interfaces, as well as the identification of potential limitations and ways of overcoming them.

Categories and Subject Descriptors
H.1.2 [**User/Machine Systems**]: Human factors, Human information processing; H.5 [**INFORMATION INTERFACES AND PRESENTATION**]: Multimedia Information Systems, User Interfaces.

General Terms
Algorithms, Performance, Design, Reliability, Experimentation, Human Factors, Theory.

Keywords
Multiparty Interaction, Multimodality, Modeling, Human-Computer Interaction, Workshop, Summary.

1. INTRODUCTION
Analysis and understanding of human-human conversations has stressed the importance of modeling all available verbal and non-verbal signals occurring in conversations to develop human-machine interfaces that are capable of interpreting multimodal signals as well as generating natural, coordinated responses. While the focus of research has been primarily on dyadic interactions, multiparty interactions as communicative setups involving more than two participants are a complex, yet challenging construct that merits attention.

Understanding and modelling the multiparty configuration and the underlying affective and social behavior of the participants address the design of interfaces that:

- can follow and participate in the conversation,
- present interactional skills to control the interaction flow,
- respond to it in the appropriate timing and as naturally as possible,
- keep track of the multimodal conversation of the participants, as well as
- guarantee a high and balanced level of involvement between them.

Related applications, such as socially aware and affective spoken dialogue systems and social robots, aim at stimulating natural, fluent and spontaneous spoken behavior from the users and decode the multimodal signals providing significant information about the participants' states, intentions, and verbal or non-verbal actions. Research on multimodal and multiparty interaction with respect to analysis, modelling and interface design encompasses the following challenges:

a) Interpretation of conversational behavior in terms of identifying the intended addressees and understanding the conversational status of the participants according to the turn-taking structure, their conversational roles and their social and affective state as expressed in their speech and non-verbal modalities.

b) Modeling the multimodal strategies and regulatory actions reflected through the participants' verbal and non-verbal signals and psychological variables.

c) Generating and displaying the appropriate timed and natural multimodal behavior, including feedback and turn-taking signals.

ICMI '14, Nov 12-16 2014, Istanbul, Turkey
ACM 978-1-4503-2885-2/14/11.
http://dx.doi.org/10.1145/2663204.2668321

2. OBJECTIVES

UM3I 2014 [1] aims to explore this growing field of multiparty multimodal interaction by bridging this multidisciplinary area and bringing together researchers from domains of multimodal signal processing, dialog systems, human-computer interaction, human-robot interaction, multimodal conversation analysis and multimodal user interfaces.

3. TOPICS OF INTEREST

The workshop will address topics that highlight recent developments and adopted methodologies in the analysis and modeling of multiparty interaction, the design and implementation principles of related human-machine interfaces, as well as the identification of potential limitations and ways of overcoming them, to conclude with the shaping of future lines of research.

Workshop topics include, but are not limited to:

- Models of multimodal & multiparty human-human, human-computer, human-robot interaction.
- Multiparty and multimodal dialogue modeling and systems.
- Modeling engagement in multiparty interactions.
- Modeling group/social relationships and dynamics.
- Models of multiparty collaboration.
- Design principles and best practices in human-machine interfaces tackling multiple modalities in multiparty interaction.
- Evaluation methodologies for multiparty interactions.
- Multiparty and multimodal turn-taking models.
- Multi-human & multi-machine models of multiparty interaction.
- Creating resources of multimodal & multiparty interactions (data capturing, corpus annotation, etc.).
- Multimodal social and affective aspects in multiparty interaction.

4. COMMITTEES AND REMARKS

4.1 Organising Committee

Samer Al Moubayed, Disney Research, USA

Dan Bohus, Microsoft Research, USA

Anna Esposito, Second University of Naples, Italy

Dirk Heylen, University of Twente, The Netherlands

Maria Koutsombogera, Institute for Language and Speech Processing /"Athena" R.C., Greece

Harris Papageorgiou, Institute for Language and Speech Processing /"Athena" R.C., Greece

Gabriel Skantze, KTH Royal Institute of Technology, Sweden

4.2 Program Committee

Rieks op den Akker, University of Twente, The Netherlands

Jonas Beskow, KTH Royal Institute of Technology, Sweden

David DeVault, USC Institute for Creative Technologies, USA

Joakim Gustafson, KTH Royal Institute of Technology, Sweden

Stefan Kopp, Bielefeld University, Germany

Jill Lehman, Disney Research, USA

Vincent Müller, Anatolia College-ACT, Greece

Sebastian Pannasch, Technische Universität Dresden, Germany

Spyros Raptis, Institute for Language and Speech processing /"Athena" R.C., Greece

David Schlangen, Bielefeld University, Germany

Björn Schuller, Imperial College London, UK

Carl Vogel, Trinity College Dublin, Ireland

Andreas Wendemuth, Otto von Guericke University Magdeburg, Germany

4.3 UM3I 2014 Program

UM3I will be a one-day workshop held on November 16, 2014. The eight accepted papers to be presented (each of which received three reviews) tackle challenging issues in various aspects of multiparty and multimodal interaction. The workshop features a keynote talk from Yukiko Nakano on designing conversational agents based on multimodal & multiparty interaction modeling.

5. ACKNOWLEDGMENTS

UM3I 2014 is being partially supported by the FP7-REGPOT-2011-1 Project LangTERRA [2] under grant agreement 285924, and the Dutch national program COMMIT [3]. We would like to thank all authors and the keynote speaker for their contributions, the program committee members for their excellent work to review the papers and the ICMI workshop chairs for their support.

6. REFERENCES

[1] http://ummmi.ilsp.gr/

[2] http://www.langterra.eu/

[3] http://www.commit-nl.nl/

Author Index

www.ingramcontent.com/pod-product-compliance
Ingram Content Group UK Ltd.
Pitfield, Milton Keynes, MK11 3LW, UK
UKHW051416290926
15471UKWH00009B/1633

9 781450 333870